Great Events from History

The Middle Ages

477 - 1453

Volume 1
477-1149

Editor
Brian A. Pavlac
King's College
Wilkes-Barre, Pennsylvania

Consulting Editors
Byron Cannon, *University of Utah*
David A. Crain, *South Dakota State University*
Jeffrey W. Dippmann, *Central Washington University*
Catherine Cymone Fourshey, *Susquehanna University*
Richard N. Frye, *Harvard University*
Katherine Anne Harper, *Loyola Marymount University*
Franklin Ng, *California State University, Fresno*
John A. Nichols, *Slippery Rock University*
Herbert Plutschow, *University of California at Los Angeles*

Salem Press
Pasadena, California Hackensack, New Jersey

Editor in Chief: Dawn P. Dawson
Editorial Director: Christina J. Moose
Project Editor: Rowena Wildin
Developmental Editor: Leslie Ellen Jones
Copy Editor: Desiree Dreeuws
Assistant Editor: Andrea E. Miller
Editorial Assistant: Dana Garey
Photograph Editor: Philip Bader
Acquisitions Editor: Mark Rehn
Research Supervisor: Jeffry Jensen
Production Editor: Cynthia Beres
Graphics and Design: James Hutson
Layout: Eddie Murillo

Cover photos: PhotoDisc, Corbis

∞ The paper used in these volumes conforms to the American National Standard for Permanence of Paper for Printed Library Materials, Z39.48-1992 (R1997).

Some of the essays in this work originally appeared in the following Salem Press sets: *Great Events from History* (1972-1980, edited by Frank N. Magill), *Chronology of European History: 15,000 B.C. to 1997* (1997, edited by John Powell; associate editors, E. G. Weltin, José M. Sánchez, Thomas P. Neill, and Edward P. Keleher), *Great Events from History: North American Series, Revised Edition* (1997, edited by Frank N. Magill; associate editor, John L. Loos), *Great Events from History: Ancient and Medieval Series* (1972, edited by Frank N. Magill; associate editor, E. G. Weltin), and *Great Events from History: Modern European Series* (1973, edited by Frank N. Magill; associate editors, Thomas P. Neill and José M. Sánchez).

Library of Congress Cataloging-in-Publication Data

Great events from history. The Middle Ages, 477-1453 / editor, Brian A. Pavlac ; consulting editors, Byron Cannon, . . . [et al.].

p. cm.

Some of the essays were previously published in various works.

Includes bibliographical references and indexes.

ISBN 1-58765-167-X (set : alk. paper) — ISBN 1-58765-168-8 (v. 1 : alk. paper) — ISBN 1-58765-169-6 (v. 2 : alk. paper)

1. Middle Ages — History. 2. Civilization, Medieval. I. Title: Middle Ages, 477-1453. II. Pavlac, Brian Alexander 1956- III. Cannon, Byron, 1940-

D119.G74 2004

909.07—dc22

2004016640

First Printing

PRINTED IN THE UNITED STATES OF AMERICA

Contents

701-800 C.E.

801-900 C.E.

901-1000 C.E.

1001-1100 C.E.

1101-1200 C.E.

Publisher's Note

Great Events from History: The Middle Ages, 477-1453 is the second installment in the ongoing *Great Events from History* series, which was initiated in 2004 with the two-volume *Great Lives from History: The Ancient World*. The series is projected to extend to the twenty-first century, with *The Renaissance & Early Modern Era, 1454-1600*, *The Seventeenth Century*, *The Eighteenth Century*, *The Nineteenth Century*, and *The Twentieth Century* to appear in sequential installments.

Expanded Coverage

Like the rest of the series, the current volumes represent both a revision and a significant expansion of the twelve-volume *Great Events from History* (1972-1980), incorporating essays from the *Chronology of European History: 15,000 B.C. to 1997* (3 vols., 1997), *Great Events from History: North American Series, Revised Edition* (4 vols., 1997), *Great Events from History: Ancient and Medieval Series* (3 vols., 1972), and *Great Events from History: Modern European Series* (3 vols., 1973).

Each installment in the new series is being enlarged with a significant amount of new material—often more than half the contents. For *The Ancient World*, new essays numbered roughly two-thirds of the set's contents, and the same is true here: The current two volumes of *The Middle Ages, 477-1443* add 200 new essays to the original 122, for a total of 322 events. These essays were commissioned especially for the new series and appear here for the first time. In addition, the new series features a new page design, expanded and updated bibliographies, internal and external cross-references, a section containing maps of the medieval world, new appendices and indexes, plus sidebars, tables, and numerous illustrations throughout.

Scope of Coverage

The date 477 was selected because it follows *The Ancient World*'s end date, 476 (the fall of Rome), and 1453 was selected because it is the year in which several important developments—notably the proliferation of documents issuing from the newly invented printing press, the end of the Hundred Years' War, and the fall of Constantinople—draw a dividing line between the late Middle Ages and the early modern world. Within this period, the events are arranged strictly chronologically, essentially forming a time line without regard to region. Hence, students can trace world history comparatively, with events in Asia, Africa, Europe, and the Americas comingled. To facilitate location of time periods within the publication, right-hand pages contain date range tabs.

The events—which range from "5th or 6th century: Confucianism Arrives in Japan" to "1453: Fall of Constantinople"—fall into one or more of the following categories: Agriculture (9); Architecture (18); Communications (6); Cultural and Intellectual History (87); Diplomacy and International Relations (5); Economics (12); Education (10); Engineering (8); Environment (5); Expansion and Land Acquisition (66); Exploration and Discovery (5); Government and Politics (129); Health and Medicine (7); Historiography (9); Laws, Acts, and Legal History (24); Literature (28); Mathematics (2); Organization and Institutions (12); Philosophy (11); Religion (103); Science and Technology (15); Social Reform (15); Trade and Commerce (27); Transportation (4); and Wars, Uprisings, and Civil Unrest (83).

The scope of this set is equally broad geographically, with essays on events associated with one or more of the following locales: Africa (35); Albania (1); Arabia (5); Australia (1); Bohemia (2); Bulgaria (3); Byzantine Empire (17); Central America (7); Central Asia (18); China (49); Egypt (10); England (21); Europe, general (24); Flanders (3); France (31); Germany (14); Greece (1); Greenland (1); Hungary (2); India (24); Iran (10); Iraq (11); Ireland (5); Israel/Palestine (14); Italy (24); Japan (20); Korea (7); Macedonia (1); Middle East (3); Moravia (2); Netherlands (1); New Zealand (2); North America (8); Pacific Islands (1); Poland (1); Portugal (2); Romania (1); Russia (5); Scandinavia (2); Scotland (1); Serbia (3); South America (4); Southeast Asia (18); Spain (10); Switzerland (2); Syria (4); Tibet (6); Turkey (17).

Essay Length and Format

Each essay averages 1,600 words (2-3 pages) in length and follows a standard format. The top matter to every essay prominently displays the most precise available *date or date range* for the event, followed by the name of the event and the following ready-reference data:

• A *summary* paragraph, encapsulating the event's significance.

• *Locale*, or where the event occurred, including both medieval place-names and modern equivalents if the locale's name has changed.

• *Categories*, or the type of event covered, from "Agriculture" to "War and Conquest."

• *Key Figures*, a list of the major individuals involved in the event, with birth and death dates, a brief descriptor, and reign dates for rulers.

The text of each essay is divided into standard sections:

• *Summary of Event*, devoted to a chronological description of the facts of the event.

• *Significance*, assessing the event's historical impact.

• *Further Reading*, an annotated list of sources for further study.

• *See also*, cross-references to other essays within the set.

• *Related articles*, which lists essays of interest in Salem's companion publication, *Great Lives from History: The Middle Ages, 477-1453* (2 vols., 2005).

SPECIAL FEATURES

Eleven maps depicting portions of the medieval world appear grouped together in the front of each volume for easy reference. Accompanying the essays are approximately 118 additional sidebars, tables, lists, and maps, along with about 201 illustrations—photographs of artworks, battles, busts, sculptures, coins, paintings, and drawings.

A *Keyword List of Contents* appears in the front matter to both volumes and alphabetically lists all essays, permuted by all keywords in the essay's title, to assist students in locating events by name.

In addition, several research aids appear as appendices at the end of Volume 2:

• The *Time Line* lists major events in the Middle Ages; unlike the Chronological List of Entries (see below), the Time Line is a chronological listing of events by subject area; it contains both those events covered by the entries and also a substantial number of other events and developments during the Middle Ages.

• The *Glossary* defines medieval terms and concepts.

• The *Bibliography* cites major sources on the Middle Ages.

• *Web Sites* provides URLs and descriptions of Internet sites devoted to medieval studies.

• The *Chronological List of Entries* organizes the contents chronologically in one place. Because this is the same order in which the contents appear, this is essentially a full table of contents for ease of reference across volumes.

Finally, four indexes round out the set:

• *Category Index* lists essays by type of event (Agriculture, Architecture, Arts, and so on).

• *Geographical Index* lists essays by region or country.

• *Personages Index* lists major personages discussed throughout.

• *Subject Index* lists persons, concepts, terms, events, organizations, artworks, and many other topics of discussion, with cross-references to the Category and Geographical indexes.

USAGE NOTES

The worldwide scope of *Great Events from History* resulted in the inclusion of many names and words that must be transliterated from languages that do not use the Roman alphabet, and in some cases, more than one transliterated system exists. In many cases, transliterated words in this set follow the American Library Association and Library of Congress (ALA-LC) transliteration format for that language. However, if another form of a name or word was judged to be more familiar to the general audience, it was used instead. The variants for names of essay subjects are listed in ready-reference top matter and are cross-referenced in the subject and personages indexes. The Pinyin transliteration is used for Chinese topics, with Wade-Giles variants provided for major names and dynasties; in a few cases, a common name that is not Pinyin has been used. Sanskrit words generally follow the ALA-LC transliteration rules, although again, the more familiar form of a word is used when deemed appropriate for the general reader.

Titles of books and other literature appear, upon first mention in the essay, with their full publication and translation data as known: an indication of the first date of publication or appearance, followed by the English title in translation and its first date of appearance in English. If no translation has been published in English, and if the context of the discussion does not make the meaning of the title obvious, a "literal translation" appears in roman type.

In the listing of Key Figures and in parenthetical material within the text, the editors have used these abbreviations: "r." for "reigned," "b." for "born," "d." for "died," and "fl." for flourished. Where a date range appears appended to a name without one of these designators, the reader may assume it signifies birth and death dates.

The Editors and Contributors

In compiling the table of contents, Salem enlisted a group of scholars who provided their knowledge on different areas of the medieval world: Brian A. Pavlac (general editor), Department of History, King's College, Wilkes-Barre, Pennsylvania; Byron Cannon (Middle East), Department of History, University of Utah; David A. Crain (the Americas), Department of History, South Dakota State University; Jeffrey W. Dippmann (China), Department of Philosophy, Central Washington University; Catherine Cymone Fourshey (Africa), Department of History, Susquehanna University; Richard N. Frye (Central Asia), Emeritus Professor of Iranian, Harvard University; Katherine Anne Harper (India), Art and Art History Department, Loyola Marymount University; Franklin Ng (East Asia), Coordinator, Asian Studies, California State University, Fresno; John A. Nichols (Europe), History Department, Slippery Rock University; and Herbert Plutschow, Department of History, University of California at Los Angeles.

Salem Press would like to extend its appreciation to these editors and to all who have been involved in the development and production of this work. Each essay was written by an academician who specializes in the area of discussion, and without their expert contribution, a project of this nature would not be possible. A full list of contributors and their affiliations appears in the front matter of this volume.

Contributors

Amy Ackerberg-Hastings
Independent Scholar

Mark Aldenderfer
University of California, Santa Barbara

Peggy E. Alford
Eastern Oregon University

Bryan Aubrey
Independent Scholar

James T. Baker
Western Kentucky University

Carl L. Bankston, III
Tulane University

Martin J. Baron
Columbia University

Xavier Baron
University of Wisconsin Milwaukee

Blake R. Beattie
University of Louisville

Milton Berman
University of Rochester

Cynthia A. Bily
Adrian College

Nicholas Birns
New School University

David W. Blaylock
Eastern Kentucky University

Steve D. Boilard
Western Kentucky University

William S. Brockington, Jr.
University of South Carolina—Aiken

David L. Browman
Washington University

David D. Buck
University of Wisconsin—Milwaukee

Joseph P. Byrne
Belmont University

Aileen Carlson
Independent Scholar

Donald E. Cellini
Adrian College

Frederick B. Chary
Indiana University Northwest

Michael M. Chemers
Carnegie Mellon University

Douglas Clouatre
Mid Plains Community College

Daisy Conduah
Independent Scholar

Weston F. Cook, Jr.
University of North Carolina at Pembroke

M. Joseph Costelloe
Creighton University

David A. Crain
South Dakota State University

John Francis Daly
Saint Louis University

Frank Day
Clemson University

Joanna Debella
Independent Scholar

Rene M. Descartes
SUNY, Cobleskill

M. Casey Diana
University of Illinois at Urbana-Champaign

Giuseppe C. Di Scipio
Hunter College

Barbara M. Fahy
Albright College

Randall Fegley
Pennsylvania State University

Richard Fink
Independent Scholar

Edward Fiorelli
St. John's University

Alan M. Fisher
California State University, Dominguez Hills

Richard D. Fitzgerald
Onondaga Community College

Dale L. Flesher
University of Mississippi

James Flynn
Western Kentucky University

James H. Forse
Bowling Green State University

Catherine Cymone Fourshey
Susquehanna University

Robert J. Frail
Centenary College

C. George Fry
Lutheran College

Gloria Fulton
Humboldt State University

Michael J. Galgano
James Madison University

K. Fred Gillum
Colby College

Karen Gould
Independent Scholar

Daniel G. Graetzer
University of Washington Medical Center

David B. Haley
University of Minnesota

Irwin Halfond
McKendree College

Gavin R. G. Hambly
University of Texas at Dallas

Travis Hamilton
Independent Scholar

Katherine Anne Harper
Loyola Marymount University

John J. Healy
Saint Joseph Seminary

Diane Andrews Henningfeld
Adrian College

Hal Holladay
Simon's Rock of Bard College

Blaine Horrocks
Independent Scholar

Marian T. Horvat
University of Kansas

Patrick Norman Hunt
Stanford University

Raymond Pierre Hylton
Virginia Union University

John Quinn Imholte
University of Minnesota, Morris

Robert Jaques
Emory and Henry College

Mary Evelyn Jegen
University of Dayton

Albert C. Jensen
Central Florida Community College

Jeffry Jensen
Independent Scholar

Bruce E. Johansen
University of Nebraska at Omaha

Amy J. Johnson
Berry College

Philip Dwight Jones
Bradley University

Richard Jones
Stephen F. Austin State University

Charles L. Kammer, III
The College of Wooster

Marguerite Keane
J. Paul Getty Museum

Edward P. Keleher
Purdue University—Calumet

Dwight Kieffer
Independent Scholar

Bokyung Kim
University of California, Los Angeles

Leigh Husband Kimmel
Independent Scholar

Gayla Koerting
University of South Dakota

Grove Koger
Boise (Idaho) Public Library

Paul E. Kuhl
Winston-Salem State University

Julian E. Kunnie
University of Arizona

Philip E. Lampe
University of the Incarnate Word

Ralph L. Langenheim, Jr.
University of Illinois at Urbana-Champaign

Lawrence N. Langer
University of Connecticut

Eugene Larson
Los Angeles Pierce College

Joseph Tse-Hei Lee
Pace University

Elizabeth Leighton
Independent Scholar

Thomas Tandy Lewis
Anoka Ramsey Community College

David Lindsay
Independent Scholar

Victor Lindsey
East Central University

Frances R. Lipp
Washington University

Herbert Luft
Pepperdine University

R. C. Lutz
CII

William P. McDonald
Tennessee Wesleyan College

Thomas McGeary
Independent Scholar

James Edward McGoldrick
Cedarville College

John F. McGovern
University of Wisconsin—Milwaukee

Douglas J. McMillan
East Carolina University

James P. McNab
Virginia Polytechnic Institute and State University

Katherine S. Mansour
Jacksonville University

Chogollah Maroufi
California State University, Los Angeles

Thomas C. Maroukis
Capital University

Lynewood F. Martin
Lindenwood College

Jennifer P. Mathews
Trinity University

Ralph W. Mathisen
University of South Carolina

Timothy May
University of Wisconsin—Madison

Ruben G. Mendoza
California State University, Monterey Bay

Hwa-Soon Choi Meyer
Seton Hall University

Randall L. Milstein
Oregon State University

Christina Moose
Independent Scholar

Alice Myers
Simon's Rock College

Walter Nelson
Independent Scholar

Carol Olausen
Independent Scholar

Patrick P. O'Neill
University of North Carolina at Chapel Hill

Robert J. Paradowski
Rochester Institute of Technology

Brian A. Pavlac
King's College

Zena Pearlstone
California State University, Fullerton

Matthew Penney
Independent Scholar

Andy Perry
Independent Scholar

Marilyn Elizabeth Perry
Independent Scholar

James Persoon
Grand Valley State University

R. Craig Philips
Michigan State University

George R. Plitnik
Frostburg State University

Edmund Dickenson Potter
Independent Scholar

Luke Powers
Tennessee State University

Victoria Price
Lamar University

Carolyn V. Prorok
Slippery Rock University

Kevin B. Reid
Henderson Community College

Edward A. Riedinger
Ohio State University Libraries

Carl F. Rohne
Southern Methodist University

Carl Rollyson
Baruch College

Joseph R. Rosenbloom
Washington University

John Alan Ross
Eastern Washington University

Robert L. Ross
University of Texas at Austin

Joseph R. Rudolph, Jr.
Towson University

Jason D. Sanchez
Tulane University

Raymond H. Schmandt
Saint Joseph College

William C. Schrader
Tennessee Technological University

Elizabeth L. Scully
University of Texas at Arlington

Rose Secrest
Independent Scholar

Evan Scott Shuey
Independent Scholar

R. Baird Shuman
University of Illinois at Urbana-Champaign

Narasingha P. Sil
Western Oregon University

Shumet Sishagne
Christopher Newport University

Thomas Sizgorich
University of California, Santa Barbara

John Edward Skillen
Gordon College

Roger Smith
Independent Scholar

Larry Smolucha
Benedictine University

Sonia Sorrell
Pepperdine University

Brian Stableford
King Alfred's College

Barbara C. Stanley
East Tennessee State University

Mary N. Storm
Jawaharlal Nehru University

Fred Strickert
Wartburg College

Glenn L. Swygart
Tennessee Temple University

Bart L. R. Talbert
Salisbury University

Robert D. Talbott
University of Northern Iowa

Cassandra Lee Tellier
Capital University

Louis P. Towles
Southern Wesleyan University

Qui-Phiet Tran
Schreiner University

William L. Urban
Monmouth College

Sem Vermeersch
Keimyung University

Joseph M. Victor
Syracuse University

Peter L. Viscusi
Central Missouri State University

Gilmar E. Visoni
Queensborough Community College

Carl A. Volz
Concordia Seminary

Jamese Celia Wells
Independent Scholar

Winifred Whelan
St. Bonaventure University

John D. Windhausen
Saint Anselm College

Michael Witkoski
University of South Carolina

Fatima Wu
Loyola Marymount University

Richard J. Wurtz
Southern Illinois University

Kristen L. Zacharias
Albright College

Yunqiu Zhang
North Carolina A&T State University

Lowell H. Zuck
Eden Seminary

Keyword List of Contents

List of Maps and Tables

Eastern Hemisphere c. 800 C.E.

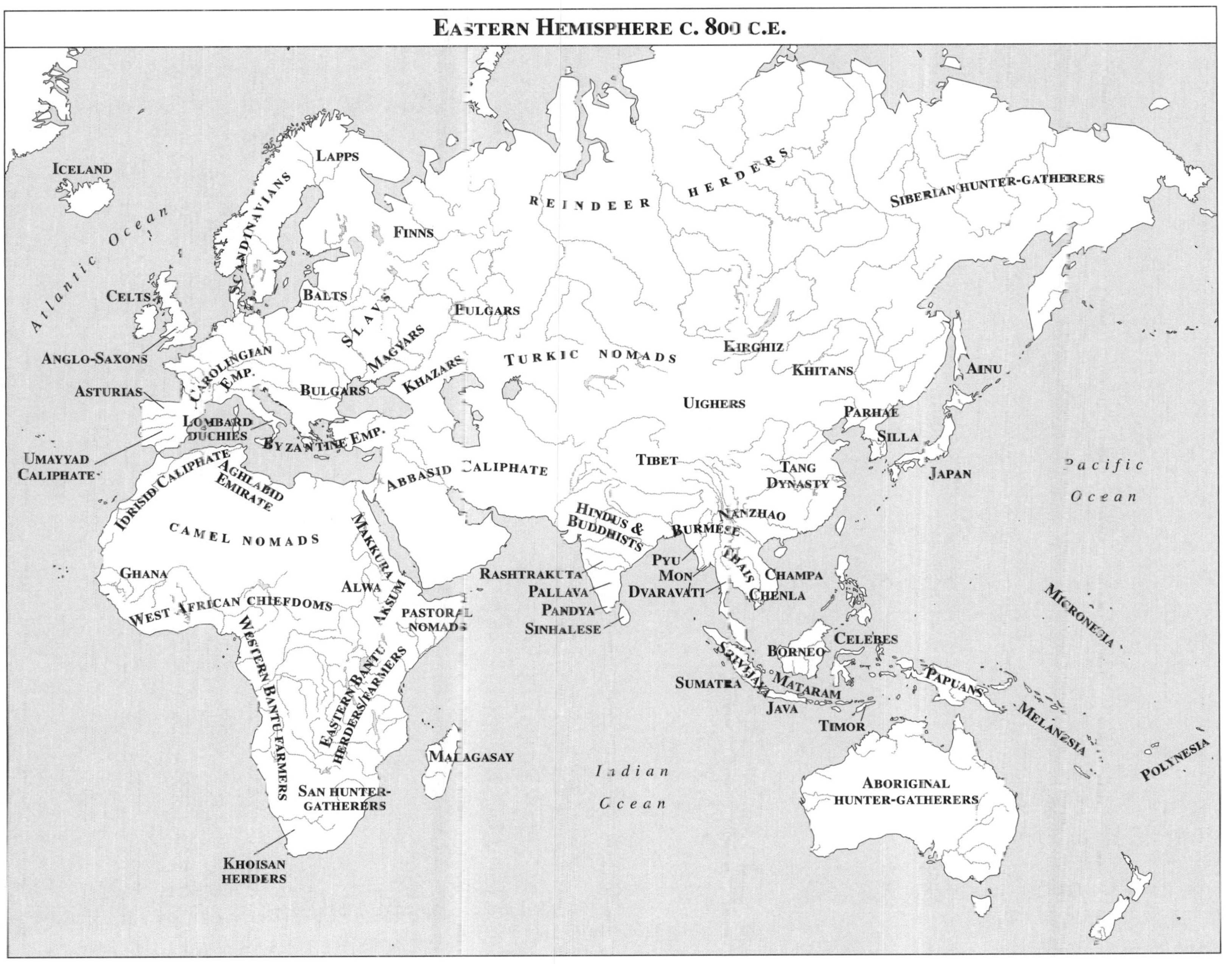

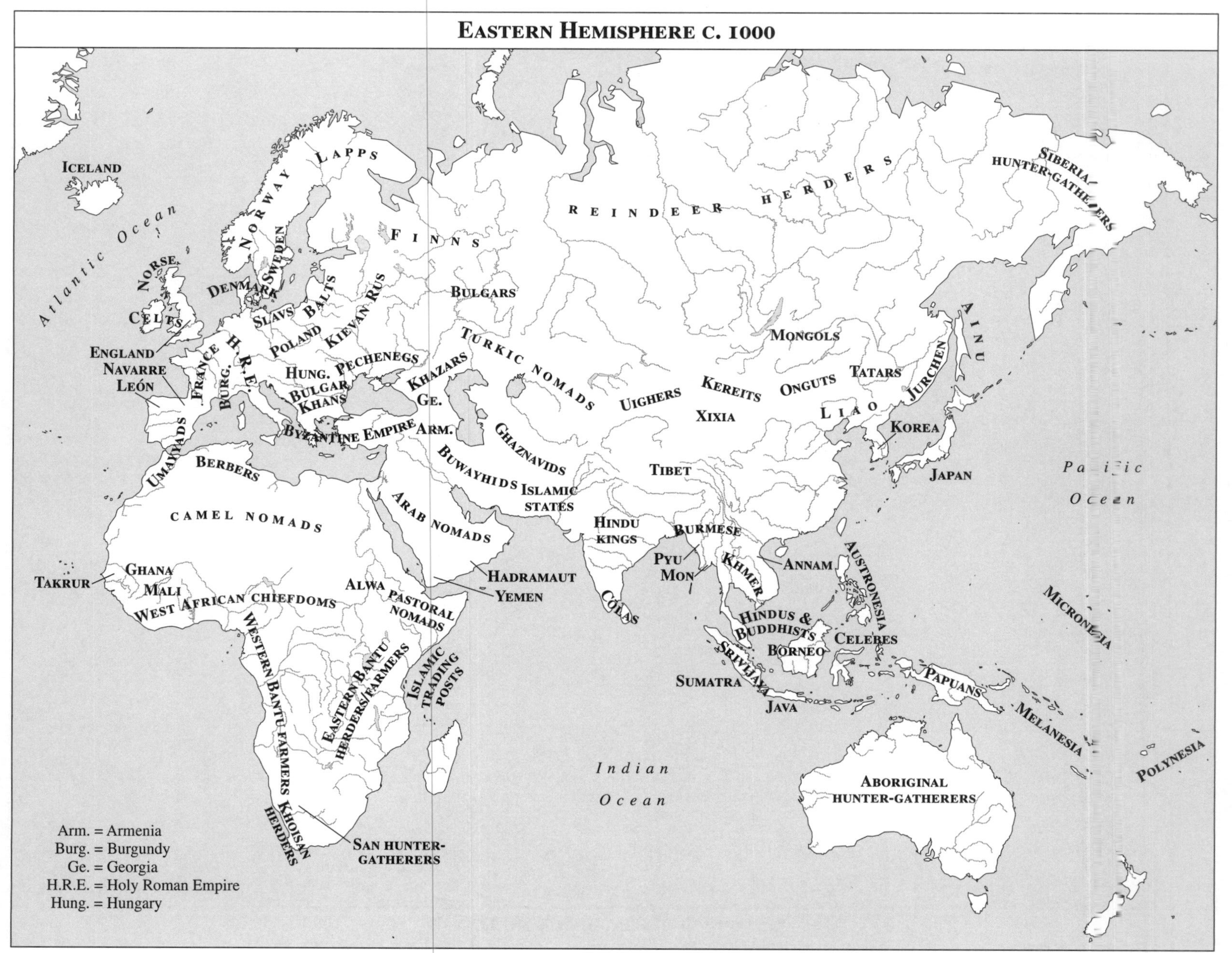

Eastern Hemisphere c. 1000
Iceland
Atlantic Ocean
Norse
Celts
England
Navarre
León
Norway
Lapps
Sweden
Denmark
Slavs
Balts
Finns
Kievan Rus
Poland
H.R.E.
France
Burg.
Hung.
Pechenegs
Bulgar Khans
Khazars
Ge.
Arm.
Byzantine Empire
Bulgars
Umayyads
Berbers
Camel Nomads
Takrur
Ghana
Mali
West African Chiefdoms
Alwa
Pastoral Nomads
Arab Nomads
Hadramaut
Yemen
Western Bantu Farmers
Eastern Bantu Herders/Farmers
Islamic Trading Posts
Khoisan Herders
San Hunter-Gatherers
Turkic Nomads
Ghaznavids
Buwayhids
Islamic States
Reindeer Herders
Siberian Hunter-Gatherers
Uighers
Kereits
Xixia
Mongols
Onguts
Tatars
Jurchen
Ainu
Liao
Korea
Japan
Tibet
Hindu Kings
Burmese
Pyu
Mon
Colas
Khmer
Annam
Hindus & Buddhists
Srivijaya
Sumatra
Java
Borneo
Celebes
Austronesia
Papuans
Melanesia
Micronesia
Polynesia
Pacific Ocean
Indian Ocean
Aboriginal Hunter-Gatherers
Arm. = Armenia
Burg. = Burgundy
Ge. = Georgia
H.R.E. = Holy Roman Empire
Hung. = Hungary

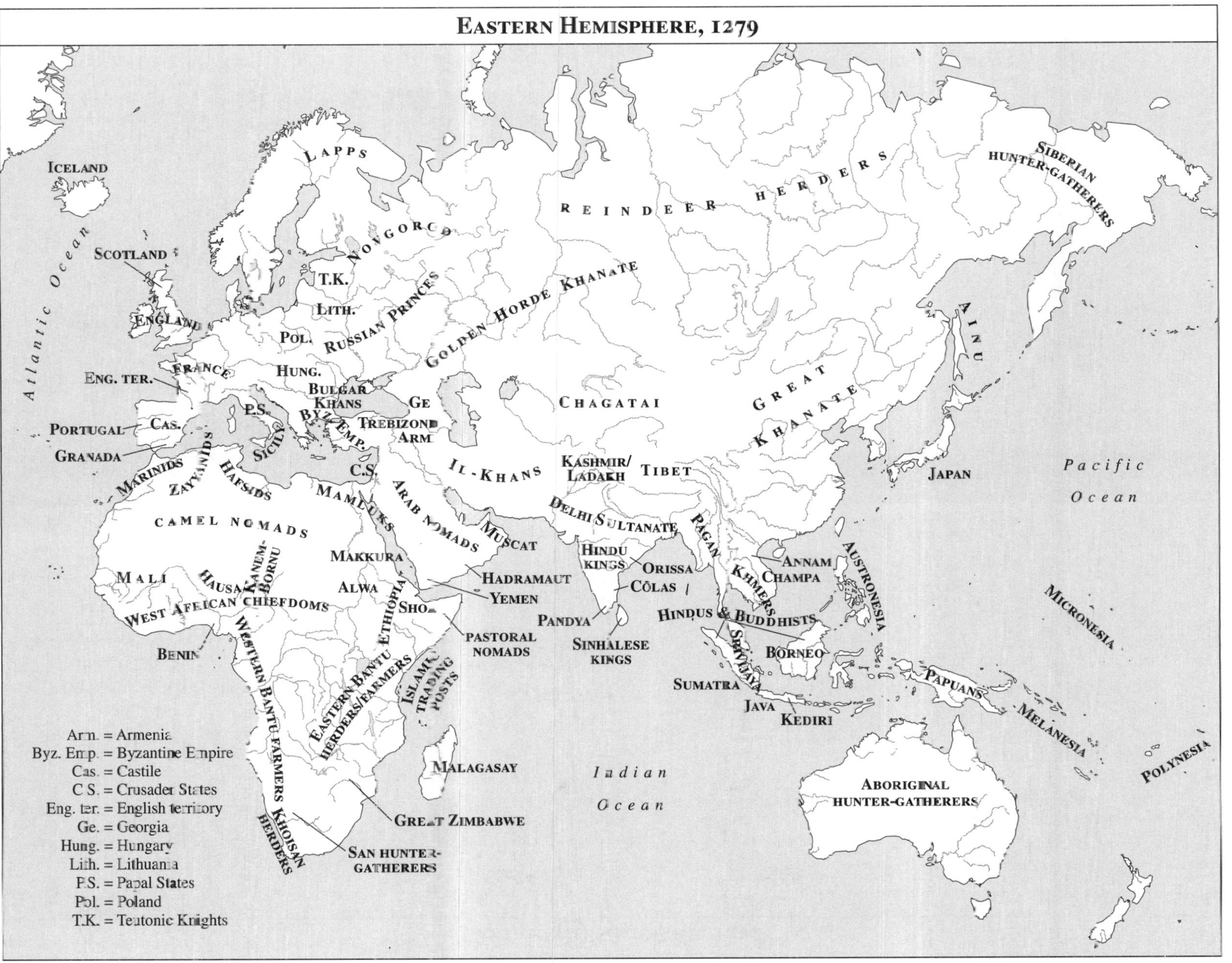
Eastern Hemisphere, 1279
Iceland
Atlantic Ocean
Scotland
England
Eng. ter.
France
Portugal
Cas.
Granada
Marinids
Zayyanids
Hafsids
Lapps
Novgorod
T.K.
Lith.
Pol.
Russian Princes
Hung.
Bulgar Khans
P.S.
Sicily
Byz. Emp.
Ge
Trebizond
Arm.
C.S.
Golden Horde Khanate
Reindeer Herders
Siberian Hunter-Gatherers
Ainu
Chagatai
Great Khanate
Japan
Pacific Ocean
Il-Khans
Kashmir/ Ladakh
Tibet
Delhi Sultanate
Pagan
Camel Nomads
Mamluks
Arab Nomads
Muscat
Makkura
Alwa
Ethiopia
Shoa
Hadramaut
Yemen
Pastoral Nomads
Mali
Hausa
Kanem-Bornu
West African Chiefdoms
Benin
Western Bantu Farmers
Eastern Bantu Herders/Farmers
Islamic Trading Posts
Malagasay
Great Zimbabwe
San Hunter-Gatherers
Khoisan Herders
Hindu Kings
Orissa
Cōlas
Pandya
Sinhalese Kings
Annam
Champa
Khmers
Hindus & Buddhists
Srivijaya
Borneo
Sumatra
Java
Kediri
Austronesia
Micronesia
Papuans
Melanesia
Polynesia
Aboriginal Hunter-Gatherers
Indian Ocean
Arm. = Armenia
Byz. Emp. = Byzantine Empire
Cas. = Castile
C.S. = Crusader States
Eng. ter. = English territory
Ge. = Georgia
Hung. = Hungary
Lith. = Lithuania
P.S. = Papal States
Pol. = Poland
T.K. = Teutonic Knights

Eastern Hemisphere, 1492

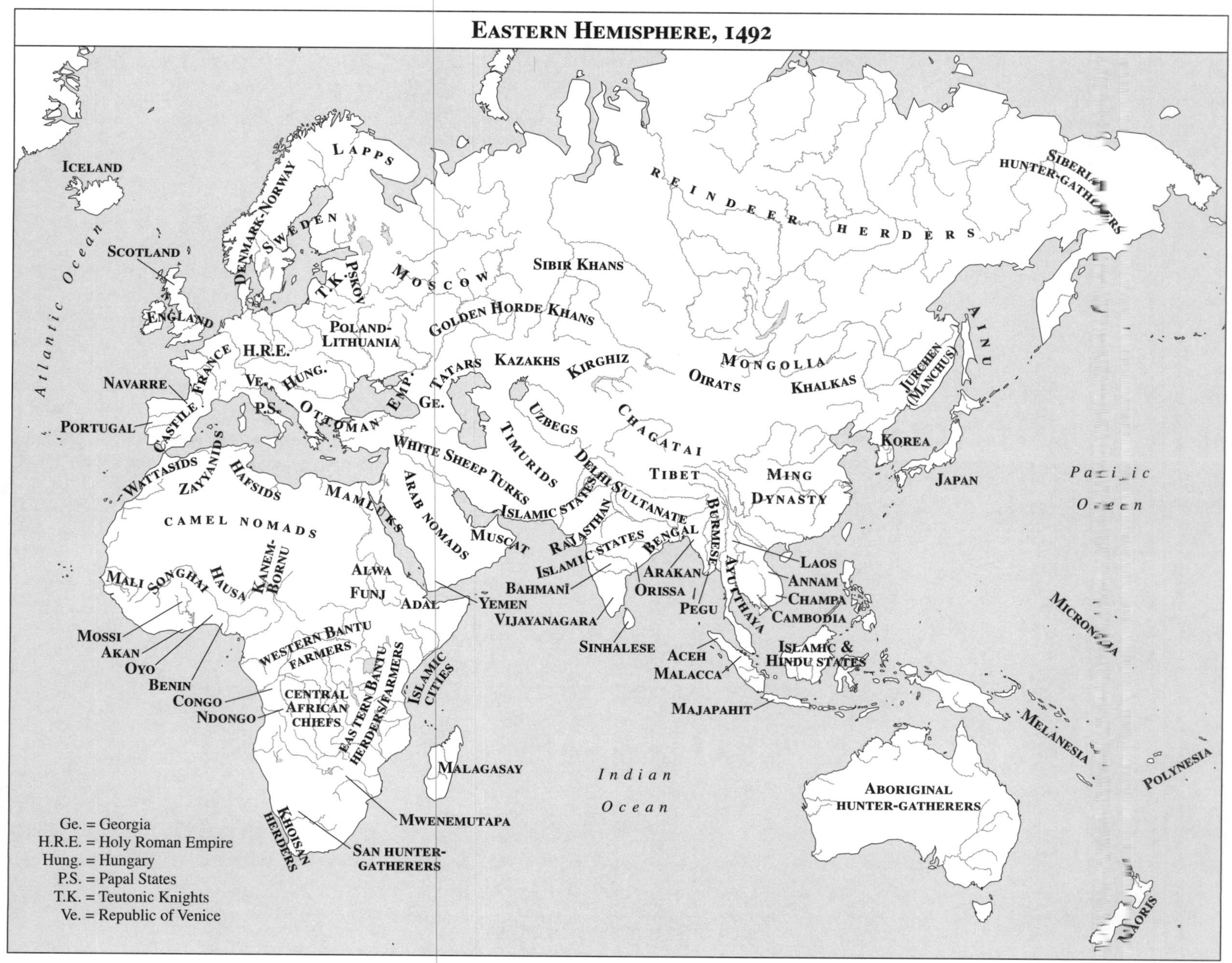

Ge. = Georgia
H.R.E. = Holy Roman Empire
Hung. = Hungary
P.S. = Papal States
T.K. = Teutonic Knights
Ve. = Republic of Venice

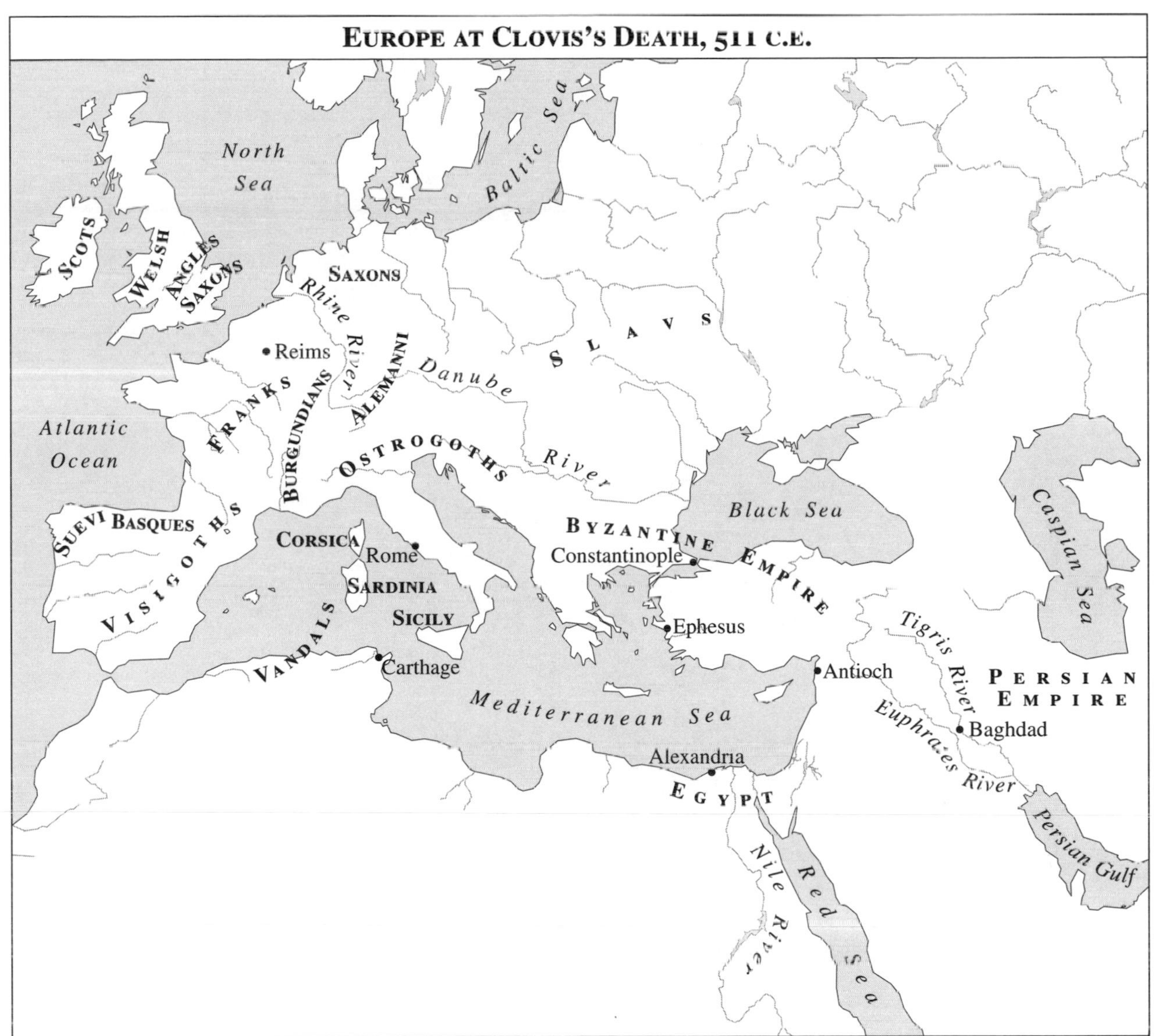
EUROPE AT CLOVIS'S DEATH, 511 C.E.
North Sea
Baltic Sea
SCOTS
WELSH
ANGLES
SAXONS
SAXONS
Rhine River
Reims
ALEMANNI
Danube River
SLAVS
FRANKS
BURGUNDIANS
Atlantic Ocean
OSTROGOTHS
Black Sea
Caspian Sea
SUEVI
BASQUES
VISIGOTHS
CORSICA
Rome
SARDINIA
SICILY
BYZANTINE EMPIRE
Constantinople
Ephesus
VANDALS
Carthage
Antioch
Tigris River
PERSIAN EMPIRE
Baghdad
Euphrates River
Mediterranean Sea
Alexandria
EGYPT
Nile River
Red Sea
Persian Gulf

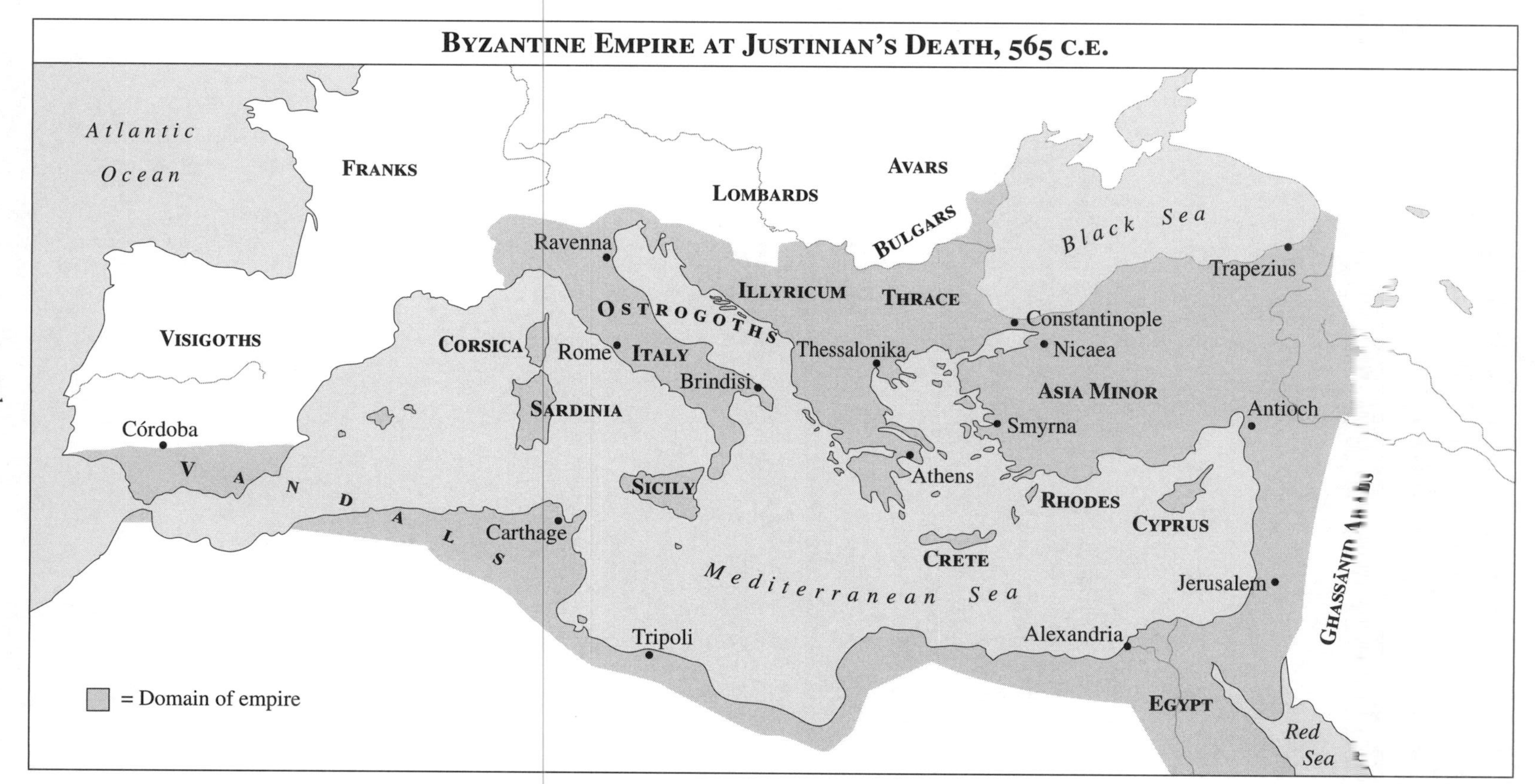
Byzantine Empire at Justinian's Death, 565 c.e.
Atlantic Ocean
Franks
Visigoths
Córdoba
Vandals
Corsica
Sardinia
Ravenna
Rome
Italy
Ostrogoths
Brindisi
Sicily
Carthage
Tripoli
Lombards
Avars
Bulgars
Illyricum
Thrace
Thessalonika
Athens
Crete
Rhodes
Constantinople
Nicaea
Asia Minor
Smyrna
Black Sea
Trapezius
Antioch
Cyprus
Jerusalem
Alexandria
Egypt
Red Sea
Mediterranean Sea
= Domain of empire

Carolingian Empire, 768-814 C.E.
North Sea
Baltic Sea
Britain
Anglo-Saxons
Danes
Abodrites
Elbe River
Wiltzites
Slavs
Frisia
Saxony
Utrecht
Thuringia
Sorbs
Cologne
Boulogne
Hérstal
Austrasia
Bohemians
Mainz
Frankfurt
English Channel
Paris
Danube River
Brittany
Neustria
Avars
Orléans
Tours
Fontenay
Alemannia
Bavaria
Pannonia
Bourges
Carinthia
Poitiers
Burgundy
Bay of Biscay
Aquitaine
Friuli
Milan
Pavia
Venice
Bordeaux
Lombardy
Ravenna
Slavs
Provence
Florence
Aix-en-Provence
Toulouse
Gascony
Septimania
Roncesvalles
Pamplona
Marseilles
Narbonne
Basques
Pyrenees
Adriatic Sea
Corsica
Rome
Saragossa
Catalonia
Barcelona
Benevento
Tortosa
Mediterranean Sea
Umayyad Caliphate
Sardinia
Carolingian Empire 768
Charlemagne's acquisitions by 814

HOLY ROMAN EMPIRE C. 1190
DENMARK
North Sea
ENGLAND
HOLSTEIN
POMERANIA
FRISIA
SAXONY
BRANDENBURG
POLAND
English Channel
LORRAINE
Rhine River
Cologne
MEISSEN
THURINGIA
BOHEMIA
FRANCONIA
MORAVIA
Ratisbon
ALSACE
AUSTRIA
Danube River
Vienna
SWABIA
FRANCE
Danube River
BAVARIA
STYRIA
CARINTHIA
CARNIOLA
HUNGARY
BURGUNDY
VERONA
Milan
Pavia
Po River
Venice
LOMBARDY
Parma
Genoa
Bologna
Pisa
Florence
TUSCANY
SERBIA
PAPAL STATES
CORSICA
Rome
BYZANTINE EMPIRE
APULIA
Naples
Salerno
SARDINIA
KINGDOM OF THE TWO SICILIES
Mediterranean Sea
Palermo
= Holy Roman Empire

Europe in the Fourteenth Century

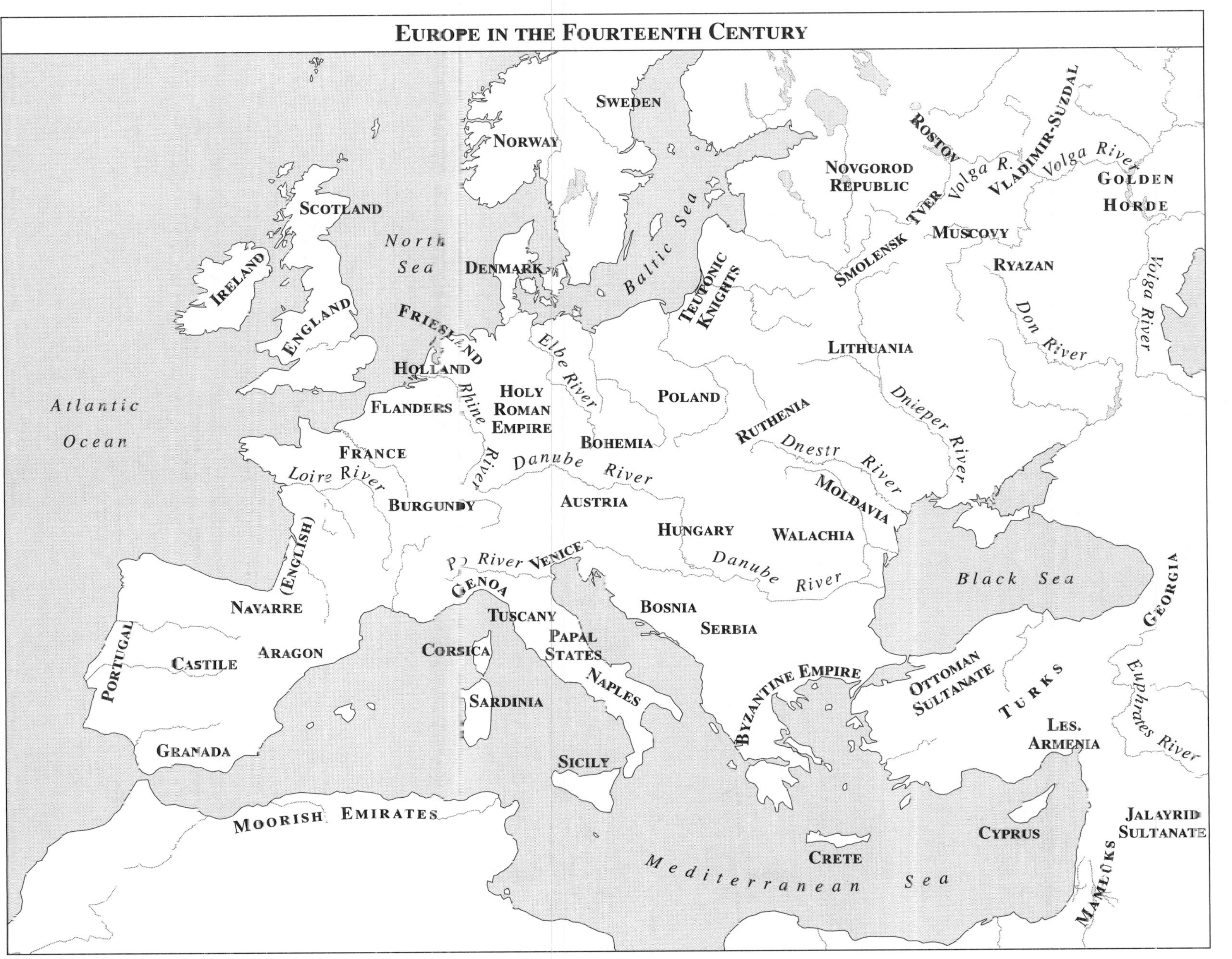

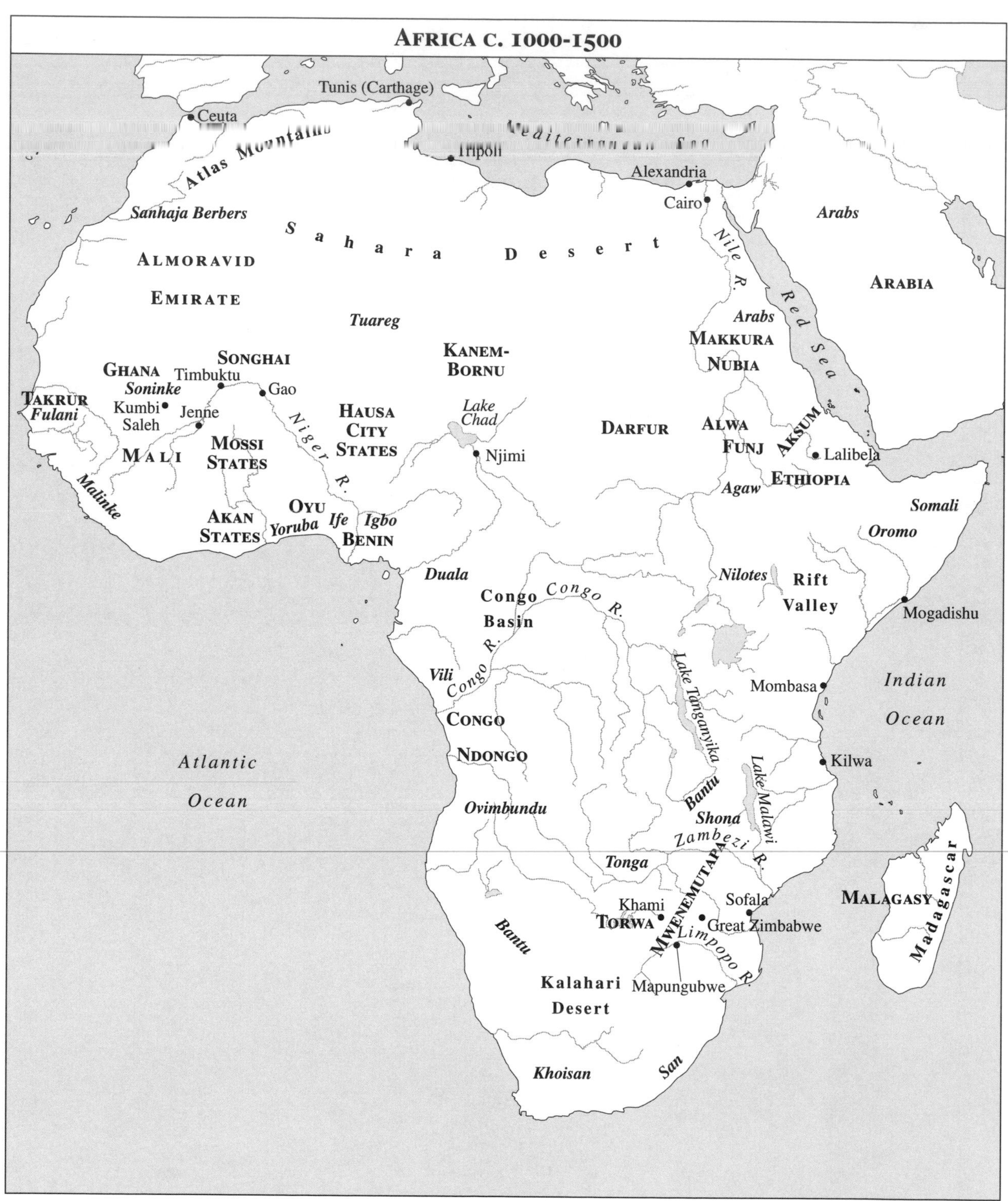
Africa c. 1000-1500
Tunis (Carthage)
Ceuta
Atlas Mountains
Mediterranean Sea
Tripoli
Alexandria
Cairo
Arabs
Sanhaja Berbers
Sahara Desert
Nile R.
Almoravid
Emirate
Red Sea
Arabia
Tuareg
Arabs
Makkura
Nubia
Kanem-
Bornu
Songhai
Ghana
Timbuktu
Soninke
Gao
Takrur
Fulani
Kumbi
Saleh
Jenne
Niger R.
Hausa
City
States
Lake
Chad
Darfur
Alwa
Funj
Aksum
Lalibela
Mali
Mossi
States
Njimi
Ethiopia
Agaw
Malinke
Akan
States
Oyu
Yoruba
Ife
Igbo
Benin
Somali
Oromo
Duala
Congo
Basin
Congo R.
Nilotes
Rift
Valley
Mogadishu
Vili
Congo R.
Lake Tanganyika
Mombasa
Indian
Ocean
Congo
Ndongo
Atlantic
Ocean
Lake Malawi
Kilwa
Bantu
Ovimbundu
Shona
Zambezi R.
Tonga
Mwenemutapa
Malagasy
Madagascar
Khami
Sofala
Torwa
Great Zimbabwe
Bantu
Limpopo R.
Kalahari
Desert
Mapungubwe
Khoisan
San

The Americas to c. 1500

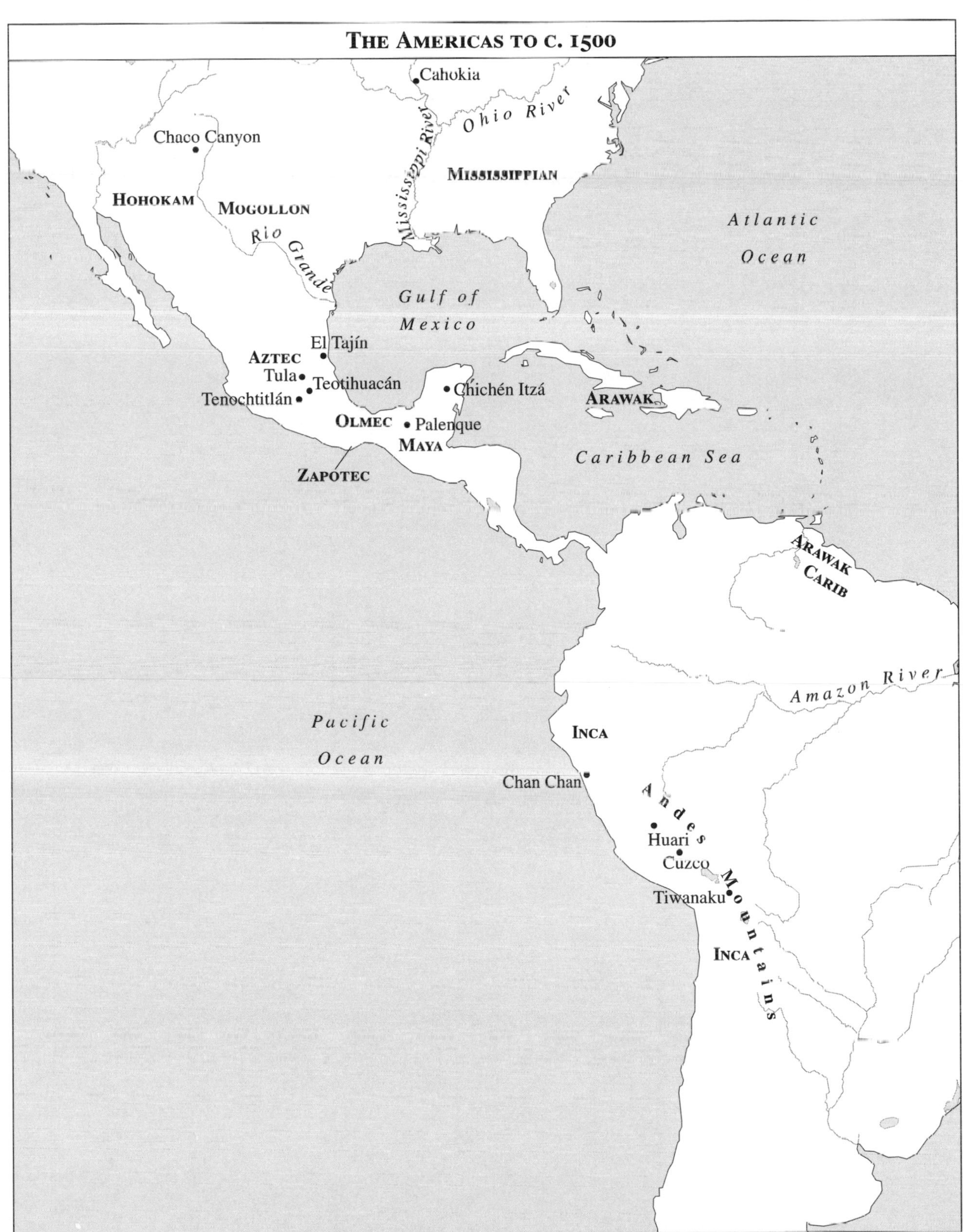

5th or 6th century
CONFUCIANISM ARRIVES IN JAPAN

Confucianism played a leading role in the attempt of Japanese rulers to centralize power in the sixth and seventh centuries and has continued to exert considerable influence on Japanese scholarship, political life, and social relations into the modern period.

LOCALE: Japan
CATEGORIES: Cultural and intellectual history; philosophy; religion

KEY FIGURES

Shōtoku Taishi (574-622), imperial prince, regent to the empress Suiko
Wani (fl. late fourth-early fifth century), Korean Confucian scholar

SUMMARY OF EVENT

The system of thought known as Confucianism in the West developed in China between 1000 and 250 B.C.E. and was introduced to Japan from Korea in the fifth or sixth century C.E., most likely in 404. The philosopher Confucius (551-479 B.C.E.) combined earlier traditions with his own innovations and interpretations to create a system of thought.

The essence of the teachings of Confucius is that there are natural forces underpinning all social relationships, including those between rulers and subjects. He taught that leaders were bound to rule by moral example, and if they did not, their countries would fall into ruin. He also put forward the idea that people should cultivate themselves by studying classical virtues as well as music and traditional rituals. The *Lunyu* (late sixth-early fifth centuries B.C.E.; *The Analects*, 1861), a collection of the philosopher's sayings complied by his disciples, is the most direct expression of Confucian philosophy. In addition, Confucius is said to have written or edited a number of other important works such as *Yijing* (eighth to third century B.C.E.; English translation, 1876; also known as *Book of Changes*, 1986), *Shujing* (compiled after first century B.C.E.; English translation in *The Chinese Classics*, Vol. 5, Parts 1 and 2, 1872; commonly known as *Classic of History*), *Shijing* (compiled fifth century B.C.E.; *The Book of Songs*, 1937), and *Chunqiu* (fifth century B.C.E.; *The Ch'un Ts'ew with the Tso Chuen*, 1872; commonly known as *Spring and Autumn Annals*). The works, along with several other volumes put together by the disciples of Confucius such as the *Xiaojing* (fifth century B.C.E.; *The Classic of Filial Piety*, 1899) and *Liji* (compiled fifth century B.C.E.; *The Liki*, 1885; commonly known as *Classic of Rituals*), became the canon that came to serve as the foundation of intellectual life across most of Asia.

During the Han Dynasty (206 B.C.E.-220 C.E.), Confucian thought became the dominant philosophical force in Chinese political life. Careful study of the Confucian classics was necessary to pursue a career in the civil service. During this period, the culture of China was widely considered to be more advanced than those of its neighbors, and Chinese thought and administrative practices were held in high regard.

During the fourth century C.E., Confucian thought spread to the Korean peninsula, where it gained considerable influence among the ruling class. Tradition states that Wani, a Confucian scholar, traveled from the Korean kingdom of Paekche to Japan in the early fifth century; one likely date accepted by most scholars is 404. Wani brought with him *The Analects* of Confucius and other important texts. According to the chronicles *Kojiki* (712 C.E.; *Records of Ancient Matters*, 1883) and the *Nihon shoki* (compiled 720 C.E.; *Nihongi: Chronicles of Japan from the Earliest Times to A.D. 697*, 1896; best known as *Nihon shoki*), Wani became an influential administrator at the court of the Yamato emperor. The books that he brought with him, however, came to have an even greater influence. They played a leading role in the diffusion of the Chinese writing system in Japan, thereby making the country literate, and they also brought a new direction to the political life of the Japanese archipelago.

The power of the imperial family at the Yamato court was limited, and influential regional clans presented an obstacle to truly centralized rule. In the sixth and seventh centuries, there was an attempt to centralize power, and Confucianism proved to be an effective tool in this struggle. In the mid-sixth century, the Soga family, a powerful regional clan, attempted to institute Buddhism, another philosophical and religious system that came to Japan from the continent, sparking a serious conflict with two other clans, the Nakatomi and Mononobe, who had a vested interest in maintaining the status quo. After a bout of fierce fighting, the Soga emerged victorious. Through their power at court, the prestige of Buddhism, and strategic marriages within the imperial family, the Soga came to hold sway over the court. Therefore, it was to their advantage to press for a stronger central government.

Confucius (551-479 B.C.E.). (Hulton|Archive by Getty Images)

In 604, Shōtoku Taishi, a member of the Soga family and the regent for the empress Suiko (r. 593-628), promulgated the Seventeen Article Constitution, designed to increase the power of the central court. Shōtoku Taishi was a devout Buddhist, and although there are many references to that faith in the document, the work's political content is obviously Confucian in character. The document enforces the idea that loyalty to one's lord and one's father, a fundamental part of Confucian ethics, is to be valued above all else. The work also stresses the idea that Japan's leaders are bound to provide just rule, another concept that can be considered a cornerstone of Confucian ideology. The presence of Confucian ideas in the Seventeen Article Constitution shows just how great a role the Chinese system of thought had come to play in Japanese political and ethical philosophy in the few centuries after Confucianism was introduced from Korea.

Within a few centuries of the introduction of Confucianism to Japan, the Chinese ideological system had become an important part of almost all aspects of Japanese political life.

SIGNIFICANCE

The impact on Japanese culture of the introduction of Confucian thought in the sixth century was as great, if not greater, than the changes brought on by contact with Western ideas in the nineteenth. Aside from its tremendous influence on Japanese politics and institutional history, Confucianism shaped Japanese social relations and such fundamentally important ideas as the concept of gender roles. Confucianism shares with Buddhism and Shintō, the native faith, a dominant role in shaping the Japanese cultural tradition.

In the sixteenth and seventeenth centuries, the ideas of the ancient Chinese philosopher came to hold sway over Japanese intellectual life in the form of neo-Confucianism. During these two centuries, a series of military leaders were trying to bring the fragmented political landscape under some type of central control. However, even before neo-Confucianism became the new intellectual orthodoxy, Confucian rhetoric had played a large role in the house laws and edicts of the various regional lords of the Warring States period (1467-1615). In addition, *bushidō*, the philosophy of the warrior class, with its emphasis on loyalty and moderation in personal conduct, bears the unmistakable mark of Confucian influence.

During the Tokugawa period (1603-1867), the influence of Confucian ideas was not limited to the political life of the nation. The Confucian texts were widely read, and many members of both the upper and lower classes used the texts to learn to read. This resulted in Confucian concepts being ingrained in the thought of all classes. Some modern-day scholars have even argued that Confucian ideas inculcated in the merchant class something akin to what German sociologist Max Weber termed the Protestant work ethic. The presence of these values in Japanese economic life has been used to explain the tremendous economic growth that the nation experienced after 1868, the beginning of the Meiji period (1868-1912). In addition, some scholars have identified aspects of Confucian ideology that have continued to influence Japanese business relationships and organization in the post-World War II period.

Finally, Confucian ideology underlay the system of imperial government that developed after the fall of the Tokugawa shogunate. The bond of loyalty that was expected to exist between citizens, soldiers, and the emperor was most often defined in Confucian terms. Important documents such as the "Imperial Rescript on Education" and the "Imperial Rescript to Soldiers and Sailors" were masterworks of Confucian rhetoric.

The strength of Confucian thought in Japanese society weakened considerably in the twentieth century. The introduction of universal male suffrage in 1926 and the liberal reforms introduced by the United States after World War II weakened the Confucian influence on politics and law.

Matthew Penney

Further Reading

Aston, W. G., trans. *Nihongi: Chronicles of Japan from the Earliest Times to A.D. 697*. 1896. Reprint. Tokyo: Charles E. Tuttle, 1972. The standard translation of one of the earliest works of Japanese history. Provides the earliest extant account of the arrival of Confucian thought in Japan.

Confucius. *The Analects*. Translated by Arthur Waley. New York: Alfred A. Knopf, 2000. A famous translation of the original sayings of Confucius.

De Bary, William Theodore, et al., comps. *Sources of Japanese Tradition*. Vol. 1. 2d ed. New York: Columbia University Press, 2001. Contains complete reprints of the Seventeen Article Constitution as well as other important documents relating to early Japanese political life.

De Bary, William Theodore, and Tu Weiming, eds. *Confucianism and Human Rights*. New York: Columbia University Press, 1998. This work deals with Confucian thought in an international context with strong background material concerning the impact of Confucian thought on the Japanese tradition.

Sansom, George. *A History of Japan to 1334*. Vol. 1. Stanford, Calif.: Stanford University Press, 1958. Decades after its initial publication, the first volume of Sansom's three-volume study of Japanese history remains a detailed and authoritative work on the subject.

Tu Weiming, ed. *Confucian Traditions in East Asian Modernity: Moral Education and Economic Culture in Japan and the Four Mini-Dragons*. Cambridge, Mass.: Harvard University Press, 1996. Traces the impact of Confucian thought in Japan with a particular emphasis on the legacy that it has left on the modern period.

See also: 538-552: Buddhism Arrives in Japan; 593-604: Regency of Shōtoku Taishi; 1156-1192: Minamoto Yoritomo Becomes Shogun.

Related article in *Great Lives from History: The Middle Ages, 477-1453*: Shōtoku Taishi.

484
White Huns Raid India

The invasions of the White Huns, a Central Asian nomadic people, disrupted the Gupta Empire of northern and north-central India.

Locale: Northern India

Categories: Expansion and land acquisition; wars, uprisings, and civil unrest

Key Figures

Skanda Gupta (d. 467), Indian prince who rallied Gupta forces against the White Huns, r. c. 455-467

Toramana (fl. early sixth century), first king of the White Huns in India

Mihirakula (fl. mid-sixth century), son of Toramana

Summary of Event

To Western readers, the word "Huns" generally brings forth images of Attila and his nomadic raiders, sweeping westward from the Central Asian plains to ravage the Roman Empire in its latter years. However, in India, the term "Huns" or "Hūṇas" is often applied to another group of Central Asian nomads who troubled northern India during the fifth and sixth centuries, at roughly the same time as Belisarius was conquering the Western Empire for Justinian of Byzantium. Those Byzantines who knew about this invasion from Persian sources referred to them as Hephthalites, and the Chinese called them the Ye-Ta or Ye-Tai.

It is uncertain if the Huns who raided India are related to the Huns who raided the Roman Empire. Little of either people's language and culture has been preserved, and without the data for comparative linguistic and anthropological studies, scholars can offer only conjecture. Because both groups arose in the region of Central Asia now occupied by Kazakhstan and southern Siberia, it is possible that they sprang from a common cultural source, but the similarities between their names and their nomadic lifestyles may be pure coincidence. One particularly telling detail is the fact that the Huns who raided In-

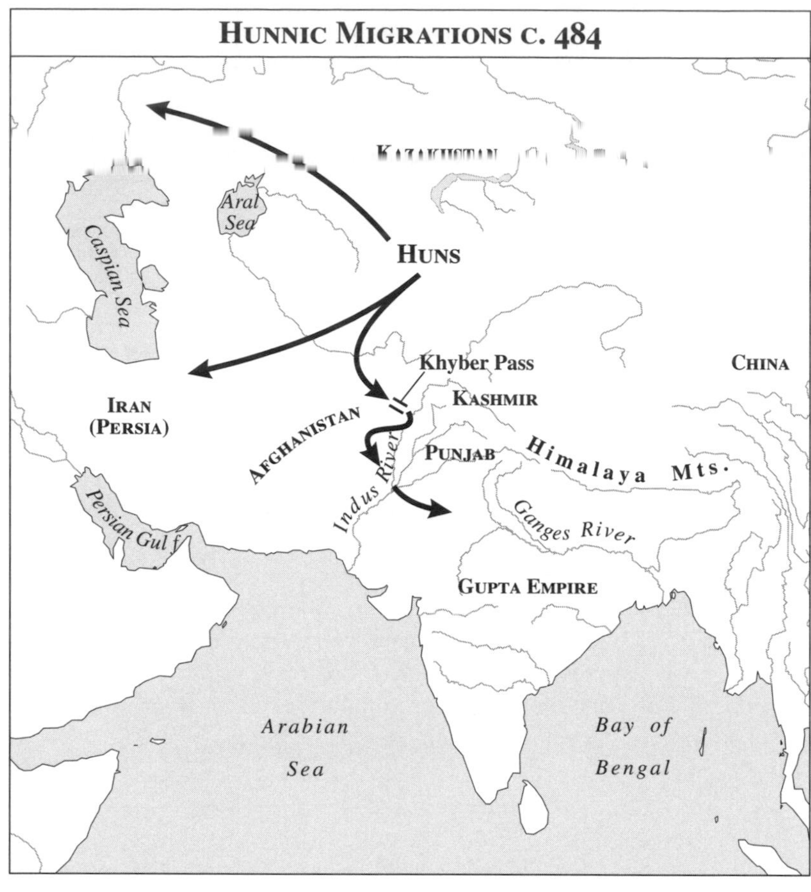

HUNNIC MIGRATIONS C. 484

dia are often referred to as the White Huns because their features were more European, without the strong epicanthic fold of the eye that marked many of the other Central Asian peoples. There are also references to their having unusually shaped heads, but this appears to have been the result of cradling, a practice of placing tight bands on the infant head so that it is forced to grow in a particular shape, rather than genetic differences.

The White Huns first invaded India near the end of the Gupta Empire (c. 312-c. 550) and are traditionally credited with having destroyed this empire. However, many modern historians have argued that there is ample evidence that the Gupta Empire was cracking from within as a result of factional struggle between various branches of the royal family and that the stress of the invasion only hastened an inevitable breakdown. As evidence, these historians point to the existence of various contradictory succession lists in the Gupta genealogies of the period, which suggest multiple rival claimants to the throne who may have engaged in wasteful competition or outright civil war. As a result, the invasion of the White Huns may have been more a matter of dividing and conquering than breaking a strong central state.

When the White Huns invaded Gupta-held territories, Skanda Gupta was able to rally the Gupta military forces for a time and hold the defenses. However, after his death, the situation deteriorated rapidly in the absence of strong leadership. In the manner typical of nomadic barbarians throughout the history of warfare before gunpowder, the White Huns ravaged every town and village they passed, destroying buildings and murdering or enslaving their inhabitants. The Gupta capital of Pataliputra, once a proud city, was depopulated and reduced to little more than a backwater village. By the middle of the sixth century, the Gupta kingdom had been reduced to a small area, and north and most of central India had fallen into Hunnish hands.

The kings of the White Huns are known primarily from inscriptions on monuments and from the coinage they ordered struck. The first king of the White Huns in India was Toramana, who lived during the early sixth century. Inscriptions bearing his name are found as far south as Eran (Madhya Pradesh), which indicate that his influence, if not his actual rule, was felt well into the subcontinent. His son Mihirakula apparently adopted some native Indian devotional practices, either alongside or in place of traditional nomadic religion. However, Buddhist traditions of the period record him as having been uncouth and cruel in his rule and warmaking habits, which indicate that he remained culturally a nomadic warrior.

By the end of the sixth century, native Indian leadership began to recover, and the White Huns were forced back north into Kashmir and Punjab. There they maintained a capital at Sakala (Sialkot, Pakistan). In time, they became assimilated and adopted sedentary agricultural patterns of life, losing their distinctive nomadic culture. Only the occasional trace of unusual religious or cultural practices among certain subcastes of the area indicated that they had descended from these invaders. However, there remained a break in the material culture of the area, and later historians would have to laboriously reconstruct the preinvasion history of the Guptas and other dynasties of the area without the aid of a continuing living tradition. Any semblance of continuity is an illusion of religious and political factors. The Brahman religious leaders had simply found it advantageous to their purposes to treat all the new aristocratic clans as though they were direct descendants of the Kḥatriyas (warrior caste) of the Vedic scriptures, whatever the truth of that particular group's social origin. In time the neologism Rājput, literally "king's son," became a synonym of the Vedic Kḥatriyas.

SIGNIFICANCE

The invasion of the White Huns put India in contact with Central Asian tribes from the area that is modern Kazakhstan. This led to cultural cross-fertilization between the two cultures as well as additional peaceful migrations of Central Asian peoples into the Indian subcontinent. For example, the Gurjaras of this period may be identified with the Khazars, a Central Asian and southern Siberian tribe that adopted a simplified form of Judaism rather than choose between Christianity and Islam. However, not all of the changes brought about by the White Huns were positive.

The invasions severely disrupted trade routes in the area and destroyed the income many northern Indian princes and merchant families had derived from it. Because of the direct and indirect effects of the invasion, many northern Indian tribes migrated to safer regions to the south, taking with them tribal customs that led to further social changes among the southern Indian peoples. The Rājput families and Kḥatriyas dynasties of central India traced their ancestry from the migration of these tribal chieftains, although for religious and political purposes they claimed descent from the Vedic Kḥatriyas classes.

—Leigh Husband Kimmel

FURTHER READING

Hiro, Dilip. *India*. London: Rough Guides, 2002. Although intended primarily as a travel guide, it provides excellent historical information on prominent sites, including a discussions of how history-changing events such as the invasion of the White Huns shaped the development of modern culture and society in India.

MacLeod, John. *The History of India*. Westport, Conn.: Greenwood Press, 2002. An overview of the history of India, including a bibliography for further research. Coverage of the period of the White Huns is primarily in terms of their effects on subsequent cultures and traditions of India.

Thapar, Romila. *Early India: From the Origins to A.D. 1300*. Berkeley: University of California Press, 2003. An overview of Indian history before the Mongol invasions, including information on the Guptas and the White Huns.

Watson, Francis. *India: A Concise History*. New York: Thames and Hudson, 2002. A good basic overview of Indian history, including this critical period in which the Gupta Empire gave way to the Central-Asian-influenced cultures of medieval India. Includes an excellent bibliography for further research.

Williams, Joanna Gottfried. *The Art of Gupta India: Empire and Province*. Princeton, N.J.: Princeton University Press, 1982. Although concentrating primarily on the art at the height of the Gupta period, it does include material on the close of the Gupta era and the influence of the White Huns.

SEE ALSO: 6th-8th centuries: Sogdians Dominate Central Asian Trade; 567-568: Sāsānians and Turks Defeat the White Huns; 740: Khazars Convert to Judaism.

496
BAPTISM OF CLOVIS

The baptism of Clovis facilitated the conversion of the pagan Germanic Franks, which eventually spread Catholicism into France and Germany.

LOCALE: France
CATEGORIES: Religion; government and politics

KEY FIGURES
Clovis (c. 466-511), king of the Franks, r. 481-511
Clotilda (c. 474-545), queen of the Franks, r. 493-511
Gregory of Tours (539-594), bishop of Tours, 573-594

SUMMARY OF EVENT

The conversion of Clovis to Christianity was one of the major events of the early Middle Ages and established a pivotal political and religious relationship between the Germanic tribe of the Franks and the Papacy. The Franks are central to much of early medieval history because they were the basis of the political and religious institutions and of the social and economic organization that distinguished the medieval world of Gaul, which became the geographic center of Charlemagne's empire and of the subsequent principalities and kingdoms of France and Germany.

The significance of Clovis's baptism was that he converted to the Nicene faith—the belief of Roman Catholicism and eastern Byzantine Orthodoxy. Most other Germanic tribes occupying the Western Roman Empire were followers of Arian Christianity. Arianism had been condemned as a heresy at the first ecumenical council in 325 because it denied the full humanity of Jesus. The Nicene faith proclaimed the Holy Trinity (Father, Son, and Holy Ghost) and declared Jesus to be both God and human. Germanic Arians included the Goths (both the Ostrogoths in Italy and the Visigoths in Spain), who were converted to Arianism by the missionary Ulfilas in the mid-fourth century; the Vandals in North Africa; the Lombards in Italy; and the Burgundians in southern Gaul. Clovis was the first important Germanic ruler to become Catholic. Others followed: The Visigoths under Recared became Catholic in 589; the Burgundians converted under Sigismund (r. 516-523); and the Lombards had a Catholic ruler, Liutprand (r. 712-744); but these groups lacked the political significance of the Franks.

In the fifth century, the Franks were probably a client state of the Romans. Frankish aid was critical in the Roman victory over the Huns in 451 near Orléans. Clovis's father, Childeric, was a protector of the Gallo-Roman population and the Catholic Church. Clovis succeeded his father in 481 and, although a pagan, continued his father's policies. This meant he sought to preserve friendly relations with and to seek the advice of the Church. During the 480's, Clovis extended his power into the kingdom of Soissons, defeating and killing Syagrius, the last Roman commander in Gaul. Until his death in 511, Clovis waged constant wars against the Armorican Celts in Brittany, the Thuringi in the lower Rhine, the Alamanni north of Trier, and the Burgundians.

The fundamental source for the conversion of Clovis is *Historia Francorum* (c. 594; *The History of the Franks*, 1927), written by Gregory of Tours a century after the event. According to Gregory, Clovis was a pagan and a plunderer of churches. Like any Germanic warrior, Clovis could be ruthless and violent. Gregory described Clovis as personally capable of splitting the head of an enemy or of anyone who demeaned his honor. Clovis worshiped Roman deities, such as Saturn, Jupiter, Mars, and Mercury. He also venerated various statues made of stone, wood, or metal, and he may have adhered to certain Celtic and Scandinavian deities as well as a sea god

GREGORY OF TOURS DESCRIBES CLOVIS'S CONVERSION

The queen [Clotilda] did not cease urging the king to acknowledge the true God and forsake idols, but all her efforts failed until at length a war broke out with the Alemanni. Then of necessity he was compelled to confess what hitherto he had wilfully denied. It happened that the two armies were in battle and there was great slaughter. The army of Clovis seemed about to be cut in pieces. Then the king raised his hands fervently toward the heavens and, breaking into tears, cried: "Jesus Christ, who Clotilde declares to be the son of the living God, . . . I now call upon thee, and I wish to believe in thee, especially that I may escape my enemies." When he had offered this prayer the Alemanni turned their backs and began to flee. . . . Clovis returned in peace to his kingdom and told the queen how he had won the victory by calling on the name of Christ.

Source: Gregory of Tours, *The History of the Franks*, quoted in *A Source Book of Mediæval History*, edited by Frederic Austin Ogg (New York: American Book Company, 1908), p. 53.

that was part man, beast, and bull. Since the powerful Burgundians, Ostrogoths, and Visigoths were all Arian, it is possible that Clovis may have considered converting to Arianism. His Burgundian wife, Clotilda, was Catholic, however, and had urged him to accept the Nicene faith. To his wife's entreaties, Clovis responded that Jesus was a god who could do nothing; perhaps Jesus was not even a god at all.

Clotilda had their infant son baptized, but he died while still in his baptismal robes. Angry, Clovis blamed the Christian god for his son's death. To his surprise, Clotilda accepted it and tried to assure Clovis that the boy was now in heaven. It was a difficult concept for Clovis to understand. A second son, Chlodomer, was born and baptized and also became ill. This only further convinced Clovis of the ineffectiveness of the Christian god, but the child recovered because of Clotilda's prayers, according to Gregory.

Clovis's war with the Alamanni had decimated both armies. In desperation Clovis now turned to Christ, calling on him to aid the Franks in battle. Only with victory, as a sign and proof of the existence and favor of Christ, would Clovis accept baptism. The Franks won the Battle of Tolbac, and Clovis informed Clotilda that he would be baptized. With the urging of Clotilda, Clovis received secret religious instruction from the bishop Remigius of Reims. Secrecy was important because Clovis was not sure of the support of his troops for such a change. Gregory glossed over the difficulty by having the Frankish leaders already willing to accept their own and the king's baptism. On Christmas Day in 496 (though 498 or even 506 is possible), Clovis was baptized in Reims by Bishop Remigius. Gregory portrayed Remigius as a learned and holy man who performed miracles and even raised a man from the dead, thereby underscoring the centrality of the Resurrection to Christianity. Three thousand Frankish warriors followed the example of their king and were baptized. Clovis affirmed the Nicene creed by accepting the Holy Trinity and by marking the holy chrism (oil) with the sign of the cross. A sister, Albofled, was also baptized. Although she died soon after, Clovis's faith held. A second sister later converted from Arianism.

The Baptism of Clovis is depicted in this woodcut from Mirouer Historial de France, *printed in Paris by Galliot du Pré in 1516.* (Frederick Ungar Publishing Co.)

Clovis's conversion made the cult of Saint Martin of Tours a central part of the religious faith of the Franks. Born around the year 316 in Pannonia (Hungary), Martin was a Roman soldier who gave half of his cloak to a beggar. His remaining half became a sacred relic of Frankish kings. Martin was in the tradition of ascetic hermits, a holy man who attracted followers and preached in central and western Gaul. In 371, he was made bishop of Tours, and though he continued to live in a solitary cell, he did travel, even as far as Rome, to defend Orthodoxy. At first the cult and monasticism of Martin did not extend much beyond the Loire River, yet Clovis was attracted to this soldier who had become an ascetic, a defender of the Nicene faith, and an administrator of a bishopric. Because of Clovis, the cult of Martin spread to Paris, Chartres,

Rouen, and other cities throughout the Frankish lands. In Gregory's *History of the Franks*, Martin and Clovis are the two pivotal figures defining Christianity in Frankish Gaul—France and Germany (now). Clovis founded the Church of the Apostles in Paris, later called Sainte-Geneviève.

SIGNIFICANCE

For Gregory, Clovis was another Constantine the Great, a pagan warrior who converted to the true faith and brought that faith to his people. As a Catholic, Clovis could also justify new wars against the heretical Arian Burgundians and Goths in Gaul. Although Gregory chronicled the bloody events and brutality of Clovis, which included the elimination of family rivals and even his expressed regret that he no longer had living relatives to kill, he still described Clovis as one who did what was pleasing to God, because Catholicism had become the official faith of the Franks.

Gregory does imply that Clovis's faith rested on the belief that Jesus was a powerful god who could aid the Franks in battle. It is not even certain whether Clovis became a strict monotheist. The consequences of the conversion, however, were immense. Unlike other Arian Germanic tribes, who stood apart from the indigenous Catholic populace, the Franks and the Gallo-Romans were not separated by religion. This allowed for a greater assimilation between the two peoples. Clovis's wars could also marshal the support of the Gallo-Roman aristocracy, particularly of those who remained under Arian domination. The conversion had therefore an important political dimension in that it was part of Clovis's political challenge against the Burgundians and the Visigoths at Toulouse.

It also helped Clovis obtain the support of the Byzantine emperor Anastasius, whose fleets prevented the Ostrogoths from aiding the Visigoths in their conflict with the Franks. Anastasius also bestowed on Clovis the honorific title of consul. Clovis probably hoped for an imperial title, because he is described as having appeared at the Cathedral of Saint Martin of Tours dressed in purple and wearing a crown. The conversion permitted a closer political and working relationship with the Merovingian bishops, many of whom were of noble birth and whose families controlled bishoprics such as Paris, Tours, and Sens.

—*Lawrence N. Langer*

FURTHER READING

Brown, Peter. "Relics and Social Status in the Age of Gregory of Tours." In *Society and the Holy in Late Antiquity*. Berkeley: University of California Press, 1982. An important analysis of religious attitudes among the Franks.

Fletcher, R. A. *The Barbarian Conversion: From Paganism to Christianity*. Berkeley: University of California Press, 1999. Looks at the history of the development of Christianity in pagan Europe during the time of Clovis.

Geary, Patrick. *Before France and Germany*. New York: Oxford University Press, 1988. A study of society in Merovingian Gaul.

Gregory of Tours. *The History of the Franks*. Translated by L. Thorpe. New York: Penguin Books, 1974. The fundamental source for the reign of Clovis.

MacMullen, Ramsay. *Christianity and Paganism in the Fourth to Eighth Centuries*. New Haven, Conn.: Yale University Press, 1997. Surveys the relationship between paganism and the Christian world in the time of Clovis.

Wallace-Hadrill, J. M. *The Frankish Church*. New York: Oxford University Press, 1983. An important study of the Frankish church.

_______. *The Long-Haired Kings*. New York: Barnes and Noble Books, 1962. The standard study of early Frankish history.

SEE ALSO: February 2, 506: Alaric II Drafts the *Breviarum Alarici*; 635-800: Founding of Lindisfarne and Creation of the *Book of Kells*; 735: Christianity Is Introduced into Germany.

RELATED ARTICLES in *Great Lives from History: The Middle Ages, 477-1453*: Charlemagne; Saint Clotilda; Fredegunde; Gregory of Tours.

c. 500-1000
RISE OF SWAHILI CULTURES

The rise of Swahili cultures demonstrates an important historical development on the African continent, which also had implications for global maritime trade and commerce. It demonstrated the remarkable capacity of indigenous African cultures to incorporate elements from Islam while maintaining the dynamism of traditional practices.

LOCALE: East African coast and adjacent islands
CATEGORIES: Cultural and intellectual history; expansion and land acquisition; trade and commerce

KEY FIGURE

ʿAbd al-Malik (c. 646-705), caliph, ruled East African Swahili coast, r. 685-705

SUMMARY OF EVENT

The term "Swahili" derives from the Arabic word *sawāḥil* (the plural of *sāḥil*, which means coast). Though it is of Arabic etymological moorings, Swahili does not imply Arabic in its roots. Sayyid Hurreiz, a Swahili scholar, contends that Swahili cultures are dynamic and that Swahili culture in Zanzibar and Kilwa Kisiwani may be different from that in Mwanza and the Comoros Islands, but is African at its roots. Just as with all cultures that have evolved through mutual exchange and interaction with other cultures, Swahili culture is no exception.

The Swahili coast traverses the East African coast and the surrounding islands and extends from Mogadishu in Somalia in the north to Cape Delgado in Mozambique in the south, covering many archipelagos and islands in the Indian Ocean, including the Comoros and Lamu archipelagos, and the islands of Mombasa, Pemba, Zanzibar, Mafia, and Kirimba.

From some of the earliest records of human civilization, the Swahili coast has featured importantly in history. Solomon from the ancient Hebrew tradition was said to have dispatched vessels to the Swahili coast. Trade in pottery, cloth, and iron implements and commercial exchanges with the nations of Arabia and India made the Swahili coast one of the most prominent geographical coastlines in the world. In the seventh century, Swahilis traded with China.

Following research conducted by coastal archaeologists in the 1980's, the towns of Shanga and Manda were unearthed and revealed a community that thrived from 700 to 1400. Shanga, divided into numerous neighborhoods called *mitaa*, was originally founded as a fishing and agricultural village and eventually was transformed into a maritime metropolis with trading ties with the Arab and Asian world. Africans on the East African coast traded ivory and tortoise shell for iron goods, perhaps as early as the second or third centuries. The heart-shaped iron hoe and the drum-type bellows are just two examples of such iron implements. The mythological work, *Periphus Maris Erythraei* (*The Periphus of the Erythraean Sea*, 1912), a work of mythology by an unknown Greek writer of the first century, described trade between the Greeks and Romans and Arabs in the north, and Africans on the East African coast. Though such accounts are not historically reliable, they do point to a flourishing exchange of cultures between East Africans and other peoples.

In direct challenge to the erstwhile Eurocentric view that portrayed Swahili civilization as an essential product of its merging with Persian and Arab cultures, archaeologists have now conceded that the presence of sun-dried clay and timber homes along the Swahili coast denotes continuity with such residential styles in other parts of Africa, which, therefore, substantiates an unequivocal African origin. Some archaeologists have insisted that the coral or clay structures do not point to an African origin because the Africans were nomadic. However, Swahili scholar Richard Wilding has demonstrated that the coastal cultures and those of the hinterland were not radically disparate in character, but rather had much in common. Findings that include ceramic motifs and similar cooking vessels, for example, establish this connection.

Wilding argues that the original Swahili coastal residents were Cushitic pastoralists and foragers and that Bantu-speaking groups merged with these pastoralists at a later period. Similarly, Sayyid Hurreiz maintains that these pastoralists migrated southward from Abyssinia (now Ethiopia) and the Nile Valley and mixed with the Bantu people on the lower East African coast whose language was Kingozi. It was the Kingozi culture and language that provided the basis of Swahili language and culture. Another theory suggests that the inhabitants of Pate Island off the East African coast are the early Swahili or proto-Swahili, who may have been speakers of proto-Sam, an African language considered to be the parent tongue of the Boni, Somali, and Rendille in East Africa.

Shungwaya was the original home of the Swahili. Two other known towns were established before 800, namely Rhapta and Kanbalu, the former located in or near the Rufiji Delta below Somalia. Around 800, the language known today as Swahili began to be spoken and people moved into Swahili settlements called *mji*.

The Swahili coast was inhabited by a diverse population, with pastoralists and agriculturists living on the northern coast in what is now Tana Delta and the Lamu archipelago and sedentary farmers and ironworkers living on the southern coast. These communities lived in interdependent economic and social relations with each other and subsequently developed the Swahili culture.

The period 300 to 1000 was a time of intense international trade along the Swahili coast. Around the seventh century, Arab communities settled in East Africa during the reign of the Islamic caliph ʿAbd al-Malik. The *Khabar al-Lamu* (*A Chronicle of Lamu*, appearing in *Bantu Studies*, vol. 12, no. 1, 1938) and other sources, not factually reliable in every manner because they are based on the fluidity of oral tradition, describe these Arab Islamic settlements. Stories abound about Arabs fleeing political and religious persecution in the Arabian peninsula, but the veracity of these accounts is difficult to confirm.

Felix Chami, a Tanzanian archaeologist, divides this period into the Azanian phase—from 300 to 600—and the Zanjian phase—from 600 to 1000. The term *zanj*, used by Arab marine traders, referred to "the land of black people." Entrepreneurial activity boomed during this period, with expanding settlements and increased imports of pottery, including ceramics from Iran, China, India, and Egypt. The sea was key in the development of Swahili society. Settlements were built on beaches or small inlets adjacent to the sea.

International cultural influences were inevitable, and the design and look of Swahili pottery changed, evidenced by findings at Tana. During the Zanjian phase, the influx of Middle Eastern and Indian styles prominently modified existing Swahili pottery design. During the Azanian phase, houses were relatively small in size and were constructed of sun-dried clay and palm fronds. People hunted game, fished, kept livestock, cultivated cereals, traded, and engaged in local and regional commerce and exchange.

Canoes and sewn planked boats were used for fishing, and anglers used hooks and lines, harpoons, nets, and basket traps. Mostly shellfish and turtles were caught. The Swahili farmed extensively, cultivating indigenous crops such as sorghum, millet, elewusine, rice, peas, beans, sugarcane, coconuts, bananas, and taro from Southeast Asia. They cultivated fields, planted seeds with sticks, weeded with hoes, and harvested crops, threshing and winnowing grain. They raised chickens and some livestock such as cattle, goats, and sheep.

Iron-smelting was another distinctive feature of this time period. Iron slags have been found at Kilwa Kisiwani, Manda, Shanga, Gedi, and Ungwana. The Swahili produced their own fishhooks, spearheads, and arrowheads and probably their own agricultural implements. They may have manufactured cotton cloth and carved pots in a unifying cultural style along the coast, trading these along with numerous other goods with other mariners from Arabia and Persia in the north and India and China in the east.

SIGNIFICANCE

Swahili peoples developed into a prosperous commercial society over the centuries as traders, farmers, and foragers all forged a common Swahili identity. The religious and cultural evolution evidenced in the Swahili culture of the Zanjian phase has come to define the very complex character of African Islam today.

The development and expansion of Swahili cultures and language furnish models of indigenous African technical and economic ingenuity from which other cultures of the period benefited and from which coastal cultures of Africa can learn today.

—*Julian E. Kunnie*

FURTHER READING

Allen, Jim. "Swahili History Revisited." Seminar Paper No. 76, Institute of African Studies, University of Nairobi, 1977. A paper that explores the debates surrounding Swahili origins.

Horton, Mark, and John Middleton. *The Swahili: The Social Landscape of a Mercantile Society*. Malden, Mass.: Blackwell, 2000. Presents a survey of Swahili society and its tradition of mercantilism and trade. Chapters on Swahili origins, Islam, the East African coast and the Indian Ocean, urbanism, governance, and more. Maps, bibliography, index.

Hurreiz, Sayyid. "Origins, Foundations, and Evolution of Swahili Culture." In *Distinctive Characteristics and Common Features of African Cultural Areas South of the Sahara*. Paris: UNESCO, 1985. This article provides a balanced account of the origins and development of Swahili culture from the perspective of a Swahili scholar.

Khalid, Abdallah. *The Liberation of Swahili from European Appropriation*. Nairobi, Kenya: East African Literature Bureau, 1977. This work offers an important critique of the Eurocentric standardization of Swahili language and culture.

Kusimba, Chapurukha M. *The Rise and Fall of Swahili States*. Walnut Creek, Calif.: AltaMira Press, 1999. A foundational and informative text for understanding the various arguments regarding the origins of Swahili states and the development of Swahili cultures.

Middleton, John. *The World of the Swahili: An African Mercantile Civilization*. New Haven, Conn.: Yale University Press, 1992. This book describes the development of Swahili culture into a formidable maritime civilization, with many of the cultural complexities emergent from such a development.

Nurse, Derek, and Thomas Spear. *The Swahili: Reconstructing the History and Language of an African Society, 800-1500*. Philadelphia: University of Pennsylvania Press, 1985. An important text that furnishes a comprehensive account of the origins, early development, and evolution of Swahili civilization to the sixteenth century.

Pearson, Michael N. *Port Cities and Intruders: The Swahili Coast, India, and Portugal in the Early Modern Era*. Baltimore: John Hopkins University Press, 1998. A discussion of the major economic, social, and religious interchange that took place on the Swahili coast and how Portugal's intrusion in the fifteenth century affected that interchange. Maps, bibliography, index.

Rosander, Eva Evers, and David Westerlund, eds. *African Islam and Islam in Africa: Encounters Between Sufis and Islamists*. Athens: Ohio University Press, 1997. Examines the effects of Islam in Africa. Includes the chapter, "Translations of the Quʾrān into Swahili, and Contemporary Islamic Revival in East Africa," by Justo Lacunza-Balda. Bibliography, index.

Were, Gideon S., and Derek Wilson. *East Africa Through a Thousand Years: A History of the Years A.D. 1000 to the Present Day*. New York: Africana, 1987. The introductory chapters of this book are informative for comprehending the foundations of Swahili civilization and culture.

Wilding, Richard. *The Shorefolk: Aspects of the Early Development of Swahili Communities*. Mobasa, Kenya, 1987. A concise overview by one of the major historians and archaeologists of Swahili and East African cultures.

See also: 630-711: Islam Expands Throughout North Africa; c. 1100: Origins of Swahili in Its Written Form; 12th century: Coins Are Minted on the Swahili Coast; 12th century: Trading Center of Kilwa Kisiwani Is Founded; 1270-1285: Yekuno Amlak Founds the Solomonid Dynasty; 1333: Kilwa Kisiwani Begins Economic and Historical Decline.

Related articles in *Great Lives from History: The Middle Ages, 477-1453*: ʿAbd al-Malik; al-Idrīsī; al-Masʿūdī.

c. 500-1000
Tiwanaku Civilization Flourishes in Andean Highlands

The Tiwanaku civilization became the second great empire in the Andean highlands, flourishing because of its unique agricultural methods, which adapted to extremely cold weather, and because its political system sought to unify and incorporate rather than transform or remake outlying territories.

Locale: Lake Titicaca basin, border of Peru and Bolivia, South America

Categories: Religion; cultural and intellectual history; expansion and land acquisition

Summary of Event

Tiwanaku, located more than 12,500 feet (3,810 meters) above sea level in the Central Andes, was the capital of a civilization situated at the highest elevation of any world empire for more than five hundred years. Its origins lie in the Early Intermediate period, from c. 200 B.C.E. to c. 200 C.E. (also named Tiwanaku phases I, II, and III). During this period, Tiwanaku began as one of several small temple dominions, political clusters that united agropastoral communities around Lake Titicaca. Subsistence was based on the cultivation of tubers (potato, oca, ullucu) and native grains (quinoa, cañihua), supplemented with meat from herds of llamas and alpacas and fish and waterfowl. Villagers lived in rectangular and circular houses of stone set in mud mortar, with thatched roofs.

The Pajano religious tradition dominated the area, with a variety of local religious practices and cosmologies, but during the Early Intermediate period, there was a syncretic convergence into a more uniform, standardized religious tradition, with particular emphasis on dualism, metamorphosis, and fundamentalism, known as Yaya-Mama. Religious observances were centralized in the larger villages, where ritual structures included platform mounds, sunken rectangular temples, and associated plazas with stone monoliths, sculptures, and plaques depicting the deities.

During this period, there was additional investment in landscape capital, especially the increased construction of raised fields and canals. The canals were built either parallel or at right angles to the sun's path, resulting in the maximum capture of solar energy, which, when radiated at night, protected the fields from frost and freeze losses because of the city's high elevation. The canals also mitigated the impact of both excessive rainfall and drought, greatly reducing agricultural risk.

By the latter half of the Early Intermediate period (c. 200-c. 600), Tiwanaku was flourishing. Smaller local groups began coalescing into a few hierarchical settlement clusters in the Tiwanaku region. At Tiwanaku itself, a subterranean temple was built, along with the central sunken courtyard of the Kalasasaya temple. The nearby village of Iwawe was established as a lake port, principally for the importation of andesite for construction purposes. In the adjacent pampa areas, intensive farming became more important, and large quantities of basalt hoes were being imported. By the end of the Late Formative period from about 200-500 and overlapping with the Early Intermediate, (also called Tiwanaku phases I-III), Tiwanaku had emerged as the area's primary center and had cemented its control over the religious and political spheres enough to begin its expansion out of its local valley.

The more specific time period called Tiwanaku IV (c. 500-c. 800), the first period of Tiwanaku hegemony over surrounding areas, is marked by the promotion of a state suite of ideologies, sacred symbols that served as markers of status and identity through a kind of theater state, and reciprocal relations between the elites and local groups, in which direct control of production (such as craft fabrication and agricultural activities) remained in the hands of a nested hierarchy of local groups integrated into reciprocal state obligations through elaborate feasting practices.

The theater state was centered on a series of grandiloquent public temples in the heart of the city, most of which were enclosed within a large, rectangular, moated precinct. Tiwanaku was a planned city, with its sewer system, roads, entry gates, and ritual structures laid out along cardinal axes. The architecture was aligned within a few degrees of the cardinal directions (the north-south axis usually 6 to 11 degrees east of true north), with major doorways, ramps, and entrances to these temples on an east-west axis aligned with the sun's path. The buildings displayed megalithic construction, employing stones up to 131 tons (119 metric tons) in weight. Because of the lack of mortar, large stones were held in place by gravity or secured by copper and bronze clamps set in drilled holes. Floors were constructed of red, green, or other deliberately colored clays, and walls show remnants of polychrome murals.

Images of the deities were on wall plaques and massive stone stelae up to 24 feet (7.3 meters) high. Some stelae show evidence of being covered with gold leaf and multicolored painting. The priests communed with the gods with the help of hallucinogenic drugs. One of the most typical Tiwanaku artifact assemblages is the hallucinogenic complex, comprising carved stone mortars and pestles, stone bowls and cups, wooden snuff trays, pottery incensarios and bowls, wooden and bone snuff tubes and spoons, specialized textiles, and gold and ceramic keros, all decorated with sacred images. Control of symbolic knowledge was more important than control of resources.

Politically, Tiwanaku was more an incorporating than a transforming polity. During Tiwanaku IV, the political organization was a loosely centralized, segmentary state, built on a nested hierarchy of local territorial segments called ayllus. Tiwanaku was an archaic state of limited means that carefully expanded into a few key strategic areas, beginning c. 600-650. It employed multiple strategies to integrate state and local power as the situation mandated, using both direct and indirect mechanisms for political control, employing federation, annexation, colonization, conquest, ports of trade, or locally inserted *mitmaqkuna* groups. Areas of direct control included the establishment of new sites, state intensification of agricultural production, formalization of road systems, resettlement of major portions of the population, and specialization of production, while areas of indirect control exhibited a variety of other policies utilized to co-opt local elites or secure mutual political benefit. Militarism seems to have been little employed; there are no known fortifications of Tiwanaku culture, and illustrations of warriors are rare.

The economy appears to have been based primarily on staple finance, rather than wealth. There was no apparent merchant class, and during Tiwanaku IV, there is little evidence of top-down managed state production. The city seemed to be composed initially of small multiethnic neighborhoods, swollen at periods by massive numbers of visiting pilgrims. Production was a cottage industry, rather than state organized, controlled by the household or ayllu. The cottage industries included both fancy ceremonial ceramics and quotidian daily wares; lithic workshops in which obsidian arrowheads and basalt hoes were produced; lapidary areas in which sodalite, turquoise, and other decorated items were fabricated; and possibly areas in which metal items were produced, including the tin and ternary nickel-tin bronzes that first appeared in the Andes during the Tiwanaku period. The limited distribution of these materials outside of Tiwanaku, as well as their extremely standardized forms, suggests that even though they were crafted in residential compounds, distribution was controlled by elite groups.

The relationship between elites and commoners was of reciprocal obligation. Evidence for reciprocity comes from the large quantity of serving dishes, storage jars, and refuse found near the major theater-state temples associated with the feasting events, and the evidence is supported by the fact that corn rose suddenly in importance at Tiwanaku. Corn generally cannot be grown at this altitude, but it is the main ingredient in chicha (a beer made from fermented corn), a critical component of Andean feasting events.

The end of Tiwanaku IV was marked by increasing status differences and social hierarchies. There was a gradual fragmentation and reorganization of the socioeconomic base. Early Tiwanaku V (800-1000) was typified by a period of sociopolitical, economic, and ideological consolidation and was marked by a series of massive urban renewal projects. Large sectors of both the ceremonial core and the residential zones were razed, with new structure types built in their place. Late Tiwanaku V (1000-1150) was a long phase of environmental crisis, political disintegration, and settlement dispersal.

Significance

The initial Tiwanaku state rose because of its laissez-faire political approach, which resulted in the creation of a polity that survived for an exceptionally long period. The shift in strategies in Tiwanaku V, around 1000, to seizing more direct control over certain regions, transforming their relationships from alliance or federation into state-administered provinces, began its demise. The Tiwanaku V political approach became openly exploitive and thus onerous to the subject populations. In Late Tiwanaku V, environmental conditions deteriorated, exacerbated by a severe long-term drought. Political allegiances and control slowly eroded; gradually many areas dropped their allegiances or linkages with the Tiwanaku state. The final collapse of Tiwanaku was both a cultural revolution that resulted in the formation of an entire new set of sociopolitical alliances and a corresponding new set of agropastoral productive strategies; it was as much the result of sociopolitical fragmentation as it was of environmental determinism.

—David L. Browman

Further Reading

Albarracin-Jordan, Juan. "Tiwanaku Settlement System." *Latin American Antiquity* 7 (1996): 183-210. Summary of the details of the Tiwanaku settlement system from the author's doctoral dissertation, supplemented by further work in his Bolivian homeland.

Bermann, Marc. "Domestic Life and Vertical Integration in the Tiwanaku Heartland." *Latin American Antiquity* 8 (1997): 93-112. Discussion of the development of secondary political centers in the hinterlands by the Tiwanaku polity and their relationship to the capital city.

Browman, David. "Political Institutional Factors Contributing to the Integration of the Tiwanaku State." In *Emergence and Change in Early Urban Societies*, edited by Linda Manzanilla. New York: Plenum Press, 1997. Discussion of the variety of different political strategies the Tiwanaku peoples adopted in order to control access to resources and markets.

Janusek, John. "Craft and Local Power: Embedded Specialization in Tiwanaku Cities." *Latin American Antiquity* 10 (1999): 107-131. Discussion of the various attached specialists and independent specialists found in Tiwanaku, and their socio-political integration in the state.

_______. "Out of Many, One: Style and Social Boundaries in Tiwanaku." *Latin American Antiquity* 13 (2002): 35-61. Discussion of the various political strategies that the Tiwanaku peoples employed in statecraft.

Kolata, Alan. *Tiwanaku: Portrait of an Andean Civilization*. Cambridge, Mass.: Blackwell, 1993. Summary of Tiwanaku from one of the major American excavators at the site.

Kolata, Alan, ed. *Agroecology*. Vol. 1 in *Tiwanaku and Its Hinterland: Archaeology and Paleoecology of an Andean Civilization*. Washington, D.C.: Smithsonian Institution Press, 1996. An important collection of papers that describe the ecological foundations of Tiwanaku civilization.

_______. *Urban and Rural Ecology*. Vol. 2 in *Tiwanaku and Its Hinterland: Archaeology and Paleoecology of an Andean Civilization*. Washington, D.C.: Smithsonian Institution Press, 2002. A collection of papers on the archaeology of Tiwanaku.

Moseley, Michael E. *The Incas and Their Ancestors: The Archaeology of Peru*. Rev. ed. New York: Thames and Hudson, 2001. A very useful synthesis of Andean prehistory.

Stanish, Charles. *Ancient Titicaca: The Evolution of Complex Society in Southern Peru and Northern Bolivia*. Berkeley: University of California Press, 2003. An ambitious overview of the rise of civilization around Lake Titicaca. Chapter 8 focuses on Tiwanaku, but the previous chapters are also useful in explaining the culture's historical context.

_______. "Tiwanaku Political Economy." In *Andean Archaeology I: Variations in Sociopolitical Organization*, edited by Helaine Silverman and William Isbell. New York: Kluwer Academic, 2002. Discussion of Tiwanaku political economy, as it was integrated into the broader regional context of socioeconomic contexts of the South-Central Andes.

SEE ALSO: After 850: Foundation of Chan Chan; c. 1000: Collapse of the Huari and Tiwanaku Civilizations; c. 1200-1230: Manco Capac Founds the Inca State.

6th-8th centuries

SOGDIANS DOMINATE CENTRAL ASIAN TRADE

The Sogdians, a group with a Persian culture and language, dominated Central Asian trade for more than two centuries. Their influence waned only after the conversion of the area to Islam in about 750. As Sogdian merchants plied their trade along the Silk Road, the Sogdian language developed into the common tongue among traders along the entire route.

LOCALE: Central Asia between the Zaravshan and Kashka-Darya River Valleys (now southern Uzbekistan and western Tajikistan)

CATEGORIES: Economics; trade and commerce

SUMMARY OF EVENT

The eastern and western sides of the Asian continent were connected by a series of trade routes known as the Silk Road, beginning in about 138 B.C.E. The term Silk Road is somewhat misleading in that there was no single route. The trade routes across Asia developed several branches that passed through various oases. Branches led south to India, and a northern route led to the Caspian and Black Seas and ended at Byzantium (now Istanbul). Because the northern route was considered more dangerous and expensive to traverse, much of the silk trade traveled by the middle route, which passed through the Persian Gulf and Euphrates Valley and ended in such cities as Damascus. However, no cities were more important than those of the Sogdian region.

The Sogdian civilization in what is now southern Uzbekistan and western Tajikistan was well established by the time of Alexander the Great's conquest of Central Asia in 328 B.C.E. and was apparently a subject of the kingdom of Darius the Great in 485 B.C.E. In 568 C.E., Sogdiana came under control of the Turks. Under Turkish rule, Sogdiana was essentially independent. Sogdiana, basically an oasis culture, was the point at which east, west, and south Asia met. As a result, various cultures left their imprint on Sogdian culture. Sogdiana was centrally situated between the northern and southern routes of the Silk Road and was an ideal location for traders and suppliers to the great caravans. As a result, the various oases became wealthy communities and were usually well stocked with luxury items from both Europe and China. The greatest Sogdian cities were Samarqand and Bukhara. It has been said that the Sogdians were good at commerce, loved profits, and were never reluctant to travel to any country where a profit could be made.

Because of their location, the Sogdians became great merchants who spread trade goods, ideas, language, and traditions throughout the cultures of Asia. One writer described them as "cultural bees." Even before Samarqand and Bukhara were founded, the Sogdians were active in Silk Road caravans. The Sogdian merchants adopted Buddhism and spread the Buddha's teaching along the Silk Road and throughout China. The merchants also exported cultural aspects such as Sogdian music and dance to China. In return, the merchants brought back from China the technology of paper production. Because of the large number of Sogdian merchants on the route, the Sogdian language became the common language all along the Silk Road, and the Sogdian alphabet was incorporated into later alphabets in this area.

Sogdian colonies and trade communities, often numbering more than a thousand individuals, were widespread throughout Central Asia, even in much of China. The Sogdians in China often adopted Chinese names.

Sogdian trade communities also stretched as far south as modern Sri Lanka and parts of India and as far north as the Ukraine and Mongolia. Individuals who lived in these communities worked largely in trade-related activities in a grand network of Sogdian merchants. In some cases, particularly in China, the Sogdians were appointed to official government positions overseeing the administration of foreign merchants. By the end of the eighth century, following the takeover of Sogdiana by the Arabs, these alien Sogdians began losing their recognizable identity and were absorbed into local society in the countries in which they were living.

During the Tang Dynasty (T'ang; 618-907), the Chinese defeated the Turks, and Sogdiana came under Chinese control, although the region stayed largely independent. Because of the importance of the region, the Chinese protected Sogdian trade. From 650 to 675, Sogdiana was essentially a protectorate of the Chinese, although the Turks also considered at least parts of the region as subject to their rule because the ruler of Samarqand had married a Turkish woman related to the khan. At that time, Samarqand, the capital, witnessed a vast expansion of trade, as evidenced by the quantity of coins that have survived to the present day. The Sogdian merchants dominated the Silk Road and what was sometimes called the "fur road" north to the Urals. Trade items, which have been discovered throughout Central Asia and China, included many silver and golden vessels crafted in Sogdiana in the seventh century. The Sogdians maintained favorable relationships with both the Turks and Chinese, both of whom considered them to be their subjects.

One indication of the wealth of the people, and perhaps their artistry, is the number of murals on the walls of homes. Russian archaeologists who excavated the city of Pendzhikent, located about 40 miles (64 kilometers) from the capital of Samarqand, found that at least a third of the homes had murals on the walls and carved statues, indicating a high level of wealth. Most houses were two or three stories in height and had many rooms. The murals depicted knights, holiday entertainment, nobles sitting at banquets, and hunters chasing their prey on horseback or atop elephants. The murals essentially showed a society that was cosmopolitan and affluent. Other sources indicate that the land was fertile and that horses were a major agricultural product. Many of these horses subsequently ended up in China.

During the mid-600's, the rise of Islam led to the increasing dominance of the Muslims in the Central Asian trade routes. Islamic law became dominant, and favorable tax rates and other concessions were given to Islamic traders. Between 706 and 712, Arabs under the Umayyad Dynasty took over the region, and the local rulers became servants of the Arabs. Various uprisings in the Sogdian city-states prolonged the Arab takeover. Some Sogdian villages and cities were abandoned or destroyed during the change in power. By about 750, the influence of the Sogdians had waned because of the wide conversion to Islam. Part of the reason for the Sogdians' vulnerability to the Arabs was their weak system of government. Although the people were wealthy and there was a highly developed economy, each city was essentially a city-state with its own government. There was no centralized government beyond that of the city-state.

Mud houses along a road in Afghanistan near the old trade routes, about thirty miles south of Samarqand, Uzbekistan. (Hulton|Archive by Getty Images)

SIGNIFICANCE

Even Sogdians who were not traders benefited from the proximity of trade. Sogdian artisans were admired for their craftsmanship and blend of eastern and western mo-

THE SILK ROAD: MAIN ROUTES

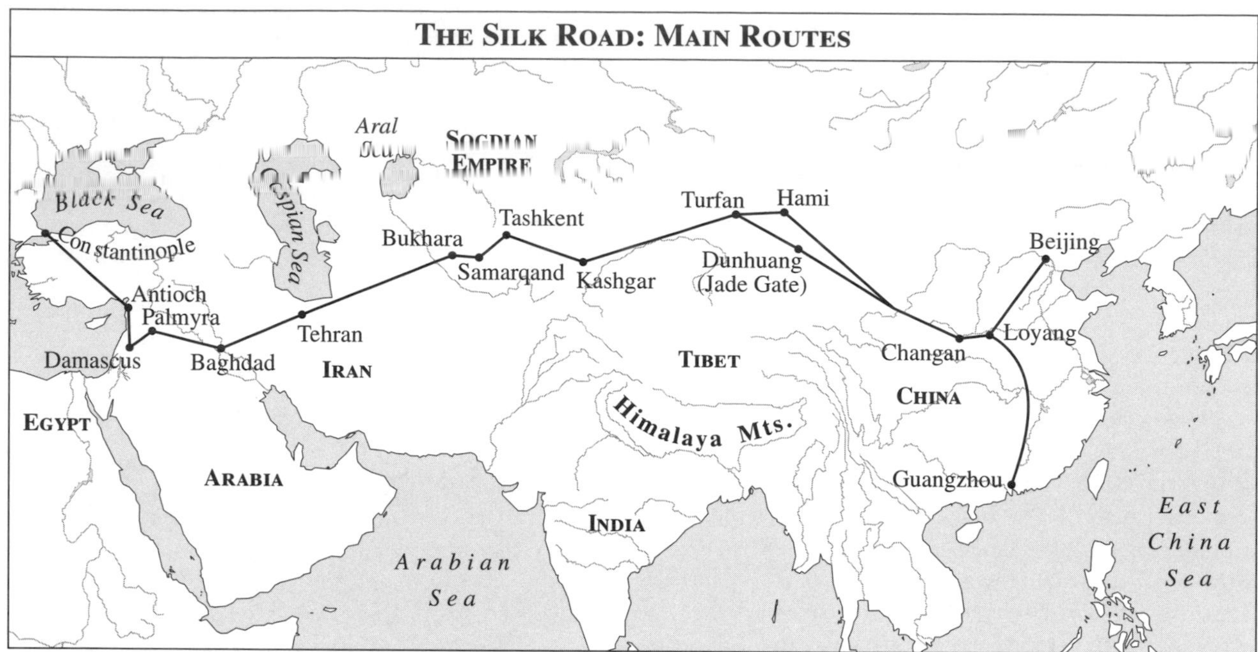

tifs. Silk weaving became a major industry, with the raw material being brought from China by the Sogdian merchants. Sogdian silk-weaving techniques were far superior to those of the Chinese, and Sogdian woven products were in great demand at the Tang court. Sogdian art motifs are quite recognizable and help pinpoint the spread of Sogdian commerce along the branches of the Silk Road.

The development of Sogdian trade and commerce did much to advance the state of civilization in the Middle Ages. A standardized language and many business practices traversed the same roads over which commodities passed, and some of those practices have continued to the present day. Varieties of fruits and vegetables traveled west from China, thus improving the agriculture of western Asia and Europe. Similarly, religions, particularly Buddhism, spread, following the path of the Sogdian merchants. Although the Sogdians were active traders along the Silk Road from as early as the third century, it was the period from the sixth through eighth centuries during which they reached their economic peak with total domination of Central Asian trade. Although it has been said that the Silk Road had a tremendous impact on Chinese culture, it was the Sogdian culture that was the instrument of that impact. In essence, China became internationalized because of the Silk Road and the activities of the Sogdian traders.

—Dale L. Flesher

FURTHER READING

Azarpay, Guitty. *Sogdian Painting: The Pictorial Epic in Oriental Art*. Berkeley: University of California Press, 1981. Classic work on Sogdian art. Includes bibliography and index.

Boulnois, Luce. *The Silk Road*. Translated by Dennis Chamberlain. New York: Dutton, 1966. Excellent work on the Silk Road, including the Sogdians' use of the trade routes.

Hopkirk, Peter. *Foreign Devils on the Silk Road*. New York: Oxford University Press, 1980. The Sogdians are among the "foreign devils" highlighted in this volume. Includes bibliography and index.

Juliano, Annette L., and Judith A. Lerner, eds. *Monks and Merchants: Silk Road Treasures from Northwest China*. New York: Harry N. Abrams, 2001. This is an illustrated catalog of a 2001 exhibition on the Silk Road organized by the Asia Society Museum in New York. The exhibit included both art and manuscripts of merchants explaining the Sogdian civilization. Includes bibliographical references and index.

Kranz, Rachel. *Across Asia by Land*. New York: Facts on File, 1991. Surveys the history of trade routes in Asia, focusing especially on the Silk Road from China to the West, but also including studies of the Ambassador's Road, Burma Road, Eurasian Steppe Route, and Russian river routes. Includes bibliographical references and index.

SEE ALSO: 7th-8th centuries: Papermaking Spreads to Korea, Japan, and Central Asia; 618: Founding of the Tang Dynasty; 629-645: Pilgrimage of Xuanzang; 791: Buddhism Becomes Tibetan State Religion; 812: Paper Money First Used in China; 1271-1295: Travels of Marco Polo.

RELATED ARTICLES in *Great Lives from History: The Middle Ages, 477-1453*: Marco Polo; Xuanzang.

February 2, 506
ALARIC II DRAFTS THE *BREVIARUM ALARICI*

Visigothic king Alaric II drafted his breviary, codifying a transmitted body of Roman statutes and jurisprudence in a form accepted by a European barbarian ruler. The breviary's existence demonstrated how Roman law and custom had a profound role in the lives of not only barbarian Europeans but also others in subsequent centuries.

LOCALE: Toulouse, France
CATEGORIES: Government and politics; laws, acts, and legal history

KEY FIGURES
Alaric II (c. 466-507), king of the Visigoths, r. 484-507
Euric (d. 484), king of the Visigoths, r. 466-484
Clovis (c. 466-511), king of the Franks, r. 481-511

SUMMARY OF EVENT
In 418, the Roman master of soldiers Constantius concluded a treaty with the barbarian Visigoths that settled them in Aquitania, the name given then and now to southwestern Gaul (now France). This marked the beginning of the so-called kingdom of Toulouse, the first of what were to become several barbarian kingdoms carved out of the Western Roman Empire. In 477, the Visigoths, under their king Euric, occupied the last Roman territory of southern Gaul, and, in Gaul at least, the Roman Empire was at an end.

The Visigoths, however, were but a drop in a Roman sea, and in many ways ruled only by the sufferance of the Roman majority. By this time, Gallo-Roman bishops had become the de facto rulers of the Roman population, and powerful Gallo-Roman senators were a force to be reckoned with. Barbarian rulers offended influential Romans at their peril.

One of the most significant areas of incompatibility between Visigoths and Romans was religion: Both peoples were Christian, but the Romans were Nicene (Catholic) and the Visigoths Arian, resulting in an insurmountable obstacle to any meaningful integration of the two societies, for each considered the other to be heretics. The ambitious Euric, in attempts to consolidate his authority, forbade the ordination of Catholic bishops as sees became vacant and, as a result, seriously antagonized the Roman aristocracy. Bishops of newly acquired Roman cities were often exiled or imprisoned.

At the same time, Euric attempted to regularize the legal affairs of his kingdom by issuing a law code known as the *Codex Euricianus* (code of Euric). He did so not only to impose his control more firmly on his Visigothic subjects, but also to assert Visigothic independence of any vestige of Roman authority. It has been suggested that the code was based on Visigothic custom and intended only for the Visigoths, but it would appear that many of the pronouncements were in fact based on Roman provincial law and applied to Visigoths and Romans equally. The surviving entries in his code, about 60 of an original 350, touch on matters of property, buying and selling, loans, and gifts. When Euric died in 484, his son Alaric II inherited a very tense social and political situation. Even though Alaric subsequently allowed vacant sees to be filled, Visigothic relations with the Gallo-Roman aristocracy continued to be strained.

In the north, meanwhile, another ambitious barbarian chieftain, Clovis, became the ruler of one of the many fragmented bands of Franks in 481. In 486, he doubled the size of his kingdom by defeating Syagrius of Soissons, the last independent Roman ruler in Gaul. In 496, Clovis adopted Nicene Christianity and was baptized, then immediately became the darling of the Gallo-Roman establishment. In the Visigothic kingdom, a number of Roman bishops were exiled or imprisoned for supposedly favoring the Franks.

By the early sixth century, Clovis had incorporated most of the other Frankish groups into his own kingdom, and it was clear that he had his eyes on the kingdom of Toulouse. Faced with this northern threat, Alaric attempted to shore up his sagging Gallo-Roman support. In 506, he permitted the Catholic bishops to summon, in the small coastal town of Agde, the first church council to be held in Aquitania since the arrival of the Visigoths.

On February 2 of the same year, Alaric sanctioned the issuance at Toulouse of yet another law code, this one strictly Roman in nature. Although described in the text simply as a *Corpus* (collection), it later became known as the *Breviarium Alarici* (breviary of Alaric), or the *Lex romana Visigothorum* (Roman law of the Visigoths). Its publication was overseen by the *vir inlustris* (illustrious gentleman) Count Goiaricus, and it was edited by the *vir spectabilis* (respectable gentleman) Anianus and distributed by the *vir spectabilis* Count Timotheus. Its heading noted, "In this body (*corpus*) are contained the laws (*leges*) and the image of justice (*ius*), selected from the Theodosian and other books and, as it was commanded, interpreted." Its prologue proclaimed that it had been issued "So that all the obscurity of Roman laws (*leges*) and ancient jurisprudence (*ius*), led into the light of a better intelligence with the assistance of bishops and the nobility, might be made clear and so that nothing might remain in doubt," and it asserted that "the assent of the venerable bishops and chosen provincials has strengthened" it.

The *Breviarium Alarici* is a typical product of Roman provincial jurisprudence. It complemented, but did not replace, the code of Euric by giving Visigothic sanction to selected elements of Roman law. In doing so, it reinforced the notion that the Visigothic kings were the direct successors of the Roman emperors. It was excerpted from the two primary sources of Roman law: the statutes (*leges*) issued by Roman emperors and the opinions (*ius*) put forth by eminent Roman jurists. In the former category were entries from the *Codex Gregorianus* (code of Gregorius) and *Codex Hermogenianus* (code of Hermogenianus), both originally issued in the 290's under the emperor Diocletian (r. 284/285-305) (and both known primarily only from their entries in the *Breviarium Alarici*); 398 constitutions (less than one-eighth of the total) from the *Codex Theodosianus* (Theodosian code), issued by the Byzantine emperor Theodosius II (r. 408-450) in 438; and the *Novellae* (new laws), which were issued between 438 and 471. The only jurists cited were Gaius, Paul, and Papinian.

Alaric II, king of the Visigoths 484-507. (Hulton|Archive by Getty Images)

Yet this is not to say that the *Breviarium Alarici* merely copied, or even summarized, the *Codex Theodosianus*. Rather, a clear selection process was at work. For example, some Roman legislation, such as that on *hospitium* (the billeting of troops), *agri deserti* (deserted lands), and heretics, was omitted. Other laws were revised: The *Breviarium Alarici* repeated the prohibition of intermarriage between Romans and barbarians dating from the 370's but substituted the words *Romani* (Romans) and *barbari* (barbarians) for *provinciales* (provincials) and *gentiles* (foreigners)—a curious instance of the Visigoths self-identifying as barbarians. Furthermore, the *Breviarium Alarici* also included, at the express request of Alaric, extensive legal *interpretationes* of the Theodosian provisions, which give an indication of the enormous scope of legal activities in late and post-Roman Gaul. Although it has been generally assumed that Alaric's Gallo-Roman legal advisers completed the task of assembling and issuing the code within the remarkably short space of a few months, it would seem more likely that the work had been going on for a very long time in private Gallic legal circles and that the politically astute Gauls merely used Alaric's dire straits to their own advantage in securing his approval for work that was already essentially complete.

It is impossible to say where Alaric's initiatives might have led. In the following year, 507, the armies of Alaric and Clovis met at Vouillé, and the result was the destruction of the Visigothic army and the death of Alaric. During the next year, Clovis occupied nearly all of the kingdom of Toulouse. All that remained to the Visigoths, now firmly entrenched in Spain, was Septimania, a coastal strip focused on Narbonne. The Gothic kingdom of Toulouse was at an end, and the history of post-Roman Gaul was to be written not by the Visigoths but by the Franks.

Significance

The *Breviarium Alarici*, however, went on to enjoy a distinguished and influential afterlife. Although other more complete sections of various parts of the Theodosian code survived elsewhere, the *Breviarium Alarici* is the only extant document that preserves the organizational structure of the entire code.

Furthermore, Alaric's initiative gave a barbarian imprimatur to Roman law that was seconded in other barbarian kingdoms that in the sixth century and later also introduced law codes heavily influenced by Roman law in general and by the *Breviarium Alarici* in particular. These include the *Lex romana Burgundionum* (Roman law of the Burgundians) of the Burgundian kingdom (which included a mere forty-seven clauses) and even the *Pactus legis salicae* (record of salic law) of the Franks.

The publication of the *Breviarium Alarici* also was one reason why subsequent Western barbarian law was based on the Theodosian code rather than the updated and expanded *Codex Justinianus* (Justinian's code), issued by the Romans at Constantinople in early 529. Other forms of the Theodosian code, perhaps based in part on the *Breviarium Alarici*, also were used in post-Roman western Europe and attest to the code's continued vitality. These include the *Lex romana curiensis* (Roman law of Chur) dating from about 800. In general, the *Breviarium Alarici* demonstrates in a microcosm the ways in which Roman law and custom had a decisive role in barbarian Europe that continues to have an effect today.

—*Ralph W. Mathisen*

Further Reading

Drew, Katherine Fischer. "The Barbarian Kings as Lawgivers and Judges." In *Life and Thought in the Early Middle Ages*, edited by Robert S. Hoyt. Minneapolis: University of Minnesota Press, 1967. Assesses the influence of the *Breviarium Alarici*, especially in southwestern Gaul and the Rhone Valley, even after it was superseded by the seventh code known as *Liber*, or *Forum Judicum*.

Harries, J., and Ian Wood, eds. *The Theodosian Code*. Ithaca, N.Y.: Cornell University Press, 1993. Provides a background for understanding the Roman legal precedents on which the *Breviarium Alarici* was based.

Mathisen, Ralph. *Roman Aristocrats in Barbarian Gaul: Strategies for Survival in an Age of Transition*. Austin: University of Texas Press, 1993. A useful study of the period.

Wood, Ian. "Disputes in Late Fifth and Sixth-Century Gaul: Some Problems." In *The Settlement of Disputes in Early Medieval Europe*, edited by Wendy Davies and Paul Fouracre. New York: Cambridge University Press, 1986. This scholarly article places the *Breviarium Alarici* in a helpful legal and historical context.

See also: 496: Baptism of Clovis.

Related articles in *Great Lives from History: The Middle Ages, 477-1453*: Clovis; Odoacer.

524
Imprisonment and Death of Boethius

The imprisonment and death of the philosopher Boethius resulted in the composition of one of the Western world's most influential books, The Consolation of Philosophy.

Locale: Pavia (Ticinum; now in Italy)

Categories: Cultural and intellectual history; government and politics

Key Figures

Boethius (c. 480-524), philosopher, theologian, Roman senator and consul

Quintus Aurelius Memmius Symmachus (d. 524 or 525), adoptive father, father-in-law, and friend of Boethius, Roman senator and consul

Theodoric the Great (c. 454-526), king of the Ostrogoths, Roman governor of Italy, and an Arian Christian, r. 474-526

Summary of Event

The philosopher, theologian, poet, and statesman Boethius was unjustly accused of treason by Theodoric the Great, king of the Ostrogoths and governor of Italy, imprisoned at Pavia, tortured, and executed in the year 524. While imprisoned, he composed what many consider to be the single most influential book for the medieval, Renaissance, and early modern Western world: *De consolatione philosophiae* (523; *The Consolation of Philosophy*, late ninth century).

Boethius, or Boece (center), with Lady Philosophy in Jean de Meung's fifteenth century translation of The Consolation of Philosophy. (Frederick Ungar Publishing Co.)

Boethius's Christian faith was orthodox according to the Roman episcopal teaching about Christ as true God and true man, whereas Theodoric's Christian faith was considered heretical, holding that Christ was neither truly God nor truly man but a being having a human body with divine essence.

The accusation of treason against Boethius occurred in 523 and took the form of four separate charges. As laid forth by Richard Green in an introduction to his translation of *The Consolation of Philosophy*, these were, by Boethius's own account: (1) that he wished to safeguard the Senate; (2) that he obstructed the use of (perjured) testimony against the Senate; (3) that he wished to preserve Rome's freedom; and (4) that he had committed sacrilege by contacting evil spirits. These charges were both politically and religiously motivated. The Senate, with a long and august tradition during the Roman Republic and Empire, probably chaffed under the new Gothic governor, Theodoric, even though he was technically under the jurisdiction of Emperor Justin I in the East. Also, Theodoric's Arianism made him a heretic to his Roman Catholic subjects. It seems likely that Theodoric might see Boethius's loyalties to the Senate and to Roman Catholicism as dangerous or at least disloyal.

Nevertheless, there seems to be universal agreement that Boethius was not guilty of the offenses of which he was accused. This innocence makes his torture, which was most unusual for a Roman senator, even more heinous. Reportedly, a strap was tied around his eyes and temples and then tightened to inflict great pain. The mode of execution itself is also clearly out of keeping with the dignity of a Roman senator; he was clubbed to death. Boethius's adoptive father and father-in-law, Quintus Aurelius Memmius Symmachus, also a Roman senator and consul, was executed under similar vague charges of treason with Boethius or within the following year.

Before the imprisonment, Boethius was not only a trusted and influential statesman but also a prominent philosopher and theologian. He learned Greek early in

Boethius belonged to an ancient, noble Roman family. He was a Roman senator, Roman consul in 510, and *magister officiorum* ("master of the palace") in 522. He had a very successful career as a statesman under Theodoric and was actually a friend of Theodoric, but the king accused him of treason, banished him from Rome, and had him imprisoned, tortured, and executed at Pavia. Theodoric, king of the Ostrogoths (the East Goths), had migrated with his whole tribe from the eastern end of the Roman Empire to Italy. In addition to being king of the Ostrogoths, Theodoric became, as a result of conquest, governor of Italy with the approbation of the Roman emperor in Constantinople.

The situation was partly a result of the fall of Rome, the change from ancient classical Rome with its emperors and senators to early medieval Rome with its barbarian overlords. Boethius was part of the old order, and Theodoric was a leader of the new order. The situation would be complicated enough if it were political alone; however, there was the further complication of religion. Boethius is believed to have been a Catholic Christian, and Theodoric was an Arian Christian. This meant that his training and had set a goal for himself to translate into Latin and to comment on all the works of both Plato and Aristotle. His further goal was to reconcile the two philosophies based on his understanding of their essential agreement with one another. Because of his political duties and particularly because of his untimely death, he did not get very far with his major project of reconciling Plato and Aristotle. He did make some important beginnings particularly with the writings of Aristotle, including the *Organon* (335-323 B.C.E.; English translation, 1812). In addition, he composed original books on logic, arithmetic, geometry, music, and astronomy as well as several Christian theological books. Although much of his work is unfinished, he left a legacy both of syntheses of ancient writings and of his own original writings. Much of what he accomplished and published became standard and basic textbook material for medieval, Renaissance, and early modern schools and universities. This alone would have made him memorable and worthy of admiration and study.

What he composed while imprisoned, however, is his true legacy. Under the shadow of torture and anticipated execution, he composed *The Consolation of Philosophy*. This work is in five books, each consisting of alternating sections of prose and poetry. The prose sections are presented as a dialogue between the persona of Boethius and the allegorical Lady Philosophy. Philosophy instructs Boethius, through a series Platonic or Socratic exchanges, leading him to understand the true nature of happiness—that it is not the result of material wealth and other worldly goods but rather the equivalent of truth, love, and indeed God. Lady Fortune also plays a role in this allegorical instruction. Lady Philosophy teaches not only about Fortune's deceptive role in human happiness but also reveals to Boethius the nature of evil, providence, free will, the supreme good, and the simplicity and perfection of divine knowledge. The Platonic and neo-Platonic character of the work is seamlessly integrated with its Christian values, and it is perhaps for this reason—as well as its treatment of the age-old problem of evil and its attacks on the undeserving (here Boethius and Job have much in common)—that the influence of *The Consolation of Philosophy* would endure into the Renaissance and still is read outside as well as inside the classroom.

LADY PHILOSOPHY DEFINES HAPPINESS

At the conclusion of Book III, Prose 10 in The Consolation of Philosophy, *Lady Philosophy leads Boethius, through a process of logic that echoes Plato's Socratic dialogues, to recognize the true nature of happiness:*

LADY PHILOSOPHY: . . . riches are sought because they are thought good, power because it is believed to be good, and the same is true of honor, fame, and pleasure. Therefore, the good is the cause and sum of all that is sought for. . . . On the other hand, things which are not truly good, but only seem to be, are sought after as if they were good. It follows, then, that goodness is rightly considered the sum, pivot, and cause of all that men desire. The most important object of desire is that for the sake of which something else is sought as a means; as, for example, if a person wishes to ride horseback in order to improve his health, he desires the effect of health more than the exercise of riding.

Since, therefore, all things are sought on account of the good, it is the good itself, not the other things, which is desired by everyone. But, as we agreed earlier, all those other things are sought for the sake of happiness; therefore, happiness alone is the object of men's desires. It follows clearly from this that the good and happiness are one and the same thing.

BOETHIUS: I cannot see how any one could disagree.

LADY PHILOSOPHY: But we have also proved [earlier] that God and true happiness are one and the same.

BOETHIUS: That is so.

LADY PHILOSOPHY: We can, therefore, safely conclude that the essence of God is to be found in the good, and nowhere else.

Source: Boethius, *The Consolation of Philosophy*, translated by Richard Green (Indianapolis: Bobbs-Merrill, 1962), pp. 64-65; labeling for speakers added.

SIGNIFICANCE

The lessons of *The Consolation of Philosophy* are closely linked to the core of medieval, Renaissance, and early modern thinking: Succeeding generations found Boethius's philosophical and poetical approach to theological questions not only intriguing but also convincing and truly consoling, and the book quickly became favorite reading for thousands of people. Early translators of the book into English included King Alfred the Great, Geoffrey Chaucer, and Queen Elizabeth I. In the realm of literary style, Boethius's use of allegorical figures would be echoed in Alain of Lille's Dreamer and Lady Nature, in the figure Reason in *Le Roman de la rose* (c. 1230; *The Romance of the Rose*, 1914-1924), in Dante's Philosophy in *Il convivio* (c. 1307; *The*

The Wheel of Fortune was a common allegory for the inconstancy of life; Lady Philosophy instructs Boethius that those who tie their happiness to Fortune are doomed to disappointment. From Jean de Meung's fifteenth century French translation of The Consolation of Philosophy. (Frederick Ungar Publishing Co.)

Banquet, 1887), in Chaucer's vision poems, in William Langland's *The Vision of William, Concerning Piers the Plowman* (c. 1362, c. 1377, and c. 1393), and more subtly in later works of literature and drama. Like the biblical Job, Boethius learns, and demonstrates, how little humans really understand about themselves and about God. Boethius's imprisonment, torture, and execution produced a major work of literature that informs not only philosophy and religion but the forms through which they have been expressed.

—Douglas J. McMillan,
revised by Christina J. Moose

FURTHER READING

Astell, Ann W. *Job, Boethius, and Epic Truth*. Ithaca, N.Y.: Cornell University Press, 1994. An exploration of Boethius's role in the history of the genres of allegory and epic.

Gibson, Margaret, ed. *Boethius: His Life, Thought and Influence*. Oxford: Basil Blackwell, 1981. A collection of fourteen major scholarly essays to celebrate the fifteen hundredth anniversary of Boethius's birth: 480-1980.

Hoenen, Maarten J. F. M., and Lodi Nauta, eds. *Boethius in the Middle Ages: Latin and Vernacular Traditions of the "Consolatio philosophiae."* New York: Brill, 1997. Translations and analysis of *The Consolation of Philosophy*. Bibliography and indexes.

Marenbon, John. *Boethius*. New York: Oxford University Press, 2003. A biography of Boethius in the Great Medieval Thinkers series. Bibliography and index.

Scott, Jamie S. *Christians and Tyrants: The Prison Testimonies of Boethius, Thomas More, and Dietrich Bonhoeffer.* New York: P. Lang, 1995. An analysis and comparison of three Christians who were imprisoned.

Varvis, Stephen. *The "Consolation" of Boethius: An Analytical Inquiry into His Intellectual Processes and Goals*. San Francisco: Mellen Research University Press, 1991. A standard historical and philosophical account of Boethius's importance.

SEE ALSO: February 2, 506: Alaric II Drafts the *Breviarum Alarici*; 590-604: Reforms of Pope Gregory the Great.

RELATED ARTICLES in *Great Lives from History: The Middle Ages, 477-1453*: Boethius; Geoffrey Chaucer; Odoacer; Theodoric the Great.

529-534
Justinian's Code Is Compiled

Justinian's code created a comprehensive, authoritative compilation of Roman law that served as the foundation of European law.

Locale: Constantinople, Byzantine Empire (now Istanbul, Turkey)

Categories: Government and politics; laws, acts, and legal history

Key Figures

John the Cappadocian (fl. 525-550), praetorian prefect of the East, c. 531-January, 532, and 532-541

Valentinian III (419-455), Western Roman emperor, r. 425-455

Theodosius II (401-450), Byzantine emperor, r. 408-450

Justin I (c. 450-527), Byzantine emperor, r. 518-527

Justinian I (c. 483-565), Byzantine emperor, r. 527-565

Theodora (c. 497-548), Byzantine empress, r. 527-548

Tribonian (c. 475-545), quaestor of the Sacred Palace, 529-532, 534-545

Summary of Event

At the time Justinian I directed its reform, Roman law was the accumulated product of Rome's history from republican times. For centuries, emperors had repeatedly issued new laws and decrees (referred to as constitutions). They also issued rescripts (official statements) regarding specific questions. Although these did not necessarily agree with the general principles of the law, they had the force of law. In addition, laws were not systematically published and the archives did not always keep copies of new legislation. This accumulation of conflicting legislation made it difficult for lawyers and judges to cite the law accurately on specific legal points. Also, jurisconsultants issued many opinions during the second and third centuries. These opinions, however, were sometimes contradictory, and many were difficult to find.

Toward the end of the third century, two different collections of laws were compiled and updating was attempted during following years. These publications, however, gradually lost their usefulness as time passed. In 426, Valentinian III, the Western Roman emperor, ordered that the opinions of only five past commentators could be cited before the courts. Opinions of earlier commentators cited by them also could be considered, but only if they were confirmed by comparison of manuscripts. If the commentators differed, the majority ruled. If they were equally divided, the authority of the group that included an opinion of Papinian, a prestigious second century jurist, was to be accepted. Theodosius II, after setting up commissions in 427 and 434 in order to prepare a collection of laws issued after 312, promulgated the Theodosian code in 438. His code, however, proved inadequate. In short, by the time of Justinian, the legal system badly needed streamlining.

Prior to succeeding the emperor Justin, who was his uncle, Justinian had long served in the emperor's administration. According to the historian Procopius, Justin appointed his nephew, Justinian, count of the Domestics, and invested him with patrician rank immediately after beginning his reign in 518. In 527, Justin, having earlier adopted him, made Justinian coemperor. Thus, Justinian became well aware of defects in the legal system and, doubtless, began formulating plans for reform.

Justinian's long-term mistress Theodora, whom he married after the death of Justin's wife, was most influential in Justinian's rule. He considered her coequal in many respects, and portions of his code, especially those relating to women's issues and rights, apparently were heavily influenced by her opinions. She appears not, however, to have been officially recognized as sharing the throne.

On February 13, 528, during the first year of his reign, Justinian appointed a commission of ten experts to produce a new code of imperial law. The chairman of the commission was John the Cappadocian, praetorian prefect of the East, the highest administrative official of the eastern empire. The commission was charged with updating the laws recorded in the existing Gregorian, Hermogenian, and Theodosian codes. In addition, the constitutions, as well as "novels" or supplementary laws, issued since promulgation of the Theodosian code, were to be included. This accumulated mass of law was systematized and simplified in the *Codex Justinianus* and published April 7, 529. An updated edition was published November 16, 534.

On December 15, 530, a second commission, under the direction of Tribonian, quaestor of the Sacred Palace (chief legal officer of the empire) and a highly qualified lawyer, set out to codify the works of Roman jurists. These works, written by Roman lawyers during the first through fourth centuries, composed 1,528 "books." Each manuscript was the length of a papyrus roll. The entire text is estimated to comprise three million lines. Tribonian, who probably was a graduate of the school at Beirut, chose the other commissioners: Constantinus, the *register libellorum*, the official whose function was to prepare cases for the supreme court, Dorotheus, dean of the Beirut law school, Anatolius, a Beirut law school professor whose father had served on the first commission; Theophilus, a professor at the Constantinople law school; and Cratinus, another Constantinople professor. In addition, eleven barristers assisted the commission. All of these were *illustres*, belonging to the highest and least numerous class of senators who were permitted to deliberate in the senate. By December 16, 533, the commission published the Panadects, or *Digest*, consisting of 9,123 separate texts contained in fifty books totaling 150,000 lines.

During their work, the commissioners found many outmoded or unjust arguments and opinions. Many of these were simply abolished, but some questions required reform, so during the first three years of his reign, Justinian issued many new laws. These then were compiled by the commission and published in late 530 or early 531 as the Fifty Decisions, the text of which has been lost. This contained only decisions promulgated before work began on the *Digest*. Tribonian's commission quickly recognized that a new edition of the code of 529 would be required, so Tribonian, Dorotheus, and three other lawyers immediately began work. The revised code, *Codex Justinianus repetitae praelectionis* or "Justinian's code of resumed reading," published in 534, replaced the *Codex Vetus* of 529.

A fragment from the Pandects of Justinian, the old Roman law that Justinian ordered to be codified. This seventh century parchment was originally housed in the library of the Medici at Florence. (R. S. Peale and J. A. Hill)

In addition, a committee consisting of Tribonian and the leading academic lawyers of Constantinople and Beirut also prepared the *Institutes*, a short textbook to be used by students of law. This was published November 21, 533, and was heavily indebted to Gaius, an earlier lawyer of the second century.

Justinian intended the entire work, *Codex*, *Digest*, and *Institutes* or *Corpus juris civilis*, as it has been known since the sixteenth century, as a unified, consistent, literal, and straightforward body of law. Commentaries on the *Digest* were prohibited, although indices and supply headings were provided. In contrast to the *Codex*, literal translations of the *Digest* into Greek also were allowed.

SIGNIFICANCE

Justinian's code seems to have little affected the mass of the empire. Civil courts were hardly used away from Constantinople. The fact that the code and *Digest* were published in Latin, a language not understood in most of the Byzantine Empire, limited the use of the *Corpus*. Local laws and institutions continued to operate in many localities even though they contradicted imperial legislation, and arbitration and mediation were favored in the provinces, generally with bishops or local holy men as arbiters. Although slightly used in the Byzantine Empire after the sixth century, the *Corpus* remained a most important philosophical contribution. In the eleventh century, rediscovery of the *Digest* led to the founding of the University of Bologna in 1088 and the revival of Roman law. Inerius's publication of the *Vulgate Digest* as a textbook for students at Bologna is, by some, considered the initial spark of the European Renaissance. In any event, Justinian's code of civil law became the de facto law in many parts of Western Europe. Furthermore, appropriate parts of Roman law were incorporated in new codes and functioned as parts of them. In this way, the influence of

Roman law persists through all subsequent European history.

—*Ralph L. Langenheim, Jr.*

Further Reading

Baker, G. P. *Justinian: The Last Roman Emperor.* 1931. Reprint. New York: Cooper Square Press, 2002. A biographical account of Justianian's reign and the history of the Roman and Byzantine Empires during his time. Maps, bibliography, index.

Borkowski, Andrew. *Textbook on Roman Law.* 2d ed. New York: Oxford University Press, 2002. Provides an exposition of Roman civil law and procedure, with the use of texts from Justinian's *Digest*. Bibliography, index.

Browning, Robert. *Justinian and Theodora.* Rev. ed. London: Thames and Hudson, 1987. A scholarly discussion of Empress Theodora's contributory role in Justinian's administration.

Bury, J. B. *History of the Later Roman Empire: From the Death of Theodosius I to the Death of Justinian.* 1923. Reprint. New York: Dover, 1958. Comprehensive scholarly history with a full chapter on Justinian's legislative works. Bury's work on the Byzantine Empire is the definitive account by an English-speaking scholar.

Evans, James Allan. *The Age of Justinian: The Circumstances of Imperial Power.* New York: Routledge, 1996. An updated political and social history of Justinian's era, including many facets of the legal system. Maps, extensive bibliography, and index.

Gerostergios, Asterios. *Justinian the Great, Emperor and Saint: Illustrious Byzantine Emperor, Legislator, and Codifier of Law.* Belmont, Mass.: Institute for Byzantine and Modern Greek Studies, 1982. Detailed account by a Greek historian of Justinian's religious policies, including the role of the *Codex*.

Moorhead, John. *Justinian.* New York: Longman, 1994. A concise biography that includes a succinct account of Justinian's legal reforms. Bibliography, index.

Thomas, J. A. C. *Textbook of Roman Law.* New York: North-Holland, 1976. A 562-page text looking at Justinian's code and its far-reaching consequences. Bibliography, index.

Vasiliev, A. A. *History of the Byzantine Empire, 324-1453.* 2 vols. 2d rev. ed. Madison: University of Wisconsin Press, 1964. Written from the point of view of czarist Russian scholarship, this comprehensive work illuminates Justinian's legal reforms and their causes and effects. Includes extensive notes and a bibliography.

See also: February 2, 506: Alaric II Drafts the *Breviarum Alarici*; 1295: Model Parliament.

Related articles in *Great Lives from History: The Middle Ages, 477-1453*: Abū Ḥanīfah; Basil the Macedonian; Henry de Bracton; Justinian I; Theodora.

532-537
Building of Hagia Sophia

The building of Hagia Sophia marked the pinnacle of Byzantine architecture and engineering, creating a cathedral whose design influenced future construction in both the Muslim and Christian worlds.

Locale: Constantinople, Byzantine Empire (now Istanbul, Turkey)

Categories: Architecture; engineering; religion

Key Figures

Justinian I (483-565), Byzantine emperor, r. 527-565

Anthemius of Tralles (c. 474-c. 534), designer and architect of Hagia Sophia

Isidore of Miletus (fl. sixth century), architect and assistant to Anthemius

Isidore the Younger (fl. sixth century), engineer who redesigned the dome

Summary of Event

When Justinian I commissioned the construction of the Cathedral of Hagia Sophia in Constantinople in 532, he envisioned the structure to be a symbol of both Christianity and his ability to civilize and rule much of the known world. The first church to occupy the site was built and dedicated by Constantine II on February 15, 360. It followed a basilica plan similar to Old Saint Peter's in Rome. During the riots that followed the banishment of John Chrysostom, the structure burned on June 20, 404. Hagia Sophia was rebuilt by Theodosius the Younger and consecrated in 415. This second church was one of many architectural victims of the riots in January, 532, begun by the uniting of Hippodrome factions against the state. Through its failure, the Nika insurrection provided Justinian the opportunity to rebuild the imperial capital and usher in a new "golden age."

As architects for the cathedral of Hagia Sophia, or "holy wisdom," Justinian chose two scholars and master builders: Anthemius of Tralles and Isidore of Miletus. Anthemius, the principal designer, authored works on conic sections and reflectors. Isidore, who taught physics and stereometry at the universities of Alexandria and Constantinople, had collected and published the works of Archimedes of Syracuse and had written commentary on the Kamarika of Heron of Alexandria concerning the construction of vaults.

Early Christian structures were built using two essentially different forms: the central plan and the rectangular basilica, with its focal point at one end. The inspiration for the first type of structure came from such buildings as the Pantheon in Rome and the mausoleums of Diocletian in Split and resulted in centralized churches such as San Stefano Rotundo in Rome (468-483) and San Lorenzo in Milan (founded c. 350 and rebuilt in the fifth century). The rectangular church form dominated in the West, where attention focused on the altar and presbyterium. Its secular predecessors were the basilica facing the forum in Pompeii and the Basilica Julia in Rome. The Cathedral of Hagia Sophia represented a fusion of these forms employing a daring and complexity that had never before been attempted.

One of the major feats of construction was the erection of a dome on a square base. This dome rested on a crown formed by the conjuncture of the tops of four arches and four pendentives rising from four massive piers. The thrust of the dome to the east and west was taken up by two semidomes abutting the arches, and these in turn discharged it on vaults and piers still farther to the east and west. The lateral pressure to the north and south, on the other hand, was absorbed by the piers. This technical skill and balance of thrusts would be copied, but not equaled, for centuries. The construction began on February 23, 532, with two teams of workers with a combined force of ten thousand men. Following traditional Roman practice, Hagia Sophia was built of brick and mortar except for the eight main piers, which were made of large blocks of stone. The use of standardized materials in conjunction with a sense of competitiveness between the work crews enabled the structure to be com-

A nineteenth century depiction of the Hagia Sophia at Constantinople. (Frederick Ungar Publishing Co.)

pleted on schedule for its dedication on December 27, 537. The rebuilt cathedral's magnificent scale pleased Justinian to such a degree that he stated, "Glory to God who has deemed me worthy to complete such a work. O Solomon, I have surpassed thee."

Worshipers enter the sanctuary by first passing through a forecourt and two vestibules, each 200 feet (61 meters) wide that fulfill the function of a narthex. Beyond is the large oval area 225 feet (68.5 meters) in length and 107 feet (32.5 meters) in width. Over the center of this open space, the architects placed a relatively shallow dome the same width as the nave, rising to a height of 160 feet (49 meters). Light for the church came through many apertures, including forty windows that puncture the great dome. The combination of a gold ceiling, multicolored marble columns, walls, and pavement and large areas decorated with mosaics gave the church's interior a luminous effect.

The exaggerated thrust of the shallow dome, the haste with which it was constructed, and severe earthquakes in 553 and again in 557 contributed to a split in the arch to the east, so that on May 7, 558, part of the central dome collapsed. As both Anthemius and Isidore had died, the task of restoration was given to Isidore the Younger, who strengthened the arches to the north and south and filled in their spandrels with windowed walls. To diminish the lateral thrust of the central dome, he raised its center some 20 feet (6 meters). Isidore's work was necessary and remarkably successful, but he was more an engineer than an artist. The resulting inner shell of the dome is no longer as brilliantly illuminated, as the walls beneath the north and south arches, even though pierced with windows, cut off the light that once filled the nave.

Significance

Following the completion of Isidore the Younger's work, Hagia Sophia changed little even as the power of the Byzantine Empire waned. In 1453, Constantinople fell to the Ottoman Turks, and the Christian Orthodox cathedral became both a royal mosque and an architectural model for Muslim religious structures throughout the Ottoman Empire. Beginning in the second half of the fifteenth century, a dramatic shift took place in the architecture of the Islamic world as designers strove to create mosques equal to the empire their masters ruled.

Throughout its existence, Hagia Sophia has required repeated restorations to combat the effects of regional earthquakes. The work of repairing the structure in the years after the fall of Constantinople gave Muslim architects the opportunity to study the cathedral's vaulting system. As early as 1463, the combination of a dome flanked by a semidome was used at the mosque of Mehmed II in Istanbul. By 1505, two semidomes were used in the construction of the city's second imperial mosque of Bayezit II. It was the late sixteenth century architect Sinan, however, who sought to create works that directly competed with Justinian's masterpiece in the mosques of Süleyman and Kilic Ali Pasha.

In the West, Saint Mark's Cathedral in Venice, the repository of much of the wealth of Constantinople stolen in the Fourth Crusade, bears the most direct relationship to Hagia Sophia. After Hagia Sophia was converted to a mosque, access to the building became restricted for nonbelievers. Only in the twentieth century were Westerners allowed to study Hagia Sophia's mosaics, which had long been covered for religious reasons. After the fall of the Ottoman Empire, following World War I, funding for the structure's preservation diminished. On February 1, 1935, Kemal Atatürk, president of Turkey, had Hagia Sophia converted into a museum in order to permit the restoration of both its interior and exterior. Although much of the ornament of Justinian's cathedral is lost, what remains provides testament to both the artist and architectural skills of the Byzantine Empire.

—M. Joseph Costelloe,
updated by Edmund Dickenson Potter

Further Reading

Calkins, Robert G. *Medieval Architecture in Western Europe: From A.D. 300 to 1500*. New York: Oxford University Press, 1998. Explores the history of Western European architecture of the Middle Ages, including the buildings of Justinian. Illustrations, extensive bibliography, index.

Kinross, Lord. *Hagia Sophia*. New York: Newsweek, 1972. Provides a large collection of commentaries made by visitors to Hagia Sophia in the many centuries since its consecration.

Krautheimer, Richard. *Early Christian and Byzantine Architecture*. 4th ed. New Haven, Conn.: Yale University Press, 1986. Demonstrates Hagia Sophia's importance in the history of architecture by illustrating church development in the first five hundred years of Christianity.

Macaulay, David. *Building Big*. Boston: Houghton Mifflin, 2000. Provides the younger reader with a chapter on the Hagia Sophia in the context of other large architectural works from around the world. Colored illustrations, maps.

Mainstone, Rowland J. *Hagia Sophia: Architecture,*

Structure, Liturgy of Justinian's Great Church. 1988. Reprint. London: Thames and Hudson, 1997. Using archaeological evidence, seeks to separate Justinian's cathedral from later restoration and to demonstrate how it was used in religious ceremonies. Also explores the cathedral's design, construction, character, influence, and changes over time. Includes architectural plans, elevations, and sections, as well as photographs, bibliography, and an index.

Mango, Cyril. *The Mosaics of Saint Sophia at Istanbul*. Washington, D.C.: Dumbarton Oaks Research Library, 1962. The author is regularly cited as an expert of Hagia Sophia's mosaics, which were an integral part of the building's design.

Mark, Robert, and Ahmet S. Cakmak. *Hagia Sophia: From the Age of Justinian to the Present*. New York: Cambridge University Press, 1992. Examines the cathedral's structure, design, and material through a series of essays by leading scholars. The work addresses Hagia Sophia's influence on Muslim architects and how restoration and stabilization of the building has changed its design since the fall of Constantinople.

Parkyn, Neil, ed. *The Seventy Wonders of the Modern World: Fifteen Hundred Years of Extraordinary Feats of Engineering and Construction*. London: Thames and Hudson, 2002. An introduction to the technology and aesthetics of great engineering and construction projects from around the world, including Hagia Sophia. Illustrations, index.

Procopius. *Buildings*. Translated by H. B. Dewing. Cambridge, Mass.: Harvard University Press, 1960-1962. As the first historian to document Justinian's reign, Procopius provided the only surviving account of Hagia Sophia's construction. This work is volume 7 in the collected works of Procopius published as part of the Loeb Classical Library.

SEE ALSO: 685-691: Building of the Dome of the Rock; c. 710: Construction of the Kāilaṣanātha Temple; 775-840: Building of Borobuḍur; 972: Building of al-Azhar Mosque; 11th-12th centuries: Building of Romanesque Cathedrals; 1009: Destruction of the Church of the Holy Sepulchre; c. 1150-1200: Development of Gothic Architecture; 1204: Knights of the Fourth Crusade Capture Constantinople; 1399-1404: Tamerlane Builds the Bibi Khanum Mosque; May 29, 1453: Fall of Constantinople.

RELATED ARTICLES in *Great Lives from History: The Middle Ages, 477-1453*: Justinian I; Mehmed II; Theodora.

538-552
BUDDHISM ARRIVES IN JAPAN

Buddhist images and scriptures sent to Japan as a form of tribute from the Korean kingdom of Paekche caused factional strife and bloodshed among the Japanese nobility but began the process by which Buddhism became a major influence on the cultural life of the Japanese court and eventually a popular religion.

LOCALE: Central Japan
CATEGORIES: Religion; cultural and intellectual history

KEY FIGURES

Sŏng (d. 554), king of the Korean kingdom of Paekche, r. 523-554
Kimmei (509-571), emperor of Japan, r. 539-571
Soga Iname (d. 570), court noble
Soga Umako (d. 626), court noble

SUMMARY OF EVENT

Tradition states that Siddhārtha Gautama, the historical Buddha, was born around 566 B.C.E. in what is now Nepal. It was not until one thousand years later, however, that Buddhism, after having spread through most of Asia, found its way to Japan.

Buddhism first spread to China in the first and second centuries C.E., then began to take root on the Korean peninsula because of the heavy Chinese cultural influence on this area. During this period, Korea was divided into three kingdoms—Paekche, Koguryŏ, and Silla. Paekche, in the southwest part of the peninsula, was under constant military threat from its neighbours, so in the sixth century, it turned to Japan, at that time in the first stages of the consolidation of central power, for military and political support. Although the scholarly theories concerning the relationship between Japan and Paekche differ, it is widely believed that the Korean kingdom was the subordinate power. Although Paekche was militarily subordinate to Japan, because of its proximity to China, the kingdom was more advanced culturally. The Paekche king Sŏng, reportedly the first leader of his country to become an ardent Buddhist, sent a delegation to the Japanese court bearing Buddhist images and scriptures as a form of tribute. The images were of the historical Buddha, shaped in copper and gold, and the scriptures were a number of sutras containing the basic teachings and traditions of Buddhism.

According to the *Nihon shoki* (compiled 720 C.E.; *Nihongi: Chronicles of Japan from the Earliest Times to A.D. 697*, 1896; best known as *Nihon shoki*), a collection of oral traditions, the mission from Korea arrived in the year 552. There are very few surviving sources of information concerning this embassy, and at present, many scholars have doubts concerning the validity of the date given in the *Nihon shoki*. There are a number of ongoing debates, but the year 538 is widely regarded as the likely date.

However, despite this confusion regarding the date, the *Nihon shoki* gives valuable details regarding the initial reception of the new religion in Japan. It reports that King Sōng sent a memorial along with the mission, describing the Indian origins of Buddhism and the transmission of the faith to China and stating that despite the difficulty of understanding its philosophy, Buddhism was superior to all other doctrines. The king of Paekche also boasted that even Confucius, the most important figure in the Chinese intellectual tradition, had not attained a knowledge of the faith. He also promised that Buddhism offered worldly benefits of unimaginable magnitude, fulfilling all the prayers and wishes of its believers.

The chronicle also states that the Japanese emperor Kimmei was overjoyed at the arrival of the new faith and asked his ministers if it should be adopted officially. The representatives of the Soga family favored the official adoption of the faith, but conservative forces, including two other powerful families, the Mononobe and Nakatomi, opposed it. These clans supported the national faith, Shintō, a form of ancestor and nature worship that lacked the complex doctrines and iconography of the newly introduced Buddhism. The Nakatomi and Mononobe advised against the worship of foreign deities for fear of incurring the wrath of the gods of Japan. The Nakatomi, in particular, opposed the new faith because

Buddhas carved into a rock in Nara, Honshu. (Hulton|Archive by Getty Images)

their position of influence at court was largely through their traditional role in Shintō religious observances. The Soga, on the other hand, wielded their influence at the imperial court through the important role that they played in financial and political dealings. Therefore, they were interested in increasing central power at the expense of the other clans, and their interest in the new religion had political dimensions.

The Japanese court decided that the Buddhist images should be given to the Soga, who were free to worship them. The court noble Soga Iname converted his residence at Mukuhara into a temple and enshrined the sacred image there. However, at the same time, an epidemic broke out in central Japan. The *Nihon shoki* reports that it did not abate for an extended period and caused many deaths. The court decided that the outbreak of disease was a result of the presence of the Buddhist images. The Mononobe and Nakatomi officials responded by burning the temple that the Soga had created to house the images and discarding the statue in a canal. However, this chain of events was followed by other catastrophes that were interpreted as ill omens. As a result, the new faith and the Soga clan alike gained more and more influence at the imperial court. Soga Umako, the son of Imane, received permission to restore the temple and sacred image. The struggle between the various clans for influence over the imperial court intensified after this point, and Buddhism was to remain a point of contention for the next fifty years. However, the new religion had taken root in Japan and proceeded to gain converts, first among the imperial family and members of the court and eventually among the population at large.

Significance

The arrival of Buddhism in Japan had the immediate effect of touching off a power struggle between the influential Soga family and the Mononobe and Nakatomi families who favored Shintō, the native faith. By the early seventh century, the Soga had effectively gained power over the imperial court and resorted to armed conflict in order to break the Mononobe family. It was not until 645, however, that the power of the Soga was brought to an end with the assassination of the family's leaders as a result of a plot by the Nakatomi, supported by the imperial prince Naka no Ōe. By this time, however, Buddhism had become a major part of the cultural life of the imperial court and was no longer tied to the fate of the Soga family. By the eighth century, Buddhism had surpassed the philosophical and cultural influence of Shintō among members of the Japanese court.

Despite its popularity, however, in the early stages of Japanese Buddhism, the faith was pursued mainly for its potential for producing worldly benefits, and a real appreciation of the philosophical complexities of the religion was missing. The Buddhist images, for example, were thought to offer protection against disease. Gradually, Japanese Buddhism developed increasing philosophical complexity as Chinese and Korean monks made the journey to the Japanese islands and Japanese monks traveled to the continent to learn more about the faith. Several hundred years after the introduction of Buddhism in Japan, the monk Saichō founded the Tendai sect, and Kōbō Daishi (Kūkai) founded Shingon; these sects offered an eclectic mix of continental ideas and the monks' own philosophical innovations. Centuries later, monks such as Shinran and Nichiren founded popular sects that caused Buddhist teachings to spread rapidly among the masses, and the Zen sect, which took root in Japan in the late twelfth century, had an immeasurable impact on the warrior society that was bringing the entire country under its power. From a single Korean delegation in the mid-sixth century came a religion that can now claim more than 95 million believers in a country whose total population is a little more than 125 million, remaining one of the dominant religious and philosophical forces in Japanese life.

—*Matthew Penney*

Further Reading

Aston, W. G., trans. *Nihongi: Chronicles of Japan from the Earliest Times to A.D. 697*. 1896. Reprint. Tokyo: Charles E. Tuttle, 1972. The standard translation of one of the earliest works of Japanese history. Provides details about the arrival of Buddhism in Japan and the cultural climate of the times.

Sansom, George. *A History of Japan to 1334*. Vol. 1. Stanford, Calif.: Stanford University Press, 1958. Decades after its initial publication, the first volume of Sansom's three-volume study of Japanese history is still a detailed and authoritative work on the subject.

Sonoda, Kōyū. "Early Buddha Worship." In *The Cambridge History of Japan*, *Ancient Japan*, edited by Delmer M. Brown. New York: Cambridge University Press, 1993. A detailed summary of the events surrounding the introduction of Buddhism to Japan as well as the historical debates surrounding the issue.

Tamura, Yoshio. *Japanese Buddhism: A Cultural History.* Translated by Jeffrey Hunter. Tokyo: Tuttle, 2001. A detailed assessment of the cultural implications and historical development of Japanese Buddhism from the introduction of the faith to modern times.

See also: 5th or 6th century: Confucianism Arrives in Japan; 593-604: Regency of Shōtoku Taishi; 607-839: Japan Sends Embassies to China; March 9, 712, and July 1, 720: Writing of *Kojiki* and *Nihon Shoki*; 792: Rise of the Samurai; 1175: Hōnen Shōnin Founds Pure Land Buddhism.

Related articles in *Great Lives from History: The Middle Ages, 477-1453*: Kōbō Daishi; Nichiren.

563
Silk Worms Are Smuggled to the Byzantine Empire

A delegation of Eastern Orthodox monks under Emperor Justinian I broke the monopoly of the East—especially China's on silk production and Persia's on the silk trade routes—by smuggling silkworms into the Byzantine Empire, ensuring new Western silk production. This change made silk more accessible and less expensive in the West.

Locale: Constantinople, Byzantine Empire (now Istanbul, Turkey), and routes through Asia Minor, Greece, and the Levant

Categories: Agriculture; science and technology; trade and commerce

Key Figures

Justinian I (483-565), first Byzantine emperor, r. 527-565

Justin II (c. 540-578), nephew of Justinian and second Byzantine emperor, r. 565-578

Summary of Event

Silk was perhaps the most desirable luxury good in the ancient world after gold, although there have been times when it was even more valuable than gold. Although the imperial city of Constantinople was the single largest consumer of silk and other precious goods such as spices and gems, it was also the most important trade and shipping center for all luxury goods flowing to the West. It was a superb place geographically, located at the junction between two continents (Europe and Asia), which ensured its commanding trade position in the eastern Mediterranean world.

Control of the silk industry in the early Byzantine Empire was a state monopoly. The Byzantine Empire's imperial silk workshops were within the precincts of the Royal Palace at Constantinople. The early Byzantine world had several problems acquiring silk, much of which in Justinian I's time derived from Persian control of the eastern silk trade under the Sāsānian king Khosrow I (r. 531-579). The source of silk before this time was distant China (more than 3,500 miles, or 5,500 kilometers, away), known to the Byzantine Empire as Serinda, a word related to *sericus*, the Roman word for silk. Silk was expensive because middlemen along the way added their profit margins to the original cost. Thus, the greater the distance, the greater was the cost. The caravan land routes crossed daunting and notoriously inhospitable mountain passes, which were rife with brigands. Great deserts with horrific sandstorms and few oases were also along the route. The shipping routes to sea were no less dangerous, being pirate-ridden or difficult to cross even in good sailing weather. Furthermore, the many different cultures along these routes were not always friendly to Byzantine interests. The average length of the journey to bring silk directly from Wei and Zhou China was about 230 days, or nearly two-thirds of a year, and the indirect journey from Persia took months and was more costly.

Justinian had inherited these silk trading problems from his uncle Justin I (r. 518-527), the Byzantine emperor, but the appetite for luxury goods and especially silk did not diminish. Rather, it increased partly because of its revered status in Constantinople and because of the demand for silk by the emerging powers of mainland Europe.

Up to the sixth century, the Sāsānian Persians and their kings controlled the intermediate territory of Mesopotamia between the Byzantine Empire and the East. Ruling from their capital of Ctesiphon (south-southeast of modern Baghdad), King Khosrow I and the Persians dominated most of the southern access of the Byzantine Empire to the silk trade, including the so-called Silk Road via the Persian Gulf and the Tigris-Euphrates watersheds. Even most sea routes terminated in the Persian Gulf, which the Sāsānians controlled. Justinian seems to have broken some of this impasse by establishing partial access over the northern land and sea routes. The Byzantine Empire was situated at the western end of the Black

Sea through the Bosporus. Thus, along the northern route, Justinian began to use the Lazican kingdom on the Caucasus as his intermediary for silk, and his envoys began asserting control over northern routes—beyond Persian hegemony—by utilizing the Gobi Desert, the route to the north of the Elburz Mountains, the route along the Caspian Sea and the Caucasus Mountains, and the route to the Black Sea along its northern, Crimean side and farther west. Using the Ethiopian merchants from the kingdom of Aksum as intermediaries, Justinian's southern trade route temporarily bypassed the Persian Gulf by sailing instead into the Red Sea. But even though the northern route was more successful, the Persians still dominated the silk trade coming through and out of India and the Indian Ocean.

The event of smuggling silkworms to the Byzantine Empire in 563 is not easily reconstructed. There is some controversy over when the Byzantine silk industry was established. Scholar John Norwich believes the event occurred a decade earlier, around 552, and not in 563. Others also place the event before 561. True raw silk is produced only by the silkworm (*Bombyx mori*), which consumes vast amounts of mulberry leaves. The Byzantine historian Procopius described how several Byzantine monks, after returning from India, reported to Justinian that the Byzantines could bypass Persia and India by dealing directly with China. Then acting on an imperial mission, the monks returned to China and smuggled back either silkworm eggs or, more likely, larvae, possibly hidden in bamboo canes, to Constantinople in 563. The young mulberry plants were also needed, and they either had already been imported or were part of this mission. Because the nascent homegrown silk industry was not fully developed by Justinian, within a few years Berytus (Beirut) became the center of the Byzantine silk industry, beginning with Justin II and subsequent emperors. Later, the Morea district in the Peloponnesus of southern Greece became the most important place to grow mulberry trees.

Several of the famous mosaics at San Vitale in the old Byzantine Adriatic port city of Ravenna in eastern Italy commemorate Justinian's reign and the construction of the church under Maximianus in the sixth century. Justinian's wife, Empress Theodora (r. 527-548), and others—including the Paleochristian martyr Saint Vitale himself—appear in the apse wearing what must be shimmering silk garments. If these are indeed new homegrown Byzantine products, it could suggest an earlier date for smuggling the silkworms, but this date is not as important as the imperial rationale demonstrating that these portrait figures required silk garments to present themselves as images of imperial propaganda at their best and most powerful.

After the sixth century, silk became one of the most important diplomatic gifts of the Byzantine Empire to the West, used for royal clothing, ceremonial robes and vestments of the highest clergy, burial wraps for both royalty and clergy, and protective wrapping for the most valuable religious reliquaries of pilgrimage cathedrals and basilicas. Some of the most important extant examples of Byzantine silk are found in shrines, such as the probably early seventh century fragment from the Byzantine emperor Heraclius (r. 610-641) at Saint Madeberte's in Liège, Belgium; the seventh to eighth century silk fragment of the Annunciation in the Vatican Sancta Sanctorum; the famous eighth century fragment of samite silk with the quadriga emblem found in Holy Roman Emperor Charlemagne's (r. 800-814) reliquary of the Aachen treasury (now in the Cluny Museum, Paris); the eleventh century triumphal Byzantine emperor silk wall-hanging found in the tomb of Bishop Gunther of Bamberg (d. 1065); and the Byzantine silk found in Saint Lambert's shrine in Liège, dating from 1142. These are only a few examples of how the Byzantine silk industry made the West look to the Byzantine Empire for its fabled luxuries.

SIGNIFICANCE

Although some raw silk and sewn cloth were still imported, the now indigenous Byzantine silk trade and its concomitant monopoly in the West gradually became one of the Byzantine Empire's most important economic resources. Before the homegrown silk industry, only members of the imperial family were allowed to import or wear silk, and only relatives who were mercantile associates were allowed to export what little silk was not directly used. With Byzantine silk now locally produced, access to silk became much greater for the entire West.

—Patrick Norman Hunt

FURTHER READING

Franck, Irene M., and David M. Brownstone. *The Silk Road: A History.* New York: Facts On File, 1986. Comprehensive study of the history of the Silk Road as a crucial communication, trade, and travel route from the Mediterranean to Central China.

Liu, Xinru. *Silk and Religion: An Exploration of Material Life and the Thought of People, A.D. 600-1200.* New York: Oxford University Press, 1996. Explores the religious significance of silk and the silk trade in the Byzantine, Buddhist, Islamic, and Christian worlds of the Middle Ages. Maps, bibliography, and index.

Major, John S. *The Silk Route: Seven Thousand Miles of History*. New York: HarperCollins, 1995. Traces the history and purpose of the legendary trade route between China and the Byzantine Empire during the Tang Dynasty. Especially for young readers. Colored maps.

Norwich, John Julius. *A Short History of Byzantium*. New York: Knopf, 1997. Places Byzantine history and trade in context with imperial policy and changes taking place throughout the Eastern Roman Empire.

Procopius. *History of the Wars of Justinian*. Translated by H. B. Dewing. London: Heinemann, 1928. Describes how Justinian procured silk from China through direct contact with monks. A very reliable account of the smuggling of silkworms from China.

_______. *Secret History*. New York: Folio Society, 2000. Procopius's contemporary sixth century biography of Justinian provides firsthand accounts of the life of this emperor and his trade and economic policies, including discussion of the silk industry under imperial monopoly.

Rice, Tamara Talbot. *Everyday Life in Byzantium*. 1967. Reprint. New York: Barnes and Noble, 1994. Extensive account of Byzantine silk consumption and trade and the imperial monopoly.

Rodley, Lyn. *Byzantine Art and Architecture*. New York: Cambridge University Press, 1994. Discusses how the early Byzantine silk trade was a vital link between East and West.

Stockwell, Foster. *Westerners in China: A History of Exploration and Trade, Ancient Times Through the Present*. Jefferson, N.C.: McFarland, 2003. Examines the history of the West's trade with China, including the time of the silk trade into the Byzantine Empire. Also discusses "China's First Contacts with the West" and the history of the Silk Road. Map, bibliography, and index.

Wood, Frances. *The Silk Road: Two Thousand Years in the Heart of Asia*. Berkeley: University of California Press, 2002. Presents a history of trade routes in Asia, specifically the Silk Road. Maps, bibliography, and index.

Wyatt, James C. Y. *When Silk Was Gold: Central Asian and Chinese Textiles*. New York: Metropolitan Museum of Art, 1997. Describes Chinese and Central Asian medieval silk technology and discusses Central Asia's influence on production and exportation.

SEE ALSO: 6th-8th centuries: Sogdians Dominate Central Asian Trade; 751: Battle of Talas River; 1150: Venetian Merchants Dominate Trade with the East; 1271-1295: Travels of Marco Polo.

RELATED ARTICLES in *Great Lives from History: The Middle Ages, 477-1453*: Justinian I; Khosrow I; Taizong; Theodora.

567-568
SĀSĀNIANS AND TURKS DEFEAT THE WHITE HUNS

From the third through the fifth centuries, the White Huns repeatedly invaded eastern Persia until they were finally crushed by a combined force of Sāsānians and Turks. At times an uneasy alliance between the Sāsānians and White Huns developed out of political or military necessity because of threats from the Byzantine and Roman empires in the west.

LOCALE: Persia (now Iran, Iraq, Afghanistan, Pakistan, and parts of Russia)

CATEGORIES: Expansion and land acquisition; wars, uprisings, and civil unrest

KEY FIGURES

Kavadh I (d. 531), Sāsānian king, r. 488-531, who maintained a military alliance with the White Huns

Khosrow I (c. 510-579), Kavadh's son and Sāsānian king, r. 531-579, who finally defeated the White Huns

SUMMARY OF EVENT

The Parthians ruled Persia for four hundred years until the Sāsānians succeeded in overthrowing Artabanus V in 224, when he was killed in battle. The Sāsānian Dynasty ruled Persia from the third through the seventh centuries with the goal of diminishing Greek influence in the area. They centralized power by constructing roads and buildings; created a hierarchal social structure dependent on a king, followed by nobility (priests and warriors) and commoners (merchants, artisans, farmers, and slaves); established a code of law; and adopted Zoroastrianism, the belief that life was a continuous struggle between good and evil, as the designated state religion. The power of Sāsānian nobles also increased, and the king grew financially and militarily dependent on them, especially in their ongoing struggles against the White Huns (also known as the Hephthalites

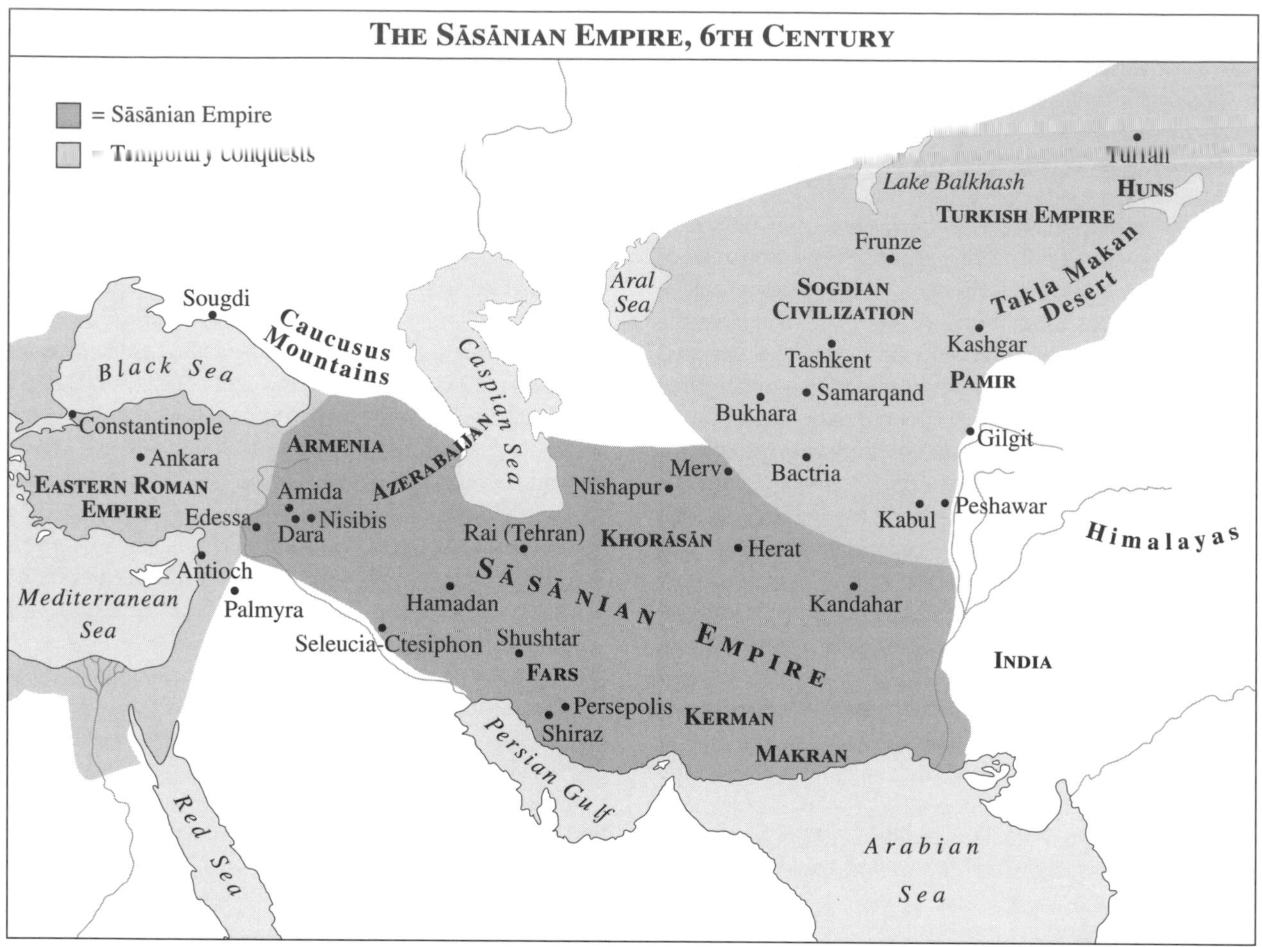

Ephthalites, or Hūṇas) during the next two hundred years.

The White Huns were an agricultural people who left no settlements or cities, nor written records. Famine was the reason they began to invade eastern Persia in the 390's. The White Huns also captured cattle for food and took people as slaves. They followed the Tigris and Euphrates Rivers to Ctesiphon (south of modern Baghdad), one of Persia's three capital cities. The White Huns managed to get to the outskirts of the city before Persian forces attacked them. Throughout the next two decades, the White Huns became a serious threat to Sāsānian rule in the region.

In 421, Barham V (r. 421-439) held various campaigns against the White Huns and was able to keep them from expanding farther into the Sāsānian kingdom. After his death, Persia experienced setbacks because of a series of severe droughts that caused the government to impose heavy taxes on the population.

Such issues helped the White Huns become victorious against Barham's successor, King Peroz (r. 459-484). Peroz was taken prisoner and released after the Sāsānian government paid a huge tribute for his return. However, Peroz was forced to leave his son, Kavadh I, as a hostage with the White Huns. Kavadh I did assume the throne in 488 and tried to implement socialist reforms in the distribution of goods and the elimination of private property. Members of Kavadh I's administration had him imprisoned, but he escaped and sought refuge with the White Huns in 499. Kavadh I eventually married the daughter of the Hunnish king and, with military support from the White Huns, recaptured the throne from his brother, Zamasp. He quickly abandoned his reform policies but continued to pay tribute to the White Huns. Kavadh I died in 531, and his son, Khosrow I, succeeded him to the throne.

Khosrow I proved to be a strong ruler who dealt the final blow to the White Huns. He began a series of administrative reforms that included taxes on land and a head tax. He also reorganized the military by forming four divisions under a separate commander, ordering compulsory service for peasants, reinforcing the infantry, and making nobles equip the army at their own expense. Khosrow I decided to stop the payment of tribute to the White Huns in 540 and built a line of defensive forts on the Gorgān Plain. He finally succeeded in destroying the White Huns' kingdom with the help of Turkish tribes that came into the region from the east, particularly from Central Asia. In 563, the Turks and Sāsānians defeated an army of White Huns near the Oxus River (now the Amu Dar'ya River).

The White Huns' threat had been eliminated for good; the few remaining White Huns were absorbed into tribes such as the Avars in eastern Iran. The Avars were Mongolians known to the Chinese as the Juan-juan. However, economic, political, and social turmoil would plague Sāsānian Dynasty during the next one hundred years. The administration in the Byzantine Empire, the new Roman capital, noticed the increasing strength of Persia. In 568, conflicts arose in Armenia when Roman Mesopotamia was invaded, and the Sāsānians successfully fought against the Byzantine army. However, Khosrow I died during peace negotiations.

SIGNIFICANCE

Khosrow's death sparked the downfall of the Sāsānian Empire over the next century, and a succession of incompetent rulers followed him. Repeated wars had left the Sāsānian Dynasty weak, undermining the state's economic, social, and religious stability. In 637, an Arab force destroyed the Sāsānians at Qadisiyah, and by 651, the Sāsānian Dynasty had completely collapsed under Yazdegerd III (r. 633-651). The Turkish khan, Istemi, received the share of the White Huns' lands after allying with the Persians. However, Turk power diminished in the region because of internal dissension and political problems. The Turks lost much of their eastern territory to China's Tang Dynasty, and the end came when they, along with Chinese forces, were defeated by the Arabs at the Battle of Talas in 751.

Gayla Koerting

MAJOR RULERS OF THE LATER SĀSĀNIAN EMPIRE, 309-651

Reign	*Ruler*
309-379	Shāpūr II
421-439	Barham V
459-484	Peroz
488-531	Kavadh I
531-579	Khosrow I
590-628	Khosrow II
633-651	Yazdegerd (Yazdgard) III

FURTHER READING

Bausani, Alessandro. *The Persians from the Earliest Days to the Twentieth Century.* Translated by J. B. Donne. London: Elek, 1971. Overview of the development of Persia from its origins to the early 1970's. Chapter 3 discusses the Sāsānid period. Includes illustrations and maps.

Bournoutian, George A. *A History of the Armenian People, Vol. 1. Pre-History to 1500 A.D.* Costa Mesa, Calif.: Mazda, 1993. Surveys the political history of the Armenian people from prehistory to 1500, with a focus on Armenian history in the context of world history. Includes maps, bibliography, and a good index.

Curtis, John. *Ancient Persia.* Cambridge, Mass.: Harvard University Press, 1990. A good overview of Persian history for general readers. Includes color photographs of British Museum artifacts, a list of rulers with reign dates, and a color map.

Ghirshman, Roman. *Persian Art: The Parthian and Sassanian Dynasties, 249 B.C.-A.D. 651.* New York: Golden Press, 1962. Discusses the artwork of the Parthians and the Sāsānians. Rejects the traditional view that Parthian art copies that of the Roman Empire, and argues instead that the works are Greco-Iranian-inspired and quite distinctive. Work includes numerous black-and-white and color plates with fold-out pages depicting sculptures and paintings.

Keegan, John. *A History of Warfare.* New York: Alfred A. Knopf, 1993. Author is a renowned military historian. Includes a select bibliography and sixty-three illustrations.

Rawlinson, George. *The Seven Great Monarchies of the Ancient Eastern World.* New York: B. Alden, 1885. Classic, scholarly three-volume work with detailed endnotes, chronological tables, illustrations, and fold-out maps.

Wiesehofer, Josef. *Ancient Persia: From 550 B.C. to 650 A.D.* Translated by Azizeh Azodi. New York: I. B. Tauris, 1996. A comprehensive study of the Persian Empire under the Achaeminids, the Parthians, and the Sāsānians. Focuses primarily on Persian written and archaeological sources rather than inaccurate Greek or Roman accounts. Includes black-and-white plates, bibliographical essays, a chronological table, and a list of dynasties and kings.

Windrow, Martin, ed. *Rome's Enemies 3: Parthians and Sassanid Persians*. London: Osprey, 1986. Focuses on armies of the Parthians and the Sāsānid Persians. Contains color plates of uniforms and insignia by artist Angus McBride.

Yarshater, Ehsan, ed. *The Seleucid, Parthian, and Sasanian Periods*. Vol. 3 in *The Cambridge History of Iran*. London: Cambridge University Press, 1983. Part of a seven-volume survey of essays on Iranian history, which provides political, military, and cultural information. Divided into themes such as institutions, religious history, art history, and languages and literature. Includes an extensive bibliography and a good index.

SEE ALSO: 484: White Huns Raid India; 563: Silk Worms Are Smuggled to the Byzantine Empire; 606-647: Reign of Harṣa of Kanauj; 890's: Magyars Invade Italy, Saxony, and Bavaria.

RELATED ARTICLE in *Great Lives from History: The Middle Ages, 477-1453*: Khosrow I.

568-571
LOMBARD CONQUEST OF ITALY

The conquest of Italy by the Lombards made the Byzantine reconquest ephemeral and underlined the permanent political separation of the eastern and western halves of what had once been the Roman Empire.

LOCALE: Italy

CATEGORIES: Expansion and land acquisition; wars, uprisings, and civil unrest

KEY FIGURES

Narses (c. 480-574), Byzantine general who had conquered Italy from the Ostrogoths

Alboin (d. 572), king of the Lombards who led the invasion of Italy, r. 565-572

Cunimund (d. 567), king of the Gepids defeated by Alboin in a fierce struggle

Rosamund, daughter of Cunimund; forced to marry Alboin

Justin II (d. 578), Byzantine emperor during whose reign Italy was lost to the Lombards, r. 565-578

Sophia, wife of Justin II

Longinus, Byzantine governor of Italy dispatched by Justin II

SUMMARY OF EVENT

From 535 to 552, Italy had been ravaged by the war between the Byzantine (East Roman) army, which was trying to reconquer the Italy lost by the Roman Empire in 476, and the Ostrogothic tribal leadership, which had dominated Italy for the previous sixty years. The Byzantine army, commanded by the aged Armenian eunuch Narses, had been ultimately victorious. Both the army and the finances of the Byzantine Empire itself, however, were exhausted, leaving Italy easy prey for future invaders.

The Lombards were one of numerous Germanic tribes of obscure origin and even more obscure subsequent migrations that played an unexpected political role in Europe in the wake of the dissolution of the Roman Empire. The Lombards called themselves the Longobards or "long-beards"; they are called the Lombards by modern-day historians because they settled in a part of Italy later known as Lombardy. In Italian, their name is "I Langobardi." Although the Lombards were among the last to make their historical mark, they had lived for centuries on the northeastern borders of the empire, most lately in the area of Pannonia (modern Hungary). By the mid-sixth century, they were serving as Byzantine allies against the Ostrogoths. Most of their military energies, though, were devoted to a bitter and protracted struggle against their fellow Germanic tribesmen and eastern neighbors, the Gepids. This struggle, taking place in a wooded region that later passed into Germanic legend as "Mirkwood," culminated when Alboin, the Lombard chieftain, slew his hated rival, the Gepid leader Cunimund, in 567. Alboin forced Rosamund, the daughter of Cunimund, to marry him; reportedly, he fashioned a drinking cup out of the skull of Cunimund and made Rosamund drink from it on the day of their wedding.

This anecdote and many others relating to the Lombard invasion may or may not be historically reliable: The problem is that the only real written source for Lombard history is the work of Paul the Deacon, which was written more than two hundred years after the events in question. Archaeological evidence, though, has proven much of Paul's account to be reasonably accurate. It is known from other sources that the Lombards were not able to rest easy in Pannonia after the defeat of the Gepids, as the area was shortly invaded by the powerful Asiatic tribe, the Avars. The Lombards had previously allied with the Avars to assure the defeat of the Gepids, but they now found themselves confronted by the far stronger Avaric power. From their longtime status as allies of the Byzantine Empire, Alboin knew that, despite the recent imperial successes in Italy, the Byzantine army was far weaker than it appeared. The combination of Lombard self-confidence, the Avar threat, and Byzantine vulnerability made the Lombards decide to invade Italy in 568.

A nineteenth century depiction of Alboin's entrance into Pavia. (F. R. Niglutsch)

The situation in Byzantine-occupied Italy was unstable because of the recent retirement of Narses, the eighty-five-year-old eunuch who had proved an improbably brilliant general, conquering much of Italy from the fierce Ostrogoths. Several historical accounts (of unsure reliability) report that this was because Narses was disliked by Sophia, the wife of Justin II, the new Byzantine emperor. Justin, who had succeeded his uncle, Justinian I, on the throne in Constantinople in 565, was an incompetent ruler, and Sophia made many of the decisions during his regime. Reportedly, Sophia had said that Narses, as a eunuch, was not entitled to be a general; instead, she believed he should have been stationed in the women's quarters of the palace at Constantinople. Behind this perhaps apocryphal story lies the very real suspicion that the new emperor and his wife were wary of Narses's power and prestige; there also exists evidence that they thought he had taken too many of the revenues of the Italian province for himself. Narses is then supposed to have invited the Lombards to invade Italy as a final form of retaliation against Constantinople.

Whatever the reasons, Narses was recalled (though he never left Italy, dying there in retirement in 574), and a man named Longinus was appointed to take his place. Before Longinus even reached the Italian administrative capital of Ravenna, however, the Lombards had marched into Italy. Alboin and his men had begun the march two days after Easter. The Lombard retinue included not only the Lombards but also the recently defeated Gepids, a few Alamanni, and a group of thousands of Saxons whom Alboin had invited along to share the booty. The Lombards were not a tightly organized army but rather an unsystematic group of warriors; however, they were militarily effective. The Lombards encountered little opposition as they entered Italy because the province was exhausted from the Gothic war as well as from a severe plague that had occurred in 565. The Lombards quickly occupied such key northern Italian cities as Milan, Modena, and, after a lengthy siege, Pavia. The only cities that stood successfully against the Lombards were the imperial capital of Ravenna, which was practically impregnable, and the city of Rome itself, protected by the authority of the pope.

The Lombards received a mixed welcome from their

LOMBARD KINGS, 565-774

Reign	*Ruler*
565-572	Alboin
572-575	Cleph
575-584	[illegible]
584-590	Authari
590-591	Theodelinda
591-615	Agilulf
615-625	Adaloald
625-636	Arioald
636-652	Rotharis
652-661	Aribert I
661-662	Godipert
662-671	Grimoald
671-674	Garibald
674-688	Bertharit
688-700	Cunibert
701	Raginpert
700-701	Liutpert
701-712	Aribert II
712-744	Liutprand
744-749	Rachis of Friuli
749-756	Aistulf of Friuli
756-774	Desiderius
774	Frankish conquest

new subjects. The Italians were unenthusiastic about Byzantine overlordship and welcomed a strong government that would offer them a respite from constant war. However, the Italians were overwhelmingly Catholic Christians (except for a few residual Ostrogoths), and the Lombard conquerors were predominantly Arian heretics, although there were Catholic and even pagan factions within Alboin's people. The Lombards were eventually to convert to Catholicism a century and a half later under the leadership of King Liutprand (r. 712-744), but until then, religion was a constant source of tension between them and their subjects.

The new Byzantine governor, Longinus, arrived soon enough to protect Ravenna and the area around it, which bordered the Adriatic Sea and was called the Pentapolis. Rome remained loosely associated with the Byzantine dominions, and the Byzantines also preserved Naples and some areas near the extreme south of Italy that were to remain under Byzantine rule until the eleventh century. The Lombards, though, ended up occupying the majority of the peninsula, and the Byzantines could do nothing to dislodge them, though they tried by intrigue, armed assaults (one of them led by Justin's son-in-law), and attempted cooperation with the Frankish rulers of Gaul in order to catch the Lombards in a kind of pincer movement.

SIGNIFICANCE

The Lombard invasion had permanently punctured the dream of restoring the Roman Empire in the west; from this point on, the Byzantine Empire was to be only a weak and limited force in Italy. The Lombards established a strong realm in the north with its capital at Pavia. They also ruled two separate duchies to the south of the thin Byzantine corridor stretching between Ravenna and Rome. These duchies, centered at Spoleto in Umbria and Benevento in the southeast respectively, were subject to the Lombard king in Pavia but not under his total control. This arrangement lasted for more than two centuries.

Alboin, however, was not to enjoy the fruits of his victory. He was assassinated at Verona in 572 in a conspiracy launched by Rosamund, still intent on avenging Alboin's cruelty to her and his murder of Cunimund, her father. Rosamund was aided by a henchman, Helmechis, and was also subsidized by the Byzantine governor, Longinus, who hoped to marry Rosamund. Rosamund was murdered shortly after, however, and Lombard rule was consolidated under the leadership of the kings Authari and Agilulf.

—*Nicholas Birns*

FURTHER READING

Christie, Neil. *The Lombards: The Ancient Langobards.* Oxford: Blackwell, 1995. An accessible survey of the history of the Lombard peoples, both before and after their settlement in Italy.

Fauber, Lawrence. *Narses: Hammer of the Goths.* New York: St. Martin's Press, 1990. This entertaining biography of the aged Byzantine general gives needed background.

Goffart, Walter. *The Narrators of Barbarian History: A.D. 550-800.* Princeton, N.J.: Princeton University Press, 1988. In discussing Paul the Deacon's account of Lombard history, Goffart also discusses that history itself.

Paul the Deacon. *History of the Langobards.* Translated by William Dudley Foulke. Philadelphia: University of Pennsylvania Press, 1974. Valuable primary source.

Schutz, Herbert. *The Germanic Realms in Pre-Carolingian Central Europe, 400-750.* New York: Peter Lang, 2000. An examination of the Germanic peoples who lived in Europe and invaded Rome and other areas.

Provides insights into the interactions between the Lombards and other groups. Bibliography and index.

Tabacco, Giovanni. *The Struggle for Power in Medieval Italy*. Cambridge, England: Cambridge University Press, 1989. Places the invasion in the context of the sweep of medieval Italian history.

SEE ALSO: February 2, 506: Alaric II Drafts the *Breviarum Alarici*; 532-537: Building of Hagia Sophia; 590-604: Reforms of Pope Gregory the Great; 1127-1130: Creation of the Kingdom of Sicily.

RELATED ARTICLE in *Great Lives from History: The Middle Ages, 477-1453*: Alboin.

581
SUI DYNASTY REUNIFIES CHINA

The Sui Dynasty reunified China, introduced administrative reforms, and created the Grand Canal system, laying the foundation for the Tang Dynasty and many Chinese institutions that lasted until the twentieth century.

LOCALE: China

CATEGORIES: Government and politics; wars, uprisings, and civil unrest

KEY FIGURES

Wendi (Wen-ti; 541-604), founder and first emperor of the Sui Dynasty, r. 581-604

Yangdi (Yang-ti; 569-617), second emperor of the Sui Dynasty, r. 604-617

Gongdi (Kung-ti; c. 611-618), third emperor of the Sui dynasty, r. 618

SUMMARY OF EVENT

After the breakup of the Western Jin Dynasty (Chin; 265-316), the Chinese Empire was plunged into more than one hundred years of turmoil and divided between north and south. The north was ruled by a series of barbarian, non-Chinese dynasties known as the Northern Dynasties, and in the south were the Southern Dynasties. In 577, the Northern Zhou Dynasty (557-581) defeated the Northern Qi (550-577) for control of the north. In 581, Yang Jian (Yang Chien), an aristocratic military officer affiliated with the Northern Zhou and acting as regent, claimed the mandate of heaven (spiritual authority to rule) and founded the Sui Dynasty (581-618), reigning as Wendi.

In 583, Wendi moved to a new capital, Chang'an (modern Xi'an), which he rebuilt with forced labor, making it the largest city in the world. To secure the empire's borders, Wendi eliminated the Turkish threat on the western border by supporting the Western Turks and encouraging division in the Eastern Turks; to secure the north, he repaired the Great Wall between 586 and 587.

With the north secured, he moved to reunify China. In 587, he conquered the Later Liang Dynasty (557-587) located in modern Hubei Province. By this time, the last of the Southern Dynasties, the Chen Dynasty (Ch'en; 557-589), had become weak, corrupt, disorganized, and inefficient. Wendi easily overran it in 589 by a swift invasion. North and south China were reunited once again.

Wendi was a strong, hardworking administrator. He made important and lasting administrative and legal reforms, beginning with a new legal code in 581 (revised in 583) that was simpler and more lenient than the previous one and became the pattern for the code of the following dynasty. He began to consolidate Sui power over China by centralizing civil and military power and incorporating the southern ruling class into the Sui bureaucracy. He simplified and reorganized the administrative structure—eliminating layers of officials, reducing the number of counties, and appointing local officials through the central government—to increase the control of the central government over the countryside. He eliminated the claims of hereditary privilege by reestablishing a civil service system based on appointment and promotions based on a merit system. The military system was reorganized as generally self-supporting militias, whose soldiers served periodic terms of duty but otherwise lived at home.

In the late 580's, Wendi carried out a new census of each household in the empire; he then reimposed the northern equal-field land allocation system. He reintroduced the old head tax system levied in grain and silk, and reduced the period of compulsory labor service. By improving the efficiency of the tax collection, Wendi accumulated great wealth for the empire. The resulting revenues were spent by later emperors on great public works projects and military campaigns.

In 583, he established a system of four state granaries to keep China supplied in times of drought or flood. To facilitate grain transport to the food-poor capitals, between 584 and 589, he constructed a canal eastward from Chang'an to the Tong Pass.

Wendi was a careful and economical ruler. He worked successfully to heal the political and cultural divisions between the north and south. He used Confucianism, Buddhism, and Daoism religions to legitimate himself as emperor and to unify a people long divided by various races, classes, religions, and regions. A new streamlined legal code of five hundred articles drew on both southern and northern legal principles. By the end of his reign, the Sui had become the greatest empire since the Han. Unfortunately, his successor squandered this legacy in extravagant construction projections, personal extravagance, and ambitious and failed military campaigns.

Wendi's second son Yang Guang (Yang Kuang) became viceroy of the south in 591. He plotted and schemed against his elder brother, who was demoted to commoner status, and was proclaimed the successor. He reigned as Yangdi from 604 to 617. Yangdi furthered the assimilation of the south into the empire and took more interest in its affairs, marrying a princess from the south. He weakened the hold of the northern aristocrats on the government by establishing an examination system based on the Confucian teachings. He also increased the south's importance by building a second capital at Luoyang (Lo-yang). This new capital and its palaces and gardens were built quickly with vast numbers of forced laborers (reportedly two million) employed in their construction and the transport of timber. Yangdi later added another southern capital on the Yangtze River.

Another part of Yangdi's efforts to unify the empire involved his plan to extend the Grand Canal system begun by his father. In 605, the canal connected Luoyang with the Huai River and then the Yangtze. In 610, the system was extended south to Hangzhou. Another canal was built northward from the Yellow River to the vicinity of modern-day Bejing. The canal system linked all the major rivers of the eastern plain from the Yangtze to the northern frontier, and canals allowed easy movement of grain and troops.

These canal construction projects were extremely expensive and caused great suffering among the population, who, one million workers at a time, provided the forced labor under conditions of great hardship. It is often said that these projects were done out of a desire to aggrandize Yangdi's own splendor and indulge his own pleasures. Vast amounts of forced labor were also employed to rebuild and strengthen the Great Wall in 607-609. In one year, one million men were sent out on this task, at great cost to human life: Five or six out of every ten workers died. Although these canals caused great hardship and misery among the people, they contributed greatly to the empire's unity and commerce.

MAJOR RULERS OF THE SUI DYNASTY

Reign	*Ruler*
581-604	Wendi
604-617	Yangdi
618	Gongdi

Yangdi's military adventures, however, were less successful. His military expeditions were successful at extending the empire southward into Vietnam, Taiwan, and Tonkin and westward along the trade route (the Silk Road), which opened up a prosperous trade with Central Asia and the West. However, other foreign adventures were futile and disastrous. Yangdi's agent unsuccessfully attempted to overthrow the Eastern Turk khan, which turned the powerful Eastern Turks into a hostile neighbor. The most disastrous ventures were Yangdi's campaigns against Korea. The most powerful of the Korean kingdoms, Koguryŏ, was hostile to China and refused to pay homage to Yangdi, who undertook a punitive campaign. After completing the Grand Canal from Luoyang to Bejing in 611, the emperor assembled a large army and great amounts of supplies. The first campaign was delayed by flood, but campaigns were launched in 612, 613, and 614. The first two were unsuccessful and cost hundreds of thousands of lives and resulted in desertion and banditry in the troops and outbreaks of rebellions in the provinces; these were put down by severe repression, which in turn led to further rebelliousness throughout the empire. The third campaign reached the Korean capital but withdrew without victory. These Korean campaigns brought great hardship and suffering to the people.

The empire was demoralized and ruined financially, and more uprisings and rebellions took place. Yangdi retreated to his southern capital on the Yangtze in 616 to live in luxury, while the northern part of his empire was taken over by local rebel warlords. In 617, Li Yuan, one of the powerful rebels, had a great victory over the Turks; he then seized the capital, overthrew other rebels, and occupied Sichuan and the Han River Valley. A Sui prince, Gongdi, was installed as a puppet, while Yangdi was "retired." After Yangdi's assassination in 618, Li Yuan deposed Gongdi and set himself up as emperor with the name Gaozu (Kao-tsu; r. 618-626) and founded the Tang

Dynasty (T'ang; 618-907), which would rule united China for nearly three hundred years.

SIGNIFICANCE

The impact and contributions of the Sui Dynasty to Chinese history far outweigh its brief life-span of less than forty years. Likewise, the harshness of the rulers and the overambitious failed military campaigns and grandiose building projects of the second emperor should not overshadow the dynasty's political and cultural achievements. The Sui reunited China, ending almost three hundred years of divided political authority and regional cultures (northern and southern). It unified the country not by new innovations but by fusing various legal and religious traditions of the north and south.

The dynasty established a strong, central political authority, revised the taxation and administrative systems, and expanded China's borders—thus laying the foundations for the even stronger Tang Dynasty and ultimately many of the institutions that held sway during the imperial period up to 1912. These measures to achieve administrative control over the empire also created political and cultural unity for China. The Grand Canal system allowed easy transport and travel throughout the empire.

Wendi's rule is noted for its reforms, prosperity, and high morale—which were all undone by his son, Yangdi. The second emperor's cruelty to his people and the excesses of his projects, which drained the populace and its wealth and disrupted the economy, finally led to popular resentment and rebellions and ultimately to the ruin of the Sui Dynasty.

—*Thomas McGeary*

FURTHER READING

Bingham, Woodbridge. *The Founding of the T'ang Dynasty.* 1941. Reprint. New York: Octagon Books, 1970. Contains a lengthy account of the Sui Dynasty, especially as it leads up to the Tang Dynasty.

Ebrey, Patricia B. *The Cambridge Illustrated History of China.* New York: Cambridge University Press, 1996. Brief account of the period, but good maps, illustrations, coverage of the arts and culture of the period, and further readings.

Gernet, Jacques. *A History of Chinese Civilization.* Translated by J. R. Foster. New York: Cambridge University Press, 1990. Extended account of history of the period, along with full treatment of culture and civilization.

Hook, Brian, ed. *The Cambridge Encyclopedia of China.* 2d ed. New York: Cambridge University Press, 1991. Brief chronological entries with numerous maps, charts, illustrations, and tables.

Huang, Ray. *China: A Macro History.* Armonk, N.Y.: East Gate, 1988. Good overview of the history of the period with attempts at a historical explanation of events.

Paludan, Ann. *Chronicle of the Chinese Emperors: The Reign-by-Reign Record of the Rulers of Imperial China.* London: Thames and Hudson, 1998. Thumbnail sketches of all the emperors with numerous other articles and illustrations.

Roberts, J. A. G. *A Concise History of China.* Cambridge, Mass.: Harvard University Press, 1999. As title suggests, a very concise presentation.

_______. *Prehistory to c. 1800.* Vol. 1 in *A History of China.* New York: St. Martin's, 1996. Good summary survey of the Sui Dynasty.

Rodzinski, Witold. *A History of China.* Vol. 1. Oxford, England: Pergamon Press, 1979. A concise account.

Schirokaur, Conrad. *A Brief History of Chinese Civilization.* New York: Harcourt Brace Jovanovich, 1991. Textbook that gives a good historical survey, as well as treatments of arts, society, science, religion, and technology.

"Sui Dynasty." In *Encyclopedia of Asian History.* Vol. 4, edited by Ainslie T. Embree. New York: Charles Scribner's, 1988. Good short overview.

Wright, Arthur F. *The Sui Dynasty.* New York: Alfred A. Knopf, 1979. Lengthy and very readable account of the dynasty, with special emphasis on biographies of the emperors.

_______. "The Sui Dynasty (581-617)." In *Sui and Tang China, 589-906.* Vol. 3 in *The Cambridge History of China.* New York: Cambridge University Press, 1979. Lengthy but very readable account.

SEE ALSO: 605-610: Building of the Grand Canal; 618: Founding of the Tang Dynasty.

RELATED ARTICLE in *Great Lives from History: The Middle Ages, 477-1453*: Taizong.

590-604
REFORMS OF POPE GREGORY THE GREAT

Pope Gregory the Great initiated reforms that established papal primacy and provided for a reorganization of Church practices and activities.

LOCALE: Italy and the Roman Empire
CATEGORY: Religion

KEY FIGURES

Pelagius II (d. 590), Roman Catholic pope, 579-590
Gregory the Great (c. 540-604), Roman Catholic pope, 590-604
Peter the Deacon (d. c. 605), Gregory's friend and fellow monk
Augustine of Canterbury (d. 604-605), prior of the monastery of Saint Andrew and missionary to England

SUMMARY OF EVENT

In the early Christian centuries, disputes about theology agitated the Church and threatened to divide it irreparably. Influential bishops took the lead in resolving such controversies, and the bishops of Rome thereby acquired a reputation as defenders of orthodoxy and authoritative teachers of doctrine. Among such powerful personalities was Gregory the Great, who became bishop at a time when the primacy of authority within the Church was much debated and church-state relations were still undefined. The capital of the Roman Empire had moved to Constantinople, and Italy was in danger from barbarian attacks.

Gregory came from an aristocratic Roman family; his ancestors included popes Felix III (483-492) and Agapetus (535-536). He obtained a fine education, especially in the law, and in 570, he became prefect of Rome, a position in which he led the senate and supervised matters of defense, finances, and internal security. Civil service did not satisfy him, however, so he abandoned this secular pursuit around 575 and became a monk. His family's estate became a renowned monastery, known as a site of learning and rigorous asceticism. Gregory intended to spend his life there pursuing monastic virtues.

Soon, however, Pope Benedict I made Gregory a deacon to administer charity in Rome, the next pontiff, Pelagius II, dispatched Gregory to Constantinople for seven years to be his legate at the imperial court. In 585, Gregory returned to his Roman monastery, hoping to enjoy its seclusion. Devastating floods and an epidemic of plague propelled him into public life again. When Pelagius died in the midst of the crisis, public acclaim demanded that Gregory succeed him as bishop of Rome.

In addition to the miseries that resulted from disease, Italy suffered from barbarian attacks, and Rome received numerous refugees. Gregory used crops from Church lands to feed hungry people, and he purchased more grain from Egypt. He was a skillful economic and political leader, and his deep sense of charity led him to ransom prisoners taken by the Lombards and to pay tribute in order to discourage further attacks.

Gregory did more than any previous Roman bishop to advance papal primacy. As a theologian, he had a profound influence because he was the first to present a well-formulated doctrine of Purgatory, which became a major theme in medieval belief. Gregory was rather naïve, however, in spiritual matters, accepting reports of miracles without substantiation. As one who believed in the imminent approach of the Apocalypse, which would mark the destruction of the world, he sometimes discouraged study of secular learning despite his own knowledge of classical literature.

Although Catholic rulers had sometimes compelled

GREGORY ON THE PREACHER'S RESPONSIBILITY TO SET A GOOD EXAMPLE

[I]t is surely necessary that those who give utterance to words of holy preaching should first be well awake in earnesteness of good living, lest they arouse others with their voice while themselves torpid in performance; that they should first shake themselves up by lofty deeds, and then make others solicitous for good living; that they should first smite themselves with the wings of their thoughts; that whatsoever in themselves is unprofitably torpid they should discover by anxious investigation, and correct by strict self-discipline, and then at length set in order the life of others by speaking; that they should take heed to punish their own faults by bewailings, and then denounce what calls for punishment in others; and that, before they give voice to words of exhortation, they should proclaim in their deeds all that they are about to speak.

Source: Gregory the Great, *Pastoral Care*, quoted in *A Source Book of Mediæval History*, edited by Frederic Austin Ogg (New York: American Book Company, 1908), p. 96.

pagans to accept Christianity, Gregory decried the practice of forced conversion. He contended that compulsion produced hypocrites, not converts. Among his most significant achievements was the extension of papal jurisdiction through missions to evangelize pagans and establish the authority of Rome in parts of Christendom where it did not prevail, particularly in Britain. In his desire to subject churches to the rule of bishops obedient to his authority, Gregory dispatched Augustine, a monk from the monastery of Saint Andrew in Rome, to England in 597 to seek the salvation of the Anglo-Saxons and to bring the British church to accept pontifical rule. Gregory rewarded Augustine's success by making him first archbishop of Canterbury. In a similar way, Gregory improved his position in Gaul and Spain, and he insisted that Italian bishops confer with him and submit to his supervision. He was highly successful in establishing the authority of the Vatican over broad areas of Christendom.

In a fifteenth century missal, Gregory is shown conducting what came to be known as the "miraculous Mass," in which Christ's real presence in the Eucharist is depicted here by his rising from the altar. (Frederick Ungar Publishing Co.)

Gregory was pope at a time when relations between the Papacy and the patriarchs of the Eastern churches were undefined and sometimes hostile. Gregory recognized the right of the patriarchs of Constantinople, Antioch, Alexandria, and Jerusalem to govern their own jurisdictions, but he asserted his own primacy and at times entertained appeals from clergy within those patriarchates. He disapproved of the archbishop of Constantinople's use of the title "ecumenical patriarch," and he declared unequivocally the universal extent of papal authority, asserting that the Church of Rome was "the head of all churches."

In addition to his success in cementing papal rule, Gregory exerted broad influence through his theological writings, some of which were composed before he became pope. *Liber regulae pastoralis* (591; *Pastoral Care*, 1950), *The Four Books of Dialogues on the Lives of the Italian Fathers and on the Immortality of Souls* (594), and a collection of his letters were all produced while he was pope.

In *Pastoral Care*, the pontiff explained his conception of a bishop's duties with regard to the spiritual well-being of his people, among which he emphasized the ministry of preaching as incumbent on all bishops, for only through that medium could they fulfill their responsibilities as successors to the apostles, the preeminent preachers of the New Testament. Gregory opposed the belief that a clergy member's main duties were ceremonial. *Pastoral Care* enjoyed wide circulation during the Middle Ages and appeared in Greek and Old English. Just as the rule of Saint Benedict served as a guide for monks, Gregory's work became the manual for bishops.

The Four Books of Dialogues on the Lives of the Italian Fathers and on the Immortality of Souls was addressed to general readers as well as to clerics. Gregory composed this work in the form of a conversation with Peter the Deacon, and therein he extolled the pious lives of saints from the sixth century (to whom he was quick to attribute miracles). The second dialogue deals with Saint Benedict of Nursia (c. 480-c. 547), founder of the Benedictine order, and is the main source of information about the most influential figure in Western monasticism. Gregory believed that the intercession of Benedict was responsible for numerous miracles, but he hastened to add that some of the finest saints had no miracles to their credit, their holy lives being the attestation to their sanctity.

In thus acclaiming the saints, Gregory encouraged the practice of invoking their intercession with God, a practice that became customary in medieval devotion. In the same way, Gregory promoted the veneration of relics and images of the saints. In letters to various bishops, the pontiff reprimanded clerics who denigrated the use of images in Catholic worship, even when ignorant people worshiped them in violation of the divine law against idolatry. Gregory held that the duty of the clergy was to teach against superstition while not contending that the use of images per se was sinful.

Gregory's formulation of the doctrine of Purgatory is an especially significant feature of his dialogues on the lives of the Italian Fathers. He taught that judgment comes right after death and that a purgation by fire awaited believers as a means to purify them of offenses that did not merit damnation. The prayers of living Christians could benefit souls in Purgatory because the good deeds of people on Earth could be reckoned to those in torment. The fourth dialogue includes graphic depictions of Hell as well as Purgatory, and it portrays Heaven as the realm of eternal bliss. Gregory's teaching about life after death promised immediate entry into Heaven for those souls who were worthy. According to him, these worthy souls would not have to wait until judgment day, as previous theologians had affirmed.

SIGNIFICANCE

Gregory's pontificate occurred during Europe's transition from classical to medieval times. His influence helped carry that movement forward in church organization, missions, moral and doctrinal theology as well as in mystical and ascetical practices of devotion. Eventually, the church arranged masses on thirty consecutive days and assigned a special indulgence for all who participated. The series became known as the "Gregorian Masses," named after a story that appeared in Gregory's dialogues in which a monk obtained release from Purgatory after people on earth had transferred the benefits to his soul. Medieval authors cited Gregory as the author of chants that became popular in that era. His exact role in their development is not clear, but the influence of Gregorian chants on church music is undeniable. In 1298, Pope Boniface VIII declared Gregory a doctor of the Church, thus laying the foundation for the custom of referring to him as Gregory the Great.

James Edward McGoldrick

FURTHER READING

Bremmer, Rolf H., Jr., Kees Dekker, and David F. Johnson, eds. *Rome and the North: The Early Reception of Gregory the Great in Germanic Europe*. Sterling, Va.: Peeters, 2001. A look at how Gregory the Great was perceived in early Germanic literature. Bibliography and indexes.

Cavadini, John D. *Gregory the Great*. Notre Dame, Ind.: University of Notre Dame Press, 1996. A biography of Gregory the Great that also examines early church history. Bibliography and index.

_______, ed. *Gregory the Great: A Symposium*. Notre Dame, Ind.: University of Notre Dame Press, 1995. A collection of essays on Gregory the Great and the early Church. Topics include the pope's holiness, his knowledge of Greek, and his influence on astronomy and early Middle Age doctrines on the artistic image.

Dudden, F. Holmes. *Gregory the Great*. 2 vols. New York: Russell & Russell, 1969. The classic biography of Gregory, Dudden's work established a benchmark to which all subsequent scholarship has responded.

Markus, R. A. *Gregory the Great and His World*. New York: Cambridge University Press, 1997. A discussion of Gregory the Great that focuses on his theology and his relations with religious and secular leaders as well as discusses the environment in which he functioned.

Straw, Carole. *Gregory the Great*. Brookfield, Vt.: Variorum, 1996. A concise introduction to Gregory's life and work. Bibliography.

_______. *Gregory the Great: Perfection in Imperfection*. Berkeley: University of California Press, 1988. Marked by its erudite scholarship, Straw's work is an excellent analysis of Gregory.

SEE ALSO: 596-597: See of Canterbury Is Established; 731: Bede Writes *Ecclesiastical History of the English People*; 12th-14th centuries: Social and Political Impact of Leprosy.

RELATED ARTICLES in *Great Lives from History: The Middle Ages, 477-1453*: Saint Benedict of Nursia; Boniface VIII.

593-604
REGENCY OF SHŌTOKU TAISHI

Shōtoku Taishi, a prince and a member of the influential Soga family, carried out a number of reforms that transformed the Japanese court between 593 and 604. Among his many innovations were a system of court ranks and the Seventeen Article Constitution, which gave a new ideological direction to Japanese political life.

LOCALE: Central Japan
CATEGORIES: Government and politics; laws, acts, and legal history

KEY FIGURES

Shōtoku Taishi (574-622), regent of Empress Suiko's government, 593-622
Suiko (554-628), empress of Japan, r. 593-628
Soga Umako (d. 626), court noble
Yōmei (d. 587), emperor of Japan, r. 585-587

SUMMARY OF EVENT

In the late sixth century, the Japanese court was dominated by the powerful Soga family. Soga Umako, the head of the clan, had managed to gain power over the imperial family through intrigue and by defeating other influential families such as the Mononobe in battle. The Soga further entrenched their power by forcing the emperors to take Soga women as their consorts, thus ensuring that future heirs to the throne would have ties to the Soga. Shōtoku Taishi, a son of the emperor Yōmei, was a member of the Soga family and was appointed as regent of the empress Suiko by Soga Umako in 593. Scholars believe that Umako recognized the young prince's ability and gave him the position despite the fact that he was just nineteen years old. This decision, and Shōtoku Taishi's extraordinary ability as a scholar and administrator, ushered in what is thought to be one of the most important reform movements in Japanese history.

Most of the traditions concerning Shōtoku Taishi's life are clearly fantastic in nature. As is common in mythologies of this type, his birth was said to have been auspicious and completely without effort for his mother, the empress-consort Anahobe no Hashibito. He reportedly could speak like an adult shortly after being born. As an adult, his fame as a wise and capable administrator was so great that it was said that he could hear ten lawsuits at one time and decide them all without error. His mastery of Buddhist and Confucian doctrines was also legendary. He is said to have had premonitions. Although these traditions obviously are exaggerated, it is clear that Shōtoku Taishi was a capable scholar and administrator and that both his father and Soga Umako trusted him implicitly.

The Seventeen Article Constitution is traditionally thought to have been created by Shōtoku Taishi in 604. Recently, some scholars have come to question the authenticity of the document, insisting that it was written decades after Shōtoku Taishi's death in dedication to his memory. Whatever its origins, however, the ideas behind the Seventeen Article Constitution, whether they were codified in Shōtoku Taishi's lifetime or not, were no doubt popularized by him and created a major turning point in Japanese political and intellectual history. The document reflects the chaotic nature of Shōtoku Taishi's times and the attempt to use continental philosophy to come to terms with these events and to promote the centralization of power. Although Shōtoku Taishi is known as a devout Buddhist, he found the political ideas that were to form the basis of the authority of the Japanese court in Chinese Confucianism.

The Seventeen Article Constitution opens with a statement to the effect that harmony is to be valued above all else, and opposition to the power of the imperial family is always to be avoided. This is both a direct quotation from the Confucian *Lunyu* (late sixth-early fifth centuries B.C.E.; *The Analects*, 1861) and an obvious attempt to quiet resistance to central authority in Japan. In the Confucian tradition, the ruler is responsible for providing moral guidance to his people. Their obedience to him is considered to be a natural part of a reciprocal relationship. In attempting to present the imperial institution in these terms, Shōtoku Taishi not only aimed to increase the prestige of the Japanese court by associating it with the majesty of the Chinese emperors but also sought to promote loyalty to the central government in a period in which factions, each vying for power and influence, had become the political norm.

Despite the Confucian emphasis, however, Buddhist ideas are not entirely absent from the text. Buddhism was very much a political issue in seventh century Japan. The Soga family, to which Shōtoku Taishi belonged, managed to increase its power by establishing itself as the defender of the Buddhist faith. The second article of the seventeen appeals to followers to revere the three treasures—the Buddha, the law, and the monastic orders—which are the main objects of faith in Buddhist belief. This was an obvious attempt by Shōtoku Taishi, himself a devout Buddhist, to associate the religion with the central government of Japan. However, in the end, the message of the constitution, even when couched in religious terms, is purely secular. The document orders vassals to scrupulously obey imperial commands and to keep their duties in mind at all times. In the rhetoric of the document, vassals are compared to the earth and the lord to heaven. It is not difficult to see how this type of thought, Chinese in origin, helped to foster the establishment of a strong central government in Japan.

Although Shōtoku Taishi clearly had a great deal of respect for China and its government—aside from his own studies of Chinese philosophy and political procedure, he sent scholars to the Chinese court to study—his tenure in power is also important in that it represents the first real attempt by the Japanese court to assert its equality with China. As is recorded in the Chinese dynastic histories, one of the letters that Shōtoku Taishi sent to the Chinese emperor was addressed from "the Son of Heaven of the Land of the Rising Sun to the Son of Heaven of the Land of the Setting Sun." This displeased the Chinese government but stands as the first real attempt by a Japanese leader to distinguish the Japanese islands from the other tributary territories that existed on the periphery of the Chinese empire.

Shōtoku Taishi died in 622 at the age of forty-eight, and Soga Umako died four years later. This turn of events eventually led to the Soga family's fall from power, but Shōtoku Taishi's legacy served as the inspiration for the Taika reforms of 645-646. Despite his associations with the unfortunate Soga family, Shōtoku Taishi became something of a mythical figure and continued to be remembered as a wise and capable administrator.

MAJOR EMPERORS OF THE ASUKA (538-710) AND NARA (710-794) PERIODS

Reign	*Ruler*
539-571	Kimmei
572-585	Bidatsu
585-587	Yōmei
587-592	Sushun
593-628	Suiko (f)
629-641	Jomei
642-645	Kōgyoku (f)
645-654	Kōtoku
655-661	Saimei (f)
661-672	Tenji
672	Kōbun
673-686	Temmu
686-697	Jitō (f)
697-707	Mommu
707-715	Gemmei (f)
715-724	Genshō (f)
724-749	Shōmu
749-758	Kōken (f)
758-764	Junnin
764-770	Shōtoku (Kōken; f)
770-781	Kōnin
781-806	Kammu

Note: (f) indicates an empress.

SIGNIFICANCE

The reforms carried out during Shōtoku Taishi's life were the first major step in the development of a centralized state in Japan. He established and codified both the institutional and ideological framework of central power in the Japanese archipelago. The basis that he established was further built on in the years after his death and served as the source of power of the Japanese court society until it was superceded by regional warrior families more than five hundred years later. Even after the evolution of samurai society eclipsed the authority of the court, the ideological and institutional developments of Shōtoku Taishi's tenure in power continued to exert a great influence over the art of government and scholarship in Japan. Shōtoku Taishi was the first Japanese scholar administrator to become well versed in both Buddhist and Confucian teaching, and his support of both ideological systems would ensure that the two traditions would continue to have a great influence on the Japanese culture and political system.

Shōtoku Taishi's emphasis on social harmony has made him a popular figure throughout Japanese history. Today he is viewed as a symbol of *wa*, or "harmony." His valuable maxim that decisions on important matters should not be made by one person alone and that they should be discussed with many is reflected in the consensus-type decision making favored by Japanese business and political leaders. In addition, Shōtoku Taishi appears as an important character in numerous Japanese films and works of fiction.

—*Matthew Penney*

FURTHER READING

Aston, W. G., trans. *Nihongi: Chronicles of Japan from the Earliest Times to A.D. 697*. 1896. Reprint. Tokyo: Charles E. Tuttle, 1972. The standard translation of one of the earliest works of Japanese history. Provides details about the life of Shōtoku Taishi and the impact of his reforms.

De Bary, William Theodore, et al., comps. *Sources of Japanese Tradition*. Vol. 1. 2d ed. New York: Columbia University Press, 2001. Contains complete reprints of the Seventeen Article Constitution as well as other important documents relating to Shōtoku Taishi's life.

Sansom, George. *A History of Japan to 1334*. Vol. 1. Stanford, Calif.: Stanford University Press, 1958. The first volume of Sansom's three-volume study of Japanese history remains one of the most detailed and authoritative works on the subject.

Tamura, Yoshio. *Japanese Buddhism: A Cultural History*. Translated by Jeffrey Hunter. Tokyo: Tuttle, 2001. A detailed assessment of the cultural implications and historical development of Japanese Buddhism from the introduction of the faith to modern times, including details of Shōtoku Taishi's life and his place in the development of the Buddhist religion in Japan.

See also: 5th or 6th century: Confucianism Arrives in Japan; 538-552: Buddhism Arrives in Japan; 607-839: Japan Sends Embassies to China; 645-646: Adoption of *Nengo* System and Taika Reforms; 701: Taihō Laws Reform Japanese Government; March 9, 712, and July 1, 720: Writing of *Kojiki* and *Nihon Shoki*.

Related articles in *Great Lives from History: The Middle Ages, 477-1453*: Shōtoku Taishi; Suiko.

595-665
Invention of Decimals and Negative Numbers

The development of a decimal place-value system made numbers easier to use, while acceptance of negative numbers aided with the development of algebra and new physical applications. The best evidence available points to India as the locale for the most significant steps in the process.

Locale: India, China

Categories: Cultural and intellectual history; mathematics; science and technology

Key Figures

Āryabhaṭa the Elder (c. 476-c. 550), Indian mathematician and astronomer

Brahmagupta (c. 598-c. 660), Indian mathematician and astronomer

Mahāvīra (c. 800-c. 870), Jaina mathematician

Bhāskara (1114-c. 1185), Indian mathematician and astronomer

al-Khwārizmī (c.780-c. 850), Indian mathematician

Summary of Event

The awareness of the "number" concept and its applications is fundamental to civilization and the building of knowledge. Indeed, many ancient cultures around the world developed the ability to count, measure time and space, and make arithmetical and geometric calculations for astronomy and other scientific endeavors. The various numeral systems that resulted generally denoted numbers by words or by a large set of symbols. Only positive numbers were considered.

Place-value systems—meaning that each "digit" in a number represented a multiple of the base—existed in Babylonia at least in part around 2000 B.C.E., in China by 200 B.C.E., and in the Maya Empire between 200 and 665 C.E. Sometime between 200 B.C.E. and 600 C.E., however, Indian mathematicians and scribes began writing numbers in true place-value notation with symbols for the numerals 1 through 9, which had evolved from the middle of the third century B.C.E. Writers gradually discarded the separate symbols they had for 10, 100, 1000, . . . ; 20, 30, 40, . . . 90; and 200, 300, 400, . . . 900. For example, Āryabhaṭa the Elder wrote a mathematics and astronomy textbook called *Āryabhaṭīya* (499; *The Aryabhatiya*, 1927) that contained numbers in place-value form with nine symbols (but no zero). A donation charter of Dadda III of Sankheda in the Bharukachcha region prepared in 595 is the oldest known dated Indian document containing a number in decimal place-value notation including zero.

Indeed, a symbol for zero is necessary for a fully decimal-positional system. Empty spaces in numbers may have been marked in ancient Egypt, Babylonia, and Greece. The Maya certainly used zero as a placeholder in their base-20 system by 665. In India, a dot as a zero to mark an empty place appeared in the Bakhshali manuscript, which may date to the 600's or earlier. Other Indian texts used ten symbols in a decimal place-value system to facilitate such tasks as multiplication. The word *kha* was sometimes used instead of a zero symbol, and the empty circle was widely adopted late in the ninth century.

Unlike Maya numerals, which were confined to that civilization, the Indian system quickly spread into other regions of the world. Inscriptions that date to 683 and 684 and employ zero as a placeholder have been found in Cambodia and in Sumatra, Indonesia. Indian astronomers used their numerals in the service of the Chinese emperor by 718. Arab scholars and merchants learned of the nine-sign Indian system in the 600's and 700's. All ten digits had reached Baghdad by 773, and they were used for positional notation in Spain by the 800's.

However, the symbols used to represent the numbers evolved separately in the western and eastern regions of the Arab Empire, with the symbols in the west (North Africa and Spain) remaining more like the original Indian versions by 1000. These symbols were standardized into today's form with the advent of printing in the 1400's. Many European scholars were introduced to the decimal place-value system through a book on the Indian symbols written in 825 by al-Khwārizmī, which was anonymously revised and translated into Latin in the 1100's as *Algoritmi de numero Indorum* (al-Khwārizmī on the Indian art of reckoning; "Thus Spake al-Khwarizmi," 1990). Some European Christians were already familiar with Indian number symbols, though; for example, they have been found in the *Codex Vigilanus*, which was copied by a Spanish monk in 976.

Negative numbers most likely first appeared in China. The anonymous work *Jiuzhang suanshu* (nine chapters on the mathematical art), which dates approximately to the second century, provides correct rules for adding and subtracting with both negative and positive numbers. The concept of negative numbers was apparently transmitted to India in the second century, where mathematicians developed true fluency in handling negatives, including the ability to multiply and divide these numbers. These Indian advancements were then transmitted back to China by the 1300's. For instance, Brahmagupta introduced negative numbers to an Indian audience in 628 through the astronomy text *Brahmasphuṭasiddhānta* (the opening of the universe). His arithmetical rules of operation were updated by Mahāvīra in *Ganita sara sangraha* (850; compendium of the essence of mathematics). In the twelfth century, the six books by Bhāskara represented the peak of contemporary mathematical knowledge. He improved notation by placing a dot over a number to denote that it was negative. He accepted negative solutions and encouraged others to accept them as well, providing several word problems to test the reader's calculating skills.

Many of these works were also notable for their authors' efforts to treat zero as an abstract number and to understand its properties. Brahmagupta and Bhāskara agreed that any number minus itself was zero and that any number multiplied by zero was zero. They disagreed on the result when dividing by zero. Brahmagupta said the result when dividing zero by zero was zero. Bhāskara realized that Brahmagupta was incorrect, but he concluded that *(a.0)/0* is *a* in his work on mathematics, *Līlāvatī* (c. 1100's; the beautiful). In a later book on algebra, *Bījaganita* (c. 1100's; seed counting or root extraction), he suggested that *a* divided by zero yielded infinity. This would force zero multiplied by infinity to equal every number *a*, or to prove that all numbers are equal. Bhāskara did not attempt to resolve this issue or to admit that dividing by zero is impossible.

SIGNIFICANCE

Although the decimal place-value system facilitates arithmetical computation, it was not easily accepted as it moved outward from India. The dissemination of Indian numeral symbols was necessarily slowed by the complex paths of transmission that roughly followed medieval trade routes. Additionally, even though writers such as al-Uqlīdisī trumpeted the utility of decimal numbers in *Kitāb al-fuḥūl fi al-ḥisāb al-Hindī* (952-953; *The Arithmetic of al-Uqlidisi*, 1978), artisans and merchants often saw no compelling reason to give up their existing numerical practices, such as finger reckoning. Indian number symbols also sometimes mixed with existing symbol sets as they entered new cultures. Finally, it took time for mathematicians to understand and adopt ten-character decimal symbols (rather than nine) that employed zero first as a placeholder and then as an abstract number in its own right.

Negative numbers also aroused the foundational concerns, definitional difficulties, and philosophical baggage of the number zero. Although writers such as al-Khwārizmī did not recognize negative numbers or zero as algebraic coefficients, this stumbling block was perhaps especially prevalent in Europe, where the rules for decimal and negative numbers in Leonardo of Pisa's *Liber abaci* (English translation, 2002), were widely read but not always taken up immediately. In fact, European mathematicians into the eighteenth century questioned the validity of negative numbers and often made computational errors when they did work with these numbers. Such influential Renaissance and early modern mathematicians as Regiomontanus, Gerolamo Cardano, and François Viète went so far as to discard negative solutions. Nevertheless, these numbers simultaneously enabled the development of modern algebra. In the end, the decimal and negative numbers that arrived in Europe from India via Islam revolutionized and algebraized mathematics. They became the basis of the European number system and were key components of the new mathematical discipline—including analytical geometry, mechanics, and differential and integral calculus—that emerged in the early modern period.

—*Amy Ackerberg-Hastings*

FURTHER READING

Calinger, Ronald. *A Contextual History of Mathematics*. Upper Saddle River, N.J.: Prentice Hall, 1999. History of mathematics with significant discussions of the development of arithmetic and numbers.

Gupta, R. C. "Spread and Triumph of Indian Numerals." *Indian Journal of History of Science* 18, no. 1 (1983): 23-38. Classic work on the subject with many examples of early uses of the symbols outside India, although Gupta's claim that the numerals entered Europe by 500 is wrong.

Joseph, George Gheverghese. *The Crest of the Peacock: The Non-European Roots of Mathematics*. London: Tauris, 1991. Standard reference on the history of non-Western mathematics.

Kaplan, Robert. *The Nothing That Is: A Natural History of Zero*. New York: Oxford University Press, 2000. Entertaining account that can by enjoyed even by readers who like numbers but not mathematics.

Martzloff, Jean-Claude. *History of Chinese Mathematics*. Translated by Stephen S. Wilson. Berlin: Springer, 1987. Comprehensive introduction to Chinese mathematics.

Pycior, Helena M. *Symbols, Impossible Numbers, and Geometric Entanglements: British Algebra Through the Commentaries on Newton's Universal Arithmetick*. New York: Cambridge University Press, 1997. Details how struggles with the concept of negative numbers continued through early modern Europe.

SEE ALSO: c. 1100: Arabic Numerals Are Introduced into Europe.

RELATED ARTICLES in *Great Lives from History: The Middle Ages, 477-1453*: Āryabhaṭa the Elder; Brahmagupta; al-Khwārizmī; Leonardo of Pisa.

596-597
SEE OF CANTERBURY IS ESTABLISHED

The See of Canterbury facilitated the conversion of the Kentish kingdom to Christianity by bringing England back into the Catholic Church and firmly reestablishing English ties to the Continent.

LOCALE: Kent, England

CATEGORIES: Organizations and institutions; religion

KEY FIGURES

Gregory the Great (c. 540-604), Roman Catholic pope, 590-604, who sent out a missionary party to Kent in 596

Augustine (d. 604/605), head of Gregory's missionary party and first archbishop of Canterbury, 597-604/605

Æthelbert I (d. 616), king of Kent, r. 560-616, and chief English ruler south of the Humber River, converted by Augustine

Bertha (d. 612), queen of Kent, Frankish Christian wife of Æthelbert I

Saint Paulinus (c. 584-644), Roman priest and head of a mission from Canterbury to Northumbria in 625

SUMMARY OF EVENT

Although the Church in England was sufficiently well established by the fourth century to be represented by bishops at church councils on the Continent, it survived the Anglo-Saxon invasion only in remote areas in the west and north and, like other aspects of English culture, failed to influence the heathen Germanic settlers to any significant extent. Nearly a century and a half after the first settlements, the conversion of the English was undertaken by an abbot named Gregory, who would later become Pope Gregory the Great. Saint Bede the Venerable recorded that Gregory's interest in the English was aroused by the sight of English youths sent to Rome to be sold as slaves. Gregory was impressed by their fair complexions and was moved to inquire about their origin, expressing a desire that their people be saved from the darkness of heathenism. As a consequence of this encounter, Gregory is said to have sought permission to undertake the mission himself. The pope granted permission, but popular demand forced Gregory to abandon the project and remain in Rome.

Canterbury Cathedral in Kent, England. (PhotoDisc)

In 595, five years after he became pope, Gregory wrote to a priest to arrange for the education of Anglo-Saxon boys in monasteries in Gaul, perhaps so that they could later contribute to missionary work in their native land. In the following year, he dispatched a missionary party from Rome to preach to the English in Kent, the chief kingdom south of the Humber River. Augustine, prior of Saint Andrew's, a monastery that Gregory founded and where he served as abbot, was put in charge of a party of about forty monks. In southern Gaul, the mission lost heart and sent its leader back to ask Gregory to give up his plan. The pope ordered the group to continue and gave Augustine absolute authority by making him abbot over the monks. Gregory also provided commendatory letters to influential secular and ecclesiastical officials in Gaul so that the dangers of the journey might be lessened.

In 597, Augustine and his party arrived in Kent and met King Æthelbert I on the Isle of Thanet. Æthelbert was acquainted with Christianity, for he had married a Christian Frankish princess, Bertha, some nine years before. Bertha had brought with her a priest, Luithard, and had continued to practice her religion in her new country, using a church that had survived from Roman times. Moreover, Kentish merchants engaged frequently in trade with their Frankish neighbors and must have brought back information about Christianity. Whatever the influence of these political and economic ties may have been, Æthelbert received Augustine with hospitality and granted the missionaries permission to preach, endowing the group with land for churches.

Some scholars speculate that Æthelbert welcomed the mission from Rome so quickly because it provided him with a means of showing his independence from the growing power of the Franks, giving allegiance to Gregory in Rome instead. Scholars disagree about the date of Æthelbert's conversion. Some place it in 597, soon after Augustine's arrival; others believe that it was postponed until as late as 601. The date of Augustine's consecration as archbishop of Canterbury is also in dispute. Most scholars agree that it took place at Autun late in 597, when the success of the mission seemed assured, but a few maintain that Augustine was consecrated before he arrived in Kent.

The work in Kent apparently went well, for in one of his letters written in 598, Gregory mentioned that ten thousand Anglo-Saxons had been baptized. This information he doubtless received from messengers whom Augustine sent to Rome that year to report on the progress of the mission and to request additional help and answers to questions about the new church. Gregory's response to Augustine was delayed until 601, when he sent competent men to join the mission, a pallium for Augustine, letters to Æthelbert and Bertha urging their support of the church, answers to Augustine's questions, and instructions for the episcopal organization of all England. In answering Augustine's questions, the pope instructed his archbishop to bring the native church in England under the authority of Rome because, during its long isolation from Rome, it had developed practices that differed from those of the Western church as a whole and that distinguished Celtic from Roman Christianity. Gregory's desire for a Christian England, unified in its acceptance of Roman Catholic doctrine and having a well-defined and efficient episcopal structure, was not realized for many years. In addition, the archbishopric he established at Canterbury did not play a major role in the Catholic Church in England until more than seventy years after Augustine's landing. Augustine and his successor, Lawrence, attempted to extend the Christian faith outside Kent into the neighboring kingdoms of Essex and East Anglia, but the results proved to be superficial and short-lived.

A later mission to Northumbria under Saint Paulinus was dramatically successful for a brief period but was brought to an end by a resurgence of heathenism. The manner of Paulinus's conversion of the Northumbrians, however, remained significant in the development of Christianity in England. In his instructions to Paulinus regarding the best way to proceed in his mission, Gregory counseled him not to destroy the pagan temples or their customs and observances but rather to transform what he found, baptizing or Christianizing the old observances to make them new.

The story is told memorably by Bede. A Northumbrian counselor, listening to Paulinus preach, counsels his king that this life on earth is like warriors feasting in a hall when, at one door, a sparrow flies in from the dark and cold, circles the warmth and light for a few minutes, and then is gone out the other door into darkness again. Christianity, the counselor argues, unlike their paganism, offers an answer to what lies beyond the two doors. The chief priest then rides into the temple and pulls down the idols worshiped there, but the temple remains and is consecrated to Christian worship.

Most of the work of conversion outside Kent fell to others, primarily to the Irish, who, like the Britons, were adherents of Celtic Christianity. Augustine's effort to enlist the support of the Celtic church merely aggravated hostility in southern England between the two churches. Here, too, the lead was eventually taken by others.

Augustine's success was limited to the establishment of the See of Canterbury. With its establishment and survival, written learning and written law, Latin architecture, liturgy, and civilization were established in England. Despite a strong revival of heathenism under Eadbald, Æthelbert's successor, the see remained occupied and the succession of archbishops was uninterrupted until 664. Christianity in Kent was soon well established.

SIGNIFICANCE

Although it did not play a major role for many years, the see was the traditional center for Roman Christianity in England and provided a model to others in its organization and in its school for bishops. When, in 669, Theodore arrived from Rome to fill the vacancy at Canterbury,

THE PARABLE OF THE SPARROW

As told by Bede in his Ecclesiastical History of the English People, *one of King Edwin of Northumbria's counselors tells this story to persuade Edwin to accept Christianity:*

The present life of man, O king, seems to me, in comparison with that time which is unknown to us, like to the swift flight of a sparrow through the room wherein you sit at supper in winter amid your officers and ministers, with a good fire in the midst, whilst the storms of rain and snow prevail abroad; the sparrow, I say, flying in at one door and immediately out at another, whilst he is within is safe from the wintry storm; but after a short space of fair weather he immediately vanishes out of your sight into the dark winter from which he has emerged. So this life of man appears for a short space, but of what went before or what is to follow we are utterly ignorant. If, therefore, this new doctrine [Christianity] contains something more certain, it seems justly to deserve to be followed.

Source: Saint Bede the Venerable, *Ecclesiastical History of the English People*, quoted in *Readings in European History*, edited by James Harvey Robinson, abridged edition (Boston: Ginn & Company, 1906), pp. 48-49.

he made use of the foundations that had already been laid for the organization of the Church under the leadership of Canterbury and for the establishment of centers of learning that were to make England the intellectual leader of the Western world in the eighth century.

Canterbury's emergence from its struggle for primacy with the rival see of York in the later Middle Ages and its close association with the English monarch as spiritual father, adviser, and consecrator elevated its power further in English national life until the advent of the Reformation in the sixteenth century, when the monarch emerged not only as protector of the Church but as its head as well. In succeeding centuries, the see of Canterbury continued to be inseparably linked with king and country in national life.

—*Frances R. Lipp, updated by James Persoon*

FURTHER READING

Bede. *A History of the English Church and People.* Translated by Leo Sherley-Price. New York: Penguin, 1981. Originally written in Latin in the eighth century, this work constitutes the chief source of written information about the early English Church.

Edwards, David L. *Christian England: Its Story to the Reformation.* New York: Oxford University Press, 1980-1984. A multivolume narrative giving a long-range view of the English Church, from the Romans through the Reformation.

Gallyon, Margaret. *The Early Church in Eastern England.* Lavenham, England: Terence Dalton, 1973. Gallyon provides a scholarly but readable account of the earliest missions in Kent, Sussex, Essex, and East Anglia, including those of Augustine and Saint Wilfrid. Illustrated.

Godfrey, John. *The Church in Anglo-Saxon England.* New York: Cambridge University Press, 1962. A general and fairly comprehensive account of the early English Church.

Green, Michael A. *St. Augustine of Canterbury.* London: Janus, 1997. Historical analysis of Augustine's journey to England, his missionary work, and the reverberating effects on the history of religion and life in Britain.

Hillerbrand, Hans J., ed. *The Oxford Encyclopedia of the Reformation.* 4 vols. New York: Oxford University Press, 1996. Covers the Reformation in the context of European church history and theology.

Sims-Williams, Patrick. *Religion and Literature in the West of England, 600-800.* New York: Cambridge University Press, 1990. Although it does not specifically cover the founding of the See of Canterbury, this work demonstrates how a concentrated examination on the regional level of all the evidence can reconstruct a fuller picture.

Yorke, Barbara. *Kings and Kingdoms of Early Anglo-Saxon England.* London: Seaby, 1990. Yorke provides a detailed discussion of the origins of the Anglo-Saxon kingdoms and the relations between king and church.

SEE ALSO: 731: Bede Writes *Ecclesiastical History of the English People.*

RELATED ARTICLES in *Great Lives from History: The Middle Ages, 477-1453*: Saint Bede the Venerable; Gregory the Great.

c. 600-950
EL TAJÍN IS BUILT

The ancient civic-ceremonial complex of El Tajín expanded its sphere of influence well beyond the Mexican Gulf coast to become a key mercantile interest and expansionist state of the Mesoamerican Epiclassic or Late Classic period.

LOCALE: Veracruz, Puebla, and Tlaxcala, Mexico
CATEGORIES: Architecture; expansion and land acquisition; wars, uprisings, and civil unrest

KEY FIGURE
13 Rabbit (fl. 700), a Classic Veracruz warlord

SUMMARY OF EVENT
During the course of the Mesoamerican Epiclassic or Late Classic period (c. 600-950), the peoples of El Tajín, Veracruz, established one of the most distinctive civic-ceremonial centers and far-reaching mercantile enterprises of ancient Mesoamerica. With an initial impetus toward the formation of state-level social and political complexity borne of the Late Preclassic, or Proto-Classic era (c. 100), the site of El Tajín initially developed as a Gulf coast outpost or trading partner of the Teotihuacán empire in the period after 250. The preponderance of Teotihuacán ceramics at the site of El Tajín during this period appears to support the inferred relationship. Beginning with the decline of Teotihuacán military and commercial interests on the Mexican Gulf coast in the sixth century, the site of El Tajín experienced exponential growth as a civic-ceremonial complex and epicenter of the Classic Veracruz stylistic tradition.

Unquestionably, El Tajín's role as a key player in the development of a pan-Mesoamerican sphere of social, political, and commercial interactions—extending well into the Huastec region to the north, and southeast into the heart of Central America—was a critical variable in the sociopolitical and commercial transformation of El Tajín. Ultimately, this extraordinary period of growth culminated with the construction of some two hundred platform-mounds and seventeen ball courts occupying a total area of some 150 acres (61 hectares). The emergence of a civic-ceremonial tradition produced a host of architectural innovations, including chiaroscuro niches, *talud-tablero* (talus-table) facades, monolithic wall panels, corbelled vaults, stucco relief, and concrete masonry construction.

Perhaps the site's most culturally distinctive, sculpturally eclectic, and readily identifiable feature remains the Pyramid of the Niches, the final construction phase of which dates to c. 600. An earlier monument dated to c. 300 lies at the core of the Pyramid of the Niches and makes clear the Early Classic (c. 300-600) affinities and origins of the site of El Tajín. Researcher Michael Edwin Kampen noted that the Pyramid of the Niches is the source of some of the most diverse and eclectic forms of sculpture available from any architectural source available for the region. The six primary platforms, steps, or levels that constitute the structure are composed of a veneer of yellow-brown limestone that raised the structure to a height of 59 feet (18 meters) with a base measuring 85 feet (26 meters) on each side. The sandstone façade in turn incorporates a purported 364 to 365 niches—if one takes into account those niche features buried beneath the 33-foot-wide (10-meter-wide) staircase that fronts the eastern flank of the monument. As noted, this single structure has produced an eclectic body of sculpted panels and monuments that include Mayoid or Maya-like, Zapotec, Teotihuacán, Cholollan, and related Gulf coast influences.

Even with glyphic and iconographic decipherment, the dynastic history of ancient El Tajín remains shrouded in mystery. Despite this fact, the individual whose name recurs most frequently, and prominently, on the monuments of El Tajín is that of 13 Rabbit, whose name is derived from the Aztec calendar. Although little is known of the lives and exploits of the leaders of El Tajín, the many monuments that commemorate the exploits of 13 Rabbit are such that it is quite likely that he and his immediate successors were responsible for kindling the renaissance in architectural and artistic development defining the site's transformation and elaboration in the period extending from c. 600 to 950. If the highly militaristic contexts within which 13 Rabbit appears are any indication, then his rise to power and the expansion of the site's influence were very likely predicated on the expanding role of the martial arts and the emergence of a conquest state centered on the northern margins of the Mexican Gulf coast.

The principal civic-ceremonial monuments, such as the Pyramid of the Niches and the Hall of Columns, date to the Epiclassic exploits of 13 Rabbit, and the seventeen or so monumental ball courts that dominate the site's core area are in turn dated to this period. The largest of these, the South Ball Court, measures 197 feet (60 meters) in length and 59 feet (18 meters) in width. Its elaborately carved stone panels measure 6.5 feet (2 meters) in height. Where Tajín's principal ball courts—mainly, the North and South Courts—are concerned, the distinctive Classic Veracruz style (with its double-volute scroll pattern and highly ornate narrative format) provides a wealth of pictorial and iconographic imagery available for future study and interpretation. However, little progress has been made toward the decipherment of those glyphic and iconographic conventions in evidence on the monolithic blocks of sandstone and basalt that form the walls of the immense North and South ball courts of El Tajín.

Researcher Arturo Pascual Soto's noteworthy attempts at deciphering the glyphs and iconography of El Tajín are flawed by the assumption that the original language of El Tajín was necessarily the same as that of contemporary Totonac peoples who have inhabited the region since the demise of El Tajín. Significantly, scholars generally agree that the Totonac were but the most recent of pre-Columbian émigrés to the region, and, therefore, their role at El Tajín postdates the advent of Classic Veracruz developments at that site. The ethnic affiliation of the original inhabitants of El Tajín, therefore, remains largely open to debate; however, the presence of a hybrid Huastec, Otomí, Nahua, and Mayoid or Maya-like presence in the region during the Epiclassic provides one additional point of departure for inferring origins and affinities.

Elaborately carved ball-game paraphernalia, consisting of monolithic stone *yugos* (yokes), *yuguitos* (small yokes), *hachas* (axes), *manoplas* (gauntlets), and *palmas* (palm fronds), depict the ball-game belts, chest protectors, and other protective gear employed in those combat sports conducted within the ball courts and arenas of the civic-ceremonial core of El Tajín and other allied sites. The use of rubber game balls, like the Mexica Aztec and Maya paraphernalia of the later Postclassic era (c. 1250-1521), is similarly apparent from monuments and related iconography recovered at El Tajín. The elaborate carvings on many of these ball-game paraphernalia characterize the Classic Veracruz style, and their appearance in pan-Mesoamerican contexts ranging from northern Veracruz through to the Guatemalan highlands—some 1,450 kilometers (900 miles) distant—speaks to the far-

The Pyramid of the Niches at El Tajín. (Corbis)

ranging influence of the ball-game cult and its epicenter at El Tajín.

The stone yokes (*yugos*) and related ball-game paraphernalia were very likely too heavy to have been effectively used in the ancient ball games of El Tajín. It is likely that the stone representations were used as the stone molds or models on which leather ball-game belts, pads, and related equipment were fashioned or molded for use in the early variation of the game known to the Maya as *pok-ta-pok* or to the later Mexica Aztec as *tlachtli*. If the stone yokes recovered from Xochicalco, Cacaxtla, Cholula, Kaminaljuyu, and related ball-game sites serve as any indication, then it is likely that the production of ball-game paraphernalia and the proliferation of craftspersons or leather workers identified with El Tajín's far-ranging economic and political interactions were equally widespread. As in later versions of the game, human sacrifice and decapitation rituals were pivotal elements of the Classic Veracruz version.

SIGNIFICANCE

El Tajín's phenomenal civic-ceremonial developments and the exponential growth of its pan-Mesoamerican economic and political interactions make clear its significance to the Epiclassic world order. Evidence of this influence is clear from archaeological evidence recovered at such important Late Classic and Epiclassic Mesoamerican centers as Cholula, Xochicalco, Cacaxtla, Monte Albán, and Kaminaljuyu. Moreover, mercantile and political outposts such as Yohualichan, Puebla, which lies approximately 37 miles (60 kilometers) southwest of El Tajín, is architecturally and culturally identical to the much larger site of El Tajín. Yohualichan, then, provides one additional line of evidence for the presence of Tajín outposts and allied centers extending from north-central Veracruz into the Sierra de Puebla corridor and into the region of the ancient states of Cantona and Cholula, Puebla. What roles Tajín entrepreneurs and militarists such as 13 Rabbit may have played in this expansion remains unclear, but the iconographic, stylistic, and cultural dimensions of El Tajín's pan-Mesoamerican impact are unmistakable.

—*Ruben G. Mendoza*

FURTHER READING

Brueggemann, Juergen, Sara Ladrón de Guevara, and Juan Sánchez Bonilla. *Tajín*. Photographs by Rafael Doniz. Mexico City: El Equilibrista/Turner Libros, 1992. A beautifully illustrated and detailed overview of the art, architecture, and civilization of the ancient metropolis of El Tajín by one of the principal archaeologists charged with the site's excavation and restoration.

Kampen, Michael Edwin. *The Sculptures of El Tajín, Veracruz, Mexico*. Gainesville: University of Florida Press, 1972. A detailed analysis and insight-filled overview of the art history and cultural contexts within which the monuments of El Tajín were recovered.

Ochoa, Lorenzo. "El golfo durante el clásico." In *Atlas Histórico de Mesoamérica*. Coordinated by Linda Rosa Manzanilla and Leonardo López Luján. Mexico City: Larousse, 1989. An annotated time line and cultural history of Classic era developments on the Mesoamerican Gulf coast during the era of El Tajín.

Weaver, Muriel Porter. *The Aztecs, Maya, and Their Predecessors: Archaeology of Mesoamerica*. 3d ed. San Diego, Calif.: Academic Press, 1993. A comprehensive overview of the civilizations of Mesoamerica as understood from the perspective of archaeology and ethnohistory.

Wilkerson, Jeffrey K. "Classic Veracruz Architecture: Cultural Symbolism in Time and Space." In *Mesoamerican Architecture as a Cultural Symbol*, edited by Jeff Karl Kowalski. New York: Oxford University Press, 1999. A scholarly overview of the architectural traditions of Classic Veracruz, with an emphasis on the site and culture of El Tajín.

_______. "In Search of the Mountain of Foam: Human Sacrifice in Eastern Mesoamerica." In *Ritual Human Sacrifice in Mesoamerica*, edited by Elizabeth H. Boone. Washington, D.C.: Dumbarton Oaks Research Library and Collection, 1984. A detailed discussion of the cult of human sacrifice as manifest on the Mexican Gulf coast with a specific emphasis on evidence for human sacrifice, including heart excision and decapitation, in the ball-court panels from the site of El Tajín.

SEE ALSO: 7th-8th centuries: Maya Build Astronomical Observatory at Palenque; c. 700-1000: Building of Chichén Itzá; c. 950-1150: Toltecs Build Tula; 1325-1519: Aztecs Build Tenochtitlán.

RELATED ARTICLE in *Great Lives from History: The Middle Ages, 477-1453*: Itzcóatl.

7th-early 8th centuries
MAYA BUILD ASTRONOMICAL OBSERVATORY AT PALENQUE

The multistoried observatory tower in this prominent Mayan ruin is testimony to the activity of this civilization's scientific elite, who developed an impressive body of astronomical and mathematical knowledge.

LOCALE: Southeast Gulf coast region of modern Chiapas, Mexico
CATEGORIES: Cultural and intellectual history; science and technology

KEY FIGURE

Pacal (603-683), best known among the dynastic rulers at Palenque, r. 615-683

SUMMARY OF EVENT

The Maya were an advanced Mesoamerican culture noted for their achievements, skills, and knowledge in areas such as architecture, engineering, artistic design, mathematics, and astronomy, and for their elaborate hieroglyphic writing system with phonetic elements.

Located on the western fringe of the Maya area, Palenque is now one of the more popular archaeological sites associated with that great ancient American civilization. Palenque's ruins, stretching for about 2 miles (3.2 kilometers) east to west, lie in the humid, lush green foothills of the southern Sierra Madre range, bordering plains stretching down to the Gulf coast. The haunting beauty of Palenque's partially restored and surprisingly well-preserved ruins is enhanced by the backdrop of a highland tropical forest from which steaming mists rise and by its spectacular dawns and dusks.

The site's history as a permanent center spans the period from around 100 B.C.E. to the early ninth century C.E. Palenque expanded in size during the Early Classic period (c. 300-600) and flourished as a major Maya center in the Epiclassic or Late Classic period (c. 600-950), which witnessed the construction of its now famous ruins. At its peak, Palenque held political sway over much of present-day Chiapas and the neighboring state of Tabasco.

Palenque's harmoniously proportioned buildings and monuments represent the work of some of the Maya's most talented architects and sculptors. A few of Palenque's significant monuments are the Temple of the Inscriptions, the Palace with its famous tower, the Temple of the Cross, Temple of the Sun, and Temple of the Foliated Cross. Some of these structures are associated with the long reign of King (or Lord) Pacal (Jaguar Shield), one of the center's most influential rulers. Pacal, born in 603, ruled sixty-eight years, between 615 and 683, and died at age eighty. The Temple of the Inscriptions is an attractive pyramid containing Pacal's magnificent tomb, and it includes an elaborate sarcophagus. The burial chamber near the base is reached by a long hidden internal stairway leading from the top platform.

Another very important structure partially linked with Pacal's reign is the Palace with its famed tower. This elaborate complex of buildings, galleries, and courtyards dominates the site's central area and rests on a platform about 300 feet (91.5 meters) long and 240 feet (73 meters) wide, accessible by two stairways leading up from a courtyard. Nearly all these structures were built in stages under several rulers over a period extending from around 600 to 720.

The most prominent and central feature of the Palace complex is its four-story tower, unique in Maya architecture. Inside the tower is a stairway leading from the second story to the top. The three upper rectangular levels contain four large doorlike openings for external viewing in each cardinal direction. Many experts believe that the tower, which commands a good long-distance view of the surrounding region, including nearby plains that descend northward toward the Gulf coast, probably performed the dual function of watchtower and astronomical observatory.

Mayan scientific and religious leaders dedicated much time to observing the night skies and identifying the most prominent stars, the planets, the sun and moon, major constellations, and the Milky Way. The recurring cyclical movements of these celestial objects were carefully recorded with mathematical formulas. In this manner, a body of celestial knowledge was constantly expanded to the point where the Mayan intellectual elite could gauge the orbits of major heavenly bodies with astounding accuracy and successfully predict solar and lunar eclipses. The elite's monopoly on this type of knowledge legitimized their power over the masses of farmers and ordinary believers whose labor constructed the great Maya centers. This responsibility for keeping track of solstices, equinoxes, and other significant solar or lunar occurrences also allowed the ruling class to direct major activities, such as determining the optimal times for planting, cultivating, harvesting, performing various necessary rituals, and conducting military campaigns.

The Maya believed that celestial bodies were linked with deities who influenced natural phenomena and human destiny. Mayan astronomy and cosmology were integrated with religious beliefs and, therefore, were often used for astrological purposes. This outlook contributed to an obsession on the part of the intellectual elite with the concept of time, chronology, and recurring celestial patterns. To measure time accurately and to predict future possible cataclysmic developments, the class of priestly astronomers utilized higher mathematics to conduct time probes that could determine cyclical alignments of celestial bodies at given periods in the distant past and project them into the future.

The Maya developed a solar calendar whose eighteen months each contained twenty days. Five so-called unlucky days were attached at the end and additional corrections were made periodically so that the calendar conformed closely with the actual solar year of approximately 365.25 days. Linked with this accurate solar calendar was a more important ritual or sacred calendar of 260 days that guided and influenced human activity. Each day was assigned a name and number and connected with a particular deity shown bearing time (the burden of the day) on his back. After the passage of 260 days, the two calendars would no longer mesh until completing a 52-year cycle, an event that indicated the possibility of a traumatic event, such as the destruction of the world.

The Maya had a dot-bar numbering system based on divisions of twenty to record statistical material and dates. Dates could be determined using a system called the long count. The year equivalent to 3114 B.C.E. in what is now the Western world's calendar system was used as a reference point. Contemporary events were then dated by subtracting a sum obtained from adding and multiplying Mayan numerical symbols arranged in rows from the number representing this starting point in time.

In Mayan cities and ceremonial centers, the alignment and placement of buildings as well as features of monuments were symbolic representations of the Mayan worldview. In the case of Palenque, its Palace tower was located so that it could also have served as a vantage point

Ruins at Palenque. (Digital Stock)

MESOAMERICA: MAJOR SITES

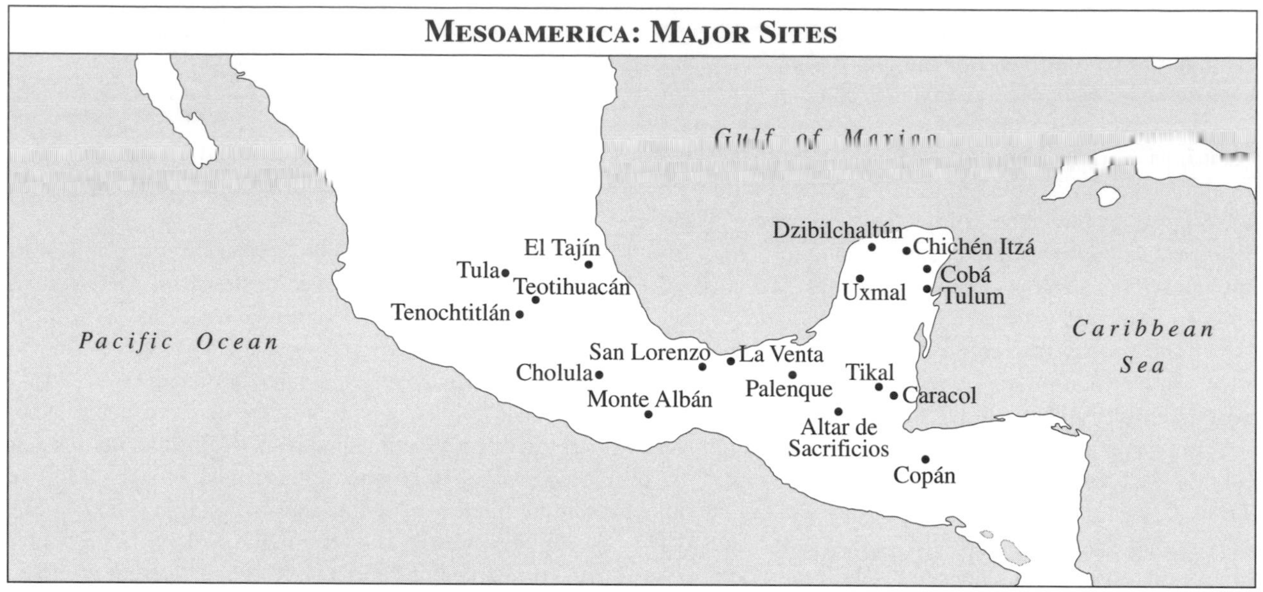

from which the ruler and his top officials observed the arrival of the winter solstice. At sunset on each December 22, these royal dignitaries could observe a glowing orb (the sun) seemingly "drop" into the Temple of the Inscriptions containing Pacal's tomb.

Also, many modern scholars of Mayan civilization believe that Mayan art, such as that found at Palenque, often represented a map of the sky and that local rituals were timed in accord with this pictorial symbolism. The imagery adorning Pacal's elaborately decorated sarcophagus may be interpreted as a picture of the sky on August 31, 683, the very night he died. Moreover, the symbolism depicting the ruler's death conforms closely with the Maya creation myth. Pacal is shown entering the Road to Xibalba by passing through the jaws of a monster and falling down the Milky Way into the Great Hole in the south. In accord with the creation myth, he will lose his struggle with the lords of death in the underworld, and his son will then need to ensure his resurrection and continue the royal line through a ritual ball game.

SIGNIFICANCE

Although Palenque was a large Maya ceremonial site, it is rather small in comparison with great Classic period urban centers such as Tikal. Although its multistoried Palace observatory tower is a unique architectural structure, observatories are also found at other centers. Palenque's importance is enhanced, however, by the well-preserved state of its abundant records in stone and stucco bas-reliefs. Advances in deciphering Mayan hieroglyphics have allowed archaeologists to learn much from these texts in stone about the names, dates, and accomplishments of Palenque's rulers, the political and diplomatic highlights of the site's past, and valuable cultural information about its sacred rituals, calendar, and mythology. Scholars probably know more about the history of Palenque and its rulers than any other Mesoamerican center. Recorded information at the site includes a complete listing of a nearly four-hundred-year-old dynasty of seventeen kings with data on dates of birth, dates of ascension to the throne, and death dates. The last recorded ruler took office on November 7, 799, and may have been connected with Palenque's downfall, which probably occurred within the next two or three decades.

—*David A. Crain*

FURTHER READING

Andrews, George F. *Maya Cities: Placemaking and Urbanization*. Norman: University of Oklahoma Press, 1975. An informative overview of the major Mayan ceremonial and urban centers and the rationale behind their layout and organization.

Aveni, Anthony F., ed. *The Sky in Mayan Literature*. New York: Oxford University Press, 1992. Anthology of scholarly articles on Mayan astronomical practices.

_______. *Skywatchers*. Rev. ed. Austin: University of Texas Press, 2001. A comprehensive, pioneering overview of Mesoamerican astronomical practices.

Ferguson, William M., and John Q. Royce. *Maya Ruins of Mexico in Color*. Norman: University of Oklahoma

Press, 1979. Descriptive guide to Palenque and other major Mayan archaeological sites.

Freidel, David, Linda Schele, and Joy Parker. *Maya Cosmos: Three Thousand Years on the Shaman's Path.* New York: W. Morrow, 1993. Includes some new findings and information on the celestial content of Mayan inscriptions and iconography.

Milbrath, Susan. *Star Gods of the Maya: Astronomy in Art, Folklore, and Calendars.* Austin: University of Texas Press, 1999. Treatise on Mesoamerican calendrical and astronomical knowledge.

SEE ALSO: c. 600-950: El Tajín Is Built; c. 700-1000: Building of Chichén Itzá; c. 950-1150: Toltecs Build Tula; 1325-1519: Aztecs Build Tenochtitlán.

RELATED ARTICLE in *Great Lives from History: The Middle Ages, 477-1453*: Itzcóatl.

7th-8th centuries
PAPERMAKING SPREADS TO KOREA, JAPAN, AND CENTRAL ASIA

Although paper was invented in ancient China, it did not become known to the rest of the world until the medieval period, when papermaking diffused first eastward, then westward, especially to Samarqand where, around 750, Arabs learned the craft from captured Chinese artisans.

LOCALE: Lei-yang (now in Hunan province), Loulan (now in Sinkiang), Korea, Japan, and Samarqand (now in Uzbekistan)

CATEGORIES: Science and technology; communications

KEY FIGURES

Cai Lun (Ts'ai Lun; 50-121), Chinese official attributed with the invention of paper

Damjing (known as Doncho in Japan; 579-631), Korean Buddhist monk who brought papermaking to Japan

Gao Xianzhi (Kao Hsien-chih; d. 755), Chinese general whose defeat in 751 resulted in the capture and employment of Chinese papermakers in Samarqand

SUMMARY OF EVENT

Despite the computer and other modern electronic devices, the combination of paper and printing still constitutes humankind's most widespread communication device. Beginning in the ancient and continuing through the medieval and modern periods, paper proved to be the most satisfactory material on which ideas, stories, political records, and business transactions could be communicated—first through writing, then through printing. According to many scholars, paper as a medium of communication helped create the modern world.

The name "paper" derives from the Latin *papyrus*, an aquatic plant that, along with woven cloth and parchment, provided ancient Egyptians, Greeks, and Romans with writing material. However, paper, with its intertwined cellulose fibers, is a substance very different from papyrus. Some scholars accept the ancient Chinese tradition that the eunuch Cai Lun, a court official in Guiyang (present-day Chenzhou, Hunan Province), invented paper in 105, the year he reported his discovery to the emperor. Other scholars trace papermaking in China back to the second century B.C.E. They see papermaking's invention as an evolutionary process rather than a single innovation. The anonymous artisans who developed the techniques of maceration, screening, and drying in the centuries before 105 became symbolized in Cai Lun, who was the personification of what had been a complex series of technological developments.

One problem confronting scholars is the large time lag between the Chinese invention of paper in the second century and its diffusion outside China to such eastern countries as Korea and Japan in the seventh century and to such western cities as Samarqand and Baghdad (now in Iraq) in the eighth century. Some scholars have explained this five-century lag by theorizing that Chinese artisans and officials kept papermaking techniques secret to protect their monopoly on what was a very valuable resource. On the other hand, the Sinologist Joseph Needham believes that the very slow diffusion of papermaking away from China was because of its geographical and cultural separation from neighboring countries, although China formed close cultural ties with Korea, Japan, and Vietnam during the medieval period.

The evidence for the rapid diffusion of papermaking within the Chinese empire is strong. For example, a Buddhist document on paper found in Loulan has been dated to 264, and other discoveries of paper fragments found in Central Asia reveal that papermaking techniques improved as they spread westward. Knowledge of papermaking also spread eastward. Korea was the first country outside China to which papermaking technology diffused. Because the northern part of Korea was under Chinese control, paper was imported into Korea in the third century, though native papermaking did not begin until the sixth century.

Buddhist monks were often the conduit for this technology transfer from China to Korea, as they were for the diffusion of papermaking from Korea to Japan in 610. Damjing, a Korean Buddhist monk known to the Japanese as Doncho, has traditionally been credited with bringing papermaking to Japan. Papermaking quickly spread throughout the country because the Japanese had a deep appreciation for paper, the artisans who made it, and the calligraphers who wrote on it.

Some scholars have questioned the traditional story of when, where, and how papermaking diffused from China to Western countries. Archeologists have found paper fragments in eastern Turkistan that have been dated to the third, fourth, and fifth centuries. Although some of this paper may have been brought from China, evidence exists that other paper samples were manufactured locally because these documents bear the names of non-Chinese papermakers. After studying the archeological evidence, Chinese scientists have concluded that papermaking was being done in countries on China's western borders by the fifth century.

The traditional story has the transfer of papermaking technology to the West occurring three centuries later, but paper had already diffused into Central Asia and Persia before 750 by a route used by traders and travelers (and later by Marco Polo). A century before the Battle of Talas River (751), paper was already in Samarqand. Despite linguistic and archeological evidence that paper had existed in the Arab world before the eighth century, the historical event of the Chinese defeat at Talas River near Samarqand helps explain how paper made by Chinese techniques rapidly replaced papyrus and parchment in the Arab world.

Agreement exists in Chinese and Arab sources that a battle occurred in 751 between invading Chinese and defending Turkic-Tibetan forces on the banks of the Talas River and that the Chinese army led by Gao Xianzhi was defeated, but in the Chinese sources, no mention is made of captured papermakers (though the names of captured weavers, goldsmiths, and painters are mentioned). In Arab accounts, Samarqand's governor pursued the fleeing Chinese, captured certain prisoners skilled in papermaking, and forced them to teach their techniques to the Arab artisans in the city of Samarqand. In China, the craftspeople had used the bark of mulberry trees in making paper, but this Central Asian region was rich in flax and hemp, which the artisans used instead of mulberry bark to make paper, which proved to be popular not only in Samarqand but also throughout the Middle East. The "paper of Samarqand" became a highly desired commercial product and an important step in the transfer of this Chinese technology of communication to the West.

SIGNIFICANCE

Paper served similar significant purposes in the East and West, but its ultimate impact on Western societies was revolutionary, whereas in China, paper had become an integral part of a highly stable bureaucratic system. Unlike the slow diffusion of papermaking technology eastward, the westward diffusion was rapid. At the end of the eighth century, papermaking was being practiced in Baghdad, then the religious and cultural center of Islam. In the ninth century, Damascus became a successful papermaking center, and by 900, the technique had crossed from Asia into Africa, and paper began to be made in Cairo, where it replaced papyrus as the principal writing material. During the tenth century, papermaking diffused westward across northern Africa, reaching Morocco around 1100.

Spain was the first European country to develop a papermaking industry. With the Iberian Peninsula under Moorish control, much interaction took place between the Spanish Christians and African Muslims, and this included the transfer of scientific and technological knowledge. Paper made its initial appearance in Spain in the tenth century, and the first paper mill was built in Játiva, in the province of Valencia, around 1150. Paper mills were then established in Italy in the thirteenth century, in France and Germany in the fourteenth century, and in England in the fifteenth century.

Though paper was not as durable as papyrus or parchment, it was much less expensive and time-consuming to produce. However, it was in association with another pivotal Chinese invention—printing—that paper participated in the revolutionary changes sweeping across Europe in the fifteenth and sixteenth centuries. Printed books and other documents played important roles in the Protestant Reformation and the Scientific Revolution. In China, printed works on paper helped to sustain traditional cultural and political institutions, whereas in Europe, books, pamphlets, and other printed documents stimulated the significant intellectual, religious, social, and political changes that made the modern Western world.

—*Robert J. Paradowski*

FURTHER READING

Bloom, Jonathan M. *Paper Before Print: The History and Impact of Paper on the Islamic World*. New Haven, Conn.: Yale University Press, 2001. Though focusing on the spread of paper from China to Muslim lands, the first chapter analyzes the invention of paper in China and the early history of its diffusion. Illustrated, with a bibliographical essay and a twelve-page "Works Cited" section.

Carter, Thomas Francis. *The Invention of Printing in China and Its Spread Westward*. Rev. ed. New York: Ronald, 1955. This book, originally published by Columbia University Press in 1925 and revised and enlarged by L. Carrington Goodrich in 1955, was for many years the classic source on the thousand-year odyssey of papermaking and printing from China to Europe. Though its importance has been diminished by later discoveries or archeologists and other scholars, it remains a valuable resource.

Hunter, Dard. *Papermaking: The History and Technique of an Ancient Craft*. New York: Dover, 1978. This Dover reprint of a work originally published in 1947 makes available to general audiences the achievement of a distinguished scholar who has published many books and articles on papermaking in various cultures. It has a 120-page chronology on paper and papermaking, a bibliography of two hundred books, and an index.

Tsien Tsuen-Hsuin. *Paper and Printing*. Part 1 in *Chemistry and Chemical Technology*, Vol. 5 in *Science and Civilisation in China*, translated and edited by Joseph Needham. New York: Cambridge University Press, 1985. This work, part of Needham's massive scholarly project, was not written by him but by Tsien Tsuen-Hsuin, an expert who spent his academic life at the University of Chicago. Tsien describes the book as a "study of the origin and development of papermaking and printing in Chinese culture from their earliest known beginnings to the end of the nineteenth century." Extensive bibliographies of books and articles written in both Eastern and Western languages, and an index.

SEE ALSO: 713-741: First Newspapers in China; 751: Battle of Talas River; 812: Paper Money First Used in China; 868: First Book Printed; c. 1045: Bi Sheng Develops Movable Earthenware Type; 1271-1295: Travels of Marco Polo.

RELATED ARTICLE in *Great Lives from History: The Middle Ages, 477-1453*: Mi Fei.

7th-13th centuries

MOGOLLONS ESTABLISH AGRICULTURAL SETTLEMENTS

The Mogollon were one of the earliest and most successful of the Pueblo peoples. Although traceable to well before the common era, Mogollon culture changed slowly until around the seventh or eighth century.

LOCALE: Southwest United States and northern Mexico

CATEGORIES: Agriculture; cultural and intellectual history

SUMMARY OF EVENT

The Mogollon people were named for the Mogollon Mountains, the southern parts of Arizona and New Mexico where remnants of their culture were first discovered. Prior to 1930, what is now recognized as Mogollon culture was considered a regional variation of Anasazi or Pueblo culture. In the 1930's, Harold Gladwin and Emil Haury recognized the Mogollon as a separate people from the Anasazi and Hohokam, who together constituted the three primary cultural divisions of what are commonly referred to as the Pueblos. Mogollon civilization flourished between approximately 300 B.C.E. and 1300 C.E.

Mogollon culture evolved from a seminomadic hunting, gathering, and agrarian way of life into one that was village-centered. In addition to cultivated foods, the Mogollon consumed a variety of wild plants, such as piñon nuts, walnuts, juniper beans, and cactus, as well as small animals and deer. There was, of course, some regional variation in the food that was available to them, variations between the hotter, drier desert regions and the cooler, wetter mountainous regions.

For centuries, the Mogollon hunter-gatherers had supplemented their diet with cultivated food. By the sixth century, cultivated produce, particularly maize, formed a large portion of their daily diet. However, around this time, for some unknown reason, the amount of cultivated food consumed appears to have decreased by as much as 80 percent, while the amount of wild plants and animals consumed increased proportionally. During the eighth century, this trend was reversed, as cultivated foods such as maize, beans, and squash once again constituted a larger part of the diet. Tobacco was also cultivated and used both socially and ceremonially. Along with this resurgence in agriculture came significant changes in the size, construction, and location of Mogollon villages. Early settlements were generally located in high, easily defensible sites but later were found in lower, more arable locations.

The Mogollons developed pit houses, roundish, excavated pits that were 2 to 5 feet (1 to 2 meters) deep and covered with an elevated roof of poles, brush, and mud. Early single-room pit houses began to evolve into multiroom, above-ground dwellings in the late tenth and early eleventh centuries. Whereas earlier settlements were small and usually consisted of fewer than a dozen structures, by the thirteenth century, the size and number of structures had increased to form villages. However, most villages contained no more than thirty or so houses, although some villages, especially in the southern region, did have two-story multifamily structures. Located at the heart of each settlement was a plaza that served as a place for both domestic and ceremonial activities. In addition to family dwellings there were storage and ceremonial structures. The latter are known as kivas, some of which were small, circular, and subterranean, whereas others, known as great kivas, were larger, rectangular structures. Around the eleventh century, single-story, multifamily dwellings, which contained from fifty to two hundred rooms, were constructed in some Mimbreno villages. The Mimbreno, renowned for their pottery, were a subgroup of the Mogollon who lived along the Mimbres River and several smaller distributaries in southwestern New Mexico.

The Mogollon were among the first people in the Southwest to make pottery, possibly influenced by their Mesoamerican neighbors to the south. The earliest pottery consisted of plain and polished red- or brown-colored vessels made by the coil-and-scrape method. This entails forming the clay into long strips and building the vessel by placing one coil on top of the other to create the desired shape, then smoothing the surface with a scraper. This type of pottery making continued through the entire existence of the Mogollon people. Around the fifth century, a red-on-brown design was added, and several centuries later, a type called Three Circle red-on-white appeared. During the tenth and eleventh centuries, a type of indented, corrugated brown pottery became popular. Paints used on this pottery were generally produced from minerals rather than by boiling plants (a method of the neighboring Anasazi), although the Mimbreno did use the extract of dried plants. What is generally considered the most beautiful and prized pottery is the pottery developed along the Mimbres River, a type believed to have been influenced by the Anasazi.

This pottery, which became popular between the tenth and thirteenth centuries, was black-on-white with stylized depictions of humans, birds, fish, insects, and mythical creatures along with geometric designs. The human depictions were often narrative in nature, showing aspects of daily life. Some pottery depicted human sacrifice, or even a horned or feathered serpent, important in Mesoamerican and southwestern cosmology. Mimbreno bowls from the eleventh and twelfth centuries sometimes depicted prayer sticks with feathers attached, similar to those used by modern Pueblo peoples. Certain designs appear to be more common in certain areas, leading to speculation that these may identify or represent particular lineages or communities. Pottery was often "killed" (deliberately broken) by punching a single hole at its bottom and placing it in the grave of its former owner. At the height of the Classic Mimbreno period (1000-1150), the population of Mimbres Valley settlements was estimated at five thousand. The Mimbreno population peaked and then declined in the twelfth century, along with the production of their distinctive pottery.

Trade between neighboring peoples appears to have been common throughout the area, and unprecedented population growth took place from the eleventh to the thirteenth centuries. However, the greater numbers and higher density put a strain on the area's limited natural resources. Not only was there competition for wild foods, but the increased depletion of trees for building and fuel would have had an impact on the plant and animal life that was part of the ecosystem supplementing the often precarious harvest.

Ironically, the growth in population ultimately appears to have been a factor in the decline of the Mogollon civilization, a decline that occurred around the twelfth and thirteenth centuries. During this time, some people abandoned the more densely inhabited areas. By the end of this period, many villages had been abandoned, including those along the Mogollon Rim and the Little Colorado River and its southern distributaries. Some people moved north into Anasazi territory and others moved back to the more elevated sites and constructed perimeter walls, possibly for defensive reasons. By the thirteenth century, Mogollon culture was increasingly exhibiting characteristics of the Anasazi culture. It appears the Mogollons eventually merged with their Anasazi neighbors to the north.

Significance

The Southwest is the region with the oldest continuous record of human habitation in what is now the United States. Pueblo peoples such as the Mogollon have been, and continue to be, important inhabitants who have adapted to, rather than attempted to change, the nature of the region.

The changes in Mogollon culture that began in the seventh century, including an increase in population, affected not only the people at the time but also to some degree the present-day Pueblos. Over time the Mogollon adapted to this population increase by developing settlements from subsurface to surface and single-family to multifamily structures. Their agricultural practices improved, as did their pottery making.

Aspects of Mimbreno culture can be seen in modern Pueblo villages of the Taos, Acoma, and Hopi of northern New Mexico and Arizona. Mimbreno pottery is prized by both collectors and museums, and their designs can be found today on such items as posters and T-shirts. Accumulated knowledge and experience has been passed on to succeeding generations, and it is believed that the modern Zuñi may be descendants of the Mogollon. The Mogollon and Mimbreno are sometimes included with the Gila Apache, along with the Gileno and Tonto.

—*Philip E. Lumpe*

Further Reading

Cordell, Linda S. *Ancient Pueblo Peoples*. Washington, D.C.: Smithsonian Books, 1994. A brief cultural history and description of the various civilizations referred to as Pueblo.

Haury, Emil W. *The Mogollon Culture of Southwestern New Mexico*. Medallion Paper 20. Globe, Ariz.: Gila Pueblo, 1936. A description of Mogollon culture according to archaeological evidence.

Lekson, Stephen. "Prodigies of Prehistory: The Southwest's Remarkable Mimbres People." *Archaeology* 43 (November/December, 1990): 46-48. Brief description of Mimbreno culture and influence.

Plog, Stephen. *Ancient Peoples of the American Southwest*. London: Thames and Hudson, 1997. Broad coverage of the peoples of the region from prehistoric to modern times. Focuses on the Hohokam, Anasazi, and Mogollon. Supplemented by 150 illustrations, including maps, drawings, and photographs.

Shafer, Harry. "Life Among the Mimbres: Excavating the NAN Ruin." *Archaeology* 43 (November/December, 1990): 48-51. Description of excavation of ruins from the Classic period. Includes photographs and three diagrams of floor plans revealing settlement growth during a seventy-five-year period.

See also: 8th-14th centuries: Cahokia Becomes the First North American City; 8th-15th centuries: Hohokam Adapt to the Desert Southwest; c. 800-1350: Mississippian Mound-Building Culture Flourishes; 9th-15th centuries: Plains Village Culture Flourishes.

605-610
BUILDING OF THE GRAND CANAL

Yangdi, the second emperor of the Sui Dynasty, integrated the fragmentary waterways between the Yellow and Yangtze Rivers into a nationwide water transportation system known as the Grand Canal.

LOCALE: China, Yellow and Yangtze Rivers, Luoyang, Dadu (Xi'an), Beijing, Hangzhou, Yangzhou
CATEGORIES: Transportation; engineering; economics

KEY FIGURES
Wendi (Wen-ti; 541-604), founder and first emperor of the Sui Dynasty, r. 581-604
Yangdi (Yang-ti; 569-617), second emperor of the Sui Dynasty, r. 604-617

SUMMARY OF EVENT
Yang Guang (Yang Kuang), known as Yangdi, the second emperor of the Sui Dynasty (581-618), is often associated with canal building, but it was his father, Wendi, who initiated construction of the canal system. In 584, Wendi decided to build a canal from the capital at Chang'an (present-day Xi'an) eastward to the strategic Tong Pass near the confluence of the Wei and Yellow Rivers. This canal, known as Guangtong Qu ("canal for expanded communication"), allowed the government to resolve the problem of food shortage by transporting grain from the fertile plain in eastern China to the capital region, a food-deficient and heavily populated area. Wendi also constructed a granary at the eastern end of the canal to serve as a center of grain storage for distributing food supplies to the capital and other regions during famines.

Shortly after he succeeded to the throne, Yangdi expanded the canal system. By 610, he had completed the Grand Canal (Dayunhe), the world's largest manmade waterway stretching more than 1,000 miles (1,600 kilometers) in length. Because the major rivers in China flow from west to east, the Grand Canal, running north to south, was significant in that it integrated several regional waterways into an empire-wide system of water communication. Tongji Qu, Han Gou and Jiangnan He were the three canals that were built between the Yellow and Yangtze rivers, and Yongji Qu was the only section constructed north of the Yellow River.

Tongji Qu (canal for effective communication), built under the order of Yangdi in 605, linked the newly established eastern capital at Luoyang on the Yellow River with the Huai River Valley and connected with another old canal to the Yangtze River. All the links in this canal followed the courses of earlier waterways and transformed the Yellow and Yangtze Rivers into a well-integrated network of inland river communication. As many as five million men and women were mobilized to carry out the construction work, and an imperial road was built along the canal banks. To further expand into Yangzhou city on the Yangtze River, Yangdi incorporated into this canal the ancient Han Gou (Han waterway), first built in the early fifth century B.C.E. and restored by Wendi as Shanyang Qu (Shanyang canal) in 587.

The portion of the Grand Canal south of the Yangtze River was Jiangnan He (canal in the Lower Yangtze Valley). Completed in 610 and more than 270 miles (435 kilometers) long, this canal was built on existing rivers in the Lower Yangtze Valley. It reached the eastern side of Lake Tai and connected Hangzhou Bay with the Yangtze River.

These three canals directly connected the Yellow and Yangtze River systems, two of the greatest and most changeable rivers in the world. Using the canals, boats could easily transport grain from the rice-growing fields of the area south of the Yangtze River to the capital region without having to sail along the East China coast. Granaries were built at many places along the route so that grain could be stored if flood or low water levels hindered transportation.

The longest section of the Grand Canal was Yongji Qu (canal for everlasting prosperity), north of the Yellow River and more than 620 miles (998 kilometers) in length. This canal followed the course of a river descending southward from the Taihang Mountains and merged with the Wei River to flow northeastward to Beijing. Built largely for strategic reasons and finished in 609, the canal allowed the government to supply the troops stationed at China's northeastern frontier. Between 611 and 614, Yangdi sent huge expeditionary forces along this canal to attack the kingdom of Koguryŏ, which controlled the part of Manchuria east of the Liao River and the north of the Korean peninsula.

SIGNIFICANCE
The Grand Canal was of great political, economic, and social significance. After many decades of civil war and political disintegration, China had recently become unified under the Sui government. The Grand Canal demonstrated the wealth and power of the dynasty. In times of crisis, the government could easily distribute re-

A stretch of the Grand Canal in 2001, in Yangzhou, Jiangsu Province. (AP/Wide World Photos)

sources and send large numbers of soldiers to the troubled regions. Strategically, the canal system integrated the southern and northern frontiers into the heart of China and laid the framework of a highly centralized imperial state.

As a great work of hydraulic engineering in seventh century China, the Grand Canal was the first fully integrated nationwide water transportation system and performed the same function as the River Nile did for Egypt and the Mediterranean Sea for Constantinople in the medieval era. This inland river system formed the basis of a unified economy. Although the Lower Yangtze Valley was the major economic area, the political center was located at the food-deficient region in the north. The canal system enabled the government to transport grain from the rest of the country to support the growing population in the capital region. In the long run, it laid the foundation for the brilliant epoch of the Tang Dynasty (T'ang; 618-907), widely regard as China's golden age. Parts of the Grand Canal are still in use today, especially the sections south of the Yangtze River.

Despite these advantages, Confucian scholars who wrote the dynastic history were very critical of Yangdi for building the Grand Canal. They often compared Yangdi with Shi Huangdi, the first emperor of the short-lived Qin Dynasty (Ch'in; 221-206 B.C.E.), who created a unified and centralized imperial state but exhausted national resources in building the Great Wall. They also regarded the Grand Canal as a key factor leading to the collapse of the Sui Dynasty. The *Kaihe zhi* (seventh century; record of the opening of the canal), an anonymous Sui text, throws light on the effect of canal construction on the people. Reportedly, more than five million workers had been mobilized to work, and every fifth family had been required to send one person to supply and prepare food for the workers. Those who failed to comply with the official regulations were severely punished, and more than two million people were said to have died. These figures reveal the tremendous loss of human life that occurred as a result of the construction. Because Yangdi completed the Grand Canal in such a quick and ruthless manner, he provoked much discontent against his rule and failed to attain a long period of peace and stability. It was the succeeding Tang Dynasty that enjoyed all the benefits from and owed much of its prosperity to the Grand Canal.

—*Joseph Tse-Hei Lee*

FURTHER READING

Needham, Joseph, and Wang Ling. *Introductory Orientations*. Vol. 1 in *Science and Civilisation in China*. New York: Cambridge University Press, 1965. The brief section on the Sui Dynasty is recommended as an introduction for the general reader.

Needham, Joseph, Wang Ling, and Lu Gwei-Djen. *Civil Engineering*. Part 3 in *Physics and Physical Technology*, Vol. 4 in *Science and Civilisation in China*. New York: Cambridge University Press, 1971. The section on hydraulics discusses the significance of the Grand Canal from historical, environmental, and technological perspectives.

Roberts, J. A. G. *A Concise History of China*. Cambridge, Mass.: Harvard University Press, 1999. Contains a concise overview of the Sui and Tang Dynasties.

_______. *Prehistory to c. 1800*. Vol. 1 in *A History of China*. New York: St. Martin's Press, 1996. Contains a summary of the Sui Dynasty.

Wright, Arthur R. "The Sui Dynasty (581-617)." In *Sui and T'ang China, 589-906*. Vol. 3 in *The Cambridge History of China*, edited by Denis Twitchett and John K. Fairbank. New York: Cambridge University Press, 1979. Provides a concise account of the major events in the Sui Dynasty, including the construction of the Grand Canal.

_______. *The Sui Dynasty: The Unification of China, A.D. 581-617*. New York: Alfred A. Knopf, 1978. Presents a comprehensive analysis of the history of the Sui Dynasty.

SEE ALSO: 581: Sui Dynasty Reunifies China; 618: Founding of the Tang Dynasty; 907-960: Period of Five Dynasties and Ten Kingdoms.

RELATED ARTICLE in *Great Lives from History: The Middle Ages, 477-1453*: Taizong.

606
NATIONAL UNIVERSITY AWARDS FIRST DOCTORATE

Yangdi, the second Sui emperor, set up a civil service examination system that made appointments to political offices by merit. This system, which culminated in the doctoral, or jinshi *title, lasted into the twentieth century.*

LOCALE: China
CATEGORY: Education

KEY FIGURE

Yangdi (Yang-ti; 569-617), second emperor of the Sui Dynasty, r. 604-617

SUMMARY OF EVENT

Beginning in the Han Dynasty (206 B.C.E.-220 C.E.), there were only two ways for a learned man to enter officialdom: by recommendation or by examinations. The Han rulers started a government-operated academic institution called *taixue*, equivalent to a national university today. The *taixue* served two purposes: to help cultivate and educate scholars and talented people who could serve as elite officials and to act as a political censor for the emperors. At the *taixue*, diligent and gifted individuals were able to receive an education in the Confucian classics from the nation's best professors and officials appointed by the ruler. These scholar-officials made annual recommendations to the emperor, who used these recommendations to directly and immediately appoint the officials in his court. This system enabled the ruler to keep watch over the intellectuals and, at the same time, to concentrate the appointments of administrative and judiciary officials in the hands of the central government. The system of recommendation had its downside. Corruption and monopoly were rampant, especially among rich landholders.

Wei Dynasty (220-265) emperor Cao Pei (Ts'ao P'ei, r. 220-226), who reigned as Wendi, introduced a new recruitment system called *jiupin zhongzheng zhi*, or the nine-rank equity system, because of his need for political support from the official-gentry class. Instead of relying on recommendations from the *taixue*, Wendi ordered equity officers to be selected and placed in each county and province; these officers then selected qualified candidates for recommendation to official posts ranging from the first to the ninth rank, with the ninth being the lowest. The criteria for selection were academic talent and family background, both of which were to be of equal importance. In the end, however, family background took priority over talent and education, chiefly because of Wendi's need to please the powerful gentry class who usurped land as well as political power, taking advantage of the social upheaval that was occurring. By practicing this system, Wendi was acknowledging that these illustrious families possessed the exclusive right to officialdom.

During the Sui Dynasty (581-618), China was once again unified. The first emperor of Sui, Yang Jian (Yang Chien; 541-604), who reigned as Wendi (Wen-ti; r. 581-604), wanted to rejuvenate higher education and do away with the disparity of the nine-rank equity system. He started the *guozijian*, the inspectorate of education, which was similar to the modern-day ministry of education. This institution, headed by a high-ranking official, had control over the four colleges of advanced studies in the capital. To recruit new talent, the emperor demanded that each prefecture send in candidates annually. About nine hundred men were summoned to the capital each year, to be screened by the *guozijian*. In 601, disappointed by the results achieved by the *guozijian*, the emperor closed some of the colleges and local schools.

Wendi's son Yang Guang (Yang Kuang, known as Yangdi after his succession to the throne), saw education as the basis for rebuilding a nation and made it a priority at the beginning of his reign. At the time, the entrenched families had begun to decline in power as the middle class had begun to flourish and demand equal opportunity to serve as officials. The emperor, in an attempt to strengthen his royal power with popular support, satisfied the demand of the majority by creating the *jinshi*, or presented scholar, an equivalent of a doctorate degree in 606, ending the long practice of recruitment by recommendation.

Yangdi combined the endowment of the doctorate with the recruitment system. In other words, when a candidate passed the examination, he would receive the doctorate title as well as an official title in court. Historians named this system *keju*, or civil service examination. To obtain this prestigious degree, a candidate first had to pass the district examination in his area, then another one at the provincial level. The third step was a national examination at the capital. Scoring high in the national examination would earn him the *jinshi* degree, the highest academic recognition available. However, if he chose to work for the government, the new *jinshi* had to take yet another examination in court before he was assigned an official position.

Although Yangdi set up the civil service examination system, it was interrupted and ignored after the emperor became caught up in his other endeavors, one of which was the building of an eastern capital at Luoyang, a symbol and a center of power for him. His other major projects included improving and extending the canal system started by his father and the reconstruction of the Great Wall, all of which required great cost and extensive labor. These projects, combined with Yangdi's attempt to subdue Koguryŏ (present-day Korea), caused education to suffer. The *keju* system was introduced and practiced in the Sui Dynasty, but it never reached maturity.

Most of what is known about the civil service examination comes from records of the Tang Dynasty (T'ang; 618-907), when the *keju* system reached its height. The national examinations covered mostly Confucian classics, which the candidates were expected to have memorized. In the examination, parts of the Confucian text would be blocked out, sometimes a paragraph and other times an inch off both sides of the margin, and the candidates were required to fill in the missing portions verbatim. In addition, the candidates also took examinations on contemporary affairs in which they were asked to express their opinions on socio-political issues. The doctorate, or *jinshi*, was awarded in two categories: A and B, with A signifying a high score in all exams and B meaning the candidate had scored at least 80 percent. The *jinshi* was the highest academic degree available at that time. During the Tang, there were, on the average, about thirty *jinshi* awarded each year. Some of the renowned *jinshi* in Chinese history include the celebrated poet Bo Juyi (Po Chü-yi; 772-846), the court historian Sima Guang (Ssu-ma Kuang; 1019-1086), the literary giant Su Dongpo (Su Tung-p'o; 1036-1101), the legendary judge Bao Zheng (Pao Cheng; 999-1062), and the Song minister Wang Anshi (Wang An-shih; 1021-1086).

SIGNIFICANCE

The *keju* system pioneered by the Sui emperor had both good and bad points. For the ruler, the new system restored the recruitment of talented people to the central government and removed this power from the local equity officers. The system was also good news to the poor but talented. The examination system made it possible for intellectuals from far and wide, Chinese or non-Chinese, and with insignificant backgrounds or social qualifications to aspire to official positions. It was not only a model of educational parity but also a powerful impetus toward higher education for all. For these reasons, the examination system continued to prosper in the subsequent dynasties of Tang, Song (Sung; 960-1279), part of Yuan (1279-1368), Ming (1368-1644), and most of Qing (Ch'ing, 1644-1911). The last year of the civil service examination was 1905, when Manchu power was moribund and China was influenced by westernization and modernization.

Over the centuries, the examination system spawned many problems. To obtain the *jinshi* degree, the candidate needed to be well acquainted with the topics and curricula designated by the inspectorate of education. These fields encompassed the Confucian classics, literature, and political theory and strategy. Although these were practical and useful subjects, the focus on these areas meant the exclusion of other fields, such as mathematics. This issue led to a second problem within the system: Young men studied only for the examinations, which acted as a stepping stone to political power and fame, and ignored other, potentially more useful subjects. In addition, private institutes sponsored by the local gentry began to emerge, all with the single goal of helping their students succeed in the examination.

This formulaic approach to education dictated the curricula of schools and converted scholastic establishments into extensions of the examination system. Students were only instructed in the subjects needed for the examinations. This not only defeated the purpose of education but also encouraged cheating and dishonesty. There were numerous cases of cheating in the examination halls in which candidates were discovered wearing undershirts on which they had made full copies of Confucian classics. Switching examination books with some other, more competitive candidate was another common way of cheating; in addition, rich families bribed examination officers so that their sons would pass. As a result, many talented candidates were not chosen, and mediocre students from illustrious backgrounds were awarded the degree. Whatever its imperfections, the *keju* system was a tool used by the imperial rulers to recruit talented men who would devote their lifetime to assisting the emperors in their propagation and maintenance of political power.

—Fatima Wu

FURTHER READING

Roberts, J. A. G. *A Concise History of China.* Cambridge, Mass.: Harvard University Press, 1999. Contains a concise overview of the Sui and Tang Dynasties.

_______. *Prehistory to c. 1800.* Vol. 1 in *A History of China.* New York: St. Martin's Press, 1996. Contains a summary of the Sui Dynasty.

Williams, S. Wells. *The Middle Kingdom: A Survey of the Geography, Government, Education, Social Life, Arts, Religion, Etcetera of the Chinese Empire and Its Inhabitants, with a New Map of the Empire.* Vol. 1. New York: John Wiley and Sons, 1876. Although much of the work is outdated, chapter 9, "Education and Literary Examination," gives an overview of Chinese higher education through the centuries.

Wright, Arthur R. "The Sui Dynasty (581-617)." In *Sui and T'ang China, 589-906.* Vol. 3 in *The Cambridge History of China*, edited by Denis Twitchett and John K. Fairbank. New York: Cambridge University Press, 1979. Wright, formerly Charles Seymore Professor of History, Yale University, covers the short-lived Sui Dynasty and its major rulers; Wendi and Yangdi. Wright's discussion includes the political and personal problems of the rulers during their region.

_______. *The Sui Dynasty.* New York: Alfred A. Knopf, 1978. The restoration of cultural hegemony during the reign of Wendi and Yangdi is discussed in detail.

SEE ALSO: 581: Sui Dynasty Reunifies China; 605-610: Building of the Grand Canal; 618: Founding of the Tang Dynasty.

RELATED ARTICLE in *Great Lives from History: The Middle Ages, 477-1453*: Taizong.

606-647
Reign of Harṣa of Kanauj

During the first half of the seventh century, Harṣa, a Buddhist leader, successfully, if only temporarily, united all of northern India under his rule.

Locale: Northern India
Category: Government and politics

Key Figures

Harṣa (c. 590-c. 647), ruler of Northern India, 606-c. 647
Bāṇa (fl. seventh century), contemporary chronicler of Harṣa's early reign
Xuanzang (Hsüan-tsang; 602-664), Chinese Buddhist monk, traveled in India from 630 to 643
Prabhākaravardhana (d. 605), raja of Thānesar and father of Harṣa
Rājyavardhana (d. 606), brother of Harṣa
Rājyasrī (fl. sixth century), sister of Harṣa and queen of Maukhari
Pulakeśin II (d. 642), Cālukya king, c. 610-642

Summary of Event

During the first half of the seventh century, Harṣa united North India under his rule, a reign that lasted for forty-one years. He ascended the throne of Thānesar, north of the present city of Delhi, in 606 at about sixteen years of age. The half century preceding his accession had been an era of anarchy, the result of the decline and fall of the Gupta Empire (c. 312-c. 550). The Gupta era had been a golden age in India, in both politics and the arts, but the invasion of the nomadic White Huns (Hūṇas or Hephalites) toward the end of the later fifth century led to the demise of the Gupta Dynasty a century later. Early Indian history is the story of the rise and fall of empires, notably the Mauryan (c. 321-185 B.C.E.) and the Gupta, followed by periods of political fragmentation, during which, as the Indian proverb states, the "big fish eat the little fish." Under Harṣa, political unity was restored, although only temporarily.

Unlike many other rulers in Indian history, Harṣa is known through two significant literary sources that can be used to reconstruct portions of his life and times. *Sri Harṣacarita* (seventh century; *The Harshacharita of Banabhatta*, 1892), written by Bāṇa, a member of India's Brahman or priestly caste, was the first biography of an Indian ruler to be written in Sanskrit. However, Bāṇa relates Harṣa's life only from his birth c. 590 to shortly after he ascended the throne in 606. The second literary account is that of Xuanzang

A number of petty North Indian kingdoms had emerged from the ashes of the Gupta Empire, all frequently engaged in warfare against each other. In the late sixth century, the kingdom of the Pushyabhutis was ruled by Prabhākaravardhana, the raja, or king, of Thānesar. When Prabhākaravardhana died in 605, his two sons were absent: The eldest, Rājyavardhana, was at war against the White Huns (Hūṇas), and Harṣa, the younger, was away hunting. According to Bāṇa, on his death bed, Prabhākaravardhana named his youngest son, Harṣa, as his heir, but Harṣa said nothing about his father's deathbed decision, and therefore, his elder brother, Rājyavardhana, ascended the throne.

Prabhākaravardhana's daughter, Rājyasrī, had been married to the Maukhari king, Grahvarman of Kanauj, establishing an alliance between Thānesar and Kanauj. Shortly after Prabhākaravardhana's death, Devagupta, king of Malwa (Malava; in west-central India), attacked Maukhari. Grahvarman died in battle, and his queen, Rājyasrī, was captured. Rājyavardhana freed his sister by defeating Devagupta, but during truce negotiations, Rājyavardhana was treacherously slain by Ṣaṣāṇka, raja of Gauḍa (modern Bengal), who was allied with the king of Malwa. After Rājyavardhana's untimely death in 606, Harṣa succeeded his elder brother as raja of Thānesar. He was sixteen years old.

Rājyasrī, Harṣa's sister, was freed but fled with the intent to commit suttee, or self-immolation on the funeral pyre of one's husband, as was expected of widows. After Harṣa thwarted her suicide attempt, Rājyasrī wanted to become a Buddhist nun, but Harṣa needed her in her public role to sanction his takeover of the Maukhari kingdom, of which she was the queen. After consolidating his rule over Maukhari, he moved his capital from Thānesar in the north to Kanauj, further east and better situated to dominate the Gangetic plain. Under Harṣa's reign, Kanauj replaced Pataliputra as the great imperial city of North India, a position it would hold until the establishment of the Muslim Delhi sultanate in the twelfth century.

Harṣa then embarked on a series of wars in order to secure his rule, most of which were conducted after the Brahman Bāṇa concluded his narrative. Harṣa's earliest campaigns were to the east of Kanauj against several states or petty kingdoms. He defeated Ṣaṣāṇka, although Ṣaṣāṇka continued to rule Gauḍa until his death in the 620's. Eventually Harṣa gained control of all north India, from the Arabian Sea in the west to the Bay of Bengal in the east. He was less successful as he moved south, and his incursion into the western Deccan, in the region of present-day Bombay, or Mumbai, was aborted by Pulakeśin II of the Cālukya Dynasty. At its height, Harṣa's empire embraced more than half of the landmass of the Indian subcontinent.

There is no surviving narrative of the middle years of Harṣa's rule, but some of his later years are covered in the account written by Xuanzang, who traveled to India with the goal of obtaining Buddhist manuscripts to take back to China. While in India, Xuanzang traveled widely, not only throughout Harṣa's realm in the north but into the south, where he was received at the court of Pulakeśin II. He also visited a number of religious and historical sites associated with the Buddha and studied at the Buddhist monastery at Nalanda. Harṣa was ostensibly a Buddhist, but like many others during that era, he also prayed to various Hindu gods, including Śiva. Harṣa invited Xuanzang to visit his court, and impressed by the Chi-

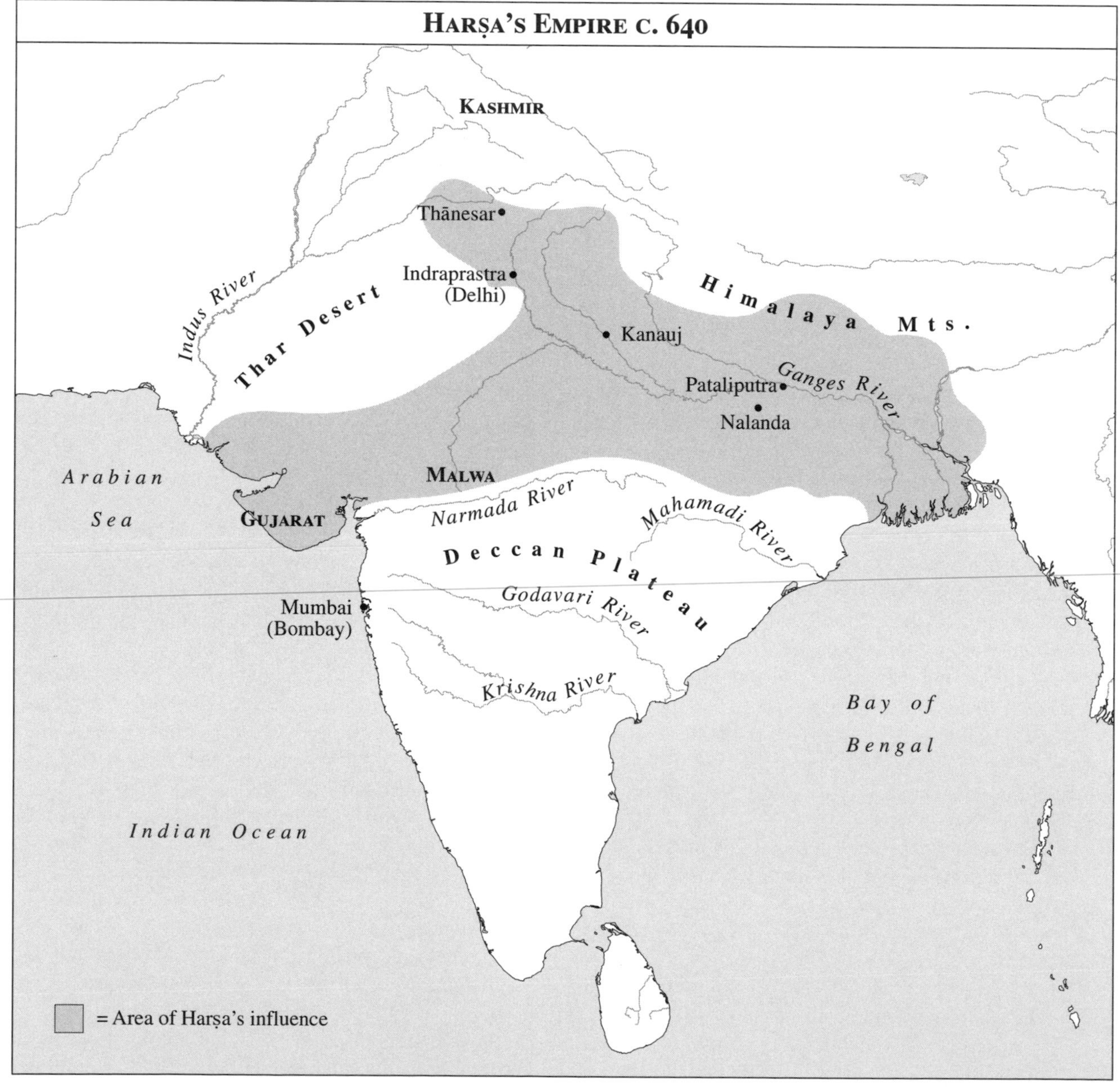

nese monk's knowledge of Buddhism, in 642, he organized a great gathering at Kanauj, the capital, where eighteen vassal kings, three thousand Buddhist monks, and three thousand Hindus and Jains debated their religious differences. After five days, Harṣa declared Xuanzang the victor, a decision that supposedly led to a failed assassination attempt by Hindu Brahmans on the king. Harṣa wanted Xuanzang to stay in India, but in 643, the monk began his homeward journey, with Harṣa providing elephants and gold to ease the monk's return to China, where he later wrote *Datang xiyouji* (629; *Buddhist Records of the Western World*, 1884), an account of his travels, including his contacts with Harṣa.

Harṣa traveled widely throughout his long reign. He had a reputation of making himself accessible to his numerous peoples. A patron not only of Buddhism but also of Hinduism, Harṣa was noted for his charitable contributions. A poet, he also wrote several dramas. He died c. 647, apparently of natural causes. As he left no heir, there would be no Vardhana dynasty to replicate the earlier Maurya and Gupta Dynasties. Harṣa's death symbolized the end of India's classical age, and once again, India became a land of big fish eating little fish.

SIGNIFICANCE

Harṣa was the last Buddhist or Hindu ruler to control a majority of the subcontinent until Indian independence in 1947. By the 900's, Islam had begun to penetrate northern India, culminating in the establishment of the Mughal Dynasty in 1526. Mughal rule was followed by that of the British, beginning in the 1700's. Buddhism, favored by Harṣa, was replaced by Hinduism and Islam and all but died out in the land of its birth. Unlike the earlier Mauryan rulers but similar to the Guptas, Harṣa's kingdom lacked a centralized bureaucratic structure. A system of feudalism developed wherein the local ruling elite was given land rather than salaries and thus often became largely independent of the royal government. It took the energy and the will of a Harṣa to maintain the unity of the kingdom. Without him, the parts became greater than the whole. Nevertheless, Harṣa's reign was significant in its own time, and because of the writings of Bāṇa and Xuanzang, it remained an example of Indian unity for later generations of Indians.

—*Eugene Larson*

FURTHER READING

Bāṇa. *The Harṣa carita of Bāṇa*. Translated by E. B. Cowell and F. W. Thomas. London: Royal Asiatic Society, 1897. A translation of Bāṇa's prose romance of the life of Harṣa.

Bose, Bela, trans. *Harsavardhana, King of Thanesar and Kanauj*. Allahabad, India: Ketabistan, 1948. A translation into English of Harṣa's three dramas.

Devahuti, Deva. *Harsha: A Political Study*. Delhi, India: Oxford University Press, 1998. 3d ed. The major biography of Harṣa available in English. Includes genealogical tables and twelve plates.

Goyal, Shankar. *History and Historiography in the Age of Harsha*. Jodhpur, India: Kusumanjali Prakashan, 1992. A history of India during the era of Harṣa's rule.

Goyala, Srirama. *Harsha and Buddhism*. Meerut, India: Kusumanjali Prakashan, 1986. A study of Harṣa's relationship with Buddhism.

Srivastava, Bireshwar Nath. *Harsha and His Times*. Varanasi, India: Chowkhamba Sanskrit Series Office, 1976. An account of the political history of India during the 600's.

Wriggins, Sally Hovey. *Xuanzang: A Buddhist Pilgrim on the Silk Road*. Boulder, Colo.: Westview Press, 1996. A readable and accessible biography of Xuanzang.

SEE ALSO: 484: White Huns Raid India; 567-568: Sāsānians and Turks Defeat the White Huns; c. 610-632: Muḥammad Receives Revelations; c. 611-642: Reign of Pulakeśin II; 629-645: Pilgrimage of Xuanzang; 973: Foundation of the Western Cālukya Dynasty; 1206-1210: Quṭ al-Dīn Aybak Establishes the Delhi Sultanate.

RELATED ARTICLE in *Great Lives from History: The Middle Ages, 477-1453*: Xuanzang.

607-839
JAPAN SENDS EMBASSIES TO CHINA

For more than two hundred years, Japan maintained a steady flow of diplomatic missions to China, sending envoys, priests, and scholars to learn more about Buddhism and China's imperial government system and to represent the achievements of Japanese civilization.

LOCALE: Japan and China
CATEGORY: Diplomacy and international relations

KEY FIGURES

Suiko (554-628), empress of Japan, r. 593-628
Shōtoku Taishi (574-622), imperial prince and regent for empress Suiko, 593-622
Ono no Imoko (fl. early 600's), chief envoy of the first Japanese embassies
Yangdi (Yang-ti; 569-617), second emperor of the Sui Dynasty, r. 604-617
Pei Shiqing (P'ei Shih-ch'ing; fl. early 600's), first Sui Dynasty envoy to Japan
Ennin (794-864), the last priest to travel to China on the final embassy

SUMMARY OF EVENT

By 600, several conditions motivated the Japanese imperial court to send an official embassy to China for the first time in several centuries. First, Empress Suiko and her regent, Shōtoku Taishi, both heavily promoted Buddhism, which had come to Japan from China. Second, Shōtoku and others were impressed by the renewed stability of China's government. Third, Japan's involvement in the wars of three Korean kingdoms also involved the Chinese.

Curiously, the first embassy in 600 is mentioned only in Chinese but not in Japanese sources. This leads some scholars to believe that it was only a regional mission from a besieged Japanese stronghold in southern Korea.

The formal Japanese embassy to China sent out in the fall of 607 is the first to be documented in Japanese chronicles. Empress Suiko and Prince Shōtoku charged Ono no Imoko to travel to China. Ono no Imoko was accompanied by an official translator and left for a sea and land journey of more than 1,300 miles (2,100 kilometers).

When Ono no Imoko reached the Chinese court, he presented an official letter to Yangdi, the emperor of the Sui Dynasty (581-618). The Chinese considered foreign embassies to be tributary offers by "barbarians." Yangdi considered Suiko insolent because she had sent her greetings as the ruler of the land in which the sun rises (Japan) to him, the ruler in whose land the sun sets (China), implying equality. Some historians believe that Yangdi's reply to Suiko was so harsh that Ono no Imoko deliberately lost the first letter. At any rate, the empress pardoned Ono no Imoko for this loss. Ironically, Japanese sources make no reference to Yangdi's anger. They report instead that Suiko used the letter's greeting later, with no negative reactions.

On his return in 608, Ono no Imoko was accompanied by the Chinese envoy Pei Shiqing. Suiko received the envoy at court and listened to Yangdi's letter. There were problems: Yangdi called Japan "Wa," while the Japanese insisted on "Nippon," meaning "originating from the sun." When Japan's status rose, at least from 670 on, the Chinese used Nippon.

In 608, Ono no Imoko was sent out again. In a pattern that would become standard, the embassy included students, monks, and priests. Many Japanese of this and subsequent missions would stay for an extended period of years to learn about China's religion and government.

The fall of the Sui Dynasty and the deaths of Shōtoku and Empress Suiko meant that the next embassy was sent to the new Tang Dynasty (T'ang; 618-907) by Emperor Jomei (r. 629-641) in 630. One of its goals was to escort home many of the Japanese who had been studying abroad since 608.

The next embassy was sent out in 653, when relations between Japan and China had become critical. The two nations found themselves supporting different warring Korean states. Until 669, four or perhaps five more embassies followed, all trying to make the difficult voyage to the coast of China and inland to the Tang capital of Chang'an (now Xi'an). Many missions now consisted of two ships, with up to 120 people on one vessel. Sadly, this precaution proved necessary because violent seas occasionally led to ships lost at sea.

Japan's defeat by Chinese-allied Koreans gave the embassies an urgent political character. After 669, Japan worried about Chinese expansion and focused on strengthening domestic defense; official embassies were not sent for three decades.

The 700's saw an active and regular pattern of Japanese missions to China, with whom relations had improved once Japan was no longer involved in Korea. Increasingly, the Japanese created more lavish missions, with up to four ships and more than six hundred voyagers. The lead envoys were selected to impress the Chinese with their knowledge of Buddhism and Confucian-based principles of centralized government and their ability to perform elegant court ceremonies. The Chinese responded with envoys of their own and generally received warmly the Japanese monks, priests, scholars, court officials, traders, and artisans.

Yet the voyages remained dangerous. Japanese captains had insufficient knowledge of the prevailing winds in the East China Sea, and vessels were barely adequate for the mission. Once ships could no longer hug the coast of western Korea on their way to China because of that country's hostility, the direct sea voyage from the eastern tip of Ryūkyū to the mouth of China's Yangtze River proved difficult to master. Some Japanese ships were blown off course, driven as far down south as Vietnam.

The last embassy sailed in 838, transporting the eminent priest Ennin to the Tang court. One of its ships sunk, but Ennin made it to Chang'an. The envoys had to return on Korean boats. Their obvious danger made the missions rather unpopular among those destined to go. Ono no Takamura had refused to lead the 838 mission and was sent to exile for his stubbornness. However, he was pardoned a year later.

A final embassy was planned for 894, but its proposed leader persuaded the court to abandon it, arguing that the Tang Dynasty was declining. Overall, at least twenty-three missions had been sent. Yet for the next few centuries, Japan would not send an official mission to China.

Significance

Ever since the introduction in the fifth and sixth centuries of writing, Confucianism, and Buddhism to Japan from China through Korea, the Japanese had begun to look at Chinese civilization with admiration and a desire to copy its achievements. The first eight scholars and Buddhist monks who accompanied Ono no Imoko brought back many books and rich firsthand knowledge and quickly influenced Japanese society.

The scholar Takamuko no Kuromaro (d. 654) and the Buddhist priest Minabuchi no Shōan (fl. 600's) sailed with Ono no Imoko's second mission in 608 and stayed for thirty-two years. On their return, they were instrumental in the Taika reforms of 645-646 that established a Chinese-style government in Japan. However, the Japanese discarded as unsuitable the Tang military system and the Chinese belief in dynastic change and merit-based court promotions.

Architectural knowledge of Chang'an led Empress Gemmei (r. 707-715) to order construction of the Japanese capital at Heijōkyō (modern-day Nara) based on the Chinese model. When conscripted peasants ran away from the construction site, their unrest caused the government to modify its Chinese-style Taihō code in 718.

During the eighth century, some Japanese envoys were employed as high officials in China. Abe no Nakamaro (698-770) arrived in China in 717, rose in rank, and in 766 was made Chinese governor of Vietnam, which China then occupied. A poet himself, he befriended China's Li Bo (701-762). Fujiwara no Kiyokawa (706?-779?) arrived on the same mission as Abe and impressed the Chinese emperor with his exact knowledge of ceremony. Indicative of Japan's esteem as a civilized country was its success in receiving preferential treatment over China's Korean allies at a state banquet for the embassy in 752. Yet in the Heian period (794-1185), Japan's interest in China waned, and it ended the embassies.

During their heyday, the Japanese embassies significantly helped change Japanese culture, state, and society along Chinese models. Once Japan developed an impressive culture of its own, the embassies were discontinued. However, classic Chinese literature and institutions retain an imaginative hold over contemporary Japanese culture, comparable to the influence that ancient Rome and Greece have on Western culture.

—*R. C. Lutz*

Further Reading

Aston, W. G., trans. *Nihongi: Chronicles of Japan from the Earliest Times to A.D. 697*. 1896. Reprint. Tokyo: Charles E. Tuttle, 1972. Contains the oldest Japanese historical accounts of the first embassies, through the year 696, when this history of Japan ends. Introduction, illustrations, and index.

Brown, Delmer M., ed. *Ancient Japan*. Vol. 1 in *The Cambridge History of Japan*. New York: Cambridge University Press, 1993. Chapter 3, by the late Inoue Mitsusada, discusses the Japanese embassies in light of the reforms in Japan in the seventh century.

Goodrich, L. Carrington, ed. *Japan in the Chinese Dynastic Histories*. Translated by Ryūsaku Tsunoda. South Pasadena, Calif.: P.D. and Ione Perkins, 1951. Translations of ancient Chinese descriptions of the Japanese embassies. Valuable to show how China perceived the Japanese missions.

Herbert, Penelope Ann. *Japanese Embassies and Students in Tang China*. Perth, Australia: University of Western Australia Centre for East Asian Studies,

601 - 700

1978. Excellent, detailed brief book on the subject. Maps, notes, and chronological table.

Murphey, Rhoads. *East Asia: A New History*. 2d ed. New York: Longman, 2001. The chapter "Buddhism, Barbarians, and the Tang Dynasty" discusses the Japanese embassies to China. Illustrations, maps, references, and index.

Sansom, George B. *A History of Japan to 1334*. Vol. 1. Stanford, Calif.: Stanford University Press, 1958. Chapter 7, "Reaction Against Chinese Influence," offers a concise review of the Japanese embassies and focuses on the reasons for their eventual termination. Chapters 3 and 4 show how Japan's contact with China changed Japanese society and government structure. Illustrated with index, very readable.

SEE ALSO: 5th or 6th century: Confucianism Arrives in Japan; 538-552: Buddhism Arrives in Japan; 593-604: Regency of Shōtoku Taishi; 645-646: Adoption of *Nengo* System and Taika Reforms; 701: Taihō Laws Reform Japanese Government; March 9, 712, and July 1, 720: Writing of *Kojiki* and *Nihon Shoki*.

RELATED ARTICLES in *Great Lives from History: The Middle Ages, 477-1453*: Shōtoku Taishi; Suiko.

c. 610-632
MUḤAMMAD RECEIVES REVELATIONS

Muḥammad, a Meccan merchant, had visions in which God commanded him to preach. Muḥammad considered himself chosen by God to be Prophet to the Arabs. The Qurʾān, the holy Islamic text in which Muḥammad's teachings are collected, reveals the word of God, or Allah.

LOCALE: Mecca and Yathrib (now Medina), Arabia (now Saudi Arabia)
CATEGORY: Religion

KEY FIGURES

Muḥammad (c. 570-632), Prophet, founder of Islam
Khadīja (d. 619), first convert to Islam and Muḥammad's first wife
Fāṭimah (c. 605-633), Khadīja and Muḥammad's daughter
ʿAlī (c. 600-661), Fāṭimah's husband, fourth caliph
Abū Bakr (c. 573-634), early convert to Islam
Abū Ṭālib (fl. sixth century), Muḥammad's uncle

SUMMARY OF EVENT

Muḥammad was the son of ʿAbd Allāh ibn ʿAbd al-Muṭṭalib, who died shortly after Muḥammad's birth, and his wife, Āminah bint Wahb, but was raised by his uncle, Abū Ṭālib. When Muḥammad was about twenty-five, he married Khadīja, a merchant who had inherited her father's business and wealth.

In the year 610, Muḥammad had a vision, the first of many revelations that came to him during the next two decades. In this first vision, the archangel Gabriel appeared to him in the desert north of Mecca. Gabriel, according to Judeo-Christian tradition, had appeared earlier to Daniel and Zacharias as well as to the Virgin Mary in the Annunciation. Before Muḥammad, the Arab world had no prophet comparable to the Judeo-Christian prophets Adam, Abraham, Moses, Elijah, and Jesus. In this first revelation, Muḥammad concluded that God was commanding him to preach to the Arabs. He considered himself the Prophet of the true religion. It was this first revelation that marked the beginning of Islam, from the Arabic word *islam*, meaning "submission to" or "having peace with God." Islam contends that there is one god, Allah, and that Muḥammad is his Prophet.

The new religion originally was rejected by most Arabs. Muḥammad was shunned by a people—mostly nomadic Bedouins—who for centuries had believed in *jinn* (plural *jinni*, also rendered *jin*, *djin*, and *djinn*), hidden or mysterious creatures. They had for many centuries attributed various inscrutable events to the *jinni*. Muḥammad's teaching that there is but one God to whom all people must submit alienated most Arabs. They felt so strongly about Muḥammad's teachings that, in the summer of 622, some of them plotted to kill him. Learning of this plot, Muḥammad fled to Yathrib, the only place where his teachings had enjoyed a degree of acceptance. At that time, Muḥammad's major followers were Khadīja, Khadīja's daughter Fāṭimah and her husband ʿAlī, and Abū Bakr.

People in Mecca were troubled particularly because the city received substantial income from pilgrims to its renowned shrine, the Kaaba. They feared that the introduction of Muḥammad's beliefs would threaten the Kaaba's appeal and would substantially affect one of the city's major sources of income. The plot to kill Muḥammad most likely was hatched more for financial than religious reasons.

Muḥammad preached that the nations of the world had been punished for disobedience to Allah, the creator of all things, who expected humans to manage his creations, and for their worship of false deities. Early Arabs, who had experienced sandstorms, earthquakes, and plagues, attributed such natural phenomena to the vengeance of their *jinni* or, as Islam developed, to a displeased Allah. A follower of Islam, a knower of God, is called a Muslim, which in Arabic means "one who submits."

The religion Muḥammad established through his revelations contained a strict system of rewards and punishments. It clung to the notion that at the end of the world, the dead would be resurrected and judged according to their past deeds. They would be dispatched to heaven or hell according to Allah's final judgments. Those who had lived according to Islamic principles were promised an afterlife of unimaginable joy and splendor, earned through their earlier behavior. Soldiers of Islam who protected and promoted the faith through *jihad* (holy war) received unique benefits after they died. Those unworthy of such posthumous rewards would suffer eternal and excruciating punishment in a terrifying underworld. Muḥammad foresaw through revelation that the world would come to an end with a final judgment. The just would be rewarded, the unjust punished.

Muḥammad, like most people during his lifetime, was probably illiterate. As his revelations proliferated, news of the principles of Islam that resulted from these revelations circulated orally among Arabs. Shortly after Muḥammad's death, however, his followers collected his pronouncements in a book they called the Qurʾān (also known as the Koran). It became and remains the holy text of Islam.

Muḥammad, through the revelations he received, established the five fundamental pillars of Islam (*arkan al-Islam*). They are *Shahadah*, the belief that Allah is the one and only God, *al-salat*, the daily ritual of five prayers recited at specified hours as Muslims prostrate themselves facing Mecca; *al-zakah*, or charitable giving; *al-sawm*, fasting during Ramadan; and *al-hajj*, the pilgrimage to Mecca expected of all Muslims at least once in their lifetimes.

Although followers of Islam are expected to make at least one trip to Mecca before they die, many make such pilgrimages year after year. Fasting takes place during Ramadan, the ninth month in the Islamic calendar, when Muslims are expected to refrain every day for the entire month from eating between sunrise and sunset. The specified times at which Muslims pray are dawn, noon, mid-afternoon, sunset, and after darkness has fallen. In Arab countries, calls to prayer are broadcast in the streets through loudspeakers.

Muslim leaders (caliphs) are both religious and social leaders. They do not actively proselytize. They do, however, focus on influencing society morally and politically. In the Arab world, where Islam is most prevalent, the Qurʾān is essentially the law of the land. Islam, more than any other world religion, is a religion of the book. It regards the Qurʾān as the word of God as dictated through revelations to Muḥammad, his earthly representative and his Prophet. Although Islam does not repudiate the teachings of Moses or Jesus, both of whom it considers prophets, it regards the Qurʾān as the revision, correction, and completion of all religious documents that preceded it, including the Torah and the Bible.

Islam distinguishes clearly between creatures and the Creator. The role of the Muslim is to worship and venerate Allah. Muslims do not come to Allah requesting favors. Rather, they pray to Allah in a spirit of adoration and thanksgiving for all that he, as the Creator, has provided for them. They do not question the veracity of what Muḥammad has revealed through his revelations. They regard revelation to be statements of Allah's will rather than Allah's disclosure about himself. Shortly after the Qurʾān was transformed into written form, it was supplemented by the Sunna or sayings and deeds of Muḥammad, brought together as the Hadith. Branches of Islam, such as the Sunni, the Shīʿite, and Sufism, interpret the Qurʾān differently and are often at odds with each other.

SIGNIFICANCE

Although it was the last of the world's three great religions to develop, Islam has had an enormous impact on the world, particularly in the Middle East, in North Africa, and in such countries as Albania, Turkey, Russia, and Indonesia. It is the majority religion in Egypt, Iran, Iraq, Saudi Arabia, Syria, the United Arab Emirates, Turkey, Algeria, Tunisia, Libya, and Morocco. Each of these countries varies in how strictly it observes the dictates of the Qurʾān.

In 1990, there were an estimated 935 million Muslims in the world, with few in the Americas but with large concentrations in the countries of the Middle East, Asia, North Africa, and parts of northeast Europe. The religion has grown since 1990. The number of practicing Muslims was reported to be 1.1 billion when the new millennium dawned, with 804 billion in Asia and 307 billion in Africa.

—*R. Baird Shuman*

FURTHER READING

Armstrong, Karen. *The Battle for God: Fundamentalism in Judaism, Christianity, and Islam*. New York: Alfred A. Knopf, 2000. A carefully researched comparative study of the world's three major religions. Bibliography, index.

Esposito, John L., ed. *The Oxford History of Islam*. New York: Oxford University Press, 2002. This reader-friendly, comprehensive resource is valuable for those who wish to look up specific information about aspects of Islam. Chronology, bibliography, index.

_______, ed. *What Everyone Needs to Know About Islam*. New York: Oxford University Press, 2002. A lucid explanation of Islam geared to the general reader. The short section on the origin of Islam is particularly relevant. Bibliography, index.

Glubb, John Bagot. *The Life and Times of Muḥammad*. 1970. Reprint. New York: Cooper Square Press, 2001. This sympathetic work by a British writer, who for some time was the commander of the Arab Legion in Jordan, is of interest partly for its depiction of Arabian life and customs and for its reconstruction of desert battles. Bibliography, index.

Green, Joey, ed. *Jesus and Muḥammad: The Parallel Sayings*. Berkeley, Calif.: Seastone, 2003. This text presents quotations from the New Testament and the Qurʾān that demonstrate similarities between Christianity's core values and the tenets of Islam. Topics include love, God, *jihad*, faith, wisdom, law, and charity. Bibliography and an index of quotations.

Rogerson, Barnaby. *The Prophet Muḥammad: A Biography*. London: Little, Brown, 2003. Presents a biographical account of the life of Muḥammad. Chapters discuss his early life, the cities of Mecca and Medina, Arabia, his first revelations, and more. Bibliography, index.

Rubin, Uri, ed. *The Life of Muḥammad*. Brookfield, Vt.: Ashgate, 1998. A comprehensive account of the Prophet from a variety of perspectives, exploring the social, political, and religious angles of his life. Part of the Formation of the Classical Islamic World series. Bibliography, index.

Waardenburg, Jacques. *Islam: Historical, Social, and Political Perspectives*. New York: Walter de Gruyter, 2002. Places Islam in historical, social, and political context, revealing its continuing social impact worldwide. Bibliography, index.

Wadud, Amina. *Qurʾān and Woman: Rereading the Sacred Text from a Woman's Perspective*. 2d ed. New York: Oxford University Press, 1999. The author's unique reading of the Qurʾān sheds light on the role of women and relations between women and men presented in the book of Islam. Chapters explore the biases of earlier interpretations and its effects on tradition and Islamic culture and society, equality between men and women, and more. Includes a list of women mentioned in the Qurʾān, a bibliography, and an index.

SEE ALSO: 630-711: Islam Expands Throughout North Africa; 637-657: Islam Expands Throughout the Middle East.

RELATED ARTICLES in *Great Lives from History: The Middle Ages, 477-1453*: Khadīja; Muḥammad.

c. 611-642
Reign of Pulakeśin II

Pulakeśin II was the greatest king of the Cālukya Dynasty of Bādāmi and one of the greatest warrior kings of ancient India. He forged a huge and formidable kingdom that endured in its homeland for more than two centuries.

Locale: Deccan and southwestern region of India
Categories: Expansion and land acquisition; government and politics

Key Figures
Pulakeśin II (d. 642), Cālukya king, r. 610-642
Maṇgaleśa (d. 610), Cālukya king, r. 598-610

Summary of Event
The fourth king of the Cālukya Dynasty, Pulakeśin II was named after the founder of the line. A fearless and mighty warrior, his name meant "great lion" or possibly "tiger-haired." The appellation suited his warrior personality. The Cālukyas and particularly Pulakeśin II played a pivotal role in the politics and historical circumstances of the seventh century in the Deccan and southernmost region of India. The first Pulakeśin, by building an imposing fortress on a hill at Vāṭāpi (modern Bādāmi) in northern Mysore sometime around 543, embarked on an age of Cālukyan ascendancy that was to last until the middle of the eighth century. Declaring Vāṭāpi his capital, the first ruler established an important precedent in performing the *aśvamedha* (horse sacrifice) and other important Vedic rituals. The Cālukyas were an indigenous Kṣatriya (warrior caste) family from the Kanara area who claimed a glorious and ancient lineage connected to the Mānavya *gotra* (clan).

Pulakeśin I's son Kīrtivarman I (r. c. 566-597) expanded the dynasty's land holdings considerably by warring against the neighboring states ruled by the Nalas, the Mauryas, and very powerful Kadambas. In doing so, he carved out a sizeable kingdom that included the very important port at Revatidvipa (modern Goa). The second king who is referred to in one inscription as "Night of Destruction," also conducted several important Vedic sacrifices. At the time of Kīrtivarman's death, his son Pulakeśin II was still a minor and too young to rule. Thus, Kīrtivarman's brother, Maṇgaleśa, took the throne and initiated a series of raids far to the north, in modern-day Gujerat, Khandesh, and Malwa, but was unsuccessful in permanently securing the region. By the time Pulakeśin II came of age, Maṇgaleśa relished his power too much to relinquish the throne to his nephew. He also wanted his own son to inherit his position. Furious with his uncle, Pulakeśin left the court, taking with him many loyal supporters. Sometime around 609-610, the prince and the loyalists initiated a civil war that rent the central part of the kingdom and left the outlying provinces and the borders unsecured. Maṇgaleśa was killed, and the rightful heir assumed the throne.

Immediately on assuming his new position, however, Pulakeśin faced serious challenges. The civil war had left the kingdom in a state of chaos and anarchy; even the capital province was in danger of attack. The new king was equal to the threat, and within a short time, he secured the homeland and subjugated the rebellious provinces. In the Meguti Temple at Aihole, a detailed account of his conquests is provided in an inscription; dated to 634, the lengthy record was composed by the court poet, a Jain named Ravikīrtti. Pulakeśin not only kept in check rebels attempting to break with Cālukya rule but also embarked on a bellicose expansionist policy that was characteristic of the Cālukyas. First, he extended the empire northward into Gujerat, overrunning the Lāṭas, Malwas, and Gurjaras. He then met Harṣa of Kanauj, the famous king of north India, in battle, an event recorded by the Chinese Buddhist pilgrim Xuanzang (Hsüan-tsang; c. 602-664). The struggle between the two kings seems to have ensued from the attempts of both to extend their control over the Deccan.

The reputation of the ferocious king of the Cālukyas spread well beyond the subcontinent of India. A Muslim historian named al-Ṭabarī wrote that King Khosrow II (r. 590-628) of Persia received an embassy from Pulakeśin in 625. Al-Ṭabarī gives the name of the king as Prmesha (Parameśa), one of Pulakeśin's alternate names. Unfortunately, it is not clear if the purpose of the visit was for trade or other reasons.

After his victories in the north, Pulakeśin turned his ambitions toward the eastern Deccan, where he brought under his control the Kosalas and the Kaliṇgas and the ruling house of Piṣṭapura. Placing his younger brother in charge of the newly acquired territories, he founded the Eastern Cālukya Dynasty, which persisted for more than four hundred years. At that point in time, Cālukya rule extended over enormous tracts of land spanning the Deccan between the Indian Ocean and the Bay of Bengal and from Gujerat in the north to southern Mysore. In one inscription he is referred to as "lord of the eastern and

MAJOR RULERS OF THE FIRST CĀLUKYA DYNASTY, 543-757

Reign	*Ruler*
543-566	Pulakeśin I
c. 566-597	Kīrtivarman I
598-610	Maṇgaleśa
610-642	Pulakeśin II
655-680	Vikramāditya I
680-696	Vinayāditya
696-733	Vijayāditya
733-746	Vikramāditya II
747-757	Kīrtivarman II

western waters," a description that confirms the breadth of his empire. With the dream of taking the entire subcontinent south of the Vindhya Mountains, the warrior king directed his army to turn south and follow the coastline into the adjacent realm of the Pallava King Mahendravarman I. A fierce battle ensued, in which the Pallava king eventually was forced to retreat behind the ramparts of his capital city at Kanchipuram, a fact that both Pallava and Cālukyan records confirm.

The record as to what occurred next is not clear, but soon afterward, Pulakeśin returned to Vāṭāpi without securing the Pallava lands. With his initial invasion, Pulakeśin inaugurated a period of protracted warfare between the two empires that lasted for generations, and whatever success he had in his rivalry with the Pallavas was short-lived. Narasiṃhavarman I Mahāmalla, the son of Mahendravarman I, avenged his father's humiliation by repeatedly attacking the Cālukyas and finally capturing and occupying Vāṭāpi for a period of thirteen years, a fact supported by an inscription left by the Pallava king at Vāṭāpi. Pulakeśin II was killed around 642 while defending his capital.

In 641, the year before the fall of Vāṭāpi, Xuanzang traveled through the Cālukya kingdom and left a valuable description of the land and its people. He found the populace stern and vindictive as well as honest, simple, and willing to aid anyone in distress. When insulted, they were quick to avenge themselves in fair fights. Many were fond of learning and grateful to their benefactors. The Buddhist pilgrim also recorded a rare account of ancient Indian warfare that is as chilling as it is fascinating. He claimed that the Cālukyas had a large group of champion warriors who, before engaging in battle, would become intoxicated with wine. Thus, fortified in the face of death, the warriors would readily take on any and all challengers. The troops advanced to the beat of drums. Particularly grim is Xuanzang's report that many hundreds of elephants were given wine to drink so that they too became inebriated and infuriated. An awesome spectacle followed in which troops of drunken warriors riding intoxicated elephants rushed en masse to stampede and trample the enemy; it was a compelling and diabolical ancient war machine.

Pulakeśin was both a warrior and an empire builder, and certainly part of his responsibility as king was to ensure divine blessings by building temples. Previously, Cālukya kings had supported the excavation of cave temples from rock. The capital city Vāṭāpi has four excellent early caves carved along the scarp of an imposing hill. The Ravula Phadi cave temple at nearby Aihole is another fine example of an early Cālukyan artistic endeavor. After his victories in the north, Pulakeśin seems to have been inspired by the religious architecture he had seen, and he supported the building of temples. The Meguti Temple, a small Jaina structure built in 634 by Pulakeśin's court poet, is the earliest stone structural temple in the region. The Upper Śivālaya Temple was constructed at the north end of the fort at Bādāmi, and soon after, the Mālegiti Śivālaya was built part way down the hill. Although small and modest, the structures are important in that they were pioneering examples of a new movement toward making permanent houses for the divine; previously, temples in the region had been made of impermanent materials, usually brick or wood.

SIGNIFICANCE

The impact of the Cālukya Dynasty and particularly the powerful king Pulakeśin II on the history of India is significant. Pulakeśin forged one of India's truly vast empires. He created it by continuously subjecting neighboring states and even those far beyond to swift and decisive war campaigns. Despite the ongoing conflict, Pulakeśin fostered a thriving kingdom that was innovative and prosperous.

—*Katherine Anne Harper*

FURTHER READING

Majumdar, R. C. *The Classical Age*. Bombay: Bharatiya Vidya Bhavan, 1954. An excellent and thorough resource on Indian history, the treatise provides expert and detailed information on political events and inscriptions. Bibliography.

Michell, George. *Pattadakal*. New Delhi: Oxford University Press, 2002. An excellent survey of the religious monuments of a major Cālukya site with a brief historical introduction.

Nilakantha Sastri, A. K. *A History of South India from Prehistoric Times to the Fall of Vijayanagar.* Bombay: Oxford University Press, 1966. This compilation of the author's many studies of South India treats not only political history in a coherent historical narrative but also social life, commerce, religion, philosophy, literature, and the arts.

Rajasekhara, S. *Early Chālukya Art at Alhole.* New Delhi: Vikas Publishing House, 1985. Provides a brief political history as background to temple building at an important Cālukya religious center. Bibliography.

See also: 606-647: Reign of Harṣa of Kanauj; 629-645: Pilgrimage of Xuanzang; 630-668: Reign of Narasiṃhavarman I Mahāmalla; 973: Foundation of the Western Cālukya Dynasty.

Related articles in *Great Lives from History: The Middle Ages, 477-1453*: Harṣa; al-Ṭabarī; Xuanzang.

618
Founding of the Tang Dynasty

A newly reunified China became the most powerful state in East Asia. Its material wealth allowed first for an explosion of culture and later a flourishing of Buddhism.

Locale: China

Categories: Government and politics; cultural and intellectual history

Key Figures

Wendi (Wen-ti; 541-604), founder and first emperor of the Sui Dynasty, r. 581-604

Li Yuan (Li Yüan; 566-635), founder and first emperor of the Tang Dynasty, r. 618-626

Xuanzang (Hsüan-tsang; c. 602-664), Chinese monk and religious leader

Huang Chao (Huang Ch'ao; 852-884), rebel leader

Summary of Event

When the Han Dynasty (206 B.C.E.-200 C.E.) collapsed, China slipped into 350 years of political and social chaos. This period of instability eventually ended when the Sui Dynasty (581-618) came to power and set China back on the road toward political unity. The new emperor, Wendi, set in motion a series of public works projects; among the most notable was the construction of the Grand Canal. To create this waterway, Wendi's civil engineers essentially connected a series of preexisting canals that would form a 1,200-mile (1,930-kilometer) corridor linking the economies of northern and southern China.

The Sui also launched a series of military expeditions against China's mainland neighbors and eventually invaded the Korean peninsula. The initial success of these campaigns was short-lived, and a series of tactical reverses, especially in Korea, resulted in the deaths of thousands of soldiers. These military failures, coupled with years of high taxes and forced labor related to the emperor's public works projects, led to rebellion and to the eventual defeat of Sui forces.

One of the leaders of the rebellion, Li Yuan, capitalized on the destruction of the Sui Dynasty and declared that the mandate of heaven (heavenly approval of rule) had passed into his hands, and he established a new dynasty known as the Tang (T'ang; 618-907). This new government would usher in an era of Chinese dominance in East Asia.

Like most of the Tang emperors, Li Yuan, who is known as Gaozu (Kao-tsu), created a political philosophy that was a blend of Confucianism and Legalism. This philosophical synthesis actually mirrored the personal characteristics of Gaozu and his successors. The emperor was more than willing to execute anyone who posed a potential political threat, and this "Legalist" attitude enabled him to structure a stable political environment. Once power was assured, Gaozu installed a Confucian system that created a governmental bureaucracy based on the merit of competitive civil service exams. These actions created an environment of peace and prosperity that formed the foundation of China's next golden age.

One of the Tang Dynasty's greatest developments was the restructuring of the Chinese economy. In the agricultural sector, the government introduced the equal-field system that allocated land according to the needs of the individual Chinese family. The impact of the system was twofold. It guaranteed that every Chinese household would be working on rich fertile land; this ensured that the people's labor would be rewarded with bountiful harvests and economic security for their families. Most important, the equal-field system prevented the accumulation of large tracts of land by wealthy aristocrats that was the root cause of the peasant rebellions during the Han Dynasty.

The productive potential of the equal-field system was unleashed at the same time that the government introduced a new, fast-ripening strain of rice into the Chinese agricultural sector. This new species allowed for multiple harvests that significantly increased the supply of food, which in turn had an important impact on Chinese demography. The population of China increased from 45 million to 115 million between 600 and 1200. This agricultural security and increased population affected the Tang Dynasty in two important ways. The number of peasants needed to produce rice was reduced, and this in turn allowed many Chinese to specialize in certain cash crops that accelerated the commercialization of Chinese agriculture.

Regions began to specialize in certain fruits and vegetables, and the same expanded transportation network that distributed these luxury crops throughout the empire also supplied these same regions with rice. This set the stage for the world's first integrated national economic system.

Increased population also led to the growth in urbanization. In numbers unprecedented in Chinese history, people moved into cities across the empire. Initially, this expansion took place in cities along major transportation routes and in centers of governmental authority. Most historians today believe Chang'an (now Xi'an), the capital of the Tang Empire, had the largest concentration of people on the face of the earth at the time. Demographers estimate some two million people lived within the confines of the city.

In conjunction with this vast agricultural explosion, China also experienced significant growth in its industrial sector. The dynasty's metallurgic industry grew significantly during this period. Strong, inexpensive iron provided the agricultural sector with highly efficient farm implements and supplied the military with the latest advances in weaponry. Technologically, this period witnessed the Tang's introduction of the use of gunpowder and the magnetic compass.

The wealth of the Tang Empire set the stage for a magnificent cultural explosion. The growth of cities had a deep impact on the culture of the Tang Dynasty. The combination of trade and great wealth created one of history's great cosmopolitan societies. Merchants, scholars, and diplomats from all over the Eurasian land mass could be found in China's great cities. Great restaurants, teahouses, and theaters catered to the varied interests and tastes of this multicultural society. A diversity of religious, political, and philosophical views intermingled and, on many occasions, challenged traditional Chinese cultural practices and beliefs.

Buddhism, which was the most important competitor to established Chinese belief systems, was introduced to the Middle Kingdom (China) by merchants traveling along the Silk Road during the Han period. Not unlike Christianity during the decline of the Roman Empire, Buddhism gained an important following during the great period of self-doubt at the end of the Han Dynasty. The traditional Confucian system seemed to be failing; consequently, this new religion offered a comforting alternative during this period of societal collapse.

The same held true during the Tang period of great wealth. When China began to experience the corruption and moral decline that often accompanies material excess, many people from all levels of Chinese society began to look for antidotes to their spiritual malaise. Buddhism offered an attractive alternative to the traditional

MAJOR RULERS OF THE TANG DYNASTY

Reign	*Ruler*
618-626	Gaozu (Li Yuan)
627-649	Taizong
650-683	Gaozong
684	Zhonggong
684-690	Ruizong
690-705	Wu Hou
705-710	Zhongzong
710-712	Ruizong
712-756	Xuanzong
756-762	Suzong
762-779	Daizong
779-805	Dezong
805	Shunzong
805-820	Xianzong
820-824	Muzong
824-827	Jingzong
827-840	Wenzong
840-846	Wuzong
846-859	Xuanzong
859-873	Yizong
873-888	Xizong
888-904	Zhaozong
904-907	Aizong

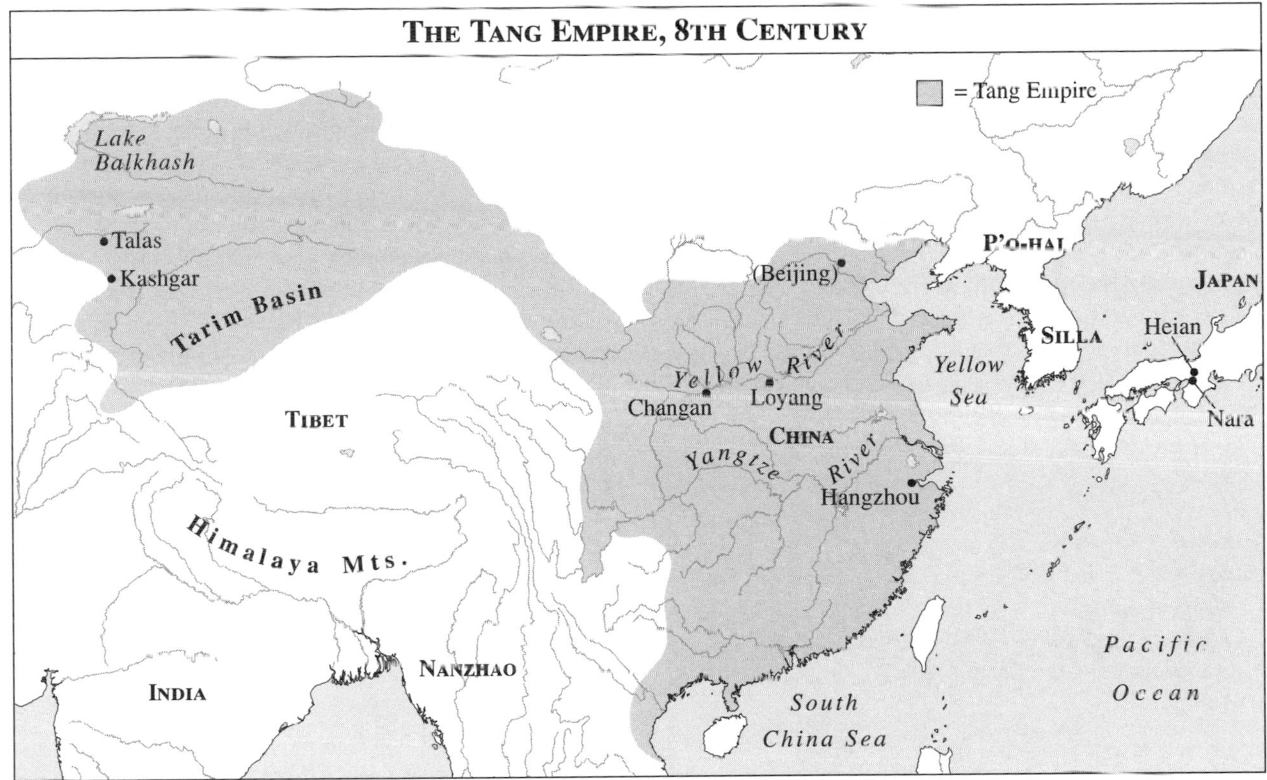

The Tang Empire, 8th Century

Chinese belief system. Members of the elite were impressed with the religion's intellectual sophistication. They were also attracted to the belief of salvation in another life based on the moral and ethical actions of the individual in this life.

The most important proponent of Buddhism in China was Xuanzang, a neo-Confucian scholar. After training and studying in India, Xuanzang returned to China and advanced the cause of Buddhism in East Asia. His greatest contribution was his translation of major Buddhist texts into Chinese.

In addition, the great economic strength of the Tang allowed the government to develop a successful and highly aggressive military and foreign policy. The Tang believed that they controlled the mandate of heaven and that China was truly the Middle Kingdom at the center of the cosmos. Taken literally, this meant that the rest of the world was beneath the status of China and should be treated accordingly. Tang international policy was essentially based on a Confucian superior/subordinate relationship. The government implemented a tributary system in which other nations paid homage to the emperor through taxes, gifts, and acts of loyalty. Tang armies conquered Korea and transformed the peninsula into a political and cultural satellite. The new Korean bureaucracy was established on the Confucian model, with its new capital, Kumsong, constructed along the lines of the Tang center of government at Chang'an. Confucianism became the dominant belief system of the Korean upper class, with its political philosophy dominating Korean education. This Confucian connection led to a cultural exchange system that helped cement Chinese culture on the peninsula. Buddhism, which had challenged Confucianism on the mainland since the fall of the Han Dynasty, became widely accepted by the Korean peasants.

The Tang Dynasty also made incursions into Southeast Asia. Most important, the empire attempted to reestablish control over Vietnam. Sino-Vietnamese diplomatic and military conflicts had been a part of Chinese history extending as far back as the Han Dynasty. Chinese emperors found that the Vietnamese jealously guarded their independence; as a result, many a Chinese general felt the sting of Vietnamese military power.

Significance

Over time, the Tang Dynasty's civil and military leadership became careless and corrupt. Uprisings occurred throughout the empire; the most prominent of these was led by Huang Chao and lasted from 875 to 884. Faced with widespread decline in the dynasty's centralized authority, the empire splintered and collapsed in 907. Subsequently, China entered into a period in which regional military governors ruled independent feudal kingdoms. Most important, Chinese intellectuals would begin to question the aggressive attitudes and policies of the Tang military. By the rise of the Song Dynasty (Sung; 960-1279), the Confucian elite succeeded in putting the military under civilian control. This new bureaucracy was to be governed by the conservative Confucian ethical system that would successfully reduce the power and prestige of the Chinese military.

—*Richard D. Fitzgerald*

FURTHER READING

Bol, Peter K. *This Culture of Ours: Intellectual Transitions in T'ang and Sung China*. Stanford, Calif.: Stanford University Press, 1992. An excellent overview of Tang and Song intellectual history. Index and bibliography.

Gernet, Jacques. *A History of Chinese Civilization*. New York: Cambridge University Press, 1990. The best single-volume account of Chinese cultural history. Maps, index, and bibliography.

Graff, David A. *Medieval Chinese Warfare, 300-900*. New York: Routledge Press, 2002. An excellent overview of medieval Chinese military history. Maps, index, and bibliography.

Graff, David A., and Robin Higham. *A Military History of China*. Cambridge, England: Westview Press, 2002. The best survey of Chinese military history on the market. Maps, index, and bibliography.

SEE ALSO: 581: Sui Dynasty Reunifies China; 605-610: Building of the Grand Canal; 606: National University Awards First Doctorate; 629-645: Pilgrimage of Xuanzang; Mid-9th century: Invention of Gunpowder and Guns; 960: Founding of the Song Dynasty; 960-1279: Scholar-Official Class Flourishes Under Song Dynasty.

RELATED ARTICLES in *Great Lives from History: The Middle Ages, 477-1453*: Taizong; Xuangzang.

627-650
REIGN OF SONGTSEN GAMPO

Known as the first Buddhist king of Tibet, Songtsen Gampo took the throne of what was to become the central Tibetan Empire in 627 and led its expansion across Central Asia.

LOCALE: Central Tibetan plateau (now the Tibet Autonomous Region, People's Republic of China)
CATEGORIES: Government and politics; religion

KEY FIGURES

Songtsen Gampo (617-650), ruler of Tibet, r. 627-650
Namri Songtsen (d. 618), ruler of small Yarlung polity, father of Songtsen Gampo
Taizong (T'ai-tsung; 599-649), second emperor of the Tang Dynasty, r. 627-649

SUMMARY OF EVENT

Reliable information about the history and activities of the early Tibetan kings and rulers is scarce, but those sources of information that do exist suggest that the political landscape of central and western Tibet in the early seventh century appears to have been dominated by small states. These were probably kin-based, either by clans or lineages, and they controlled relatively limited areas around the major river drainages and their tributaries. In some cases, these polities owed allegiance to larger states. One such state was the Zhang-zhung confederacy, which was said to control much of Tibet from its capital, Kyunglung, located near Mount Kailash in western Tibet.

Around 600, Namri Songtsen, a ruler of a small polity in the Yarlung Valley of the portion of Tibet known as Ü (now central Tibet in the vicinity of Lhasa), forged a secret alliance with petty rulers to the north and west of Yarlung and nominally sworn to fealty with the local overlord of the Zhang-zhung confederacy. This alliance succeeded in defeating this Zhang-zhung ruler, and buoyed by this outcome, Namri and his followers pushed even further to the west, conquering another confederacy dependent. This series of conquests led to the establishment of the Spurgyal, which is best seen as the nascent Tibetan empire, and which now controlled most of the Tibetan plateau with the exception of the northeast (Amdo, now known as Qinghai) and extreme eastern Tibet. Namri sent an embassy to the Sui Dynasty (581-618) emperor in China in an apparent attempt to ally his growing state with them against the Aza of Amdo, but it met with little success and instead aroused Chinese suspicions about his territorial ambitions.

On the death of his father in 618, Songtsen Gampo quickly suppressed all opposition to his rule on the Tibetan plateau. He first put down a rebellion and then moved forcefully against his remaining enemies, especially the remnants of the Zhang-zhung. His first strategy was to marry his sister to the Zhang-zhung king. He and his sister then plotted an ambush of the unsuspecting king and killed him. This established Songtsen Gampo as the undisputed ruler of the plateau, and through this, he gained the grudging respect of the Chinese. He further consolidated his rule through a series of political arrangements, including a marriage of his son to a Nepali princess. By 635, he had proposed to the Tang emperor, Taizong, that he be permitted to wed a Chinese princess, but this request was refused. Songtsen Gampo had watched with growing concern the expansion of the Tang into the Amdo regions and decided to act, most likely using the refusal of his request for a princess as a convenient pretext.

From 637 to 638, he conquered the Chinese Amdo vassal states, and in the fall of 638, his forces raided Chinese colony towns on the extreme eastern margin of the Tibetan plateau in what is now Sichuan Province. After a series of minor military engagements on this frontier, the Tibetans and Chinese declared a peace, which was cemented by the marriage of Songtsen Gampo to the Chinese princess Wenzheng (Wen-cheng), who left for the Tibetan capital of Lhasa in 641. This peace lasted well after the deaths of both Songtsen Gampo and Taizong in 649. As an indication of the respect in which the Chinese

Potala Palace, above Lhasa Valley in Tibet. Songtsen Gampo is reputed to have built the original palace, which in the seventeenth century was expanded into the large compound that still stands today. (PhotoDisc)

held Songtsen Gampo, Gaozong (Kao-tsung; r. 650-683), the third Tang emperor, bestowed on him just before his death the title Precious King.

Songtsen Gampo is known as the first Buddhist king of Tibet because under his rule, Buddhism was formally introduced to the plateau. The indigenous, pre-Buddhist religion of Tibet is poorly known, but it appears to have been based on the shamanic propitiation of local spirits, deities, demons, ghosts, and other entities. Many of these lived in specific landscape features, such as rivers or bodies of water, mountains, especially peaks and passes, and other locations. Folk religion, practiced by the common people, involved rituals designed to ward off evil or to ask for special benefits. Ritual specialists performed many of these rites. Later Buddhist texts describe how important figures in the diffusion of Buddhism "tamed" or "subjugated" these demons and spirits and bound them to the service of the Buddha. In practice, this meant that these local spirits were incorporated into the Buddhist belief system as subordinate or protector deities.

A number of authors describe what they call court religion, which would have been practiced by the ruling elites and nobles of the small-scale polities before the formation of the Tibetan empire. Kings (local rulers) were considered divine and returned to heaven each night by means of a special connecting cord. According to myth, the cord of one of these kings was severed in combat, thus making him mortal. Elaborate funerary traditions, including animal sacrifice and mound construction, became part of court religious activity. Kings were further identified with mountains and the deities on them, who were thought to be their ancestors. Ritual specialists, usually diviners (or often described as the "chief shaman"), attended the court and directed its rituals. Ancient texts refer to this class of priestly figures as *bön* or *shen*, and many authors use the term Bonpo (or Bon) to describe Tibetan religion at this time. However, it is clear that Bon was much more complex than this simple attempt at equivalence. The priestly class shared power with two other factions: the king and his followers and the leaders of the noble families.

Tibetan Buddhist scholars of later periods have ascribed to Songtsen Gampo a major role in promoting Buddhism in his nascent empire. He is said to have constructed twelve temples, with at least one in Nepal, and also to have promulgated a Buddhist ethical code. During his reign, the Tibetan script was developed. Some authors have even written that he was converted to Buddhism through the efforts of his wife, Wenzheng. However, his actual accomplishments are in some dispute. There is no question that Buddhism established a foothold on the plateau during his reign and that he did in fact create a context of tolerance for its diffusion, at least at the level of the royal court. The Jokhang, perhaps Tibet's holiest place, was built to house the statute of Śākyamuni (the historical Buddha, also known as the *Jo bo*), that was brought by Wenzheng to Lhasa. Other small temples were constructed at this time. The influence of Buddhism at this time was not widespread, and it is best to see it as one of a number of cults or religions that operated on a small scale, primarily at the level of the nobles and elites, but had little political importance or power. Nor is there a sense that as yet, Buddhism had made inroads into folk religious practice, as it was to do over the next 250 years.

SIGNIFICANCE

Songtsen Gampo consolidated the process of political centralization on the Tibetan plateau begun by his father, Namri Songtsen. From his relatively small polity in the Yarlung Valley, he was able through alliance building, threat, marriage, and outright conquest to lay the foundations of what became the Tibetan Empire, which controlled much of Central Asia in the 250 years following the end of his reign. His efforts made Tibet, along with the Arabs, Chinese, and Turks, one of the most powerful states in all Central Asia. The extent of his influence on the introduction of Buddhism to the plateau is open to question, but it is clear that he created a context into which Buddhism was accepted by the royal court and that he assisted in its early growth through temple construction, patronage, and tolerance. Buddhism soon grew in both secular and religious power such that it overshadowed traditional religious practice in the hands of the *bön* and *shen* priests, which in time laid the basis for reaction and ultimately, the collapse of Buddhist fortunes, which paralleled the eventual collapse of the empire itself.

—*Mark Aldenderfer*

FURTHER READING

Beckwith, Christopher S. *The Tibetan Empire in Central Asia*. Princeton, N.J.: Princeton University Press, 1987. The definitive treatment of the expansion of the Tibetan empire into Central Asia.

Haarh, Erik. *The Yarlung Dynasty*. Copenhagen: Gad, 1969. A highly detailed discussion of the myth and history of the royal Tibetan lineage.

Richardson, Hugh. "How Old Was Srong-brtsan Sgampo?" *Bulletin of Tibetology* 2, no. 1 (1965): 5-8. A well-reasoned analysis of records documenting Songtsen Gampo's life.

Samuel, Geoffrey. *Civilized Shamans: Buddhism in Tibetan Societies*. Washington, D.C.: Smithsonian Institution Press, 1993. A comprehensive examination of the development of Buddhist thought on the Tibetan plateau.

Stein, R. A. *Tibetan Civilization*. Stanford, Calif.: Stanford University Press, 1972. An excellent and accessible overview of Tibetan history, culture, and civilization.

SEE ALSO: 763: Tibetans Capture Chang'an; 791: Buddhism Becomes Tibetan State Religion; 838-842: Tibetan Empire Dissolves; 1368: Tibet Gains Independence from Mongols.

629-645
PILGRIMAGE OF XUANZANG

Xuanzang's long journey from China to India and back again had a major impact on the spread of Buddhism in China and elsewhere in Asia.

LOCALE: China, Central Asia, and India
CATEGORIES: Religion; cultural and intellectual history

KEY FIGURES

Xuanzang (Hsüan-tsang; c. 602-664), Buddhist monk
Taizong (T'ai-tsung; 599-649), Tang Dynasty emperor, r. 627-649

SUMMARY OF EVENT

One scholar has called the Buddhist monk Xuanzang the greatest traveler in all history. His journey from China to India and back again has long been known in China, India, and much of Asia, both in history and myth. Since the monk passed that way in the years between 629 and 645, many other adventurers have followed his route over deserts and mountains.

Xuanzang was born into a family of scholars and officials, a class highly esteemed in imperial China with its long tradition of the centrality of the ancient sages such as Confucius to the cultural, intellectual, and political life. The scholar gentry were invariably of higher status than either successful military officers or wealthy merchants. Xuanzang's grandfather was president of the Imperial College of Beijing, and he was sufficiently rewarded economically so that his descendants could rely on inherited wealth rather than having to pursue other, less prestigious occupations.

As with many influential figures, the earliest biographies of Xuanzang are more hagiography than objective history. As a child, he is portrayed as preferring his studies to playing games, and as an adult he was described as tall, handsome, and charming. He could have followed his family's scholarly profession, achieving a high level governmental position, but instead he chose to follow the path of Siddhārtha Gautama, the Buddha (c. 566-c. 486 B.C.E.).

In the centuries that had elapsed since the death of the Buddha, Buddhism had evolved into numerous movements, some mainly philosophical, others moral and ethical, still others primarily religious. Some stressed extensive study of Buddhist texts, others found enlightenment through the immediacy of individual insight, and some through ritual and chanting. Suffering and ignorance kept one bound to the wheel of birth and rebirth, but it was possible to escape reincarnation through enlightenment and to achieve nirvana, likened to the blowing out of a candle. In Mahāyāna Buddhism, the prevailing form of Buddhism in China, a few figures who had achieved enlightenment, bodhisattvas, postponed progressing to nirvana in order to assist and to save others on the path to enlightenment and bliss.

Introduced to Buddhism by an elder brother, by the age of thirteen Xuanzang had already become a noted preacher and explicator of Buddhist texts, works that he mastered after only two readings. Because of the chaos and violence engendered by the fall of the Sui Dynasty (581-618), he and his brother moved to Sichuan Province. During these years, he had come to question some of the available Buddhist texts, believing that many were corrupted and unintelligible because of inadequate translations from Sanskrit into Chinese.

After the Tang Dynasty (T'ang; 618-907) had restored order, Xuanzang moved to the Tang capital of Chang'an (now Xi'an), soon to become the world's largest city. Even though he was only about twenty years old, Xuanzang believed he could be Buddhism's savior. To accomplish this, he decided to journey to India, the Buddha's birthplace. There, he would obtain additional Buddhist manuscripts not available in China, bring them back to China, and translate them from Sanskrit into Chi-

XUANZANG'S JOURNEY, 629-645

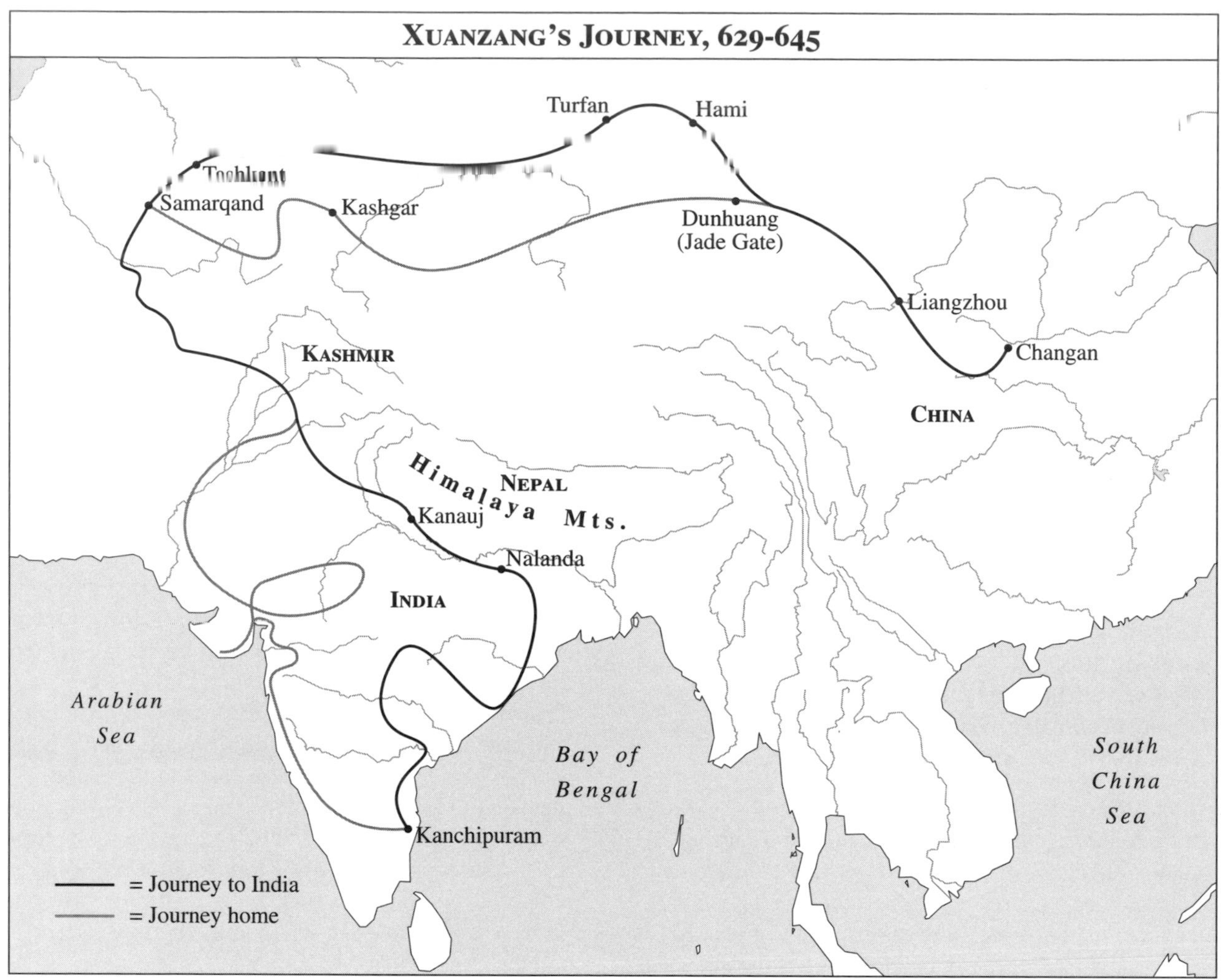

nese, thus bringing greater truth and clarity to Chinese Buddhism.

Xuanzang left Chang'an for India in 629, when he was about twenty-seven years old. The new Tang Dynasty was consolidating its authority, and the emperor, Taizong, had forbidden anyone to travel beyond China's borders, particularly to the west into areas then under the rule of Huns, Mongols, and Turks. Xuanzang was not the first Chinese Buddhist monk to travel to India, but he became the most famous and the most influential.

Because of Taizong's prohibitions, Xuanzang traveled secretly, often at night. Beyond the fabled Jade Gate, little but desert and occasional oases could be found in what became today's Xinjiang Province, then largely controlled by Turkish-speaking peoples, usually Buddhist and thus often willing to assist Xuanzang in his travels. Beyond the deserts were the mountains, equally challenging, with cold, ice, and high mountain passes to traverse. It took the monk about a year before he reached the lands of the Buddha after traveling through a number of Central Asian republics as well as what would become modern-day Afghanistan and Pakistan.

After arriving in the Indian subcontinent, Xuanzang is believed to have spent two years in Kashmir, mastering Sanskrit. He also visited numerous Buddhist sites in northern India, including the Buddha's birthplace, Lumbinī, near Kapilavastu (now Rummindei, Nepal); Bodh Gayā, where Siddhārtha found enlightenment while sitting under the bodhi tree, and the Deer Park at Sarnath, the site of the Buddha's first sermon where he elucidated the Middle Path between extreme asceticism and excessive sensual pleasure. Many of Xuanzang's years in India were spent at Nalanda, the intellectual and spiritual center of Buddhism for many centuries. Students numbered in the many thousands at this school, where Xuanzang studied and debated with other Buddhist scholars. He also traveled through southern India, and much of what is known about Indian society and culture during the seventh century is because of Xuanzang's writings about his travels.

One of the major events that occurred during his long stay in India was his victory in a debate among Buddhist scholars held in the presence of Harṣa (r. 606-647), the ruler of most of northern India. King Harṣa urged Xuanzang to remain at his court, but the monk had never intended to stay in India, and by 645, he had returned to China's western borders, again overcoming the obstacles of geography and climate and attacks by bandits. In the interim between the monk's departure from China in 629 and his return, Emperor Taizong had extended Chinese rule over many Turkish and other states that Xuanzang had traveled through earlier. Unsure about his reception, given that he had ignored the emperor's decree not to leave China, Xuanzang sent a letter to the emperor, justifying his journey to India. After a wait of several months, Taizong responded, informing the monk that his arrival was eagerly anticipated.

By 645 or 646, Xuanzang was back in Chang'an. He had brought with him nearly six hundred Buddhist manuscripts. The Wild Goose Pagoda was constructed to house the manuscripts, and the emperor ordered other scholars to assist Xuanzang in the task of translating the many texts. Taizong had hoped to glean useful military information from Xuanzang about potential enemies in the west, but the monk was unable or unwilling to provide this information. However, he did write the story of his travels, *Datang xiyouji* (629; *Buddhist Records of the Western World*, 1884). Xuanzang continued his translations and his studies until his death in 664 at Jade Flower Palace Monastery. Five years later, a five-story brick pagoda was constructed in Chang'an to house his remains.

SIGNIFICANCE

Xuanzang's importance cannot be overemphasized. His *Buddhist Records of the Western World* is not only an exciting adventure story but also a crucial historical source about the lands to the west of China and of India during the seventh century. Because of his fame as a scholar, Xuanzang was influential in the development of Buddhism in China and beyond. The texts he brought to China were the last major additions of Indian Buddhist writings into China. Many Japanese and Koreans monks journeyed to Chang'an to study with Xuanzang, their studies subsequently having an influence in their own countries.

In China, thanks in part to the contributions and influence of Xuanzang, Buddhism retained its dominant religious position for several centuries. His translations of the Buddhist *Heart Sutra* and the *Diamond Sutra* remain the standard texts. The travels of Xuanzang and others to the west and India also influenced the direction of Chinese art and architecture, then and in the future. Lastly, he became the inspiration for one of China's greatest literary epics. In the early sixteenth century, Wu Cheng'en wrote a marvelous literary work titled *Xiyouji* (c. 1570-c. 1580, oldest surviving edition, 1592; *Journey to the West*, 1977-1983), which relates in a magical-realism style the mythic and legendary travels of Xuanzang.

—*Eugene Larson*

FURTHER READING

Bernstein, Richard. *Ultimate Journey: Retracing the Path of an Ancient Buddhist Monk Who Crossed Asia in Search of Enlightenment*. New York: Alfred A. Knopf, 2001. The author, a respected journalist, followed the route of Xuanzang in the late 1990's.

Devahuti, D. *The Unknown Hsüan-tsang*. New York: Oxford University Press, 2001. A collection of translations of Xuanzang's translations into Chinese, with a biographical account of the monk by an Indian scholar.

Hui-li. *The Life of Hsüan-tsang*. Translated by Li Yuanghsi. Bejing: Chinese Buddhist Association, 1959. Early biography of Xuanzang by one of his contemporaries.

Watters, Thomas. *On Yuan Chwang's Travels in India*. Delhi: Munshi Ram Manohar Lal, 1961. A classic nineteenth century account of Xuanzang's travels.

Wriggins, Sally Hovey. *Xuanzang: A Buddhist Pilgrim on the Silk Road*. Boulder, Colo.: Westview Press, 1996. A readable and accessible biography of Xuanzang.

Wu-Ch'eng-en. *Monkey*. Translated by Arthur Waley. New York: John Day, 1943. A translation by a noted scholar of one of China's most famous novels.

SEE ALSO: 618: Founding of the Tang Dynasty; 845: Suppression of Buddhism; 1193: Turkish Raiders Destroy Buddhist University at Nalanda.

RELATED ARTICLES in *Great Lives from History: The Middle Ages, 477-1453*: Harṣa; Taizong; Xuanzang.

630-668
REIGN OF NARASIṂHAVARMAN I MAHĀMALLA

Narasiṃhavarman I Mahāmalla was the fourth Pallava king and a brilliant military leader, but he is primarily remembered as the patron and builder of the many rock-cut caves and temples and monumental sculptures at Mahabalipuram.

LOCALE: South India
CATEGORIES: Cultural and intellectual history; government and politics

KEY FIGURES

Narasiṃhavarman I Mahāmalla (d. 668), Pallava king, r. c. 630-668
Mahendravarman I (d. 630), Pallava king, r. c. 600-630

SUMMARY OF EVENT

Narasiṃhavarman I Mahāmalla was the fourth king of one of South India's most glorious dynasties. The Pallavas of Kanchipuram claim descent from Simhavarman (r. c. 550-575), but the true founder of the dynasty was his successor, Simhavishnu (r. c. 575-600), because it was he who rose above the political confusion of the late sixth century in Tamil Nadu and began to shape a strong political state. The third king, Mahendravarman I (r. c. 600-630), extended Pallava control southward as far as the Kaveri River. In doing so, he came into conflict with the Pāṇḍyas and the rulers of Ceylon who mounted regular resistance to the Pallavas.

Mahendravarman, a talented genius, was originally a Jain who converted and made Śiva his patron deity after he met Appar, the great Shaivite saint. After his conversion, the king boldly inaugurated the creation of temples in south India that were dedicated to Hindu deities and carved from stone rather than formed from the traditional materials of wood or brick. His first rock-cut cave temple at Mandagapattu bears an inscription stating that the king "caused to be constructed a temple of Brahma, Īśvara and Viṣṇu without using bricks, timber, metal, and mortar." Mahendravarman also wrote plays in Sanskrit, two of which have survived. *Mattavilāsa prahasana* (seventh century) is a delightful farce full of wit and satire about a dispute between a Buddhist and a drunken Kāpālika (Tantric Shaivite worshiper). The second play, *Bhagavadajjuka prahasana* (seventh century) is another hilarious farce that makes fun of hypocrisy and extreme religious behavior. Mahendravarman's creativity and originality were inherited by his son Narasiṃhavarman I.

In his early reign, Mahendravarman extended Pallava rule northward into modern Andhra Pradesh as far as the Krishna River. The Pallavas' rivals, the Cālukyas, feared the increasing strength of the Pallavas. The Cālukya king Pulakeśin II, ruling from the capital at Bādāmi, began a formidable assault on Mahendravarman's kingdom as early as 616. Some time later (although the exact date is unknown), Pulakeśin II led a campaign far into the Pallava realm, seizing Pallava lands no more than a few miles north of the capital city at Kanchipuram. It was the beginning of protracted warfare between the two powers.

Narasiṃhavarman I Mahāmalla, on assuming the throne, retrieved land lost to the Cālukyas. Narasiṃhavarman's rule marked the summit of Pallava power; it was a time of unrivaled prestige for the Pallavas. Sometime after Narasiṃhavarman ascended the throne, the ambitious Pulakeśin made a second attempt to overthrow the Pallavas, and once again threatened the capital. However, the Cālukya king was defeated at Manimangala about 20 miles (30 kilometers) east of Kanchipuram and in several other battles. Narasiṃhavarman, who had the help of the Sinhalese prince Mānavaram in the battles, decided to seek revenge. Known in the annuls of Indian history as the mighty king who captured and destroyed the Cālukya capital at Bādāmi, he was given the title Vāṭāpikoṇḍa or conqueror of Vāṭāpi (Bādāmi); the destruction of the capital took place around 641.

A declaration regarding Narasiṃhavarman's successful campaign is recorded in an inscription at the Mallikārjunadeva Temple at Bādāmi in the florid Pallava Grantha script. In this inscription, dated to 642, Narasiṃhavarman I Mahāmalla states that in his thirteenth regnal year, after he captured the city, he created there a victory pillar (*dvajaṣṭhambha*).

Although Pulakeśin was killed defending his capital, the Cālukyas eventually were able to take back their traditional land holdings. The two powerful rivals continued to engage in warfare for generations. Ancient records show that Narasiṃhavarman vanquished the neighboring Cōlas, Cheras, Kalabhras, and Pāṇḍyas. The Pallavas were probably a maritime power at this time because the Sinhalese epic, the *Mahāvaṃsa* (fifth century; *The Mahāvaṃsa*, 1837, 1909) mentions two successive naval expeditions by Narasiṃhavarman to take back the Sinhalese throne for his friend, the disenfranchised prince Mānavarman.

During Narasiṃhavarman's reign, the Chinese pilgrim Xuanzang (Hsüan-tsang; c. 602-664) visited the

Pallava capital, Kanchipuram, possibly in 640 sometime before the expedition against Bādāmi. The pilgrim spent the rainy season in the capital city before he embarked on a planned journey to Ceylon. While in Kanchipuram, the Chinese monk studied the works of the great Buddhist theologian Dharmapāla whose teachings on metaphysics and logic were to influence Xuanzang's life and work. The monk also reported that the capital was about 6 miles (10 kilometers) in circumference. He described the people as being courageous, trustworthy, and public spirited. In addition, he reported that there were more than one hundred Buddhist monasteries with more than ten thousand monks. Xuanzang never realized his dream of visiting Sri Lanka; before leaving for that region, he encountered three hundred Sinhalese monks who had fled a civil war at home and who implored him to abandon his plan.

The seventh century in south India was an exhilarating and creative time. The Tamils were undergoing a period of Hindu revivalism that swept through the region in response to the very successful spread of Jainism and Buddhism in previous centuries. The early saints of the south, the Shaivites Appar and Sambandar and the Vaishnavites Peyar, Poykai, and Pūtān, spearheaded the *bhakti* (devotion) movement. They created poignant devotional literature that professed total surrender to the deity. Poykai in particular created beautiful and moving linked verses (groups of one hundred) called *antati* in which the final verse became the beginning of the next verse. The verses were regarded as "garlands" of devotional songs that honored the deity. Kanchipuram had long been an important religious center, and by the seventh century, the temples and monasteries had become illustrious centers of advanced philosophical speculation, a fact confirmed by Xuanzang.

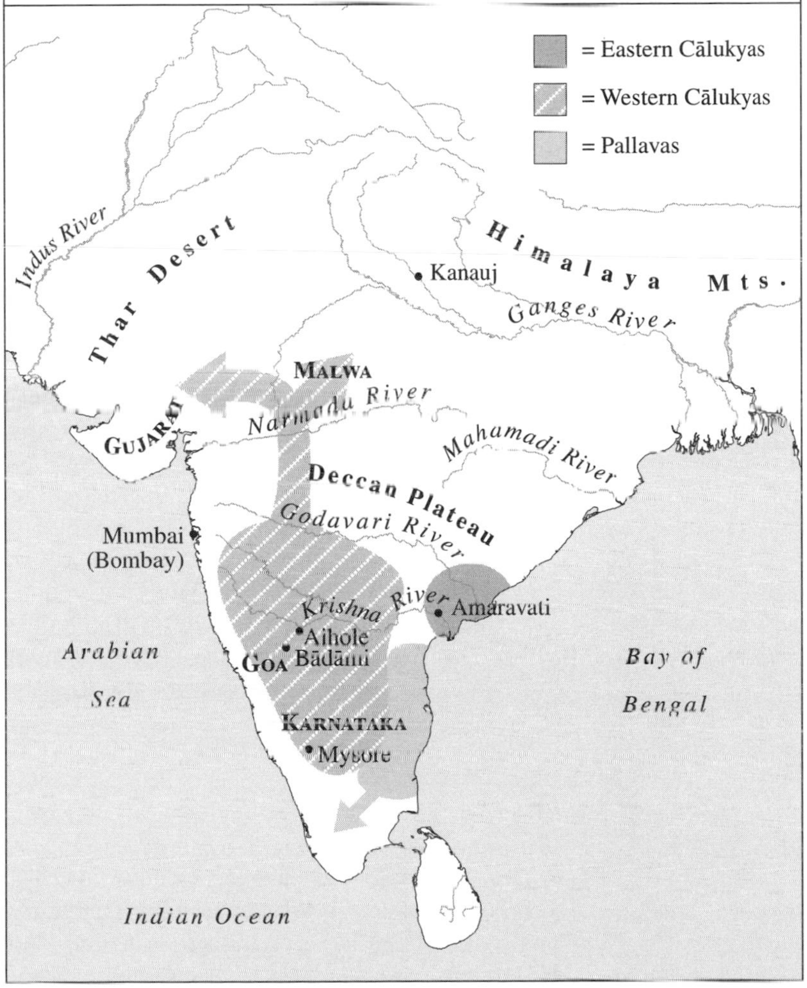

Among Narasiṃhavarman's many great feats, the creation of the marvelous architecture laden with splendid ornamentation and sculpture at Mahābalipuram was his crowning achievement. Originally called Māhamallapuram after its founder, the port city of Mahabalipuram was located about 30 miles (50 kilometers) east of the capital at Kanchipuram. It was once a thriving trading center and undoubtedly the home of the Pallava navy. The port city was not only a strategic military and mercantile center but also a remarkable religious center. Narasimhavarman instructed his craftspeople to sculpt unique houses of worship from the enormous natural boulders of granite located along the shore. Included are ten rock-cut caves and six monolithic temples called *rathas* (chariots).

Cutting from the top and working downward, the artisans sculpted rather than constructed life-sized temples. The sculptures covering the façades of the *rathas* are memorable for their youthful grace, elegant and slim proportions, and soft, rounded faces. The *rathas* are examples of the southern or Dravidian style of architecture,

CĀLUKYAS AND PALLAVAS, 7TH CENTURY

= Eastern Cālukyas
= Western Cālukyas
= Pallavas

THE PALLAVA KINGS

Reign	*King*
c. 550-575	Simhavarman (some sources give c. 436)
c. 575-600	Simhavishnu
c. 600-630	Mahendravarman I
c. 630-668	Narasiṃhavarman I Mahāmalla
c. 668-670	Mahendravarman II
c. 670-700	Paramesvaravarman I
c. 695-728	Narasiṃhavarman II
c. 728-731	Paramesvaravarman II
c. 731-796	Nandivarman

which had previously used less durable materials. The many sculptures at Mahābalipuram are some of the earliest representations of Hindu divinities in the Tamil region. In addition, the clothing and ornaments worn by the deities provide a glimpse of courtly Pallava fashions and are a valuable resource for historians.

At Mahābalipuram is a monumental sculpted panel measuring approximately 90 by 25 feet (30 by 8 meters). In an excellent state of preservation and formed from a single massive rock, the surface is sculpted to exhibit a crowded assembly consisting of representatives from the divine, human, and animal world.

The subject of the work is controversial. Some scholar have contended that it relates to the hero Ārjuna from the epic *Mahābhārata* (400 B.C.E.-400 C.E., present form by c. 400 C.E.; *The Mahabharata of Krishna-Dwaipayana Vyasa*, 1887-1896), who assumes a yogic posture as he does penance while praying to the god Śiva for a powerful weapon for destroying his enemies. Others argue that it portrays the Hindu myth about the descent of the celestial River Gaṇgā (Ganges) as it plunges to Earth. According to the legend, an ascetic king named Bhagīratha prayed to Śiva for the divine river Gaṇgā to wash over the cremated remains of his ancestors. Lending support to the second identification is a great stone tank positioned at the top and just behind the wall of sculpture. Scholars speculate that water may have been released and allowed to flow over the panel's central crevice, which is filled with sculpted water creatures, to enhance the realism of the myth.

Whatever the event portrayed, the artists have created a great assembly gathered to witness it, including a family of monumental elephants, a newborn elephant just rising to its feet, a family of monkeys grooming themselves, and a scrawny ascetic cat performing a one-legged yogic stance accompanied by worshipful mice. Such original and charming subjects are unusual in Indian art.

SIGNIFICANCE

The brilliant reign of Narasiṃhavarman ended with his death in 668; his son Mahendravarman II succeeded him but spent no more than two years on the throne. The impact of Narasiṃhavarman's life and reign are incalculable. Like his father, he was highly creative and original as well as a devout Hindu. His patronage resulted in the creation of some of India's finest and most memorable art and architecture, works that were seminal in the region and were to inspire the magnificent Hindu temples of south India. His heroic defeat of his aggressive enemy, Pulakeśin II, ensured him a prominent position as a great warrior king. The diary of the Chinese pilgrim Xuanzang and many other contemporary records attest to the breadth and wealth of Narasiṃhavarman's vast empire and his able administration. Although he was a superb warrior who maintained an impressive empire, one that endured as a model for later rule in south India, he will be remembered most of all for his stunning monuments at Mahābalipuram.

—*Katherine Anne Harper*

FURTHER READING

Lockwood, Michael. *Māmallapuram and the Pallavas*. Madras, India: Christian Literature Society, 1982. An excellent work that includes a series of articles on Pallava art and inscriptions at Māmallapuram. Extensive notes and bibliography.

Lockwood, Michael, Gift Siromoney, and P. Dayanandan. *Mahābalipuram Studies*. Madras, India: Christian Literature Society, 1974. An important work on Pallava art in general and the authorship of the intriguing monuments at Mahābalipuram. Bibliography.

Nilakantha Sastri, K. A. *A History of South India from Prehistoric Times to the Fall of the Vijayanagar*. Bombay: Oxford University Press, 1966. An important and careful reconstruction of the history of Tamil Nadu from earliest times through its last great dynasty. Bibliography.

SEE ALSO: 606-647: Reign of Harṣa of Kanauj; c. 610-632: Muḥammad Receives Revelations; c. 710: Construction of the Kāilaśanātha Temple; 770-810: Reign of Dharmapāla; 915: Parāntaka I Conquers Pāṇḍya; 973: Foundation of the Western Cālukya Dynasty.

RELATED ARTICLES in *Great Lives from History: The Middle Ages, 477-1453*: Harṣa; Xuanzang.

630-711
ISLAM EXPANDS THROUGHOUT NORTH AFRICA

The expansion of Islam beyond the Middle East came with the conquest and conversion of Berber tribes in North Africa by Muslim forces. This expansion influenced the cultural and intellectual shaping of both the Islamic world and the European world beginning in the Middle Ages.

LOCALE: North Africa
CATEGORIES: Expansion and land acquisition; religion; trade and commerce; wars, uprisings, and civil unrest

KEY FIGURES

ʿAmr ibn al-ʿAṣ (d. 663), a Muslim commander in Egypt
ʿUthmān ibn ʿAffān (d. 656), third Orthodox caliph, r. 644-656
ʿAbd Allāh ibn Saʿd ibn Abū Sarḥ (d. 656), governor of Egypt under ʿUthmān
Muʾāwiyah I (d. 680), Umayyad caliph, r. 661-680
ʿUqbah ibn Nāfiʿ (d. 683), general who fought to convert the Berbers and founded an Islamic base at al-Qayrān
Abū al-Muhajir, Muslim general who briefly replaced ʿUqbah and successfully converted Berbers
Kasila, a Berber chieftain who converted to Islam
ʿAbd al-Malik (646/647-705), Islamic caliph, r. 685-705
Mūsā ibn Nuṣayr (640-716/717), the Muslim commander who oversaw the Muslim conquest of North Africa after c. 700
Damia al-Kāhina (d. 701), Berber queen and military commander
Ḥassān (d. after 704), Muslim military commander

SUMMARY OF EVENT

By the time of the Islamic conquests, most of interior of North Africa was either in the hands of or under the influence of powerful Berber tribes and tribal coalitions. It was these tribal bodies that controlled the massive trade networks that transported precious resources and products from sub-Saharan Africa to trade centers and commercial ports on the Mediterranean, most of which were controlled by the Byzantine Empire.

The Byzantines had regained control of such coastal cities as Carthage and Tripoli after having lost these to Vandal armies during the sixth century. After returning to North Africa, the Byzantines never managed to reestablish the kind of direct control over wide swaths of territory they had enjoyed in previous centuries. Instead, they depended upon their capacity to control certain crucial trade routes, sheltered in fortresses, and sought cooperation and exchange with the Berber tribes.

Following the Muslim conquest of Egypt, which concluded with the Treaty of Alexandria in 642, ʿAmr ibn al-ʿAṣ (d. 663), the Muslim commander in Egypt, sought to protect his new holdings by countering the threat posed by Byzantine naval power in the Mediterranean. To do so, he deemed it necessary to launch a series of campaigns into the lands to the west (*al-maghrib*) of his Egyptian frontiers—the Maghreb Desert area in northwest Africa. He began by dispatching troops to Barka, the main city of the region of Cyrenaica (now in Libya). ʿAmr then continued along the coast, concluding treaties with some cities, and eventually taking Tripoli as the Byzantine defenders escaped by sea or down the coast to smaller cities.

In 645, ʿAmr was relieved of his duties in Egypt and north Africa. The caliph ʿUthmān ibn ʿAffān (r. 644-656) appointed another governor over Egypt, ʿAbd Allāh ibn Saʿd ibn Abī Sarḥ. ʿUthmān's policy as caliph called for continued expansion of Islam through the conquest of the territories of Iran and North Africa. When the Muslims took the field against Byzantine forces at ʿAqūba, Abī Sarḥ's troops killed the Byzantine exarch Gregory and routed his army. When the alarmed Byzantines offered a reported tribute of 2.5 million dinars to the Muslims if they would withdraw from North Africa, Abī Sarḥ took the money and returned to Egypt.

Over the next thirteen years, the Arabs avoided open conflict with the Byzantines in North Africa but began building a navy to counter the Byzantine Mediterranean fleet. When the first Muslim civil war ended in 661, the new caliph, Muʾāwiyah I (r. 661-680), returned to a policy of conquests on the frontiers of the Muslim world, and ʿAmr returned to Egypt as governor and began again the process of subjecting North Africa to Muslim rule.

The first expeditions in this project were intended to subdue the powerful Berber tribes, who were now less willing than before to submit to the Muslims because they now doubted that the Arab armies were capable of maintaining rule in the region after their long absence. After a series of early successes, ʿAmr died in 663 and his brother ʿUtba bin Abū Sufyān was put in command of Egypt and military operations in North Africa. For the

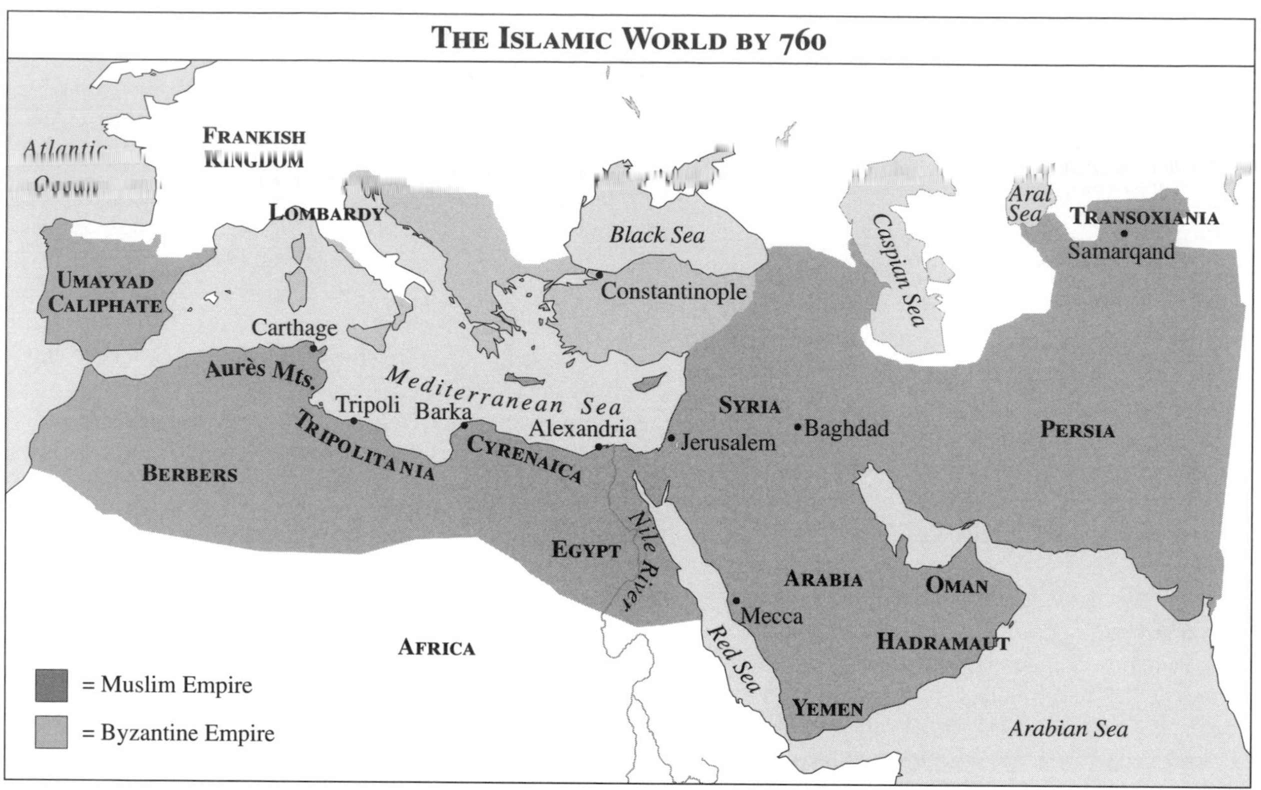

THE ISLAMIC WORLD BY 760

next three years, raids were carried out against the Byzantines and Berber tribesmen, but no sustained effort toward definitive conquest of the region seems to have been undertaken.

Beginning in 666, the Muslim armies began a new series of raids under the leadership of ʿUqbah ibn Nāfiʿ (d. 683), a veteran of many campaigns in North Africa since the days of ʿAmr. ʿUqbah understood that subduing and converting the Berbers was key to control of the region. He then allied with the Berbers against the Byzantines and established a base at al-Qayrān, situated at a distance from the coast that was beyond the reach of Byzantine forces. The city he founded there was built by 675, but in that year he was suddenly dismissed from power. His replacement, Abū al-Muhajir, faced a growing alliance of Berber warriors under the command of a Christian leader.

Shortly after taking command in North Africa, Abū al-Muhajir defeated Kasila, who had previously been an ally of the Byzantines. Little is known about the battle itself, but in its wake, the defeated Kasila was treated equitably by Abū al-Muhajir, and the Berber chieftain converted and formed an alliance with the Muslims. Additionally, Abū al-Muhajir set in place a policy of converting and assimilating Berber tribesmen into the Muslim forces. He understood that the Arabs alone would never be numerous enough to conquer and maintain control over the entire region. His policy met with considerable initial success. In 678, he began operations against the Byzantines.

Abū al-Muhajir was by some accounts a converted former Coptic Christian. If this is true, his personal experience with conversion and assimilation into the Islamic community may have helped him understand the importance of the shift in policy with regard to the Berber tribes that his actions initiated. In any case, beginning with the period of Abū al-Muhajir's command in North Africa, the conversion and assimilation of Berber tribesmen would facilitate the Islamic conquest of North Africa and would eventually shape the intellectual and cultural life of not only the Islamic world, but that of Western Europe as well.

Despite some successes against the Byzantines, Abū al-Muhajir was replaced in 681 by ʿUqbah. Upon retaking command, ʿUqbah set out on a long and hard-fought campaign against a combined Byzantine and Berber force. During his tenure, however, ʿUqbah rejected Abū al-Muhajir's egalitarian policies with regard to the new

Berber Muslims, a choice for which he was to pay a heavy price. The powerful recent convert Kasila eventually abandoned and then attacked ʿUqbah, finally killing him in battle near the fortress of Tahūda. The crushing defeat led the Arabs to partially and, in some cases, completely abandon their recently conquered territories in North Africa.

In 688, however, the Arabs were back. Kasila was soon killed in battle, but so was the new Muslim commander, Zuhayr bnu Qays al-Balawī. His death alarmed Caliph ʿAbd al-Malik, who dispatched forty thousand troops to root out the Byzantine forces in North Africa. The commander of these troops was Ḥassān. Ḥassān was a tried and proven warrior and administrator, and in 695 he entered the Byzantine provinces of Cyrenaica and Tripolitania and took the strategic and commercial capital of Carthage.

A new leader had now arisen among the Berbers, however. She was Damia al-Kāhina (the priestess or the soothsayer), a member of the Jarawa tribe, one of the leading tribes of the mighty Butr confederation. Al-Kāhina's tribe had previously converted to some form of Judaism, and there is some evidence to suggest that she herself was either Christian or Jewish. She proved a formidable opponent for Ḥassān in the last stages of the conquest of North Africa. During the first clash, al-Kāhina routed Ḥassān's forces and chased them back to the coast. Then she made a fatal mistake. Assuming that the Arabs were out on yet another raiding expedition, she ravaged the surrounding countryside so that there would be nothing for which the Arabs would return. These actions earned her the animosity of many Berber tribes, who invited the Arabs back and assisted them in their future campaigns.

When Ḥassān returned to the field, al-Kāhina was defeated and eventually killed after fleeing to the Aurès Mountains. Free to turn his attentions to the coast and the Byzantine contingents there, Ḥassān expelled the Byzantines again from Carthage, effectively ending the Byzantine presence in North Africa. To preserve his gains, Ḥassān re-adopted the policy of Abū al-Muhajir, treating defeated Berber tribesmen equitably, even generously, and sending missionaries among the tribes to seek converts. The newly converted tribesmen—among them the sons of al-Kāhina—were promised full and equal shares of all future conquests.

The next commander of North Africa, Mūsa ibn Nuṣayr, found it necessary to continue Ḥassān's policy as he attempted to consolidate Ḥassān's achievements and bring North Africa under stable administration. Troops assisted in bringing the rest of North Africa under Muslim control, and they also participated in raiding expeditions outside of Africa. As Musa and his Berber allies subdued the remaining portions of North Africa, they met and slowly assimilated such powerful tribes as Kutama, Hawwara, Zanata, and Musmuda. Their practice was to invite these tribes to accept Islam, and if they refused, to attack and fight them stubbornly until they agreed to convert. On conversion, the tribes would contribute troops to the Arab armies and their native chiefs would be confirmed by the Muslim authorities. Increasingly, the Muslim army in North Africa was becoming mostly Berber rather than Arab.

601 - 700

Significance

Following the Muslim conquest of North Africa, the region would remain part of the larger Islamic world, and it continues to be a part of that world into the twenty-first century. The conquest of North Africa did not end the resistance of local peoples to foreign domination, however. Although the Berbers converted to Islam, they did not quietly join the growing Muslim empire. Instead, they frequently adopted strains of Islam that lent an Islamic aura to continued resistance, most notably within the Ibādi Khārijite community. However, the most profound impact of the conquest of North Africa may have been its sequel, the conquest of Iberia with the revival of Sunni Islam in the eleventh century.

—Thomas Sizgorich

Further Reading

Bogle, Emory C. *Islam: Origin and Belief*. Austin: University of Texas Press, 1998. A concise look at Islam and its expansion between 570 and 1517. Also includes discussion of Muḥammad and Islam's beginnings. Maps, bibliography, index.

Brett, Michael. "The Arab Conquest and the Rise of Islam in North Africa." In *The Cambridge History of Africa*, edited by J. D. Fage. Vol. 2. New York: Cambridge University Press, 1979. One of the best analyses available of the conquests and their consequences, written by the field's leading authority. Bibliography, index.

_______. "The Islamisization of Morocco from the Arabs to the Almoravids." *Journal of the Society for Moroccan Studies* 2 (1992): 57-71. A study of the process whereby North Africa developed a distinct Islamic character.

Jandora, John Walter. *Militarism in Arab Society: An Historiographical and Bibliographical Sourcebook.*

Westport, Conn.: Greenwood Press, 1997. A detailed history of Arab military culture, with a discussion of Muʿāwiyah and his descendants and "Muslim warriors of medieval times." Illustrations, maps, bibliography, index.

Kenny, Joseph. *The Spread of Islam Through North to West Africa, Seventh to Nineteenth Centuries: A Historical Survey with Relevant Arab Documents*. Lagos, Nigeria: Dominican, 2000. Although this text might be difficult to locate, it is a valuable collection of Arab and other sources on the expansion of Islam into North and West Africa, beginning in the seventh century. Illustrations, maps, bibliography, index.

Levtzion, Nehemia, and Randall L. Pouwels, eds. *The History of Islam in Africa*. Athens: Ohio University Press, 2000. A comprehensive examination of the history of Islam in Africa, including a chapter on the period immediately following the initial conquest in the seventh century. Introductory chapter looks at the "Patterns of Islamization and Varieties of Religious Experience Among Muslims of Africa." Illustrations, maps, bibliography, index.

Mones, H. "The Conquest of North Africa and Berber Resistance." In *General History of Africa*, edited by Ivan Hrbek. Vol. 3. Abridged ed. Berkeley: University of California Press, 1992. A study of the conquest that emphasizes the reasons and means of Berber resistance to Arabicization. Illustrations, maps, bibliography, index.

Taha, Abdulwahid Dhanun. *The Muslim Conquest and Settlement of North Africa and Spain*. New York: Routledge, 1989. A narrative guide to the conquest and settlement. One of relatively few serious histories of this topic by a modern Arab scholar, a work that relies heavily on Arabic sources. Bibliography, index.

Watt, William Montgomery. *A Short History of Islam*. Boston: Oneworld, 1996. Provides a concise history of Islamic expansionism, the formation of the caliphate, and the politics of Islam. Bibliography, index.

SEE ALSO: c. 610-632: Muḥammad Receives Revelations; August 15-20, 636: Battle of Yarmūk; 637-657: Islam Expands Throughout the Middle East; April or May, 711: Ṭārik Crosses into Spain; October 11, 732: Battle of Tours; 10th-11th centuries: First Hausa State Established; 969-1171: Reign of the Fāṭimids; 11th century: Expansion of Sunni Islam in North Africa and Iberia; 1048: Zīrids Break from Fāṭimid Dynasty and Revive Sunni Islam.

RELATED ARTICLES in *Great Lives from History: The Middle Ages, 477-1453*: ʿAbd al-Malik; Charles Martel; al-Ḥasan al-Baṣrī; Heraclius; Damia al-Kāhina; Khadīja; Maḥmūd Ghāzān; Muḥammad; Ṭāriq ibn-Ziyād; ʿUmar I.

635-800
FOUNDING OF LINDISFARNE AND CREATION OF THE *BOOK OF KELLS*

The founding of Lindisfarne and the creation of the Book of Kells *established a monastic community that in turn became the inspirational source for much of the religious, educational, and cultural renewal of the Dark Ages in Europe.*

LOCALE: Northern Britain and Ireland
CATEGORIES: Cultural and intellectual history; literature; religion

KEY FIGURES

Saint Columba (c. 521-597), missionary monk who founded the monastery at Iona
Oswald (c. 605-641), Northumbrian king, r. 633-641, who sponsored the founding of Lindisfarne
Saint Aidan (d. 651), first bishop of Lindisfarne, 635-651
Saint Colman (c. 605-676), third abbot of Lindisfarne who represented the Irish position at the Synod of Whitby, 661-664
Saint Cuthbert (635?-687), abbot, hermit, and bishop of Lindisfarne who was its most illustrious saint, 683-687

SUMMARY OF EVENT

Since its settlement before the seventh century, the small island of Lindisfarne, located a mile off the northeast coast of England, has been accessible from the mainland only by a causeway exposed at low tide. The monastic community first established on "Holy Island" in 635 was one of the key sites of the encounter between two different Christian missions to pagan Saxon England during the 600's.

The establishment of Lindesfarne's monastery can

A page from the illuminated manuscript known as the Book of Kells *shows the Virgin and the Christ child.* (Hulton|Archive by Getty Images)

best be understood within the historical context of the Roman settlement of Britain. The withdrawal of Roman troops from Celtic Britain in the early fifth century allowed the successful colonization of Britain by invading Germanic peoples from the northern European mainland, isolating the indigenous Celts in the "fringes" of Wales, Ireland, and Scotland. Those Celts who had been Christianized were largely cut off from regular intercourse with the continental Church under the authority of Rome. Nevertheless, the vibrancy of the Irish church during the 500's is evidenced by its fame for scholarship, by the evangelizing missions back to the Continent by people such as Saint Columbanus, and by the number of admired founders of monastic communities. One of these was Saint Columba, born of Irish nobility, who journeyed across the Irish Sea in the 560's to establish a monastic community on the tiny island of Iona off the western coast of Scotland.

The several tribal kingdoms of the Anglo-Saxon invaders engaged in their own jockeying for power. In the rivalry between two northern kingdoms, for instance, Æthelfrith of Bernicia forced Edwin of Deira into exile in the early 600's and became sole overlord over a combined Northumbria. After Æthelfrith's death in battle in 616, Edwin regained power and forced Æthelfrith's two sons Oswald and Oswy into exile among the Irish and Scottish peoples to the northwest.

Into the context of this tribal rivalry, a new evangelistic mission arrived in southeastern England in 597, sent by Pope Gregory the Great and led by an Italian monk named Augustine. After converting the Kentish king Æthelbert and establishing a bishopric at Canterbury,

Augustine and his successors sent missions northward during the early seventh century to other Saxon kingdoms. Paulinus's mission to Edwin's Northumbria in 625 is described in considerable detail by the monk and scholar, Saint Bede the Venerable, on whose work *Historia ecclesiastica gentis Anglorum* (731; *Ecclesiastical History of the English People*, 1723) every account of the period depends.

When the now-converted Edwin was defeated in 633 by Cædwalla (also known as Cædwallon), king of the Welsh Britons, Æthelfrith's exiled sons Oswald and Oswy returned to reestablish their family's overlordship in Northumbria. Yet Oswald and Oswy had themselves been converted by the Irish Christians among whom they had lived in exile, in all likelihood under the influence of the Irish mission on Iona, whose founder Columba had died in the year of Augustine's arrival at Canterbury. Soon after establishing his authority in Northumbria, Oswald invited the Ionan church to send a mission to oversee the evangelization of his kingdom. From Iona came Saint Aidan, to whom Oswald gave the island of Lindisfarne as a base of operations.

The half century following the founding of Lindisfarne in fact saw a complex web of Christian enterprise moving in all directions throughout Britain, and involving people from Augustine's Roman mission, from Ireland or the indigenous Welsh church directly, and from the Irish mission based at Lindisfarne. Nevertheless, historians commonly identify Lindisfarne as the most influential center of ecclesiastical influence through the 660's, even as the church throughout Britain became increasingly aware of the importance of bringing itself into conformity with the Church of Rome.

In 664, a church counsel was called at Whitby to address the main points of conflict between the Irish and Roman "camps." Underlying issues involved the differences between the Irish monastic system of church government and the Roman diocesan system. Yet one of the critical sticking points concerned different means of calculating the date of Easter. The resolution of these matters in favor of Roman custom represented a watershed moment of reorientation toward Catholic unity with the continental Church. Nevertheless, respect for the virtues and piety of the Irish tradition remained strong.

To be sure, there occurred among Irish diehards a reorientation back toward Ireland. Saint Colman, the abbot of Lindisfarne and leading spokesperson for the defeated Irish position, resigned his abbacy and led a group of monks (some of whom were certainly English) to Ireland to establish a new community at Mayo. Ireland remained a pilgrimage direction for many who found Irish scholarship preeminent. Thus the Irish church was invested with significant new vibrancy during the 700's in large part through the intercourse sought by Saxon converts. The threads of mutual influence become so difficult to separate as to warrant the modern term "Hiberno-Saxon." For example, the Celtic elements in the products of the Lindisfarne scriptorium clearly demonstrate Irish influence, yet the brilliant synthesis of Celtic, Germanic, Mediterranean, and even Coptic elements found in the Lindisfarne Gospels also influenced the design of later Irish manuscripts.

Lindisfarne became the northern Irish pole of an axis reaching southward to the developing family of monasteries under Roman influence, including those established in 674 and 682 by Saint Benedict Biscop only thirty miles down the coast at Wearmouth and Jarrow. Clearly the monasteries collaborated collegially with one another. Lindisfarne also continued as the eastern pole of an axis oriented westward toward Iona and the family of monastic communities throughout Ireland. This axis accounts for Lindisfarne's connection with the problematic second subject of this entry: the *Book of Kells*, the most famous of the surviving Hiberno-Saxon gospel books whose unfathomable intricacy of ornamentation marks it as one of Ireland's national treasures.

Although datable to somewhere around 800, the *Book of Kells* remains a mystery text. Where was it made, and by whom? The longest surviving tradition associates the book with Columba and Iona, although it is clearly of later provenance than the sixth century. Most scholars accept the likely relevance of the fact that Iona was attacked by Viking raiders in the late 700's (as were the Northumbrian monasteries) and that a band of Ionan monks seeking refuge established a daughter house at Kells in County Meath. By the eleventh century, the gospel book that became known as the *Book of Kells* was associated with this monastery. Many questions remain. It is possible that it was created by the monks there, or it may have been created at the scriptorium at Iona and then brought with the monks escaping the Vikings. Another theory claims that it was begun at Iona and completed at Kells. One of the most controversial yet respected arguments suggests that it was produced at Lindisfarne or at one of the northern English monasteries but was at some point brought back to Kells, which an Irish faction might have considered to be its proper keeping-place.

SIGNIFICANCE

Bede, who spent his entire life at Jarrow, was invited by the Lindisfarne community to compose the biography of its most illustrious saint, Cuthbert. The elaborately illuminated gospel books, of which the Lindisfarne Gospels is the most splendid survivor, clearly represent a synthesis—both textual and artistic—of sources from Irish tradition and from the continental scholarship imported by Benedict Biscop and other leading seventh century churchmen such as Wilfrid and Archbishop Theodore. In turn, Lindisfarne influenced the production of such manuscripts as the *Codex Amiatinus*, a complete Bible sent to Italy in 718 as a gift to the pope from Wearmouth and Jarrow, and for centuries supposed to be of Italian, not Northumbrian, origin.

—*John Edward Skillen*

FURTHER READING

Blair, Peter Hunter. *The World of Bede*. 2d ed. New York: St. Martin's Press, 1990. While focusing on Bede, this eminent historian of Saxon England provides the layperson with an overview of the entire Hiberno-Saxon world.

Brown, Michelle P. *The Lindisfarne Gospels: Society, Spirituality, and the Scribe*. Toronto: University of Toronto Press, 2003. This study provides a good overview of the early illuminated gospel books. Includes bibliography and index.

De Hamel, Christopher. *A History of Illuminated Manuscripts*. London: Phaidon, 1994. The chapter "Books for Missionaries" emphasizes the intended uses of the splendid illuminated gospel books such as the *Book of Kells*.

Mayr-Harting, Henry. *The Coming of Christianity to Anglo-Saxon England*. 3d ed. University Park: Pennsylvania State University Press, 1991. Oriented toward the general reader, this study includes the Irish and Mediterranean influences on early English Christianity.

Meehan, Bernard. *The "Book of Kells": An Illustrated Introduction to the Manuscript in Trinity College, Dublin*. New York: Thames and Hudson, 1994. This richly illustrated popular guide is written by one of the foremost contemporary Kells scholars.

SEE ALSO: 731: Bede Writes *Ecclesiastical History of the English People*; June 7, 793: Norse Raid Lindisfarne Monastery.

RELATED ARTICLE in *Great Lives from History: The Middle Ages, 477-1453*: Saint Bede the Venerable.

August 15-20, 636
BATTLE OF YARMŪK

Muslim forces besieged and captured the holy regions of Syria and Palestine from the Byzantine Empire and continued their conquest and expansion of the Middle East.

LOCALE: Sea of Galilee, near the border of Syria and Jordan

CATEGORY: Wars, uprisings, and civil unrest

KEY FIGURES

Heraclius (c. 575-641), Byzantine emperor, r. 610-641

Khālid ibn al-Walīd (d. 642), Muslim field commander

Theodore Trithourios (c. 600-636), commander of Byzantine forces in Syria

Abū ʿUbaidah (c. 600-636), commander of Muslim forces in Syria

Vahān (c. 600-636), Byzantine field commander

Jabala bin al-Ayham (c. 600-636), Ghassānid king, commander of Byzantium's Arab allies

SUMMARY OF EVENT

In 628, the Byzantine emperor Heraclius successfully concluded a war against the Sāsānid Dynasty of Persia. This Persian War, waged since 603, left both empires exhausted just when a new and soon to be powerful Islamic state was rising to the south. Islam, which means "submission to God," was the new religion created by the Prophet Muḥammad. A follower of Islam is called a Muslim, "one who submits."

After Muḥammad died in 632, his successors (caliphs) began to expand the borders of the state in a series of *jihads* (holy wars). The town-based Muslims needed to control their Arab cousins to the north; if not consolidated, these independent nomads, who were such an integral part of the region's economy and culture, would threaten the survival of the state. The Muslims were also drawn north because they considered Syria and Palestine to be holy regions; Muḥammad was the last and greatest Prophet of Islam, but the religion also counted Adam,

Noah, Abraham, Moses, and Jesus as early Prophets. The fact that the region contained rich trading cities was a further and perhaps greater inducement.

Syria, Palestine, and Egypt had been part of the Greco-Roman world for centuries but enjoyed only a thin Hellenistic veneer. Greek- and Latin-speaking Europeans dominated the westward-looking coastal cities, but the green agricultural belt and desert fringe beyond were dominated by Jews, Arabs, and other minorities. They spoke Semitic languages and were at odds with the Orthodox Christianity of the Byzantines.

Heraclius. (Library of Congress)

The southern borders of Byzantine Syria and Palestine were protected by the Ghassānid tribes. These Arab bedouin allies, like the Lakhmid tribes who protected the southwestern flank of Iraq for the Persians, were ruled by "client kings." At the time of the Muslim invasion, Heraclius was rebuilding the Ghassānid tribal coalition destroyed during the Sāsānian occupation of 611 to 630.

Arab and Byzantine sources are sketchy concerning the campaigns in Syria. Nevertheless, scholars have been able to reconstruct the basic sequence of events. Muslim raids into Byzantine territory had begun in 629, but in 633, Abū Bakr, Muḥammad's father-in-law and successor, launched four Arab armies totalling twenty-four thousand men into southern Syria and Palestine. In the spring of 634, Heraclius, in northern Syria keeping an eye on the Persians, sent sizable reinforcements down the coast under his brother Theodore. In response, Abū Bakr ordered his best general, Khālid ibn al-Walīd, campaigning in Iraq, to cross the desert to Syria. Khālid's small but elite force came in behind Theodore's army in May, joined the other Muslim columns, and met the Byzantines head on for the first time on July 30, west of Jerusalem at Ajnadain. Theodore, abandoned by the local Arabs and outnumbered two to one, was routed after a bloody two-day battle. Some Byzantine forces were chased into the fortified coastal cities while others retreated northward.

After Ajnadain, Heraclius sent Theodore back to Constantinople in disgrace while the Arabs ravaged the countryside of southern Palestine. Theodore Trithourios, the *sakellarios* (state treasurer) and probably *magister militum per Orientem* (master of the soldiers in the East), was then put in charge of the retreating Byzantines. Following the death of Abū Bakr, the new caliph ʿUmar I (r. 634-644) replaced Khālid in regional command with Abū ʿUbaidah, a pious and more conciliatory man. Khālid continued to lead the field army and pressed the Byzantines northward, defeating them near Pella in late January of 635 and again at Marj al-Saffar in February. Greeted as liberators for the most part, the victorious Muslims confined the Byzantines to a small coastal strip after they took Damascus in September and Emesa (Homs) in November.

Heraclius, though suffering from dropsy (edema), began amassing a new army at Antioch. Elite troops from the capital, which included men from the Balkans, Anatolia, and Germanic Lombards from Italy, were combined with local forces, various Armenian contingents,

After Muḥammad: The Early Caliphs

Reign	Caliph
632-634	Abū Bakr
634-644	ʿUmar I
644-656	ʿUthmān ibn ʿAffan
656-661	Alī ibn Abī Ṭālib

and allied Arab tribes to form a large but eclectic mercenary force. Heraclius was probably able to gather seventy thousand for the defense of Syria, forty thousand of whom would be available to oppose the Muslims. The Byzantine army, like the Muslim, was two-thirds infantry armed with bows, spears, swords, and shields. Byzantine mounted troops, mostly Arab auxiliaries, were augmented by an elite core of heavily armored cavalrymen known as cataphracts. Field operations against Khālid were given to Vahān, an Armenian who had commanded at Emesa and knew the area best. Outnumbered and fearful of being flanked by Byzantine seaborne forces, the Muslims abandoned Emesa and Damascus in the spring of 636 and settled that summer near the Yarmūk River, a strong defensive position a day and a half's march south of Damascus. The Yarmūk anchored their left and the Harra, a vast lava rock plain, protected their right. The population there, mostly Arabs and Jews, was anything but friendly to the Byzantines and the position afforded Khālid a clear route to the safety of the desert in case of a defeat.

The Muslims, inspired by their new faith, proved impervious to the usual Byzantine attempts to bribe enemy leaders and sow dissension in their ranks. In fact, it was the Byzantine army that was suffering from desertions and infighting among its different ethnic groups. When he realized that his army was getting weaker and Khālid's was receiving reinforcements from Arabia, Vahān decided to attack. The armies, probably very close to equal by then, faced each other on a plain north of the Wadi Yarmūk. (A wadi is a deep stream bed or gorge that remains mostly dry except during the rainy season.) Vahān entered the plain from the west by crossing the Wadi Ruqqad, a tributary of the Yarmūk, via the old Roman bridge on the road to Damascus. He divided his army into four main divisions; his left, consisting of the Christian Arab Ghassānid contingent under their "king," Jabala bin al-Ayham, stretched north. His left-center was led by the *buccinator* Ibn al-Qanātir and consisted of Byzantine units stationed in Syria before the Muslim invasion. (*Buccinator* was an old East Roman military title revived by Heraclius and given to local officials.) Vahān commanded his right-center division of mostly Armenians, and Gargis (George) commanded another Armenian division that anchored the right. Khālid formed his men into four infantry and four cavalry divisions, one cavalry division behind his left, right, and center and a larger one in reserve under Zarrar, a young and fearsome cavalry leader.

The first day of the battle, August 15, saw the infantry of both sides spar inconclusively until sunset. On the second day, the Byzantines caught the Muslims at dawn prayers and drove back both wings. Muslim legend has it that the Arab retreat was halted and the front stabilized when their womenfolk rushed from the camps, abused their men for running, and helped repel the Byzantines by using tent poles and rocks.

After a similar engagement on day three, the fourth and decisive day began with the Byzantine center and Ghassānid cavalry pushing back the right-center Muslim division under Shurahbil. Khālid countered with his mounted reserve, striking the Byzantine flanks and separating their infantry from their cavalry. While the Byzantine center and right unsuccessfully assaulted the camps again, Zarrar chased the Ghassānid cavalry north, turned Vahān's left flank, and seized the old Roman bridge over the Wadi Ruqqad. After resting a day, the Muslims, now facing south, started to force the Byzantines into a corner formed by the deep gorges of the Yarmūk and the Ruqqad. Vahān tried to open an escape route by driving north to regain the bridge, but his army panicked after Gargīs was killed on the right and the left of the *buccinator* was driven in on the center. Some tried to surrender, but the Muslims, after their own heavy losses, were in no mood to take prisoners; some fell to their deaths in the deep gorges while others scrambled to safety. Of the Byzantine leaders, only Jabala escaped. Overconfidence had caused the Byzantines to forget their usual caution in dealing with invaders. They gambled all on a decisive battle and lost.

With no major force left to oppose them, the Muslims besieged and captured the major cities in the region one by one. By 645, Syria, Palestine, and Egypt were firmly in Muslim hands. Most of the Arab population converted to Islam rather quickly, but the Christians and Jews were shown toleration, and life went on much as it had under the Byzantines. Syria became the staging area for attacks on Byzantine-held Asia Minor and the center of later Islamic expansion. The holy places of Christendom were in the hands of the Muslims and would remain so until retaken during the First Crusade in 1099.

SIGNIFICANCE

The Byzantine defeat at Yarmūk and the subsequent loss of Syria heralded the beginning of a thousand-year struggle between Muslims and Christians. Had the Byzantines prevailed at Yarmūk, it is doubtful that the Arabs would have enjoyed their fantastic run of conquests that followed. From Damascus, armies of the Umayyad caliphs, mainly Arab and mostly Syrian, spread Islamic control to India and across North Africa into Spain by 750. Later Muslim armies would make serious inroads into the heart of Europe, threatening the very existence of Christian civilization. Despite being slowly pushed out of Spain after the eighth century and losing temporary control of the Holy Land to Western Crusaders between 1099 and 1254, Muslim armies remained a serious threat to Christian Europe through the seventeenth century. They destroyed the last vestiges of the Byzantine Empire when they took Constantinople in 1453 and surged up to the gates of Vienna in 1683.

—Bart L. R. Talbert

FURTHER READING

Bogle, Emory C. *Islam: Origin and Belief.* Austin: University of Texas Press, 1998. A concise look at Islam and its expansion between 570 and 1517. Also includes discussion of Muḥammad and Islam's beginnings. Maps, bibliography, index.

Collins, Roger. *The Arab Conquest of Spain, 710-797.* London: Blackwell, 1994. This work focuses specifically on the eighth century in Spain, and is particularly valuable for its evaluation of original sources.

Donner, Fred McGraw. *The Early Islamic Conquests.* Princeton, N.J.: Princeton University Press, 1981. A look into the origin and nature of the Islamic conquest movement and the conquest of Syria and Iraq. Bibliography, index.

Haldon, John. *Warfare, State and Society in the Byzantine World, 565-1024.* London: UCL Press, 1999. An examination of the relationship between Byzantine society, its armies and warfare. Maps, bibliography, index.

Jandora, J. W. "The Battle of Yarmūk: A Reconstruction." *Journal of Asian History* 19 (1985). An attempt to sort out anomalies of the battle concerning names, places, the size of the armies, and dates.

Kaegi, Walter E. *Byzantium and the Early Islamic Conquests.* New York: Cambridge University Press, 1995. This work explores how and why the Byzantine Empire failed to contain Islam and how and why it lost many valuable provinces to the Arab conquests. Maps, bibliography, index.

Nicolle, David. *Warriors and Their Weapons Around the Time of the Crusades: Relationships Between Byzantium, the West, and the Islamic World.* Burlington, Vt.: Ashgate/Variorum, 2002. Presents a history of the weaponry of the Byzantines and the Muslims during the time of the Crusades, a period of ongoing tension precipitated by the seventh century battle at Yarmūk. Illustrations, bibliography, index.

_______. *Yarmūk 636 A.D.: The Muslim Conquest of Syria.* Oxford: Osprey, 1994. An excellent volume in the Osprey series that provides an in-depth look into the background of the campaign, the fighting, and its consequences.

Sicker, Michael. *The Islamic World in Ascendancy: From the Arab Conquests to the Siege of Vienna.* Westport, Conn.: Praeger, 2000. Presents a history of the rise and expansion of the Islamic empire. Concludes with a chapter on the end of the ascendancy. Bibliography, index.

Treadgold, Warren. *Byzantium and Its Army, 284-1081.* Stanford, Calif.: Stanford University Press, 1995. An examination of the Byzantine army's role and structure within empire's history. Maps, illustrations, bibliography, index.

SEE ALSO: c. 610-632: Muḥammad Receives Revelations; 630-711: Islam Expands Throughout North Africa; 637-657: Islam Expands Throughout the Middle East; April or May, 711: Ṭārik Crosses into Spain; October 11, 732: Battle of Tours; November 27, 1095: Pope Urban II Calls the First Crusade; c. 1145: Prester John Myth Sweeps Across Europe; 1147-1149: Second Crusade; 1189-1192: Third Crusade; 1204: Knights of the Fourth Crusade Capture Constantinople; 1217-1221: Fifth Crusade; 1227-1230: Frederick II Leads the Sixth Crusade; 1248-1254: Failure of the Seventh Crusade; May 29, 1453: Fall of Constantinople.

RELATED ARTICLES in *Great Lives from History: The Middle Ages, 477-1453*: Firdusi; al-Ḥasan al-Baṣrī; Heraclius; Khadīja; Maḥmūd Ghāzān; Ṭāriq ibn-Ziyād; ʿUmar I.

637-657
ISLAM EXPANDS THROUGHOUT THE MIDDLE EAST

The original Arab campaigns of expansion began as a way to keep nomadic tribes faithful to Islam, but they became conquests for lands to tax and rule. After early successes, the Arabs kept moving until they had conquered the Persian Empire and much of the eastern Byzantine Empire. The price of this expansion was a deep rift within Islam and the first civil war that pitted Muslim against Muslim.

LOCALE: Byzantine Empire, Lycian Coast (now the southern coast of Turkey), Medina, Arabia, Persian Empire, and Sind (now in Pakistan)

CATEGORIES: Expansion and land acquisition; religion; wars, uprisings, and civil unrest

KEY FIGURES

Muḥammad (c. 570-632), the Prophet and founder of Islam

Abū Bakr (c. 573-634), first caliph, r. 632-634, early convert to Islam

ʿUmar I (c. 586-644), second caliph, r. 634-644, early convert to Islam

ʿUthmān ibn ʿAffān (d. 656), third caliph, r. 644-656, early convert to Islam

ʿAlī ibn Abī Ṭālib (c. 600-661), fourth caliph, r. 656-661, early convert to Islam

ʿĀʾishah (614-678), leader of the forces opposing ʿAlī at the Battle of the Camel

Muʿāwiyah I (c. 602-680), governor of Syria

SUMMARY OF EVENT

The Arab army, by 637, was poised to destroy what remained of the Persian Empire and further expand the new Islamic Empire. Begun in 632 when nomadic Arab tribesmen strayed from Islam at the death of Muḥammad, the early military campaigns waged by the first caliph and Muḥammad's close friend, Abū Bakr, successfully subdued the errant tribes and reenforced their faithfulness to Islam. To keep the tribes faithful, Abū Bakr continued the military campaigns and moved his forces northward into Byzantine and Persian lands. They met with little resistance and were able to subdue the subjects of both empires easily.

ʿUmar I, the second caliph and a close companion to Muḥammad, continued these successful military forays, and ʿUmar's forces defeated Byzantine forces in Syria. During the next twenty years, the Arabian armies continued to expand the Islamic territories and the caliphs consolidated power within the empire. The Arabic successes were not without price, however. The expansion of empire and consolidation of power led to the first civil war, which pitted Muslim against Muslim and created an enduring rift within Islam.

In the spring of 637, the Arabian army destroyed the Persian army at the Battle of al-Qadisiyah (Kadisiya), captured the Persian capital, Ctesiphon, and soon took the rest of Iraq north to Mosul. This victory, coupled with the Arabian victory over the Byzantine forces at the Yarmūk River in Syria, left the Arabs in control of two rich, fertile lands.

In Syria and Iraq, many people were of Arab origin and quickly adjusted to the new rulers. Christians and Jews had been persecuted by Byzantine and Persian rulers. Under Islam, they were considered *ahl al-kitab* (peoples of the book) who had received authentic scriptures from God and were allowed to practice their faiths freely according to stipulations in the Qurʾān. Subjects of the new Islamic Empire paid both a poll and a land tax that were lower than those paid to the previous rulers. As protected subjects, they were treated fairly, which increased their acceptance of their Arab rulers.

The Arab forces continued their successful conquests. Between 639 and 642, they invaded Egypt, vanquished the Byzantine forces at Heliopolis, and conquered the port city of Alexandria. Before the end of 644, ʿUmar's forces controlled much of the Persian Empire and had wrested Egypt from the Byzantine Empire.

As the Islamic Empire grew, ʿUmar created the *amsar* (armed garrison camps) for housing Arabs, separate from the conquered, non-Muslim peoples. The most important *amsar* were Basra and Al-Kufa in Iraq; Al-Fusṭāt (now part of Cairo), Egypt; Qum, Iran; and Damascus, Syria, which was already a bustling city when the Arab garrison moved in. These camps controlled the surrounding areas, which grew into bustling cities around the newly built governor's palace and mosque.

Caliph ʿUmar did not give fiefdoms to occupying forces. Instead, he doled out state pay to the military from the taxes and plunder obtained from conquered areas. ʿUmar's system of pay, according to military service and date of conversion to Islam, created an elite group of Arabs who would eventually split over questions of power and wealth.

Between 642 and 644, ʿUmar's forces moved from Iraq into the western reaches of Iran. They defeated the

The murder of ʿUthmān. (H. Bricher and B. F. Waitt)

Persian army at the Battle of Nahavand (642) and continued eastward, taking Eşfahān, Hamadān, Rayy, and Qazvīn in turn. Meanwhile, the Arab forces in the west conquered Tripoli in North Africa. ʿUmar was stabbed to death by a Persian prisoner-cum-servant while in the mosque at Medina in 644. The third caliph, ʿUthmān ibn ʿAffān, was one of the Prophet's earliest converts and his son-in-law, but was also a member of the rich Umayyad family who had originally spurned Muḥammad and his message. Many Muslims could not forgive this.

ʿUthmān further damaged his image and outraged the emirs (territorial governors) by requiring that they send all revenues back to Medina to be tallied and allotted by his administrators. ʿUthmān offended many of the religious authorities when he ordered that a single version of the Qurʾān be prepared and used. He also offended most of the powerful Medinan families, including Muḥammad's own Quraysh, by appointing members of his own Umayyad family to government positions.

The third caliphate was not a complete failure, however. Between 649 and 650, Muʿāwiyah I, governor of Syria, conquered Cyprus with the newly formed Arab navy and seized the formerly invulnerable island of Aradus (Arwād). By 651, Arab forces had secured much of Armenia, parts of the Caucasus, Iran as far as the Oxus River, Herāt in Afghanistan, the Sind in India, and Nishapur, the capital of the eastern Iranian province of Khorāsān. The rest of Khorāsān capitulated by 654. The next year, the Arab navy ousted the Byzantine navy from the eastern Mediterranean at the Battle of the Masts near the Lycian coast.

Despite these territorial gains, ʿUthmān was still unpopular. A group of Muslim soldiers, angry because they felt they were not receiving just rewards for their services, stormed ʿUthmān's house in 656, intent on raising their complaints in person. In the attack, ʿUthmān was wounded and subsequently died. Immediately after ʿUthmān's death, a small group of followers proclaimed ʿAlī ibn Abī Ṭālib, Muḥammad's cousin and son-in-law, the fourth caliph. Because of his close familial ties to Muḥammad, his followers felt ʿAlī could be a religious and political successor to the Prophet. ʿAlī stressed equality among all Muslims, and his supporters hoped for a return to the true Islam under his leadership.

ʿUthmān's family and followers, indeed many Muslims, questioned ʿAlī's election. Because ʿAlī had failed to avenge ʿUthmān's murder and because the Quraysh believed their standing in Medina was threatened by ʿAlī's policy of equality among all Muslims, ʿĀʾishah, the Prophet's favorite wife, mustered an army for the first *fitna* (civil war). In December, 656, at the so-called Battle of the Camel, ʿAlī's forces attacked and defeated ʿĀʾishah's army outside Basra, sustaining his claim to the caliphate.

Seeking to avenge ʿUthmān's murder, his kinsman, Syrian governor Muʿāwiyah I, mustered forces in 657 and brought them to meet ʿAlī's army at Siffin on the upper Euphrates River. The two forces fought until Muʿāwiyah's men requested arbitration according to the Qurʾān. ʿAlī agreed, but the arbitration over ʿUthmān's murder devolved into a dispute over the caliphate. The outcome was an agreement that the caliph would henceforth be selected by committee following the historic precedent set by selection of the first three caliphs.

ʿAlī lost much of his support during the arbitration because of his compromise over the succession and because many felt that he was subjecting the will of Allah to human judgment. As ʿAlī's position weakened, Muʿāwiyah claimed the caliphate of Jerusalem for himself, deepening the Islamic rift that had begun during ʿUthmān's caliphate.

SIGNIFICANCE

The early Arab expansion, initiated to occupy the restless nomadic tribes, evolved into a conquest of land and wealth for Islam. Arab success led to the formation of an Islamic Empire that continued to expand until it reached its zenith in the eighth century.

Between 637 and 656, both ʿUmar and ʿUthmān oversaw the growth of this empire. With conquest came plunder, new peoples to rule and tax, old families and tribes to appease, power to consolidate, cities and administrations to build, and, inevitably, a rising discontent among Muslims over the distribution of power and wealth. ʿUthmān's murder caused this dispute to erupt into an ugly struggle for power that rent the Empire in two within a year of his death.

ʿAlī was proclaimed caliph as a reaction to Umayyad power in the Islamic Empire under ʿUthmān. His claim to the caliphate caused the first Islamic civil war, ripping Islamic unity apart and engendering continued hostility between Syrian and Iraqi Muslims. The Khāijites splintered off into an Islamic extremist group, setting a precedent for politics to force the formation of new theology. ʿAlī's own supporters eventually formed a minority religious group, the Shīʿites. The ultimate consequence of the first expansion of Islam and the power struggles it engendered occurred between 657 and 661, when the Islamic Empire was split between two rival Muslim groups: ʿAlī and Muʿāwiyah.

Islam had united the Arabs for the first time. Soon, however, the entire empire stood divided. The faithful were concerned by how far the Islamic Empire had strayed from the teachings of the Prophet, and they became just as determined to find a way back.

—*Peggy E. Alford*

FURTHER READING

Armstrong, Karen. *Islam: A Short History*. New York: Modern Library, 2002. Explores the philosophical, religious, and political movements that have driven the Muslims throughout their history. Maps, bibliography, index.

Bogle, Emory C. *Islam: Origin and Belief*. Austin: University of Texas Press, 1998. A concise look at Islam and its expansion between 570 and 1517. Also includes discussion of Muḥammad and Islam's beginnings. Maps, bibliography, index.

Gabrieli, Francesco. *Muḥammad and the Conquests of Islam*. Translated by Virginia Luling and Rosamund Linell. New York: McGraw-Hill, 1968. A narrative account of the rise of the Prophet and Islam. Also explores the resulting Islamic conquests in the Middle East, Africa, Asia, and Europe. Illustrations, maps, bibliography.

Hodgson, Marshall G. S. *The Venture of Islam: Conscience and History in a World Civilization*. 3 vols. Chicago: University of Chicago Press, 1974. This work provides a comprehensive investigation of the establishment of an international Islamic Empire. Volume 2 examines Islamic expansionism in the Middle Ages. Bibliography, index.

Hourani, Albert. *A History of the Arab Peoples*. Cambridge, Mass.: Belknap Press, 2002. This seminal work covers Arab history from the pre-Islamic through the twentieth century, including empire building, societal structures, religion, art, and popular culture. Illustrations, maps, extensive bibliography, index.

Jandora, John Walter. *Militarism in Arab Society: An Historiographical and Bibliographical Sourcebook*. Westport, Conn.: Greenwood Press, 1997. A detailed history of Arab military culture, with a discussion of Muʿāwiyah and his descendants and "Muslim warriors of medieval times." Illustrations, maps, bibliography, index.

Kaegi, Walter E. *Byzantium and the Early Islamic Conquests*. New York: Cambridge University Press, 1995. This work explores how and why the Byzantine Empire lost many valuable provinces to the Arab conquests. Map, bibliography, index.

Lewis, Bernard. *The Arabs in History*. Rev. ed. New York: Oxford University Press, 2002. Provides a narrative overview of the Arabs and their historical significance, with a concentration on social and economic history. Focuses mostly on the social, everyday impact of historical events.

Tritton, A. S. *The Caliphs and Their Non-Muslim Subjects: A Critical Study of the Covenant of ʿUmar*. 1930. Reprint. London: F. Cass, 1970. This study documents ʿUmar's endeavors to deal administratively with nonconverted subjects of the Islamic state, both in terms of guarantees of religious practice and fiscal responsibilities. Bibliography.

Watt, William Montgomery. *A Short History of Islam*. Boston: Oneworld, 1996. Provides a concise history of Islamic expansionism, the formation of the caliphate, and the politics of Islam. Bibliography, index.

SEE ALSO: c. 610-632: Muḥammad Receives Revelations; 630-711: Islam Expands Throughout North Africa; August 15-20, 636: Battle of Yarmūk; 969-1171: Reign of the Fāṭimids; 11th century: Expansion of Sunni Islam in North Africa and Iberia; 1048: Zīrids Break from Fāṭimid Dynasty and Revive Sunni Islam.

RELATED ARTICLES in *Great Lives from History: The Middle Ages, 477-1453:* al-Ḥasan al-Baṣrī; Heraclius; Khadīja; Maḥmūd [illegible]; Muḥammad; ʿUmar I

645-646
ADOPTION OF *NENGO* SYSTEM AND TAIKA REFORMS

After the assassination of the leaders of the Soga family, Imperial Prince Naka no Ōe and his supporters proceeded to enact a series of reforms that attempted to bring Chinese institutional innovations to the Japanese islands and create a more powerful and centralized government.

LOCALE: Central Japan
CATEGORIES: Laws, acts, and legal history; government and politics

KEY FIGURES

Soga Emishi (d. 645), court noble
Soga Iname (d. 645), court noble
Naka no Ōe (626-671), imperial prince, then emperor Tenji, r. 661-671
Fujiwara Kamatari (614-669), court noble

SUMMARY OF EVENT

In the first half of the seventh century, the Soga, a powerful aristocratic family, were the main source of power at the Japanese court. Through their support of Buddhism and other continental innovations, they were able to eclipse the power of other major clans such as the Nakatomi and Mononobe and to hold sway over the court. Between 622 and 645, the imperial family was under the direct influence of Soga Emishi, who became the head of the clan as well as great minister in 622. The power of the Soga family over the court was so great that Emishi was able to appoint imperial successors and ensure that they were married to Soga daughters. Emishi continued to flaunt his power by building a tomb of a magnitude that had previously been reserved for members of the imperial family and by murdering rivals who stood in his way.

This behavior as well as the reportedly crude and arrogant conduct of Emishi's son Soga Iname, coupled with the desire of other important families such as the Nakatomi to restore the power that the Soga had usurped, fomented a conspiracy against the Soga that took shape in 644. Prince Naka no Ōe, interested in restoring the power of the imperial family, and the head of the Nakatomi family, better known as Fujiwara Kamatari, who had seen his family's influence eclipsed by the Soga, decided to act. Tradition holds that they had met at a kickball gathering, and the conspiracy developed from there. The pair planned to have the Soga leaders murdered and to gain control of the throne. It did not take them long to put their plan into action.

Emishi's son Iruka was murdered, while at court and in the presence of the empress, by the henchmen of the conspirators. Within days, Emishi's other supporters were rounded up and executed. Emishi then took his own life. The reigning empress, Kogyoku, was compelled to abdicate, and Imperial Prince Karu was enthroned. Naka no Ōe, who had played a leading role in the conspiracy, was named heir and effectively wielded power over the government. This chain of events paved the way for a series of reforms that would transform the nature of the Japanese government.

In 645, Japanese society existed in a relatively undeveloped state. The aristocracy was formed from the leaders of influential provincial families, the interests of which were often at odds. The imperial institution, which was the theoretical center of power in the country, did not have the legal or martial power to exert its influence over the whole of the land. The conspirators who took action against the Soga family were well aware of the weaknesses of this system and were well versed in the political theory of neighboring China, a philosophy that stressed order and strong central power. These theoretical precepts served as the basis for a wide reform movement that has come to be known collectively as the Taika reforms.

The name Taika, itself meaning "great reform," was chosen as the reign name of Imperial Prince Karu when he was placed on the throne in 645. The process of adopting reign names for emperors, known as the *nengo* system, was used to play up the idea that dramatic change was at hand. The basis of these reforms was promulgated before the great nobles on June 19, 645, and they were forced to take an oath that they would serve the emperor with loyalty and not attempt to build up their own power at the expense of the central government. This enforced the idea that the emperor was now firmly at the center of Japanese political life and that the assembled ministers and nobles were his servants, and it is perhaps even more important than the specific institutional reforms that were to follow.

A generation before the conspiracy that ended the power of the Soga family, Shōtoku Taishi, himself both a Soga and an imperial prince, held power over the government as regent. Shōtoku Taishi introduced a number of reforms that brought Confucian and Buddhist ideas to Japanese politics. These earlier ideas served as the inspiration for the much more ambitious social reconstruction that Naka no Ōe and Fujiwara Kamatari introduced. In 646, a more direct and detailed reform edict than the previous precepts, outlining concrete reforms, was promulgated. Private ownership of land was abolished. In theory, all farmland in Japan belonged to the throne. This land, however, was to be evenly distributed among the people based on a survey of population. A new, more organized system of taxation was introduced as was a more logical system of impressed labor, designed to spare farmers the burden of extra work in the harvest and planting seasons. There were also regulations concerning common use of ponds and water and dealing with the garrisoning of areas of the countryside. Finally, the edict established a region in the middle of the country that was to act as a center of government, the first step toward the establishment of a permanent capital, a necessary precondition for the centralization of power. In addition, a system of prefecture governorships was established. Regulations as to the conduct of governors and what to do in cases of bribery and the like were also outlined. Smaller administrative districts—villages and townships—were also established. These reforms were all based on the Chinese administrative system. Other important reforms introduced during this period, including a fixed scale of court ranks, each with prescribed regalia and duties, were also based on Chinese models. In the short term, the Taika reforms succeeded in increasing the power of the imperial institution. However, there were many long-term consequences as well.

SIGNIFICANCE

The Taika reforms had many faults. China was a far more advanced society than was the Japan of this period. The reforms, patterned largely on Chinese models, were in some ways unsuited to the political and geographical realities of the Japanese islands. Enforcing the egalitarian distribution of land proved troublesome. In addition, transient elements of the population proved impossible to register and tax. Despite their weaknesses, however, the impact of the Taika reforms was widespread.

Although the basic content was revised on a number of occasions and superceded in some respects, the reforms remained the theoretical basis for the administration of the Japanese archipelago until the early modern period. Despite the fact that the imperial family soon found itself under the influence of the Fujiwara, the new name of the Nakatomi family who had helped to overthrow the Soga, the imperial court was now unquestionably the center of political life in Japan. The reforms also provided the impetus for the establishment of Japan's first permanent capital at Nara in 710.

The provision that farmers and administrators on the northern frontier should be allowed to keep weapons in order to defend themselves against raids by an indigenous people who were referred to as Emishi, gives scholars some insight into how a warrior culture was able to develop away from court influence. In addition, the concept of the illegality of private ownership of land also proved to be an important one in later years as it provided the basis for the complex system of landholding that emerged when provincial warrior families gained influence and came to dominate the court in the eleventh and twelfth centuries. In short, the Taika reforms not only created a strong imperial institution but also helped form the warrior society that was to become the main force in Japanese political life during the medieval period.

—*Matthew Penney*

FURTHER READING

Aston, W. G., trans. *Nihongi: Chronicles of Japan from the Earliest Times to A.D. 697*. 1896. Reprint. Tokyo: Charles E. Tuttle, 1972. The standard translation of one of the earliest works of Japanese history. Provides details about the plot that led to the downfall of the Soga family and the Taika reforms.

Farris, William. *Population, Disease, and Land in Early Japan, 645-900*. Cambridge, Mass.: Harvard University Press, 1995. A detailed analysis of the impact of the Taika reforms on landholding in Japan.

Friday, Karl. *Hired Swords: The Rise of Private Warrior Power in Early Japan*. Stanford, Calif.: Stanford University Press, 1992. Provides details concerning the military consequences of the Taika reforms and how they set the institutional basis for warrior power.

Sansom, George. *A History of Japan to 1334*. Vol. 1. Stanford, Calif.: Stanford University Press, 1958. The first volume of Sansom's three-volume study of Japanese history remains a detailed and authoritative work on the subject.

SEE ALSO: 593-604: Regency of Shōtoku Taishi; 701: Taihō Laws Reform Japanese Government; March 9, 712, and July 1, 720: Writing of *Kojiki* and *Nihon Shoki*; 792: Rise of the Samurai; 858: Rise of the Fujiwara Family.

RELATED ARTICLES in *Great Lives from History: The Middle Ages, 477-1453*: Fujiwara Michinaga; Shōtoku Taishi.

652-c. 1171
CHRISTIAN NUBIA AND MUSLIM EGYPT SIGN TREATY

The treaty (or baqt*) between Christian Nubia and Muslim Egypt was a territorial rights agreement and an agreement of exchange between two great and seemingly irreconcilable powers infused with powerful new faiths. This skillful baqt, which ensured the survival of Nubia, proved to be one of history's longest lasting treaties.*

LOCALE: Nubia (northern Sudan and southern Egypt)
CATEGORIES: Diplomacy and international relations; government and politics;

KEY FIGURES

ʿAbd Allāh ibn Saʿad ibn Abū Sarḥ (fl. seventh century), governor of Egypt, r. 644-656
Kalidurut (fl. seventh century), Makurian king

SUMMARY OF EVENT

Nubia stretches along the Nile River from Aswān in Egypt to Khartoum in what is now called Sudan (roughly one-third in Egypt and two-thirds in Sudan). Named after the Nobatae who settled along the Nile during the reign of Roman emperor Diocletian, Nubia was the scene of a flourishing medieval Christian culture.

This region was the site of the great ancient empire of Kush and the iron-working state of Meröe. Following Meröe's collapse in the fourth century, three Christian kingdoms took shape. The northernmost, Nobatia, stretched from Aswān to the second cataract. Farther south was Makuria, which extended south to the confluence of the Atbara and Nile. Its capital was Dongola, now known as Old Dongola to distinguish it from a nearby Turkish-built town of the same name. Farthest south and least known was Alodia, which dominated the region where the Blue and White Niles meet.

The three kingdoms converted to Christianity between 543 and 580. This conversion was a major cultural stimulus. Centuries of church influence are apparent in inspirational art, fine manuscripts, elaborately decorated pottery, and huge stone churches. While Greek, Coptic, and, later, Arabic were common tongues along the Nile, a written language called Old Nubian developed and was used widely in biblical texts, administrative and legal documents, and letters. However, religious controversy was also part of Nubia's history. Popular in Nobatia and Alodia, Monophysite Christianity, which emphasized Christ's divine nature, had been considered heretical by the official or Melkite church after the Council of Chalcedon in 451. Separating Nobatia and Alodia, Makuria adhered to the Melkite rite.

Following the Arab conquest of Egypt, led by ʿAmr ibn al-ʿAṣ in 640, hostilities broke out between the newly Christianized Nubians, who had ruled Upper Egypt at times, and the newly Islamized Arabs, whose armies were sweeping across north Africa. As a result of these first contacts with Muslims, Nubians promised not to attack Egypt and began to pay tribute in slaves and livestock. Muslim armies reached the plain north of Dongola but failed to capture the city. Forestalling the conversion of Nubia to Islam for more than seven centuries, Nubian soldiers gained a reputation as *rumat al-hadaq* (eye-smiters), skillful archers who specialized in shooting at their opponents' eyes. Arab attacks in 652 penetrated as far as Dongola, where the principal church was destroyed with stones shot from catapults. Makurian king Kalidurut sued for peace.

The conflict was settled by a *baqt*, a bilateral agreement (or treaty) negotiated with ʿAbd Allāh ibn Saʿad ibn Abū Sarḥ, Umayyad governor of Egypt. The term *baqt* derived from the Greek *pakton*, which is also the root of the English word "pact." Both diplomatic and commercial in nature, this accord fixed territorial rights and provided for a regular exchange of four hundred male slaves from Makuria in return for two specially bred horses, thirteen hundred *kanyr* of wine, and fixed quantities of grain, lentils, and cloth from Egypt. The exchange of these commodities was to be made annually at the border town of Al-Qasr, near Philae Island, south of Aswān. At Al-Qasr, a stone archway known as the Gate to Nubia, stood as the physical interface of the two cultures throughout the medieval era. Each side was to protect travelers from the other and return runaway slaves. In subsequent years, several revisions were made to the treaty's terms. A second *baqt* was negotiated between the Egyptians and the Blemmyes (Beja) in 720.

However, given the changing fortunes of politics, the *baqt* was not always observed. In 745, King Cyriacus of Dongola laid siege to the Umayyad capital at Al-Fusṭāṭ (now near Cairo). By 758 Egypt's ʿAbbāsid rulers complained that *baqt* payments were not being made, and the Blemmyes attacked Upper Egypt. In 819 both the Makurian king and the Beja refused to make their payments and mounted attacks on Egypt. Despite these violations and Nubian raids on Egypt in 951, 956, and 962, the *baqt* secured a measure of peace and stability until 1275.

Eventually, Nobatia and Makuria became a single federated kingdom that lasted some six hundred years under Makurian kings. The Makurian king Merkurios, sometimes referred to as the "new Constantine," may have conquered Nobatia, which nevertheless maintained its own identity with a royal governor, known to the Arabs as Sahib el Jebel (lord of the mountain) and to the Nubians by the Greek title *eparch*. This unification was important, as it enabled a stronger Nubia to resist later Arab raids. Long-distance trade brought prosperity.

While never a power on the scale of Kush or Meröe, Christian Nubia was of great significance. Its rulers were treated as equals by their Egyptian and Arabian counterparts. One of the greatest of Makuria's kings, George I, even traveled to Baghdad and Cairo. Nubian kings were regarded as protectors of the Coptic patriarch of Alexandria, sometimes intervening on behalf of Egypt's Christians. Bishops and other church officials of the kingdom's seven dioceses were appointed with royal approval. Nubians served as mercenaries in the Umayyad and later Ṭūlūnid armies.

At the height of Makurian power, the era from 909 to 1171, the Nubians lived in peace with Egypt's Fāṭimid rulers, following an initial attack on Egypt by Makurian king George II and a counterattack on Nubia by al-ʿUmari. The Faṭimids restored the Melkites in Nobatia's capital Faras, and possibly in all of Nubia.

The Fāṭimid army employed as many as fifty thousand Nubians. When the last Fāṭimid was defeated by Kurdish general Saladin, however, Makuria's fortunes changed. Fearing a Nubian-Crusader alliance, Saladin's brother, Turanshah, campaigned against Nubia, occupied Qaṣr Ibrīm in 1172, and exterminated Nubians in Egypt two years later. Nubia was fully cut off from the rest of Christendom. The region's most recent Greek inscription dates from 1181 and the last priest sent to Nubia from Alexandria arrived in 1235.

The power of Nubian kings gradually eroded during the fourteenth and fifteenth centuries, when internal disputes abounded and unfriendly Mamlūk Turks ruled Egypt and claimed Lower Nubia. In 1264, following attacks by the Turks, Nubians reinstated their *baqt* payments, now paid to Mamlūk sultan Baybars I. In 1276 Mamlūk armies sacked Dongola, forced conversion to Islam, and captured Nubian king Dawud who had abrogated the *baqt* and raided Aswān the year before. Increasing Arab migration also seems to have been both cause and effect of much insecurity along the Nile's middle reaches. Abdullah Barshambu, the first Muslim king of Makuria, was enthroned in 1317. He reestablished the *baqt* and built Dongola's first mosque. Kudanbes, the last Christian king of Makuria, was replaced by a Muslim, Kanz al-Dawla, and the royal palace at Dongola was converted into a mosque in 1323. Constantinople's fall to the Turks in 1453 reinforced Nubia's isolation. Finally, the Christian era in Nubia ended around 1504 with Alodia's fall to the Muslim Fung sultanate, based at Sennar farther south on the Blue Nile.

SIGNIFICANCE

Although Nubia's Christian millennium has been largely overlooked in favor of the glorious history of its northern neighbor Egypt, much evidence shows that Nobatia, Makuria, and Alodia established themselves as major political, religious, and cultural powers in their own right. The *baqt* allowed for Nubia's flourishing.

Modern Nubians, though Arabized and Muslim, have retained distinctive languages, architectural forms, and folk traditions from their distant Christian past. Numerous archaeological and historical studies have demonstrated that despite isolation from the rest of Christendom, the Nubians maintained their unique Christian faith and Byzantine-influenced art for centuries. The Makurian royal palace still towers over the Nile near El Ghaba and the frescoes of the cathedral at Faras can be found in museums in Khartoum and Warsaw. Even greater than these magnificent pieces of artistic expression, however, is the record of the *baqt*.

—*Randall Fegley*

Further Reading

Adams, William Y. *Nubia: Corridor to Africa*. Princeton, N.J.: Princeton University Press, 1977. Although many findings have changed much of the body of scholarship on Nubia, this work remains the most thorough reference on Nubian archaeology and history.

Holt, P. M., and M. W. Daly. *A History of the Sudan: From the Coming of Islam to the Present Day*. London: Longman, 1988. Though not primarily about the Christian era, this excellent work has useful information on medieval Nubia.

Hrbek, Ivan, ed. *General History of Africa*. Vol. 3. Abridged ed. Berkeley: University of California Press, 1992. Contains the chapter, "Christian Nubia at the Height of Its Civilization." Bibliography, index.

Spaulding, Jay. "Medieval Christian Nubia and the Islamic World: A Reconsideration of the Baqt Treaty." *International Journal of African Historical Studies* 28, no. 3 (1995): 577-594. Another look at the *baqt* between Nubia and Egypt.

Sundkler, Bengt, and Christopher Steed. *A History of the Church in Africa*. New York: Cambridge University Press, 2000. The first part of this comprehensive study explores Nubian Christianity. Maps, bibliography, index.

Vantini, Giovanni. *Christianity in the Sudan*. Bologna, Italy: EMI, 1981. The best survey of the history of Christianity in Sudan from ancient times to 1980.

_______, trans. *Oriental Sources Concerning Nubia*. Warsaw: Polish Academy of Sciences, 1975. Provides resources for further study about Nubia.

See also: 630-711: Islam Expands Throughout North Africa; 969-1171: Reign of the Fāṭimids; 972: Building of al-Azhar Mosque: 1340: Al-ʿUmarī Writes a History of Africa; May 29, 1453: Fall of Constantinople.

Related articles in *Great Lives from History: The Middle Ages, 477-1453*: Baybars I; Saladin.

668-935
Silla Unification of Korea

The Silla unification of the Korean peninsula heralded a golden age in Korean history, culture, and arts. Many aspects of classical culture—ceramics, music, poetry, and philosophy—developed at this time continue to give great pride to the Korean people.

Locale: Korean peninsula

Categories: Government and politics; cultural and intellectual history

Summary of Event

Unified Silla had its roots in an earlier Silla Dynasty that controlled the southeastern part of the Korean peninsula. This earlier dynasty, one of three kingdoms on the peninsula, lasted from 57 B.C.E. until 668 C.E., when it completed the process of conquering the other kingdoms (Paekche and Koguryŏ). A key strength of that earlier Silla kingdom was the walled town of Saro (now Kyŏngju), where the dynasty began. From this small city-state, Silla slowly but surely expanded until it controlled the whole peninsula.

At first, this expansion occurred because Silla felt threatened by the incursions of its neighbors, including the Japanese to the southeast. As a result, its leaders developed a militaristic culture called the *hwarang*. The *hwarang* was an institution of elite soldiers that had a strong sense of chivalry and had made an unquestioned commitment to the king. The *hwarang* was so successful in responding to attacks from all directions that Silla eventually was able to expand the kingdom by absorbing the other states. In the process, the people of Silla were exposed to Chinese culture.

The Chinese of the Tang Dynasty (T'ang; 618-907) had allied themselves with the original Silla Dynasty in order to claim large parts of the Korean peninsula for themselves. Once the old kingdoms were conquered, the Tang laid claim to the northern region, but the Silla encouraged the local people to rebel against the Chinese with their help. After several years, the Silla recovered the northern region, although the Tang did not officially acknowledge Silla control until 735. Despite this political tension, much cultural information flowed from China to Korea.

Chinese ideas and technology had a strong impact on the Silla culture; however, the people of Silla transformed the Chinese imports into uniquely Korean artforms. One of the lasting effects of the United Silla was the development of Buddhism as the state religion. With the support of the government, many temples and hermitages were built, and much artwork was commissioned. The Silla built the most famous Korean Buddist temple, Pulguksa (Bulguksa), in Kyŏngju, and the equally famous hermitage of Sokkuram just outside of Kyŏngju. Pulguksa is still standing today, although the temple has many fewer buildings. At its height in the eighth century, the temple had eighty buildings made of carved wood and fine stonework that blended beautifully into the surrounding hillside. In 1592, much of the temple, which represents the pinnacle of Silla architecture, was looted and burned by invading Japanese forces. The modern Korean government has restored the eight most important of these structures, and they are identified as national treasures. The Sokkuram hermitage is situated high above Kyŏngju and built directly into the hillside. It is modeled on the hermitage caves in India that contain great sculptures of the Buddha. The sculptures of Buddha at Sokkuram, which face east to protect Korea from invasion, are considered the best examples of Korean art. Most of them are intact, and they, too, have been named national treasures.

In addition to the development of religion and art, United Silla is famous for the development of Korea's earliest urban center. Today Kyŏngju is a modest-sized city with only 150,000 people, but in the eighth and ninth centuries, it was one of the largest cities in the world, home to more than a million people. Kyŏngju rivaled Nara, Japan, and Chang'an (Xi'an), China, as a political center and was the site of many of Korea's advancements in ceramics, including early celadon and stoneware. Today, a number of modern kilns in Kyŏngju produce ceramics in the Silla manner in order to preserve this style. The city was also the site of Ch'omsongdae, the earliest known astronomical tower to be built in eastern Asia; established by Queen Sondok, it is still standing today.

The United Silla had already begun to collapse when Kyŏngju was ravished by Mongol invasions in the thirteenth century, and the dynasty had ended before the Japanese invasions in the sixteenth century, when the city lost much of its glory. Therefore, in the early twentieth century, when archaeologists began excavations at Kyŏngju, they uncovered tombs and other sites containing magnificent artifacts. So many of Korea's national treasures, national historic sites, and great natural monuments are found in the city that Kyŏngju is known as the museum without walls. Most of the tombs have yet to be excavated, and they may be left untouched because the entire town would have to be moved to reach them. The United Nations counts Kyŏngju as one of the ten most important World Heritage sites for its wealth of cultural artifacts and contribution to the understanding of historic cultures.

The Silla Dynasty and the United Silla came to an end in 935 in part as a result of increasing corruption and the oppression of its people. Earlier in the dynasty, Silla rulers had given land allotments to peasants and developed an excellent irrigation system. However, by the ninth century, corruption and greed caused an increase in taxes and a decline in the maintenance of the agricultural infrastructure. Private merchants began to trade on their own with China and Japan, and bandits began taking over large parts of the countryside.

By the end of the ninth century, peasant revolts led to the creation of small, rival states within United Silla terri-

MAJOR RULERS OF THE UNIFIED SILLA DYNASTY, 661-935

Reign	*Ruler*
661-681	Munmu Wang
681-692	Sinmun Wang
692-702	Hyoso Wang
702-737	Sŏngdŏk Wang
737-742	Hyosŏng Wang
742-765	Kyŏngdŏk Wang
765-780	Hyesong Wang
780-785	Sŏndŏk Wang
785-798	Wŏnsŏng Wang
798-800	Sosŏng Wang
800-809	Aejang Wang
809-826	Hŏndŏk Wang
826-836	Hŭngdŏk Wang
836-838	Hŭigang Wang
838-839	Minae Wang
839	Sinmu Wang
839-857	Munsŏng Wang
857-861	Hŏnan Wang
861-875	Kyŏngmun Wang
875-886	Hŏn'gang Wang
886-887	Chŏnggang Wang
887-896	Queen Chinsŏng
897-912	Hyogong Wang
912-917	Pak Sindŏk Wang
917-924	Kyŏngmyŏng Wang
924-927	Kyŏngae Wang
927-935	Kyongsun Wang

601 - 700

tory. It was only a matter of time before a state became strong enough to overthrow the Silla and form a new dynasty. In what later became Kangweondo Province, Kung-ye formed the Later Koguryŏ kingdom (901-935; the first Koguryŏ kingdom had been absorbed by the Silla).

In 918, one of Kung-ye's generals, Wang Kŏn, overthrew him and renamed the kingdom Koryŏ, from which the English name of Korea is derived. By 935, he had peacefully taken control of the remaining Silla territory through a number of agreements with its leaders. It would take several years of serious battles before he could take control of the smaller peasant-based states that had formed in the dying days of Silla.

The Koryŏ Dynasty (918-1392) would distinguish itself by creating metal-cast movable type (two hundred years before Gutenberg) and completing the *Tripitaka Koreana* (thirteenth century), a great work of Korean Buddhist philosophy of which many copies were printed.

SIGNIFICANCE

The significance of the United Silla in Korean history goes beyond its great artistic and cultural achievements, although these alone would be reason enough to remember it. The United Silla made Buddhism its state religion, transforming Chinese Buddhist ideas into Sŏn Buddhism, which was characterized by different meditation techniques. This version of Buddhism was transmitted to the Japanese, who developed it into Zen Buddhism.

Another significant impact of the Silla was the unifying of the peoples of the peninsula. Without this unification, the creation of a classical Korean culture would have been confined to one area. Moreover, because United Silla became the first kingdom to rule the entire peninsula in 668, its development of classical Korean culture gradually was transmitted to people throughout the entire peninsula and provided the basis for a common Korean identity that has lasted to this day. Later developments of the Koryŏ and Yi (Chosŏn; 1392-1910) Dynasties built on the strengths established by the United Silla, thereby creating the basis for the modern people known as Koreans.

—*Carolyn V. Prorok*

FURTHER READING

Adams, Edward B. *Korea's Golden Age: Cultural Spirit of Silla in Kyongju*. Seoul: Seoul International Publishing House, 1991. Adams reveals the extraordinary cultural development of the Silla in their capital city of Kyŏngju through detailed descriptions and hundreds of photos. Index.

Covell, J. Carter. *Korea's Cultural Roots*. Elizabeth, N.J.: Hollym International, 1981. Covell presents the ancient roots of Korea's culture through its artwork and religious materials. Index.

Kim, Duk-Whang. *A History of Religions in Korea*. Seoul: Daeji Moonhwa-sa, 1990. Kim describes the history and beliefs of the many religious traditions in Korea from ancient times to the current era.

SEE ALSO: 918-936: Foundation of the Koryŏ Dynasty; 958-1076: Koreans Adopt the Tang Civil Service Model; 1145: Kim Pu-sik Writes *Samguk Sagi*; 1196-1258: Ch'oe Family Takes Power in Korea; July, 1392: Establishment of the Yi Dynasty.

RELATED ARTICLE in *Great Lives from History: The Middle Ages, 477-1453*: Wang Kŏn.

October 10, 680
MARTYRDOM OF PROPHET'S GRANDSON ḤUSAYN

The betrayal and massacre of the Prophet Muḥammad's grandson and dozens of his followers at the Battle of Karbalāʾ is one of the most significant events in the history of Islam's electrifying early expansion, contributing to the split between the Sunni and Shīʿite sects of Islam.

LOCALE: Karbalāʾ, Al-Kufa (now in Iraq)
CATEGORIES: Religion; wars, uprisings, and civil unrest

KEY FIGURES
Ḥasan (624-680), grandson of Muḥammad and second imam of Islam
Ḥusayn (626-680), brother of Ḥasan and third imam of Islam
Muʿāwiyah I (c. 602-680), founder of the Umayyad Dynasty, caliph, r. 661-680
Yazīd I (c. 645-683), second caliph of the Umayyad Dynasty, r. 680-683

SUMMARY OF EVENT
With the death of the Prophet Muḥammad in 632, the burgeoning Islamic Empire lost its charismatic leader and began to show signs of internecine strife that, within a generation, would see intrigues, assassinations, and massacres. The reigns of the "ideal" or "rightly guided" caliphs (Abū Bakr, r. 632-634; ʿUmar I, r. 634-644; ʿUthmān ibn ʿAffān, r. 644-656; and ʿAlī ibn Abī Ṭālib, r. 656-661) kept these struggles to a minimum until the succession of ʿAlī, son-in-law of Muḥammad and the last of the ideal caliphs.

ʿAlī's moral and spiritual authority as caliph was challenged by Muʿāwiyah I, the wealthy and politically puissant governor of Syria. The resulting bloody battles and politics left a bad taste in the mouths of some who were used to the relative purity of the Islamic world under Muḥammad. When ʿAlī was assassinated by the Khāijites, a group of warriors, his elder son, Ḥasan, succeeded ʿAlī as caliph. Ḥasan soon abdicated in favor of Muʿāwiyah, retiring to Medina. In 680, Ḥasan was poisoned, possibly by his wife at the behest of Muʿāwiyah. With Ḥasan out of the way, Muʿāwiyah founded the Umayyad Dynasty, which would dominate Islam until 750.

Although Muʿāwiyah was now the legitimate caliph, or political head, of Islam, the imamate (spiritual authority) of Islam remained with Ḥasan until his death, when it passed to his brother Ḥusayn. Ḥusayn, by all accounts a thoughtful and pious man, felt bound by his brother's oath and made no challenge to Muʿāwiyah. Muʿāwiyah's rule ended with his death in 680, and his son Yazīd I succeeded to the caliphate. Muslim leaders across the peninsula were made to sign oaths of allegiance to Yazīd; Ḥusayn refused to do this on the grounds that the caliphate should not become a hereditary monarchy, mimicking the Persian and Byzantine patterns. With supporters and his family, Ḥusayn fled his home in Al-Kufa for the relative safety of Mecca.

The Kufans, however, chafing under Syrian rule, soon invited Ḥusayn to return. They promised he would find vast support for a reassertion of his rights as caliph. Ḥusayn sent an emissary, Muslim ibn Aqeel, to gather intelligence. Muslim sent word assuring Ḥusayn that some twelve thousand Kufans had sworn allegiance to him. Against the advice of his friends in Mecca, Ḥusayn undertook the three-week journey back to Al-Kufa, accompanied only by his household and entourage of some one hundred persons, many of whom were women and children.

Yazīd's governor in Al-Kufa, Ubaydullah ibn Ziyad, responded to this news with a campaign of threat, coercion, bribery, and violence against any dissenters. By the time Ḥusayn reached Zubalah, about halfway to Al-Kufa, word was waiting for him that his support had melted away. Nevertheless, Ḥusayn pressed on, joined by some Bedouins from the desert and some loyal refugees from Al-Kufa, until stopped by an Umayyad army of one thousand men commanded by the young Hur al-Riyahi.

Hur al-Riyahi approached Ḥusayn's band and explained to him that he had been ordered to prevent Ḥusayn from entering any town in Iraq. Ḥusayn showed Hur al-Riyahi the letters from Al-Kufa begging him to return, then shared his water with Hur al-Riyahi's soldiers and invited the Umayyads to pray with him. Moved, Hur al-Riyahi permitted Ḥusayn to travel on while his army followed, awaiting further instructions from Al-Kufa.

On the second day of the month of Muharram in 680, Ḥusayn's party reached the plain of Karbalāʾ, skirting the Euphrates River. The following day, a war band of four thousand Umayyad soldiers, led by ʿUmar ibn Saʿad, appeared and blocked Ḥusayn's access to the water. Ibn Saʿad explained to Ḥusayn that he would not allow his party to leave Karbalāʾ until Ḥusayn had signed an oath of loyalty to Yazīd.

Ḥusayn refused, although his party was all but defenseless and beginning to die from thirst. On the tenth of Muharram, a day now known as ʿĀshūrāʾ, the Umayyads advanced against Ḥusayn's loyal followers, who had refused any opportunity to abandon him. Hur al-Riyahi, who still lurked behind Ḥusayn, joined the battle against ibn Saʿad, adding his thousand to the armed men (that tradition numbers at 72) and the women and children who followed the Prophet's grandson. This addition would avail but little against the four thousand Umayyad archers and cavalry that stood between them and the life-giving Euphrates.

The resulting series of forays against Ḥusayn's camp was a massacre. Hur al-Riyahi was among the first to fall, and the remainder of Ḥusayn's supporters were subjected to heavy fire from ibn Saʿad's archers. Ḥusayn at last approached the Umayyads, begging for water, holding his infant son before him. The baby was killed by an arrow in the throat, and Ḥusayn was then set on by the Umayyad cavalry. According to tradition, he was struck by a blow that forced him to the ground facedown, but the Umayyads hesitated before striking the coup de grace until Shamir, an emissary from Ubaydullah, stepped forward and slew the helpless imam.

All the male members of Ḥusayn's party were decapitated, and the women were taken prisoner. The sole male survivor of the massacre was Ḥusayn's son ʿAlī (later known as Zayn-al-ʿĀbidīn) who, afflicted with fever, had not joined the battle. Ḥusayn's body was trampled by horses, and his head was brought back to Al-Kufa, where it was subjected to further violence by Ubaydullah, until an old man from the crowd called out that he had seen the lips of the Prophet kiss the very face that Ubaydullah was mutilating.

SIGNIFICANCE

The savagery of this atrocity had immediate consequences in popular uprisings in Mecca and Medina. Yazīd was forced to divert his energies to suppressing these revolts and avenged himself by plundering the holy cities. In addition, Yazīd's violence and appetite for worldly things is reckoned by some historians to have sewn the seeds of the ʿAbbāsid revolution that would unseat the Umayyads in 750. The more significant result of Ḥusayn's martyrdom, though, was the creation of the Shīʿite minority in Islam.

Among both Sunni and Shīʿite Muslims, amazingly, the basic facts of this tragic tale, even down to Yazīd's cruelty and Ḥusayn's sanctity, are not disputed. For Shīʿite Muslims, however, the root of an unjust and catastrophic history is manifested in the massacre at Karbalāʾ. Most Shīʿites believe that ʿAlī, husband of the Prophet's daughter Fāṭimah, should have immediately succeeded Muhammad, and that Abū Bakr and ʿUmar I plotted to keep ʿAlī out of power as long as possible (although many scholars consider this unlikely, since Abū Bakr was famous for carrying out the Prophet's orders even if it went against his own better judgment or safety). For the Shīʿites, this alleged political machination began to corrupt the purity of Islam even before the Prophet's death. This corruption was made tragically visible in the massacre, when the keepers of the central principles of Islam were brutally cut down by a worldly tyrant. Among Sunni's, the tale of Ḥusayn is a chastisement and a warning against the temptations of temporal power. For the Shīʿites, however, the story incorporates the quest for a pure Muslim identity defined by sacrifice and suffering.

During the month of Muharram, Shīʿite communities re-enact the sacred story of Ḥusayn in a powerful mass ritual, called a Taziyeh or Karbalāʾ play, involving a complicated procession of public grief and self-flagellation. The participants in the play enact the main events of the story and slash their own heads with swords. Participation in these ceremonies is held to be a sacred and redemptive act that will earn the intercession of Ḥusayn, keeper of the keys of Heaven, at the Last Judgment. Akbar Ahmed writes that

> The immense sacrifice [of Ḥusayn] ensured the perpetuation of the myth of Karbalāʾ; its political content has made it a powerful and emotional rallying point against tyranny and oppression.

An Urdu poet summed it up in verse: *"Islam zinda hota hay har Karbalāʾ key bad"* ("Islam is reborn after every Karbalāʾ").

—Michael M. Chemers

FURTHER READING

Ahmed, Akbar S. *Discovering Islam: Making Sense of Muslim History and Society.* Rev. ed. New York: Routledge, 2002. A thoughtful, easy-to-read, comprehensive analysis of Islam. Map, chronology, glossary, bibliography, index.

Halm, Heinz. *Shia Islam: From Religion to Revolution.* Translated by Allison Brown. Princeton, N.J.: Markus Wiener, 1997. A concise history of Shiism, from its beginnings during the time of the massacre of Ḥusayn and his followers through the twentieth century. Highlights the massacre, Shiism's historical development, and its rituals of mourning and atonement, including the Karbalā' play and self-flagellation. Illustrations, bibliography, index.

Hitti, Philip K. *History of the Arabs*. 10th ed. New York: St. Martin's Press, 1974. This is still the standard text for the entire spectrum of Arab history. Illustrations, genealogical tables, maps, bibliographical references.

Jafri, Syed Husain Mohammad. *The Origins and Early Development of Shia Islam*. New York: Oxford University Press, 2000. A thoroughly researched study of Shiism's formative period using contemporary and near-contemporary sources. Includes chapters on Al-Kufa, Ḥusayn's martyrdom, and the after effects of Karbalā'. Bibliography, index.

Jandora, John Walter. *Militarism in Arab Society: A Historiographical and Bibliographical Sourcebook*. Westport, Conn.: Greenwood Press, 1997. A somewhat-slanted but detailed military history of Arab military culture focusing on Muʿāwiyah and his descendants.

Lewis, Bernard. *The Middle East: A Brief History of the Last Two Thousand Years*. New York: Scribner, 1997. An erudite, comprehensive, controversial text from one of the most prolific Western authors on Islamic history.

Momen, Moojan. *An Introduction to Shii Islam: The History and Doctrines of Twelver Shiism*. New Haven, Conn.: Yale University Press, 1985. A balanced and detailed approach to understanding an oft-misunderstood Muslim minority. Bibliography, index.

Rahman, Fazlur. *Islam*. Chicago: University of Chicago Press, 1979. A detailed and extensive study on the institutions of Islam by a Pakistani expert. Bibliography, index.

Schacht, Joseph, and C. E. Bosworth, eds. *The Legacy of Islam*. 2d ed. New York: Oxford University Press, 1979. An unusual text that traces the debt the Western world owes to Islamic thought and civilization. Illustrations, bibliography, index.

SEE ALSO: c. 610-632: Muḥammad Receives Revelations; 637-657: Islam Expands Throughout the Middle East; 869-883: Zanj Revolt of African Slaves; 969-1171: Reign of the Fāṭimids.

RELATED ARTICLES in *Great Lives from History: The Middle Ages, 477-1453*: ʿAbd al-Malik; al-Ḥallāj; al-Ḥasan al-Baṣrī; Muḥammad; ʿUmar I.

682-1377
EXPANSION OF ŚRIVIJAYA

Śrivijaya was for many years the most important seagoing power in Southeast Asia, and it may have played a part in the spread of Buddhism.

LOCALE: Modern-day Indonesia and Malaysia, primarily the Indonesian islands of Sumatra and Java
CATEGORIES: Expansion and land acquisition; government and politics

KEY FIGURES

Yijing (I-tsing; 635-713), widely traveled Chinese Buddhist pilgrim

Jayanasa (fl. late seventh century), king of Śrivijaya, r. late seventh century

Sanjaya (d. 750), king of Mataram in Java, r. 732-750

Chulamanivarmadeva (dates unknown), king of Śrivijaya, r. late tenth to early eleventh century

Rājendracōla Deva I (d. 1044), king of Cōla in South India, r. 1014-1044

Airlangga (c. 990-c. 1060), founder and king of Kahuripan kingdom in eastern Java, r. 1019-c. 1060

SUMMARY OF EVENT

During the late seventh century, Śrivijaya rose to become one of the most important states in Southeast Asia. It was a center of Buddhism, with close ties to the Buddhist schools of India. A seagoing power, Śrivijaya had ships that traveled throughout the region, and it maintained ties with China and the major powers in the Middle East and South Asia.

The rapid rise of the kingdom of Śrivijaya began at the end of the seventh century and was largely the product of two developments in Southeast Asia. First, this historical period showed a marked expansion in seagoing traffic. Merchants, many of them Arabs, used improved methods of navigation to trade around the islands and the mainland coasts. Taking advantage of advances in navigation, the Chinese empire began communicating with countries to its south, sending and receiving embassies. The island of Sumatra, lying just southwest of the Malay Peninsula and just northwest of the island of Java between the straits of Malacca and Sunda, was a natural stopping point for ships traveling from China with the monsoon winds. Second, the kingdom of Funan broke apart. Funan had dominated the waters of Southeast Asia from its base in present-day Cambodia, and the decline of this kingdom left a political vacuum to be filled by a new power.

The pilgrimage of the Chinese Buddhist Yijing (also I-Ching) to India at the end of the seventh century left some of the earliest written records of the political organization of Sumatra. On his way to India in 671, Yijing stopped for about six months in a city that he called Fo-shih, located at Palembang on the Musi River. He described this city as a center of the Buddhist religion, with more than a thousand monks. Yijing also mentioned a city just to the north of Fo-shih that he called Mo-lo-yu, which is believed to have been Malayu, alongside the Batang River near the eastern coast of Sumatra. At the end of the seventh century, Yijing went back to China and he wrote that Mo-lo-yu had become part of what he called Shih-li-fo-shih.

Inscriptions in stone written in the Old Malay language have provided some details of the early growth of Śrivijaya during Yijing's time. In 682, the Śrivijayan King Jayanasa began a series of military campaigns against his neighbors. Scholars have debated whether Jayanasa's kingdom grew from native people at Palembang or whether it was created by the conquest of Palembang by invaders from elsewhere. However, Jayanasa ap-

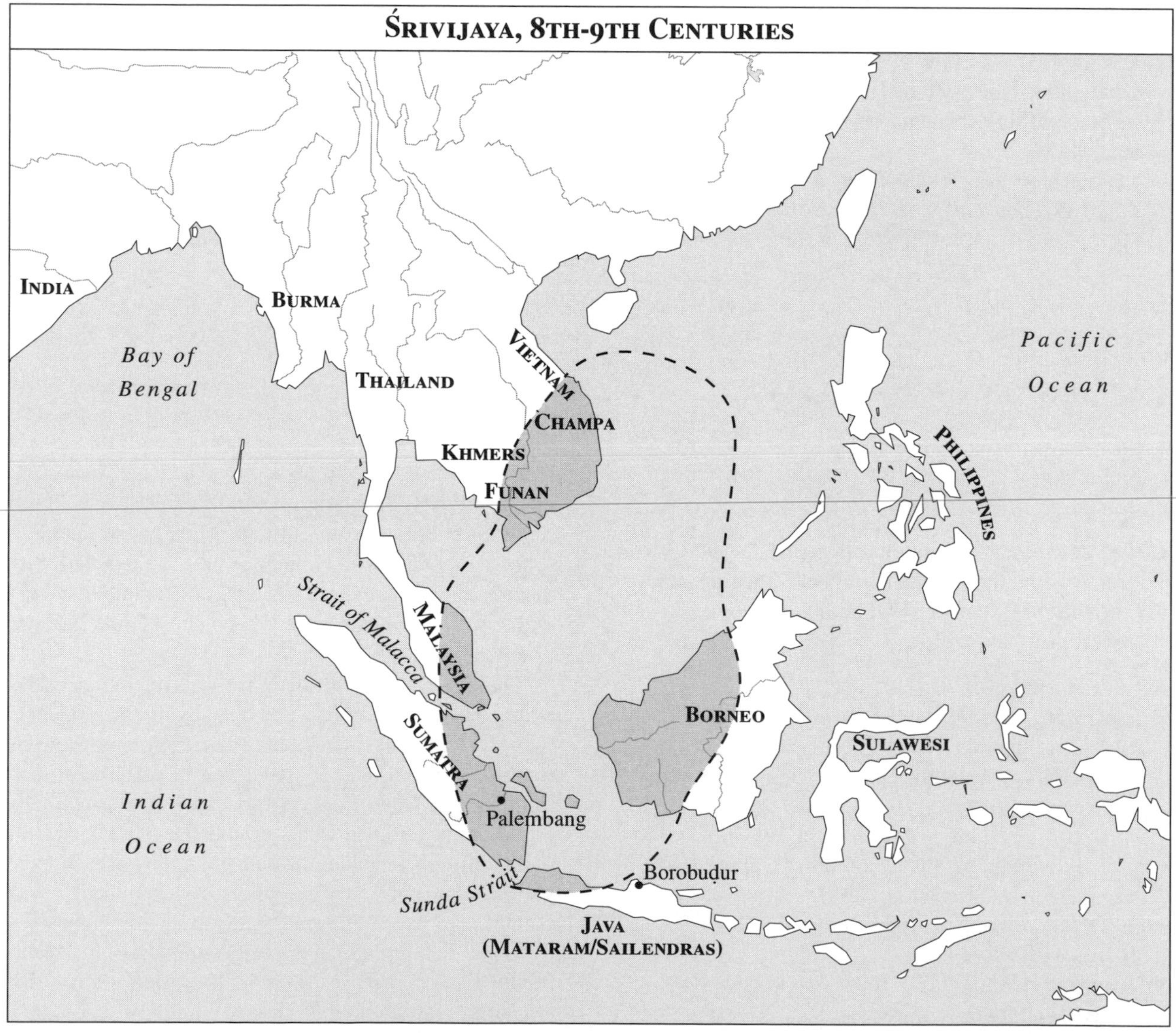

parently brought Malayu and the island of Bangka, just off the coast of Sumatra, under his rule. Other lands also fell quickly under Śrivijayan power. By 686, the kingdom had sent expeditions against kingdoms in Java, brought all of Sumatra under its control, and extended its power up the Malay Peninsula.

Both Yijing's writings and the inscriptions emphasize the importance of the Buddhist religion for Śrivijayan society. The inscriptions indicate that the king was seen as a religious teacher and perhaps even a bodhisattva (an enlightened being remaining on Earth to lead ordinary humans toward salvation). These writings in stone also provide clear evidence that the Tantric school of Buddhism was already influential in Śrivijaya during the seventh century. Tantric Buddhism involved a heavy reliance on magical practices and symbols. It is generally thought to have developed in India after about 600 as a result of the blending of Hindu chants and incantations with Mahāyāna Buddhist philosophy. Its early appearance in Śrivijaya is a testimony to the close ties between the island kingdom and India.

Scholars believe that Śrivijayan influences on religion and art spread up the Malay Peninsula and into what is now Thailand. Some scholars also point to Yijing's own Buddhist studies in Śrivijaya as evidence that the kingdom played a valuable part in the development of Chinese Buddhism.

Two major challengers to Śrivijayan power emerged in the region. The first of these was the kingdom of Mataram in central Java. Mataram's king Sanjaya undertook attacks against Sumatra, Bali, Cambodia, and southern China. Also in Java, the dynasty of the Sailendras emerged. The Sailendras, or "kings of the mountain," erected some of the most impressive works of sculpture and architecture in the Indonesian lands, including the Javanese monuments of Borobuḍur. A branch of the Sailendras also became the rulers of Śrivijaya.

How the Sailendras reached the Śrivijayan throne is not clear; possibly, the Śrivijayans and the Sailendras initially became allies against Sanjaya because the former two were Buddhists and Sanjaya was a worshiper of the Hindu god Śiva. The Sailendras may well have received aid from Śrivijaya in establishing themselves in Mataram at the end of the eighth century. It may have been as a result of marriages between the two royal families that a Sailendra became king of Śrivijaya by 860.

Despite these ties between Śrivijaya and Java, enmity developed between the two. The Sailendras at Mataram apparently converted to the Shaivite faith, the worship of Śiva. Śrivijaya remained resolutely Buddhist. About 992, King Chulamanivarmadeva of Śrivijaya sent a mission to China to request the Chinese emperor's help in resisting attacks from Java. A few years later, in 1006, Chulamanivarmadeva attacked Mataram, burned its palace, and killed its king.

During the tenth and eleventh centuries, Śrivijaya went into a period of steady decline. This was probably at least partially a result of problems with the seagoing trade that had earlier brought it to power. Serious political difficulties in China and in the Middle East meant a decrease in economic activity for the region of Southeast Asia. In addition, the continual warfare brought disorder to Java and Sumatra.

Śrivijaya came into conflict with the Cōla kingdom in South India as a result of competition to control the seas. In 1025, King Rājendracōla Deva I attacked Śrivijaya; eventually he took some of the lands of the Malay peninsula and invaded Sumatra. Śrivijaya survived these assaults, but it was forced to pay tribute to the Cōlas for a number of years.

While Śrivijaya was struggling with the Cōlas, it came under the sway of a new power in Java. King Airlangga founded the Kahuripan kingdom in eastern Java in 1019. Through marriage, Airlangga brought Śrivijaya into his lands. Airlangga's kingdom broke up when he divided it among his sons, but Śrivijaya continued to play a much less influential part in the region than it had in earlier years. The Sumatran kingdom of Malayu, previously absorbed into Śrivijaya, rose to prominence again and dominated Śrivijaya. The kingdom remained under Malayu for the next two centuries, and it never again established a powerful presence in the waters of the region. When the famous Italian traveler Marco Polo reached Sumatra in 1292, the island was no longer under a single ruler. It had broken into eight different states, with none laying claim to the name of Śrivijaya.

A year after Marco Polo's visit, Mongol invaders reached Java. A new regional power, Majapahit, emerged in the fight against the Mongols. Over the course of the following century, Majapahit spread its control over the region. In 1377, Majapahit conquered Palembang in Sumatra, the apparent original capital of the Śrivijayan empire. By modern times, the powerful state of Śrivijaya had disappeared so completely that scholars could only reconstruct its history from archeological remains and references in ancient documents.

SIGNIFICANCE

Śrivijaya's central geographic location enabled it to link cultural areas throughout Asia. Scholars theorize that

Śrivijayan culture, particularly its religion and art, spread up the Malay Peninsula and into what is now Thailand. In addition, Śrivijaya may have helped Buddhism and Indian culture spread through the region. Some scholars also point to Yijing's Buddhist studies in Śrivijaya as evidence that the kingdom played a valuable part in the development of Chinese Buddhism.

—Carl L. Bankston III

FURTHER READING

Coedès, George. *The Indianized States of Southeast Asia.* Translated by Susan Brown Cowing. Honolulu: East-West Center Press, 1968. The classic work on Southeast Asian history.

Coedès, George, and Louis-Charles Damais. *Sriwijaya: History, Religion, and Language of an Early Malay Polity.* Monograph of the Malaysian Branch, Royal Asiatic Society 20. Kuala Lumpur, Malaysia: MBRAS, 1992. A collection of studies on the history of Śrivijaya.

Hall, Kenneth R. "An Economic History of Early Southeast Asia." In *Cambridge History of Southeast Asia.* Vol. 1, edited by Nicholas Tarling. Cambridge, England: Cambridge University Press, 1992. Traces the economic origins of early kingdoms, including Śrivijaya.

Spencer, George W. *The Politics of Expansion: The Chola Conquest of Sri Lanka and Sri Vijaya.* Madras, India: New Era, 1983. This examination of the Cōlas' conquests looks at Rājendracōla Deva I's attack on Śrivijaya.

Wolters, Oliver William. *Early Indonesian Commerce: A Study of the Origins of Śrivijaya.* Ithaca, N.Y.: Cornell University Press, 1970. Looks at the role of maritime trade in the rise of Śrivijaya.

_______. *The Fall of Śrivijaya in Malay History.* Ithaca, N.Y.: Cornell University Press, 1970. A key work on the end of Śrivijaya.

SEE ALSO: 775-840: Building of Borobuḍur; 780: Rise of the Sailendra Family; c. 985-1014: Reign of Rājarāja I; 1204: Genghis Khan Founds Mongol Empire; 1225: Tran Thai Tong Establishes Tran Dynasty; 1271-1295: Travels of Marco Polo.

RELATED ARTICLES in *Great Lives from History: The Middle Ages, 477-1453*: Ngo Quyen; Marco Polo.

685-691
BUILDING OF THE DOME OF THE ROCK

The Dome of the Rock, a spectacular octagonal monument to Islam that still dominates the landscape of the holy city of Jerusalem, was constructed to affirm the Umayyad Dynasty and to demonstrate the arrival of Islam in Jerusalem.

LOCALE: Jerusalem
CATEGORIES: Architecture; engineering; religion

KEY FIGURES

ʿAbd al-Malik (646 or 647-705), caliph, r. 685-705
ʿUmar I (c. 586-644), caliph, r. 634-644

SUMMARY OF EVENT

In the year 685, the Muslim caliph ʿAbd al-Malik commissioned the construction of a domed monument on a rocky outcropping on the platform of Jerusalem known as the Al-Haram al-Sharif, or the Temple Mount. An inscription on the inside wall credits ʿAbd al-Malik and dates the work to 72 A.H. (*anno Hegirae*), an early period in the Islamic era. The founding of Islam is dated from the year of the *Hijra*, or Hegirae, the migration of Muḥammad and his followers to Medina (dated in the Western calendar to 622). Calculating a lunar year of 354 days, a date of about 691 is reckoned for the construction.

It was during the initial visit by the caliph ʿUmar I to Jerusalem that the seeds were sown for building this monument. The story of the city's surrender to ʿUmar by the Christian patriarch Sophronius (c. 560-638) is filled with legend. Nevertheless, a number of basic themes persist.

Jerusalem had always held a special place in Islam. The Qurʾān mentions that prayers once were directed toward that city before Muḥammad established the *qibla* (the direction of prayer) at Mecca. The subject of prayer arose during ʿUmar's visit. Sophronius invited the caliph to pray in the Church of the Holy Sepulcher. ʿUmar declined, not wanting to set a precedent for the possible Muslim takeover of this historic Christian site. Instead, ʿUmar wandered the city until he came to the raised platform where the Jewish temples of Solomon and Herod had once stood—the latter destroyed by the Romans in 70. The Christians had never showed interest in develop-

The Dome of the Rock, also known as ʿUmar Mosque. (Hulton|Archive by Getty Images)

ing this site. It was then a pile of ruins, the perfect place for the caliph's prayers.

Muslims had also understood Jerusalem as the location of "the farthest mosque" (Masjid al-Aqsa) where Muḥammad had begun his night journey into heaven. According to one report, Muḥammad had shared with ʿUmar a description of the site. Thus, ʿUmar carefully explored the site by turning over stones, removing rubble and placing it in the folds of his robes, and dumping it over the side of the wall. Eventually he discovered the unusual outcropping of rock that today lies at the center of the Dome.

ʿUmar was ready for prayer. Rejecting a suggestion that he kneel to the north of the rock where he could face both the rock and Mecca, he apparently chose to say his prayers from the southern edge of the platform. It was there that the Muslims built the Dome of the Rock.

The year 661 began a shift of power in the Islamic empire from Medina to Damascus and then to Baghdad, with the rule of the Umayyads and the ʿAbbāsids respectively. Jerusalem as a city received a boost in recognition and significance when the first Ummayad Muʿāwiyah I (r. 661-680) was proclaimed caliph in Jerusalem, receiving the homage of Arab-Muslim leaders. The city soon became known among Muslims as Bayt al-Maqdis—the house of the holy.

Although Jerusalem was still predominantly Christian, the Muslim population continued to grow. Some Jews also were invited to return to Jerusalem to serve as menial laborers on the Al-Haram al-Sharif. There are written reports that laborers were sent from Egypt to work on a mosque, presumably the dome, in Jerusalem, and that funds were made available from Egyptian taxes. The pilgrimage report of the Gallic (Frankish) bishop Arculf in c. 690, the first major Christian to observe Islam's rise, described a mosque that could hold as many as three thousand people for prayer. However, he described it as a simple wooden mosque of poor quality.

ʿAbd al-Malik became caliph following a period of turmoil within the Islamic empire, with the Shīʿite movement split. The city of Medina also rejected the Umayyads and named their own caliph: ʿAbd Allāh ibn al-Zubayr (r. 683-692). Under these circumstances, the Ummayad caliph turned his attention to Jerusalem. He repaired the city walls and gates and built a new governor's residence. However, the crowning achievement was the Dome of the Rock, a structure that, according to the tenth century writer, geographer, and native of Jerusalem, al-Maqdisī (c. 946-c. 1000), was to be "unique and a wonder to the world."

Little is known about the actual construction of the Dome of the Rock and how long it took. No contemporary journals documented the construction. Some have suggested that the work was commissioned in 685 and completed in 691, the date mentioned in the inscription. This range makes sense because the inscription would have been added during a later stage of the project. However, in 691, the caliph had just returned from Iraq, where he had been working to unify the empire. It also is likely that 691 marks the beginning of the project. Dated milestones showing road construction between Jerusalem and Damascus all suggest that building activity flourished throughout the 690's. It is likely that the project consumed most of the decade.

The construction became a building of extreme simplicity. An octagonal structure surrounded a circular drum that raised the dome three times the height of the ring. Colorful mosaics in geometric and floral motifs covered the walls inside. A single Arabic inscription some 787 feet (240 meters) in length with phrases from the Qurʾān led visitors in a walk around the ancient rock at the center.

SIGNIFICANCE

First, the construction of the Dome of the Rock helped establish Islam as a legitimate religion, on a level with Christianity. A number of later Muslim sources suggest that the dome's purpose was to establish spiritual superiority, but that interpretation probably reflects the mood of later times. Seventh century social attitudes in Jerusalem were more likely about cooperation.

The style of the Dome of the Rock was not based solely on Islamic architecture but also on Christian buildings throughout the east. The octagonal shape imitated numerous churches from Bethlehem to Byzantium. The dome reflected the nearby Church of the Holy Sepulcher. The construction itself was carried out by Christian artisans: The architects came from Byzantium and the marble workers had completed a decade of work at the Church of the Nativity in Bethlehem.

The Arabic inscriptions clearly state the primary theological difference between Islam and Christianity, denying the divinity of Jesus. However, the primary focus may well be the praise of the one God and not a polemical attack against Christians. There are no comments questioning the death and resurrection of Jesus symbolized by the nearby Church of the Holy Sepulchre. Ultimately, the Dome of the Rock did not replace the Christian churches of Jerusalem: It stood alongside them. Also, the construction of the dome served to unify the Muslim world. A number of later writers suggest that ʿAbd al-Malik constructed the Dome of the Rock to draw pilgrims (*hajji*) away from Mecca. It is true that a separate caliph ruled Arabia from Medina. However, ʿAbd al-Malik continued to send pilgrims to Mecca even after the dome's construction.

A more important argument is that the design of the Jerusalem structure was never intended for large numbers to circle the rock inside. It was never intended to be a mosque for prayer. When its construction was complete, ʿAbd-al Malik went one step further and commissioned the building of the al-Aqsa mosque, which was then completed by his son al-Walīd I (r. 705-715). Its position on the south side of the Haram platform directed worshippers toward Mecca.

ʿAbd al-Malik and his architects provided a monument so unique that visitors are absorbed in the contemplation of the divine. The geometric precision, the use of light, the curves, and the floral designs all lead the visitor from focusing on humanity and its differences and toward the unity of the creator and creation. Architects refer to its "annular" character—there is a sense of circular movement with no hint of hierarchy, no point of beginning or end.

Finally, the Dome of the Rock has become symbolic of Jerusalem. Until the twentieth century, nearly every depiction of the city (mostly by Western Christians) highlighted the dome. Travel brochures and other images still depict the dome as Jerusalem's civic centerpiece. The Dome of the Rock, though a Muslim monument, signifies a city in which three monotheistic faiths—Judaism, Islam, and Christianity—come together.

—Fred Strickert

FURTHER READING

Armstrong, Karen. *Jerusalem: One City, Three Faiths.* New York: Ballantine Books, 1997. An overview of the history of Jerusalem with emphasis on the interaction of three major monotheistic faiths. Illustrations, map, bibliography, index.

Bloom, Jonathan, ed. *Early Islamic Art and Architecture.* Burlington, Vt.: Ashgate, 2002. A historical overview of the art and architecture of Islam, including the Dome of the Rock in Jerusalem. Illustrations, bibliography, index.

Duri, Abdul Aziz. "Jerusalem in the Early Islamic Period: Seventh-Eleventh Centuries A.D." In *Jerusalem in History,* edited by K. J. Asali. Brooklyn, N.Y.: Olive Branch Press, 2000. Covers the period in Jerusalem's history during which the Dome was constructed. Illustrations, bibliography, index.

Grabar, Oleg. *The Shape of the Holy: Early Islamic Jerusalem.* Princeton, N.J.: Princeton University Press, 1996. A carefully detailed study of Islam in Jerusalem prior to the start of the Crusades (1099), based on both literary texts and archaeological evidence. Includes a chapter on the Dome of the Rock and an appendix listing dome inscriptions. Illustrations, plans, bibliography, index.

Makiya, Kanan. *The Rock: A Tale of Seventh-Century Jerusalem.* New York: Pantheon Books, 2002. A historical novel by an Iraqi-born architect about the Dome of the Rock and those associated with its construction and legend, revealing a shared history between Islam, Judaism, and Christianity in Jerusalem. Best for readers with some knowledge of the three major world religions.

Murphy-O'Connor, Jerome. *The Holy Land: An Oxford Archaeological Guide.* 4th rev. ed. New York: Oxford University Press, 2001. A guide for the general reader to the sites of the Holy Land. Illustrations, maps, index.

Nuseibeh, Saïd. *The Dome of the Rock.* New York: Rizzoli, 1996. A comprehensive collection of photographs of the Dome of the Rock, with an essay by Oleg Grabar. Bibliography, index.

Raby, Julian, and Jeremy Johns, eds. *Bayt-al-Maqdis: ʿAbd al-Malik's Jerusalem.* 2 vols. New York: Oxford University Press, 1992-1999. Explores the architecture of ʿAbd al-Malik and the history of religious architecture in Jerusalem. Some text in French. Bibliography.

Rosovsky, Nitza, ed. *City of the Great King: Jerusalem from David to the Present.* Cambridge, Mass.: Harvard University Press, 1996. Examines the significance of Jerusalem to Islam in chapters on the spiritual meaning of the city to Muslims, the city in medieval Islamic literature, and Islamic construction plans for the Haram platform. Illustrations, maps, plans, bibliography, index.

SEE ALSO: c. 610-632: Muḥammad Receives Revelations; 972: Building of al-Azhar Mosque; 1009: Destruction of the Church of the Holy Sepulchre; c. 1181-1221: Lalibela Founds the Christian Capital of Ethiopia; 1410-1440: Florentine School of Art Emerges.

RELATED ARTICLES in *Great Lives from History: The Middle Ages, 477-1453*: ʿAbd al-Malik; Filippo Brunelleschi; Melisende; Muḥammad.

690-705
REIGN OF EMPRESS WU

Originally a royal concubine, Wu Hou became the only female emperor in Chinese history. Historians portray her as a ruthless autocrat, but her reign also saw great achievements in both domestic and foreign affairs.

LOCALE: China
CATEGORY: Government and politics

KEY FIGURES
Wu Hou (625-705), Tang Dynasty empress, r. 690-705
Taizong (T'ai-tsung; 599-649), second emperor of the Tang Dynasty, r. 627-649
Gaozong (Kao-tsung; 628-683), third emperor of the Tang Dynasty, r. 650-683

SUMMARY OF EVENT
Wu Zhao (Wu Chao; later Wu Hou) was born into a family from Wenshui in the province of Shanxi. Her father was a wealthy Chinese general who had served Li Yuan who reigned as Gaozu (Kao-tsu, r. 618-626), the first emperor of the Tang Dynasty (T'ang; 618-907). As a child, she learned to write, play music, and read the classics. She became respected for her intelligence as well as her physical beauty. In 638, Taizong, the second Tang emperor, invited Wu Zhao to the palace, and she joined his harem with the rank of concubine of the fifth grade. The emperor was impressed by her scholarship and placed her in the imperial study, where she became familiar with official documents.

In 649, Taizong died, and his son Li Zhi (Li Chih) became emperor as Gaozong. As was customary, all the imperial concubines, including Wu Zhao, went to live the rest of their lives in a convent. There was speculation that the new emperor had already fallen in love with Wu Zhao, even before his father had died. At any rate, after three years of mourning, Gaozong visited the nunnery and later summoned Wu Zhao to live in the palace as *zhaoyi*, a second grade concubine. This was with the blessing of the childless empress Wang, who felt threatened by Xiao Shufei (Hsiao Shu-fei), the emperor's favorite concubine and mother of one of his sons. Empress Wang believed that Wu Zhao could distract the emperor from his affections for Xiao Shufei.

Wu Zhao herself, however, soon took over the role of the emperor's favorite companion, and in 652, she had a son by him. She became influential in the court, so a power struggle followed, with Empress Wang and her former rival Xiao Shufei now conspiring together against Wu Zhao. In 654, Wu Zhao gave birth to a daughter, who died suddenly in her crib. She blamed the death on Empress Wang, who had often held the newborn. Some historians suggest that Wu smothered her own infant so that Empress Wang would be blamed for the killing. The emperor believed Wu Zhao, but senior statesmen would not depose Empress Wang, who came from a powerful aristocratic family.

However, there were less powerful officials who saw an opportunity to advance, so they supported the arguments for change put forth by Gaozong and Wu Zhao. In 655, Empress Wang and Xiao Shufei were accused of trying to poison the emperor. As a result, Empress Wang was deposed, Wu Zhao was promoted to empress, and her son became the heir apparent. Empress Wang and Xiao Shufei were imprisoned and eventually murdered, possibly on orders from Wu Zhao. As time passed, an increasing number of Empress Wu's opponents were sent into exile.

In 660, Gaozong suffered the first of many crippling strokes, which left him unable to rule. With each illness, he allowed Empress Wu to assume more power and make more decisions for him, although she could hold court only from behind a screen, in keeping with the Confucian tradition for empresses and empress dowagers. Eventually, she took over his whole administration. It is generally acknowledged by even her worse detractors that she ruled with intelligence. However, she was also ruthless in her will to power and removed, exiled, or executed anyone, even family members, who threatened her position.

In 674, the emperor and empress adopted new titles that placed them above their predecessors: heavenly sovereign (*tian huang*) and heavenly empress (*tian hou*). The empress's popular and intelligent son and heir apparent, Li Hong (Li Hung; 653-675) often disagreed with his mother. In 675, he argued publicly with her about the brutal treatment of Xiao Shufei's two daughters. He died suddenly and mysteriously. Contemporary and later historians believed that he had been poisoned on orders from the empress. Then her second son, Li Xian (Li Hsien; 655-684) was proclaimed the crown prince. In 680, the empress accused him of plotting against his parents, and he was exiled.

On December 27, 683, Emperor Gaozong died, and in 684, Empress Wu's third son, Li Zhe (Li Che) ascended the throne as Emperor Zhongzong (Chung-tsung; r. 684), with Wu Zhao as the dowager empress. However, the empress could not control her third son, and he attempted to give his father-in-law a high bureaucratic post. Six weeks after ascending the throne, he was sent to prison. Now her fourth son, Li Dang (Li Tang), became Emperor Ruizong (Jui-tsung, r. 684-690), but he was weak and incompetent. He was secluded in a different palace and was sovereign in name only; Empress Wu actually ruled.

Soon there was a plot by princes and other imperial family members in the Yangtze Valley. They issued a proclamation accusing the empress of killing her own children, amongst other crimes. The rebels were disorganized and eventually subdued by imperial armies. To crush any further opposition, Wu Zhao set up a system of rewards and promotions for informants who would advise the authorities about anyone plotting against her.

In 689, she appeared carrying the imperial scepter and wearing the imperial robes. She had the support of a group of Buddhist monks, who claimed that the Great Cloud Sutra, a Buddhist work, contained the prophecy of Empress Wu's rise to the imperial throne. In 690, Ruizong abdicated in favor of his mother, and the high ministers asked her to ascend the throne. She named the new dynasty Zhou (Chou) and assumed the title of sage and divine emperor.

Eventually, as she grew older, there was the question of who would be her successor because there had never been a female monarch before. In 698, she decided to bring Zhongzong back from exile and proclaim him as her successor, instead of Ruizong. At the same time, there was increasing criticism of her dependence on sorcerers and young male concubines.

On February 22, 705, after a palace coup, she was forced to abdicate. The Tang Dynasty was restored, and Zhongzong became the emperor again on February 23, 705. He would remain emperor until 710. Wu was given the title "Zetian," which means "supreme empress." On December 16, 705, she died and was buried next to Emperor Gaozong in the Qianling Tomb.

Wu Hou's achievements were numerous and significant. Between 655 and 675, she negotiated with Korea and persuaded that country to become an ally of China. She decreased military spending and operations and replaced the government's military aristocracy with a scholarly bureaucracy based on merit examinations. She also lowered taxes, increased agricultural production, and constructed majestic buildings in the capital. Wu Hou also built Buddhist temples, cave sculptures, and hospitals. Chinese Buddhism thrived during her reign. At the same time, she was a patron of Chinese art, literature, and culture. Not surprisingly, she elevated the position of women, challenged the Confucian position against women rulers, and commissioned scholars to to write biographies of famous women.

SIGNIFICANCE

Wu Hou was the only female emperor in Chinese history. Many of the stories about her portray a cruel and ruthless despot, yet she was also a remarkable and successful ruler of the Chinese empire during one of its most glorious and peaceful periods.

Sources of information about her reign include the official Tang Dynasty histories, which were compiled by state-appointed historians as aids to government administration. Another source is the *Zizhi tongjian* (1084; comprehensive mirror for aid in government), the great imperial history by the Confucian scholar, Sima Guang (Ssu-ma Kuang; 1019-1086). The official Confucian histories about her were written several hundred years after her death, and these tended to be unfavorable. This is not surprising because her reign as emperor was completely contrary to Confucian and traditional Chinese political theory. However, perhaps because of these obstacles against her rise to power, it is plausible that she did plot, scheme, and eliminate opponents in order to succeed. Many male rulers took similar actions. Empress Wu remains a mysterious and controversial figure, the subject of debate and fascinating stories.

—*Alice Myers*

FURTHER READING

Fitzgerald, C. P. *The Empress Wu*. 2d ed. London: Cresset Press, 1968. A detailed, interesting biography of Empress Wu. This 263-page book includes maps, tables of relationship, an "Annual Table of Events," notes on the chapters, and an index and bibliography in Chinese.

Guisson, R. W. L. *Wu Tse-Tien and the Politics of Legitimation in T'ang China*. Bellingham: Western Washington University, 1978. In-depth study dealing with the question of the legitimation of Empress Wu's position, the tension between Confucian state theory and the contradiction of a female ruler, and a nontraditional historiography.

Hibbert, Eloise. *Embroidered Gauze: Portraits of Famous Chinese Ladies*. 1941. Reprint. Freeport, N.Y.: Books for Libraries Press, 1969. The frontispiece is an illustration of Empress Wu, and the work includes a 33-page chapter on her.

Paul, Diana. "Empress Wu and the Historians: A Tyrant and Saint of Classical China." In *Unspoken Worlds:*

Women's Religious Lives in Non-Western Cultures, edited by Nancy Falk and Rita Gross. 3d ed. Belmont, Calif.: Wadsworth/Thomson Learning, 2001. Paul analyzes Empress Wu's relationship to the Buddhist and Confucian traditions. She discusses the possible reasons for the often negative historical views and presents a more balanced portrait of Empress Wu.

Willis, John E. *Mountain of Fame: Portraits in Chinese History.* Princeton, N.J.: Princeton University Press, 1994. One of the chapters is an interesting, general biography of the empress.

SEE ALSO: 581: Sui Dynasty Reunifies China; 606: National University Awards First Doctorate; 618: Founding of the Tang Dynasty.

RELATED ARTICLES in *Great Lives from History: The Middle Ages, 477-1453*: Taizong; Wang Wei; Yan Liben.

c. 700
BOW AND ARROW SPREAD INTO NORTH AMERICA

The bow and arrow, introduced from Asia into North America, became important tools of hunting and warfare among nearly all of the native North American cultures. Favored especially by early nomadic groups, use of the bow and arrow spread southward with migrating peoples and proved instrumental both in deciding conflicts with the more settled groups and in aiding the nomads' survival through the acquisition of game.

LOCALE: Plains of Northwestern Canada and North America
CATEGORY: Science and technology

SUMMARY OF EVENT

The use of the arrow alone, in the form of a dart or light throwing spear, is believed to predate the use of the combined archery bow and arrow. The efficacy of these earliest hand-propelled missile weapons was later improved by the introduction of a separate launching tool in the form of a corded sling or notched throwing stick, such as the Australian woomera (wooden rod with a hooked end), which added greater impetus to the throw. The development of the archery bow as a specialized tool for launching arrows is thought by some anthropologists to represent a separate and distinct stage of cultural development as important as the discovery of fire. The first recorded use of archery bows occurred quite early in human history. Images from Paleolithic and Mesolithic cave paintings (c. 10,000-5000 B.C.E.) in Spain and France depict groups of simple silhouette figures using the bow as both a weapon of combat and the hunt. One such image from Castellón, Spain, shows an archer nocking an arrow with one hand while clasping a bow and three extra arrows in his other fist.

Evidence suggests that Subarctic peoples first brought the archery bow with them to North America from Asia (c. 30,000-10,000 B.C.E.). Its use gradually spread throughout the coastal regions, then southeastward following the principal migratory routes of nomadic hunters. Critical to the development and use of the bow was the availability of certain key natural materials. These included wood of sufficient tensibility (Osage orange, yew, hickory, ash) for the bow and arrow shafts, stone or malleable metal (flint, obsidian, iron, copper) for the arrow points, sinew or plant fiber for the bowstring, and feathers for fletching. As a consequence of these resource needs, the adoption of the archery bow, with slight regional variations in its structure, naturally progressed through those geographic regions in which such materials were plentiful. By c. 700, the archery bow was used throughout North America.

One case in point will serve as an illustration: The Mogollon people were the first to adopt the bow in the Southwestern region of what is now called the United States (c. 100-200). Subsequent Mogollon trade with the Hohokam people (southern Arizona area) brought the bow farther into the continental interior. Sometime between 400 and 500, the bow was introduced into the Great Plains and found use among the Arapaho, Blackfoot, and Cree peoples (all descendants of the Lenape). Later, between 500 and 600, the Lenape, now allied with the Wyandotte Iroquois, defeated the Talega of the Great Lakes region, extending their influence south into the Ohio Valley. Ironically, when offered a chance to acquire eighteenth century flintlocks, many tribes of the Great Lakes region refused, preferring the bow and arrow for their stealth and rapid fire capabilities.

The bow of the Plains Indians, familiar to many from its appearances in Western films and nineteenth century illustrations, is actually a later form (after c. 1500) shortened for use on horseback. This shortened form came into use following the introduction of horses to North America by the Spanish in the sixteenth century. Before that time, the most common Plains bows resembled more closely, both in their size and draw strength, the European longbows used by archers in the Battle of Agincourt (1415). A surviving specimen of one such Plains longbow, measuring 57 inches (145 centimeters) in length, was recovered from Blanco Canyon in northwest Texas in the 1980's. Found alongside a skeleton and some stone implements, the bow was part of a burial cache located under the lip of a caprock escarpment.

The physical characteristics of this bow are striking in several respects. In addition to its surprising length, the limbs of the bow are recurved, rather than straight as one might expect, imparting a graceful gull-wing appearance. Most surprising of all, the bow is almost round in cross section, except for a shallow quarter-inch groove that runs the length of its inner (or belly) surface, a distinct departure from the rectangular cross sections of most European and modern bows. Also, the bow features two sets of string nocks at each tip, the purpose of which may have been to increase the draw weight of the bow by shortening the limbs and, thus, making the bow more powerful. Another possible explanation may be that because animal fiber bowstrings are affected by moisture, the second set of nocks may have been added to allow the hunter to adjust the string tension to compensate for the inevitable stretching of the sinew or rawhide in damp weather.

As the bows of the Anasazi and the Pueblo people are known to be round in cross section, it is believed that this bow originated not in the heart of the Plains, but farther west, perhaps in northwestern New Mexico. It is known that from prehistoric times onward, people of the Pueblos made periodic autumn and winter migrations to hunt the Plains buffalo for meat and hides. It may have been one of these journeys that the ill-fated hunter and his bow were left behind.

A second prehistoric bow more than 75 inches (190 centimeters) in length, with limbs 1.75 inches (4.5 centimeters) wide tapering to 1.25 inches (3 centimeters) at the tips, was found leaning against a cave wall in central Texas, along the eastern boundary of the Plains, during the later years of the nineteenth century. Apparently made of hickory—although the great age of the wood precludes exact identification—the bow incorporates what appears to be an arrow shelf or rest, a finger-sized notch cut into the handle. Firing the arrow through the resulting notch would result in a partial reduction of the archer's paradox—the tendency of an arrow's shaft to oscillate, flexing along its long axis in flight—thereby increasing the weapon's accuracy.

It is important to note that in both of these instances, the bows came to the Texas Plains from areas further west and northeast, respectively.

SIGNIFICANCE

Although widely adopted by almost all North American Indian cultures, the use of the archery bow is not an absolute universal. Among the Haida of the Northwest coast, for example, the principal hunting strategy was the spearing of fish and seals at close range, and, thus, the bow and arrow never found an enduring niche there. Likewise, the great warrior cultures of early Mexico eschewed the bow in favor of the club and sword, which proved themselves highly effective when wielded by massed warriors in large, tightly organized formations. The bow and arrow seems to have been favored by more loosely organized peoples that tended to hunt and fight as individuals or in small groups. In such a context, the bow became a powerful tool, lending more force to small groups by effectively extending the range, accuracy, and power of their primitive missile weapons—the stopping power of even the short Plains bows being sufficient to fell large animals such as the buffalo when wielded by an experienced archer. In warfare, the Apache further enhanced the arrow's killing potential, making the arrows poisonous by dipping them into decomposing liver or into scorpion or snake venom or by rubbing them with the poison spines of the common cacti (*Opuntia*) mixed with grease.

Following the introduction of the horse, the mounted Apache and Comanche archers became as potent a military force as their Mongolian forebears, whose sweeping raids of conquest devastated medieval Europe. It remains a testament to these Indian archers' skill with the bow and arrow that they won many engagements against better equipped U.S. Cavalry troops before being subjugated in the late nineteenth century.

—*Larry Smolucha*

601 - 700

FURTHER READING

Allely, Steve, and Jim Hamm. *Encyclopedia of Native American Bows, Arrows, and Quivers*. New York: Lyons Press, 1999. Focuses exclusively on the North American bow and arrow. Includes illustrations and maps.

Baker, Tim, et al. *The Traditional Boyer's Bible*. Vol. 3. New York: Lyons Press, 1994. A collection of essays on the origins, design, construction, and proper use of a variety of wooden bows and arrows. This book is highly recommended for those seeking to create replicas. Includes a discussion of bows and arrows found at several significant North American archeological sites.

Francis, Leo, III. *Native Time: An Historical Time Line of Native America*. New York: St. Martin's Press, 1996. A comprehensive historical survey presented in time line format across several simultaneous developmental dimensions: historical, cultural, philosophical, and biographical. Traces related developments in material culture, including the cultural dispersion of the bow and arrow. The time line ranges from the prehistoric Calico culture of the Mojave Desert (c. 200,000 B.C.E.) to the contemporary epoch.

Hamilton, T. M. *Native American Bows*. 2d ed. Columbia, Mo.: Missouri Archaeological Society, 1982. Includes an appendix on making bows, photographs of horn bows and other illustrations, a bibliography, and an index.

Harding, David, ed. *Weapons: An International Encyclopedia from 5000 B.C.E. to 2000 A.D.* New York: St. Martin's Press, 1980. A visual cross-cultural survey of weaponry development (from c. 10,000 B.C.E.), tracing the evolution of hand-thrown missiles to missile throwers (bows) in their diverse forms among world cultures. Well illustrated with detailed, schematic drawings, engravings, and photographs.

Laubin, Reginald. *American Indian Archery*. Norman: University of Oklahoma Press, 1980. Part of the Civilization of the American Indian series, examines the history of the use of the bow and arrow. Includes illustrations, bibliography, and an index.

McGee, W. J. *Seventeenth Annual Report of the American Bureau of Ethnology*. Washington, D.C.: Government Printing Office, 1895-1896. Treats the genesis of the bow and arrow in a representative western coastal culture, the Seri tribe of Sonora and of Tiburón Island (Gulf of California). Traces the origin of the archery bow and establishes parallels between the aim-at-draw postures used by archers of the Seri and African cultures. Scholarly and diverse in scope.

SEE ALSO: Mid-9th century: Invention of Gunpowder and Guns; 11th-12th centuries: First European-Native American Contact; August 26, 1346: Battle of Crécy.

c. 700-1000
BUILDING OF CHICHÉN ITZÁ

Occupied primarily between 700 and 1000, the Chichén Itzá core consists of structures such as the Castillo, the Observatory, and the Great Ball Court. Architectural similarities between Chichén Itzá and the Toltec capital of Tula in Hidalgo, Mexico, have spurred debates about foreign influence, and while once thought to be a Late Postclassic site, many believe it was occupied earlier.

LOCALE: North-central Yucatán, Mexico
CATEGORIES: Architecture; cultural and intellectual history

SUMMARY OF EVENT

Located in the north-central portion of the state of Yucatán in Mexico, the site of Chichén Itzá is situated in the midst of a karstic limestone environment. There are no rivers or lakes nearby, and the primary water source besides rainfall includes karstic sinkholes known as *cenotes*. Caves abound in the region, and the major cave site of Balankanche is located about 2.5 miles (4 kilometers) from Chichén Itzá.

The name Chichén Itzá is Yucatec Mayan for "the mouth of the well of the Itzá." According to legend, the site of Chichén Itzá was founded by the Itzá and ruled by three brothers, one named K'ak'upakal (or Fiery Shield). There are several ideas about where the Itzá originated, including the northern Yucatán coast, the Tabasco/Campeche coast, and the central Mexican Toltec region; however, they most likely originated in the southern Maya lowlands. Major wars and defeats in the south involving kingdoms such as Tikal, Naranjo, and Dos Pilas during the Classic period (between 672 and 692) may have led to the deaths of kings, a loss of power by the noble class, and mass migrations to the north, perhaps resulting in the populating of Chichén Itzá.

Although minor occupation of the site of Chichén Itzá is first thought to have started in the Preclassic and Early

Classic periods (350 B.C.E.-250 C.E.), it has long been thought to have been a primarily early Postclassic site (900-1200) that came to power after other major Maya centers were abandoned. This Postclassic settlement was associated with a Toltec "invasion" stemming from the capital site of Tula in Hidalgo, about 1,000 miles (about 1,600 kilometers) away. The French explorer Claude-Joseph-Désiré Charnay was the first to note the similarities between the style of architecture, art, and iconography of Chichén Itzá and Tula during an 1857-1861 expedition. Supporting the idea of a foreign conquest is the myth of a once great Toltec king known as Quetzalcóatl (Feathered Serpent; also known as Kukulcan in the Maya area), who, after years of successful rule of the Toltecs, fell from power and led them to ruin. He left Tula in shame and is believed to have headed to the east. Spanish bishop Diego de Landa, who wrote about Chichén Itzá during the contact period, noted that a foreign ruler known as Kukulcan arrived to conquer the site. Modern interpretations have interpreted this legend as reflecting a Toltec conquest of Chichén Itzá.

Additionally, this foreign conquest was believed to have occurred because of the distinct architectural styles that were once thought to have represented different chronological periods and cultural influences. Old Chichén, which includes the elaborate mosaic stonework of the Puuc-style architecture such as the Nunnery Palace and the Red Deer House, was thought to represent the earlier "Maya" occupation. In contrast, New Chichén architecture, such as the Castillo and Great Ball Court, was thought to represent the later Toltec-style architecture. These "foreign" structures exhibit few Maya inscriptions, are generally larger, and include images that appear to have Central Mexican influence. However, radiocarbon dating and a reassessment of the ceramics indicate that the site of Chichén Itzá rose to power around 700 and was in decline by around 1000. Additionally, most archaeologists recognize that Old Chichén and New Chichén were actually contemporary and everything was constructed before 1000. As the Toltec occupation at Tula is thought to date to 950-1150, this would indicate that Chichén Itzá was occupied long before Tula rose to prominence.

The Pyramid of Kukulcan (Quetzalcóatl) at Chichén Itzá. (Digital Stock)

The layout of the site core includes major architecture that radiates out from the Cenote of Sacrifice, which measures 150 feet (46 meters) across. A second, smaller *cenote*, known as Xtoloc, is also located in the site center and probably served as a water source. The Cenote of Sacrifice served a primarily ritual function and was the site of ceremonies and offerings to the gods. The *cenote* was dredged by American archaeologist Edward Herbert Thompson in 1904, during which he recovered objects made of jade, obsidian, gold, and pottery. Evidence suggests that a large number of human sacrifices were offered and included men, women, and children.

The site core also contains amazing constructions that exhibit jaguar, sacrifice, and feathered serpent imagery, as well as elaborate stone mosaics. The most prominent structure at the site is the Castillo (or Temple of Kukulcan), located in the main plaza. This four-sided pyramid has a stairway on each side and a large amount of feathered serpent imagery. An earlier pyramid was found inside, with a beautiful jaguar throne painted red and with jade spots and eyes. A reclining *chacmool* figure, representing a Mayan fertility or rain god, a captive noble coaxing the rains, or a figure holding a receptacle for receiving sacrificed hearts, was located nearby. The Temple of the Warriors consists of a temple located on top of a stepped platform surrounded by square columns carved with soldiers who exhibit non-Maya regalia. Two feathered serpent sculptures are found at the entrance to the temple, and a *chacmool* is located at the top of the stairs.

Another important structure, known as El Caracol (or "the snail," named for the spiral staircase inside), is a round structure located on square platforms. It is also known as the Observatory and is believed by many to have astronomical alignments, in which the rising and setting sun, moon, and Venus can be tracked from the doors and windows. Other important structures include the Red House (the Chichanchob), the Nunnery Palace (Casa de las Monjas), the High Priest's Grave (or Osario), the *tzompantli* (skull rack), the Venus platform, the Lower Temple of the Jaguars, and the Great Ball Court, the largest known ball court in Mesoamerica. It should be noted that large numbers of raised roads or *sacbeob* ("white roads" or "white ways") made of stone also radiate throughout the site.

The limestone that is ubiquitous in the region was used to construct the architecture, and plaster made of *sascab* (soft limestone) covered the outside of the buildings. Structures often had elaborate masks and were painted in bright pigments such as red, green, yellow, and blue. However, it should be noted that the site of Chichén Itzá includes a large amount of settlement outside the site core and included perishable structures made of pole and thatch. Although this is where the largest portion of the population lived, small, round rock rings and associated artifacts (such as tools and ceramics) are often the only remnants of this nonelite occupation.

SIGNIFICANCE

Chichén Itzá controlled much of the surrounding area during its reign, including major trade ports on the north coast. After 1000, the site's importance waned, construction stopped, and squatters made up the majority of the settlement. The importance of this site was recognized long after it was in decline. The conqueror Francisco de Montejo (senior) and his soldiers established a temporary settlement in the site center in 1533. Later they were forced out after continued attacks by the Maya. Bishop Diego de Landa visited the site in 1566 and noted that the Cenote of Sacrifice was still a pilgrimage site where visitors went to throw offerings. Other important outside visitors included American adventurer John Lloyd Stephens and British artist Frederick Catherwood in 1842.

A major archaeological project was conducted by the Carnegie Institution in the 1920's in which many of the structures were reconstructed, including the Castillo and the Temple of the Warriors. Today, archaeologists of Mexico's Instituto Nacional de Antropologia e Historia continue to research the site, and thousands of visitors flock to this great center every year.

—*Jennifer P. Mathews*

FURTHER READING

Coe, Michael D. *The Maya*. 6th ed. New York: Thames and Hudson, 1999. Coe argues the traditional view that Chichén Itzá is a Postclassic site that was invaded by the Toltecs.

Coggins, Clemency Chase, and Orrin C. Shane III, eds. *Cenote of Sacrifice: Maya Treasures from the Sacred Well at Chichén Itzá*. Austin: University of Texas Press, 1984. Exhibition catalog of objects recovered from the Cenote of Sacrifice.

De Landa, Diego, and Alfred Tozzer, ed. "Landa's 'Relación de las Cosas de Yucatán': A Translation." *Papers of the Peabody Museum of Archaeology and Ethnology* 18. Cambridge, Mass.: Harvard University Press, 1941. A translation of Bishop de Landa's study of Mayan culture at the contact period, including Chichén Itzá and its continued use as a pilgrimage site.

Jones, Lindsay. *Twin City Tales: A Hermeneutical Reassessment of Tula and Chichén Itzá*. Niwot: University Press of Colorado, 1995. This volume examines the way in which scholars have created a polarized view of the Maya versus the Toltecs, and critically examines the arguments for the similarities between the two sites.

Krochock, Ruth J. "Women in the Hieroglyphic Inscriptions of Chichén Itzá." In *Ancient Maya Women*, edited by Traci Ardren. Walnut Creek, Calif.: AltaMira Press, 2002. Argues that while women rarely are included in the inscriptions of the site, they were nonetheless powerful and provided legitimacy to the male rulers of Chichén Itzá.

Schele, Linda, and Peter Mathews. "Chichén Itzá: The Great Ballcourt." In *The Code of Kings: The Language of Seven Sacred Maya Temples and Tombs*. New York: Scribner, 1998. Describes the debate about the Toltec invasion, discusses information about who founded the site, and focuses on the imagery and inscriptions associated with the Great Ball Court.

See also: c. 600-950: El Tajín Is Built; 7th-8th centuries: Maya Build Astronomical Observatory at Palenque; c. 950-1150: Toltecs Build Tula; 1325-1519: Aztecs Build Tenochtitlán.

Related article in *Great Lives from History: The Middle Ages, 477-1453*: Itzcóatl.

c. 700-1000
Heavy Plow Helps Increase Agricultural Yields

The use of the heavy plow increased agricultural yields, eliminating the need for cross plowing and allowing for the cultivation of rich, damp soils in northern Europe.

Locale: Northern Europe
Categories: Agriculture; economics; environment; science and technology

Summary of Event

Throughout the Middle Ages, farming remained the most important economic activity in Europe. It absorbed the daily labor of nearly all inhabitants and determined social customs and practices. Development and widespread use of the heavy plow, which began gradually in Europe between the eighth and eleventh centuries, was the principal transformation in rural life during this period.

The new wheeled plow, fitted with a coulter or heavy knife fixed to the pole to cut vertically into the soil, a flat, asymmetrical plowshare set at right angle to the coulter to cut the earth horizontally at the root level, and a moldboard to turn the sliced turf to the left or right and create furrows, did not immediately supplant the earlier scratch plow that was fitted with a symmetrically shaped share that merely broke the ground and threw the earth to either side depending on where the "ears" were attached.

The advantages of the scratch plow were its lightness, ease of assembly and handling, and low cost. A single plowman could fit together its wooden pieces that were sometimes reinforced with metal strips. The scratch plow could be pulled by a team of oxen and operated by a lone plowman. This plow remains in use in the Mediterranean areas of Europe where the soils are thinner and the climate more arid. In these regions, the heavier wheeled plow brings too much precious moisture to the surface and thereby reduces fertility. Although it was easier to manipulate and cheaper to operate, the scratch plow required intense manual labor and could not be used efficiently on the heavier soils of northern Europe. Also, because it left a wedge between furrows, cross plowing was necessary. Thus, each field had to be plowed twice. In addition, the fields had to be dug with spades as often as every four years.

The wheeled plow overcame these disadvantages and proved suitable to the heavier turf and damper climate of the north. Its origins can actually be traced to imperial Roman times. Pliny refers to its presence in the lands south of the upper Danube and archaeological evidence indicates its use in the areas inhabited by Slavs, Bulgarians, and Byzantine peoples on the lower Danube, as well as along the North Sea. A hoard of tools uncovered at Osterburken, dating from the fifth century, includes a smaller, similar version, possibly a precursor to the heavy plow. Comparable in shape, the Osterburken plowshare differs only in the worn symmetry of its coulter. Plowshares dating from Carolingian and Anglo-Saxon times were worn on one side indicating use of a moldboard that forced the plow to cut at an incline and create a furrow.

Peasant farmers ploughing c. 1250, from Joseph Strutt's 1775 work, Horda Angel-Cynnan: Or, A Compleat View of the Manners, Customs, Arms, Habits, and of the Inhabitants of England. (Hulton|Archive by Getty Images)

Changes in the rural environment occasioned by the end of the Roman Empire in the west led to the temporary abandonment of the heavier wheeled plow. Roman *latifundia* (landed estates) ceased to exist and villages were more scattered. As monarchical states formed and monastic foundations settled wastelands, the rural population first stabilized then grew, larger fields were once again cultivated, and the heavier wheeled plow became desirable. The Benedictines were particularly important in promoting settled agriculture. Saint Benedict emphasized the virtues of manual labor and many of his followers wore a pruning hook in their girdles symbolic of their agrarian labor. According to Benedictine tradition, Theodulf, from a monastery near Rheims, operated a plow daily for twenty-two years. After his death, his fellow monks venerated his plow at the church of Saint-Thierry.

Archaeological discoveries of plows from Poland, Bohemia, the Rhineland, and Savoy place the redevelopment of the heavy plow between the eighth and tenth centuries. While there is scattered earlier evidence from Cornwall and Wales, the heavy plow was not widely used across England and Wales until the eleventh century. Fossilized furrows from other parts of Europe support the idea of a gradual transformation in plow technology.

The heavy wheeled plowshare reduced manual labor by eliminating the need to cross plow and spade fields by hand. Its weight, coupled with the nature of the soil, demanded greater reliance upon animal power. The single team of oxen gave way to teams of eight or more and ultimately to teams of horses once the fixed wooden head collar was developed. Horses could work a field more rapidly than oxen, though they were more expensive to maintain. The Bayeux Tapestry shows a horse-drawn harrow, and its presence there may help explain the reluctance of English farmers to abandon the oxen for the horse.

While manual labor was saved, it hardly disappeared. An Anglo-Saxon plowman described his daily routine:

> O my lord, I work very hard: I go out at dawn, driving the cattle to the field, and I yoke them to the plow. Nor is the weather so bad in winter that I dare to stay at home, for fear of my lord: but when the oxen are yoked, and the plowshare and coulter attached to the plow, I must plow one whole field a day, or more.

The plowman's fear was well-founded. He had to remain in the field as his tax was tied to the plowing he was expected to perform during the year. The English plowland or hide came to be the unit of assessment, and eventually the day's plowing was standardized at an acre.

The new wheeled plow also improved drainage and increased crop yields. The moldboard turned the furrow to one side only, piling the soil to the center of the field and creating shallow trenches between plowlands. These trenches improved drainage. The better drained fields ensured greater yields in wet and dry years. In wet years, crops flourished on the drier crest of each ridge while in dry ones, crops grew in the furrows. Deeper plowing brought richer soil to the surface, also enhancing soil productivity. At a minimum, fields in France produced four times what had been customary in Charlemagne's time. Slowly, knowledge of marling and manuring became more widespread, and eventually farmers devised the three-field rotation with one field lying fallow every third year. As a result of these changes, all tied to the widespread adoption of the heavier wheeled plow, crops of wheat, rye, spelt, barley, and oats—staples of the European bread diet—rose dramatically across the continent.

Finally, the heavier wheeled plow altered field shape and necessitated agrarian cooperation. Cross plowing resulted in square Roman field types; furrow plowing, especially with large teams of animals, was more suited to longer fields. As farms were divided into the lands of the lord and those of the tenant, field shape adapted to the new technology. The expense of a plow team forced most peasants to either share teams or borrow them from wealthier neighbors in exchange for labor. Thus, even tenurial relationships were revised by the plow as fewer tenants could maintain a purely independent status. Cooperation enhanced and stabilized community.

SIGNIFICANCE

The end result of the heavy wheeled plow was economic growth, a rise in population, the expansion of trade, and the growth of towns and cities. In a very real sense, the heavy wheeled plow nourished the feudal and religious establishments of medieval Europe.

—Michael J. Galgano

FURTHER READING

Astill, Grenville, and Annie Grant, eds. *The Countryside of Medieval England*. Oxford, England: Basil Blackwell, 1988. Essays blend multidisciplinary and traditional scholarship to examine how the countryside was cultivated in medieval England.

Astill, Grenville, and John Langdon, eds. *Medieval Farming and Technology: The Impact of Agricultural Change in Northwest Europe*. New York: Brill, 1997. Treats farming in the Middle Ages from the point of view of the history of technology. Looks at the broad social and economic effects of technological advances in farming, and discusses local, region-specific developments in agriculture of the period.

Campbell, Bruce M. S. *English Seigniorial Agriculture, 1250-1450*. New York: Cambridge University Press, 2000. An in-depth study of the technologies, methods, and effects of late medieval agriculture in England.

Duby, Georges. *Rural Economy and Country Life in the Medieval West*. Translated by Cynthia Postan. 1968. Reprint. Philadelphia: University of Pennsylvania Press, 1998. This work is a valuable introduction to the European rural economy from the Carolingian period to the fourteenth century by a leading French *Annales* historian.

Fossier, Robert. *Peasant Life in the Medieval West*. Translated by Juliet Vale. Oxford, England: Basil Blackwell, 1988. Synthesis of recent scholarship by a modern French scholar to defend the controversial argument that lasting agricultural improvements began only after the tenth century.

Hamerow, Helena. *Early Medieval Settlements: The Archaeology of Rural Communities in North-West Europe, 400-900*. New York: Oxford University Press, 2002. Culls together the evidence of many archaeological excavations to create an overview of rural life in medieval Europe. Includes discussions of agricultural practices and development from 400 to 900.

Rösener, Werner. *Peasants in the Middle Ages*. Translated by Alexander Stützer. Urbana: University of Illinois Press, 1992. Most comprehensive modern synthesis of the difficult and challenging world of European peasants by a leading German scholar.

Slicher Van Bath, B. H. *The Agrarian History of Western Europe, A.D. 500-1850*. Translated by Olive Ordish.

601 - 700

London: Edward Arnold, 1963. Surveys agrarian history from the fall of Rome to industrialization. Good treatment of agricultural productivity based upon statistical evidence.

Speed, Peter, ed. *Those Who Worked: An Anthology of Medieval Sources*. New York: Italica Press, 1997. This collection of primary historical sources includes three sections on agriculture. It presents letters, chronicles, notebooks, scientific treatises, and other medieval texts.

Sweeney, Del, ed. *Agriculture in the Middle Ages: Technology, Practice, and Representation*. Philadelphia: University of Pennsylvania Press, 1995. Collection of essays place changes in agriculture and economics in a cultural context and examine how societal changes shaped views of peasants and their labor.

White, Lynn, Jr. *Medieval Technology and Social Change*. Oxford, England: Oxford University Press, 1980. Sound introduction to the relationship between technology and social change.

SEE ALSO: March 21, 1098: Foundation of the Cistercian Order; c. 1200: Scientific Cattle Breeding Developed.

RELATED ARTICLE in *Great Lives from History: The Middle Ages, 477-1453*: Saint Benedict of Nursia.

c. 700-1100
SETTLEMENT OF THE SOUTH PACIFIC ISLANDS

Between the eighth and twelfth centuries, Polynesians settled most of the islands and island groups in the central and eastern Pacific Ocean. The discovery of New Zealand was one of the last in a long series of deliberate voyages of colonization across the Pacific, which had begun from Southeast Asia or, some scholars hypothesize, South America, some five thousand to seven thousand years earlier.

LOCALE: Cook Islands, Austral Islands, and New Zealand

CATEGORIES: Expansion and land acquisition; exploration and discovery

KEY FIGURES

Kupe (fl. c. 925), a mythical Polynesian navigator who arrived in New Zealand c. 925

Toi (fl. c. 1350), a mythical Polynesian who, according to oral legend, arrived in New Zealand c. 1350

SUMMARY OF EVENT

The Cook-Austral volcanic chain is located on the southern part of the Pacific plate, in a region of shallow seafloor known as the South Pacific superswell. The first settlers of New Zealand (also known as Aotearoa) and many other island groups in the South Pacific were the Polynesians. Archaeological evidence indicates that the Polynesians discovered New Zealand sometime after 800 C.E. Some Central Pacific islands, such as the Marquesas, were probably populated by about 1000 B.C.E., but the earliest vestiges of civilization there date back to only 150 B.C.E. From the Marquesas, the Polynesians branched out to other settlements. The Cook Islands and Austral Islands were settled by the Polynesians sometime shortly before or after they reached New Zealand. Some theories argue that New Zealand was settled first, while others state that the Maoris of New Zealand began their voyage on Rarotonga, the capital island of the sixteen-island Cook group, possibly as early as the fifth century C.E. The southern Cook Islands were apparently settled by Tahitians around 800, while the northern islands were settled a little later by Tongans and Samoans.

The Austral Islands are a seven-island volcanic group sometimes known as the Tubuai Islands. Archaeological diggings in these isolated islands have uncovered habitation sites, council platforms, and marae temples on Rurutu, showing man's presence around the year 900. Tubuai and Rimatara also have the ruins of open-air stone temples, and giant stone tikis have been found on Raivavae that resemble those in the Marquesas Islands and on Easter Island. On Rapa there are remains of seven fortresses on superimposed terraces; such fortresses are found nowhere else in Polynesia except New Zealand, where the Maori people settled. Exquisite wood carvings, now in museums, tell of an artistic people highly evolved in their craft, who were also superb boat builders and daring seafarers.

Scholars believe that the population of these islands occurred by way of long, island-hopping voyages made in large, wood-hulled canoes that enabled the voyagers to take plenty of food, food plants, domesticated animals, and other supplies with them. Opinions concerning why these people spread across the Pacific usually center on ecological factors: limited or declining resources in the homeland, competition for resources, predation, and political motivations such as intertribal strife and religious beliefs. In fact, overpopulation may have been the chief motive for exploration. Some scholars, alternatively, believe that deliberate exploration, such as that undertaken by Europeans in the sixteenth through eighteenth centuries, also motivated the voyages.

Although the names of the early voyagers have been lost to history, the legends still tell of certain individuals who may or may not have been real. One mythical Polynesian navigator was Kupe, who arrived in New Zealand around 925. Another was a mythical Maori named Toi, who was estimated to have arrived in New Zealand around 1350. The latter individual came with the Great Fleet, supposedly composed of eight giant canoes, which transported a mass of Polynesian settlers. Like many other Polynesian legends, this story is open to debate; some authorities question the date of 1350, while others question whether the expedition ever happened.

It is likely, however, that because the first Polynesians settled on the east coast of New Zealand, the settlers may have come from islands to the east, such as Tahiti or the Marquesas. On arrival, the Polynesians found New Zealand to be the home of many large, flightless birds, particularly the moa. The eleven species of moa varied in size, from the size of a turkey to that of the giant moa, which stood over 10 feet (about 3 meters) tall. Today, most authorities think the Polynesians originated between five thousand and seven thousand years ago in Southeast Asia.

A variety of theories have been posited to account for the Polynesian migrations. In the mid-twentieth century, the Norwegian explorer and archaeologist Thor Heyerdahl posited that the Polynesians had originated from South America. Although linguistic and physical characteristics of the Polynesians differ from those of South American Indians, Heyerdahl proved in 1947, with his now-famous Kon-Tiki expedition, that a raft could have traveled from South America to the South Pacific islands in 101 days. Heyerdahl's theory is best suited to the settlement of New Zealand, since one of the staple cultivated food crops of pre-European New Zealand, the kumara—a type of sweet potato—originates from central South America.

However, Heyerdahl's and other theories positing a South American origin have now been largely abandoned because of the faunal, floral, and linguistic similarities between the Polynesians and Southeast Asians. The early adzes and fishhooks of New Zealand seem clearly to have precursors in other parts of Polynesia. Also, the fact that the Polynesian islands and island groups were essentially settled in a west-to-east chronology indicates that the people most likely came from Southeast Asia. Thus, the preponderance of evidence linking the Polynesians with Southeast Asia is perhaps an indication that the Southeast Asians traveled as far east as South America, where they discovered the kumara and took it back to the islands.

SIGNIFICANCE

Some have attributed the discovery of various Pacific islands to luck, but colonization of the Austral and Cook Islands and New Zealand is largely a testimony to the development of navigational skills among ancient and medieval Southeast Asian peoples. Although the oral tradition of the South Pacific islands does not provide much information, the Polynesians' knowledge of navigation was probably based on observation of the winds, stars, marine currents, birds, and migration routes. The journeys undertaken by the Polynesians in their fragile craft dwarf the voyages of exploration boasted of by the later European explorers. In a sense, the colonization of the South Pacific island groups represents the more important "age of exploration": These migrations led to the peopling of new continents, and the fact that Stone Age peoples had the wherewithal to journey thousands of miles is remarkable in itself. Considering their small seacraft and the daunting odds they overcame in traveling such great distances on the open seas, these Polynesians may have been the greatest navigators and sailors in the history of the world—even more advanced than the Vikings or other European explorers of a later era.

—Dale L. Flesher

FURTHER READING

Barrow, Terence. *The Art of Tahiti and the Neighbouring Society, Austral and Cook Islands.* New York: Thames and Hudson, 1979. A specialized work on Polynesian art.

Heyerdahl, Thor. *American Indians in the Pacific: The Theory Behind the Kon-Tiki Expedition.* Chicago: Rand McNally, 1953. A scholarly explanation of why Polynesians might have originated in South America.

_______. *Kon-Tiki: Across the Pacific by Raft.* Chicago: Rand McNally, 1950. Heyerdahl's famous story of his adventures as he replicated the route that he theorized that early South American Indians made across the

Pacific in search of what are now known as Polynesian islands.
Irwin, Geoffrey. *The Prehistoric Exploration and Colonisation of the Pacific*. New York: Cambridge University Press, 1992. Suggests that the Pacific Islanders could have taken advantage of seasonal wind patterns to sail around the open ocean and would then have had a reasonable chance of getting back to where they started without incurring too much risk.
McLean, Mervyn. *Weavers of Song: Polynesian Music and Dance*. Honolulu: University of Hawaii Press, 1999. An overview of Polynesian music and dance.
Siikala, Jukka. *Akatokamanava: Myth, History, and Society in the Southern Cook Islands*. Auckland, New Zealand: Polynesian Society, in association with the Finnish Anthropological Society, 1991. A good general history of the Cook Islands.

SEE ALSO: Late 13th century: Maoris Hunt Moa to Extinction.

c. 700-1253
CONFEDERATION OF THAI TRIBES

Loose confederations of tribes of people speaking Thai or Tai languages enabled the ancestors of the modern Thai, Lao, and other groups to maintain ties while migrating into Southeast Asia.

LOCALE: Southern China, Laos, and Thailand
CATEGORIES: Expansion and land acquisition; government and politics

KEY FIGURES

Pilaoko (c. 700-750), king of Nanzhao, r. 728-750
Kublai Khan (1215-1294), Mongol khan, r. 1260-1294; Yuan Dynasty ruler, r. 1279-1294
Sri Indraditya (Bang Klang Hao; c. 1200-1257), Thai chieftain, first king of Sukhothai, r. c. 1239-1257
Ramakhamhaeng (c. 1235-c. 1317), son of Sri Indraditya, king of Sukhothai, r. c. 1279-c. 1317
Mangrai (1239-1317), king of Lan Na, r. 1259-1317

SUMMARY OF EVENT

Centuries before the development of Siam (Thailand) and Laos, tribes of the ancestors of the Thai and Lao were grouped into *muangs*, or principalities, that maintained alliances. These alliances may have led to the creation of the ancient kingdom of Nanzhao in Yunnan, and they enabled migrants into Southeast Asia to unite against the Cambodian empire.

Scholars disagree on the origins of the Thai people. Some argue that the Thai have lived on the lands now known as Thailand since prehistoric times. Most maintain that they migrated into Southeast Asia from some other location. The most common view on the origin of the Thai is that they moved south from China and that the Thai and Lao nations grew out of a loose and shifting confederation of tribes over the course of several centuries.

The Thai (also known as Siamese); the Lao; and the Shan, who are located mainly in contemporary northeastern Burma, are three of the largest groups of people who speak Tai, or T'ai, languages. Ancient Chinese documents refer to these people as the Ailao. According to some accounts, the Ailao moved up into south China from the Indian subcontinent and established a federation of *muangs* (*muong* or *meuang*). The word *muang* in modern Thai refers to a country or a people, and Thailand itself is often known as Muang Thai. The ancient word appears to have meant something along the lines of a tribe or a principality, a collection of scattered villages. A *chao*, or lord, led each *muang*. Leadership was based on personal ties between the lord and those who followed him, and the personal qualities of lords gave them their authority.

According to this view of history, the Thai tribes were based mainly in the mountainous plateau of modern Yunnan Province, south of the Yangtze River in China. They would frequently join together against some common enemy, such as the Chinese. This kind of union may have led to the first Thai kingdom, Nanzhao (Nanchao), located mainly in Yunnan.

The Chinese had established their sovereignty over the Ailao or Thai tribes by about the middle of the third century. Some of the tribes moved south in response. The view of many historians is that Nanzhao continued to serve as a central starting point for the migration of bands out of southern China. During the middle of the seventh century, the tribes who remained in Yunnan joined together to revolt against Chinese rule. The confederation resulted in the rise of King Sinulo, supposedly the first Thai ruler of the kingdom of Nanzhao. The Chinese Tang Dynasty (Tan'g; 618-907) accepted the existence of the new kingdom and established a treaty with it. The ties between Nanzhao and China resulted in many lasting Chinese cultural influences on the Thai.

Political connections between the Thai of Nanzhao and the Chinese became stronger with threats from the Tibetans. King Pilaoko, who came to the throne of Nanzhao in 728, allied himself with the Chinese emperor Xuanzong (Hsüan-tsung; r. 712-756) and agreed to defend the borders of China from all enemies, especially from Tibet. Pilaoko then turned to attack Tibet, and he seized several Tibetan settlements.

Pilaoko's son Kolofeng reportedly turned against the Chinese. Kolofeng struck an alliance with the Tibetans and invaded China. In response, the Chinese invaded Nanzhao once again, in 752-754, but failed to impose their will on the rebellious state. Over the next 150 years, Nanzhao maintained troubled relations with China. However, after about 900, the kingdom received little mention in the Chinese annals, indicating that these years may have been peaceful ones.

In 1253, Kublai Khan, chief of the Mongols in China, invaded and conquered Nanzhao. This brought an end to the kingdom. Some historians have claimed that the rulers of Nanzhao were not Thai at all, but members of some other ethnic group. Whatever the ethnicity of those at the top, though, the Mongol conquest apparently set off another large wave of migration. Although some Tai-speaking people remain in modern-day southern China, many tribes left for other locations with the breakup of Nanzhao.

The Thai migrants who moved southward found *muangs* already established in what is now Thailand. These tribal settlements were under the rule of the Cambodian (Khmer) empire, but some of them, such as the states of Lan Na and Phayao, in modern northern Thailand, had already placed themselves under Thai leadership. The most famous early Thai state, Sukhothai, was originally a tribal chiefdom under the political and cultural direction of the Cambodians. The earliest monuments of Sukhothai, which means "dawn of happiness," were built in the style of the Cambodians. Because the Cambodians had been heavily influenced by Indian civilization, India ultimately replaced China as a cultural model for the Thai.

Traveling along the banks of rivers and streams, the migrating Thai tribes entered a Cambodian empire that was open to the rise of new powers. Following the death of the Cambodian ruler Jayavarman VII around 1220, there appears to have been a great deal of political disorder in the lands to the south of China. Thus, although the Mongol invasion provided pressure to move out of Yunnan, new opportunities seem to have arisen around the Mekong and Chao Phraya rivers. The Mongols may also have served as something as an inspiration for the loosely confederated Thai tribes. According to the famous French scholar George Coedès, the military feats of the Mongols had captured the imagination of the Thai rulers.

In addition to the existing Thai *muangs* in the south, new principalities came into existence at about this time. The principality of Muang Nai was founded on a tributary of the Salween River in 1223. Even Assam, in the far eastern part of modern-day India, became Thai territory.

At the beginning of the twelfth century, the Thai tribes who had settled in the upper basin of the Chao Praya River grew in strength and political organization. In the early years of the thirteenth century, just before the Mongols invaded Nanzhao, the Thai chiefs of Chieng Rung and Chieng Suen on the upper Mekong, the river that now separates Thailand and Laos, entered into a marriage alliance between their children. This can be seen as a new expression of the old confederation of Thai tribes that may have led to the emergence of Nanzhao in earlier years.

In 1238, an alliance between Thai chiefs enabled them to attack and defeat a Cambodian garrison at Sukhothai, which was at that time the capital city of the northwestern section of the Cambodian empire. One of those chieftains, Bang Klang Hao, took the Indian name of Sri Indraditya. He became the first king of Sukhothai and the father of the most celebrated early Thai ruler, Ramakhamhaeng (literally, "Rama the brave").

During the first half of the thirteenth century, a confederation of Thai rulers of Sukhothai defeated their Cambodian overlords and set up an independent Thai kingdom. Driving the Cambodians southward, the Thais, under the leadership of Sukhothai, expanded their power in all directions. In addition to conquest, the rulers of Sukhothai used the common bonds of language and ethnicity to establish networks of marriage alliances with the ruling families of other Thai states. Religion also served to cement their union because the Thai tribes had adopted Theravāda Buddhism, the school of Buddhism that continues to predominate in Burma, Thailand, Laos, and Cambodia.

Thai historians usually date the origin of their nation from the reign of Ramakhamhaeng. This son of Sri Indraditya continued to forge alliances with other Thai princes. In particular, he formed pacts with Mangrai, king of Lan Na in northern Thailand, and with Ngam Muang, the prince of the Thai *muang* of Phayao. However, as Sukhothai spread its power over a large number of Thai tribes, many of the tribes began to become part of a single state and to move from a confederation to the beginnings of a unified nation.

SIGNIFICANCE

The confederations formed by Thai tribes allowed these groups to maintain a common identity during the migration from China into Southeast Asia. They also enabled these groups to defend themselves against other groups, including the Mongols and Chinese. These tribal alliances also served to promote the creation of kingdoms that became larger states.

—*Carl L. Bankston III*

FURTHER READING

Coedès, George. *The Indianized States of Southeast Asia*. Translated by Susan Brown Cowing. Honolulu: East-West Center Press, 1968. The classic work on Southeast Asian history.

Freeman, Michael. *Lanna: Thailand's Northern Kingdom*. London: Thames and Hudson, 2001. Traces the settlement of northern Thailand by different ethnic groups and describes the artifacts and architecture of the region.

Higham, Charles, and Rachanie Thosarat. *Prehistoric Thailand: From Early Settlement to Sukhothai*. London: Thames and Hudson, 1998. The last section discusses the arrival of the Thai and the rise of Sukhothai.

Wyatt, David K. *Thailand: A Short History*. New Haven, Conn.: Yale University Press, 1986. Provides an introduction to Thai history, including some coverage of the early centuries.

SEE ALSO: 618: Founding of the Tang Dynasty; 729: Founding of Nanzhao; 832: Nanzhao Subjugates Pyu; 863: Nanzhao Captures Hanoi; 877-889: Indravarman I Conquers the Thai and the Mons; 1259: Mangrai Founds the Kingdom of Lan Na; 1271-1295: Travels of Marco Polo; 1295: Ramkhamhaeng Conquers the Mekong and Menam Valleys; 1350: Ramathibodi I Creates First Thai Legal System.

RELATED ARTICLE in *Great Lives from History: The Middle Ages, 477-1453*: Kublai Khan.

8th-14th centuries
CAHOKIA BECOMES THE FIRST NORTH AMERICAN CITY

At its height between 1050 and 1150, Cahokia was the largest city in North America before the arrival of Europeans.

LOCALE: Cahokia (now near East St. Louis, Missouri)
CATEGORIES: Cultural and intellectual history; environment; trade and commerce; architecture

SUMMARY OF EVENT

The extensive village of Cahokia, whose remains lie 8 miles (13 kilometers) east of present-day East St. Louis, Missouri, was the largest and most influential settlement in precontact (pre-European) North America, boasting great earthen mounds, an "urban" population, sophisticated artwork, and an extensive trade network. It was one component in the large and long-lived mound-builder complex whose influence spread over what is now the eastern United States, and it developed from the artistic and conceptual legacy of the Northeastern Archaic and Woodlands periods that preceded it. When the center of power of the eastern half of the country moved south, beginning about 700, a new southern culture was created that is today called Mississippian. The Mississippian peoples of the American Southeast carried mound building, the burial of the dead, and artistic creativity to new levels. Each of the major power centers, of which Cahokia was the greatest and the earliest, was a ceremonial hub for a large area of the surrounding countryside, including dozens of satellite communities and scores of smaller villages, whose inhabitants paid tribute to a ruling class.

Founded around 600, Cahokia grew during a four-hundred-year-period into a large settlement. The city, including its "suburban" populations, covered about 6.5 square miles (17 square kilometers). Population estimates at its zenith, c. 1050-1150, range from eight thousand to more than forty thousand people, although most estimates fall between ten thousand and twenty thousand.

The city was ideally situated at the confluence of the Mississippi and Missouri Rivers on a floodplain 80 miles (130 kilometers) long, known as the American Bottom. This location provided the population with fertile soil, extensive forests, and abundant fish and game. Settlements spread slowly and grew in size between 800 and 1000 and then expanded rapidly in the Mississippian period (1000-1400), as more intense farming, especially of corn, made rapid population growth possible.

Cahokia's location was also optimal to transport and control the trade goods that were moved along lakes and rivers, some possibly connected by canals. Historic accounts tell of 50-foot canoes carrying tons of goods. Merchants traded with cultures from the Gulf coast to the Great Lakes and from the Atlantic coast to Oklahoma, as Mississippian culture spread across that vast area. Goods were imported from many locations; copper came from the area around Lake Superior, mica from the southern Appalachian Mountains, shells from the Atlantic and Gulf coasts, and galena, ocher, hematite, chert, fluorite, quartz, and finely made ceramics from the lower Mississippi Valley. Salt and stone hoes were among the items exported.

Mississippian settlements are distinguished by mounds. Flat-topped examples are the most prominent, followed by conical mounds and rectangular ridge top mounds. Cahokia had about 120 earthen mounds, possibly more than six times as many as the next largest Mississippian settlement, that of Moundville in Alabama. Some with flat tops supported civic buildings and the residences of Cahokia's elite. One provided the foundation for the charnel house, a funeral-processing center where the honored dead were prepared for burial. Some conical mounds accommodated burial places for the elite, as did ridge top mounds. One conical mound in the central area appears to have been the resting place of the aristocracy.

The preeminent structure at the site is Monks Mound, so called because early in the nineteenth century a group of Trappist monks were growing wheat and fruit trees on the tremendous earthen structure that stood at the center of the site. They planned to build a monastery, but disease and poverty forced them to leave in 1813. Monks Mound, which contains 6.6 million cubic meters (22 million cubic feet) of earth, is the largest structure in precontact North America and the largest precontact earthen structure in the New World. Situated at the northern edge of the 16-hectare (40-acre) Grand Plaza (the primary gathering and ceremonial area), it covers 5.6 hectares (14 acres) at the base and rises in four terraces to a height of 30.5 meters (100 feet). Excavations and core samples indicate that it was built in stages between 900 and 1200 and went through fourteen different building phases.

Some scholars believe that each new leader may have been responsible for an enlargement of the mound. At the summit there was a clay floor, posts 1 meter (3 feet) thick, and a wooden building 31.5 meters long and 14.5 meters wide (104 by 48 feet). If Cahokia resembled better-documented Southeast mound settlements, its leaders may have governed from this summit or lived here, or bones of the deceased may have been stored in a temple.

Tourists climb the steps of Monks Mound at Cahokia. (AP/Wide World Photos)

In the thirteenth century, a stockade consisting of about fifteen thousand logs the size of telephone poles was constructed enclosing a central area containing sixteen mounds including Monks Mound. Towers with raised platforms were created from which arrows could be shot, even though there is little evidence of invasion. This area of about 80 hectares (200 acres) was presumably a sacred precinct where the elite lived and were buried. In or near this central precinct, at least five circles of posts once stood, the largest 130 meters (427 feet) in diameter. Because of the resemblance to England's Stonehenge, the circles of standing wooden posts became known as Woodhenge. The circles were almost certainly linked with posts placed along the horizon to mark solstice and equinox sunrises and sunsets and other important dates. The Grand Plaza, noted above, was predominant over six major plazas within village boundaries. As Cahokia's plazas are aligned on the cardinal directions with Monks Mound at the crossing, some scholars think it is clear that Cahokia is a landscape cosmogram. Monks Mound itself is aligned with the position of the sun at the equinoxes.

Between 1200 and 1300, Cahokia began to decline. The village may have become exhausted through a shortage of physical resources because of an ever-growing population. Also, shifting climate patterns between 1150 and 1350 were not conducive to growing corn. There was a decrease in the number of houses and the amount of pottery. Some scholars feel that the growing pressures led to political failure and subsequent population abandonment. The village's population declined to about four thousand individuals by 1400, and when French explorers reached the area around 1700, they found nothing but a few overgrown mounds.

SIGNIFICANCE

The first archaeological excavations at Cahokia took place in the 1920's under the direction of Warren K. Moorehead of the R. S. Peabody Museum in Andover, Massachusetts. Moorehead's work put to rest nineteenth century imaginings that the mounds had been built by colonists from Europe or even by mysterious wanderers such as the lost tribes of Israel. Even though Hernando de Soto had described the construction of Southeastern mounds in 1539, it took until the early twentieth century for Moorehead to illustrate conclusively that these were packed earth mounds made by the hands and feet of American Indian men and women. In the 1940's and 1950's, archaeologists from the University of Michigan, the Illinois State Museum, the Gilcrease Institute of Tulsa, and elsewhere conducted scattered excavations at the site. The most intensive work began in the 1950's when Interstates 55 and 70 were routed though the site.

The 1967 to 1971 excavation of Mound 72, a ridge top mound just south of Monks Mound, yielded spectacular findings. The mound, originally three separate smaller mounds, contained about 280 burials dating to 1000-1050. Many of the practices paralleled those of the Natchez, a Mississippian people who survived into the contact period and who were described by late-seventeenth century Europeans. Some of the dead at Cahokia were clearly elite citizens, carried and buried in litters or wrapped in mats. Others seemed to have been hastily deposited. In one lavish burial, a man about forty years of age had been placed on a bird-shaped platform of nearly twenty thousand marine shell beads. Around him were other bodies, some reburied, perhaps servants to aid him in the next world, or relatives to accompany him. On top of six nearby burials were two caches of more than eight hundred newly made arrowheads, fifteen large concave ground-stone discs (chunky stones used in a ceremonial game), a roll of unprocessed mica, a three-foot-long roll of copper (possibly a ceremonial staff), and more marine-shell beads. Several mass burials, most of females between the age of 15 and 25, appear to have been sacrificial victims.

Since the 1950's, much of the site, including more than forty mounds, has been destroyed. Land has been plowed for farms and bulldozed for subdivisions, minimalls, and highways. Sixty-eight of the mounds are preserved within the 890 hectare (2,200 acre) Cahokia Mounds State Historic Site, managed by the Illinois Historic Preservation Agency. In 1982, the United Nations Educational, Scientific, and Cultural Organization (UNESCO) named the Cahokia Mounds a World Heritage Site.

—*Zena Pearlstone*

FURTHER READING

Chappell, Sally A. Kitt. *Cahokia: Mirror of the Cosmos*. Chicago: University of Chicago Press, 2002. A look at the geological, historical, and cultural history of Cahokia. Includes photographs, maps, prints, and drawings.

Emerson, Thomas E. *Cahokia and the Archaeology of Power.* Tuscaloosa: University of Alabama Press, 1997. A study of power relations at Cahokia and its surroundings.

O'Connor, Mallory McCane. *Lost Cities of the Ancient Southeast*. Gainesville: University Press of Florida, 1995. An account of the Mississippian period with an informative chapter on Cahokian art.

Pauketat, Timothy R., and Thomas E. Emerson, eds. *Cahokia: Domination and Ideology in the Mississippian World*. Lincoln: University of Nebraska Press, 2000. Explores various aspects of Cahokian life and history, including religion, trade, social organization, and mound construction.

Young, Biloine Whiting, and Melvin L. Fowler. *Cahokia: The Great Native American Metropolis*. Urbana: University of Illinois Press, 2000. A popular account of Cahokia, surveying more than two centuries of general questions and scientific investigation.

SEE ALSO: 7th-13th centuries: Mogollons Establish Agricultural Settlements; 8th-15th centuries: Hohokam Adapt to the Desert Southwest; 9th-15th centuries: Plains Village Culture Flourishes; c. 800-1350: Mississippian Mound-Building Culture Flourishes.

8th-15th centuries

HOHOKAM ADAPT TO THE DESERT SOUTHWEST

The agriculture-based Hohokam adapted to a challenging desert environment, utilizing an innovative hydroagricultural economy. Their successful, productive economy allowed for a rich cultural apparatus, including sophisticated ceramics, stonework, and shell jewelry, in addition to features that mirror a Mexican stimulus: ball courts and pyramid mounds.

LOCALE: North American Southwest
CATEGORIES: Agriculture; architecture; cultural and intellectual history; science and technology

SUMMARY OF EVENT

The Hohokam were an agriculture-based people who successfully adapted to a desert environment not suited for food cultivation. There exists no consensus among current archaeologists regarding Hohokam origins or the chronological sequence of development. Some scholars have suggested that the Hohokam were migrants from the south. In this model, the migrants displaced an earlier indigenous culture in the southwestern desert. Other fieldworkers interpret the Hohokam as being indigenous, and their roots are traced to an archaic hunting and gathering tradition that evolved into a sedentary agricultural society.

Pioneering archaeological work on the Hohokam began in 1888 when Frank Hamilton Cushing excavated at the Los Muertos and Los Guanacos sites in the Salt River Valley. In 1891, Cosmos Mindeleff worked at Casa Grande, a large Hohokam dwelling near the Gila River. A number of archaeologists, including J. W. Fewkes and Frederick Hodge, excavated numerous sites in the late nineteenth and early twentieth centuries, in an attempt to understand spatial distribution and cultural traits. Work at the large pueblo of Snaketown on the Gila River by Harold Gladwin and Emil Haury, among others, began in 1934, with excavations continuing into the mid-1960's. In the twentieth century, archaeologists focused on varied aspects of Hohokam society and culture, including canal irrigation, ceramics manufacture, settlement pattern, chronology, and the diffusion of cultural traits from Mesoamerica, as well as the institutional framework of Hohokam society, which remains poorly understood.

Although debate persists over the chronological sequence, a general framework suggests that the Hohokam were farming in the river valleys by 300 B.C.E. By 300 C.E., significant changes were discernible in the cultural apparatus, which included sunken ball courts and earthen platform mounds. The large canal systems, essential for a successful agricultural rather than hunter-gatherer life, were well established by 700. Between 1250 and 1450 Hohokam occupation was greatly restricted, and it ultimately led to the abandonment of sites. In some cases, sites such as Snaketown were abandoned by 1200.

The Hohokam inhabited an area of about 45,000 square miles (120,000 square kilometers). Much of this region, including the Sonoran Desert, exhibits variability in elevation, hydrology, and vegetation. Summer temperatures regularly exceed 100 degrees, and annual rainfall for much of the region is often less than 30 centimeters (12 inches).

Within this region a great variety of flora and fauna supplemented an agricultural economy. Remains of prickly pear cactus, little barley grass, amaranth, and tansy mustard, among numerous other plants, have been recovered from Hohokam archaeological sites. Fauna that were hunted, trapped, and collected included rabbits, rodents, deer, and reptiles.

The primary subsistence strategies of the Hohokam, however, were agricultural and were linked to an irrigation technology. Among the crops produced, maize was the most important. Maize production began about 300 B.C.E. at the large community of Snaketown. Drought-resistant strains were probably developed and planted over a great period of time. Cotton was produced for its consumable seeds as well as for its fibers, which Hohokam weavers made into cloth. Beans of various types were cultivated, and varieties of domesticated squash were probably an important cultigen. However, very little evidence exists that attests to the cultivation of native plants. Also, domesticated livestock were unknown.

Canalization allowed for agriculture. By ensuring harvests in an environment prone to drought, the significant amount of labor required for food-gathering tasks could be channeled into producing a sophisticated material culture.

Hohokam waterworks channeled water from the rivers to individual fields. Canals could be quite extensive: Several near what is now Phoenix, Arizona, were 10 miles (16 kilometers) in length. Some canals exceeded 30 miles (50 kilometers) in length and crisscrossed the desert floor. Smaller branches directed water to individual fields. Canal gates that functioned to open and close off the flow of water were probably designed from woven grass mats. By 1200, Hohokam waterworks were very complex; some canals were up to 30 feet (9 meters) wide and 10 feet (3 meters) deep. Earthen dams on rivers directed water into the canals, and canal walls were occasionally lined with a clay mixture to prevent leakage. Construction incorporated a slight grade to facilitate water flow: The main canal at Snaketown dropped slightly more than 5 feet per mile (1 meter per kilometer).

Domestic architecture consisted of pit houses, the primary domestic form through much of the Hohokam sequence. Houses averaged about 27 square yards (23 square meters) in area and were about 1 foot (about one-third of a meter) deep. Poles were set in the ground and supported the roof, which was constructed of reeds or grass. Walls were designed from rush or reeds and slanted inward. A covering of earth completed the dwelling. Late in the Hohokam sequence (post-1300), large multistoried buildings such as Casa Grande were constructed. Casa Grande, about 60 miles (about 37 kilometers) from Phoenix, Arizona, measured about 40 by 60 feet (about 12 by 18 meters). The adobe walls were 4 feet (slightly more than 1 meter) thick at ground level.

The Casa Grande ruins, the most important Hohokam site, under its protective cover near the Gila River in Arizona. (AP/Wide World Photos)

The Hohokam funerary complex centered around cremation. After a body was burned, ashes and bones were gathered and buried in a ceramic vessel. There is little evidence from funerary practices to infer evolving status or social rank.

Villages of the period around 600 were small, probably never exceeding two hundred individuals. Snaketown may have held a maximum population of two thousand people by the end of the period (twelfth century). Hohokam architecture included raised earthen platforms and ball courts. One platform at Snaketown measured 26 yards long by 21 yards wide and nearly 3 yards high (29 meters long by 23 meters wide and about 3 meters high). Presumably community-wide ceremonial activities occurred atop these low earthen mounds. Ball courts were sunken with raised walls. These were oval depressions constructed in the ground about 55 yards long (about 50 meters) with sloping walls about 3.5 to 5.5 yards high (about 3 to 5 meters) on each side. The presence of ball courts has led archaeologists to suggest cultural diffusion from Mexico. The Mesoamerican ball game, or a variant, may have been played in these courts.

Ceramic technology included a number of different decorative patterns and motifs such as plain red ware, red on gray, and red on buff. Vessel shapes included animal and human effigy forms, plates, jars, and bowls of different sizes.

Hohokam stonework was extraordinarily sophisticated. Examples included effigy forms, a range of animals and birds, tools, metates (grinding stones) used in food processing, polished stone vessels, and stone palettes.

The Hohokam shell industry produced exquisite items and demonstrated a high level of specialization. Bracelets, rings, necklaces, and acid-etched shell were produced from a variety of shell species, most of which came from the Gulf of California.

SIGNIFICANCE

In fifteen hundred years of residency in the Sonoran Desert and river valleys, the Hohokam achieved a remarkable adaptation to a difficult if not unfriendly environment. Their agricultural engineering skills permitted the creation of a delicate and sophisticated material culture. The reality of their engineering achievements becomes increasingly remarkable when compared to other preindustrial cultures, especially as the Hohokam lacked the wheel, draft animals, and metals such as bronze or iron.

The Hohokam most likely were products of significant amounts of cultural diffusion from central and northern Mexico over a great period of time. The demand for exotic bird plumage, the plant complex, ear spools, effigy vessels, copper bells, and artistic motifs, in addition to civic architecture, suggests powerful southern contacts. However, the centralized political administration that was necessary for various projects utilizing controlled labor in Mexico appears not to be a feature of Hohokam society. Family units and loosely coordinated groups of farmers could have provided the necessary labor for the construction and maintenance of the great waterworks systems. No evidence exists for a developed bureaucratic class among the Hohokam. This fact makes the Hohokam achievement even more unique.

—*Rene M. Descartes*

FURTHER READING

Abbott, David R. *Ceramics and Community Organization Among the Hohokam*. Tucson: University of Arizona Press, 2000. Discusses the chemistry of Hohokam ceramics, the canal system, social and cultural organization, and more. Includes a bibliography and an index.

Crown, Patricia L., and W. James Judge, eds. *Chaco and Hohokam: Prehistoric Regional Systems in the American Southwest*. Santa Fe, N.M.: School of American Research Press, 1991. An exhaustive analysis of Hohokam archaeology. Includes a bibliography and an index.

Doyel, David E., Suzanne K. Fish, and Paul R. Fish, eds. *The Hohokam Village Revisited*. Glenwood Springs, Colo.: American Association for the Advancement of Science, 2000. Topics include the origins, chronology, village structure, demography, and regional diversity of Hohokam culture.

Fish, Paul R. "The Hohokam." In *Dynamics of Southwest Prehistory*, edited by Linda S. Cordell and George J. Gumerman. Washington, D.C.: Smithsonian Institution Press, 1989. A survey article synthesizing information on the Hohokam from a number of perspectives. Includes bibliographies and an index.

Haury, Emil W. *The Hohokam, Desert Farmers and Craftsmen: Excavations at Snaketown, 1964-1965*. Tucson: University of Arizona Press, 1976. An indispensable study of the Hohokam that analyzes the Snaketown excavations. Includes appendixes and a bibliography.

McGuire, Randall H., and Michael B. Schiffer, eds. *Hohokam and Patayan: Prehistory of Southwestern Arizona*. New York: Academic Press, 1982. A multifaceted study dealing with the natural environment, archaeological history, theory, and issues of chronology. Includes appendixes and a bibliography.

Patterson, Berniece. "The Art and Achievements of the Hohokam." *Arts and Activities* 126, no. 5 (2000): 42-43. Discusses the history of Hohokam arts.

SEE ALSO: 7th-13th centuries: Mogollons Establish Agricultural Settlements; 8th-14th centuries: Cahokia Becomes the First North American City; 9th-15th centuries: Plains Village Culture Flourishes; c. 800-1350: Mississippian Mound-Building Culture Flourishes.

701
TAIHŌ LAWS REFORM JAPANESE GOVERNMENT

The Taihō laws revised earlier legal codes and formed the basis for the ritsuryō system, the foundation of Japanese legal and governmental practice until the tenth century. In addition, the bureaucratic system created by the Taihō code continued to provide the basis for the organization of the Japanese aristocracy until the nineteenth century.

LOCALE: Japan
CATEGORY: Laws, acts, and legal history

KEY FIGURES

Awata no Mahito (d. 719), imperial bureaucrat
Fujiwara Fuhito (659-720), great councillor and minister of the right
Prince Osakabe (d. 719), imperial prince

SUMMARY OF EVENT

The Taika reforms of 645-646 transformed the Japanese state and produced the legal foundation of centralized government. The legal precepts put forward in the Taika reform edict of 646 were limited in scope, however, and some scholars believe that even these were later inventions designed to make the Taika reforms seem to be more important than they actually were. In any case, a more detailed legal code known as the Asuka Kiyomihara code was promulgated in 689 as a way to restore order after a period of domestic strife. At this time, Japan's political system was relatively undeveloped and the Japanese administration looked to Tang China for inspiration.

China's Tang Dynasty (T'ang; 618-907) was at its height in the second half of the seventh century, and Chinese law, philosophy, and religion, three important components of good government during this period, were held in great esteem by the Japanese nobility. Many scholars believe that in the years after the fall of the Roman Empire, Tang China was the most complex and advanced society on earth. The Tang state consisted of a highly centralized court supported by an elaborate and efficient bureaucracy. Order was maintained through the enforcement of a complex body of penal law, and the entire system was buttressed by a system of conscription and taxation by which the productive might of the lower classes was harnessed. Japan, which had yet to establish a permanent capital when the Taihō code came into effect in 701, clearly looked up to the great continental civilization. As a result, Tang legal concepts came to exert a dominant influence over the Asuka Kiyomihara code and the more important legal developments that followed.

In the early eighth century, the decision was made at the Japanese court to strengthen imperial legal authority, and a commission was appointed to produce a revised code of laws. Notable courtiers such as Prince Osakabe, Fujiwara Fuhito, and Awata no Mahito all had a hand in the compilation of the new document. The code went into effect during the second year of the Taihō era from which it took its name. Including both penal and administrative laws, the Taihō code consisted of seventeen volumes in all. No original copies of the code survive, but other sources have given scholars an idea of its contents.

The penal sections of the work were very elaborate. A wide variety of punishments, including beatings and public execution, were allowed. This level of detail is an indication of the Chinese influence on Japanese legal history. In addition, it is also obvious that the criminal sections of the Taihō code show the unmistakable mark of the influence of continental philosophy, in particular, Confucianism. For example, Confucian philosophy is famous for the weight given to the values of loyalty and filial piety. As a result of Confucian ideology, the Taihō code prescribed severe punishment for crimes such as patricide, while injuries inflicted on children by a parent were less severely punished. An aristocratic bias is also evident. There were many clauses that exempted those of high rank, including courtiers and influential monks, from corporal and capital punishment.

The administrative sections of the Taihō code were about twice as long as the penal ones. The main preoccupation of this side of the code was the structure of the imperial court and the bureaucracy that existed within it. It articulated an elaborate system of ranks and duties that governed almost every aspect of aristocratic life. It also established widespread systems of conscription and taxation.

Clearly, the Taihō code served to entrench the privileges of the aristocratic class that compiled it. Under the system created by the code, courtiers served in the imperial government as part of an elaborate bureaucracy modeled after that of Tang China. Scholars have pointed out, however, that there were notable differences between the Chinese system and the one that developed in Japan under the guidance of the Taihō code. Unlike the meritocracy that existed at the Tang court, the Japanese system played up inherited privilege. Although there was potential for advancement for members of the aristocracy, only members of the most powerful and influential families could hold the most important offices in the new system. This aspect of the Taihō code had a notable impact on Japanese political life and relations between different social classes.

Another important aspect of the Taihō code was its entrenchment of the economic obligations of the lower classes. A large measure of economic control was necessary in order to end the period of civil strife that preceded the consolidation of central power in the hands of the imperial court. The system of laws collected in the Taihō code enforced an elaborate system of taxation, conscription, and forced labor that enabled the establishment of a dominant political center. Although the imperial Japanese state was never able to establish a system of taxation as efficient as that which existed in China, scholars currently acknowledge that the system established in the Taihō legislation was important in Japanese economic and political development as it allowed national production to be harnessed in the interests of defense and created the circumstances by which an elaborate capital city and an equally elaborate aristocratic culture were created.

SIGNIFICANCE

In 718, the second year of the Yōrō period, Fujiwara Fuhito, one of the authors of the Taihō code, and his assistants, compiled a new legal code that came to be known as the Yōrō code. Scholars believe that it was similar both in content and character to the Taihō code. The Yōrō code was not put into effect until 757, but from that time until the tenth century, its influence, patterned on the legal foundations set by the Taihō code, remained strong.

Aside from its importance in a legal sense, the obvious Chinese and, more specifically, Confucian character of the Taihō code and the revisions that followed is also important within the context of Japanese intellectual and philosophical history. While Confucian philosophy was studied by the small minority of Japanese raised in the aristocratic circle, the vast majority of the population was not literate and had no significant contact with philosophical ideas. However, because the morality that underlies the penal section of the Taihō code is Confucian, ideas of this philosophy were inculcated among the population at large by a spread in the awareness of the central legal precepts as well as the obligations spelled out in the administrative sections of the code. To this day, Confucian thought continues to have a significant impact on Japanese socialization and political life, and the Taihō code is significant in that it played a leading role in diffusing these ideas throughout the Japanese population.

Even after the seizure of power by the warrior class in the twelfth century, the administrative laws originally promulgated in the Taihō code continued to have great influence. The system of government, law, and land distribution adopted by the government of the Minamoto shogunate took several cues from the earlier Taihō code. In additon, the Taihō code continued to be the most important legal document at the now relatively powerless imperial court and continued to spell out the hierarchy that lasted until the modernizing reforms of the nineteenth century.

—*Matthew Penney*

FURTHER READING

Aston, W. G., trans. *Nihongi: Chronicles of Japan from the Earliest Times to A.D. 697*. 1896. Reprint. Tokyo: Charles E. Tuttle, 1972. The standard translation of one of the earliest works of Japanese history. Provides accounts of the compilation of the Taihō code and details concerning the cultural and political background of its creation.

Bentley, John. *Historiographical Trends in Early Japan*. New York: Edwin Mellen Press, 2002. The historiography of ancient Japan in general with a particular focus on the era of the Taihō laws and the way in which surviving accounts of their enactment may have been manipulated for political purposes.

Brown, Delmer, ed. *Ancient Japan*. Vol. 1 in *The Cambridge History of Japan*. New York: Cambridge University Press, 1993. The most up-to-date collection of articles by leading scholars on pre-Heian Japanese history. The work contains a great deal of information on legal traditions and the political circumstances that led to their foundation.

De Bary, William Theodore, et al., comps. *Sources of Japanese Tradition*. 2d ed. Vol. 1. New York: Columbia University Press, 2001. Contains abridged translations of Japanese legal documents as well as other important documents relating to early Japanese political life.

Friday, Karl. *Hired Swords: The Rise of Private Warrior Power in Early Japan*. Stanford, Calif.: Stanford University Press, 1992. Contains details of how the laws established in the Taihō code contributed to the rise of warrior society.

Sansom, George. *A History of Japan to 1334*. Vol. 1. Stanford, Calif.: Stanford University Press, 1958. The first volume of Sansom's three-volume study of Japanese history remains a detailed and authoritative work on the subject.

SEE ALSO: 593-604: Regency of Shōtoku Taishi; 645-646: Adoption of Nengo System and Taika Reforms.
RELATED ARTICLE in *Great Lives from History: The Middle Ages, 477-1453*: Shōtoku Taishi.

c. 710
CONSTRUCTION OF THE KĀILAŚANĀTHA TEMPLE

The monumental Kāilaśanātha Temple at Kanchipuram, built by Pallava king Narasiṃhavarman II Rājasiṃha, is important because it was the first major structural stone temple in southern India. The numerous sculptures formed an iconographical program exalting both the god Śiva and the king who built it.

LOCALE: Kanchipuram, Tamil Nadu, India
CATEGORY: Architecture

KEY FIGURES

Narasiṃhavarman II Rājasiṃha (d. 728), Pallava king, r. 700-728
Mahendravarman III (eighth century), Pallava king
Raṅgapatākā (eight century), Pallava queen

SUMMARY OF EVENT

Kāilaśa is the Himalayan mountain home of the god Śiva to whom Narasiṃhavarman II Rājasiṃha's grand temple complex is dedicated. The Kāilaśanātha Temple, also known as the Rājasiṃheśvara Temple, was the first structural stone temple in southern India; previously temples in the south were constructed in either brick or wood. Although Narasiṃhavarman II's royal predecessors had cave temples excavated from stone and monolithic temples carved from boulders, it was Narasiṃhavarman II who took the decisive step of ordering his artisans to construct a sacred building entirely of quarried stone. Built on a grand scale, the enormous temple was an attempt to recreate Śiva's mountain abode.

King Narasiṃhavarman II's reign was relatively peaceful and free from internal and external strife. At the very zenith of its power, the Pallava Dynasty was blessed with extremely prosperous times, and the kingdom grew rich from maritime trade along India's shores with the vassal Śrivijaya kingdom in Southeast Asia and with China. Records indicate that Narasiṃhavarman sent diplomatic missions to China. He was an ardent devotee of Śiva and built several temples to the god, although he also supported construction of a Jaina temple at Tirupathikundram and a Buddhist monastery at Nagappattinam. Like his predecessors Mahendravarman I and Narasiṃhavarman I, Narasiṃhavarman II had an avid interest in all the arts. An accomplished musician, he personally directed the planning of temples and their decoration, including paintings, and provided the temples with musicians and dancers necessary for the entertainment of the deity. Of the many temples he built, the Kāilaśanātha was the most impressive and important.

The temple complex, built in sandstone and facing east, was a joint venture that included Narasiṃhavarman, his son Mahendravarman III, and Queen Raṅgapatākā, who was either Narasiṃhavarman's consort or his mother. The elaborate compound consisted of the main temple (*vimāna*), an assembly hall (*maṇḍapa*), an enclosure wall with fifty-eight attached smaller shrines, a small adjacent temple built by Mahendravarman III, and an entry courtyard fronted by six smaller shrines located in front of the entry gate. Initially, the *vimāna* and *maṇḍapa* were separate structures, but the two buildings were joined by an intervening structure built in the seventeenth century.

The *vimāna*, with its inner sanctum (*garbha gṛha*), houses the two main icons, a large fluted, faceted sixteen-sided basalt *liṅgam* (the aniconic symbol of Śiva) in the center of the cella and, carved on the back wall, the seated group called Sōmāskanda, consisting of Śiva, his wife Pārvatī, and their son Skanda seated on a throne; they are flanked by standing images of Brahma and Viṣṇu (Vishnu). The *vimāna*, a four-storied structure essentially square in plan, rose in a series of tiers (talas) to form a great tower (*śikhara*) that was crowned by an enormous octagonal stone. Each tier was distinguished by a row of carved miniature shrines.

Artists covered the walls of the *vimāna* with many Hindu deities, mythological scenes, and fantastic rearing creatures called *vyālas*. Originally, all the walls of the compound were covered with plaster and paintings. Rare fragments of the early, perhaps original, paintings can be seen in some of the smaller shrines along the south and west enclosure walls. There are more than 120 major icons as well as a host of subordinate images, all of which provide a tangible and permanent record of important religious movements of the early eighth century in southern India. The temple's many images of Śiva were indicative of the king's devotion as well as Śiva's immense popularity in the Tamil region. The vast collection of Shaivite iconography, symbols, and legends depicted in bas-reliefs may be the largest and most complete in India. Several of the icons in the complex appear for the first time in southern India as official members of the southern Hindu pantheon. The Dikpālas (guardians of the directions), the Saptamātṛkās (seven mothers), and Jyeṣṭha (goddess of misfortune) are noteworthy examples.

The *vimāna* walls also bear several fascinating icons of Śiva that appear for the first time in Indian art. The various dance poses of Śiva, the *nṛtyamūrtis*, created by Pallava artists for this temple are an important achievement. The energetic representations of the dancing lord convey his mighty cosmogonic function as provider of the power that causes the universe's evolution, maintenance, and dissolution. His dance, wild but full of grace, is meant to affect all nature and its creatures. According to the Āgamas (texts sacred to Śiva), the mighty god has 108 dance forms; only nine, however, are portrayed in the sculptural program of the Kāilaśanātha. One of the most interesting is the icon called Urdhva Taṇḍava that, according to a southern Indian legend, represents a famous dance competition between Śiva and the goddess Kālī. Whatever dance pose Śiva assumed, Kālī repeated it with ease. When Śiva, however, lifted one leg straight up the side of his head, Kālī was forced to concede, because, as a woman, she was not willing to assume a posture so indiscreet that her genitalia would be exposed. A few other stunning iconic representations of Śiva debuted at the Kāilaśanātha Temple, including Śiva as Tripurāntaka, or the Destroyer of Three Cities; Lingodbhavamūrti, or Śiva emerging from a flaming *liṅgam*; and Śiva as Gajāsura Saṃharamūrti, which shows the forceful god destroying a terrible elephant demon.

The walls of the temple bear many of Narasiṃhavarman II's inscriptions; they provide the king's mythological and real genealogies, his many alternate names, his accomplishments, and numerous accolades. According to one inscription, the temple was built for the sake of a queen named Raṇgapatākā, either the king's consort or mother, who was famous for her beauty and chastity.

Raṇgapatākā seems to have played an active role in the construction of the temple. Some experts believe that what appear to be portraits of Śiva and Pārvatī carved on the back wall of the shrine actually may be portraits of the king and queen. Another of the inscriptions praises Narasiṃhavarman as an *āgamapriya*, or one who is versed in the Āgamas. The king clearly adopted some of the conventions stated in the Āgamas for his temple. For example, the layout of the complex with its smaller shrines along the cloister walls is based on a scheme mentioned in the Amṣumadbhedāgama (eighth century). The temple also reflects the development of ritual worship and evolving Hindu iconography.

There is another important dimension to understanding the temple and its royal builder recently recognized among scholars. The temple complex seems to have been a religious center for a cult of a divine king. There are hints that previous Pallava rulers may have regarded themselves as god-kings and that the tradition of a rudimentary form of divine kingship was indigenous in ancient Tamil society. It is apparent from Narasiṃhavarman II's inscriptions on the Kāilaśanātha Temple that he regarded himself as divine, a role that no doubt facilitated his control over his vast empire. Narasiṃhavarman's personal inscriptions were particularly informative and instructive on the subject; for example, in one, he called his temple "The Holy Rājasiṃha-Pallesvara." In a subtle play on words, he named the temple after himself, not as its builder, but as the divine resident.

One of the temple's names, Rājasiṃheśvara, can be translated two ways: (Śiva) the lord of (king) Rājasiṃha; the lord (god/king) Rājasiṃha. The double entendre is intentional. Similarly, Pallava specialists have recognized that the temple's many icon panels of Sōmāskanda, Śiva, and his family members also were intended to represent the Pallava royal family. Thus, icons of Śiva also represented the king; Pārvatī, the queen; and Skanda, a Pallava prince. Both poetic inscriptions and imagery corroborate the idea of a god being incarnate in human form and specifically the god taking a royal incarnation. The religious doctrine of the time supported the idea of the merging of Śiva and the king, as the god's supreme devotee, into a single entity. According to Śaiva Siddhānta, the popular religious movement of the seventh and eighth centuries in southern India, the goal of the devotee was to unite with Śiva in a state of absolute oneness. The king, most worthy and accomplished of mortals, naturally assumed the state of divine oneness with Śiva. Thus, while asserting assiduously again and again that he was the devotee of Śiva, Narasiṃhavarman simultaneously embraced and merged with the divine.

SIGNIFICANCE

The Kāilaśanātha Temple is one of the most important sacred buildings in south India. Its construction was revolutionary in the region, and the temple was monumental and elegantly decorated. Narasiṃhavarman II encouraged experimentation and inventiveness in the temple's iconography. His visionary approach ensured that the Kāilaśanātha would become a model for later Shaivite temples: the Shore Temple at Mahabalipuram, the Virūpākśa Temple at Pattadakal, and the very famous Kāilaśanātha Temple at Ellora all were directly inspired by Kanchipuram's famous temple. Narasiṃhavarman laid down such a standard of excellence that later kings vied to surpass his spectacular achievement. In addition, his legacy has provided tangible proof that he was regarded as a divine king and that the Kāilaśanātha Temple was a monument dedicated not only to Śiva but also to Narasiṃhavarman II as an earthly manifestation of that powerful deity.

—*Katherine Anne Harper*

FURTHER READING

Lockwood, Michael. *Mamallapuram and the Pallavas*. Madras, India: Christian Literature Society, 1982. An excellent work that includes a series of articles on Pallava art and material on Narasiṃhavarman II and his monument at Kanchipuram. Bibliography.

Lockwood, Michael, Gift Siromoney, and P. Dayanandan. *Mahabalipuram Studies*. Madras, India: Christian Literature Society, 1974. An important work on Pallava art in general, with some interesting materials on the Kāilaśanātha at Kanchipuram. Bibliography.

Longhurst, A. H. *Pallava Architecture*. New Delhi: Cosmo Press, 1982. A pioneering and detailed study on important Pallava monuments. Bibliography.

SEE ALSO: 630-668: Reign of Narasiṃhavarman I Mahāmalla.

RELATED ARTICLE in *Great Lives from History: The Middle Ages, 477-1453*: Rāmānuja.

April or May, 711
ṬĀRIK CROSSES INTO SPAIN

Ṭārik's crossing into Spain began the Muslim political conquest that allowed Muslim influences to pervade all aspects of Spanish life.

LOCALE: Western North Africa and Iberian Peninsula
CATEGORIES: Expansion and land acquisition; wars, uprisings, and civil unrest

KEY FIGURES

Mūsa ibn Nuṣayr (640-716/717), Arab governor of North Africa and commander of Arab troops
Ṭārik ibn-Ziyād (d. c. 720), Berber lieutenant of Mūsā
Roderick (d. 711), last king of Visigothic Spain, r. 710-711
Count Julian (fl. c. 710), ruler of the Christian city of Ceuta
Witiza (d. 710), king of Visigothic Spain, r. 697-710

SUMMARY OF EVENT

The entire question of the Muslim conquest of Spain is shrouded in mystery and romance. Some historians think it was the result of religious zeal on the part of newly converted Arabs; others maintain that the invasion of Spain was part of a grand strategy planned by the Islamic caliphs and aimed at the subjugation of Europe. The latter school points to the Muslim siege of Constantinople in 717 and to the entry into Spain in 711 as opposing eastern and western pincer movements. Still others see an economic motive only.

Scholarship shows that the caliph of Damascus actually had little control over Mūsā ibn Nuṣayr, his governor in North Africa, and that the latter's push from Egypt was the result of his personal ambition and only incidentally led to independent raiding parties bent on plundering Spain.

The first of these expeditions across the Strait of Gibraltar did little more than report the ease with which booty could be obtained. Mūsa accordingly outfitted a larger raiding party led by his lieutenant, Ṭārik ibn-Ziyād, a Berber and a former slave. With about seven thousand Berber warriors, none from Mūsa's army, Ṭārik landed in April or May, 711, on the great rock that has since borne his name, the Jebel Ṭārik or Gibraltar. King Roderick, a usurper of the Visigothic throne from the sons of his predecessor Witiza, marched south with between 40,000 and 100,000 men to intercept Ṭārik.

At the seven-day Battle of La Janda fought between the Barbate River and the Sierra de Retin, treachery by members of the disposed Visigothic line assured Ṭārik of

Ṭārik laying his conquests at the feet of Mūsa. (F. R. Niglutsch)

victory. King Roderick became a figure in Spanish legend. Although his horse and sandals were found on the river bank, the body of Roderick was not with them. He undoubtedly was killed and his body washed out to sea. In Spanish legends, King Roderick would return in triumph to lead the Christians against the Moors.

Fearful and jealous of his lieutenant, Mūsa led another army across the strait to complete the subjugation of the peninsula. He degraded Ṭārik publicly and moved north, taking city after city, and finally driving the Visigothic nobles under Christian leaders such as Pelayo into the mountainous region of Asturias in the northwest. These Christian pockets were destined to hold isolated fortresses for more than three hundred years. They ultimately coalesced into the Christian kingdoms of León, Castile, and Navarre and began to reconquer the peninsula from Muslim control.

Most historians regard much of the Visigothic version of the conquest as legend. King Roderick, largely unknown, appears to have reigned for only one year. Evidence that the sons of Witiza played some part in Ṭārik's success is only partly credible. The identities of Count Julian, the governor of Cueta, and his daughter Florinda are either vague or fanciful.

According to Spanish legend, Count Julian sent his beautiful daughter to the court of King Roderick at Toledo to be educated. Instead of protecting her as he was honor bound to do, Roderick seduced her. Because Julian's wife, the daughter of deposed King Witiza, was of royal blood, the disgrace was even greater. Count Julian revenged himself by aiding Ṭārik. Although the legend may not be true, it is known that Julian supplied the four ships used by Ṭārik to cross to Gibraltar and those used by Mūsa in the second invasion. Another explanation for Julian's action is his desire to retain his position of governor in Cueta after the inevitable Muslim conquest of the city.

Instead of such colorful and romanticized accounts, historians prefer to cite the disorganized internal situation in Visigothic Spain to explain its sudden collapse. The kingdom had been weak since the fifth century, when the Visigoths seized the area from the Romans. The Visigoths remained a minority because they would not be assimilated into the hostile local population, whom they cruelly exploited. The serfs were legally tied to the land and without rights or recourse. The middle class was burdened with crushing taxes, and slaves, who had no hope of betterment or freedom, labored on the large estates owned by a small group of nobles.

The Visigoths were Arian Christians when they conquered Spain, and most of their subjects were staunch orthodox Christians. Furthermore, the Visigoths sporadically persecuted a large Jewish element who had made their homes in the peninsula. Finally, in the sixth century, the Visigothic king and most of his followers converted to orthodox Christianity, but the monarchy fell under the domination of Spanish bishops. By the time of Roderick, the kingship was almost powerless, insecure, and still regarded as an alien influence by most of the population.

When Ṭārik arrived, the kingdom was incapable of united action in any form. The native population did not seem to care one way or the other. The Jews threw in their lot with the Arabs and actually held the city of Toledo for the invaders. The nobles were jealous and disorganized, and the high-ranking clergy, including the archbishop of Toledo, were interested only in saving their treasures and themselves. The result was that Christian Spain disintegrated and collapsed.

The Spanish people found scant consolation in the fact that Mūsa ibn Nuṣayr fell into disfavor. Summoned to Damascus by the caliph, he was stripped of his rank and possessions and forced to retire to Medina, where he died penniless. Ṭārik ibn-Ziyād journeyed to Damascus with his master, but he returned to live out his days on the riches he had gained from his unexpected and phenomenal conquest.

SIGNIFICANCE

The Iberian Peninsula was dominated by Muslims for the next four hundred years, with the Muslim presence continuing until the fall of Granada in 1492. During this period, Arabic learning flourished at Muslim courts, and Spain became one of the primary sources from which western Europeans in the twelfth century drew much of their knowledge of mathematics, medicine, astronomy, and particularly Aristotelian philosophy. Muslim culture has been one of the continuing influences in many aspects of Spanish life. In the face of Islamic penetration, Spain developed an aggressive devotion to orthodox Christianity, a characteristic that has been typical of Spain through the Reformation and through today.

—*James H. Forse, updated by Robert D. Talbott*

FURTHER READING

Chejne, Anwar G. *Muslim Spain: Its History and Culture*. Minneapolis: University of Minnesota Press, 1974. The author gives a panoramic view of Hispano-Arabic culture.

Christys, Ann. *Christians in Al-Andalus, 711-1000*. Richmond, England: Curzon, 2002. Considers Christianity coexisting with Islam in Moorish Spain. Chapters on chronicles of the time, the city of Toledo, martyrdom, and more.

Coppée, Henry. *History of the Conquest of Spain by the Arab-Moors: With a Sketch of the Civilization Which They Achieved and Imparted to Europe*. 2 vols. Piscataway, N.J.: Georgia Press, 2002. This work, originally published in 1881, explores Ṭārik's conquest of Spain and the resulting Arab influences on European civilization.

Fregosi, Paul. *Jihad in the West: Muslim Conquests from the Seventh to the Twenty-first Centuries*. Amherst, N.Y.: Prometheus Books, 1998. A history of Muslim conquests, including Ṭārik's crossing into Spain. Includes chapters titled "The Mountain of Tarik: Spain 711" and "A Conqueror's Fate: Spain 711-715."

Hitti, Philip K. *History of the Arabs: From the Earliest Times to the Present*. 10th ed. New York: Palgrave Macmillan, 2002. Argues that the Arabs carried the torch of culture to Spain and to Europe. Includes a complete description of Arab culture in Spain.

Kennedy, Hugh. *Muslim Spain and Portugal: A Political History of al-Andalus*. New York: Longman, 1996. Chapters on the 711 conquest, emir leadership, the caliphates, and the end of al-Andalus. Includes an appendix on ruling dynasties, a bibliography, and an index.

Marín, Manuela, and Julio Samsó, eds. *The Formation of al-Andalus*. 2 vols. Brookfield, Vt.: Ashgate, 1998. Vol. 1 looks at Andalusian history and society, and Vol. 2 explores Andalusian language, religion, culture, and science. Includes a bibliography and an index.

Trend, J. B. "Spain and Portugal." In *The Legacy of Islam*, edited by Thomas Arnold and A. Guillaune. New York: Oxford University Press, 1952. A summary of the views of leading Spanish historians of the importance of the Moorish invasion.

SEE ALSO: October 11, 732: Battle of Tours; c. 950: Court of Córdoba Flourishes in Spain; 1031: Caliphate of Córdoba Falls; November 1, 1092-June 15, 1094: El Cid Conquers Valencia; c. 1150: Moors Transmit Classical Philosophy and Medicine to Europe; 1230: Unification of Castile and León.

RELATED ARTICLES in *Great Lives from History: The Middle Ages, 477-1453*: ʿAbd al-Raḥmān III al-Nāṣir; Alfonso X; Charles Martel; El Cid; Saint Isidore of Seville; Damia al-Kāhina; Ṭārik ibn-Ziyād.

March 9, 712, and July 1, 720
WRITING OF *KOJIKI* AND *NIHON SHOKI*

The publication of two Japanese histories known as the Kojiki *and the* Nihon shoki, *the oldest in existence, greatly contributed to a national self-consciousness, helped legitimize the imperial system, and solidified the positions of the noble families by tracing their ancestors to the gods and the mythical creation of Japan.*

LOCALE: Japan
CATEGORY: Historiography

KEY FIGURES

Temmu (d. 686), emperor of Japan, r. 673-686, ordered the recording of the history of Japan

Hieda no Are (fl. seventh century), court attendant who memorized Japan's earliest myths and documents

Ō no Yasumaro (d. 723), nobleman who transcribed the *Kojiki* from Are's memorized material

Prince Kawashima (657-691), nobleman, along with eleven others, ordered to begin what would become the *Nihon shoki*

Ki no Kiyohito (d. 753) and

Miyake no Fujimaro (fl. eighth century), noblemen added in 714 to the writers of the *Nihon shoki*

Prince Toneri (677-735), presented the finished *Nihon shoki* to Empress Genshō (680-748, r. 715-724)

Gemmei (661-722), Japanese empress, r. 707-715, received the finished *Kojiki*

SUMMARY OF EVENT

Writing came to the Japanese through the Korean scribe Wani, who flourished in the late fourth-early fifth century C.E. When Wani arrived, most likely in 404, he brought with him a collection of Chinese classics, from which the Japanese devised a system of writing their own language. One of the oldest inscriptions, in which spoken Japanese is recorded using the pronunciations of Chinese characters, has survived on a Japanese iron sword, inscribed in 471 and re-deciphered in 1978.

After contact with the literate societies of China and Korea and adopting the Chinese writing system, the Japanese developed a desire to record their own history. By recording an official history of Japan, the imperial family, which traced its origins to the sun goddess of Amaterasu, hoped to justify its rule through its claim to divine ancestry. Similarly, the noble clans wanted to record that they had been founded by ancient princes or princesses, or followers of the earliest, mythical rulers.

Prince Shōtoku (574-622), with a friend, wrote the earliest Japanese history in 620. It focused on the imperial line and its relationship to the nobles and lower ranks of people. However, a fire destroyed most of the text in 645, and the surviving remnants disappeared during the Jinshin War of 672. Some scholars theorize that it was deliberately destroyed by rebels who wanted to erase detrimental records.

In his preface to the *Kojiki*, Ō no Yasumaro writes that around 680, Emperor Temmu became concerned about Japanese history. Various noble families possessed different, sometimes partial copies of the *Imperial Chronicles* (*teiku*) and Fundamental Pronouncements (*kyūji*). The emperor also rightfully suspected that there were many forgeries. Temmu charged the courtier Hieda no Are with discovering the true history of Japan and memorizing its text.

Perhaps as backup, in the spring of 681, Temmu ordered Prince Kawashima and eleven other nobles to write an authorized, official version of the Imperial Chronicles and other important Japanese historical events. This included the earlier mythical accounts of Japan's past, then believed to be real.

Before the completion of Are's oral and Prince Kawashima's literary efforts, Emperor Temmu died in 686. Empress Jitō (645-703, r. 686-697) continued to support the project. In 691, she ordered eighteen noble clans to furnish their ancestral records, obviously as sources.

Probably to preserve Are's work for posterity, Empress Gemmei commanded Ō no Yasumaro to write down the memorized historical text on November 3, 711. Working speedily, Yasumaro presented the empress with the *Kojiki* (*Records of Ancient Matters*, 1883; best known as *Kojiki*) on March 9, 712.

Contemporary scholars still debate how the *Kojiki* was written. Yasumaro's preface states that it is a mere compilation of true tales of the past. However, with stakes so high for the imperial line and the noble clans, who wanted to prove their ancestry, and with so many forgeries in circulation, Are and Yasumaro must have done careful research and editing and been subject to political pressure.

The *Kojiki* offers a unified history of Japan's past. It is divided into three sections, the first of which deals with the "Jindai no maki" (book on the age of gods) and covers the creation of the universe with Japan at its center. The

MAJOR PERIODS IN JAPANESE HISTORY

Dates	*Period*
538-710	Asuka Period
710-794	Nara Period
794-1185	Heian Period
1185-1333	Kamakura Period
1333-1336	Kemmu Restoration
1336-1573	Muromachi Period
1336-1392	Nanboku-cho Period
1476-1615	Sengoku (Warring States) Period
1573-1603	Azuchi-Momoyama Period
1603-1867	Tokugawa (Edo) Period
1868-1912	Meiji Period

second section covers the period from Japan's first legendary emperor Jimmu to that of Ōjin, the first emperor who can be verified. The third part continues up to the reign of Empress Suiko (554-628, r. 593-628), which ends the book. The *Kojiki* is written in Chinese characters whose sounds correspond to the Japanese language, and it contains a glossary for the correct pronunciation of proper names.

The *Kojiki*, however, it is not a history in the modern sense. It includes large amounts of mythology, legend, and imaginary speeches mixed in with real historical facts. To give the Japanese empire an older and more auspicious date for its foundation, all but the most recent historical dates of the *Kojiki* are backdated. This has been proven by comparison with Korean and Chinese histories describing the same events at verifiably later dates.

For reasons still hotly debated by scholars, in 714, Empress Gemmei added Ki no Kiyohito and Miyake no Fujimaro to the team that was working on the *Nihon shoki*. On July 1, 720, Prince Toneri, one of Temmu's sons, officially presented the thirty volumes of the finished history, plus one book of genealogical charts, to Empress Genshō. The book soon was called the *Nihon shoki* (*Nihongi: Chronicles of Japan from the Earliest Times to A.D. 697*, 1896; best known as *Nihon shoki*), even though its official title is *Nihongi*.

The *Nihon shoki* is written in classical Chinese. Only its first two books deal with the mythological age. The others cover the time from Jimmu to Jitō's abdication. The different writing styles of its books show that it was composed by many authors, with Prince Toneri an honorary editor. Although more focused on historical events than the *Kojiki*, the *Nihon shoki* similarly presents divine events as real and backdates Japanese history. It also contains passages from Chinese and Korean histories and sometimes gives more than one narrative of the same event. However, the *Nihon shoki* becomes reliable and detailed history as it moves closer to the time of its writing

SIGNIFICANCE

For more than a thousand years, the Japanese considered the *Kojiki* and *Nihon shoki* a true account of the origin and early times of their nation. The oldest surviving copy of the *Kojiki* dates from 1371-1372, and its subject has been an integral part of Japanese national historical self-consciousness. Under the influence of Motoori Norinaga (1730-1801), the *Kojiki* became highly esteemed as a literary classic. Because it is not written in Chinese, it has often been regarded as the purer of the two ancient histories. Contemporary scholars value the *Kojiki* as an exemplary literary text that showcases how medieval Japan viewed its history and the origin of its society.

Ever since its publication, the *Nihon shoki* has been treated as a valuable official document. History lectures were given based on it in the eighth century, and public readings and lectures continued to 1185. Numerous medieval commentaries exist on this work, which was considered a standard history long into the modern era. The oldest existing manuscripts date from the late 700's or early 800's.

The events told in the two histories have been part of Japanese historical belief until the cultural cataclysm following defeat in World War II. In the 1960's, radical Japanese intellectuals tried to discredit the two ancient histories based on modern standards of historiography. In the early twenty-first century, Japanese national consensus focused on their value as literature and as historical record for the later parts of their chronicle.

Still, the two texts have a powerful imaginative impact on Japanese cultural thought and tradition. The *Nihon shoki* is considered the oldest of the "six national histories of Japan." February 11, the legendary day when, as told in these oldest histories, in 660 B.C.E. Jimmu founded the Japanese empire, is celebrated as a national holiday.

—*R. C. Lutz*

FURTHER READING

Aston, W. G., trans. *Nihongi: Chronicles of Japan from the Earliest Times to A.D. 697*. 1896. Reprint. Tokyo: Charles E. Tuttle, 1972. Still the only English translation of the *Nihon shoki*. Introduction, illustrations, index.

Brown, Delmer M., ed. *Ancient Japan*. Vol. 1 in *The Cambridge History of Japan*. New York: Cambridge

University Press, 1993. Chapter 9, by Edwin Cranston, and chapter 10, by Brown, deal with the writing of the two texts and show their impact on Japanese literacy and historical consciousness.

Brownlee, John S. *Political Thought in Japanese Historical Writing: From Kojiki (712) to Tokushi Yoron (1712)*. Waterloo, Ontario: Wilfrid Laurier University Press, 1991. The first two chapters deal with the two oldest extant histories, their writing, and their meaning for Japanese society. Appendix, notes, bibliography, and index.

Motoori, Norinaga. *Kojiki-den Book 1*. Translated by Ann Wehmeyer. Ithaca, N.Y.: Cornell East Asia Program, 1997. The text of the first of Mootori's forty-four books of commentary on the *Kojiki*, written from 1764 to 1798, which argue that this history is to be preferred because of its more purely Japanese style than the *Nihon shoki*. Introduction, notes, bibliography, and index.

Philippi, Donald L., trans. *Kojiki*. Princeton, N.J.: Princeton University Press, 1968. Most generally available English translation. Philippi's unique transcription of ancient Japanese names alters their common English spellings.

Robinson, G. W. "Early Japanese Chronicles: The Six National Histories." In *Historians of China and Japan*, edited by W. G. Beasley and E. G. Pulleyblank. Oxford, England: Oxford University Press, 1961. Relatively unsympathetic view of the Japanese writers of the *Kojiki* and *Nihon shoki*, who are considered less accomplished than their earlier Chinese counterparts.

Sakamoto Tarō. The Six National Histories of Japan. Translated by John S. Brownlee. Vancouver: University of British Columbia Press, 1991. Translation of the 1970 Japanese study of the oldest Japanese histories. Chapter 2, on the *Nihon shoki*, contains an excellent discussion on the source materials used by Japanese historiographers and a summary of the historical text. Appendix, bibliography, and index.

SEE ALSO: 5th or 6th century: Confucianism Arrives in Japan; 538-552: Buddhism Arrives in Japan; 593-604: Regency of Shōtoku Taishi; 607-839: Japan Sends Embassies to China; c. 800: Kana Syllabary Is Developed.

RELATED ARTICLE in *Great Lives from History: The Middle Ages, 477-1453*: Shōtoku Taishi.

713-741
FIRST NEWSPAPERS IN CHINA

What may be considered the world's first newspapers appeared in China during the Tang Dynasty.

LOCALE: China
CATEGORIES: Communications; cultural and intellectual history

SUMMARY OF EVENT

Given the vast expanse of the ancient Chinese empire, government officials, both in the provinces and in the capitals, had a constant need to keep informed of events and to disseminate official information and decrees. Perhaps because of this need, China was the first nation in the world to develop what may be considered newspapers.

By the end of the Han Dynasty (206 B.C.E.-220 C.E.), the Chinese empire had almost everything in place to establish a system of newspapers: a well-developed system of communication, paper, and printing. Pre-Han Dynasty emperors had created a communications system for reasons of military necessity. They had built a system of roads and post relays, with stations at regular intervals, which were also used by imperial couriers. Messages could also be carried on rivers or canals. The invention of paper traditionally is attributed to the eunuch Cai Lun (Ts'ai Lun) in 105, but crude paper fragments from several centuries earlier, probably not suited for writing, have been discovered. Paper was probably not used for writing until the first century, and the earliest samples of writing on paper date from the second century. By the Han Dynasty, seals, small wooden stamps, and rubbings were used to reproduce religious charms or textile patterns. By the seventh century, the Chinese had probably begun printing on paper from wooden blocks, and the first surviving examples date from between 704 and 751.

To get news from the Chinese capital, almost all important local rulers of large frontier territories established official residences in the capitals, staffed by their own representatives, who sent back handwritten news accounts and reports of events over the empire's system of roads and couriers. These official residences or mansions in the capitals were called *di*. The distances were so great that imperial officials had to rely on these private, handwritten reports instead of word of mouth to convey information to the local rulers. The imperial court created an office to convey its orders to these representatives, and it used the system of roads and couriers to collect information about events that transpired in the empire.

In the Tang Dynasty (T'ang; 618-907), these private newsletters developed into official handwritten newspapers, known as *dibao*, from *di* plus *bao*, or "report." The first dibao is known to appeared between 713 and 741. Titled *Kaiyuan zabao*, after the Kaiyuan Dynasty, it was sent from the capital at Chang'an (now Xi'an). The oldest surviving court newspaper, and the oldest in world, was issued in 876 and is now in the Bibliothèque Nationale, Paris. In it, a correspondent in the capital describes to a general the activities celebrating the New Year.

The *dibao* were published at regular intervals and were filled with official and court news: promotions, demotions, dismissals, edicts, government memoranda, and reports of other activities. Some of the memoranda were learned essays giving the opinion of scholars on political or social reforms, so the *dibao* contained some official opinions about issues of the day, in addition to just news. By 777, a number of *dibao* were being issued by different publishing offices in the capital, including the *chao bao* ("court newspaper") and the *gongmenchao* ("imperial court newspaper"). Therefore, the central government created a bureau of official reports responsible for all the news going in and out of the capital. It combined all the *dibao* going out of the capital into the provinces into a single, official newspaper.

The *dibao* were distributed to enough local rulers that at some time during the Tang Dynasty, some of the newsletters began to be printed. Printing had begun in China in the seventh century, and the printing of the *dibao* was probably done at first from a clay block and then from wooden blocks.

After the Five Dynasties Period (907-960), another period of instability and warfare, China was again united under the Song Dynasty (Sung; 960-1279), and again *dibao*—both government-sponsored and private—flourished.

News publishing had become an important institution, and the *dibao* reached a wide circulation that consisted of officials, scholars, and intellectuals throughout the country. Reading the *dibao* for entertainment and to hear the latest rumors and gossip seems to have been popular, leading to the development of unofficial *xiaobao* ("small newspapers"), a type of tabloid newspaper containing sensational news. The news in the *xiaobao* was considered so inaccurate, misleading, and injurious to the government that one official asked the emperor to prohibit publishing such "sensational news" because it was "misleading the public." In effect, he called for censorship of the news.

The Song emperors took heed, retaining government control of the *dibao* and censoring and suppressing the *xiaobao*. In 1090, a law was promulgated giving a two-year punishment to anyone printing a *xiaobao* and a reward for whoever reported the printer. The central government also suppressed unfavorable military news, a development that brought an objection from one official. Later, in the Ming Dynasty (1368-1644), news of murders, appointments, and dismissals that would suggest corruption in the government was also suppressed.

The early handwritten or printed *dibao* are a far cry from the modern concept of a newspaper. In the modern sense, a newspaper is published regularly, is available to a significant part of the public, includes a variety of stories or articles, serves as an organ of public opinion, and helps shape a sense of community among readers, printers, and editors. However, the first *dibao* were primarily a means of distributing official government information. These newsletters circulated only among a closed circle of government officials and bureaucrats, who were among the small literate elite. They were not intended for the masses, though they might learn of news from the capital by word of mouth from those officials who had read the *dibao*. Unlike the Roman *acta*, the *dibao* do not seem to have been posted in public places.

SIGNIFICANCE

China had an early and important role in the history of journalism and newspapers. Papermaking and the process of printing—on which Western Europe's own newspapers depended—were invented in China. Although the *dibao* were the first "newspapers," they should not be considered journalism or public newspapers in the modern sense. They were not objective publications that served the people and acted as a check on government. They were closer to a government press service developed for the use of bureaucrats. In their content, there is little or no sense of gathering, selecting, and editing news for the broad general public. Nor was there any means—by editorials or news stories—of offering expression to the voice of the people to shape public opinion and social or political events. In this sense, the *dibao* are closest to modern newspapers in countries in which the press is rigidly controlled and heavily censored by the government.

Whatever their relation to modern newspapers, the *dibao*, part of a system of collecting news from the provinces and disseminating information throughout the empire, enabled the Chinese to administer a large empire. The government's involvement in their publication and its later censorship of the *xiaobao* illustrates the government's major purpose in developing these "newspapers," which was to convey the official story throughout the empire.

—*Thomas McGeary*

FURTHER READING

Lin Yutang. *A History of the Press and Public Opinion in China*. Shanghai: Kelly and Walsh, 1936. Classic and most thorough account of the origin of newspapers.

Smith, Anthony. *The Newspaper: An Introductory History*. London: Thames and Hudson, 1979. Brief mention of the Chinese press in its world context.

Stephens, Mitchell. *A History of News*. Fort Worth, Texas: Harcourt Brace, 1997. Textbook with a good account of the history of Chinese journalism and newspapers.

Tsien Tsuen-Hsuin. "Paper and Printing." Part 1 in *Chemistry and Chemical Technology*, Vol. 5 in *Science and Civilisation in China*, translated and edited by Joseph Needham. New York: Cambridge University Press, 1985. Thorough and up-to-date account of the history of paper and printing in China.

SEE ALSO: 7th-8th centuries: Papermaking Spreads to Korea, Japan, and Central Asia; 618: Founding of the Tang Dynasty; 812: Paper Money First Used in China; 868: First Book Printed; 907-960: Period of Five Dynasties and Ten Kingdoms; c. 1045: Bi Sheng Develops Movable Earthenware Type; 1115: Foundation of the Jin Dynasty.

726-843
ICONOCLASTIC CONTROVERSY

The Iconoclastic Controversy, a major religious crisis, divided Byzantium and caused a split between the Christian centers of Constantinople in the east and Rome in the west.

LOCALE: Constantinople and Rome
CATEGORY: Religion

KEY FIGURES

Saint Gregory II (669-731), Roman Catholic pope, 715-731
Leo III (c. 680-741), Byzantine emperor, r. 717-741
Constantine V Copronymus (718-775), Byzantine emperor, r. 741-775
Leo IV (749-780), Byzantine emperor, r. 775-780
Leo V (d. 820), Byzantine emperor, r. 813-820
John of Damascus (c. 675-749), Eastern monk and theologian
Saint Irene (c. 752-803), Byzantine empress, r. 797-802
Charlemagne (742-814), king of the Franks, r. 768-814
Theodora (c. 810-862), Byzantine empress, r. 842-858

SUMMARY OF EVENT

The Iconoclastic Controversy constituted a profound religious and political crisis within Christendom. It divided the religious worlds of the Western Roman Catholic Church from Eastern Orthodoxy, and it shook the religious, political, and military foundations of Byzantium.

First, the controversy concerned the use and religious significance of icons. Icons became very popular in the sixth century, when imperial images were replaced by those of Jesus. Icons were perceived as more than simply paintings. They were holy objects, capable of working miracles to heal the sick or to offer divine protection against foreign invasion. They represented the Christian belief in intercession, offering a way by which human fears and aspirations, suffering and pain, joy and faith, and common superstition could reach God. Icons stood at the intersection of the human and divine worlds. The difficulty, however, was that icons might appear as objects of idolatry, thereby violating one of the sacred Ten Commandments.

The problem of idolatry was compounded by the rise of Islam in the seventh and early eighth centuries. Islam adhered to a strict monotheism and rejected the concept of intercession and the use of images in worship. The Arabs conquered vast Byzantine territories stretching from Syria, Palestine, Egypt, and through North Africa. Many Byzantines believed the explanation for their defeats was God's punishment for idolatry. Although political and military issues became intertwined with iconoclasm, the central question remained religious.

Emperor Leo III was an iconoclast who, like Jews and Muslims, considered icons to be idol worship. Leo broke the great Arab Siege of Constantinople in 717 and promulgated an important law code (*Ecloga*). Because of his hostility to icons, he was called "Saracen-minded." In 726, Leo III ordered the removal of the image of Jesus to the entrance of the imperial palace and banned the worship of icons. Despite opposition from the patriarch, elements of the army, and even the populace in Constantinople, he reaffirmed his decision to ban icons in 730 in a kind of council (Silentium). Pope Gregory II and his successor Gregory III (d. 741) refused to recognize Leo's imperial authority in such religious matters. Gregory III condemned iconoclasm in 731. The emperor responded by removing Dalmatia from the ecclesiastical jurisdiction of Rome to that of Constantinople—an action that would later bring many Balkan Slavs under the Eastern Orthodox Church.

Leo was succeeded by his son Constantine V Copronymus. For his first two years, Constantine fought a civil war with his father-in-law Artavasdus, who supported icons. Constantine triumphed with loyal troops from Anatolia. At times, though not always, the eastern provincial armies (*themes*) were more sympathetic to iconoclasm than European troops.

Although it was not attended by any eastern patriarch or papal legate, Constantine called a council in 754 to condemn icons as the work of the devil and to place offending believers under imperial laws. This change allowed the administration to begin a widespread persecution of monks, some of whom were forced to wear secular dress, to marry, or to march through the hippodrome holding the hands of women. Torture and executions of icon worshipers—Saint Stephen the Younger of Mount Saint Auxentius being the best-known victim—were not uncommon. Monastic lands were confiscated and monasteries turned into military barracks; thousands of monks were said to have fled the empire, particularly to Cyprus, southern Italy, and Sicily. It is probable that Constantine wished to destroy the entire Byzantine monastic order.

Not all monks opposed Constantine, especially those who had a formal religious education and resided in urban monasteries, or who came from aristocratic families. The most fervent opponents of Constantine were usually popular holy men, often poor and uneducated, who were the focal point of popular unrest. These holy men were largely responsible for bringing icons into Church liturgy.

The concept of the incarnation of Jesus (Jesus as both God and man) was at the heart of the theological dispute over icons. Constantine may have been a dualist (perhaps even a Manichean), one who believed that matter (the wood of icons) was created in sin by a lesser deity, or he may have been a Monophysite, one who believed Jesus to be only divine. (Monophysite doctrine was declared heretical and denounced in the Fourth Ecumenical Council held at Chalcedon in 451.) Constantine argued that icons could never depict what was divine in Jesus because divinity cannot be limited in paint and wood. On the other hand, if icons portray only what is human in Jesus, then they divided what could not be separated. For Constantine, only the miracle of the Mass transformed matter into spirit.

The theological defense of icons was given by John of Damascus. Jesus as God, having taken on flesh, had sanctified the flesh as holy. Therefore, icons could not be condemned simply because they were made of matter. Icons were an imitation (*mimesis*) and not of the same substance or essence (*ousia*) of the divine. By themselves, icons had no independent significance, but through imitation they partook of the divine.

Constantine's successor, Leo IV, halted the assault on monasticism, and Empress Irene, his wife, was an advocate of icons. After Leo's death, Irene ruled as regent for her ten-year-old son Constantine VI. In 787, the Council of Nicaea (the seventh ecumenical council) sanctioned icons, excommunicated those who declared icons to be idols, condemned seizure of monasteries, and declared that Christians could give reverence (*proskynesis*) to icons but could not literally worship (*latreia*) them.

In August of 797, Irene deposed her son and had his eyes put out; he died shortly thereafter. Her reign coincided with that of Charlemagne in the West. At the Frankfurt Council in 794, Charlemagne attacked the council of 787 and the Byzantines as too iconodule and as idolatrous. Icons were useful only for didactic purposes. From the point of view of Charlemagne and Pope Leo III (795-816), the fact that a woman reigned in Constantinople meant that the Byzantine throne was effectively empty. Pope Leo III hoped to unite East and West under Charlemagne by crowning him emperor on December 25, 800. To solidify his claim as emperor of Rome, Charlemagne proposed marriage to Irene, but her fall from power in 802 ended any possibility of such a union. In 812, Byzantine emperor Michael I (r. 820-829) recognized Charlemagne as emperor but not of the Romans, a title that belonged only to the Byzantine East.

As with the Arab conquests, icons may have been once more associated with apostasy and foreign victory. Emperor Nicephorus I (r. 802-811) was killed by the Bulgars in 811 and had his head turned into a victorious drinking cup. In the council of 815, Leo V condemned icons and ushered in the second iconoclastic era. He was opposed by the abbot Theodore Studites of the Studius monastery in Constantinople. Theodore became a leader of the iconodules and struggled for Church independence from imperial power. He had the support of Pope Paschal I (817-824), who offered asylum to Greek monks and sent legates in an unsuccessful attempt to end iconoclasm.

Iconoclasm continued to divide Byzantium. A terrible revolt from 821 to 823 by Thomas the Slav (d. 823) sought to restore icons. The Arab conquest of Crete in 826, the appearance of Arab forces in Sicily in 827, and the Arab sack of Amorian in Anatolia in 838 argued against the idea that Christ favored iconoclasm.

SIGNIFICANCE

After the death of the emperor Theophilus (r. 829-842), Empress Theodora restored icons on March 11, 843—the date marks the Byzantine Feast of Orthodoxy, celebrated to this day on the first Sunday of Lent. Icons were to remain an integral part of the faith of the Eastern Orthodox Church, but they had created a schism between the churches of the East and West. The Roman Church could not accept the right of an emperor to interfere and define religious doctrine.

—*Lawrence N. Langer*

FURTHER READING

Alexander, P. J. *The Patriarch Nicephorus of Constantinople: Ecclesiastical Policy and Image Worship in the Byzantine Empire*. Oxford, England: Oxford University Press, 1958. An important study on Byzantine church policy and the worship of images and icons in the Eastern Orthodox Church.

Brown, Peter. "A Dark Age Crisis: Aspects of the Iconoclastic Controversy." In *Society and the Holy*. Berkeley: University of California Press, 1989. An interpretation of the controversy as an issue concerning the nature of the holy in the Middle Ages.

Cavarnos, Constantine. *Guide to Byzantine Iconography: Detailed Explanation of the Distinctive Characteristics of Byzantine Iconography, with a Concise Systematic Exposition of Saint John Damascene's Defense of Holy Icons*. Boston: Holy Transfiguration Monastery, 1993. An excellent resource on the icons of the Eastern Orthodox Church, explaining the theology of icons. Bibliography, index.

Kaegi, Walter. "The Byzantine Armies and Iconoclasm." *Byzantinoslavica* 27 (1966): 48-70. A study of the role the Byzantine Empire's armies played in iconoclasm and in the controversy.

Magoulias, Harry J. *Byzantine Christianity: Empress, Church and the West*. Chicago: Rand McNally, 1970. A good introduction to the beliefs of the Eastern Orthodox Church as it compares to the Western Church.

Martin, E. J. *A History of the Iconoclastic Controversy*. London: S.P.C.K., 1930. An older work but still an excellent overview of iconoclasm and the controversy.

Parry, Kenneth. *Depicting the Word: Byzantine Iconophile Thought of the Eighth and Ninth Centuries*. New York: E. J. Brill, 1996. Surveys intellectual contributions defending the veneration of icons, controversial literature on iconoclasm, and more. Bibliography, index.

Schönborn, Christoph. *God's Human Face: The Christ-Icon*. Translated by Lothar Krauth. San Francisco: Ignatius Press, 1994. An exploration of the nature and history of iconoclasm and the Iconoclastic Controversy, the theology of images, the representation of the body, and much more. Chapters also cover "The Icon as Grace-Filled Matter: John Damascene" and the second Council of Nicaea. Bibliography, index.

SEE ALSO: 630-711: Islam Expands Throughout North Africa; 637-657: Islam Expands Throughout the Middle East; April or May, 711: Ṭārik Crosses into Spain; 1054: Beginning of the Rome-Constantinople Schism.

RELATED ARTICLES in *Great Lives from History: The Middle Ages, 477-1453*: Charlemagne; Saint Irene; John of Damascus.

729
FOUNDING OF NANZHAO

The founding of the kingdom of Nanzhao may have represented the establishment of the first major Thai state. A major power, Nanzhao both allied with and fought against China, eventually falling to the invading Mongols.

LOCALE: Modern-day Yunnan Province in southern China

CATEGORY: Government and politics

KEY FIGURES

Sinulo (d. 674), first king of Nanzhao, r. c. 650-674

Pilaoko (c. 700-750), king of Nanzhao, r. 728-750

Kolofeng (d. 779), son of Pilaoko and king of Nanzhao, r. 750-779

Kublai Khan (1215-1294), Mongol ruler, r. 1260-1294; Yuan Dynasty ruler, r. 1279-1294

SUMMARY OF EVENT

Nanzhao apparently emerged from several Thai states in southern China. It was a major power for several centuries, extending its control over parts of Burma and even attacking Hanoi, in northern Vietnam. Nanzhao sometimes allied itself with China against Tibet and sometimes fought against China. It finally fell to the Mongol invasion in 1253, touching off increased migration of Thai and related people to the south.

Although scholars accept the existence of the kingdom of Nanzhao (Nanchao or Nan Chao), there is some disagreement on whether it really was the first Thai state, or the first state led by Tai-speaking people, as the speakers of Thai, Shan, Lao, and other related languages are often called. According to historian Keith W. Taylor, Nanzhao was actually led by Tibeto-Burmans, and the Thai or Tai peoples played only a marginal role in the kingdom. However, other historians have long held that Nanzhao was the first known major Thai state and that although its leaders may have been heavily influenced by the Chinese and Tibetan cultures, those leaders were of the same ethnic and linguistic heritage as their followers.

People of Thai ethnicity are thought to have settled in southern China by the first century of the common era. Their region was bounded by the Red River in the east, by the Yangtze River in the north, and by the upper Mekong in the west. Ancient Chinese documents refer to these people as the Ailao. According to some accounts, the Ailao moved up into southern China from the Indian subcontinent and established a federation of *muangs* (*muong* or *meuang*). The word *muang* in modern Thai refers to a country or a people; Thailand itself is often known as Muang Thai. The ancient word appears to have meant something along the lines of a tribe or a principality, a collection of scattered villages. Each *muang* was led by a *chao*, or lord. Leadership was based on personal ties between the lord and those who followed him, and the lords' authority came from their personal qualities.

The Chinese emperors had brought the region under their control by about the third century. However, disorder in China enabled many local chieftains to establish their independence. During the middle of the seventh century, struggle with China inspired many *muangs* to join together into larger groupings. Reportedly, as many as six Thai states came into existence. Nanzhao, which means "the southern principality," took shape as one of these states. By about 650, Nanzhao was ruled by King Sinulo. The Chinese Tang Dynasty (Tan'g; 618-907) accepted the existence of the new kingdom and established a treaty with it. The ties between Nanzhao and China resulted in many lasting Chinese cultural influences on the Thai.

After Sinulo died in 674, he was succeeded first by his son, Loshengyen, and then, in about 712, by his grandson, Shenglope. In 728, Pilaoko, the king who apparently led the rise of Nanzhao as a powerful kingdom, came to the throne. Pilaoko allied himself with the Chinese emperor Xuanzong (Hsüan-tsung; r. 712-756) and agreed to defend the borders of China from all enemies, especially from Tibet. Pilaoko then turned to attack Tibet, seizing several Tibetan settlements. He also used his position as a vassal of the Chinese to dominate the neighboring states and to extend the territory of Nanzhao. Fortifying himself in the Tali Lake Plain, which is surrounded by mountains and gorges, Pilaoko was able to build his dominion into a place that was easy to defend and difficult to attack. In 735, Pilaoko formally accepted Chinese sovereignty over Nanzhao. In turn, the Chinese recognized Pilaoko as the lord of Yunnan.

Pilaoko's son, Kolofeng, reportedly turned against the Chinese. Kolofeng struck an alliance with the Tibetans and invaded China. In response, the Chinese invaded Nanzhao once again, in 752-754, but failed to impose their will on the rebellious state. Over the next 150 years,

Nanzhao maintained troubled relations with China, but the former did send missions and tribute to the powerful Chinese empire. Kolofeng also turned his attention south, where the main power in the Irawaddy River basin was the ancient Pyu Empire. The Pyu derived their wealth from trade between India and China. By shifting the trade route away from the Irawaddy, Nanzhao reduced the the strength of the Burmese empire. The Pyu became vassals of Nanzhao by about 800, when Chinese records reported that Nanzhao had sent Pyu musicians to the imperial court of China.

After the death of Kolofeng in 779, his son, Imoshun, tried to invade China but was defeated. In the years that followed, Imoshun reconsidered his enmity with the Chinese. He sent a letter to the emperor repudiating his alliance with Tibet, and the Chinese, in turn, recognized Imoshun as king of Nanzhao. Imoshun, however, died in 808. Imoshun's successor reportedly attacked China once again, capturing several provinces and bringing captive artisans and scholars back to Nanzhao. In about 832, Nanzhao turned on the weakened empire of the Pyu, already a vassal, and conquered the Burmese state.

Chinese records report that in 859, Tsuiling became king of Nanzhao and took on the title of emperor. This angered the Chinese emperor Yizong (I-tsung; r. 859-873), because that title was supposed to represent supremacy over all other rulers and to belong to the ruler of China alone. Warfare broke out once again between Nanzhao and China, and Nanzhao invaded China, laying siege to Chengdu. At this time also, the armies of Nanzhao moved to the southeast to invade northern Vietnam, then a part of the Chinese empire. In 862 and 863, the forces of Nanzhao attacked and occupied the Vietnamese city of Hanoi. The presence of Nanzhao in Vietnam was short-lived, however, because a Chinese general retook the region about 866.

Kublai Khan, from a Chinese engraving. (Library of Congress)

Taiking became king of Nanzhao in 877 and made peace with China. With his death, about 902, the dynasty that had begun with Sinulo came to an end. Nanzhao continued to exist, but little information is available on its history. There is little mention of it in the Chinese records, the chief source for modern historians. The silence probably indicates continued good relations between the two countries.

In 1253, Kublai Khan, the ruler of the Mongols in China, invaded and conquered Nanzhao. This brought an end to the kingdom. Some historians have claimed that the rulers of Nanzhao were not Thai at all, but members of some other ethnic group. Whatever the ethnicity of those at the top, though, the Mongol conquest apparently set off another large wave of migration. Although some Tai-speaking people remain in modern-day southern China, many tribes left for other locations with the breakup of Nanzhao.

Significance

If Nanzhao was a Thai kingdom, as many believe, then it was the first appearance of a major state organized by people of an ethnic group that later came to occupy an important place in Southeast Asian history. It may also have been a central source of immigrants to the lands that are now known as Laos and Thailand.

—Carl L. Bankston III

Further Reading

Coedès, George. *The Indianized States of Southeast Asia.* Translated by Susan Brown Cowing. Honolulu: East-West Center Press, 1968. A classic work on Southeast Asian history. Several chapters in the book refer to Nanzhao.

Tapp, Nicholas, and Andrew Walker, eds. *The Tai World: A Digest of Articles from the Thai-Yunnan Newsletter.* Canberra: Australian National University, 2001. A collection of articles first published in a newsletter devoted to folklore, history, rituals, and beliefs among the Thai, Lao, and people of Yunnan. These demonstrate the continuing close connections between the tribes in Yunnan and the Thai people.

Taylor, Keith W. "The Early Kingdoms." In *Cambridge History of Southeast Asia*. Vol. 1, edited by Nicholas Tarling. Cambridge, England: Cambridge University Press, 1992. The author rejects the idea that Nanzhao was primarily a kingdom of Tai-speaking people.

Wyatt, David K. *Thailand: A Short History*. New Haven, Conn.: Yale University Press, 1986. Provides an accessible introduction to Thai history.

SEE ALSO: 618: Founding of the Tang Dynasty; c. 700-1253: Confederation of Thai Tribes; 832: Nanzhao Subjugates Pyu; 863: Nanzhao Captures Hanoi; 877-889: Indravarman I Conquers the Thai and the Mons; 1271-1295: Travels of Marco Polo; 1295: Ramkhamhaeng Conquers the Mekong and Menam Valleys; 1350: Ramathibodi I Creates First Thai Legal System.

RELATED ARTICLE in *Great Lives from History: The Middle Ages, 477-1453*: Kublai Khan.

730
RISE OF THE PRATIHĀRAS

The Gurjara-Pratihāra Dynasty ruled a large area of north-central India for three hundred years, successfully preventing the Muslim conquest and making significant contributions in cultural areas such as art and architecture.

LOCALE: North-central India
CATEGORIES: Government and politics; architecture

KEY FIGURES

Nāgabhaṭa I (d. c. 756), founder of the second line of the Gurjara-Pratihāra Dynasty, r. c. 730-c. 756
Mihira Bhoja (d. c. 885), the most illustrious of the Gurjara-Pratihāra kings, r. c. 836-c. 885
Mahendrapāla (d. 910), Mihira Bhoja's successor, r. c. 890-c. 910
Maḥmūd of Ghazna (971-1030), the founder of the Ghaznavid Dynasty in Delhi, r. 997-1030

SUMMARY OF EVENT

The rivalry between Indian dynasties and the threat of foreign invasion dominated the history of northern India from the death of Harṣa c. 647 until 1526, when at the Battle of Pānīpat, a victory over the Delhi sultan by the Mughal leader Bābur enabled him to consolidate rule under a Muslim dynasty.

During these troubled times, between the seventh and eleventh century, the Rajput Gurjara-Pratihāra Dynasty (c. 730-c. 1027) ruled a large area of the north-central Indian subcontinent. Gurjara refers to the ethnic affiliation of the family and Pratihāra to the dynastic designation. The Gurjaras were a nomadic people of western Rajasthan who may have been related to the White Huns (Hūṇas or Hephalites), those nomadic marauders who entered India in the fifth century. The Gurjara-Pratihāra political rivals, the Rāśṭrakūṭa, claimed that the Pratihāra were mere doorkeepers (pratihāra), a reference that may imply that the Pratihāra were minor palace officials who had usurped the throne, historically a not uncommon Indian political event. Although the insult may have been only adversarial hyperbole, it is true that the social origins of the Pratihāra remain obscure.

At the height of its power, the Gurjara-Pratihāra Empire was as great as that of the Guptas. The Pratihāra ruled an area consisting of segments of the modern states of Rajasthan, Gujarat, Madhya Pradesh, and Uttar Pradesh and stretching even further into parts of eastern and western India under systems of vassalage. At their apogee, their territory, albeit under loosely allied vassals, reached from Gujarat to Bengal. They made their headquarters first at Ujjayini (modern Ujjain) and then at Kanauj (just north of modern Kanpur).

The later Gurjara-Pratihāra period represented a Hindu cultural bulwark against the attempted Islamic domination of northern India. The Prophet Muḥammad died in 632; within twenty years, his followers had formed an organized religion around his teachings. By the early eighth century, Arab invaders had successfully entered the Indian subcontinent, first to plunder, then later with the goal of converting the population to Islam. The first Delhi sultanate was formed by the Turkish Ghaznavids. Subüktigin of Ghazna, a former slave, entered India in 991, and his son Maḥmūd (r. 997-1030) established the Ghaznavid Dynasty in Delhi. This was the first of a series of Islamic dynasties that would control large areas of north India for the next eight hundred years.

The Gurjara-Pratihāra Dynasty had two major lines of descent. The first, the line of Brahamana Haricandra

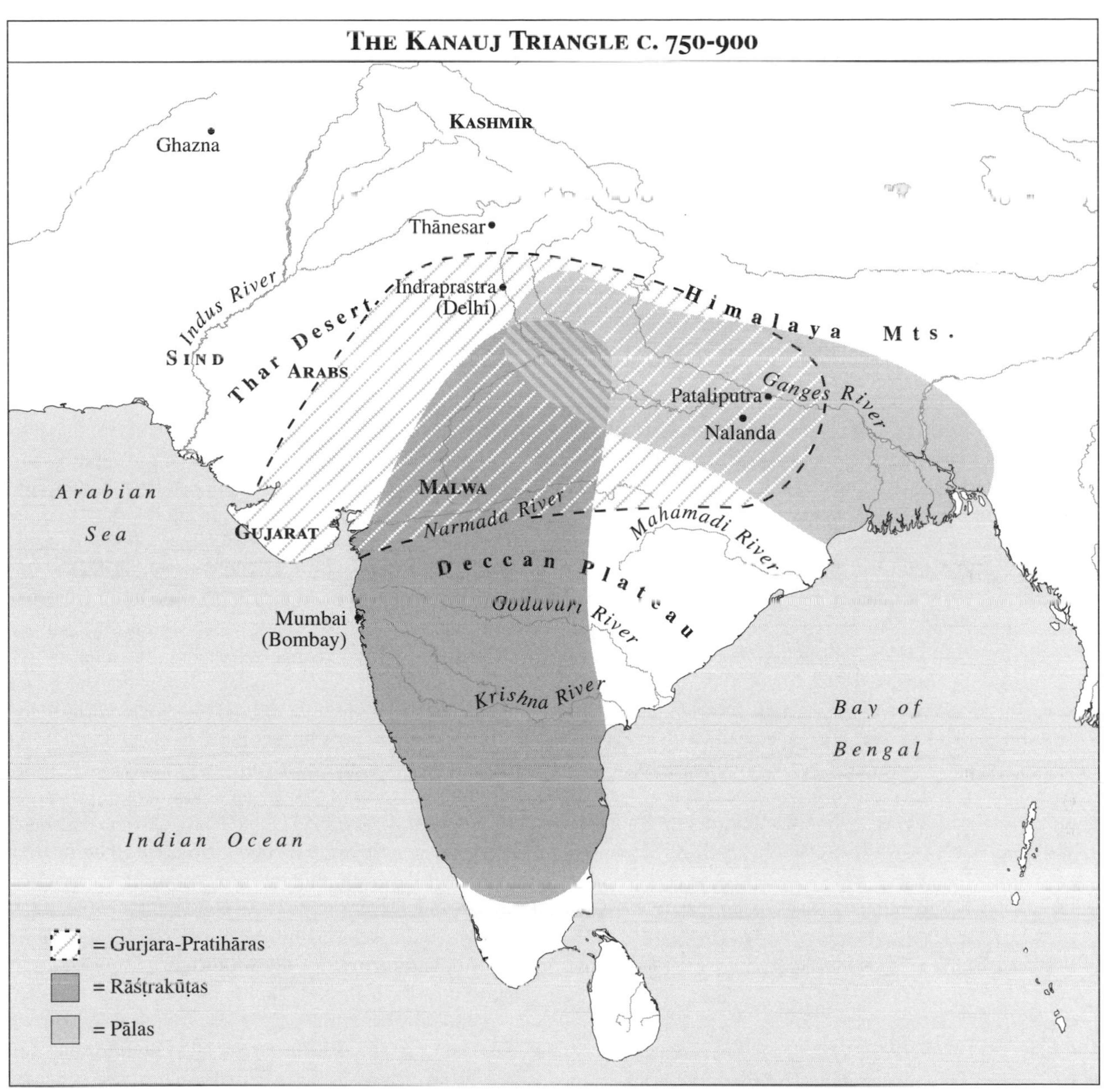

(c. 550) and his Kṣatriya wife Bhadri, ruled from Mandor in Rajasthan (north of the city of Jodhpur), then from Nandipuri (near Broach), and later from Bhinmal. The Chinese pilgrim Xuanzang

The second line, that of Nāgabhaṭa I (r. c. 730-c. 756) ruled from Ujjayini and then from Kanauj from the eighth until the eleventh century. Nāgabhaṭa I was famous for his military prowess, most probably against the Muslim invaders. In a c. 875 inscription from Ujjain, Nāgabhaṭa is described as "having crushed the large armies of the powerful Mlechchha [barbarian] king," according to R. C. Majumdar in *The Age of Imperial Kanauj* (1984). Although not specified by name, this non-Indian king was most likely either the Arab governor of Sind, Junaid, or his successor, Tamin. Nāgabhaṭa, despite conflicts with his neighbors, was able to leave to his descendants a stable and powerful territory consisting of areas of Malwa, Rajasthan, and Gujarat.

Nāgabhaṭa's grandson Vatsarāja (r. c. 778-c. 794) lost this territory to the Rāṣṭrakūṭas, his powerful rivals to the south, and was forced to accept their domination, but he was able to defeat the Pālas in their attempts to conquer Pratihāra territory. His son Nāgabhaṭa II (r. c. 794-c. 833) eventually threw off the Rāśṭrakūṭa yoke and pushed the Pālas further back into eastern Bihar. Nāgabhaṭa II was able to reconquer former Gurjara-Pratihāra territory so that by 816, he took possession of Kanauj. Nāgabhaṭa is also credited in an inscription from Gwalior with defeating the Turuksa (probably a reference to the Arabs).

The constant threat of foreign invasion from the west and conflicts with the Rāśṭrakūṭas from the Deccan, as well as a contentious relationship with the Pālas in the east, must have kept the Gurjara-Pratihāra Dynasty in a state of perpetual tension. All three dynasties vied for the hegemony of vast territories in northern India, as well as the control of Kanauj, which was desired not only for its position as a wealthy trading city but also for its status as the former imperial city of Harṣa.

Under the most famous of the Pratihāra kings, Mihira Bhoja (r. c. 836-c. 885) and his successor Mahendrapāla I (r. c. 890-c. 910), the dynasty reached its zenith of power and prestige. The Arab historian Sulaiman (851) refers to Bhoja in respectful terms, noting his large army, his fine cavalry and camel corps, the wealth of his empire, and its safe roads, according to scholar A. K. Majumdar.

Ruling from his imperial seat at Kanauj, Mihira Bhoja was able to firmly hold back the Arab menace from the west but also occupied much of his time in a nearly continuous series of battles with the Rāśṭrakūṭas and the Pālas. The Arab visitor al-Masʿūdī, visiting Kanauj in 915-916 under the reign of King Mahipāla, wrote that the king was in a state of unremitting enmity with the Deccan, noting that the king's vassals and feudatories were in a constant state of battle readiness, according to scholar Romila Thapar. He also noted that the king had four armies of 800,000 men each, which, even if these numbers are exaggerated, probably indicates that a huge part of the royal revenues were used in warfare. The Rāśṭrakūṭas, under Indra III, sacked Kanauj in 915 and again in 918. Mahipāla held onto his kingdom only with the help of his feudatory Harṣa Chandelā, who by then had grown stronger than his liege.

This situation did not improve over the next century. Ultimately the rivalry proved to be reciprocally destructive, weakening all opponents to such an extent that they fell prey to the familiar Indian pattern of revolt by former feudatories. By the mid-tenth century, the Gurjara-Pratihāra Dynasty was so weakened that it fell victim to its former vassals. An 954 inscription credits the Chandelā under Dhanga (c. 950-1002) with a defeat of the Gurjara-Pratihāra, although several other Rajput princely families continued to acknowledge Gurjara-Pratihāra suzerainty. Newly arising Rajput families such as the Haihaiyas of north-central India, the Paramaras of Malwa, and the Solaṇkis of Gujarat filled the power vacuum left by the decline of the Gurjara-Pratihāras.

With the sack and destruction of Kanauj in 1018 by Maḥmūd of Ghazna, the Gurjara-Pratihāra light was all but eclipsed. Trilocanapāla, the last Gurjara-Pratihāra king for whom there are records, ruled at least until 1027, the date of the last Pratihāra inscription. After that period, Muslim dynasties dominated the political climate of northern India, and no Indian Hindu or Buddhist king was able to form sufficiently strong and harmonious alliances to fend off foreign domination.

Although it is tempting to see Indian kingdoms in terms equivalent to European feudal systems, it may not be entirely accurate. It is hard to determine just how much power individual kings wielded. Scholars such as Burton Stein (studying the Cōlas) and Ronald Inden (studying the Rāśṭrakūṭas) argue that the king was important as a symbolic figure, but that his authority was in a constant process of contest and reconfiguration. It is therefore difficult to say what impact these shifts in Gurjara-Pratihāra power and prestige ultimately had on the local population.

Despite the tensions with neighboring rulers and the inevitable dissipation of monies and energy in warfare, the Gurjara-Pratihāras were great patrons of the arts, or at least, they created an atmosphere conducive to patronage

MAJOR RULERS OF THE GURJARA-PRATIHĀRA DYNASTY, C. 730-C. 1027

Ruler	*Reign*
c. 730-c. 756	Nāgabhaṭa I
n.d.	Devaraja
c. 778-c. 794	Vatsarāja
c. 794-c. 833	Nāgabhaṭa II
c. 836-c. 885	Mihira Bhoja I
c. 890-c. 910	Mahendrapāla I
c. 914-?	Mahipāla
n.d.	Mihira Bhoja II
n.d.	Vinayakapāla
c. 946-c. 948	Mahendrapāla II
c. 948-c. 960	Devapāla
c. 960-?	Vijayapāla
n.d.	Rājyapāla
c. 1018-c. 1027	Trilocanapāla

by members of the landed aristocracy or wealthy merchant classes. During the Gurjara-Pratihāra rule, patronage of temple architecture, in particular, was prolific and lavish. The temples constructed during their rule are usually small but sumptuously sculpted, indicating a sophisticated and generous patronage. These temples reflect the logical stylistic interlude between their two more famous termini, the earlier Gupta period and the later Chandelā period. The sculptural style is fluid, coherent, and elegant. Gurjara-Pratihāra period style is more sinuous and voluptuous than Gupta style and less hardened and formulaic than the Chandelā style. Gurjara-Pratihāra style imbues the human form with full-bodied vigor; there is a refined crispness in the facial features and great elaboration of detail in the treatment of jewelry, hairstyles, and ornamentation.

The temples reveal a great deal about the life of the period. The iconographic programs of certain temples show that Tantrism was practiced. The cults of Tantrism were often concerned with the acquisition and maintenance of power, according to scholar Vidya Dehejia. It is known that the great King Bhoja was a Śākta, most likely because his tutelary goddess, Bhagavati, was perceived to be powerful and protective. Terahi, a small temple of the mid-tenth century, has a highly elaborate Tantric iconographic program that demonstrates that dangerous but powerful Tantric rites must have been performed for the acquisition of power. This temple was a reflection in art and religion of the stressful political times, during which all means must have been employed to maintain and enhance the stability of the throne.

SIGNIFICANCE

For three hundred years, the Gurjara-Pratihāra Dynasty held back the Arab invaders from the west. The cultural achievements and political failures of the dynasty reflect medieval Indian civilization. Its contributions to Indian art and architecture were of lasting beauty and sophistication and were indicative of the high level of Pratihāra culture, but the dynasty's inability to form permanent and effective alliances with its rivals left it weak and vulnerable to eventual foreign conquest.

—*Mary N. Storm*

FURTHER READING

Dehejia, Vidya. *Yogini Cult and Temples: A Tantric Tradition*. New Delhi, India: National Museum, 1986. A study of the rare tantric Hindu temples dedicated to the yogini goddesses. It includes interesting speculation on patronage. Well illustrated.

Inden, Ronald B. *Imagining India*. Oxford, England: Blackwell, 1990. Analyzes the modern Western and colonial constructs of Indian empire and kingship.

Kalia, Asha. *Art of Osian Temples: Socio-economic and Religious Life in India, Eighth-Twelfth Centuries A.D.* Atlantic Highlands, N.J.: Humanities Press, 1982. A study of the early and most famous Gurjara-Pratihāra temple site at Osian, Rajasthan.

Majumdar, A. K. *Political History*. Vol. 1 in *Concise History of Ancient India*. 2d ed. New Delhi, India: Munshiram Manoharlal, 1992. Contains a helpful section on the rise and fall of the Gurjara-Pratihāra dynasty.

Majumdar, R. C., ed. *The Age of Imperial Kanauj*. 3d ed. Bombay, India: Bhartiya Vidya Bhavan, 1984. A general survey of the "classical period" of Indian history, including the rise of the Gurjara-Pratihāras.

Puri, Baij Nath. *The History of the Gurjara-Pratihāras*. Bombay, India: Hind Kitabs, 1957. An early study of the dynasty.

Stein, Burton. *Peasant State and Society in Medieval South India*. Oxford, England: Oxford University Press, 1980. This analysis of traditional Indian patterns of kingship and governance questions the assumptions of established historical interpretation.

Thapar, Romila. *From the Discovery of India to 1526*. Vol. 1 in A History of India. Baltimore: Penguin Books, 1991. A general and easily accessible introduction to Indian history written by a great contemporary scholar of the field.

Willis, Michael D. *Temples of Gopaksetra: A Regional History of Architecture and Sculpture in Central India, A.D. 600-900*. London: Trustees of the British Museum, 1997. A very scholarly and dense text on the architectural heritage of the Gurjara-Pratihāra heartland. Well illustrated.

SEE ALSO: 606-647: Reign of Harṣa of Kanauj; 770-810: Reign of Dharmapāla; 973: Foundation of the Western Cālukya Dynasty; 998-1030: Reign of Maḥmūd of Ghazna; 1206-1210: Quṭ al-Dīn Aybak Establishes the Delhi Sultanate.

RELATED ARTICLES in *Great Lives from History: The Middle Ages, 477-1453*: Harṣa; Maḥmūd of Ghazna.

731
BEDE WRITES *ECCLESIASTICAL HISTORY OF THE ENGLISH PEOPLE*

Bede completed his Ecclesiastical History of the English People, *creating both a spiritual document and a contemporary history of Anglo-Saxon England that popularized the system of dating events from the birth of Christ rather than by the years of a ruler's reign.*

LOCALE: Jarrow, Northumbria, England
CATEGORIES: Cultural and intellectual history; historiography; literature; religion

KEY FIGURES

Saint Bede the Venerable (672/673-735), a scholar-priest of Jarrow later considered the father of English history
Benedict Biscop (c. 628-689/690), founding abbot of Jarrow
Ceolfrith (c. 642-716), second abbot of Jarrow
Ceolwulf (c. 695-764), king of Northumbria, r. 729-737, to whom Bede's *Ecclesiastical History of the English People* is dedicated

SUMMARY OF EVENT

Elevated after his death by the Church to sainthood and honored by the secular world as the father of English history, Saint Bede the Venerable was born into unlikely circumstance for such honors. Northumbria, in the psychological geography of the times, was a remote part of a remote island on the very edge of a fallen Roman Empire. The Anglo-Saxon king Edwin, who had first received Christianity at the hands of Saint Paulinus some forty-five years before Bede's birth in 672 or 673, was killed soon after by a pagan claimant to the throne. Politically and religiously, Northumbria was an unsettled place.

Into this unsettled time and peripheral place, Bede was born, most likely to a noble family. Nothing further is known about his origins, for he was given at the age of seven to the abbot Benedict Biscop to be educated. Benedict was a former Northumbrian thane who had left secular life around the age of twenty-five to go on a pilgrimage to Rome. Returning with books, religious relics, and skilled stonemasons from France, Benedict was granted land first at Wearmouth and later at Jarrow to found monasteries. He recruited Ceolfrith, another Northumbrian nobleman turned monk, to help; it was Ceolfrith who, more than anyone, became Bede's spiritual father.

Benedict made six visits to Rome during his life, each time returning to England with copied books, vestments, and even pictures. As a result, the twin monasteries of Wearmouth and Jarrow grew as centers of learning, with Bede as their greatest jewel. Under Ceolfrith, a revised and edited version of the Bible was produced based on the best available manuscripts. This work to produce a good text of the Bible made Bede's writings on biblical interpretation and meaning possible. In his lifetime, Bede wrote prolifically: biblical commentaries; histories of the saints; books of homilies, of hymns, of epigrams, and of martyrology; books on time, on poetry, and on orthography; and, in five books, the church history of his island and people.

This latter work, *Historia ecclesiastica gentis Anglorum* (731; *Ecclesiastical History of the English People*, 1723), completed when Bede was fifty-nine years old, is considered his masterpiece. One reason for this is his system of dating events. Bede created a cumulative dating system beginning with *annus domini*, the year of Christ's birth, rather than with *annus mundi*, the year of the Creation, used by Eusebius of Caesarea, Saint Jerome, and Saint Isidore of Seville in their histories. This change required a massive effort of calculation, taking into account previous chronicles with different starting points, imperial Roman regnal years in the East and the West, and the regnal years of six or more Anglo-Saxon kings ruling at the same time. It also required a knowledge of the multitude of starting points for various systems of calculating a year, such as the calendar year, which might begin on January 1, in September, or at Christmas; or the Indiction beginning dates of September 1, September 25, or January 25; or the date in a particular kingdom when a king took up his reign. With so much variation possible, complete accuracy could never be achieved by anyone, resulting in uncertainties that neither Bede nor those who followed him could resolve. Bede's own birth date, for example, is uncertain. Given these small variations in accuracy, however, Bede produced a trustworthy chronology, a monumental achievement.

Bede's careful method in seeking out sources for past events, as well as the near-contemporaneity of many of the events he wrote about, is a second reason his history is so remarkable. It has an importance as a historical document unmatched by anything else of the time. The history begins with a prefatory letter to the Northumbrian king Ceolwulf, telling readers that the king already had a draft copy of the work and wanted to have this revised version for copying. Albinus of Canterbury, whom Bede named as his source for information on the Kentish church, also had a copy for review. Scholars know that when Bede wrote a life of Cuthbert, he sent it on to the monastery at Lindisfarne, where Cuthbert had been abbot, so that those still alive who knew Cuthbert could comment on it. Bede relied on interviews he conducted and on those conducted for him by others. A priest of London visited Rome to search the archives there and copy out for Bede the letters of Pope Gregory the Great concerning the mission of Saint Augustine and Paulinus to convert the English. Eanflæd, daughter of Edwin, the first king of Northumbria to receive Christianity, was still alive during Bede's lifetime and served as the abbess of Whitby. As an infant, Eanflæd had actually been the first person to be baptized by Paulinus. Some of the most interesting stories—for example, how the pagan Bretwalda (overlord) of East Anglia kept both a pagan altar and a Christian one side by side—most likely came to Bede from royal family history, in this case through King Ceolwulf or through Saint Hilda, founding abbess of Whitby. Thus Bede was dealing in his history with events whose witnesses were still alive.

An engraving of the Venerable Bede from a French history. (Library of Congress)

The *Ecclesiastical History of the English People* is divided into five books. The first book begins with a description of Britain as a rich, almost paradisiacal land, in the tradition of the garden before the Fall in the book of Genesis. It then moves to the Roman history of Britain, its despoiling by the Anglo-Saxon invaders of the fifth century, and the mission of Augustine to re-Christianize Britain. The second book concentrates on Paulinus's mission to Northumbria, down to the death of King Edwin and the failure of the mission. Book 3 deals with the second planting of Christianity in Northumbria from Ireland and its spread to Mercia and East Anglia, with the Easter controversy and the Synod of Whitby in 664, which resolved the controversy in favor of the Roman way over the Irish. Book 4 treats the life of Cuthbert, who began his life's work as an Irish monk but moved firmly into the Roman camp, and of Hilda, who founded Whitby and made it a center of learning.

In its recounting of the successions of various abbots and bishops, book 5 moves the story up to 731, but it is given over much more to miraculous visions and healing than were the first four books. Book 5 includes stories of the afterlife: One man returns from the dead to tell of the dreadful and desirable things he saw, and another is given a preview by devils of the fate awaiting him for his sins. Thus one can see in Bede's history the general movement of the Bible from the book of Genesis to the book of Revelation and of the Christian soul from baptism to the afterlife.

SIGNIFICANCE

Although a competent history, Bede's text is first and foremost a spiritual document. It is an ecclesiastical history that sought to tell the details of Britain and its peoples only insofar as those details helped tell the story of God's providence. Thus Bede focused on the mission from Rome and the conversion of the English to Christianity, with the subsequent history of church establishments, abbots, and bishops, but also included political history, pagan and Christian, to illustrate the workings of divine providence. Hagiography, or the lives of saints and holy persons, as well as the recording of miracles, was also necessary, fitting his larger purpose. Bede's particular genius was weaving all these disparate elements into a cohesive story.

—*James Persoon*

FURTHER READING

Bede. *A History of the English Church and People.* Translated by Leo Sherley-Price. New York: Penguin Books, 1985. Bede's famous work.

Blair, Peter Hunter. *The World of Bede.* 2d ed. New York: St. Martin's Press, 1990. A thorough evocation of Bede's times by an eminent historian of Anglo-Saxon England.

Chance, Jane. *Woman as Hero in Old English Literature.* Syracuse, N.Y.: Syracuse University Press, 1986. A discussion of the treatment of women in Bede's *History* and in Old English literature in general.

Mayr-Harting, Henry. "Bede's Ecclesiastical History." In *The Coming of Christianity to Anglo-Saxon England.* University Park: Pennsylvania State University Press, 1991. Chapter 2 gives a readable and succinct judgment of Bede's place in the larger context of church history.

Sims-Williams, Patrick. *Britain and Early Christian Europe: Studies in Early Medieval History and Culture.* Brookfield, Vt.: Variorum, 1995. A collection of scholarly articles on Bede and his contemporaries.

Wallace-Hadrill, J. M. *Bede's "Ecclesiastical History of the English People": A Historical Commentary.* New York: Oxford University Press, 1993. Extended scholarly notes and a bibliography accompany this serious study of Bede's History.

SEE ALSO: 596-597: See of Canterbury Is Established; 635-800: Founding of Lindisfarne and Creation of the Book of Kells; 781: Alcuin Becomes Adviser to Charlemagne; June 7, 793: Norse Raid Lindisfarne Monastery.

RELATED ARTICLES in *Great Lives from History: The Middle Ages, 477-1453*: Saint Bede the Venerable; Cædmon; Saint Hilda of Whitby; Priscian; Saint Sergius I.

October 11, 732
BATTLE OF TOURS

The Battle of Tours discouraged further Muslim incursions beyond the Pyrenees mountains—incursions that were part of the extensive Islamic Empire—after the Muslims were defeated by Christian Frankish forces.

LOCALE: Near Poitiers, France

CATEGORIES: Religion; wars, uprisings, and civil unrest

KEY FIGURES

Charles Martel (c. 688-741), Frankish mayor of the palace, c. 719-741

ʿAbd al-Rahman (d. 732), Muslim governor of Spain

Eudo (665-735), duke of Aquitaine, c. 714-735

SUMMARY OF EVENT

A Christian army under the Frankish ruler Charles, later nicknamed Martel (hammer), defeated a Muslim army under the governor ʿAbd al-Rahman, most likely on October 11, 732. Little else is known about the Battle of Tours, a battle that should be more accurately called the Battle of Poitiers because it was fought closer to Poitiers than Tours, but it is convenient to use the traditional name to distinguish this battle from ones fought near Poitiers in 507 and 1356. Contemporary accounts are so sketchy, and sometimes so unbelievable, that accounts by modern historians vary in details.

By the end of 725, the Islamic empire spread from central Asia through North Africa into Spain and even across the Pyrenees into Septimania, in southern Gaul. Meanwhile, in that part of Gaul still under Christian rule, central military and political power lay not with the Frankish king, a figurehead, but with Charles, his mayor of the palace. Among the noblemen more or less under Charles's rule was Eudo, the duke of Aquitaine, who had defeated the Muslims at Toulouse in 721 but gave his daughter as a bride in 730 to the Muslim ruler of Septimania to form an alliance to secure Eudo's own position against both Charles and the Spanish Muslims. In 731, Eudo declared himself independent of Charles, but Eudo's son-in-law died that year in a revolt against ʿAbd al-Rahman, who gave the young widow to his own master, the caliph in Damascus.

Then Eudo learned that ʿAbd al-Rahman had crossed the western Pyrenees and was heading into Aquitaine. Trying to divert Christian forces by sending a small army east toward Arles, ʿAbd al-Rahman himself led a bigger force north. Arriving too late to keep the Muslims from pillaging and burning Bordeaux, Eudo's soldiers then lost in battle to ʿAbd al-Rahman's soldiers at the Dordogne. Humbling himself, Eudo appealed to Charles for help as perhaps seventy thousand Muslims went toward the rich abbey at Tours. When Charles's probably smaller army of Franks and their German allies eventually crossed the Loire River near Tours, ʿAbd al-Rahman led his men back toward Poitiers, near which the battle occurred at a site now unknown.

The two armies that faced each other were different in more than religion. The Franks and their allies were mainly an infantry force relying on shields, chain mail, and helmets for armor, and on axes, javelins, daggers, and swords for weapons. Charles's personal troops were experienced and probably better armed and armored than the militias raised by his vassals; even so, the discipline and organization of the army as a whole was poor by the standards of most modern nations. ʿAbd al-Rahman's army, which had more Berbers than actual Arabs, was similar in armor and weaponry to the Arab armies that had won so many victories in the century since Muḥammad's death. Most of the men rode horses and carried little armor, forgoing shields and preferring turbans to helmets. Their typical weapons were lances and swords.

The Franks at Tours, searching the Arab camp. (F. R. Niglutsch)

The different armies faced each other for six days with little fighting. On the seventh day, the Muslims, primarily an offensive force, attacked the Christians, who had taken a defensive position. Although at first the Muslim cavalry could not penetrate the massed Christian infantry, eventually the horsemen broke through in a few places. After a while, however, many Muslims heard a rumor that Christians were stealing the goods the Muslims themselves had earlier stolen in the invasion, and a number of Muslim squadrons rode off to protect their camp. Then, thinking their comrades were fleeing, many other Muslims started riding away from the battle, to the dismay of ʿAbd al-Rahman, who, in his attempt to stop the chaotic retreat, died at his enemies' hands. On the eighth day, when no Muslims came to fight, Charles sent scouts to the enemy camp. They reported that the Muslims had fled and taken some of their loot with them. Aware of the enemy tactic of feigned retreats, the severity of his own losses, his soldiers' fatigue, and the ease with which horsemen could outdistance infantrymen, Charles decided not to pursue.

The significance of the battle is debatable. For Edward Gibbon and many other historians who have followed his lead, the battle changed world history because, had Charles not led his Christian army to victory, Muslim conquerors might have reached Poland and Scotland, and Islamic theology would have been taught in Gibbon's own day to an entirely Muslim student body at Oxford.

Such events might indeed have happened had the Christians lost the Battle of Tours, but evidence suggests that, while important to the men who fought there, especially those who died, the battle did not have by itself all the importance Gibbon claims for it. In reality, the spread of Islam through war had not been one fast victory after another. In 642, only ten years after Muḥammad's death, Muslims had conquered Egypt, but not until 709 did they conquer the rest of North Africa. Before the Battle of Tours, two Muslim sieges of Constantinople had failed; the Christian victory under Leo III in the second siege, which ended in 718, was probably more important than the victory under Charles fourteen years later in the West. Furthermore, by 732, Muslim soldiers often lacked the zeal that had led their predecessors to fight and risk death for God and were generally more concerned with pillaging than with winning Europe for Islam. That loss of belligerent fervor, combined with civil strife in Muslim Spain and a revolt of the Berbers in North Africa, worked against an extension of Muslim territory in western Europe. A final indication of the relative unimportance of the Battle of Tours is that the Muslims later were militarily successful in Charles's territory and held Arles and Avignon a while. Only by 759, eighteen years after Charles's death, did the Franks end the Muslim occupation of Gaul.

SIGNIFICANCE

The Christian triumph in the Battle of Tours did, however, discourage Muslim raids deep into Gaul and let Muslim generals know that conquering the Franks would be harder than conquering the Visigoths in Spain, and Charles's success at the Battle of Tours and elsewhere against Muslims strengthened the position of his son Pépin the Short, who actually became king, and led to the celebrated rule of Pépin's son Charlemagne.

—*James H. Forse, updated by Victor Lindsey*

FURTHER READING

France, John. "Recent Writing on Medieval Warfare: From the Fall of Rome to c. 1300." *Journal of Military History* 65, no. 2 (April, 2001): 441-475. Offers a detailed discussion of scholarship on medieval warfare from the fall of the Roman Empire through the end of 1300, including battles between Muslim forces of the Islamic Empire and Frankish soldiers.

Fregosi, Paul. *Jihad in the West: Muslim Conquests from the Seventh to the Twenty-first Centuries*. Amherst, N.Y.: Prometheus Books, 1998. Surveys the history of the Islamic empire, including its reaches into Spain and France and the Battle of Tours. Illustrated, with a bibliography and an index.

Fuller, J. F. C. *A Military History of the Western World: From the Earliest Times to the Battle of Lepanto*. Vol. 1 in *A Military History of the Western World*. 3 vols. New York: Funk and Wagnalls, 1954-1956. Considers Charles's victory significant as an epilogue to Leo's.

Gibbon, Edward. *The History of the Decline and Fall of the Roman Empire*. 6 vols. 1776-1788. Vol. 5. Philadelphia: John D. Morris, n.d. This text possibly overstates the significance of the battle, but the description of the consequences of a Christian defeat is classic.

Lewis, Archibald R. *Naval Power and Trade in the Mediterranean, A.D. 500-1100*. Princeton, N.J.: Princeton University Press, 1951. Argues that the battle was a thwarting of only a raiding party.

Mitchell, Joseph B., and Sir Edward S. Creasy. *Twenty Decisive Battles of the World*. New York: Macmillan, 1964. A detailed description of the battle's action.

Oman, Charles. *The Dark Ages, 476-918*. 6th ed. London: Rivingtons, 1919. Argues against historian Gibbon's interpretation of the battle.

SEE ALSO: April or May, 711: Ṭārik Crosses into Spain; 786-809: Reign of Hārūn al-Rashīd; c. 950: Court of Córdoba Flourishes in Spain; 1031: Caliphate of Córdoba Falls.

RELATED ARTICLES in *Great Lives from History: The Middle Ages, 477-1453*: Charlemagne; Charles Martel; Hārūn al-Rashīd.

735
CHRISTIANITY IS INTRODUCED INTO GERMANY

Christianity's introduction into Germany expanded the borders of Christendom beyond the boundaries of the Roman Empire.

LOCALE: Hesse, Thuringia, and Bavaria (now in Germany), and Frisia (now in the Netherlands)
CATEGORY: Religion

KEY FIGURES

Saint Willibrord (658?-739), apostle of Frisia, bishop of Utrecht
Saint Boniface (c. 675-754), apostle of Germany, archbishop of Mainz, 747-754
Saint Gregory II (669-731), head of the Roman Catholic Church, 715-731, patron of Saint Boniface

SUMMARY OF EVENT

From 500 to 700, Irish and later English missionary monks under religious conviction attempted to create a new Europe out of its wreckage from previous wars. Anglo-Saxon monks and the Papacy were hard at work in the mission field during the eighth century in a dual attempt to transform the Frankish church and to convert the pagan continental Germanic tribes.

An early evangelical pioneer was Willibrord, a Northumbrian monk, who began a minimally successful forty-year effort to convert the Frisians in approximately 690 in the area around the town of Utrecht (now in the Netherlands). Willibrord was later joined in Frisia by one of his missionary associates, Wynfrith, a celebrated English nobleman and Benedictine monk. Wynfrith would later be renamed Saint Boniface and be given the title apostle of Germany from his patron, Pope Gregory II, who called him in 718 to preach in Germany. Wynfrith's personal call by the Papacy, however, did not come immediately as Gregory II was initially disturbed to see a member of the Roman Church trying to organize a band of pilgrims instead of settling in a monastery permanently. Only after Wynfrith produced an episcopal letter of recommendation and explained his intentions did Gregory II authorize him to go into the German mission field and represent the Roman Church.

Wynfrith, born in a noble Anglo-Saxon family in Kirton, Devonshire, and christened as Winfrid, labored at making converts for three years before the pope made him bishop for all of Germany east of the Rhine River in 723 and gave him the name Saint Boniface. In approximately 743, Saint Boniface founded the Abbey of Fulda, which later became one of the most famous monasteries in Germany, and served as archbishop of Mainz from 747 to 754. Visiting the Frankish ruler Charles Martel on his way to minister in the rebellious heathen province of Hesse, Saint Boniface was granted protection by Frankish officials. This civil protection greatly assisted his ability to further institute and strengthen papal authority in France and allowed his missions to succeed where others had previously failed. Ten years of missionary work in the areas of Hesse and Thuringia followed, during which tradition relates that Saint Boniface felled a famous oak tree sacred to the pagan gods at Geismar to reinforce one of his teachings and then used the timber to build a church in honor of Saint Peter.

Saint Boniface's work among the heathen was later opposed by Frankish bishops and Irish monks who ac-

Saint Boniface converting the Saxons. (Hulton|Archive by Getty Images)

cused him of working in regions under their jurisdiction. News of this resistance to his work brought numerous English volunteers to his aid, which served to advance the young German church but at some cost to the Church of England. When Gregory III became pope in 732, Saint Boniface was granted metropolitan rank with power to consecrate other bishops, although he remained without an episcopal see until he secured the chair of Mainz. With great organizing skill and loyalty to the Holy See, Saint Boniface founded missionary works for Bavaria in Salzburg, Regensburg, Freising, and Passau. By 742, he had established episcopal seats for Hesse and Thuringia at Wurtzburg, Buraburg, and Erfurt.

Saxons undergoing baptism after being conquered by Charlemagne. From a miniature in a fifteenth century manuscript in the Burgundy Library, Brussels. (Frederick Ungar Publishing Co.)

Saint Boniface visited Rome in 738 for the third time when the structure and organization of the German church was completed. Even though Saint Boniface enjoyed the numerous advantages of papal support during his missionary projects, his work among the heathen Saxons resulted in very limited success. He had apparently underestimated the difficulties of converting the Saxons, his continental blood brothers, and met such fierce resistance that military efforts by Charlemagne a half-century later were necessary to make them permanent converts. Although Christianity is founded on the teachings of Jesus Christ, who sought to prepare his disciples to convert followers for the coming kingdom of God, Saint Boniface found through his studies and struggles that the Bible includes very few organizational instructions on how to accomplish this. After his failure with the Saxon tribes, Pope Gregory III instructed Saint Boniface to continue the organization of the church in southern Germany on a diocesan basis, which he accomplished with tremendous skill and dedication.

History will remember Saint Boniface being clearly more successful as a missionary than other notable missionaries during the Middle Ages such as Saint Augustine, apostle to the English nation and first archbishop of Canterbury. One contributing factor may have been that Saint Boniface had considerably more military protection and financial support from Charles Martel and Pépin III the Short than Saint Augustine did from King Ethelbert of Kent (d. 616). Saint Boniface also had the advantage of working among people less different from himself than missionaries either before or after him. Additionally, the previous attempts by Irish monks to convert the Saxons and other Germanic tribes in the area had undoubtedly helped prepare the way for Saint Boniface and his talent for attracting helpers and financial support.

SIGNIFICANCE

Saint Boniface left his mark on German religion and culture by starting the Benedictine-dominated German church of the early Middle Ages and, to some extent, the Carolingian monarchy of the eighth and ninth centuries. Saint Boniface's love for and devotion to the Papacy also contributed to the final emancipation of the Papacy from the Roman Empire in the East, to the penetration of the idea of the theocratic monarchy into Western Europe, and to the legal founding of the papal states. Willibrord, Wilfred, and Saint Boniface are credited by most historians as "heroes whose labor established the Roman Church as the ultimate standard in the heart of Europe." The festival of Saint Boniface is celebrated in both the Catholic and Anglican churches on June 5, the anniversary of his death in 754 at the hands of an angry pagan mob.

The Roman Catholic form of Christianity continued to prosper in all German lands until the advent of the Protestant Reformation. A majority of the Protestants of the sixteenth century followed the teachings of Martin Luther, which were based on the scripture "the just shall live by faith," and thus became known as Lutherans. Other German Protestants followed the teachings of the French Protestant reformer John Calvin and thus organized Reformed and Evangelical churches. Many of the Polish-speaking people of eastern Prussia remained in the Roman Catholic faith, as did many peoples of Austria, Bavaria, and some of the Rhineland cities of western Prussia. Most of Prussia, Saxony, and northern and central Germany increasingly turned away from the Roman Catholic form of Christianity to the Protestant church after the Great Reformation.

—Daniel G. Graetzer

FURTHER READING

Brown, Peter. *The Rise of Western Christendom: Triumph and Diversity, A.D. 200-1000*. 2d ed. Malden, Mass.: Blackwell, 2003. A survey of the development and spread of Christianity during the first millennium, focusing especially on the different types of Christianity in different parts of Europe and the Middle East and the interactions of believers.

Deanesly, Margaret. *The Pre-Conquest Church in England*. New York: Oxford University Press, 1961. This volume contains excellent and well-organized chapters on Boniface and other English missionaries to Germany in the eighth century.

Duckett, Eleanor Shipley. *Anglo-Saxon Saints and Scholars*. 1947. Reprint. Hamden, Conn.: Archon Books, 1967. A biographical account of numerous Anglo-Saxon saints and scholars who shaped the religious development of Europe during their time.

Egmond, Wolfert von. "Converting Monks: Missionary Activity in Early Medieval Frisia and Saxony." In *Christianizing Peoples and Converting Individuals*, edited by Guyda Armstrong and Ian N. Wood. Turnhout, Belgium: Brepols, 2000. Explores the encounter between missionaries and non-Christians in two medieval German regions.

Godfrey, John. *The Church in Anglo-Saxon England*. Cambridge, England: Cambridge University Press, 1962. Eulogizes Boniface as a creator of Europe, a founder of German Christianity, a reformer of the Frankish church, and a chief architect of the monumental alliance between the Papacy and the Carolingian family.

Greenaway, George W. *Saint Boniface*. New York: Humanities Press, 1955. A brief account of the life, struggles, and dedication of Boniface.

Levison, Wilhelm. *England and the Continent in the Eighth Century*. Oxford, England: Oxford University Press, 1946. A text that contains a full, standard, and learned account of the work of English missionaries in the time of Boniface.

Logan, F. Donald. *A History of the Church in the Middle Ages*. New York: Routledge, 2002. Covers the spread and development of medieval Christianity, beginning with the conversion of the Celts and of the Germanic tribes.

Schnurer, Gustav. *Church and Culture in the Middle Ages: Volume I, 350-814*. Paterson, N.J.: Saint Anthony Guild Press, 1956. Emphasizes the numerous difficulties Boniface had to overcome and calls him "probably the most able missionary ever produced by a north European country."

Talbot, C. H., ed. *The Anglo-Saxon Missionaries in Germany: Being the Lives of SS. Willibrord, Boniface, Sturm, Leoba, and Lebuin, Together with the Hodoeporicon of Saint Willibald and a Selection from the Correspondence of Saint Boniface*. New York: Sheed and Ward, 1954. An excellent write-up on the "Life of Saint Boniface" is included in this well-edited text, with all sources translated into English.

SEE ALSO: 496: Baptism of Clovis; 596-597: See of Canterbury Is Established; c. 850: Development of the Slavic Alphabet; 864: Boris Converts to Christianity; 988: Baptism of Vladimir I; 1136: Hildegard von Bingen Becomes Abbess; 1228-1231: Teutonic Knights Bring Baltic Region Under Catholic Control; 1414-1418: Council of Constance; July 6, 1415: Martyrdom of Jan Hus.

RELATED ARTICLES in *Great Lives from History: The Middle Ages, 477-1453*: Saint Boniface; Boris I of Bulgaria; Charlemagne; Charles Martel; Saint Clotilda; Clovis; Gregory of Tours; Hildegard von Bingen; Jan Hus; Louis the German; Saint Sergius I; Vladimir I.

740
KHAZARS CONVERT TO JUDAISM

The Khazar kingdom in southern Russia dominated major worldwide trade routes from the eighth to the eleventh century. The conversion of a large part of the population to Judaism makes this little-known kingdom intriguing historically and of controversial significance to the issue of the Jewish Diaspora.

LOCALE: Southern Russia from the Black Sea to the Caspian Sea, north of the Caucasus Mountains
CATEGORIES: Cultural and intellectual history; religion; trade and commerce

KEY FIGURES

Bulan (fl. mid-ninth century), king of the Khazars, converted the kingdom to Judaism, r. c. 740's
Obadiah (d. 909), king of the Khazars, r. 886-909, built synagogues, Jewish schools, and institutionalized Jewish religious practices
Joseph (fl. mid-ninth century), Khazar king, r. mid-ninth century, corresponded with Muslims about the Khazars

SUMMARY OF EVENT

Bulan, king (kagan) of Khazaria, had an important decision to make in 861. His people, the Khazars, controlled a vast area stretching from the Black and Caspian Seas to the Ural Mountains. This empire traversed important north-south and east-west trade routes affecting major world trading centers in the Islamic and Byzantine worlds from which goods as far away as China and India were shipped along the Silk Road.

Because the Silk Road was blocked by Muslims, trade was directed through Khazaria. For more than a century, Muslim expansion into eastern Europe had been blocked by formidable Khazar military might. Bulan, however, needed an official religion for his expanding and strategically important kingdom.

As part of a confederation of Turkish tribes, which once were part of the Western Turkish Empire, the Khazars practiced shamanistic and animistic beliefs. The disintegration of the Western Turkish Empire led the Khazars to invade the Caucasus, where they gained control of southern Russia and the Ukraine. Conquest did not change the basic Khazar agricultural existence. Sheepherding and fishing supplemented a staple diet of barley, wheat, and rice. However, considerable wealth was generated from duties on trade (particularly with the Byzantine Empire) and taxes on subject peoples such as the eastern Slavs, Magyars, Bulgars, and Pechenegs. Control of the gold and silver mines in the Caucasus also contributed to Khazar wealth.

Khazar tax money was channeled into the building of commercial and administrative cities. The earliest capital was Balanjar. A new capital, Samander, was built in 720 on the coast in the north Caucasus. Finally, Atil (Itil) was built in 750 on the Volga River and remained the Khazar capital for more than two centuries. Also a large fortress, Sarkel (834), was built of stone and brick along the Don River to control a major trade route.

Located between the ever-expanding Islamic world and the ever-shrinking but still economically important Byzantine Empire, the Khazars by 740 were a strong, major power. In a series of wars (the first from 642 to 652 and the second from 732 to 737), the Khazars proved successful in stopping Islamic expansion in southern Russia. By 740, the Khazars also received large numbers of Jewish immigrants fleeing Byzantine and Persian persecution and leaving disruptions in the Arab world for economic opportunities in Khazaria.

Historical sources designate 740 as the earliest possible date that the Khazars converted to Judaism as the major state religion. Other historians point to several dates during the first half of the ninth century. There is a strong probability that the process had been taking place for more than a century when the Byzantine missionaries Cyril and Methodius arrived in 860 to try to convert the remainder of the population to Orthodox Christianity. They had no success but may have convinced King Bulan to declare an official state religion.

In 861, King Bulan invited representatives from Christian, Islamic, and Jewish faiths to speak on the merits of their respective beliefs. The decision to select Judaism most likely was made to avoid political or religious control by either the Muslim caliphate in Baghdad, the Byzantine emperor in Constantinople, or the pope in Rome. Lacking anything resembling a power center, Judaism clearly guaranteed the kagan's autonomy over Khazaria. Tradition says that when Bulan asked the Christian and Islamic representatives which religion they would accept after their own, they each identified Judaism. Bulan's decision is described in a letter written by King Joseph of Khazaria, a century after the event.

As the court religion, Judaism rapidly spread among the Khazar nobility and then among large numbers of common people. Under Bulan's successor, King Obadiah, synagogues and Jewish schools were established after the rabbinical form of Judaism was embraced. The Talmud, Torah, and Mishnah were well-received, along with Saturday worship, circumcision, and the following of major Jewish holidays. Biblical names such as Joseph and Aaron became common.

However, the Khazars also exhibited extreme tolerance for all religions among the many different peoples populating the Crimea. Consequently, while establishing a Jewish state, the Khazars were open to the extensive practice of other religions. In Atil, a supreme court of seven members was established to represent religious diversity. Two Jewish, two Christian, two Islamic, and one pagan judge sat on the court. Khazaria established a reputation of tolerance in the Arab and Christian world, attracting merchants across Eurasia. Also, to signal a ready acceptance of diversity, Khazar nobles sent their sons to study in the scholastically advanced academies in Islamic Spain.

Khazaria's prosperity was affected first by Viking raids and then by wars by the Bulgars and Pechenegs who struck at the Khazar's Magyar allies. Ultimately the Magyars were pushed into the area that is now Hungary. The Viking reorganization of the Kievan state hit hard at Khazar power. Military threats caused a change in Khazar government. The kagan became a spiritual and figurehead leader while power was transferred to the hands of the *bek*, a civilian in command of military forces.

In 965, the prince of Kiev, Svyatoslav I (r. 945-972), defeated a Khazar force and was able to capture the major Khazar fortress of Sarkel. By 987, Prince Vladimir I of Kiev (r. 980-1015), who had married Anna, the sister of the Byzantine emperor, converted both himself and the people of Rus to Orthodox Christianity in the late tenth century. In 1016, a joint Russian-Byzantine force defeated the Khazars in a major battle. From this point, Khazaria entered into rapid decline and ultimate disintegration. The correspondence of King Joseph of Khazaria around 960 with Caliph ʿAbd al-Raḥmān III al-Nāṣir (r. 912-961) of Córdoba (Muslim Spain) sheds important light on this period as well as general Khazar history. Domination of lucrative trade routes would henceforth be in the hands of the princes of Kievan Rus.

SIGNIFICANCE

From the eighth to the eleventh century, the Khazars played a critical role in early Russian national development and world trade. As a strong military state, Khazaria was instrumental in blocking the spread of Islam north of the Caucasus Mountains. Juxtaposed between the conflicting Islamic and Christian worlds, the Khazars introduced a third force into the power struggle. Moreover, by the mid-ninth century, they had established the only Jewish state between the biblical kingdoms of Israel and Judah and the modern nation of Israel. Along with places such as Andalusia (Muslim Spain), Khazaria still stands as a model of religious tolerance.

Finally, the relationship of the Khazars in the evolution of Jewish populations in Europe remains a source of considerable contemporary controversy because it calls into question the relationship of many contemporary Jews of European ancestry to the Jews of biblical times. Many ethnologists believe that the Khazars are very much a part of the gene pool of Russian and East European Jews.

—*Irwin Halfond*

FURTHER READING

Brook, Kevin Alan. *The Jews of Khazaria*. Northvale, N.J.: Jason Aronson, 1999. A well-written study that includes reference to recent archaeological finds. Contains a bibliography, footnotes, time lines, and maps.

Christian, David Gilbert. *Inner Eurasia from Prehistory to the Mongol Empire*. Vol. 1 in *A History of Russia, Central Asia, and Mongolia*. Oxford, England: Blackwell, 1998. Chapter 11 offers an excellent account of the broader perspective of the early development of Russia. Bibliography, footnotes, and chronologies.

Franklin, Simon, and Jonathan Shepard. *The Emergence of Rus, 750-1200*. London: Longman, 1996. Provides strong background material and a good analysis of the historical role of the Khazars. Bibliography, footnotes.

Koestler, Arthur. *The Thirteenth Tribe: The Khazar Empire and Its Heritage*. New York: Random House, 1976. A landmark study in popularizing the Khazars and bringing to the forefront the issue of the social heritage of modern Jewry. Informational footnotes and bibliography.

Soteri, Nicholas. "Khazaria: A Forgotten Jewish Empire." *History Today* 45, no. 4 (April, 1995): 10-12. An excellent introduction to the "forgotten" history of the Khazars.

SEE ALSO: c. 850: Development of the Slavic Alphabet; 850-950: Viking Era; 890's: Magyars Invade Italy, Saxony, and Bavaria; c. 950: Court of Córdoba Flourishes in Spain; c. 960: Jews Settle in Bohemia; 988: Baptism of Vladimir I; c. 1150-1200: Rise of the Hansa Merchant Union; 1290-1306: Jews Are Expelled from England, France, and Southern Italy.

Related articles in *Great Lives from History: The Middle Ages, 477-1453*: Anna, Princess of the Byzantine Empire; Saint Cyril and Saint Methodius; Judah ha-Levi; Rurik; Vladimir I.

744-840
Uighur Turks Rule Central Asia

By consolidating their power over the Central Asian steppe in the second great Turkic empire, the Uighur Turks were able to introduce stable government systems to the region.

Locale: China, Mongolia, Kyrgyzstan, Tajikistan
Categories: Expansion and land acquisition; government and politics

Key Figures

Guli Peiluo (Ku-li p'ei-lo, also known as Kutluk Bilgé Kül; d. 747), founder of Uighur Empire, r. 744-747

Moyanchuo (Mo-yen-ch'o, also known as Bayan Chor; d. 759), son and heir of Guli Peiluo, who consolidated Uighur dominance in Central Asia and in relations with China, r. 747-759

Mouyu (Mou-yü, also known as Bügü; d. 779), second son of Moyanchuo, who brought Uighur power to apex and converted Uighurs to Manichaeanism, r. 759-779

Xie Yujiasi (Hsieh yü-chia-ssu; also known as Kutluk; d. 805), oversaw military, political, and Manichaean revival in Uighur Empire, r. 795-805

Summary of Event

In the sixth and seventh centuries, numerous peoples of Turkic ethnicity dominated the vast steppe regions to the north and west of China. Around 550, the Tuque (T'u-chüeh) established loose domination of the area stretching from Korea to Karashar. A confederation of nine western tribes known as the Tiele (T'ieh-le) broke away from Tuque control in the mid-seventh century and moved east to provide military aid to the government of the Chinese Tang Dynasty (T'ang; 618-907). In 647, the Chinese took the tribes under their official protection, but by the end of the century, the Tuque khaghan (ruler) Mochuo (Mo-ch'o) had again subjugated them. The Uighur (Uyghur) tribe, one of the nine Tiele, led a successful rebellion and overthrew Tuque rule. The leader was the Uighur Guli Peiluo of the Yaloge, one of the ten Uighur clans. He allied the Uighur with the Basmil and Kharlukh tribes and sent the severed head of the last Tuque khaghan to the Chinese emperor as proof of the coup. The Kharlukh and Uighurs soon turned on the Basmil, scattering them. The Kharlukh were next, and they, too, were forcibly absorbed into the new Uighur state. In 744, Guli Peiluo declared the founding of his Uighur Empire and his own position as khaghan.

The son of Guli Peiluo, Moyanchuo, finished off the Basmil and Kharlukh resistance and began the process of changing Uighur—and steppe—culture. Before 744, the Uighur were purely nomadic herders who lived in constant motion. They had no experience with farming or city life except through visits to China or the Iranian regions to the west. They were fierce horsemen and master mounted bowmen. However, Moyanchuo chose not to rule from horseback and established a brand new capital city, Ordu Balik (Karabalghasun), on the upper Orkhon River. Its centerpiece was the khaghan's palace, on the flat top of which a golden tent was erected; a wall with twelve great iron gates surrounded the palace. The city itself was 4 by 1.5 miles (7 by 2.5 kilometers) in area and grew from empty grassland to thriving emporium virtually overnight. It was an administrative center, a major local and long-distance market center, and a hive of craftspeople of all sorts. The Uighurs were beginning to see themselves as rivals of the Chinese and consciously avoided imitating them. Ordu Balik and Bay Balik (Rich City), built on the Selenga River, were steppe cities without the form or feel of Chinese urban centers. In many ways, the Uighurs would look westward for models even as Moyanchuo married the Tang emperor's daughter in 758.

Chinese losses at the Battle of Talas River (751) against a Muslim army in the west and in wars against Korea in the east spawned the rise of the Turkic/Sogdian general An Lushan, who united the northern Chinese and many Turks against the Tang. The rebellion began in December, 755, and by spring, four thousand Uighur horsemen led by Mouyu, second son and heir of Moyanchuo, were aiding the Tang government armies to great effect.

After a year, An Lushan was assassinated, but the war continued under Shi Chaoyi (Shih Ch'ao-I) until 763. The rebels had taken both Chinese capitals of Chang'an (now Xi'an) and Luoyang, and with Uighur aid, both were taken. To the Uighurs, however, a captured city was a captured city, and a three-day sack should have been their reward. Chang'an was spared, but Luoyang was looted.

In 759, Mouyu had become khaghan on his father's death. While in Luoyang for four months, Mouyu became strongly affected by the Manichaean religion, which was hated by the Chinese and adhered to by many Sogdians. On returning to Ordu Balik, he and his court debated the wisdom of converting to the western religion and abandoning their ancient Turkic nature-religion. His acceptance of Manichaeanism for his people alienated many, but he enforced it by using the Mongolian military measure of having one person in charge of nine: in this case, for preaching and practicing the new faith. This also meant much tighter ties with the Sogdian merchants and their western way of life. The Sogdians quickly filled important positions at court and gained great trade concessions within the empire.

To the Chinese, for whom the Uighurs were merely powerful barbarians, the Sogdian influence was entirely unwelcome. Even though the Uighurs continued to aid the Tang, as against the Tibetans in 764-765, anti-Uighur (and anti-Sogdian) violence in Chinese territory grew in frequency and brutality. In 779, on the death of Emperor Daizong (Tai-tsung, r. 762-779), Mouyu was convinced by the Sogdians at court to attack China. This drove the khaghan's cousin and main minister, Dun Mohe (Tun Mo-ho), to assassinate Mouyu, many of his family, and as many Sogdian Manichaeans as he could. Ruling as khaghan (779-789), Dun reinstated the traditional Turkic religion and strengthened relations with the Chinese (he married a Chinese princess).

After Dun, Uighur power waned, and the position of the Yaloge clan became precarious, Tibetans got the best of them militarily in the west but were checked by General Xie Yujiasi of the Xiedie clan. When the khaghan died without an heir in 795, Xie Yujiasi took the position and began a new dynasty. Known as Kutluk (r. 795-805), he brought back the Sogdian/Manichaean influence and reestablished a strong central court. He also expanded Uighur domination to Sogdian Ferghana. His successor was Baoyi (Pao-i) khaghan (r. 805-821), under whose rule the Uighur economy prospered and whose court became noted for its luxury. Uighur tribesmen and their allies throughout the empire were directly governed by their tribal leaders, known as *tutuk*, who managed affairs among the nomadic folk and collected taxes for the khaghan's court. As that court grew more detached from its roots, it lost something of the loyalty on which it based its power. Should the *tutuk* be lost, central authority would crumble.

The Chinese were none too happy with the Sogdian/Manichaean renaissance, the Tibetans were seeking revenge, and a new force of nomadic horsemen, the Kirghiz, was harassing the empire's northern fringes. In 822, the Chinese refused an offer of Uighur cavalry support, a sign of both Chinese power and strained relations. By the later 840's, the strains were too great: A poor crop was followed by a livestock-killing freeze. A Uighur rebel helped the Kirghiz gain entry into Ordu Balik and kill the khaghan. The center was shattered, and the empire disintegrated.

SIGNIFICANCE

Uighur domination of the steppe established important precedents and planted important seeds. Unlike the earlier Turks, the Uighurs were remarkably stable as rulers. Tribalism seems to have been subordinated to central rule, and mere assassinations replaced bloody civil wars marking transitions in political power. This facilitated the flow of goods and people between east and west through the empire. The Uighurs themselves demonstrated an adaptability rarely seen in the region before, as some built and peopled cities and others became agriculturalists. Similar flexibility and stability attended the experiment with Manichaeanism.

The Sogdian influence was important in enabling the Uighurs to insulate themselves from the Chinese and yet to develop the forms and institutions of civilized life. From the Sogdians, the Uighurs borrowed a script that would also serve the Mongolians half a millennium later. The steppe could be controlled, tolls and taxes collected, records kept, and stable government maintained from a capital city.

Joseph P. Byrne

FURTHER READING

Barfield, Thomas J. *The Perilous Frontier: Nomadic Empires and China, 221 B.C. to A.D. 1757*. New York: Blackwell, 1992. Overview of the larger issue of Chinese relations with its border peoples that views Uighurs as a major stabilizing force in the region.

Christian, David. *A History of Russia, Central Asia, and Mongolia*. Vol. 1. New York: Blackwell, 1998. Provides a broad treatment of the region. Places Uighurs in the context of their Turkic heritage and traces the cultural effects of their contacts with Sogdians and Chinese during their imperial period.

Mackerras, Colin. *The Uighur Empire According to the T'ang Dynastic Histories: A Study in Sino-Uighur Relations, 744-840*. 2d ed. Columbia: University of South Carolina Press, 1972. A concise introduction to Uighur history is followed by translations from contemporary Chinese histories of the period. Attention is clearly on relations with China, but this is the only work in English specifically on Uighurs.

_______. "The Uighurs." In *The Cambridge History of Early Inner Asia*, edited by Denis Sinor. New York: Cambridge University Press, 1990. Short introduction to their history and culture during the imperial period.

SEE ALSO: 6th-8th centuries: Sogdians Dominate Central Asian Trade; 618: Founding of the Tang Dynasty; 751: Battle of Talas River; 840-846: Uighur Migrations.

c. 750-1240
RISE AND FALL OF GHANA

Ghana was one of the earliest and most important empires of West Africa, controlling trans-Saharan trade from its capital, Kumbi, and lasting nearly five hundred years.

LOCALE: Ancient Empire of Ghana (Western Africa), Sudan, Mali.
CATEGORY: Government and politics

KEY FIGURES

Sumanguru (d. c. 1235), ruler of the Susu kingdom
Sundiata (c. 1215-c. 1255), founder and king of Mali, r. 1235-1255
Tilutane (fl. ninth century), Berber tribal leader

SUMMARY OF EVENT

Ghana was founded about 750 by the Soninke people in a region of West Africa settled as early as five hundred years before. It was the first great trading empire of West Africa, lying between the Senegal and Niger Rivers. The empire earned its name from the Wagadu word *ghana*, which means "war chief" and was applied to the warrior kings who controlled the gold trade. Such chiefs were absolute monarchs, overseeing princes who ruled adjacent areas annexed by Ghana. The name Ghana was first applied to the state and its culture around 770, when it was recorded by an Arab geographer who also referred to Ghana as the "land of gold."

Ancient Ghana derived power and wealth mostly from its control of the gold fields of Bambuk and Buré. The introduction of the camel allowed trans-Saharan trade to increase the quantity of goods that were transported in and out of the El-Ghaba forest region. The route taken by traders of the Maghreb to Ghana started in North Africa in Tahert. Trade came down through Sjilmasa in southern Morocco. From there, the trail went south and inland, running parallel with the coast, continuing southeast through Awdaghust, and terminating in Kumbi, the royal capital of Ghana. Thus the coast, the Sahara, and the West African forest were all networked in an extensive trade system.

Kumbi was first uncovered by archaeologists in 1914. It was a unique city, formed by two townships roughly 4 miles (about 6 kilometers) apart. One of these townships was inhabited by Muslims, and it boasted twelve mosques—an indication of how important the Islamic religion was in Ghana. The other township, called El-Ghaba (Arabic for "the woods"), was inhabited by the non-Muslims. This township also contained a palace, built of stone and wood, where the king resided. World traveler al-Bakri documented during his stay in El-Ghaba in the early thirteenth century that Kumbi was one of the greatest and most populous cities of the world. According to al-Bakri, "Around the town are wells of sweet water from which they drank and near which they grew vegetables."

Kumbi was at the crossroads of the trans-Saharan trade and therefore became the center for control of the gold and salt exports and imports. As a result, Ghana became wealthy and achieved widespread and effective power and greatness. As Ghana grew, it became an enormous empire, threatening the independence of its West African neighbors. Surrounding states were motivated to put a halt to Ghana's reign of power not only to defend themselves but also to secure control of Ghana's gold mines and the trans-Saharan trade.

In 990, Tilutane, a leader of a local Berber tribe, united a number of Berber units into a confederacy aimed at challenging Ghanaian hegemony in West Africa. Although unsuccessful, Tilutane did briefly gain control of Awdaghust, although it was retaken in 992 by Ghana's king, Tounka. Although a failed mission, the Berbers' attempt and brief victory set the stage for the eventual downfall of the great civilization of Ghana.

As a result of the continual efforts of the Berbers to overthrow Ghana, many nations within Ghana became fearful that their demise was near. As a result, the nation was plunged into chaos as many vassal states such as Silla, Tekrur, and Anbara began to declare their independence. In an effort to achieve independence, they attacked Kumbi, forcing the Arab merchants within the city to flee to a new place called Walata in 1224 and establish a new commercial city.

The flight of the Arab merchants out of Kumbi slowed the volume of trans-Saharan trade flowing through Ghana. Deprived of gold wealth and trade, both the government and its citizens became impoverished. The destabilized army failed to restrain the increasing rebellions and continuous assaults from foreigners.

One foreigner who attempted to expand into Ghanian territory was Sumanguru, chief of the Susu (or Soso), another West African people. During his campaigns in the late twelfth century, Sumanguru attacked the established trade routes and was able to weaken the remnants of the empire. Finally, in 1203, he attacked and successfully took control of Kumbi, thus asserting himself as the new king of Ghana. He molded the nine provinces of Ghana into a sizable but short-lived empire. During his reign of terror, his heavy-handed tactics, though initially successful, ultimately resulted in resentment against him and his Susu people.

SIGNIFICANCE

Because Sumanguru was primarily a war leader and did not have the experience needed to be a king, his rule did little to restore prosperity and political stability to the empire, which had been disrupted by years of warfare among rival kingdoms. Hence, Sumanguru proved to be the last king of remnants of ancient Ghana.

According to legend, Sumanguru controlled all the Ghana lands except for Manding. There, he managed to kill all the sons of the king except one, Sundiata, who was spared because he was frail and weak. Sumanguru would later live to regret leaving Sundiata alive. After hiding in exile for many years, Sundiata gained strength and, with some help from the king of Mema, received a force of troops to take back the Ghana Empire.

Oral tradition relates that Sundiata grew stronger and began to rule the Mali kingdom while steadily gaining power and troop strength. In 1235, at the Battle of Kirina, Sundiata and Sumanguru met and fought. African tradition maintains that both were sorcerers, and thus their magic would determine the outcome of the fight. Sundiata snarled at the troops of King Sumanguru, who became terrified and ran for cover. Sumanguru retaliated, however, and the heads of eight spirits magically appeared above his own. Unfortunately for Sumanguru, Sundiata had the stronger magic, and the spirits were defeated. Sundiata then aimed an arrow at Sumaguru, and although it only grazed Sumanguru's shoulder, it drained him of all his magic, and Sumanguru was defeated.

Whether true or not, this legend confirms the fact that Ghana's power declined in the mid-thirteenth century, and the power vacuum was filled by another empire, the great empire of Mali. The tradition of the legendary Sundiata demonstrates the importance of trade and commerce in the ancient empires of western Africa. Those who controlled luxury items and trade routes secured economic prosperity and political strength.

—*Richard Fink, Aileen Carlson, and Joanna Debella*

FURTHER READING

Crowder, Michael. *West Africa: An Introduction to Its History.* 2d ed. Harlow, England: Longman, 1987. A well-known history that has seen two editions and several printings. Illustrations, maps, bibliography, index.

Davidson, Basil. *A History of West Africa, 1000-1800.* Rev. ed. London: Longman, 1977. Another standard history. Illustrations, maps, bibliography, indexes.

Fage, J. D. *Ghana: A Historical Interpretation.* Madison: University of Wisconsin Press, 1959. Although dated, still useful as a concise overview in English. Bibliographic references, index.

Greene, Sandra. *Sacred Sites and the Colonial Encounter: A History of Meaning and Memory in Ghana.* Bloomington: Indiana University Press, 2002. Examines myth, legend, and oral tradition; "shows how ideas from outside forced sacred and spiritual meanings associated with particular bodies of water, burial sites, sacred towns, and the human body itself."

Koslow, Philip. *Centuries of Greatness, 750-1900: The West African Kingdoms.* New York: Chelsea House, 1995. Designed for younger readers (grades 7-10), an overview of more than a millennium of African history from art to warfare. Includes maps, black-and-white photographs, bibliographies, chronologies.

Levtzion, Nehemia. *Ancient Ghana and Mali*. 1973. Reprint. New York: Africana, 1980. A classic and substantial study of nearly three hundred pages, with maps, bibliography, and index.

McKissack, Patricia, and Frederick McKissack. *The Royal Kingdoms of Ghana, Mali, and Songhay: Life in Medieval Africa*. New York: H. Holt, 1994. Designed for young readers, an introduction to these three major empires by reference to folklore, contemporaneous accounts, and scholarly research, covering roughly the period 500-1700. Includes a timeline, notes, and a substantial bibliography.

Munson, Patrick J. "Archaeology and the Pre-historic Origins of the Ghana Empire." *Journal of African History* 21 (1980): 457-466. Examines the history of western Africa with specific attention to the origins of the Ghana Empire.

Prussin, Labelle. *The Medieval Age: West African Empires*. Berkeley: University of California Press, 1986. Covers art, architecture, and religion in three West African empires. Contains a chapter on the Ghana Empire.

SEE ALSO: 992-1054: Ghana Takes Control of Awdaghust; c. 1010: Songhai Kingdom Converts to Islam; 1076: Almoravids Sack Kumbi; c. 1100: Founding of Timbuktu; 1230's-1255: Reign of Sundiata of Mali.

RELATED ARTICLE in *Great Lives from History: The Middle Ages, 477-1453*: Sundiata.

751
BATTLE OF TALAS RIVER

Arab forces defeated the Chinese troops in the Battle of Talas River, resulting in the closing of the Silk Road for about five hundred years and a substantial weakening of the central power of the Tang Dynasty.

LOCALE: Talas River, in modern Kazakhstan and Afghanistan, near the cities of Tashkent and Taraz (Dzhambyl)

CATEGORY: Wars, uprisings, and civil unrest

KEY FIGURES

Gao Xianzhi (Kao Hsien-chih; d. 755), Korean-born general of the Chinese army at Talas River

Xuanzong (Hsüan-tsung; 685-762), Tang emperor, r. 712-756

An Lushan (An Lu-shan; 703-757), general who led a rebellion against the Tang Dynasty

SUMMARY OF EVENT

The Battle of Talas River was the only major military battle between Chinese and Arab forces. During the Tang Dynasty (T'ang; 618-907), the Chinese succeeded in regaining and stabilizing control in regions near the Talas River, particularly the trade routes. The Chinese had taken back the Tarim Basim region from the Tibetans in 738, and these outermost provinces agreed to become vassals of the Chinese empire with the promise of protection against enemy invasion. However, a disagreement arose between the rulers in the states of Tashkent and Ferghana, both Chinese vassals.

The heir of the Tashkent province wanted to seek revenge against his family's honor after his father was slated for execution by a leading Chinese general. He asked for support of the Arabs at Bukhara and Samarqand. The Muslim Arabs, a group that had rapidly spread from the Iberian Peninsula into Central Asia during the seventh century, intervened on behalf of Tashkent. To stop an Arab invasion in this region, 30,000 Chinese forces, under General Gao Xianzhi, engaged the Arabs near Atlakh on the banks of the Talas River. The Chinese army suffered a devastating military defeat when their western Turkish (Qarluq) allies deserted them on the battlefield, resulting in their ground support being spread too thin. Arab rule, Islamic civilization, and power would dominate the area during the next 150 years; however, this conflict ended Arabic expansion eastward. The battle also signified the beginnings of military, political, and economic turmoil that would plague the Chinese government throughout the next two centuries.

SIGNIFICANCE

The ramifications of the Battle of Talas were enormous for China. The Arabs captured many Chinese papermakers who worked in factories near the river. The Arabs proceeded to learn the art, keeping the papermaking process a secret, and began to export paper from distribution points outside Baghdad at inflated prices to European markets. Chinese silk workers, who were also taken as prisoners after the Battle of Talas, passed on their craft to the Arab world as well, but the quality of silk produced in the Near East never equaled that of China.

Moreover, the loss of these provinces marked the decline in power of the Tang Dynasty under Emperor Xuanzong. China lost control of its main trade route, the Silk Road, for the next half century. Due to the turmoil in the area, trade routes to the south began to suffer. Tibetans also reestablished control of the Tarim Basin and Kansu Corridor, and they took the city of Dunhuang in 766, continuing to spread a Lamaist version of Buddhism in Central Asia. The Chinese army in the north was not able to divert repeated attacks from a Mongol tribe known as the Khitan. The Khitan were able to settle in the northeast near Beijing (Peking) and sacked the city of Kaifeng.

Because of these disturbing developments, civil unrest ensued in China, and the outcome was a rebellion that broke out four years after the Battle of Talas. An Lushan, a general of Sogdian-Turkish origins, rose quickly through the ranks of the army to become a favored member of the Tang court. Emperor Xuanzong gave him a military governor post in the 740's. In 755, An Lushan used his powerful position in the border areas to amass a large army and led a rebellion against the empire. The general attacked the capital city of Luoyang, forcing the royal family to flee southwest of the mountain region of Sichuan (Szechuan). An Lushan then proclaimed himself emperor, and six months later, he captured the city of Ch'angan (modern Xi'an). An Lushan was killed in 757, and the rebellion was quelled in 763 with the help of a hired Uighur army. However, the rebellion weakened the central Tang government, resulting in the collapse of the dynasty.

The state of political division continued in the Five Dynasties and Ten Kingdoms period (907-960) because of the rise of powerful warlords and several independent states. The emphasis on militarism contributed to the decline of the Tang, a lesson not lost on the founder of the Song Dynasty (Sung; 960-1279), who was a former general. He based the government on civil ideals rather than military virtues. The Song Dynasty absorbed these autonomous states over time, unifying the empire and shifting the geographical base of the government near the Wei and Huang Rivers.

—*Gayla Koerting*

FURTHER READING

Cowley, Robert, and Geoffrey Parker, eds. *The Reader's Companion to Military History*. New York: Houghton Mifflin, 1996. General reference work that lists important battles, leaders, and military terminology in alphabetical order. The work also features forty battle maps and an extensive index.

Franck, Irene M., and David M. Brownstone. *The Silk Road: A History*. New York: Facts On File, 1986. Comprehensive study of the history of the Silk Road as a crucial communication, trade, and travel route from the Mediterranean to Central China. Extensive research that uses primary and secondary source materials.

Kennedy, Hugh. *The Armies of the Caliphs: Military and Society in the Early Islamic State*. New York: Routledge, 2001. Kennedy looks at the early Islamic conquests from 600 to 945. The ʿAbbāsid caliphs fought for dominance in an empire that went from Spain to the borders of India. He explains how the army influenced the political system through recruitment, payment, weaponry, and fortifications. The author focuses heavily on the relationship between the army, society, and culture.

_______. *The Prophet and the Age of the Caliphates: The Islamic Near East from the Sixth to the Eleventh Century*. New York: Longman, 1986. An introduction to the Near East from the end of the sixth century, with the birth of Islam with Muḥammad, until the rise of Islamic society in 1050. The author also discusses Arab conquests during the seventh century and the age of Umayyad and ʿAbbāsid caliphates. Includes list of genealogical tables and four maps.

Muqi, Che. *The Silk Road, Past and Present*. Beijing: Foreign Languages Press, 1989. The author recounts his journey along the oldest section of the Silk Road in this memoir. The account also explains the historical importance of the ancient road from a political and economic perspective.

Perkins, Dorothy. *Encyclopedia of China: The Essential Reference to China, Its History and Culture*. New York: Facts On File, 1999. Entries in this one-volume reference work are presented in alphabetical order. Categories include cities/provinces, government and politics, important leaders, traditions, literature, language, family structure, religion, and traditional events.

Shouyi, Bai, ed. *An Outline History of China*. Beijing: Foreign Languages Press, 1982. Shouyi is a professor of Chinese history. The work focuses on the history of Chinese dynasties; chapters 7 and 8 are devoted to the Tang and Sung. Includes a foldout map of China and an extensive index.

Weiss, Bernard G., and Arnold H. Green. *A Survey of Arab History*. Rev. ed. Egypt: The American University in Cairo Press, 1987. Work is a comprehensive overview of Arab history from 600 to 1916. Authors address trade routes, caliphates, Arab expansion, the rise of Islam, European imperialism, nationalism, and the emergence of independent Arab nations in the early 1900's. Includes twenty illustrations but lacks an index.

SEE ALSO: 7th-8th centuries: Papermaking Spreads to Korea, Japan, and Central Asia; 618: Founding of the Tang Dynasty; 637-657: Islam Expands Throughout the Middle East; 755-763: Rebellion of An Lushan; 907-960: Period of Five Dynasties and Ten Kingdoms; 936: Khitans Settle Near Beijing; 960: Founding of the Song Dynasty.

RELATED ARTICLE in *Great Lives from History: The Middle Ages, 477-1453*: An Lushan.

754
CORONATION OF PÉPIN THE SHORT

Pépin's coronation marked the first time a European dynasty was given formal religious sanction.

LOCALE: Ponthion, France
CATEGORIES: Government and politics; religion

KEY FIGURES

Pépin the Short (c. 714-768), mayor of the palace under the Merovingians from 741, son of Charles Martel, and father of Charlemagne
Stephen II (d. 757), Roman Catholic pope, 752-757
Zacharias (d. 752), Roman Catholic pope, 741-752
Childeric III (d. 754), last Merovingian king, r. 743-751, deposed by Pépin

SUMMARY OF EVENT

The Franks conquered much of France under the leadership of Clovis, who founded the dynasty of kings known as the Merovingians. They continued to rule during the seventh and eighth centuries, assisted by officials called mayors of the palace. Because of periods of minorities, dwindling royal resources, and the physical deterioration of the dynasty, the mayors of the palace eventually became the actual power behind the throne, although they were careful to cloak their actions behind the formal prerogative of the Merovingian kings, who were held in quasi-sacred respect by the Frankish people. In time, the mayoral power became concentrated in the Arnulfing family. In 750, Pépin the Short, mayor of the palace and son of Charles Martel (mayor of the palace before Pépin), sent two messengers to Pope Zacharias to inquire whether it was right that a ruler with no power should continue to be called "king." The pope replied that it was better for the man who actually possessed power to be the legal ruler, and he authorized Pépin to assume the title. Historians have debated whether this was a spontaneous interchange or the enactment of a carefully choreographed script. The Merovingians were so established as a dynasty that nothing less than the pope's explicit approval could have sanctioned their removal. As a result, Childeric III and his son, the last remaining Merovingians, were sent to a monastery in November, 751, and Childeric was ritually shorn of his long hair, long a symbol of kingship in Frankish eyes. Pépin thus became king of the Franks. This new dynasty of Arnulfing rulers later became known as the Carolingians, after the most illustrious representative of the line: Charlemagne, son of Pépin.

Meanwhile, the Lombards under King Aistulf had conquered Ravenna, expelled the emperor's viceroy, and directed their armies toward Rome. Pope Stephen II dispatched messengers to Pépin requesting an escort for the pope to visit the Frankish kingdom in person. Pépin agreed to cooperate. The emperor in Constantinople likewise dispatched an envoy to the pope, insisting that he negotiate with Aistulf the Lombard. Stephen did stop briefly in Pavia to confer with Aistulf, but he proceeded to the meeting with Pépin at Ponthion on January 6, 754. The pope's biographer later reported that Pépin prostrated himself on the ground and then held the bridle of the papal horse. He vowed to reconquer papal territories that had been taken by the Lombards. At the monastery of Saint-Denis, the pope anointed Pépin and his wife and sons, and bestowed on him the title "Patrician of the Romans." Stephen also prohibited, under pain of excommunication, the choice of a king other than from the line of Pépin. With the papal-Frankish alliance firmly concluded, Pépin entered Italy, defeated Aistulf, and, in 756, gave to the pope all the territories of the exarchate around Ravenna, which had formerly been the possession of the emperor. This bequest has come to be known as the Donation of Pépin.

Pépin's coronation ceremony. (R. H. Pease)

Traditionally, the pope had regarded the emperor in Constantinople as his secular counterpart and protector. This was true even after the Lombard invasion disturbed the imperial hold over much of Italy. During the eighth century, however, the Iconoclastic Controversy in the Byzantine Empire alienated the Papacy and made the popes conscious of the distinctly Western foundation of the spiritual culture over which they presided. Therefore, the popes began to look across the mountains toward the Frankish kingdom for their secular sponsors.

Controversy over the significance of Pépin's coronation continued for centuries. Papal theorists contended that by appealing to Zacharias for an opinion, Pépin was actually acknowledging papal superiority over kingship; by accepting the unction from Stephen II, Pépin recognized the right of the pontiff to create kings. By accepting the Donation of Pépin, the pope was merely receiving back his own land from a loyal son of the Church. Supporters of the emperor in Constantinople challenged the right of the pope to create kings or bestow titles because this was solely the prerogative of the emperor. Furthermore, they maintained that the Donation of Pépin was illegal because the exarchate around Ravenna had belonged to the emperor. Pépin's successors, on the other hand, pointed out that the pope came to France as a suppliant seeking aid against the Lombards, and that Pépin was in no way dependent on the pope. They said that by defeating Aistulf and bestowing land, Pépin was actually patronizing the pope. He never used the title of patrician conferred by the pope, nor did he return to Rome after 756.

SIGNIFICANCE

No matter how the event is interpreted, Pépin's coronation resulted in an intimate relationship between kings and popes. The ambiguities implicit in this relationship were the cause of papal-imperial tensions for the remainder of the medieval period. In a concrete way, the episode raised the question of ultimate sovereignty, creating a precedent for the coronations of Charlemagne and of Otto the Great.

—*Carl A. Volz, updated by Nicholas Birns*

FURTHER READING

Bachrach, Bernard S. *Early Carolingian Warfare: Prelude to Empire*. Philadelphia: University of Pennsylvania Press, 2001. A history of the art and science of

A MONK'S ACCOUNT OF PÉPIN'S CORONATION

In the year of the Incarnation of our Lord, 750 [*scribal error*], Pépin sent ambassadors to Pope Zacharias to ask his opinion in the matter of the kings of the Franks, who, though of the royal line, and called kings, enjoyed in truth no power in the realm except that official documents were issued in their name. Otherwise they were destitute of power, and did only what the mayor of the palace told them. . . . Pope Zacharias, therefore, in virtue of apostolic authority, told the ambassadors that he judged it better and more advantageous that he should be king and be called king who had the power [Pépin] rather than he who was falsely called king [Childeric]. The said pontiff accordingly enjoined the king and the people of the Franks that Pépin . . . should be called king and raised to the throne. And this was done by Saint Boniface, the archbishop, who anointed him king in the City of Soissons.

Source: Milton Viorst, *The Great Documents of Western Civilization* (Philadelphia: Chilton Books, 1965), pp. 17-18.

military campaigns at the time of Pépin. Extensive bibliography and index.

Barraclough, Geoffrey. *The Medieval Papacy.* London: Thames & Hudson, 1968. Barraclough views the coronation of Pépin as an incident in the centuries-old East-West tension. The Donation of Pépin established the Papacy as a temporal power.

Ganshof, François Louis. *The Carolingians and the Frankish Monarchy.* Translated by Janet Sondheimer. London: Longman, 1971. Somewhat old-fashioned and underestimates the importance of religious issues, but still a helpful basic source.

Herrin, Judith. *The Formation of Christendom.* Princeton, N.J.: Princeton University Press, 1987. Describes the evolution of a distinctively Western idea of a Christian commonwealth which underlay the coronations of both Pépin and Charlemagne.

McKitterick, Rosamond. *The Frankish Kings and Culture in the Early Middle Ages.* Aldershot, England: Variorum, 1995. Essays on the period by the leading late twentieth century historian of the Carolingians.

Moreira, Isabel. *Dreams, Visions, and Spiritual Authority in Merovingian Gaul.* Ithaca, N.Y.: Cornell University Press, 2000. A look at the religious aspects of the early Christian church before and during the time of Pépin. Extensive bibliography and index.

Nelson, Janet. "Kingship and Empire in the Carolingian World." In *Carolingian Culture: Education and Innovation*, edited by Rosamond McKitterick. Cambridge, England: Cambridge University Press, 1994. Scholarly look at the significance of coronation rituals and the royal prerogatives that emanated from them.

Riché, Pierre. *The Carolingians.* Philadelphia: University of Pennsylvania Press, 1993. Very detailed, reliable, and reflective account of the origins of the Carolingian dynasty. Compares the political skill of Pépin in displacing the Merovingians to his less accomplished ancestors.

Scherman, Katherine. *The Birth of France: Warriors, Bishops, and Long-Haired Kings.* New York: Random House, 1987. Written for the general reader, and good on the nature of the Merovingian Dynasty and its decline and fall.

Schutz, Herbert. *The Germanic Realms in Pre-Carolingian Central Europe, 400-750.* New York: P. Lang, 2000. Sets the context of the Germanic influence on the Carolingian realm.

Wood, Ian N., ed. Franks and Alamanni in the Merovingian Period: An Ethnographic Perspective. Rochester, N.Y.: Boydell Press, 1999. Surveys the Church history—through the tenth century—of the Germanic peoples and the Franks. Includes a bibliography and index.

SEE ALSO: 568-571: Lombard Conquest of Italy; 726-843: Iconoclastic Controversy; October 11, 732: Battle of Tours.

RELATED ARTICLES in *Great Lives from History: The Middle Ages, 477-1453*: Charlemagne; Charles Martel.

755-763
Rebellion of An Lushan

The rebellion of An Lushan undermined the stability of the Tang Dynasty, planting the seeds of the dynasty's ultimate fall.

Locale: China
Category: Wars, uprisings, and civil unrest

Key Figures

An Lushan (An Lu-shan; 703-757), Tang general who led a rebellion against the dynasty
Xuanzong (Hsüan-tsung; 685-762), Tang emperor, r. 712-756
Li Linfu (d. 752), a leading Tang minister during the 740's
Yang Guifei (Yang Kuei-fei; 719-756), Xuanzong's young, beautiful concubine
Yang Guozhong (Yang Kuo-chung; d. 756), a relative of Yang Guifei
Suzong (Su-tsung; 711-762), Tang emperor, r. 756-762, third son of Xuanzong
Daizong (Tai-tsung; 727-779), emperor, r. 762-779, eldest son of Suzong

Summary of Event

The rebellion of An Lushan was one of the seminal events in China's long history, an event that not only led to the ultimate fall of the Tang Dynasty (T'ang; 618-907) but also generated a story filled with romance, betrayal, and tragedy.

An Lushan was a Chinese general of non-Chinese origin. His father, a Sogdian from Central Asia, was a soldier in the Tang armies and his mother was of Turkish origin. His rebellion began in 755 and was not put down by imperial authorities until 763, although An Lushan was murdered in 757. The rebellion was a consequence of a number of factors that long preceded the uprising. The Tang Dynasty is often considered to be China's greatest dynasty. Its capital, Chang'an (now Xi'an), was the largest city in the world, a cosmopolitan city with links to the Mediterranean Sea, the Middle East, and India (because of the Silk Road), as well as to Korea, Japan, and elsewhere in Asia. Under the Tang, China ruled territories that reached across much of Central Asia. Among the greatest of the Tang emperors was Xuanzong, who ascended the throne in 712.

As emperor, Xuanzong reduced the corruption of the previous reign, appointed well-qualified and hard-working ministers generally selected through a public examination system based on the writings of China's ancient sages such as Confucius, reformed the laws and made them more humane, and attempted to shift the tax burden from the peasants to the landowners. Commerce expanded, canals were rebuilt, and foreign trade increased. A patron of artists and intellectuals, he established the Imperial Academy of Letters, or the Hanlin Academy. Although he had fifty-nine children, he was largely successful in excluding the relatives of his numerous consorts and concubines as well as the palace eunuchs from political power.

However, in the 730's, Xuanzong abandoned many of his public responsibilities, retreating into religious pursuits, notably Daoism and Tantric Buddhism. Li Linfu became the chief minister, engendering much controversy by purging his opponents. In the 740's, the sixty-year-old emperor became infatuated with the much younger Yang Guifei, the beautiful wife of one of his sons. For Xuanzong, political power and responsibility were cast aside in favor of his captivating concubine.

However, with Yang Guifei came her family and their ambitions, a phenomena not unusual in China, where the emperor was the focus of wealth and power. By the early 750's, Yang Guozhong, a relative of Yang Guifei and a regional military governor, was rivaling Li Linfu as the dominant figure at court, a position he solidified with Li's death in 752. A year earlier, in 751, the emperor's favorite, Yang Guifei, adopted An Lushan as her son, although rumors circulated that she was more his mistress than his mother, thus scandalizing many at court.

An Lushan had achieved a position of considerable authority as a Tang general, serving in the western frontier region. The Tang Empire stretched far beyond China's traditional borders, requiring an army of 600,000, divided into nine zones or provinces, each headed by a military governor. The soldiers and officers, like An Lushan, often were not Chinese. During the early decades of Xuanzong's reign, the border area was secure, with China at peace with most of its western neighbors.

However, by the mid-eighth century, imperial calm was shattered and China's security was threatened from several quarters, most notably by Islamic Arabs. After the overthrow of the Umayyad caliphate by Abū al-ʿAbbās as-Saffāḥ in 750, Baghdad became the capital of the ʿAbbāsid caliphate dynasty. The following year, 751, Abū al-ʿAbbās defeated a large Tang army at the Talas River in present-day Kazakhstan, severing China's routes to India and installing Muslims in place of Chinese as the rulers along the Silk Road across Asia.

Whether the defeat at the Battle of Talas River was a key factor leading to An Lushan's rebellion is difficult to ascertain. It did lead to the eventual loss of China's Central Asian empire and indicated that Tang military supremacy had declined. However, the pre-existing policy of giving military governors considerable authority was a more important factor in explaining the rebellion. An Lushan, like other regional military governors, had established his own power base, and by 755, he had an army at his disposal numbering 160,000 soldiers, ostensibly to defend the empire from foreign attack, but which could also be turned against the central government. For any government, to have allowed control of the military to slip from the hands of the emperor and the imperial bureaucracy to the generals was fraught with potential danger. It has also been suggested that An Lushan's non-Chinese origins explain his rebellion against a Chinese ruler, and that if he were Chinese, he would have remained loyal to the Tang Dynasty.

What is certain is that Xuanzong had allowed power to be seized by Yang Guifei's family, notably Yang Guozhong. Although Yang Guifei continued to give support to An Lushan, Yang Guozhong saw him as a dangerous rival and warned the emperor about An Lushan's ambitions. Xuanzong, still enthralled by his concubine, ignored Yang Guozhong's warnings. In 755, An Lushan rebelled, justifying his actions on the grounds that Yang Guozhong had usurped the emperor's authority.

An Lushan's mounted cavalry overwhelmed the royalist forces, and after capturing the eastern capital of Luoyang in only thirty-three days, An Lushan declared himself emperor of a new dynasty. He halted after the fall of Luoyang, and by failing to attack Chang'an, he gave the royalist forces the opportunity to regroup, but when Yang Guozhong's imperial armies attempted to recapture Luoyang, they suffered a disastrous defeat, forcing the emperor and the court to flee Chang'an.

While in flight, Emperor Xuanzong's guard murdered Yang Guozhong and his family, blaming him for the defeat. The emperor was forced to order the execution of his beloved Yang Guifei, which became the subject of one of China's most famous poems, written by Bo Juyi (Po Chü-yi; 772-846).

> The emperor could not save her, he could only cover his face
> And later when he turned to look, the place of blood and tears
> Was hidden in a yellow dust blown by a cold wind.

With the fall of Chang'an, the emperor relocated in China's southwest while his son and heir, Li Yu, fought the rebels in the north. Believing Xuanzong incapable of governing, the prince assumed the throne in 756 as Emperor Suzong. An Lushan was murdered the following year by his son, who in turn was killed by another rebel. Chang'an was recaptured from the rebels in 757, as was Luoyang, briefly, but with the weakening of Tang authority, the Tibetans invaded, sacking Chang'an in 763. Suzong died in 762, with his eldest son becoming Emperor Daizong. The royal armies gradually overcame the rebels, and by 763, the An Lushan rebellion was at an end, but Tibetan forces remained a threat until 777. Both Suzong and Daizong practiced a policy of clemency toward the rebels, but by leaving rebel leaders in power in various provinces, the dynasty planted the seeds for further problems.

SIGNIFICANCE

Tang China never recovered from An Lushan's rebellion. Emperor Daizong died in 779, having retreated into mystical Buddhism, and by the time of his death, several border provinces had broken away from imperial control. By the mid-ninth century, civil war had broken out in China, and in 907, the Tang Dynasty ended.

Most historians agree that An Lushan's rebellion did not in itself cause the fall of the Tang, although it was a major turning point. In the aftermath, China was left without its Central Asian territories and was continuously threatened by foreign invaders. Internally, China was subject to the ambitions of ruthless warlords similar to An Lushan, with their semi-independent armies. A series of weak emperors left the central government controlled by royal eunuchs. Tang China after An Lushan's rebellion was a different China.

—*Eugene Larson*

FURTHER READING

Chiu Tang-shu. *Biography of An Lushan*. Translated by Howard S. Levy. Berkeley: University of California Press, 1960. A brief but readable biography of An Lushan.

Paludan, Ann. *Chronicle of the Chinese Emperors*. New York: Thames and Hudson, 1998. Includes an account of Xuanzong's reign and the An Lushan episode.

Pulleyblank, Edward G. "The An Lu-shan Rebellion and the Origins of Chronic Militarism in Late T'ang China." In *Essays on T'ang Society*, edited by John Curtis Perry and Bardwell Smith. Leiden, the Netherlands: E. J. Brill, 1976. A shorter discussion of the An Lushan rebellion.

_______. *The Background to the Rebellion of An Lushan*. London: Oxford University Press, 1955. The major study of An Lushan's rebellion.

Roberts, J. A. G. *A History of China*. Vol. 1. London: Alan Sutton, 1996. Includes an excellent brief examination of An Lushan's rebellion.

See also: 606: National University Awards First Doctorate; 690-705: Reign of Empress Wu; 751: Battle of Talas River; 907-960: Period of Five Dynasties and Ten Kingdoms.

Related article in *Great Lives from History: The Middle Ages, 477-1453*: An Lushan.

763
Tibetans Capture Chang'an

For a brief period, the forces of the Tibetan Empire occupied the Tang Dynasty capital of Chang'an (Xi'an).

Locale: Tibetan plateau (now the Tibet Autonomous Region, People's Republic of China), western China, and Central Asia

Category: Wars, uprisings, and civil unrest

Key Figures

Me Agtsom (704-755), emperor of Tibet, r. ?-755

Trisong Detsen (742-797), emperor of Tibet, r. 755-797

Xuanzong (Hsüan-tsung; 685-762), Tang emperor, also known as the Brilliant Emperor, r. 712-756

Suzong (Su-tsung; 711-762), Tang emperor, son of Xuanzong, r. 756-762

Daizong (Tai-tsung; 727-779) Tang emperor, r. 762-779

An Lushan (An Lu-shan, d. 757), Chinese general, leader of the great rebellion of 755

Summary of Event

By 730, an uneasy peace had settled on Central Asia. The four major powers of the region—the Arab states to the far west, the Tibetans to the south, the Turks to the northeast in what is now known as Mongolia, and the Chinese to the southeast—had fought themselves to a temporary standstill. Each power had similar goals: to maintain dominance over or parity with the others and to either control or maintain access to the major trade routes that crossed Central Asia from China to the west. To accomplish these goals, they had engaged in outright conquest of small, independent polities; established colonies along trade routes; created vassal states through alliance and treaty; and fomented rebellion whenever necessary. Both the Tibetans and the Turks had formal peace treaties with the Chinese but also maintained a military and political alliance with each other and sought as allies to control far western Central Asia.

The Chinese learned of this alliance from small vassal states that sought protection from the incursions of Tibetan and Turkic forces after 734. Xuanzong, the Tang Dynasty (T'ang; 618-907) emperor, ordered the administrators of his colonies to the north and west of the Pamir Mountains to begin negotiations for a military alliance with the Arab states of that region despite long-standing hostilities between them. The Chinese attacked both beginning in 737, defeating first the Turks and then the Tibetans. By 740, the Chinese had crippled Tibetan ambitions in the far west and had taken over large parts of northeastern Tibet, which, despite constant battles, remained in Chinese hands for the next decade.

Indeed, the Tang Dynasty had reached the peak of its political and military power by 750. The Tang had established colonies in the Tarim Basin, ruled a series of vassal states from the east into the Pamirs, and fully dominated the weakened Turks both militarily and politically. The Arabs in the far west had recovered from their earlier defeats and a series of local rebellions, such that they once again became a serious rival to Chinese hegemony of Central Asia. Tibet, meanwhile, had succumbed to the endemic problem of factional politics at the royal court, where the emperor, Me Agtsom, had attempted to promote Buddhism but was fiercely resisted by Bonpo priests and their allies. By 755, he had been assassinated during these struggles, and Tibetan fortunes had reached their lowest ebb. Tang China seemed invincible.

Chinese fortunes collapsed dramatically, however, in 755. An Lushan, a Chinese general and military administrator of the northeastern frontier, and of Sogdian and Turkic descent, led a massive rebellion against the Tang. An Lushan had been deeply involved in court politics, and Xuanzong's favorite concubine, Yang Guifei (Yang Kuei-fei), adopted him as her son. A power struggle broke out between various factions, and An Lushan led his army against loyalist forces, inflicting defeat after defeat on them. The emperor and his court fled Chang'an (now Xi'an) in 756 en route to Sichuan. He sent his son, Suzong, northward with a small force; Suzong, on arrival at his destination, declared himself emperor. Xuanzong abdicated on hearing the news. Suzong wasted little time in consolidating his forces and recaptured Chang'an in 757, the same year in which An Lushan was killed by his own son. Although this was a major blow to the rebellion, it by no means ended it, and conflict between rebels and loyalists raged for another five years.

To counter the An Lushan rebellion, loyalist troops had been pulled from their posts in northeastern Tibet as well as the most important garrisons in Central Asia, and it did not take long for the Tibetans and others to take advantage of this newly created power vacuum. Former vassal states now paid homage and tribute to the Tibetan court, and the Tibetans began almost immediately to attack the remaining Chinese forces. After retaking their northeastern territories long held by the Chinese, they moved further to the east to the Chinese border towns in Sichuan and other areas in China proper along the margins of the plateau. By 763, they had moved far to the east and entered Chang'an late in the year. The newly installed Tang emperor, Daizong, son of Suzong, fled just in time to avoid capture. The Tibetans plundered the capital, and continued raiding further to the east.

Although they abandoned Chang'an after a few weeks, their military power continued unchecked, and by c. 780, they had overrun what is now the Chinese province of Gansu, which lies along the main path of the Silk Route. The Tibetans also re-established themselves as a force farther to the west, and through a series of alliances with Arabs, Qarluqs, and others, they made trade and travel on the major trade routes in Central Asia far safer. They, of course, benefited from this through heavy taxation of caravans.

Daizong, despite these setbacks, did not remain idle. He concluded a peace treaty in 783 with Trisong Detsen, the Tibetan emperor, and actually proposed a bilateral military agreement with the Tibetans, which they accepted based on a number of lavish promises made to them. However, well before that, he actively courted the Uighurs, a large nomadic polity in northern Central Asia, with hopes of making them an ally in his struggles with both the Tibetans and the rebels. In contrast to earlier emperors, who simply manipulated nomadic tribes for military or political advantage on the frontiers of empire, Daizong followed a course of appeasement and accommodation with the Uighurs so that they would help him maintain his position within China. They thus became intricately involved with the internal politics of the Chinese state. Although they did agree to align themselves with the Chinese, they proved to be fickle and rebelled, causing Daizong to invoke the treaty with the Tibetans, which they honored. However, the emperor failed to follow through with his promises, and this led to new hostilities with the Tibetans, who forced the Chinese to accept a peace treaty in 783. Although Daizong was able to hold onto his throne despite his conflicts with the Tibetans and rebellions of the Uighurs, the political and military power of the Tang Dynasty was broken, and it never recovered from the loss of its Central Asian colonies and access to the west.

SIGNIFICANCE

The capture of Chang'an by the Tibetans in 763 was of little practical significance in the power struggles of the mid-eighth century in Central Asia. The Tibetans did not linger, and Daizong was able to restore his court fairly rapidly. However, the capture of Chang'an had a deeper geopolitical significance in that it represented the total collapse of Chinese political, military, and economic power in Central Asia. In the years after 755, China had no direct, unimpeded route to the west, and what trade did flow into it from that direction was carefully regulated by the Arabs, Tibetans, and others. China in fact lost a significant source of wealth with the closure of the trade routes. However, perhaps of even greater significance is the change in the relationship the Chinese had enjoyed with the nomadic tribes to the north. For most of its history, the Chinese used these tribes as political pawns and manipulated them from afar for their geopolitical ends. However, the An Lushan rebellion changed this relationship and created a pattern whereby nomadic tribes, first the Uighurs, then a series of others until the Mongols, became intimately involved in the internal politics of the Chinese state. The Chinese emperors thus increasingly relied on foreigners to maintain internal political stability.

—*Mark Aldenderfer*

FURTHER READING

Beckwith, Christopher S. *The Tibetan Empire in Central Asia*. Princeton, N.J.: Princeton University Press, 1987. The definitive treatment of the expansion of the Tibetan Empire into Central Asia.

Pulleyblank, Edwin G. *The Background of the Rebellion of An Lu-shan*. London: Oxford University Press, 1955. The definitive analysis of the rebellion that changed the face of Central Asia and China after 755.

Stein, R. A. *Tibetan Civilization*. Stanford, Calif.: Stanford University Press, 1972. Useful and accessible historical overview of Tibet's history and culture.

SEE ALSO: 618: Founding of the Tang Dynasty; 627-650: Reign of Songtsen Gampo; 744-840: Uighur Turks Rule Central Asia; 755-763: Rebellion of An Lushan; 791: Buddhism Becomes Tibetan State Religion; 840-846: Uighur Migrations.

RELATED ARTICLES in *Great Lives from History: The Middle Ages, 477-1453*: An Lushan; Taizong.

770-810
REIGN OF DHARMAPĀLA

By the middle of the eighth century, northern India was in political chaos. Gopāla, a new king, and his dynasty, the Pāla, exerted control over the region. On Gopāla's death, his son Dharmapāla expanded the empire from the Bengal region across northern India to the modern Afghan city of Qandahār.

LOCALE: Northern India (the region that is now Bengal and Bangladesh)
CATEGORY: Expansion and land acquisition

KEY FIGURES

Gopāla (d. 770), founder of the Pāla Dynasty, r. 750-770
Dharmapāla (d. 810), Gopāla's son and successor, the most powerful ruler of the Pāla Dynasty, r. 770-810

SUMMARY OF EVENT

During the medieval period of Indian history, northern India was a collection of small states stretching from the Himalayas to the Ganges River and west to the border of modern Afghanistan. Much of the knowledge of this era is fragmentary and based on archaeological findings all over northern and eastern India. Many of the sources for the period are literary in nature, sometimes leading to distortions in the facts and portrayals of the people and events of the time.

Indian history is filled with tales of the battles among the many states in the Indian subcontinent. Monarchs of small states and tribes battled each other to gain control over their neighbors or to fend off the advances of those same neighbors. Frequently these mini-states would ally themselves with a dominant state in order to maintain their independence and the protection of the dominant state. Then, when the tide turned, they would switch alliances just as easily with a new, more powerful leader.

Such a revival of the fortunes of northern India was begun under the Pāla Dynasty. The Pāla followed the Gauḍa Dynasty. When the last Gauḍa ruler, Śaśāṅka, died, chaos ensued in the region. The Gauḍa Empire broke up into numerous mini-states that proved unable to protect their citizens from outside powers.

In an effort to produce stability, the rulers of the region chose a king, Gopāla, who was the first of the Pāla rulers. The word *pāla* is interpreted to mean "protector," which is an appropriate description of the role played by the dynasty. Gopāla was one of the era's more effective leaders. He first secured his kingdom and then expanded it. Unlike most monarchs in India, Gopāla did not claim divine heritage but rather was a ruler with an ordinary past. The Pāla Dynasty would continue for more than four centuries, finally falling in 1161.

In 750, Gopāla's kingdom was in the Vanga region of East Bengal. East Bengal was located in the Ganges Delta region of modern Bangladesh. Gopāla began expanding his kingdom by advancing northward and defeating several kings and their armies. He established a set of vassal kingdoms with rulers who paid tribute to him. Gopāla's conquests involved him in a series of wars that continued even past his death.

Gopāla died in 770 and was succeeded by his son Dharmapāla. Almost immediately on taking his father's throne, he was forced to fight off several challenges to his authority. His first victory was against the Kanauj tribe and its prince, Indrayadha. With this victory Dharmapāla called a *durbar*, or meeting, at Kanauj. He met with his allied kingdoms including Punjab, Rayputana, Malava, and Berar. Establishing his authority among those tribes, Dharmapāla felt strong enough to challenge his neighbors. He attempted to extend his dynasty's control westward into north-central India.

In battling his western neighbors, Dharmapāla proved to be an effective leader who was able to recover from defeats and take advantage of opportunities to expand his kingdom. One of his first wars was with the Pratihāra, a neighboring tribe led by Vatsarāja, an accomplished general who was able to defeat Dharmapāla. After his vic-

MAJOR PĀLA KINGS	
Reign	*Ruler*
750-770	Gopāla
770-810	Dharmapāla
810-850	Devapāla
854-908	Narayanpāla
c. 988-1038	Māhipāla I
c. 1077-1120	Rāmapāla
1143-1161	Madanpāla

tory, though, Vatsarāja found himself under attack from another tribe fearful that the Pratihāra would acquire too much power. Vatsarāja was forced to fight King Dhruwa of neighboring Rāṣṭrakūṭa. Vatsarāja was defeated and fled the field. Dhruwa did not attempt to advance, leaving the area open for Dharmapāla, who moved his control west toward the Deccan plain.

Under a new leader, Nāgabhaṭa II, the Pratihāra returned to challenge Dharmapāla, defeating him at the Battle of Monghyr, throwing Dharmapāla's armies back eastward to their home territory. The Pratihāra then invaded Kanauj and overthrew Dharmapāla's handpicked leader, Chakrayudha. The Pratihāra occupied Kanauj and made it a vassal state for Nāgabhaṭa II.

Dharmapāla moved quickly to expel them from Kanauj. He allied himself with another powerful king, Govinda II, who was able to attack and defeat the Pratihāra. In exchanged for Govinda's aid, Dharmapāla agreed to become a junior partner in a loose confederation of the two kingdoms.

SIGNIFICANCE

Dharmapāla's reign saw the focus of power in India move to the north and east. His empire stretched from the foothills of the Himalayas in Nepal to modern Pakistan. He established his capital in Pataliputra, making it a cultural and political center for the region.

Dharmapāla played a major role in the cultural development of the region. A Buddhist, he was responsible for constructing the Vikramasila monastery. He also built the Odantapurī monastery in Bihar. He was a patron for the famous Buddhist author Haribhadra. He supported learning by founding nearly fifty religious schools in his kingdom and spending considerable funds to advance religious learning.

As the second ruler of the Pāla Dynasty, Dharmapāla expanded on his father's conquests. During his reign, he established control over the region from Nepal to Afghanistan. Medieval writers described him as presiding over a huge army and an overwhelming navy. His army was thought to have numbered in the thousands, with hundreds of elephants that were used to move men and equipment quickly and to intimidate less well-equipped opponents.

Dharmapāla's legacy includes the continued use of the Pāla name in the modern state of Nepal and the construction of Buddhist temples in northeast India. He succeeded in passing his empire to his son Devapāla, and the Pāla Dynasty continued to rule northern India until 1161.

—*Douglas Clouatre*

FURTHER READING

Ali, Daud. *Culture and Politics in the Courts of Medieval India*. Cambridge, England: Cambridge University Press, 2002. A detailed work on the internal politics of medieval Indian kings.

Chandra, Satish. *Essays on Medieval Indian History*. New York: Oxford University Press, 2003. A series of articles by a renowned student of Mughal history, analyzing the social, economic, state, and religious facets of India's medieval history and their interrelationships.

Crewe, Tara Boland, and David Lea. *The Territories and States of India*. New York: Europa Press, 2002. Details the development of the many Indian states from the north and south of the country.

McLeod, John. *A History of India*. Westport, Conn.: Greenwood Press, 2002. A broad-ranging work on ancient through modern India with focus on the various states and dynasties that ruled the country.

Metcalf, Barbara, and Thomas Metcalf. *A Concise History of India*. New York: Cambridge University Press, 2002. A survey of the entire history of the subcontinent that places the various dynasties that ruled India in context.

Nizami, Khaliq Admad. *Royalty in Medieval India*. New Delhi: Munshoriam, 1997. Discusses the various monarchies in south, central, and northern India during its medieval period.

Saha, B. P., and K. S. Behera. *Ancient History of India from Earliest Times to 1200 A.D.* New Delhi: Vikas, 1988. Focuses on ancient through medieval India with emphasis on the social and political development of the people.

Sandha, Gurcharn Singh. *A Military History of Medieval India*. New Delhi: Vision Books, 2003. Discusses the weapons, tactics, and battles that occurred during India's medieval history.

Sengupta, Nitish. *A History of the Bengali Speaking People*. New Delhi: UBS, 2001. Examines the Bengal region of northeast India and the development of the separate Bengali people.

Thapar, Romila. *Early India: From the Origins to A.D. 1300*. London: Allen Lane, 2002. Describes the development of civilization in India and the rise of the dynasties that came to rule it.

SEE ALSO: 484: White Huns Raid India; 606-647: Reign of Harṣa of Kanauj; c. 610-632: Muḥammad Receives Revelations; 630-668: Reign of Narasiṃhavarman I Mahāmalla; c. 710: Construction of the Kāilaśanātha Temple; 730: Rise of the Pratihāras; 788-850: Śaṇkara Expounds Advaita Vedānta; 915: Parāntaka I Conquers Pāṇḍya; 973: Foundation of the Western Cālukya Dynasty; c. 985-1014: Reign of Rājarāja I.

RELATED ARTICLES in *Great Lives from History: The Middle Ages, 477-1453*: Harṣa; Mahmūd of Ghazna.

775-840
BUILDING OF BOROBUḌUR

The Buddhist monument Borobuḍur, located in Central Java (Indonesia), was built during 775-840. It has been suggested that it was built by the Sailendra family as an expression of Sailendra's pious devotion to Buddhism. Its stepped pyramid shape, beautiful bas-reliefs covering a total surface of more than half an acre, and large size have captured scholars' attention for nearly a century.

LOCALE: Central Java (now in Indonesia)
CATEGORIES: Architecture; engineering; religion

SUMMARY OF EVENT

Borobuḍur is a Buddhist monument built over a natural hill located in the middle of the fertile Kedu plain 25 miles (40 kilometers) northwest of Yogyakarta on the island of Java, Indonesia. The monument, made out of dark volcanic rocks, is a solid structure with no interior space, unlike other Buddhist temples. It is a stepped pyramid with projections on four sides and crowned by a large dome-shaped structure known as a stupa. Each side measures approximately 400 feet (122 meters), and the monument at its highest point reaches about 103 feet (about 31 meters). Overall, the structure is divided into two parts: five lower concentric square terraces and three upper circular platforms. Walls and balustrades at each lower level form a pathlike space, where circumambulation might have taken place, and seventy-two perforated stupas are placed on concentric circular platforms at the upper level.

Unfortunately, there is no written documentation concerning the construction of Borobuḍur, its use in worship, or its religious background. Therefore, it is extremely difficult to determine how this monument was built, how it was used in worship, what it represents, and even who built it. Most scholars suggest that the Sailendra (Lord of the Mountain) family must have been involved in the building of Borobuḍur. The Sailendras were devout followers of Buddhism who (as evidenced by many Javanese inscriptions) were active from the late eighth century to the mid-ninth century in erecting Buddhist temples and images. Borobuḍur is thus assumed to be one of the Sailendras' achievements.

701 - 800

It is still uncertain whether "Borobuḍur" is the ancient name of the monument. At the early stages of the studies on Borobuḍur, it was suggested that because *boro* is a derivative of Sanskrit *vihāra* (monastery) and *budur* means "to emerge (from the plain)" in a modern Indonesian dialect, "Borobuḍur" thus means "hill monastery." However, this theory has been widely rejected because the latter part of the name, *budur*, means nothing in Javanese. The ninth century historian Casparis argued that the phrase *Bhūmisambhāra Bhudhara* (which literally means "mountain of the accumulation of virtue in passing through [ten] stages of a Bodhisattva"), which appeared in one Javanese inscription, might have been the original name of the monument. Like many mysteries surrounding Borobuḍur, that regarding the name itself is unsolved.

What is most striking at Borobuḍur is the presence of an extensive series of bas reliefs on the walls and the balustrades of the monument. Almost 1,460 stone panels depict famous Mahāyāna Buddhist texts, including *Mahākarmavibhanga* (great classification of actions), *Lalitavistara* (life of Śākyamuni Buddha), *Avadānas* (heroic deeds), *Gandhavyūha* (Sudhana's search for wisdom), and *Jātakas* (birth stories). Because the circumambulation is done in a clockwise direction, these bas-reliefs are meant to be read from right to left. The *Mahākarmavibhanga* is depicted in a "hidden foot" at the outer wall of monument's lowest level, which was completely covered at some point in its construction. The reason the original foundation was covered is unknown. However, the most convincing explanation is a technical one: At some point during its construction and after the depiction of the *Mahākarmavibhanga* had been finished, an additional terrace must have been added to the original outer wall to prevent the building from collapsing under the weight of the monument. This process resulted in the covering of a series of the *Mahākarmavibhanga* bas-reliefs and the construction of a wide pilgrimage path around the monument.

The original foundation was accidentally discovered in 1885, and soon after the entire series of 160 bas-reliefs was photographed in 1890-1891, it was covered again to prevent any tragic collapse. Therefore, today only photographs of the *Mahākarmavibhanga* bas-reliefs remain, with the exception of several panels at the southeastern corner that were uncovered by the Japanese during the Japanese occupation of Indonesia in the 1940's. The *Mahākarmavibhanga* reliefs illustrate various actions of human beings. They were meant to teach visitors which actions are good or bad and which kind of rewards or punishment would follow a specific action, such as robbery, laziness, or the killing of a living creature. It also has been suggested that the hidden foot was intentionally covered because the scenes of these earthly lives were thought to be inappropriate for worshipers to view.

Moving up the monument, the next stories depicted are *Jātakas* and *Avadānas*, which can be found on the second and third levels of the monument. The *Jātakas* are "birth stories" that are mainly related to the self-sacrifices performed by Buddha in his previous lives, and the *Avadānas* are about the heroic deeds of various people from nobles to merchants. Another important Mahāyāna Buddhist text depicted at Borobuḍur, called *Lalitavistara*, tells the life story of Śākyamuni Buddha. Meanwhile, the walls and balustrades from the second to the fourth levels are devoted to the story of a young practitioner, Sudhana, in search for wisdom. This text is called the *Gandhavyūha*, and it is one of the most popular Mahāyāna Buddhist texts in Asia.

One unfinished Buddha image, now kept at a museum next to the monument, is thought to have been originally enshrined inside the larger stupa at the very top of the monument, yet it should be noted that it is still controversial whether this image was originally placed inside the larger stupa. More than 432 other Buddha images are kept in the decorated niches on the four sides of the mon-

A Buddha at Borobuḍur. (AP/Wide World Photos)

ument facing outward. The features of these Buddha images are all alike, but their *mudrās* (hand gestures) mark their different locations: a gesture of the seal of the touching the earth, or *bhūmisparśa-mudrā*, in the east; a gesture of having no fear, *abhaya-mudrā*, in the west; a meditation pose, *dhyāni-mudrā*, in the north; and a pose of charity, *vara-mudrā*, in the south. In addition, 64 Buddha images in the niches at the fifth level display a teaching gesture, *vitarka-mudrā*, and those inside the perforated stupas at the upper circular platforms make a gesture of turning the wheel of the wisdom, *dharmacakra-mudrā*.

Interpreting the architectural form of Borobudur is a very difficult task. In the early 1930's, the historian Paul Mus once suggested that Borobuḍur represents a huge stupa, a place to keep Buddha's relics, but no relic has been found at Borobuḍur. Some scholars have tried to explain it as a *mandala*, a diagram of the cosmic world in Buddhism, because the architectural plan of Borobuḍur is reminiscent of the form of a *mandala* with its combination of circles and squares. Specific Buddhist texts such as *Avatamsaka-sūtra* (flower adornment sutra, or lotus sutra) have also been suggested as the basis for the monument's architectural design. None of these theories, however, has been confirmed.

It is generally agreed that the route from the bottom to the top of the monument symbolizes the religious path that Buddhist worshipers should follow. Starting from the earthly lives of the *Mahākarmavibhanga*, worshipers are meant gradually to find the ultimate truth of Buddhism as they ascend the monument, and at the top level they can finally see Buddha images through the small holes of the perforated stupas. Borobudur is therefore often read as the embodiment of the Buddhist cosmic world, which is composed of three spheres: the *kāmadhatu* (sphere of desire), the *rūpadhatu* (sphere of form), and the *arūpadhatu* (sphere of formlessness), each of which corresponds to the bas-reliefs at the hidden foot, the four square levels, and the three circular platforms, respectively.

Two other small Buddhist temples, Candi Pawon and Candi Mendut (*candi* means "temple" or "monastery"), stand on the route toward Borobuḍur and share artistic and architectural styles with Borobuḍur. These temples must have served as places to welcome pilgrims who visited Borobuḍur. The type of Buddhist ceremony that might have taken place at Borobuḍur is unknown.

SIGNIFICANCE

Considered by many to be one of the wonders of the world, Borobuḍur represents a wholly distinct form of architecture, restricted to Central Java and built under the Sailendras' rule. It is larger in scale, more elaborately decorated, and more complex in plan than Hindu architecture dated prior to the 780's. Similar ideas of representing the Buddhist world as a form of architecture as in Borobuḍur were applied to other Javanese Buddhist temples, such as Candi Sewu and Candi Kalasan in Central Java.

—*Bokyung Kim*

FURTHER READING

Chihara, Daigoro. *Hindu-Buddhist Architecture in Southeast Asia*. Leiden, the Netherlands: Brill, 1996. A good survey of Southeast Asian architecture.

Dumarçay, Jacques. *Borobuḍur*. Translated by Michael Smithies. New York: Oxford University Press, 1978. A good survey of Central Javanese architecture, including Borobuḍur.

Fontein, Jan. *The Sculpture of Indonesia*. Washington, D.C.: National Gallery of Art, 1990. The catalog for a 1990 exhibition, including three very good introductory essays on Indonesian art and architecture by three eminent scholars.

Frédéric, Louis. *Borobuḍur*. Photographs by Jean-Louis Nou. New York: Abbeville Press, 1994. Contains photographs of all of Borobuḍur's bas-reliefs.

Gómez, Luis O., and Hiram W. Woodward Jr., eds. *Barabuḍur: History and Significance of a Buddhist Monument*. Berkeley: Regents of the University of California, 1981. A collection of nine articles written by eminent scholars, presented at the International Conference on Borobudur held on May 16-17, 1981, at the University of Michigan. Glossary, bibliography, index.

Miksic, John. *Borobuḍur: Golden Tales of the Buddhas*. Photographs by Marcello and Anita Tranchini. Singapore: Periplus, 1990. Miksic's text on Borobuḍur's architecture, art, and history, and on each of its bas-reliefs, offers an excellent accompaniment to the photographs.

SEE ALSO: 682-1377: Expansion of Śrivijaya; c. 700-1253: Confederation of Thai Tribes; 729: Founding of Nanzhao; 802: Founding of the Khmer Empire; 832: Nanzhao Subjugates Pyu; 877-889: Indravarman I Conquers the Thai and the Mons.

RELATED ARTICLE in *Great Lives from History: The Middle Ages, 477-1453*: Suryavarman II.

780
BEGINNING OF THE HAREM SYSTEM

By the late eighth century, the rights of Muslim women during the ʿAbbāsid Dynasty had been suppressed, combined with the start of the harem system. This repression was caused in part by an increase in urbanization, social stratification, the influx of other cultures, and a growing rigidity in the development of Islamic law.

LOCALE: Baghdad (now in Iraq)
CATEGORIES: Cultural and intellectual history; laws, acts, and legal history

SUMMARY OF EVENT

Leila Ahmed has written that women in ʿAbbāsid society were explicitly excluded from the public life of the dynasty by being made absent. "In the records relating to this period," she continues, "they are not to be found, as they were in the previous era, either on battlefield or in mosques, nor are they described as participants in or key contributors to the cultural life and productions of their society." So, Ahmed concludes, "women of the elite and bourgeois classes would live out their lives in seclusion, guarded by eunuchs if wealthy."

The ʿAbbāsid caliphate was an Islamic state centered in Baghdad; it succeeded the Damascus-based Umayyad caliphate in 749 and lasted until the Mongols sacked Baghdad and killed the caliph in 1258, although ʿAbbāsid caliphs continued to lead as figureheads in Cairo until the Ottoman conquest of Egypt in 1517. The ʿAbbāsid rulers adopted a different style of government than the Umayyads, a dynasty whose downfall was due largely to its rulers' harshness and unpopularity. The ʿAbbāsid caliphate, named after an uncle of the Prophet Muḥammad, was characterized by the inclusion of Persian traditions; a more cosmopolitan atmosphere; numerous achievements in the sciences, art, literature, and medicine; urban revival; economic prosperity; and much more decentralized rule (particularly beginning in the tenth century). The new rulers presented themselves as the rightful heirs of the Prophet and as rulers who would wash away the impiety and improper practices of their predecessors.

Despite the fact that the new ʿAbbāsid caliphs claimed to be purifying the Muslim community, their style of rule was not consistent with the simplicity of the first four caliphs, or successors to Muḥammad, who had preceded the Umayyad caliphate. Rather, their rule was more despotic and more in the style of the shahs of Persia than it was reflective of the early years of Islam in Arabia. This is particularly true with respect to the status of women.

During the time of the Prophet and the first four caliphs, women were held in high esteem. The Prophet consulted women and sought their advice, and they contributed to the compilation of the Qurʾān, added to the Hadith reports, prayed in mosques alongside men, and were involved in religious affairs. Women were educators and students, were market officials and were engaged in economic activities, participated in caliphal rulings, made independent oaths, and were not segregated from men. Women had a broad range of rights and freedoms under Islam, but as time progressed, as the Muslim community was transformed into centralized states, as the society became more urbanized, and as other customs, cultures, and peoples were absorbed into those states, women's status began to change.

As Islamic expansion continued into the Byzantine Empire and Iran, Muslims came into contact with societies where the veiling and seclusion of women of the urban upper classes was practiced; this practice was then adopted by Muslims. While some argue that the veiling and seclusion of women is religiously required by the Qurʾān, the interpretation of the verses addressing this issue is disputed, and many historians stress the changing economic, political, and social circumstances of the Muslim community as the cause of the development of these practices in the Islamic context.

Conquests, political expansion, and military victories brought vast wealth and huge numbers of slaves to the ruling elite. Expansion also meant that the population of the state became much more diverse ethnically, culturally, and religiously; some caliphs assimilated the Sāsānid Persian custom of rulers having hundreds or thousands of concubines. By the late Umayyad and early ʿAbbāsid period, elite men had the economic resources to buy as many concubines and slaves as they desired—an option often much more attractive than marriage to a woman of equal social status, who would insist on her rights in the marriage contract.

Slaves, concubines, and wives of the elite were kept within the harem, defined both as a place of seclusion and as the group of women secluded, wherein each woman generally sought to improve her position vis-à-vis the others. Children born to slaves or concubines were free, but if a woman bore the child of the master, she could not be sold. She also could be elevated to the position of wife. Therefore, it was in the interest of harem women to bear children for their masters; likewise, it was in the interest of the master to prevent such births (because it negated his economic investment), and it was in the interest of the wives of the master to prevent them as well (because the slave or concubine could become a rival wife and because additional children became rivals to the wives' children as potential inheritors and successors to their father).

An eighteenth century depiction of the interior of a harem. (Hulton|Archive by Getty Images)

This vast increase in wealth and the adoption of local customs resulted in a significant decline of the status of women during the ʿAbbāsid period. The buying and selling of women, primarily for sexual "use," became common and accepted practice. This reality, so different from that of the time of the Prophet and the first four caliphs, influenced the development of Islamic law and the interpretation of religious texts. Practices that were permitted in Islam, such as polygamy (designed to make provision for remarriage for women whose husbands had died in battle) and male-initiated divorce, were thus interpreted and legislated in a historical context in which women were seen as property and sexual slaves. Orthodox Islam under the ʿAbbāsids thus developed to endorse the prevailing view of women; others interpreted the same religious texts very differently, in ways that prohibited practices such as concubinage and child marriage. Among other things, such sects stressed what the developing ʿAbbāsid orthodoxy did not—the equality of all believers and the fair and equitable treatment of women.

SIGNIFICANCE

During the ʿAbbāsid period, the government formally recognized the four developing Sunni schools of legal thought, sponsored them, and adopted their doctrines as legitimate interpretations of the law. By the tenth century, the legal thought developed in the four Sunni schools was considered to be authoritative; henceforth, legal decisions were to be based on precedent.

Enshrined within the authoritative Sunni legal code is the orthodox view of women developed within the context of the ʿAbbāsid period. Thus, the rapid expansion of the ʿAbbāsid state, the vast increase in wealth and access to slaves and concubines, and the contact with other societies and their traditions of veiling, seclusion, and views of women as sexual objects combined not only to decrease the status of women in ʿAbbāsid culture significantly, but also to color the interpretations given to the emerging body of Islamic law, including the portions of law that apply to women's rights and status.

—*Amy J. Johnson*

701 - 800

FURTHER READING

Ahmed, Leila. *Women and Gender in Islam*. New Haven, Conn.: Yale University Press, 1992. This book discusses the changing roles and norms of Muslim women throughout history, from the pre-Islamic Middle East to the modern period. One of the most important works of its kind.

Barlas, Asma. *"Believing Women" in Islam: Unreading Patriarchal Interpretations of the Qurʾān*. Austin: University of Texas Press, 2002. This work explores different ways in which one can read the Qurʾān: to stress either the subordinate position of women or the equality of believers. It is useful particularly for those interested in doctrinal issues. Bibliography, index.

Denny, Frederick Mathewson. *An Introduction to Islam*. 2d ed. New York: Macmillan, 1994. This book discusses the religion of Islam and its history, including different sects' views of women and the change in those views over time. Bibliography, index.

Keddie, Nikki R., and Beth Baron, eds. *Women in Middle Eastern History: Shifting Boundaries in Sex and Gender.* New Haven, Conn.: Yale University Press, 1991. Chapters 1-4 of this volume will be most useful for the reader, as they explore sources on the topic and discuss the early Islamic centuries. Bibliography, index.

Kennedy, Hugh. *The Early ʿAbbāsid Caliphate: A Political History*. Totowa, N.J.: Barnes and Noble Books, 1981. A good source for information on the caliphate and its political affairs. Gives the reader a good background in the politics of the time period. Maps, bibliography, index.

Lassner, Jacob. *The Shaping of ʿAbbāsid Rule*. Princeton, N.J.: Princeton University Press, 1980. Excellent source for information on the politics and government of the ʿAbbāsid period, including discussion of the role religion played therein. Bibliography, index.

Roded, Ruth, ed. *Women in Islam and the Middle East: A Reader.* New York: I. B. Tauris, 1999. Provides a collection of original sources on women in Islam in the Middle East, from the Middle Ages through the twentieth century. Looks at the legal, cultural, political, religious, and domestic contexts of women's experience in a discussion of the Qurʾān, the foundations of Islam, and the selective quotation of the Prophet's words. Bibliography, index.

Wadud, Amina. *Qurʾān and Woman: Rereading the Sacred Text from a Woman's Perspective*. 2d ed. New York: Oxford University Press, 1999. The author's unique reading of the Qurʾān sheds light on the role of women and relations between women and men presented in the book of Islam. Chapters explore the biases of earlier interpretations and their effects on tradition and Islamic culture and society, equality between men and women, and more. Includes a list of women mentioned in the Qurʾān, a bibliography, and an index.

SEE ALSO: c. 610-632: Muḥammad Receives Revelations; 637-657: Islam Expands Throughout the Middle East; 786-809: Reign of Hārūn al-Rashīd; 834: Gypsies Expelled from Persia; 869-883: Zanj Revolt of African Slaves; c. 1250-1300: Homosexuality Criminalized and Subject to Death Penalty; 1290-1306: Jews Are Expelled from England, France, and Southern Italy.

RELATED ARTICLES in *Great Lives from History: The Middle Ages, 477-1453*: Abū Ḥanīfah; Aḥmad ibn Ḥanbal; Hārūn al-Rashīd; Muḥammad.

780
RISE OF THE SAILENDRA FAMILY

The significant number of Buddhist temples dating from the eighth and ninth centuries in Central Java, Indonesia, has been associated with the rise of the Sailendra (Lord of the Mountain) family, credited with establishing Buddhism in modern Indonesia and constructing, among other temples, the world-famous Borobuḍur.

LOCALE: Java (now in Indonesia)
CATEGORY: Cultural and intellectual history; government and politics; religion

KEY FIGURES

Panamkarana (fl. eighth century), presumably the second king of Mataram, r. c. 760-c. 780
Sanggrāmadhanaójaya (fl. eighth century), one of the early Sailendra kings, r. c. 782

SUMMARY OF EVENT

Writing an ancient history of Indonesia is very difficult because of the paucity of written sources. In fact, scholars still do not agree on the exact details of most historical events in ancient Indonesia. Several issues surrounding the Sailendra family, which ruled Indonesia in the eighth and ninth centuries, remain uncertain. It is still difficult to determine who the Sailendras really were, where they originated, and where their kingdom was actually located.

In the early stages of their studies of the Sailendra family, scholars noticed that two Central Javanese inscriptions written in Sanskrit in the late eighth century contained a brief narrative of the Sailendras' Buddhist activities; this activity was roughly contemporaneous with the period when most Buddhist monuments in Central Java were beginning to be built. Thus, most scholars believe this to be the moment when the Sailendras first appeared in Javanese history. However, it is still unclear how they suddenly appeared without any hint of their presence prior to 778, when the Sailendra family is first mentioned in a Sanskrit inscription.

In fact, the existence of the Sailendra family can be traced back to the seventh century by looking at various Chinese sources, such as Ouyang Xiu's *Xin Tang shu* (1060; the new Tang history) and Yijing's (I-Ching's) *Datang xiyu qiufa gaoseng zhuan* (wr. c. seventh century; *Chinese Monks in India: Biography of Eminent Monks Who Went to the Western World in Search of the Law During the Great Tang Dynasty*, 1986). From these Chinese sources, scholars infer the existence of a country named Heling (Ho-ling) in Java, which sent missionaries ten times to the Chinese court from 640 to the Daihe era (827-835), which was a kingdom of the Sailendras in Java. From the fact that Heling is usually used as a translation of Kaliṅga, a region in East India, it was once suggested that Heling might have been built by immigrants from Kaliṅga.

However, this theory of considering the Sailendras as Indian immigrants was soon rejected by scholars who sought the origin of the Sailendras in Malaysia, Cambodia, or Java. George Coedès, an eminent scholar in the field, tried to relate the Sailendras with Funan, an ancient kingdom in southern Cambodia, by arguing that the name of the kingdom, Funan (its ancient pronunciation is bu-nam), bears a meaning of "mountain" in Khmer and is related to "Sailendra," meaning "king of the mountain."

Most Indonesian scholars have tried to find the Sailendras' origin in the local context by using the inscription discovered in 1963 at Sodjomerto, Central Java, as evidence. This inscription, written in Old Malay, mentions a person, an ardent Sivaite, named Selenda with a title of *dapunta*. The historian Sidi Ibrahim Boechari, who first reported this inscription, suggested that Selenda could have been an Indonesianized form of Sailendra. The inscription is sometimes dated back to as early as the fifth or sixth century, yet it is reasonable to date it to the seventh to early eighth centuries, if one considers its paleographical characteristics. If this interpretation is correct, the inscription at Sodjomerto could be considered as valuable evidence to prove the fact that the Sailendra family was locally evolved and converted from Hinduism to Buddhism at some point. For now, however, the question of the Sailendras' origin must be left open until further studies can provide more information on their political, economic, and artistic activities.

Although scholars still do not have exact dates of when the Sailendras founded their kingdom, two Sanskrit inscriptions discovered in Central Java clearly show that the Buddhist Sailendras already were powerful enough in Central Java to build many astonishing Buddhist temples from the late eighth century. The earliest inscription was discovered in the village of Kalasan, to the east of Yogyakarta. It tells about a group of people who met in 778 to build a Tārā temple on a site that had been granted by the Sailendra kings in a village named Kālasa. These Sailendra kings called themselves *rājasimha* (the lion of kings) and appointed three local officials as witnesses to this gathering. At the end of the inscription, it is written that Mahārāja (a great king) Panamkarana requested future kings of Sailendra to maintain the Tārā temple in a proper way. For many years Panamkarana has been read as one of Sailendra kings. Yet, if one considers the context, it is more reasonable to read him not as a Sailendra king but as a king of a different family.

The second inscription, dated to 782, also contains the word "Sailendra." This inscription, called the Kelurak inscription, was discovered north of Candi Loro Jonggrong in Prambanan (Central Java). Interestingly, it designates a specific Sailendra king, Sanggrāmadhanañjaya (the killer of enemy heroes), as the person who erected a Buddhist image of Manjuśrī.

In addition to these two early inscriptions, much Buddhist architecture and sculpture date stylistically to this period. Not only did the number of Buddhist temples increased dramatically from the late eighth century, but these temples also became more complex in their architectural plan and more elaborately decorated in their artistic design when compared with Hindu temples dated prior to 780.

How to define the relationship of the Sailendra rulers with their neighboring kingdoms is another focus of study. The unfinished Sanskrit inscription discovered at Ligor (775) on the Malay Peninsula suggests that the kings from Śrivijaya, a maritime kingdom in Sumatra, and the Sailendra family in Java were related somehow, although the nature of that relationship is still a topic of debate. Whereas one side of the inscription says that an anonymous king of Śrivijaya built a Buddhist foundation in 775, its other, unfinished side states that a king Viṣṇu with the title mahārāja is a descendant of the Sailendra. If the two sides were written at the same time, one can presume that the power of the Sailendra king in Java had reached into Sumatra in the late eighth century.

However, many unanswered questions remain to call this interpretation into question: whether the two sides of the inscription were contemporaneously written, who the two kings mentioned in the inscription were, and how these two kings were related. Unfortunately, none of these questions has been answered clearly. Many scholars have attempted to connect the identities of the two kings with rulers mentioned in other inscriptions, such as the Kalasan and Kelurak inscriptions and the Nalanda Copper Plate (c. 860); yet, the interpretation of the Ligor inscription and the definition of the Sailendras' relation to the Sumatran kingdom are still open to discussion.

SIGNIFICANCE

The emergence of the Sailendra family in Indonesian history had a major impact on the establishment of Buddhism and Buddhist art in Java. The astonishing examples of Buddhist temples dating from the late eighth century to the ninth century in Central Java show unique features of art and architecture under the Sailendras' rule. Borobuḍur (c. 785-c. 845), located in the Kedu plain, is the best-known example among them. This monument, a stepped pyramid crowned by a large stupa, is decorated with 1,460 stone reliefs, 432 Buddha images, and 72 small stupas. Unique in scale and architectural and artistic styles, it is often regarded as the pinnacle of the Sailendras' ardent devotion to Buddhism and the embodiment of their understanding of Buddhism. The Sailendra kings were actively involved in the promotion of Buddhism in Java in other ways as well, providing Buddhist pilgrims with a place to stay and making a donation for the construction of the monastery at Nalanda, a center of Mahāyāna Buddhism in India, as is stated in the Nalanda Copper Plate.

—*Bokyung Kim*

FURTHER READING

Coedès, George. *The Indianized States of Southeast Asia*. Edited by Walter F. Vella, translated by Sue Brown Cowing. Honolulu: University of Hawaii Press, 1968. A history of Southeast Asia from the beginning of the Christian era up to the early sixteenth century, written by an eminent historian in the field who used extensive Chinese and Sanskrit sources.

Fontein, Jan. *The Sculpture of Indonesia*. Washington, D.C.: National Gallery of Art, 1990. The catalog for a 1990 exhibition, including three very good introductory essays on Indonesian art and architecture by three eminent scholars.

Sakar, H. B. *Corpus of the Inscriptions of Java up to 928 A.D.* Vols. 1-2. Calcutta: K. L. Mukhopadhyay, 1971. Useful if somewhat dated; includes full translations of major Javanese inscriptions to 928. Footnotes.

Tarling, Nicholas, ed. *From Early Times to c. 1800*. Vol. 1 in *The Cambridge History of Southeast Asia*. New York: Cambridge University Press, 1992. An excellent survey of Southeast Asian history with several different thematic approaches.

SEE ALSO: 682-1377: Expansion of Śrivijaya; 775-840: Building of Borobuḍur; c. 985-1014: Reign of Rājarāja I.

RELATED ARTICLE in *Great Lives from History: The Middle Ages, 477-1453*: Suryavarman II.

781
ALCUIN BECOMES ADVISER TO CHARLEMAGNE

When the abbot Alcuin became an adviser to Charlemagne, he initiated a flowering of intellectual and cultural achievement that is known as the Carolingian Renaissance.

LOCALE: Parma (now in Italy)
CATEGORIES: Cultural and intellectual history; education; government and politics

KEY FIGURES

Alcuin (c. 735-804), head of Charlemagne's palace school and abbot of Saint-Martin at Tours
Charlemagne (742-814), king of the Franks and Carolingian emperor, r. 768-814
Peter of Pisa (d. c. 800), grammarian
Paul the Deacon (c. 720-800), historian
Paulinus (726-802), patriarch of Aquileia
Theodulf (c. 760-821), abbot of Saint-Benoît-sur-Loire, Saint Aignan, and bishop of Orléans
Einhard (c. 770-840), historian and biographer of Charlemagne

SUMMARY OF EVENT

Alcuin was a scholar and teacher. He was educated at the cathedral school at York, where he remained first as a scholar in residence and later as head of the school and its library.

In 780-781, the Northumbrian king Elfwald sent Alcuin on a mission to Rome to ask for papal confirmation of Eanbald as the new archbishop of York. Around Easter, 781, as Alcuin was returning from Rome to York, he met Charlemagne in northern Italy at Parma. Because Charlemagne was eager to foster a program of education for clergy and laypersons throughout his kingdom, he urged Alcuin, who was famous for his educational endeavors at York, to join his court. Although Alcuin hated to leave his native York, Charlemagne persuaded him. Alcuin arrived at the Frankish court of Charlemagne in 782. With the exception of several visits to England, Alcuin remained in the Frankish kingdom, first connected with the court and later, from 796 until his death in 804, as abbot of the great Carolingian monastery of Saint-Martin at Tours.

With the fall of the Roman Empire in 476 C.E., classical culture, including Latin literature, education, literacy, and the arts, declined. In the various Germanic kingdoms that succeeded the Roman Empire in Europe, monasteries became the primary centers of literate culture. In some areas, such as Northumbria in England, monks and scholars such as Saint Bede the Venerable (672/673-735) continued to study classical literature and write works of theology and history. Alcuin was trained in this tradition.

When Charlemagne became king of the Franks in 768, the levels of education and literacy were low. During the first decade of his reign, Charlemagne was primarily occupied with securing his rule through military conquest, which eventually made him ruler of most of Europe, including lands in France, Germany, and Italy. Around 780, his concerns turned toward governing his extensive territories. As a Christian ruler, he assumed responsibility for the spiritual welfare of the Church and the people throughout his empire, a concept that drew on the imperial heritage of the later Roman emperors. Charlemagne's encouragement of a widespread program of education and cultural development in literature and the arts had both practical and idealistic components. Because it looked to classical Greco-Roman culture for many of its models, modern historians have called this movement the Carolingian Renaissance.

Alcuin. (Library of Congress)

When Charlemagne recruited Alcuin to join his court in 781, he had already embarked on various initiatives to improve education and to promote cultural literacy. Several scholars and intellectuals were in residence at Charlemagne's court. Peter of Pisa focused particularly on grammar. Paul the Deacon was a Lombard who spent four years at the court. He wrote on grammar, but his interests also included history, poetry, and mathematics. Another Italian, Paulinus, also taught grammar at the court for a time until he became patriarch (bishop) of Aquileia in 787. Theodulf, a Visigoth from Spain, joined the court in the late eighth century. He became involved with several theological debates, particularly concerning the Iconoclastic Controversy. These scholars formed a core of the various intellectuals and students who maintained an ongoing and changing group of literati who enlivened and edified the court and spread the educational program and cultural ideals of the Carolingian Renaissance to many parts of Charlemagne's empire.

Although Alcuin was only one among many intellectuals who constituted a "palace school," he became Charlemagne's chief adviser on matters relating to education and culture. Alcuin's career during his years in the Frankish kingdom exemplifies many of the key facets of the Carolingian Renaissance under Charlemagne's leadership.

Above all, Alcuin was a teacher. He instructed members of Charlemagne's family, especially his children. Other young people, usually from noble families, also received an education at the court of Charlemagne. Einhard presents an example of someone who benefited from this educational opportunity. After Charlemagne's death, Einhard wrote a life of Charlemagne modeled on the biographical writing of the Roman historian Suetonius, which became one of the best-known literary works of the Carolingian Renaissance.

Alcuin's influence on education was not confined to his personal instruction at the palace school. He also wrote a number of pedagogical treatises that became popular books of instruction for schools in the Carolingian period. Alcuin was also responsible for organizing the educational curriculum of the seven liberal arts into three basic disciplines, the trivium, consisting of

Charlemagne was crowned emperor at Rome in the year 800, establishing the Frankish dominance in Europe and setting the foundation for the Holy Roman Empire. (F. R. Niglutsch)

The Seven Liberal Arts	
The Trivium	**The Quadrivium**
Grammar	Arithmetic
Dialectics	Geometry
Rhetoric	Astronomy
	Music

grammar, dialectics, and rhetoric, and four advanced subjects, the quadrivium, composed of arithmetic, geometry, astronomy, and music.

Although educational training utilized classical foundations of the seven liberal arts, the ultimate goal of learning and literacy was in the service of the Christian religion. Through several treatises and many letters, Alcuin articulated the emperor's position on several important theological debates. He argued against adoptionism (the belief that Jesus was God's adopted son) and iconoclasm (the prohibition against images). His theological position on the Trinity in the filioque controversy supported the view that the Holy Spirit proceeded from both God the Father and Christ the Son. Alcuin's most important and long-ranging contribution to religious practice in the Carolingian empire was his revision and standardization of liturgy in developing the lectionary of biblical readings for church services and bringing the sacramentary used by the priest in performing the sacrament of the Mass in accord with usage of the Church in Rome.

In 796, Alcuin became abbot of the monastery of Saint-Martin at Tours. Although he remained in close contact with Charlemagne's court, he directed his primary attention toward the text of the Bible, chiefly clarifying passages that had become corrupted through scribal transmission of the text. The monastery at Tours became a center for copying manuscripts of the Bible with a corrected text that were disseminated throughout the Carolingian empire. These manuscripts were written in a script known as Caroline minuscule. Although Alcuin did not personally develop the script, the clarity of the letters and the spacing between words and lines was a visual embodiment of the goals of the Carolingian Renaissance in the improvement of literacy.

Alcuin and the circle of court scholars were primarily concerned with literature and education, but the Carolingian Renaissance also encompassed the visual arts and music. Architecture, especially of churches and monasteries, revived Roman plans of basilicas and baptisteries, as well as the structure and aesthetics of arches and columns. Wall paintings and mosaics decorated these buildings. Although few of these edifices have survived, one example is the small church with apse mosaic at Germigny-des-Prés, whose construction and iconographical program probably were guided by Alcuin's colleague, Theodulf of Orléans. Manuscripts of Bibles, liturgical texts, and secular books preserve miniatures whose figure style and decorative patterns recall Roman paintings. Sumptuous ivory and jeweled bindings on many of these books also revive the style and magnificence of late antique ivory carving and metalwork. Music supported the liturgy with the Roman practice of Gregorian chant.

Significance

In political terms, Charlemagne's empire did not survive the division among his heirs, but the Carolingian Renaissance that Alcuin and his contemporaries promoted was passed down through several generations of scholars who continued these literary traditions even while the political fabric of the Carolingian empire disintegrated. Indeed, the Carolingian Renaissance has had a long-lasting influence. It preserved and transmitted much of the classical Roman literature that has survived. It established standards for an education in the liberal arts. Its texts were copied in a clear, legible script that remains the foundation of typographical letters to the present. The text of the Bible owes much to the work of Alcuin and the Carolingian dissemination of biblical manuscripts. The collaboration of Alcuin and Charlemagne, along with other intellectuals and artists, thus had a major impact on the cultural heritage of Western civilization.

—*Karen Gould*

701 - 800

Further Reading

Becher, Matthias. *Charlemagne*. Translated by David S. Bachrach. New Haven, Conn.: Yale University Press, 2003. A biography of Charlemagne, the emperor whom Alcuin advised. Bibliography and index.

Duckett, Eleanor Shipley. *Alcuin, Friend of Charlemagne*. 1951. Reprint. Hamden, Conn.: Archon Books, 1965. Written by an important medieval historian, this study remains the only complete biography of Alcuin.

Einhard. *Charlemagne's Courtier: The Complete Einhard*. Edited and translated by Paul Edward Dutton. Peterborough, Ont.: Broadview Press, 1998. A translation of Einhard's biography of Charlemagne. Shows the influence of Alcuin's teachings. Bibliography and index.

Houwen, L. A. J. R., and A. A. Macdonald, eds. *Alcuin of York: Scholar at the Carolingian Court*. Groningen, the Netherlands: E. Forsten, 1998. A collection of papers presented at the Third Germania Latina Conference at the University of Groningen in 1995. Examines his role as a scholar and his influence.

McKitterick, Rosamond, ed. *Carolingian Culture: Emulation and Innovation*. New York: Cambridge University Press, 1994. Contains eleven essays by leading scholars that discuss the literary and artistic contributions of the Carolingian Renaissance.

_______. *The Carolingians and the Written Word*. New York: Cambridge University Press, 1989. Examines the extent and uses of literacy and education in the Carolingian period.

Morrissey, Robert John. *Charlemagne and France: A Thousand Years of Mythology*. Translated by Catherine Tihanyi. Notre Dame, Ind.: University of Notre Dame Press, 2003. A study of Charlemagne and the stories about him that attempts to separate fiction from fact. Bibliography and index.

SEE ALSO: 496: Baptism of Clovis; 726-843: Iconoclastic Controversy; 1100-1300: European Universities Emerge.

RELATED ARTICLES in *Great Lives from History: The Middle Ages, 477-1453*: Alcuin; Saint Bede the Venerable; Charlemagne.

786-809
REIGN OF HĀRŪN AL-RASHĪD

Hārūn al-Rashīd's reign marks one of the high points in the power and authority of the ʿAbbāsid caliphate and the Golden Age of the Islamic Empire centered on the capital at Baghdad. He encouraged thriving intellectual and cultural activities and saw to the caliphate's rise in industry and trade.

LOCALE: Islamic Empire, primarily Mesopotamia, Syria, and Asia Minor.

CATEGORIES: Cultural and intellectual history; government and politics

KEY FIGURES

Hārūn al-Rashīd (766-809), caliph, r. 786-809
Khayzurān (fl. eighth century), mother of caliphs Hārūn al-Rashīd and al-Hādī
Yaḥyā ibn Khālid al-Barmakī (d. 805), vizier and head of the Barmakid clan
Saint Irene (c. 752-803), Byzantine empress, r. 797-802
Nicephorus I (d. 811), Byzantine emperor, r. 802-811
Charlemagne (742-814), king of the Franks, r. 768-814, and Holy Roman Emperor, r. 800-814

SUMMARY OF EVENT

In 750 the ʿAbbāsid family, which claimed descent from the Prophet Muḥammad's paternal uncle, ʿAbbās (566-c. 653), overthrew the reigning Umayyad Dynasty and assumed leadership over the vast Islamic Empire. The second ʿAbbāsid caliph, al-Manṣūr (r. 754-775), in 762-763 developed the site of the village of Baghdad (literally, "the gift of God") in Mesopotamia into the imperial capital and, ultimately, a sprawling metropolis. Al-Mahdī, who followed his father al-Manṣūr as the third caliph (r. 775-785), numbered among his children two sons: al-Hīdī and Hārūn al-Rashīd.

As the eldest, al-Hādī was in line for succession to the caliphate ahead of the younger Hārūn. However, it was Hārūn who was to distinguish himself as a brilliant military commander. At the age of eighteen, he led ʿAbbāsid forces against the Byzantine Empire and penetrated into the Byzantine capital of Constantinople. This exploit is said to have been the occasion on which al-Mahdī conferred on his son the title of "al-Rashīd" (or "the Upright"). Hārūn's campaign forced the empress Irene, who was then acting as regent for her son Emperor Constantine VI (r. 780-797), to capitulate to a one-sided treaty in which her government agreed to pay the caliphate an annual tribute of up to ninety thousand dinars. In 786, after only a year on the throne, al-Hādī died, and Hārūn al-Rashīd became the fifth ʿAbbāsid caliph.

The strongest influences during the early years of Hārūn's reign were his mother, al-Khayzurān, and Yaḥyā ibn Khālid al-Barmakī, the vizier and patriarch of the powerful eighth to ninth century Barmakid family. Both had been very supportive of Hārūn's claims to succession and had urged him to resist pressure from Caliph al-Hādī to surrender these claims in favor of al-Hādī's son. Yaḥyā was imprisoned by the caliph, who died shortly thereafter. Al-Khayzurān was later suspected by some of having connived at al-Hādī's untimely death in order to elevate Hārūn to the throne. Al-Khayzurān, who had been a slave, continued to exert tremendous behind-the-scenes influence at the ʿAbbāsid court.

THE ʿABBĀSID CALIPHATE C. 800

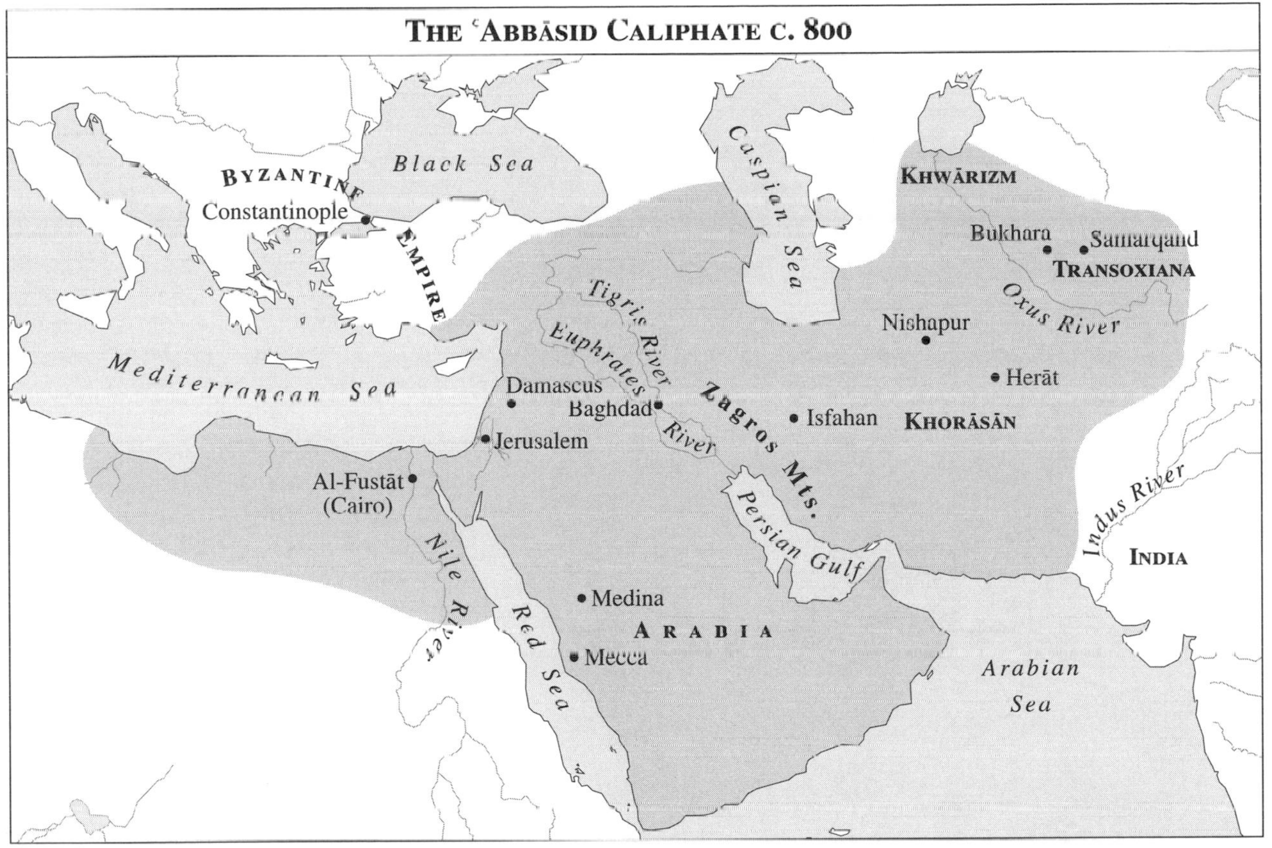

The Barmakids were of Persian origin: Yaḥyā's father Khālid had served as vizier to al-Manṣūr and Yaḥyā had been Hārūn's mentor before becoming vizier in his turn. The Barmakids, under the leadership of Yaḥyā and his sons Jaʿfar and al-Faḍl, amassed fortune, power, and prestige that were second only to those of the ʿAbbāsids themselves. As the Barmakids waxed ever stronger, however, Hārūn became alarmed and broke them. In 803, Jaʿfar was killed by Hārūn's order, while Yaḥyā and al-Faḍl (d. 808) were incarcerated for the rest of their lives. Persian influence, however, would continue to overshadow and dominate the Arabic element in the ʿAbbāsid state.

Until 802, the major source on international conflict facing the ʿAbbāsid Empire had been the rival Umayyad caliphate centered on Córdoba, Spain, and the breakaway Idrīsid regime in Morocco. In that year, however, Empress Irene was overthrown in a palace coup by an administrative official, who assumed the imperial title as Nicephorus I. Nicephorus repudiated the annual tribute to the caliphate and went so far as to demand restitution. Hārūn responded by leading a military campaign, forcing Nicephorus to sue for peace. Though the Byzantine emperor agreed to resume tribute payments, he went back on his word as soon as the ʿAbbāsid armies left. A second campaign was launched, with similar results, and issues with the Byzantines remained unresolved at Hārūn's death.

The caliph initiated an alliance with Charlemagne, king of the Franks and Holy Roman Emperor, sending him lavish gifts, including an elephant named Abūl ʿAbbās. The two had common adversaries in the Córdoba Umayyads and the Byzantines. Hārūn, who is credited with having introduced the game of chess from Persia into the Arab world, is further said to have included a chessboard and chessmen among his presents to Charlemagne, and may thus have also brought chess into Europe.

In 809, while at the border town of Ṭūs, preparing for a military drive against the rebellious Khāijite religious sect in Khorāsān (now northeastern Iran), Hārūn suffered what was probably a stroke and died shortly thereafter.

SIGNIFICANCE

In the years following Hārūn's death, particularly after 847, when ʿAbbāsid power had visibly deteriorated,

Hārūn al-Rashīd's embassy delivers gifts to Charlemagne. (F. R. Niglutsch)

Hārūn's reign would take on a nostalgic glow as a time of glory and prosperity, and the caliph was considered a paragon of wisdom and cultural enlightenment. Though Baghdad's fabled "House of Wisdom" was not established until around 820, achievements were still impressive. The Chinese technology of papermaking was first evident in the Middle East during Hārūn's reign; the caliph's head librarian, al-Faḍl ibn Nawbakht, began actively translating a large number of Persian manuscripts into Arabic; Ibrāhīm al-Mawsili and ibn-Jami Mukhariq brought Islamic music to new heights; and Muḥammad ibn Irāhīm al-Fazārī conducted the first scientific astronomical studies in the Muslim world.

In poetry, the time of Hārūn's reign produced two outstanding individuals: Abū al-Nuwās and ʿAbd al-ʿAtāhiyah. Abū al-Nuwas, whose verses extol good living and carousing and are often bawdy in content, was said to have been a favorite drinking companion to both Hārūn and his son and successor, al-Amīn (r. 809-813). ʿAbd al-ʿAtāhiyah's poetry was ascetically religious in nature.

There also were significant advances in medicine. Hārūn authorized the first medical field hospital (with "ambulance" service by camel transport) and the first public hospital (in Baghdad) in the Islamic Empire. Included among the era's noteworthy literary accomplishments were *Kitaāb al-kharāj* (*Islamic Revenue Code*, 1979), by Abū Yūsuf, and Ahmad ibn Abdullah ibn Salām's translation of the Bible into Arabic.

The extent of Hārūn's connection to the collection of Indian, Persian, African, and Arabic lore known as *Alf layla wa-layla* (fifteenth century; *The Arabian Nights' Entertainments*, 1706-1708; also known as *The Thousand and One Nights*) is uncertain. The work was centuries in the making and not compiled into its final form until the fifteenth century. The frame story of Scheherazade and some of the tales date back to a Persian work called *Hazar Afsana*, prior to the ʿAbbāsid caliphate. Some of the stories apparently originated during the reign of al-Manṣūr, others during that of Hārūn or shortly thereafter (including those that use Hārūn and his court as a backdrop). Still others were incorporated during the Mamlūk era in Egypt.

Hārūn's reign is heralded as a time of exceptional cultural and intellectual vitality, though it is sometimes difficult to draw the line between fact and legend. Hārūn's prestige is so remarkable that he is traditionally credited with many advances that may have occurred not in the course of his reign but during those of his sons, al-Amīn and al-Maʾmūn (r. 813-833).

It cannot be denied that tangible advances and contributions in the fields of literature, jurisprudence, philology, Arabic grammar, science, medicine, and music were realized during the reign of Hārūn. The extent of the caliph's personal role in this, however, is debatable. Much of the credit must undoubtedly be attributed to, or at least shared with, the disgraced but brilliant Barmakid family. Nonetheless, as head of state and religion, Hārūn would have been a crucial supporter of the arts throughout his realm.

—*Raymond Pierre Hylton*

THE ʿABBĀSID CALIPHS TO 861

Reign	*Caliph*
750-754	Abū al-ʿAbbās al-Saffāḥ
754-775	al-Manṣūr
775-785	al-Mahdī
785-786	al-Hādī
786-809	Hārūn al-Rashīd
789	Beginning of ʿAbbāsid breakup
809-813	al-Amīn
813-833	Maʾmūn the Great
833-842	al-Muʿtaṣim
842-847	al-Wathīq
847-861	al-Mutawakkil
861	Turkish Guard assassinates al-Mutawakkil; beginning of military domination of caliphate

FURTHER READING

Bishai, Wilson B. *Islamic History of the Middle East: Backgrounds, Development, and Fall of the Arab Empire.* Boston: Allyn and Bacon, 1969. Fine chronological work with a very readable format. The reigns of the different caliphs are discussed, with a full section devoted to the career of Hārūn. Maps, bibliography.

Brockelmann, Carl. *History of the Islamic Peoples.* Translated by Joel Carmichael and Moshe Perlmann. New York: Routledge, 2000. This reprinted volume is still the classic work on Islamic history, its civilization, and its main dynasties, including the ʿAbbāsid period. The synopsis on Hārūn is among the most developed and useful case studies in the book. Maps, bibliography, index.

Goldston, Robert. *The Sword of the Prophet: The History of the Arab World from the Time of Mohammed to the Present.* New York: Dial Press, 1979. A good fundamental study, though it somewhat underplays the cultural achievements of the ʿAbbāsids.

Hibri, Tayeb el-. *Reinterpreting Islamic Historiography: Hārūn al-Rashīd and the Narrative of the ʿAbbāsid Caliphate.* New York: Cambridge University Press, 1999. Argues that past historical accounts of the eighth and ninth century caliphate were not written as portraits of the time, but instead as a means to convey the religious, political, and social issues that were then prominent. Bibliography, index.

Hitti, Philip K. *History of the Arabs.* New York: St. Martin's Press, 1979. Remains one of the definitive works on the subject. Devotes much attention to the "Golden Age" idea as it pertains to Hārūn and his reign.

Hodgson, Marshall G. S. *The Classical Age of Islam.* Vol. 1 in *The Venture of Islam.* Chicago: University of Chicago Press, 1974. The outstanding features of this study are the tables, maps, and explanatory notes that make it ideal for all readers.

Kennedy, Hugh. *The Prophet and the Age of the Caliphates: The Islamic Near East from the Sixth to the Eleventh Century.* New York: Longman, 1986. A crisp account that is somewhat critical of Hārūn and focuses a great deal on the fall of the Barmakids.

SEE ALSO: 7th-8th centuries: Papermaking Spreads to Korea, Japan, and Central Asia; 637-657: Islam Expands Throughout the Middle East; 751: Battle of Talas River; 755-763: Rebellion of An Lushan; 780: Beginning of the Harem System; 809: First Islamic Public Hospital; c. 950: Court of Córdoba Flourishes in Spain; c. 1150: Moors Transmit Classical Philosophy and Medicine to Europe.

RELATED ARTICLES in *Great Lives from History: The Middle Ages, 477-1453*: Charlemagne; Saint Irene; al-Jāḥiẓ; al-Ṭabarī.

788-850
ŚAṄKARA EXPOUNDS ADVAITA VEDĀNTA

In his highly influential system of Advaita Vedānta, Śaṅkara synthesized disparate elements in medieval Indian religious thought, including elements of Mahāyāna Buddhism and the popular forms of devotion known as the bhakti *cults.*

LOCALE: India
CATEGORIES: Philosophy; religion

KEY FIGURE

Śaṅkara (c. 700-c. 750), religious philosopher, exponent of the school of thought known as Advaita Vedānta

SUMMARY OF EVENT

Although Śaṅkara's life was short, he exerted a huge influence on Indian philosophical and religious thought, both during his life and after his death. He had a gift for assimilating ideas from other schools of thought in order to strengthen the system known as Advaita Vedānta. In particular, he assimilated elements of Mahāyāna Buddhism into his system, as well as steering a middle path between two established strands of Hindu thought, that of Yoga (one of the classical systems of Indian philosophy), which emphasized ascetic contemplation, and the many *bhakti* cults, which emphasized the importance of religious devotion.

The essence of Śaṅkara's nondualistic philosophy, which he based on his interpretations of the Upaniṣads (c. 1000-c. 200 B.C.E.), lies in the identification of the inner essence of human beings, the *ātman*, with the universal spirit, Brahman. There are no separate, individual souls. The only reality is Brahman, which is absolute and eternal. For Śaṅkara, nothing could be described as real if it was impermanent. It therefore follows that the transient universe that is perceived by the human senses is not real. It is *māyā*, or illusion, the force that makes Brahman, the One, appear as Many. *Māyā* is what deceives the human senses. Only by turning away from the sensual world and engaging in contemplation of Brahman can the illusion be overcome. A person who has realized, as a direct experience rather than an intellectual idea, the identity of *ātman* and Brahman, lives in the unalloyed eternal bliss that is Brahman. The *ātman*, wrote Śaṅkara in *Vivekachudamani* (early eighth century, authorship questionable; *The Crest Jewel of Wisdom*, 1890), "never ceases to experience infinite joy. It is always the same. It is consciousness itself. . . . [It] is birthless and deathless. It neither grows nor decays. It is unchangeable, eternal." However, those whose attention still follows the senses are caught in a cycle of suffering, because the senses only incite desires and cravings, which, once satisfied, only give rise to more cravings. People who do not understand this cycle go to destruction, said Śaṅkara, ignorant of the bliss of Brahman and ignorant of reality.

This doctrine of *māyā* and the illusion of the senses has much in common with the Mādhyamika school of Mahāyāna Buddhism, which was founded in the second century C.E. by Nāgārjuna. Nāgārjuna was a Brahman who adopted Buddhism, and his school retained some affinities with Brahmanism or Vedānta. According to the Mādhyamika school, humans are prevented from recognizing the ultimate truth of nirvana because they are deceived by the false appearances of the world. They must engage in meditation and contemplation in order to realize the essential nothingness of the things that only appear to be real.

Because of such similarities in doctrine, in his lifetime Śaṅkara was accused of being a Buddhist in disguise. However, he viewed himself as an opponent of Buddhist doctrines and even disparaged the Buddha himself. Whenever he could, Śaṅkara either attacked Buddhist beliefs or integrated them into his own system. For example, he rejected the Buddhist idea that the individual was nothing more than an insubstantial stream of consciousness, because this would exclude entirely the *ātman*, the inner consciousness and true self.

Śaṅkara did not directly attack the popular *bhakti* (devotion) cults, which emphasized service or surrender to God. *Bhakti* does not figure prominently in his system, which is one of knowledge rather than love. Because there is no separation between the *ātman* (humans) and God (Brahman), there is no need for worship or devotion. Some commentators argue that what Śaṅkara referred to as the highest *bhakti* was simply another term for the impersonal self-knowledge that comes from conscious awareness of the identity of the *ātman* with Brahman. However, part of Śaṅkara's genius was to accommodate existing beliefs, and to satisfy the ordinary worshiper, he developed the idea of two levels of truth. At the highest level of truth, *ātman* is identical with Brahman, and for the one who has attained this knowledge, practices of religious worship and devotion have no meaning. However, if that truth has not yet been realized, such practices may serve a useful function. Thus, for the ordinary person who has not attained the higher knowledge, it would be acceptable for him or her to offer devotion and rituals to a personal God.

SIGNIFICANCE

Although Buddhism in India was already fading when Śaṅkara began his teaching, Śaṅkara has sometimes been referred to as the architect of the decline of Buddhism in India. Śaṅkara's philosophy also forced the advocates of *bhakti* to develop defenses of their own position because they perceived Śaṅkara's philosophy as a threat. The most influential of these did not come until the twelfth century and is associated with Rāmānuja. Rāmānuja's system set out to redress what he perceived as an imbalance in Śaṅkara's thought. He emphasized the personal aspect of God and the necessity of ritual, devotion, and adoration, while upholding the value of the ascetic life of contemplation.

Whatever the influence of Rāmānuja's qualified nondualism, as well as another school of Vedānta founded by Madhva in the thirteenth century, which included a distinction between God and the individual soul, Śaṅkara's philosophy became the dominant spiritual teaching in India.

Śaṅkara laid the basis for this dominance by establishing monastic settlements all over India to preserve and propagate his teaching, as the Buddhists had earlier. This establishment of the monastery as a spiritual center became a characteristic of medieval Hinduism. There were four main monasteries, Sringeri, Dwaraka, Puri, and Badrinatha, established in the south, west, east, and north (respectively) of the country. These monasteries are still in existence today, and they are able to trace an unbroken line of teachers, or Śaṅkarācāryas, from Śaṅkara's time to the present. The monasteries today are centers of spiritual education and also serve as destinations for pilgrimages. Major Hindu temples are either attached to them or stand nearby. During the twentieth century, eleven centuries after Śaṅkara lived, the vitality of the tradition he established continued to thrive, mainly because of the strong leadership of the Śaṅkarācāryas. The fact that most educated, nonsecular Indians adhere to the Advaita Vedantic philosophy is a tribute to Śaṅkara, who more than any other philosopher or teacher in Indian history is considered to have brought this about.

—*Bryan Aubrey*

FURTHER READING

Bader, Jonathan. *Conquest of the Four Quarters: Traditional Accounts of the Life of Śaṅkara*. New Delhi, India: Aditya Prakashan, 2000. Focuses on how Śaṅkara is portrayed in eight hagiographies written seven hundred years after his death.

Cenkner, William. *A Tradition of Teachers: Śaṅkara and the Jagadgurus Today*. Columbia, Mo.: South Asia Books, 1983. A study of the tradition of gurus established by Śaṅkara and described in his writings. Tests the ideal outlined by Śaṅkara against the reality of present-day gurus who follow in his tradition.

Cronk, George, Worth Hawes, and Steve Wainwright. *On Shankara*. Belmont, Calif.: Wadsworth Publishing, 2002. Offers a concise yet comprehensive introduction to Śaṅkara's most important ideas.

Isayeva, Natalia. *Shankara and Indian Philosophy*. New York: State University of New York Press, 1993. Sketches Śaṅkara's life and creative activity, and provides a consistent exposition and interpretation of his teaching.

Masih, Y. *Shankara's Universal Philosophy of Religion*. New Delhi, India: Munshiram Manoharlal, 1987. Gives a new interpretation of Śaṅkara's religious philosophy and gives a defense of Advaitism in the current language of Western philosophy.

Pande, Govind Chandra. *Life and Thought of Śaṅkarācārya*. Delhi, India: Motital Banaresidass, 1994. Reconsiders Śaṅkara's writings in the context of his textual sources, answering such questions as how Śaṅkara represented the essential truth of Vedānta while also meeting the philosophical and religious challenges of his time.

Śaṅkara. *Crest-Jewel of Discrimination*. Translated with an introduction by Swami Prabhavanda and Christopher Isherwood. 3d ed. Hollywood, Calif.: Vedanta Press, 1978. A classic Vedantic text regarding the path to God through knowledge. Lucid and informative introduction.

SEE ALSO: c. 710: Construction of the Kāilaśanātha Temple; 1193: Turkish Raiders Destroy Buddhist University at Nalanda; c. 1380: Compilation of the Wise Sayings of Lal Ded.

RELATED ARTICLES in *Great Lives from History: The Middle Ages, 477-1453*: Rāmānuja; Śaṅkara.

791
BUDDHISM BECOMES TIBETAN STATE RELIGION

The emperor of Tibet, Trisong Detsen, established Buddhism as the official state religion and created a pattern of royal subsidy for its religious institutions that persisted into the twentieth century.

LOCALE: Central Tibetan plateau (now the Tibet Autonomous Region, People's Republic of China)
CATEGORIES: Government and politics; religion

KEY FIGURES

Me Agtsom (704-755), father of Trisong Detsen and emperor of Tibet, r. ?-755
Trisong Detsen (742-797), emperor of Tibet, r. 755-797
Padmasambhava (Guru Rinpoche; fl. mid-eighth century), founder of the Nyingma order of Tibetan Buddhism
Hashang Mahāyāna (fl. eighth century); Chinese monk, presented the case for a Tantric and Zen approach to Buddhism at the Council of Samye
Kamalaśīla (fl. eighth century); Indian monk, presented the case for clerical Buddhism at the Council of Samye

SUMMARY OF EVENT

Although the Tibetan Empire was firmly established as a major political power in Central Asia by Songtsen Gampo and his successors during the seventh century, the freedom of the emperor to rule was constantly challenged and compromised by competing factions. One faction was the Bonpo priests, who strove to maintain their position and extend the reach of their religious practice. The second faction was the great noble families, who supplied the lay ministers of the king's government and tended to use their positions to extend the power and wealth of their families and diminish that of their rivals. The third faction was the king and his supporting families, who strove to maintain a strong central government for both personal and political ends. Alliance, treachery, and even murder were common as these factions jockeyed for advantage. This tension between centralization and fragmentation was the central theme of Tibetan politics until the collapse of the empire in the mid-ninth century. Political leaders, then, whenever possible sought advantage to maintain their positions and influence.

Trisong Detsen's father, Me Agtsom, had a turbulent reign. Relations with China were under constant strain, and the empire fought battles across all Central Asia in an effort to maintain its political position. Internal politics were likewise troublesome, and he was beset with rebellions and unfavorable alliances for most of his reign. Although his true motivations are not clear, it seems that he moved to support Buddhism as a tool to be used against the Bonpo priests and their ministerial supporters. He invited Indian masters to teach Buddhism to the court, but these requests were apparently declined. He also sponsored the foundation of a number of small temples in Tibet, and later Buddhist authors write that Me Agtsom had promulgated edicts attempting to establish Buddhist ethics as the moral foundation of his rule. His attempts to push Buddhism forward, however, were thwarted by both priests and ministers.

Me Agtsom was assassinated in 755 while Trisong Detsen was a minor, and an anti-Buddhist faction rose to power. Trisong Detsen survived the intrigue around him through the help of powerful protectors, and on taking the throne, he began a systematic, if low-key, process of promoting Buddhism in the court. It is probable that he learned of and developed his affinity to Buddhism through his father. Under his patronage, both Indian and Chinese sources of Buddhist thought were translated into the Tibetan script and were widely disseminated. With his allies, he began to sponsor the construction of Buddhist temples. He also invited Indian teachers to Tibet. One of these, Padmasambhava, helped establish the Nyingma order of Buddhism and was also instrumental in founding the first monastic community, Samye, c. 775. A few years later, members of high-ranking families (a number fixed at seven in the legends surrounding this history) were ordained as monks in this order, with Samye as their base. Tibetan histories give the sense that many noble families saw contributing to the new monastery as a distinct honor, but the primary impetus for its founding was Trisong Detsen, who directed that 150 families were to support the temple and its activities, while a similar number were ordered to support the growing monastic community.

Despite low-level hostilities along the borders and in far-flung places in Central Asia, Tibet and China had reached an uneasy peace. Noble families sent sons to China for their education, and all things Chinese were in vogue among the Tibetan elite. The Chinese used this situation to advance their own political agenda of maintaining peaceful borderlands and sent Chinese Buddhist monks of the Chan tradition (similar to Japanese Zen Buddhism) to Tibet to further these ends. This path to enlightenment (or nirvana) stressed the possibility of achieving instantaneous nirvana as opposed to the growing clerical and scholarly tradition of Indian Buddhist thought that maintained enlightenment could be attained only through long study and rigorous discipline. Clerical Buddhism also promoted a belief in karma and the doctrine that through continuous good works, one could achieve a good rebirth and thus move ever closer to enlightenment. In contrast, Tantric approaches to Indian Buddhism emphasized the use of magic and shamanistic techniques and were little interested in promoting good works. Bonpo, with its own shamanistic past, saw Chan and Tantric Buddhism as potential allies in the ongoing power struggle surrounding the king.

These traditions co-existed for a period, but it appears that Trisong Detsen began to favor the clerical and scholarly tradition of Buddhism. From his perspective, this would have made good political sense, because the clerical approach promoted strong ethical concepts and could be seen as a controlling force that would assist his long-term political goal of state centralization. In contrast, Tantrism and Chan were often destabilizing. Support of clerical Buddhism would also undercut the Bonpo priests, which would further strengthen his grip on his domain. To this end, in 791, Trisong Detsen issued an edit that made Buddhism the official state religion with specific reference to the strict moral code of clerical Buddhism and erected a stone pillar at Samye marking the event. This edict was clearly staged, for a number of nobles took religious vows and promises were made by the king for their support. Although many great families supported this edict, it created even stronger animosity among those who opposed Buddhist thought and its growing political power.

Aware of this enmity and the threat it posed to his rule, Trisong Detsen convened what has become known as the Council of Samye sometime between 792 and 794 in an attempt to create both popular support and an intellectual foundation for his edict. The council took the form of an academic debate in which the participants hurled questions and responses back and forth in a dramatic and theatrical manner. According to tradition, so-called "Chinese" Buddhism (in reality an amalgam of Tantric and Chan beliefs) was defended by a Chinese monk named Hashang Mahāyāna, while clerical Buddhism was defended by Kamalaśīla, an Indian monk invited to Samye by the king. Tradition asserts that Kamalaśīla handily defeated his rival, and through this victory, a moral and ethical approach to Buddhism was proven to be superior to all other forms. Although the debate may have quieted Trisong Detsen's opponents temporarily, it did not eliminate them entirely. Within fifty years, the opponents of clerical Buddhism proved victorious.

Significance

Trisong Detsen established Buddhism as the state religion of Tibet. Moreover, through his patronage of the monastery at Samye, he created a pattern of royal or elite subsidy for these religious institutions that persisted into the twentieth century. This example of monastic foundation and support was widely emulated in the Buddhist world after his reign. Although he was undoubtedly a devout Buddhist, it is important to stress that his support of Buddhism was a part of a political strategy designed to consolidate his rule in the midst of competing factions. Although the monastic institutions he created were his allies, over time, they became politically dominant on the plateau and were in fact the true origin of the lamaist state that ruled Tibet beginning in the sixteenth century.

—*Mark Aldenderfer*

Further Reading

Beckwith, Christopher S. *The Tibetan Empire in Central Asia*. Princeton, N.J.: Princeton University Press, 1987. The definitive treatment of the expansion of the Tibetan Empire into Central Asia.

Samuel, Geoffrey. *Civilized Shamans: Buddhism in Tibetan Societies*. Washington, D.C.: Smithsonian Institution Press, 1993. A comprehensive examination of the development of Buddhist thought on the Tibetan plateau.

Snellgrove, David. *Indo-Tibetan Buddhism: Indian Buddhists and Their Tibetan Successors*. Boston: Shambhala, 1987. A detailed discussion of important practitioners of Buddhism from India and the influence they had on Tibetans and the evolution of Buddhist thought on the Tibetan plateau.

Stein, R. A. *Tibetan Civilization*. Stanford, Calif.: Stanford University Press, 1972. Useful and accessible historical overview of Tibet's history and culture.

Tucci, Giuseppe. *The Religions of Tibet*. Berkeley: University of California Press, 1988. First published in 1970, this volume provides a masterful and very detailed overview of Tibetan religious thought from its origins to the modern era. It also describes important aspects of ritual practice and its interpretation.

See also: 618: Founding of the Tang Dynasty; 627-650: Reign of Songtsen Gampo; 763: Tibetans Capture Chang'an; 838-842: Tibetan Empire Dissolves.

792
RISE OF THE SAMURAI

In 792, the emperor Kammu abolished armies conscripted from peasants and created a system whereby the sons of noble families were recruited to serve as aristocrat-warriors. Members of this group eventually became known as samurai.

LOCALE: Japan
CATEGORIES: Government and politics; wars, uprisings, and civil unrest

KEY FIGURE

Kammu (737-806), emperor of Japan, r. 781-806, who created the military system that evolved to the privileged samurai class

SUMMARY OF EVENT

When Nara became the capital of Japan in 710, a new system of government was fabricated along with the city. An emperor, reigning with absolute authority, ruled through a centralized bureaucracy over three distinct classes: the emperor's immediate family, free subjects (officials and state tenants), and slaves. This new social system, designed to improve the efficiency of land management and increase state revenue, also inculcated Buddhism into the new government as a means of keeping the subjects peaceful and subservient. Each province was required to build monasteries and temples, eventually resulting in forty-eight Buddhist temples in Nara alone. As these temples amassed great wealth, monks endowed with high political positions increasingly began to meddle in secular affairs and drain resources from the state. Civil and religious establishments became so hopelessly entwined and corruption so prevalent that a strong reaction against Buddhistic political influence arose.

When Kammu, who had no Buddhist leanings, became emperor in 781, he resolved to solve the problem in a typically Japanese roundabout manner by deserting Nara for a new capital city from which the Nara temples would be physically excluded. By this means, Kammu could sever political connections to temples, escape the control of meddlesome priests, and re-establish a secular government far removed from possible competitors for the throne. Although he abandoned Nara in 784, he was unable to establish a new capital until 794, when Heian (present-day Kyoto) became the seat of government. Buddhist monasteries were prohibited from transferring their headquarters, and priests were forbidden to interfere in affairs of state; Buddhism was allowed to serve only as a religion.

During the Nara period (710-794), because less than 10 percent of the population were slaves, the largest and most important group of freemen were the farmers. Each male child was granted a state-owned rice field to cultivate, but the government levied a 3 percent tax on the produce as well as a head tax on adult males. Although the rice tax was low, the head tax, payable in rice or other commodities, imposed a heavy burden. A further burden was imposed because the farmers bore the full responsibility for transporting their tax from the provinces to the capital, an enormous encumbrance on those living far away. In addition, all adult males were obliged to provide labor of up to sixty days yearly for public works and to serve in the military. Up to one-third of mature males in a province could be conscripted into service during their years of eligibility (ages twenty through fifty-nine). Each was obligated to serve one year at the capital and three years on the frontier. While on active duty, a soldier was required to provide his own equipment and provisions, this burden falling on his local province. One's service could be commuted by produce, or one could pay for a substitute. The resulting armies, reluctantly conscripted from the lower classes and lacking discipline and fighting spirit, degenerated into little more than labor gangs.

In 792, Kammu abolished conscription so that he could replace the cumbersome and ill-trained armies with a more efficient system for expanding the frontier wars in the provinces of the still growing nation. Local militia henceforth were to be recruited from among the sons of local government officers and the provincial gentry. Volunteers were to be paid or have their family taxes remitted in lieu of service. The emphasis changed from an obligation of peasants to a service loyally contributed to the nation and the emperor by the noble class.

These aristocratic warriors (*bushi*), who came to prominence in the subsequent Heian period (794-1185), eventually came to be known as samurai, from the Japanese verb "to serve." They followed *bushidō*, a moral code of chivalry that stressed integrity, justice, courage, benevolence, politeness, sincerity, honor, unswerving loyalty to one's feudal lord, and stoicism in suffering. Samurai warriors scorned death (a constant threat during the feudal period) and held their personal honor in such high esteem that they would atone for errors by willingly committing ritual suicide by disembowelment (*seppuku*) rather than face possible disgrace. The *sakura* (cherry blossom), with its short-lived beauty, came to epitomize the samurai's glorious but brief life.

During the tenth and eleventh centuries, powerful landowners came to control most of the country's wealth. These aristocrats led a life of luxury on proceeds from their vast estates. Lower-ranking aristocrats unable to acquire land near the capital would assume posts in the provinces, where they could establish their own power bases. To protect and increase their land holdings, they allowed the local peasants to join the ranks of the samurai and trained them to become superb swordsmen. The system was effective and was to have far-reaching influence on the political development of provinces. Although the court had wealth and power in the environs of the capital, centralized control over the country weakened, and military aristocracies, controlled by influential families, ruled in the provinces. With huge armies of highly trained samurai warriors, the slightest incident would provoke armed conflict as these powerful earls vied with each other to amass power and property. Samurai did not own land but were totally dependent on their *daimyō* (feudal barons), who provided their support. In return, the samurai placed loyalty to their *daimyō* above all other personal or family commitments. The great age of samurai warfare raged in Japan for some four hundred years, finally ceasing in 1603 when Ieyasu Tokugawa unified the country and became the first national shogun.

Samurai warriors in the late nineteenth century. (Hulton|Archive by Getty Images)

Significance

Originally used to denote the aristocratic warriors (*bushi*), the samurai caste was to dominate the Japanese government through the almost constant warfare of the Middle Ages. It was under samurai leadership that many of the distinctive features of Japanese culture evolved; these characteristics have remained characteristic traits of Japanese society, particularly for political and industrial leaders, down to the present.

The samurai code had three main sources: Confucianism, Buddhism, and Shintō. The ethical elements, emphasizing political loyalty, obligation, and always adhering to the proper rules of etiquette, were thoroughly Confucian. Samurai were trained to suffer affliction with patience and self-control, and to never expose their emotions. They were expected to repudiate money and commercial transactions and to abhor underhanded dealings. Samurai labored for justice and strove to always show compassion and benevolence toward the oppressed. They were presumed to always speak the truth, to sustain an unblemished honor, and to avoid disgrace.

Buddhism provided the warrior with the recognition that life is impermanent and that one must always be ready to submit stoically to the inevitability of death. Zen Buddhism, with its emphasis on effective mind and body control through a life of disciplined simplicity and earnest labor, became an integral aspect of a samurai's training. He learned to make decisions quickly and to prefer action above argument.

From the Shintō tradition, samurai came to champion loyalty to their *daimyō* and to the emperor, the spiritual guardian of the nation. Political loyalty was considered more important than family loyalty and national honor a higher purpose than personal honor.

During the peaceful Tokugawa period (1603-1867), the samurai class, with no more battles to fight, became stewards and chamberlains of the baron's estates. The Tokugawa shogunate solidified the feudal system and created a highly stratified bureaucratic society; every detail of the class system was scrupulously regulated. Admittance to the bureaucracy was limited to the former warriors, who were placed on stipends and whose privileged caste position was protected by law. Because samurai were the highest of four classes (samurai, farmers, craftspeople, and merchants, in descending order), they engendered great respect. Consequently, unique forms of art, literature, and drama congenial to the samurai emerged. Although samurai cultural dominance ended about 1700, members of the class did not lose their privileged status until 1871, when feudalism was officially abolished.

—*George R. Plitnik*

FURTHER READING

Dunn, Charles. *Everyday Life in Traditional Japan*. Rutland, Vt.: Charles E. Tuttle, 1989. Although this book concentrates on Japanese life during the Tokugawa Era (1600-1867), it includes an entire chapter devoted to the samurai class.

Nitobe, Inazo. *Bushido: The Soul of Japan*. 1904. Reprint. Rutland, Vt.: Charles E. Tuttle, 1994. *Bushidō* embodies the samurai's governing code of honor throughout Japan's long feudal age, which set the criteria of manners, ideals, and moral codes of obligation that have come to characterize Japanese culture.

Schirokauer, Conrad. *A Brief History of Japanese Civilization*. New York: Harcourt Brace Jovanovich, 1993. A compact but comprehensive survey of Japanese history from its origins through the late twentieth century.

Varley, H. Paul. *Japanese Culture*. 4th ed. Honolulu: University of Hawaii Press, 2000. A concise survey of two thousand years of Japanese history with an emphasis on the distinctive elements of Japanese culture.

SEE ALSO: 794-1185: Heian Period; 1156-1192: Minamoto Yoritomo Becomes Shogun; 1219-1333: Hōjō Family Dominates Shoguns, Rules Japan; 1336-1392: Yoshino Civil Wars.

RELATED ARTICLES in *Great Lives from History: The Middle Ages, 477-1453*: Minamoto Yoritomo; Taira Kiyomori.

June 7, 793
NORSE RAID LINDISFARNE MONASTERY

The raid of Lindisfarne by Vikings foreshadowed large-scale Scandinavian migrations that permanently altered the culture and politics of the British Isles.

LOCALE: Northeast coast of Northumbria, northern England

CATEGORIES: Religion; wars, uprisings, and civil unrest

KEY FIGURES

Alcuin (c. 735-804), Northumbrian-born monk and religious adviser to Charlemagne

Charlemagne (742-814), king of the Franks, r. 768-814

Higbald (d. 802), bishop of Lindisfarne

Ethelred I (763-796), king of Northumbria, r. 774-779 and 790-796

Offa (d. 796), king of Mercia, r. 757-796

SUMMARY OF EVENT

On June 7, 793, three ships beached on the small island of Lindisfarne, a few hundred meters off the east coast of northern Northumbria, just south of modern England's border with Scotland. A band of warriors, about one hundred strong, disembarked and attacked the monastery at the southern tip of the island. They looted the church and surrounding buildings, killed the old monks who had not fled, and captured the young for slavery. Packing the booty and captives into their ships, they sailed back in the direction whence they had come, the north.

Nothing else definite is known about the Lindisfarne raid from the fragmentary records that survived this turbulent period in Anglo-Saxon England. Its immediate effects, however, are well attested. Contemporaries, especially churchmen, reacted with shock and outrage at the sacrilege to the Lindisfarne monastery, one of England's wealthiest and most distinguished religious institutions, where Saint Cuthbert, a patron saint of the Anglo-Saxons, lay buried. They blamed "heathen northmen" who were taking advantage of the moral and political degeneration of the northern English kingdom of Northumbria and worried that more such piratical bands might follow. The worries were well founded. Although probably not the first appearance of northern marauders, the Lindisfarne incident traditionally begins a period of escalating raiding and then large-scale invasion of the British Isles and western France. Scholars called this period the Scandinavian migration age, the Viking age, or, as Anglo-Saxons thought of it, the Viking terror.

Based on archaeological evidence and histories written late in the Anglo-Saxon period (450-1066), scholars have conjectured further details about the Lindisfarne raid. Originally from southern Norway, the raiders operated out of a base in the Orkney Islands, north of Scotland. They called themselves *v'kingar* (or *vikingar*), an Old Norse word of obscure origin. To the English they were "northmen" or "shipmen," names that immediately became synonymous with pirates. These pirates were probably berserkers (an ancient Scandinavian term), members of a pagan warrior cult known for their battle frenzy. In fact, although they might fight like madmen, they were raiders who planned their attacks carefully based on information gathered from traveling merchants: a Viking band typically sought a wealthy monastery easily accessible from the sea; they preferred to hunt in areas in which the local rulers were weak or fighting among one another; and they tried to maximize their profits by plundering during church festivals when people thronged together and were not on their guard. The Vikings carried away anything that could be resold, but gold, silver, and slaves were their chief goals.

The monks of the Lindisfarne monastery were far from helpless. A mixture of Anglo-Saxons, Irish, and British Celts, they frequently came from the warrior class themselves, performed hard physical labor farming the monastery's holdings, and were almost certainly capable of mounting a spirited defense. Yet, even though outnumbering the Vikings, they stood little chance. The northmen wielded swords, axes, and pikes with devastating skill as they charged, all the while shouting a blood-

An artist's rendition of Vikings come ashore at Lindisfarne island off Northumberland in northeastern England. (Library of Congress)

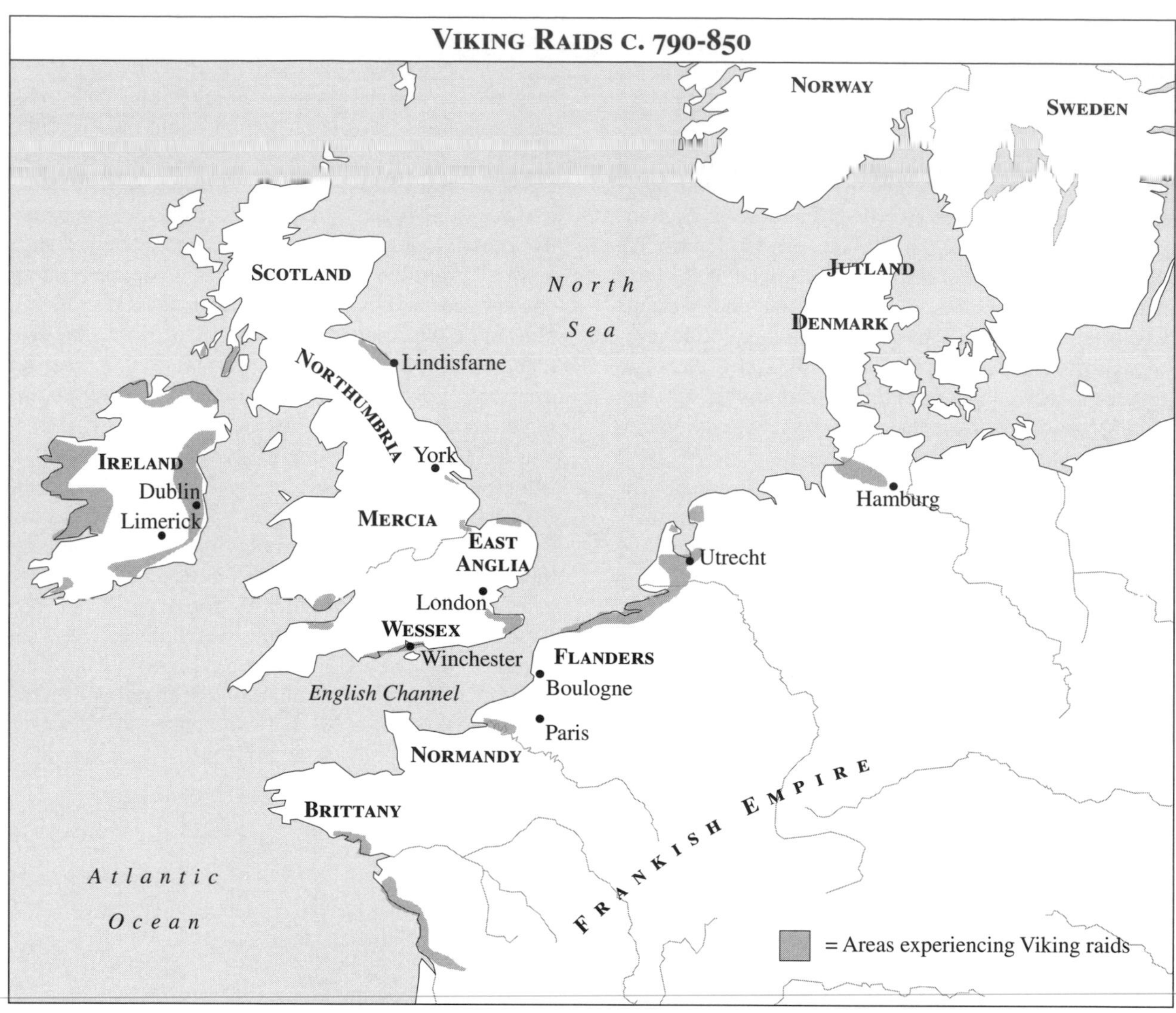

chilling berserker battle cry that was famous for unnerving opponents. Moreover, the monks were almost certainly caught by surprise, thanks to the Viking longship. The finest vessel in northern waters during the early Middle Ages, the longship could be rowed or sailed swiftly, and because it had a shallow draft and a strong keel, its crew could run the vessel aground close to shore to discharge warriors and horses for a quick assault into the hinterland.

According to local tradition, the Vikings landed on the north side of the island and charged across farm fields, routing the monks as they went, to the monastery grounds. There, they found two churches, a guest house, and a dormitory, all surrounded by an earthen wall. The monastery's considerable wealth consisted primarily of adornments for the main church. The Vikings took chalices, candelabra, crucifixes, and other ritual objects, made of silver and often having inlaid gold and amber, and stripped the golden ornamentation from the altar and holy books. Yet the destruction, while great, was not complete. The Lindisfarne Gospels, an ornately decorated vellum manuscript similar to the Book of Kells, survived, as did the remains of Saint Cuthbert, the single most valuable possession to the monastery. Most significantly, the monastery remained in operation.

The names of the Vikings are lost to history, and there is no indication that Anglo-Saxons tried to identify them. What mattered, especially to ecclesiastical leaders, was that the raiders were pagans. That pagans could succeed in robbing and killing servants of God was horrifying and ominous. The most outspoken about the danger was Alcuin, an adviser to Charlemagne, king of the Franks. Alcuin had been born in Northumbria and trained in monasteries there. He viewed the attack on his homeland as a sign of moral and political corruption. In a series of letters, he suggested to Higbald, the bishop in charge of Lindisfarne, that monastic discipline had slipped and darkly hinted that some monks must have secretly sinned and brought on God's displeasure. The Vikings performed God's punishment. Alcuin also upbraided the Northumbrian king, Ethelred I, accusing him of self-indulgent habits and lack of valor. To Alcuin's great disgust, the raid went entirely unpunished. The anonymous writers of the *Anglo-Saxon Chronicle* entries for 793 also saw the raid as a moral portent, along with famine, strange flashes of lightning, and fiery dragons reportedly seen the same year.

Whatever the moral conditions of Northumbria, Alcuin was right that the kingdom was weak. Once the strongest kingdom of England, it had degenerated during the previous one hundred years because of infighting among claimants to the throne. The feuding had left the coasts undefended, as the Vikings surely knew. Alcuin vaguely promised Bishop Higbald military help from Charlemagne, but the Frankish king soon had Viking troubles of his own. Viking attacks on trading ports in Frisia (now in the Netherlands) and France prompted Charlemagne to build a coastal fleet and harbor defenses. In Northumbria, Ethelred seemed to have taken no such measures. Yet in Mercia, the kingdom to the south, King Offa was already preparing coastal defenses in 792.

In any case, the Vikings soon shifted their hunting grounds. After 800, raids on England declined, and those on the west coast of Scotland and on Ireland dramatically increased, as the Norse sea raiders took advantage of the incessant feuds that obsessed Celtic kings. Vikings repeatedly plundered the monastery founded by the Irish saint Columba at Iona, an island establishment as prestigious as Lindisfarne. Soon the northmen were raiding far inland, and in 841 they established a permanent town, Dublin, to support their trade in slaves and stolen goods.

SIGNIFICANCE

Historians have cited a variety of social and political causes for the sudden outburst of Scandinavian raiders in the late eighth century. Population pressure and political instability in parts of Norway probably supplied the main impetus for warrior bands to seek their fortune in the rich Christian islands to the south, and improvements in weaponry and the longship gave the Vikings considerable tactical advantage. When northmen returned to England, they did so in army-sized invasions. Following 865, they began to settle the areas that they had conquered and eventually controlled most of northern England, permanently affecting the political balance, social structure, legal system, language, and arts of England. Overall, the Scandinavian migration age should not be seen in isolation. It was the last in a series of Germanic migrations, including that of the Angles and Saxons to Britain in the fifth century, that spread tribes throughout Europe after the dissolution of the Roman Empire.

—*Roger Smith*

FURTHER READING

Farrell, R. T., ed. *The Vikings*. London: Phillimore, 1982. A collection of articles by scholars considering the causes of the Viking Age, the Viking image, Vikings in the British Isles, and northern art, history, and literature.

Haywood, John. *The Penguin Historical Atlas of the Vikings*. New York: Viking Press, 1995. An illustrated look at the history of the Vikings, their origins, and their infamous raids. Includes a time line, color maps, a bibliography, and an index.

Jones, Gwyn. *A History of the Vikings*. Rev. ed. New York: Oxford University Press, 1984. The most comprehensive and readable treatment available, describing Scandinavian history and culture from prehistoric times to 1066. The Lindisfarne raid receives brief attention.

Logan, F. Donald. *The Vikings in History*. 2d ed. New York: Routledge, 1992. A general history of the Vikings, with one chapter devoted to the raids on the British Isles. Helpful illustrations and maps.

Loyn, H. R. *The Vikings in Britain*. Rev. ed. Cambridge, Mass.: Blackwell, 1995. The author devotes three chapters to the early raids and subsequent large-scale invasions of England by Scandinavians. A highly regarded history of the Viking Age.

Marsden, John. *The Fury of the Northmen: Saints, Shrines, and Sea-Raiders in the Viking Age, A.D. 793-878*. New York: St. Martin's Press, 1995. Details Viking depredations on monasteries, particularly Lindisfarne, quoting medieval sources extensively. Views the Vikings as barbarian pirates and the monasteries as repositories of civilization.

O'Sullivan, Deirdre, and Robert Young. *Book of Lindisfarne: Holy Island*. London: B. T. Batsford, 1995. A look at Lindisfarne monastery as an archaeological site. Includes illustrations and maps.

SEE ALSO: 635-800: Founding of Lindisfarne and Creation of the Book of Kells; 731: Bede Writes *Ecclesiastical History of the English People*; 850-950: Viking Era; 11th-12th centuries: First European-Native American Contact.

RELATED ARTICLES in *Great Lives from History: The Middle Ages, 477-1453*: Alcuin; Saint Bede the Venerable; Charlemagne.

794-1185
HEIAN PERIOD

During the Heian period, Japan experienced a golden age of literature, philosophy, and religion in which it developed a unique culture and sense of national identity.

LOCALE: Central Japan
CATEGORIES: Cultural and intellectual history government and politics

KEY FIGURES
Fujiwara Michinaga (966-1028), noble who was the most successful head of the Fujiwara clan
Murasaki Shikibu (c. 978-c. 1030), noblewoman who wrote *The Tale of Genji*
Kōbō Daishi (Kūkai; 774-835), powerful Buddhist monk

SUMMARY OF EVENT

Much of early Japanese culture was influenced by the intellectual systems of China. This cultural diffusion reached a high point during the Tang Dynasty (T'ang; 618-907). Once the Tang solidified their power on the mainland, they launched a series of military expeditions against Korea and Vietnam. Tang foreign policy was based on the Confucian principle of superior/subordinate relationships and the belief that China was truly the Middle Kingdom at the center of the earth. Thus, the Tang Dynasty established a tributary relationship with the governments in Korea and Vietnam. This international system was based on the model of hierarchy, obedience, and discipline. The Tang emperor was at the top of the power pyramid, and every other official paid tribute to his rank.

In time, Confucianism and Buddhism established themselves on the Korean peninsula. The aristocratic and intellectual elite of Korea were attracted to Confucian philosophy and its ethical code of conduct. At the same time, much of Korean society was also influenced by the Buddhist belief in personal salvation based on people's conduct during their lifetimes. Korean intellectuals would travel to China and study at Confucian academies or Buddhist temples. On their return to the peninsula, they would establish schools modeled on the academies found in China. In time, these belief systems reached Japan from Korea; throughout history, the Korean peninsula has served as a cultural, political, and military "bridge" connecting mainland East Asia to Japan. Most historians believe that the Korean-Japanese connection was first established in the fourth or fifth century when the Korean military launched a series of expeditions in an attempt to conquer the Japanese mainland. Under the leadership of the Korean emperor, Silla, Chinese culture was introduced to the Japanese people.

In 710, the Japanese officials instituted a series of political policies that brought much of Japan under the control of a central government; this marks the beginning of what historians refer to as the Nara period (710-794). A new universal legal code was adopted that placed everyone in a Confucian hierarchy and established a set of legal procedures that would have a significant impact on the development of Japanese society. This code both established a well-ordered civil society and accelerated economic growth by making Japanese society a much safer place to conduct commerce.

The leaders of the new government also realized that they needed to create a historical narrative that would act as a societal adhesive to connect the different regions of Japan to a common heritage. The Nara government instituted a series of historical and literary projects that would form the foundation of a Japanese cultural heritage. In the area of historical writing, scholars produced three important works. The first work, a collection of the most ancient Japanese myths, legends, and folk tales, is the *Kojiki* (712 C.E.; *Records of Ancient Matters*, 1883; best known as *Kojiki*). This was followed by the *Nihon shoki* (compiled 720 C.E.; *Nihongi: Chronicles of Japan from the Earliest Times to A.D. 697*, 1896; best known as *Nihon shoki*), which attempted to give an accurate account of early Japanese history. Finally, in 713, these same scholars began compiling the *Fudoki* (*Records of Wind and Earth*, 1997; best known as *Fudoki*), a collection of provincial histories. This was the first Japanese attempt to bring provincial history, geography, and folklore to a national audience.

The government followed these publications with two literary anthologies. The first, the *Manyōshū* (c. 750; *Manyōshū*, 1929-1964; also known as *The Ten Thousand Leaves*, 1981), contains the first collection of Japanese poetry. This anthology included works from unknown authors, government officials, and even former emperors. The last major work of the Nara period was the *Kokin wakashū* (c. 905; also known as *Kokinshū*; English translation, 1970), a poetry anthology of old and new poems specifically commissioned by the emperor. Its creation that firmly established government support of the arts.

The intellectual elite of the Nara period also adopted many of the concepts of Confucianism and Buddhism, drawn, like the Korean intellectuals, largely because of the concept of individual ethical accountability. Despite the widespread acceptance of Confucianism and Buddhism, many Japanese intellectuals still embraced their native Shintō, a religion based on an animistic view of nature. Japan at this time was still very much a rural nation, and the concept of a spiritual connection with the natural environment still played a major role in Japanese culture.

By the late 790's, the aristocratic class began a series of bloody uprisings in an attempt to gain control of the government. To quell this violence, the capital was transferred to Heian-kyō (near modern-day Kyoto) in 794; it was during this period that the Fujiwara family came to power. Thus began the second great period of classical Japanese culture, known as the Heian period (794-1185).

MAJOR EMPERORS OF THE HEIAN PERIOD

Reign	*Ruler*
781-806	Kammu
806-809	Heizei
809-823	Saga
823-833	Junna
833-850	Nimmyō
850-858	Montoku
858-876	Seiwa
876-884	Yōzei
884-887	Kōkō
887-897	Uda
897-930	Daigo
930-946	Suzaku
946-967	Murakami
967-969	Reizei
969-984	En'yu
984-986	Kazan
986-1011	Ichijō
1011-1016	Sanjō
1016-1036	Go-Ichijō
1036-1045	Go-Suzaku
1045-1068	Go-Reizei
1068-1073	Go-Sanjō
1073-1087	Shirakawa (cloistered, 1086-1129)
1087-1107	Horikawa
1107-1123	Toba (cloistered, 1129-1156)
1123-1142	Sutoku
1142-1155	Konoe
1155-1158	Go-Shirakawa (cloistered, 1158-1192)
1158-1165	Nijō
1165-1168	Rokujō
1168-1180	Takakura
1180-1185	Antoku

The Fujiwara clan established a feudal economic and political model based on the operation of self-sufficient agricultural estates known as the *shōen* system. Through a series of strategic marriages, Fujiwara women became the brides of the heirs of the most powerful *shōen* estates; thus, the clan was able to establish itself as the most powerful force in Japanese politics for three centuries. The most successful practitioner of the concept of strategic marriage was Fujiwara Michinaga, who had four of his daughters married to members of the royal family.

During the Heian period, Japan began to develop its distinct culture and identity, which incorporated some Chinese concepts and practices but were removed from those of Tang China. The two areas of Japanese intellectual life that most significantly reflect these phenomena were the development of Japanese literature and the growth of Buddhism.

The eleventh century was the start of a golden age in Japanese literature, and aristocratic women played a primary role in the development of this art form. The most notable of these female authors was Murasaki Shikibu, who wrote a fifty-four-chapter masterpiece known as *Genji monogatari* (c. 1004; *The Tale of Genji*, 1925-1933). Like many works of literature in Europe during this time period, *The Tale of Genji* reflects the social mores of contemporary aristocratic society. Many fathers from the nobility encouraged their daughters to become well educated. If one's daughter aspired to become a member of the royal court, she had to be conversant in both Chinese and Japanese literature. Minor aristocrats also used their attractive, well-educated daughters to elevate their family's social status by marrying them into the most powerful of Japan's noble families.

Buddhism played a central role in Japanese life during the Heian period. One of the major factors in the rise of Buddhism was its close connection to the spiritual beliefs of Japan's nature-based religion, Shintō, because both belief systems sought a harmony between the forces of society and those of nature. Buddhist monks constructed great monasteries throughout the country, especially around the capital. The monks who occupied these great complexes were among the best-educated members of Japanese society, and over time, these Buddhist priests became very active in Japanese society. One of the most important of the Buddhist intellectuals was Kōbō Daishi. His ideas on the importance of developing an esoteric lifestyle had a deep and lasting impact on the development of Japanese music, art, literature, and poetry.

The decline of Heian Japan was the result of the chaotic conditions brought about by the failure of the nation's agriculture system and the great social unrest resulting from the accumulation of most of the fertile farmland by a few prominent clans of aristocrats. Two of the most powerful of these families were the Taira and Minamoto. These two noble families began a series of bloody wars in an attempt to gain control of the government. These wars of conquest were fought by a new segment of Japanese society known as samurai. These professional warriors created so much carnage that Japan slipped into a state of civil war, and the resulting chaos brought an end to the Heian Era.

SIGNIFICANCE

Japan emerged from this classical golden age with a unique culture and strong sense of national identity. Japan's rejection of Chinese cultural supremacy would eventually allow it to become the dominant force in East Asia, and this would be especially true in the nineteenth and twentieth centuries. Unlike China, where Confucian conservatism blocked any acceptance of Western technology and prevented rapid modernization, Japan had a strong sense of nationhood that allowed it to incorporate selected aspects of Western technology and culture. During the Meiji Restoration of 1867, Japanese scholar-officials created a model in which the basic tenets of Japanese culture were preserved at the same time that the nation was embracing Western science and technology.

—Richard D. Fitzgerald

FURTHER READING

Cleary, Thomas. *The Japanese Art of War: Understanding the Culture of Strategy.* Boston: Shambhala Press, 1992. An excellent account of the development of Japanese military strategy. Index.

Keene, Donald. *Seeds in the Heart.* New York: Columbia University Press, 1999. The first volume of Donald Keene's history of Japanese literature, this work deals with Heian period literature.

Sansom, George. *A History of Japan.* 3 Vols. Stanford, Calif.: Stanford University Press, 1958-1963. An excellent three-volume history of Japan. Index, bibliography, and maps.

Varley, Paul. *Japanese Culture.* Honolulu: University of Hawaii Press, 2000. An outstanding historical overview of Japanese culture. Index and bibliography.

_______. *Warriors of Japan: As Portrayed in the War Tales.* Honolulu: University of Hawaii Press, 1994. The best literary account of Japanese warfare. Index and bibliography.

SEE ALSO: 5th or 6th century: Confucianism Arrives in Japan; 538-552: Buddhism Arrives in Japan; March 9, 712, and July 1, 720: Writing of *Kojiki* and *Nihon Shoki*; 792: Rise of the Samurai; c. 1001: Sei Shōnagon Completes *The Pillow Book*; c. 1004: Murasaki Shikibu Writes *The Tale of Genji*; 1336-1392: Yoshino Civil Wars.

RELATED ARTICLES in Great Lives from History: The Middle Ages, 477-1453: Fujiwara Michinaga; Jōchō; Kōbō Daishi; Minamoto Yoritomo; Murasaki Shikibu; Nijō; Sei Shōnagon; Taira Kiyomori; Unkei.

c. 800
Kana Syllabary Is Developed

The creation of the kana *syllabaries made it possible to write the Japanese language, laying the foundation for a unique Japanese literature during the tenth and eleventh centuries.*

Locale: Japan
Category: Cultural and intellectual history

Key Figure

Kōbō Daishi (Kūkai; 774-835), Buddhist monk credited with the invention of *kana*

Summary of Event

Three main types of written characters are used to represent the Japanese language: *kanji*, *hiragana*, and *katakana*. *Kanji* are ideograms originally imported from China in about the fifth century because Japan lacked a written language. These characters were adopted as a crude way to record the Japanese language, even though they were unsuitable because of the structural differences of these two unrelated tongues. Chinese is monosyllabic and terse, with no grammatical inflections; tense and mood are either ignored or expressed by means of syntax and word position within a sentence. The Japanese language is polysyllabic, diffuse, and highly inflected and has its own peculiar sentence structure.

During the eighth century, phonetic characters developed to better approximate Japanese syllables; by the ninth century, these had simplified into the *hiragana* and *katakana* systems. Each *kana* system has forty-six characters, with each character representing a single syllable and each system independently representing all the sounds of spoken Japanese. Although both are derived from Chinese characters, each system serves a different purpose and looks somewhat different. The angularly shaped *katakana* are used primarily for foreign words, and the more cursive *hiragana* performs grammatical functions necessitated by Japanese inflections impossible to express with *kanji*. Foreign sounds that cannot be represented by syllables native to Japanese are attempted by using whatever *katakana* symbols most closely approximate the sound.

With the development of the phonetic *kana* system, it became possible to write Japanese using *hiragana* exclusively, but by this time, many Chinese words had been incorporated into the Japanese language. These words were best written with Chinese ideograms, even though they were pronounced quite differently in Japanese. Ultimately this evolved to the mixture of Chinese characters and *kana* that is employed today. Chinese *kanji* are used for nouns, verb roots, adjectives, and certain common words, while *hiragana* is employed for grammatical markers (verb and adjective endings indicating tense), auxiliary verbs, particles, and adverbs. The *katakana* are reserved for foreign names or loan words. Arguably, modern Japanese, burdened with Chinese characters, is the most complex written language in the world, yet these characters have undoubtedly enriched Japanese society and provided a deep cultural connection between China and Japan. The use of Chinese characters has influenced modes of expression and led to an association between literary composition and calligraphy lasting many centuries.

Although about fifty thousand Chinese characters exist, in 1945, the Japanese government officially specified about two thousand *kanji* as the principal characters every high-school graduate must know. However, one must know considerably more to read newspapers and books because many personal names and place-names are not included in this list.

Although the *kana* syllabaries were most likely the result of evolution rather than invention, the Buddhist monk Kōbō Daishi has been credited as the inventor of *kana* as well as the person who first introduction tea to Japan. Founder of the Shingon sect of Buddhism, this brilliant scholar's study of Sanskrit during a three-year sojourn in China may have provided the inspiration that led to kana.

During the Heian period (794-1185), Japanese authors were primarily ladies of the court who had the leisure time for reading and writing. Although there were men with literary inclinations, prose literature was considered the domain of women. So strong was this interdiction that, when Ki no Tsurayuki (869-945) composed the *Tosa nikki* (935; *The Tosa Diary*, 1912), he pretended it was written by a woman. Men continued to be educated in Chinese, which enjoyed undiminished prestige and remained the official language for all purposes except speech (similar to the manner in which Latin was used in Europe during the Middle Ages). The study of Chinese was an exclusively male domain from which women were excluded. Even if a woman learned Chinese, it was not considered proper for her to write in this language, so instead women used *kana* to represent their thoughts in their native tongue; in the process, they composed classic works of Japanese prose.

SIGNIFICANCE

From the late sixth century until the mid-ninth century, Japan was learning and copying from China. During the ninth century, however, a subtle change occurred. The emphasis shifted from borrowing to adapting and assimilating what had already been acquired. One of the clearest signs of the divergence of Chinese and Japanese culture was the development, during the ninth and tenth centuries, of an adequate way of writing Japanese. The *kana* system evolved from simplifying certain Chinese characters into simple phonetic symbols, devoid of any specific meaning, each representing an entire syllable, such as *ka*, *te*, or *no*. The result was a syllabary, not an alphabet. Although more clumsy than alphabets, *kana* are quite efficient for writing Japanese because this language utilizes fewer phonemes than most languages. Because the *kana* system perfectly represented the spoken language, writing in the national tongue became facile enough to allow complex ideas to be readily expressed. Consequently, a unique literature, written in the Japanese language, emerged concurrently with the *kana*. Courtiers and their ladies wrote and exchanged poems, many of which are still extant, on every conceivable occasion.

Kana also made more extensive literary works possible. By the tenth century, stories, travel dairies, and essays written in Japanese appeared. Although most educated men scorned the use of their native tongue for any serious literary purpose (writing only in Chinese), women of the imperial court, blocked from learning Chinese, had only Japanese *kana* (referred to as "woman's hand") as a medium for literary expression. While the men were pompously writing bad Chinese, the ladies consoled themselves by writing good Japanese and, in the process, created Japan's first great prose literature. Private collections of poetry in *kana* began to be compiled about 880. In about 905, *Kokin wakashū* (also known as *Kokinshū*; English translation, 1970), the first major work of *kana* literature, was compiled by poet Ki no Tsurayuki and others. The preface by Tsurayuki is the oldest work of sustained prose written in *kana*. The golden age of this venue was the late tenth and early eleventh centuries. The most eminent accomplishment of the period, as well as the world's first novel, was *Genji monogatari* (c. 1004; *The Tale of Genji*, 1925-1933), written by Murasaki Shikibu, a court woman, early in the eleventh century.

One may wonder why written Japanese remains burdened with Chinese characters when the phonetic *kana* characters alone can represent the entire language. One possible explanation is the long-term continuing prestige that Chinese culture and language has commanded throughout Asia. For a long period after the introduction of *kana*, most learned Japanese men continued to write in Chinese, but as the knowledge of this tongue decreased, more *kana* crept into their bastard Chinese texts. Moreover, thousand of technical and scholarly words were created out of Chinese lexical elements (similar to Western use of Greek and Latin roots to form new words) as the need arose. Unfortunately, many of the compound words created in this manner are identical when pronounced in Japanese. For this reason, in modern Japan, new words, particularly technical terms, are typically derived from the more distinct English words and written in *katakana*.

The Japanese writing system may be complex, but it cannot now be easily changed. Chinese characters have worked themselves deeply into the entire culture and have acquired artistic and psychological values the Japanese are loathe to abandon. Since World War II, the number of characters in daily use has declined somewhat, and many have been superficially simplified, but their use as a major component of written Japanese is unlikely to change significantly in the near future.

—George R. Plitnik

FURTHER READING

Cortazzi, Hugh. *The Japanese Achievement*. New York: St. Martin's Press, 1990. Cortazzi analyzes and discusses this intriguing culture from a Western perspective, from its prehistoric origins through contemporary Japan.

Keene, Donald. *Seeds in the Heart*. New York: Columbia University Press, 1999. The first volume of Donald Keene's history of Japanese literature, this work deals with the women's literature produced in Japanese.

Reischauer, Edwin O. *Japan: The Story of a Nation*. 4th ed. New York: McGraw-Hill, 1990. A first-rate text that traces the history of Japan from its origins to the world power it became. The development of *kana* and its influence on Japanese culture can be seen in the context of the country's long and fascinating history.

Schirokauer, Conrad. *A Brief History of Japanese Civilization*. New York: Harcourt Brace Jovanovich, 1993. A compact but comprehensive survey of Japanese history from its origins through the late twentieth century, this concise history includes the development of thought and literature and their contingency on the evolution of *kana*.

Varley, H. Paul. *Japanese Culture*. 4th ed. Honolulu: University of Hawaii Press, 2000. A concise survey of two thousand years of Japanese history with an emphasis on Japan's cultural peculiarities, including the evolution of Japan's complex system of writing.

See also: March 9, 712, and July 1, 720: Writing of *Kojiki* and *Nihon Shoki*; 794-1185: Heian Period; c. 1001: Sei Shōnagon Completes *The Pillow Book*; c. 1004: Murasaki Shikibu Writes *The Tale of Genji*.

Related articles in *Great Lives from History: The Middle Ages, 477-1453*: Murasaki Shikibu; Nijō; Sei Shōnagon.

c. 800-1350
Mississippian Mound-Building Culture Flourishes

Mississippian culture, the last and most advanced of the mound-building cultures, made up the final and most advanced stage of the prehistoric Late Woodlands peoples, who originated in the eastern part of North America.

Locale: Lower Mississippi, Southeast, and upper midwestern North America
Category: Agriculture

Summary of Event

"Mississippian culture" is a term denoting the late period of Native American prehistory and an advanced stage of indigenous cultural development in North America. "Mississippian" is the name used to describe the new era because the initial area of development was largely centered along the Mississippi River between modern St. Louis and Vicksburg and later along tributary streams in the Southeast, such as the Cumberland and Tennessee Rivers.

Earlier mound-building cultures, such as the Adena (which flourished c. 800 B.C.E.-200 C.E.) and the Hopewell (c. 300-700), were noted for their permanent village settlements, their impressive earthwork constructions (including burial and effigy mounds), their interregional trade networks, their high-quality craftwork, and (by around 500 B.C.E.), some agricultural activity. While sharing these traits, Mississippian societies were, by contrast, predominantly agricultural. Moreover, they were organized into centralized political entities called chiefdoms. They were governed by elites in large population centers that contained larger and more complex monumental constructions than those of preceding eras. A trend toward increased territoriality and warfare also developed among Mississippian peoples.

Factors contributing to the rise of the Mississippian culture include the introduction of the bow and arrow (during the late Hopewell period), the flint hoe, and a hardy variety of maize known as eastern flint corn. The latter was resistant to cold weather and had a shorter growing season. In the three to four centuries following 800, food production dramatically expanded as a result of intensive cultivation along rich bottomlands and other fertile areas connected to population centers by both water and land routes. Maize, which had originated in Central America, was a more productive and more easily stored crop than the native plant foods cultivated by the earlier Hopewell peoples and therefore spurred population growth. By 1200, maize, beans, and squash formed the basis of the diet, supplemented by hunting, fishing, and gathering.

Mississippian peoples shared a number of features with the high civilizations of Mesoamerica. In addition, the Mississippians probably traded, and to some degree intermingled, with Mesoamerican peoples. Nevertheless, some scholars see the impact of Mesoamerican cultures on the Mississippian as minimal and stress the largely independent development of Mississippian culture.

The period of the Mississippians' initial growth witnessed the rise of some spectacular ceremonial centers and even true urban complexes, with wattle-and-daub, rectangular buildings. These were centers of political, social, religious, and economic power, as well as a rich artistic ceremonial life, fortified by log palisades and containing residences, public buildings, and elevated central plazas with great temple mounds topped by shrines and dwellings for rulers and other elite members of society. Subordinate and outlying settlements paid tribute to the noble elites in these centers.

Mississippian society was stratified and dominated by an elite class from whose ranks came all-powerful male and female hereditary, theocratic rulers known as Great Suns. These exalted leaders, who may have been revered as deities or representatives of deities, were richly adorned and surrounded with great ceremony. Priestly

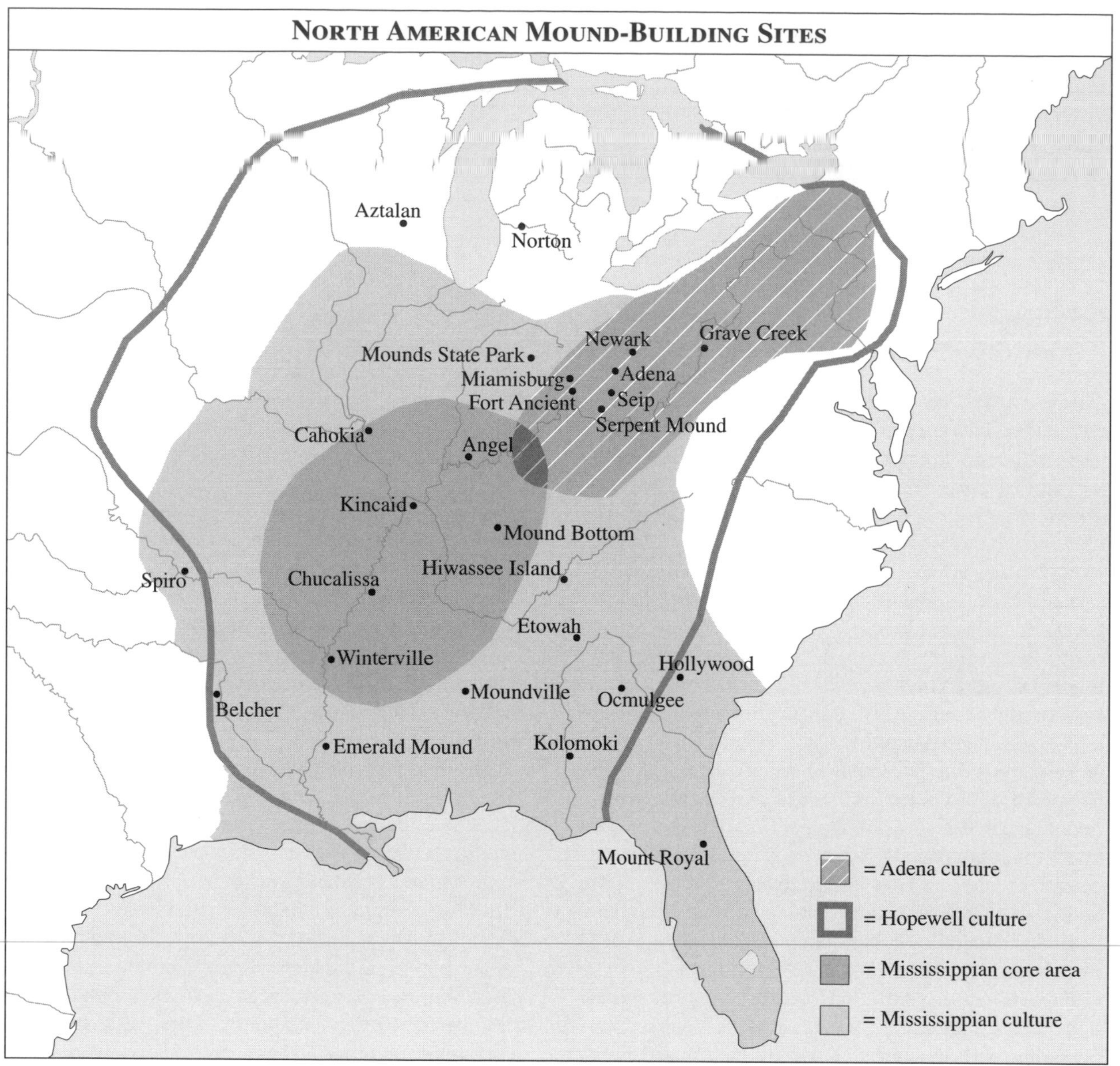

religions oriented toward agriculture exercised a powerful and central role in maintaining this social, economic, and political order. Many anthropologists believe that the top elite lineages and mound-building centers arose in locales best suited to producing a reliable supply of food and strategically placed for trade, which in turn served to secure political allies who occupied less favorable locations.

For many centuries, the heart of the Mississippian civilization was the great city of Cahokia, located about 8 miles (13 kilometers) east of modern St. Louis on the fertile Mississippi floodplain. Established as early as the eighth or ninth century, the city reached its peak of influence between 900 and 1150. The largest prehistoric metropolis north of Mexico, Cahokia (also called City of the Sun because Sun symbols, Sun calendars, and indications of Sun worship have been unearthed there) occupied an area of 5 square miles (13 square kilometers) and at its height was home to a population of twenty thousand or more people, according to some estimates. Thousands more lived in small, "suburban" settlements and farmsteads.

Cahokia contained more than one hundred ceremonial mounds. The largest and most spectacular earthwork, Monk's Mound, towered over the city's central plaza. The earthen base of this monumental construction is larger than those of the largest pyramids of Egypt and Mexico, measuring 1,100 by 790 feet (335 by 240 meters) and covering 16 acres (6.5 hectares), with a total volume of 804,608 cubic yards (618,929 cubic meters). The top tier served as a platform for a large temple and residence of Cahokia's priestly ruler. Surrounding this ceremonial area was a timber palisade. which extended for more than 2 miles (3 kilometers). Nearby, builders also laid out an observation area with wooden poles placed in a circle. This structure, today known as Woodhenge, was probably used to keep track of the movements of the sun and other heavenly bodies.

Cahokia's strategic location near the Mississippi River and its junctures with major tributary river systems made it a great commercial hub of the continent during the tenth, eleventh, and twelfth centuries. Dugout canoes laden with highly valued trade items arrived from both local and distant waterways. Mississippian craftspeople obtained products such as obsidian from distant mountain areas of the American West, copper from the Great Lakes, mica from the Appalachians, seashells from the Gulf coast, quartz from Arkansas, and silver from southern Canada. Using these and local materials, Mississippian artisans produced ornaments and jewelry, a unique pottery tempered with crushed mussel shells, effigy jars, cult figurines in human and animal form, ceremonial costumes, and items made from feathers, leather, stone fibers, wood, and beaten copper.

In addition to Cahokia, Mississippian civilization gave rise to other notable population centers and small chiefdoms. Some have been excavated, including Moundville in Alabama, Etowah and Okmulgee in Georgia, and Spiro on the Arkansas River in eastern Oklahoma. Although all were considerably smaller than Cahokia in both territory and population, they nevertheless were active and thriving centers of population, craft production, and a rich artistic and ceremonial life.

Neighboring regions of the Midwest, including sites in the Great Lakes area and the Ohio Valley, have been linked to the Mississippian cultural complex. Migrations of Mississippian peoples from the Southeast also brought new groups westward into the Great Plains, where they established agricultural villages in favorable areas along major streams and gave rise to a Plains Mississippian culture.

The power of the various southeastern chiefdoms and regional centers ebbed and flowed. A period of decline occurred after 1350, prior to the arrival of the Spaniards. The great mound-building projects ceased, and the major centers gradually disappeared. Rivalries and power struggles, as evidenced by an increase in fortifications, weaponry, and a glorification of the warrior in religious art, may have been part of several factors contributing to this decline. An exception was the Natchez chiefdom, which survived in pristine Mississippian form until its destruction at the hands of the French and their local native allies in the early eighteenth century. Incursions of European explorers and gold seekers into the Southeast during the early 1500's brought new pressures, especially the fatal epidemic diseases against which the indigenous populations had no immunity. The result was a precipitous decline in the Mississippian population from millions of people to a few hundred thousand.

SIGNIFICANCE

Many tribal cultures of the historic southeastern United States retained Mississippian traditions after the culture's decline. These groups include indigenous nations such as the Muskogee Creek, Choctaw, Chickasaw, Alabama, Cherokee, Shawnee, and Caddo. Remnants of the prehistoric culture survived in permanent agricultural settlements, a reverence for mounds as sacred symbols, strong matrilineal clans, some social stratification, the

A frog effigy pipe found in Ross County, Ohio, dating to the Hopewell tradition. (Photograph courtesy of National Museum of the American Indian, Smithsonian Institution)

Green Corn ceremony (a purification ritual performed at harvesttime), and ball games such as "chunky," which was played with a rounded stone disk. The power of Mississippians on land and water, which impressed the Spaniard Hernando de Soto's expedition (1539-1542) to the Mississippi River area, delayed the European conquest of North America. Many of the aforementioned tribal nations retained their independence until as late as the early nineteenth century.

—*David A. Crain*

FURTHER READING

Emerson, Thomas E. *Cahokia and the Archaeology of Power.* Tuscaloosa: University of Alabama Press, 1997. Argues that the Cahokian elite used a cosmology and worldview to support their dominant position.

Emerson, Thomas E., and R. Barry Lewis, eds. *Cahokia and the Hinterlands: Middle Mississippian Cultures of the Midwest.* Urbana: University of Illinois Press, 2000. Collection of articles dealing with the appearance of Cahokian Mississippian cultural patterns in Midwest fringe areas.

Mehrer, Mark. *Cahokia's Countryside: Household Archaeology, Settlement Patterns, and Social Power.* De Kalb: Northern Illinois University Press, 1995. Synthesizes Mississippian settlement and social systems using recent data and an anthropological theoretical model.

Milner, George R. *The Cahokia Chiefdom: The Archaeology of a Mississippian Society.* Washington, D.C.: Smithsonian Institution Press, 1998. Reconstructs what life must have been like in the Cahokian-dominated Mississippian period society.

Morse, Dan F., and Phyllis A. Morse. *Archaeology of the Central Mississippi Valley.* London: Academic Press, 1983. Chapters 10-12 center on Mississippian cultural development. Stresses importance of environmental factors in this process.

O'Connor, Mallory McCane. *Lost Cities of the Ancient Southeast.* Gainesville: University of Florida Press, 1995. More than twenty ceremonial sites are represented. Also discusses sculpture, ceramics, engravings, and other artifacts associated with each era.

Pauketat, Timothy R., and Thomas E. Emerson, eds. *Cahokia: Domination and Ideology in the Mississippian World.* Lincoln: University of Nebraska Press, 1997. Collection of articles examining Cahokia's powerful position in the Mississippian world. Agriculture and appropriation, production and power, ideology and authority, monuments and mobilization are cited as factors.

Shaffer, Lynda Norene. *Native Americans Before 1492: The Moundbuilding Centers of the Eastern Woodlands.* Armonk, N.Y.: M. E. Sharp, 1992. Examines the historical development and features of the great centers of the Mississippian phase and previous Woodlands cultures.

Smith, Bruce D. "Mississippian Patterns of Subsistence and Settlement." In *Alabama and the Borderlands,* edited by B. Reid Badger and Lawrence A. Clayton. Tuscaloosa: University of Alabama Press, 1985. This chapter in a work on the prehistoric and early historic periods of the Southeast examines a variety of Mississippian settlement patterns.

Young, Biloine W. *Cahokia: The Great Native American Metropolis.* Urbana: University of Illinois Press, 2000. An archaeological overview of the prehistory of Cahokia and mound excavations during the life of the settlement, including a discussion of Cahokia's "place in the pre-conquest world." Illustrations, maps.

SEE ALSO: 7th-13th centuries: Mogollons Establish Agricultural Settlements; 8th-14th centuries: Cahokia Becomes the First North American City; 8th-15th centuries: Hohokam Adapt to the Desert Southwest; c. 700: Bow and Arrow Spread into North America; 9th-15th centuries: Plains Village Culture Flourishes.

9th-14th centuries
RISE OF THE TOUTSWE KINGDOM

Archaeological evidence shows that the Toutswe kingdom existed in a territory flanked by the Zambezi River in the north and the Limpopo River in the south, from approximately the early ninth century to the fourteenth century.

LOCALE: Southern Africa (now Botswana)
CATEGORIES: Agriculture; government and politics

SUMMARY OF EVENT

The Toutswe culture of southern Africa developed from a group of Bantu people whose language derived from the Sala-Shona branch of languages. The Bantu populations that came to be known by historians as the Toutswe seem to have inhabited lands also utilized by the Khwe (non-Bantu-speaking) populations of livestock-herding, wild-food-gathering peoples.

Archaeological excavations carried out by James Denbow demonstrate that early cattle raisers, who practiced many of the lifeways indistinguishable from the later Toutswe, began to settle Toutswe sites beginning in the seventh century. These sites are characterized by hilltop settlements, scattered homesteads, and evidence of cattle raising. The evidence indicates that the region occupied by the Toutswe state was previously occupied for several centuries by Bantu speakers, coinciding with the Iron Age developments that were occurring in the late first millennium in many regions of Africa.

The Toutswe economy was agropastoral, with a population inhabiting communities that were organized as scattered homesteads. These separated settlements probably were a response to sparse food sources and limited natural resources, which were unable to support denser settlements. The settlements were also typically located near water sources—probably another reason that the homesteads were scattered.

The Kalahari Desert is believed to have served as one of the hunting grounds for the Toutswe people. The most important sources of meat for the Toutswe were domesticated cattle, sheep, and goats, but large bovids, such as the zebra, the eland, and the wildebeest, enhanced the main sources of meat for the Toutswe. Other sources of food were cultivated crops: millet, sorghum, nuts, and melons.

The headwaters of the Limpopo River served as the primary settlement grounds for the Toutswe. Here they settled in large hilltop communities in locations that offered security: Hilltops are easily defended against attacking enemies. Their settlements were arranged in a circle, and the buildings themselves were circular.

Large Toutswe settlements and villages have been identified by the presence of a grass, *Cenchrus ciliaris*, whose reflective properties make it easy to identify in aerial photographs. It is believed that these grasses thrive in the soil left by cattle in kraals (pens or enclosures), where the animals' dung has enriched the soil with nutrients especially favorable to the grass's growth. The grass thus became a marker for Toutswe settlements. The presence of *Cenchrus ciliaris* has also pointed to three main settlements—Toutswemogala (which means Toutswe Hill), Bosutswe, and Shoshong—at three main hilltop sites. Evidence suggests that these three dominant subkingdoms of the Toutswe existed by the twelfth century.

Each of the three main hilltop sites encompassed an area covering just over 1.5 square miles (more than 40,000 square meters). At these main hilltop sites, archaeologists have uncovered enormous dung deposits and remains of trade items from the Indian Ocean and elsewhere. The largest site, Toutswemogala, was occupied for approximately five hundred years and covers more than nearly 4 square miles (100,000 square meters).

Secondary sites covered an area half that of the three main hilltop sites. Typical of these sites are Mmadipudi, Thatswane, and Taukome, occupied for approximately two hundred to three hundred years. The kraal deposits of the secondary sites were large but not comparable in size or volume to that of the main site, Toutswemogala. Trade items have also been found at the secondary sites.

Yet smaller, tertiary sites include Maipethwane and Kgaswe, which range from about about 2,400 to 6,000 square yards (2,000 to 5,000 square meters) in area. The tertiary sites contain small kraals usually around 33 yards (30 meters) in diameter. Numerous ceramics and stone artifacts have been found at these tertiary sites.

There has been speculation of a fourth-level site, which arose from the finding of stone concentrations indicating that certain elements of the Toutswe milieu focused on hunting and gathering rather than herding and farming. The stone concentrations include stone tools and spears, used particularly for hunting. Whether these were Bantu or non-Bantu populations within the realm of Toutswe rule remains unknown.

Various organizational features distinguish the three tiers of the site: length of occupation, size of cattle kraals, proportion of exotic trade items, relative numbers of domestic stock, the area of land covered by houses, and additional variations in features of the settlement communities.

From the various sites and archaeological evidence, it is clear that the Toutswe kingdom was a hierarchal society, consisting of three primary economic or social classes, determined by the quantity and quality of cattle possessed. Cattle announced the class and wealth and were used for significant social and political transactions. Those with the most cattle occupied the top of the social hierarchy and lived on the hilltops in elaborate homesteads that were capable of housing hundreds of cattle. Local chiefs possessed fewer cattle and lived in smaller homesteads, typically 7,000 square meters (about 8,400 square yards) in size. At the bottom of the hierarchy were the majority of the Toutswe people. Their homesteads were approximately 1,000 square meters (836 square yards) in size, and they were fortunate if they possessed a small livestock pen. In some of the smaller hilltop villages and all of the capital towns, there were the essential large community cattle kraals.

The increase in trade across the Indian Ocean after the commencement of gold mining in the twelfth century greatly affected the value of cattle to the Toutswe culture. Although cattle retained their value as a food source, they began to decline as a form of wealth as surrounding states de-emphasized the value of cattle. With luxury items such as gold and imported foreign goods in circulation, cattle were no longer the most important means to gain social power and political importance. Higher-order Toutswe sites began to see a decline in the value of cattle, which in turn led to a reorganization of cattle herding. The cattle were shifted from core centers to lower-order communities as the higher-order classes began to accumulate other forms of wealth.

The Toutswe kingdom came to an end between the thirteenth and fourteenth centuries. Although the reasons are unclear, the Toutswe people evidently moved elsewhere and abandoned their homesteads. Various explanations have been put forward: A drought may have caused the Toutswe to move eastward, or too many cattle may have caused a drain on resources and finances. The scattered hierarchical layout of the kingdom may have contributed to the demise of the Toutswes, as well. The greater population had continuously growing herds of cattle whose grazing was more than the land could support, evidenced in remains at Taukome, where the Toutswe often slaughtered juvenile and postreproductive animals to help control herd maintenance.

SIGNIFICANCE

The exact cause of Toutswe decline is unknown, but scholars hypothesize that severe environmental degradation from cattle raising, environmental shifts from desertification (expansion of the Kalahari), dissensions within the state, or a combination of these are the most likely causes of the collapse. Another distinct possibility is that Toutswe's decline was the result of the increasing power of Great Zimbabwe to the east. As resources were drawn toward Great Zimbabwe, neighboring states may have found it difficult to compete or maintain their established standards of living.

Toutswe was one of the few centralized states of interior southern Africa. While there were many populations of nonsedentary hunter-gatherers in this region prior to the emergence of the Toutswe state, at the cusp of the first and second millennia, there is little material evidence of those populations. Thus the archaeological evidence on Toutswe sites provides important insights into the probable lifeways of earlier populations in the Botswana region of southern Africa, including with which other communities the Toutswe may have had social or economic interactions.

—*Dwight Kieffer, David Lindsay, and Carol Olausen*

FURTHER READING

Denbow, James R., and Edwin N. Wilmsen. "Paradigmatic History of San-Speaking Peoples and Current Attempts at Revision." *Current Anthropology* 5 (1990): 489-524. Discusses the importance of food gatherers in Botswana.

Isichei, Elizabeth. *A History of African Societies to 1870*. New York: Cambridge University Press, 1997. A general history of Africa that includes ethnographic descriptions.

McIntosh, Susan Keech, ed. *Beyond Chiefdoms: Pathways to Complexity in Africa*. New York: Cambridge University Press, 1999. Contains a section on the excavation of Bosutswe from 1990. Demonstrates how the enclosed towns were laid out, where vitrified dung was located, and where granaries were located.

Phillipson, David W. *African Archaeology*. New York: Cambridge University Press, 2000. A survey of African history through archaeological data. Includes a small section on Toutswe and maps that identify the kingdom's location.

Shaw, Thurstan, Paul Sinclair, Bassey Andah, and Alex Okpoko. *The Archaeology of Africa: Foods, Metals, and Towns*. New York: Routledge, 1993. Covers a number of historical topics in ancient and medieval African history, from climate and geography to Iron Age tools and economies. Draws heavily on archaeological data, with a section on Toutswe archaeological traditions.

SEE ALSO: 11th-15th centuries: Great Zimbabwe Urbanism and Architecture; c. 1075-1220: Emergence of Mapungubwe.

9th-15th centuries
PLAINS VILLAGE CULTURE FLOURISHES

The classic Plains Village culture of the eastern U.S. plains region developed permanent villages along river bluffs and was devoted to agriculture and gathering, supplemented by seasonal hunts.

LOCALE: Eastern plains, United States
CATEGORIES: Agriculture; expansion and land acquisition; cultural and intellectual history

SUMMARY OF EVENT

The classic image of the Native American—of the Indian on horseback hunting buffalo or fighting the U.S. Cavalry and living in circular tipi villages—is only true of a short period of Native American life, that of the High Plains Indian after the mid-1800's. Indispensable to the High Plains period, the culmination of the Plains Village period that remained relatively unchanged until the nineteenth century, was the widespread and transformative introduction by Europeans of the horse and the rifle.

Inhabiting the Plains for more than seven hundred years, however, were the Plains Village Indians, who lived in the Great Plains region of what is now the United States, an area of about 1.5 million square miles (4 million square kilometers) from central Alberta and Saskatchewan (in Canada) to central Texas, between the Rocky Mountains and the Mississippi River. The area was mostly treeless grassland: short grass in the west and longer grass on the eastern prairies. There were wooded areas along the many river valleys. The high plains to the west had little rainfall and were very hot in the summer, which did not favor agriculture; but the prairies to the east received more rain and were more humid, a good climate for agriculture.

The first bands of nomadic hunter-gathers probably reached North America across the Bering Strait connecting Siberia with Alaska, probably about 18,000 B.C.E. As shown by evidence from the Folsom and Clovis sites, by about 11,000 B.C.E., ancient peoples were hunting the huge now-extinct mammals (mammoth and bison) in the American Southwest. For a long period, the hot and dry high plains were largely deserted of people. The change from hunter-gatherer to farmer was gradual. By about 6,000 B.C.E., groups on the eastern plains and in valleys along the Missouri and Mississippi Rivers and tributaries began living in permanent villages to exploit fish and gather edible plants. Indians living on the Plains from about 500 B.C.E. to 1000 C.E. are called the Plains Woodland Indians. The principal archaeological sites are along the Missouri River and its tributaries, a main site being the Kansas City Hopewell site. Along the rivers of the eastern plains, from about 200 B.C.E. to 200 C.E., corn (maize), beans, and squash, and cultural influences including burial mounds and elongated pottery with cone-shaped bases, were introduced by farmers to the east.

As early as the ninth century, as agricultural efficiency improved, the Plains Woodland cultures changed into the Plains Village cultures on the eastern Plains. The Indians adopted a semisedentary lifestyle, living in permanent houses and small villages, with their subsistence divided between crops and hunting-gathering. Surviving parts of the villages are near fertile river floodplains. Village culture seems to have spread westward and northward, up the Missouri, Republican, Red, Arkansas, and Platte Rivers and their tributaries. Initially, the settlements were scattered and only semipermanent, giving way eventually to larger permanent villages located on the bluffs and terraces overlooking river valleys. Farming took place on the river lowlands.

Unlike the mounds of the earlier Woodland and Mississippian cultures of the Midwest, or the cliff dwellings and pueblos of the southwestern Indians, the archaeological remains of the thousands of Plains Indians villages are now buried and barely noticeable along the river terraces and bluffs. Many sites are now buried by reservoirs created by later dam-building projects. What can be learned from archaeological evidence is supplemented or confirmed by observations and artifacts collected by anthropologists in the nineteenth and twentieth centuries. Archaeological evidence has led to the identification of numerous cultural areas, traditions, phases, and complexes.

Archaeological evidence for Plains Village dwellings consists of occasional stone wall foundations, major interior support post and smaller-wall pole holes (often filled with wood dust or charred wood), central hearths, cache pits, and refuse heaps. Burial remains have been found beneath house floors. This evidence indicates the villagers lived in domed, square, or rectangular multifamily lodges, up to 60 feet (18 meters) across, that could hold up to thirty or sometimes even fifty people. The lodges were covered with earth, grass, bark, mats, or hides, and entered by covered passages. Some tribes excavated the floor, so the lodges were partly subterranean. Many villages seem to have been laid out with no concern for defense. However, some villages in the Dakotas were fortified by ditches and pole stockades.

Stone artifacts found at house and village sites include arrowheads and spear points, knives, drills, reamers, scraping tools, elbow pipes, shaft abraders, and grinding tools. Artifacts made from bone include tips for digging-sticks and hoes, awls, beads, sickles, and fishhooks. Pottery shards, beads, and other ornaments are also common. Other more rarely found items include clay pipes, shell beads, and objects made from obsidian and turquoise, indicative of trade with Indians of the Southwest.

Food was dried and stored in underground (cache) storage pits, and could remain edible for months. Corn was ground on stone metates. Agriculture was always risky: Crops could fail from too much or too little rain, high winds, storms, hail, grasshoppers, birds, and animals. Even if there was a good crop, there was always the danger of loss of stored food from rotting, rodents, or theft by other tribes when villagers were away on hunts. Trading was common, especially trading agricultural goods for products of the hunt, primarily buffalo hides.

The villagers also depended to varying degrees on hunting (the able-bodied members of the village took part in two hunts per year) and gathering, including the gathering of berries, fruits, and nuts. It appears, however, that cultivated crops remained the major source of food. The success of all these methods ensured the availability of food throughout the year.

Buffalo meat from the hunts was eaten fresh, dried and stored, or turned into pemmican, which could last four to five years. The buffalo hunt provided clothing, materials for shelter, and a variety of tools, containers, ropes, belts, spoons, and cups. Dried buffalo droppings made excellent fuel.

Plains Indian society was ranked and stratified, based on one's wealth or spiritual powers. Men could achieve status through deeds of bravery in war. The position of chief was often mostly honorific, and an individual held the authority as long as he commanded respect. Older men often formed councils, which led the tribe.

In their spiritual beliefs, the Plains Indians did not make sharp divisions between the sacred and the secular. They believed in the importance of visions (dreams), which were a way of connecting with the spirit world. Success in life depended upon the guidance of friendly spirits. Individuals held "vision quests" to beg for assistance, which were accompanied by self-inflicted deprivation or punishment. If the suppliant was successful, a spirit (often in the form of an animal or bird) would appear with instructions.

Tribes had medicine men, or shamans. With their supernatural powers, they were a bridge between the sacred and secular world, and could cure illness (although herbal remedies could be used for less serious illness). Rituals and ceremonies varied among tribes, and some could last up to four days. Important ritual artifacts usually included sacred medicine bundles.

Early anthropologists estimated the entire Plains area population to be between 130,000 and 300,000 people. Recently, the population of all Indians on the Great Plains at about the year 1520 was estimated to be more than two million. Later reports by Europeans of the sparsely populated plains probably do not reflect the great reduction of the population by disease during that time.

Migration of groups in response to droughts and possibly hostile groups led to the demise of the Plains Village tradition. By 1400, the Plains Villagers on the eastern periphery of Nebraska and Iowa had departed, drought being one likely reason, and had been replaced by the Oneota people. Likewise, because of major droughts and an unpredictable climate, the areas along the western periphery of Nebraska, Kansas, and Colorado, and the Texas and Oklahoma panhandles, had been depopulated by 1400. By 1500, the southern plains of Texas and Oklahoma were abandoned and its peoples dispersed, again possibly because of poor climate. The Central Plains villages of Nebraska and Iowa had been abandoned by the mid-1500's.

SIGNIFICANCE

An increasing reliance on agriculture and on bison hunting led to the full development of the Plains Village culture. Significantly, villagers slowly began living in large, permanent, self-sufficient locales and balanced agriculture with seasonal hunting trips, helping the stable and conservative culture to survive for almost seven hundred years. Plains Village culture might have survived and thrived indefinitely, except for the effects of climate change and the arrival of Europeans, which occurred in 1541 in Kansas with the explorations of the Spaniard Francisco Vásquez de Coronado.

—Thomas McGeary

FURTHER READING

Fagan, Brian M. *Ancient North America: The Archaeology of a Continent*. 3d ed. New York: Thames and Hudson, 2000. A well-organized textbook, with ample illustrations.

Holder, Preston. *The Hoe and the Horse on the Plains: A Study of Cultural Development Among North American Indians*. Lincoln: University of Nebraska Press, 1970. A classic and very readable account of Plains Village life.

Johnson, Michael. *Macmillan Encyclopedia of Native American Tribes*. 2d ed. New York: Macmillan, 1999. A brief introduction to Plains Village Indians, with sections on major tribes. Good illustrations, some in color.

Meyer, Roy W. *The Village Indians of the Upper Missouri: The Mandans, Hidatsas, and Arikaras*. Lincoln: University of Nebraska Press, 1977. A thorough study of three village peoples.

Pritzker, Barry M. *A Native American Encyclopedia: History, Culture, and Peoples*. New York: Oxford University Press, 2000. General survey of Great Plains Indians, followed by section on major tribes.

Schlesier, Karl H., ed. *Plains Indians, A.D. 500-1500: The Archaeological Past of Historic Groups*. Norman: University of Oklahoma Press, 1994. A collection of scholarly articles about Indian cultures of the Plains region.

Sturtevant, William C., ed. *Handbook of North American Indians*. Vol. 13, *Plains*, edited by Raymond J. Demallie. Washington, D.C.: Smithsonian Institution Press, 2001. A general survey, followed by detailed discussions of village cultures and regions.

Sutton, Mark Q. *An Introduction to Native North America*. Boston: Allyn and Bacon, 2000. A general introduction to the Plains peoples, with a study of the Pawnees.

Wood, W. Raymond, ed. *Archaeology on the Great Plains*. Lawrence: University of Kansas Press, 1998. Several detailed chapters on Plains Village cultures.

SEE ALSO: 7th-13th centuries: Mogollons Establish Agricultural Settlements; 8th-14th centuries: Cahokia Becomes the First North American City; 8th-15th centuries: Hohokam Adapt to the Desert Southwest; c. 800-1350: Mississippian Mound-Building Culture Flourishes.

802
FOUNDING OF THE KHMER EMPIRE

Jayavarman II combined the many kingdoms that existed during the Chenla period of Khmer history and formed a dynasty that would last more than five centuries.

LOCALE: Modern-day Cambodia
CATEGORY: Government and politics

KEY FIGURES

Jayavarman I (c. 635-681), a Khmer king during the Chenla period, r. 657-681

Jayavarman II (c. 770-850), founder and first king of the Khmer state, r. 802-850

SUMMARY OF EVENT

The Khmer state in modern-day Cambodia dominated its neighbors for more than six centuries and built some of the greatest architectural works of Southeast Asia, including the Angkor Wat and Angkor Thom complexes. The state began at the start of the ninth century, but its creation involves a mix of Chinese and Indian history that influenced how the Khmers viewed their monarchs and how the monarchs viewed themselves. The state's exact beginnings are a matter of dispute and based on fragments of writings composed centuries later.

The region now known as Cambodia was initially influenced by the two largest powers in Asia: India and China. The creation of the cult of the god-king in Khmer history can be traced back to an Indian folktale about the creation of the original Khmer nation and monarchy. According to the story, a Brahman by the name of Kaundinga was looking for a wife. He shot an arrow into the boat of a dragon princess, which enabled him to convince her to marry him. Her father, the dragon king, proceeded to swallow all of the water that covered the land and gave that land to the couple to rule. The name given them, Kambuja, became the name of the territory they ruled, and from it derives the English word *Cambodia*, the modern name for Khmer.

From the third through the sixth century, the Chinese had control over what they called Funan province. Funan did not contain all of Cambodia and was focused more on the southern towns, which were used by the Chinese as ports for their trading ships sailing to India and other portions of Asia. Not much is known about the Funan period, and what was written by Chinese historians contains exaggerated accounts of Chinese accomplishments and the extent of Chinese control.

A sculpture at Angkor Thom, built in the twelfth century by Jayavarman VII. (PhotoDisc)

The Funan period ended after the sixth century, and the Cambodian state fragmented into several smaller kingdoms. This period became known as the Chenla. During the Chenla, Cambodia was divided between coastal kingdoms with a trading economy and the inland kingdoms, which were agriculturally based. Most of these kingdoms were located along the Mekong River flowing north and along the Tonle Sap or Great Lake and the Tonle Sap River. From 600 to 800, various kings attempted to combine these kingdoms into a single state. In 620, Isanavaraman was able to seize control over several kingdoms along the Mekong and create a larger state. His successor, Jayavarman I, expanded on this control and included a portion of the Tonle Sap region. However, this kingdom collapsed after his death, and during the eighth century, there was a tendency for the small states to resist any attempts to form them into a single state.

At the end of the eight century, however, a leader emerged who would draw the kingdoms together into a united Khmer state. Jayavarman II most likely came from the Malay peninsula. He was chosen to lead one of the kingdoms in the south of the country, probably near the town of Prei Veng. He began consolidating his power along the Mekong River, militarily conquering several states and, in one instance, marrying a princess so as to take over her father's territory. Once his control over the Mekong was assured, Jayavarman II moved westward, to the Tonle Sap River and the Great Lake. His movement west was marked by a succession of capital cities that followed him. In his conquests, Jayavarman demonstrated that he had a larger goal than his predecessors. He sought to build a more permanent state, one that would combine all the Khmer people and would allow them to defeat invaders, conquer weaker peoples outside their borders, and build a civilization that would be uniquely Khmer.

Once his conquests were secure, Jayavarman II sought to establish that central Cambodian state and a permanent dynasty that could be handed down through his family. He arranged for a ritual in which he would be crowned as king of the Khmers and would assume a god-like status among the people. In 802, Jayavarman received a Brahman or priest who was given the task of performing the necessary rituals. Most scholars place this event at Mount Makendrapavata, a sacred mountain of the Śiva cult. Although the exact rituals are not known, the Brahman utilized those from several local religions, including the worship of Śiva and Viṣṇu (Vishnu), two cults from India, and Buddhism. All the rituals were intended to prevent invaders from attacking the Khmer people. The rituals also established Jayavarman and his successors as the king of kings, a deity on earth not only to be obeyed but also to be worshiped by his people.

Jayavarman II extended this idea into the cult of Devaraja, or the worship of the god-king. No longer were kings mortal men who could be defeated or killed or would share power with others. Instead, Jayavarman II and his successors attained the status of divine rulers. Part of the development of the cult required creating a priesthood and a ritual structure with temples and sacred objects for worship. One such object was the Linga. Each ruler following Jayavarman II would build a new temple on a hill, mountain, or mound as protection for the sacred Linga. Jayavarman II was also responsible for the hereditary priesthood in the cult. He appointed a head priest, Sivakawalya, who appointed the rest of the priests. He created the rituals used for worshiping the new god-king and had strict oversight to ensure the priests were performing the rituals properly and treating the beliefs with sufficient regard.

Beyond his creation of the god-king, Jayavarman II proved to be a shrewd and, at times, brutal leader. He swiftly eliminated opposition to his rule either by using lower officials to carry out his policies or executing those who refused to accept his offer. Jayavarman constructed a new capital city on a mountain near the Tonle Sap. The location provided security for his rule and was close to some of the best fishing and agricultural lands in Cambodia. Jayavarman also began constructing temples in the region, construction that through the centuries would produce the Angkor Wat complex.

Jayavarman II ruled his new kingdom until 850, but unlike previous rulers, who had allowed others to choose their successors, Jayavarman chose his and anointed him as the next god-king. This began the Angkorean period of Cambodian history. The period lasted until 1431 when the Khmers were defeated by Siam (Thailand). However, even after defeat, the Khmers continued the tradition of the god-king, which still existed in the twentieth century with the last king of Cambodia, Norodom Sihanouk.

SIGNIFICANCE

Jayavarman II's crowning as the king of kings and the rituals performed on Mount Makendrapavata created a new nation and a form of government that would last for more than eleven hundred years. The Khmer state, under a single monarch after 802, would develop into a major economic and military power in southeast Asia. Its armies swept north into what is now Laos and west into modern-day Vietnam. The Khmer form of king worship made the Khmer leader one of the most absolutist in the region. In addition to military power, the Khmers proved to be economically strong and used their wealth to construct some of the greatest architectural sites in Southeast Asia. The Angkor Wat and Angkor Thom sites were built in the twelfth century by one of Jayavarman II's successors, Jayavarman VII. These temples and palaces have existed under the attack of nature and the many wars that have plagued modern Cambodia.

—*Douglas Clouatre*

FURTHER READING

Audric, John. *Angkor and the Khmer Empire*. London: Robert Hale, 1992. A story about the building of the Angkor Wat complex and its meaning within Khmer cultural and political history.

Chandler, David. *A History of Cambodia*. Boulder, Colo.: Westview Press, 1992. A wide-ranging description of the history of Cambodia starting with the influence of the Chinese and Indians and continuing into the modern-day genocide of the Khmer Rouge.

Higham, Charles. *The Civilization of Angkor.* Berkeley: University of California Press, 2001. A book with a plethora of pictures detailing the Angkor Wat complex and text on how the civilization grew and flourished during the medieval period.

Mabbet, Ian, and David Chandler. *The Khmers*. Oxford, England: Blackwell Press, 1995. A more limited look at the Khmer empire and the various leaders before Jayavarman II and the cultural and economic growth of the empire and its people.

SEE ALSO: 877-889: Indravarman I Conquers the Thai and the Mons; 982: Le Dai Hanh Invades Champa.

RELATED ARTICLE in *Great Lives from History: The Middle Ages, 477-1453*: Suryavarman II.

809
FIRST ISLAMIC PUBLIC HOSPITAL

Doctors and physicians of the early Islamic Empire provided medical attention to the ruling class and those who could afford their care. The poor often resorted to using leeches, herbs, or magic to find relief, until the first Islamic public hospital opened to all who needed medical treatment, changing the face of medicine.

LOCALE: Baghdad, Mesopotamia (now Baghdad, Iraq); Damascus, Syria; and Jund-i-Shapur, Persia (now near Ahvāz, Iran)

CATEGORIES: Health and medicine; organizations and institutions; social reform

KEY FIGURES

al-Rāzī (c. 864-c. 925), Muslim philosopher and physician

Avicenna (980-1037), Persian physician, scientist, and philosopher

Hārūn al-Rashīd (766-809), ʿAbbāsid caliph of Baghdad, r. 786-809, had hospital built

Jibrāʾīl ibn Bukhtishu (fl. eighth century), Christian physician, first director of the hospital

SUMMARY OF EVENT

In the pre-Islamic Middle East, popular medicine centered around magical charms, incantations, medicinal herbs and plants, ashes, and leeches as cures for illness caused by evil spirits. According to pre-Islamic medical lore, both *jinn*, or evil spirits, and *al-ayn*, the evil eye, were the cause of illness, fevers, madness, infection, children's diseases, and epidemics. When afflicted by an illness or infection, common people often visited barbers, who would use leeches to bleed out evil spirits, or they patronized herbalists for infusions to expurgate the afflicting spirit. If leeches or herbs did not help, people would seek out the magic of diviners, seers, or charmers for help in ending their suffering and warding off future illness. Learned doctors and physicians were retained by those who could afford them; they were not available to the common people.

As Islam developed into a formalized faith, traditional medicine came under fire because of its animistic bent. The *jinn* was not something that could coexist with a monotheistic faith in which Allah was the progenitor of all things, including diseases. Islam taught that Allah sent no malady without also sending a cure. The Qurʾān does remark on ablutions before prayer, the practice of proper hygiene, dietary practices, and honey's power to heal but it says nothing about medicine and medical practices. Until the early ninth century, knowledge of internal medicine was almost nonexistent in the Islamic world.

At age twenty-two, Hārūn al-Rashīd became the ʿAbbāsid caliph in Baghdad and ruled until his death in 809. His reign was marked by peace and a great cultural renaissance, which included a major acceleration in translations of non-Islamic works into Arabic. *Dhimmis* (Christians and Jews who were believers in God but who refused to accept the prophethood of Muḥammad, and who were protected minorities of Islam) translated philosophical and medical texts, including the works of Galen and Hippocrates, from Greek and Syriac into Arabic. Once Arabic doctors had access to this information, they were eager to build on it. So was Hārūn.

In 805, Hārūn commissioned the first public Islamic hospital and had it set up in his city. Hospitals were initially inspired by the precedent of sick-relief services offered in Christian monasteries. Although Hārūn had a court physician, Jibrāʾīl ibn Bukhtishu, a Christian doctor from Jund-i-Shapur, he was aware that his subjects had little recourse beyond leech keepers and seers.

Ibn Bukhtishu, brought the knowledge of monastic sick-relief services and information gleaned from his time studying in Jund-i-Shapur to Baghdad and his patron. By the early ninth century, Jund-i-Shapur, near the ancient city of Susa (now Shūsh) in southern Persia, had become a meeting place for Arab, Greek, Syrian, and Jewish intellectuals. An academy and hospital existed at Jund-i-Shapur and it became famous as a seat for the exchange and acquisition of scientific knowledge. Hārūn appointed Ibn Bukhtishu as the new hospital's first director. The hospital was completed in 809.

The Baghdad hospital was set up along the same lines as the academy and hospital at Jund-i-Shapur. The new hospital included wards for different physical and mental diseases, and surgery, dispensary, library, and lecture rooms. It became the hub of medicine and the center for the rise of Islamic medical training and study. It also served as a model for the later hospitals in both Baghdad and other Muslim cities such as Damascus.

In the Islamic Empire, medicine was taught in the madrasas, the Qurʾānic schools, as an art rather than as solely a form of knowledge. Students apprenticed with master physicians to learn the art of medicine. The new public hospital combined the apprenticeship method along with classroom studies. Study in the new hospital was keyed to mathematics, logic, and Galen's work on medicine. The Qur'ān prohibited dissection as a violation of the dead, so students had to rely on Galen's writings and illustrations in their study of anatomy.

In the public hospital, students could observe and describe the course of many different diseases. Apprentices made the rounds with their masters. Physicians used patients to illustrate diseases, problems, symptoms, and cures. Chief physicians and surgeons lectured to both students and graduates at the hospital. They used a variety of manuals, available in Arabic for the first time, as they lectured. Students had to master their texts by memory. They also had to participate in classroom work. They sat with their master doctor, who posed questions and explained complex concepts.

At the end of their apprenticeships, students had to pass a rigorous examination given by the master physicians; licenses were issued based on the results. No man could legally practice medicine without passing an examination and receiving a diploma. The chief physicians of the hospital also inspected and regulated leech keepers (who were mostly barbers), druggists, and orthopedists.

SIGNIFICANCE

Research and practice at Islamic public hospitals led to profound medical discoveries, methods, and techniques, including cauterization, the diagnosis of stomach cancer, the development and use of antidotes for poisoning, the treatment of eye diseases, the understanding that the bubonic plague could spread through clothing, the use of anesthetics, cataract surgery, and humane treatment for the mentally ill. Doctors and physicians also developed new surgical techniques, produced new drugs from medicinal plants, and came to understand the chemistry and effects of drugs.

Two of the greatest medical minds of the Islamic Empire trained at the Baghdad hospital: al-Rāzī and Avicenna. Al-Rāzī, a philosopher and physician, was the first to diagnose the difference between smallpox and measles. He developed the discipline of pharmacology and wrote a multivolume encyclopedia of medicine that

The tenth century Persian physician al-Rāzī (Rhazes), in his laboratory in Baghdad, depicted here by Louis Figuer in Vies des savants Moyen Âge *(1867). Razi produced an important treatise on the causes and treatment of smallpox.* (Hulton|Archive by Getty Images)

Baghdad doctors examine a distinguished patient c. 1350. (Hulton|Archive by Getty Images)

became a critical medical text in the Islamic Empire and in Medieval Europe.

Avicenna, also a physician and philosopher, wrote a canon of medicine that became the main medical textbook in Europe until sixteenth century. Through research at the hospital, he discovered the contagious nature of tuberculosis and developed an understanding of how disease can spread through contamination of soil and water.

Soon after the first public hospital opened in Baghdad, dozens of hospitals began to appear in other major Islamic cities. The foundation laid by the hospital in Baghdad fostered the growth of modern medicine in medieval Europe as well.

—*Peggy E. Alford*

Further Reading

Bakar, Osman. *The History and Philosophy of Islamic Science*. Cambridge, England: Islamic Texts Society, 1999. Discusses questions of methodology, doubt, spirituality and scientific knowledge, the philosophy of Islamic medicine, and how Islamic science influenced medieval Christian views of the natural world.

Bonner, Michael, Mine Ener, and Amy Singer, eds. *Poverty and Charity in Middle Eastern Contexts*. Albany: State University of New York Press, 2003. A collection that includes the chapter "The Functional Aspects of Medieval Islamic Hospitals," which looks at how concerns of poverty and charity were addressed in Islamic hospitals. Bibliography, index.

Bos, Gerrit. "Ibn al-Jazzar on Medicine for the Poor and Destitute." *Journal of the American Oriental Society* 118, no. 3 (July-September, 1998). Traces the world of Islamic medicine and medical care during the Middle Ages through a history of a literary genre called "medicine for the poor." Uses the tenth century Islamic medical treatise, "Medicine for the Poor and Destitute" as an example of this type of literature. Bibliographical footnotes.

Conrad, Lawrence I., et al., eds. *The Western Medical Tradition: 800 B.C. to 1800*. New York: Cambridge

University Press, 1995. A history of medicine in the West and Middle East, including a chapter on the Arab-Islamic medical tradition. Maps, bibliography, index.

Durant, Will. *The Age of Faith: A History of Medieval Civilization—Christian, Islamic, and Judaic—From Constantine to Dante: A.D. 325-1300*. New York: Simon and Schuster, 1950. The author's extensive work includes an in-depth look at the practice and development of medicine in the early Islamic empire. Part of the author's Story of Civilization series. Illustrations, maps, bibliography, index.

Johnstone, P. "Traditions in Arabic Medicine." *Palestine Exploration Quarterly* 107 (1975): 23-37. This article provides a good overview of the medical traditions in the Islamic world and their origins.

Nasr, Seyyed Hossein. *Islamic Science: An Illustrated Survey*. London: World of Islam Festival, 1976. A carefully researched photographic record of the tools of Islamic science. Provides an overview of the development of science in the Islamic world, including the development of medicine, pharmacology, and hospitals.

Porter, Roy. *The Greatest Benefit to Mankind: A Medical History of Humanity*. New York: W. W. Norton, 1997. A comprehensive history that includes an examination of Islamic medicine and hospitals and their practices and origins. Bibliography, index.

Rahman, Fazlur. *Health and Medicine in the Islamic Tradition: Change and Identity*. Chicago: ABC International, 1998. A brief survey on Islamic medical practice and health care in the context of religious faith. Discusses the concept of prophetic medicine, medical ethics, sexual ethics, and Islamic attitudes on death and dying. Bibliography, index.

Ullmann, Manfred. *Islamic Medicine*. 1978. Reprint. Edinburgh: Edinburgh University Press, 1997. This short work provides an overview focusing on the impact of the translation of Greek medical texts into Arabic on the practice of medicine in the Islamic world. Bibliography, index.

SEE ALSO: 786-809: Reign of Hārūn al-Rashīd; c. 1010-1015: Avicenna Writes His *Canon of Medicine*; c. 1150: Moors Transmit Classical Philosophy and Medicine to Europe.

RELATED ARTICLES in *Great Lives from History: The Middle Ages, 477-1453*: Pietro d'Abano; Alhazen; Arnold of Villanova; al-Ashʿarī; Avicenna; Jacqueline Félicie; Guy de Chauliac; Hārūn al-Rashīd; Abū Mūsā Jābir ibn Ḥayyān; Moses Maimonides; al-Rāzī; Trotula.

812
PAPER MONEY FIRST USED IN CHINA

The innovation of using paper money—a type of fiat money—was critical in underpinning the economics of the modern world.

LOCALE: Chang'an (now Xi'an), Shaanxi Province, China

CATEGORIES: Trade and commerce; economics

KEY FIGURES

Taizong (T'ai-tsung; 599-649), Tang Dynasty emperor, r. 627-649

Xianzong (Hsien-tsung; 778-820), Tang Dynasty emperor, r. 805-820

SUMMARY OF EVENT

A popular story associated with Marco Polo (c. 1254-1324) is that when he returned to Italy from China, he brought with him paper money to show the Venetians. His incredulous companions burned the paper, costing him a small fortune, and Polo wept at the naïveté of the Europeans.

The story is almost certainly apocryphal. Even in the thirteenth and fourteenth centuries, Chinese paper money was comparatively rare, despite the fact that it had existed for more than five hundred years. The use of paper money was strictly limited within China, and it is unlikely Polo would have carried useless paper with him except as a curio. The increasing use of paper money within China reflected the growing economy throughout the Tang Dynasty (T'ang; 618-907).

In the early 620's, the second emperor of the Tang Dynasty, Taizong, introduced a new Chinese currency, the *Kaiyuan tongbao*. This coin, the "new era commercial money," was a copper coin that became accepted as legal tender throughout virtually all of Asia, from Japan to Afghanistan, and as far away as Mongolia to parts of Indonesia. The currency greatly improved trade, as these

Taizong leaving for his campaign against the Tatars (based on a Chinese print). Taizong introduced a new Chinese currency, the kaiyuan tongbao, *or "new era commercial money."*(F. R. Niglutsch)

cause silk was one of the chief commodities of the Silk Road and could easily be resold to foreign merchants for silver, the substitution of silk for coins did not pose a major problem for Chinese authorities. The tax system was restructured to accept coins, silk, or rice for payment of taxes or other levies.

The threat of Buddhist statue making, coupled with the already shrinking supply of metal, would have been enough to threaten the amount of coinage in China, but several disruptions during the Tang Dynasty exacerbated the situation. From 755 to 763, the empire was struck by an enormous civil war known as the An Lushan Rebellion. This brutal civil war resulted in the deaths of more than 30 million people, and the ensuing destruction cut off trade and brought about an economic slowdown as the country recovered from the devastation of the war.

An important result of the rebellion was the great increase in the power of the individual provinces relative to the central government. No longer able to assert fully its independent authority, the central government was forced to rely on provincial tax levies for revenue.

The provinces themselves relied on their merchant classes as the main providers of tax revenues to the central government. In particular, merchants involved in the new trade of tea became the primary source of tax revenue payments through a method known as *fei qian*, or "flying money." The *fei qian* were paper notes that signified that a merchant had made a deposit of silver with the local provincial government. Rather than send the physical silver, a *fei qian* note was sent to the capital, where the provincial authority's capital office received the *fei qian* and performed the physical payment. *Fei qian* became extremely attractive to tea merchants because they could be used not only for paying taxes but also for remitting their profits back to their home provinces. This was of particular use to the tea industry, as it could not rely on

coins became accepted as a standard by many different peoples across numerous borders.

Although the new coins were in high demand, the *Kaiyuan tongbao* was always in short supply. Existing copper mines in China were rapidly being exhausted, leading to a shortage of metal that could be used to cast coins. In addition, the popularity of Buddhism during the Tang Dynasty threatened coinage. As many Chinese citizens converted to Buddhism, monks asked the newly religious to build statues of Buddha using copper. The resulting coin shortages forced civil authorities to accept standard sizes of rolled silk cloth as money instead. Be-the fact that silk was already accepted as a form of money.

Although some Chinese sources seem to imply that *fei qian* may have been available as early as the sixth century, the first certain use of them began in 812, during the reign of Xianzong. The imperial government may have used paper money internally, but Xianzong's decree marked the first time that it was given wider usage outside the imperial administration.

Because the *fei qian* represented a financial compact that was limited to a named merchant and the issuing provincial authority, they were not negotiable. Referring to *fei qian* as the first paper money, therefore, is not accurate. What the *fei qian* really represented was a form of bankers' acceptances, which are still used today in international trade.

The real innovation that led to paper money was instead a form of credit acceptance that began to be used at about the same time. These credit instruments were known as *jingui* or *jifupu*, notes issued by goldsmiths or silversmiths, often against a deposit of precious metals made by a customer. Unlike the *fei qian*, the credit instruments were freely negotiable. A person who had deposited gold or silver with a silversmith in his own town could have a *jingui* written against the deposit by his own or another silversmith, and exchange it for goods or services. Because the note was negotiable, the receiver could exchange it for another note, sell it, or redeem the silver at the silversmith's. These credit instruments thus behaved much more like checks and paper money than did the *fei qian*, especially as they were freely negotiable.

Despite these early innovative forays into paper money, the Tang Dynasty did not seem to appreciate their use as a monetary policy tool. *Fei qian*, *jingui*, and *jifupu* were issued by private lenders and were cleared privately and, therefore, did not represent a government issue of any sort. The first government issues of paper money in China would not come until two hundred years later, during the Song Dynasty (Sung; 960-1279), and even then were limited to regional use. The national usage of paper money on a broad scale in China did not occur until the late nineteenth and early twentieth century.

SIGNIFICANCE

The evolution of the *fei qian* and *jingui* allowed the Chinese economy to continue to expand, even when its *tongbao* monetary base was quite restricted. The gradual development from bankers' acceptances to promissory notes to credit instruments and finally to true paper money would take many more centuries of growing familiarity between the public and the government.

The use of *fei qian* notes moved in and out of fashion. The *jingui* and *jifupu* increased in use throughout the next several centuries. At times, they were used extensively, but it is difficult to assess from the few written records extant what role they had in the overall monetary economy. Surviving credit instruments that exist primarily date from the Ming Dynasty (1368-1644). The American Numismatic Society in New York has many on display to the public, and the *fei qian* notes remain highly sought-after today by collectors of coins and currencies. There are extremely few known specimens of *jingui* notes, and none from the ninth century are currently known to survive.

MARCO POLO'S STORY

A popular story told by Marco Polo in the thirteenth century relates the use of paper money in the kingdom of Kublai Khan—probably exaggerated, but an early indication of the manufacture and use of what would eventually become the most common form of currency:

In this city of Kanbalu [in modern Burma] is the mint of the Great Khan, who may truly be said to possess the secret of the alchemists. . . . The coinage of this paper money is authenticated with as much form and ceremony as if it were actually of pure gold or silver; for to each note a number of officers, specially appointed, not only subscribe their names, but affix their seals also. When this has been regularly done by the whole of them, the principal officer, appointed by his Majesty, having dipped into vermilion the royal seal committed to his custody, stamps with it the piece of paper, so that the form of the seal tinged with the vermilion remains impressed upon it. In this way it receives full authenticity as current money, and the act of counterfeiting it is punished as a capital offence. . . . [T]his paper currency is circulated in every part of the Great Khan's dominions; nor dares any person, at the peril of his life, refuse to accept it in payment. All his subjects receive it without hesitation, because, wherever their business may call them, they can dispose of it again in the purchase of merchandise they may require; such as pearls, jewels, gold, or silver. With it, in short, every article may be procured.

Source: Marco Polo, *The Travels of Marco Polo*, edited and revised from William Marsden's translation by Manuel Komroff (New York: Modern Library, 2001), pp. 134-135.

Bankers' acceptances were innovated not solely in China but also in many countries throughout the world; China, however, was the first country that made a deliberate attempt to shift the population to paper, although it was unsuccessful. The early lead China had in developing paper money did not last. Europe began to use paper money on a widening scale during the eighteenth and nineteenth centuries, whereas China did not use paper money on a wide scale until later in the twentieth century. Today, paper money is familiar to most residents of the world, but in the twenty-first century, society is in a transition from paper to electronic money. Many stores of wealth today—such as the common stock of a listed corporation—have no physical presence at all but instead exist virtually, often exchanged as payment for goods and services.

—Jason D. Sanchez

FURTHER READING

Gernet, Jacques. *Buddhism in Chinese Society: An Economic History from the Fifth to the Tenth Centuries.* Translated by Franciscus Verellen. New York: Columbia University Press, 1995. An invaluable work that points out the relationship between economy and Buddhism. Contains a superb bibliography and references many previously unknown fragments from Dunhuang.

Jen, David. *Chinese Cash: Identification and Price Guide.* Iola, Wis.: Krause, 2000. Primarily of interest to the coin collector. Jen also includes references to history works.

Peng Xinwei. *A Monetary History of China*. Translated by Ed Kaplan. 2 vols. Bellingham: Western Washington University Press, 1994. A translation by a scholarly economist of the seminal Chinese study on monetary economy. Despite its age—the original was written during the 1940's—the work has a stunning bibliography and its conclusions remain robust decades later.

Twitchett, Denis. *Financial Administration Under the T'ang Dynasty*, 2d ed. New York: Cambridge University Press, 1970. Twitchett's work is the single most importance source on Tang Dynasty economic affairs.

Von Glahn, Richard. *Fountains of Fortune: Money and Monetary Policy in China, Tenth to Seventeenth Cenutries*. New York: Cambridge University Press, 1996. This study looks at the transition from a coin-based economy to a silver-based economy in China; this work is also useful for looking at the changing industrial base of China.

SEE ALSO: 618: Founding of the Tang Dynasty; 755-763: Rebellion of An Lushan; 907-960: Period of Five Dynasties and Ten Kingdoms; c. 1045: Bi Sheng Develops Movable Earthenware Type; 12th century: Coins Are Minted on the Swahili Coast; 1115: Foundation of the Jin Dynasty; 1271-1295: Travels of Marco Polo.

RELATED ARTICLES in *Great Lives from History: The Middle Ages, 477-1453*: An Lushan; Marco Polo; Taizong.

832
NANZHAO SUBJUGATES PYU

The Nanzhao completed their conquest of Pyu, forcing the Pyu to migrate northward, and eventually formed a cultural center at Pagan, which became the center of the Pagan Empire, the first organized kingdom of Burma.

LOCALE: Burma (Myanmar), Yunnan Province, Prome (modern Pye), and Pagan

CATEGORIES: Expansion and land acquisition; government and politics

KEY FIGURES

Kolofeng (d. 779), king of Nanzhao, r. 750-779

Kublai Khan (1215-1294), Mongol ruler, r. 1260-1294; Yuan Dynasty ruler, r. 1279-1294

Anawrahta (d. 1077), first king of Pagan Empire, r. 1044-1077

SUMMARY OF EVENT

During the eighth and ninth centuries, China's imperial domination began to wane, resulting in the rise of independent city-states such as the Shan kingdom of Nanzhao (modern-day Yunnan Province), the Mon in lower Burma, and the Pyu in the Irrawaddy Valley. The Nanzhao began to consolidate their kingdom during this period, and they emerged as a threat to Chinese territory during the Tang Dynasty (T'ang; 618-907).

The Pyu, a Tibetan-Burmese tribe, established city-kingdoms in the Irrawaddy Valley during the first century

B.C.E. By 128 B.C.E., they offered an alternative route for goods traveling between China and India, a network that would be used extensively by the Chinese and Roman empires. Their chief capital city and the base of their political power was Shrikshetra, located at the mouth of the Irrawaddy River. The city acted as a crucial portage stop for ships in the Gulf of Siam because it was a shorter route to India. This trade network helped make Pyu culture flourish and facilitated the development of a lucrative economy. The Pyu economy was essentially agricultural; the major cash crop was rice. However, trade in precious metals allowed the Pyu to erect elaborate brick palaces and pagodas with gold-decorated interiors and lead-tile roofs. Artisans also honed their skills with works made from crystal, gold, silver, jade, and tin. The Pyu eventually claimed sovereignty to eighteen tribes.

The Mon lived to the south of the Pyu and spoke an Austro-Asiatic language. The port of Thaton was their capital and became an important trade city to India through the Malay peninsula. Between the first and fourth centuries, prosperity increased, and the Mon readily embraced Indian culture, law, and Theravāda Buddhism. The Mon shifted their political center to a delta region near the Pegu River, taking complete control of the trade network in southern Burma. The Mon never were able to form an empire but instead formed a loose confederation of states. They reached their peak of power during the seventh and eighth centuries.

By the eighth century, the Nanzhao state had evolved into the dominant power in southwestern China. In 751, Nanzhao broke off relations with China, and forty years later gained complete autonomy. In the late 700's, the Nanzhao, led by King Kolofeng, penetrated northern Burma, spreading their rule throughout the Irrawaddy River Valley and gradually coming into contact with the Pyu. By the 800's, the Nanzhao had made Pyu a vassal state. In 802, both Nanzhao and Pyu sent emissaries to the Tang court, opening up political relations and the negotiation of commercial agreements. However, over the next fifty years, the Nanzhao's expansionist policies allowed them to defeat the Pyu, obtain crucial trade routes, capture Hanoi, and raid adjacent territories controlled by the Mon, a kingdom in lower Burma. Nanzhao was not able to take over the Mon, but the Pyu were not so fortunate. In 832, Nanzhao completed its capture of Pyu, already a vassal. The Nanzhao also invaded the Chinese portion of Sichuan but were defeated in 875. The Nanzhao would remain independent until they were conquered by the Mongols under Kublai Khan in 1253.

SIGNIFICANCE

The downfall of the Pyu in 832, the continuous plundering by the Nanzhao, and the decline of the Tang Dynasty disturbed the balance of trade and political power in the region. The Pyu were forced to migrate farther north, and a subsequent merger of local tribes led to the rise of the first Burmese empire, which endured from the eleventh to the thirteenth century. With the decline of Prome, the Pyu moved two hundred miles north and formed a new cultural center at Pagan. The Burmese took the opportunity for political unification of the region.

In 1044, Anawrahta seized power and reigned for thirty-three years over the Pagan Empire (1044-1287). Anawratha consolidated power by various means. First, he captured the Mon capital and forcibly relocated the royal family, craftspeople, and monks to Pagan. Then, he strengthened northern military defenses against the Nanzhao, created marriage alliances, explored new economic resources, and adopted Theravāda Buddhism in order to stabilize the empire. The Pagan Empire became the first organized kingdom of Burma, and it remained strong until 1287, when it was defeated by Mongol armies. Reunification would not occur until the sixteenth century.

—*Gayla Koerting*

FURTHER READING

Aung, Maung Htin. *The History of Burma*. New York: Columbia University Press, 1967. Traces the history of Burmese social, political, and religious institutions from Burma's earliest kingdoms through the advent of British colonization and the regaining of independence. Includes a chronological table; a king list, 1044-1885; and bibliographical notes.

Cowan, C. D., and O. W. Walters, eds. *Southeast Asian History and Historiography: Essays Presented to D. G. E. Hall*. Ithaca, N.Y.: Cornell University Press, 1976. A series of essays dedicated to Hall, an emeritus professor of Southeast Asian history at the University of London and Cornell University. The papers reflect a wide range of topics, including anthropology, history, economics, linguistics, and literature.

Hall, D. G. E. *A History of Southeast Asia*. 4th ed. New York: St. Martin's Press, 1981. Hall traces the history of Southeast Asia from its earliest tribal kingdoms in the eighth century to European expansion and dominance from 1500 to 1950. Includes an extensive index, bibliography, colored maps, and illustrations. The appendix "Dynastic Lists" is particularly helpful.

Harvey, G. E. *History of Burma: From Earliest Times to 10 March 1824, the Beginning of the English Conquest*. 1925. Reprint. London: Frank Cass, 1967. Harvey concentrates his scholarship on the political aspects of Burmese history, focusing on kingdoms and dynasties. Contains an extensive notes/bibliography section and an index.

Holcombe, Charles. *The Genesis of East Asia, 221 B.C.-A.D. 907*. Honolulu: University of Hawaii Press, 2001. Holcombe explains the political, economic, and social history of East Asia. He argues that the region developed a distinct cultural identity because of its physical geography, diverse ethnic groups, and political interaction between states. Holcombe also asserts that a major unifying factor was the system of writing.

Htoo, Aung. "Ethnic Issues in Burma, Part One: The Fourth Burman Empire." *Legal Issues on Burma Journal* no. 5 (April, 2000): 1-21. The author explains the history of ethnic groups and peoples in Burma. This is the first of three articles on the topic.

Stargardt, Janice. *Early Pyu Cities in a Man-made Landscape*. Vol. 1 in *The Ancient Pyu of Burma*. Cambridge, England: Cambridge University Press, 1990. This work contains the results of data formulated by archaeologists over the past forty years for the early Pyu civilization. It showcases the economic and social dimensions of the Pyu culture; a major portion of Stargardt's book focuses on the complex irrigation system the Pyu developed in Burma's Dry Zone.

Steiger, G. Nye. *A History of the Far East*. 2d ed. New York: Ginn, 1944. Steiger outlines the history of eastern and southeastern Asia from ancient times to the end of World War II, focusing on China, India, Korea, and Japan. The work includes a list of maps and an impressive bibliography of primary and secondary sources divided into subject categories by country.

SEE ALSO: 729: Founding of Nanzhao; 863: Nanzhao Captures Hanoi; 877-889: Indravarman I Conquers the Thai and the Mons; 1295: Ramkhamhaeng Conquers the Mekong and Menam Valleys.

RELATED ARTICLE in *Great Lives from History: The Middle Ages, 477-1453*: Kublai Khan.

834
GYPSIES EXPELLED FROM PERSIA

With the death of the ʿAbbāsid Dynasty caliph al-Maʾmūn, Baghdad's rule over Persia began to crumble. Local dynasties less tolerant of outsiders gained control of the region and expelled the Gypsies, also known as the Roma, from Persia. The expulsion launched the nomadic spread of the Gypsies into Europe and initiated centuries of persecution.

LOCALE: Central Persia (now in Iran)

CATEGORIES: Cultural and intellectual history; wars, uprisings, and civil unrest

KEY FIGURES

al-Maʾmūn (786-833), last ruler of the ʿAbbāsid Dynasty, r. 813-833

Firdusi (between 932 and 941-between 1020 and 1025), Iranian poet and historian

Rudolph IV (c. 1289-1348), ruler of Baden, ordered Gypsy enslavement, r. 1335-1348

Maḥmūd of Ghazna (971-1030), Muslim sultan of Ghazna, r. 997-1030

SUMMARY OF EVENT

The precise origin of the Roma people, popularly if somewhat inaccurately known as the Gypsies, is still unclear. The current consensus is that they originated as a series of nomadic, warrior, and farming tribes, gathered in or around the Gujarat area of northwest India. By the sixth century, large numbers had found a second home in Persia. The events leading to their arrival in Persia are disputed and are known through a mixture of folklore and history. One version maintains that they first arrived as low-caste mercenary warriors, hired to protect Persia from the Arab threat to its west. Another dates their arrival from the ninth century, viewing their migration from India as an effort to escape India's invasion by Mongols from the east.

The explanation favored by Roma themselves, and the one that contains a harbinger of their future, originates with Firdusi, a tenth or eleventh century Iranian poet and historian. In his *Shahnamah* (c. 1010; the book of kings), Firdusi writes that in approximately 420, the Persian king Bahrām V (r. 420-438) asked the ruler of India to send twelve thousand Dom musicians to deflect his people's attention from the drudgery of their daily lives. These Doms—one of the many names by which these people were then known—were rewarded for their musical entertainment with grain and land so that they could prosper. In this legend, however, the Dom were considered lazy; they ate the grain but shunned working the land. Ultimately, the king was forced to expel them to a life of ceaseless roaming and supporting themselves through smuggling and begging.

Legends aside, it is clear that life in Persia had a significant impact on the Roma, affecting their language (now classified in the Indian-Iranian group) and their subsequent tribal structure. It was during their sojourn in Persia that the Roma split into the three major tribal groups that still characterize their European social structure, the most important being the Gitanos, a group whose name derived from the misconception that its members came from Egypt. The commonly used word "gypsy" comes from the term Gitano. The word gypsy, however, is considered derogatory by many and, in 1995, the Council of Europe approved the use of the term Roma as the official designation for Gypsies in its documents and usage.

In 651, the Arabs conquered Persia, installed Islam as the official faith of the state, and brought it under the rule of the ʿAbbāsid Dynasty (750-1258) centered in Baghdad. While Baghdad controlled Persia, the Roma were tolerated even as their numbers grew. The first recorded Roma state (the Zott state) survived along the Tigris River near the juncture of the border of what is now Iran and Iraq between 1820-1833.

With the death of Caliph al-Maʾmūn in 833, however, Gypsy fortunes sank. Al-Maʾmūn was a great believer in law as a means of resolving conflict, but on his death, de facto power fell into the hands of Baghdad's governors in Persia's provinces. The governors quickly proved to be neither tolerant nor inclined toward legal solutions to social problems. The following year, Persia's Roma communities were expelled from Persia. In the centuries that followed, expulsion—along with persecution—would become a way of life for the Roma.

The expulsion of the Roma from Persia marked the beginning of their long trek westward. Some traveled through Iraq and eventually into Syria, where large numbers were taken prisoner during the Byzantine Empire's attack on Syria in 855; some migrated to Egypt and North Africa. The majority, though, traversed the famous Silk Road that was used by traders moving between Asia and Europe, arriving first in Constantinople, the gateway to Europe. From there they wandered into the Balkans (by the early thirteenth century), which still contains the largest concentration of Roma in the world, and then into southern, western, and northern Europe by the fifteenth century. Along the way, what began as linguistically and ethnically mixed groupings developed into a common ethnic background and form of language that links modern Europe's Roma communities.

The bulk of India's Roma tribes followed others from Persia, in the early eleventh century primarily. This was a time when India was invaded by Muslim Afghan, Turkish, and Persian warriors under the leadership of Maḥmūd of Ghazna, who forced India's Roma communities to relocate westward en masse. They relocated into the Middle East, marking the first great Gypsy migration, and then into Europe, in what historians consider to be the second great migration of Roma.

By the early 1300's, Roma people had begun to appear in eastern and central Europe in sizable numbers. It was an unfortunate moment for their arrival. The Crusades (1095-1270) had just concluded, and intolerance toward non-Christians was growing throughout Europe. Gypsies—described most often as very dark in complexion and with black hair—were perceived as clearly non-Christians and sometimes as hated Muslims. Thus, following a brief moment in which their metalworking skills earned them a place in local economies suffering from a depletion of workers brought on by the Crusades, Roma settling in eastern and central Europe were abused by local communities. Abuse quickly turned to widespread oppression when Rudolph IV established during his reign Europe's first recorded system of Roma slavery.

SIGNIFICANCE

Rudolph IV's system consigned to slavery approximately 20 percent of the Roma in his realm, most of them slaves to local landlords and monasteries. During the following centuries, until its elimination between 1856 and 1861, Roma slavery became nearly universal in parts of central Europe, affecting nearly half of Europe's total Roma population. Sexual unions with Roma altered the appearance of their offspring, lightening their complexion and leaving Europe's Roma population with an average genetic makeup that is 60 percent Caucasian-European. Unwilling and forced couplings also increased their numbers. Children born of Roma women were born into slavery. In turn, Roma girls with light skin were usually raised as house servants and, hence, were coupled with their "owners" for sexual unions.

Meanwhile, Roma who continued to migrate farther west, in part to evade slavery, encountered substantially the same pattern: arrival followed by persecution and often exile. In 1407, for example, Roma arrived in what is now Germany; nine years later they were expelled from its Meissen region. Not until 1761, during the reign of Maria Theresa (1740-1780), queen of Hungary and Bohemia, was an effort made to settle and assimilate Roma. However, that effort died with Maria Theresa in 1780. The nineteenth century ushered in Roma hunts as a popular "sport" in Germany.

The darkest days for the Roma occurred during the twentieth century, when Adolf Hitler ordered the extermination of all Roma falling under Germany's control during World War II. By the war's end, 70 percent to 80 percent of Europe's Roma population had perished. Central Europe's still-surviving Roma population then fell under the control of communist regimes and their assimilationist policies. Those efforts ended with the fall of Communism (1989-1991) and the rapid reassertion of the old patterns of discrimination against the Roma.

—Joseph R. Rudolph, Jr.

FURTHER READING

Appiah, Kwame Anthony, and Henry Louis Gates, Jr., eds. *Identities*. Chicago: University of Chicago Press, 1995. A social and cultural history of the idea of ethnic identity, with a chapter called "The Time of the Gypsies: A 'People Without History' in the Narratives of the West." Bibliography, index.

Chaman Lal. *Gipsies: Forgotten Children of India*. Delhi, India: Ministry of Information and Broadcasting, 1962. An early but highly useful study of the topic from the perspective of the country from which Gypsy migrations began. Illustrations, bibliographical footnotes.

Crowe, David M. *A History of the Gypsies of Eastern Europe and Russia*. New York: St. Martin's Press, 1994. Excellent advanced reading on the Roma in twentieth century Europe and the Soviet Union and Russia. Illustrations, bibliography, index.

Fraser, Angus. *The Gypsies*. 2d ed. Cambridge, Mass.: Blackwell, 1995. An exhaustive collection that discusses early Roma migrations to, from, and within Persia, the Balkans and the Byzantine Empire, and other regions of Europe. Illustrations, maps, bibliography, index.

Hancock, Ian. *Handbook of Vlax Romani*. Columbus, Ohio: Slavica, 1995. Although primarily a book on Romani (Gypsy) languages, this text includes a helpful discussion of Romani migration from India to the regions of Europe. Bibliography, index.

Kenrick, Donald. *Gypsies: From India to the Mediterranean*. Toulouse, France: CRDP, 1993. A short history of the Roma focusing on their migration from India to Persia and life there under Arab rule before moving on to Constantinople. Written by the English language authority.

_______. *Historical Dictionary of the Gypsies (Romanies)*. Lanham, Md.: Scarecrow Press, 1998. A concise collection exploring the history and culture. Intended as a tool for educators, students, and political activists. Includes a collection of biographies, notes on spelling, a glossary of terms, and a list of organizations, museums, and relevant academic and other journals. bibliography.

Lucassen, Leo, Wim Willems, and Annemarie Cottaar. *Gypsies and Other Itinerant Groups: A Socio-Historical Approach*. New York: St. Martin's Press, 1998. Excellent advanced reading, with chapters on the history of the study of Gypsies, the representation of Gypsies in encyclopedias, and their place in the formation of European nations beginning in the fourteenth century. Includes an outstanding bibliographical list for further research.

Rudolph, Joseph R., Jr. "Central Europe: The Romany, a Stateless Minority in a World of States." In *Encyclopedia of Modern Ethnic Conflicts*, edited by Joseph R. Rudolph, Jr. Westport, Conn.: Greenwood Press, 2003. Good introductory reading to the broad topic of the Roma, from their origin to their continuing outsider status in contemporary Europe.

SEE ALSO: c. 960: Jews Settle in Bohemia; 998-1030: Reign of Maḥmūd of Ghazna; 1010: Firdusi Composes the *Shahnamah*; 1290-1306: Jews Are Expelled from England, France, and Southern Italy.

RELATED ARTICLES in *Great Lives from History: The Middle Ages, 477-1453*: Firdusi; Maḥmūd of Ghazna.

838-842
Tibetan Empire Dissolves

A series of regicides plunged the Tibetan Empire into a period of disunity and fragmentation.

Locale: Lhasa, Tibet
Categories: Government and politics; religion; wars, uprisings, and civil unrest

Key Figures

Songtsen Gampo (617-650), first Dharma king of Tibet, r. 627-650
Trisong Detsen (c.742-797), second Dharma king of Tibet, r. 755-797
Ralpachen (806-838), third Dharma king of Tibet, r. c. 815-838
Lang Darma (d. 842), last king of Tibet, r. 838-842

Summary of Event

Although the line of Tibetan kings, or *tsenpos*, begins with the legendary Nyatri in 127 B.C.E., a reliable historical record of the dynasty begins in the seventh century C.E. with the reign of Songtsen Gampo (r. 627-650), who consolidated the petty states of the Tibetan plateau under a single monarchy based in Lhasa. The first of the nation's three Dharma kings (Buddhist warrior-rulers who for three hundred years led Tibet to a material and spiritual golden age), Songtsen extended Tibet's influence across Central Asian and China through military conquest and strategic marriage alliances. He also shifted the focus away from the native shamanistic Bon religion to the Indian based Buddhism. For the new religion, he built the Jokhang and Ramoche Temples (in honor of his Nepalese and Chinese queens, respectively), as well as the Potala Palace. He also authorized the creation of a Tibetan alphabet based on Sanskrit in order to translate key Buddhist texts.

Trisong Detsen (r. 755-797), the second Dharma king, expanded on his predecessor's military and religious accomplishments. He triumphed over Tibet's traditional enemy China, managing to capture the capital Chang'an (modern Xi'an) and briefly installing a puppet emperor in 763. He also institutionalized Buddhism as the state religion and established the Samye, the nation's first monastery. The influx of foreign Buddhist missionaries such as the Indian pandit Padmasambhava proved a mixed blessing for the kingdom. Although they provided practical skills such as the administration and record keeping necessary for an expanding empire, they also incited a backlash among Tibetans devoted to the traditional Bon religion, which Buddhism was rapidly replacing. In particular, aristocratic elements of the traditional Tibetan society saw themselves being displaced in the social organization by a rising Buddhist bureaucracy.

This political-religious conflict came to a head during the reign of the third Dharma king Ralpachen (r. 815-838). His very elevation to kingship, over the claims of his elder brother Lang Darma, is evidence of the power of the ascendant Buddhist priesthood. In their role as government ministers, Buddhist priests were in a position to promote the selection of the pro-Buddhist Ralpachen over that of Lang Darma, a follower of the Bon religion. As his first name suggests, Lang (Tibetan for "bull") was noted for his aggressiveness and, from the Buddhist perspective, irreligiousness.

Once in power, his younger brother Ralpachen was a strong proponent of Buddhism, commissioning the translation of sacred texts from Sanskrit into Tibetan and the codification of these works into a form that remains in use in modern times. His commitment to the faith and his personal subordination to its priesthood is commemorated in his custom of allowing monks to meditate on prayer rugs attached to the long braided locks of his hair.

More controversially, Ralpachen introduced a system of domestic taxation to provide revenues for the expanding priesthood an action that only spurred the growth of an anti-Buddhist faction centered around Lang Darma. In foreign affairs, however, he maintained the strength of Tibet's military and political influence. In 821, he concluded a peace treaty with China that confirmed the nation's borders much in accordance with Tibetan claims. A stone pillar in the Jokhang, still standing, commemorates this achievement.

Court intrigue, spearheaded by Lang Darma, proved to be Ralpachen's undoing. Lang Darma first created a rumor that the king's minister Bande Dangka, a Buddhist monk, was having an affair with the queen. After the suspicious Ralpachen dismissed the minister, Lang Darma had the monk murdered. Meanwhile, the innocent queen was so upset by the accusations that she committed suicide by leaping from the palace walls. In the climate of such instability, Ralpachen himself became the next victim. He was assassinated in 836 by a pair of secretly pro-

Bon ministers, working in league with Lang Darma; they strangled him as he drank beer.

Upon Ralpachen's death, Lang Darma ascended the throne. He initiated a campaign to reinstate Bon as the state religion with himself as a kind of god-king. He also ruthlessly persecuted Buddhism, passing laws that forbid the teaching of the religion, and requiring priests to marry. He closed up the temples and, in an early form of negative advertising, even ordered crude drawings of drunken priests painted on the exteriors.

Buddhism in Tibet was effectively forced underground for the next few years. Monks retreated to mountain caves in the hinterlands. The situation became so dire that a monk named Lhalung Palgye Dorje decided to take action in 842. He blackened a white horse with charcoal and dressed himself in a long flowing black robe with a white interior. He rode to Lhasa and met Lang Darma in front of the Jokhang with a party of ministers. Using a bow and arrow he had concealed up his sleeve, he shot Lang Darma, killing him. In the tumult following, he escaped on his horse, inverting his robe to show white and riding his horse through a river to wash off the charcoal. While the king's ministers sought a man wearing a black robe on a black horse, the white-robed monk on a white horse fled to safety.

Lang Darma left behind two queens. As the younger was already pregnant with an heir, the older suddenly claimed to be pregnant as well. According to tradition, the older queen presented an orphaned infant as her own child. The court ministers were dubious about the child and dubbed him Yumtan (Depending on Mother). The younger queen gave birth to a son, O-sung (Guarded by Light), who was recognized as the legitimate heir. Yumtan, however, failed to accede to the authority of his half-brother and set up a rival monarchy based in the Yarlung Valley. Further fragmentation occurred when O-sung's heirs established rival lineages in the provinces of Tsang and Purang. Without the centralized authority in Lhasa, Tibet's military and political power waned, and its borders fell prey to its powerful neighbors. Without the intellectual and social sophistication provided by Buddhist priesthood, the nation receded culturally into a dark age.

SIGNIFICANCE

The most immediate result of the assassinations of Ralpachen and Lang Darma was the end of a single dynastic line and the fragmentation of a unified Tibet into petty states. These petty states soon fell prey to the depredations of their powerful neighbors, culminating in their conquest by the Chinese Yuan Dynasty (1279-1368) in the thirteenth century. Yuan emperor Kublai Khan reunited the country as a client-state in 1248 and installed the first high lama as priest-king. This historical subordination serves as the primary justification for China's current claim to Tibet, following its invasion and occupation of the country in 1959.

Although official suppression of Buddhism in Tibet continued for almost two hundred years after the assassination of Lang Darma, the faith took on a distinctly Tibetan cast during its years "underground": It synthesized elements of traditional Bon magic with esoteric Indian Tantrism when it reemerged as a public faith in the middle of the eleventh century. Indeed, the political and religious organization of the nation under a high lama in the thirteenth century owed as much to the Bon tradition of the god-king as to Buddhist faith.

—Luke Powers

FURTHER READING

Baumer, Christopher. *Tibet's Ancient Religion: Bon*. Tokyo: John Weatherhill, 2002. A good introductory examination of Tibet's traditional religion and its syncretic relationship with Tibetan Buddhism.

Beckwith, Christopher. *The Tibetan Empire in Central Asia*. Princeton, N.J.: Princeton University Press, 1993. Focuses on the golden age of the Tibetan Empire and its conflicts with the Arabs, Turks, and Chinese for control of the Silk Road.

Bsod-Nams-Rgyal-Mtshan, ed. *The Clear Mirror: A Traditional Account of Tibet's Golden Age*. Ithaca, N.Y.: Snow Lion, 1996. An anthology of traditional documents in English translation from the Tibetan golden age, including a royal history and genealogy.

Feigon, Lee. *Demystifying Tibet: Unlocking the Secrets in the Land of Snows*. Blue Ridge Summit, Pa.: Ivan R. Dees, 1995. This broad cultural history of Tibet explores the nation's cultural roots in its golden age and examines its complex historical relationship with China.

Hambly, Gavin, ed. *Central Asia*. New York: Delacorte Press, 1966. Offers an excellent overview on the foundations of Tibetan society in the context of other Central Asian states.

Ray, Reginald, and Tulku Thondup. *The Secret of the Vajra World: The Tantric Buddhism of Tibet*. New York: Shambhala, 2001. Includes a lengthy history of the evolution of Tibetan Buddhism through periods of suppression.

Shakabpa, Tsepon. *Tibet: A Political History*. New Haven, Conn.: Yale University Press, 1967. Though unaffectedly pro-Buddhist, this work provides a readable and at times novelistic account of the tsenpo line.

SEE ALSO: 618: Founding of the Tang Dynasty; 627-650: Reign of Songtsen Gampo; 763: Tibetans Capture Chang'an; 791: Buddhism Becomes Tibetan State Religion.

840-846
UIGHUR MIGRATIONS

After their defeat by the Khirghiz, the Uighur Turks migrated into eastern Turkistan and western China, established new homelands, and continued their development as a nation.

LOCALE: Turkistan and Western China
CATEGORIES: Cultural and intellectual history; expansion and land acquisition

KEY FIGURE

Ughe Tegin Khan (d. 856), leader of the Uighurs who migrated to Tarim Basin, r. 840-846

SUMMARY OF EVENT

The Uighur Turks, a branch of the Huns, are first mentioned in Chinese documents dating from the third century B.C.E. They shared their early history with other Turkish tribes living in Mongolia and Central Asia until the eighth century, when they built their own state after the collapse of the Göktürk Empire. Under great leaders such as Guli Peiluo (Kutluk Bilgé Kül; r. 744-747), Moyanchuo (Bayan Chor; r. 747-759), Mouyu (Bügü; r. 759-779), and Xie Yujiasi (Kutluk; r. 795-805), they established a state along the Orkhun River that eventually extended from Mongolia to India. In the ninth century, however, this early Uighur empire declined and, in 840, was conquered by the Khirghiz.

Groups of Uighurs then migrated eastward—some to the western banks of the Yellow River in Gansu, others to eastern Turkistan in the Tarim Basin at Tian Shan, and the largest group to the north of Tian Shan, where their descendants live today. The Kunchou Uighurs on the Yellow River never established themselves as a great power, although some of their leaders earned the respect of the Chinese. The Tankuts absorbed the kingdom in 1028. A small group called the Yellow Uighurs, who practice Buddhism, still exist today.

The second group, living in the Tian Shan in eastern Turkistan, formed the Karakhoja Uighur Kingdom near the present-day city of Turfan, where they absorbed the indigenous population in the region. The kingdom began in 846 and was recognized by the Chinese, who sent ambassadors in the tenth century. The first ruler was Ughe Tegin (r. 840-846), followed by Enian Tegin (r. 846-847). Most of the Karakhoja Uighurs practiced Buddhism, converting from Manichaeanism, although some were Nestorian Christians. In this area, the Uighur civilization thrived, creating large, prosperous Buddhist monasteries and towns. The Uighurs were remarkable writers and artists, and their position along the famed Silk Road contributed to their economy. Many of the stronger Turkish states in the region formed marriage alliances with the Uighur rulers.

The third kingdom, the Qarakhanid kingdom, in the southern part of east Turkistan with its capital at Kashgar, began in 840 after the fall of the earlier kingdom. The ruler at that time was Bilge Kur Kadir. This kingdom included other Turkish tribes such as the Karluks, Turgish, and the Basmils. In 999, the Qarakhanid conquered Bukhara from the Sāmānids but were checked from advancing further by the Ghaznavids. In 1040, the Qarakhanids lost control of west Turkistan, where other Turkish tribes established their own states. In 1397, the two east Turkistan kingdoms united and remained independent of the Sāmānid Dynasty of western Turkistan until the Qing Dynasty (Ch'ing, 1644-1911) of China conquered them in 1759.

During their first empire, the Uighurs had developed their own script and literature—initially, translations of Manichaean and Buddhist religious texts. With the coming of Islam, they changed to the Arabic script and made great contributions to Muslim theology and scholarship. Among the most notable is *Kutadgú biliğ* (1070; *Wisdom of Royal Glory*, 1983) by Yūsuf Khāss Hājib, which was written for the education of princes but also describes Uighur society and politics in the writer's era. In the same period, Maḥmūd Kāshgarī wrote his dictionary of Turkic dialects, *Dīwān lughāt al-Turk* (1074; *Compendium of the Turkic Dialects*, 1982-1985), a comprehensive study of the various Turkish dialects and customs as well as the geographical locations in which the dialects were spoken. Kāshgarī's work is based on extensive travels and personal investigations and is a major source for the study of Uighur civilization. Another well-known work is poet Ahmet Yukneki's *Atabetülhakayik.*

The earliest Uighurs were Shamanists, but adopted Buddhism, Brahmanism, and Manichaeanism. In 934, the Uighurs converted to Islam under Satuq Bughra Khān, the first Turkish ruler to adopt the Muslim faith. Over the next few centuries, the khans built hundreds of mosques. More than three hundred were established in Kasgar alone, the most famous being the Azna (twelfth century), the Idgah (fifteenth century), and the Appak Khoja (eighteenth century) mosques. The government also established schools (madrasas), creating eighteen major schools in the capital that taught Muslim theology and also secular subjects such as logic, arithmetic, geometry, ethics, astronomy, medicine, and astronomy. Almost two thousand students attended at any one time. In the fifteenth century, the capital's Mesudi library had a collection of two hundred thousand books.

The Uighurs were farmers, growing wheat, millet, sesame, grapes, melons, sugar beets, cotton, and other produce. They built canals to bring water from distant sources for irrigation. Some of these canals are still used today. Cotton was a source of great commercial wealth as were the carpets woven by the Uighurs. The early Turks wove carpets using knotted fibers. Uighur carpets, which were first made in the third century, were woven from cotton, wool, and silk imported into China and displayed many different colors and patterns. Cities such as Hoten, Kashgar, and Turfan became quite renowned as centers of Turkish carpets. The Uighurs created metal objects of various kinds as well. They also made and played more than sixty different musical instruments.

The oldest Turkish burial grounds are found at Hun Kurgans near the Altai Mountains. These were small mounds over a hidden chamber. During the Göktürk Empire, the graves were simple stones over the graves surrounded by statues (balbal), which stood for the persons killed by the deceased in battle. The Uighurs, however, covered their dead with a dome known as a stupa.

Chinese visitors to Turkistan expressed their admiration of Uighur civilization. For example, ambassador Wang Ye De, addressing the Karakhoja Uighurs in the 980's, wrote "I was impressed with the extensive civilization I have found in the Uygur [sic] Kingdom. The beauty of the temples, monasteries, wall paintings, statues, towers, gardens, housings and the palaces built throughout the kingdom cannot be described. The Uygurs are very skilled in handicrafts made from gold and silver, vases and potteries. Some say that God has infused this talent into these people only."

The Uighurs were well known for their medical knowledge. During the Song Dynasty (Sung; 960-1279), an Uighur physician, Nanto, visited China, bringing with him medicines and knowledge unknown to the Chinese. The Chinese scholar and physician Li Shizen (1518-1593) records in his medical text that Uighurs used more than a hundred different herbs in their medical practice, and Uighur documents reveal descriptions of acupuncture with graphic anatomical examples. Indeed, some scholars have argued that acupuncture was a Turkish invention perfected by the Uighurs, rather than a Chinese creation.

SIGNIFICANCE

The Uighur migration into eastern Turkistan and western China after the fall of their empire led to the survival of their ethnicity and its further cultural development. The Uighurs never again created as great of an empire; however, the literary, scholarly, scientific, and spiritual achievements in this phase of Uighur history contributed greatly to its own society and that of other communities in Central and East Asia. Uighur manuscripts discovered in the caves of Turkistan have revealed the development of Turkish writing and literature. The Uighurs' religious diversity allowed religious dissidents such as the Nestorian Christians to preserve their churches, and the Uighurs' later conversion to Islam helped to spread that faith into the Far East. The Uighurs left their name in the Uighurstan region of China, where a Muslim minority called Uighurs (or Uyghurs) exists until today. However, there is a scholarly debate if these are descendants of the medieval Uighurs or later migrants who adopted the name.

—Frederick B. Chary

FURTHER READING

Beller-Hann, Ildiko. *The Written and Spoken: Literacy and Oral Transmission Among the Uighur.* Berlin. Das Arabische, 2000. A scholarly book describing Uighur literature and folklore.

Rudelson, Justin Jon. *Oasis Identities: Uighur Nationalism Along China's Silk Road.* New York: Columbia

University Press, 1997. Describes Uighur roots in the Tarim Basin.

Sinor Denis, ed. *The Cambridge History of Early Inner Asia.* New York: Cambridge University Press, 1990. Has a chapter on the Uighur Empire and references to their subsequent fate.

Wei, Ts'ui-i. *Uighur Stories from the Silk Road.* Lanham, Md.: University Press of America, 1998. A collection of Uighur folktales.

SEE ALSO: 744-840: Uighur Turks Rule Central Asia; Early 10th century: Qarakhanids Convert to Islam.

843
TREATY OF VERDUN

The Treaty of Verdun provided rough lines of territorial demarcation within Charlemagne's empire and established a temporary measure of stability for nascent France and Germany.

LOCALE: Northern France

CATEGORIES: Diplomacy and international relations; expansion and land acquisition; government and politics; laws, acts, and legal history

KEY FIGURES

Charlemagne (742-814), king of the Franks (r. 768-814), king of the Lombards (r. 774-814), Holy Roman Emperor (r. 800-814)

Louis the Pious (778-840), emperor of the Franks, r. 814-840, and successor of Charlemagne

Lothair I (795-855), son of Louis the Pious and coemperor, r. 817-855

Pépin I (c. 803-838), second son of Louis the Pious and king of Aquitaine, r. 817-838

Louis the German (c. 804-876), youngest son of Louis the Pious and heir to the eastern part of the Frankish empire, r. 843-875

Charles the Bald (823-877), Holy Roman Emperor, r. 875-877, son of Louis the Pious by his second wife, Judith

Gregory IV (d. 844), Roman Catholic pope, 827-844, and supporter of Lothair

SUMMARY OF EVENT

More than almost any event of early European history, the Treaty of Verdun of 843 is intriguing because it not only established the broad boundaries of modern France and Germany but also gave political and legal recognition to an area that became a matter of tension and dispute between the two nations ever after.

The Treaty of Verdun, however, did not provide for the resolution of national rivalries. In 843, neither France nor Germany, as such, existed. What happened at Verdun was, rather, a temporary settlement of a family feud of

The Treaty of Verdun temporarily resolved the dispute among the heirs to the Frankish empire, resulting in three kingdoms: France in the west, Germany in the east, and a corridor between that included northern Italy. (F. R. Niglutsch)

some twenty-six years' standing, in which each of the major parties was supported by a sizable following with vested interests in the land.

Louis the Pious, Charlemagne's sole surviving son, succeeded him as king of the Franks and Italy, and as emperor of the West. Father of three legitimate sons when he took over the throne in 814, Louis made immediate provision for two of them. Although neither of the boys was old enough to rule the territory granted him, Lothair was named king of Bavaria and Pépin was named king of Aquitaine. Louis, the youngest son, known later as Louis the German, was not assigned a portion of the empire at this first division.

Three years later, Louis the Pious modified this arrangement. By the *Division Imperii* of 817, Lothair was made coemperor with his father. Louis the German received Bavaria, which had been Lothair's, and Pépin added Gascony, Toulouse, and some Burgundian counties to Aquitaine, his original holding. On the death of Louis the Pious, the rest of the empire was to go to Lothair. Although each of the sons was sovereign in his own domain and was recipient of its revenues, the emperor's supremacy was ensured by the requirements that they consult him on all occasions of importance, that they obtain his consent before waging war or making treaties, and that they seek his approval for their marriages. A further provision required the brothers to attend the emperor's court every year to confer with him on public affairs. Finally, disputes among the brothers were to be settled by a general assembly of the empire.

The first test of the 817 arrangement came not from one of the sons but from the emperor's nephew Bernard, king of Italy. Seeing his own position threatened, Bernard crossed the Alps and staged an abortive revolt against Louis. After the revolt was crushed, Louis retaliated by having his nephew blinded. Bernard died a few days later. Louis's remorse led him to make a public confession and penance at Attigny in 833. The public humiliation that followed put Louis under the power of the ecclesiastics who supported Bernard and whose loyalties changed with the conflicting ambitions of Louis's sons. Meanwhile, Louis's wife died, and he married Judith, the daughter of a Swabian magnate. In 823, Judith bore Louis a son, Charles the Bald, a key player in the power struggle that was temporarily resolved by the Treaty of Verdun.

In 829, after an assembly at Worms, Louis issued an edict giving Charles a portion of the empire that had belonged to Lothair. Lothair was sent to Italy, and charters ceased referring to him as coemperor. What followed was a struggle between Louis's three sons by his first wife and the party of Judith's son Charles.

In this phase of the struggle, the emperor succeeded in wooing Louis the German and Pépin away from Lothair by promising them additional territories. Soon, however, the emperor had to face Louis and Pépin in separate battles. Aquitaine was wrested from Pépin for Charles, but the Aquitanians refused to accept the new arrangement and drove the emperor's forces out in 833. In his next bid, Lothair found an ally in Pope Gregory IV, who crossed the Alps on Lothair's behalf but returned disillusioned by the opportunism he witnessed on all sides of the struggle. Louis the Pious's fortunes reached a low ebb in 833, when he was again subjected to public penance and for all practical purposes was deposed, only to be restored to power in 835.

THE STRASBOURG OATHS

In 842, Charles and Louis swore fealty to each other in the language familiar to the subjects of their opposite: Louis in lingua romana *(a precursor to French, Italian, and Spanish) and Charles in* lingua teudisca *(an early form of German). Their subjects, in response, swore their oaths in their respective languages. These oaths solidified the brothers' alliance against Lothair, enabling them to overwhelm Lothair's claim to the empire and forcing the provisions of the Verdun treaty, concluded the following year. The divisions set forth in the treaty presaged political borders reflected in modern Europe.*

Louis and Charles swore to each other:

For the love of God, and for the sake as well of our peoples as of ourselves, I promise that from this day forth, as God shall grant me wisdom and strength, I will treat this my brother as one's brother ought to be treated, provided that he shall do the same by me. And with Lothair I will not willingly enter into any dealings which may injure this my brother.

Louis's and Charles's subjects swore:

If Ludwig [Charles] shall observe the oath which he has sworn to his brother Charles [Ludwig], and Charles [Ludwig], our lord, on his side, should be untrue to his oath, and we should be unable to hold him to it, neither we nor any whom we can deter, shall give him any support.

Source: Milton Viorst, *The Great Documents of Western Civilization* (Philadelphia: Chilton Books, 1965), pp. 24-25.

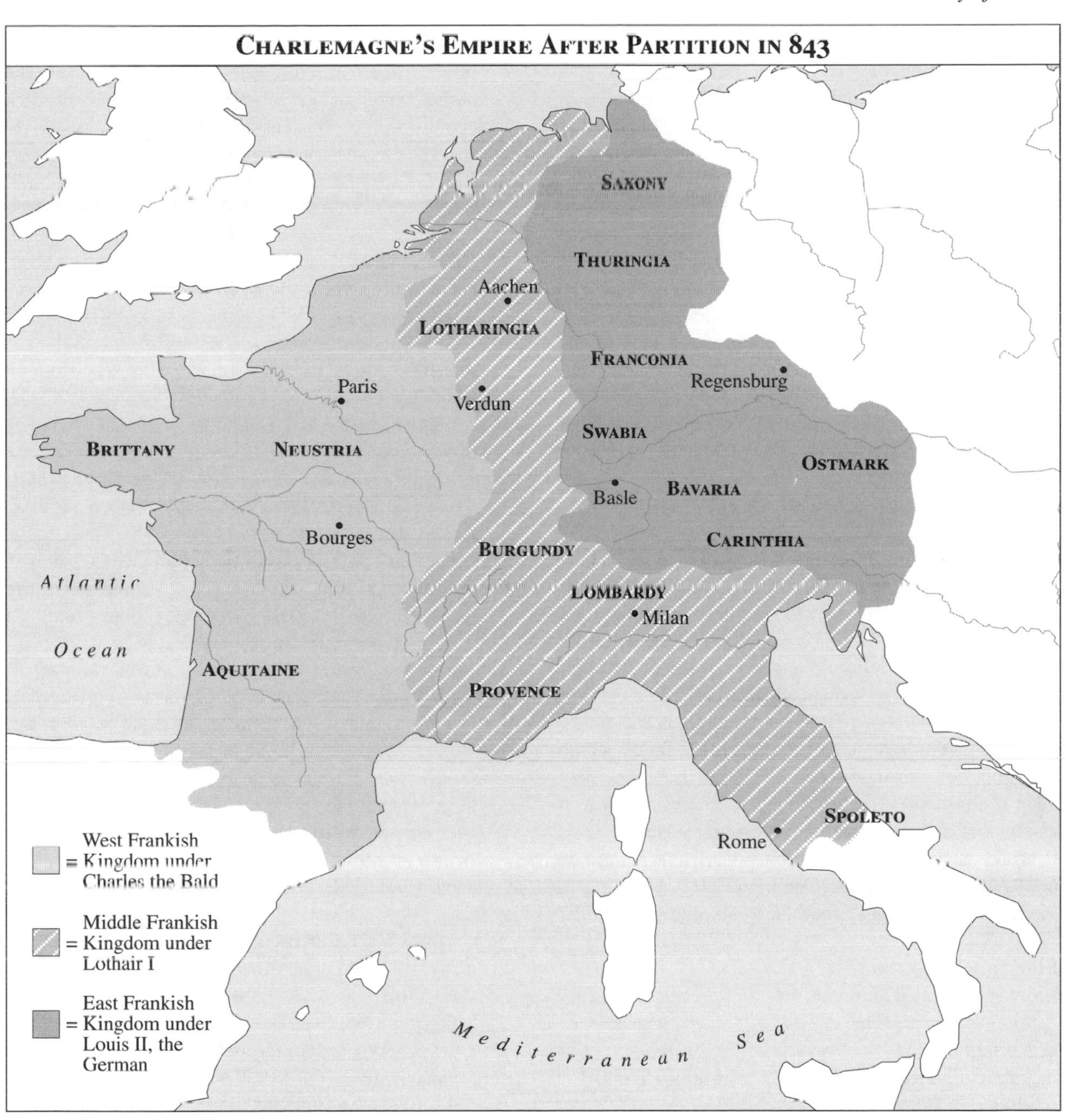

In 838, Pépin died and Aquitaine went to Charles, but again, partisans of Pépin resisted in favor of Pépin's son, Pépin II. When Louis the Pious died in 840, he could have had small consolation in knowing that he had succeeded in having Lothair proclaimed emperor once more.

It was after the death of his father that Lothair attempted to press vigorously the provisions of the *Divisio Imperii* of 817. He was supported by ecclesiastics but not by a large enough number of lay magnates and therefore was doomed to lose. With all these personal feuds, it is impossible to interpret the complicated struggle as a nationalistic one, although Louis the German's followers were predominantly residents of what was to become Germany, and Charles's followers were from what was to become France. Both Louis the German and Charles found themselves opposed to the imperial claims of Lothair.

When Lothair failed to appear at Attigny in 841 for peace negotiations, his cause was for all practical purposes finished. Although there was a major battle at Fontenoy that proved indecisive, it was fatigue rather than military action that brought a willingness to talk peace late in 842. The division was concluded in 843, after consideration by 120 representatives selected to arrange the partition. Lothair was able to hold out for the middle portion of the old empire, a territory including northern Italy and a narrow corridor, about 150 miles (240 kilometers) wide, running to the North Sea. Louis the German received the territories east of the Rhine River and the dioceses of Spires, Worms, and Mainz on the west side. Charles received all else as far as Spain. The brothers swore to secure one another's shares, a promise that was to be honored only when convenient.

SIGNIFICANCE

With the exception of Lothair's "middle kingdom," which was geographically and culturally unnatural, the divisions established at Verdun have essentially lasted throughout the course of European history. It is significant that in the later phase of their struggle and in the presence of their followers, Louis the German and Charles swore oaths in each other's languages. These are the famous Strasbourg Oaths, which provide one of the earliest examples of the emerging German and French languages. In this incident there is a reminder that what can be seen primarily as a war ending in the temporary settlement by Verdun was a struggle colored by cultural differences so deep as to be reflected in diverging languages.

—*Mary Evelyn Jegen, updated by John Quinn Imholte*

FURTHER READING

Brown, Warren. *Unjust Seizure: Conflict, Interest, and Authority in an Early Medieval Society*. Ithaca, N.Y.: Cornell University Press, 2001. Covers religious and political disputes between the Carolingians and the emerging German nation.

Cantor, Norman F. *Medieval History: The Life and Death of a Civilization*. New York: Macmillan, 1963. The author's section on Europe in the eighth and ninth centuries places the Treaty of Verdun in perspective.

Deanesly, Margaret. *A History of Medieval Europe: 476-911*. New York: Barnes and Noble Books, 1962. Argues that only Charlemagne could command a united Frankish effort. Neither Louis the Pious nor Lothair could prevent the internal disintegration of the empire.

Ganshof, F. L. *The Carolingians and the Frankish Monarchy: Studies in Carolingian History*. Ithaca, N.Y.: Cornell University Press, 1971. This scholarly and readable account presents some brief observations on Charlemagne's failure, Louis the Pious's intellectual strengths, and the origin and importance of the Treaty of Verdun.

Innes, Matthew. *State and Society in the Early Middle Ages: The Middle Rhine Valley, 400-1000*. New York: Cambridge University Press, 2000. Discusses social and political conditions of the middle Rhine valley in the time preceding the Treaty of Verdun and up to the year 1000. Includes a chapter on the "zenith of Carolingian politics" in the area.

Previte-Orton, Charles W. *The Shorter Cambridge Medieval History*. Vol. 1, *The Late Roman Empire in the Twelfth Century*. Cambridge, England: Cambridge University Press, 1952. The author argues that the Carolingian Empire weakened because it was too large, its agrarian economy was unable to produce the necessary leadership, and its "Frankish custom" of dividing an estate among all sons amounted to self-destruction.

SEE ALSO: 735: Christianity Is Introduced into Germany; 890's: Magyars Invade Italy, Saxony, and Bavaria; July 15, 1240: Alexander Nevsky Defends Novgorod from Swedish Invaders.

RELATED ARTICLES in *Great Lives from History: The Middle Ages, 477-1453*: Charlemagne; Charles the Bald; Louis the German.

845
SUPPRESSION OF BUDDHISM

Pogroms against Buddhism marked the beginning of its loss of power and position as the dominant religion in China, at which point Daoism re-emerged as the dominant religion, and Chan Buddhism gained ground.

LOCALE: Chang'an (modern Xi'an), Shaanxi Province, China
CATEGORY: Religion

KEY FIGURES

Wuzong (Wu-tsung; 814-846), Tang Dynasty emperor, r. 840-846
Xuanzang (Hsüan-tsang; c. 602-664), Buddhist monk
Taizong (T'ai-tsung; 599-649), Tang Dynasty emperor, r. 627-649

SUMMARY OF EVENT

During the Tang Dynasty (T'ang; 618-907), Buddhism made a triumphant emergence from being a minor, foreign religion to becoming the dominant belief of the Chinese people, including the ruling class. The transition had taken many centuries to complete. Among the attractions of Buddhism was its tenet of offering to all people a form of salvation in the form of nirvana, a state of transcendence in which the individual leaves the world of suffering behind. Previously, an imperial cult of Confucianism and Daoism had held sway over the minds of the Chinese, but Buddhism gradually made inroads, and during the Tang Dynasty, it became the most prevalent religion in the country.

In 845, the Tang emperor Wuzong announced that he was proscribing the practice of the religion. During this time, monasteries were burned to the ground, monks were killed, and statues of the Buddha were melted down. At first glance, this might seem an overreaction of the part of a single ruler, but the imperial house had been struggling with the question of what to do about the religion for more than one hundred years. Although the religion did no harm to its followers, it subverted the power of the emperor and caused numerous economic problems for the empire.

The establisment of the Tang Dynasty, with its orderly road systems, communications, and organization, greatly facilitated the Buddhist religion. In particular, the travels of the monk Xuanzang to India from 629 to 645 and his subsequent patronage by the emperor Taizong brought millions of converts to the religion. Xuanzang's grand trip, which he wrote about in *Datang xiyouji* (629; *Buddhist Records of the Western World*, 1884), captured the hearts and minds of the empire. Xuanzang's role in converting the common people to Buddhism was so important that even today, the story of Xuanzang's journey is retold in East Asia in books, cartoons, stage plays, films, and video games—and forms the basis for an extensive portion of popular culture in China, Hong Kong, Singapore, Korea, Japan, and Taiwan. The conversion of vast numbers of Chinese to Buddhism caused problems for the empire in many areas, including decreases in the amount of tax collected, hoarding that created coin shortages, and an increase in exemptions from work projects.

Perhaps the most serious consequences Buddhism had on the Chinese empire were economic. As Buddhist monasteries were established, they created "inexhaustible treasuries." The purpose of the treasuries was to create a reserve fund that could be used to purchase food for the poor during times of famine or to provide help for adherents to Buddhism in times of distress. The treasuries served as depositories for the donations that were made to the monasteries. Sometimes these donations took the form of a simple string of cash in gratitude for a safe delivery of a child or a recovery from a long illness. Other donations involved large tracts of land, usually granted at the death of the landowner, which the monastery could lease out to small sharecroppers. Because monasteries did not pay taxes to the central government, whatever was raised on monastery land was also untaxed. This allowed the monasteries to raise silk and sell it via the Silk Road at an enormous profit to the monastery, without paying taxes to the central government.

To the central government, even more worrisome than the monasteries' receipt of tax-free income was the fact that most monasteries hoarded coins and silver, which had catastrophic consequences on the fiscal and monetary system. Throughout China's history, the country had been plagued by the problem of not having enough coins to transact business. During the Tang Dynasty, the lack of money had been alleviated somewhat by the introduction of a new, nearly pure copper coin, the *Kaiyuan tongbao*. When monasteries received strings of coins and deposited them into their inexhaustible treasuries, the central government was not informed that these coins were effectively no longer in circulation. In fact, many of the monasteries were saving the coins to melt them down and cast statues of the Buddha. This action removed the coins from circulation and meant that the central government would have to mint more coins to make up for those that had gone into the creation of statues. In effect, this meant that the central government was financing the creation of the statues of the Buddha. Occasionally, even during the reign of emperors who supported Buddhism, the coinage shortage was so severe that statues had to be removed from temples, melted down, and reissued as coinage.

Another economic problem that Buddhism posed to the imperial house involved the laity. Lay members were Buddhists who did not join the order as ordained monks or nuns but devoutly served their local monastery or temple. Although many lay members of the Buddhist religion were simply pious believers, their numbers soon swelled as many people attempted to declare themselves lay members in order to avoid mandatory military service, official conscription on work projects, and heavy tax burdens. The number of dubious converts to the religion was probably small at first but by the late Tang Dynasty had grown to several million. The situation made staffing army positions so difficult that officials on occasion had to enter monasteries and completely empty them of followers, ordering some to enter military service immediately and others simply to revert to taxable status.

The leaders of the monasteries could perhaps have saved themselves from the coming backlash if they had found ways to moderate the monasteries' seemingly insatiable appetite for worldly goods, an ironic state of affairs given Buddhism's precepts against materialism. However, the monasteries did not seem to be aware of the drain that they imposed on the central administration, and at the same time, the religion of the emperors was changing.

The Tang Dynasty had supported both Buddhism and Daoism for reasons of legitimacy. Members of the Tang ruling class had the surname Li, which was the same as that of the legendary founder of Daoism, Laozi (Lao-tzu; 604-sixth century B.C.E.). As a result, Tang emperors frequently experimented with Daoism, which promised (though did not deliver) eternal life to the devout emperor. In fact, many emperors probably killed themselves by drinking elixirs of immortality, which often contained deadly poisons. Among the Daoists was Wuzong. Early in life, he had become a strict Daoist, preferring the traditional Chinese religion to the foreign import of Buddhism. Faced with numerous financial crises that could be conveniently blamed on the Buddhists, Wuzong eagerly and actively pursued policies that led to the destruction of hundreds of monasteries and the returning of millions of Buddhist lay members to civilian life.

SIGNIFICANCE

The sanctions imposed by Wuzong signified the beginning of the end for Buddhism as the dominant religion in China. The collapse of the Tang Dynasty and the resultant disruption of imperial power effectively spelled the end of imperial Buddhism. The pogroms that were imposed on Buddhism in China had two major effects: First, they caused the Buddhist leaders to gradually turn inward; the religion began to focus on internal enlightenment rather than existing in the national conscience. This furthered the development of the Chan (Zen) form of Buddhism. Today Zen Buddhism is the dominant religion of Japan. Second, the Chinese government developed a distrust of organized religion, an attitude that remains a hallmark of the government, which has gradually permitted more religious activity among its population in the twenty-first century but maintains very strict controls over the practice of religion.

—*Jason D. Sanchez*

FURTHER READING

Ch'en, Kenneth. *The Chinese Transformation of Buddhism.* Princeton, N.J.: Princeton University Press, 1973. Examines how the religion changed as it increasingly became Sinicized. Special emphasis on the foundations of Zen.

Gernet, Jacques. *Buddhism in Chinese Society: An Economic History from the Fifth to the Tenth Centuries.* Translated by Franciscus Verellen. New York: Columbia University Press, 1995. Points out the relationship between Buddhism and the economy of China. Contains a bibliography and references many fragments from Dunhuang.

Lopez, Donald, ed. *Buddhism in Practice.* Princeton, N.J.: Princeton University Press, 1995. Devoted purely to the religion of Buddhism, this anthology compares the practice of the religion in China, India, Tibet, and certain regions of Southeast Asia.

_______. *Religions of China in Practice.* Princeton, N.J.: Princeton University Press, 1996. An excellent anthology that examines Confucianism, Daoism, and Buddhism and includes references to anthologies, autobiographies, and other texts not usually available. Compares and contrasts the thoughts and beliefs of the three religions, along those of popular religion.

Zurcher, Eric. *The Buddhist Conquest of China*. 2 vols. Leiden, the Netherlands: E. J. Brill, 1972. The classic study of how Buddhism flexed its muscle in Confucian China.

SEE ALSO: 618: Founding of the Tang Dynasty; 629-645: Pilgrimage of Xuanzang; 12th century: Wang Chongyang Founds Quanzhen Daoism.

RELATED ARTICLES in *Great Lives from History: The Middle Ages, 477-1453*: Taizong; Xuanzang.

Mid-9th century
INVENTION OF GUNPOWDER AND GUNS

Originating in Daoist alchemy, gunpowder's invention and development was one of the greatest achievements of medieval China.

LOCALE: China
CATEGORIES: Science and technology; wars, uprisings, and civil unrest

SUMMARY OF EVENT

Gunpowder, a mixture of potassium nitrate, sulfur, and carbon, was the first chemical explosive discovered, and it was momentously significant in the history of both East and West. Its discovery was serendipitous because the Daoist alchemists, who first blended saltpeter, sulfur, and charcoal, were searching not for explosives but for the elixir of life. Long before these alchemists, ancient Chinese had been adept in creating amalgamations of substances that produced smoke for religious and hygienic purposes. As early as the seventh century B.C.E., the annual purification of homes and public buildings with these fumigants was carried out to rid them of evil spirits and harmful insects. By the seventh century C.E., incendiary mixtures had been concocted that produced a variety of colored effects in public celebrations but because these pyrotechnic displays did not derive from gunpowder, it would be anachronistic to call them fireworks.

Before gunpowder could be made, saltpeter (potassium nitrate) had to be recognized as a specific substance. Buddhist monks of the sixth century noticed a crystalline white material on certain soils, and this saltpeter later became part of the array of substances that Daoist alchemists systematically mixed together in their endeavor to discover a mixture that would confer longevity. In the early ninth century, these alchemists found that a mixture of sulfur, saltpeter, and dried organic matter was extremely flammable, but because it did not actually explode, modern scholars have called these early mixtures proto-gunpowder. Evidence exists that, during the second half of the ninth century, alchemists devised mixtures with genuinely explosive properties because accidental ignition led to injuries and destruction of property. During the tenth century, references to a "fire chemical" (*huo yao*), which scholars later identified as gunpowder, became widespread. A popular misconception is that gunpowder was initially used by the Chinese in fireworks, but the evidence is overwhelming that gunpowder's initial applications were military. For example, in 919, it was used as an igniter for flame-throwers.

During the last years of the Tang Dynasty (T'ang, 618-907), the country was fragmented into several warring states, and in the early decades of the Song Dynasty (Sung; 960-1279), soldiers used gunpowder in such new weapons as bombs and grenades, some of which they threw by hand at the enemy, others of which were catapulted by trebuchets.

The first book containing a formula for gunpowder appeared in 1044. This and later gunpowder formulas resulted in weak explosions, but as the saltpeter proportion was increased in the next two centuries, the explosive power of gunpowder increased as well. In the early eleventh century, gunpowder became an essential component of primitive rockets. A bamboo tube filled with gunpowder was attached to an arrow, and ignition of the gunpowder powered the flaming arrow to its target. In this same period, gunpowder-filled bamboo tubes were attached to lances and used as flame-throwers. Metal scraps or broken porcelain were sometimes mixed with the gunpowder, and these fire-lance projectiles played an important role in the wars between the Song Chinese and the Jin Tatars in the eleventh and twelfth centuries. Some scholars see these bamboo-tube devices as precursors to the gun. They were also related to firecrackers, and references to these characteristically Chinese gadgets multiply during this time.

SIGNIFICANCE

Gunpowder did not appear in the West until the late thirteenth century. Therefore, it is probable that gunpowder was a Chinese invention, and that its first military applications were also made by the Chinese. However, the first use of gunpowder in guns and cannon is controversial. Some scholars, such as Sinologist Joseph Needham, believe that the transition from bamboo tube to metal barrel to gun and cannon occurred in China in the thirteenth century. Others argue that these weapons are European inventions. Still others trace them to Arab inventors. Evidence for a Chinese origin consists of the late appearance of gunpowder in the West and the evolution of the bamboo tube to the metal gun barrel in China. Furthermore, the thirteenth and fourteenth centuries were a time of cross-cultural contacts between China and Europe, and a large number of other Chinese inventions passed from the East to the West, including paper, printing, and the magnetic compass. The devastating impact that gunpowder, the gun, and cannon had on Europe is well known. For centuries, historians have recognized the role that these technologies played in the downfall of European aristocratic military feudalism. Castles fell easily to cannon fire, and mounted knights with lances were no match for guns. What is not so well known is the role that these technologies played in China. For example, they helped preserve the Ming Dynasty (1368-1644) from conquest, and the empire's defenses depended heavily on guns and cannon.

However, these weapons did not homogenize East and West, and significant differences between these cultures led to the rise of the West and the decline of the East in the centuries after the scientific and industrial revolutions in Europe. Because of their advanced scientific knowledge of materials and techniques, Europeans were able to develop weapons that were far superior to those produced in China. Furthermore, technologies associated with gunpowder led to societal revolutions in Europe, whereas in China, they failed to revolutionize the culture. The Chinese bureaucratic system proved able to absorb these new technologies without radical disruptions. Nevertheless, gunpowder, though it had its peaceful uses (in mining and road construction, for example), continued to power projectiles that caused the deaths of millions of soldiers, sailors, and civilians. Thus, an invention that began with the search for a way to extend life had the ironic consequence of becoming the means of prematurely ending millions of lives during the more than a thousand years of its existence.

—*Robert J. Paradowski*

FURTHER READING

Arrault, Alain, and Catherin Jami, eds. *Science and Technology in East Asia: The Legacy of Joseph Needham*. Turnhout, Belgium: Brepoplis, 2001. A collection of papers from the International Congress on the History of the Sciences, held in 1997 and dealing with Needham's work on China.

Dawson, Raymond, ed. *The Legacy of China*. 1964. Reprint. Boston: Cheng and Tsui, 1990. This book is part of a series surveying the impact that various civilizations have had on the world. Chapter 5, "Science and China's Influence on the World," written by Joseph Needham, contains a survey of his research on Chinese science and technology, including the invention of gunpowder.

Needham, Joseph. *Military Technology: The Gunpowder Epic*. Part 7 in *Chemistry and Chemical Technology*, Vol. 5 in *Science and Civilisation in China*. New York: Cambridge University Press, 1986. The fullest treatment of the massive amount of work that Needham and his collaborators have done on proto-gunpowder, gunpowder, and the military uses of gunpowder in China. This volume has an excellent and extensive bibliography.

_______. *Science in Traditional China: A Comparative Perspective*. Cambridge, Mass.: Harvard University Press, 1981. This book's second chapter, "The Epic of Gunpowder and Firearms, Developing from Alchemy," gives the general reader a concise account of the research that the author and his collaborators have done on gunpowder in China.

_______. *Spagyrical Discovery and Invention: Apparatus, Theories and Gifts*. Part 5 in *Chemistry and Chemical Technology*, Vol. 5 in *Science and Civilisation in China*. New York: Cambridge University Press, 1980. This volume contains the author's analysis of the origins of gunpowder in Daoist alchemy. It has an excellent and extensive bibliography.

Temple, Robert K. G. *The Genius of China: Three Thousand Years of Science, Discovery, and Invention*. 1986. Reprint. New York: Prion Books, 1999. This overview of China's early scientific and technological developments includes a discussion of gunpowder.

Wang Ling. "The Invention and Use of Gunpowder and Firearms in China." *Isis* 37 (1947): 160. Though this account is more than fifty years old, it is by a Chinese scholar whose ideas on this subject are still interesting and relevant.

SEE ALSO: 618: Founding of the Tang Dynasty; 907-960: Period of Five Dynasties and Ten Kingdoms; 960: Founding of the Song Dynasty; 960-1279: Scholar-Official Class Flourishes Under Song Dynasty; 1115: Foundation of the Jin Dynasty; 1271-1295: Travels of Marco Polo.

c. 850
DEVELOPMENT OF SLAVIC ALPHABET

The creation and development of the Slavic alphabet played a critical role in spreading Christianity and promoting the cultural identity of the Slavic peoples.

LOCALE: Moravia and southeastern Europe
CATEGORIES: Cultural and intellectual history; literature; religion

KEY FIGURES

Saint Cyril (c. 827-869), possible creator of the Slavic alphabet
Saint Methodius (c. 825-884), brother and associate of Cyril
Rotislav (d. 869), prince of Great Moravia, r. c. 846-869
Vladimir I (c. 956-1015), grand prince of Kiev, r. 980-1015

SUMMARY OF EVENT

One of the most important linguistic developments in medieval Europe was the building of the Slavic alphabet. This alphabet, uniquely adaptable to the richness of the spoken Slavic tongues, has been paramount in promoting the cultural identity of the Bulgarians, Serbs, Ruthenians, Ukrainians, and Russians. It was also forcibly adopted by non-Slavic peoples under Russian and Soviet domination in the nineteenth and twentieth centuries until the breakup of the Soviet Union's republics into separate countries in the late 1980's and early 1990's.

Little is known of the Slavs prior to their adoption of a written language, although they did have a notch-and-stick system of communication. The earliest evidence of their settlements is in and about the region between the Oder and Vistula Rivers. Their expansion in all directions from this area was noted by Greek and Latin writers. Their southern and western movement was eventually restricted in the late eighth century by the nascent Germanic *Drang nach Osten* (push to the east) of Charlemagne and the Magyar incursion in the next century. This resistance to Slavic expansion explains the division of the southern Slavs of the Balkan peninsula and the western Slavs of east central Europe, who managed on their own to expand slowly eastward, a process not completed until the Russian settlement on the Bering Sea in the late nineteenth century.

The development of writing among the Slavs had its origin in their conversion to Christianity beginning in the later ninth century. Traditionally, the brothers Cyril and Methodius, two Greek priests from Salonika in upper Macedonia, have been recognized as the apostles of the Slavs. Both were well prepared for their mission, coming as they did from that part of the Eastern Empire with the greatest exposure to Slavic peoples and culture. Cyril had studied and taught philosophy at Constantinople, and both brothers had served in court in a mission to the Khazars beyond the Black Sea in 860-861.

Soon after their return, they came to Great Moravia at the request of Prince Rotislav. This mission had religious as well as political overtones, because Rotislav wished to curb the influence among his people of Roman-rite German missionaries from Salzburg and Passau led by Bishop Wiching, a symptom of the stress developing between Rome and Constantinople in the battle for souls in Slavic territories. Moreover, because of the long-term economic relationship between the Slavs and Constantinople and the security that Constantinople provided from a Frankish invasion, Rotislav was politically motivated to request missionaries from Constantinople. Cyril and Methodius were to spread the Christian message among the pagan Slavs by preaching in the vernacular, training a native clergy, and providing a written Slavic language for the transmission of the Scriptures and liturgical texts. In the process, their efforts would underscore the need for a Slavic alphabet.

Unfortunately, the immediate success of the Byzantine mission was limited because of the ecclesiastical debate between Rome and Constantinople. Cyril and Methodius's efforts were, however, ultimately recognized by Rome; the former died in 869 while on a mission to Rome and the latter was created archbishop of Sirmium and papal legate. Even so, Methodius's work was thwarted at nearly every turn in Moravia by the efforts of Bishop Wiching and the German party. Following Methodius's death in 884, his disciples were persecuted and driven from Moravia. The brothers' influence proved more effective among the Slavic people of the Balkans, where their orthodox form of Christianity prevailed as well as their Slavic alphabet.

The spread of the Slavic alphabet was limited because of ethnic, regional, and political differences. With the acceptance of Christianity as the state religion by the Kievan prince Vladimir I in 988, however, the use of the Slavic alphabet grew. Although almost exclusively limited to religious sermons, tracts, and church service books, these documents formed the backbone of the Russian literary language until the seventeenth century.

The appearance of two alphabets presents a problem in early Slavic literature: the Cyrillic, with its forty-three letters, and the Glagolitic, with its thirty-eight or forty characters, depending how diphthongs were counted. While differing widely in the form of their letters and their eventual development, both alphabets were admirably suited for representing the many Slavic sounds and subtle nuances of pronunciation. Scholarship is much divided over which was the creation of Cyril, although it seems likely that the more primitive Glagolitic was developed by him, while the Glagolitic alphabet was modified by the followers of Cyril and Methodius, probably in Bulgaria, into the Cyrillic alphabet, named in honor of Saint Cyril. The shapes of the Glagolitic letters are unlike any known variety of Greek, and the general impression of its nonligatured quadrangles, squares, and appended circles is that they have an Ethiopian, Samaritan, Armenian, or even Hebrew base.

This appearance may have been a deliberate attempt on Cyril's part to create a unique and original alphabet to document the Slavic culture, while yet maintaining a similarity to the alphabets of other civilized nations of his time. Nevertheless, the Glagolitic characters had a numerical and phonetic value nearly identical to the Cyrillic letters, and in the early stages of Slavic writing Glagolitic was an important rival of the Cyrillic. This Bulgarian Glagolitsa, as it is called, was used widely in northern and eastern Balkan areas until the thirteenth century, when it was superseded by the Cyrillic alphabet. There did remain, however, some localized use of Glagolitsa in Dalmatia and Montenegro until early modern times.

Saint Cyril helped to Christianize the Slavs, using a new alphabet to translate the Scriptures into their native tongue. The Slavic alphabet, Cyrillic, was named for him. (Library of Congress)

SIGNIFICANCE

The basis for the Cyrillic is clearly the Greek script found in Salonika in the ninth century. Adaptations of this script to correspond to the sounds of the Slavic language of the day were so effective that it has been considered one of the most complete systems of writing in the family of languages. This Cyrillic alphabet became the vehicle for the religious literature, devotional and scriptural, of those Slavic peoples who received their Christianity from Constantinople.

Although the script was modified in the early eighteenth century by Peter the Great, and again by the Bolshevik Revolution of 1917, the Cyrillic alphabet itself remained the basic tool used to express the literary aspirations of the Russians, Ukrainians, Bulgarians, and White Russians, as well as those countries that fell under Soviet domination after the Russian Revolution. The Slavic peoples of central and southeastern Europe who accepted their Christianity from Rome adapted their language to the Roman alphabet. The alphabetic break with their Slavic brethren to the east is not complete, however, for the Glagolitic characteristic of diacritical marks is found in several of the western Slavic languages.

—*Richard J. Wurtz, updated by Elizabeth L. Scully*

FURTHER READING

Christin, Anne-Marie, ed. *A History of Writing: From Hieroglyph to Multimedia*. Paris: Flammarion, 2002. This comprehensive history of ideograms and alphabets includes essays on the Slavic alphabet.

Diringer, David. *The Alphabet: A Key to the History of Mankind*. 2 vols. London: Hutchinson, 1968. This two-volume work provides a brief treatment of the Slavic alphabet.

Duichev, Ivan, ed. *Kiril and Methodius, Founders of Slavonic Writing: A Collection of Sources and Critical Studies*. Translated by Spass Nikolov. New York: Columbia University Press, 1985. Series of monographs covering various aspects of the development of the Slavic alphabet.

Dvornik, Francis. *Byzantine Missions Among the Slavs: Saints Constantine—Cyril and Methodius*. New Brunswick, N.J.: Rutgers University Press, 1970. Considers the development of the Slavic alphabet as an outgrowth of religious missions.

Entwistle, W. J., and W. A. Morrison. *Russian and the Slavonic Languages*. 2d ed. London: Faber and Faber, 1974. First published in 1964, this work provides a detailed examination of the historical and cultural development of all Slavonic languages. The introductory chapters are important for the general reader.

MacKenzie, David, and Michael W. Curran. "Kievan Rus: Economic Life, Society, Culture, and Religion." In *A History of Russia, the Soviet Union, and Beyond*. 4th ed. Belmont, Calif.: Wadsworth, 1993. A brief overview of the bonds between religion, politics, economics, and the development of the Slavic alphabet.

Obolensky, Dimitri. *Byzantium and Slavic Christianity: Influence of Dialogue?* Berkeley, Calif.: Patriarch Athenagoras Orthodox Institute, 1998. This work, published as part of a lecture series, looks at the lives and works of Saints Cyril and Methodius, focusing on how they influenced the Slavs.

Vukcevich, Ivo. *Rex Germanorum, Populos Sclavorum: An Inquiry into the Origin and Early History of the Serbs/Slavs of Sarmatia, Germania, and Illyria*. Santa Barbara, Calif.: University Center Press, 2001. This voluminous history of the Slavic peoples includes discussion of their language and alphabet.

SEE ALSO: 864: Boris Converts to Christianity; 890's: Magyars Invade Italy, Saxony, and Bavaria; 893: Beginning of Bulgaria's Golden Age; 988: Baptism of Vladimir I.

RELATED ARTICLES in *Great Lives from History: The Middle Ages, 477-1453*: Boris I of Bulgaria; Saint Cyril and Saint Methodius; Saint Olga; Vladimir I.

850-950

VIKING ERA

The Vikings were Scandinavian Norsemen who explored, raided, and settled distant lands and whose actions have had a lasting social, political, and cultural impact on areas from the shores of North America to Kiev in modern-day Ukraine.

LOCALE: Northeastern coast of North America, North Atlantic, northern and eastern Europe
CATEGORY: Expansion and land acquisition

KEY FIGURES

King Godfred (d. c. 810), Danish Viking
Guthrum (d. 890), Danish Viking king, r. late ninth century
Rurik (d. 879), Swedish Viking
Erik the Red (c. 950-1001?), Norwegian Viking
Leif Eriksson (c. 970-c. 1035), Norwegian Viking, son of Erik the Red

SUMMARY OF EVENT

The Norsemen were inhabitants of Scandinavia, which consists of Norway, Sweden, and Denmark. They were Germanic in origin and had the same basic lifestyle of other Germanic tribes. Norse social structure, however, was more individualistic, perhaps leading to greater tolerance for a more adventurous, rugged spirit. As pagans, too, they were free from the moral restraints of Christianity.

The word Viking, which probably means "those who go away" (and also, perhaps, "sea king"), applied to the Norsemen who left their homeland beginning in the eighth century and took to the sea. Some became mercenaries and traders. The majority became adventurers, raiders, and invaders.

The infamous Viking method was to sweep in from the sea unexpectedly and attack villages by looting, burning, and raping. They would then retreat before any resistance could be mounted. The first raids to have a permanent, resounding impact were those along the coasts of England. As early as 792, churches in Kent, in southeastern England, were forced to contribute to coastal defenses against "pagan seamen." On June 7, 793, the famous Lindisfarne monastery on a small island off the northeast coast, was sacked by Vikings from Denmark. Some villages tried offering tribute to the Vikings to prevent being looted. In 845, the monastery of Saint-Denis in France offered a sizable tribute. The Vikings accepted the tribute and looted what was left anyway. The monks could only pray, "From the fury of the Norsemen, Good Lord, deliver us!"

Soon there were raids as far west as the island of Iona between Ireland and Scotland. By 870, much of eastern and central England was ruled under Danelaw (Danish law). The climax of the raids was the conflict between Danish king Guthrum and Alfred the Great, king of England. Alfred founded the English navy to stop future invasions, but the invasions were not stopped. Before Guthrum's death in 890, Danelaw had been expanded and officially recognized by Alfred, and Guthrum in return had agreed to become a Christian.

The first Norse king to take an active role in the raids was Danish king Godfred. In 810, a large fleet under Godfred's direction attacked Frisia, now the Netherlands, and forced the people to pay tribute. However, the immediate threat ended when Godfred was assassinated and a struggle for succession ensued between his sons.

Vikings from Norway began raiding along the northern coast of France. In 841, they invaded the Seine Valley north of Paris, and in 845, Paris was ransomed for seven thousand pounds of silver. In 852, the Vikings spent the winter in the Seine Valley. Like the Danes, the Norwegian Vikings soon began establishing permanent settlements. They were concentrated along the coast in the area still called Normandy.

Swedish Vikings expanded to the east. They crossed the Baltic Sea into eastern Europe and were soon making raids into what is now Russia. By about 800, the Vikings, whom the Slavic peoples of the area called Varangians, were being hired as mercenary guards by the Slavs. For about fifty years, the Varangian guards protected the Slavs from other potential invaders. In 856, the Slavs, tired of instability, reportedly issued a call for the Varangians to become their rulers. *Povest vremennykh let* (c. 1113; *The Russian Primary Chronicle*, 1930), com-

Artist's rendition of the funeral of Rurik, who led a force into Russia and set up headquarters in Novgorod near what is now St. Petersburg, becoming its grand prince. (F. R. Niglutsch)

VIKING, MAGYAR, AND MUSLIM INVASIONS, 9TH CENTURY

piled over a period of several centuries, recorded the words, "Our land is great and abundant, but there is no order to it. Come rule and reign over us." *The Russian Primary Chronicle* also calls the Vikings "rus" ("beyond the sea"), most likely the origin of the word Russia. Because the Vikings normally did not wait for an invitation, the call was probably a means of justifying the Viking takeover. Viking chief Rurik answered the call about 859. He led a force into Russia and set up headquarters in Novgorod near what is now St. Petersburg, becoming its grand prince. Rurik and his followers left Russia in 873 and a new band led by Prince Oleg took control. Oleg captured the city of Kiev in 882 and made it the capital. When Oleg died in 912, Igor, the grandson of Rurik, took over. The House of Rurik that began with Igor ruled Russia for several centuries.

From Kiev, the Varangian mercenaries had gone into other areas of service. Their fighting ability soon led them into the service of the Greek emperors in Constantinople. After spending much of the tenth century fighting the emperors' battles in Mesopotamia, Crete, southern Italy, and other areas, the Varangians were organized into the famous Varangian Guard, which became the personal guard unit of the emperors in about the year 1000.

About 860, the Vikings began voyages west into the north Atlantic. Improvements in shipbuilding and seamanship made possible more adventurous journeys. They reached Iceland in 874. Within a short time, they were establishing settlements and claiming the island as their own. The island's nonindigenous inhabitants, most likely exiles from Ireland, could not resist the Viking takeover. The Vikings had heard about the Faroe Islands, between the British Isles and Iceland, from the Irish. Irish monks had settled on the island in about the seventh century. From the Faroes, news about Iceland came quickly.

Iceland served as both a home and a refuge for the Vikings. Pasture and cultivatable lands were satisfactory during the summer months. Lakes and rivers were full of trout and salmon. By about 930, most of the habitable land, primarily near the east coast of Iceland, was occupied.

Erik the Red (Erik Thorvaldson), a Norwegian Viking, was banished from his homeland for manslaughter and left Norway for Iceland in about 982. However, his still-murderous ways led to a three-year banishment from his new home, a time spent exploring farther west into the north Atlantic. About fifty years earlier land had been spotted by a sailor driven west by a storm, and Erik set out to find it. In about 985, Erik discovered a large island full of game animals, but apparently devoid of human occupation. Although applied primarily to the coastal regions, he named the new land Greenland, believing that the name would help attract settlers. With his banishment soon over, he first returned to Iceland and prepared to colonize the new land.

The western limits of Viking exploration were marked about the year 1000. Leif Eriksson led an expedition across Baffin Bay to Baffin Island, then down the North American coast to Labrador. He then established a colony called Vinland, which was probably in what is now Newfoundland. The colony lasted only about twenty years, but the forests of Labrador provided timber for Greenland for many years following.

SIGNIFICANCE

The impact of the Vikings on North America was short lived. Following the collapse of the colony of Vinland about 1020, knowledge of the area was mostly forgotten. Vague accounts written about Vinland in the thirteenth century provided little aid to later European explorers. However, the Viking impact between Greenland on the west and Russia on the east was far greater. In England, Danelaw became a permanent part of English law and custom. Normandy in France retained its Viking character for many centuries. The "axe-bearing barbarians" of the Varangian Guard protected Greek emperors of the Byzantine Empire until the thirteenth century. In Russia, the House of Rurik (Rurik Dynasty) did not end until the death of Fyodor, the son of Ivan the Terrible, in 1598. Viking culture has been preserved through tradition in its Scandinavian homelands, and still, legend surrounding the seafaring and exploring Vikings resonates around the world.

—*Glenn L. Swygart*

FURTHER READING

Barrett, James H., ed. *Contact, Continuity, and Collapse: The Norse Colonization of the North Atlantic*. Turnhout, Belgium: Brepols, 2003. Presents an analysis of the discovery, exploration, and colonization of the North Atlantic by the Vikings. Bibliography and index.

Franklin, Simon, and Jonathan Shepard. *The Emergence of Rus, 750-1200*. New York: Longman, 1996. A comprehensive work that places Rurik and his successors in the general context of the Viking eastward expansion. Maps, extensive bibliography, list of genealogies, and excellent index.

Graham-Campbell, James, ed. *Cultural Atlas of the Viking World*. New York: Facts on File, 1994. This atlas is an overview of the Vikings and their cultural impact on the world. It has an excellent chronological table comparing the events of each area.

_______. *The Viking World*. London: Frances Lincoln, 2001. A succinct account with a brief but helpful bibliography.

Konstam, Angus. *Historical Atlas of the Viking World*. New York: Checkmark Books, 2002. This atlas covers the entire period of Viking history. It traces Viking expansion from Russia to the north Atlantic.

Loyn, H. R. *The Vikings in Britain*. Rev. ed. Cambridge, Mass.: Blackwell, 1995. The author devotes three chapters to the early raids and subsequent large-scale invasions of England by Scandinavians. A highly regarded history of the Viking Age.

Page, R. I. *The Chronicles of the Vikings*. Toronto: University of Toronto Press, 1995. This book about Vikings, by Vikings and as interpreted by modern historical scholarship, covers Viking records, memorials, and myth.

Roesdahl, Else. *The Vikings*. 2d ed. Translated by Susan M. Margeson and Kirsten Williams. New York: Penguin Books, 1998. Provides a solid, meticulous survey. Includes maps, illustrations, an extensive bibliography, a general index, an index of names, and an index of places.

Sawyer, Peter, ed. *The Oxford Illustrated History of the Vikings*. New York: Oxford University Press, 2001. With the aid of numerous color plates, maps, and other figures, this book presents a comprehensive picture of the Vikings and their impact on the world.

SEE ALSO: June 7, 793: Norse Raid Lindisfarne Monastery; 878: Alfred Defeats the Danes; 988: Baptism of Vladimir I; 11th-12th centuries: First European-Native American Contact; April 23, 1014: Battle of Clontarf; 1016: Canute Conquers England; c. 1250: Improvements in Shipbuilding and Navigation; 1405-1433: Zheng He's Naval Expeditions.

RELATED ARTICLES in *Great Lives from History: The Middle Ages, 477-1453*: Æthelflæd; Alcuin; Alfred the Great; Charlemagne; Edward the Elder; Egbert; Leif Eriksson; Ethelred II, the Unready; Harold II; Rurik.

After 850
FOUNDATION OF CHAN CHAN

Chan Chan, the capital of the Chimú Empire, ruled the north coast of Peru for several hundred years and established a political and economic administration later used by the Incas. It was the largest city of northern Peru in pre-Inca times, and it developed a high level of artistic achievement and urban planning.

LOCALE: Moche Valley on the north coast of Peru
CATEGORIES: Architecture; government and politics; science and technology

SUMMARY OF EVENT

The ruins of the Chimú city Chan Chan are located on the desert coastal plain of the Pacific at the mouth of the Moche River, about 330 miles (530 kilometers) northwest of Lima. The first king of the Chimú Empire began to build Chan Chan sometime after the fall of the Moche Empire (c. 850), but the city did not begin to flourish until about 1000.

There were four types of structures that reflected a caste-like social system, a system the Incas used as a model for their own civilization: royal palaces or *ciudadelas*, elite structures for the nobles, small irregularly agglutinated rooms for commoners, and basic living quarters for laborers brought into the city from other areas of the empire.

The ruins of the city cover 14 square miles (36 square kilometers) and are dominated by ten large, citadel-like enclosures called *ciudadelas*. The 30-foot-high (9-meter-high) adobe walls are 6 feet (2 meters) wide at the base. Each is orientated on a north-south axis and arranged in roughly a rectangle around the center of the site. The *ciudadelas* vary in size, but all have a north section, a central section, and a *chanchón* or wing on the south. This wing was the living quarters of the servants and retainers. A narrow passage led from the one door in the north wall to an audience chamber, a series of courtyards, a reservoir, and a large number of storerooms.

There is a complicated pattern of narrow corridors, courtyards, U-shaped rooms called *audiencias* (administrative control points), and storerooms. For security reasons, wells and storerooms were in the most interior part of the structure. The storerooms held large quantities of goods and could be reached only by a series of corridors that passed by the *audiencias*. Open courtyards with benches along one, two, or three sides served as *audienca* chambers.

Each *ciudadela* was a royal residence, an administrative center, and bureaucratic headquarters of the Chimú Empire. All *ciudadelas* contained a royal burial chamber. The Chimú used a system of split-inheritance, which meant the heir to the throne inherited only the position of ruler, not the wealth of the dead king. His wealth was left to other members of the royal family, who lived in the former king's *ciudadela* and preserved it as a shrine. The new king had to acquire his own wealth, usually by conquest, and build a new *ciudadela*.

Another form of structure at Chan Chan is the elite compound. There are thirty-five of them, each enclosed by an adobe wall with only one door leading into a series of narrow corridors. The elite compounds vary in size, number of wells, and internal divisions, or arrangement of rooms. As with *ciudadelas*, elite compounds had open courtyards with benches, *audiencias*, wells, and storerooms. Elite compounds did not contain burial chambers.

The nobles who lived in the elite compounds controlled space and especially water, scarce commodities in an urban area. This control gave them status and power just below the king. They were responsible for the distribution of food and other goods and for supervising the labor, called *mit'a*, required of the commoners, who constructed the structures and irrigation canals of the Chimú Empire.

Adjacent to or near elite compounds were compounds for commoners called small irregularly agglutinated rooms (SIARs). Most of the SIAR compounds were concentrated in the south, west, and northwest sections of the city, but one was in the middle of the city and another along the east side. Both of them were small and isolated without apparent association with other structures and lacking easy access to a well. The centrally located SIAR unit was constructed on an artificial platform. The other SIAR units were associated with elite compounds, wells, or large adobe-walled enclosures thought to be cemeteries. All had easy access to a well. The units seemed to be organized into self-contained wards. Interior walls were less massive than the walls around the compound and showed signs of remodeling, apparently as needs changed.

Rooms within the SIAR included one or more kitchens, work and sleeping rooms, and storage rooms. The storerooms were very small and also held items used in the manufacturing of goods; little food was stored in the SIARs. The inhabitants had to have supplies provided them on a regular basis. Redistribution of goods was a responsibility of the government and was administered by the bureaucracy. All supplies probably came from storerooms in the elite compounds. Refuse was piled in interior rooms or in the alleys between compounds. Over time, as the refuse collected, the ground level in the SIAR rooms and alleys became higher.

SIAR units served as residences for the lower class and were workshops for metalworking, weaving, and woodworking. The quality of the goods, especially gold work, was very high. In some units, llamas and guinea pigs were kept as part of the food supply. The dung was tamped down to form the floor.

Basic housing was provided for a few outsiders, who lived in communal barracks-like buildings constructed by *mit'a* labor. One of these buildings was located in the southeast corner and the other near the center of the city, in what seems to have been an area set aside for trading. The building had direct access to the main route leading into the center of the city. A group of traders lived in the central building. The other outsiders were probably laborers brought in from the countryside to work on construction projects.

Chan Chan was the center of the political and economic system of the Chimú Empire. The king, the chief political and religious leader, was isolated from the masses in his *ciudadela* and appeared in public only on special occasions. The nobles who lived in elite compounds were the bureaucrats who administered the king's business. Control of water, food, space, and conscript labor was the basis of their power.

The Chimú believed in supernatural gods who could become visible to the faithful and be persuaded to help humans who asked for help, but only if the individuals would abstain from salt and pepper and from sexual relations.

Chan Chan controlled three administrative cities located in strategic areas of the empire, which extended at the height of its power from northern Peru to Lima but did not extend into the mountains. The administrative centers directed agricultural production and maintained and constructed new irrigation canals. They stored food until it was moved to Chan Chan.

Trade between the various areas of the empire provided a variety of both raw materials and manufactured products. Trade with areas outside the empire was not an important part of the general economy, but it did provide mostly luxury goods for the royal family and the nobles.

The Chimú successfully resisted conquest by the Incas until 1465, when Chan Chan finally fell. The king of the Chimú was taken to Cuzco and treated with great honor. His son then governed the Chimú territory as a puppet of the Incas. The city was abandoned shortly after its conquest, perhaps as a result of destruction caused by heavy battering rams.

SIGNIFICANCE

Chan Chan was the capital of the largest empire that existed before the Inca. It was the seat of an extensive bureaucracy that efficiently controlled a large population and the economy of all the territory of northern Peru. The Incas later copied the Chimú administration, the conscript labor system, the caste-like social structure, and the incorporation of conquered territories into the empire. The economy, based on agriculture, was made possible by the extensive irrigation canal network. The Incas also copied the excellent metalworking and weaving of the Chimú.

—*Robert D. Talbott*

FURTHER READING

Kosok, Paul. *Life, Land, and Water in Ancient Peru*. New York: Long Island University Press, 1965. Discusses how land and water affected the political and economic development of Chan Chan and the Chimú Empire.

Lumbreras, Luis G. *The Peoples and Cultures of Ancient Peru*. Translated by Betty S. Meggers. Washington, D.C.: Smithsonian Institution Press, 1974. Describes the economic, political, religious, and cultural aspects of the Chimú Empire. Includes several illustrations.

Moseley, Michael E. *The Incas and Their Ancestors: The Archaeology of Peru*. 1992. Rev. ed. New York: Thames and Hudson, 2001. Covers the Moche Valley and the development of the Chimú Empire.

Moseley, Michael E., and Kent C. Day, eds. *Chan Chan: Andean Desert City*. Albuquerque: University of New Mexico Press, 1982. A series of articles about the economic, political, territorial, and architectural growth of the Chimú Empire.

Pillsbury, Joanne, ed. *Moche Art and Archaeology in Ancient Peru*. Washington, D.C.: National Gallery of Art, 2001. Covers the artistic achievements of the Chimú Empire. Includes bibliography and index.

SEE ALSO: c. 1000: Collapse of the Huari and Tiwanaku Civilizations; c. 1200-1230: Manco Capac Founds the Inca State.

858
RISE OF THE FUJIWARA FAMILY

The Fujiwara family rose to power in the Heian period, securing dominion by creating marriage alliances and establishing a hereditary claim to the position of regent.

LOCALE: Central Japan
CATEGORY: Government and politics

KEY FIGURES

Fujiwara Yoshifusa (804-872), founder of the Fujiwara regency
Fujiwara Mototsune (836-891), leader who solidified the power of the Fujiwara regency
Oye Masahira (952-1012), Confucian scholar

SUMMARY OF EVENT

The rise of the Fujiwara clan coincided with the establishment of the Heian period (794-1185). At this time in Japanese history, the Fujiwara family was one of many aristocratic clans vying for power in the newly established capital at Heian-kyō (modern-day Kyoto). Initially, the Fujiwara clan consisted of four main families, and over the next half century, the Hokke branch of the family established itself as the dominant power within the clan.

The family's rise to national power began under the leadership of Fujiwara Yoshifusa, who became great minister of state in 857. He acquired this prestigious position as the result of his marriage to the daughter of the Japanese emperor. Yoshifusa took advantage of this opportunity to establish the Fujiwara family as an up-and-coming power in the Japanese aristocracy. The following year, he had his nine-year-old grandson, Seiwa (r. 858-876), placed on the throne and made himself regent.

Upon Yoshifusa's death, Fujiwara Mototsune assumed his role as head of the Fujiwara and became regent when the child emperor Yōzei ascended the throne. Soon after Mototsune had secured his political power, the Japanese government experienced a grave crisis when it was discovered that the young emperor was mentally ill.

The royal family removed Yōzei from his position of leadership and placed a very old and feeble relative, Kōkō (r. 884-887), on the throne. The new emperor had neither the strength nor the character to become a major force in Japanese politics. Mototsune took advantage of this situation and quickly became the dominant figure at the Japanese court. He instituted the position of *kampaku* (chancellor, or regent to an adult emperor) in 884. Because Mototsune possessed considerable talent, energy, and character, Japan prospered under his rule. When the old, feeble emperor died, he was replaced by a young and vigorous monarch, Uda, who was actually the child of an aristocratic woman from the Fujiwara clan. The new emperor clashed with Mototsune and initiated a number of palace intrigues in an attempt to wrest power away from the Fujiwara family. Mototsune's power and ability were too great; therefore the new emperor had to allow Mototsune to remain in power until his death in 891.

Mototsune's time in power was a major turning point in the history of the Fujiwara family. To maintain his powerful position, Mototsune had to battle the royal family constantly; this helped establish the image of the Fujiwara clan as a powerful political force in the eyes of the Japanese monarchy. It also helped solidify the primacy of the Fujiwara family in the eyes of the other aristocratic clans who had been defeated by Mototsune's great skill in the power struggles at the Japanese court.

The rise of the Fujiwara clan also coincided with the establishment of a new Japanese political philosophy that emphasized high moral character and great dedication to duty. This new political worldview is best represented in the document known as the Kampyō testament. This philosophical thesis reflected the political and cultural dominance of the Chinese Tang Dynasty (T'ang; 618-907) and the Confucian ethic that dominated its government bureaucracy. To protect a bureaucrat from the perils of materialistic excess, the author of the Kampyō testament emphasized a life of following simple tastes and of dedication to duty. Although the Fujiwara clan vastly expanded its family's wealth, the majority of its members who rose to great positions of power made their decisions according to what was in the best interest of the Japanese state. Thus, the Fujiwara ministers were perceived as outstanding examples of Kampyō era (889-897) bureaucrats.

The Fujiwara family also benefited from the fact that Japan was moving into a decentralized feudal period. During the Heian period (794-1185), the royal family was increasingly unable to control events in the nation's countryside. The violent state of affairs in the provinces pushed the peasants into a traditional feudal existence, in which they exchanged taxes and loyalty for the protection of a powerful member of the landed gentry, the most prominent being the Fujiwara family.

The ability of the Fujiwara clan to provide this security was the result of a technological and social revolution that had taken place in the Japanese countryside. Widespread violence forced the rural aristocrats to develop their own military protection. This coincided with the introduction of new military technology from Tang China. Among the most important examples of this new technology were strong and highly accurate weapons that increased the military efficiency of both infantry and cavalry.

Many provincial aristocratic families took advantage of the new weaponry to protect themselves from the chaos of the countryside. Beginning in the ninth century, a new aristocratic military class arose in Japan that would

MAJOR FUJIWARA REGENTS, 866-1184

Reign	*Regent (position)*
866-872	Fujiwara Yoshifusa (sessho)
872-884	Fujiwara Mototsune (sessho)
884-891	Fujiwara Mototsune (kampaku)
930-941	Fujiwara Tadahira (sessho)
941-949	Fujiwara Tadahira (kampaku)
967-969	Fujiwara Saneyori (kampaku)
969-970	Fujiwara Saneyori (sessho)
970-972	Fujiwara Koretada (sessho)
973-977	Fujiwara Kamemichi (kampaku)
977-986	Fujiwara Yoritada (kampaku)
986-990	Fujiwara Kaneie (sessho)
990	Fujiwara Kaneie (kampaku)
990-993	Fujiwara Michitaka (sessho)
993-995	Fujiwara Michitaka (kampaku)
995	Fujiwara Michikane (kampaku)
996-1017	Fujiwara Michinaga (kampaku)
1016-1017	Fujiwara Michinaga (sessho)
1017-1020	Fujiwara Yorimichi (sessho)
1020-1068	Fujiwara Yorimichi (kampaku)
1068-1075	Fujiwara Norimichi (kampaku)
1075-1087	Fujiwara Morozane (kampaku)
1087-1091	Fujiwara Morozane (sessho)
1091-1094	Fujiwara Morozane (kampaku)
1094-1099	Fujiwara Moromichi (kampaku)
1106-1107	Fujiwara Tadazane (kampaku)
1107-1114	Fujiwara Tadazane (sessho)
1114-1121	Fujiwara Tadazane (kampaku)
1121-1123	Fujiwara Tadamichi (kampaku)
1123-1129	Fujiwara Tadamichi (sessho)
1129-1142	Fujiwara Tadamichi (kampaku)
1142-1151	Fujiwara Tadamichi (sessho)
1151-1158	Fujiwara Tadamichi (kampaku)
1158-1165	Fujiwara Motozane (kampaku)
1165-1166	Fujiwara Motozane (sessho)
1166-1173	Fujiwara Motofusa (sessho)
1173-1179	Fujiwara Motofusa (kampaku)
1184	Fujiwara Moroie (sessho)

Note: Some Fujiwara were regents more than once or for more than one emperor. The position of *sessho* indicates regency for an underage emperor, that of *kampaku*, regency for an adult emperor.

eventually play an important role in the nation's history. These new aristocratic warriors took the title of samurai and developed their own ethical code of conduct known as *bushidō*. This new professional warrior class valued above all else loyalty, martial talent, and strict discipline. Failure in any of these areas meant great dishonor that could only be rectified by ritual suicide, or *seppuku*. This unbending code of conduct made the new class of samurai a powerful force and key element to the success of the major aristocratic families. A significant portion of the Fujiwara achievement stemmed from the fact that the vast majority of the families of this new warrior class remained loyal to the Fujiwara clan.

The Fujiwara family used the loyalty and skill of these military families to defeat various warrior tribes that had been ravaging the provinces of northern and western Japan. The inability of the royal family to deal effectively with this problem added to the lack of confidence in the central government. Subsequently, when these rebel armies were defeated by forces loyal to the Fujiwara clan, the family's power and prestige increased dramatically and allowed them once again to challenge the royal family for power.

In spite of the close connection between the military class and the Fujiwara clan, the family leadership always emphasized the importance of family ties as the true basis of its political power. For this reason, the leaders of the clan focused on the importance of developing and maintaining power through the marriage of their daughters to the royal household. Japanese political culture had historically linked family ties to the ability to hold high political office. Those family members who were most closely tied to the royal family were the ones who had the most opportunity to serve. This was especially true when it came to the children of those marriages. A truly successful marriage was one that produced offspring that someday might be elevated to the office of emperor. Healthy children were so important to the success of the Fujiwara clan that on many occasions, the family would bring their expectant daughter back to the family residence in order to provide both the mother and the newborn with the best medical care. One of the great examples of the power of the Fujiwara clan was the fact that it could obtain better medical care for its women than the royal family could. The family also spared no expense in educating its children. One of the most important reasons daughters of the Fujiwara family were so successful in gaining opportunities to marry into the royal family was the fact they were among the most educated women in Japan.

At the height of the Fujiwara regency (which lasted from 886 to 1184), Japan experienced a period of unprecedented prosperity that was a combination of international and domestic factors. Internationally, the success of the Tang Dynasty helped establish a peaceful and prosperous East Asian system whereby trade in material goods and cultural ideas flowed freely. Domestically, the Fujiwara regency established an environment based on good government and economic security.

Over time, Japanese society became overtly materialistic and culturally corrupt. Oye Masahira, a great Japanese Confucian scholar, confronted the nation's aristocracy with the reality of their corruption. He called for the rejection of material excess and the adoption of a Confucian ethic that placed duty and the well-being of the Japanese nation over personal fame and fortune. Japanese leaders, including the Fujiwaras, refused to abide by his directive, and eventually the regency collapsed.

SIGNIFICANCE

The Fujiwara regency created a model of government that brought political stability to the Japanese nation. Generation after generation of talented Fujiwara regents ruled with great skill; therefore, the impact of this famous family was felt in every corner of Japanese society.

The Fujiwara clan's great political leadership created an environment that increased trade and industrial and agricultural productivity. This economic revival was the foundation of what would become a Japanese intellectual renaissance. This great cultural explosion manifested itself in the creation of a literary golden age that is best represented in the two famous works from the Japanese aristocracy, Sei Shōnagon's *Makura no sōshi* (c. 994-c. 1001; *Pillow Book*, 1929; best known as *The Pillow Book of Sei Shōnagon*, 1967, or *The Pillow Book*) and Murasaki Shikibu's *Genji monogatari* (c. 1004; *The Tale of Genji*, 1925-1933).

—*Richard D. Fitzgerald*

FURTHER READING

De Bary, William Theodore, et al., comps. *Sources of Japanese Tradition*. Vol. 1. 2d ed. New York: Columbia University Press, 2001. An excellent source of primary materials dealing with the history of Japan. Index and bibliography.

Holcombe, Charles. *The Genesis of East Asia: 221 B.C.-A.D. 907*. Honolulu: University of Hawaii Press, 2001. An excellent one-volume history of the early development of East Asia. Index and bibliography.

Sansom, George. *A History of Japan to 1334*. Vol. 1. Stanford, Calif.: Stanford University Press, 1958. The best history of Japan during its developmental period. Index and bibliography.

Varley, H. Paul. *Japanese Culture*. 4th ed. Honolulu: University of Hawaii Press, 2000. An excellent overview of Japanese culture. Index and bibliography.

SEE ALSO: 792: Rise of the Samurai; 794-1185: Heian Period; 927: Compilation of the *Engi Shiki*; c. 1001: Sei Shōnagon Completes *The Pillow Book*; c. 1004: Murasaki Shikibu Writes *The Tale of Genji*.

RELATED ARTICLES in *Great Lives from History: The Middle Ages, 477-1453*: Fujiwara Michinaga; Jocho, Murasaki Shikibu; Nijō; Sei Shōnagon.

863
NANZHAO CAPTURES HANOI

Ironically, the temporary capture of Hanoi by the Nanzhao people, who defeated the Chinese occupiers of Vietnam, served to reinforce Vietnamese cultural ties to China, while loosening Chinese power over a soon-to-be independent Vietnam, distinct from the Nanzhao raiders.

LOCALE: Northern Vietnam
CATEGORY: Wars, uprisings, and civil unrest

KEY FIGURES

Do Ton Thanh (d. 854), governor of Ai province, whose death, ordered by the Chinese, started the Nanzhao war

Do Thu Trung (d. 860), son of Do Ton Thanh, whose execution inflamed the Vietnamese

Li Cho (fl. ninth century), Chinese protector general of Vietnam, 854-857, who had Do Ton Thanh killed

Wang Shi (fl. ninth century), Chinese protector general of Vietnam, 858-860, who achieved a partial peace

Li Hu (fl. ninth century), Chinese protector general of Vietnam, 860-861, whose mistakes intensified the war

Cai Xi (Ts'ai Hsi; d. 863), Chinese protector general of Vietnam, 862-863, who drowned after the fall of Hanoi

Gao Pian (Kao P'ien; fl. ninth century), Chinese general who recaptured Hanoi in 866

SUMMARY OF EVENT

By the middle of the ninth century, Chinese rule over the Vietnamese was increasingly challenged. By 679, China's Tang Dynasty (T'ang; 618-907) had reorganized its Vietnamese possessions, conquered in 111 B.C.E., into the Protectorate of Annam. China ruled the area then occupied by the Vietnamese, which corresponds roughly to northern Vietnam.

Around 850, the Vietnamese had become strong enough that Chinese rule was effective only when the Chinese protector general, the highest administrator in the Pacified South, as China called Vietnam, collaborated with his Vietnamese subjects. The Vietnamese themselves felt divided by the situation. There were those who lived in the agriculturally rich heartland along the Red (Hong) River draining into the Gulf of Tonkin. Their old capital, then called La Thanh and much later rebuilt as Hanoi, had become a center of administration, learning, and cultivated urban living. The Vietnamese of the city and the region were those most deeply touched by Chinese civilization and did not oppose Chinese rule when it was not hostile. However, in the mountains to the north and west, the rough life far from the capital led to greater political and spiritual independence. The same was true for the southern frontier, where the Vietnamese traded with Champa and the Khmer.

In the eighth century, the kingdom of Nanzhao (Nanchao, Nam Chieu in Vietnamese) had arisen to the northwest of Vietnam, in the present-day Chinese province of Yunnan. Called "yellow grotto barbarians" by the Chinese, the Nanzhao were a fierce, independent mountain people. As dissatisfaction with the Chinese grew, some Vietnamese started to look toward Nanzhao as a potential ally.

In 854, Li Cho was appointed protector general of Annam. Greedy and cruel, with a violent temper, Li quickly became unpopular. To enrich himself, he changed the terms of trade between the Vietnamese and the Lao mountain chiefs. The Lao resisted this change, and Li attacked them, suffering substantial losses. The mountain chiefs then allied themselves with the king of Nanzhao and the anti-Chinese Vietnamese.

Do Ton Thanh was one of the Vietnamese opposed to the Chinese. Do was the military governor of Ai Province, which had a reputation for being most resistant to Chinese rule and influence and would become a center of

Vietnamese nationalism in the next century. The degree of Do's anti-Chinese sentiments is not known, but Li became enraged. In 854, he had Do killed, an act that inspired fierce opposition to his rule. The Nanzhao, who had become firmly allied with the local mountain chiefs, raided Vietnam, and the Nanzhao war began.

From 858 to 860, Wang Shi, the new protector general, succeeded in firming up China's position. He completed the fortification of La Thanh, persuaded Nanzhao raiders to return to their homes with an apology, and defeated an invasion by the mountain chiefs. He tried to alienate his followers from Do Thu Trung, son of the executed governor of Ai, who became a leader of the Vietnamese resistance. In 860, the able Wang was recalled to fight rebels in another part of China.

His successor, Li Hu, quickly reversed Wang's accomplishments. He executed Do Thu Trung, enraging the Vietnamese. Next, Li left to fight the Nanzhao in China, which they had invaded from Yunnan. In his absence, the Do family recruited thirty thousand soldiers, including allies from Nanzhao. They met the returning Li with this force. In December, 860, the Do army captured La Thanh. Li fled to China, gathering a new army. By mid-861, Li had recaptured La Thanh but failed to destroy the enemy, who moved into China. For his failures, Li was exiled to Hainan Island and replaced with Wang Guan by the end of the year.

Wang Guan attempted reconciliation. The Chinese court sent a letter of apology for the execution of both Do Ton Thanh and his son Do Thu Trung, honoring the father with a posthumous title and officially acknowledging that Li Hu had acted wrongly.

In early 862, Nanzhao launched a full-scale invasion of Vietnam. Wang Guan asked for reinforcements but was replaced as protector general by Cai Xi, who managed to stop the Nanzhao with thirty thousand fresh troops in the summer. Then, Cai Xi fell victim to a personal intrigue. A rival recommended to the emperor that his army be dissolved as the threat from Nanzhao had vanished. Cai Xi's true assertions to the contrary were not believed, and his army was withdrawn. Encouraged, Nanzhao decided to attack La Thanh, trapping Cai Xi there with a small force.

In January, 863, after a siege of twenty-four days, La Thanh fell to the Nanzhao. Cai Xi fought to the end. Wounded, he drowned in the Red River, and his men were encircled and killed. Contemporary Chinese sources estimate that the Nanzhao killed and captured 150,000 Chinese soldiers in 862 and 863, with many of these troops being Vietnamese recruits.

After their victory, Nanzhao soldiers poured into Vietnam to pillage and plunder. Terrified Vietnamese and Chinese refugees fled into the caves and ravines of the inhospitable mountain regions and crossed the border into China. In fortified towns, Vietnamese commanders fought against the Nanzhao and successfully defended their people. It became clear to the Vietnamese that the Nanzhao had come not as liberators but as raiders and invaders.

With the Nanzhao occupying La Thanh and Vietnam with twenty thousand troops and fighting the Chinese to the north, those Vietnamese who had allied with them felt betrayed by the plundering, and the pro-Chinese faction felt abandoned by their protectors. China slowly reorganized its southern army. In the summer of 865, General Gao Pian attacked fifty thousand Nanzhao soldiers foraging in Vietnam and defeated them with only five thousand soldiers. Yet Gao Pian, too, nearly fell victim to a court intrigue, as news of his victory was not forwarded to the emperor.

Reinforced by seven thousand soldiers, Gao Pian defeated a new Nanzhao army in the spring of 866. Just as he had laid a siege to recapture La Thanh, he heard that he had been replaced. While Gao sent an aide to the court to clear up the situation, his officers refused to obey his successor. They lifted the siege of La Thanh, letting half of the Nanzhao escape.

Officially reinstated, Gao Pian returned to capture La Thanh later in 866, and he beheaded the thirty thousand Nanzhao who had not yet escaped. The Tang Dynasty reorganized its rule in Vietnam. China abolished the Protectorate of Annam, calling the land the Peaceful Sea Army and assigning its rule to a military governor, Gao Pian being the first. After his victory, Gao Pian rebuilt the city of La Thanh, calling it Dai-la. His rule became very supportive of local Vietnamese customs, traditions, and beliefs. He was well liked when he left for another position in 868.

Significance

The capture of the Vietnamese capital by the "yellow grotto barbarians" of Nanzhao served as a significant turning point. As Chinese power weakened, there rose strong Vietnamese opposition to Chinese rule, particularly at the frontier. The Do family of Ai represents those elements who were ready to shake off Chinese domination.

Yet the Nanzhao war also showed the Vietnamese the dangers of allying themselves with foreign people. The brief Nanzhao conquest even led to rumors that the

Chams also were rampaging through Vietnam in the wake of the fleeing Chinese. The pro-Nanzhao elements in Vietnam, such as the Muong-Viet of the frontier, decided to leave the country with the Nanzhao.

Ironically, the Vietnamese adopted more of the culture and civilization of the Chinese after the Nanzhao war. As China grew weaker, the Vietnamese distinguished themselves from the surrounding mountain people and looked to Chinese culture to enrich their own cultural identity. Chinese rule began to slowly dissolve, giving some real power to Vietnamese leaders while maintaining official rule. The next century would see full Vietnamese independence.

—R. C. Lutz

FURTHER READING

Huard, Pierre, and Maurice Durand. *Viet-Nam, Civilization and Culture*. 2d ed. Hanoi: École Française d' Extrême Orient, 1994. Useful general history of Vietnam, its people, culture, and customs. Richly illustrated, maps, bibliography, and index.

Lockard, Craig A. "The Unexplained Miracle: Reflections on Vietnamese National Identity and Survival." *Journal of Asian and African Studies* 29 (January-April, 1994): 10-35. Framework for the Vietnamese attitude toward the Chinese and Nanzhao as they struggled for their independence.

Taylor, Keith Weller. *The Birth of Vietnam*. Berkeley: University of California Press, 1983. The standard historical work of the era in English. Detailed and readable, based on the author's knowledge of primary historical sources in Vietnamese and Chinese. Maps, glossary, bibliography, and index.

_______. "An Evaluation of the Chinese Period in Vietnamese History." *The Journal of Asiatic Studies* (Korea University) 23 (January, 1980): 139-164. Concise article analyzing the rise and fall of China's one-thousand-year rule over Vietnam. Notes.

Wiens, Harold. *Han Chinese Expansion in South China*. Hamden, Conn.: Archon Books, 1967. Useful background information on China's earlier conflict with the Nanzhao people.

SEE ALSO: 729: Founding of Nanzhao; 802: Founding of the Khmer Empire; 832: Nanzhao Subjugates Pyu; 939-944: Reign of Ngo Quyen; 1225: Tran Thai Tong Establishes Tran Dynasty; 1428: Le Loi Establishes Later Le Dynasty.

RELATED ARTICLE in *Great Lives from History: The Middle Ages, 477-1453*: Ngo Quyen.

864
BORIS CONVERTS TO CHRISTIANITY

The conversion to Christianity of the Bulgarian khan Boris I anchored Bulgaria to a civilized, Christian Europe in a way that determined its national destiny.

LOCALE: Bulgaria
CATEGORIES: Government and politics; religion

KEY FIGURES

Boris I of Bulgaria (830-907), khan of the Bulgarians, r. 852-889
Michael III (838-867), Byzantine emperor, r. 842-867
Saint Cyril (c. 827-869), Byzantine missionary to the Slavs and Bulgars
Saint Methodius (c. 825-884), Byzantine missionary to the Slavs and Bulgars
Nicholas the Great (c. 819/822-867), Roman Catholic pope, 858-867, sought to convert Bulgarians
Photios (820-893), patriarch of Constantinople, intellectual architect of Bulgarian conversion

SUMMARY OF EVENT

The Bulgarians were originally a Turkic people residing to the northeast of the Sea of Azov and ruled, according to legend, by the house of Dulo. Under a semilegendary figure, Kubrat, they entered history in the seventh century as a powerful tribal confederation. Kubrat's grandson, Asperukh, led a portion of the people south across the Danube River in 681, deemed the founding date of Bulgarian nationhood.

Asperukh and his heirs soon found themselves in conflict with the mighty Byzantine Empire, which yearned to reoccupy its former possessions in the Thracian territories the Bulgarians now held. The ferocious Bulgarian leader, or khan, Krum so annihilated a Byzantine army in 811 that Byzantium became convinced it did not have the strength to conquer Bulgaria. Krum's son and successor, Omortag, was more conciliatory to the Byzantines. By 852, with the accession of Khan Boris I, Byzantine-Bulgar relations were more amicable. In particular, whereas the ferocious Krum had been an unrelenting pagan, rejoicing in drinking blood out of the skulls of his enemies, Boris began to understand the air of sanctity and authority that Christianity provided to the Byzantine ruler.

Christianity also appealed to Boris for more local political reasons. The Turkic-descended Bulgars ruled over a majority of Slavs who were beginning to acquire increasing political power in the kingdom. Boris was interested in appealing to these Slavs as he wished to weaken the power of the Bulgar nobles or "boyars." The Slavs and Bulgars were beginning to become one people. Yet the Slavs would never subscribe to the traditional Bulgar religion, and therefore the supraethnic nature of Christianity became a decided boon in Boris's eyes.

Though desirous of converting to Christianity, Boris was also conscious that he had more than one version of Christianity from which to choose. Although Bulgaria was geographically closer to the Eastern church at Constantinople, that very proximity made the Western church centered at Rome a potentially less controlling alternative. Yet it was the Eastern church that had begun to realize the importance of missionary activity among the Slavic peoples. In the late 850's, the Byzantine emperor, Michael III, had approved the sending of the missionaries Cyril and Methodius to preach Christianity in the kingdom of Great Moravia, a kingdom to the northwest of Bulgaria whose exact location is disputed by historians. Seeing Moravian power as a threat, especially if exercised in concert with the Byzantine Empire, Boris sought an alliance with the German emperor as a counterweight, a potential alliance that entailed, as well, acceptance of the Western form of Christianity. This frightened the Byzantines into action, and a frantic rivalry began between East and West as to which would be the one to convert the Bulgars.

Both the Eastern and Western churches were blessed with excellent leadership in this period. The Eastern patriarch at this time was Photios, one of the greatest intellects of Byzantine history and possibly the most gifted individual ever to occupy his position. The Roman Catholic pope was the capable and energetic Nicholas the Great, who was the most assertive pope the West was to have in the ninth and tenth centuries. Both Photios and Nicholas fully realized the importance of Bulgaria to the power of their churches. Photios, though, had the immediate advantage of the Byzantine army being ready to assist his cause. Michael sent his troops into Bulgaria and welcomed Boris's rapid surrender in order to impose terms consisting of Boris's adoption of Eastern Christianity for his nation. In a diplomatic turnabout, Boris was not only baptized but also accepted the sponsorship of the emperor and thereby received the symbolic name Michael.

Yet all was not harmonious in the newly Christian Bulgaria. The boyars sensed that Boris's enthusiasm for Christianity stemmed partially from his eagerness to centralize power in the monarchy and thus revolted bloodily, a revolt Boris quelled only with much effort. Boris also was vexed by the rigor of the Eastern rite, with its seemingly minute and arcane modes of observation. Especially, he was annoyed by the sudden irruption of Greek-speaking clergy into his kingdom, since he realized that the priests would have no loyalty to him but only to the emperor and would limit the effectiveness of the Bulgarian church as a national organ. Thus the continuing entreaties of Pope Nicholas took on a renewed appeal to Boris.

In a letter to the pope, Boris inquired as to the necessity of the various practices of Eastern Christianity, as well as the extent to which he had to reform pagan practices, such as polygamy, that still flourished among his people. Nicholas's response was firm in its insistence on the basic truths of Christianity but pleasingly flexible on certain details.

Because Nicholas and Photios were simultaneously quarreling on a massive scale over the theological issue of whether the Holy Spirit proceeded from both the Father and the Son, an issue that would lead to schism between the Eastern and Western churches centuries later, their duel over Bulgaria took on an added urgency. Nicholas sent in a detachment of bishops and priests, and the Greek supremacy in the Bulgarian church was overturned. Although Boris was pleased by the fact that the new clergy owed allegiance only to the pope and therefore were unlikely to provide support for a rival sovereign, he still was uneasy about the amount of local control Rome would permit. Nicholas made some vague promises of a future autonomous Bulgarian church, but, on further pressure from Boris, retrenched and made it clear that the only permissible model for the Papacy was a centralized church hierarchy completely controlled by Rome. Boris decided that he preferred Eastern Christianity because of its tendency to leave political matters to the monarch and concentrate on spiritual questions alone.

The Byzantines, meanwhile, had decided to change their tactics. A new and more energetic emperor, Basil the Macedonian, succeeded Michael and decided to fire Photios as patriarch in order to repair relations with the Western church. The new patriarch smoothed over matters with Rome sufficiently to obtain grudging consent to Bulgaria being within the Eastern sphere. The Byzantines had made a huge concession: They sanctioned the liturgy being preached not in Greek but in Bulgarian, a language that by that time had a heavy admixture of Slavic syntax and structure. This would ensure that the priests would themselves be Bulgarian and thus owe allegiance to the Bulgarian king. After 870, Boris enthusiastically promulgated the new order and, as a symbol for the evolution of his people, prepared to move the seat of government from the old capital, Pliska, with its pagan associations, to the new city of Preslav. Although his conversion was motivated by political expediency, Boris became personally pious and ended his days as a monk.

SIGNIFICANCE

The new Bulgarian liturgy flourished, as did the Cyrillic alphabet especially developed for the Slavic languages by the missionaries Cyril and Methodius and propagated by their disciples, such as Saint Clement of Ohrid. This liturgical language eventually came to be called Old Church Slavonic and was the basis for the church language used in Slavic countries, such as Russia, which followed Bulgaria in converting to Eastern Christianity. Perhaps the most far-reaching effect of Boris's conversion was to sanction the use of vernacular languages in Orthodox Christianity, which had previously permitted worship in only the three "sacred" languages of Hebrew, Greek, and Latin.

The Bulgarians, like their contemporaries the Anglo-Saxons in England, had managed to keep their own language and culture while fully participating in the classical and Christian heritage. It is for this that Bulgarians are often termed the Englishmen of the Balkans. After Boris's conversion, Bulgaria was to hold a permanent place in the framework of European civilization.

—*Nicholas Birns*

FURTHER READING

Bowlus, Charles R. *Franks, Moravians, and Magyars: The Struggle for the Middle Danube, 788-907*. Philadelphia: University of Pennsylvania Press, 1995. Radical revision of early Central European history that highlights relations between Bulgaria and the West.

Browning, Robert. *Byzantium and Bulgaria*. Berkeley: University of California Press, 1975. Accessible account of Bulgarian-Byzantine relations.

Crampton, R. J. *A Concise History of Bulgaria*. New York: Cambridge University Press, 1997. Contains a brief but useful treatment of Boris in the chapter on medieval Bulgaria, as well as an extensive bibliography.

Fine, John. *The Early Medieval Balkans*. Ann Arbor: University of Michigan Press, 1983. Learned and comprehensive work aimed at the advanced student.

Lang, David Marshall. *The Bulgarians*. Boulder, Colo.: Westview Press, 1976. A convenient overview of early Bulgarian history.

Norris, Frederick W. *Christianity: A Short Global History*. Oxford, England: Oneworld, 2002. Places Boris in the context of the medieval spread of Christianity.

Obolensky, Dimitri. *The Byzantine Commonwealth*. Crestwood, Ill.: Saint Vladimir's Seminary Press, 1971. This epochal book describes how Byzantine Christianity was spread to the emerging nations of Eastern Europe.

Runciman, Steven. *The First Bulgarian Empire*. London: Bell, 1930. Although dated, this work is still the best narrative account of the period in English.

Tsvetkov, Plamen. *A History of the Balkans*. San Francisco: Mellen Press, 1993. A densely written account that situates Bulgarian history in a regional context.

SEE ALSO: c. 850: Development of the Slavic Alphabet; 893: Beginning of Bulgaria's Golden Age; 1054: Beginning of the Rome-Constantinople Schism.

RELATED ARTICLES in *Great Lives from History: The Middle Ages, 477-1453*: Árpád; Basil the Macedonian; Boris I of Bulgaria; Saint Cyril and Saint Methodius; Nicholas the Great; Saint Olga.

868
FIRST BOOK PRINTED

Although other books had been printed in previous centuries, the Chinese Diamond Sutra *of 868 is the earliest extant and complete printed book.*

LOCALE: Dunhuang, Gansu Province, China
CATEGORIES: Communications; literature

KEY FIGURES

Wang Jie (Wang Chieh; fl. ninth century), printer of the *Diamond Sutra*

Feng Dao (Feng Tao; 881-954), prime minister once revered as the inventor of printing

SUMMARY OF EVENT

Like papermaking, the technique of woodblock printing (xylography) was first discovered in China. Though scholarly consensus exists on the Chinese provenance of the printed book, less agreement exists on what constitutes a book. The word "book" has come to have many meanings, including a rolled scroll or a set of paper sheets bound together. Some of today's publishers distinguish a book from a pamphlet by limiting the term "book" to works of more than sixty-four pages, but this would eliminate the *Jin gang jing* (868; *Diamond Sutra*, 1912) as the first printed book as it was only seven pages long. The sutra was translated into Chinese from the Sanskrit version, the *Vajracchedikā-prajñāpāramitā Sūtra*.

As in ancient Mesopotamia and Egypt, books proliferated in China because they fulfilled a need to transmit to others what people had thought and felt about a variety of subjects. The book became a repository of human knowledge, an important means of communication, and an instrument of socialization. Because the development of block printing in China was gradual, pinpointing its exact date is problematic. From the sixth century, the Chinese were printing pictures, such as portraits of the Buddha, from wooden blocks, and during the Tang Dynasty (T'ang; 618-907), several methods were invented in Buddhist monasteries for the reproduction of sacred texts. The Sinologist Joseph Needham emphasized the Buddhist desire for multiple copies of devotional works as being responsible for early printed books. Although many early books were related to the three traditional religions of China—Confucianism, Daoism, and Buddhism—secular books were also printed.

The story of the earliest extant printed book is fascinating. Nine miles (fifteen kilometers) south of Dunhuang, a Chinese town near Turkistan, is a great cliff containing numerous caves. Beginning in the fifth century, holy men lived in and pilgrims visited these caves, known as the Caves of a Thousand Buddhas. During a turbulent period in the eleventh century, some monks collected many sacred texts and concealed them in a walled-up chamber to prevent their destruction. These treasures remained undisturbed for nine hundred years, until 1900, when a Daoist priest restoring one of the caves discovered the plaster of a fresco had eroded to reveal not the expected stone wall but layers of brick. After removing the bricks, he found a secret room piled high with thousands of wrapped scrolls.

Information of this important find gradually diffused to Europe, stimulating the British archaeologist Aurel Stein to travel to Dunhuang in 1907. He examined many of the 13,500 scrolls (along with numerous fragments), and he purchased about three thousand rolls as well as more than five thousand fragments from the Daoist priest. Stein brought these scrolls and fragments back to England, where they eventually became part of the British Museum's collection. Most of the documents were written in Chinese, though some rolls were in Tibetan, Sanskrit, and other languages. The scrolls averaged around 16 feet (5 meters) in length, though some were more than 90 feet (27 meters). The scrolls had been written over a period of six centuries, and the most important one had a Chinese date that was equivalent to November 5, 868. This scroll was a Chinese version of the Buddhist *Diamond Sutra*, whose subject was a series of discourses by Buddha to a disciple on the ephemeral nature of material reality.

Because of the dry climate and isolation from the elements, the *Diamond Sutra* was well preserved. The scroll is 17.5 feet (5.3 meters) long and about 1 foot (30 centimeters) wide. It consists of seven sheets of paper pasted end to end, six of them containing the text and a short seventh sheet containing a woodcut of Buddha as a teacher. Each 2.5-foot (77-centimeter) sheet of the scroll was printed using a large block on which the Chinese ideograms were carved. An inscription on one of the sheets reads that Wang Jie printed this book for the enlightenment of ordinary people.

Though the *Diamond Sutra* is the most famous of the cave scrolls, the others also proved interesting to scholars. About eight thousand of the scrolls ended up at the National Library in Beijing, and the remaining scrolls went to the Bibliothèque Nationale in Paris and other ar-

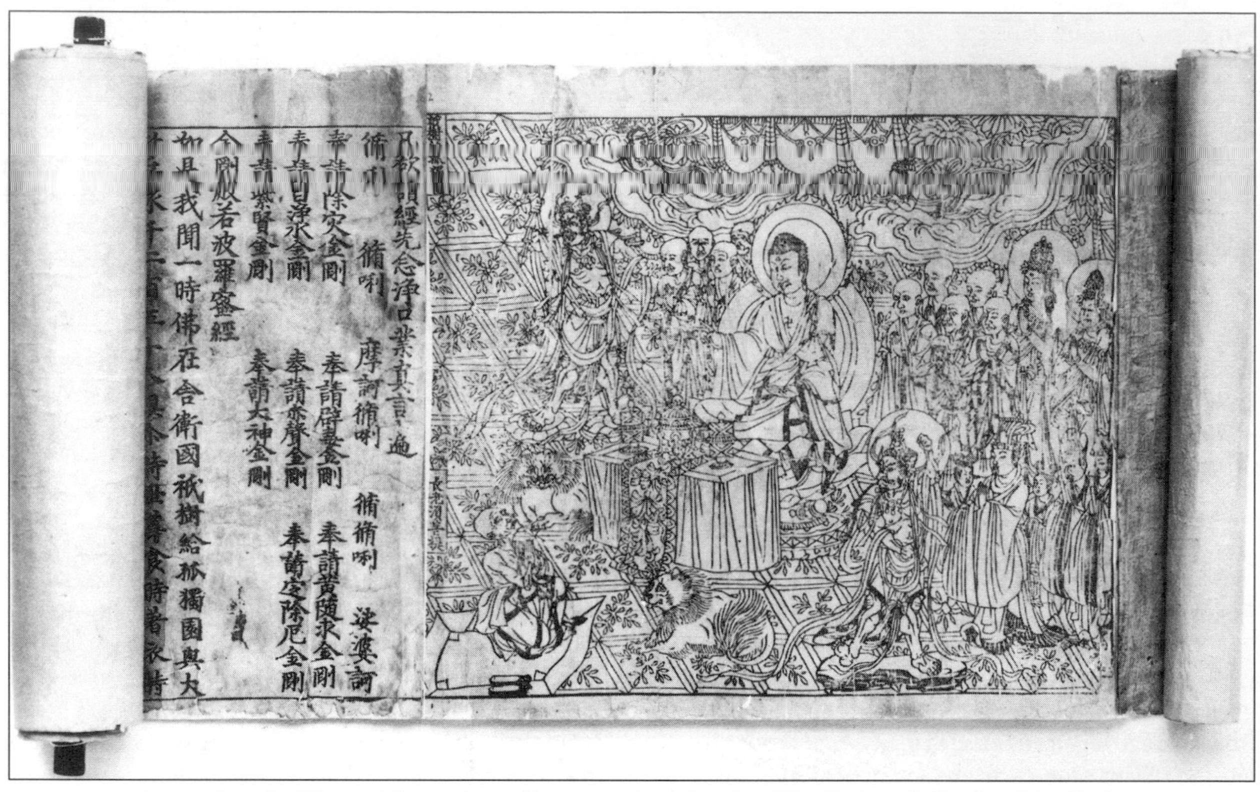

A page from the Diamond Sutra, *the earliest extant book in print.* (The Granger Collection, New York)

chives. Because of the sophisticated printing techniques exhibited in many of these scrolls, which date from the ninth and tenth centuries, scholars realized that less sophisticated books must have existed before them. Some evidence of such books has surfaced, for example, fragments of books printed in Sichuan. Furthermore, the scroll was not the only form for the printed book. Some books were folded into accordion pleats, and they, like the scrolls, were printed on only one side.

In Chinese history, the most famous printed books were the Confucian classics. These works, so influential in Chinese religious, political, and intellectual life, emphasized ethical precepts needed for the proper functioning of society. In the tenth century, the emperor ordered all these works to be inscribed on wooden blocks and multiple copies to be printed. Feng Dao and his associates completed the twenty-one-year task of printing the 130 volumes of the Confucian corpus in 953. For many years, the Chinese wrongly attributed the invention of printing to Feng Dao. In the West, he has been compared to the fifteenth century German printer Johann Gutenberg. Block printing and typography existed before Gutenberg, but his printing of the Bible ushered in a new era of European civilization. Similarly, printed books existed in China before Feng Dao, but his printing of the Confucian classics ushered in the renaissance of the Song Dynasty (Sung; 960-1279).

SIGNIFICANCE

Though the Chinese developed xylography in the Tang Dynasty and typography (movable type printing) in the Song Dynasty, the revolutionary significance of the printed book has often been attributed to fifteenth century Europeans. Because of the ideographic nature of the Chinese language and the alphabetic nature of European languages, xylography was more important in the East and typography was more important in the West. Similarly, the impact of the printed book on China was different from its impact on Western countries. The Chinese language has been and continues to be spoken differently in various regions, but the written language is the same everywhere. It was therefore difficult for books to have the fragmenting effect on Chinese regions that mass-produced books had on European countries during the Renaissance. During the Middle Ages, handwritten books in Latin helped unify Christian European civilization, but in the fifteenth and sixteenth centuries, books written in different languages began circulating widely, and these helped establish national identities and foster nationalism.

Because of the Reformation and the Scientific Revolution of the sixteenth century, it has been customary to credit the printed book with great powers of cultural change and individual liberation. On the other hand, some scholars have seen the printed book as an instrument of servitude. For example, books continued the domination of the illiterate by the literate. Despite these critics, most scholars recognize the importance of books for the enrichment of life, work, and leisure.

—*Robert J. Paradowski*

FURTHER READING

Carter, Thomas. *The Invention of Printing in China and Its Spread Westward*. Rev. ed. New York: Ronald, 1955. First published by Columbia University in 1925, this is a historical analysis of papermaking and printing in China. Carter thinks it is likely that European block printing came from China, and it is possible that European movable type was influenced by Chinese techniques, especially through the reports of travelers. Each chapter has notes and an extensive bibliography. Includes a chronological chart and an index.

Shubao, Luo, ed. *An Illustrated History of Printing in Ancient China*. Kowloon, Hong Kong: City University of Hong Kong Press, 1998. Beautifully illustrated chronicle of the history of printing in China from its origin to its later development. Index in English and Chinese.

Soeng, Mu. *The Diamond Sutra: Transforming the Way We Perceive the World*. Boston, Mass.: Wisdom Publications, 2000. Part 2 contains a translation of the *Diamond Sutra* into English. Part 1 analyzes the historical and cultural context of this great Buddhist text, including Aurel Stein's discovery of its significance in the history of the printed book. Bibliography and index.

Tsien Tsuen-Hsuin. *Paper and Printing*. Part 1 in *Chemistry and Chemical Technology*, Vol. 5 in *Science and Civilisation in China*. Translated and edited by Joseph Needham. New York: Cambridge University Press, 1985. Unlike previous volumes in this series, this book was not written by Needham. Though the emphasis is on the origin and development of papermaking and printing in China, the author also discusses early books, printed scrolls, and the influence of Chinese books on East and West. Illustrated with substantial bibliographies and a detailed index.

SEE ALSO: 7th-8th centuries: Papermaking Spreads to Korea, Japan, and Central Asia; 713-741: First Newspapers in China; c. 1045: Bi Sheng Develops Movable Earthenware Type; 1403-1407: *Yonglo Dadian* Encyclopedia Is Compiled.

869-883
ZANJ REVOLT OF AFRICAN SLAVES

A ninth century uprising and prolonged revolt of black African slaves proved the most serious threat the ʿAbbāsid caliphate faced in a period remarkable for the wide array of challenges to caliphal power.

LOCALE: Basra (now in Iraq)
CATEGORY: Wars, uprisings, and civil unrest

KEY FIGURES

ʿAlī ibn Muḥammad (d. 883), rebel leader
Abū al-ʿAbbās (d. 902) Muslim commander, caliph as al-Muʿtaḍid, r. 892-902
al-Muwaffaq (d. 892), father of Abū al-ʿAbbās, Muslim commander

SUMMARY OF EVENT

The history of the early Islamic world is frequently one of rebellion and revolt. The ambiguous nature of authority within the early Muslim *ummah* (community of believers) following the death of the Prophet stemmed in part from the fact that Muḥammad never clearly designated a successor. This, combined with the inevitable disaffection of those unable to compete for wealth or power within the evolving Islamic hierarchy, produced persistent factional strife within the community. It was the nascent ʿAbbāsid Dynasty's ability to harness and focus discontent that proved important in the overthrow of the Umayyad caliphate, but once in power, the ʿAbbāsids themselves faced the effects of the social and political turbulence that undid their predecessors.

It is thus against a backdrop of precarious central power and insurgencies nourished by personal disappointment and led by charismatic prophetic figures that the so-called Zanj revolt, which began in 869, should be understood. The slaves involved in the revolt, which was directed by a self-styled Arab prophet, were almost exclusively men of sub-Saharan and East African extraction, the Zanj. It began and progressed while the ʿAbbāsid regime faced local challenges to its authority and power from the Sāffārids in Khorāsān, the Ṭūlūnids in Egypt and Syria, the Sāmānids in Transoxiana, and Khāijite rebels dispersed throughout Iraq and Iran. In addition, the ʿAbbāsid regime faced an ongoing conflict with the Byzantine Empire on its western frontiers.

Although the revolt was finally put down in 883, during the conflict, the Zanj army took several major cities, including Wasit and, in 871, the cultural, religious, and commercial center of Basra. In so doing, Zanj troops committed long-remembered acts of brutality and vandalism. In narrating these events, the normally dispassionate contemporary historian al-Ṭabarī referred to the leader of the revolt, ʿAlī bin Muḥammad, as "the accursed one." It is impossible to know how many died during the campaigns of the Zanj, although estimates range from 500,000 to 2 million people. Basra never recovered its former wealth or importance as a trading center, and the memory of the revolt may have shaded Arab perception of blacks, long after the last former Zanj guerrilla was mustered into the ʿAbbāsid army following the collapse of the revolt.

For more than a century before the outbreak of the Zanj rebellion, thousands of black African slaves were employed removing unusable topsoil from extensive tracts of southern Iraqi marshland. Islamic law held that anyone who made land productive would thereafter own it, and transforming otherwise unusable Iraqi marshland into arable farmland seems to have been an industry deemed worthy of the investment of large-scale capital in the form of slave cadres. For the men who labored in the salt marshes, however, conditions were miserable. Such conditions led to smaller Zanj uprisings under the Umayyads in 689-690 and 694.

The catalyst for the rebellion of 869 seems to have been the appearance of ʿAlī ibn Muḥammad, a charismatic would-be Arab prophet. Before reaching Basra prior to the revolt, ʿAlī had drifted from employment as a poet and teacher in the orbit of the caliphal court at Sāmarrāʾ to the desert regions of Bahrain, where he presented himself to the Bedouin tribes as a descendant of Abū Ṭālib (d. 619), Muḥammad's uncle. He claimed to receive revelations from God in the form of poetry that came tripping off his tongue, and he badgered the desert tribes for their "moral laxness." Moreover, he rallied his followers against the power of the caliphate, a project in which he enjoyed some patchy success.

After a series of defeats and close scrapes with the authorities in Bahrain, Basra, and Baghdad, however, ʿAlī returned to the Basra region posing as a well-to-do merchant. Having captured a trader whose business was the transportation of flour to the labor camps arrayed throughout Iraq's southern salt marshes, ʿAlī seems to have recognized immediately the slaves working in those camps as potential followers. After inquiring about the condition of the slaves, ʿAlī sent the merchant to recruit as many of the Zanj as he could to his cause.

The revolt began as a series of local riots whose focus was the acquisition of provisions and armaments and whose targets were local villages. The residents of these villages were unable to field an effective defense against the rebels, and they were quickly joined by Basrans determined to protect their movable property and to regain control of their slaves. Through a series of guerrilla-style operations, the Zanj routed or evaded their enemies consistently and made a habit of collecting the banners and severed heads of their defeated foes and delivering them to their leader.

As they made their way through the Iraqi countryside, the Zanj also rallied other black slaves to their cause and rejected offers of payment from local officials and citizens to leave the area. On October 22 and 23, 869, the Zanj fought a pair of climactic battles with the people of Basra among the canals south of the city. The first day was a serious defeat for the Zanj, but on the second day the Basrans were decisively routed, many prominent members of the community were killed, and their former slaves took their heads as trophies. Following the battle, the Zanj established a base camp in the salt marshes and set about plundering and massacring the surrounding villages. The people of Basra immediately appealed to the caliph for help against the rebels.

Meanwhile, the rebellion spread. The Zanj took the cities of Ubulla and Abbadan, Jubba and Ahvāz. The caliph al-Muʿtamid dispatched his brother, al-Muwaffaq, to deal with the rebellion, but it nevertheless continued unabated. Complicating matters was the fact that the revolt had taken on a nebulous quality and manifested itself where least expected before dissipating and re-forming again elsewhere. In 872, al-Muwaffaq took personal command of a large army and set out to crush the Zanj once and for all. The resulting battles were inconclusive, however, and each side took away its share of victories before disease in the ranks forced al-Muwaffaq to withdraw.

During this and directly preceding periods, the vicious excesses of the Zanj crescendoed into the sack of Basra on September 7, 871. Having defeated the ʿAbbāsid contingent on hand, the Zanj set about pillaging and burning the city while indiscriminately murdering men, women, and children. The rich were stripped of their wealth before being murdered, while the poor were butchered immediately. Throughout the environs of the city, people tried to hide from the Zanj, and they were reportedly reduced to cannibalism after the supply of rats and feral dogs had been exhausted.

Distracted with other matters following the collapse of al-Muwaffaq's campaign, the ʿAbbāsids remained content with a policy of containment with regard to the Zanj. This strategy lasted from 873 to 879. When the caliphate was once again free to deal exclusively with the Zanj, al-Muwaffaq, now caliph, sent his son Abū al-ʿAbbās to crush the Zanj. Abū al-ʿAbbās proved a talented and tenacious commander. Having learned from his own failure, al-Muwaffaq instructed his son to undermine the Zanj's ability to wage the style of warfare at which they had proven most adept: the use of guerrilla tactics in the salt marshes using home terrain and small boats for swift mobility and amphibious assaults. Beginning in 879-880, Abū al-ʿAbbās slowly ground away the capacity of the Zanj to wage war in the swaps, destroying boats and cutting off supplies while pushing the Zanj out of captured cities and territories.

SIGNIFICANCE

ʿAlī ibn Muḥammad was killed in battle on August 11, 883, and the Zanj revolt collapsed. When the rebel leader's head was carried in triumph through the streets of Baghdad by Abū al-ʿAbbās, the city was jubilant. The Zanj revolt had come to represent for the ʿAbbāsid caliphate not just a challenge to its authority but also a threat to the existence of the community it headed. Carried on in the Iraqi heartland and by a group of people the ʿAbbāsids could neither negotiate with nor co-opt, the revolt was of a character distinct from those of other, less radical challenges to ʿAbbāsid authority. Basra, however, would never recover from the ravages of the revolt, and southern Iraq thereafter entered a long period of neglect, poverty, and despair.

Less easily quantified are the effects of the rebellion on perceptions of blacks among Muslims. Such perceptions had never been overly positive. Al-Jāḥiẓ (c. 776-868), for example, an Arabic satirist who died the year before the Zanj revolt broke out, reveals in his tongue-in-cheek essay "The Superiority of Blacks to Whites" (English translation, 2002) that despite arguments made on their behalf, blacks were thought by his contemporaries to be stupid, ugly, and uncultured. In other writings, al-Jāḥiẓ suggests that blacks are, in his own estimation, crude, vicious, and "dim." Other Arab writers were less generous. Blacks, they declared, were not only lacking in intelligence, but also violent, malodorous, and, as one put it, "beggars when hungry and rapists when fed." While it is not difficult to understand how the excesses of the Zanj revolt might have nourished such stereotypes, the grim consequences of the prejudices that underlie such stereotypes carried grave implications for the millions of black Africans who were to come into contact with Islam in the ensuing centuries as converts and slaves.

—*Thomas Sizgorich*

FURTHER READING

Goldenberg, David M. *The Curse of Ham: Race and Slavery in Early Judaism, Christianity, and Islam.* Princeton, N.J.: Princeton University Press, 2003. A thoroughly researched study of the topic of race, slavery, and anti-black sentiment—and the portrayal of black Africans—in the major world religions and in the Bible. Focuses on the belief that the biblical figure Ham and his descendants, including black Africans, had been cursed by God with eternal slavery. Extensive bibliography, index.

Hunwick, John, and Eve Troutt Powell. *The African Diaspora in the Mediterranean Lands of Islam.* Princeton, N.J.: Marcus Wiener, 2002. Provides primary sources on the topic of the enslavement of black Africans by Muslims in the Mediterranean region during a one-thousand-year span of history. Illustrations, map, bibliography.

Jāḥiẓ, al-. *Sobriety and Mirth: A Selection of the Shorter Writings of al-Jāḥiẓ.* Translated by Jim Colville. New York: Kegan Paul, 2002. Writings on social and moral issues by the Islamic satirist of the ninth century, including "The Superiority of Blacks to Whites."

Kennedy, Hugh. *The Prophet and the Age of the Caliphates: The Islamic Near East from the Sixth to the Eleventh Century.* New York: Longman, 1986. A clear and accessible guide to the events of the age of the Zanj revolt. Genealogical tables, maps, bibliography, index.

Lewis, Bernard. *Race and Color in Islam*. New York: Harper and Row, 1970. Explores the topic of race, color, and racism in the context of Islam. Illustrations, bibliography.

_______. *Race and Slavery in the Middle East: An Historical Enquiry*. New York: Oxford University Press, 1990. Explores the legacy of slavery in the Middle East, focusing on the relationship between the institution of slavery and racial prejudice and oppression. Illustrations, bibliography, index.

Popovic, Alexandre. *The Revolt of African Slaves in Iraq in the Third/Ninth Century*. Translated by Léon King. Princeton, N.J.: Marcus Wiener, 1999. A translation of the author's 1976 classic and exhaustive study of the revolt. Includes a new introduction by scholar Henry Louis Gates, Jr. Maps, bibliography, index.

Waines, David, trans. *The Revolt of the Zanj*. Vol. 36 in *The History of al-Ṭabarī*. Albany: State University of New York Press, 1985. An important historical work by the Arab historian al-Ṭabarī, author of a multivolume treatise on Islam before and during the Middle Ages, up to the year 915.

_______. *The ʿAbbāsid Recovery*. Vol. 37 in *The History of al-Ṭabarī*. Albany: State University of New York Press, 1985. Discusses the end of the revolt and the "recovery" of the ʿAbbāsids. Bibliography, index.

SEE ALSO: October 10, 680: Martyrdom of Prophet's Grandson Ḥusayn; 780: Beginning of the Harem System; 872-973: Publication of the *History of al-Ṭabarī*; 1377: Ibn Khaldūn Completes His *Muqaddimah*; 1415-1460: Prince Henry the Navigator Promotes Portuguese Exploration.

RELATED ARTICLES in *Great Lives from History: The Middle Ages, 477-1453*: al-Jāḥiẓ; Muḥammad; al-Ṭabarī.

872-973
PUBLICATION OF *THE HISTORY OF AL-ṬABARĪ*

The publication of al-Ṭabarī's massive work provided a historical narrative both for Muslims and for students of Islamic history. It also marked the advent of one of the great works of world historiography.

LOCALE: Baghdad (now in Iraq)
CATEGORIES: Cultural and intellectual history; historiography; literature; philosophy; religion

KEY FIGURE
al-Ṭabarī (c. 839-923), Arab historian

SUMMARY OF EVENT
Much of what is known of the first three centuries of Islamic history is the result of the publication of al-Ṭabarī's *Taʾrīkh al-rusul wa al-mulūk* (872-973; *The History of al-Ṭabarī*, 1985-1999, 39 vols.). The chronicle covers the period from the history of the early Semitic patriarchs, prophets, and rulers through the reign of the caliph al-Muqtadir, a period ending in the year 915. It does so in the dominant idiom of early medieval Muslim historiography, as an assemblage of reports, or *akhbar*, ostensibly passed down through oral and written retellings and then fashioned into an overarching narrative by al-Ṭabarī.

The narrative so fashioned by al-Ṭabarī is that of a community instituted on earth by the God of Abraham and his last Prophet, Muḥammad, but one also frequently torn by factionalism and individual ambition. This was the narrative with which premodern Muslims would reckon the history of their community and the narrative that, with minor alterations, was taken over as Western scholars began to compose their own histories of the early Islamic world. Despite this, the *Taʾrīkh al-rusul wa al-mulūk* was not published in English translation until the last two decades of the twentieth century, this the result in part of its imposing dimensions—the English translation consists of thirty-nine volumes.

Much of the information that was to find its way into al-Ṭabarī's work was collected by the scholar during wide-ranging travels made as a young man to various parts of the Islamic world. Prior to the advent of the madrasa system of education, and to a lesser degree thereafter, such travels were an expected part of a young Muslim intellectual's training. To "go in search of wisdom" was reminiscent of the *hijra* or "setting out (from home)" enjoined on Muslims by the Prophet, and students customarily traveled to such intellectual centers as Baghdad in search of teachers with whom they might study traditions of the Prophet and his companions (Hadith), the elements of Islamic law and jurisprudence (*shariah*), or Qurʾānic commentary (*tafsir*). In so doing, they would listen to lectures and take copious notes, thus collecting books of tradition and knowledge. It was during travels to Syria, Egypt, and Iraq, and throughout his extended period of residence in Baghdad that al-Ṭabarī collected much of the information he would craft into his historical text.

Just as al-Ṭabarī roamed a wide portion of the medieval Muslim world in order to collect material for his history, his work should be understood as a product of its author's voracious intellect and prodigious creative capacity and as a text informed by the central scholarly and religious concerns of his culture. Al-Ṭabarī himself produced a corpus of work that modern scholars have estimated would have required an output of fourteen handwritten folios per day during a period of fifty years of literary activity. In addition to his history, al-Ṭabarī produced a massive and magisterial work of Qurʾānic commentary, texts on topics ranging from ritual purity to various forms of prayer to the firing of arrows and works of poetry and biography.

For medieval Muslim intellectuals, the wide range of interests manifested in al-Ṭabarī's corpus represented less discrete disciplines than mutually dependent bodies of knowledge, all of which, ideally, supported and cast light on the others. The history of the early Muslim community, for example, was indispensable for formulating law and understanding the Qurʾān, while one's day-today actions and comportment helped to maintain a link with the community's foundational moments, in which it was believed God instituted a polity that was to rule the world in his name. For al-Ṭabarī and his contemporaries, to understand the past meant to better understand the present and future, and indeed to better understand human relations with the divine and eternal.

The importance for modern readers of al-Ṭabarī's work resides in part in the mix of materials with which it was composed, and also in part for the brilliance of the composite whole. Al-Ṭabarī frequently preserves information that does not otherwise survive. This is due in part to the success of the work itself: Al-Ṭabarī's history supplanted many of the works on which it relied for material. Demand for copies of these earlier works slackened with the advent of al-Ṭabarī's work, and those earlier books were no longer copied or collected. For later medieval and early modern Muslim historians, al-Ṭabarī's history exercised influence at second or third hand as these historians crafted their own works relying on earlier histories that in turn owed their central narrative and information to al-Ṭabarī.

The work itself is, as necessitated by its subject matter, a sprawling narrative that shifts in focus from the dramas of cosmic creation to the tensions and passions that guide the actions of individual men and women. At the work's outset, al-Ṭabarī informs his reader that he shall pass on information he has attributed to an original source only, preferring eyewitness testimony because, he says, no knowledge of the past is available to those who did not witness the events of that past except through the reports of those who did. This notion of the past and its recovery in works of history, with which many modern empiricist historians would readily assent, was in accord with evolving practices among Muslim traditionalists who specialized in collecting and analyzing "sayings" of the Prophet as models for Muslim behavior and law.

Al-Ṭabarī will thus frequently provide several reports describing the same event. Often subtle differences occur among these individual reports, and occasionally they vary considerably in both content and implication. In such cases al-Ṭabarī will sometimes indicate one version that he prefers, while elsewhere he will conclude with an ambiguous "but God knows best the truth of the matter." In addition to his pledge to rely on eyewitness reports as the basis for his history, al-Ṭabarī also assures his reader that he will only rarely exercise his own judgment in arranging his material. The plausibility (or even desirability) of such practice may be regarded with skepticism by modern readers, of course, and in any case a distinct authorial voice is detectable throughout al-Ṭabarī's chronicle.

Given al-Ṭabarī's pledge to witness "statements of fact," and the sheer volume of information he assembles, it might be assumed that the knowledge of the early Islamic centuries is fairly complete owing to his efforts. In fact, quite the opposite is true. Among medieval Muslims, the dependability of the sources available to al-Ṭabarī or any other historian were subjected to rigorous scrutiny and frequently found wanting. Among modern historians, unease has been prompted by the fact that the earliest of the sources on which al-Ṭabarī depended for the events and personalities of the primordial Muslim world (the Qurʾān excepted) date from around 150 years after the *hijra*. The so-called eyewitness reports on which al-Ṭabarī relies cannot be accounted for before the middle of the second century.

In any society at any time, there may be any number of reasons for historians and storytellers to amend, revise, or otherwise distort the historical narratives they pass on. In addition to simple variances of perspective or writing style, individual biases, personal or communal prejudices and other agendas will inevitably help to shape the ways in which different historians edit and interpret their material. In societies such as early Islam, where questions of political and religious authority were predicated on questions of history, the engines historians know to shape and even distort historical information churn incessantly. Partisan concerns and sectarian chauvinism have thus colored the narratives with which al-Ṭabarī was to construct his history. The question that has bedeviled medieval and modern scholars alike has been how much and in what ways the surviving material in al-Ṭabarī's book may have been affected.

In addition, as suggested previously, medieval and modern scholars have debated endlessly the merits of al-Ṭabarī's individual sources. Among these sources are Ibn Isḥāq (c. 704-767), author of the earliest extant biography of the Prophet, and the historians al-Wāqidī (747-823), Abū Mikhnaf (d. 774), and the notorious Sayf bin ʿUmar, whose dependability was doubted by both medieval Arab scholars and modern Western Arabists, but who has been generally rehabilitated in recent research. What one finds reported in al-Ṭabarī's history concerning the very early Islamic community is therefore less dependably "what really happened" than "what was imagined to have happened" as the Muslim community began to circulate and record stories about the initial decades and centuries of its history.

SIGNIFICANCE

Despite these concerns, however, the consensus among historians of the early Muslim world is that al-Ṭabarī's history represents the single most valuable repository of information regarding the formation of the first Islamic empires. Indeed, whether it is al-Ṭabarī's depiction of the crucial battles of the conquest period or his close and nuanced study of persistent struggles of the Khāijite movement or the Zanj revolt or the slow but sure ascendancy of Turkish military elites over their ʿAbbāsid Dynasty masters, the stories contained in *The History of al-Ṭabarī* are the stories that medieval historians and modern historians alike have told and will continue to tell about the early Muslim world. In this sense, al-Ṭabarī is and will likely remain, as one nineteenth century German admirer put it, "the father of Arabic history."

Al-Ṭabarī's history thus allows modern scholars to understand, if only imperfectly, the birth and early development of the Islamic polity. Perhaps more important, however, al-Ṭabarī's work has provided generation upon generation of Muslims an essential core of stories and ideas with which to craft their communal selves. Alongside the most important Islamic works of religion and law, then, al-Ṭabarī's history has proven one of the Islamic world's foundational documents.

—*Thomas Sizgorich*

FURTHER READING

Donner, Fred M. *Narratives of Islamic Origins: The Beginnings of Islamic Historical Writing*. Princeton, N.J.: Darwin Press, 1998. A crucial study of the process whereby the narratives one finds in the works of al-Ṭabarī and other early Islamic historians evolved as well as the role these narratives played in the formation of the community itself. Extensive bibliography, index.

Hibri, Tayeb el-. *Reinterpreting Islamic Historiography: Hārūn al-Rashīd and the Narrative of the ʿAbbāsid Caliphate*. New York: Cambridge University Press, 1999. Argues that past historical accounts of the eighth and ninth century caliphate were not written as portraits of the time, but instead as a means to convey the religious, political, and social issues that were then prominent. Bibliography, index.

Khalidi, Tarif. *Arabic Historical Thought in the Classical Period*. New York: Cambridge University Press, 1994. Traces the history of Muslim historiography, especially its focus on the documentation of scholars, scholarship, and learned society. Quotes historians and historical texts of the time period. Bibliography, index.

Noth, Albrecht, and Lawrence Conrad. *The Early Arabic Historical Tradition: A Source Critical Study*. Princeton, N.J.: Darwin Press, 1994. A revision of the author's pioneering study of early Islamic historiography.

Robinson, Chase F. *Islamic Historiography*. New York: Cambridge University Press, 2003. A concise guide to early Islamic historiography suitable for both the specialist and nonspecialist. Bibliography, index.

Rosenthal, Franz. "General Introduction." In *The History of al-Ṭabarī: Volume I: General Introduction and From the Creation to the Flood*, translated by Franz Rosenthal. Albany: State University of New York Press, 1989. This lengthy introduction is one of the most concise and focused studies yet available in English of al-Ṭabarī as an author.

_______. *A History of Muslim Historiography*. 2d rev. ed. Leiden, the Netherlands: E. J. Brill, 1968. One of the foundational studies of the early practice of Islamic history and its composition. A broad survey with a bibliography.

Ṭabarī, al-. *The History of al-Ṭabarī*, translated by Franz

Rosenthal. 39 vols. Albany: State University of New York Press, 1985-1999.

Tayob, Abdelkader I. "Ṭabarī on the Companions of the Prophet: Moral and Political Contours in Islamic Historical Writing." *Journal of the American Oriental Society* 119, no. 2 (April-June, 1999). An examination of an early motif in the writing of Islamic history, that of the status and roles of the Prophet's companions. Shows how al-Ṭabarī considers the companions as moral, and not political, beings.

SEE ALSO: c. 610-632: Muḥammad Receives Revelations; 869-883: Zanj Revolt of African Slaves; 972: Building of al-Azhar Mosque; 1340: Al-ʿUmarī Writes a History of Africa; 1377: Ibn Khaldūn Completes His *Muqaddimah*.

RELATED ARTICLES in *Great Lives from History: The Middle Ages, 477-1453*: Aḥmad ibn Ḥanbal; Avicenna; al-Ghazzālī; Ibn Khaldūn; al-Masʿūdī; Muḥammad; al-Ṭabarī; Yaqut.

877-889
INDRAVARMAN I CONQUERS THE THAI AND THE MONS

Based on stone inscriptions praising rule, military prowess, and conquests of Indravarman I that have been found in northeastern Thailand, many scholars believe that this Khmer king conquered the Thai and Mon peoples and enlarged the boundaries of his empire.

LOCALE: Khmer (now Cambodia) and other parts of Southeast Asia

CATEGORIES: Expansion and land acquisition; government and politics; wars, uprisings, and civil unrest

KEY FIGURES

Jayavarman II (c. 770-850), founder of the Angkor civilization and king of Khmer, r. 802-850

Jayavarman III (d. 877), second king of Khmer during the Angkor period, r. 850-877

Indravarman I (d. 889), king of Khmer, r. 877-889

SUMMARY OF EVENT

Much of the exact nature of Indravarman I's military conquests is still a mystery to contemporary historians. From stone inscriptions, archaeological evidence, and foreign sources, it is known that during his reign, this Khmer king at Angkor ruled over an area in northeastern Thailand and lower Laos peopled by Thai and Mons. Unfortunately, the names and dates of the battles have not been discovered, so that the individual events of Indravarman I's conquest remain unknown.

Indravarman I was not the son of his predecessor, Jayavarman III, but the great-nephew of Jayavarman II, the founder of Khmer's Angkor civilization. This illustrious great-uncle had established a new Khmer dynasty by conquest. He finally moved the capital to the area where later kings would build the impressive temple complex of Angkor Wat. It lies next to the present town of Siem Reap at the Tonle Sap, or great lake, in the heart of Cambodia.

How Indravarman I became ruler of Khmer remains unclear. His own inscriptions claim that his grandfather, Rudravarman (fl. late eighth/early ninth century) was a local king. However, nothing is known of such a kingdom, and he may have been just a chieftain. One of Rudravarman's nieces became one of Jayavarman II's wives and bore him the future king, Jayavarman III. Some scholars believe that Jayavarman III himself fought his way to the throne, eliminating his half brothers. Because early royal succession may have been rather violent, some historians believe that Indravarman I usurped kingship and might even have killed his predecessor, but there is no concrete historical proof of this.

Most likely, Indravarman I's family had allied itself with Jayavarman II. Jayavarman II's initial push northwest out of a likely starting point in the upper Mekong Delta, near today's Vietnamese city of Long Xuyen, in all likelihood continued after his death around 850. Very little is known about any concrete events in the reign of his successor, Jayavarman III. Even the beginning of his rule is disputed. Man Chu (Man Ch'u), a Chinese chronicler, visited Khmer from 861 to 863 and reported that its king ruled over vast Thai and Lao lands. For 875 or 880, the Arab traveler Ya Kubi attests to the power of the Khmer king, who received homage from local Thai and Lao lords.

This contemporary historical evidence helps establish the fact that the Khmer kings had conquered Thai and Mon lands by the time of Indravarman I's reign. When Indravarman I became king in 877, he followed the ritual established by Jayavarman II in 802 and declared himself

A detail from the Leper King Terrace at Angkor Wat, built in the twelfth century during the reign of Jayavarman VII, who ruled the Khmer empire three centuries after Indravarman. (PhotoDisc)

devaraja. This Sanskrit phrase can be translated as "god-king," "king of gods," or "universal monarch." Obviously exaggerated, the claim is nevertheless grounded in the holder's rule over a significant part of Southeast Asia.

The third Angkorian king, Indravarman I was the first to extensively commission inscriptions celebrating his glory and achievements. Because his predecessors left no such records, it is hard to distinguish their individual contributions to the rise of the Khmer empire of the Angkor era. This era is commonly dated from 802 to 1431, when Angkor Wat was abandoned. However, by the time Indravarman I became king, or very shortly after, he ruled over vast stretches of Thai and Mon territory.

As king, Indravarman I lived in a palace at Hariharalaya (now Roluos). It lies very close to the later Angkor Wat. Two years after he became king, Indravarman I completed the temple complex Preah Ko (Sanskrit for "sacred cow"). The temple honored his parents and ancestors, and its inscriptions contain the earliest records of his military achievements.

The inscriptions at Preah Ko state that Indravarman I came to power through successful conquest and military valor. He is described as a fierce yet compassionate warrior:

> The right hand of this prince, long and powerful, was terrible in combat when his sword fell on his enemies, scattering them to all points of the compass. Invincible, he was appeased only by his enemies who turned their backs in surrender, or who placed themselves under his protection.

Another inscription at the temple reads: "In battle, which is like a difficult ocean to cross, he raised a pathway, made up of the heads of his arrogant enemies; his own troops passed over on it." However, it is not written who these enemies were. Some scholars believe that the passages could refer to both external adversaries such as the Thai and Mons and Khmer rivals.

The clearest indication for Indravarman I's victories over other people in Southeast Asia also comes from Preah Ko: "It seems that the creator [Indra], tired of making so many kings, had fashioned this king Indravarman to form the joy of the three worlds, uniquely."

The new king's very name means "protected by Indra," with Indra the name of the creator in Hinduism. Indravarman I may have used a name that expresses his rule over many different people in his empire, whose many kings he replaced with himself alone.

A different inscription at a temple far away from the capital attests the reality of territorial conquest not so much by its words but by its geographical location in recently conquered territory. The inscription calls Indravarman I "ruler of the entire world" and claims that "atop the lordly heads of the kings of China, Champa, and Yavadvipa his reign was like a flawless crown," meaning that these kings obeyed him. Historians have fiercely debated this claim. The Khmer state did not rule over China; most likely the area meant was in Laos, a country that borders China to the south, and included land in northern Thailand. Champa refers to an indigenous kingdom in present-day southern Vietnam. Scholars hotly discuss where Yavadvipa was located. Some think it is Java, in Indonesia, others believe it lies in the Mekong Delta.

Because the remaining inscriptions of Indravarman I's reign speak of peace and the prosperity of his subjects, it appears that any conquests made by this king must have occurred either during the reign of Jayavarman III, in a period of civil war following Jayavarman III's death, or in the two years from 877 to 879 when Preah Ko was completed. Most scholars believe that Indravarman I fought to successfully expand the Khmer empire under its second king, whom he may have deposed by force, and celebrated his victories by crowning himself king in 877.

Significance

Regardless of the exact historical circumstances of Indravarman I's conquest and the exact degree of his military contribution to the rise of Cambodia's Angkorian empire, it is clear that this king ruled over a large stretch of Southeast Asian land that included many Thai and Mons who had been conquered. By the time of his death in 889, Khmer had established a strong empire that would flourish for more than five hundred additional years. His ambitious building program and his commission of inscriptions celebrating his glory created a pattern for his successors.

The Khmer conquest of Thai and Mon people and their territory created the material base for the rise of a remarkable civilization. Indravarman I solidified the young empire and established the styles for the religious buildings through which its rulers sought to immortalize themselves.

However, the violence of his early years also contained the seeds for the eventual fall of the Angkor civilization. Conquered people fought to free themselves. Another ongoing problem was the recurring violent struggle for royal succession that may have also plagued Indravarman I's rise. Civil wars among princely contenders disrupted society, and foreign allies of the fighting factions would claim parts of the empire.

Indravarman I left behind a strong empire. Through his inscriptions and stone reliefs depicting life during his reign, much of his culture has survived for posterity. Conquered foreign workers aided his building program. Soon, the Khmer would build one of humanity's most astonishing temple complexes at Angkor Wat, close to Indravarman I's temples.

—R. C. Lutz

Further Reading

Briggs, Lawrence Palmer. *The Ancient Khmer Empire*. 1951. Reprint. Bangkok: White Lotus Press, 1999. Groundbreaking description of the Angkor kings and the basis of much later writing. Discusses all of Indravarman I's inscriptions with a map of their location. Genealogical table, strong focus on art and architecture. Illustrated.

Chandler, David P. *A History of Cambodia*. 3d ed. Boulder, Colo.: Westview Press, 2000. Chapter 2 provides a very informed and readable portrayal of the early Angkor kings. Maps, illustrations.

Coedès, George. *The Indianized States of Southeast Asia*. Translated by Walter Vella and Susan Brown Cowing. Honolulu: East-West Center Press, 1968. Influential study. The chapter on "The Kingdom of Angkor" offers a useful overview. Illustrated, maps.

Ghosh, Manomohan. *A History of Cambodia*. Rev. 2d ed. Calcutta, India: Calcutta Oriental Book Agency, 1968. Portrait of Indravarman I's reign from a non-Western perspective.

Hall, Daniel. *A History of Southeast Asia*. London: Macmillan, 1981. 4th ed. The chapter on "The Khmers and Angkor" reveals a solid survey of the rise of the Angkor civilization.

Higham, Charles. *The Civilization of Angkor*. London: Weidenfeld and Nicolson, 2001. Competent portrayal of Indravarman I and his reign, places the king well in the context of his rising civilization. Photos, maps.

See also: c. 700-1253: Confederation of Thai Tribes; 802: Founding of the Khmer Empire.

Related article in *Great Lives from History: The Middle Ages, 477-1453*: Suryavarman II.

878
ALFRED DEFEATS THE DANES

King Alfred defeated the Danes at Edington, encouraging further Anglo-Saxon resistance against Viking invasion and establishing the foundation for his transition from king of Wessex to king of the English.

LOCALE: Wiltshire, Wessex, England
CATEGORIES: Expansion and land acquisition; wars, uprisings, and civil unrest

KEY FIGURES

Æthelred I (d. 871), king of Wessex, r. 866-871, and elder brother of Alfred the Great
Alfred the Great (849-899), king of Wessex, r. 871-899
Asser (d. c. 909), Alfred's biographer, a monk from St. David's (Wales), and later bishop of Sherborne (Somerset)
Guthrum (d. 890), self-appointed Danish king of East Anglia, r. 880-890
Ragnar Lothbrok (fl. ninth century), Viking leader
Halfdan (fl. ninth century), son of the Viking chief Ragnar Lothbrok, conqueror of York
Ivar the Boneless (fl. ninth century), Halfdan's brother and conqueror of East Anglia

SUMMARY OF EVENT

The Vikings, invaders from Denmark, Norway, and Sweden, first arrived in England in 789 and raided Dorchester, Wessex, then under Mercian control. The raiders did not commit any plunder but exhibited their superior strength. When the royal reeve from Dorchester commanded them to meet the king (Brihtric), he was killed on the spot. In 793, the Vikings sacked the monastery of Lindisfarne off the coast of Northumbria. The following year, they hit the monastery of Jarrow at the mouth of the Don. Nearly half a century later, in 835, a Danish raiding party devastated the Isle of Sheppey in the Thames estuary. In 836, thirty-five Viking ships landed at Carhampton (Somerset), but King Egbert put up a stiff resistance. Two years later, a Viking fleet joined forces with the Britons of Cornwall, but the allies were defeated by Egbert's West Saxon army at Hingston Down.

A more serious phase of Viking operations in England

An artist's dramatization of Danes preparing for a raid on the English. (F. R. Niglutsch)

began when they took to wintering on island bases in the river mouths, conveniently situated for quick resumption of campaigning at the onset of spring. In 851, after wintering on the Isle of Thanet, an army of 350 ships stormed Canterbury and London. It routed the army of King Berhtwulf of Mercia but was defeated by Æthelwulf, king of Wessex, and his son Æthelbald at Aclea ("oak field") in Surrey.

The *Anglo-Saxon Chronicle* for 865 records how the people of Kent promised the Viking army at Thanet protection money, or Danegeld, and how the heathens broke their promise. In 866, a Great Army of Danes commanded by two brothers, Halfdan and Ivar the Boneless, took up winter quarters in East Anglia, and the East Angles paid them money to buy their peace. For fifteen years, this army terrorized England. According to Scandinavian folklore, the two young Danes wished to avenge the horrible murder of their father Ragnar Lothbrok, "Hairy Breeches," the most notorious Viking of his time. Evidently some years earlier, Ragnar's ships had been wrecked by a great storm off the Northumbrian coast. He was captured by the Northumbrian king, Ælle, and flung into a pit of adders where the violent Viking met a horrible death.

The Great Army conquered York in 866, East Anglia in 868, and by 870 had seized Reading at the junction of the Thames and Kennet Rivers. In January, 871, they were checked by Alfred the Atheling, brother of King Æthelred I of Wessex, who, as Asser, a monk from St. David's, writes, charged the enemy "acting courageously, like a wild boar," cutting them down at Ashdown. Although the Vikings were vanquished, they held their own and fought nine more battles that year. In April, 871, Alfred became king of Wessex on his brother's death and decided to make peace by paying protection money to the Danish host. The Danes then turned to Mercia, forced King Burhred to abdicate in 874, and in his place appointed one of the royal *thegns*, Ceolwulf II, "a foolish king's *thegn*," in the contemptuous phraseology of the *Anglo-Saxon Chronicle*.

The peace that Alfred bought from the Danes gave his kingdom a respite for reorganizing its defense, though it must be recognized that the West Saxon army, the *fyrd* (national militia), was nothing more than an emergency force, though quite effective and expedient. Neither ealdorman nor king could keep it in the field indefinitely nor lead it far beyond the borders of the shire (county) of its origin. The inability to keep a battle-worthy army constantly at hand resulted in the near-destruction of Wessex when the second Viking invasion began toward the end of 875. This was the southern division of the army, commanded by the three kings: Oscetel, Anwend, and the foremost and most forceful, Guthrum (Godrum). Under Guthrum's leadership, the Danes quickly settled themselves at Wareham on the Dorset coast in 876 before the West Saxons could intercept them in the open country.

Unable to dislodge them by force, Alfred soon came to terms with the Danes, who promised to leave the West Saxon kingdom. In actuality, however, they merely transferred their camp farther west and took up winter quarters for 876 to 877 at Exeter. Again, Alfred offered terms; this time, the Danes actually honored the agreement. In August, 877, they crossed the border into Mercia and es-

ANGLO-SAXON CHRONICLE, YEAR 878

In this year in midwinter after twelfth night the enemy army came stealthily to Chippenham, and occupied the land of the West Saxons and settled there, and drove a great part of the people across the sea, and conquered most of the others; and the people submitted to them, except King Alfred. He journeyed in difficulties through the woods and fen-fastnesses with a small force.

And the same winter the brother of Ivar and Healfdene [Halfdan] was in the kingdom of the West Saxons [in Devon] with 23 ships. And he was killed there and 840 men of his army with him. And there was captured the banner which they called "Raven."

And afterwards at Easter, King Alfred with a small force made a stronghold at Athelney, and he and the section of the people of Somerset which was nearest to it proceeded to fight from that stronghold against the enemy. Then in the seventh week after Easter he rode to "Egbert's stone" east of Selwood, and there came to meet him all the people. . . . And then the enemy gave him preliminary hostages and great oaths that they would leave his kingdom, and promised also that their king should receive baptism, and the most important in the army came . . . and the king stood sponsor to him at his baptism there. . . . And he was twelve days with the king, and he honored him and his companions greatly with gifts.

Source: The *Anglo-Saxon Chronicle*, quoted in *Readings in Medieval History*, edited by Patrick J. Geary (Lewiston, N.Y.: Broadview Press, 1989), p. 269.

tablished camp at Gloucester. Here they proceeded to share some of the land and to give some to King Ceolwulf II of Mercia, their protégé. The Viking settlement covered an extensive region of central and eastern Mercia comprising the Five Boroughs—Lincoln, Stamford, Nottingham, Leicester, and Derby—as well as the land further south and southeast, around Northampton, Bedford, and London. Ceolwulf's share lay in the southwesterly part of the kingdom, including the towns of Gloucester, Worcester, and Warwick.

The settlement of parts of Mercia in the autumn of 877 must have diverted Viking manpower, but still they had enough fighting men to undertake a third invasion of Wessex. The English had, on the other hand, mistakenly believed that their invaders followed a single method of attack: campaigning in summer and holding up in a fortified lair in winter. After departing from Exeter in August, 877, Guthrum's army tarried for five months and then "in midwinter" 878, descended on Chippenham. Guthrum chose a surprise attack when the land of the West Saxons had hibernated for the winter and its army long dispersed. Chippenham was the royal residence, and probably the invaders attempted to kill Alfred and his body of councilors at one stroke. Although the attempt failed and Alfred decamped, this winter descent of the Danes surprised, confused, and appalled the West Saxons, who thought their king to be dead and thus lay at the mercy of the intruders.

Alfred actually fled southeast into the heart of Somerset, where he set up a guerrilla base on the Isle of Athelney and began mounting periodic incursions against the Vikings. His preparations were severe and precarious. He could not raise the full muster of Wessex but had to make do with the *fyrds* of Somerset, Wiltshire, and western Hampshire. In any case, in the late spring of 878, he rode to Egbert's Stone east of Selwood, took command of the host, and led his men toward the northern fringe of the Salisbury Plain, where Guthrum's men paused on their march through Wessex. At Ethundune (Edington), as the *Anglo-Saxon Chronicle* records, Alfred drove the entire Danish army away from the battlefield, and they promised to quit Wessex and have their king Guthrum baptized. Accordingly, "three weeks later King Guthrum with thirty of the men . . . came [to] Athelney, and the king [Alfred] stood sponsor to him at his baptism there." Guthrum may have faced growing unrest among his battle-weary host, who compared their uncertain and unstable condition on the field to the peaceful and settled life of Halfdan's men in Northumbria and thus looked for a peace with the Christians of the south so that they would be free to pursue a normal settled life in East Anglia and southern Mercia.

SIGNIFICANCE

Alfred's flight to Athelney and triumphant return to Egbert's Stone, "where men were fain of him," as well as his victory at Edington followed by Guthrum's conversion to Christianity have become part of the folk history of England. These episodes showed Alfred in his magnificent best and glorified Christianity as a civilizing force for the pagan and nomadic Vikings who were to be Christianized and civilized. The immediate threat to Wessex was eliminated. Edington led to the eventual creation of a united Christian, Anglo-Scandinavian kingdom. To cite the concluding remarks of a distinguished historian, "whatever Alfred's shortcomings as a military commander in the future might prove to be, Edington was truly his finest hour."

—Narasingha P. Sil

FURTHER READING

Asser, John. *Alfred the Great: Asser's Life of King Alfred and Other Contemporary Sources*. Translated by Simon Keynes and Michael Lapidge. New York: Penguin Books, 1988. Meticulous, scholarly, indispensable account of Alfred's life.

______. *The Medieval Life of King Alfred the Great*. Translated by Alfred P. Smyth. New York: Palgrave, 2002. A translation of Asser's classic ninth-century text, *De Rebus gestis Aelfredi*. Includes extensive bibliography and index.

Graham-Campbell, James. *The Viking World*. London: Frances Lincoln, 2001. A succinct account with a brief but helpful bibliography.

Loyn, H. R. *The Vikings in Britain*. Rev. ed. Cambridge, Mass.: Blackwell, 1995. A concise and highly regarded history of the Vikings and Viking Age by a renowned medievalist.

Smyth, Alfred P. *King Alfred the Great*. New York: Oxford University Press, 1995. Erudite critical study of Alfred. Chapter 3 is especially pertinent to an understanding of the Battle of Edington.

Sturdy, David. *Alfred the Great*. London: Constable, 1995. In an effort to counterbalance prevailing accounts, Sturdy's biography is extremely critical of Alfredian myths and legends.

Whitelock, Dorothy. "The Importance of the Battle of Edington." In *From Bede to Alfred: Studies in Early Anglo-Saxon Literature and History*. London: Variorum Reprints, 1980. This lecture to the Society of Friends of the Priory Church of Edington comments on the long-term significance of the Battle of Edington.

Whitelock, Dorothy, David C. Douglas, and Susie I. Tucker, eds. *The Anglo-Saxon Chronicle: A Revised Translation*. New Brunswick, N.J.: Rutgers University Press, 1961. An authoritative annotated translation of an important primary source from the period.

SEE ALSO: 635-800: Founding of Lindisfarne and Creation of the *Book of Kells*; June 7, 793: Norse Raid Lindisfarne Monastery; 850-950: Viking Era.

RELATED ARTICLES in *Great Lives from History: The Middle Ages, 477-1453*: Alfred the Great; Canute the Great.

890's
MAGYARS INVADE ITALY, SAXONY, AND BAVARIA

The Magyar invasions of Italy, Saxony, and Bavaria introduced a new ethnic element into the Central European population. Eighty years after the Magyar incursions, a Central Asian ethnic presence was firmly established in the heart of Europe, altering the ethnic mix of the European continent.

LOCALE: Central Europe
CATEGORIES: Cultural and intellectual history; expansion and land acquisition; wars, uprisings, and civil unrest

KEY FIGURES

Árpád (d. 907), leader of the Magyars, c. 890-907
Arnulf (c. 850-899), king of Germany, r. 887-899
Lambert of Spoleto (d. 898), claimant to the throne of Italy, Holy Roman Emperor, r. 892-898
Zwentibald (c. 840-894), king of Great Moravia, r. 871-894

SUMMARY OF EVENT

The origin of the Magyars is obscure and half-legendary. Yet historians have surmised that the Magyars were originally a Finno-Ugric people, related to the Finns, the Estonians, and the Mordvinians. These peoples tended to be sedentary forest-dwellers. Sometime in the earlier centuries of the first millennium, the Magyars abandoned their sedentary way of life and adopted the nomadic habits of the Turks and other Altaic peoples of the steppes. It was at this time that they were given the name "On-Ogur" or "ten tribes," which later was corrupted by Europeans into "Hungarian" even though they always called themselves "Magyars" and continued to do so.

In this era, the steppes were in constant turmoil, and nomads constantly invaded westward toward Europe in search of food and territory. The most famous of these incursions was by the Huns in the mid-fifth century. Although Hungarian tradition sees the Huns as ancestors of the Hungarians, and although the famous Hunnish name Attila is a popular Hungarian given name, there is no evidence that the Huns were anything more than collateral relatives of the Magyars.

After the Huns, steppe people such as the Avars and Bulgars continued to pour into central Europe. Whereas the Bulgars occupied a corner of southeastern Europe and settled there permanently, the Avars, although amassing a large realm that included what is now Hungary and that posed a threat to the Byzantine Empire in the seventh century, never jelled into a sovereign nation-state. The Avar realm soon collapsed and was replaced by the state of Great Moravia, the first major Slav-dominated political entity. Traditionally, historians assumed that Great Moravia was in the area of Moravia (in what is now the Czech Republic). Lately, though, some scholars have claimed that Great Moravia actually lay in portions of Serbia stretching toward the Hungarian border and that only that location explains why Great Moravia had as much to do with Byzantium as with the Latin West. This is important because the location of Great Moravia explains exactly where the lands were that the Magyars initially conquered.

At the time of the height of Great Moravia's power, the Magyars were still living on the steppes, as vassals of the ethnically Turkish (and Jewish by religion) Khazar empire. Despite their Turkish lifestyle, the Magyars had retained their Finnish-related tongue, which enabled them to preserve their tribal identity. Because the Magyars had no written language and did not keep their own records, historical sources for the early Magyars are sparse, relying on Arabic, Greek, and Latin accounts far removed from the action. Nonetheless, a bare narrative of events can be pieced together. The Magyars left the Khazar confederation about 830 and moved westward to the Ukraine. They were just about to put down roots in this fertile breadbasket when pressed from the east by a ferocious Turkic tribe, the Pechenegs. The Pechenegs, who were later to establish an impermanent state on the shores of Romania and Moldova, also expelled some Khazar tribes who became attached to the Magyars in a grand federation. Recognizing the need to defend themselves against their opponents and secure a permanent home for all the tribes, the federation established a more stable leadership structure than was customary among the steppe peoples. The person chosen to lead this federation was a man named Árpád, a senior chief of the most powerful Magyar tribe.

The opportunities for the Magyars to attack central Europe had increased because of the decline of the Carolingian Empire, which had conquered the region under Charlemagne. By the 890's, the empire had been divided and subdivided into several states. The eastern, German portion was ruled by Arnulf, who had only a peripheral connection to Carolingian ancestry and whose legitimacy was thus questioned. Arnulf lay claim to the symbolic center of the empire in Rome, but his authority was strongly challenged by Lambert of Spoleto, the young son of the late Italian count Guido of Spoleto, who was not a Carolingian at all but who nevertheless mani-

An artist's rendition of Árpád, c. 896, leading the Magyar tribes to their new home in the Danube basin. (Hulton|Archive by Getty Images)

fested a claim to the throne of, at least, Italy. The Magyars probably could have taken advantage of this dissension to invade, but there was no need for this.

In a manner so often repeated throughout history, Arnulf willingly risked barbarians on his own soil in order to gain a temporary advantage over his opponent by asking the aid of the Magyars against Lambert. The Magyars swept into the central European plain in 892 and completely conquered Great Moravia, which had been attacking Arnulf on his east just as he was trying to subjugate Lambert on his south. King Zwentibald and much of the Moravian aristocracy were killed. Árpád and the other Magyar leaders were impressed by the space and fertility of the flatlands to the west of the Carpathian range and, given the presence of the Pechenegs on the Black Sea coast, decided to move the entire Magyar people there in 895 now that there was a vacuum after the end of the Moravian state. Arnulf was too busy with his other problems to prevent this.

The Magyars did not become vassals of Germany; they did not convert to Christianity or adopt Latin institutions. All this was to come later. Indeed, for several decades thereafter the Magyars lived and behaved like traditional steppe warriors, launching swift and massive invasions of Italy, Germany, France, and Serbia (often, as in the case of Arnulf, at the behest of embattled rulers of these countries who required aid) during which they captured booty and then quickly withdrew. A German attempt to conquer the Magyars was handily rebuffed at a battle near Bratislava in 907.

Significance

For Western Europeans, the Magyars represented as much of a problem as the ubiquitous Viking raids taking place at the same time, as is evidenced by the apparent derivation of the word "ogre" from "On-Ogur." A new wave of terrible barbarian invasions seemed set to undermine Carolingian culture much as late Roman culture had been disjointed by the Germanic tribes centuries before.

Yet what happened to the Magyars turned out to be different. Whereas the Huns, for instance, had amassed a large territory during the lifetime of Attila only to see it totally collapse with his death, the Magyars settled a more compact, easily cultivated territory in which they established a permanent stake and identity. Instead of merely subjugating the Slavic populace that remained from Great Moravia, the Magyars integrated the Slavs into their tribal structure and, to some extent, assimilated them. This was symbolized by the marriage of Árpád's son Zolta to a Moravian princess in 904.

A stabilizing secondary element in the ethnic mix were the Szekelers, a people related to the Avars who occupied a small but defined role in the Magyar realm. Historians are unsure whether the Szekelers had been part of the original Avar state or traveled in with the Magyars from the steppes.

—*Nicholas Birns*

Further Reading

Barraclough, Geoffrey. *The Crucible of Europe: The Ninth and Tenth Centuries in European History.* Berkeley: University of California Press, 1976. A general history of the period that places some emphasis on the Magyar invasion.

Bobula, Ida Miriam. *Origin of the Hungarian Nation.* Gainesville, Fla.: Danubian Research and Information Center, 1966. A speculative account heavily influenced by Hungarian nationalism, but has useful background information.

Bowlus, Charles R. *Franks, Moravians, and Magyars: The Struggle for the Middle Danube, 788-907.* Philadelphia: University of Pennsylvania Press, 1995. Controversial in its contention that Great Moravia was actually located in modern Serbia and a lightning rod for renewed debate about early Magyar history.

Kosztolnyik, Z. J. *Hungary Under the Early Árpáds, 890's to 1063.* Boulder, Colo.: East European Monographs, 2002. A historical survey of the House of Árpád. Discusses the early years of the Magyars, their migrations and settlement patterns, military campaigns, and more. Genealogical tables, maps, bibliography, index.

Lázár, István. *Hungary: A Brief History.* Translated by Albert Tezla. 6th ed. Budapest: Corvina Press, 2001. Presents a brief but concise history of Hungary, from its beginnings during the days of Árpád through the present day. Maps, index.

Lendavi, Paul. *The Hungarians: A Thousand Years of Victory in Defeat.* Translated by Ann Major. Princeton, N.J.: Princeton University Press, 2003. Comprehensively traces the history of the Hungarians from the Magyars' entry into the Carpathian region in the 890's to the end of the Cold War in the late twentieth century. Includes a summary, maps, chronology, bibliography, and an index.

McCartney, C. A. *The Magyars in the Ninth Century.* London: Cambridge University Press, 1968. Exhaustively detailed, scholarly account that is quite reliable and informative.

Riché, Pierre. *The Carolingians*. Philadelphia: University of Pennsylvania Press, 1993. Useful on the roles of Arnulf and Lambert in the events of the 890's.

Róna-Tas, András. *Hungarians and Europe in the Early Middle Ages: An Introduction to Early Hungarian History*. New York: Central European University Press, 1999. A comprehensive survey of the history of Hungary and a good introduction for general readers unfamiliar with the region. Maps, extensive bibliography, index.

Sugar, Peter F., ed. *A History of Hungary*. Bloomington: Indiana University Press, 1990. A readable and reliable account that is good for an elementary overview of Hungarian history.

SEE ALSO: 740: Khazars Convert to Judaism; 850-950: Viking Era; 893: Beginning of Bulgaria's Golden Age; August 10, 955: Otto I Defeats the Magyars; 1442-1456: János Hunyadi Defends Hungary Against the Ottomans.

RELATED ARTICLES in *Great Lives from History: The Middle Ages, 477-1453*: Árpád; Boris I of Bulgaria; Charlemagne; János Hunyadi; Saint László I; Otto I; Stephen I.

893
BEGINNING OF BULGARIA'S GOLDEN AGE

The beginning of Bulgaria's golden age, from the ascension of Symeon to the end of his reign in 927, witnessed Bulgaria's cultural and intellectual flowering, its territorial expansion, and its aspirations to capture the imperial city of Constantinople.

LOCALE: Bulgaria

CATEGORIES: Cultural and intellectual history; expansion and land acquisition; government and politics

KEY FIGURES

Boris I of Bulgaria (830-907), Bulgarian khan, r. 852-889

Symeon (863-927), czar of Bulgaria, r. 893-927

Leo VI (866-912), Byzantine emperor, r. 886-912

Alexander (870-913), Byzantine emperor, r. 912-913

Nicholas the Mystic (852-925), patriarch of Constantinople, 901-907 and 912-925

Constantine VII Porphyrogenitus (905-959), Byzantine emperor, r. 913-959

Zoe Karbonopsina (d. c. 920), Byzantine empress, r. 914-919

Romanus I Lecapenus (c. 870-948), Byzantine emperor, r. 920-944

SUMMARY OF EVENT

Bulgaria's golden age began with the reign of Symeon, following a church council convened in Preslav in 893. Boris I, the Bulgarian ruler who had first accepted Christianity in 864, left his kingdom to his eldest son Vladimir in 889 in order to retire to a monastery. Vladimir, however, consorted with the aristocratic Bulgar boyars to overturn the Christian religion that Boris had introduced. Clergy were persecuted, the alliance with Byzantium was dropped in favor of one with King Arnulf of Germany, and a revival of paganism seemed imminent.

After four years of this retrograde regime, Boris reappeared in Pliska, the capital, recovered the crown, and deposed and blinded his son. Boris then called a church council in 893, which recognized Vladimir's deposition and proclaimed Symeon the new ruler and Christianity the state religion, with Slavonic the state language instead of Greek. The new capital was to be Preslav instead of the former capital Pliska.

Symeon, the younger son of Boris, was trained for a religious vocation, having spent almost ten years as a novice at a Byzantine monastery in Constantinople. While there, he had also received a secular education and was well versed in the philosophical and literary culture of his day. He had returned to Bulgaria in 888 to pursue Greek studies and to oversee the translation of Greek religious and historical texts into Bulgarian. In 893, he became czar of Bulgaria.

By this time also, the Slavicization of the Turkic Bulgars, the conquerors of the indigenous Slavic population, was practically complete, the more numerous Slavs having assimilated the Bulgars both linguistically and culturally. This assimilation had come about through intermarriage, trade, Christianization, and the numerical superiority of the Slavs.

Soon after his accession, Symeon came into conflict with the Byzantine Empire over the expulsion from Constantinople of Bulgarian merchants trading there. He invaded the imperial domains in Thrace and let his troops

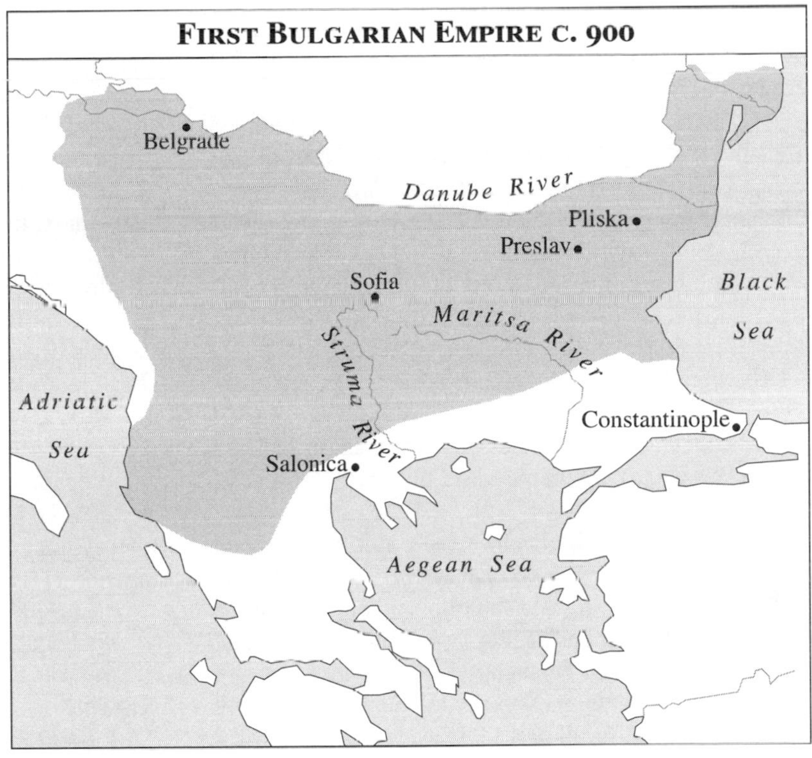

lay waste to the countryside. When the Byzantine emperor retaliated, his troops were defeated by those of Symeon. The emperor then mobilized a larger force, including the Magyars, which caused Symeon to sue for peace. Symeon's secret negotiations with the Pechenegs, a central Asian nomadic people, however, served to divert the Magyars from the Bulgarian flank and enabled him to continue his quarrel with Leo VI, the Byzantine emperor. Symeon demanded the return of all Bulgarian captives and, unsatisfied, engaged the imperial army at Bulgarophygon in Thrace and triumphed.

The Bulgarians and Byzantines signed a treaty in 897, whereby the Byzantines agreed to pay the Bulgarians tribute, commercial rights of Bulgarian traders were restored in Constantinople, and Symeon was given some territory along the frontier.

From 902 to 904, the Arabs were depredating the Aegean area, especially the coast of Thessaly and the Peloponnesus. In 904, they captured Thessaloniki but later withdrew with prisoners and booty. Symeon used this opportunity to garner further territory from the Byzantine Empire in return for refraining from attacking the devastated city. He acquired parts of Thrace and obtained Byzantine recognition for Bulgarian dominion over most of Macedonia. This allowed Bulgaria to claim sovereignty over Slavic tribes west of the original Bulgarian state.

With Emperor Leo VI's death in 912 and the ascension of his brother Alexander, a number of new political figures came into power, among them the former patriarch Nicholas the Mystic. Nicholas had been deposed by Leo for refusing to acknowledge his fourth marriage, from which the future emperor, Constantine VII Porphyrogenitus, had sprung.

Alexander alienated Symeon by refusing to pay tribute to his envoys under the terms of the 897 treaty. This refusal gave Symeon the pretext he needed for launching an attack on Byzantium, which he did by spring of 913. Shortly thereafter, the degenerate Byzantine emperor Alexander died, leaving the seven-year-old Constantine VII under the regency of Nicholas the Mystic, with Constantine's mother Zoe Karbonopsina exiled to a monastery.

In August of 913, Symeon led his army to the massive walls surrounding Constantinople, claiming the emperor's crown for himself. Symeon, educated in Constantinople, sometimes called the half-Greek, and filled with imperial ambition, wished to be recognized as the sole "Roman" emperor of a combined Greek-Bulgarian state. Like so many of his precursors, however, Symeon was unable to break through the thick walls surrounding the city.

The patriarch and regent Nicholas agreed to meet and confer with Symeon, and, in so doing, placed a crown on Symeon's head. Nicholas also agreed to a marriage between the young Constantine and Symeon's daughter. Whether this coronation was genuine or a sham is disputed by scholars, as is the nature of the crown with which Symeon was honored. At any rate, Symeon believed that he, as future father-in-law of the future Byzantine emperor, had come closer to the throne of the Byzantine Empire, his ultimate goal.

Shortly after this "coronation" early in 914, Constantine's mother Zoe Karbonopsina returned to the capital, led a palace coup, replaced Nicholas as regent, and reversed Symeon's marriage plans for her son. The infuriated Symeon, frustrated in his hopes, retaliated by resuming his war against the empire, which he continued for the next decade.

For the next five years, Symeon's campaign in the Balkans was largely successful as he moved from one conquest to another. Symeon and the Byzantine army clashed at Anchialos on the Black Sea on August 20, 917. The Byzantines were routed. Then Symeon invaded Serbia, which had earlier been consorting with the Byzantines, and placed his own candidate, Pavel, on the Serbian throne. He then proceeded to attack Greece.

Then, in 919, the regent Zoe was deposed in Byzantium by the admiral Romanus I Lecapenus, who married his own daughter to the hapless Constantine. He then had himself crowned coemperor with Constantine VII in December, 920.

Disappointed in his own imperial ambitions, Symeon overran Thrace. Now the Serbian crown went to Zaharije, the Bulgarian's candidate. Zaharije, however, proved to be unreliable and turned against his kingmaker, defeating Symeon's troops and beheading his officers.

Symeon then attempted to create a navy by proposing an alliance with the Fāṭimid Dynasty in North Africa. When the Byzantines subverted this plan, he finally agreed to meet with Romanus. His imperial designs foiled, Symeon turned a large army against Serbia in 924 and annexed it, greatly increasing his state, and reoccupied several cities in Thrace. In 926, he launched an invasion against his new neighbor to the west, Croatia, then at the height of its fortunes under its king, Tomislav. This attack was repelled, and Symeon made peace with Tomislav.

In 927, Symeon set out once again against the Byzantine Empire, but died on the road, never having achieved his ultimate goal of becoming emperor of the Romans.

SIGNIFICANCE

Under Symeon's military leadership, Bulgaria failed to capture Constantinople, but in the cultural realm, Symeon's reign saw the flourishing of the new Bulgarian capital Preslav, which became a monastic, cultural, and crafts center. Also, the Bulgarian Orthodox Church first became independent of Greek clergy. Symeon fully supported the adaptation of Greek liturgical texts to the Slavic vernacular, as well as the translation of numerous secular literary texts. Bulgaria at this time was experiencing a flourishing of the literary arts, not only continuing and expanding on the mission of the disciples Cyril and Methodius but even carrying this work to other Slavic nations within the Byzantine sphere of influence. The new capital, Preslav, rivaled Constantinople in the splendor of its royal palace, which the new czar constructed by importing builders and artists from the imperial capital.

—*Gloria Fulton*

FURTHER READING

Browning, Robert. *Byzantium and Bulgaria: A Comparative Study Across the Early Medieval Frontier.* Berkeley: University of California Press, 1975. Focuses on the ninth and tenth centuries and the relationship between Byzantium and Bulgaria.

Crampton, R. J. *A Concise History of Bulgaria.* New York: Cambridge University Press, 1997. Includes a brief discussion of Symeon in the chapter on medieval Bulgaria.

Fine, John. *The Early Medieval Balkans: A Critical Survey from the Sixth to the Late Twelfth Century.* Ann Arbor: University of Michigan Press, 1983. A scholarly work stressing the many uncertainties about the historical sources for the earliest Bulgarian period. Chapter 5 examines the reign of Symeon.

Obolensky, Dimitri. *The Byzantine Commonwealth: Eastern Europe, 500-1453.* New York: Praeger, 1971. Historical and geographical study of the nations of Eastern Europe, particularly the Slavs, during the Byzantine Empire.

Runciman, Steven. *A History of the First Bulgarian Empire.* London: Bell, 1930. A classic history of the first Bulgarian Empire, focusing on religious and political developments from the earliest times to 1014.

Shepard, Jonathan. "The Ruler as Instructor, Pastor, and Wise: Leo VI of Byzantium and Simeon of Bulgaria." In *Alfred the Great: Papers from the Eleventh-Centenary Conferences*, edited by Timothy Reuter. Burlington, Vt.: Ashgate, 2003. A discussion of the relationship between the two rulers and their governance of their respective peoples.

Tzvetkov, Plamen. *A History of the Balkans: A Regional Overview from a Bulgarian Perspective.* 2 vols. San Francisco: Edwin Mellen Press, 1993. Volume 1 covers the early period, giving the Bulgarian version of the historical events.

SEE ALSO: c. 850: Development of the Slavic Alphabet; 864: Boris Converts to Christianity; 890's: Magyars Invade Italy, Saxony, and Bavaria; 1054: Beginning of the Rome-Constantinople Schism.

RELATED ARTICLES in *Great Lives from History: The Middle Ages, 477-1453*: Basil the Macedonian; Boris I of Bulgaria; Saint Cyril and Saint Methodius.

Early 10th century
QARAKHANIDS CONVERT TO ISLAM

Satuq Bughra Khān of the Eastern Turkish Qarakhanid Dynasty compelled his people to adopt Islam. They were the first Turks to be drawn into the Islamic world.

LOCALE: Xinjiang (Sinkiang), China
CATEGORIES: Cultural and intellectual history; religion

KEY FIGURES

Satuq Bughra Khān (d. c. 955), Qarakhanid ruler, r. ?-c. 955
Abū'l-Naṣr Sāmāni (fl. tenth century), Sufi mystic and teacher

SUMMARY OF EVENT

During the ninth century, and coinciding with the decline in authority of the Tang Dynasty (T'ang; 618-907), in the region now known as Xinjiang (Sinkiang), various Turkish peoples—Karluk, Yaghma, and Chighil—began to coalesce around a ruling family, known to modern scholars as the Qarakhanids (Karakhanids), who themselves may have been descended from one of the prominent clans among the Karluk. Like previous Eastern Turkish tribal confederacies, such as the Uighurs (744-840), Kirghiz, and Karluk, the majority of Qarakhanids were pastoral nomads practicing a shamanism tinged in the oases by Buddhism, Nestorian Christianity, and Manichaeanism. The earliest history of the Qarakhanids is unrecorded, but between 992 and 1211, they ruled a vast swathe of territory, comprising the Tarim Basin (Xinjiang, China), the western Tian Shan, Semirechye (southeastern Kazakhstan), the Farghana valley (Kyrgyzstan/Tajikistan), and Transoxiana (Uzbekistan/Kazakhstan). Their headquarters were at Balasaghun in the Chu River Valley, but following their conversion to Islam, Kashgar increasingly served as a religious and cultural center.

No medieval Islamic dynasty has a more obscure history. There are no surviving dynastic chronicles, and the course of events has to be reconstructed from accounts by hostile neighbors. Even the chronology is uncertain, because the dynasty observed a system of decentralized rule, with a supreme khaghan taking precedence over family members who held separate territorial appanages. When the khaghan died, appanage rulers moved up the hierarchy in a game of musical chairs made more complicated by internecine strife among familial rivals, a process that makes the numismatic history of the dynasty exceptionally confusing.

The term "Qarakhanid" is a construct of nineteenth century European Orientalism, based on the fact that, according to the eleventh century lexicographer Maḥmūd Kāshgarī, the Turkish word *kara* ("black," also meaning "northern" and "powerful"), occurring frequently in their titulature, denoted a rank among these rulers, as did the term *ilek-khan* (or *ilig-khan*), by which they are also known. Contemporary Islamic writers referred to them as al-Khakaniyya, and the Persian literary tradition styled them al-i Afrasiab, linking them to the legendary Afrasiab, king of Turan, in *Shahnamah* (c. 1010; the book of kings).

The Qarakhanids were the first Turkish people to become Muslims. Islamization came to them through four distinct processes. First, they were exposed to *jihads* (holy wars) by their Muslim neighbors. An example of this was the campaign of 893 by the Persian Sāmānids against the Turks of Talas (Dzhambul, Kyrgystan), in which the Nestorian church was converted into a mosque, as related in the *Tārīkh-i Bukhārā* (ninth century; history of Bukhara) by Abū Bakr Muḥammad ibn Jafar Narshakhī. Second, they could be influenced by the religious practices of itinerant Muslim merchants through a process of osmosis. Third, the same process could operate very powerfully through the presence of Muslim Sufis (mystics), some of whom were quietists but others *ghāzīs* (holy warriors) in the Muslim borderlands. Finally, and perhaps most effectively, an already converted Turkish chieftain might compel his followers to subscribe to his newly acquired beliefs. This was what happened in the case of the Qarakhanids.

During the first half of the tenth century, a Qarakhanid ruler, Satuq Bughra Khān, a descendant and possibly the grandson of the first Qarakhanid khaghan, became a convert to Islam, taking the Muslim name of ʿAbd al-Karim and vigorously imposing his beliefs on his followers. Although he was undoubtedly a historical figure, the facts of his life became overlaid with legendary material, preserved in Sufi devotional works such as the *Tadhkira yi Bughra Khani* (history of Bughra Khān) or *Tadhkira-yi Uwaysiyya* (c. 1600; history of the Uwaysis) of Ahmad Uzgani. Linked with his conversion was another, possibly legendary, figure, Abūʾl-Naṣr Sāmāni, whose name points to a connection with the Sāmānid Dynasty of Bukhara (819-1005) or with the Sāmānid realm (Transoxiana). According to tradition, Abūʾl-Naṣr combined the occupations of merchant, man of learning, and missionary. In a dream, the Prophet Muḥammad instructed him to search out and convert a man from Turkistan, who would thereafter spread the faith among the Turks. After much wandering, Abū'l-Naṣr learned that the person for whom he was searching was a boy living in Kashgar. This was Satuq Bughra Khān.

Satuq Bughra Khān's father died when he was seven, and in accordance with Turkish custom, his mother then married her late husband's brother, Hārūn Bughra Khān. At the age of twelve, Satuq Bughra Khān, although still a pagan, one day encountered a hare (among the shamanist Turks, animals, especially the hare, were venerated as transmitters of wisdom to humans). In one account, it then transformed itself into a Sufi master (in other accounts, it became Khidr, the Green Man of ancient folklore, or an angel), teaching him to say "there is no God but God and Muḥammad is his Prophet" and alerting him to the coming of Abū'l-Naṣr.

While he was out hunting with his companions, Satuq Bughra Khān encountered Abū'l-Naṣr, made the full declaration of faith, and acknowledged Abū'l-Naṣr as his teacher. For a while, he and his companions practiced Islam secretly, but his uncle and stepfather, Hārūn Bughra Khān, got wind of his conversion and plotted his death. When divine intervention purportedly caused the unbelievers to fall into a deep sleep, Satuq Bughra Khān entered his uncle's room with the intention of killing him. His conscience, however, restrained him, as his uncle had been like a father to him, but his dilemma was solved when God caused the ground to open and his uncle was swallowed up. In an alternative account of these events, related by a Qarakhanid envoy in Baghdad in 1005 and preserved in the writings of the Ottoman historian Ahmed Dede Müneccimbaşi (c. 1702), Satuq Bughra Khān obtained a *fatwa* (legal opinion) from a *faqih* (religious scholar) in Bukhara authorizing him to commit parricide.

Having overcome all opposition, Satuq Bughra Khān compelled the people of Kashgar to accept Islam, subsequently spending his summers waging war against the unbelievers in the borderlands and his winters at his devotions in Kashgar. A near-contemporary historian, Ibn Miskawayh, reported that within a decade of the ruler's death, 200,000 Turkish tents (households) had adopted Islam, and his tomb became a place of pilgrimage, which it remains to this day.

Thereafter, the Qarakhanid realm was regarded as a fully fledged Muslim state, but under Satuq Bughra Khān's grandsons, two separate khanates emerged. One grandson ruled the eastern khanate, consisting of Kashgaria, Semirechye, and eastern Farghana, while the other ruled the western khanate, encompassing Transoxiana and western Farghana. Their descendants quickly assimilated the Perso-Islamic traditions long established in Transoxiana, building mosques and caravansaries, and emulating as literary patrons the Sāmānids, whom they had ousted from Bukhara in 992. The twelfth century belleletrist Neẓāmī lists thirteen Qarakhanid court-poets writing in Persian.

Unlike such Turkish dynasties as the Ghaznavids (997-1186) and the Seljuks (1038-1194), the Qarakhanids preserved many aspects of traditional pre-Islamic Turkish culture, such as those that still survived in the Uighur kingdom of Qocho (850-1250), near Turfan (Xinjiang). From Qarakhanid times come two of the earliest Turkish literary texts, Maḥmūd Kāshgarī's *Dīwān lughāt al-Turk* (1074; *Compendium of the Turkic Dialects*, 1982-1985), a Turkish-Arabic dictionary written to show that Turkish was the equal of Arabic as a vehicle of literary expression, still invaluable for the study of early Turkish dialects; and *Kutadgú biliğ* (1070; *Wisdom of Royal Glory*, 1983) by Yūsuf Khāss Ḥājib of Balasaghun, a Turkish "mirror for princes" saturated with Sufi thought and imagery. One of the charismatic Sufi shaykhs who lived under the Qarakhanids was Ahmed Yesevi (d. 1166), founder of the dervish-order of the Yasawiyya. His *Dīwān-i hekmet*, an anthology of short mystical poems written in Turkish in a genre of mystical folk literature, contributed powerfully to the diffusion of Islam among the Central Asian steppe peoples.

SIGNIFICANCE

Through Satuq Bughra Khān, the Qarakhanids were the first Turks to be drawn into the Islamic world. Their melding of Islamic high culture with elements of indigenous pre-Islamic folklore as well as Sufism gave a distinctive character to the beliefs and practices of the Muslim Turks of this part of China, who continue to maintain them to this day.

—*Gavin R. G. Hambly*

FURTHER READING

Baldick, Julian. *Imaginary Muslims: The Uwaysi Sufis of Central Asia*. New York: New York University Press, 1993. Essential for the Sufi dimension.

Dankoff, R. *Wisdom of Royal Glory: A Turko-Islamic Mirror for Princes*. Chicago: University of Chicago Press, 1983. Translation of *Kutadgú biliğ*.

Dankoff, R., and J. Kelly. *Compendium of the Turkic Di-*

alects. 3 vols. Cambridge, Mass.: Harvard University, 1982-1985. Translation of *Dīwān lughāt al-Turk*.

Golden, Peter B. "The Karakhanids and Early Islam." In *The Cambridge History of Early Inner Asia*, edited by Denis Sinor. Cambridge, England: Cambridge University Press, 1990. Most detailed account in English.

Soucek, Svat. *A History of Inner Asia*. Cambridge, England: Cambridge University Press, 2000. Useful additional account that also provides background.

SEE ALSO: 744-840: Uighur Turks Rule Central Asia; 840-846: Uighur Migrations; 956: Oğhuz Turks Migrate to Transoxiana.

10th century
CULT OF QUETZALCÓATL SPREADS THROUGH MESOAMERICA

Worship of the feathered serpent god of regeneration, Quetzalcóatl, intensified with the end of the stability and prosperity of the Classical period in Mesoamerican cultures, a decline that started around the ninth century.

LOCALE: Mesoamerica (central highlands of Mexico to Guatemala and Honduras)

CATEGORIES: Cultural and intellectual history; religion

KEY FIGURES

Quetzalcóatl, deity

Topiltzin-Quetzalcóatl (935 or 947-c. 987), evangelist and prophet of the cult of Quetzalcóatl

SUMMARY OF EVENT

The earliest hunter-gatherers settling in Mesoamerica came upon an environment rich in flora and fauna. Most intimidating and impressive among the local animals were the jaguar and the snake. Almost three thousand years ago the Olmec culture, along the fertile coast of the Gulf of Mexico, produced a surplus of food that allowed the development of a more complex social and cultural organization.

Along with many other animals, the Olmecs came to worship a snake whose scales were enlarged and considered feathers. This feathered serpent represented a union of the forces of the earth and the air, of wind and life, and became a symbol of vital force and regeneration. The richest manifestation of this symbol was the serpent (*cóatl* in the later Nahuatl language) with the rare and beautiful long green tail feathers of the *quetzalli* bird. Thus emerged the feathered or plumed serpent god, Quetzalcóatl. The mouth of the serpent acquired the fierce features of a beast, akin to a Chinese dragon, with especially prominent teeth emphasizing its force or power. The feathered serpent deity penetrated into all subsequent Mesoamerican cultures and was a core motif of the Classical flowering of Mesoamerican culture from the fourth to seventh centuries.

The cultures of this region produced numerous achievements in agriculture, commerce and trade, urban organization, religion, warfare, and science. However, for reasons not wholly clear, their stability and achievements diminished and disappeared during the seventh to ninth centuries.

Successive attempts were made to restore the classic wealth and stability of the past. The Toltecs were singularly successful in this effort. Toltec culture grew along the northern edge and then through the fertile Valley of Mexico. During the tenth to twelfth centuries, the Toltecs revived, consolidated, and refined the religious, cultural, and technical achievements of the previous age.

Central to this revival was the Toltec high priest and ruler Ce Acatl Topiltzin, born in 935 or 947. His name referred to the time of his birth—Acatl means the year "one reed"—and the honorific Topiltzin means "young lord or prince." He trained in the great religious and commercial center, Teotihuacán, which was reviving Classical learning. Among its many prominent buildings was the noted temple to Quetzalcóatl. In an era eager to revive stability and prosperity, a cult emerged that deified Quetzalcóatl as a principal god. Ce Acatl Topiltzin identified himself with this god to the point that he changed his name to Topiltzin-Quetzalcóatl, or Lord Quetzalcóatl.

However, as Teotihuacán declined, the Toltecs assumed a central role in Mesoamerican culture and the Classical revival. North of Teotihuacán, they founded their own capital, Tula, which developed as the most authoritative and influential center for the revival and spread of renewed Classical culture. As the high priest-ruler of Tula, Topiltzin-Quetzalcóatl grounded its religious beliefs in his namesake deity. He insisted, however, that worship of the god Quetzalcóatl not include human

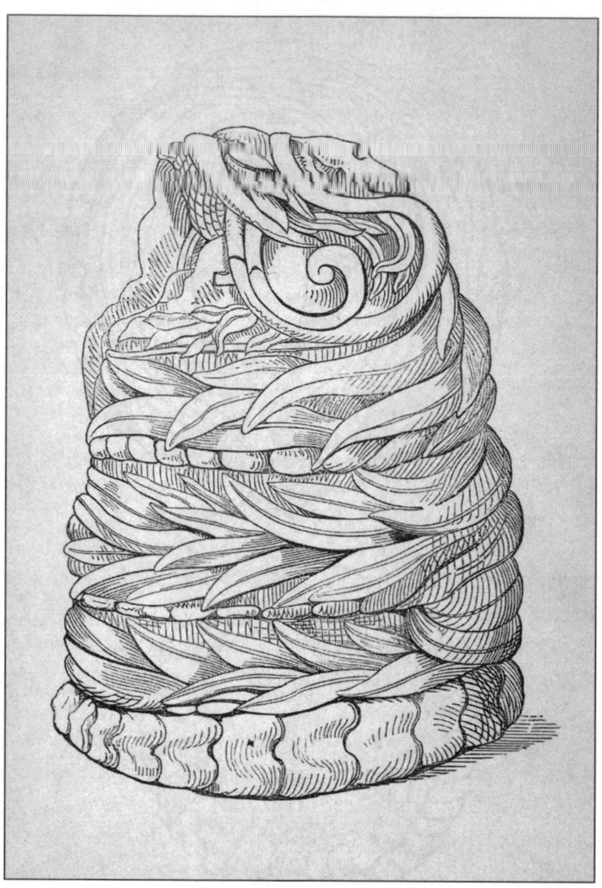

The cult of Quetzalcóatl worshiped the life force as a snake (cóatl) *with the feathers of the quetzalli bird.* (Hulton|Archive by Getty Images)

sacrifice. Against this heresy, orthodox forces mounted a campaign against him and a loyal core of followers that resulted in their exile from Tula. This flight led to an evangelical advance of the cult of Quetzalcóatl and of Topiltzin-Quetzalcóatl as the god's evangelist.

Moving eastward toward the Gulf of Mexico, Topiltzin-Quetzalcóatl remained for some time in Cholula, an ancient religious center noted for its mammoth pyramid. At some point, Lord Quetzalcóatl, or someone with a similar name, then advanced as far as the Yucatán peninsula, the center of northern Maya culture. Here the deity Quetzalcóatl and his prophet came to be worshiped under the name Kukulcán and were incorporated into the temple complex at Chichén Itzá. Penetrating farther south into Guatemala, this identity changed to Gucumatz and was incorporated into the Maya epic *Popol Vuh*, written by an unknown Maya author (or authors) between 1554 and 1558.

Written in Quiché Mayan hieroglyph, *Popol Vuh* is the creation myth of the Maya people, recounting their origins and the legends of their gods and heroes. Quetzalcóatl (or Gucumatz) and his prophet appear prominently in this work. Worship of this god was reaching its peak as *Popol Vuh* achieved its final written form. The Mayan legends of the previous centuries were incorporated into this climactic text to preserve them against the cultural onslaught of the Spanish conquest in the early sixteenth century. This epic, therefore, has become a crucial document in preserving the historical sweep of the legend and worship of Quetzalcóatl.

Another significant advance of the cult occurred back in the Valley of Mexico. Much as the Toltecs had replaced Teotihuacan, the Aztecs now replaced the former when Tula was destroyed in 1168. In the following century, the Aztecs centered their culture in the southern reaches of the great lake dominating the Valley of Mexico. Their capital of Tenochtitlán emerged as a rich agricultural region that resulted from draining surrounding swamp land. It became a hallowed center of Quetzalcóatl. Moreover, all rulers had to claim descent from Topiltzin-Quetzalcóatl, and they did so until the time of the conquest.

SIGNIFICANCE

Quetzalcóatl and his evangelist Topiltzin-Quetzalcóatl present an exceptional microcosm of religious evolution within the changing circumstances of economic, religious, cultural, and social conditions in Mesoamerica over two millennia.

Topiltzin-Quetzalcóatl and his efforts to advance the worship of Quetzalcóatl recall significantly other events in religious and cultural history. The waning classical culture of Greece was revived and spread as Hellenism throughout the ancient world by the conquering hero, Alexander the Great. During almost the same period as Topiltzin-Quetzalcóatl, the Spanish hero El Cid advanced Catholicism and Castilian Spanish against the Moors in Iberia. The flight of Topiltzin-Quetzalcóatl from Tula recalls that of Muḥammad from Mecca to Medina.

The development of the cult worship of Quetzalcóatl and of his prophet Topiltzin-Quetzalcóatl reflects critical conditions in the culture of late medieval Mesoamerica. Instability and impoverishment had replaced the glories of the Classical period. A divine force of regeneration was sought, and a forceful agent to harness that energy amassed faithful adherents. This renewed native religious revival was defeated, however, by foreign invaders, subsumed under the religion of the conqueror. Nonetheless, as the colonial power itself waned, Topiltzin-Quetzalcóatl re-emerged as a symbol of enduring force against occupation and submission.

—*Edward A. Riedinger*

FURTHER READING

Anaya, Rudolfo A. *Lord of the Dawn: The Legend of Quetzalcóatl*. Albuquerque: University of New Mexico Press, 1987. Narrative recounting of the life and exploits of Topiltzin-Quetzalcóatl with a glossary of Nahuatl terms and names.

Brundage, Burr Cartwright. *The Phoenix of the Western World: Quetzalcóatl and the Sky Religion*. Norman: University of Oklahoma Press, 1982. Traces various meanings and manifestations of Quetzalcóatl as a religious phenomenon in Aztec and other Mesoamerican cultures. Contains numerous black-and-white illustrations.

Carrasco, Davíd. *Quetzalcóatl and the Irony of Empire: Myths and Prophecies in the Aztec Tradition*. Rev. ed. Boulder: University Press of Colorado, 2000. A noted revisionist scholar of Quetzalcóatl and of Mesoamerican religions examines the ongoing interest in Quetzalcóatl in Mexican history. Some black-and-white illustrations.

Florescano, Enrique. *The Myth of Quetzalcóatl*. Translated by Lysa Hochroth. Baltimore: Johns Hopkins University Press, 1999. Reviews Quetzalcóatl as myth and history, emphasizes his sustaining role as a cultural hero, and reviews historic texts showing the development of the legend over time.

Lafaye, Jacques. *Quetzalcóatl and Guadelupe: The Formation of Mexican National Consciousness, 1531-1813*. Translated by Benjamin Keen. Chicago: University of Chicago Press, 1987. Traces competing social and political forces in Mexico regarding the use of key religious figures as expressions of national spirit and objectives.

Meyer, Michael C., William L. Sherman, and Susan M. Deeds. *The Course of Mexican History*. 6th ed. New York: Oxford University Press, 1999. A 732-page history of Mexico, including the time of Quetzalcóatl. Maps, bibliography, and index

Nicholson, Henry B. *Toplitzin Quetzalcóatl: The Once and Future Lord of the Toltecs*. Boulder: University Press of Colorado, 2001. A thorough analysis of surviving primary sources, from the pre- and post-conquest periods, of the Quetzalcóatl phenomenon.

SEE ALSO: c. 610-632: Muḥammad Receives Revelations; c. 700-1000: Building of Chichén Itzá; c. 950-1150: Toltecs Build Tula; November 1, 1092-June 15, 1094: El Cid Conquers Valencia; 1325-1519: Aztecs Build Tenochtitlán.

RELATED ARTICLES in *Great Lives from History: The Middle Ages, 477-1453*: El Cid; Itzcóatl; Muḥammad.

10th-11th centuries
FIRST HAUSA STATE ESTABLISHED

Hausa city-states, which were economically and politically autonomous and independently governed, serve as examples of state building far different from the more typical empire building in western African history. Also, the Hausa were among the earliest Africans to convert to Islam because of their connections with Saharan traders.

LOCALE: Hausa states (northern Nigeria and southern Niger)

CATEGORY: Government and politics

KEY FIGURE

Bayajidda (fl. tenth-eleventh century), probable legendary founder of the Hausa city-states

SUMMARY OF EVENT

Archaeological, linguistic, and written records indicate that the Hausa people, culture, and language emerged in northern Nigeria and southern Niger by the early tenth century. Unlike other parts of the western Sudan that commonly employed centralized kingdoms and empire-building strategies, the Hausa relied on a system organized around political self-sufficiency and autonomy.

The Hausa population is viewed as a single ethnic group in modern times, but in the tenth century, the people speaking the Hausa language and practicing customs associated with Hausa culture came from a variety of ethnic and social backgrounds. This diversity among the Hausa includes not only the Chadic inspiration but also Sudanic influences. Hausa, a language from the Chadic branch of the Afro-Asiatic family of languages, became significant in the Niger-Nigeria borderlands and encompassed a cultural domain that distinguished the Hausa from their neighbors.

With the centralization of settlement and the rise of the city-state, the Hausa culture began to take root. One of the primary urban centers in Hausa history is Kano. Archaeological evidence demonstrates that Kano was a site of ironworking as early as the seventh century, indicating that it was inhabited permanently or intermittently by people even before the city-states arose in the tenth century.

According to Hausa oral traditions, the political founder of the Hausa city-states was a man named Bayajidda, who traveled to what is now Nigeria from the east in an attempt to escape his father's control after they quarreled. This Hausa account of the origins of their political leadership links them to an important hero. According to tradition, Bayajidda was the son of the king of Baghdad and a Muslim, linking the Hausa to an important medieval Islamic state.

The tradition surrounding Bayajidda is significant because it indicates the Hausa were Islamized after the tenth century. Tradition says that Bayajidda first went to the city of Gaya, where he commissioned several blacksmiths to create a powerful knife for him. He then proceeded to Daura, which was near what is now called Kano in northern Nigeria. In Kano, Bayajidda learned of a sacred snake guarding a well, which kept the Daura residents from drawing water. Wielding his powerful knife, Bayajidda slew the mighty serpent. The queen of Daura married Bayajidda to demonstrate gratitude for his assistance. The couple produced seven healthy sons who went on to rule each of the seven Hausa city-states, collectively called Hausa Bakwai.

For the Hausa people, the choice of political rulers was determined by ancestry. Anyone with the ability to trace their family lines to Bayajidda was considered of the royal lineage. Thus the traced line of Bayajidda typically ruled Hausaland. Knowing whether these hereditary ties were authentic or fashioned to advance social status is less significant than understanding how important the Islamic connection was to this emerging Muslim polity.

Scholars have uncovered data that link the Hausa to the history, populations, and geography of the Lake Chad region. Historians contend that in ancient times the Hausa ancestors migrated westward into northern Nigeria-southern Niger (Hausaland) after Lake Chad receded, with some populations migrating to new lands. This implies that the Hausa ancestors came from a tradition of river- and lake-based economies and cultures. The Kanem-Borno populations, just east of Hausaland, share many cultural elements with the Hausa, such as oral traditions, music, and riding horses. Scholars have also discovered evidence that places Hausa origins to the north of Hausaland. This theory contends that the people who settled northern Nigeria were an offshoot of populations who utilized the resources of the Sahara Desert as nonsedentary pastoralists.

The competing theories on the early Hausa as either aquatic- and agricultural-based or pastoralists herding livestock indicate that the early populations that settled in the regions that became the Hausa city-states were from several different economic, cultural, and ethnic backgrounds. It also would mean that the Kano (and other Hausa city-state) settlers adopted a single language (Hausa) and over time adopted a body of common cultural practices.

The seven states of Hausaland were named Kano, Rano, Katsina, Zaria, Biram, Daura, and Gobir. Each of the city-states was known for its specialized and particular trade products. Kano and Rano were known as cities of the "chiefs of indigo." Geographically, these areas were made up of plains, ideal for growing cotton. The people of Kano and Rano were renowned weavers and indigo-cloth dyers. They wove and dyed the cloth into the famous indigo that is a trademark of the Hausa people. This indigo-dyed cloth was a commodity in high demand and was sent far beyond the borders of Hausaland on trade caravans. The indigo cloth produced in the states of Kano and Rano made these places strong economically. Hausa traders accumulated wealth by controlling the transfer of trade between regions without forming a strong centralized, vastly powerful state, unlike many of their neighbors to the west and south.

Biram became the center of government. The greater political administration of the Hausa confederation was maintained from Biram. Zaria became the "chief of slaves," as it provided slave labor to all parts of Hausaland. Zaria was densely populated and could most afford to export labor. Katsina and Daura were the "chiefs of the market" because their northern location was ideal for receiving caravans from the Sahara. Trans-Saharan trade that came into Hausaland first passed through one of these two northern city-states. Gobir was the "chief of war" because its western location put it closer to rival empires such as Ghana and Songhai. The people of Gobir were responsible for raising the military force for the defense of Hausaland on the western frontier and beyond.

SIGNIFICANCE

The formation of the Hausa city-state exemplifies a political confederation of independent and small but powerful and successful polities. The commercial activity of each of the city-states created a profitable market in Hausaland that benefited each of the independent and economically competing cities.

An undated Egyptian sword was uncovered at a Hausa palace in Daura, demonstrating trade connections or some type of relationship between the Hausa traders and Egypt. Hausaland's trade connections reached far beyond Sudanic Africa.

The Hausa adopted Islam very early as Islam migrated through Africa, but it was the specific Hausa style of syncretic worship that was greatly responsible for the widespread purification of Islam in the *jihads* of Usman de Fodio in the nineteenth century. After a series of *jihads*, Hausaland was unified under the Islamic leadership of de Fodio. A millennium after the founding of the Hausa city-states, Hausaland underwent a process of full Islamic conversion for the vast majority of its population.

—*Evan Scott Shuey and Catherine Cymone Fourshey*

FURTHER READING

Augi, Abdullahi Rafi. "A Consideration of the Relations Between Kano and Western Hausaland Before the Nineteenth Century." In *Kano and Some of Her Neighbours*, edited by Bawuro M. Barkindo. Kano, Nigeria: Ahmadu Bello University Press, 1989. An examination of Hausa culture and history in precolonial times.

Collins, Robert O. "Kano Chronicle." In *Western African History*. Princeton, N.J.: Wiener, 1997. An oral account of Hausa history. Primary document.

Hansen, Mogens Herman, ed. *A Comparative Study of Thirty City-State Cultures: An Investigation*. Copenhagen, Denmark: Kongelige Danske Videnskabernes Selskab, 2000. This work is an examination of how to define the city-state and its culture. Draws examples from various parts of the world and includes a chapter on Hausa city-states of the fifteenth century.

Smith, M. G. *Government in Kano, 1350-1950*. Boulder, Colo.: Westview Press, 1997. This work surveys Hausa political history between the fourteenth and twentieth centuries.

SEE ALSO: 11th-15th centuries: Development of the Ife Kingdom and Yoruba Culture; c. 1010: Songhai Kingdom Converts to Islam; c. 1100: Founding of Timbuktu; 1230's-1255: Reign of Sundiata of Mali.

RELATED ARTICLE in *Great Lives from History: The Middle Ages, 477-1453*: Mansa Mūsā.

907-960

PERIOD OF FIVE DYNASTIES AND TEN KINGDOMS

After the collapse of the Tang Dynasty, China entered into a period of social and political chaos.

LOCALE: China

CATEGORIES: Government and politics; wars, uprisings, and civil unrest

KEY FIGURES

Huang Chao (Huang Ch'ao; d. 884), Chinese intellectual who began a rebellion that would eventually bring down the Tang Dynasty

Zhu Wen (Chu Wen; 852-912), founder of the Later Liang Dynasty, r. 907-912

Li Cunxu (Li Ts'un-hsü; d. 926), founder of the Later Tang Dynasty, r. 923-926

Shi Jingtang (Shih Ching-t'ang; d. 944), founder of the Later Jin Dynasty, r. 936-944

Liu Zhiyuan (Liu Chih-yüan; d. 948), founder of the Later Han Dynasty, r. 947-948

Guo Wei (Kuo Wei; d. 954), founder of the Later Zhou Dynasty, r. 951-954

Zhao Kuangyin (Chao K'uang-yin; 928-976), founder of the Song Dynasty, r. 960-976

SUMMARY OF EVENT

In 907, the Tang Dynasty (T'ang; 618-907) fell as a result of a series of uprisings that were caused by high taxes that had forced peasants off their lands and had also led to widespread poverty and starvation. The first and most important of these rebellions was led by Huang Chao, a Chinese intellectual who was enraged because he had failed to pass a series of civil service examinations that would have placed him at the highest levels of power in the Tang bureaucracy.

Huang Chao's forces targeted two important groups for extermination during the uprising. The first was the old imperial bureaucracy that had rejected his application for service. Huang Chao's purge of this important organization was so extensive that the Tang civil service literally disappeared, creating widespread social and political chaos. His forces also targeted the landed aristocracy in the provinces. Over centuries of Tang rule, these powerful members of the nobility had provided the majority of candidates for the Tang bureaucracy. These families were also the champions of the Tang Empire in the provinces, and their loyalty served the Tang government in these important areas. In time, the rebel forces were defeated and the surviving members of the Tang Dynasty attempted to restore order by claiming the mandate of heaven (heavenly authorization of rule), but by this time, the political situation had become too unstable and China slipped into a time of great political chaos known as the Period of Five Dynasties and Ten Kingdoms.

The southern part of China had divided into ten kingdoms: Wu, Min, Chu (Ch'u), Former Shu (also Qian Shu), Nanping (Nanp'ing; also Jingnan), Southern Tang (T'ang), Later Shu, Wu-Yue, Southern Han, and Northern Han. In northern China, especially in the area bordering the Yellow River Valley, five separate dynasties unsuccessfully attempted to gain control of the region. China suffered under a series of corrupt officials who used their positions of power to enrich themselves at the expense of civil society. This governmental abuse caused the destruction of the agricultural infrastructure, which in turn led to widespread peasant rebellions.

This series of uprisings brought on new attempts to unify the nation and to centralize the Chinese government. The first attempt to reestablish central authority was made by Zhu Wen, who established one of the most important dynasties of the period, the Later Liang Dynasty (907-923). Zhu Wen had been a highly successful army officer during Huang Chao's rebellion, and once in power, he initiated a series of actions to reestablish a well-functioning civil bureaucracy. He began by replacing any official who had any ties to the old Tang Dynasty. He filled these positions with men who had distinguished themselves in recent military service. The long-term impact of this move was to link loyal service in the army to future opportunity in the central bureaucracy.

Zhu Wen also created two powerful ministries to oversee the day-to-day operations of the central government. The Ministry of Civil Office regulated and controlled public works and services and made sure they were done in a professional and timely manner. The recruiting and training of the Imperial Army was regulated by the Ministry of War, which also controlled all the strategic, tactical, and logistical decisions made by the general staff.

THE FIVE DYNASTIES AND THE TEN KINGDOMS

FIVE DYNASTIES

Later Liang

Reign	*Ruler*
907-912	Zhu Wen
912-923	Modi (Zhu Zhen)

Later Tang

Reign	*Ruler*
923-926	Zhuangzong (Li Cunxu)
926-934	Mingzong (Li Siyuan)
933-934	Minzong (Li Congxu)
934-936	Feidi (Modi)

Later Jin

Reign	*Ruler*
936-944	Shi Jingtang
944-947	Chudi

Later Han

Reign	*Ruler*
947-948	Liu Zhiyuan
948-951	Yindi

Later Zhou

Reign	*Ruler*
951-954	Taizu (Guo Wei)
954-960	Shizong

TEN KINGDOMS

Kingdom	*Dates*
896/907-951	Chu
903/907-925	Former Shu (Qian Shu)
926/933-965	Later Shu
898/909-945	Min
907/924-963	Nanping (Jingnan)
951-979	Northern Han
917-971	Southern Han
937-975	Southern Tang
902-937	Wu
893/907-978	Wu-Yue

Finally, Zhu Wen created a new financial department that reformed both tax collection and the distribution of government funds. After he reformed the imperial bureaucracy and armed forces, he moved to establish control over the rebellious provinces. He began by entering into a number of military alliances through a series of marriages between his daughters and the sons of the more important provisional governors. These marriages created an important connection between the central government and the provincial nobility; however, the ties were not strong enough to assure Zhu Wen of the complete loyalty of the provincial governors.

In reaction to this strategic reality, the emperor sent his most talented generals to occupy and fortify the borderlands between the central government and the provinces, and he gave these commanders both civil and military power. Zhu Wen's actions set off a series of rebellions because the provincial governors believed the emperor was attempting to undermine their political status. In spite of the deep animosity on the part of the governors, Zhu Wen's forces were successful in defeating the provincial armies because their generals were unable to mount a unified attack against the emperor's forces.

The emperor's success was cut short when he was assassinated by one of his sons, who was executed in turn by another son. This began a period of political chaos in which one dynasty rapidly followed another in northern China. Later Liang general Li Cunxu, with the assistance of his father, Li Keyong, overthrew the Later Liang and founded the Later Tang Dynasty (T'ang; 923-935). Then a Later Tang general, Shi Jingtang, with the help of the Khitans, founded the Later Jin Dynasty (936-947). The Khitans later withdrew their support, and the Later Jin was followed by the creation of the Later Han Dynasty (947-951) by Liu Zhiyuan, a general of the Later Jin, who pushed back the Khitans. The fifth dynasty, the Later Zhou (Chou; 951-960), was founded by Guo Wei, another general. The new emperor established an elite corps of highly trained soldiers known as the emperor's army. The most accomplished served as his personal bodyguards, protecting him from the culture of assassination that had plagued and undermined the central government for decades.

Throughout Chinese history, periods of great chaos have also created conditions that have stimulated cultural advances. The Period of Five Dynasties and Ten Kingdoms generated important attempts at economic and political reform. Political philosophers, as well as government bureaucrats, took action to deal with the plight of the peasants who had suffered from the effects of constant warfare. They initiated land redistribution and significant tax reform to alleviate the widespread suffering of the displaced peasants. They also took steps to control political corruption. A series of strict laws and harsh punishments were instituted by many regional kingdoms in an attempt to reform their local bureaucrats.

China also experienced a neo-Confucian revival that coincided with a growing nationwide rejection of Buddhism. A number of prominent philosophers began to publish scholarly works calling for a return to traditional Confucian ideals. China's publishing industry was inundated with orders for copies of Confucius's *Lunyu* (late sixth-early fifth centuries B.C.E.; *The Analects*, 1861) to meet the needs of students studying at a growing number of Confucian academies. At the same time, most of the regional governments were rejecting applications for military deferments from men applying to become Buddhist monks. These actions sent an important signal that the Buddhist tradition was losing its power and prestige throughout the Chinese culture.

Confucianism in turn received a serious challenge from another ancient Chinese belief system, Daoism, which was its intellectual antithesis. Daoists believed that any attempt to systematize human action conflicted with the natural laws of the universe and, thus, was doomed to failure. Philosophers of the Daoist school stated that humanity should strive to become one with nature and to adopt its rhythms and patterns. This neo-Daoist movement was also the intellectual foundation of a new school of art known as Wadai painting. Practitioners of this art form held the Daoist belief that mountains were the most sacred places on earth. Artists of the Wadai school created ink landscape paintings using these natural cathedrals as the focus of their work. These intellectual and artistic movements reflected a culturewide attempt to find a "Chinese" solution to the problems facing China at this time.

In 951, the Later Zhou Dynasty came to power in northern China, and under the leadership of Zhao Kuangyin it set into motion a series of reforms that redistributed land to the peasants, controlled excessive taxation, and removed corrupt officials from positions of power. These measures reinvigorated the economy and allowed the dynasty to create a strong military establishment. The new emperor was able to reunify China; this set the stage for the start of China's next "golden age" under the leadership of the Song Dynasty (Sung; 960-1279).

SIGNIFICANCE

The Period of Five Dynasties and Ten Kingdoms refocused Chinese culture on the importance of political and social stability. China's leadership looked to the nation's neo-Confucian academia to find a solution to the country's problems. These scholars created a bureaucratic model based on the traditional Confucian belief that through proper study and training, a class of superior men could be created that would develop an environment of peace and prosperity. This neo-Confucian system would eventually become the basis of the Song bureaucracy, and its overwhelming success would form the foundation of China's next "golden age."

The Confucian rejection of military culture, as well as the violent experience of the Period of Five Dynasties and Ten Kingdoms, would lead the Song to place antimilitary civilian bureaucrats in charge of the nation's armed forces. This decision would weaken Song security and would eventually allow nomadic tribes to conquer China.

—*Richard D. Fitzgerald*

FURTHER READING

Bol, Peter. *This Culture of Ours: Intellectual Transitions in Tang and Sung China*. Stanford, Calif.: Stanford University Press, 1912. An excellent overview of Chinese intellectual history from the Tang through Song Dynasties. Index and bibliography.

Gernet, Jacques. *A History of Chinese Civilization*. New York: Cambridge University Press, 1990. The best single-volume account of Chinese cultural history. Maps, index, and bibliography.

Graff, David A. *Medieval Chinese Warfare, 300-900*. New York: Routledge Press, 2002. An excellent overview of medieval Chinese military history. Maps, index, and bibliography.

Graff, David A., and Robin Higham. *A Military History of China*. Cambridge, England: Westview Press, 2002. An excellent survey of Chinese military history. Maps, index, and bibliography.

SEE ALSO: 618: Founding of the Tang Dynasty; 936: Khitans Settle Near Beijing.

915
PARĀNTAKA I CONQUERS PĀṆḌYA

Parāntaka's defeat of the powerful neighboring state of Pāṇḍya was part of a remarkable reign of nearly fifty years and provided the basis for Cōla control of southern India for the next two centuries. This golden age in the development of Tamil culture was an era of prosperity derived from extensive trade and successful agriculture.

LOCALE: Pandi-nadu, Madurai, Kaveri River Basin, Thanjavur, Sri Lanka, and southern India beginning just below the Deccan region

CATEGORIES: Expansion and land acquisition; government and politics; wars, uprisings, and civil unrest

KEY FIGURES

Parāntaka I (d. 955), Cōla king, r. 907-955

Rājasiṃha II (d. 915), Pāṇḍya king, r. 913-915

Udaya IV (d. 950), Sinhalese king defeated by Parāntaka, r. 942-950

Vijayālaya (d. 870), grandfather of Parāntaka and founder of revived Cōla kingdom, r. c. 850-c. 870

SUMMARY OF EVENT

In the early tenth century, the lower half of the Indian subcontinent was a loosely organized conglomerate of semifeudal states. These Tamil-speaking states, separated from the Aryan-dominated Sanskrit-speaking north by the mountainous uplands of the Deccan region, preserved ancient Hindu cultural values. Three of the most powerful states, the Pallava (controlling the Madras region), the Pāṇḍyas (dominating Pandi-nadu and the city of Madurai), and the Cōlas (centered around the Kaveri River basin), competed with each other for dominance. Hegemony meant a major share of the rich overseas trade with Southeast Asia. Under Parāntaka I, major steps were taken to establish Cōla supremacy over southern India, ushering in a golden cultural age for the region.

As a ruling family, the Cōlas dated back to the first century; however, by the third century, their importance had waned. In following centuries, the Cōlas occupied a small territory in the Tanjore and Triconopoly districts. The Cōlas emerged from obscurity in 850 when Parāntaka's grandfather, Vijayālaya, after first aiding the Pallavas in war to weaken the Pāṇḍyas, seized Tanjore from the Pallavas and made it the capital city of the revived Cōla kingdom. Additional victories against the Pallavas and consolidation of Cōla power took place under the administration of Parāntaka's father, Āditya I (r. 871-907). However, it was Parāntaka who greatly expanded the territory under Cōla control and laid the foundation for Cōla domination of southern India for succeeding centuries.

On coming to power, Parāntaka formed alliances with regional chieftains such as the Gangas and Kerala. He then launched a victorious war against the Pāṇḍyas, winning the decisive Battle of Vellur in 915. Parāntaka captured the Pāṇḍya capital city of Madurai, thus forcing the Pāṇḍya king, Rājasiṃha II, to flee south to Sri Lanka. Consequently, the territory under his control expanded southward toward the island of Sri Lanka. Additional victories against the Pallavas extended Cōla control northward as well. The Pāṇḍyas conspired with the Sinhalese king of Sri Lanka, Kasyapa VI, to weaken Parāntaka's control of the south.

In the war of 917-918, Sinhalese and Pāṇḍyan forces were soundly defeated. Ultimately, Parāntaka invaded Sri Lanka. In 943, Sri Lankan forces under their new king, Udaya IV, were soundly defeated, and the royal palace sacked. Udaya was forced to flee to Ruhuna in the southern part of Sri Lanka, as Parāntaka occupied the north. Parāntaka's well-organized army, organized into elephant and cavalry divisions as well as regular infantry and swordsmen, seemed unstoppable. The formation of a powerful naval fleet also allowed Parāntaka to extend his power southward and to protect Cōla merchant ships.

Parāntaka's success was based not only on a comparatively efficient military but on sound administrative reforms as well. His kingship was used to grant a large degree of autonomy to village assemblies. Decrees were passed to encourage election of capable and relatively honest individuals to village assemblies and committees. Separate assemblies were formed for general tax-paying farmers, merchants, and craftspeople, and tax-exempt Brahmans. The end result was a policy of inclusiveness on the local level. At the same time, Parāntaka greatly increased the number and nature of positions in the central administration, based in the Cōla capital city of Thanjavur, where an elaborate palace was built and run on a lavish scale. His kingdom was divided into nine provinces, each of which was subdivided into districts, which in turn were subdivided into groups of villages. This administrative structure made tax collecting more efficient. It also created a force of central administrative agents who could act as advisers on the local level. These local leaders could act to produce cohesiveness without the outward appearance of intrusion on local decisions.

MAJOR RULERS OF THE CŌḶAS, c. 850-1279

Reign	*Ruler*
c. 850-c. 870	Vijayālaya
871-907	Āditya I
907-955	Parāntaka
956	Arinjayā
956	Parāntaka II
956-969	Āditya II
969-985	Madhurantaka Uttama
985-1014	Rājarāja I
1014-1044	Rājendracōla Deva I
1044-1052	Rājadhirāja I
1052-1060	Rājendracōla Deva II
1060-1063	Ramamahendra
1063-1067	Virarājendra
1067-1070	Adhirājendra
1070-1122	Rājendra III
1122-1135	Vikrama Cōla
1135-1150	Kulottuṅga II Cōla
1150-1173	Rājarāja II
1173-1179	Rājadhirāja II
1179-1218	Kulottuṅga III
1218-1246	Rājarāja III
1246-1279	Rājendra IV

Agriculture was improved by government-sponsored projects for irrigation and the turning over of virgin lands for increased agricultural production. Parāntaka also encouraged the growth of port cities and the expansion of merchant guilds to stimulate the extension of trade between the Cōlas, Southeast Asia, and China. Trade not only contributed to general prosperity but also generated significant tax revenues.

Parāntaka emphasized patronage of the arts and crafts, pioneering the development of bronze sculpture as an important art form. He catalyzed an extensive program of temple building, using stone instead of brick to guarantee permanency and, perhaps, to symbolize the benevolence of Cōla rule. Many of the historical records are based on inscription stones contained in the newly built temples, many of which were designed as an elaboration of Pallavan styles. By making temple life an important part of village life and building magnificent structures such as Tirumundeeswaram, located near Tiruvenneinallur and dedicated to the god Śiva, Parantaka undoubtedly sought to stabilize and popularize his regime. Temples were also intended to be educational and literary centers, where Tamil poets and writers were patronized to produce literature of a religious nature. Temples were centers for the planning of religious festivals, the celebration of which were vital for well-functioning village life. Temples, which received large grants of prime lands, were also intended to be productive units aiding in the development of agriculture.

SIGNIFICANCE

Ultimately, Parāntaka was forced to retire from Sri Lanka because of the invasion of Cōla territory to the north by the Rāṣṭrakūṭas of the Deccan region. In the ensuing battles, the northern Cōla districts were lost. The final years of Parāntaka's reign witnessed a rollback of Cōla power, which continued under the reigns of Parāntaka's immediate successors. However, the foundation of Cōla power had been laid by Parāntaka, and by 985, thirty years after his monarchy ended, Cōla fortunes were on the rise. Capable successors such as Rājarāja I (r. 985-1014), Rājendracōla Deva I (r. 1014-1044), and Rājendra III (r. 1070-1122) recreated the expansive Cōla kingdom that existed under Parāntaka and organized it along administrative lines established by Parāntaka. Support of commerce and the arts as well as efficient central and local government were long-standing trademarks of Cōla rule.

In many areas, Parāntaka's successors were able to expand Cōla influence. A reinvigorated naval fleet was able to defeat the Śrivijaya fleet in 1025 and to establish dependency states in the Malayan peninsula. Commerce flourished, as did the building of magnificent temples and patronage of the arts. Consequently, the golden age continued for Tamil culture in southern India. Lucrative trade with Southeast Asia expanded, and Cōla trading missions visited China. Cōla trading ventures extended to East Africa and Arabia; however, its highest profits appear to have been reached in trade with Europe. By 1000, the Cōlas were minting their own gold and silver coins.

Unfortunately, given the continual pressure exerted by feudal chieftains, political unity was a fragile commodity in medieval India, where political division and incessant warfare were dominant themes. The rise of the Hoysaḷas in the west and the rebirth of Pāṇḍyan military power caused a serious shrinkage of Cōla dominion during the thirteenth century. The expansion of Islamic rule in northern India also produced additional stresses on southern Indian states. In 1279, the last successor of Parāntaka died, and Cōla territory came under the rule of the Pāndyas.

The architecture of the Cōlas, particularly in the building of temple complexes, is perhaps the single greatest permanent Cōla contribution to Indian civilization. The inscriptions left behind in these temple complexes preserved a large part of the historical record of the commercial and agricultural prosperity that the Cōlas fostered in southern India.

—*Irwin Halfond*

FURTHER READING

Balasubrahmanyam, S. R. *Early Chola Temples: Parantaka I to Rajaraja I (A.D. 907-985)*. Bombay, India: Orient Longman, 1971. Concentrates on temples but reveals Cōla political and cultural involvements as derived from temple inscriptions.

Karashma, Noboru. *History and Society in South India: The Cholas to Vijayanagar.* New Delhi, India: Oxford University Press, 2001. A tedious but definitive account, using much statistical data, of Cōla administrative and agricultural policies, and their effects.

Nilakanta Sastri, K. A. *A History of South India from Prehistoric Times to the Fall of Vijayanagar.* Madras, India: Oxford University Press, 1966. An excellent treatment of the development of Southern India.

Spencer, George W. *The Politics of Expansion: The Chola Conquest of Sri Lanka and Sri Vijaya*. Madras, India: New Era, 1983. A study of late Cōla warfare and foreign policy accomplishments.

Swaminathan, S. *The Early Cholas: History, Art, and Culture*. Delhi, India: Sharada Publishing House, 1998. The best overall analysis of the rise and fall of the Cōlas.

Thapar, Romila. *From the Discovery of India to 1526*. Vol. 1 in *A History of India*. Baltimore: Penguin Books, 1991. A readable account of the general development of India to the sixteenth century.

Wolpert, Stanley. *A New History of India*. New York: Oxford University Press, 1999. Provides excellent contextual background for the development of India.

SEE ALSO: 682-1377: Expansion of Śrivijaya; 730: Rise of the Pratihāras; c. 985-1014: Reign of Rājarāja I.

RELATED ARTICLE in *Great Lives from History: The Middle Ages, 477-1453*: Harṣa.

918-936
FOUNDATION OF THE KORYŎ DYNASTY

At the end of Korea's Unified Silla Dynasty, the kingdom was divided into three states—Silla, Later Paekche, and Later Koguryŏ—giving rise to the Later Three Kingdoms period. In 918, Wang Kŏn took over Later Koguryŏ and renamed it Koryŏ, completing the reunification of the three kingdoms in 936.

LOCALE: Korean peninsula
CATEGORY: Government and politics

KEY FIGURES

Kyŏn-hwŏn (c. 867-936), founder and king of Later Paekche, r. 892-935

Kung-ye (d. 918), founder of Later Koguryŏ; king of Majin, r. 904-911; king of T'aebong, r. 911-918

Wang Kŏn (T'aejo; 877-943), founder of Koryŏ, reunified the Later Three Kingdoms, king, r. 918-943

SUMMARY OF EVENT

The last half century of the Unified Silla (668-935) period was a time of chaos. Since 780, the royals had been engaged in a century-long struggle for the throne. During that period, fourteen kings ascended the throne, three kings were assassinated, and one committed suicide. Royals and aristocrats led extravagant lifestyles in the city of Kyŏngju, where, it is said, the sound of music never stopped.

Although the central government was weak and unable to pay much attention to the local governments, local aristocrats grew independent and became ever more powerful. In the countryside, disaffected farmers were heavily weighed down by grain taxes and corvée duties to support both the local and central governments. Many fled their farms and roamed the country, some joining bandits and others being absorbed by the increasingly powerful local landed lords who took them in as slave laborers. The local elites ran their own governments independent of the capital, owned private armies of various sizes, and were commonly referred to as generals and castle lords.

Unable to collect taxes, the national economy was in a desperate state. In 889, when Queen Chinsŏng (r. 887-896) tried to collect taxes by force, farmers and robbers throughout the country rose up in arms. The most prominent generals leading the insurgents were Kyŏn-hwŏn from Wansan (now Chŏnju) in North Chŏlla Province, and Yang-gil from Pukwŏn (now Wŏnju) in Kangwŏn Province. By 892, Kyŏn-hwŏn, a young Silla general, carved out a territory in Chŏlla Province and asserted his independence from the Silla government. He presented himself as the successor of the former Paekche, made Chŏnju the capital, and, in 900, proclaimed himself the king of Later Paekche (900-936).

Another prominent figure was Kung-ye, who was born a Silla prince. There are interesting reports regarding his birth. As the story goes, the king, his father, ordered him thrown out of the palace because of his inauspicious birth. His nurse saved the baby and raised him. At the age of ten, Kung-ye entered a Buddhist monastery, and in 891 he enlisted in the camp of the bandit Ki-hwŏn. After being ill treated, Kung-ye moved to the camp of another bandit, Yang-gil of Pukwŏn, and served as his lieutenant. Being resourceful and courageous, he won many battles and soon commanded a sizable army. One of the men who joined Kung-ye was Wang Kŏn (895), a member of the local gentry from Songak (or Song-do, now Kaesŏng), who later would become the founder of the Koryŏ Dynasty (918-1392).

Yang-gil, becoming suspicious and envious of his lieutenant's success, attacked Kung-ye but was soundly defeated and subsequently lost all his territory. In 901, Kung-ye founded a state and named it the Later Koguryŏ (901-918), indicating that his dynasty was the legitimate continuation of the former Koguryŏ kingdom. He declared Songak his capital and proclaimed himself king. This period, from c. 900 until 936, is known as the Later Three Kingdoms period.

As his domain expanded, Kung-ye changed the name of his state twice, first to Majin, then to T'aebong, and moved the capital to Ch'orwŏn. He now held the largest territory among the three kingdoms. His territory extended beyond the Taedong River to the city of P'yŏngyang in the north, in effect occupying the whole southern part of the former Koguryŏ, or almost all of the northern part of Silla.

After his military success, he turned to Buddhism, with the intention of devoting the rest of his life to the religion. He declared himself a Maitreya Buddha, proclaimed both of his sons Buddhists, and named them bodhisattvas, thus trying to present his family as a true Buddhist family. He authored twenty volumes of Buddhist scripture and showed them to the most revered monk at the time, Sŏckch'ŏng. When the latter criticized them as heretical nonsense, Kung-ye killed him. After

MAJOR RULERS OF THE KORYŎ DYNASTY, 918-1392

Reign	*Ruler*
918-943	T'aejo (Wang Kŏn)
944-945	Hyejong
946-949	Chŏngjong
949-975	Kwangjong (Wang So)
975-981	Kyŏngjong (Wang Yu)
981-997	Sŏngjong (Wang Ch'i)
997-1009	Mokshong
1009-1031	Hyŏngjong
1031-1034	Tokjong
1034-1046	Chŏngjong
1046-1083	Munjong (Wang Hwi)
1083	Sunjong
1083-1094	Sŏnjong
1094-1095	Hŏnjong
1095-1105	Sukjong
1105-1122	Yejong I
1122-1146	Injong I (Wang Hae)
1146-1170	Ŭijong
1170-1197	Myŏngjong
1197-1204	Sinjong
1204-1211	Hŭijong
1211-1213	Kangjong
1214-1259	Kojong I
1260-1274	Wŏnjong
1274-1308	Ch'ungugŏl Wang
1308-1313	Ch'ungsŏn Wang
1313-1330	Ch'ungsuk Wang
1330-1332	Ch'unghye Wang
1332-1339	Ch'angsuk Wang
1339-1344	Ch'unghye Wang
1344-1348	Ch'ungmok Wang
1348-1351	Ch'ungjŏng Wang
1351-1394	Kongmin Wang
1374-1388	U (Sin-u)
1389	Sinch'ang
1389-1392	Kongyang Wang

the incident, Kung-ye became more violent and unpredictable and turned into a neurotic psychopath. Kung-ye even accused his queen of infidelity and killed her. When their sons tried to intervene, he killed them as well.

The officials under him were genuinely alarmed by the king's erratic behavior and implored Wang Kŏn to replace him. Understandably, everyone under Kung-ye's rule feared for his life. In 918, Wang Kŏn came with ten thousand soldiers and surrounded the royal palace. Kung-ye fled for his life but was eventually captured and killed.

Wang Kŏn, now King T'aejo (although this title was given posthumously), renamed his state Koryŏ and moved his capital back to his town of Songak. He established good relations with Silla while remaining hostile toward Later Paekche. When Kyŏn-hwŏn invaded deep into Silla's capital in 927, King Kyŏng-ae asked for Koryŏ's help. Wang Kŏn set out immediately, personally leading his troops. However, Kyŏn-hwŏn arrived at the capital first and ravaged the city.

Oblivious to the crisis at hand, King Kyŏng-ae, his queens and concubines, and other royal families were dining sumptuously near the capital at the outdoor banquet place known as P'osŏkjŏng when the Later Paekche forces fell on the city. Paekche soldiers killed and plundered. King Kyŏng-ae was captured and forced to commit suicide. Then, Kyŏn-hwŏn violated the queen and allowed his soldiers to do likewise with the king's consorts and concubines. Before leaving the city, Kyŏn-hwŏn placed a relative of the former king on the throne. He was King Kyŏngsun, the last monarch of Silla.

Although he was too late to prevent the sacking of the capital city, Wang Kŏn came to Silla's aid and engaged Kyŏn-hwŏn's returning forces. During the next two years of battles, Wang Kŏn lost many men and two generals, and once could barely extricate himself from Kyŏn-hwŏn's formidable forces.

An internal discord was Later Paekche's undoing. Kyŏn-hwŏn took many wives and sired ten sons. Among them, he most favored his fourth son, Kŭmgang, and chose him as his successor. This decision sowed the seeds of family discord. The eldest son, Sin-gŏm, in collusion with two younger brothers, kidnapped and imprisoned his father in a Buddhist monastery, killed Kŭmgang, and made himself king (935). After three months, the imprisoned monarch escaped and made his way to his old archenemy, Wang Kŏn, and surrendered. Wang Kŏn received him and treated him royally.

In the same year, the last king of Silla, Kyŏngsun, discussed with his officials a possible surrender to Koryŏ, as Silla was no longer viable. Silla had been reduced to the territory just around the capital city of Kyŏngju. The only dissension came from the crown prince, who argued that a nation's rise and fall depended on the mandate of heaven (heavenly authority to rule) and it was imprudent to surrender a country that had lasted a thousand years.

Regardless, the king decided to surrender and lead his nobles and ministers from Kyŏngju to Songak in a procession that stretched out for miles. In despair, the crown prince bid farewell to the king and retreated to the mountains. There, he lived eating grass and wearing hemp cloth until he died. In Korean history, he is known as the Hemp Prince (Ma-ŭi T'ae-ja). Thus ended the Silla Dynasty, which had seen fifty-six kings and lasted (through its early and United phases) from 57 B.C.E. to 935 C.E., just eight years short of a millennium.

Koryŏ's Wang Kŏn had his two former adversaries under his wing. In 936, Kyŏn-hwŏn convinced Wang Kŏn to attack his own sons in Later Paekche; after a fierce battle, Wang Kŏn defeated Sin-gŏm and his brothers. Some accounts say Kyŏn-hwŏn died on the battlefield, while others say he died shortly thereafter. Thus ended Kyŏn-hwŏn's Later Paekche in 936.

SIGNIFICANCE

Koryŏ's Wang Kŏn unified Korea for the second time in its history, and it remained one entity until the twentieth century. The name he gave his kingdom, Koryŏ, from which the English name for Korea originated, was chosen to recall the greatness of the earlier Koguryŏ kingdom.

—*Hwa-Soon Choi Meyer*

FURTHER READING

Hulbert, Homer B. *History of Korea*. 2 vols. Richmond, Surrey, England: Curzon, 1999. Written in the manner of annals, this history contains the most detailed account. Covers up to 1904.

Joe, Wanne J. *Traditional Korea: A Cultural History*. Rev. ed. Edited by Hongkyu A. Choe. Elizabeth, N.J.: Hollym, 1997. Comprehensive and well-written history of Korea.

Lee, Ki-Baik. *A New History of Korea*. Translated by Edward W. Wagner. Cambridge, Mass.: Harvard University Press, 1984. Very succinct overview of Korean history. The "Dynastic Lineages" section is particularly helpful.

Rutt, Richard. *James Scarth Gale and His History of the Korean People*. 2d ed. Seoul: The Royal Asiatic Society, Korea Branch, 1983. Based on the history written by James Gale, a contemporary of Homer B. Hulbert. Gale and Hulbert were born a month apart and served together at the court of the emperor Kojong (r. 1864-1907) at the end of the Yi Dynasty. Often they have similar views, yet they complement each other in details.

SEE ALSO: 668-935: Silla Unification of Korea; 958-1076: Koreans Adopt the Tang Civil Service Model; 1145: Kim Pu-sik Writes *Samguk Sagi*; 1196-1258: Ch'oe Family Takes Power in Korea; July, 1392: Establishment of the Yi Dynasty.

RELATED ARTICLE in *Great Lives from History: The Middle Ages, 477-1453*: Wang Kŏn.

927
COMPILATION OF THE *Engi shiki*

The Engi shiki*, a legal code compiled under the orders of the emperor Daigo, represented an attempt by the imperial family to reassert its authority in the Japanese political world and to press for the more effective implementation of earlier legal concepts. It also contained important information relating to Shintō, the native Japanese faith.*

LOCALE: Japan

CATEGORIES: Laws, acts, and legal history; government and politics; religion

KEY FIGURES

Daigo (885-930), emperor of Japan, r. 897-930

Fujiwara Mototsune (836-891), regent

Uda (867-931), emperor of Japan, r. 887-897

SUMMARY OF EVENT

Since the seventh century, the Fujiwara family had held a great deal of power over the imperial court through its monopolization of high posts in the central administration and close relationship with the imperial family. The emperor Uda was one of the first sovereigns who attempted to assert his authority outside the administrative context that had been developed by the Fujiwara regents. The Fujiwara had pursued a strategy of intermarriage with the imperial family in order to gain authority over the throne, and Uda was one of the first sovereigns in more than one hundred years who did not have close blood ties to the Fujiwara. Uda's confrontational attitude led to a power struggle between him and the Fujiwara regent Fujiwara Mototsune. When Mototsune died in 891, Uda refused to appoint another regent, in the interest of increasing the power of the imperial family. Uda retired to a monastery in 897, and his son Daigo came to power. Daigo's reign also was characterized by his attempt to increase the power of the imperial family. Uda, who continued to wield considerable power from behind the scenes assisted his son in this endeavor.

To increase the power of the imperial family and the central court in general, in 905, the fifth year of the Engi period (901-922), Daigo ordered the compilation of a new series of supplementary legal precepts and regulations. The undertaking was completed in 927, and the result was the code known as the *Engi shiki* or "procedures of the Engi era." The *Engi shiki* cannot be considered an original legal work as its purpose was not to revolutionize Japanese law but rather to provide for the more effective enforcement of earlier legal codes. It contains both penal and administrative details as well as a religious focus—a reminder that religion was a central feature of Japanese administration at that time—and touched on many aspects of the lives of Japanese commoners and aristocrats alike.

Although earlier Japanese legal documents such as the Taihō code of 701 contain detailed regulations for the creation of bureaucratic hierarchies, the *Engi shiki* served to reorganize the institutions of government in the tenth century. Some of the most important administrative policies contained in the document consist of a detailed statement of the duties of the *dajōkan*, the "great council of state," which was effectively the main policy-making organ in the Japanese government. It was through control of the great council of state that the Fujiwara had managed to usurp administrative authority from the imperial family. These regulations were, in part, designed to rectify this situation. Changes to the central government did not stop there, however. In total, forty books of the fifty total deal with procedures for the various government ministries and bureaus. It is clear that the emperor, Daigo, and his retired father were attempting to consolidate imperial control over the government through the introduction of a more detailed system of political control.

In addition to the adjustment of the legal duties and functions of the central administration, one of the main goals of this new legal code was to limit the expansion of *shōen*, estates that were slipping outside imperial rule. By the early tenth century, powerful families and several influential Buddhist sects, such as the Tendai sect centered on Mount Hiei, had amassed large amounts of tax-free land. These tracts were organized into *shōen* and were directly administered by bailiffs and other extra-governmental authorities for the profit of important aristocratic families. Just as earlier legal codes such as the Taihō code had attempted to strengthen central power, Daigo's *Engi shiki* attempted to curtail and reverse the erosion of that power. Although this was a brave step on the part of the imperial family to assert its authority over the entire country, the process of *shōen* formation continued unabated until the entire system of land control and taxation was co-opted by the new warrior government in the late twelfth century.

Despite the abundance of secular content, the *Engi shiki* had important religious aspects as well. In fact, the first ten books of the work are devoted to the conduct of festivals and worship related to Shintō, the native Japanese faith. In essence, the Japanese imperial family owed its privileged position to its claim of direct descent from the sun goddess Amaterasu. By promoting the native faith and organizing its various festivals and ceremonies into a coherent system, Daigo and his legal assistants were effectively working toward the increase in the power of the Japanese imperial family and the concept of the legitimacy of its rule.

SIGNIFICANCE

The compilation of the *Engi shiki* is a significant moment in Japanese legal and social history because it represents a direct challenge by the imperial family to the system of regency by which the Fujiwara family had managed to control the throne. Despite the fact that the Fujiwara managed to reassert their power after the death of the emperor Daigo, this early tenth century challenge formed the basis for a tradition of emperor-centered thought that proved to be a very important stream in the Japanese intellectual tradition. When the code was compiled, the assertion of the importance of the role of Shintō in the government of the state represented a challenge to the continental philosophical and religious systems of Buddhism and Confucian thought.

The *Engi shiki*, as a revision of earlier aspects of the law of the Japanese court, continued to have an impact on the conduct of court life even after the power of the old capital was eclipsed by the rise of warrior clans in the east. The procedures for worship as well as details concerning the court hierarchy continued to have a great influence on court life throughout the period of warrior rule and until the modernizing reforms of the nineteenth century. The ceremonial details and the regulations concerning the religious role of the imperial family continue to have an influence on Shintō and are still considered to be part of the sacred text of that religion. Elements of the religious functions carried out by members of the imperial family at present can be traced back to the religious guidelines laid out in detail in the *Engi shiki*.

Although the *Engi shiki*'s importance as a legal document was overshadowed as a result of later developments, its status as a philosophical and cultural statement continued to be important. Although the *Engi shiki* did not bring about a restoration of imperial authority, and the Fuijwara—who later would be eclipsed by the power of provincial warrior families—maintained their authority, the code came to be considered a high point in the political and cultural history of classical Japan. During the Tokugawa period (1603-1867), scholars who were dissatisfied with orthodox Confucian scholarship began to look more closely at Japan's own classical traditions. Influential authors such as Motoori Norinaga (1730-1801) launched a *kokugaku* ("national learning") movement that popularized the study of the ancient chronicles as well as documents such as the *Engi shiki*. This provided the basis for a stream of thought in Japanese intellectual culture that stressed the desirability of imperial restoration and the primacy of Shintō as a national religion. These developments provided the intellectual and philosophical foundation of the Meiji Restoration of 1867 and had a great influence on the subsequent development of Japanese civilization.

—*Matthew Penney*

Further Reading

Crump, Thomas. *The Death of an Emperor.* London: Constable, 1989. A discussion of the maintenance of the Shintō rites described in the *Engi shiki* in modern Japan.

De Bary, William Theodore, et al., comps. *Sources of Japanese Tradition*. 2d ed. Vol. 1. New York: Columbia University Press, 2001. Contains abridged translations of Japanese legal documents as well as other important documents relating to early Japanese political life.

Littleton, Scott. *Shintō: Origins, Rituals, Festivals, Spirits, Sacred Places*. New York: Oxford University Press, 2002. Traces the history of Shintō and includes both a detailed discussion of the origins of the religious sections of the *Engi shiki* and the impact that it had on subsequent Japanese traditions.

Ono, Sokyo. *Shintō: The Kami Way*. Tokyo: Charles E. Tuttle, 1997. An excellent general account of the Shintō faith touched on in the *Engi shiki*.

Sansom, George. *A History of Japan to 1334*. Vol. 1. Stanford, Calif.: Stanford University Press, 1958. The first volume of Sansom's three-volume study of Japanese history remains a highly detailed and authoritative work on the subject.

Shively, Donald, ed. *Heian Japan*. Vol. 2 in *The Cambridge History of Japan*. Cambridge, Mass.: Cambridge University Press, 1999. A detailed history of the period written by leading scholars. Particular attention is paid to the development of legal traditions.

See also: 645-646: Adoption of *Nengo* System and Taika Reforms; 701: Taihō Laws Reform Japanese Government; 794-1185: Heian Period; 858: Rise of the Fujiwara Family.

Related article in *Great Lives from History: The Middle Ages, 477-1453*: Fujiwara Michinaga.

936
KHITANS SETTLE NEAR BEIJING

The Khitans moved into northern China and founded the Liao Dynasty. They retained their ethnic identity, and their dualistic administration set the pattern for later conquering dynasties.

LOCALE: Northern China
CATEGORIES: Expansion and land acquisition; government and politics

KEY FIGURES

Abaoji (A-pao-chi; 872-926), chief of the Yila tribe and founder of the Khitan Liao Dynasty, r. 907-926
Deguang (Tö-kuang, Yao-ku; 902-947), second Liao Dynasty emperor, r. 926-947, expanded Khitan control into China
Zhao Kuangyin (Chao K'uang-yin; 927-976), first Sung Dynasty emperor, r. 960-976, who unified and strengthened Chinese resistance to Khitans

SUMMARY OF EVENT

The Khitans were a Mongol nation of eight tribes whose homeland lay along the eastern slopes of the Greater Xing'an Mountains in Manchuria, north of China. Chinese sources record relations with the Qidan (Khitans) as early as the fifth century. They were nomadic pastoralists who raised horses and cattle and fought as mounted cavalrymen in the steppe tradition. They shared borders to the west with other nomadic Mongols, to the north with the forest hunters of the Jurchen tribes, and to the east with the hunters, farmers, and fisherfolk of the Bohai (Po-hai) state of northern Korea.

With the breakup of the Uighur state, to which they had been subject during the Tang Dynasty (T'ang; 618-907), many of these Turkish people entered Khitan society. The position of *khan*, or leader of the Eight Tribes, emerged in the mid-eighth century and rotated among various tribal chieftains for 150 years. In 905, the chief of the Yila tribe, Abaoji, led seventy thousand cavalry in the conquest of the Chinese borderland of Datong. This bold and aggressive move ensured his "election" as Khitan *khan* in 907, which in turn established the Khitan Liao Dynasty (so named in 947, Chinese style, for a homeland river; 907-1125). China's imperial administration and armies failed to respond effectively because of the disarray that followed the collapse of the Tang Dynasty in 907. This inaugurated a period of Chinese weakness known as the Five Dynasties and Ten Kingdoms (907-960). Khitan foreign policy throughout this time aimed at keeping the Chinese pot stirred and its imperial administration unstable.

Under the leadership of Abaoji, now the emperor Taizu (T'ai-tsu), Khitan armies brought their western, northern, and eastern neighbors under submission. These groups were administered in typical steppe fashion, with garrisons of faithful troops studding the landscape. Conquest of northern Chinese-settled areas prompted Abaoji to adopt a novel, dual model for ruling his territories. He established a northern chancellery that was Khitan, was military in emphasis, and concentrated on the shifting non-Chinese populations as well as a primarily civil southern chancellery that was largely Chinese and oversaw the collection of taxes and the application of Chinese law in the settled, ethnically Chinese areas.

He went further, adopting Chinese court rituals in 916 and founding a capital city, Shangjing, on the Chinese model, in 918. The Khitans soon established more than thirty new Chinese-style cities for administration and manufacturing, in which ethnic Chinese dominated. Abaoji also declared primogeniture—rule by the first-born male—mimicking the Chinese yet again. Despite Abaoji's wishes, he was succeeded in 926 by his second son, Deguang, who was heavily supported by his powerful mother, Yingtian. The elder brother, Bei, was considered too "Chinese" by the ethnic Khitans at court, and indeed, he spent the last ten years of his life writing Chinese poetry in China.

The early 930's witnessed a deepening of Chinese disunity. The Chinese rebel leader Shi Jingtang attacked the rump Tang power base with Khitan assistance, emerging as a Khitan puppet. In 936, armies of mounted archers belonging to Deguang, who ruled as Taizong (T'ai-tsung), carved out a swath of northern Chinese territory for their emperor. This territory ranged from 70 to 100 miles (110 to 160 kilometers) in depth and became known as the Sixteen Prefectures (though there were actually nineteen). Deguang ruled these prefectures from his new capital at Yen near the site of modern Beijing.

Like his father, Deguang retained most elements of the Chinese administrative system and relied heavily on the natives both to remain productive members of society and to serve as administrators. His dual system had two prime ministers and six ministries: war, justice, revenues, works, rites, and personnel. In 988, the Khitan administration in the south instituted the Chinese examination system for bureaucrats, a requirement that remained applicable only to the southerners. Both Deguang and his father may have envisioned Khitan rule over all of China, but frequent campaigning along the Mongol and Jurchen frontiers proved a constant distraction. The success of this northern policy reduced the number of unabsorbed tribes, prefiguring the greater consolidations under Genghis Khan's horde. According to scholar F. W. Mote, the core structure of the northern Khitan state rose from eight tribes to sixty-two.

The unsuccessful Chinese attempt in 960 to regain the lost prefectures resulted in the death of the Chinese emperor and the rise of Zhao Kuangyin, founder of the Song Dynasty (Sung; 960-1279) in China. Zhao, who ruled as Taizu (T'ai-tsu), spent two decades consolidating his power in China before turning on the northern Turkic Han, a client state of the Liao. In 979, the Han fell to the Chinese, who proceeded against weak resistance to Yen (Beijing). Though the Song army besieged the city, they were crushed at the Battle of the Gaoliang River (979). The Chinese formally recognized the Khitan state and its hold on Chinese territory in early 1005, when annual tributes were set and the emperors recognized each other as "brothers." This ushered in a century of relative peace and Khitan prosperity.

MAJOR RULERS OF THE LIAO AND WESTERN LIAO DYNASTIES

LIAO DYNASTY

Reign	*Ruler*
907-926	Abaoji (Taizu)
926-947	Deguang (Taizong)
947-951	Shizong
951-969	Muzong
969-982	Jingzong
982-1031	Shengzong
1031-1055	Xingzong
1055-1101	Daozong
1101-1125	Tianzuodi

WESTERN LIAO DYNASTY

Reign	*Ruler*
1125-1144	Dezong
1144-1151	Empress Gantian
1151-1164	Renzong
1164-1178	Empress Chengtian
1178-1211	The Last Ruler

Khitan society and culture changed considerably with the infusion of Chinese culture. Abouji had Confucians, Buddhists, and Daoists at court, but he preferred the Confucian beliefs and rituals. After his death, Buddhism replaced Confucianism, and the Khitan imperial family, known as the Liao after 947, became great patrons of monks and scribes. This provided the Khitans with ties to other Buddhist cultures in Xixia, Korea, Tibet, China, and even Japan. Beginning with Deguang, the Khitans fostered cultural contacts and exchanges, and Yen became a center of Buddhist creative activity from the 990's. Among the steppe folk to the north, however, the animistic tribal religions and warrior ethic remained dominant. Nonetheless, important Buddhist texts were translated into Khitan through a new written language that borrowed from both the Turkic and Chinese.

The early twelfth century saw the rise of the Jurchen leader Aguda, whose ascent to power paralleled that of Abaoji. From about 1115, Aguda was able to unify his people and gain useful allies among disaffected Khitans and many of those under Khitan rule. His invasion of the Khitan state swept through the tribal areas, and the northern capital fell in 1120. The Chinese portions of the Khitan state fell just as rapidly. Aguda marched into Yen in 1122, though the disappearance of the Liao state is generally dated to 1125.

SIGNIFICANCE

The Khitan model of bringing the steppe and Chinese settled areas under a single if dualistic administration set the tone for later "conquest dynasties"—including the Mongols—and influenced the region until the seventeenth century. Khitan recognition of the need for ethnic and cultural division extended to a long-standing prohibition against intermarriage. The Khitans retained their ethnic identity despite heavy borrowing from the Chinese, demonstrating that "barbarians" could not only conquer but also rule. In addition, they could rule not only according to their own steppe traditions but also in accord with "civilized" Chinese practice.

—Joseph P. Byrne

FURTHER READING

Barfield, Thomas J. *The Perilous Frontier: Nomadic Empires and China, 221 B.C. to A.D. 1757*. Cambridge, Mass.: Blackwell, 1992. Places Khitan achievements in the context of Chinese relations with the "Manchurian candidates"of the period.

Hansen, Valerie. *The Open Empire: A History of China to 1600*. New York: W. W. Norton, 2000. This cultural history moves beyond dynastic labels to view interactions that both enriched and spread Chinese culture. Places especially strong emphasis on the Tang and Sung Dynasties.

Mote, F. W. *Imperial China, 900-1800*. Cambridge, Mass.: Harvard University Press, 1999. Several chapters cover the rise of the Khitans and their administration, society, and culture.

Sinor, Denis, ed. *The Cambridge History of Early Inner Asia*. New York: Cambridge University Press, 1990. The final essay provides a brief overview of Khitan and Jurchen society.

Twitchett, Denis, and Klaus-Peter Tietze. "The Liao." In *Alien Regimes and Border States, 907-1368*. Vol. 6 in *The Cambridge History of China*, edited by Denis Twitchett and Herbert Franke. New York: Cambridge University Press, 1994. An extensive analysis of the Khitan Liao Dynasty, especially in its relations with China.

Wittfogel, Karl A., and Feng Chia-sheng. *History of Chinese Society: Liao (907-1125)*. Philadelphia: Transactions of the American Philosophical Society, 1949. The standard work in English on the Khitans, based on an exhaustive study of Chinese sources.

SEE ALSO: 618: Founding of the Tang Dynasty; 744-840: Uighur Turks Rule Central Asia; 907-960: Period of Five Dynasties and Ten Kingdoms; 960: Founding of the Song Dynasty; 960-1279: Scholar-Official Class Flourishes Under Song Dynasty.

RELATED ARTICLES in *Great Lives from History: The Middle Ages, 477-1453*: Genghis Khan; Kublai Khan.

939-944
REIGN OF NGO QUYEN

With his decisive defeat of a Chinese army at Bachdang River, Ngo ended one thousand years of Chinese rule over the Vietnamese, freed his nation, and became its king.

LOCALE: Northern Vietnam
CATEGORIES: Government and politics; wars, uprisings, and civil unrest

KEY FIGURES

Ngo Quyen (c. 898-944), rebel leader and first king of the liberated Vietnamese, r. 939-944
Duong Dien Nghe (d. 937), key fighter against the Chinese, assassinated in 937
Kieu Cong Tien (d. 937 or 938), assassin of Duong, allied with the Chinese against Ngo
Liu Yan (Liu Yen; d. 942), emperor of the Southern Han, r. 917-942
Liu Hongcao (Liu Hung-ts'ao; d. 938), leader of the Chinese invasion fleet, son of Liu Yan
Dinh Bo Linh (923-979), first king after the fall of the Ngo Dynasty, r. 965-979

SUMMARY OF EVENT

The fall of China's powerful Tang Dynasty (T'ang; 618-907) provided the Vietnamese with a unique chance to regain their independence. Since 111 B.C.E., China had ruled over the Vietnamese. The Vietnamese lived in the fertile Red (Hong) River delta, the mountainous interior, and along the coast. In spite of occasional Vietnamese revolts, such as the famous one by the Trung sisters in 40-43 C.E. and the Nanzhao wars of the mid-ninth century, Chinese rule had not yet been eliminated.

The Chinese had organized the Vietnamese lands into a province that they called Annam, or Pacified South. They ruled from their capital of Dai-la (La Thanh), near present-day Hanoi. In 906, with China in chaos, a Vietnamese man, Khuc Thua Du, managed to get appointed as China's military governor of Annam. He, his son, and his grandson, My, governed the Vietnamese for China. In 930, the new emperor of the Southern Han Dynasty (909-971), Liu Yan, decided to impose a more direct rule. He sent an army to occupy Dai-la. My was captured, apparently without a fight, and sent to Canton (Guangzhou) in southern China, submitting to the emperor. In his place ruled Li Chen (d. 932).

At this time, the Vietnamese rebellion against Chinese rule began in earnest. One of My's generals, Duong Dien Nghe, refused to be co-opted by the Chinese. Although the Chinese made him a nobleman, he organized a Vietnamese army of three thousand soldiers. He refused a bribe by the desperate Li Chen to dissolve his forces. Instead, he captured Dai-la in battle in 931. He defeated the Chinese reinforcements, killing their general. Li Chen fled to Canton, where he was beheaded for his failure. Dien Nghe established his rule at Dai-la by his own power. Eventually, the emperor nominally

VIETNAM: INDEPENDENT GOVERNMENTS, 10TH-20TH CENTURIES

Dates	*Government*
939-965	Ngo Dynasty (Ngo Quyen, founder)
968-980	Dinh Dynasty
980-1009	Le Dynasty
1009-1225	Ly Dynasty
1225-1400	Tran Dynasty
1400-1407	Ho Dynasty
1428-1789	Later Le Dynasty
1790-1802	Chinese occupation

recognized him as military governor. Yet Dien Nghe governed in his own right, and his family became very important.

Ngo Quyen was one of Duong Dien Nghe's most loyal and capable generals. Ngo Quyen had been born in the heartland of Vietnamese civilization in about 898, the son of a provincial magistrate. Later, legends related that he was born bathed in luminescent light with three moles on his back, traditional signs of a great person. His given name, Quyen, means "strength of command and power" in Vietnamese. Ancient sources describe him as extremely handsome, with keen eyes and the walk of a tiger. He was considered intelligent, courageous, and sturdy in battle. After the conquest of Dai-la, Ngo Quyen married one of the daughters of Dien Nghe and was appointed governor of the ruler's home province of Ai, to the south of the Red River.

In March, 937, Dien Nghe was assassinated by Kieu Cong Tien. The assassin hoped to gain sympathy by aligning his rule with Chinese power and interests, reflecting remnants of pro-Chinese attitudes among some ruling elites. Immediately, Ngo Quyen gathered an army and led it against the assassin. Cong Tien begged the Chinese for help, and this alliance gave Ngo Quyen's quest a nationalistic character.

Emperor Liu Yan decided to send his own son, Liu Hongcao, to lead an army that should defeat the Vietnamese. Liu Hongcao was eager to load his army on warships and sail to Ha Long Bay, at the mouth of the Red River Delta. However, before any Chinese forces could assist Cong Tien, Ngo Quyen captured him and had him executed. He next prepared to battle the invaders.

In the fall of 938, Ngo Quyen employed a brilliant plan. He correctly guessed that Liu Hongcao was eager to invade by the fastest, most northern river of the delta, the Bach-dang. He placed sharpened wooden stakes, reinforced with tips of iron, just below the waterline at high tide in the river. When the Chinese fleet appeared at the mouth of the Bach-dang, the Vietnamese pretended to attack it from light, shallow boats with minimal draft, at high tide. Hongcao immediately pursued the attackers up the river. As the tide receded, the heavy Chinese troop ships were suddenly impaled on the stakes and lost all capability to move or maneuver. Then, Ngo Quyen's troops attacked again from their light boats and utterly defeated the immobilized Chinese. Liu Hongcao drowned, together with more than half of his assault troops. Emperor Liu Yan wept at his losses, and his Southern Han Dynasty abandoned its plans to conquer the Vietnamese.

Ngo Quyen's decisive victory meant full independence for his people. In 939, Ngo Quyen crowned himself king of the Vietnamese and radically broke with the past. He moved his capital out of the town associated with the Chinese governors. He established a new palace farther north at Co-loa, the city of the ancient, pre-Chinese Vietnamese kings.

Yet to some extent, Ngo Quyen could not yet escape the Chinese influence. He organized his court system along Chinese patterns and relied on a feudalistic, rather than nationalistic, order of society. He generally left in peace those nobles who had collaborated with the Chinese, and his newly liberated people looked up to their charismatic leader.

Ngo Quyen died suddenly in 944, aged only forty-six. If he had further plans to reform and remodel the Vietnamese state and its society, he died too soon to implement them. After a thousand years, Vietnam had gained independence, yet the domestic situation would reveal itself as far from stable.

SIGNIFICANCE

Ngo Quyen's decision to eliminate the assassin who had tried to usurp power and return to Chinese hegemony led to the decisive Battle of Bach-dang River. The total defeat of the Chinese fleet and army reestablished Vietnamese independence. From this time on, with a very brief interlude of twenty years in the fifteenth century, Vietnam would remain independent until the advent of the French in the late nineteenth century.

Ironically, in 1287, the Vietnamese would defeat an invading Mongol army on the Bach-dang River with virtually the same strategy employed by Ngo Quyen. Some of the stakes from both of the battles have survived and are on display at the Museum of History in Hanoi.

Political stability, however, did not accompany freedom. Instead, Ngo Quyen's succession led to a period of civil war and chaos in Vietnam. His brother-in-law attempted to reign instead of his eldest son, who fled into a cave; his second son eventually overthrew his uncle. An attempt by the two brothers to rule together failed. When the younger brother was killed in action against rebellious villagers in 963, the Ngo Dynasty began its demise.

After two years of civil war during the "period of twelve warlords," Dinh Bo Linh successfully seized power. He founded a new kingdom, which he named Dai Co Viet ("great empire of the Vietnamese"), and solidified Vietnamese independence. Yet he, too, fell victim to an assassin, in 979. Anarchy broke out until the establishment of the Early Le Dynasty in 980.

Vietnamese historians have been divided in their estimation of who should be given credit of being their first truly independent ruler. Toward the end of the fifteenth century, Ngo Quyen's fame was most celebrated. Later on, his reign was judged too brief, and the anarchy that ended his dynasty was regarded as too deep, so that Dinh Bo Linh has been given more historic credit. Maybe the fact that the latter claimed the title of "emperor" helped his posthumous credentials, even though he fell victim to an assassin.

Without Ngo Quyen's determination, ingenuity, and success in battle, the Southern Han could have reestablished authority over the Vietnamese. Instead, the people were freed from foreign domination. In the fifteenth century, they would become conquerors themselves, pushing far south to the Mekong Delta.

—*R. C. Lutz*

FURTHER READING

Huard, Pierre, and Maurice Durand. *Viet Nam: Civilization and Culture*. Translated by Vu Thiên Kim. 2d ed. Hanoi: Ecole Française d'Extrême-Orient, 1994. This general overview provides a survey of history and is richly illustrated.

Lockard, Craig A. "The Unexplained Miracle: Reflections on Vietnamese National Identity and Survival." *Journal of Asian and African Studies* 29 (January-April, 1994): 10-35. Provides framework for Ngo's regard as national hero, as it contemplates the strategies and triumphs of the Vietnamese in the face of foreign attempts to eradicate their culture.

Shih-Peng, Lü. *Vietnam During the Period of Chinese Rule*. Monograph Series 3. Hong Kong: Chinese University of Hong Kong, 1964. Useful overview of the one thousand years of Chinese rule over the Vietnamese; uses Wade-Giles transcription for both Chinese and Vietnamese names.

Taylor, Keith Weller. *The Birth of Vietnam*. Berkeley: University of California Press, 1983. The authoritative study of the period of and leading up to Ngo Quyen's reign. Makes accessible groundbreaking studies of Vietnamese and Chinese historical sources in English. Maps, appendices.

SEE ALSO: 729: Founding of Nanzhao; 832: Nanzhao Subjugates Pyu; 863: Nanzhao Captures Hanoi; 982: Le Dai Hanh Invades Champa; 1225: Tran Thai Tong Establishes Tran Dynasty; 1428: Le Loi Establishes Later Le Dynasty.

RELATED ARTICLE in *Great Lives from History: The Middle Ages, 477-1453*: Ngo Quyen.

c. 950
COURT OF CÓRDOBA FLOURISHES IN SPAIN

The flourishing of the court of Córdoba produced cultural and intellectual accomplishments in al-Andalus (Andalusia) that had a profound significance for Western Europe.

LOCALE: Córdoba, Spain
CATEGORIES: Cultural and intellectual history; education; government and politics; religion

KEY FIGURES

ʿAbd al-Raḥmān I (731-788), founder of the Umayyad Dynasty at Córdoba and emir of Córdoba, 756-788
ʿAbd al-Raḥmān II (788-852), emir of Córdoba, 822-852
ʿAbd al-Raḥmān III al-Nāṣir (891-961), emir of Córdoba, 912-929, and first caliph of Córdoba, 929-961
Al-Hakam I (770-822), emir of Córdoba, 796-822
Al-Hakam II (d. 976), caliph of Córdoba, 961-976
Hishām I (757-796), emir of Córdoba, 788-796
Abū ʿĀmir al-Manṣūr (c. 938-1002), vizier of Hishām II, 976-1002

SUMMARY OF EVENT

The foundation of the court of Córdoba, which in the tenth century became one of the greatest centers of learning in Europe, reads like a story out of *Alf layla wa-layla* (fifteenth century; *The Arabian Nights' Entertainments*, 1706-1708; also known as *The Thousand and One Nights*). In 750, a revolution by the ʿAbbāsid family against the Umayyad caliph broke out in Iraq and Syria. A young Umayyad prince, ʿAbd al-Raḥmān, escaped the proscription and traveled to North Africa, where he gained the support of his Berber relatives. He eventually went to Spain, where he established himself at Córdoba as an independent ruler.

After his death in 788, civil wars and revolts threatened the state he had created. In 912, a strong successor came to the throne: ʿAbd al-Raḥmān III al-Nāṣir, who firmly established control over Muslim Spain and carried on successful campaigns against small Christian outposts in the North. He and his successors al-Hakam II and Hishām II brought Muslim Spain to its greatest heights until the ambition of Hishām's vizier, Abū ʿĀmir al-Manṣūr, caused dynastic difficulties that brought about the collapse of the caliphate of Córdoba in 1031. About the same time, the long Reconquista of Spain by the Christians began.

The Umayyads of Damascus had been notable patrons of art and learning, and their descendants at Córdoba continued the family tradition. Cultural and intellectual edification at the new court was so emphatic that its spiritual impact outlived its political life. While ʿAbd al-Raḥmān I was still struggling to secure control of Spain, he found time to promote such artistic endeavors as initiation of the construction of the great mosque of Córdoba, which became the model for future Moorish mosques. He wrote poetry extolling the beauties of his Syrian homeland, imported fruit trees and vegetables from the eastern Islamic lands, and built the Rusafah Palace in the midst of gardens that were regarded as a wonder. Under his successors Hishām I and al-Hakam I, the great mosque was enlarged and extensive building campaigns were undertaken. ʿAbd al-Raḥmān II, a poet him-

CÓRDOBA'S UMAYYAD RULERS

Reign	*Ruler*
756-788	ʿAbd al-Raḥmān I
788-796	Hishām I
796-822	al-Hakam I
822-852	ʿAbd al-Raḥmān II
852-886	Muḥammad I
886-888	al-Mundhir
888-912	ʿAbd Allāh
912-961	ʿAbd al-Raḥmān III al-Nāṣir
961-976	al-Hakam II al-Mustanṣir
976-1008	Hishām II al-Muayyad
1008-1009	Muḥammad II al-Mahdī
1009	Sulaimān al-Mustaʿīn
1010-1013	Hishām II (restored)
1013-1016	Sulaimān (restored)
1016-1018	Alī ben Hammud
1018	ʿAbd al-Raḥmān IV
1018-1021	al-Qasim
1021-1022	Yaḥyā
1022-1023	al-Qasim (restored)
1023-1024	ʿAbd al-Raḥmān V
1024-1025	Muḥammad III
1025-1027	Yaḥyā (restored)
1027-1031	Hishām III
1031	End of Umayyads; dissolution of Umayyad Spain into small states

Note: Until 929 the Umayyad rulers were emirs; thereafter, with the ascendancy of ʿAbd al-Raḥmān III, they were caliphs.

self, imported scholars and artisans from the East and carried on an extensive building program.

This early activity came to fruition during the reign of ʿAbd al-Raḥmān III, called "the Great," and his immediate successors. Once he had centralized his authority over Muslim Spain and coastal areas of North Africa, forcing the powerful Fāṭimid Dynasty to move eastward to Egypt, he determined that his court would surpass that of his ʿAbbāsid rivals in Baghdad, who were on the decline. Perhaps for political reasons, ʿAbd al-Raḥmān III was the first Andalusian Umayyad dynast to declare himself "caliph," establishing throughout his reign absolute authority and increased isolation from his subjects, circumscribed by complex court etiquette. He brought prosperity as well as political unity to al-Andalus; during his reign Córdoba was the most prosperous city in Europe and foreign delegates marveled at the splendors of his court. He introduced new agricultural techniques and carried on a massive building program in and around Córdoba, including the lavish all-inclusive government city, Madinat al-Zahra, on the outskirts of Córdoba. He was a dedicated patron of the ever-increasing body of poets, historians, physicians, geographers, astronomers, mathematicians, musicians, and philosophers who gathered at his court. His son al-Hakam II continued such patronage, as did the powerful vizier of Hishām II, Abū ʿĀmir al-Manṣūr. The Córdoban tradition of scholarship based on Greco-Arabic learning was so strong that even as late as the twelfth century, long after the fall of the caliphate, the old capital produced two celebrated medieval thinkers, the Islamic philosopher Averroës and the Jewish scholar Moses Maimonides.

The court of the Córdoban emirate and caliphate, and the al-Andalus it ruled, was culturally heterogeneous. Although the rulers maintained the eastern Umayyad ideal of Arab supremacy, in reality the population consisted of large numbers of Berbers, Hispanic Jews and Christians, Slavs, and others, many of whom rose to positions of prominence. This unique blend of cultural and religious elements contributed to the ease with which Andalusian accomplishments were disseminated throughout the West.

As early as the tenth century, certain concepts of Arabic mathematics and astronomy were apparently introduced into Western Europe through contacts with Córdoba and Islamic Spain. John, a monk from the abbey of Gorze, was sent as ambassador to Córdoba by Emperor Otto I of Germany and returned with books on mathematics that soon made Gorze and other Lotharingian monasteries centers of study in this field. Gerbert of Aurillac, a young monk who later became Pope Sylvester II, owed much to Islamic learning when he became one of the greatest Western European scholars of the tenth century. When he visited Barcelona, he absorbed much mathematical and astronomical knowledge, which had spread northward from Muslim centers. Many scholars believe that, as the most learned mathematician of his

The interior of the cathedral at Córdoba, with its 106 pillars. Originally it was a mosque, built during the rule of the Umayyad sultans. (Frederick Ungar Publishing Co.)

time, Pope Sylvester introduced the abacus and also Arabic numerals into Europe. Because he was familiar with superior Islamic learning, legends after his death pictured him as a wizard created by Saracen sorcery and magic.

SIGNIFICANCE

The dissemination of Islamic learning in Spain had its greatest impact on Europe in the twelfth and thirteenth centuries, when Latin translations of Arabic texts and treatises on Aristotle began to appear in the North. Such translations spurred the development of Scholasticism, and the philosophical works of Averroës and his school at Córdoba played an influential role in the process.

The intellectual impact of Muslim scholarship was wide and varied. The works of Avicenna, the eleventh century Islamic medical theorist, became standard texts for Western physicians. The colorful stonework of the Romanesque churches of Auvergne bears striking resemblance to the variegated patterns of Moorish architecture; development of the Gothic arch can possibly be traced to the colonnades and horseshoe arches of Islamic Spanish masterpieces such as the mosque of Córdoba and the Alhambra. Considering the close contacts between southern France and northern Spain, the similarity between the themes and descriptions of Arabic love poetry is not surprising, and the roots of medieval courtly love poetry and music may be found in Moorish prototypes. One Spanish scholar, Miguel Asin-Palacios, maintains that Muslim legends about heaven and hell influenced that supreme poetic creation of medieval Western Europe, Dante's *La divina commedia* (c. 1320; *The Divine Comedy*, 1802).

—*James H. Forse, updated by Katherine S. Mansour*

FURTHER READING

Chejne, Anwar G. *Muslim Spain: Its History and Culture*. St. Paul: University of Minnesota Press, 1974. Written as a text for graduate students, this work provides a well-written and interesting overview of the history, culture, and intellectual life of al-Andalus.

Fletcher, Richard A. *Moorish Spain*. New York: Henry Holt, 1992. This work incorporates current scholarship on al-Andalus and offers a concise treatment of the Moors in Spain.

Hayes, John R., and George N. Atiyeh, eds. *The Genius of Arab Civilization: Source of Renaissance*. 3d ed. New York: New York University Press, 1992. A lively collection of essays, suitable for the general reader, discussing Arab intellectual and cultural accomplishments. Includes a bibliography and an index.

Jayyusi, Salma Khadra, ed. *The Legacy of Muslim Spain*. New York: E. J. Brill, 1992. A massive, one thousand-plus page collection on the artistic and cultural heritage of Muslim Spain. Includes maps, a bibliography, and an index.

Menocal, Maria Rosa, Raymond P. Scheindlin, and Michael Sells, eds. *The Literature of Al-Andalus*. New York: Cambridge University Press, 2000. Surveys the literature, including poetry, of the Andalusian period. Includes illustrations, a bibliography, and an index.

Reilly, Bernard F. *The Contest of Christian and Muslim Spain: 1031-1157*. Cambridge, Mass.: Blackwell, 1995. Enlightening use of primary sources to provide insight into the political and cultural changes in Iberia during this critical period.

Robinson, Cynthia. *In Praise of Song: The Making of Courtly Culture in al-Andalus and Provence, 1005-1134 A.D.* Boston: Brill, 2002. Explores Andalusian and Muslim influences on the rise of courtly culture, namely courtly love music. Includes some color illustrations, a bibliography, and an index.

Sordo, Enrique. *Moorish Spain*. New York: Crown, 1963. A work that concentrates on the three greatest cultural centers of Islamic Spain: Córdoba, Seville, and Granada.

SEE ALSO: April or May, 711: Ṭārik Crosses into Spain; 969-1171: Reign of the Fāṭimids; c. 1010-1015: Avicenna Writes His *Canon of Medicine*; 1031: Caliphate of Córdoba Falls; c. 1100: Arabic Numerals Are Introduced into Europe; c. 1100: Rise of Courtly Love; c. 1150: Moors Transmit Classical Philosophy and Medicine to Europe; c. 1150-1200: Development of Gothic Architecture; 1190: Moses Maimonides Writes *The Guide of the Perplexed*.

RELATED ARTICLES in *Great Lives from History: The Middle Ages, 477-1453*: Pietro d'Abuno; ʿAbd al-Raḥmān III al-Nāṣir; Abū Ḥanīfah; Alfonso X; Alhazen; Averroës; Avicenna; Roger Bacon; al-Bīrūnī; Dante; Fakhr al-Dīn al-Rāzī; al-Ghazzālī; al-Ḥallāj; Judah ha-Levi; Moses Maimonides; Otto I; al-Rāzī; Sylvester II; Thomas Aquinas.

c. 950-1100
Rise of Madrasas

From the tenth through the beginning of the twelfth century, a system of self-contained and privately funded institutions of higher learning called madrasas appeared throughout the Islamic world, becoming centers for the production of knowledge and normative practices in Islamic society.

Locale: Iraq, Iran, and other parts of the Islamic world

Categories: Cultural and intellectual history; education; organizations and institutions; religion

Key Figure

Niẓām al-Mulk (1018 or 1019-1092), Iranian government administrator and patron of madrasas

Summary of Event

The rise of the madrasa system marked the confluence and culmination of several defining aspects of medieval Islamic culture, among these traditions of rigorous scholarly inquiry, the rise of specifically Islamic forms of jurisprudence and the fields of intellectual activity that complemented and assisted these, and the practice of pious personal donation as a form of worship. The madrasa (literally "a place of study") became a site for the production of knowledge, and for the production of a knowledgeable subculture, that of the *ʿulama*. The madrasa shaped the character of Muslim intellectual and religious life, effectively circumscribing the range of questions that could be legitimately posed, pondered, and answered within Islamic society.

The advent of the madrasa system took place as part of a series of developments in medieval Islamic learning. Since the eighth and ninth centuries, groups of scholars had met in mosques throughout the Islamic world to discuss matters crucial to the formation of an Islamic identity and community. These meetings of study circles, which were known as *halaq* (singular *halqa*) or *majalis* (singular *majlis*), were presided over by an acknowledged teacher or authority in topics of formal religious study, including those of law, Hadith, or the sayings of the Prophet, and Qurʾānic commentary and interpretation. These "Islamic sciences" were set in opposition to the "foreign sciences" of philosophy and rational inquiry into the natural world, both of which represented the intellectual legacy of Hellenistic scholarship and study.

During the ninth century, four schools or *madhabs* of Islamic law—the Shafi, Hanafi, Maliki and Hanbali—developed separate but equally orthodox modes of legal interpretation among Sunni Muslims. The doctrine of these schools evolved as part of widespread advancements in Islamic law, and the study of law itself became more complicated. Legal education thus required more intensive and more prolonged efforts on the part of students and steady, stable venues for their teachers. Thus the study and teaching of the increasingly complex nuances of Islamic law each became full-time vocations.

Over time, hostels for students and teachers known as khans sprang up in proximity to mosques in which legal studies took place. In this way, local communities of scholars and students took shape, and students and masters from around the Muslim world were able to come together, thus fostering continuity of legal theory and practice. Khans were frequently built as communal gifts by rich Muslims. Such foundations combined the imperatives of local hospitality—khans were frequently at the disposal of travelers and pilgrims as well as students and teachers—with the religious obligations enjoined upon Muslims regarding the sharing of wealth with other Muslims.

The advent of the madrasa system proper is perhaps best understood as the intersection of the educational trends in the Arab world with the distinctively Islamic institution known as the *waqf*. From the time of the earliest Arab conquests, one question that consistently confronted the Muslim community was the disposal of communal wealth and the rights and obligations of individual Muslims with regard to the needs of other individual Muslims and the Muslim community as a whole. Among the doctrines that evolved out of these concerns was that of the *waqf*. A *waqf* is a pious donation of private funds to the community of Muslims. Often these funds went to mosques, libraries, Sufi monasteries, or hospitals; to ransom prisoners of war; or as simple alms for the poor. The religious objective in making such a donation was to attain greater nearness to God. Of course, other, more worldly objectives might prompt the donor as well. For whatever reason a *waqf* donation was made, however, its purpose and conditions could be laid out very specifically by the donor prior to the giving of the gift, but once the capital was turned over to its overseer (typically a respected *qadi* or judge), the *waqf* became "like an emancipated slave," free of its founder's direct control.

Increasingly during the tenth and eleventh centuries, *waqf* donations were earmarked for the foundation of what came to be known as a madrasa. This trend was exemplified by the foundation of madrasa complexes throughout the heartlands of the Islamic empire, and especially in Iraq by the powerful Seljuk executive officer Niẓām al-Mulk. Among Niẓām's most noteworthy foundations was the Madrasa Nizamiya in the intellectual hub of Baghdad, which was an immensely rich and prestigious institution that attracted the brightest and most revered scholars in Islam and that also housed vast collections of books.

The madrasa combined the elements of the *majlis* and khan and became a venue in which students and teachers alike could take up more or less permanent residence. The conditions of the *waqf* foundations varied from madrasa to madrasa—sometimes they provided a salary for teachers and stipends for students, sometimes only salaries for teachers, sometimes only the physical facilities themselves. It was not uncommon for the funds associated with the madrasa's initial foundation to derive from an orchard or some other form of productive capital.

The madrasa itself was devoted first and foremost to the study and transmission of Islamic law, although such subsidiary (and necessary) pursuits as the study of Arabic grammar, prophetic tradition, and Qur'ānic commentary might also be taught. The method of instruction was typically a lecture by a respected master of a given field of knowledge, during which his students would surround him and take notes. The master would frequently recite from memory his own works on questions of jurisprudence, religious doctrine, traditions of the Prophet, or other topics. In addition, he would cite, also from mem-

A madrasa in Samarqand, Uzbekistan, c. 1950. (Hulton|Archive by Getty Images)

ory, important works of other masters, including his own teachers. Memory was highly prized in this setting, and students were encouraged to memorize the knowledge they "collected" and free themselves of the need for the written word.

Although within the madrasa, the study of Islamic law was exalted above all other pursuits, including the study of literature and the foreign sciences, these realms of knowledge systematically made their way back into the madrasa through the extracurricular activities of resident students and teachers who studied these "lesser" disciplines away from the madrasa. In this way, the methods and modes of disputation encountered in Greek philosophy, for example, affected the discussion and debate of points of Islamic law profoundly (if covertly). Similarly, histories, biographies, and other works of belles-lettres were read to enhance the students' and teacher's imagination and capacity for analogous reasoning.

Learning was understood as a lifelong process, and there are numerous anecdotes that depict famous Muslim scholars taking the time on their deathbeds to learn one last prophetic saying or one last poem. Once a student had mastered one science, there were always more to study and always more knowledge to acquire. Learning was thought to leave its imprint on the individual, and through diligent study, individuals were understood to refine themselves and become better Muslims and more honorable social beings. As one scholar put it, learning shone out from the learned man and not only illuminated those around him but also marked him as a communal exemplar.

Perhaps the most important function of the madrasa from the point of view of the Islamic community was that it served as a venue for the creation of consensus in a society ruled by custom and common public assent. Medieval Islamic society had no organizing bodies with which to produce such consensus, or with which to interpret or refine custom. In other societies, such functions may be fulfilled by ecclesiastical hierarchies or by formal public judicial bodies. In medieval society, questions of law and normative custom were regulated by a dialectical process by which propositions were either popularly assented to or objected to. The madrasa became the site in which the legal scholars whose voice was authoritative in such matters debated matters of custom and law, and the site in which they determined the acceptability or permissibility of thousands on thousands of questions and propositions large and small, all of which would manifest themselves in the day-to-day lives of millions of Muslims over the space of generations.

SIGNIFICANCE

During the centuries of the Crusades, and following the overthrow of the Shīʿite governments of the eastern Muslim world in the tenth and eleventh centuries, the madrasa became a center for the production of specifically Sunni, and increasingly militant, ideologies. During the same period and in later centuries, the madrasa was also a site for the forging of relationships between what were often non-Arab ruling elites and the intellectual and spiritual leaders of the communities over whom they held sway. Thus, despite the inherent separation between madrasas and secular leaders, they became and would remain crucial meeting points between the worldly power of their founders and patrons and the spiritual and moral authority wielded by the scholars whose work they fostered.

—*Thomas Sizgorich*

FURTHER READING

Berkey, Jonathan. *The Transmission of Knowledge in Medieval Cairo: A Social History of Islamic Education*. Princeton, N.J.: Princeton University Press, 1992. A concise and vivid study of the relationship between secular elites and institutions of learning and culture in medieval Cairo. Bibliography, index.

Ephrat, Daphna. *A Learned Society in a Period of Transition: The Sunni "ʿUlama" of Eleventh Century Baghdad*. Albany: State University of New York Press, 2000. A study of the intellectual circles of Baghdad that were inspired by the founding and success of the madrasas. Chapters discuss the arrival of the madrasas, the ʿulama in the context of scholarly networks beyond Baghdad, and the *halqa*. Maps, bibliography, index.

Huff, Toby E. *The Rise of Early Modern Science: Islam, China, and the West*. 2d ed. New York: Cambridge University Press, 2003. Provides a strong cross-cultural background on madrasas and their role in the rise of science and scientific knowledge in the Muslim world. Illustrations, bibliography, index.

Leiser, Gary. "The *Madrasa* and the Islamization of the Middle East: The Case of Egypt." *Journal of the American Research Center in Egypt* 22 (1985): 29-47. A study of the role played by madrasa institutions in producing and disseminating Islamic identity and communal mores.

_______. "Notes on the Madrasa in Medieval Islamic Society." *Muslim World* 73 (1983): 165-181. Considers the situation of the early madrasa system in its historical and social setting.

Makdisi, George. *Religion, Law, and Learning in Classical Islam*. Brookfield, Vt.: Variorum, 1991. These collected articles of the author represent the evolution of his scholarship regarding the intellectual milieu in which the madrasa system was born. An indispensable source. Bibliography, index.

_______. *The Rise of the Colleges: Institutions of Learning in Islam and the West*. Edinburgh: Edinburgh University Press, 1981. The standard work on the rise of the madrasa and one of the foremost works on the intellectual culture to which the madrasa was home. Bibliography, index.

SEE ALSO: 972: Building of al-Azhar Mosque; 1100-1300: European Universities Emerge; c. 1150: Moors Transmit Classical Philosophy and Medicine to Europe.

RELATED ARTICLES in *Great Lives from History: The Middle Ages, 477-1453*: Abū Ḥanīfah; Aḥmad ibn Ḥanbal; al-Ashʿarī; al-Ghazzālī; al-Ḥasan al-Baṣrī; Niẓām al-Mulk.

c. 950-1150
TOLTECS BUILD TULA

Tula was the capital of the Toltec Empire, the most powerful and influential civilization of pre-Hispanic Mexico's Early Post-Classic period.

LOCALE: Highland Central Mexico (now Tula de Allende, Hidalgo, Mexico)

CATEGORIES: Architecture; cultural and intellectual history; expansion and land acquisition; trade and commerce

KEY FIGURE

Quetzalcóatl (fl. tenth century), legendary Toltec ruler of Tula and high priest of the Quetzalcóatl cult

SUMMARY OF EVENT

The archaeological site known as Tula (or Tollán) is associated with the powerful Toltec civilization that appeared after the fall of the great Classic period metropolis of Teotihuacán around 650. Tula is located about 50 miles (80 kilometers) north of what is now Mexico City on the northern fringes of the Central Plateau region. The ancient city's ruins lie on a ridge flanking a rather arid plain. The ancient name appearing in early chronicles was Tollán (Place of the Reeds).

Following the destruction of Teotihuacán, migrating groups from the north began to settle in the Valley of Mexico and adopt the more settled life of agriculturalists. The Toltecs who occupied Tula were apparently an amalgamation of several ethnic groups speaking a variety of languages and most likely coming from various regions of ancient Mexico. Although northern elements were most dominant and the main language was Nahuatl, the tradition of the former highly advanced urban cultures represented by some associated ethnic groups aided the rise of Toltec civilization at Tula.

Settlement at Tula began as early as 700-750 and continued for more than four centuries. There are two clusters of ruins at the site. Tula Chico represents the earliest occupation. The ruins of Tula Grande, a larger civic-religious center, are located three-quarters of a mile (a little over a kilometer) southwest of the earlier site on a large mesa. Here, the Toltec capital grew and reached its peak of influence during the period c. 950-1150. These are the excavated ruins now seen by visitors to the site.

A fully accurate reconstruction of the history of the Toltecs and Tula is complicated by contradictory sources. Aided by Aztec pupils and converts, scholarly Spanish friars such as the Franciscan missionary Bernardino de Sahagún produced written accounts of this earlier era that contain some factual material mixed with fanciful tales and exaggeration. Later interpretations of Tula's past, based on archaeological excavations, differ on some points, including Sahagún's chronology of events.

The Toltec foundation myth speaks of an early mythological Toltec leader called Mixcóatl (Cloud Serpent) who conquered much of the Valley of Mexico and established a capital at Culhuacán. Mixcóatl's son, Quetzalcóatl (named Ce Acatl Topiltzin, Our Prince One Reed, at birth), became a high priest of the Quetzalcóatl (Feathered Serpent) cult. As was common in this profession, he also took on the name of the god he served. In later accounts, this mortal hero became transformed into this same deity and is credited with introducing many of the arts and inventions of civilized life during his leadership in Tula. According to the legend, Quetzalcóatl moved the capital of the Toltecs to Tula, where under his wise and benevolent leadership as a religious reformer, it developed into the mythical paradise described in later

The Toltec statues at Tula, Mexico. (Digital Stock)

Aztec legends. Chronologies based on the early post-conquest Spanish sources (mid-sixteenth century) place this event close to the beginning of the Tula Grande or Tollan archaeological phase. However, the old sources also complicate matters in connecting the same cultural hero with events in Tula's collapse around the mid-1100's. Modern specialists differ widely on the chronological context for Quetzalcóatl's presence in Tula. One well-known treatise places Mixcóatl and Quetzalcóatl in the period associated with Tula's fall rather than its beginning. Others suggest the old story may be connected with the earlier Tula Chico site and its collapse.

By 1100, Tula had evolved into the largest urban center in Mesoamerica. The city covered 6 square miles (15.5 square kilometers) and had a population of at least thirty-five thousand. Some experts give even larger figures. The major structures and monuments include I-shaped ball courts, pyramid temples, and huge buildings with colonnaded halls that surround a great open plaza. Atop Pyramid B, also called the Temple of Quetzalcóatl, are spectacular 15-foot-high (4.5-meter-high) Atlantean figures representing Toltec warriors armed with atlatls (spear throwers). These gigantic sculptures probably served as columns supporting a roof. One of the carved reliefs on the temple is a feathered serpent image and could possibly represent Quetzalcóatl. The so-called Burnt Palace to the west of Pyramid B contains a forest of rectangular and circular columns. A stone bench extends around three sides. Despite its name, this great structure most likely served as a meeting place for the elite rather than a residence for rulers. Other distinctive features at the site are large sculpted, reclining figures representing a male deity or a captive noble with raised head and knees. On the stomachs of these *chacmools* was a bowl, which may have served as a receptacle for hearts taken from human sacrificial victims. Other features are a skull rack on a 160-foot-long (49-meter-long) low platform near one of the ball courts and a 131-foot-long (40-meter-long) free-standing Serpent Wall with motifs that include rattlesnakes devouring human skulls. Toltec art and architectural decorations at Tula emphasize militarism and themes of death and destruction.

Excavations at Tula have uncovered thousands of well-made houses. Most were built on raised platforms and had stone or adobe walls and flat roofs. Features such as stucco floors and underground storm drains were also present. Rectangular or square buildings with several rooms formed residential complexes with up to five houses that faced interior courtyards containing a small shrine. Causeways and streets linked the city's distinct neighborhoods. In some cases, neighborhoods were made up of people specializing in the same occupation.

Many residents of Tula were engaged in craft production, and the term *toltec* later meant master craftsperson or artisan. Many of the valuable materials craftspeople used in their trades were obtained through extensive long-distance commerce. Goods arrived from far-off regions such as Central America, the Gulf and Pacific coasts, and the far northern frontier in what is now the southwestern United States. Some exclusively Mexican trade items appear at ancient Anasazi sites such as Chaco Canyon in what is now northern New Mexico.

Tula was also the capital of an empire state. The motivation for empire building was probably collecting tribute from subjugated peoples. Although precise boundaries are difficult to determine, Toltec control most likely encompassed most of central Mexico and regions to the north. There is also some historical and architectural evidence that a freelance band of Toltecs under a cultural hero known Quetzalcóatl (also known as Kukulcan, a Maya term for Feathered Serpent) may have occupied some sites in the Yucatán Peninsula, such as Chichén Itzá, around 1000. Many monuments, sculptured figures, and Maya artwork at that famous site are replicas of those found in Tula's central precinct.

The exact cause of Tula's sudden mysterious collapse around the mid-to-late 1100's remains a mystery. The colorful mythical account found in Sahagún's work depicts an epic conflict between rival factions resulting in the downfall and expulsion of the humanistic and benign Quetzalcóatl. Going into exile with a group of followers, this deified cultural hero eventually sailed eastward from the Gulf coast, vowing to return on a predicted future date. Meanwhile, the legendary rule of Quetzalcóatl's evil nemesis Tezcatlipoca (God of the Night Sky) possibly led to Tula's demise. The city's ruins show evidence that it was laid to waste and burned. Most specialists today attribute Tula's collapse to a combination of external enemies and internal pressures.

Some groups who left Tula before and during its final stressful period settled in communities of the nearby Valley of Mexico such as Culhuacán, Mixcóatl's old center.

SIGNIFICANCE

Tula's destruction and the collapse of Toltec power in the twelfth century was by no means the final chapter in the history of this powerful pre-Aztec civilization. Later Mesoamerican peoples with imperial ambitions sought to claim the mantle of the Toltec legacy and embellished the legends about its greatness. The Aztec ruling classes linked themselves with royal Toltec bloodlines through marriages to Toltec descendants in neighboring Culhuacán. Also, the compound at Tula described above was a prototype for the central precinct of the Aztec capital Tenochtitlán (now Mexico City). Artifacts that Aztec peoples systematically looted from Tula's ruins centuries after its fall have turned up in excavations of Tenochtitlán. Finally, the legend of Quetzalcóatl's return from the east in a year coinciding with 1519 in the European calendar, his reportedly non-Indian physical characteristics, and other coincidental factors contributed to the downfall of the Aztecs at the hand of Spanish conqueror Hernán Cortés, beginning in 1519.

—*David A. Crain*

FURTHER READING

Davies, Nigel. *The Toltec Heritage: From the Fall of Tula to the Rise of Tenochtitlán*. Norman: University of Oklahoma Press, 1980. Examines the lingering importance of this civilization's legacy to successor groups such as the Mexica/Aztecs.

_______. *The Toltecs, Until the Fall of Tula*. Norman: University of Oklahoma Press, 1977. Attempts to resolve frequently conflicting historical and archaeological evidence on the prestigious ancient Toltec civilization.

Diehl, Richard A. *Tula: The Toltec Capital of Ancient Mexico*. London: Thames and Hudson, 1983. Important overview on the Toltecs and the archaeological investigations at Tula.

Healan, Dan M., ed. *Tula of the Toltecs: Excavations and Survey*. Iowa City: University of Iowa Press, 1989. Detailed treatise on the archaeological activity and findings conducted at Tula by a team of scholars from the University of Missouri.

Mastache, Alba Guadalupe, Robert H. Cobean, and Dan M. Healan. *Ancient Tollan: Tula and the Toltec Heartland*. Boulder: University Press of Colorado, 2002. A work on origins and development of Tula and the Toltec civilization based on the extensive archaeological research on Tula.

SEE ALSO: c. 600-950: El Tajín Is Built; 7th-8th centuries: Maya Build Astronomical Observatory at Palenque; c. 700-1000: Building of Chichén Itzá; 1325-1519: Aztecs Build Tenochtitlán.

RELATED ARTICLE in *Great Lives from History: The Middle Ages, 477-1453*: Itzcoatl.

August 10, 955
OTTO I DEFEATS THE MAGYARS

Otto I's defeat of the Magyars halted their raids of Central Europe and encouraged their peaceful settlement in the plains of Hungary as a settled and Christianized nation.

LOCALE: Lechfeld, near Augsburg, Germany
CATEGORIES: Religion; wars, uprisings, and civil unrest

KEY FIGURES

Otto I (912-973), king of Germany, r. 936-973, and Holy Roman Emperor, r. 962-973
Saint Adelaide (931-999), widow of King Lothair of Lombardy and second wife of Otto I
Berengar II (c. 900-966), marquis of Ivrea
John XII (c. 937-964), Roman Catholic pope, 955-964

SUMMARY OF EVENT

Otto I, whom contemporaries named the Great, has been called the Charlemagne of Germany proper. His reign marked the beginning of Germany's First Reich, known for almost a thousand years (until 1806) as the Holy Roman Empire of German Nations.

Otto I inherited the kingship from his father, Henry I, the Fowler. Although exercising little royal power over the strong and independent tribal dukes, Henry nevertheless increased the prestige of the Crown by his charismatic personality. His successor, the twenty-four-year-old Otto, took a different view of the German kingship than his father. The great Frankish emperor Charlemagne was his model. Consequently, he held his coronation at Charlemagne's favorite residence, Aix-la-Chapelle (Aachen). The ceremony was attended by all the tribal dukes of Germany, who unanimously elected him king. The archbishop of Mainz anointed him king and invested him with Charlemagne's gigantic crown, scepter, sword, and golden mantle.

King Henry's death became a signal of revolt among the Slavic and Hungarian peoples to the east of the kingdom. In 895, the Magyars, a nomadic people, began taking possession of the ancient Roman province of Pannonia, from which they raided central Europe for more than half a century. In 937, they made their first incursion into Germany during Otto's reign, raiding Saxony and ransacking their way to the borders of France. They were defeated by forces led by Otto himself at a place unknown.

In addition, the early part of Otto's reign was fraught with insurrection and challenges to his crown by the independent-minded dukes of Germany, aided by archbishops and his own brother, Henry, and half brother, Tankmar. Otto was able to defeat these rebellious nobles and consolidate his power by giving their territories to faithful relatives and other followers. In addition to these internecine challenges, Otto had to fight incursions of the Danes to the north, the Slavs and Wends to the east, Bohemians and Hungarians to the southeast, and the duke of Lorraine on the western frontier. Being the embodiment of the Germanic warrior king at the head of his troops, he succeeded in beating back these onslaughts. In many instances he was able not only to secure the borders but also to subjugate and Christianize these pagan peoples and bring them into the orbit of the German realm. During his reign, Germany extended its colonization of Slav territory from the Elbe to the Oder River. These policies, in imitation of Charlemagne, earned Otto the title "the Great."

His most decisive victory came over the marauding Magyars, who had made repeated incursions into Germany in 937, 944, 948, and 950. In 955, they were invited into Germany by some Bavarian nobles as part of their civil strife against Otto. The Hungarian hordes, arrogant of success on account of their sheer numerical strength (contemporaries estimated 100,000 horsemen; the Hungarians boasted that their horses could drain every river in Germany), laid siege to the city of Augsburg, which was heroically defended by its bishop. Badly outnumbered and with only dilapidated walls to protect it, the city seemed incapable of withstanding the assault. When Otto heard of the Magyar invasion, he hastily assembled an army from all parts of Germany and hurried to Augsburg. The decisive Battle of Lechfeld took place on August 10, 955, outside the city on the Lech River. Before the battle started, Otto and his armies consecrated themselves in a mass where they took the Holy Eucharist and the king vowed to found a bishopric at Merseburg if God granted him victory. The upcoming battle took on the characteristic of a crusade.

In the scorching heat of August, the Magyar troops were attacked by three waves of Bavarians, followed by a wave of Franks, a fifth wave of elite Saxon troops led by the king himself, followed by five lines of Swabians and a rear guard composed of Bohemians, under the banner of the archangel Michael. At first, the Magyars were able to avoid the direct attack, even causing havoc by falling into the rear of Otto's army. Nevertheless, valor saved the day. Sword in hand, Otto himself fought in the thick of battle. Conrad of Lorraine, the most valiant warrior of the day who led the Franks in combat, died from an arrow in his throat while lifting his helmet to wipe his face and catch some air. As the tide of battle turned, the Hungarians tried to escape across the Lech River, where many of them drowned. The rest of the Magyar invaders were routed and killed. If one can believe the statistics of the age, some 100,000 Hungarians died.

SIGNIFICANCE

So decisive was the victory at Lechfeld, the Magyars gave up their wandering, accepted Christianity, peacefully settled on the plains of Hungary, and eventually became allies of the Holy Roman Empire.

With his prestige enhanced by this victory, Otto tried to further consolidate the German monarchy by seeking to extend his influence to Italy and eventually to be crowned Holy Roman Emperor. Adelaide, widow of the Lombard king, had lost her northern Italian kingdom to the local pretender Berengar II. In 951, Otto, in response to a call for help, crossed the Alps and defeated Berengar. A widower himself at the time, Otto married Adelaide and reincorporated her lands into the empire. This began Germany's fateful involvement in the chaotic affairs of Italy. In an attempt to win an empire, the German emperors lost Germany, as later history was to witness.

While Otto's attention was absorbed with his rebellious and disloyal vassals in Germany and his defense against the Magyars, Berengar had reconquered the Lombard kingdom, seeking independent sovereignty in Italy. Consequently, in 961, Otto crossed the Alps again, expelled Berengar, and continued on to Rome, where the reluctant Pope John XII on February 2, 962, crowned him Holy Roman Emperor. This union of Germany and Italy under the imperial crown created the Holy Roman Empire.

This coronation marked the apex of Otto's emulation of Charlemagne. Yet with it he also had set the agenda for the Holy Roman Empire for the remainder of the Middle Ages. His successors would see the need to keep the reluctant northern Italians in the empire as the rationale to obtaining the Roman Crown. Their dream of an empire would prevent the consolidation of the monarchy in Germany.

The eastward expansion of Germany into Slavic territory became a constant theme of German history, as did the colonization of eastern central Europe, where the Poles, Bohemians, and Hungarians remained in the orbit of the Holy Roman Empire. The Battle of Lechfeld, however, not only ended Hungarian incursion into central Europe but also marks the beginning of the Magyars as a sedentary people and Christian nation.

—Herbert Luft

FURTHER READING

Arnold, Benjamin. *Medieval Germany, 500-1300*. Buffalo, N.Y.: University of Toronto Press, 1997. This survey of medieval German history emphasizes both the fragmented, provincial nature of that history—a history divided between different peoples with different customs and social structures—and the global nature of the Western Roman Empire that had Germany at its center. Includes significant discussion of the role of Otto I in developing and strengthening the empire.

Falco, Georgio. *The Holy Roman Empire*. Westport, Conn.: Greenwood Press, 1980. This general history of the Holy Roman Empire profiles the Middle Ages in German history.

Fichtenau, Heinrich. *Living in the Tenth Century: Mentalities and Social Order*. Chicago: University of Chicago Press, 1991. A survey of the Carolingian and post-Carolingian era in the *Annales* style.

Hill, Boyd H., Jr. *Medieval Monarchy in Action: The German Empire from Henry I to Henry IV*. New York: Barnes and Noble Books, 1972. A history of the reigns of German emperors with emphasis on their domestic and foreign policies.

Leyse, Karl J. *Rule and Conflict in Early Medieval Society: Ottonian Saxony*. Bloomington: Indiana University Press, 1979. This collection of studies includes a discussion of Otto I and his enemies.

Macartney, C. A. *Studies on Early Hungarian and Pontic History*. Edited by Lóránt Czigány and László Péter. Brookfield, Vt.: Ashgate, 1998. Provides crucial background information on the early Magyars and the developments leading up to the Battle of Lechfeld.

Reuter, Timothy. *Germany in the Early Middle Ages*. London: Longman, 1991. A largely political history of medieval Germany and its realm.

Róna-Tas, András. *Hungarians and Europe in the Early Middle Ages: An Introduction to Early Hungarian History*. New York: Central European University Press, 1999. This highly technical historiography includes detailed discussion of the encounter between the Magyars and medieval Germanic peoples.

SEE ALSO: c. 850: Development of the Slavic Alphabet; 864: Boris Converts to Christianity; 890's: Magyars Invade Italy, Saxony, and Bavaria.

RELATED ARTICLES in *Great Lives from History: The Middle Ages, 477-1453*: Charlemagne; Otto I.

956
OĞHUZ TURKS MIGRATE TO TRANSOXIANA

The conquering and occupation of the Transoxian region of Central Asia, or Transoxiana, marked the beginning of the Turkic people's control of much of the Middle East. The Oğhuz people, led by the Seljuk tribe, swept south from Central Asia, defeated the old Muslim Empire, and created a new one that would eventually become the Ottoman Empire.

LOCALE: Transoxian region of Central Asia
CATEGORY: Expansion and land acquisition

KEY FIGURES

Subüktigin (d. 990), a Turkish general who took the Sāmānid city of Ghazna

Maḥmūd of Ghazna (971-1030), son of Subüktigin and founder of a Turkish empire in modern Afghanistan, r. 997-1030

SUMMARY OF EVENT

Central Asia has always been a place where civilizations have met and clashed. Bordered by China in the east, Europe in the west, and the Islamic states in the south, it has been conquered and controlled by several large empires. During medieval times, the steppes of Central Asia were home to two competing groups, the Islamic caliphate headquartered in Baghdad (soon to be replaced by the Persian Empire) and the Turks, or Oğuz Confederation, north of the Oxus River.

The Oğuz Turks originated in the region of Mongolia and were pushed westward and southward by the Mongols during the sixth century. They settled in the region between Lake Baikal and the Aral Sea in the northern portion of Central Asia. The Oğuz were part of a loosely based confederation of tribes who had different cultures, languages, and political systems. The broad plains in the north and mountainous areas of the south also prevented a central authority from establishing itself over the tribes. Yet the Oğuz had the reputation of being fierce fighters, a quality favored by the powers that controlled Central Asia south of the Oxus. It was the need for these fierce fighters that eventually led the Oğuz to move south of the Oxus and invade the Middle East.

The Transoxian region refers to the territory between the Oxus and Jaxartes Rivers. This piece of land was the dividing line between the territory controlled by the nomadic Oğuz and the Muslim Persian Empire. The Oxus River (today known as the Amu Dar'ya River) flowed through the entire Central Asian region. It began in the high Pamir Mountains, a range near the Chinese border, and flowed northward to the Aral Sea. Immediately to its north is the Jaxartes, which also flowed from the Pamir Mountains, through the modern country of Uzbekistan and into the Aral Sea. North of this territory were the wild steppes of inland Asia. South of the line was the more mountainous territory controlled by different Persian empires. The region between the two rivers could best be described as the Fertile Crescent of Central Asia. It was a trading center for the Silk Road from Europe to China.

The Oxus was a wild river, frequently shifting course and making it a dangerous crossing for any invader. For this reason, it served as the ideal barrier against invasion by those north of the river who might attack the Persian Empire. The Transoxian region resembled the Roman Empire's Rhine and Danube River borders. The Turkic tribes to the north were considered barbarians in Muslim civilization because of the Turks' nomadic lifestyle.

When the ʿAbbāsids had conquered the Persians in the mid-eighth century, they halted at Transoxiana and did not challenge the power of the Oğuz tribe. The ʿAbbāsids and their successors, the Sāmānids, controlled the region for two centuries and ensured that the Middle East was secure from the marauding bands.

Although the Oxus was an effective physical barrier to invasion, the Oğuz Confederation also had its own difficulties. Composed of several tribes, the Oğuz were not powerful enough on their own to challenge the empires to the south and were unwilling to combine their strength. It was only when the southern empires became weak and dependent on the Oğuz for mercenary troops that the Oğuz were able to challenge their neighbors to the south.

The Oğuz were constantly moving, pushed from the north and east by the Mongols and other Asian tribes. As the tribes of the Oğuz federation moved south, they faced two different empires. The ʿAbbāsid caliph controlled the massive Muslim armies that conquered much of the Middle East, including the Persian Empire. The caliphate extended its power to and beyond the Oxus River, controlling the cities of Samarqand and Bukhara, which had served as trading posts and economic centers in Central Asia for centuries. It was between the Oxus and Jaxartes Rivers that the Oğuz came into contact with the ʿAbbāsid Dynasty.

The ʿAbbāsids ruled for several centuries and used members of the fierce tribes to their north as surrogate troops. Eventually, the power of the ʿAbbāsids declined, and they were defeated by a new Persian dynasty, the Sāmānids. This dynasty ruled Persia, and their empire stretched from Mesopotamia to India and to the region between the Oxus and Jaxartes Rivers.

However, the Sāmānids were not as powerful as the ʿAbbāsid caliphs and came to rely increasingly on surrogate troops from the Oğuz to maintain their control in Central Asia. By the middle of the tenth century, the Sāmānids had established much of their government in Transoxiana. They made Bukhara their capital city, increasing the vulnerability of their government to the Oğuz.

The Oğuz Confederation's close proximity to the ʿAbbāsid and Sāmānid Empires led to a conversion of many of the Turkic tribes to Islam. The Seljuks were converted in 956, and during this time there were mass conversions of tens of thousands of Turkic people.

Even with their shared religious beliefs, however, the Sāmānids and the Oğuz experienced a deteriorating relationship during the middle of the tenth century. High taxes, a clumsy and overbearing government bureaucracy, and a growing dependence on the Turks for the defense of Sāmānid territory weakened the empire.

A series of small rebellions revealed the Sāmānid vulnerability to attack. In Afghanistan, the fortress city of Ghazna fell to the Turkish general Subüktigin, who declared the city independent of the Sāmānid Dynasty. His son, Maḥmud, began the Ghaznavid Dynasty in Central Asia. Maḥmūd would lead his Turkic followers south and east into India, spreading the Muslim faith into that region. The loss of Ghazna and its establishment as an independent empire led to further attacks between the Oxus and Jaxartes Rivers.

As the tribes of the Oğuz Confederation moved into Transoxiana, then south of the river, they began to use the Persian officials to operate their growing empire. At the end of the tenth century, the Seljuks and other Turkic tribes moved south and west into Persia and toward the Mesopotamian region.

SIGNIFICANCE

The penetration of the Transoxian region marked the decline of the river Oxus as a boundary between the civilized Muslim civilizations south of the area and the "barbarian" tribes to the north. The movement south also exposed the weaknesses of the Sāmānids, opening the Middle East to conquest and control by the nomadic Seljuk Turks, who were fierce warriors and rulers. The successors to the Seljuks would eventually create the Ottoman Empire, which would rule the Middle East for centuries.

—*Douglas Clouatre*

FURTHER READING

Baldick, Julian. *Animal and Shaman: Ancient Religions of Central Asia*. New York: New York University Press, 2000. Describes the earliest belief systems of the Central Asian tribes and their replacement by Islam.

Di Cosmo, Nicola, ed. *Warfare in Inner Asian History*. Boston: Brill, 2002. Discusses the means and tactics of warfare among the early tribes that settled in Central Asia.

Gordon, Matthew. *The Breaking of a Thousand Swords*. Albany: State University of New York Press, 2001. Details the tribes, conflicts, and cultures of Central Asia during medieval times.

Grotenhuis, Elizabeth, ed. *Along the Silk Road*. Washington, D.C.: Smithsonian Institution, 2002. Provides pictures of modern Central Asia and text detailing the Silk Road and its path through Central Asia.

Kafesogla, Ibrahim. *A History of the Seljuks*. Carbondale: Southern Illinois University Press, 1988. Covers the rise of the Seljuks within the Oğuz Confederation and their eventual domination of much of the Islamic world.

Richards, D. S., trans. *The Annals of the Seljuk Turks*. London: Routledge Curzon Press, 2002. A modern translation of the stories and myths surrounding the rise of the Seljuk Turks in Central Asia.

Soucek, Svatopoluk. *A Short History of Central Asia*. New York: Cambridge University Press, 2002. A concise overview of the Central Asia region from ancient to modern times.

SEE ALSO: 744-840: Uighur Turks Rule Central Asia; 998-1030: Reign of Maḥmūd of Ghazna; 1010: Firdusi Composes the *Shahnamah*; 1040-1055: Expansion of the Seljuk Turks; 1077: Seljuk Dynasty Is Founded.

RELATED ARTICLES in *Great Lives from History: The Middle Ages, 477-1453*: Alp Arslan; Maḥmūd of Ghazna; Niẓām al-Mulk; Tamerlane.

958-1076
KOREANS ADOPT THE TANG CIVIL SERVICE MODEL

The Korean kings Wang So and Wang Ch'i created a new governing structure modeled on that of the Chinese Tang Dynasty in order to achieve greater centralization and a stronger monarchy.

LOCALE: Korean peninsula
CATEGORY: Government and politics

KEY FIGURES

Wang So (posthumous title King Kwangjong; 925-975), king of Koryŏ, r. 949-975
Wang Yu (posthumous title King Kyŏngjong; 955-981), king of Koryŏ, r. 975-981
Wang Ch'i (posthumous title King Sŏngjong; 960-997), king of Koryŏ, r. 981-997
Wang Hwi (posthumous title King Munjong; 1019-1083), king of Koryŏ, 1046-1083

SUMMARY OF EVENT

Government reform in Koryŏ started with Kwangjong, the fourth king of the Koryŏ Dynasty (918-1392) and a son of the dynastic founder T'aejo (Wang Kŏn). T'aejo's reign (r. 918-943) had failed to establish a strong, centralized monarchy. Instead, the dynasty was more of a confederation of various strongmen with local power bases, who leaned heavily on the throne and meddled in the royal succession. As a result, a violent succession struggle erupted following the death of T'aejo's chosen successor, King Hyejong (r. 944-945), in 945. After another of T'aejo's sons failed to consolidate the dynasty, Kwangjong took the throne.

Kwangjong was endowed with sufficient character and vision to leave an indelible imprint on the dynasty. One of his chief concerns was to strengthen royal authority and reduce the influence of the powerful families that had helped T'aejo ascend to the throne. Kwangjong looked to the Chinese bureaucratic system of government to replace the unstable coalition of warlords with people who would be loyal to the dynasty and state rather than to their vested regional or family interests. To some extent, he could draw on the experience of the Chinese Later Zhou Dynasty (Chou; 951-960), which at that time was also implementing a program of administrative reform aimed at overcoming the independent military governors who had wrestled power from the imperial bureaucracy in the second half of the Tang Dynasty (T'ang; 618-907). In fact, Kwangjong hired an émigré from Later Zhou, Shuang Chi (Shuang Ch'ih), who had experience in implementing administrative reforms and who helped the king organize the first civil service examination in Koryŏ (958).

The examination was the cornerstone of the imperial bureaucracy as it had matured in Tang China. It tested people on their knowledge of Confucian classics and composition skills, thus providing objective criteria to use as a basis to recruit people for administrative and government work. In Koryŏ, the composition test was organized separately from the classics test and was the chief means of recruitment, suggesting that the examination was more functional and less ideologically slanted than its Chinese model. The Koryŏ examinations organized by Kwangjong selected only a few people. Although the examinations gave Kwangjong the opportunity to select people who did not have a strong power base and were thus dependent on their office for income, the small number of people who passed the examination indicates that the pace of reform was very slow.

Either to speed things up or to overcome resistance to his reforms, Kwangjong started to purge members of the old elite in 960. The purges were bloody and unsettling and led to the elimination of many merit subjects, people awarded government posts for their service in the founding of the dynasty. According to the *Koryŏsa* (1451; history of Koryŏ), the purges were conducted randomly, in a climate of terror in which subordinates were encouraged to accuse their superiors. Whether Kwangjong was forced to resort to such drastic measures or whether he willingly indulged in excessive cruelty is impossible to determine, but ultimately these measures had the desired effect in that the examination system became the main avenue toward reaching government posts.

The gradual pace of the reforms is perhaps a measure of the amount of resistance that had to be overcome and the enormity of the task, which was carried out step by step. The next stage was to create a remuneration system for officials. Kwangjong had already tried to attack the economic basis of the old elite through the Slave Investigation Act (956), which forced them to manumit people who had been illegally enslaved. This had the effect of increasing the class of commoner peasants, who could then be taxed by the state. In 976, Kyŏngjong initiated the Stipend Land Law, a law giving officials certain rights to land use as a reward for office. The land grant was not permanent and often no more than an entitlement to collect rent. It was intended both as an incentive to attract people and as a step toward asserting state control of the means of production.

The administrative reforms were virtually completed by Sŏngjong, who created the main government institutions. In 983, he instituted a structure that was almost identical to that of the Tang Dynasty, consisting of three departments and six ministries. The secretariat, chancellery, and executive departments respectively were responsible for drafting, reviewing, and implementing policy. The executive department also oversaw the six ministries, each of which had a different area of competence (personnel, military affairs, taxation, justice, rites, and public works). The only other organs that could rival the power of these institutions were the royal secretariat, responsible for transmitting royal commands and military emergencies, and the censorate, which had the power to investigate what went on at all the other institutions. Each of these institutions was headed by officials of the first or second grade in a system consisting of nine main grades.

Sŏngjong's reforms put in place an administrative structure that, in theory, would help create a centralized state that was the sole arbiter of power and influence in the country. In effect, however, consensus building and compromise with regional elites remained part of the system. The central government never managed to achieve even nominal control over all its counties and prefectures. Even at the height of its power, it was able to centrally appoint magistrates only to roughly one-third of all counties and prefectures. Also, the taxation and remuneration system continued to undergo numerous revisions and was not finalized until 1076, when King Munjong established the final salary levels. However, despite his efforts to make the state control the distribution of wealth, in effect officials and gentry retained a considerable degree of control over land, both that held in private and that obtained through office holding.

SIGNIFICANCE

The changes wrought by the implementation of the Tang civil service system were part of a process that profoundly changed the politics and society of the Korean peninsula. Previously, society and politics had been dominated by the Silla Dynasty (668-935) bone-rank system, in which office holding, status, and profession were all determined by one's descent group. With the collapse of this societal system in the transition from the Silla to the Koryŏ Dynasty, there was an urgent need for a new system to integrate the various local and central elites on the peninsula. The examination system made it possible for local elites to gain entry to the capital aristocracy, initially dominated by a coalition around the dynastic founder. Although the examination never became the sole avenue to office holding, it did give talented individuals without a previous foothold in the administration the opportunity to help shape policy and govern.

However, the civil service examination was not open to everyone, but only to those with at least the status of village or town head. Thus a new status group formed in early Koryŏ, much broader than the Silla elite, consisting of those families who formed the gentry at the local level but who could also gain access to the central aristocracy. The examination became an important additional avenue to improve one's status, but unlike in China, it was never the sole marker of qualification for office holding. Because classical Chinese was the language used for the examination, the examination system helped spread knowledge of Chinese language and culture. Previously, an indigenous writing system, based on Chinese but adapted to write Korean words and syntax, had coexisted with classical Chinese. Now this writing system, known as *hyangch'al*, gradually disappeared. Although the adoption of the Tang civil service model meant an increase in the impact of Chinese civilization, the institutions borrowed from China did not necessarily operate in the same way as they did in China. For instance, despite the checks and balances built into the three departments system, political decisions were usually made by a special council consisting of the top-ranking officials of all the departments.

—*Sem Vermeersch*

FURTHER READING

Duncan, John B. "The Formation of the Central Aristocracy in Early Koryŏ." *Korean Studies* 12 (1988): 39-61. Investigates the actual functioning of the new bureaucracy by looking at the social background of those in power.

_______. *The Origins of the Chosŏn Dynasty.* Seattle: University of Washington Press, 2000. The first chapter contains a good introduction to the Koryŏ political system.

Kang, H. W. "Institutional Borrowing: The Case of the Chinese Civil Service Examination System in Early Koryŏ." *Journal of Asian Studies* 34, no. 1 (1974): 109-126. Still the only study of the introduction of the new examination system.

Palais, James. "Land Tenure in Korea: Tenth to Twelfth Centuries." *Journal of Korean Studies* 4 (1982-1983): 75-205. An analysis of critical literature in Korean on the land reforms attempted in the first half of Koryŏ.

_______. "Slavery and Slave Society in the Koryŏ Dynasty." *Journal of Korean Studies* 5 (1984): 173-190. Examines the nature and economic importance of slavery in Koryŏ.

SEE ALSO: 668-935: Silla Unification of Korea; 918-936: Foundation of the Koryŏ Dynasty; 1145: Kim Pu-sik Writes *Samguk Sagi*; 1196-1258: Ch'oe Family Takes Power in Korea; July, 1392: Establishment of the Yi Dynasty.

RELATED ARTICLE in *Great Lives from History: The Middle Ages, 477-1453*: Wang Kŏn.

960
FOUNDING OF THE SONG DYNASTY

The founding of the Song Dynasty ushered in a period in which the economy expanded rapidly, literature flourished and reached unprecedented numbers of readers, and landscape painting, architecture, pottery, sculpture, and music reached some of the highest artistic levels in Chinese history under the emperors' patronage.

LOCALE: China
CATEGORIES: Cultural and intellectual history; government and politics

KEY FIGURE

Zhao Kuangyin (Chao K'uang-yin; 927-976), first Song emperor, r. 960-976

SUMMARY OF EVENT

By the beginning of the tenth century, China was divided into numerous kingdoms. During the Five Dynasties and Ten Kingdoms period (907-960), emperors of five different dynasties held power in one of the largest kingdoms, which had a capital at Kaifeng. In 951, General Guo Wei (Kuo Wei) established the last of these short-lived dynasties, which is known as the Later Zhou Dynasty (Chou; 951-960). Guo Wei managed to unify most of northern China and began to expand southward. Zhao Kuangyin, a military inspector general for the Later Zhou Dynasty, seized power after Guo Wei's death. Zhao took the imperial name Taizu (T'ai-tsu) and gave his dynasty the name "Song" after a district he had governed in the province of Henan.

The first Song emperor was an able diplomat and administrator as well as a successful military man. He used gifts of honors and position to persuade many of his rivals to become his followers. He established a competent civil service with a firm basis in Confucian philosophy. He took the administration of territory away from the army and placed his lands under the supervision of civilian officials.

The expansion of the land under the control of the dynasty owed as much to its efficient civilian administration as to its military successes. Two southern kingdoms agreed to submit to the Song as a result of diplomatic negotiations. Several other kingdoms surrendered after brief military struggles.

Although the Song enjoyed a series of successes in unifying much of China, they continued to be threatened

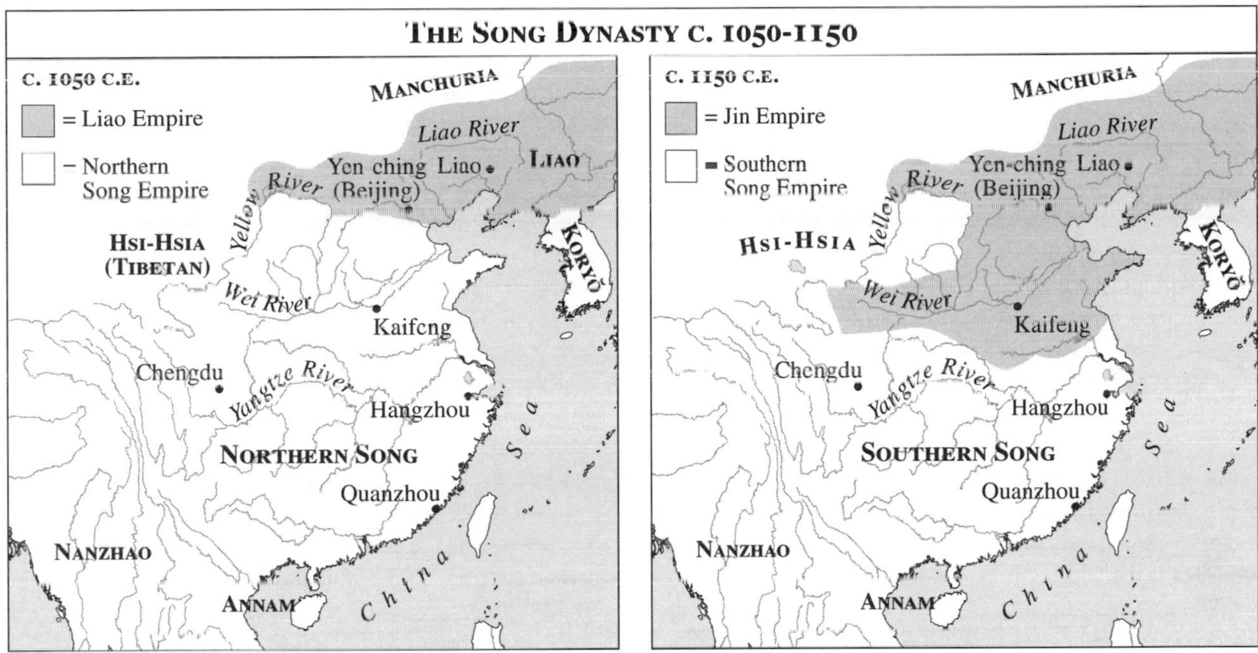

THE SONG DYNASTY C. 1050-1150

from the north by a Manchurian tribe known as the Khitans. The Khitans had pushed southward from Manchuria and occupied part of the province of Hebei, on the Chinese side of the Great Wall. In 979, the second Song emperor, Taizong (T'ai-tsung; r. 976-997), attempted to retake part of Hebei and suffered defeat at the hands of the Khitans. For the rest of the dynasty's reign, the Song were constantly on the defensive against fierce northern neighbors.

Under the first two Song emperors, the dynasty developed a workable, highly centralized governmental system. At the core of this system, the emperor chaired a council of state consisting of five to nine members that made general policy decisions. The central government beneath the council of state was divided into three departments. The first of these dealt with matters of the economy and was known as the "three services" because it was composed of three mutually independent bureaucracies: the service of state monopolies, the budget service, and the population service. The second department was military and controlled the armies. The third, known as the secretariat, administered justice and handled recruitment for government offices and promotions.

Historians regard the civil service as the greatest governmental accomplishment of the Song. A civil service system consisting of officials recruited through competitive examinations had taken shape under the emperors of the Tang Dynasty (T'ang; 618-907), but the Song period saw the highest development of this system. From the end of the tenth century through the eleventh century, the Chinese government created three levels of testing that could recruit civil servants from around the empire. Tests were held in local districts known as prefectures, in the capital under the administration of the secretariat, and in the palace in the presence of the emperor. Each prefecture set up public and private schools to prepare men for the tests. The "mandarins," the learned civil servants who had earned their positions through examination, had more control over state affairs during the Song period than at any other time in Chinese history.

Wang Anshi, who came from a family of prosperous farmers in Jiangxi, may have been the most outstanding Song civil servant. After he rose through a variety of posts to the council of state, Wang attempted to reform the laws to improve management of the national income and to strengthen military defenses. He also tried to give practical subjects, such as geography, economics, and law, a greater place in the civil service examinations. Wang's opponents forced his resignation in 1076, however, and most of his reforms were reversed.

One of the departments of the Chinese state, the department of the "three services," was chiefly concerned with matters of finance and the economy. The reign of the Song Dynasty was a time of rapid commercial development. Traders organized trade guilds, and the use of paper money encouraged business activities.

Agricultural expansion fueled this economic progress. Progress in rice cultivation in the Yangtze Basin and in southern China produced a surplus of food that enabled a growing proportion of the population to engage in trade and in industries such as mining, textiles, and ceramics. The merchant class of China's cities grew in size and wealth.

Each region of China became known for its own special product. Sichuan and Zhejiang were famous for the paper they produced. Changdu and Hangzhou were noted for their printed books. Fujian produced cane sugar. Several towns in Henan were known for ceramics. Southern Hebei produced iron.

The unification of China made possible trade among all these regions, making a variety of goods available throughout the empire. Ships and boats traveled along China's immense inland network of rivers and waterways. Vessels carrying merchandise made their way up and down the coast.

The expansion of waterborne trade made China a maritime power. The high-seas junk, a big sailing ship, was probably developed during the Song era. Song junks made voyages to Southeast Asian and the Indian Ocean, and books about voyages during this period contained information even about faraway Europe.

The Song period was a time of remarkable artistic, literary, and intellectual achievement. Dreamy, impressionistic landscape and nature painting on silk and paper became the period's characteristic form of visual expression. Each painting was believed to be a microcosm, a self-contained representation of the whole of the natural world. In the later part of the Song era, known as the Southern Song (1127-1279), Chan (Zen) Buddhism inspired paintings of Buddhist deities and birds. Song sculpture was also primarily religious, concentrating on images of the Buddha.

The ceramics and related industries made possible the production of beautiful artifacts for everyday use. Porcelain ware became common in the homes of the well-to-do. The patronage of the emperor helped foster the art of architecture, so that the imperial capital at Kaifeng was filled with temples and multistoried pagodas built with brick and colorful tiles.

Woodblock printing presses came into wide use, and the earliest full-length printed books in existence were produced during the Song Dynasty. The works of essayists and historians found a wider readership than ever before as a result of printing, and earlier literary works, such as the Confucian classics, were printed and widely distributed. The encyclopedia, a form of literature that came to occupy an important place in Chinese culture, first appeared during the dynasty.

The philosophers Zhu Xi (Chu Hsi) and Lu Jiuyuan (Lu Chiu-yüan) developed neo-Confucianism into a coherent system during the twelfth century. Neo-Confucianism was based on the teachings of Confucius, which stressed the importance of hierarchical, obedient social relations, government by virtue, and an educated bureaucracy. Neo-Confucianism, however, combined these teachings with elements of Buddhist and Daoist thinking.

Although the Song Dynasty was culturally brilliant, it was never militarily secure. A Manchurian people known as the Jurchen were subordinate to the Khitans. The Jurchen allied themselves with the Song Chinese, however, and forced the Khitans into Central Asia. The alliance was an unfortunate one for the Song, however, because the Jurchen became an even greater threat. The Jurchen extended their power southward, and the Song court fled to the southern capital of Nanjing in 1127 and then established its capital in Hangzhou in 1132. Historians refer to the larger empire, which existed from 960 to 1126, as the Northern Song. The southern remnant, which survived until 1279, is known as the Southern Song.

MAJOR RULERS OF THE SONG DYNASTY

NORTHERN SONG

Reign	*Ruler*
960-976	Taizu (Zhao Kuangyin)
976-997	Taizong
998-1022	Zhenzong
1022-1063	Renzong
1064-1067	Yingzong
1068-1085	Shenzong
1086-1101	Zhezong
1101-1125	Huizong
1125-1126	Qinzong

SOUTHERN SONG

Reign	*Ruler*
1127-1162	Gaozong
1163-1190	Xiaozong
1190-1194	Guangzong
1195-1224	Ningzong
1225-1264	Lizong
1265-1274	Duzong
1275-1275	Gongdi
1276-1278	Duanzong
1279	Bing Di

Despite economic and military problems in the diminished Southern Song Dynasty, the bureaucracy continued to function, and cultural achievements did not cease. At the beginning of the thirteenth century, however, a new threat appeared in the north: the Mongols under Genghis Khan. In 1211, the Mongols attacked the northern Chinese empire of the Jurchen, and by 1215, they had managed to conquer Beijing.

The Southern Song held the Mongols off for most of the thirteenth century. Genghis Khan's grandson, Kublai Khan, invaded the Song regions in 1250. In 1279, Kublai Khan defeated the last Song emperor and established a Chinese-style Mongol dynasty, known as the Yuan (1279-1368) that ruled China for almost a century.

SIGNIFICANCE

Under the Song emperors, China achieved a high degree of cultural unity that helped to hold the large empire together. Despite changes in dynasties, China maintained relative social stability from the Song era until the twentieth century. The civil service, restored and improved during the dynasty, remained a central part of Chinese governmental life for centuries. Neo-Confucian philosophy continued to be the empire's official ideology.

The cultural and technical innovations of the period made China one of the world's most advanced societies. Woodblock printing, for example, helped make books widely available in China centuries before Europe developed the printing of books. The contact the Chinese made with other societies through trade also helped enrich Chinese culture. The concept of zero, an essential aspect of mathematical thinking, was borrowed from India during the Song Dynasty.

The social stability and high cultural level attained during the Song Dynasty may eventually have worked against China. By the time Europeans became involved with China in the nineteenth century, the empire's ancient institutions could not change quickly enough to adapt to new circumstances. The faith of Chinese officials in tradition and their belief that China was the center of world civilization may have made China vulnerable to European domination.

—*Carl L. Bankston III*

FURTHER READING

Chaffee, John W. *Branches of Heaven: A History of the Imperial Clan of Sung China*. Cambridge, Mass.: Harvard University Press, 1999. An examination of the ruling class during the Song Dynasty. Illustrations, maps, bibliography, and index.

Ebrey, Patricia B. *The Cambridge Illustrated History of China*. New York: Cambridge University Press, 1996. Contains information on the Song Dynasty.

Gernet, Jacques. *A History of Chinese Civilization*. Translated by J. R. Foster. New York: Cambridge University Press, 1990. A detailed introduction to the history of China. Part 5 is dedicated to the Song "renaissance."

Jay, Jennifer W. *A Change in Dynasties: Loyalties in Thirteenth Century China*. Bellingham: Western Washington University Press, 1991. A study of Song Dynasty loyalists, Song government officials who resisted the Mongol conquest.

Liu Shu-hsien. *Understanding Confucian Philosophy Classical and Sung-Ming*. Westport, Conn.: Greenwood Press, 1998. A discussion of the development of Confucian thought from the viewpoint of a contemporary neo-Confucian. Contains a section on Zhu Xi.

Murck, Alfreda. *Poetry and Painting in Song China: The Subtle Art of Dissent*. Cambridge, Mass.: Harvard University Press, 2000. Examines the poetry of Du Fu and Su Dongpo and the painting of Wang Hong, among others.

Roberts, J. A. G. *A Concise History of China*. Cambridge, Mass.: Harvard University Press, 1999. Provides an overview of the Song Dynasty.

Walton, Linda A. *Academies and Society in Southern Sung China*. Honolulu: University of Hawaii Press, 1999. A study of the academies active during the Sung Dynasty and their role in society.

SEE ALSO: 618: Founding of the Tang Dynasty; 907-960: Period of Five Dynasties and Ten Kingdoms; 936: Khitans Settle Near Beijing; 960-1279: Scholar-Official Class Flourishes Under Song Dynasty; c. 1000: Footbinding Develops in Chinese Society; 1012: Rice Is Introduced into China; c. 1045: Bi Sheng Develops Movable Earthenware Type; 1069-1072: Wang Anshi Introduces Bureaucratic Reforms; 1115: Foundation of the Jin Dynasty; 1130: Birth of Zhu Xi.

RELATED ARTICLES in *Great Lives from History: The Middle Ages, 477-1453*: Genghis Khan; Kublai Khan; Wang Anshi; Zhu Xi.

c. 960
Jews Settle in Bohemia

The settlement of Jews in Bohemia, particularly in Prague, marked the establishment of one of the most important centers of Judaism and Jewish culture in the European world.

Locale: Prague, Bohemia (now in the Czech Republic)

Categories: Cultural and intellectual history; religion

Key Figures

Otakar II (1230-1278), king of Bohemia, r. 1253-1278

Isaac ben Moses of Vienna (c. 1180-c. 1250), Jewish scholar

Summary of Event

The origin of the Jews of Bohemia is shrouded in myth and legend. A Czech legend relates that in the eighth century, the mythological Bohemian princess Libuse had a vision of a new people who were about to come to the land bringing the Czechs good luck, and soon after the Jews arrived. Jews were allowed to stay in Prague because they helped the Christian Czechs defend against attacks by the pagans. Another legend states that the Jews came to the Carpathian Mountains after the destruction of the temple in 70. Historians believe the Jews of Bohemia descended from the Cumans and Quadi, but that they did so in the tenth century.

There is only a small amount of precise documentation concerning the arrival of the Jews, and only in the thirteenth century does a history of the Jews in Bohemia emerge in writing. However, in 965, Ibrahim bin Jakub, a Jewish merchant and diplomat from Spain who was traveling in Prague, described Bohemian Jews as essential to the city's life and economy. Documents indicate that in Prague the Jews lived north of the old town square and perhaps in other regions of the city alongside Christian merchants, which was convenient for local markets. Historians also speculate that Bohemian Jews were involved in trade with Germany, the East, the Byzantine Empire, and Kievan Rus.

Jews also settled in two suburbs of Prague, one near Prague castle and the second in the south near Vyšehrad castle. In the tenth century, Jews were probably masters of the royal mint. In 1142, fire destroyed Prague castle, forcing Jews to move to the famous Jewish quarter on the right bank of the Vltava River, also near the Altschule (old school) synagogue and cemetery. In the 1170's, Prince Sobolev gave the Jews legal status equivalent to other foreigners in Bohemia; however, this was soon lost as the Church conducted a campaign against the European Jews, which reduced their status.

The Crusades, which began in 1095, brought anti-Semitism to central Europe. In that year, a pogrom broke out in Prague, killing many Jews and forcing others to convert to Christianity. The medieval chronicler Cosmas of Prague (1045?-1125) described the experience of the Jews in Bohemia and Moravia during this time period.

In 1215, reflecting the beginning of change in the European economy from feudalism to commercial capitalism, the Fourth Lateran Council put limitations on Jews, decreeing that they must wear distinctive clothing and banning them from public office. The council prescribed by law the amount of interest on Jewish loans. The Bohemian princes, however, initially paid little attention to these decrees. Otakar II, in 1254, eased many of these restrictions and allowed Jews to run their own affairs. He answered the Church's complaints by affirming the medieval law stating the Jews were *servi camerae* (servants of the king) and therefore under his protection. Otakar II and his successors were given monetary gifts in exchange for these privileges. As a result, Jews governed their own community. They provided education for their children, cared for the sick, and administered justice in traditional rabbinic courts.

Prague became a center of Jewish culture, and many scholars such as Abraham ben Azriel and Isaac ben Moses of Vienna came to study and teach there. The latter wrote his commentary on the law in the Czech language. In his important twelfth century work *Or Zaru'a* (light is sown), which expounded on Jewish law, he referred to Bohemia as the land of Canaan and the Czech language as the language of Canaan.

In the thirteenth and fourteenth centuries, the Czech kings gave permission to the Jews to live in other towns. However, in the second half of the fourteenth century, anti-Semitic backlashes occurred as local authorities tried to wrest control of the Jews from the kings. Local authorities and priests accused Jews of blasphemy and desecration of the sacred host. Recalling the era of the Crusades, crowds incited by the accusations attacked Jews, killing many and once more forcing many to convert to Christianity. Especially because of the Hussite wars of the 1420's, the situation worsened. Although the community remained vibrant in succeeding centuries, many areas, especially in Moravia, were closed to them, and they faced new restrictions.

Significance

The history of the Jews of the Czech Republic, especially in Prague, has attracted much interest and sparked curiosity throughout the ages. The Hebrew folktale of the golem, the poetic jumble of the ancient cemetery, and the writings of Franz Kafka are just part of the myth and history of the Bohemian Jews.

The famous old cemetery with its twelve thousand graves and gravestone crowns standing one upon the other in a confined space dates back to the fifteenth century. It includes the graves of Rabbi Judah Loew, the reputed creator of the golem legend. There are several versions of the legend, but, according to one, Rabbi Loew made a giant out of clay and branches and brought it to life by placing the forbidden name of god under its tongue in order to forever combat and protect against anti-Semitic pogroms in Prague.

—*Frederick B. Chary*

Further Reading

Kieval, Hillel J. *Languages of Community: The Jewish Experience in the Czech Lands*. Berkeley: University of California Press, 2000. Chapter 1 covers the experiences of the Czech Jews in the medieval period, and Chapter 2 discusses the golem of Prague in the context of Jewish culture and tradition. Bibliography, index.

Putik, Alexandr, and Olga Sixtová. *The History of the Jews in Bohemia and Moravia*. Prague: Maisel Museum, 2002. A guide to the historic exhibition housed in the Maisel Synagogue in Prague, one of the best resources for the early history of the Czech Jews.

Sadek, Vladimir. *The Ghetto of Prague*. Prague: Olympia. 1992. A book of photographs and text about the Jewish "ghetto" in Prague.

Vilimkova, Milada. *The Prague Ghetto*. Prague: Aventinum, 1993. A description of the Jewish quarter in Bohemia's capital.

See also: 740: Khazars Convert to Judaism; c. 850: Development of the Slavic Alphabet.

Related articles in *Great Lives from History: The Middle Ages, 477-1453*: Gershom ben Judah; Saint Ludmilla.

960-1279
Scholar-Official Class Flowers Under Song Dynasty

During the Song Dynasty, neo-Confucianism rose to a place of prominence in Chinese society and dominated Chinese intellectual life for the next eight centuries.

Locale: China

Category: Cultural and intellectual history

Key Figures

Zhao Kuangyin (Chao K'uang-yin; 927-976), first Song emperor, r. 960-976

Zhu Xi (Chu Hsi; 1130-1200), neo-Confucian philosopher

Summary of Event

By the middle of the eighth century, the Tang Dynasty (T'ang; 618-907) began to fall victim to bureaucratic corruption and military weakness. Years of governmental inefficiency and the decline of the equal-field system led to widespread peasant unrest. A series of devastating rebellions weakened the dynasty's ability to maintain a peaceful and prosperous environment.

The Tang Dynasty also faced a renewed threat from its nomadic neighbors to the north. Over time, the entire northern part of the empire deteriorated into a series of regional kingdoms, and the last Tang emperor resigned in 907. China then drifted into a half century of political chaos, known as the Five Dynasties and Ten Kingdoms period, in which feudal warlords fought among themselves in bloody wars of conquest.

In 960, a young army officer, Zhao Kuangyin, became the first emperor of the Song Dynasty (Sung; 960-1279), ruling as Taizu (T'ai-tsu). He was able to claim the mandate of heaven (heavenly authorization of rule) when his men overwhelmingly proclaimed him emperor. Their loyalty was based on his exceptional honesty and leadership ability. His strong character enabled him to convince his political rivals to accept his power, and he set in motion a series of reforms that would return China to a place of prominence in East Asia.

Taizu instituted a series of governmental reforms that increased the power of the emperor and made him a truly autocratic ruler. He accomplished this by creating a bureaucracy that was totally under his control. Different sections of the bureaucracy were given similar duties to perform. This duplication created competition among the different agencies, which allowed Taizu to play one group against another. This not only increased efficiency but it also prevented any group from becoming strong enough to challenge the power of the emperor.

Taizu also took advantage of the preceding half century of chaos to weaken the aristocracy. During the years of decentralized rule after the fall of the Tang Dynasty, much of the land controlled by the aristocracy had been confiscated by regional warlords. This reduced their wealth and drove the noble class into large metropolitan areas with the intent of obtaining a position in the government. The new emperor controlled these nobles through the allocation of jobs in his bureaucracy. Taizu also opened the civil service examination system to a large segment of Chinese society; this action had three long-lasting effects on Chinese society. First, it established a system of permanent competition for the aristocracy, which enhanced the emperor's power over them. Second, the reforms created a large pool of candidates; thus, only the best and the brightest of Chinese society were appointed to important bureaucratic posts. Third, this open examination system created a vibrant, energized society in which men knew they had the chance to be socially upwardly mobile. For the first time in Chinese history, talent accounted for more than accident of birth. This energy of accomplishment would infuse Chinese society with a power that did not exist in any other major civilization at this time in history.

The most significant aspect of the Song Dynasty was the development of a new philosophical system known as neo-Confucianism. This philosophy was the result of a synthesis of basic Confucian principles and the cosmic metaphysical concepts of Buddhism. From the fall of the Han Dynasty (206 B.C.E.-220 C.E.) through Buddhism's apex during the Tang Dynasty, the religion provided a powerful alternative to traditional Chinese belief systems. By the time of the Song Dynasty, a new class of intellectuals, driven by a nationalistic and ethnocentric vision of past and future greatness, rejected Buddhism as a debilitating foreign influence. China's new intellectual elite believed the strength of the Song Dynasty should be based on the traditions found in the Confucian system.

Zhu Xi was the leading proponent of neo-Confucianism, and his teachings would help create a philosophy that would dominate Chinese society until the end of the nineteenth century. Zhu Xi, like important Confucians before him, sought to develop a system of behavior that would curtail the suffering caused by the perpetual rise and fall of China's empires. This "dynastic cycle" of growth, maturity, decline, and fall had dominated Chinese history since the Zhou Dynasty (Chou; 1066-256 B.C.E.). Neo-Confucians believed that emperors lost their right to rule because dynasties failed to solve the problem of bureaucratic corruption, which over time inflicted pain and suffering on the Chinese people.

The Zhu Xi model was centered on the traditional Confucian principle that society and the cosmos were a wholly integrated, harmonious system. This principle stated that the laws of nature and proper ethical principles both emanated from the mind of heaven. Zhu Xi believed this linkage between humanity and heaven allowed society to discover these proper cosmic principles through the use of reason. This knowledge could then be used to create a harmonious, well-functioning society in which peace and prosperity would reign. Zhu Xi also believed that this important knowledge could be found in such classical Confucian texts as *Chunqiu* (fifth century B.C.E.; *The Ch'un Ts'ew with the Tso Chuen*, 1872; commonly known as *Spring and Autumn Annals*) and *Lunyu* (late sixth-early fifth centuries B.C.E.; *The Analects*, 1861). He further believed that the writings of the Confucian scholar Menicius were an important source for neo-Confucian scholars. Zhu Xi especially embraced Mencius's belief that people were basically good and had an inherent propensity toward ethical behavior.

Zhu Xi understood that if the neo-Confucian system were to be successful, its teachings would have to permeate all levels of Chinese society and be applied to every aspect of life. Personal morality had to be continually cultivated; thus, every aspect of Chinese society, from the family to the most powerful government bureaucracy, had to be based on these principles.

The first tenet was that every Chinese citizen would be born into a family that acted as an incubator for Chinese civil society. Next, the patriarchical hierarchy of the family was to mirror the power pyramid of the Song Dynasty. Thus, children grew up inculcated with a deep respect for rank based on age and gender. The father was the emperor of the family and, as such, was to be respected without question. Older male siblings mirrored the power of the emperor's civil servants; respect was based on their rank and accomplishments within the family structure. Women were regarded as second-class citizens and would remain marginalized in Chinese society for the next eight hundred years. Finally, the best and the brightest of the male children would be educated to prepare to take a series of national exams that would determine whether they would gain entrance into the national university system.

In addition, Zhu Xi helped establish a national educational system that would train future candidates for the Chinese civil service. The curriculum of these Confucian academies was based on the traditional classical texts and the most recent commentaries by neo-Confucian scholars. Even though the primary focus of this educational system was to train candidates for the civil service tests, scholars such as Zhu Xi believed that the system would ultimately fail if it focused only on exam preparation. He understood that any successful government needs virtuous as well as intelligent men in positions of power. To be successful, every generation of bureaucrats had to accept the premise that they had to place personal power and accomplishment second to the well being of the nation. In the past, it was the narcissistic pursuit of power by highly skilled, intelligent men that had led eventually to the corruption, decline, and fall of dynasties.

Neo-Confucianism had an important impact on Song military policy. The basic Confucian belief in nonaggressive behavior, along with its traditional ethnocentric, isolationist stance, forced the Song Dynasty to make fundamental and drastic changes in its military establishment. The aggressive and expansionist military establishment of the Tang Dynasty was replaced with a neo-Confucian, antimilitary elite that downplayed the importance of the armed services. As the military became weaker, China adopted an appeasement policy for dealing with its aggressive neighbors, especially with the nomadic tribes to its north. The Song Dynasty used a series of very generous economic agreements to appease its potential adversaries. By the end of the Song Dynasty, the Chinese military had been transformed into an ineffective fighting force.

SIGNIFICANCE

During the Song Dynasty, the neo-Confucian philosophy weakened the cultural energy of Chinese civilization. Its conservative stance, which questioned any change, prevented Chinese intellectuals from implementing the reforms needed to ensure the future of the dynasty. The systematic weakening of the empire's military establishment by neo-Confucian bureaucrats eventually allowed the Mongols to conquer China.

—*Richard D. Fitzgerald*

FURTHER READING

Bol, Peter K. *This Culture of Ours: Intellectual Transitions in Tang and Song China*. Stanford, Calif.: Stanford University Press, 1992. An excellent overview of Tang and Song intellectual history. Index and bibliography.

Gernet, Jacques. *A History of Chinese Civilization*. New York: Cambridge University Press, 1990. The best single-volume account of Chinese cultural history. Maps, index, and bibliography.

Graff, David A. *Medieval Chinese Warfare, 300-900*. New York: Routledge Press, 2002. An excellent overview of medieval Chinese military history. Maps, index, bibliography.

Graff, David A., and Robin Higham. *A Military History of China*. Cambridge, England: Westview Press, 2002. The best survey of Chinese military history on the market. Maps, index, and bibliography.

SEE ALSO: 606: National University Awards First Doctorate; 618: Founding of the Tang Dynasty; 845: Suppression of Buddhism; 907-960: Period of Five Dynasties and Ten Kingdoms; 1069-1072: Wang Anshi Introduces Bureaucratic Reforms; 1115: Foundation of the Jin Dynasty.

RELATED ARTICLES in *Great Lives from History: The Middle Ages, 477-1453*: Wang Anshi; Zhu Xi.

963
FOUNDATION OF THE MOUNT ATHOS MONASTERIES

The Mount Athos monasteries provided a cultural and intellectual center for the Eastern Orthodox religion particularly during the prolonged period of Ottoman Turkish domination of the Balkan Peninsula.

LOCALE: Mount Athos, on the Chalkidike Peninsula in northern Greece

CATEGORIES: Organizations and institutions; religion

KEY FIGURES

Leo VI (866-912), Byzantine emperor, r. 886-912

Nicephorus II Phocas (912-969), Byzantine emperor, r. 963-969

Athanasios of Athos (925-1001), saint and founder of Great Lavra monastery

John I Tzimisces (925-976), Byzantine emperor, r. 969-976

Gregory of Sinai (c. 1268-1346), Hesychast monk and writer

SUMMARY OF EVENT

Although the legend of Mount Athos as a Christian religious sanctuary goes back to a purported visit to the Holy Mount by the Virgin Mary in 49 C.E., this area has a religious tradition that predates Christianity. Named after Athos, son of Poseidon, according to tradition, it was the home of the Greek gods before Olympus.

Throughout the early Middle Ages, Athos held a reputation as a holy place. In the ninth century, it was the home of Saint Peter the Athonite, a semilegendary hermit who lived there in a cave for thirty-five years. By the end of the ninth century, there were several small *lavras* (monasteries) there. A *chrysobul* (imperial document) from the Byzantine emperor Leo VI was issued around 900 C.E., confirming the possession of the entire peninsula by certain hermits already there.

Around 961, the Byzantine general Nicephorus II Phocas and his adviser, the monk Athanasios, decided to build a great monastery on Athos to which they might retire from public life. However, Nicephorus became the emperor instead, leaving Athanasios to complete the monastery. This monastic establishment, the Great Lavra, still stands as the oldest and largest monastery on Athos, although Athanasios was killed supervising its construction.

The hermits living on Athos at that time were not pleased by the rise of the Great Lavra, and they complained to Nicephorus's successor John I Tzimisces about its size and worldliness. The latter reconfirmed the monastery, however, and increased the number of monks allowed to live there. He established a common council of hermit-monks who would meet regularly in Karyes, a small town in the center of the peninsula.

By the end of the tenth century, several more monasteries, including Iveron, Vatopedi, Chilandar, Esphigmenou, Pantaleimon, Xenophontos, and Zographou, had been built. At about this time, monks from other nations, including Georgia, Italy, and Armenia, began to come to Athos, and the following two centuries saw the addition of Slavic monks from Serbia, Bulgaria, and Russia. New monasteries were founded during the next hundred years with a steadily increasing population of monks and hermits. This continued until the fall of Constantinople, in 1453, which slowed the building impetus. Many of these larger monasteries became wealthy from royal subsidies, as well as the sale of agricultural products produced by the monks and of trees from the forests.

The later Middle Ages represent the most active era in the establishment of the monasteries of Mount Athos. All of the Ruling Monasteries had been established by 1540, less than a century after the fall of Constantinople to the Turks. The largest monasteries had extensive libraries and treasure houses, as well as archives relating to the founding of each of the monastic houses. The purpose of the monastic establishments was to provide a place for prayer and contemplation away from the tribulations of everyday life. These monasteries were usually supported by gifts from various rulers or by donations solicited from the faithful. The monks themselves took responsibility for the daily tasks involved in the upkeep of their own monastic communities.

Among issues of importance to the monasteries on Athos was the question as to whether the Byzantine emperor or the Orthodox patriarch had supreme authority over the Mount. Another matter of importance was the proscription of eunuchs, beardless youths, women, and in fact all female creatures from the area. Although traditionally at the behest of the Virgin Mary, this proscription was instituted in 1045 under the constitution approved by Constantine Monomachus, the Byzantine emperor.

In 1204, when the Byzantine Empire was invaded and pillaged by the legions of the Fourth Crusade, there was great danger that the treasures on Mount Athos, which included a great jeweled Bible, a reliquary of the True Cross, and many priceless manuscripts, might be seized by the crusaders. Pope Innocent III, however, guaranteed the autonomy of the mount, which prevented this disaster from occurring. After the restoration of the Byzantine emperors to the throne, however, and the consequent attempt to end the schism between the Eastern and Western Catholic Church by recognizing the supremacy of the pope of Rome, many of the monks on Athos were executed by inquisitors.

Another disaster that befell the inhabitants of Mount Athos occurred in 1307, when the Grand Company of Catalans, mercenaries who had been hired by Andronicus II Palaeologus to defend the Byzantine Empire against the Turks, turned to devastation against their host and pillaged the monasteries on Athos, despoiling their treasures and slaughtering many of the monks.

Up to that point, the monastic organization of Mount Athos had been cenobitic, with all of the monks living in a communal environment. After the Catalans departed, for the first time arose the alternative idiorrhythmic style of monasticism. Based on the Christian ideal of brotherly love, the cenobitic example of monastic living, as developed by Saints Pachomius and Basil in the fourth century, stressed the desirability of living together in a rule of poverty, chastity, and obedience, with all meals, worship, and living space in common. The idiorrhythmic principle, on the other hand, allowed the possession of personal property, the solitary taking of food, and worship in private if desired. It also allowed for a much more rigorous eremetic existence and thus appealed to those monks who wished to become more fervent practitioners of the monastic ideal.

Of the twenty Ruling Monasteries on Athos, nine eventually adopted the idiorrhythmic way of life. It was forbidden for any more monasteries to choose the idiorrhythmic organization, although the formerly idiorrhythmic monasteries were allowed to opt for the cenobitic style.

In monastic governance, the idiorrhythmic monasteries are governed by a committee of three elected representatives and a permanent council of elders, while the cenobitic houses are governed by an abbot, who is elected for life and may assume almost dictatorial power.

The Hilandarion Monastery on the Mount Athos peninsula in northern Greece. (AP/Wide World Photos)

The Hesychast regimen, based on a movement introduced to Athos by Gregory of Sinai in the early fourteenth century, was adopted by some of the Athonite monks. Basically, the Hesychasts believed in perpetual prayer and self-illumination from within, and joy through meditation. This mystical approach to spiritual communion with God later became associated with social and political movements that led to a civil war within the Byzantine state. This issue was not resolved until John VI Cantacuzenus presided over a council that upheld the Hesychasts.

SIGNIFICANCE

Of the twenty Ruling Monasteries on Athos, one is Serbian (Chilandar), one is Russian (Pantaleimon), one is Bulgarian (Zographou), and the remainder are Greek. They are each represented by one member at the Holy Synod at Karyes, the parliament of Athos. For those desiring it, however, there are other options besides the Ruling Monasteries. There are a dozen or so *sketes*, both cenobitic and idiorrhythmic, where a more austere lifestyle and an interest in trade or handicraft obtains. Smaller than the *sketes* are the *kellia*, usually occupied by two to four monks, and usually following agricultural pursuits. Then there are the true hermits. They are in the tradition of the earliest eremitic inhabitants of Athos, leading an ascetic existence in caves and single huts, spending their days in prayer, self-mortification, and solitude.

During the almost half-millennium of Turkish occupation of the Balkans, the cultural legacy of the past survived almost entirely because of the influence of the Orthodox Church. Athos because of its independence was a great center of Byzantine and Hellenistic thought, and because of its isolated location was as well a refuge for those seeking to escape from Ottoman disfavor. Because the Ottomans were tolerant of other religions and because the monks did not politically display their lack of sympathy for the Turkish authorities, they were largely left alone to pursue their intellectual and religious endeavors.

The monasteries on Mount Athos continued to exist into the twenty-first century, although the number of monks was much smaller than during its flourishing in the Middle Ages.

—*Gloria Fulton*

FURTHER READING

Fine, John V. A. *The Early Medieval Balkans: A Critical Survey from the Sixth to the Late Twelfth Century.* Ann Arbor: University of Michigan Press, 1991. Covers the development of Mount Athos in the context of the events of the Balkans.

________. *The Late Medieval Balkans: A Critical Survey from the Late Twelfth Century to the Ottoman Conquest.* Ann Arbor: University of Michigan Press, 1994. Discusses the later development of Mount Athos in the context of general developments in the Balkans.

Hussey, J. M. *The Orthodox Church in the Byzantine Empire.* Oxford, England: Clarendon Press, 1986. An exhaustive work on the history, principles, and organization of the Eastern Orthodox religion as it developed under the Byzantines.

Norwich, John Julian, and Reresby Sitwell. *Mount Athos.* New York: Harper & Row, 1966. An account of the monasteries and their history arising from visits to Mount Athos by Norwich and Sitwell.

Obolensky, Dimitri. *The Byzantine Commonwealth: Eastern Europe, 500-1453.* 1971. Reprint. Crestwood, N.Y.: St. Vladimir's Seminary Press, 1982. Chapter 10 discusses monasticism under the Byzantines, particularly as practiced by the Slavs at Athos and elsewhere.

Pavlikianov, Cyril. *The Medieval Aristocracy on Mount Athos: The Philological and Documentary Evidence for the Activity of Byzantine, Georgian, and Slav Aristocrats and Eminent Churchmen in the Monasteries of Mount Athos from the Tenth to the Fifteeenth Century.* Sofia, Bulgaria: Center for Slavo-Byzantine Studies, 2001. A look at the ruling elite on Mount Athos in the Middle Ages.

Zimbardo, Xavier. *Monks of Dust: The Holy Men of Mount Athos.* New York: Rizzoli, 2001. An examination of the monasteries at Mount Athos.

SEE ALSO: 976-1025: Reign of Basil II; 1054: Beginning of the Rome-Constantinople Schism; 1204: Knights of the Fourth Crusade Capture Constantinople; 1233: Papal Inquisition.

RELATED ARTICLE in *Great Lives from History: The Middle Ages, 477-1453*: Innocent III.

969-1171
REIGN OF THE FĀṬIMIDS

The Fāṭimids, an Islamic movement of Ismāʿīlī Shīʿite dissidents from North Africa, conquered Egypt and created their own caliphate there to rival the Sunni ʿAbbasid caliphate of Baghdad. The Fāṭimid caliphs lived two centuries of splendor until they succumbed to internal factionalism, civil strife, and foreign incursions.

LOCALE: Cairo, Egypt

CATEGORIES: Government and politics; expansion and land acquisition; religion

KEY FIGURES

ʿUbayd Allāh al-Mahdī (d. 934), leader of an Ismāʿīlī Shīʿite movement, founded the Fāṭimid caliphate in North Africa

al-Muʾizz (c. 930-975), fourth Fātimid caliph and conqueror of Egypt, r. 953-975

al-Ḥākim (985-1021), sixth Fāṭimid caliph, r. 996-1021

Ḥasān-e Ṣabbāḥ (d. 1124), political-religious dissident, founder of the Nizari Ismāʿīlī, known to their enemies as the Assassins

Saladin (1138-1193), Sunni sultan, r. 1174-1193, ended Fāṭimid rule over Egypt as part of his campaign against the Crusaders in Palestine

SUMMARY OF EVENT

During the late-800's, Ismāʿīlī Shīʿite Muslims launched an unprecedented challenge against the ʿAbbāsid caliphate for rule of the Islamic world. The ʿAbbāsid caliphs of Baghdad, although still the symbolic leaders of Sunni Islam and claiming authority over all Muslims, had lost real political control over almost all the Islamic empire except Iraq. As the empire fragmented, local military governors ran their provinces like independent enterprises, often for the benefit of their own tribe or ethnic group.

In this decadent environment, followers of an Ismāʿīlī leader named ʿUbayd Allāh al-Mahdī convinced a Berber tribe, the Kutama, to embrace his revolutionary religious doctrines. Decrying the ʿAbbāsids as usurpers and tyrants, ʿUbayd presented himself as a direct descendant of the Prophet Muḥammad and the great champions of Shīʿite Islam, ʿAlībū Abū Ṭālib and Ismāʿīl. In 909, ʿUbayd's forces swept out of Algeria and conquered Tunisia, and he declared himself the true and divinely ordained caliph of Islam. Taking the name of Fāṭimah, Muḥammad's daughter and ʿAlī's wife, his regime came to be called the Fāṭimids.

Decades later, the fourth Fāṭimid caliph, al-Muʾizz, not only completed the pacification of North Africa and Sicily but also swept into Egypt. Exhausted by famine, taxation, and harsh rule, the Sunni Muslims of Egypt lacked the energy and will to resist the Ismāʿīlī forces. In July, 969, Fāṭimid armies entered the Nile Valley and established their ruling center at a massive troop camp that eventually became the city of Cairo. Caliph al-Muʾizz himself entered Egypt in 973. A vigorous leader, he made Cairo the imperial capital and created an efficiently centralized administrative hierarchy.

Through a mix of state industry, commercial subsidies, and patronage of private merchant initiatives, the caliph laid the foundations for Egypt's dramatic economic recovery. Ismāʿīlī Shīʿite Islam now became the ruling religion, taking over the major mosques, schools, and judicial posts throughout Egypt. However, since Ismāʿīlī Muslims remained a tiny minority of the population, al-Muʾizz extended official toleration to Sunni Muslims as well as Christians and Jews so long as they remained docile. In fact, many of them joined the Fāṭimid civil service. Nonetheless, the caliph regarded Egypt as the base from which Ismāʿīlī Shiism must spread through the Muslim world. To this end, he established a grand mosque, al-Azhar, to become the religious, political, and intellectual training center for Ismāʿīlīsm. Fāṭimid military expeditions also extended eastward, bringing much of Palestine, Lebanon, southern Syria, and the holy cities of Mecca and Medina under Cairo's power.

The caliphs who succeeded al-Muʾizz inherited a complex, volatile legacy and thus achieved contradictory results. On the positive side, Fāṭimid economic policies made Egypt the commercial hub of the eastern Afro-Eurasian continent for more than two centuries and rewarded Egyptians with considerable prosperity. Local manufactures such as textiles, glassware, and foodstuffs were exchanged for raw materials from Europe and luxuries from the Indian Ocean emporium. Italian ports in particular profited richly.

Ismāʿīlī doctrine encouraged not only religious scholarship but the study of astronomy, optics, mathematics, and medicine as well. The luxuriant image of the Fāṭimid state often combined with the appeal of Ismāʿīlī propagandists to inspire revolts and subversion in lands outside

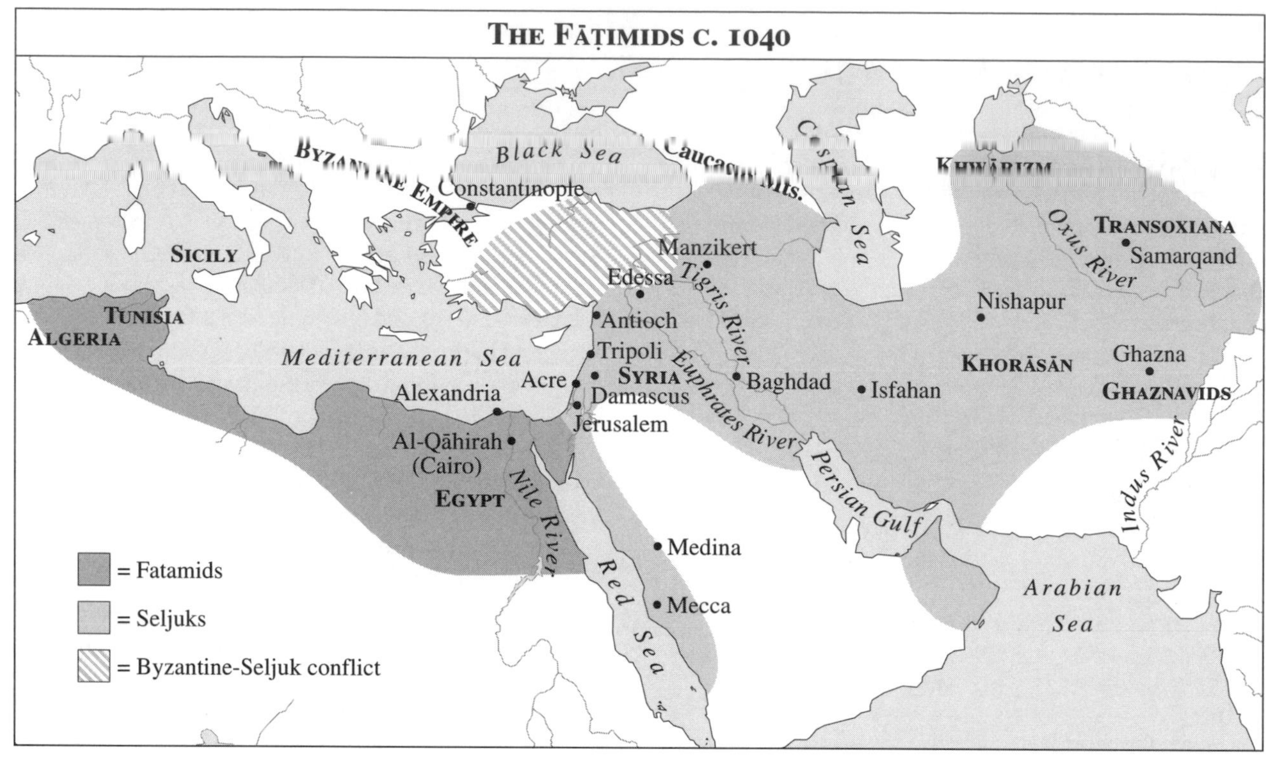

Cairo's control. In 1054, for example, conspirators took over Baghdad for a month and almost overthrew the beleaguered ʿAbbāsid caliphate.

Nonetheless, instability haunted and enfeebled the Fāṭimid caliphate throughout its existence. Ironically, certain aspects of Ismāʿīlī practice that might have been sources of strength contributed directly to weakening the system. For Ismāʿīlīs, the caliphs were divinely guided authorities, answerable only to God and ruling in response to God's direction. For the traditionalist Sunni majority, however, such claims were at best arrogant posturing and at worst blasphemous and tyrannical. Either way, both North Africans and Egyptians viewed Ismāʿīlī Fāṭimid rule with sullen resentment and, sometimes, as worse. In the 1020's, Sunni Muslim revolts began in North Africa that, by the 1050's, finally forced the Fāṭimids to abandon their hold over everything except Egypt and parts of Libya.

Another development in the 1020's underscored two further dangers that Fāṭimid religious ideology invited—dictatorial personalities and child rulers. The sixth caliph, al-Ḥākim, invoking his inspired powers, launched a host of radical measures offensive to many of the traditional landowners, to urban non-Muslims, and even to his own clergy. Depicted by many chroniclers as brutal, even deranged, he disappeared under mysterious circumstances, probably assassinated. (The Druze Muslims, now prominent in Lebanon, arose from the preaching of some of al-Ḥākim's most devoted followers.) Like several later caliphs, al-Ḥākim had been ordained to rule while still a child. Because the quality of spiritual insight that conferred true power purportedly passed from father to son, a child might be designated heir and thus require a regency until maturity. Regencies, by their nature, promoted factionalism and internal conflicts within religious, military, and bureaucratic cadres. Some of al-Ḥākim's actions undoubtedly reflected his struggles to surmount and subjugate these interest groups.

Fāṭimid military structures also bred factionalism within the ruling elites. Essentially, Cairo's army was a loose constellation of slave soldiers and mercenary units, recruited, organized, and run on the basis of ethnic identity. Under Ubayd Allāh, Berber tribes, supplemented by recruits from port towns to serve the navy and Bedouin mercenaries, provided the original fighting forces. After Egypt fell, however, the state gained access to Turkish, Daylam (from northern Iran), Slavic, and black African recruits from the Middle East to balance off Berber warriors. To control these diverse units, the state often played one ethnic group off against the others, gradually wrecking its ability to command any real loyalty among any of them. Rivalries between different commanders and garrisons intensified, sometimes leading to disruptions, riots, and mutinies. The military became undisciplined, hostility destroyed cohesiveness and morale, and fighting capability slackened. Officers made alliances with ambitious civilian politicians, steadily reducing the caliph to a passive and increasingly pathetic figurehead.

In 1094, on the eve of the First Crusade, a clique of courtiers and officers seeking to protect their selfish interests blocked the designated heir, al-Nizār, and replaced him with his eight-year old brother, al-Mustaʿlī. This coup led one of the rightful caliph's allies, Ḥasān-e Ṣabbāḥ, to organize a religious countermovement within the Ismāʿīlī faith known as the Nizaris. His enemies, however, called Nizaris Assassins because, among other tactics, they used lone attackers to menace or murder opponents.

The loss of Jerusalem, Palestine, and most Levantine ports to the Crusaders combined with Nizari attacks to humiliate the Fāṭimids and expose their military ineptitude. Such losses also plunged Egypt into economic recession and threatened urban famine. By 1118, the Europeans raided regularly along the Egyptian coast while caliphs became pawns in civil wars between the military factions. In 1154, a uniquely vicious coup massacred most of the royal family. Another infant caliph was placed on the throne but, in reality, the Fāṭimid caliphate was in virtual collapse.

In the last decade of the caliphate's life, foreign powers sought to subvert Egypt by manipulating one of the contending domestic commanders. It was a Kurdish general known as Saladin who finally succeeded by first gaining control of a garrison on the Nile and bringing in reinforcements to help repulse two Crusader invasions. After his victories, Saladin compelled the sickly young caliph to give him complete power over the government, which he set about to quietly reshape. Except for some Sudanese troops, public resistance to the transformation was scant. In 1171, when the caliph died, Saladin simply refused to allow a successor and declared himself loyal to the ʿAbbāsid caliph of Baghdad. The Fāṭimid caliphate was gone.

SIGNIFICANCE

The Fāṭimid movement and dynasty played a vital role in medieval history. For a time, the Fāṭimids united all of North Africa, Egypt, and much of the western Middle East under one ruler. Not since the time of the pharaohs had Egypt been an imperial center. The economic revival stimulated by Fāṭimid trade helped to finance the rebirth of urban commerce in medieval Italy and had a positive impact on western Europe. Cairo became one of the great cities of the Mediterranean, a center of power, culture, and wealth. Ismāʿīlīsm, however, failed to become dominant in Islam, and Fāṭimid decline opened Palestine to Crusader invasion. Saladin's elimination of the Fāṭimid caliphate in 1171 ensured that Sunni Islam in Egypt would survive both Ismāʿīlīs and Crusaders.

—*Weston F. Cook, Jr.*

FURTHER READING

Brett, Michael. *The Rise of the Fāṭimids: The World of the Mediterranean and the Middle East in the Fourth Century of the Hijra, Tenth Century C.E.* Boston: Brill, 2001. A look at the early decades of the Fāṭimid movement in Egypt, North Africa, and Syria. Maps, bibliography, index.

Halm, Heinz. *The Fāṭimids and Their Traditions of Learning*. New York: I. B. Tauris, 1997. Overview to Fāṭimid contributions to education and teaching, the humanities, and science. Bibliography, index.

Lev, Yaacov. *State and Society in Fāṭimid Egypt*. New York: E. J. Brill, 1991. The best current introduction to the subject. Part of the Arab History and Civilization series. Bibliography, index.

Lyons, Malcolm Cameron, and D. E. P. Jackson. *Saladin: The Politics of Holy War*. New York: Cambridge University Press, 1997. Provides insights into the final years and the fall of the Fāṭimid Dynasty. Maps, bibliography, index.

Sanders, Paula. *Ritual, Politics, and the City in Fāṭimid Cairo*. Albany: State University of New York Press, 1994. A social history that surveys the place of rituals, rites, customs, and ceremonies in the Cairo of the Fāṭimid era. Maps, bibliography, index.

Walker, Paul, E. *Exploring an Islamic Empire: Fāṭimid History and Its Sources*. New York: I. B. Tauris, 2002. A comprehensive source on Fāṭimid history, from its beginnings to its fall in 1171. Includes an introduction to the dynasty and its place in the history of the Islamic world. Especially useful as a resource for further study. Illustrations, extensive bibliography, index.

SEE ALSO: 630-711: Islam Expands Throughout North Africa; 637-657: Islam Expands Throughout the Middle East; October 10, 680: Martyrdom of Prophet's Grandson Ḥusayn; 972: Building of al-Azhar Mosque; 11th century: Expansion of Sunni Islam in North Africa and Iberia; 1009: Destruction of the Church of the Holy Sepulchre; 1048: Zīrids Break from Fāṭimid Dynasty and Revive Sunni Islam; November 27, 1095: Pope Urban II Calls the First Crusade.

RELATED ARTICLES in *Great Lives from History: The Middle Ages, 477-1453*: ʿAbd al-Raḥmān III al-Nāṣir; Alp Arslan; Abū Mūsā Jābir ibn Ḥayyān; Niẓām al-Mulk; Saladin.

972
BUILDING OF AL-AZHAR MOSQUE

The al-Azhar mosque was the first mosque constructed in the Islamic Fāṭimid Dynasty's capital city of Cairo. Soon after it was built the mosque also became a center for teaching and continued for more than one thousand years as an educational institution devoted to the study, preservation, and dissemination of Egyptian, Arabic, and Islamic culture.

LOCALE: Cairo, Egypt
CATEGORIES: Architecture; education; engineering; religion

KEY FIGURES

Jawhar (c. 900-c. 980), Fāṭimid general, conquered Egypt

al-Muʾizz (c. 930-975), fourth Fāṭimid caliph, moved dynasty's capital to Cairo, r. 953-975

SUMMARY OF EVENT

The al-Azhar mosque was built as the first congregational mosque for the city of Cairo, the capital of the Fāṭimid Empire. The city was established by the Fāṭimids in 969 to assert their control over conquered Egypt, and the mosque, completed in 972, offered a visible monumental sign of Fāṭimid power in the new city. The name al-Azhar, which translates as "radiant" or "splendid," may have been derived from the name of the daughter of the Prophet Muḥammad, Fāṭimah, to whom the Fāṭimids trace their ancestry.

In the four centuries after the death of the Prophet, the faith of Islam had spread rapidly through the Mediterranean world by virtue of the brilliant successes of Islamic armies. Two ruling dynasties dominated the Islamic world in these centuries: the Umayyads (661-750, until 1031 in Spain) and the ʿAbbāsids (750-1258). The province of Egypt was unusual in that it was often controlled by semi-independent local dynasties who merely offered allegiance to the ruling Umayyads or ʿAbbāsids, such as the Aghlabids (800-909) and Ikhshidids (935-969). The Fāṭimids ruled Egypt from 969-1171; they had built an empire beginning in the early tenth century in North Africa with a capital at Mahdia (now in Tunisia).

The Fāṭimid conquest of Egypt came about through the efforts of the capable general Jawhar who, after subduing the Ikhshidid defenses at Al-Fusṭāṭ (now near Cairo) on the Nile delta in 969, settled with his troops just north of the city. The Fāṭimids had long maneuvered to conquer Egypt. The wealthy province was highly desired throughout the ancient and medieval eras because of its geographically strategic location at the crossroads of travel between the Near East and North Africa and its ready access to the prosperous Mediterranean trade routes. Jawhar's conquest came at the behest of the fourth Fāṭimid caliph al-Muʾizz, who almost immediately moved his court to Jawhar's new city, which he called Al-Qāhirah (city of victory; now Cairo).

As the principal mosque of Cairo, al-Azhar grew exponentially in size and influence as it participated in the ever-increasing prosperity and fame of the city. It enjoyed a special relationship to the Fāṭimid caliphs, who endowed it with gifts and special patronage. The original mosque (it has been much altered and received additions over the centuries) had a traditional rectangular plan, with a large hypostyle hall to accommodate the rows of the faithful who prostrated themselves in prayer toward Mecca. Al-Azhar had other components typical of medieval mosque construction, including a central arcaded courtyard and an elaborately decorated mihrab, or niche, placed in the *qibla* wall (the *qibla* is the direction of Mecca, toward which one should pray). At al-Azhar, the mihrab bay is topped by a dome, recalling the design of the mosque in the former Fāṭimid capital of Mahdia.

The decoration of the mosque is typical of Islamic architectural decoration in its use of purely epigraphic and natural (trees and other vegetal) ornamentation.

The representation of humans or animals is nearly nonexistent in Islamic architectural decoration. Early Islamic artists were wary of representing living beings in mosques because they wanted to avoid possible connections with idol worship or with the sacred role of the divine in creating life. However, Islamic art in mosques is appropriately described as aniconic rather than iconoclastic; artists simply avoided the representation of living beings. The epigraphs at al-Azhar glorify the Fāṭimid Dynasty, and the vegetal decoration may have referred to Paradise beyond the present life promised to believers.

Al-Azhar never had a purely religious function. Prayer in a mosque specifically is not required for Muslims; for prayer it is only necessary that a space be reserved sufficient for prostration and orientation toward Mecca. Mosques were built to accommodate large numbers of the faithful, especially for the Friday congregational prayer, but also as community gathering places with political and social functions. One of these additional roles at al-Azhar was that of an educational institution. The first class was taught at the mosque in 975 and it became an official school with thirty-seven scholars teaching Islamic jurisprudence in 988-989. Institutions like al-Azhar eventually gave rise to madrasas, or religious schools, which were founded around mosques to accommodate the demand for religious instruction.

The Fāṭimid caliphate reached its pinnacle of wealth and power in the century following the foundation of Cairo, with an empire extending to Algeria in the west and to Arabia in the east. By the middle of the eleventh century, the Fāṭimid caliphate was severely weakened by military setbacks and famine in Egypt, and in 1171, the last Fāṭimid was suppressed by the first ruler of the new Ayyūbid Dynasty (1169-1250), Saladin (r. 1174-1193); by 1174, he was sultan. Al-Azhar suffered under the Ayyūbid caliphs, who ruled Egypt until 1252. The Ayyūbids were Sunni Muslims who transferred caliphal patronage away from Shīʿite institutions such as al-Azhar to traditionally Sunni establishments such as the al-Ḥākim mosque in Cairo. Al-Azhar enjoyed a resurgence as a center for education under Sultan Baybars I in the thirteenth century and during the Ottoman rule of Egypt al-Azhar had such great fame that students were drawn to it from all over the empire.

SIGNIFICANCE

Al-Azhar remained one of the premier educational institutions in the Islamic world. In the modern age it expanded from a mosque with a number of associated religious schools to a modern university teaching all subjects. It has also developed a network of educational institutions, including a system of primary and secondary schools. Many schools outside of this network as well as beyond Egypt also are staffed by al-Azhar graduates, extending even further the educational philosophy of the mosque-school.

Al-Azhar participates in the tradition of great medieval universities, of centers of education established because students flocked to these cities to study under famous masters. Other such historic educational institutions are Oxford University in England and the University of Paris. These universities are sources of great nationalistic pride because of their long teaching traditions and their connections to their country's history and identity. Al-Azhar intellectuals are extremely influential in Egyptian public life and in the greater Islamic world because they represent the authority of the past; they place the imprimatur of tradition on their decisions.

The long tradition of al-Azhar as a religious and educational center has established it as a repository of the history of the city of Cairo, of the Fāṭimid Dynasty that built it, and as a symbol of Egyptian, Arab, and Islamic identities.

Marguerite Keane

FURTHER READING

Behrens-Abouseif, Doris. *Islamic Architecture in Cairo: An Introduction*. Leiden, the Netherlands: E. J. Brill, 1989. Analyzes the artistic style of Islamic monuments in Cairo, with a chapter on the early history of the city as well as a detailed description of its Fāṭimid era architecture.

Berkey, Jonathan Porter. *The Transmission of Knowledge in Medieval Cairo: A Social History of Islamic Education*. Princeton, N.J.: Princeton University Press, 1992. Investigates the Islamic educational system under the medieval Mamlūk Dynasty, including the rise in importance of madrasas, the subjects studied, and the system for training teachers. The al-Azhar mosque is discussed briefly as one of the early Fāṭimid congregational mosques.

Ettinghausen, Richard, and Oleg Grabar. *Islamic Art and Architecture, 650-1250*. New Haven, Conn.: Yale University Press, 1987, 2001. A survey of Islamic art and architecture from the Umayyad Dynasty through the end of the ʿAbbāsid period. The authors also examine the origins of Islamic art and architecture after the death of Muḥammad and study the dissemination and revision of these early styles as the Umayyad and ʿAbbāsid empires expanded.

Halm, Heinz. *The Fāṭimids and Their Traditions of Learning*. New York: I. B. Tauris, 1997. A small volume that describes the system of religious teaching and learning during the Fāṭimid rule of Egypt.

SEE ALSO: 630-711: Islam Expands Throughout North Africa; 685-691: Building of the Dome of the Rock; c. 950-1100: Rise of Madrasas; 969-1171: Reign of the Fāṭimids.

RELATED ARTICLES in *Great Lives from History: The Middle Ages, 477-1453*: Baybars I; Muḥammad; Saladin.

973
FOUNDATION OF THE WESTERN CĀLUKYA DYNASTY

In the late tenth century, the Cālukya Dynasty, first established in the 600's in southern India, experienced a revival under Taila II.

LOCALE: Southern India
CATEGORY: Government and politics

KEY FIGURES

Taila II (d. 997), first ruler of the Western Cālukyas, r. 973-997

Vikramāditya VI (d. 1126), the greatest of the Western Cālukya rajas, r. 1076-1126

SUMMARY OF EVENT

The history of southern India is complex and often obscure, not least in the area known as Karnataka, or the northern region of the Western Ghats in the Deccan peninsula. That complexity is something of a contrast to northern India and the Gangetic plain area, where large and often long-lasting empires such as the Mauryan and Gupta and then later the Muslim states centered at Delhi gave a semblance of continuity and focus. In comparison, the history of southern India is relatively unknown. Throughout the first millennium in the common era and well into the second, the history of the region is the history of the rise and fall of numerous dynasties and kingdoms. One of those dynasties was the Cālukya, which twice during that long period achieved significant prominence in the region, controlling considerable territory.

The earlier Cālukya Dynasty ruled much of southern India, the peninsular region known as the Deccan, from 543 to 757. Pulakeśin I (r. 543-566) founded the dynasty and established his capital at Vāṭāpi (modern Bādāmi) in the district of Bijapur. It was claimed that Pulakeśin even performed the *aśvamedha* (horse sacrifice), a ceremony associated with great rulers in a tradition going back a thousand years to earlier Aryan times. Subsequent Cālukya kings, or rajas, extended Cālukya territories, generally through military conquest, and became powerful enough under Pulakeśin II (r. 610-642), one of the most successful of the early Cālukya rajas, to supposedly inflict a military defeat on the greatest Indian ruler of the time, Harṣa of Kanauj, c. 620. The noted Chinese Buddhist pilgrim Xuanzang (Hsüan-tsang; 602-664) visited Pulakeśin's court. By the end of the century, Cālukya rule extended into the Gujarat region, north and west of the Deccan. As a consequence of that territorial expansion, one of the conquered areas was given to a brother of Pulakeśin II, which resulted in the establishment of what became known as the Eastern Cālukyas, who governed the region in what is now Andhra Pradesh, from the early 600's to the late eleventh century. The Cālukyas were Hindus but were noted for their toleration of rival creeds, notably Jainism and Buddhism. However, the original Cālukyas fell to the Rāśṭrakūṭas of Mānyakheta toward the end of the eighth century, with the Cālukyas becoming merely feudatories of the Rāśṭrakūṭas. In ancient India, it was said that the big fish ate the little fish, and the Rāśṭrakūṭas had become the bigger fish.

By the tenth century, the power and influence of the Rāśṭrakūṭas in the region was shared with the Pratihāras and the Pālas, but during that century, the three dynasties declined almost simultaneously, an event that fueled a Cālukya revival, possibly inspired or rationalized by a knowledge, historical or legendary, of the earlier Cālukya's exalted past. In any event, as a cause or a consequence of the decline of the three states, the Cālukyas again achieved independence and regional prominence under Taila II, in 973, who established what is known as the Western Cālukyas. Making Kalyani his capital, Taila restored the luster of the Cālukyas, ruling for twenty-four years until approximately 997.

Taila's reign—like that of so many kings and rajas before and after him—was made glorious by his military accomplishments, most notably his defeat of Paramāra Munja of Malwa. Taila's victories, not least his victory over Paramara, became the subject of legends and poems. One of the most notable poets of the era, Ranna of Kannada (fl. 993), a Jain and the author of the *Ajiṭa Purāṇa* (tenth century), celebrated Taila's fame and that of Taila's son, Saṭyaśraya, whom Ranna compared to Bheema, the great warrior who defeated Duryodhana in India's great epic masterpiece, *Mahābhārata* (c. 400 B.C.E.-400 C.E.; *The Mahabharata of Krishna-Dwaipayana Vyasa*, 1887-1896). Although Hindus, the Western Cālukyas were also patrons of Jainism, giving support to writers and artists and constructing temples and other religious structures.

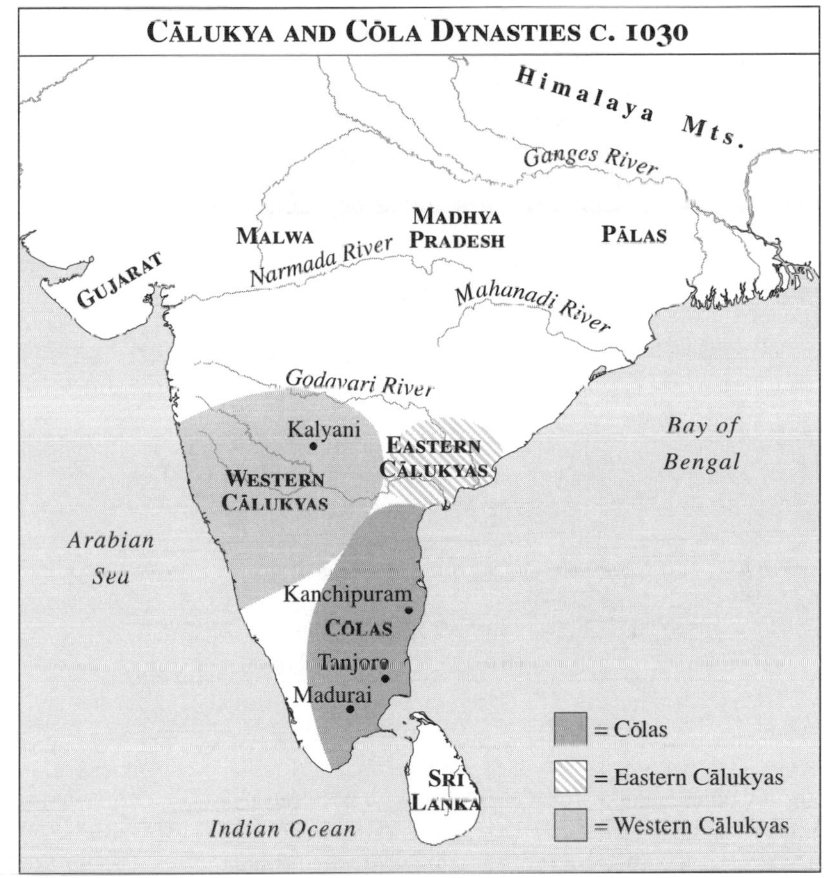

Cālukya ambitions and successes were not unchallenged. From the far south of the peninsula, the Cōlas of Tanjore, under the leadership of Rājarāja I (r. 985-1014) and his successors, had established a successful and expansionist dynasty, and in the early tenth century, the Cōlas invaded Cālukya territories. According the Calukya sources, the Cōla army was particularly brutal, killing women and children and raping young girls from the higher castes, a heinous offence in India's caste-dominated society. However, instead of defeating the Cālukyas and making them feudatories to the Cōlas, Rājarāja's assault guaranteed that the Cālukyas would become and remain bitter antagonists.

Although plunder was always a motivating factor, the Cālukya-Cola conflict was about territorial ambitions, and the continuing struggle can best be understood as repeated attempts to establish defensible frontiers or borders between the two south Indian dynasties that were relatively equally balanced in resources and strengths. Taila's son, Satyaśraya, won renown by defeating Rājarāja. Later Cālukya kings experienced invasions, suffered defeats, and won victories. Jayasimha I successfully resisted invasions from the north and from the Cōla south, led by Rājarāja's son and successor, Rājendracōla Deva I (r. 1014-1044). Jagadhekamalla supposedly defeated the ruler of the Malava confederacy as well as the king of Chedi. The Cōlas sacked the Cālukya capital of Kalyani c. 1050, but Someśvara I (r. 1043-1068) subsequently drove the Cōlas out of the city and out of Cālukya lands.

The dynasty's greatest raja was Vikramāditya VI (r. 1076-1126). The son of Someśvara I, he was his father's first choice to rule, but Vikramāditya declined in favor of his elder brother, Someśvara II. Before becoming raja in his own right, Vikramāditya defeated the Cōla king Virarājendra, who gave his daughter to Vikramāditya as a peace pledge. Vikramāditya was also victorious over the Keralas and Sri Lanka, although that claim sounds problematic. The Cālukya brothers had a falling out, and Vikramāditya ruled the southern part of Cālukya lands independently from Someśvara II, but he became raja of the Cālukyas in his own right in 1076. As other rulers before him, Vikramāditya was a patron of the arts, giving support to the writers Bhilhana and Vijnaneswara.

His successor, Someśvara III, more interested in the arts than in politics and war, allowed Viṣṇuvardhana

MAJOR RULERS OF THE SECOND WESTERN CĀLUKYA DYNASTY, 973-1189/90

Reign	*Ruler*
973-997	Taila II
997-1008	Saṭyaśraya
1008-1014	Vikramāditya I
1014-1015	Ayyana
1015-1042	Jayasimha I
1043-1068	Someśvara I
1068-1076	Someśvara II
1076-1126	Vikramāditya VI
1127-1135	Someśvara III
1135-1151	Jagadhekamalla II
1151-1154	Taila III
1155-1168	Bijjala
1168-1177	Someśvara IV
1177-1180	Saṇkama II
1180-1183	Āhavamalla
1183-1184	Singhana
1184-1189/90	Someśvara IV

Hoysaḷa to become largely independent of Cālukya rule, and Jagadhekamalla II (r. 1135-1151) saw the Hoysaḷas invade Cālukya territory. His successor, Taila III (r. 1151-1154), was captured by Prola I, of the Kākatīya. Bijjala Kalacuri, Taila III's chief general, usurped the throne, but he successfully restored the kingdom's defenses. Several brief reigns followed: Someśvara IV (r. 1168-1177), Saṇkama II (r. 1177-1180), Āhavamalla (r. 1180-1183), and Singhana (r.1183-1184). The last of the Western Cālukya rajas was Someśvara V (r. 1184-1189/1190).

SIGNIFICANCE

The dynasty came to an end perhaps the way it had begun in the late tenth century under Taila II, with the decline and fall of a kingdom and the successful takeover by an ambitious individual or family and the establishment of a new ruling dynasty. Most Indian dynasties, like many other monarchies elsewhere, were organized on a feudal basis, with local families and clans giving support to the kings and rajas in exchange for protection and privileges. Weak rulers and ambitious feudatories could and did often reverse the relationship. The Hoysaḷas, originally a family of petty hill chiefs, were ostensibly Cālukya feudatories. Long ambitious, the Hoysaḷas had assisted Vikramāditya VI against the Cōlas, and in the 1100's, they had declared their semi-independence from the Cālukyas. With the decline of the Cālukyas in the twelfth century, possibly due in part to inadequate leadership, but also because the Cālukyas were weakened by a continuing struggle with the invading Kalacuris of Madya Pradesh, the Hoysaḷas, led by Vira Ballala I, supplanted the Western Cālukyas in 1190. The Cōlas, longtime rivals of the Cālukyas, also declined in the twelfth century. The wheel of southern India dynasties had turned once more.

—*Eugene Larson*

FURTHER READING

Aruna, A. *State Formation in the Eastern Deccan, Seventh Century A.D.-Thirteenth Century A.D.* Delhi, India: Bharatiya Kala Prakashan, 2000. A political history that also discusses the Cālukya Dynasty.

Dikshit, Durga Prasad. *Political History of the Chalukyas of Badami*. New Delhi, India: Abhinau Publications, 1980. An overly detailed account of the political history of the Cālukyas, but one of the few available in English.

Gopal, B. R. *The Chalukyas of Kalyana and the Kalachuris*. Dharwad, India: Karnatak University Press, 1981. A scholarly study of the later Cālukyas.

Krishaswami Ayyangar, S. "Hindu States in Southern India." In *The Cambridge History of India*. Vol. 3, edited by Sir Wolsey Haig. Delhi, India: S. Chand, 1958. Relates in knowledgeable detail the era that includes the history of the Western Cālukyas.

Majumdar, Asoke Kumar. *Chalukyas of Gujarat*. Bombay, India: Bharatiya Vidya Bhaven, 1956. A study of Gujarat from the tenth to the end of the thirteenth century.

Murari, Krishna. *The Calukya of Kalyani from Circa 973 to 1200 A.D.* Delhi: Concept Publishing, 1977. A history of the Cālukyas written by an Indian historian.

SEE ALSO: 606-647: Reign of Harṣa of Kanauj; c. 610-632: Muḥammad Receives Revelations; 770-810: Reign of Dharmapāla; c. 985-1014: Reign of Rājarāja I.

RELATED ARTICLE in *Great Lives from History: The Middle Ages, 477-1453*: Harṣa.

976-1025
REIGN OF BASIL II

The reign of Basil II marked the apex of Byzantine power and political expansion and produced remarkable achievements in the military, religious, and economic realms, despite controversies over Basil's successor.

LOCALE: Byzantine Empire
CATEGORY: Government and politics

KEY FIGURES

John I Tzimisces (925-976), Byzantine emperor, r. 969-976
Theophano (d. after 976), empress and wife of Romanus II, Nicephorus II Phocas, and John I Tzimisces, and mother of Basil II and Constantine VIII
Basil II (c. 958-1025), Byzantine emperor, r. 976-1025
Basil the Chamberlain (d. 985), great-uncle of Byzantine emperors Basil II and Constantine VIII
Samuel (d. 1014), czar of Bulgaria, 980-1014
Vladimir I (c. 956-1015), grand prince of Kiev, 980-1015
Bardas Skleros (fl. tenth century), powerful general, challenged Basil's succession in 976 and 987
Bardas Phocas (d. 989), nephew of Nicephorus II Phocas, member of a powerful aristocratic house and general who claimed the imperial office in 987
John XVI (d. c. 1013), antipope, 997-998, bishop of Calabria, and Basil's candidate as Roman pontiff

SUMMARY OF EVENT

In spite of its bloody beginnings, the Macedonian Dynasty of the Byzantine Empire, founded by the illiterate Armenian peasant Basil I who, as imperial chamberlain and then coemperor, assassinated his rival to gain the throne, attained its zenith of power during the reign of Basil's great-great-grandson Basil II, son of Emperor Romanus II and the beautiful Empress Theophano, who may have murdered a series of emperor-husbands.

Although crowned in 960 as a child, Basil II ascended to the throne in Constantinople in 976 after fifty years of court dissension and intrigue. Always able to control his brother and joint emperor, Constantine VIII, Basil moved to control the empire by himself only in 985, when he drove his able adviser-minister and great-uncle, Basil the Chamberlain, into exile.

In the same year, according to the chief contemporary source, Michael Psellus, Basil reached another turning point in his life. Whereas in his early years, Basil had been given to the banquet table and pleasures of the flesh, he now became secretive, ascetic, and effectively autocratic. His sole concern was to forge a strong state, defending it from enemies within and without. By this time, his military skills had been sharpened in frustrated campaigns against Czar Samuel of Bulgaria in the Balkans, and his administrative and diplomatic aptitude had developed in the absence of Basil the Chamberlain. In cultural and intellectual pursuits, however, the emperor showed little interest, and during his administration government patronage of learning and the arts declined.

His rule continued to be plagued with unrest until 989 through such contenders as the general Bardas Skleros, who was raised to the imperial purple by his troops in 976, and the pretender Bardas Phocas, who in 987 tried to usurp the throne with the support of army officers and the landed aristocracy of Asia Minor. Basil put down these rebellions in 987 by the expedient of inviting Prince Vladimir of Kiev and his Varangian troops to his aid, in return for which Vladimir was promised the hand of Basil's sister, the Byzantine princess Anna. Vladimir ensured the fulfillment of this promise by seizing the Byzantine colony of Cherson in the Crimea. After the marriage, and following his own research into the Byzantine ritual, Vladimir accepted the Orthodox rite of Christianity for himself and the Russian state in 988.

In 996, Basil attacked the powerful landed aristocracy by demanding that they restore property to those whom they had dispossessed. Although this action was motivated partly out of revenge against the Bardas family and their supporters, there were legitimate economic considerations involved. These programs revived the intentions of Basil's predecessor and great-grandfather, Romanus Lecapenus, insofar as agrarian reforms were promoted and the tax base was broadened. No longer was the aristocracy able to ignore imperial assessments or transfer property to monastic establishments, for Basil threw the weight of taxation on all the propertied classes including the Church.

As commander in chief, Basil II had no equal among the Byzantine emperors before or after him. Not always a victor in battles, he was inevitably successful in wars, following a policy of careful consolidation of his victories along each step of his military campaigns. The Caucasian provinces were in a state of constant unrest as a result of the independent spirit of the Georgian and Armenian aristocracy, but a show of strength by Basil in 998 ensured imperial control. The expansionist policy in Syria of an Egyptian Fāṭimid caliph was countered by successful campaigns in 991 and 999 by the emperor himself.

Basil's greatest military triumph was against the Bulgars of Czar Samuel. The Bulgarian war occupied Basil's attention intermittently for thirty years. John I Tzimisces, Basil's usurping predecessor, had fragmented Bulgarian power in the Balkans, but it became a threat again under Czar Samuel, who in 985 ravaged Thrace to the Corinthian Isthmus and overran the strategic territory around Thessalonica. Basil himself narrowly escaped with his life after a sound defeat at the hands of the Bulgars in the summer of 986. The revolts of Bardas Phocas and Bardas Skleros between 986 and 996 interrupted the emperor's Bulgarian campaign, and Samuel was able to make himself the arbiter of the Balkans, killing or capturing with impunity the Byzantine administrative officials who attempted to drive him from Thessalonica.

In 996, however, the imperial general Nicephorus Uranus crushed Samuel's army at the Spercheus River, and the Bulgarian czar directed his attention to the more accessible goals of Dalmatia, Bosnia, and Dioclea, petty kingdoms federated to Constantinople. So successful was Samuel's campaign in the western Balkans that he was able to arrange, about 1000, the marriage of his son and successor, Gabriel Radomir, to a daughter of Stephen of Hungary.

Basil pursued a relentless policy of encirclement, negotiating a treaty with the Venetians to cut off Bulgarian access to the Adriatic, and deploying his own forces in a pincer movement along the lower and middle Danube and into the central Balkans. Although Basil surprised the army of Samuel in the spring of 1003 near Skoplje, and nearly captured him, Bulgarian resistance dragged on until 1019 as a result of the tenacious spirit of the Bulgarians and the impregnable nature of their strongholds. The turning point was Basil's summer campaign of 1014 aimed at the Bulgarian capital of Ochrid, when the emperor captured a Bulgarian force of fourteen thousand men. The eyes of ninety-nine out of every hundred were put out; the hundredth man was left with only one eye so he could lead his fellows back to their hapless czar. Samuel was so struck by this tragic sight that he suffered a seizure and died on October 6, 1014. Basil, the "Bulgar-slayer," could as a result hold the Balkan Peninsula securely in the empire.

Basil's skill as a diplomat presents a record more mixed in its success. While he himself never married and seemingly had little liking for women, he used marriage freely to cement relationships with his allies. In addition to the alliance with the Kievan Dynasty of Vladimir, another royal princess was promised in marriage to the Venetian John Urseolo in order to seal an alliance with that naval power against the Bulgarians in 998. Crown Princess Zoë (980-1050), eldest daughter of Constantine VIII (r. 976-1028), was given in marriage to the three-year-old emperor Otto III (r. 983-1002), who died before consummation. In the latter case, there was a precedence for such a foreign marriage, since the mother of Otto III was a Byzantine princess.

In regard to the Church, Basil maintained a truly autocratic policy. He personally appointed three successive patriarchs in Constantinople and controlled the appointments at Antioch and Jerusalem. Probably unappreciative of the complexity of Western papal-imperial politics, he tried to promote a Calabrian bishop, the antipope John XVI (997-998), as a rival for the German papal candidate and then pope, Gregory V (996-999). The ambitious plan failed in 998 when Philagathus was captured, mutilated, and imprisoned by Ottonian supporters.

SIGNIFICANCE

During Basil II's reign, the Byzantine Empire's political expansion and its artistic and cultural influence was at its peak. At his death in December, 1025, however, Basil was preparing an offensive against the Normans in southern Italy, the objective being to resurrect Byzantine power in the West.

Basil was a supreme nation builder and protector, and his main focus was on maintaining the powerful position the empire had attained and maintained in the region, a position that began with Constantine the Great's transformation of an old Greek port called Byzantium into Constantinople around 330, when the city was named the center of the Eastern Roman Empire.

Basil saw both the peak and the beginning of a decline of the Byzantine Empire during his lifetime. The eleventh century was marked by the Seljuk Turks attacking the eastern Mediterranean, and the Byzantines began to seek the help of Crusaders and the Papacy in Rome. The empire, however, did not collapse completely until the fall of Constantinople in 1453, when the Ottoman Turks attacked and conquered the city and established their own flourishing empire.

—Richard J. Wurtz, updated by Gloria Fulton

Further Reading

Browning, Robert. *The Byzantine Empire*. Rev. ed. Washington, D.C.: Catholic University of America Press, 1992. A history of the Byzantine Empire. Chapter 3 discusses its golden age and the reign of Basil II.

Fine, John V. A. *The Early Medieval Balkans: A Critical Survey from the Sixth to the Late Twelfth Century*. Ann Arbor: University of Michigan Press, 1991. A detailed historical survey of the entire Balkans, with a good discussion of original sources and areas of scholarly dispute. Maps, bibliography, index.

Jenkins, Romilly. *Byzantium: The Imperial Centuries, A.D. 610-1071*. 1966. New ed. New York: Barnes and Noble Books, 1993. A scholarly study of the apex of Byzantine power. Maps, bibliography, index.

Kazhdan, A. P., and Ann Wharton Epstein. *Change in Byzantine Culture in the Eleventh and Twelfth Centuries*. Berkeley: University of California Press, 1985. A scholarly treatment of the cultural, social, and economic background to the reign of Basil II and his successors. Bibliography, index.

Magdalino, Paul, ed. *Byzantium in the Year 1000*. New York: Brill, 2003. A collection that reassesses the politics and culture of the empire during Basil's time. Articles look at diplomacy, Basil's power, Byzantine provinces, law, historiography, poetry, and more. Bibliography, index.

Norwich, John Julius. *Byzantium: The Apogee*. New York: Alfred A. Knopf, 1996. A very readable account of the fortunes of the Byzantine Empire, including considerable detail on the relationship with Bulgaria. Bibliography, index.

_______. *Byzantium: The Decline and Fall*. New York: Alfred A. Knopf, 1996. Continuation of the author's account above, covering the period from the Crusades to the fall of the Byzantine Empire to the Turks in 1453. Tables, maps, bibliography, index.

Runciman, Steven. *A History of the First Bulgarian Empire*. London: Bell and Sons, 1930. The classic history of the first Bulgarian Empire, focusing on religious and political developments from the earliest times to the end of the reign of Samuel. Bibliography.

Stephenson, Paul. *The Legend of Basil the Bulgar-slayer*. New York: Cambridge University Press, 2003. A historical biography that argues Basil's reign did not mark a golden age for the empire. The author also argues that the epithet "Bulgar-slayer" was not ascribed to Basil during his time but instead a century and a half later, as political propaganda. Illustrations, maps, bibliography, index.

Treadgold, Warren. *Byzantium and Its Army, 284-1081*. Stanford, Calif.: Stanford University Press, 1995. An examination of the Byzantine army's role and structure within the empire's history. Maps, illustrations, bibliography, index.

See also: c. 850: Development of the Slavic Alphabet; 864: Boris Converts to Christianity; 893: Beginning of Bulgaria's Golden Age; 988: Baptism of Vladimir I; 1040-1055: Expansion of the Seljuk Turks; 1054: Beginning of the Rome-Constantinople Schism; November 27, 1095: Pope Urban II Calls the First Crusade; 1189-1192: Third Crusade; 1204: Knights of the Fourth Crusade Capture Constantinople; May 29, 1453: Fall of Constantinople.

Related articles in *Great Lives from History: The Middle Ages, 477-1453*: Anna, Princess of the Byzantine Empire; Justinian I; Michael Psellus; Theophanes the Confessor; Vladimir I.

982
LE DAI HANH INVADES CHAMPA

The invasion of Champa by the Vietnamese emperor Le Dai Hanh culminated in the destruction of the Champa capital of Indrapura and led to centuries of warfare between the Vietnamese and the Chams that ended with Champa's eventual elimination.

LOCALE: Northern and Central Vietnam
CATEGORY: Wars, uprisings, and civil unrest

KEY FIGURES

Dinh Bo Linh (923-979), first emperor of Vietnam, r. 965-979

Le Dai Hanh (Le Hoan, d. 1005), emperor of Vietnam, r. 980-1005

Paramesvaravarman (d. 982), king of Champa, r. ?-982

Indravarman IV (d. 986), king of Champa, r. 982-986

SUMMARY OF EVENT

When the first emperor of Vietnam, Dinh Bo Linh, was assassinated in 979, the recently independent state of Dai Co Viet ("great empire of the Vietnamese") faced a serious crisis. The assassin, Do Thich, was captured and beheaded, and his corpse cut into small pieces that were given to the people to eat. The only surviving heir was Dinh Toan, a young prince of five, who was crowned emperor. His mother, one of Dinh Bo Linh's five wives, was young and beautiful and deeply in love with the military commander in chief, Le Hoan.

Emperor Taizong (T'ai-tsung; r. 976-997) of the Chinese Song Dynasty (Sung; 960-1279) tried to use the opportunity to reestablish Chinese domination over the Vietnamese, which had lasted for more than a thousand years and had been ended in 939. Faced with this danger, the Vietnamese military supported Le Hoan's assumption of imperial power. His lover agreed to have her son give up the throne. Le Hoan became emperor in 980 and took the imperial name of Le Dai Hanh, under which he is most widely known.

The Chinese emperor refused to acknowledge Le Dai Hanh and demanded that the child Dinh Toan and his mother travel to China to pay their respects. Le Dai Hanh was unwilling to let go of his lover, so he refused the Chinese and readied for war.

In 981, the Chinese send an invasion fleet to northern Vietnam. Le Dai Hanh lost a battle on the Bach-dang, the most northern tributary of the Red River delta near modern Hanoi. However, he managed to capture and kill the Chinese commander and captured two more senior Chinese generals. Because China was busy fighting off Mongol invaders, the Chinese court accepted Le Dai Hanh's offer to exchange his prisoners in return for peace and his formal recognition as ruler of Vietnam, who officially paid tribute to China.

Having secured his and his people's position against China, Le Dai Hanh turned his attention south to deal with the kingdom of Champa. The first kingdom of Champa was founded by southern rebels against Chinese rule in 192 C.E., and it was known as Lin-yi by the Chinese and Lam Ap by the Vietnamese. In the fifth century, Malay settlers from Indonesia, especially Java, changed the ethnic nature of the Cham people and enlarged the kingdom's territory. At the height of its power, Champa stretched over a coastal area ranging south from modern Da Nang up to Cape Vung Tau just east of modern Ho Chih Minh City (Saigon). A dark-skinned people with curly black hair, the Chams had a reputation for cleanliness and survived by fishing, trading, and piracy. After its foundation, Champa maintained an uneasy relationship with its neighbors, including the Vietnamese and the Chinese. During the Nanzhao war of the ninth century, Cham raiders were seen in northern Vietnam.

In 979, after the assassination of Dinh Bo Linh, the Cham king Paramesvaravarman decided to invade Vietnam. He led a great attacking fleet north, but a fierce tempest dispersed his ships and prevented the landfall of the invaders. A year later in 980, Le Dai Hanh sent an embassy to the Cham capital of Indrapura, near modern Da Nang. Instead of receiving the Vietnamese envoy with courtesy and respect, king Paramesvaravarman threw the messengers in jail.

In 982, having successfully dealt with the Chinese, Le Dai Hanh led a Vietnamese army to invade Champa. Le Dai Hanh won in battle and killed the Cham king. The Cham capital of Indrapura was captured, plundered, and destroyed. The victorious Vietnamese took much booty and led the royal ballet troop of Champa into captivity to Vietnam.

With his people defeated and his capital razed, the new king Indravarman IV had to agree to pay tribute to Vietnam. The new capital became Vijaya, near modern Qui Nhon, 200 miles (320 kilometers) farther south. Le Dai Hanh's invasion had been a resounding success for the Vietnamese.

SIGNIFICANCE

Le Dai Hanh's victory over the Champa indicated that in the late tenth century, Vietnam had not only gained its long sought independence from China but was ready to embark on its own aggressive course of expansion. Provoked by the abortive Cham raid against Vietnamese shores in 979 and the imprisonment of his envoy in 980, Le Dai Hanh retaliated with force. His invasion of Champa and the destruction of Indrapura marked the beginning of a century-long struggle between the Vietnamese and the Chams. Eventually, warfare between the two people would end only with a set of total Vietnamese victories in the fifteenth and the early nineteenth centuries. These victories in effect eliminated Champa and erased it from the map of Southeast Asia. Much of modern central and southern Vietnam is land gained by the Vietnamese from their defeated Cham enemies.

However, up to the final dissolution of the Champa kingdom in the nineteenth century, the struggle with the Vietnamese that began in earnest with the battle of Le Dai Hanh against king Paramesvaravarman would be long and arduous. The fortunes of both sides would rise and fall, a pattern already revealed the immediate aftermath of Le Dai Hanh's initial triumph.

While the new Cham king Indravarman IV ruled from the city of Vijaya and fruitlessly asked the Chinese for help against Vietnam, a Vietnamese man, Luu Ky Tong (d. 989), seized power in northern Champa, still littered with the ruins of Indrapura. Luu, dreaming of a kingdom of his own, even defied emperor Le Dai Hanh's order to relinquish power over the Chams.

When Indravarman IV died in 986, Luu dared to proclaim himself king of Champa, an audacious move for an ethnic Vietnamese. The Chams resisted this alien ruler. Many Chams fled into southern China. They preferred to live there rather than under a Vietnamese king. Yet at Vijaya in 988, a Cham rebel proclaimed himself the true king of Champa. The rebel took the name of Harivarman II (d. 1000). When Luu died suddenly in 989, Harivarman II's authority in Champa was ensured. In 990, he defeated an attacking Vietnamese army that could not duplicate Le Dai Hanh's triumph of eight years earlier. Harivarman II and Le Dai Hanh exchanged prisoners of war, and Champa continued to pay regular tribute to the Vietnamese. Harivarman II even rebuilt Indrapura, which served again as capita of Champa.

The Chams soon resumed their raids against the Vietnamese, who responded with force. In 1000, the new Cham king, Harivarman III (d. 1021), had to abandon Indrapura for the safety of the more southern Vijaya. In the last years of Le Dai Hanh's reign, the Vietnamese again assumed the upper hand against the Chams.

Thus, beginning with Le Dai Hanh's invasion of Champa, even though the Vietnamese occasionally lost ground, their war with Champa would ultimately be successful. In addition to asserting Vietnamese power in the south, Le Dai Hanh also managed to establish a stable position for Vietnam's independence from China that enabled the Vietnamese to focus their energies south to the acquisition of new territory wrested from its weaker neighbors. From the reign of Le Dai Hanh, China recognized the Vietnamese emperor as a king who nominally paid tribute to the Chinese court but who really enjoyed full independence. This diplomatic solution saved face for the Chinese and guaranteed Vietnamese independence and expansion.

—R. C. Lutz

FURTHER READING

Chapuis, Oscar. *A History of Vietnam*. Westport, Conn.: Greenwood Press, 1995. Good history of Champa, and a concise discussion of the reign of Le Dai Hanh. Maps, bibliography, index.

Hall, Daniel George. *A History of Southeast Asia*. 4th ed. London: Macmillan Press, 1981. Still a standard work on the period. Chapter 8 surveys the history of Champa, chapter 9 that of Vietnam, from the beginnings to the sixteenth century. Illustrations, maps, bibliography, and index.

Huard, Pierre, and Maurice Durand. *Viet Nam: Civilization and Culture*. Translated by Vu Thiên Kim. 2d ed. Hanoi: Ecole Française d'Extrême-Orient, 1994. General overview that contains a historic survey and much background on Vietnamese culture through the ages. Richly illustrated.

Lockard, Craig A. "The Unexplained Miracle: Reflections on Vietnamese National Identity and Survival." *Journal of Asian and African Studies* 29 (January-April, 1994): 10-35. Provides a framework for appraising Le Dai Hanh's achievement of safeguarding Vietnamese independence in the face of foreign attempts to eradicate its culture.

Raj, Hans. *History of South-East Asia*. Delhi, India: Surjeet, 2002. Comprehensive account incorporating fresh historical, archaeological, and anthropological research and insights. Maps, bibliography, index.

SEE ALSO: 729: Founding of Nanzhao; 832: Nanzhao Subjugates Pyu; 877-889: Indravarman I Conquers the Thai and the Mons; 939-944: Reign of Ngo Quyen; 1225: Tran Thai Tong Establishes Tran Dynasty; 1323-1326: Champa Wins Independence from Dai Viet; 1428: Le Loi Establishes Later Le Dynasty.

RELATED ARTICLE in *Great Lives from History: The Middle Ages, 477-1453*: Ngo Quyen.

c. 985-1014
REIGN OF RĀJARĀJA I

Rājarāja I was the greatest of southern India's Cōla kings. In addition to creating and administering a great empire, he forged impressive commercial links with Southeast Asia that led to later kings establishing trade with China. He is remembered as a patron of the arts on an unprecedented scale.

LOCALE: South India

CATEGORIES: Expansion and land acquisition; government and politics; cultural and intellectual history

KEY FIGURES

Rājarāja I (d. 1014), king of Cōla Empire, r. 985-1014

Rājendracōla Deva I (d. 1044), his son and successor, r. 1014-1044

SUMMARY OF EVENT

The Cōla Empire marks a high point in the history of south India. The dynasty rose from obscurity with Vijayālaya (r. c. 850-c. 871), who, initially a local chieftain from the neighborhood of Uraiyur, captured the city of Tanjore around 850. Making Tanjore his capital, he founded what was to become one of India's richest kingdoms. However, it was the sixth king of the line, Rājarāja I, who transformed a relatively small kingdom into a glorious empire.

Prince Arumoḷivarman took the name Rājarāja (king of kings) at his coronation in 985. His thirty-year rule was the formative period of Cōla imperialism. At the time of Rājarāja's accession, Cōla was still a relatively small state. The king worked to extend the land holdings and to formulate a tightly knit empire efficiently administered and protected by a powerful army and navy. His earliest victory was against the confederation formed by the rulers of the Pāṇḍya kingdom to the south, the Kerala kingdom to the west, and the kingdom located in Sri Lanka. In two ground attacks, his army overran the neighboring kingdoms. In the third assault, a naval attack on the island, he took control over a large portion of northern Sri Lanka. The ancient Sinhalese capital at Anuradhapura was destroyed, and the Cōla king made Polonnaruva the new island capital.

After consolidating his newly acquired territories, Rājarāja I extended his control to the Maldive Islands and initiated diplomatic and economic links with the Sailendra rulers of the Śrivijaya kingdom located on the island of Sumatra. Although Rājarāja had created a formidable empire, he had contenders who vied to take control of his empire. His greatest enemy was the Cālukya king Satyāśraya, who, angered at the Cōla expansion northward into the Cālukya Empire, went to war in 1006. Initially successful, Satyāśraya reclaimed the Cālukya eastern capital at Vengi in Andhra Pradesh that had been taken by the Cōlas.

In response, Rājarāja I ordered his son Rājendra to lead an invasion against the Cālukyas. By striking their western territories in Mysore while simultaneously directing a second branch of the Cōla army into central Andhra Pradesh, Rājendra forced Satyāśraya to withdraw his troops from Vengi and the surrounding region, thereby ceding control of lands extending southward from modern-day Andhra Pradesh to the tip of the subcontinent to the Cōla king.

Rājarāja was not only an empire builder but also an impressive civil administrator. He devised a centralized administrative network focused on a single authority by breaking down the barriers between the traditional territorial divisions and incorporating them into his imperial administration. His leadership gave such great security to the people that a distinctive Tamil social and cultural life flourished and endured for centuries.

Perhaps in recognition of the successful achievements in the first decade of his rule, Rājarāja constructed an enormous royal temple at his capital, Tanjore, between c. 995 and 1010. Called the Rājarājeśvara initially, it later became known as the Bṛhadīśvara Temple. Funding for the enterprise came from the revenue of many villages scattered throughout the empire. A surviving inscription stipulates the amount of revenue from each village; more than forty villages in the twenty-ninth year of Rājarāja were granted to the temple, including five villages in Sri Lanka. The temple, consisting of more than 160,000 cubic feet of granite, was constructed on a monumental scale, exceeding by fivefold or sixfold the dimensions of any temple previously constructed in southern India. It rose in fifteen tiers to nearly 200 feet (60 meters). Of enormous height and elegant, elongated proportions, the temple is characterized by great clarity in design. The original temple was part of a massive complex that included a cloister wall at the periphery, a main temple dedicated to the Hindu god Śiva, a pavilion to Śiva's bull Nandi, a smaller temple dedicated to the Goddess Caṇḍikeśvara (several additional smaller shrines were constructed in subsequent centuries), and two massive gateways. Most likely, the proud and confident king played an important role in designing a temple with such bold and innovative construction and rich decoration.

Rājarāja was actively involved in organizing the daily practices and celebrations of the temple, and the model that he established became standard in south India. Generally larger Hindu temples maintained male and female singers and reciters of sacred texts who praised the deity with long cycles (garlands) of devotional songs. In his temple, Rājarāja appears to have systemized the recitation practices at the Bṛhadīśvara Temple. For the recitation of the sacred *Tiruppadigam* at the Bṛhadīśvara Temple, for example, he appointed forty musicians, including one person for playing a small drum and another for the big drum. Altogether, the temple maintained sixty-seven musicians, both men and women. The male musicians were called *gandharva*, and the female ones were called *gandharvī*.

One important function of the temple was allowing for the continuation and preservation of the arts; essentially it was a repository for the fine arts. In addition to musical performances, dance and theater productions were staged regularly. It is recorded that the play *Rājarājeśvara nāṭaka*, a production about the king himself, was enacted at the Tanjore temple during an annual festival. Other arts patronized by the temple included sculpting in stone, the bronze casting of images, painting, and jewelry making. The temple also served as the principal repository of public records. Besides collecting and conserving sacred literature, the temple carefully recorded all its affairs in the inscriptions on its walls. The inscriptions are authentic evidence serving as a primary source of valuable historical data; in addition, the inscriptions are fine examples of calligraphy in the Tamil Grantha script.

The temple as an employer played an important role in the socioeconomic life of a large number of people who were maintained to serve the temple in various capacities. Each temple had many servants, male and female, both skilled and unskilled. Skilled positions included the priests, assistants to the priests, scholars, reciters, accountants, superintendents, treasurers, gardeners, artisans, musicians, and dancers. Unskilled servants were used for sweeping, bringing water, looking after the oil lamps, and husking rice for offerings. Ever the generous patron, the king donated 2,928 cows to the Bṛhadīśvara Temple at Tanjore so that they could supply the temple with the required *ghee* (clarified butter) necessary for conducting the rituals. The cows were entrusted to sixty-one herders within and outside the city.

When Rājarāja I died in 1014, his son Rājendra, who had directed several of Rājarāja's victorious campaigns, succeeded to the Cōla throne. Rājendracōla Deva I is remembered for his continued expansion of the empire that, at one brief point in time, extended to the mouth of the Ganges River in northern India. He built his own impressive royal temple at his new capital city in the Kaveri

Major Rulers of the Cōlas, c. 850-1279

Reign	*Ruler*
c. 850-c. 870	Vijayālaya
871-907	Āditya I
907-955	Parāntaka I
956	Arinjayā
956	Parāntaka II
956-969	Āditya II
969-985	Madhurantaka Uttama
985-1014	Rājarāja I
1014-1044	Rājendracōla Deva I
1044-1052	Rājadhirāja I
1052-1060	Rājendracōla Deva II
1060-1063	Ramamahendra
1063-1067	Virarājendra
1067-1070	Adhirājendra
1070-1122	Rājendra III
1122-1135	Vikrama Cōla
1135-1150	Kulottuṇga II Cōla
1150-1173	Rājarāja II
1173-1179	Rājadhirāja II
1179-1218	Kulottuṇga III
1218-1246	Rājarāja III
1246-1279	Rājendra IV

Delta, named Gangaikondacōlapuram in honor of his victory. Curious about the world beyond Indian shores, he sent a diplomatic and commercial mission to China in 1016, and as a result, trade between the two empires was established. Rājendra's father had sustained friendly relationship with the Sailendras of the Srivijaya kingdom in Southeast Asia. A powerful maritime state, the Sailendras had ruled the Malayan peninsula, Sumatra, Java, and neighboring islands for centuries and thus controlled the seas between India and China.

At some point the Sumatran Dynasty must have posed a threat to Cōla trade, perhaps blockading the Cōlas' contact with China. Whatever the cause, Rājendra dealt with them swiftly, and in 1025, he sent out a great naval expedition against the Sailendras. His forces seized and occupied parts of Burma, Malaya, and Sumatra. Having secured the sealanes, the Cōla king sent another diplomatic mission to China in 1033.

SIGNIFICANCE

Rājarāja I and his son Rājendra were powerful kings who ruled one of India's most important and richest empires. Their reigns mark the zenith of a great overseas commercial empire as well as the florescence of Tamil culture in southern India. Rājarāja in particular is considered the greatest ruler of southern India. His conquests established the foundation of the mighty Cōla Empire, and his administrative talents set excellent standards for righteous governance that were emulated by later Cōla rulers and also served as a model for kings of subsequent dynasties.

During Cōla suzerainty, the south experienced a time of untold prosperity and cultural richness. All lands south of the Tungabhadra River were united and held as one state for a period of more than two centuries. The apex of the Cōla splendor resulted from the brilliant vision, strategic military judgment, and superior administrative talents of Rājarāja I.

—*Katherine Anne Harper*

FURTHER READING

Hernault, Fracoise L'. *The Brhadesvara Temple*. New Delhi: Indira Gandhi National Centre for the Arts, 2002. An excellent work providing a detailed survey of the iconography of Rājarāja I's great temple in Tanjore. Short bibliography.

Nilakanta Sastri, K. A. *A History of South India from Prehistoric Times to the Fall of Vijayanagar.* Bombay: Oxford University Press, 1966. An important and careful reconstruction of the history of Tamil Nadu from earliest times through its last great dynasty. Bibliography.

Pichard, Pierre. *Tanjavur Brhadisvara: An Architectural Study.* Pondicherry: École Française d'Extrême-Orient, 1995. Provides some historical facts on Rājarāja I and an extensive survey of his great temple complex at Tanjore. Bibliography.

Poongothai, Selvi T., and K. D. Thirunavukkarasu. *Rājarāja the Great: A Garland of Tributes*. Madras, India: Government Museum, 1984. A compilation of quotations by scholars commemorating Rājarāja I one thousand years after his coronation. Partial citations provided after each quotation.

SEE ALSO: 770-810: Reign of Dharmapāla; 780: Rise of the Sailendra Family; 915: Parāntaka I Conquers Pāṇḍya; 973: Foundation of the Western Cālukya Dynasty; 998-1030: Reign of Maḥmūd of Ghazna.

987
HUGH CAPET IS ELECTED TO THE FRENCH THRONE

Hugh Capet was elected to the French throne, reestablishing the principle of hereditary succession. Capet also founded the Capetian Dynasty, which ruled France continuously from 987 to 1328, perpetuating monarchal authority.

LOCALE: France
CATEGORY: Government and politics

KEY FIGURES

Hugh Capet (c. 938-996), duke of the Franks, 956-996, king of the Franks, r. 987-996
Lothair (941-986), Carolingian king of the Franks, r. 954-986
Louis V (967-987), last Carolingian king of the Franks, r. 986-987
Charles of Lorraine (953-991), duke of Lorraine, hereditary heir to the throne of the Franks and uncle of Louis V
Robert the Pious (c. 970-1031), son of Hugh Capet, king of the Franks, r. 996-1031
Adalbero of Reims (d. 989), archbishop of Reims, supporter of Hugh Capet
Gerbert of Aurillac (c. 945-1003), secretary to Adalbero, who became Pope Sylvester II in 990

SUMMARY OF EVENT

Hugh Capet was described by contemporary sources as a man of "nobility and vigor," but neither his character nor his appearance emerges from the scanty source material dating from his reign. Nevertheless, he founded a dynasty that ruled without interruption for almost three hundred years and under whose rule emerged the beginnings of the nation of France.

The situation in the region known as Western Francia was not propitious in 987 for the beginning of the reign of Hugh Capet and his Capetian successors. During the ninth and tenth centuries, the descendants of Charlemagne who ruled the territory steadily lost power to the landed nobility, especially those entrenched in large feudal principalities such as the duchies of Normandy, Burgundy, and Aquitaine, and the counties of Cham-

An artist's rendition of the election of Hugh Capet. (F. R. Niglutsch)

900 - 1000

pagne and Anjou. Clashes between the monarchs and these powerful barons were frequent, and at virtually every point the great nobles proved their determination to hamstring the authority of their king. Indeed, even before Hugh's election, the nobles had already deposed of two Carolingian monarchs and had elected three of Hugh's relatives as kings. The first, after the dethronement of Charles the Fat in 888, was Hugh's great-grandfather Odo; later, with the deposition of Charles the Simple in 922, Hugh's grandfather Robert and then Hugh's granduncle Raoul had been chosen as kings. In each case, however, the kingship had been returned to the Carolingians, but precedents for an elective monarchy had been set.

The powers of the king declined dramatically during the tenth century, as the ongoing deposition and election of monarchs by the nobles reveal. Further, the lands under royal authority continued to shrink until the royal principality included little else than the lands immediately surrounding Paris.

In 954, Lothair became king on the death of Louis IV. Because Lothair was only twelve, his uncles protected his rights. In so doing, they called on Hugh Capet for succor and support of the young king, which Hugh Capet granted. On Lothair's death, his son Louis V was elected king; however, he survived his father by only one year. Louis V's nearest blood relative was his uncle, Charles, the duke of Lorraine.

It has been suggested that Charles's claim was overlooked on the basis of his marriage to a woman of lower birth; others suggest that Charles's shifting allegiances cost him the throne. It is also possible that Hugh Capet's relationship through his mother to Otto II contributed to his appeal to the assembled nobles and Church officials responsible for electing a king. In any event, at an assembly at Senlis in 987, Hugh Capet was considered to be the more attractive candidate, and he was elected king in spite of Charles's claim. Though Charles and his few supporters tried to appeal to the concept of legitimate succession by birth, his claims were countered and frustrated by the intrigues of two of Hugh's most active supporters: Adalbero, the archbishop of Reims, and his secretary Gerbert of Aurillac, one of the most respected scholars of the tenth century and later Pope Sylvester II.

According to the sources, Adalbero of Reims flatly denied any principle of hereditary right, affirming instead that the crown was conferred only through election by the nobles of the kingdom. Ironically, Hugh himself quickly reestablished hereditary rights by installing his own son as heir shortly after his own ascension.

In 987, Hugh himself was far from being more powerful than the nobles. His county of Paris, the only realm he could call his own, was small, poor, and badly organized compared with great feudal lands such as Normandy and Champagne. Indeed, he could scarcely control the lesser nobles who were his vassals within the county of Paris, let alone the powerful dukes and counts throughout the realm. Hugh at his ac-

With the election of his son Robert the Pious as his successor in 996, Hugh Capet ensured that the kingdom would pass on to his direct descendant. In this miniature from a fourteenth century manuscript house at the Burgundy Library, Brussels, King Robert composes in Latin. (Frederick Ungar Publishing Co.)

ADALBERO, ARCHBISHOP OF REIMS, ADDRESSES THE ASSEMBLY AT SENLIS

King Louis [IV], of divine memory, left no children; we must therefore take counsel as to the choice of a successor.

. . . [L]et us endeavor, in all prudence and rectitude, not to sacrifice reason and truth to our personal likes or dislikes. We know that Charles [of Lorraine] has his partisans, who claim that the throne belongs to him by right of birth. Regarding the question from this point of view, we reply that the throne cannot be acquired by hereditary right. Nor should one be placed upon it who is not distinguished alike by nobility of body and wisdom of mind, and by his good faith and magnanimity. We see in the annals of history rulers of illustrious origin deposed on account of their unworthiness, and replaced by incumbents of equal, or even of inferior, birth. . . .

Make a choice, therefore, that shall insure the welfare of the state instead of being its ruin. If you wish ill to your country, choose Charles; if you wish to see it prosperous, make Hugh, the glorious duke, king. . . . Not only the state, but every individual interest, will find in him a protector. Who has ever fled to him for aid and been disappointed?

Source: Richer, monk of Reims, *Historiarum libri IV,* quoted in *Readings in European History*, edited by James Harvey Robinson, abridged edition (Boston: Ginn & Company, 1906), pp. 99-101.

cession was perhaps the weakest of the great lords of France, and it had been made clear at the outset that he held his throne only at the sufferance of the nobility and the Church.

SIGNIFICANCE

The election of Hugh Capet was an event of prime importance in the history of France, in spite of the fact that the decentralization of political power and the decline in royal authority continued on for another century. In the first place, he successfully defended his throne against the intrigues and armed revolts launched against him by Charles of Lorraine, thereby preserving the throne for his Capetian descendants. He apparently also continually insisted on recognition of the theoretical supremacy of the crown over the claims of nobles and upon the unique nature of the royal dignity. Furthermore, it would appear that he began the policy of gradual accumulation of power through the legal exercise of rights as feudal suzerain, directing his efforts primarily at trying to subdue the nobles within his own territory.

There is also evidence to suggest that Hugh resorted to diplomacy more frequently than to war to establish his claims. Some historians claim that this is because he knew he was likely to fail on the battlefield. Finally, in seeing to the preservation of his royal line, he encouraged the reestablishment of the principle of hereditary succession. With the election and consecration of his son Robert the Pious as his successor in 996, Hugh Capet ensured that the kingdom would pass on to his direct descendant. The facts that the Capetian kings enjoyed remarkably long reigns, the average being thirty years, and were generally able to pass the crown to mature males were, of course, caused more by chance than astuteness. The device of crowning the heir apparent during his father's lifetime was not abandoned until the reign of Philip II (1179-1223), and the practice of insistence on royal prerogatives and gradual extension of monarchical authority through the exercise of feudal law was carried on by Hugh's successors.

Hugh's greatest accomplishment was, quite simply, the founding of a dynasty. It was for his heirs to establish the centralized monarchical authority of the later Middle Ages.

—James H. Forse,
updated by Diane Andrews Henningfeld

FURTHER READING

Duby, Georges. *France in the Middle Ages, 987-1460: From Hugh Capet to Joan of Arc*. Translated by Juliet Vale. Oxford: Blackwell, 1991. A noted French historian traces the development of the French state during the Middle Ages, paying particular attention to the intellectual climate of the time.

Dunbabin, Jean. *France in the Making, 843-1180*. 2d ed. New York: Oxford University Press, 2000. A thorough political history of France, covering the end of the Carolingian Empire through the rise of the Capetian Dynasty and the formation of the French state. Includes a comprehensive bibliography and an index.

Fawtier, Robert. *The Capetian Kings of France: Monarchy and Nation, 987-1328*. Translated by Lionel Butler and R. J. Adams. Reprint. London: Macmillan, 1962. Long considered the standard text of the roles played by the Capetian kings in the creation of a French dynastic state, this book stresses Capetian continuity.

Hallam, Elizabeth M, and Judith Everard. *Capetian*

France, 987-1328. 2d ed. New York: Longman, 2001. This excellent and scholarly book is firmly grounded on the most basic and practical aspects of the Capetian era. It contains narrations of political events as well as clear analyses of social and economic conditions. Includes maps, genealogical tables, and a bibliography.

James, Edward. *The Origins of France: From Clovis to the Capetians, 500-1000*. New York: St. Martin's Press, 1982. A thorough study of the Carolingian background of Capetian France with an extensive bibliography. This work offers a counterpoint to Duby's interpretation of the same period.

SEE ALSO: 843: Treaty of Verdun; 1155: Charter of Lorris Is Written; 1305-1417: Avignon Papacy and the Great Schism.

RELATED ARTICLES in *Great Lives from History: The Middle Ages, 477-1453*: Charlemagne; Philip II; Suger; Sylvester II.

988
BAPTISM OF VLADIMIR I

When Vladimir, the prince of Kiev, converted to Orthodox Christianity through his baptism, he linked the cultural, economic, and political fortunes of the Rus with the Byzantine world.

LOCALE: Kiev (now in Ukraine)
CATEGORIES: Government and politics; religion

KEY FIGURES

Vladimir I (c. 956-1015), grand prince of Kievan Rus, r. 980-1015

Anna, Princess of the Byzantine Empire (963-1011), sister of Basil II and wife of Vladimir

Basil II (958-1025), Byzantine emperor in Constantinople, r. 976-1025

Igor (c. 877-945), grand prince of Kievan Rus, r. 912-945

Saint Olga (c. 890-969), grand princess of Kievan Rus and regent, r. 945-964

Svyatoslav I (d. 972), grand prince of Kievan Rus, r. 945-972

SUMMARY OF EVENT

In 1988, the Russian Orthodox Church celebrated the millennial anniversary of its founding. Early sources reveal that Vladimir, grand prince of Kievan Rus, was baptized an Eastern Christian in 988 and then compelled his subjects to be baptized in the Dnieper River. Christianity certainly penetrated Russian society much earlier. Russian churchmen insist that Saint Andrew visited Russia in the first century, an event used by chroniclers to show the apostolic origins of Russian Orthodoxy. In reality, he probably never got farther than the Crimea.

The Christian Church of Saint Elias existed in Kiev during the rule of Igor, and members of his military retinue were Christians when the Rus signed a treaty with Constantinople in 945. Igor's widow, Grand Princess Olga, grandmother to Vladimir, was even baptized a Christian in the Byzantine capital ten years later, although the pagan faith remained the religion of her Kievan state. A number of merchants in Kiev were known to be Christians as well, but Christianity gained official status only with Vladimir.

Born in Kiev sometime around 956, Vladimir was the son of Malusha (Malfried), a former housekeeper of his grandmother, Olga, and Svyatoslav I, grand prince of Kievan Rus. When the latter died in 972, civil wars erupted among the sons—Yaropolk, Oleg, and Vladimir—over the succession to the grand princely throne. With Viking armies, Vladimir emerged, and as grand prince he forged a new union of Novgorod and Kiev. To maintain this empire required a common religious bond.

Early in his reign, Vladimir considered the adoption of a new pagan cult to unify the realm, binding ruled and ruler. He had already created a pagan pantheon of gods, using regional cults in conjunction with the state cult of Perun, the god of thunder and lightning. He came to realize that the pagan cult could have limited use in foreign affairs and that a modern religion would best facilitate territorial expansion. The Rus were surrounded by adherents of the new religions: the Khazars adopted Judaism in the ninth century, the Volga Bulgars chose Islam in the early tenth century, and Latin Christianity was spreading among the Poles, Hungarians, and other Eastern Europeans.

Chroniclers relate the famous story of emissaries sent to investigate the various religions and the discussions the grand prince had with each of them. There is undoubtedly some truth to the prince's aversion to the fasting from drink and to the practice of circumcision among the Jews and Muslims, as well as to his particular attraction for the beauty of the Byzantine liturgy over that of the Roman and his dislike of Islamic mosques. Yet it seems that the decisive issue involved the establishment of close political and economic ties of Kiev with Constantinople, as well as strong apprehension concerning submission to the central authority of Rome.

There was yet another factor. In January of 988, Vladimir sent a bodyguard of six thousand Varangian warriors to aid Emperor Basil II to quell a rebellion in his empire. This force was the origin of the famed Varangian Guard in Constantinople. When Basil hesitated on his promise to send his sister to Vladimir in marriage, however, an angry grand prince attacked the Byzantine port of Chersonesus (Kherson) in the Crimea. The emperor relented and sent his sister, Anna, to marry Vladimir in Chersonesus on the condition that he become a Christian. The local bishop and the priestly retinue of Anna were responsible for Vladimir's formal conversion to the Christian religion that year in Chersonesus. On returning to his capital city, Vladimir ordered the statue of Perun to be dragged through the main avenue of Kiev and tossed over the falls in the Dnieper River. The populace was ordered to the river for their own baptism, and a similar command was sent to all the towns of the Kievan realm.

The early rulers of Russia (top left to bottom right): Vladimir I, Rurik, Dmitry Donskoy, Michael Romanov, Alexis, Ivan the Great, Ivan the Terrible, Fyodor III, Yaroslav the Just. (F. R. Niglutsch)

The decision of Vladimir for the Orthodox faith meant the adoption of an entire culture, replete with the artistic tradition of icon painting, Byzantine style architecture, monasticism, religious education, legal principles, and other patterns of thought. It is worth noting that one feature was absent from the legacy of the Byzantine Empire—namely, the interest in theological speculation. Several modern authorities argue that Vladimir and the Kievan Rus were so entranced by the beauty of Orthodoxy that tampering with doctrinal formulations was thought to be tampering with perfection. Another modern analysis holds that the Russians were not really converted to Christianity so much as they overlaid a shallow veneer of Christianity on a pagan base.

How much Vladimir himself was changed by the religious conversion is disputed. Chroniclers make frequent mention of his weekly feasts, wherein he invited his retinue and others to dine at court, while servants would distribute food to the poor in the streets. Notice is also made of his newfound aversion to capital punishment and the cessation of his harem. He continued to exercise little restraint in warfare, allowing his soldiers to pillage at will, although it was the usual custom of the time.

Some Western elements are found in Vladimir's religious policies, such as his introduction of the tithe to support his plans for a cathedral. Vladimir gave the Church a

KIEVAN RUS C. 900-1000

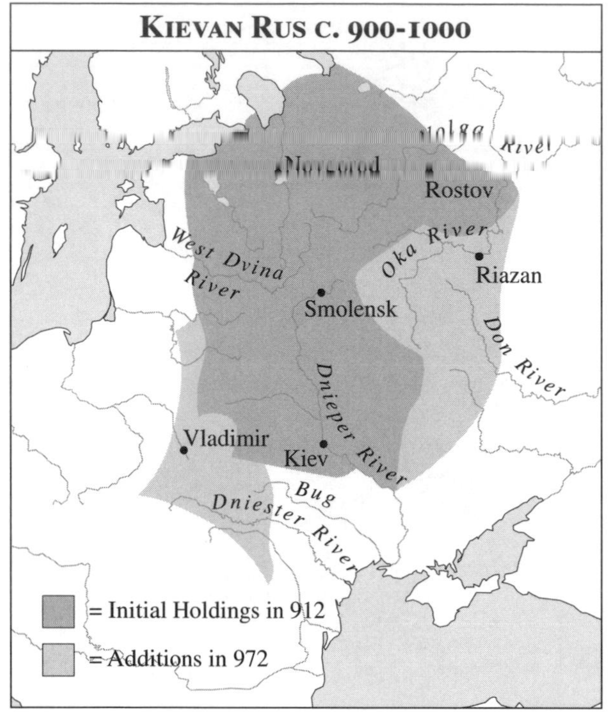

broad charter of immunity from the civil law and allowed the Church's own jurisdiction to include not only moral and liturgical matters but also family disputes and inheritances. Such issues corresponded more to Western than Greek practices.

Russian churchmen adopted two central features of the Byzantine traditions: the sacramental and mystical element of Christianity, which was best expressed in the veneration of icons; and the Platonic ideal that stressed the Spirit as reality. This last was illustrated by the strength of monasticism in Russia. In both traditions, the liturgy assumed major importance with its icon screens, chants, and a general air of the unworldly. Like the Byzantine caesar, Vladimir also assumed the role as a church leader in Kievan Russia.

Byzantine traditions sometimes blended with the Russian pagan traditions, which included the Cult of Mother Earth: the Paraskeva, when the crops, rivers, and forests were venerated, where one is lost in nature. These traditions included the Rusolki, or stories of female spirits, and the inclination to ancestor worship evident in the continued use of the patronymic. There was the residue also of other pagan customs such as beating with palms, decorating Easter eggs, and the cult of Grandfather Frost. Such a blend of Christian and pagan practices was the case in the early Roman Church as well.

SIGNIFICANCE

Russians refute the accusation sometimes made in the West that they were not Christianized before Vladimir's time because they were too savage, barbaric, and illiterate. Evidence shows the existence of a written language in Smolensk from a much earlier period. Scholars have also made note of a complicated trade agreement between the Rus and Byzantines in 907, which must have involved sophisticated language. Pre-Christian artistic traditions lasted even into the age of Andrei Rublev in the early fifteenth century. The voluminous secular graffiti and business discussions on the walls of the churches of Saint Sophia in Kiev and in Novgorod in the early eleventh century indicate that society at that time was not unsophisticated in this genre. In short, Vladimir's decision to become a Christian did not begin Russian civilization.

—*John D. Windhausen*

FURTHER READING

Cross, Samuel Hazard, and Olgerd P. Sherbowitz-Wetzor, eds. and trans. *The Russian Primary Chronicle*. Cambridge, Mass.: Medieval Academy of America, 1953. Contains the Laurentian Chronicle, the principal annals of Vladimir's era.

Dukes, Paul. *A History of Russia: Medieval, Modern, Contemporary, circa 882-1996*. 3d ed. Durham, N.C.: Duke University Press, 1998. Part 1 of this historical study introduces medieval Russia and the construction and then collapse of Kiev (882-1240). Extensive bibliography and an index.

Fedotov, George P. *The Russian Religious Mind: Kievan Christianity*. Cambridge, Mass.: Harvard University Press, 1946. A classic exploration of the historical roots of Russian Orthodoxy and its relations with the state by a writer who combines scholarship with beautiful prose.

Fennell, John. *A History of the Russian Church to 1448*. New York: Longman, 1995. This last work by a respected medieval scholar stresses the extent of Christianity in Kievan Rus as the context for Vladimir's conversion.

Franklin, Simon, and Jonathan Shepard. *The Emergence of Rus: 750-1200*. New York: Longman, 1996. This book examines the medieval origins and development of the Slavic peoples of Eastern Europe, focusing upon Scandinavian, Byzantine, and barbarian influences. Includes an important chapter on the period from 960 to 1015 and Vladimir's role in expanding and shoring up the power structure in Kiev. Maps, extensive bibliography, list of genealogies, and excellent index.

Grekov, B. A. "The Reign of Prince Vladimir Svyatoslavich." In *Kievan Rus*. Moscow: Foreign Languages, 1959. The most noted work by a Soviet scholar on the Kievan era of Russian history. In it he argues that paganism yielded to Christianity because the former was a tribal religion whereas the latter was essentially class oriented.

Grunwald, Constantin De. "Saint Vladimir." In *Saints of Russia*. New York: Macmillan, 1960. A concise, intelligent account of Vladimir's life, using many Nordic sources, which stresses Vladimir's Scandinavian ties. Argues that the conversion of the Kievan people took place in 990.

Lobachev, Valeri, and Vladimir Prevotorov. *A Millennium of Russian Christianity*. Moscow: Novosti Press, 1988. A concise view of the Soviet point of view on the question of Russian Christianity.

Korpela, Jukka. *Prince, Saint, and Apostle: Prince Vladimir Svjatoslavic of Kiev, His Posthumous Life, and the Religious Legitimization of the Russian Great Power.* Wiesbaden, Germany: Harrassowitz, 2001. This ingenious study examines how Vladimir has been described and represented in Russia since his death. It looks at how the figure of Vladimir in religious discourse was used to support and even legitimate several rulers of Russia, especially Ivan the Terrible.

Pospielovsky, Dimitry V. *The Orthodox Church in the History of Russia*. Crestwood, N.Y.: St. Vladimir's Seminary Press, 1998. Includes separate chapters on the events leading up to the conversion, the conversion itself, and its political aftermath.

Vernadsky, George. *Kievan Russia*. New Haven, Conn.: Yale University Press, 1948. The standard account of Vladimir's conversion by a well-respected scholar whose discussion of the grand prince is still not challenged.

SEE ALSO: 496: Baptism of Clovis; 740: Khazars Convert to Judaism; c. 850: Development of the Slavic Alphabet; 850-950: Viking Era; 864: Boris Converts to Christianity; 976-1025: Reign of Basil II.

RELATED ARTICLES in *Great Lives from History: The Middle Ages, 477-1453*: Anna, Princess of the Byzantine Empire; Boris I of Bulgaria; Clovis; Olaf I; Saint Olga; Rurik; Vladimir I.

992-1054
GHANA TAKES CONTROL OF AWDAGHUST

Under the leadership of King Tounka, the Wagadu Empire, called Ghana by the Arabs, was able to expand its borders and add tax revenue to its base by controlling Awdaghust, the northernmost point of the empire and the southernmost terminus of trans-Saharan trade. The capture of Awdaghust was an important feat for the expansionist state of Wagadu, especially given the city's location near the Senegal and Niger Rivers.

LOCALE: From the lower Senegal River region to the Niger River bend in the east and north to Awdaghust, near Walata

CATEGORIES: Expansion and land acquisition; wars, uprisings, and civil unrest

KEY FIGURES

Tounka (fl. tenth century), king of Wagadu, led 992 campaign to capture Awdaghust

Abū Bakr ibn ʿUmar (d. 1087), leader of the Sanhaja Berber army, seized Awdaghust from Wagadu control by 1055

SUMMARY OF EVENT

Ghana, as the Arab chroniclers referred to the state known to its Soninke population as Wagadu (king), gained its wealth and power by taxing gold and other goods that passed through its kingdom from gold mines to the west and south (Akan, Bure, and Bambuk). As the state's power increased, Wagadu began to conquer surrounding areas and kingdoms. Eventually the Wagadu kingdom was able to control the gold mines to the south and levy tribute taxes on all gold production.

Wagadu faced competition from Berbers, who sought to dominate trade in the Western Sahara. The city of Awdaghust, controlled alternately by Sanhaja and Zanata Berbers, was a significant and valuable post located northwest of the Wagadu capital at Kumbi. (It took approximately ten days by camel to travel from Kumbi to Awdaghust.) Awdaghust was the farthest southern point of trans-Saharan trade. It was linked to Niger River trade in the East, Mediterranean-Maghreb trade in the north, and Egyptian-Sudanic trade to the northeast.

Awdaghust's role as a trade hub and its central position made control of the town critical to the economic hegemony of any politically centralizing state in the region. Each political entity was vying for economic control of Awdaghust's traffic in salt and gold transregionally, as well as the opportunity to tax the urban trades. Awdaghust was a wealthy city with supplies of water in close proximity and sufficient resources to maintain cattle herds. The city of Awdaghust had much agricultural surplus from its surrounding rural and periurban neighbors as well. The nearby regions could supply the city with millet, grapes, dates, wheat, and figs. Because of its location and resources, Awdaghust was coveted by various political entities.

In 992, the Soninke king of Wagadu, Tounka, was able to capture the control of trade at Awdaghust, to the detriment of the Berbers. Because Awdaghust served as the gateway to Saharan trade, this was an important, though brief, moment for the Wagadu economy. With greater control over Awdaghust, the *ghana* (kings) of Wagadu were able to exploit the wealth of the city's trade in order to expand the Wagadu Empire. With the surplus wealth, the state experienced its greatest florescence. Between 992 and 1054, Wagadu maintained control of Awdaghust and ruled it as a province. The primary population of Awdaghust was made up of Zanata Berbers, with the Sanhaja inhabiting the outskirts. While Wagadu levied taxes on Awdaghust, the Zanata maintained independent control over trade from another urban center farther north, at Sijilmasa.

As Ghana flourished, Muslim traders continued to travel south in caravans from North Africa and moved through Awdaghust eastward to Hausaland and the Lake Chad region. They carried supplies of salt, dates, and figs as well as luxury items such as cloth, copper, steel, cowrie shells, and glass beads. The Wagadu Empire maintained trade relations with the Berber traders as well as Arab merchants. Ghana maintained control of the region and ruled over the Zanata Berbers until the mid-eleventh century. In 1054, the Sanhaja Berbers allied with the Almoravids, or *al-Murabutin*, who were influenced by a zealous religious devotion. The Muslim Almoravids sought to initiate a renewed orthodoxy among the Sahelian Berbers and their southern neighbors, whom the Almoravids perceived as practicing "unpure" forms of Islam.

Abū Bakr ibn ʿUmar, the leader of the Sanhaja army, had captured Awdaghust by 1055. In 1076, after two decades of military campaigns, the Sanhaja for a short time occupied the city of Kumbi. Although the Almoravid-Sanhaja occupation of Kumbi was short-lived, lasting only a few years, the Almoravids did maintain control of the forest-to-Sahel trade that previously had been economically dominated by Wagadu. The power of Wagadu's kings declined without the ability to manage, direct, and tax all the gold trade moving through the Sahelian centers on its northern frontier.

The written record of Muslim chroniclers (both Arab and African) reveals that the Almoravids were insulted by the Soninke people's "superficial" practice of Islam. Furthermore, notions of Sudanic sacral royalty, associating the ruler of Wagadu and political power with the will of divinity, conflicted with Almoravid interpretations of Islamic doctrine. Although the ruler's power is associated with divinity, the ruler is not a god but an intermediary between mortal and divine realms and a servant to both. For this reason, the Soninke saw the king as the defender of life and death, sickness and health.

For the Muslims of the Almoravid movement, this concept of sacral leadership was foreign and sacrilege, which motivated Islamized Berbers and Almoravids to unite against the Wagadu control of Awdaghust. A *jihad* (holy war) arose and swept across the Sahara and Sahel, as the various Berber factions, previously disunited, joined against a common rival, the Wagadu Empire. The Wagadu population converted increasingly to Islam in the later eleventh and through the twelfth centuries. The sixty years in which Wagadu had built up its economic strength came to an end as control of desert trade shifted to the Almoravids. While the Wagadu state and the Soninke population remained intact, the empire began to decline.

Vassal states and provinces began to assert their own independence as well. By 1203, the Susu province had taken control of the former patron state's capital, Kumbi.

SIGNIFICANCE

The control of Awdaghust was critical for the economic and political strength of the political entities at the crossroads of trans-Saharan and savannah forest trade in the inter-Senegal-Niger peninsula. Because there were few southern centers of trade and because competition was fierce, each state sought to monopolize the important towns. The capture of Awdaghust by the Wagadu state demonstrates the tensions that existed in a system that was highly competitive.

Soninke trade relations with Muslims were not always contentious; however, there were critical moments when competition superseded healthy trade relations. Trade did not necessarily require the absolute control of urban centers, but for centralized states, the stakes became higher and the need to establish hegemonic power increased as the state expanded and become responsible for larger populations. The state had to maximize its control of resources in order to satisfy the growing empire. The case of Awdaghust demonstrates that as states became centralized they increasingly sought to monopolize resources in order to edge out competitor states and political ideologies.

—*Jamese Celia Wells*

FURTHER READING

Levtzion, Nehemia. "Ancient Ghana: A Reassessment of Some Arabic Sources." *Le Sol, la parole et l'écrit: 2000 ans d'histoire africaine mélanges en hommage de Raymond Mauny.* Vol. 1. Paris: Société Française d'Histoire d'Outre-mer, 1981. A history of sources on ancient Ghana and the Ghana Empire.

McKissack, Patricia, and Fredrick McKissack. *The Royal Kingdoms of Ghana, Mali, and Songhay: Life in Medieval Africa*. New York: H. Holt, 1994. Provides a history of the Ghana Empire with a focus on the Middle Ages. Written for a younger readership.

Munson, Patrick J. "Archaeology and the Pre-historic Origins of the Ghana Empire." *Journal of African History* 21 (1980): 457-466. Examines the history of western Africa with specific attention to the origins of the Ghana Empire.

Prussin, Labelle. *The Medieval Age: West African Empires*. Berkeley: University of California Press, 1986. Covers art, architecture, and religion in three west African empires. Contains a chapter on the Ghana Empire.

SEE ALSO: 1062-1147: Almoravids Conquer Morocco and Establish the Almoravid Empire; 1076: Almoravids Sack Kumbi; 12th century: Trading Center of Kilwa Kisiwani Is Founded; 1333: Kilwa Kisiwani Begins Economic and Historical Decline.

RELATED ARTICLES in *Great Lives from History: The Middle Ages, 477-1453*: Lalibela; Mansa Mūsā; Sundiata.

998-1030
REIGN OF MAḤMŪD OF GHAZNA

Maḥmūd of Ghazna, founder of the Ghaznavid Dynasty, expanded his empire into Persia and India and built his capital Ghazna into an important Muslim political and cultural center.

LOCALE: Ghazna, Central Asia (now in Afghanistan)
CATEGORIES: Expansion and land acquisition; government and politics; wars, uprisings, civil unrest

KEY FIGURE

Maḥmūd of Ghazna (c. 971-1030), sultan of Ghazna, r. 997-1030

SUMMARY OF EVENT

Maḥmūd of Ghazna established a Muslim empire in the tenth century that rivaled that of the ʿAbbāsids in Persia and encompassed territory from India to Afghanistan and parts of Persia. His capital of Ghazna south of Kabul was comparable to Baghdad and became a Muslim cultural and political center.

Maḥmūd's father was a Turkish slave who seized control of Ghazna in 977. When Maḥmūd came to the throne in 971, he had already earned a reputation as a capable leader. At his ascension, his kingdom included the area of what is now called Afghanistan and Iran, but the ambitious Maḥmūd carried out a score of expeditions adding the Punjab and more of Persia.

In his first years Maḥmūd consolidated his hold on the state. He gave nominal allegiance to the ʿAbbāsids of Baghdad who supported his conquests, but he was an independent ruler. He began his frequent invasions of northern India in 1001. From then until 1026, he led seventeen expeditions, which began during the summer and retreated before the monsoon season, which would have trapped his troops. In his first campaign, he entered the Punjab, leading fifteen thousand cavalry. There he faced the region's ruler, Rajah Jaipal, who countered with twelve thousand cavalry, thirty thousand infantry, and three hundred elephants. The two armies met at Peshawar, and despite his inferior numbers, Maḥmūd

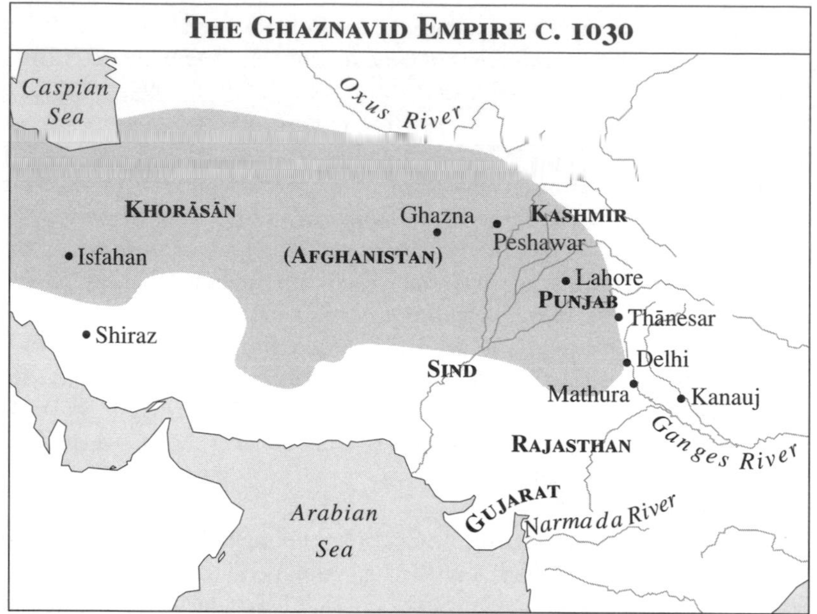

southern India, who would have proven to be a stronger match but had little interest in aiding the northern rulers.

Maḥmūd added the Punjab to his empire and returned with slaves and valuable plunder from his success in India. He then proceeded to build up Ghazna as a great cultural center of the Muslim world. He built palaces, gardens, caravansaries for travelers, mosques, and madrasas (schools). He invited artists and scholars to come to Ghazna. His noblemen also contributed by following his example as a builder and patron of the arts and scholarship. Ghazna became the most important cultural center in Central Asia.

Although he was a great conqueror, he also proved to be a wise ruler and a champion of cultural life. He did not rule his Indian subjects harshly. He saw in India an opportunity to gain great wealth for his country and his goals. He allowed his Indian subjects to be ruled by their native leaders, and the Indian troops he commanded were under Indian officers. He zealously supported Islam, but he used Indian troops to fight his Muslim enemies. Indeed, he treated Muslims he thought heretical just as fiercely as Hindus. Although some Indian authorities claim he forcibly converted Hindus to Islam, apparently this is an exaggeration because he had many Hindu subjects. A Hindu by the name of Tilak was one of his best generals.

As a champion of the arts and scholarship, Maḥmūd brought many eminent persons to Ghazna. The philosopher al-Bīrunī, also renowned as a mathematician and astronomer, came to Ghazna, as did the great Persian poet Firdusi, who wrote the national epic *Shahnamah* (c. 1010; the book of kings). Al-Bīrunī spent time in the Indian lands of the empire studying Sanskrit documents and wrote of the destruction that his patron carried out among the Indians, noting their special hatred of him.

From 1024 to 1026, Maḥmūd fought his last campaign in India. He invaded the Arabian sea port of Somnath, destroying the city and its famous Hindu temple of Shiva. The Muslim chronicles report that fifty thousand Hindus were killed in the battle and that Maḥmūd himself destroyed the idol of Śiva. Six and a half tons of gold were looted, and the famous carved doors were carried off. It is this battle in particular that

defeated the rajah and took him and a number of his entourage captive. Fifteen thousand Indians lay dead. Maḥmūd released his captives, but the despondent Jaipal abdicated and committed suicide.

Jaipal's son Rajah Anandpal prepared his revenge. He called on other Indian rulers to send aid, and many did, leading their armies. Their wives sold their jewels to finance the force. In 1008, the Indian army faced Maḥmūd again in the field between Und and Peshawar. The two forces stood opposite each other for forty days without engagement. Finally Sultan Maḥmūd drew the Indians out. The fierce Kohkar tribesmen attacked the Muslim troops with such force that the sultan considered retreat, but fortune intervened. Rajah's elephant was frightened by the battle and began to flee the field. The Indian forces, believing that their leader was deserting them, followed suit, and Maḥmūd's army won a great victory and proceeded to advance farther into India. Maḥmūd also defeated the Chandelās, the Pratihāras, and the Rājputs in his wars in India. Kanauj, Mathura, and Thaneshwar were among the cities that the sultan's forces laid to waste.

Maḥmūd's success can in part be attributed to the professionalism and egalitarian nature of the Muslim forces. Even slaves could rise to command (as did Maḥmūd's father) if they displayed ability. In contrast, the Indians maintained a caste system that militated against such nurturing of talent. Furthermore, the rajahs of the north, whom Maḥmūd fought, were inferior to the Cōlas of marked Maḥmūd as a merciless marauder for the Hindus. Afterward, he was forced to defend his empire from the north when Turkish tribes of Central Asia, notably the Seljuks, attacked him. He died in 1030. His successors continued to rule a section of northern India around Lahore until 1186.

SIGNIFICANCE

Maḥmūd was one of the most important figures in Central Asian and Afghani history. He stands among the prominent leaders of the medieval Muslim world as both a conqueror and a builder of Islamic civilization. Although his empire did not last as long as those of the ʿAbbāsids, Seljuks, or Ottomans, he still left his mark. Maḥmūd is a controversial figure. Because he brought Islam to India, Muslim historians and writers regard him as a great figure. On the other hand, the British and the Indians consider him a ruthless invader and plunderer.

Maḥmūd transformed Ghazna into an important city that approached Baghdad and Constantinople in its brilliance and importance as a center of culture, art, and scholarship. Maḥmūd's conquest of India mingled Central Asian and Indian cultures. Muslims brought the cultural and intellectual ideals of ancient civilizations to Central Asia and helped spread them throughout the subcontinent.

—*Frederick B. Chary*

FURTHER READING

Bosworth, Clifford Edmund. *The Ghaznavids: Their Empire in Afghanistan and Eastern Iran, 994-1044*. Edinburgh: Edinburgh University Press, 1963. A scholarly study of the beginning of Maḥmūd's dynasty. Maps, tables.

_______. *The Later Ghaznavids, Splendour and Decay: The Dynasty in Afghanistan and Northern India, 1040-1186*. New York: Columbia University Press, 1977. Covers the reigns of Maḥmūd's descendants. Illustrations, bibliography, index.

Flood, Finbarr Barry. "Between Cult and Culture: Bamiyan, Islamic Iconoclasm, and the Museum." *Art Bulletin* 84, no. 4 (December, 2002). Argues that the looting of the temple in Somnath by Maḥmūd was part of a complex history, one that stands in stark contrast to the traditional argument that Maḥmūd's act was indicative of a Muslim iconophobia (fear of icons) against South Asian iconophilia (love of icons). Footnotes, photographs.

Habib, Mohammad. *Sultan Maḥmūd of Ghaznin*. 2d ed. Delhi, India: S. Chand, 1967. This well-written biography provides an overview of not only Maḥmūd's life but also the cultural and political context of the time in which he lived, including major developments in the centuries immediately before and after. Bibliography.

Haig, Wolseley, ed. *Turks and Afghans*. Vol. 3 in *The Cambridge History of India*. Cambridge, England: Cambridge University Press, 1922. An exceptionally good scholarly account of Maḥmūd's era.

Hashmi, Yusuf Abbas. *Successors of Maḥmūd of Ghazna: In Political, Cultural, and Administrative Perspective*. Karachi, Pakistan: South Asian, 1988. Discusses the political, cultural, and governmental influences of Maḥmūd on Central Asia.

Nazim, Muhammad. *The Life and Times of Sultan Mahmud of Ghazna*. Lahore, Pakistan: Khali, 1971. A very detailed account, including a chapter on the sultan's political structures. Includes appendices with Persian language sources. Map, bibliography, index.

Thapar, Romila. *Narratives and the Making of History*. New York: Oxford University Press, 2000. Includes a chapter, "Somnatha: Narratives of a History," that focuses on what many regard the most symbolic act of Maḥmūd's career: his destruction of the Hindu idol in the famous temple at Somnatha. The author deconstructs various interpretations of the event. Bibliography, index.

Utbi, Abdul Nasr Muhammad bin Muhammad al Jabbar al. *Kitāb-i-Yamini*. Translated by James Reynolds. 1858. Reprint. Lahore, Pakistan: Qausain, 1975. A rare, contemporary account of Maḥmūd by a court historian, carefully translated, with copious notes.

SEE ALSO: 834: Gypsies Expelled from Persia; 956: Oğhuz Turks Migrate to Transoxiana; 1010: Firdusi Composes the *Shahnamah*; 1040-1055: Expansion of the Seljuk Turks; 1193: Turkish Raiders Destroy Buddhist University at Nalanda; 1206-1210: Quṭ al-Dīn Aybak Establishes the Delhi Sultanate; 1299: ʿAlāʾ-ud-Dīn Muḥammad Khaljī Conquers Gujarat.

RELATED ARTICLES in *Great Lives from History: The Middle Ages, 477-1453*: Alp Arslan; al-Bīrūnī; Firdusi; Maḥmūd of Ghazna; Niẓām al-Mulk.

c. 1000
COLLAPSE OF THE HUARI AND TIWANAKU CIVILIZATIONS

The two major highland states of the high Andes collapsed around the year 1000. Intense conflict signaled the end of Huari, whereas a combination of environmental and social factors appeared to signal the fall of Tiwanaku.

LOCALE: Highlands of central and southern Peru, western Bolivia, and northern Chile

CATEGORIES: Government and politics; expansion and land acquisition; wars, uprisings, and civil unrest; architecture; environment

SUMMARY OF EVENT

Around the year 500, two large polities dominated the Andean highlands: Huari (also called Wari), with its homeland in the Ayacucho basin of central Peru, and Tiwanaku (also called Tiahuanaco), in the Lake Titicaca basin of western Bolivia and southeastern Peru. Although these contemporaries had some contact and shared a number of affinities in artifact style and motif, they appear to have developed independently in their homelands.

The Huari were an expansionist people, and at the height of their power they controlled most of the Andean sierra, ranging to Cajamarca in northern Peru to the Cuzco basin in the south. They also had significant contact with coastal Peru. The capital of the Huari state was at the eponymous site of Huari, which was well in excess of 1.5 square miles (4 square kilometers) in size and had a maximum population ranging from ten thousand to seventy thousand. This center was supported by a massive irrigation and terracing system. Water was brought to the site by canals from a series of high-elevation springs and streams and was then distributed to hillside terraces into the agricultural fields. Maize was the principal crop, but it was supplemented by Andean domesticates, such as quinoa and various tubers.

Huari expansion was accomplished through a variety of means, but military conquest and domination appear to have been the most important strategy. However, Huari administration of the areas within their domain varied considerably depending on what the Huari wanted from the conquered polity and its degree of political complexity. In the highland valleys relatively close to Huari, for example, it appears that the Huari forced local populations to move their settlements to somewhat lower elevations into fertile areas suitable for growing maize. The terraces of these valleys were expanded considerably, and it is likely that the Huari imported labor from elsewhere to assist in this effort. Finally, they constructed enclosures in Huari architectural style. The function of these enclosures is uncertain, but they may have served as residences for Huari administrators, as storehouses, or both.

In more distant areas, the Huari used different strategies. Instead of intervening directly in agricultural production, they concerned themselves with the extraction of prestigious goods, such as fine ceramics, metals, textiles, and marine shells. The Huari built administrative centers according to a strict architectural canon at more than thirty locations in the Andean sierra. Importantly, none of these centers showed evidence of fortifications.

The evidence on how Huari collapsed is scant, but most signs point to imperial overextension and increased conflict. The consumption of prestigious goods in the Huari core grew substantially over time, and this forced distant Huari administrators to extract ever more production from their subjects. As demands grew, probably so too did resistance, and some have argued that subject peoples resorted to violence to overthrow the Huari. Evidence for the increased level of warfare around 1000 suggests this scenario is highly plausible. It is also possible that agricultural production in the Huari core was unable to keep up with rapid rates of population growth, and this probably led to instability and conflict in the homeland itself.

Tiwanaku emerged under very different circumstances. The Tiwanaku heartland and the site itself are found on the high Altiplano just to the east of Lake Titicaca at an elevation of more than 12,500 feet (3,810 meters) above sea level. Although cold and windswept, the environment is highly productive. Tiwanaku subsistence practice focused on a combination of resources and agricultural technologies, including raised fields, rainfed fields, camelid herding, and lake exploitation. Raised fields were especially important; in the Andean highlands, they were used where land was prone to significant flooding or was otherwise waterlogged. They have been shown to improve soil condition, trap nutrients, and improve microclimates by minimizing the risk of frost damage to crops. However, they needed large amounts of water to function effectively, and so the Tiwanaku built an extensive canal system to maintain them, requiring a substantial investment of labor for their construction and maintenance.

Tiwanaku is relatively large, about 2.5 square miles (6.5 square kilometers) in size, and composed of residential areas, platform mounds, and large sunken courts, which were the scenes of important rituals. The layout of roads and streets shows the site was carefully planned, and at its zenith, it was one of the largest urban centers in the Americas.

Tiwanaku conquered or annexed much of the southern highlands but at a relatively slow pace. Aside from its core in the Lake Titicaca basin, Tiwanaku did not control large, contiguous blocks of territory. Instead, it established trade relationships with neighbors or far-flung polities or created colonial enclaves in locations with key economic resources or high agricultural potential. The area around what is now called Cochabamba in Bolivia was one such colony, as was the Omo site in southern Peru on the western flanks of the Andes. However, they also conquered smaller polities, especially in the lake basin, as is evidenced by the trophy head iconography of the large sunken court ritual center at Tiwanaku called the Akapana. Rituals and feasting were also important ways by which Tiwanaku elites maintained their power and convinced or coerced others to submit to their control.

Two monoliths six miles from the Tiwanaku ruins in Bolivia. (Hulton|Archive by Getty Images)

There is clear evidence that c. 900 the Tiwanaku Empire began a steady decline. The Omo colony was destroyed by conflict, but it is not clear whether it was destroyed by a rebellion or by outside forces. Colonies in northern Chile were abandoned as well, and trade relationships also contracted.

The cause of this decline remains hotly debated. Some authorities have argued that the immediate cause of the Tiwanaku collapse was a long drought that began around 1000. A persistent and intense drought would have made raised field farming untenable, and if these fields were in fact the most important part of the subsistence agricultural system, the Tiwanaku elite would have been unable to maintain themselves and their people. However important the drought might have been as a cause of the Tiwanaku collapse, it is clear that it cannot be the only cause, because Tiwanaku's fortunes started declining well before the drought's onset. If this is the case, it suggests that politics, not environmental change, led to this collapse. What sort of political process may have occurred is uncertain, but there is no evidence of widespread violence, nor is there a sense that epidemic disease or hunger was a contributing factor. However, the drought after 1000 certainly hastened Tiwanaku's fall. By 1100, Tiwanaku had been abandoned, as were all of the other large Tiwanaku centers, and the population of the basin was dispersed into much smaller towns and villages.

SIGNIFICANCE

The collapse of these two highland empires created something of a power vacuum in the Andean highlands. Although coastal states continued to thrive and grow, in both the Huari and Tiwanaku homelands the collapse of political centralization led to the creation of large numbers of small politics that engaged in constant warfare with one another. In Tiwanaku's former domain, this led to population movements as some groups tried to move away from the violence. Others built large hilltop fortresses that served as refuges when enemies appeared. This situation of small-scale, endemic warfare persisted in the Andean highlands for the next three hundred years until the

Inca expanded out of their homeland in the Cuzco basin and created the largest empire in the ancient Americas.

—*Mark Aldenderfer*

FURTHER READING

Isbell, William Harris. *The Rural Foundation for Urbanism: Economic and Stylistic Interaction Between Rural and Urban Communities in Eighth-Century Peru.* Urbana: University of Illinois Press, 1977. A comprehensive and systematic discussion of the archaeology at site of Huari.

Jennings, Justin, and Nathan Craig. "Politywide Analysis and Imperial Political Economy: The Relationship Between Valley Political Complexity and Administrative Centers in the Wari Empire of the Central Andes." *Journal of Anthropological Archaeology* 20 (2001): 479-502. A clear and compelling reconstruction of how the Huari administered their empire.

Kolata, Alan L., ed. *Agroecology.* Vol. 1 in *Tiwanaku and Its Hinterland: Archaeology and Paleoecology of an Andean Civilization.* Washington, D.C.: Smithsonian Institution Press, 1996. An important collection of papers that describe the ecological foundations of Tiwanaku civilization.

_______. *Urban and Rural Ecology.* Vol. 2 in *Tiwanaku and Its Hinterland: Archaeology and Paleoecology of an Andean Civilization.* Washington, D.C.: Smithsonian Institution Press, 2002. A collection of papers on the archaeology of Tiwanaku.

Moseley, Michael E. *The Incas and Their Ancestors: The Archaeology of Peru.* Rev. ed. New York: Thames and Hudson, 2001. A very useful synthesis of Andean prehistory.

Stanish, Charles. *Ancient Titicaca: The Evolution of Complex Society in Southern Peru and Northern Bolivia.* Berkeley: University of California Press, 2003. An excellent synthesis of the prehistory of the Titicaca basin.

SEE ALSO: c. 500-1000: Tiwanaku Civilization Flourishes in Andean Highlands; After 850: Foundation of Chan Chan; c. 1200-1230: Manco Capac Founds the Inca State.

c. 1000
FOOTBINDING DEVELOPS IN CHINESE SOCIETY

The painful custom of footbinding was practiced for a thousand years in China. The bound foot was an object of erotic worship and defined feminine beauty. The custom also reflected Confucian social values and helped keep women in a subordinate social position.

LOCALE: China

CATEGORIES: Cultural and intellectual history; health and medicine

KEY FIGURES

Li Yu (Li Yü; 937-978), poet and the last Southern Tang kingdom ruler, r. 961-975

Yaoniang (Yao Niang; fl. tenth century), favorite concubine of Li Yu and believed to be the first woman with bound feet

SUMMARY OF EVENT

"Footbinding" pertains to the Chinese custom of using wrapped bandages or gauze strips to retard the natural development of a female's feet. It was practiced mainly by the Han Chinese, the majority ethnic group named after the Han Dynasty (206 B.C.E.-220 C.E.). Usually, between the ages of four and eight, a young girl would receive the initial wrappings by her mother. A few years later, the feet would be bound so as to bend all toes, except the big toe, under and into the sole. The sole and heel were forced as close together as possible. After a year of extreme pain, the feet would become numb. To keep the feet tiny, the binding continued throughout the woman's life. Special shoes for bound feet were called gilded lilies (*jinlian*), arched shoes (*gongxie*), and embroidered slippers (*xiuxie*).

The exact origin of footbinding has been controversial. Chinese folklore and oral tradition provide many origin myths. According to one story, a Shang Dynasty (1600-1066 B.C.E.) empress had a clubfoot, which made compressed feet a standard of beauty. In another version, the empress was actually a fox in human disguise, who had to hide her paws. A variation of this presents the fox as Da Ji, the favorite concubine of the king of Zhou, the last Shang emperor. Da Ji, who had been been sent by the gods to destroy the corrupt kingdom, hid her fox's feet by wrapping them in cloth.

The "golden lotus" was invented by the ruler of the state of Qi (Ch'i) and the marquis of Donghun, Xiao

Baojuan (Hsiao Pao-chüan; r. 499-501). He created gilded gold lotus petals on the floor and had his concubine, Pan, walk on them, each step resembling a lotus. Later, "golden lotus" became a poetic metaphor for bound feet.

Glorification of small feet was evident in a Tang Dynasty (T'ang, 618-907) tale that appeared in the Chinese anthology, *Yuyangzu* (c. 850-860). This story about Yexian (Yen-shen), the Chinese Cinderella, was based on an oral tradition of cave dwellers in southern China, possibly in Yongzhou in Guangxi Province. The tale relates that before the first imperial dynasty, the Qin (Ch'in, 221-206 B.C.E.), there lived a chieftain called Wu-the-Cave. His first wife, Yexian's mother, died, and his new wife was cruel to Yexian. After escaping from a party, Yexian dropped a beautiful golden slipper, which the cave people sold to the Tuohan king. The slipper was too small for anyone in his kingdom. Finally, the king found Yexian, whose tiny foot could fit into the slipper, and he married her.

The most precise and accepted account of the beginning of footbinding appears in the twelfth century writings of Zhang Bangji (Chang Panchi), who asserted that footbinding did not begin earlier than in the court of the sovereign poet Li Yu, the last ruler of the Southern Tang kingdom (937-975), one of the kingdoms in the Five Dynasties and Ten Kingdoms period (907-960). Li Yu built a six-foot (two-meter) tall, gold-gilded lotus flower as a dance platform for his favorite concubine, Yaoniang. He ordered her to bind her feet with strips of cloth into the shape of a crescent moon and then dance in the lotus flower. Small bound feet soon became fashionable among the court women and an object of erotic attention.

Archaeological evidence verifies that in the thirteenth century, footbinding was practiced among upper-class women in southern China, during the the Southern Song Dynasty (Sung, 1127-1279). In 1975, the tomb of Lady Huang Sheng (1227-1243) was discovered in the southern coastal city of Fuzhou, Fujian Province. In her tomb were tiny shoes, each with an upturned big toe and ranging in size from 5.25 to 5.5 inches by 1.75 to 2 inches (13.3 to 14 centimeters by 4.4 to 5 centimeters). A similar pair of shoes belonging to Lady Luo Shuangshuang, the first wife of a scholar, Shi Shengzu (d. 1274), was discovered in his tomb in Quzhou, north of Fuzhou. Years later, seven pairs of tiny shoes belonging to Madame Zhou (1240-1274) were discovered in a tomb in De'an, northwest of Fuzhou and Quzhou.

Therefore, footbinding, which began among imperial dancers in the tenth century, had spread to the upper class by the thirteenth century and was used to restrict women to their homes. During the Song Dynasty, neo-Confucianism and conservative views of marriage prevailed. Zhu Xi (Chi Hsi; 1130-1200), the great Song philosopher, endorsed footbinding as a means of promoting the separation of men and women in southern Fujian.

A Chinese girl with bound feet (San Francisco, California). The practice continued well into the twentieth century. (Library of Congress)

Beginning in the Yuan Dynasty (1279-1368), the Mongol dynasty founded by Kublai Khan, footbinding was an indicator of upper-class or aristocratic status. Also, according to a Yuan treatise, bound feet guaranteed female chastity.

Footbinding became even more popular during the Ming Dynasty (1368-1644). The custom was officially sanctioned and glorified in Ming literature. The footbinding process itself revolved around festival days or Daoist auspicious days and numerous other superstitions and customs. In addition, the "golden lotus" had become a prerequisite to a proper marriage, beginning with elaborate bridal shoes embroidered with sayings regarding good fortune.

SIGNIFICANCE

During the Qing Dynasty (Ch'ing, 1644-1911), the Manchu rulers were opposed to footbinding and attempted repeatedly to ban the practice, but their restrictive policy only caused the practice to become even more widespread. However, there were other forces at work that gradually helped abolish footbinding. By the beginning of the nineteenth century, many Chinese leaders were fighting for women's rights. *Jing hua yuan* (1810-1820; *Flowers in the Mirror*, 1965), the famous novel by Li Ruzhen (Li Juchen), vividly exposes the pain and humiliation of footbinding. The plot follows the travel of a merchant to a kingdom in which the sex roles are reversed, and submissive men have crippled, bound feet. In the late nineteenth century, foreign missionaries and liberal reformers openly criticized footbinding, and international condemnation spurred Chinese intellectuals to action.

Toward the end of the Qing Dynasty, antifootbinding sentiment was widespread within larger movements for gender equality and modernization. In 1894, philosopher and reform leader Kang Youwei (K'ang Yu-wei) started the Unbound Foot Association in Canton. Soon, natural-foot societies were everywhere, holding mass meetings and publishing literature and songs. In 1902, the empress dowager issued an imperial decree against footbinding. Although of a voluntary nature, it gave respectability to the natural-foot movement.

When the Nationalist government overthrew the last Chinese monarchy in 1911 and established the Republic of China (1911-1949), it banned footbinding completely. Although it was still practiced in some areas until the beginning of the Communist regime in 1949, many developments in Chinese society favored natural feet. Western-educated young men did not want old-fashioned women with bound feet, and more women became educated.

Originally a way of enhancing dance in the imperial court of the tenth century, footbinding eventually spread to even peasants. Although tortuous and unnatural, it was a popular tradition passed from mother to young daughter. The "lotus blossom" symbolized women's subservience to men in a Confucian society as the physical crippling helped restrict women to their homes. At the same time, the tiny feet represented feminine beauty and sensuality. For a thousand years, it profoundly defined and affected Chinese women's lives.

—*Alice Myers*

FURTHER READING

Drucker, Alison. "The Influence of Western Women on the Anti-Footbinding Movement, 1840-1911." In *Women in China: Current Directions in Historical Scholarship*, edited by Richard Guisso. Youngstown, Pa.: Philo Press, 1981. Looks at the influence of Western women on the tradition of footbinding.

Hong, Fan. *Footbinding, Feminism, and Freedom: The Liberation of Women's Bodies in Modern China*. London: Frank Cass, 1997. With an emphasis on social and cultural history and women's rights, this book shows the relationship between women's exercise and emancipation, including from footbinding, in modern China. Includes some illustrations and photographs, and extensive chapter notes.

Jackson, Beverley. *Splendid Slippers: A Thousand Years of an Erotic Tradition*. Berkeley: Ten Speed Press, 1997. A detailed account of the thousand-year history of footbinding, including Chinese folklore and comparisons with practices in other cultures. Contains numerous color photographs.

Ko, Dorothy. *Every Step a Lotus: Shoes for Bound Feet*. Berkeley: University of California Press, 2001. Well-researched presentation of footbinding in terms of material culture and women's status and identity in society. Presents the different view that footbinding was actually a source of pride, power, and identity for women. Includes beautiful illustrations and photos throughout the book, including color photos of shoes from the Bata Shoe Museum in Toronto.

Levy, Howard S. *The Lotus Lovers: The Complete History of the Curious Erotic Custom of Footbinding in China*. 1966. Reprint. Buffalo, N.Y.: Prometheus Books, 1992. The first complete treatment of the subject for the Western reader. Based on research into primary Chinese sources, this book includes more than one hundred photos and drawings, extensive notes, and a bibliography.

Wang, Ping. *Aching for Beauty: Footbinding in China*. Minneapolis: University of Minnesota Press, 2000. Includes a detailed chapter on the history of footbinding, with many references to literature. Generally, this book examines the subject in the context of history, literature, linguistics, and psychoanalysis.

SEE ALSO: 618: Founding of the Tang Dynasty; 690-705: Reign of Empress Wu; 907-960: Period of Five Dynasties and Ten Kingdoms; 960: Founding of the Song Dynasty; 960-1279: Scholar-Official Class Flourishes Under Song Dynasty.

RELATED ARTICLES in *Great Lives from History: The Middle Ages, 477-1453*: Kublai Khan; Zhu Xi.

c. 1000
HINDI BECOMES INDIA'S DOMINANT LANGUAGE

The language descended from Sanskrit and known as Hindi among Hindus and Urdu among Indian Muslims became a common language of the various tribes of the area, enabling wider communication and commerce.

LOCALE: Hindustan (modern Pakistan and northern India)

CATEGORIES: Communications; cultural and intellectual history; literature

SUMMARY OF EVENT

The language known as Hindi among Hindus and Urdu among Indian and Pakistani Muslims is descended from Sanskrit, the language of the Vedas and other Hindu liturgical texts. Sanskrit, a member of the Indo-Iranian branch of the Indo-European language family, is believed by historical linguists to have been brought into the Indian subcontinent from the Fars Plateau of what is now Iran by the Aryan invaders who displaced the existing civilizations of the Indus Valley between 1500 and 1000 B.C.E. Over subsequent centuries, the Sanskrit-speaking peoples developed diverse spoken languages, or Prakrits, for everyday discourse, and Sanskrit was carefully preserved as a liturgical language (the word Sanskrit means "purified" and indicates the reverence with which it was held in the Indian religious mind).

The 1000 C.E. date for the development of Hindi and Urdu is a standard reference point used by historians, but actually, the boundary between Hindi and the various Prakrits and Apabhramsas that preceded it is blurry. Many of the oldest extant texts for the development of Hindi and Urdu from their predecessor dialects are copies of copies, dating many centuries after their original composition and showing evidence of subsequent scribal alteration and editorial redaction. In India, by the time a language was considered to be worthy of scholarly attention, it was generally so far removed from the forms of everyday discourse that it no longer truly qualified as a living language. As a result, documentary evidence of language change in India is weak and questionable, being divorced from the common speech that is the primary mover of these processes.

Hindi developed from five major dialect traditions. Dingal was the language of Rajesthan's bardic tradition and was originally largely oral. The Braj dialect grew out of the Vaishava tradition of Krishna worship (a religious tradition from which the modern Hare Krishna movement can trace its ancestry) and was the vehicle for a large volume of erotic religious poetry of a somewhat Tantric nature, celebrating love as a method of growing closer to the divine. The Avadhi dialect comes from the allegorical romances of the Sufi, a mystical Muslim sect, and as such contains a larger proportion of Arabic and Turkic borrowings, particularly for terms of religious significance. The Sadhu Bhasa dialect can be seen in the texts of the western recension of the *nirgua bhakti* tradition, a subset of the *bhakti* yoga or "path of devotion" that developed as a popular way for ordinary Indians to reach spiritual enlightenment through loving devotion to a deity (a religious practice that is also ancestral to the Hare Krishna movement). The Maithili dialect grew out of the devotional traditions of northern Bihar.

Strictly speaking, Urdu is not a distinct language from Hindi but rather is the form of the Hindustani language spoken by Indian and Pakistani Muslims. The word "Urdu" comes from a Turkish word meaning "camp" (cognate to the English word "horde," borrowed from the same common Turkic root via a different branch of the Turkic migrations of the period) and originally had the sense of the binding language spoken by everyone in a military camp, as opposed to the various dialects that individuals might have spoken in their native villages. Urdu is a continuation of the Hindi spoken near Delhi, but includes large numbers of Persian, Arabic, and Turkish words, particularly terms of Muslim religious significance for which there were no theologically appropriate native terms. For example, although Sanskrit *karma* and Arabic *kismet* both have a sense of "appointed fate," they rest on very different theological underpinnings. The concept of karma is based on the idea of consequences for past actions carrying across multiple reincarnations, while kismet is a function of the divine will.

The earliest forms of Urdu are generally traced to a Hindustani dialect called Dakani, which flourished in the Deccan, a rugged region of ancient volcanic mountains. The most common literary forms in which this early form of Urdu has been preserved are the treatises and popular tracts of various Sufi sects. In contrast to later developments in Urdu, the Dakani Sufis used relatively few Persian and Arabic loanwords, even in their discussions of theological matters. Instead, they preferred to draw their terminology primarily from Sanskrit roots and from other local languages. However, later Dakani poetry and prose borrowed increasing amounts of vocabulary from Persian and Arabic, even as writers adopted various Persian literary forms. Among these forms were the *dastan*, a Persian prose romance of adventure and magic that became firmly incorporated into the Urdu literary tradition.

Because Hindi and Urdu were mutually comprehensible, the most obvious distinguishing point between Hindi and Urdu lay in the alphabets in which they are written. Early Hindi as spoken by worshipers of the traditional Indian religion was written in several related alphabets, including the Kaithi, or cursive, script, and modern Hindi came to be written in the Devanagari, the "script of the city of the gods," which is also used to write Sanskrit. Urdu is written in Arabic script, right to left, and uses thirty-six letters. All are consonantal except *alif*, which is exclusively a vowel in Urdu usage (as opposed to the classical Arabic of the Quʾrān, in which it represents a glottal stop consonant). Three other letters can indicate either a consonant or a vowel, and readers must determine from context the exact value of the letter.

The literary tradition of both Hindi and Urdu were formed and enriched by the often conflict-ridden interaction between Muslims and Hindus. Although many Indians responded to the Turkic invaders' repression of traditional Indian patterns of devotion by converting to Islam, others embraced their Hindu identity more fervently, developing Hinduism from a collection of local religious traditions into a cohesive system of practice and belief. Writers on both sides of the religious divide sought to express their devotion in the realm of letters and, as a result, produced powerful new works of poetry and prose. Among the notable works of the period was Somadeva's *Kathāsaritsāgara* (eleventh century; *The Ocean of Story*, 1924-1928), a verse epic of nested stories that drew on native Indian myth and folklore. The storytelling tradition of medieval India frequently dealt with tragic, even pathetic, plots: innocents being taken to their executions for crimes they did not commit, loyal family members being banished from their homes by unloving fathers or husbands, or other gross injustices. However, these stories inevitably culminated in happy endings, with innocence proven moments before the execution and family members joyously reunited, even if it required gross contortions of the storyline, even *deus ex machina* interventions, to achieve.

SIGNIFICANCE

The development of a widespread common tongue made trade and travel easier throughout the area of northern India, resulting in commercial and cultural growth. Its position was further strengthened by the development of a literary tradition among both Hindu and Muslim Indians. So strong was the position of this language that it survived even the imposition of English by the British Empire in the nineteenth and twentieth centuries to emerge as a unifying language after the attainment of Indian independence in the 1940's.

—Leigh Husband Kimmel

FURTHER READING

King, Christopher Rolland. *One Language, Two Scripts: The Hindi Movement in Nineteenth Century North India*. New York: Oxford University Press, 1994. A history of Hindi and Urdu, including the political and religious battles that had been simmering for centuries and came to a head during the British occupation.

Koul, Omkar N., and L. Devaki, eds. *Linguistic Heritage of India and Asia*. Mysore, India: Central Institute of Indian Languages, 2000. A collection of articles, some technical but some quite readable, on the development of the languages of India, including Hindi and Urdu.

McGregor, R. S. *Hindi Literature from Its Beginnings to the Nineteenth Century*. Wiesbaden, Germany: Harrassowitz. 1984. A historical overview of the development of Hindi as a literary language, looking particularly at the role of intercultural conflict in defining a peculiarly Hindi mode of literary development.

MacLeod, John. *The History of India*. Westport, Conn.: Greenwood Press, 2002. An overview of the history of India, including a bibliography for further research.

Singh, K. Suresh. *Languages and Scripts*. Oxford, England: Oxford University Press, in association with the Anthropological Survey of India, 1993. An analysis of the relationships among the various languages of India and the alphabets in which they were written, including the Devanagari and its descendants and Arabic.

Watson, Francis. *India: A Concise History*. New York: Thames and Hudson, 2002. A good basic overview of Indian history, including this critical period in which conflicts of religious devotion led to the development and flowering of Hindi and Urdu as literary languages.

SEE ALSO: c. 800: *Kana* Syllabary Is Developed; 997-1030: Reign of Maḥmūd of Ghazna; c. 1380: Compilation of the Wise Sayings of Lal Ded.

11th century
EXPANSION OF SUNNI ISLAM IN NORTH AFRICA AND IBERIA

Sunni Islam expanded in North Africa and the Iberian Peninsula during the eleventh and early twelfth centuries through the military and spiritual dominance of the revivalist Almoravid and Almohad Empires.

LOCALE: North Africa

CATEGORIES: Expansion and land acquisition; religion; wars, uprisings, and civil unrest

KEY FIGURES

Yūsuf ibn Tāshufīn (d. 1106), founder of the Almoravid Empire, r. 1061-1106

Ibn Tūmart (c. 1080-1130), religious leader, founder of the Almohad Empire

ʿAbd al-Muʾmin (1094-1163), Almohad successor to Ibn Tūumart, r. 1130-1163

SUMMARY OF EVENT

From the eleventh to thirteenth century, the western Islamic empire was dominated by two states: the Almoravids and Almohads. Both states began as Sunni revivalist movements among rival North African Berber tribes, split politically after the collapse of Fāṭimid domination and the invasion by Banū Hilāl Arabs, Bedouin tribes expelled from Egypt, in the twelfth century. Across the Mediterranean, Muslim Iberia (now Spain and Portugal) was divided into numerous small feuding kingdoms. North Africa remained a region of great religious diversity, despite the influence of Islam, and while Sunni Islam was strong in certain areas, Khāijism, the rejection of a caliphate based on descent from the Prophet Muḥammad, remained widespread. However, in remote mountainous regions of the Maghreb, Islam was not a dominant presence.

The Almoravids, also known as the al-Murābitūn, were Sunni reformers made up of lowland Saharan Berbers. The Almoravid movement was initiated by a Sunni scholar named Yūsuf ibn Tāshufīn, who, after a pilgrimage to Mecca, became filled with religious zeal. He returned to Saharan Africa with the goal of reforming Islam as practiced in the region; he wanted to found a "pure" state of Islam near the Senegal River.

By forming an alliance with Berber chiefs, the Almoravid movement developed a military capability they used to spread their brand of Sunnism northward with the aim of establishing proper Islamic practice among tribes and cultures they encountered, by force if necessary. Under the leadership of Tāshufīn, the Almoravids subjugated non-Islamic and non-Sunni Islamic Berbers, whom they viewed as heretical. The Almoravids also used the expansion of their forced religious philosophy as a way to place rival political groups under their domination. Conquered groups were given three choices: tribute, Almoravid Sunnism, or the sword.

Tāshufīn conquered most of what is now Morocco and western Algeria and converted the citizenry to Almoravid Sunnism. When Islamic kingdoms and city-states in the Iberian Peninsula were threatened by resurgent Christian kingdoms from the north, Tāshufīn entered Iberia to battle the invading Christians. His defeat of the Christian army at the Battle of Al-Zallāqah in 1086 kept southern Iberia from Christian invasion. While in the peninsula, Tāshufīn also deposed and incorporated many of the Muslim kings and incorporated their lands into his growing Almoravid Empire.

Though Tāshufīn's military strength kept Christian armies at bay, many Iberian Muslims resented Almoravid influence over their lives and traditions. Much of this was linked to a cultural distaste for Berber history in the region and a sense of elitism: Iberian Muslims considered their North African neighbors to be culturally unsophisticated. Another aspect of Almoravid culture that Iberians Muslims found to their dislike was the strict enforcement of Sunni Islam, including the persecution of non-Muslims and members of minor Islamic sects such as the Sufis. This persecution often included the burning of books deemed heretical by local Islamic leaders. Eventually, a revolt against the Almoravids beginning in the 1140's saw the end to Almoravid power and influence in the Iberian Peninsula.

While the Almoravids expanded their influence northward, another Sunni revivalist movement, the Almohads, began to challenge them in North Africa. The founder or the Almohads was Ibn Tūmart. Ibn Tūmart was a highland Berber who, after studying in Cordoba and the Islamic east, returned to the Berber highlands to preach a message of strict Islamic piety. In 1125, Ibn Tūmart declared himself ruler, claiming the Almoravids were impious and corrupt Muslims. Establishing a military base of operations in the Atlas Mountains of Morocco, Ibn Tūmart built an army of highland Berber converts and began a military campaign to conquer surrounding areas. Ibn Tūmart's rapid rise to power and support may have resulted from his actions conforming to traditional Berber beliefs regarding the power of charismatic holy leaders. Also, by leading attacks against the lowland

Almoravid Berbers, he played to the highland Berbers' prejudices against their lowland neighbors.

Ibn Tūmart's Almohad successor was ʿAbd al-Muʾmin. Al-Muʾmin would lead a military campaign against the Almoravids that resulted in eventual Almohad control of most of northern Morocco and western Algeria by 1147. The fall of the Almoravids developed into a political schism in Muslim Iberia. Sensing a weakening of Muslim military strength, Christian forces invaded the region. The Christian invasion was eventually repelled by Almohad forces led by al-Muʾmin. Al-Muʾmin also mounted several military expeditions that unified North Africa and stretched the Almohad Empire from Tunisia to the Atlantic Ocean, including all Islamic regions of the Iberian Peninsula.

During the late twelfth century, the Almohads were in constant military struggle with Almoravid holdouts and Iberian Christians. In 1212, the Almohads suffered a crushing defeat by a combined Christian force at Las Navas de Tolosa, resulting in their eventual loss of control over the entire Iberian Peninsula, except for the small kingdom of Granada. During this same period, the Almohad Empire in North Africa began to dissolve into a group of small independent states. In time, the Almohads were challenged and displaced by powerful regional emirs, viceroys, and nomadic invaders.

SIGNIFICANCE

The Almoravid and Almohad Empires demonstrated that

power could be built by combining tribal military units and Islamic religious ideologies to structure a formidable political entity. The key leaders of both groups won support from the superstitious Berbers by presenting themselves as miracle-working holy men touched by the hand of Islam. In the case of the Almoravids, their conquest of lands along the important Saharan trade routes allowed them to control valuable sources of gold and commerce throughout western Africa. This ability to control regional trade allowed them to project their accumulated power.

The transitory and short-lived Almoravid and Almohad Empires helped create the first unified western North Africa political unit as well as a distinct non-Arabic Islamic culture. Despite the idiosyncratic nature of their Islamic beliefs, the Almoravids and Almohads were staunchly Sunni. Their piety and religious intolerance repressed the Khāijite, Shīʿite, and heterodox forms of Islam, which, until their empire building, had dominated the region.

The rule of the Almoravids and Almohads advanced the Saharan region out of its culturally primitive standing, placing it in step with other Islamic cultures. During their occupation of the Iberian Peninsula, with its own rich Islamic traditions, the Almoravids imported many scholars and theologians from Iberia to their North African cities, especially Marrakesh, a city that had become a new center for Islamic culture.

—*Randall L. Milstein*

FURTHER READING

Bosworth, Clifford Edmund. *The New Islamic Dynasties: A Chronological and Genealogical Manual.* 1967. Rev. ed. New York: Columbia University Press, 1996. A historical and genealogical accounting of the Islamic dynasties, including those in Spain and Africa. Bibliography, index.

Brett, Michael. "The Islamisization of Morocco from the Arabs to the Almoravids." *Journal of the Society for Moroccan Studies* 2 (1992): 57-71. A study of North Africa's development into a region with a distinct Islamic character.

Brett, Michael, and Elizabeth Fentress. *The Berbers.* Cambridge, Mass.: Blackwell, 1996. This study focuses on the history of the Berber-speaking peoples. The authors establish the identity of the Berbers and analyze their traditions, while tracing their political and social history. Maps, bibliography, index.

Cleveland, W. L. *A History of the Modern Middle East.* Oxford, England: Westview Press, 1994. A concise history from pre-Islamic Arabia to the modern independent nations of the Middle East.

Esposito, John L., ed. *The Oxford History of Islam.* New York: Oxford University Press, 1999. An easily readable and accessible history of Islam. The book follows a time line that makes the complex history of Islam understandable. Bibliography, index.

Fregosi, Paul. *Jihad in the West: Muslim Conquests from the Seventh to the Twenty-first Centuries.* Amherst, N.Y.: Prometheus Books, 1998. A survey of Muslim conquests and military campaigns, including the battle at Las Navas de Tolosa and others throughout Iberia. Map, bibliography, index.

Le Tourneau, Roger. *The Almohad Movement in North Africa in the Twelfth and Thirteenth Centuries.* Princeton, N.J.: Princeton University Press, 1969. Excellent in integrating ʿAbd al-Muʾmin into the Almohad movement and showing his strengths and weaknesses. Brief but good treatment of contemporary accounts and historical studies. Bibliography, index.

Reilly, Bernard F. *The Contest of Christian and Muslim Spain, 1031-1157.* Cambridge, Mass.: Blackwell, 1995. This work is a more complete coverage of the rise of Christian Iberia and deals extensively with military struggles and dynastic history. Illustrations, maps, bibliography, index.

Schatzmiller, Maya. *The Berbers and the Islamic State: The Marinid Experience in Pre-protectorate Morocco.* Princeton, N.J.: Markus Wiener, 2000. A detailed study of the history of the Berbers in North Africa and Morocco. Includes discussion of acculturation and its legacy, developing an Islamic state and institutions, Jews in the region, and more. Bibliography, index.

SEE ALSO: 630-711: Islam Expands Throughout North Africa; October 10, 680: Martyrdom of Prophet's Grandson Ḥusayn; April or May, 711: Ṭārik Crosses into Spain; c. 950: Court of Córdoba Flourishes in Spain; 969-1171: Reign of the Fāṭimids; 1031: Caliphate of Córdoba Falls; 1048: Zīrids Break from Faṭimid Dynasty and Revive Sunni Islam; 1062-1147: Almoravids Conquer Morocco and Establish the Almoravid Empire; c. 1075-1086: Hummay Founds the Sefuwa Dynasty; 1076: Almoravids Sack Kumbi; November 1, 1092-June 15, 1094: El Cid Conquers Valencia; c. 1150: Moors Transmit Classical Philosophy and Medicine to Europe; 1230: Unification of Castile and León.

RELATED ARTICLES in *Great Lives from History: The Middle Ages, 477-1453*: ʿAbd al-Muʾmin; Afonso I; El Cid; al-Ghazzālī; Saladin; Ṭāriq ibn-Ziyād; ʿUmar I.

11th-12th centuries
BUILDING OF ROMANESQUE CATHEDRALS

Massive Romanesque cathedrals were built throughout Europe, ushering in the era of great, magnificent cathedrals that led to the Gothic period.

LOCALE: Europe
CATEGORIES: Architecture; cultural and intellectual history; engineering

SUMMARY OF EVENT

The period following the year 1000 saw an increase in the number of cathedrals constructed in Europe and England, an increase of building that was, in part, an expression of Christians' gratitude to God for the uneventful passing of the millennium, which people had feared would bring an apocalyptic end to the world. Also, the weather had been improving in Europe, helping crops flourish and populations rise, thereby increasing the need for larger churches to hold burgeoning congregations. More crops resulted in increased trade and increased wealth for the new middle class of merchants and the religious communities that had extensive landholdings. Civic leaders and church hierarchy yearned to express their religious devotion by constructing impressive cathedrals.

The eleventh century was also a time of pilgrimages to religious sites across Europe and the Holy Land. New pilgrimage centers were constructed at regular intervals along the major pilgrimage routes, each with an elaborate new church at its center. The Crusades, begun at the close of the eleventh century, opened up trade with the East, which served to bring even more wealth into Europe and to fund still more cathedrals. As one eleventh century monk commented, the world was putting on "a white mantle of churches."

It was during this period of optimism and growth that the Romanesque style developed almost simultaneously in Germany, Lombardy, France, Normandy, England, Tuscany, and Spain.

The term Romanesque was coined in the nineteenth century to describe a late medieval architectural style that was Roman-like in mass and scale. However, the term is unfortunate since it implies an architecture that is an imitation of an earlier style. Romanesque is, in fact, a unique style that reflects an important period in European history.

The time period ascribed to the Romanesque style is the eleventh through the twelfth centuries, although the exact beginning of the Romanesque is difficult to discern because it slowly evolved from earlier Carolingian and Ottonian styles. The feature that most distinguishes the Romanesque style from that of its predecessors is found in its cathedrals. Earlier cathedral styles were marked by flat timber ceilings that covered the naves, or central halls, whereas the Romanesque style had masonry vaults over the naves. The shift to masonry was most likely a style developed to prevent damage from fire, which destroyed many of the earlier timber-ceiling structures. Also, the use of masonry permitted, and may have even encouraged, Romanesque builders to experiment with various types of vaulting, which came into common use in cathedrals by the year 1000.

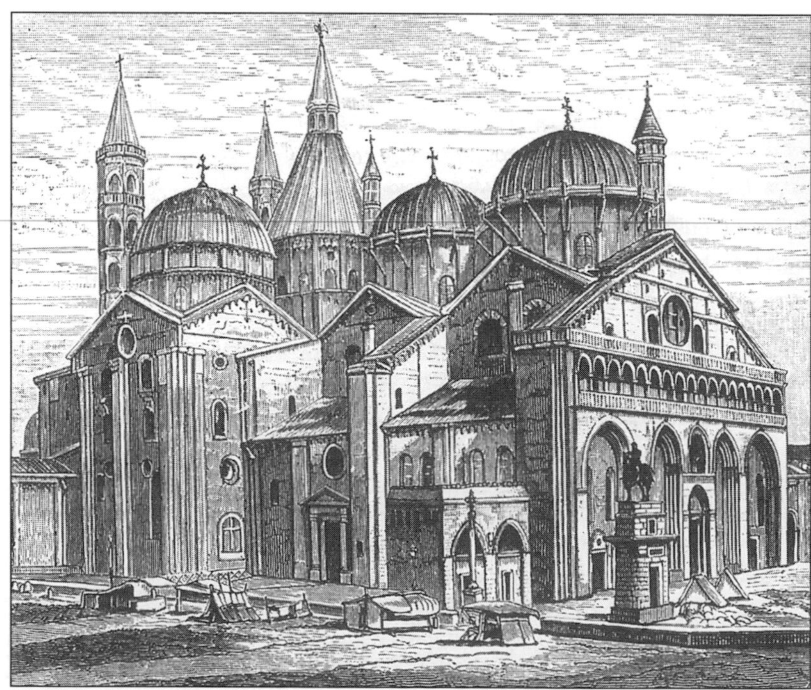

The Church of Saint Anthony, Padua, showing features typical of Romanesque architecture: rounded vaults, few windows, massiveness, and low elevation relative to later Gothic structures. (Frederick Ungar Publishing Co.)

Although there are minor regional differences, all Romanesque cathedrals share common features in their plans, elevations, and methods of construction. Romanesque cathedrals were based on the Roman basilica plan, with a long central hall, two side aisles, and a hemicycle (half circle) apse at one end. The Christian basilica plan added a transept (a smaller hall, intersecting the nave at right angles) at the apsidal end, thereby forming a Latin cross (a cross with one long and three short arms). The altars of the cathedrals were placed at the crossings of the nave and the transept and were typically covered with a dome, placed either on squinches (rectangular blocks) or on pendentives (curved triangular elements). The apse served as a choir, under which a crypt was usually located, and around the outer rim of which ran an ambulatory (walkway) for access to apsidal relic chapels. The apse is nearly always oriented east, indicating the direction of Jerusalem.

Cathedrals with apses on both ends of the nave are unusual, but examples can be found, especially in Germany. The church at Maria Laach (1093-1156) is one example of this style. The Latin cross cathedral plan developed out of the Western church's Latin style liturgy, which invited the presence of large congregations in the long nave.

The Late Romanesque Refectory at Saint Martin des Champs, Paris, now the library at the Musée des Arts et Métiers. The ribbed groin vaulting, higher ceilings, and more open windows point toward the Gothic style. (Frederick Ungar Publishing Co.)

In their interior elevations, Romanesque cathedrals were based on the Roman basilica's tripartite division of the nave walls into an arcade on the ground level (separating the nave from the side aisles), a triforium (a solid wall concealing the pitched roof over the side aisles) above the arcade, and a clerestory (window) level at the top. Romanesque builders, however, soon replaced the solid triforium with a second story gallery (viewing area and walkway) built within the pitched roof of the side aisles and opening onto the central nave. The placement of a lofty hemicycle arch at the altar end of the nave was based on the Roman triumphal arch and represents the triumphal spread of Christianity throughout the known world.

The exterior elevation of the Romanesque cathedral reflects the interior elevation, with hemicycle-arched windows on the ground level (admitting light into the side aisles), a shed roof concealing the triforium or gallery level, and hemicycle-arched windows in the clerestory level. Typical also on Romanesque cathedrals are towers covered by high-pitched roofs. The number and placement of the towers vary, but typically two towers were placed flanking the western (entrance) end of the cathedral, as at Saint Étienne at Caen (begun 1068), or one tower was placed over the crossing of the nave and the transept, as in Saint Sernin at Toulouse (c. 1080-1120).

One of the most unique features of Romanesque cathedrals, as mentioned above, was the use of masonry as the principle building material. The ancient Romans used concrete to span their great halls, creating elaborate vaulted ceilings, and the Carolingians and Ottonians used timber to create flat ceilings over their great halls. Romanesque builders, however, chose to use masonry to create lofty vaulted ceilings over their cathedral naves. There is no single explanation for the Romanesque builders' choice of masonry, which is a difficult and time-consuming method of construction. The Romanesque builders' rejection of timber for construction seems self-evident based upon the medieval records of cathedral fires. If timber was not an option, then why not use concrete? In earlier times, historians believed that the technology to create concrete was lost during the upheaval of the early Middle Ages, but it is now known that copies of an ancient Roman treatise by the architect Vitruvius, detailing how to make and use concrete, existed during the Romanesque period and were accessible to at least some of the builders of the day.

The Romanesque builders' rejection of concrete was probably based on the fact that concrete required exorbitant amounts of timber, both for scaffolding and for forms to hold the concrete in place until the concrete dried. The construction of an entire vaulting system for a large cathedral would take more timber than was affordable or attainable. The solution, then, was to use what the Romanesque builders had available and in abundance, which was masonry. The type of stone varied by location: limestone in France; marble in Italy and Province; Caen stone in Normandy, which was also shipped to Norman England; limestone, sandstone, and flint in England; and brick in lieu of masonry in Germany and the Netherlands.

The heavy masonry ceiling vaults created a problem of thrust that required the Romanesque builders to strengthen the thick walls of single-hall churches with external buttresses. The problem of thrust could also be resolved by building churches with two side aisles nearly equal in height to the nave, wherein the three vaults (nave and two side aisles) could balance one another; however that configuration meant the central nave had illumination only from the side aisle windows. In churches with two side aisles and a higher central nave, which permitted the nave to be illuminated by windows in the nave clerestory, the nave vaults were held aloft by an elaborate system of compound piers integrated into the nave arcades. The compound piers were articulated with moldings that were often carried up and onto the vaults, creating a visual continuity between the arcaded walls and the vaulted ceilings, especially effective in structures with ribbed vaults (vaults with masonry edges), as in Saint Étienne at Caen (vaulted c. 1115-1120). Typical vaults were either simple barrel or tunnel (hemicycle) vaults, as in Saint Savin-sur-Gartempe (nave 1095-1115), or groin (cross) vaults, as in Speyer Cathedral (nave vaults c. 1082-1106). Vaults became a distinguishing feature of the Romanesque style, giving the cathedral naves a vertical emphasis pointing toward Heaven and foreshadowing the Gothic style.

SIGNIFICANCE

Arising across Continental Europe and across England almost simultaneously, Romanesque architecture was the first truly international style of architecture, with representative masterpieces such as Saint Sernin at Toulouse, Autun Cathedral in Burgundy, Saint Étienne in Caen, Saint Ambrogio in Milan, Speyer Cathedral in Germany, Santiago de Compostela in Spain, and Durham Cathedral in England. Romanesque builders ushered in the great age of cathedral building that led to the Gothic era.

—*Sonia Sorrell*

FURTHER READING

Armi, C. Edson. *Design and Construction in Romanesque Architecture: The First Romanesque Architecture and the Pointed Arch in Burgundy and Northern Italy.* New York: Cambridge University Press, 2004. Focuses on the regions of Europe where the first Romanesque buildings were constructed at the beginning of the eleventh century.

Conant, Kenneth J. *Carolingian and Romanesque Architecture, 800-1200.* 4th ed. New Haven, Conn.: Yale University Press, 1992. A scholarly overview of both architectural styles. Well illustrated.

Hammett, Ralph Warner, and George H. Edgell. *The Romanesque Architecture of Western Europe: Italy, France, Spain, Germany and England.* New York: Archival Book, 1927. Offers clear descriptions and excellent black-and-white photographs that still provide a fine overview of the Romanesque style through the eyes, and camera lens, of a trained architect.

Jackson, Thomas Graham. *Byzantine and Romanesque Architecture.* New York: Hacker Art Books, 1975. A compendium of Byzantine and Romanesque architecture organized by geographical areas and illustrated with black-and-white photographs, drawings, elevations, plans, and details.

Kubach, Hans E. *Romanesque Architecture*. New York: Electa/Rizzoli, 1988. A nicely illustrated discussion of the major monuments of the Romanesque style.

Tadgell, Christopher. *Early Medieval Europe: The Ideal of Rome and Feudalism*. 1988. Reprint. London: Ellipsis, 2001. Extensively illustrated study of church architecture after the fall of Rome in both Western Europe and Russia. Compares Romanesque and late-Byzantine styles and explores their mutual influence.

Toman, Rolf, ed. *Romanesque: Architecture, Sculpture, Painting*. Cologne: Konemann, 1997. Well-balanced discussion connecting Romanesque architecture with the visual arts.

SEE ALSO: c. 1025: Scholars at Chartres Revive Interest in the Classics; c. 1150-1200: Development of Gothic Architecture.

RELATED ARTICLES in *Great Lives from History: The Middle Ages, 477-1453*: Arnolfo di Cambio; Filippo Brunelleschi; Nicholas V; Suger.

11th-12th centuries
FIRST EUROPEAN-NATIVE AMERICAN CONTACT

As Thule Inuit culture spread eastward across the Arctic and as Norse settlers established themselves in Greenland, Native Americans for the first time met, traded, and then clashed with Europeans.

LOCALE: Kalaallit Nunaat, in Greenland, and Vinland (now Atlantic coastline of eastern and northeastern Canada)

CATEGORIES: Expansion and land acquisition; exploration and discovery

KEY FIGURES

Erik the Red (c. 950-1001?), founder of Norse settlement in Greenland

Leif Eriksson (c. 970-c. 1035), son of Erik the Red, first European discoverer of Vinland

Thorvald Eriksson (d. c. 1004), brother of Leif, first Norse casualty at Vinland

Thorfinn Karlsefni (c. 980-after 1007), leader of a colonizing expedition to Vinland

SUMMARY OF EVENT

In the latter part of the first millennium, Neo-Eskimos, or Inuit, as they called themselves, spread rapidly from northern Alaska across the Arctic to Greenland. Innovative Thule culture Inuit were much better adapted to Arctic conditions than their Dorset culture predecessors. Dorset Inuit depended on heavy spears when hunting and hand-pulled their sleds. Thule Inuit developed one form of the bow and arrow and various sizes of stone-pointed harpoons, and they had dogs pull their sleds. To pursue large whales in open waters, Thule Inuit created umiaks, open skin boats holding a crew of eight, and used one-person kayaks to hunt smaller sea mammals that also were pursued by the Dorset.

Use of kayaks and umiaks in summer and dog sleds in winter permitted Inuit hunters to travel rapidly. Taking advantage of climatic warming from the ninth to the twelfth century that provided open water in the Arctic, Thule Inuit followed whales across the northern coast of Canada, probably reaching northwest Greenland around 1000.

Although Greenland is the world's largest island, only one-sixth of the land is open. Most terrain is covered by an enormous ice cap, thousands of feet deep, with many associated glaciers. The only ice-free areas are along the mountainous coasts. Smaller islands are numerous, and long fjords run far inland. The Inuit preferred to locate on the headlands, islands, and sea ice outside the fjords. Whales, seals, and other marine animals abounded there, providing food and clothing. Caribou hunts drew the Inuit inland during warm weather, but they distrusted the fjords, where even in winter the ice was treacherous. Moving south along the west coast, the Thule Inuit met another group of migrants who had arrived in Greenland at approximately the same time.

Erik the Red (Erik Thorvaldson) was the first Norseman to explore Greenland. Born in Norway, he had come to Iceland as a teenager when his father was exiled for manslaughter. Erik himself was banished from Iceland for three years in 982 for a similar crime and decided to sail west and explore land sighted earlier by a ship driven off course in a storm. Unable to approach the forbidding east coast of Greenland, Erik sailed around the southern tip of the island and discovered deep fjords with lush grass meadows at their head. Erik selected for settlement an area of southwest Greenland in which the ice cap is more than 100 miles (161 kilometers) from the coast and the climate is less harsh than elsewhere on the island. It was the only part of the island where farming was possible. During the three years that Erik and his party explored the west coast, they met no other people, though they did find evidence of previous occupants, probably Dorset Inuit.

Erik's description of the island he named Greenland to stress its attractions excited land-hungry Icelanders. When he sailed back to Greenland in 986, Erik led twenty-five ships. Fourteen vessels carrying some four hundred people arrived and created an eastern settlement in today's Julianehåb area (Qaqortoq). By 1003, three other immigrant fleets had landed, bringing the population to about one thousand and establishing a western settlement in today's Godthåb area (Nuuk, the capital of Greenland). Most of those who came were farmers seeking good grazing land for their cattle and sheep. The grassy meadows along the fjords suited the type of agriculture the settlers had practiced in Iceland. From their animals, they produced meat, milk, cheese, and butter in large quantities. To these products they added fish, along with seals, walrus, and caribou collected on annual hunts in northern Greenland. The growing season was too short for wheat, and bread was practically unknown. Trade with Norway provided badly needed timber, iron, weapons, and clothing of European style. In exchange, the settlers sent furs and hides, walrus ivory, white falcons and much-admired polar bear skins. During the colony's peak population of more than four thousand in the thirteenth century, the eastern settlement contained two-hundred fifty farms, supporting twelve parish churches, an Augustinian monastery, a Benedictine nunnery, and a cathedral at Gardar (now Igaliko). The smaller western settlement had ninety farms and four churches.

Norse exploring and hunting voyages ranged north along the Greenland coast and westward to the North American continent. The first contact between Native Americans and Norse, recorded in the Norse sagas, occurred on the coast of North America. In 1001, Leif Eriksson (also called Leif the Lucky) sailed for Greenland but instead sailed off course and reached the land he named Vinland the Good, the Atlantic coast of what is now eastern and northeastern Canada. His brother Thorvald, continuing Leif's exploration a few years later, met a party of nine natives and immediately attacked them, killing eight. A counterattack by a larger number of natives caused Thorvald's death from an arrow wound. Who these natives were is unclear—the Norse applied the contemptuous term Skraelings (possibly meaning "weak" or "sickly") to both Inuit and North American Indians. The attackers may have been Thule Inuit moving down the coast in pursuit of sea mammals or Algonquian-speaking Indians. In either case, the encounter was predictive of the violence that would mar future Native American-European relations. An attempt to colonize Vinland, led by Thorfinn Karlsefni, enacted a similar history. Although peaceful trading marked his group's first encounter with Skraelings, attacks by the natives soon forced abandonment of the settlement.

Around 1500, the Norse disappeared, while the Thule Inuit became the ancestors of the present Greenland population. When the climate turned colder after 1200, during a period of global cooling known as the Little Ice Age, conditions worsened for the Norse. Increasing drift ice along the west coast of Greenland limited the ability of Norsemen to hunt sea mammals. Despite several centuries of contact with the Inuit, the Norse never adopted the superior Arctic hunting techniques of the Thule. Shorter growing seasons meant that grassy meadows no longer supported as many grazing animals as before. Archaeologists note that later graves are shallower than earlier ones, reflecting the difficulty of digging in the frozen ground. Problems in Norway—the black plague and political turmoil—distracted Norwegians and caused abandonment of trade with Greenland. As the ice moved south, the Inuit followed in larger numbers. Their animal-skin-covered boats and their dog sleds and fur clothing perfectly adapted to the colder climate.

SIGNIFICANCE

Not all encounters between natives and Europeans were violent. Both Inuit legends and Norse sagas describe friendly meetings and trade between the two peoples. Within fifty years of their arrival on Greenland, Norse hunting parties, ranging north, came upon Thule Inuit. Archaeologists find many Norse objects in Neo-Eskimo sites; some might have resulted from raids or may represent loot from abandoned Norse areas, but many most likely came from trade. The quantity of walrus tusks and skins exported to Norway appears too large to come solely from Norse hunts and probably included additions from trading with the Inuit. Possibly the two peoples could have coexisted peacefully in Greenland as the Inuit concentrated on the coast and the Norse preferred interior fjords. Most Norse references to Skraelings, however, describe conflicts, and the main theme of Inuit legends about the Norse is how Norsemen were met and conquered.

What ultimately happened to the Norse is not clear from surviving sources. The Inuit may have wiped them out, or, as the climate worsened, the less well-adapted Europeans may have slowly declined in number and died off. Possibly the Norse used their boats to retreat to Iceland or Norway. Some scholars have suggested that the survivors may have joined the English or the Portuguese who became active in North American waters at the end of the fifteenth century. Whatever the reason, the Norse vanished, and Greenland's future belonged to the Inuit.

—*Milton Berman*

FURTHER READING

Barrett, James H., ed. *Contact, Continuity, and Collapse: The Norse Colonization of the North Atlantic*. Turnhout, Belgium: Brepols, 2003. Presents an analysis of the discovery, exploration, and colonization of the North Atlantic by the Vikings. Bibliography and index.

Gad, Finn. *The History of Greenland*. Vol. 1, *Earliest Times to 1700*. Translated by Ernst Dupont. London: C. Hurst, 1970. The standard history of Greenland. Provides a succinct account of Dorset and Thule cultures, along with a detailed narrative of the Norse settlements.

Ingstad, Helge. *Land Under the Pole Star: A Voyage to the Norse Settlements of Greenland and the Saga of the People That Vanished*. Translated by Naomi Walford. New York: St. Martin's Press, 1966. Combines a description of Greenland archaeological sites with a history of the Norse settlements.

Jones, Gwyn. *The Norse Atlantic Saga: Being the Norse Voyages of Discovery and Settlement to Iceland, Greenland, and North America*. 2d ed. New York: Oxford University Press, 1986. A careful account of Norse settlements in North America, written for the general reader. The second half of the volume contains translations of the Norse sagas *The Greenlanders' Saga* and *The Saga of Erik the Red*.

Jordan, Richard H. "Neo-Eskimo Prehistory of Greenland." In *Arctic*, edited by David Damas, Vol. 5 in *Handbook of North American Indians*. Washington, D.C.: Smithsonian Institution Press, 1984. Concise history of Thule culture in Greenland based on archaeological evidence.

Oswalt, Wendell H. *Eskimos and Explorers*. 2d ed. Lincoln: University of Nebraska Press, 1999. Descriptive account of Norse-Eskimo relations. Includes bibliographic notes and maps.

Seaver, Kirsten A. *The Frozen Echo: Greenland and the Exploration of North America, Circa A.D. 1000-1500*. Stanford, Calif.: Stanford University Press, 1996. Questions earlier interpretations of hostile contacts between Inuit and Norse. Suggests that the Norse abandonment of Greenland was probably voluntary, not due to pressure from Eskimos.

Wahlgren, Erik. *The Vikings and America*. London: Thames and Hudson, 2000. Part of the Ancient Peoples and Places series, looks at the Viking discovery of North America. Bibliography and index.

SEE ALSO: 850-950: Viking Era.

RELATED ARTICLE in *Great Lives from History: The Middle Ages, 477-1453*: Leif Eriksson.

11th-15th centuries
DEVELOPMENT OF THE IFE KINGDOM AND YORUBA CULTURE

The city of Ife became the first center of power in West Africa's forest area. It was the site from which distinctive Yoruba cultural characteristics emerged, including the development of complex trade networks, urbanization and the formation of city-states, and the creation of hereditary monarchies led by ruler-priests.

LOCALE: Yorubaland (now southwestern Nigeria and southeastern Republic of Benin)
CATEGORIES: Cultural and intellectual history; government and politics; trade and commerce

KEY FIGURE
Oduduwa, legendary first king of Ife

SUMMARY OF EVENT
Yorubaland stretches northward from the Atlantic coast to the savannahs above Nigeria's forest area. The city of Ife, located in the northern limits of the forest, is situated in the heart of Yorubaland and at the core of Yoruba life. Archaeological evidence indicates substantial settlement there from as early as 900, and it flourished as a city-state from the eleventh through the fifteenth centuries.

Ile-Ife (the homeland of Ife) is considered to be the birthplace of the Yoruba. It is their cultural and spiritual center and is the source from which all major Yoruba dynasties claim legitimacy. Yet its primacy is not easily defined and much of its past remains obscure. As most written accounts date from the nineteenth century, reconstruction of the precolonial history of Ife and the Yoruba relies on interpretation of oral traditions, linguistic studies, and archaeological evidence.

Oral traditions vary in detail but contain the same essentials, lending support to claims of a shared Yoruba past. Narratives of creation and origin all center on Ife. Tradition states that Oduduwa reigned as the first king. According to some accounts, he descended from heaven; others say he arrived from somewhere in the northeast. The narratives claim that his sons and grandsons were sent forth from Ife to establish the ruling dynasties of various Yoruba states and the neighboring kingdom of Benin.

Archaeological evidence shows that the forested areas of southwest Nigeria have been inhabited for thousands of years. Excavations southeast of Ife, for example, indicate occupation as early as the tenth millennium B.C.E. Linguistic studies of the Niger-Congo language family show that Yoruba is several thousand years old and that it has been affected by two movements of immigrants who spoke languages closely related to that of the original inhabitants of the area. It is believed that these migrations began around 700.

Examination of traditional narratives in light of archaeological and linguistic studies suggests that the stories of Oduduwa and his progeny reflect distant memories of immigrants belonging to a dominant but not alien cultural group, who established sovereignty at Ife and later established additional settlements among local inhabitants. Such studies suggest that the process of Yoruba state formation came not from conquest but from assimilation. It has been further speculated that the immigrants were originally from the grassland areas to the northeast, where methods of cultivation were more advanced and where inhabitants were familiar with Sudanic concepts of state organization and kingship.

There are few clues regarding the interaction between the immigrants and indigenous residents. It is evident that by the end of the first millennium, the emerging Yoruba had entered a new stage of development. This era was characterized by an extensive population engaged in forest farming and iron smelting. The time period was further distinguished by the emergence of the interrelated institutions of town life and the formation of large states, developments unique in the history of the forest regions.

Conditions in the forest region were not particularly conducive to the rise of urbanism and state formation. The dense undergrowth and the coastal mangrove swamps hindered agriculture and commerce. Nevertheless, although they emerged later than the savannah states of Mali, Ghana, Songhai, Bornu, or Hausa, early Yoruba polities such as Ife were established in the forest areas; later city-states were developed in the savannah areas to the north.

In the eleventh century, Ife emerged as the forest region's first major power. There were a number of contributing factors. Some have suggested that urban settlement was a result of military necessity, indicated by defensive walls built around Ife and most other Yoruba communities. Others have emphasized the evolution of metal technology, introduced in the area around 300 to 500, which provided better tools and implements for farming. The large-scale cultivation of yams, plantains, and bananas enabled the support of a large population.

Commerce played a major role in the centralization of Yoruba city-states. Ife's proximity to the forest-savannah boundary and the Niger River made it a center for the interchange of ideas and products. There is evidence that Ife produced glass beads, cotton cloth, and metal works. Those manufactures along with camwood dye, kola nuts, and various foods from the forest were exchanged for products made and grown in the grasslands.

In addition to its location for agriculture and trade, Ife was a center for specialized political and spiritual functions. Traditions claim that Ife was the site of the first monarchy. Supporting archaeological evidence indicates that it was functioning as a city-state as early as 1000, whereas other Yoruba city-states did not emerge until the twelfth and thirteenth centuries.

The positioning of Ife as the seat of early monarchy is further supported by the brass and terra-cotta sculptures discovered there. They are believed to portray the rulers, called *onis*, and members of the ruling class. They were possibly used in ceremonies for the dead. The works were created with a complex lost-wax metal technology using copper and its alloys. As copper is not now found in Nigeria, the metal was probably secured through trade. The existence of these artworks provides evidence of powerful patrons who supported skilled artists and supplied the scarce and expensive metal. The naturalistic style, which has affinities with terra-cotta images from the earlier Nok culture in central Nigeria, distinguishes it from other African art. Scientific dating places Ife's terra-cotta works in the twelfth through fourteenth centuries, and the lost-wax figures in the fourteenth and fifteenth centuries.

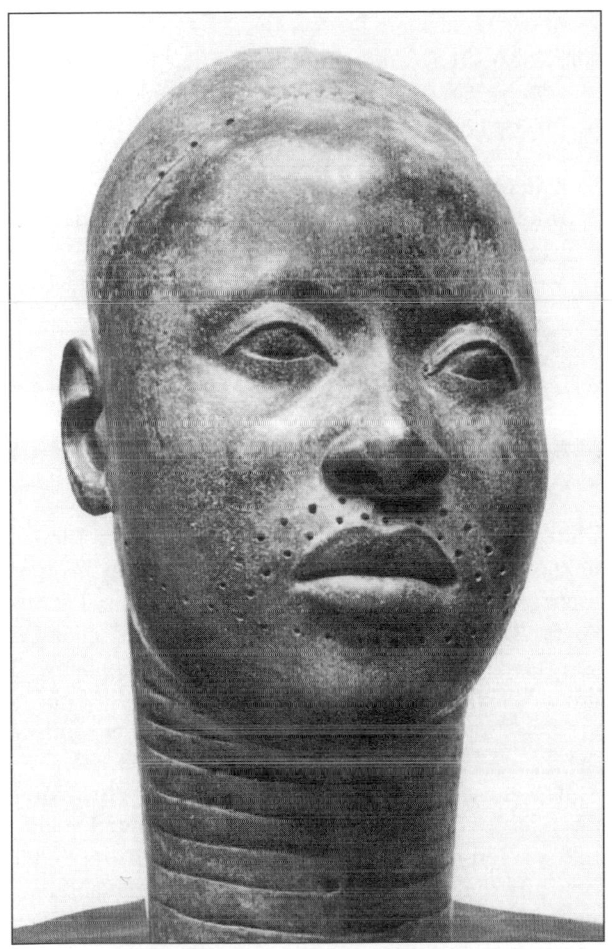

A bronze sculptured head of a Yoruba woman from Ife. (Leon Underwood, *Bronzes in West Africa*; London: Alec Tiranti, 1968)

According to traditions, the diffusion of kingship took place through the migration of royal family members from Ife. Each major city became the capital of a city-state ruled by a hereditary king, who functioned as a ruler-priest and who claimed ancestry from the deified Oduduwa. Dynastic links with Ife were critical in legitimizing claims of royalty. Lengthy king lists were recited to prove Ife origin of royal lineages, regalia from Ife were used in coronation rites, and deceased monarchs were sent to Ife for burial.

There have been several, although intermittent, archaeological studies to determine the size and scope of Ife. Although it has been suggested that the present town of Ife is not located at its original site, archaeological discoveries beneath its potsherd pavements have produced radiocarbon dates of the tenth and twelfth centuries. It is certain that the ancient town occupied a greater area than that of the present walled enclosure. Archaeologists have been impeded by dense forests, high annual rainfall, and the fact that Yoruba structures were built of mud from the site, which makes it difficult to distinguish between collapsed buildings or walls and the surrounding dirt.

Nevertheless, excavations have revealed older walls that extend beyond current structures. In addition, potsherd pavements have been discovered under the present town walls, indicating that these defenses were constructed after older structures related to the pavements were gone. Although evidence indicates that the city underwent periods of contraction, perhaps a consequence of war, Ife was a large urban center with a possible land area of 18.5 square miles (30 square kilometers).

Significance

The Yoruba developed highly nucleated villages and became the most urbanized African culture of the precolonial era. They centralized into individual city-states, each with its own capital ruled by a hereditary priest-king. Their economies were founded on commerce.

Ife was the earliest of the Yoruba city-states and the site from which many Yoruba cultural traits emerged. Located between the forest and savannah areas, it was well situated to become a major commercial center. According to tradition, the first Yoruba monarchy originated at Ife, along with the concept of hereditary rule. It was here that the renowned royal sculptures were created. By the second millennium, the Yoruba had developed a pantheon of gods and narratives, and although these took different forms, they centered on Ife—the purported site of earth's creation.

Ife tradition alleges that the city-states were linked in a spiritual and political confederation under the *oni*, who served as the senior representative of the descendants of Oduduwa. Other narratives indicate that their confederacy, if it existed at all, was a loose one. With sixteenth century military and commercial expansion of the northern city-state of Oyo and the neighboring kingdom of Benin, Ife declined. It lost commercial and political significance, but it retained the spiritual and cultural status of Ile-Ife—the homeland of Yoruba civilization.

—*Cassandra Lee Tellier*

FURTHER READING

Akinjogbin, I. A. *Milestones and Concepts in Yoruba History and Culture: A Key to Understanding Yoruba History*. Ibadan, Nigeria: Olu-Akin, 2002. Examines the history of the Yoruba people and culture. Maps, bibliography.

Davidson, Basil. *West Africa Before the Colonial Era: A History to 1850*. New York: Longman, 1998. An overview of early West African social, political, and economic history.

Falola, Toyin, ed. *Yoruba Historiography*. Madison: University of Wisconsin Press, 1991. This compilation of articles examines the issue of sources in exploring the history of Yoruba culture.

Johnson, Samuel. *The History of the Yorubas*. 1897. Reprint. London: Routledge and Kegan Paul, 1966. A traditional version of Yoruba precolonial history that has been a source of debate among historians.

Law, Robin. *The Oyo Empire, c. 1600-1936*. Brookfield, Vt.: Gregg Revivals, 1991. Although primarily concerned with Oyo, this book discusses the early history of the Yoruba and the role of Ife.

Smith, Robert S. *Kingdoms of the Yoruba*. Madison: University of Wisconsin Press, 1988. A survey of Yoruba precolonial history.

SEE ALSO: 10th-11th centuries: First Hausa State Established; 11th-15th centuries: Great Zimbabwe Urbanism and Architecture; 1400-1500: Foundation of the West African States of Benin.

11th-15th centuries
GREAT ZIMBABWE URBANISM AND ARCHITECTURE

Great Zimbabwe epitomizes the sophistication and skills of medieval African civilization. Located in the southern region of the nation of Zimbabwe, the Great Enclosure is one of many historic sites consisting of a series of walls, granaries, and fortifications built of granite blocks without mortar. The nation of Zimbabwe takes its name from this extraordinary place.

LOCALE: Zimbabwe, southern Africa
CATEGORIES: Architecture; engineering; government and politics; trade and commerce

SUMMARY OF EVENT

Crossing the Zambezi River in a southerly direction, people left the plains of eastern Africa shortly after 1000 to settle the great plateau of what is now called Zimbabwe. The exact cultural and linguistic origins of the settlers is unknown, though they most likely belonged to the great migration of Bantu-speaking peoples that spread across Africa. Descendants of these migrants formed a number of clans called Karanga, the forebears of Zimbabwe's dominant ethnic group, the Shona, who produced one of the most sophisticated, urbanized settlements south of the Sahara Desert during the medieval period.

The early settlers found many advantages to settling this plateau. First, it had a mild environment with plentiful rain, and much of the plateau region was free of the tsetse fly that spread serious illness to people and livestock. Fertile soils of the many tributaries to the Zambezi and Limpopo Rivers supported horticulture that supplied millet, sorghum, and cowpeas. The plateau is dotted with kopjes (Afrikaans term meaning hillocks). The

Karanga found the kopjes to be excellent places for settlement because they were pockmarked with caves and could be defended easily. Finally, the plateau is crossed, from north-northeast to south-southwest, by the longest linear volcanic extrusion in the world. More than 250 kinds of minerals, precious stones, and carving stones have been mined from the plateau since the time of the Karanga settlements. The Karanga depended on gold, copper, iron, and emeralds mined here. They also made good use of verdite, steatite (soapstone), malachite, and different forms of serpentine for the distinctive sculptural art now known around the world.

The Great Enclosure is one of many historic sites consisting of a series of walls, granaries, and fortifications built of granite blocks without mortar. (R. Kent Rasmussen)

During early settlement years, people made their homes and surrounding compounds from the heavy clays called *daga*, which became hard when baked in the sun. By the twelfth century, cattle herding, iron smelting, and trade in the abundant collected ivory increased wealth and led to social stratification, with royal families emerging as economic, political, and ritual centers of power.

Royals increasingly used slabs of granite, which were easily collected from the kopjes, to strengthen their compounds, provide more privacy from commoners, and symbolize their authority over trade and ritual. The granite breaks off through exfoliation (weathering) in slabs that are about 3 to 8 inches (7.5 to 20 centimeters) thick. Early in the thirteenth century, the slabs were collected and used without mortar. The slabs were leaned into each other with each layer slightly recessed in comparison to the successive layers below. This produced a balancing of weights that held the structure in place.

Some of the interior walls, the floors, and extensions to the granite walls were made of *daga*. Thus, spiraling strings of connected homes and compounds of relatives could extend for some distance from the central, and most important, home compound of the king. Farther out, in a longer ring, were the *dagas* of the commoners who supported the royal family. This settlement pattern produced unusually high concentrations of people at that time. Nearly three hundred such sites existed at the civilization's height in the late fifteenth century.

Many sites were later destroyed by warfare or colonial visitors, so only the remnants of 150 stone-wall complexes can be found throughout Zimbabwe today. In fact, the country takes its name (*zimbabwe*) from the old Shona words used to describe the stone houses. *Dzimba dza mabwe* in Shona literally means "house of stone" (plural *madzimbabwe*). Because the royal families were so powerful—controlling major rituals—and because they were buried in granite-encased graves, the term eventually took on the meanings of sacred house, ritual seat of a king, or both.

By the fourteenth century, a number of Karanga kings gained control of the gold and copper trade, but they did not do their own mining. Instead, they controlled the gold and copper trade across their territories and manipulated the trade in cattle relative to the trade in gold and copper. New trade with Swahili and Arab merchants from the coast brought Ming porcelain from China, stoneware from the Rhineland, Persian textiles, and fine glass beads from India. The extraordinary wealth derived from this new source of income resulted in the building of several massive *madzimbabwe* between the early fifteenth century and the late sixteenth century. They are located at Great Zimbabwe (near Masvingo), Khami (near Bulawayo), and Dhlodhlo (near Gweru). Great Zimbabwe and Khami became UNESCO World Heritage Sites in 1986.

Great Zimbabwe is the grandest and the first of the major granite enclosures to be built. More than one million blocks of dressed-granite masonry without mortar (which were chipped and trimmed to a desired size) are found here. This site alone most likely supported nearly twenty thousand people. It has three parts: the Acropolis, the Valley Enclosures, and the Great Enclosure. The Acropolis is atop the kopje that rises more than 260 feet (79 meters). A series of narrow and steep passageways in stone lead to enclosures with walls 16 feet (5 meters) thick and 25 feet (7.5 meters) high. They were decorated with turrets and monoliths. The Acropolis is the oldest section (three hundred years of continuous habitation) and was inhabited by the king and his family. It was the spiritual center of the Great Zimbabwe civilization and had the main ritual enclosures.

The Valley Enclosures are a series of concentric walls that connected the *daga* huts of important people close to the king and his family. Here, carved steatite birds similar in style to the chevron were uncovered. This is now the symbol of the Zimbabwe nation and found on the flag and the state seal.

The Great Enclosure is the largest single ancient structure in sub-Saharan Africa. Its circumference is 820 feet (250 meters) and its length is 290 feet (88.5 meters) (about the size of a football field) with walls 36 feet (11 meters) high and 16 feet (5 meters) thick. It has another interior wall with a passageway and a number of stone structures decorated with courses, or layers, of chevron and herringbone designs. The most famous interior structure is the conical tower. The tower is 16 feet (5 meters) in diameter at the base and tapers to about 7 feet (2 meters) in diameter at the top. It is 33 feet (10 meters) high and probably was a symbolic structure. Some archaeologists believe that it was an initiation and ritual center.

Great Zimbabwe was the seat of the first formal state to emerge in southern Africa. By the middle of the fifteenth century, another clan, near what is now called Bulawayo (western region), led by Mwene Mutapa, became strong and took over Great Zimbabwe and lands reaching to the Zambezi River and well into what is now western Mozambique.

SIGNIFICANCE

The Great Zimbabwe site, and the wide distribution of several hundred sites related to it throughout the country of Zimbabwe and just across its borders into Mozambique, Botswana, and northern South Africa, had made a significant cultural impact.

First, it is invaluable as a source regarding precolonial African societies. Stone is among the most durable of building materials, thus preserving for posterity the skill, sophistication, and beauty of the legacy of the Shona people. This legacy is evident in the name Zimbabwe and in the pride many Zimbabweans have in their ancestral culture. Second, it is an outstanding example of early engineering skills. Third, it is a clear indication that eastern and southern Africa affected and was influenced by trade with cultures as far away as China, India, Persia, and central Europe. This evidence belies the assumption colonial Europeans had of the African interior: that it was a land without civilizations and cultures. This erroneous assumption was used to justify European expansion in Africa in the late nineteenth and early twentieth centuries.

Finally, it clearly and definitively challenges colonial European assumptions about the intelligence and capabilities of indigenous peoples in general and African people in particular.

—Carolyn V. Prorok

FURTHER READING

Bahn, Paul G., ed. *Lost Cities*. New York: Barnes and Noble Books, 1997. Considers Great Zimbabwe within the context of other great world cities and sites that no longer exist. Illustrations, maps, bibliography, index.

Beach, D. *The Shona and Their Neighbours*. Oxford, England: Blackwell, 1994. This is an overview of Zimbabwe's dominant ethnic group and its historical impact on its neighbors in southern Africa.

Elleh, Nnamdi. *African Architecture: Evolution and Transformation*. New York: McGraw-Hill, 1996. Presents an overview of African architecture from antiquity through the twentieth century. Looks at Zimbabwean architecture, architectural heritage, urbanization in Africa, and laying a foundation for the history of African architecture. Illustrations, maps, bibliography, index.

Garlake, Peter. *Early Art and Architecture of Africa*. New York: Oxford University Press, 2002. Provides a chapter on Great Zimbabwe and the southern African interior. Includes a time line, illustrations, maps, a list of sources for further study, a bibliography, and index.

Herbert, E. W. *Iron, Gender, and Power: Rituals of Transformation in African Societies*. Bloomington: Indiana University Press, 1994. The author illustrates the relationship between new technologies and their impact on changing social and religious life in the African context. Zimbabwe's medieval period is highlighted.

Huffman, T. N. *Snakes and Crocodiles: Power and Symbolism in Ancient Zimbabwe*. Johannesburg, South Africa: Witwatersrand University Press, 1996. The central role of religious belief, ritual, and symbolism is put forth as the basis for the flowering of the Karanga kings, their culture, and achievements.

McIntosh, Roderick J. "Riddle of Great Zimbabwe." *Archaeology* 51, no. 4 (1998). Discusses the continuing scholarly debates about the origins of and motivations for building Great Zimbabwe.

Scarre, Chris, ed. *The Seventy Wonders of the Ancient World: The Great Monuments and How They Were Built*. London: Thames and Hudson, 1999. Discusses Great Zimbabwe and its architecture as ancient world marvels. Illustrations, some in color, bibliography, index.

SEE ALSO: 9th-14th centuries: Rise of the Toutswe Kingdom; c. 1075-1220: Emergence of Mapungubwe; 12th century: Trading Center of Kilwa Kisiwani Is Founded.

After 1000
DEVELOPMENT OF MIRACLE AND MYSTERY PLAYS

Miracle and mystery plays developed in France and England as the Catholic Church began to dramatize Mass, signaling a radical intellectual and creative break with the artistic styles of the ancient world and marking the start of the secularization of religious drama.

LOCALE: France and England
CATEGORIES: Literature; religion; cultural and intellectual history

KEY FIGURES

Jean Bodel (c. 1167-1210), French playwright
Adam de la Halle (c. 1250-c. 1285-1288), French composer

SUMMARY OF EVENT

The medieval mind brought about an almost complete break with ancient music, architecture, and poetry, and the same thing happened with drama. The germ of medieval and modern drama appeared first in the so-called liturgical drama, and it developed later in the miracle and the mystery plays.

Toward the end of the tenth century, or possibly as early as the ninth century at Saint Gall, the Catholic Church began to dramatize certain portions of the Latin Mass, especially at the major festivals. At Easter, the appearance of the risen Christ to the three Marys was so obvious a theme that the first two words of the Latin text, *Quem quaeritis?* (whom do you seek?), are used to refer to this embryonic liturgical play.

Technically, the term "miracle play" refers to those plays that dramatized the lives of saints (or those in which miracles were performed), while the term "mystery play" is used to designate plays derived from the Scriptures as opposed to those dealing with saints' lives. Miracle plays were originally associated with the celebration of saints' feast days and with religious processions (such as the Corpus Christi festival) and were performed in Latin as part of the liturgical services. Later, these plays were expanded, performed in the vernacular, and moved into the streets. Trade guilds were often responsible for the performance of a particular play, so that in time a series of performances by various guilds would create a cycle of plays.

It was inevitable that gradual secularization ensued. At first, only the clergy took part, using the Latin text inside the church building. In the second stage of development, the site of the drama was moved to the church porch or the steps of the cathedral, and laypeople began to participate, as in the twelfth century *Mystère d'Adam* (play of Adam). According to scholar

L. Cazamian, the *Mystère d'Adam* is the oldest extant *jeu* (a comedic play), in this case written in the dialect used in Normandy and southern England at that period. Its interesting and detailed stage directions indicate that it was performed outdoors. Even at this early date, lighthearted elements appear in the diverting dialogue between Eve and Satan, and in the gusto with which devils drag Adam and Eve, as well as Cain, into everlasting torment. The transition from the staging of liturgical drama to the development of short, vivid, amusing pieces outside church buildings suggests that comedy played a significant role in the transition from sacred to secular drama.

Another theory about the rise of comedy suggests that the element of humor emerged from the characterization of the devil. His grotesque costume and appearance could easily have led to the comic, and when he was constantly being outwitted, he gave the impression of stupidity. Already in the *Mystère d'Adam*, the demons provide gusto in their pantomime of selling the forbidden fruit to their victims, gleefully awaiting their opportunity to drag them off into hell. On the other hand, comedy may have been no more than the outcome of a natural tendency to introduce the commonplace, such as the appearance in early liturgical drama of the extraneous merchant selling oil to the three Marys. The commonplace easily leads to the grotesque and hence to the comic. Such scenes as the raving of Herod may have been introduced as comic relief to arouse the flagging interest of the audience. Comedy was entrenched by 1170 when the Abbess of Hohenburg denounced scenes of buffoonery even in Nativity plays.

By the thirteenth century, comedies had become sophisticated. Mansion staging—with both fixed and movable stages—was used in England and France, but more important were the settings. They were suggestive and stylized, never photographic, so that each scene in a typical mystery play had certain visible symbols that recurred over and over again: the trees in the Garden of Eden, Noah's ark, the hill where the shepherds watched over their flocks at the time of the Nativity, the Temple for the Presentation of Christ to Simeon, Herod's throne, clouds and stars suggesting Heaven from which angels descended, and the yawning chasm of Hell surrounded by grisly teeth and belching forth smoke and fireworks. The acting area remained static while these booths or mansions were mobile. They varied in size, but they could be set up behind or around the acting area, or brought to it on carts, or covered by curtains when not in use.

In a third development, the marketplace was used as a site completely detached from church buildings, as in *Le Jeu de Saint-Nicolas* (1932; *Play of Saint Nicholas of Jean Bodel*, pr. c. 1200), written by Jean Bodel of Arras.

The structure of the play itself also became more complex. Even when the *Quem quaeritis?* form was still being staged in church, the addition of dialogue between the Marys and the angel, of Peter and John to the cast, and a role for the risen Christ reflected new layers of development. The cathedral of Rouen kept a simple version of the play into the thirteenth century, but most Easter plays became more sophisticated. At Tours and other cathedrals, extra scenes were added, and an attempt was made to incorporate the Easter sequence, the hymn *Victimae Paschali*, into the dramatic action by

STAGE DIRECTIONS FOR *MYSTÈRE D'ADAM*

Let Paradise be set up in a somewhat lofty place; let there be put about it curtains and silken hangings, at such an height that those persons who shall be in Paradise can be seen from the shoulders upward; let there be planted sweet-smelling flowers and foliage; let divers trees be therein, and fruits hanging upon them, so that it may seem a most delectable place.

Then let the Savior come, clothed in a dalmatic [a wide-sleeved overgarment worn by deacons], and let Adam and Eve be set before him. Let Adam be clothed in a red tunic; Eve, however, in a woman's garment of white, and a white silken wimple . . . and in uttering the verses, let them neither add a syllable nor take away, but let them pronounce all clearly. . . . Whoever shall speak the name of Paradise, let him look back at it and point it out with his hand. . . .

Then shall the Devil come, and three or four other devils with him, bearing in their hands chains and iron shackles, which they shall place on the necks of Adam and Eve. And certain ones shall push them on, others shall drag them toward Hell [Hellmouth, a structure on stage]; other devils, however, shall be close beside Hell, waiting for them as they come . . . and they shall take them up and thrust them into Hell; and thereupon they shall cause a great smoke to arise, and they shall shout one to another in Hell, greatly rejoicing; and they shall dash together their pots and kettles, so that they may be heard without. And after some little interval, the devils shall go forth, and shall run to and fro in the square. . . .

Source: A. M. Nagler, *A Source Book in Theatrical History* (New York: Dover Publications, 1952), p. 45.

An audience England (c. 1953) watches the performance of a mystery play as it might have been staged in the twelfth or thirteenth century. (Hulton|Archive by Getty Images)

mentioning the napkin found in the tomb and introducing additional dialogue between Mary Magdalene and the angel. Soon other characters appeared, such as a merchant selling spices to the women, Thomas meeting two of the Apostles, and even Christ himself appearing eight days after the Resurrection. The singing of *Victimae Paschali* and *Te Deum Laudamus* provided a fitting conclusion to the proceedings.

The so-called miracle play is generally thought of as a delimited type based on the lives of saints and their miraculous intervention on earth. The life story of the Virgin Mary or of some saint with local claims to honor would be staged in a city as a token of gratitude or as a bid for favor. Typical is the thirteenth century play by Bodel depicting the effectiveness of Saint Nicholas in forcing some robbers to return the treasure they had stolen from a Saracen king and the resulting conversion of the Saracen host. The work breathes the genial and humorous spirit of youthful medieval scholars who produced these *jeux* and who chose Nicholas as their patron saint. Plays about Saint Catherine were also popular. A later work, *Le Miracle de Théophile* (pr. c. 1260; *Théophilus*, 1971), written by Rutebeuf in the thirteenth century, treats the popular legend of Théophilus, an ambitious priest who loses his job as financial administrator to a bishop, sells himself to the devil, later repents, and finally through the intercession of the Virgin Mary regains the original contract signed in his own blood.

Miracles de Notre-Dame (miracles of Our Lady), partly compiled by Gautier de Coincy and preserved in a French text of the fourteenth century, are considered the best examples of this form. Forty-two sketches do not distinguish between matters of faith and religious imagination. Mary, for instance, can save a woman from burning or bring about the conversion of King Clovis from paganism to Christianity. Such miracle plays must have been welcome diversions during the horrors of the Hundred Years' War.

This form of entertainment was indicted by the Parlement of Paris in November, 1548, largely because of objections by Protestants to the comic or licentious material mixed in with biblical texts. The German *Passion Play* of Oberammergau is an amazing survival of the form.

The thirteenth century *Play of Daniel* from Beauvais in northern France has again become popular. Its use of a curious mixture of French and Latin when Daniel is summoned to the court of Belshazzar, followed by a refrain in French, shows the manner in which the vernacular invaded the mystery play at that period. The vernacular predominated after 1300.

The first *opéra-comique*, or opera with spoken dialogue, was written in the mid-thirteenth century by Adam de la Halle and entitled *Le Jeu de Robin et de Marion* (pr. c. 1283; *The Play of Robin and Marion*, 1928), a charming reminder that a poet could then compose both the music and the words of a play.

SIGNIFICANCE

Despite their success, and most likely because of their secularization, miracle and mystery plays began to lose their social significance and popularity at the end of the fifteenth century and during the Reformation. It has been argued that successive Protestant governments between 1535 and 1575 resorted to ridicule, censorship, threats, and ultimately to direct prohibition in an effort to suppress the plays. Every performance represented Catholic dogma as a living, vital force, and such propaganda could not be ignored by governments struggling with the political consequences of the breach with Rome. It was inevitable that the Crown should ultimately suppress the plays.

—*Robert Jaques*

FURTHER READING

Cazamian, L. *A History of French Literature*. Oxford, England: Clarendon Press, 1955. An introduction to the development of plays in the Middle Ages.

Chambers, Sir Edmund K. "Medieval Drama." In *English Literature at the Close of the Middle Ages*. Oxford, England: Clarendon Press, 1945. An excellent introduction to the plays and the problems that surrounded them.

Craig, H. *English Religious Drama in the Middle Ages*. Oxford, England: Clarendon Press, 1955. A general expression of traditional views.

Fries, Maureen. "The Evolution of Eve in Medieval French and English Religious Drama." *Studies in Philology* 99, no. 1 (Winter, 2002): 1-16. Looks at the differing depictions in France and England of Eve as both woman and prophet, arguing "that one must almost speak of a French Eve and English Eve."

Holmes, Urban T., Jr. *A History of Old French Literature*. New York: Russell and Russell, 1962. A scholarly work that provides detailed information on various miracle and mystery plays in French.

Normington, Katie. "Giving Voice to Women: Teaching Feminist Approaches to the Mystery Plays." *College Literature* 28, no. 2 (Spring, 2001): 130-155. Although primarily focused on the teaching of women's roles in mystery and miracle plays, this article offers suggestions for overcoming problems finding resources and discusses the biased research about the lives of women in the world of mystery plays and in the Middle Ages.

Salter, Frederick M. *Medieval Drama in Chester*. Toronto: University of Toronto Press, 1955. A description of how medieval plays were presented at Chester.

Walker, Greg, ed. *Medieval Drama: An Anthology*. Malden, Mass.: Blackwell, 2000. A collection of essays surveying the history of dramatic works in England in the Middle Ages. Includes illustrations and maps.

Warning, Rainer. *The Ambivalences of Medieval Religious Drama*. Translated by Steven Rendall. Stanford, Calif.: Stanford University Press, 2001. A look at German mystery and miracles plays of the Middle Ages.

Wickham, Glynne W. *Early English Stages, 1300-1660*. Vol. 1. London: Routledge and Kegan Paul, 1959. Vol. 2. New York: Columbia University Press, 1963. This study is based on the author's work as a producer of plays, and he challenges favorite assumptions about medieval drama.

Young, Karl. *The Drama of the Medieval Church*. 2 vols. Oxford, England: Clarendon Press, 1933. A standard work on the development of liturgical drama.

SEE ALSO: 496: Baptism of Clovis; c. 1100: Rise of Courtly Love; 1337-1453: Hundred Years' War.

RELATED ARTICLES in *Great Lives from History: The Middle Ages, 477-1453*: Adam de la Halle; Clovis; Guillaume de Machaut.

c. 1001
SEI SHŌNAGON COMPLETES *THE PILLOW BOOK*

Sei Shōnagon, a lady-in-waiting to the Japanese empress Sadako, finished The Pillow Book, *a collection of anecdotes, lists, and assorted writings that is one of the best sources of information concerning the court society of the tenth century and is considered an influential landmark in the history of Japanese literature.*

LOCALE: Heian-kyō (modern Kyoto), Japan
CATEGORIES: Literature; cultural and intellectual history

KEY FIGURES

Sei Shōnagon (966 or 967-1013?), Japanese lady-in-waiting and writer
Kiyohara Motosuke (fl. tenth century), Japanese provincial official
Murasaki Shikibu (c. 978-c. 1030), Japanese lady-in-waiting and writer

SUMMARY OF EVENT

The details of the life of Sei Shōnagon are not well known to scholars. Even the date of her birth is conjecture. It is know that she was a daughter of Kiyohara Motosuke, a provincial official, and that she served as a lady-in-waiting to the Japanese empress Sadako in the 990's for nearly a decade. Some scholars have made the argument that she was married to a government official and even gave birth to a son, but this aspect of her life remains unclear. So scant are details concerning her life that even her name is unknown. *Shōnagon* ("minor councillor") is a reference to her position at court and *Sei* to the Kiyohara family.

Although the information about Sei Shōnagon's life is scant, of all the Japanese historical figures of her day, it is she whose thought and opinions concerning daily life are most intimately known. This is because of the character of her major literary work, *Makura no sōshi* (c. 994-c. 1001; *Pillow Book*, 1929; best known as *The Pillow Book of Sei Shōnagon*, 1967, or *The Pillow Book*). "Pillow book" was a common way to refer to any collection of random writings during the tenth and eleventh centuries; Sei Shōnagon probably did not give her work this title. Scholars believe that she started the work as a private endeavor and did not intend it to be read by an audience.

The work is a collection of essays, lists, anecdotes, random musings, poems, and descriptive passages with little connection to one another other than the whims of the author. *The Pillow Book* was probably written over a ten-year period while Sei Shōnagon served as the lady-in-waiting to Empress Sadako. This position placed the young woman in the inner circle of court life at what was the height of classical Japanese society, and aside from its purely literary interest, *The Pillow Book* provides the best information available about the daily realities of Japanese court society at that time.

The Pillow Book is written entirely in Japanese. During the late tenth and early eleventh centuries, Japanese men typically wrote in Chinese, using Chinese characters, while Japanese women wrote almost exclusively in their native tongue, using *hiragana*, a syllabary derived from Chinese characters. The only Chinese terms that appear in *The Pillow Book* are place-names and personal titles. *The Pillow Book* is a part of a larger tradition of women's literature. Other works of this period, such as Murasaki Shikibu's *Genji monogatari* (c. 1004; *The Tale of Genji*, 1925-1933), considered to be the first true novel in world history, are notable as works of literature, but the beauty and simplicity of Sei Shōnagon's style have resulted in it being used as an example of the finest Japanese prose to this day.

The majority of *The Pillow Book* is devoted to short anecdotes or sketches. The subject matter is amazingly varied; Sei Shōnagon provides her impressions and observations of everyday life at the court as well as descriptions of nature. Many readers have described her attitude as arrogant or confrontational; certainly, she expresses her opinions freely and employs a sharp wit. She frequently disparages other members of the court's inner circle and makes no secrets of her prejudices. One of her most famous and controversial statements comes in her description of a number of commoners who have been brought to the area of the palace as carpenters. She suggests that they are almost akin to beasts and that watching them while they eat is almost frightening. This, no doubt, is one of the most direct examples of the aristocratic prejudice of the Japanese court that is available to modern readers. It is also an invaluable indication of just how removed Japanese court society was from the lives of the people at large.

Sei Shōnagon's scorn was not reserved for members of the lower classes. In another famous section, she made known her attitude concerning the bizarre emotions of men. The aspect of men's behavior that Sei Shōnagon found most mystifying was their ability to fall in love with women viewed by others as unattractive, even leaving more beautiful women for these plain women. Modern scholars have described the society of the Japanese court as having been obsessed with appearances, and many sections of *The Pillow Book* contain comments on inappropriate clothing or actions. Passages such as the ones described show Sei Shōnagon to have been a forceful woman who was not afraid to express any type of opinion in her work.

However, most of the pieces found in *The Pillow Book* are positive in nature, inspired by curiosity and aesthetic sense. For example, in the well-known opening passage of the work, Sei Shōnagon describes what time of day is most beautiful in each season, beginning with *Haru wa akebono* ("In spring it is the dawn that is most beautiful").

In addition to the anecdotes and sketches, *The Pillow Book* contains 164 lists. They range from collections of "Things That Should Be Short" and "Things That Should Be Large" to lists of "Poetic Subjects" and "Elegant Things." Although many of these lists are of aesthetically pleasing items, some of them are, if anything, less diplomatic than her anecdotes. Under the heading of "Things Without Merit," she lists an ugly person with a bad character. Her long list of "Hateful Things" includes fleas, mosquitos at night, elderly people warming their wrinkly hands over a brazier, loud drunken men, and visitors and men who behave badly, for example, "A man with whom one is having an affair keeps singing the praises of some woman he used to know. Even if it is a thing of the past, this can be very annoying."

In the end, there is little attempt to impose any type of order on these lists and anecdotes. In assessing the quality of literature of Sei Shōnagon's time, scholars have concluded that a disorganized, whimsical approach was considered to be a virtue by many. Lack of any complex agenda or thematic purpose in the work has made it accessible to consecutive generations of readers and has contributed to the enduring popularity of the work.

Shortly after she finished writing the main body of *The Pillow Book*, Sei Shōnagon's tenure at court ended. Although it is clear that much of *The Pillow Book* was written while at court, scholars believe that parts of it were based on her memories and were set down during her later life. What is known, however, was that the book was read by many Japanese nobles during Sei Shōnagon's own lifetime. However, it is known that not all the members of the imperial court appreciated Sei Shōnagon's candor and whimsical style. Murasaki Shikibu, Sei Shōnagon's famous contemporary and the author of *The Tale of Genji*, wrote in her diary that Sei Shōnagon had the most extraordinary air of self-satisfaction and that her writings were presumptuous and flawed. She also worried about Sei Shōnagon's future, saying that her trivial writings would no doubt cause her to fall from favor.

SIGNIFICANCE

The details of Sei Shōnagon's later life are not known to scholars. Traditions tell of her dying lonely and in poverty, but many scholars consider this to be an invention. In any case, accurate information does not exist concerning the date or circumstances of her death. What is well known, however, is the influence of her work, both during her own lifetime and in later periods of Japanese history. Sei Shōnagon's *The Pillow Book* inspired a genre of Japanese writings known as *zuihitsu* (assorted or random writings). Later works such as Yoshida Kenko's *Tsurezuregusa* (c. 1330; *Essays in Idleness*, 1967) are a part of this same tradition. *Zuihitsu*, many of which share Sei Shōnagon's desire to capture the essence of everyday life and lack of concern with structure, remain a popular part of the Japanese publishing industry.

The Pillow Book itself has enjoyed enduring popularity. It continued to be circulated in court circles after Sei Shōnagon's death. Hand-copied versions were popular during the middle ages, and it was first printed and widely distributed in the seventeenth century. In modern times, *The Pillow Book* is looked to by authors, scholars, and average readers alike for insight into the everyday happenings and aesthetic insights of the classical Japanese court society as well as for the beauty of its prose and the fascinating character of its author. In this regard, it has remained not only an important historical source but also an acknowledged literary classic.

—*Matthew Penney*

FURTHER READING

Keene, Donald. *Seeds in the Heart*. New York: Columbia University Press, 1999. The first volume of Donald Keene's history of Japanese literature, which deals both with *The Pillow Book* and the literary climate of Sei Shōnagon's lifetime.

Mulhern, Chieko I., ed. *Japanese Women Writers: A Biocritical Sourcebook*. Westport, Conn.: Greenwood Press, 1994. Contains information about Sei Shōnagon and her contribution to the Japanese literary tradition. It also makes reference to other important authors of her time and provides valuable contextual information.

Murasaki Shikibu. *The Diary of Lady Murasaki*. Translated by Richard Bowring. London: Penguin, 1999. Provides insight into the lives of ladies in waiting in the Heian court and gives a context in which to understand Sei Shōnagon.

Okada, Richard. *Figures of Resistance: Language, Poetry, and Narrating in "The Tale of the Genji" and Other Mid-Heian Texts*. Durham, N.C.: Duke University Press, 1991. Focuses on the importance of literature in the lives of women during the time of Sei Shōnagon. It provides valuable background concerning the literature of the period and the daily character of the lives of the authors themselves.

Sansom, George. *A History of Japan to 1334*. Vol. 1. Stanford, Calif.: Stanford University Press, 1958. The first volume of Sansom's three-volume study of Japanese history remains a detailed and authoritative work on the subject.

Sei Shōnagon, *The Pillow Book of Sei Shōnagon*. Translated by Ivan Morris. 1967. Reprint. New York: Columbia University, 1991. A beautiful and authoritative translation of *The Pillow Book* by a famous scholar of Japanese literature, Ivan Morris.

SEE ALSO: March 9, 712, and July 1, 720: Writing of *Kojiki* and *Nihon Shoki*; 794-1185: Heian Period; c. 800: *Kana* Syllabary Is Developed; c. 1004: Murasaki Shikibu Writes *The Tale of Genji*.

RELATED ARTICLES in *Great Lives from History: The Middle Ages, 477-1453*: Murasaki Shikibu; Nijō; Sei Shōnagon.

c. 1004
MURASAKI SHIKIBU WRITES *THE TALE OF GENJI*

Written at the height of the Heian period by Murasaki Shikibu, The Tale of Genji *was the first novel ever written.*

LOCALE: Heian-kyō (now Kyoto), Japan
CATEGORIES: Literature; cultural and intellectual history

KEY FIGURES

Murasaki Shikibu (c. 978-c.1030), Japanese writer and lady-in-waiting to princess Shōshi
Fujiwara Akiko (Shōshi; fl. tenth century), princess at the Imperial Palace in Heian-Kyō

SUMMARY OF EVENT

Murasaki Shikibu was a member of the politically powerful Fujiwara family, famous in the tenth and eleventh centuries in Japan, although her particular branch of the family did not enjoy the power held by those in the upper echelon of the clan. She was the daughter of Fujiwara Tametoki, a scholar of Chinese. Although 978 is usually given as the year of her birth, she could have been born as early as 973. She had an elder sister and a younger brother, Nobunori; her mother died the same year in which her brother was born, possibly in childbirth.

Her given name is not known. *Murasaki*, which means "purple," was the name of a heroine in her novel; this may be why her contemporaries called her Murasaki. *Shikibu* is composed of two Japanese characters, *shiki,* signifying the imposition of something of a ceremonial nature, and *bu*, indicating a class or division. Thus, *shikibu* is not actually a name. There is some evidence that she was also known as Tō no Shikibu; *tō* is another reading of the character *fuji*, part of the family name Fujiwara.

Although her family may have lacked political power, Murasaki Shikibu came from a line of well-known literary figures: Her great-grandfather and her grandfather were noted poets, her father was best known as a great scholar and writer of Chinese poetry, and her elder brother was also a recognized poet. In her diary *Murasaki Shikibu nikki* (eleventh century; *Murasaki Shikibu: Her Diary and Poetic Memoirs*, 1982), Murasaki Shikibu mentions that, although women were not expected to be literate in Chinese, her father allowed her to learn to read, but she often feigned ignorance so as to not be disliked by those around her. She enjoyed advantages beyond those afforded many of her acquaintances and friends at court in that she often accompanied her father when he traveled to Senshu no Tomai and Echizen. In 999, Murasaki Shikibu married Fujiwara Nobutaka, a man twenty-five years her senior, who served as secretary to the emperor. The marriage was apparently a happy one. Her husband died in 1001, the year after a daughter was born.

Murasaki Shikibu entered the service of Fujiwara Akiko in 1007 when she was about thirty years old and apparently remained at court for the rest of her life.

> **THE DEATH OF LADY MURASAKI**
>
> Once before it had seemed that she was dying, and Genji hoped that whatever evil spirit it was might be persuaded to loosen its grip once more. All through the night he did everything that could possibly be done, but in vain. Just as light was coming she faded away. Some kind of power alone, he thought, had kept the empress with her through the night. He might tell himself, as might all the others who had been with her, that these things have always happened and will continue to happen, but there are times when the natural order of things is unacceptable. . . .
>
> "It seems to be the end," said Genji, summoning [his son Yūgiri] to Murasaki's curtains. ". . . We did not do a great deal for her in this life, but perhaps the Blessed One can be persuaded to turn a little light on the way she must take into the next. Tell them, please, that I want someone to give the tonsure. There is still someone with us who can do it, surely?"
>
> He spoke with studied calm, but his face was drawn and he was weeping.
>
> *Source:* Murasaki Shikibu, *The Tale of Genji*, translated by Edward G. Seidensticker (New York: Alfred A. Knopf, 1976), pp. 717-721.

Whether Murasaki Shikibu wrote the earliest parts of *Genji monogatari* (c. 1004; *The Tale of Genji*, 1925-1933) away from court and completed it after she began her court service is not clear. Whatever the case, the author had direct personal experience with what went on at court and used that experience to provide scrupulously accurate scenes in the novel.

The Tale of Genji is set in a period about one century earlier than the time in which Murasaki Shikibu is writing, during the Heian period, from 794, when the site of the capital was moved to Heian-kyō, to 1185, when the Taira family was defeated by the Minamoto clan. The author's deliberate vagueness is evident in the opening words of Arthur Waley's translation of the novel: "At the Court of an Emperor (he lived it matters not when)."

The story follows the life of the idealized Prince Genji, sometimes called "the shining prince," from his birth to his death, but then continues with accounts of his descendants, covering seventy-five years. Western scholars have attempted to break down the fifty-four chapters into logical divisions, and doing so is helpful for the Western reader, but it is very doubtful that Murasaki Shikibu herself did so; she followed no model and invented her structure as she went along, drawing from her personal experience as a lady-in-waiting at court.

With that disclaimer, one possible breakdown would postulate five parts. Part 1 consists of chapters 2 through 11 (chapter 1 was added later to serve as an introduction), which cover the birth of Genji and follow his growth and his amorous escapades with various women to his adolescence and young adulthood at age twenty-six. When Genji is twelve, he participates in a coming-of-age ceremony and is married off soon thereafter to Aoi, the daughter of one of the ministers. Older than he and overbearing, Aoi disappoints Genji. She produces a son, Yūguri, but dies soon afterward. He meets young Murasaki, whom he truly loves, and formalizes their relationship; marriages to concubines were the norm. Life becomes more and more difficult for Genji, and he is finally exiled to Suma.

Part 2 follows Genji's exile at age twenty-six and his return to the capital about two years later. Once restored at court, Genji is promoted and continues to rise in status. He puts a daughter by the Lady Akashi in the care of his wife, Murasaki. Genji's son Yūgiri is now of age (twelve) and enters court, but Genji elects not to confer rank on him until he has completed his university work.

Part 3, covering Genji's life from about age thirty-four to thirty-eight, focuses in particular on Tamakazura, whom many think is Genji's daughter, but who is actually the daughter of Tō no Chūjō, Genji's principal friend and often rival in things amorous and artistic.

Part 4 (chapters 32-41) may be thought of as Genji's gradual decline. Now thirty-nine, Genji has numerous wives and children, and many of the adults in the novel are aging and dying. Genji's son Yūgiri has numerous children. Murasaki has been begging permission of Genji to become a nun, but he has refused. Her health declines, and when Genji is fifty-one, she suddenly dies. Genji is so grief-stricken that he cannot take charge of her funeral arrangements and must depend on his son Yūgiri to do so. After the customary year of mourning, he plans to renounce the world and take holy orders, but near the end of his fifty-second year, he dies.

The final sections of *The Tale of Genji* move to the third generation after noting that "Genji was dead, and there was no one to take his place" (Arthur Waley's translation). Prince Genji's son Yūgiri takes over one of Genji's principal residences, but the story focuses on Niou and Kaoru, two young men who are under pressure to marry. In at least one instance, the young men become friendly rivals in pursuit of the same woman, Ukifuni. She first encourages Niou but realizes later that Kaoru is of greater worth and renounces the world to become a nun. As the long novel ends, Kaoru tries to visit Ukifuni but is allowed only to send in a note.

SIGNIFICANCE

The product of an aristocratic culture in eleventh century Japan, *The Tale of Genji* is credited with being the greatest achievement of Japanese literature. Chinese forms and ideas had dominated Japanese writing for a long time, but conditions were optimal for the emergence of an indigenous literature in Japan. *The Tale of Genji* is more than just a novel, however; it is seen by many Japanese scholars as an important resoure for information about the Heian period. Murasaki Shikibu's being in service at court was obviously one reason for her being able fo relate experiences that mirror that life, but her genius lay in her ability to observe keenly and report that life with meticulous accuracy.

Another reason for the novel's importance that Murasaki Shikibu is able to convey her theory of the novel through the character Genji. She believes that the art of the novel does not lie in just telling a story about someone, but rather, it happens because novelists have been so moved by their own experiences of the world and of people that they cannot bear to keep their experiences shut up and have them pass into oblivion.

The novel became the object of scholarly interest in the twelfth century, when Fujiwara Shunzei (1114-1204) and his son Fujiwara Teika (1162-1241) declared that it was a "scandal" that not all poets had read *The Tale of Genji*. From then on, it became essential reading. In the Tokugawa period (1603-1867), Motoori Norinaga (1730-1801) produced the first work that can truly be called literary criticism. He rejected the view that literature must be didactic and focused on the merits of *The Tale of Genji* as a masterpiece of literature.

For the Western world, except for a few scattered comments in the late nineteenth century, *The Tale of Genji* did not exist until the completion of Arthur Waley's translation in 1933. The novel's psychological insight and sophistication was considered a remarkable phenomenon.

—*Victoria Price*

FURTHER READING

Bowering, Richard. *Landmarks of World Literature: Murasaki Shikibu, "The Tale of Genji."* New York: Cambridge University Press, 1988. Includes a genealogical chart and discusses the novel and its cultural background. Examines the impact, influence, and reception of the novel.

Keene, Donald. *Seeds in the Heart*. New York: Columbia University Press, 1999. The first volume of Donald Keene's history of Japanese literature, this work discusses *The Tale of Genji* as well as many other works.

Morris, Ivan. *The World of the Shining Prince*. 1964. Reprint. New York: Kodansha International, 1994. Discusses court life in ancient Japan; helps the reader understand the world of Genji. This version contains a new introduction by Barbara Ruch.

Murasaki Shikibu. *The Diary of Lady Murasaki*. Translated by Richard Bowring. New York: Penguin, 1996. A good translation of Muraskai's other writings. Includes poetry, nonfiction, and a personal look into Lady Murasaki's life. Includes bibliographical references.

_______. *The Tale of Genji*. Translated by Edward G. Seidensticker. 1976. Reprint. New York: Knopf, 1992. In the second major English translation of *The Tale of Genji*, Seidensticker produced a translation that more closely reflected the original than did Arthur Waley's translation.

_______. *The Tale of Genji*. Translated by Royall Tyler. 2 vols. New York: Viking, 2001. A detailed yet poetic translation of the famous tale by a modern scholar.

_______. *The Tale of Genji by Lady Murasaki*. Translated by Arthur Waley. New York: Houghton Mifflin, 1925-1933. 6 vols. Waley's translation of *The Tale of Genji*, a relatively poetic, "free" translation, introduced the work to a Western audience.

Puette, William J. *"The Tale of Genji": A Reader's Guide*. Rutland, Vt.: Charles E. Tuttle, 1983. Provides a synopsis of each chapter of the novel, the cultural background, biographical data concerning Murasaki Shikibu, and a comparison of the English translations.

Waithe, Mary Ellen, ed. "Murasaki Shikibu." *A History of Women Philosophers: Medieval, Renaissance, and Enlightenment*. Vol. 2. Boston: Klewer Academic Press, 1989. Identifies *Genji Monogatari* as a work of philosophy written in the form of an epic novel. Argues that Murasaki Shikibu used the novel to trace the effects of eleventh century philosophies on Japanese society and to present her criticism of those philosophies.

SEE ALSO: 794-1185: Heian Period; c. 800: *Kana* Syllabary Is Developed; 858: Rise of the Fujiwara Family; c. 1001: Sei Shōnagon Completes *The Pillow Book*; c. 1360-1440: Kan'ami and Zeami Perfect Nō Drama.

RELATED ARTICLES in *Great Lives from History: The Middle Ages, 477-1453*: Fujiwara Michinaga; Murasaki Shikibu; Nijō; Sei Shōnagon; Zeami Motokiyo.

1009
DESTRUCTION OF THE CHURCH OF THE HOLY SEPULCHRE

The Church of the Holy Sepulchre was destroyed by Egyptian Shīʿite Fāṭimids but was later rebuilt by Byzantine emperors, inspiring the Christian conquest of the holy city of Jerusalem during the Crusades, which began in 1099.

LOCALE: Jerusalem
CATEGORIES: Architecture; religion; wars, uprisings, and civil unrest

KEY FIGURE
al-Ḥākim (985-1021), sixth caliph of the Egyptian Shīʿite Fāṭimid Dynasty, r. 996-1021

SUMMARY OF EVENT
The Holy Sepulchre is the tomb in which the body of Jesus Christ was laid after his death. No historical mention of the tomb is found until the early 300's, but converts to Christianity probably visited the Holy Sepulchre soon after the Resurrection and taught their children to venerate it.

Roman armies destroyed the city of Jerusalem in the year 70, and Christians who were in Jerusalem fled, but it was possible for them to go back in 73. No doubt there were many who knew the location of the tomb. In 135, however, Emperor Hadrian (r. 117-138) built a sanctuary of Venus (Aphrodite) at the site where the sepulchre of Christ had stood. Alexander of Jerusalem (d. 251) "visited the places for the investigation of the footsteps of Jesus and of His disciples," and by the beginning of the fourth century, the custom of visiting Jerusalem for the sake of information and devotion had become so frequent that third-fourth century scholar Eusebius wrote that Christians "flocked together from all parts of the earth." By the early 400's, two hundred hostels and monasteries had been built to accommodate pilgrims in and around Jerusalem.

According to legend, the emperor Constantine the Great (r. 306-337) sent his mother Helena to build a church on the spot. They looked for the cross of Christ but could not find it, so they decided to build on the place of the Passion and Resurrection. As they began to tear down the temple of Venus that had been built there, they found three crosses, a few nails, and Pilate's inscription. In 335, Constantine dedicated the new basilica, and it is on this site that the Church of the Holy Sepulchre now stands.

Within the basilica, the Holy Sepulchre was in the center of a rotunda 65 feet (20 meters) in diameter. It extended eastward from this to a distance of 250 feet (76 meters). An atrium and vestibule gave a total length of 475 feet (145 meters). Beyond this was a second open court, where the rock of Calvary stood in the open air, rising some 12 feet (3.7 meters) above the ground. The tomb that had been the sepulchre of Christ was enclosed by a round domed building that became known as the Anastasis because it commemorated the place of the Resurrection.

After the church was built, many Christians began to visit the Holy City. Along with Jerome and Rufinus, ascetic women from Rome, such as Paula and Melania, traveled to Jerusalem and searched out as many biblical sites as possible. Melania settled on the Mount of Olives while Paula and Jerome, along with a group of women who traveled with them, went to Bethlehem. Both established monasteries for men and women, built with money the women had inherited.

The Constantinian buildings were destroyed by fire in 614 during the Persian invasion under Khosrow II (r. 590-628); in 878, the Egyptian ʿŪlūnids annexed Palestine. In 935, a mosque was built on the site of the exterior atrium. This regime did not last long, however, because the Egyptians were soon conquered by the Fāṭimids. This administration ruled all of the lands around the Mediterranean Sea, including Egypt.

Although the Fāṭimids were generally tolerant, it was a descendant of this dynasty, al-Ḥākim, the sixth ruler (caliph) of the Egyptian Shīʿite Fāṭimid Dynasty, who came to power in Jerusalem. From 1004 until 1014, he went on a fiery rampage against churches in Syria and Palestine, burning and looting some thirty thousand before he finished. He built mosques on the roofs of those churches he did not burn. He was known for his cruelty and persecution of Christians, Jews, and even Sunni Muslims. He destroyed all dogs because their barking annoyed him, and he banned various kinds of shellfish and vegetables. It is said that al-Ḥākim took offense at the Holy Fire ceremony performed in the church annually at Easter. During famines, however, he distributed food and tried to stabilize prices. He also founded mosques and patronized scholars and poets. In 1017, he began to encourage the teachings of some Ismāʿīlī missionaries who held that he was the incarnation of the divinity.

Some authors note that the persecution only stopped when al-Ḥākim became convinced that he himself was divine. After this he changed completely and began to provide money for the rebuilding of churches and to allow those who had been forcibly converted to Islam to return to Christianity.

Al-Ḥākim is known for having initiated Druzism, which developed out of Ismāʿīlī teachings and which has thousands of devotees in southern Lebanon and the Syrian district of Hawrān. This is a relatively small Middle Eastern religious sect with a very close-knit identity. They call themselves *muwaḥḥidūn*, or monotheists. They permit no conversion, either away from or to their religion, and no intermarriage. Their religious system is kept secret from the outside world. Only an elite of initiates participate fully in their religious services and have access to the sacred teachings of the Druze religious doctrine. According to this doctrine, in times of persecution, a Druze is allowed to deny his or her faith outwardly if his or her life is in danger. Al-Ḥākim mysteriously vanished while taking a walk on the night of February 13, 1021, and it is believed by some Druze people that he will again return in triumph to inaugurate a golden age.

SIGNIFICANCE

After the devastation in 1009, very little can have remained of the tomb of Jesus. Al-Ḥākim's successors showed more tolerance. The Byzantine emperor Michael IV (r. 1034-1041) persuaded the Fāṭimid caliph in 1034 to allow the rebuilding of all the churches of the Holy Land. In 1048, Constantine IX Monomachus (r. 1042-1055) was able to reconstruct the cave in masonry, obliterating, however, the last trace of the natural state of the tomb.

An etching of the Church of the Holy Sepulchre in Jerusalem, based on an early twentieth century photograph. (Frederick Ungar Publishing Co.)

In 1099, the Crusaders found the basilica in ruins. They built a Romanesque church, which was consecrated on July 15, 1149. A rotunda at the western end rose over the Holy Sepulchre. They established Jerusalem as their capital, and the city prospered during the 1100's. Again, extensive building was undertaken, but Crusader occupation of Jerusalem meant persecution for local Muslims and Jews. The basilica built by the Crusaders was partially destroyed by fire in 1808, when the rotunda fell in on the sepulchre. A new church was built at the expense of Greeks and Armenians and was dedicated in 1810.

The modern church consists of two main sections: the chapel of Saint Helena with the cave of the Finding of the Holy Cross and the church proper with its many adjacent chapels. The sections are divided up among the Latins, the Greeks, the Armenians, the Syrians, and the Copts, but there are sections that are common to all. There are arguments as to whether the present church occupies the actual site of the original tomb. According to the Gospel, it was outside the walls of the city, whereas the present church is inside. Yet the walls have been in different places in different historical eras; it seems there is no archaeological evidence to suggest that any other site might be more accurate.

—*Winifred Whelan*

FURTHER READING

Biddle, Martin. *The Tomb of Christ*. Stroud, Gloucestershire, England: Sutton, 1999. A detailed, first-of-a-kind analysis by two archaeologists of the fragile tomb of Christ and its appearance, destructions, and rebuildings throughout its two-thousand-year history. A well-illustrated text with lengthy footnotes, a bibliography, and an index.

Biddle, Martin, et al. *The Church of the Holy Sepulchre*. New York: Rizzoli, 2000. A richly illustrated text on the church and its history, art, liturgy, and communities. Color photographs, maps, and bibliography.

Hawkins, Peter S. "Sacred Time Share: At the Church of the Holy Sepulchre." *Christian Century* 113 (January 3, 1996): 4-5. The author describes how the Church of the Holy Sepulchre was again restored under the joint direction of six churches.

Idinopulos, Thomas A. *Jerusalem Blessed, Jerusalem Cursed: Jews, Christians, and Muslims in the Holy City from David's Time to Our Own*. Chicago: I. R. Dee, 1991. A history of the city of Jerusalem. The fifth chapter, "God Wills It!" describes the particular era in which the Church of the Holy Sepulchre was destroyed by the Muslim rulers. Map, bibliography, index.

Kochav, Sarah. "The Search for a Protestant Holy Sepulchre: The Garden Tomb in Nineteenth Century Jerusalem." *Journal of Ecclesiastical History* 46 (April, 1995): 278-301. Protestants came too late to claim a stake in the Church of the Holy Sepulchre. In 1893, therefore, a committee of Englishmen bought an ancient tomb and called it the "Garden Tomb," the Protestant Holy Sepulchre.

Murphy-O'Connor, Jerome. *The Holy Land: An Oxford Archaeological Guide*. 4th rev. ed. New York: Oxford University Press, 2001. A guide for the general reader to the sites of the Holy Land. Illustrations, maps, index.

Powell, James M., ed. *Muslims Under Latin Rule, 1100-1300*. Princeton, N.J.: Princeton University Press, 1990. Shortly after the destruction of the Church of the Holy Sepulchre, the Crusaders entered Jerusalem and began to rebuild the city. This book explores the Muslim minorities and how they fared under Christian rule. Bibliography, index.

SEE ALSO: 685-691: Building of the Dome of the Rock; 969-1171: Reign of the Fāṭimids; August 26, 1071: Battle of Manzikert; November 27, 1095: Pope Urban II Calls the First Crusade; c. 1120: Order of the Knights Templar Is Founded; 1147-1149: Second Crusade; 1189-1192: Third Crusade.

RELATED ARTICLES in *Great Lives from History: The Middle Ages, 477-1453*: Saint Bernard of Clairvaux; Bohemond I; Melisende; Philip IV the Fair; Saladin; Tancred; Urban II.

1010
FIRDUSI COMPOSES THE *SHAHNAMAH*

Firdusi's long narrative poem and the national Iranian epic, the Shahnamah, *treats the legendary history of Persia from the beginning of the world to the overthrow of the Persian Empire by invading armies of Islam in the seventh century.*

LOCALE: Iran and parts of Iraq and Afghanistan
CATEGORIES: Cultural and intellectual history; historiography; literature

KEY FIGURE

Firdusi (between 923 and 941-between 1020 and 1025), Persian poet

SUMMARY OF EVENT

Firdusi was born to rich landowners (a class called *dihqan*) in a village near what is now Mashad, Iran. Though little is known of his early life, his financial independence allowed him to take up poetry as a lifelong pursuit. By the time he became interested in writing his epic, Arab influence had dominated Iran for two hundred years, having supplanted Persian rule and installing Islam as the official religion over Zoroastrianism. However, the force of Persian culture was still strong, especially when the capital of Islamic (and Arab) power was moved to Baghdad in the eighth century and the caliph himself was half Persian and was advised by a Persian minister of state.

Firdusi saw the time as ripe for both the preservation and glorification of the Persian heritage. Tales of battle and extraordinary heroism were already part of that heritage, much of it oral. Several written sources, now lost, were available to Firdusi as well. An unfinished poem by the Persian poet al-Daqīqī (d. c. 976-981), of about a thousand lines, had found its way into his hands, as well as a prose version of the history of Persian kings.

Drawing on these works, Firdusi began his own *Shahnamah* (the book of kings) in about 980. The work took him twenty-five to thirty years to complete, and is a massive, complex text of more than fifty thousand rhyming lines. Each is composed of twenty-two syllables, so that the comparable length of the poem in English is more than 100,000 lines. Its technical brilliance is unchallenged in Persian literature. The language is a purposely archaized version of Modern Persian. Although by Firdusi's time, Arabic words had significantly infiltrated the Persian vocabulary, the nationalistic intent of *Shahnamah* receives greater emphasis by the fact that hardly any Arabic loanwords or expressions are found in the work.

Tradition says that on its completion, Firdusi sent the poem to the Muslim sultan Maḥmūd of Ghazna (r. 997-1030). Perhaps for political reasons, Maḥmūd rewarded Firdusi with only one thousand units of gold, a sum the poet found insulting. He contemptuously gave it away as gratuities, and Maḥmūd angrily ordered Firdusi to be trampled by elephants. Firdusi fled and went into hiding. Months later, Maḥmūd relented and sent the poet his rightful sum, but before the money arrived, Firdusi had died.

In form and structure, the *Shahnamah* is a legendary history of Persia seen through the lives and conquests of its rulers, some fifty kings and queens—an episodic narrative poem more suggestive of medieval romance than classical Greek and Roman epics. Epics such as Homer's *Iliad* (c. 750 B.C.E.; English translation, 1611) or Vergil's *Aeneid* (c. 29-19 B.C.E.; English translation, 1553), for instance, typically began in media res, in the middle of things, relating the actions of its hero through a series of flashbacks, and then bringing the story back to the present. The *Shahnamah*, in contrast, begins with the creation of the world, and the action centers not just on an Achilles or an Aeneas but deals with scores of rulers and great individuals during a period of thirteen hundred years. In the epic, armor-clad warriors fight on horseback with shields and lances, much like the knights of medieval story and legend. Even their Persian designation as *pahlavans* evokes the image of English and French "paladins" of the Middle Ages and the pre-Renaissance courts. However, the main focus of the battles and other tales within the work is on the idea of the shah or king as the center, the source, of all significant human activity. The shah is the one constant historical reality, the benchmark of civilization, for better or for worse.

Even the wickedness of the villains comes from their roles as king or in their attempts to stay in power. In the famous tale of Rustam and Isfandiyār, for example, itself a self-contained story of more than sixteen hundred verses, Shah Goshtasp tricks his son Isfandiyār into fighting Rustam, knowing that Rustam is fated to kill Isfandiyār, thereby eliminating him from taking over Goshtasp's throne. Rustam is the quintessential Persian hero. A largely legendary warrior, he lived for more than nine hundred years and was pious, fearless and loyal. Despite his obviously mythical character, he takes on human complexity by his stubbornness and his fiery temper, like Roland in the French national epic *Chanson de Roland* (eleventh century; *Song of Roland*, 1880). Firdusi does not condone the wickedness or incompetence of a shah like Goshtasp. Despite the nationalistic ardor of the work, Firdusi is not writing propaganda, and he tells his stories with classic objectivity.

Although figures such as Rustam are invested with legendary and mythic qualities, they often are drawn with traits that make them legitimately tragic figures. In another tale, a version of which was composed by the English poet Matthew Arnold, Rustam fights and kills his son Sohrab, each unaware of the other's identity. Sohrab is young, impetuous, and proud; Rustam is old but unyielding and equally proud, as only an epic hero can be. Each pays the price for the flaw in his own character. The tragic elements in these stories gain universal significance not just in the portrayal of human strengths or weaknesses but in Firdusi's concept of justice. The tyranny of shahs like Goshtasp or the wickedness of rulers such as the last Sāsānian king, Yazdegerd III (r. 632-651), also called Yazdegerd the sinner, is not condoned or even judged by the poet. The shah as institution is a given, like earth, air, fire, and water. Implicit, however, in their conduct and subsequent fate is the Islamic view of history as divine judgment. God will eventually mete out his justice.

Textual evidence reveals that the tales and episodes of Firdusi's poem were not composed in the order in which they finally appear. One curious example of the work's diffusiveness is Firdusi's insertion late in the poem of an elegy to his dead son in which the poet insists that as an old man of sixty-five, he should have died before his son who was only thirty-seven. In spite of these occasional narrative intrusions, the poem maintains an intrinsic unity and cohesion. Fully two-thirds of the epic draw on ancient and legendary material. Some of the stories tell of events as early as 500 B.C.E. at the courts of Cyrus and King Darius III, whose reigns are depicted in the *Shahnamah* as Dara and Dārāb.

The opening section presents an account of the creation of the world "out of nothing" and quickly tells of the coming of the first shah, thereby establishing the primacy of the king as a seminal force in the shaping of the civilization that is about to emerge. The discovery of fire, for example, is said to have been made during the reign of Hūshang. Jamshīd, an early shah who has similarities to Yama, the Indian god of the Underworld, reigned for seven hundred years. These shahs are depicted as kinds of demiurges, humankind's ancestors, the shaping forces that prepare the way for humanity itself. In this respect, Firdusi's treatment of the primordial era is distinctly non-Islamic, a celebration of indigenous culture.

SIGNIFICANCE

In the final analysis, the *Shahnamah* is a celebration of Persian civilization by a brilliant melding of oral and folk traditions with the insight and grace of true poetry. It has woven and strenghtened a Persian and Iranian national consciousness, a consciousness that still holds in the twenty first century.

—*Edward Fiorelli*

FURTHER READING

Browne, Edward G. *A Literary History of Persia*. 4 vols. 1902-1924. Reprint. Cambridge, England: Cambridge University Press, 1964-1969. This is still the standard account of classical Persian literature, usefully woven into a historical narrative that places authors' lives and works in their contemporary setting. Volume 2 contains valuable information relating to Firdusi. Bibliography provided in volume 1.

Clinton, Jerome W., trans. *In the Dragon's Claws: The Story of Rostam and Esfandiyar from the Persian Book of Kings*. Washington, D.C.: Mage, 1999. The famous tale of Rustam and the shah's son rendered into English blank verse. Provides a concise introduction to the work, particularly the moral and ethical issues implicit in the tale.

Davidson, Olga. *Poet and Hero in the Persian Book of Kings*. Ithica, N.Y.: Cornell University Press, 1994. An important work focusing on Firdusi's use of the oral tradition.

Davis, Dick. *Epic and Sedition: The Case of Ferdowsi's "Shahnameh."* Washington, D.C.: Mage, 1994. A thoroughly researched exposition of the work and a study of its influence as a major literary monument.

_______. "The Problem of Ferdowsi's Sources." *Journal of the American Oriental Society* 116, no. 1 (January-March, 1996). Argues that Firdusi used mainly versified oral sources rather than written sources for his epic, and any written sources used most likely were in verse form that came from an oral tradition. Bibliographic footnotes.

Firdusi. *The Epic of the Kings: Shahnamah, the National Epic of Persia, by Ferdowsi*. Translated by Reuben Levy. Chicago: University of Chicago Press, 1967. Few translators have dared to tackle the *Shahnamah*, most of them in the nineteenth century. This volume contains the free-flowing prose translation of some of its most famous episodes.

Meisami, Julie Scott. *Persian Historiography to the End of the Twelfth Century.* Edinburgh: Edinburgh University Press, 1999. Explores the writing of Persian-Iranian history during Firdusi's time and discusses the *Shahnamah* as historical prose. Maps, bibliography, index.

Robinson, B. W. *The Persian Book of Kings: An Epitome of the Shahnama of Firdawsi.* London: Routledge-Curzon, 2002. A concise introduction to and summary of Firdusi's epic work. Illustrated with early Persian paintings depicting events and actions. Includes a list of kings addressed in the book, a bibliography, and an index.

SEE ALSO: August 15-20, 636: Battle of Yarmūk; 637-657: Islam Expands Throughout the Middle East; 834: Gypsies Expelled from Persia; 972: Building of al-Azhar Mosque; 1340: Al-ʿUmarī Writes a History of Africa; 997-1030: Reign of Maḥmūd of Ghazna; 1010: Firdusi Composes the *Shahnamah*.

RELATED ARTICLES in *Great Lives from History: The Middle Ages, 477-1453*: Jean Froissart; Hafiz; al-Jāḥiẓ; Maḥmūd of Ghazna; Omar Khayyám; Jalāl al-Dīn Rūmī; Saʿdi.

c. 1010
SONGHAI KINGDOM CONVERTS TO ISLAM

The kingdom of Songhai, with its strategically situated trading and manufacturing city of Gao on the Niger River, became the first West African kingdom to convert to Islam.

LOCALE: Songhai Empire of West Africa (now Mali), Niger River area, and Gao

CATEGORIES: Religion; trade and commerce

KEY FIGURES

Kossoi (fl. eleventh century), fifteenth *dia* (king), converted to Islam in 1010 by Muslim traders in Gao

Abū ʿUbayd ʿAbdallāh al-Bakrī (1040-1094), Andalusian geographer, informed Gao, Takrur, and Ghana about Islam

Sundiata (c. 1215-1255), Muslim founder and king of Mali, r. 1235-1255

Mansa Mūsā (c. 1280-1337), Muslim king of Mali, r. 1312-1337

Sonni ʿAlī (d. 1492), Muslim king of the empire of Gao, r. 1464-1492

Muḥammad I Askia (d. 1538), Muslim king of Mali, r. 1493-1528

SUMMARY OF EVENT

North African caravan routes that grew before the year 1000 were established as trade routes bringing goods to such commercial centers as Gao, Timbuktu, and Jenne in what is now Mali. These caravans, however, brought more than material goods to their destinations. They brought to these relatively isolated enclaves ideas, philosophies, and concepts that reflected happenings in the non-Muslim world and in the Islamic world of Tunisia, Arabia, Egypt, and Sudan.

Established caravan routes connected Gao with Tunisia via Ghadames and Air and connected with caravan routes that led to Tripoli to the north and Chad to the south. It was the tradespeople, largely nomadic Berbers, who, toward the end of the tenth century, introduced Islam into the thriving commercial and manufacturing city of Gao, whose inhabitants up to that point were largely believers in the animistic sects that were traditional in Africa and that concerned themselves with the *jinni* (mysterious creatures) and magic. People who followed these sects regarded their ancestors as sacred because they were thought to serve as intermediaries between living people and the unseen, mystical forces that controlled their destinies.

Gao enjoyed a favored location on the east bank of the Niger River just south of the Niger bend. Timbuktu was located some 150 miles (240 kilometers) to the northwest and Jenne was slightly farther to the southwest. Caravans reached Gao not only from the north but also from Arabia and Egypt via Sudan in the east. They brought with them such utilitarian items as horses, copper, weapons, cloth, as well as trinkets such as beads and bracelets. They traded these items for luxuries like gold, ivory, kola nuts and, later, ostrich feathers and leather. There was also a market in slaves from areas around Gao.

The rise of Gao, which became the official seat of the Songhai aristocracy, can be documented as early as the beginning of the ninth century. The historian Ibn Khaldūn noted that it was the birthplace of Abū Yazīd in 893.

By that time it was already a thriving trading center, sometimes referred to as Kawkaw, to which numerous Muslim traders, Arab and Berber, came to exchange their wares.

In 1010, the fifteenth *dia*, Kossoi, strongly influenced by Muslim traders, converted to Islam. The royal capital was moved from Koukya to Gao. The geographer Abū ʿUbayd Abdallāh al-Bakrī reported that when Kossoi officially became the ruler, he was called Kanda and adopted Islam as his official faith. The caliph (Muslim leader) of Baghdad provided the emblems of Kossoi's office by giving him a sword, a shield, and a copy of the Qurʾān, which established a strong official link between the ruler of Gao and Islam.

Kossoi, in accordance with the mandates of the Islamic faith, made his *hajj* (pilgrimage) to the holy city of Mecca. He recited faithfully the five daily prayers expected of Muslims, fasted during the month of Ramadan, and erected mosques in his empire. Not all of his kingdom, however, was Muslim, nor was he necessarily bent on converting those who had not accepted the faith, as was the king of Takrur, who made mandatory the conversion of his subjects to Islam.

During this transitional period, court ceremonials observed the pagan traditions of the past. When the king ate, women danced before him, and seven drums, the symbol of magical and mystical power, rolled. No one worked while the king was eating, after which his leftover food was pitched into the Niger River amidst great cheering, and then work was resumed. Although the acknowledged royal religion was Islam, a majority of the common people did not profess that faith. The official leaders had a foot in each religious camp, a necessity if they were to rule successfully.

Kossoi and the kings who followed him in Mali—Sundiata, Mansa Mūsā, and Sonni ʿAlī—followed Islamic conventions and consulted with Muslim imams, the teachers of Islamic philosophy, and with marabouts, Islamic clergymen who ministered to the sick and led their followers in prayer. They simultaneously consulted, however, with traditional animist priests, which kept Islam from becoming a divisive force within their communities.

During the eleventh century, Gao was partly a Muslim town and partly a town whose people clung to their traditional, ancestral, animistic worship. These divergent religious elements were officially separated by residential area so that the two groups could follow their religious conventions of the faith without antagonizing the other. These twin towns existed close to each other for several centuries. As a result, the religious factions within Gao were reasonably harmonious.

SIGNIFICANCE

The empire of Mali was established in the eleventh century and it reached its high point under the leadership of Sundiata, who followed the Islamic faith. Mansa Mūsā built on Sundiata's success and in the early fourteenth century extended his empire from the Atlantic Ocean in the west to the territory east of Gao. Mansa Mūsā made his *hajj* to Mecca and was regarded as an ardent follower of Islam. Officials in Egypt who met him when he was bound for Mecca considered him a pious man strict in his observance of daily prayers, recitations from the Qurʾān, and frequent reverential mention of Allah's name.

The empire of Mali began a rapid decline when several hereditary kings proved to be ineffective leaders. The Songhai Empire of Gao came into the ascendant. Sonni ʿAlī and Muḥammad I Askia, who were both Muslims, established themselves as extremely effective kings, expanding their empire substantially. By this time, Islam was much more firmly a part of society in Gao, although it still existed side by side with the traditional animistic religion of large numbers of its people.

—*R. Baird Shuman*

FURTHER READING

Esposito, John L., ed. *The Oxford History of Islam*. New York: Oxford University Press, 1999. This exhaustive study of Islam offers cogent information about Mali, particularly Gao, in relation to the development of Islam there and its course through the centuries that followed its beginnings in the early eleventh century. The text is well written and appropriate for those new to the field.

Falola, Toyin. *Key Events in African History*. Westport, Conn.: Greenwood Press, 2002. Discusses the rise of Islam beginning in the seventh century and includes the chapter, "Kingdoms of West Africa: Ghana, Mali, and Songhay, A.D. 1000-1600." Illustrations, maps, bibliography, index.

Hiskett, Mervyn. *The Course of Islam in Africa*. Edinburgh: Edinburgh University Press, 1994. Several chapters address the rise of Islam in West and Northwest Africa. Maps, bibliography, index.

Hunwick, J. O. "Religion and State in the Songhay Empire, 1464-1591." In *Islam in Tropical Africa*, edited by I. M. Lewis. 2d ed. Bloomington: Indiana University Press, 1964. Although the essay focuses largely on a later period, it does mention in succinct detail the early manifestations of Islam in Gao, showing how it ran its course over several centuries. The editor's collection of fourteen essays, including a lengthy and detailed introduction, was sponsored by the International African Institute and is well presented.

Insoll, Timothy. "Looting the Antiquities of Mali: The Story Continues at Gao." *Antiquity* 67 (September, 1993): 628-633. Tells the sad and shocking story of how impoverished thieves in Mali, working in pairs, have looted the tombs of ancient Muslims and others buried in mounds within walking distance of contemporary Gao. Using a multidisciplinary approach involving survey and surface collection, archaeologists believe the site near Gao will enable them to document the spread and acceptance of Islam in the area between 800 and 1200.

Kenny, Joseph. *The Spread of Islam Through North to West Africa, Seventh to Nineteenth Centuries: A Historical Survey with Relevant Arab Documents*. Lagos, Nigeria: Dominican, 2000. Although this text might be difficult to locate, it is a valuable collection of Arab and other sources exploring the expansion of Islam into North and West Africa, beginning in the seventh century. Illustrations, maps, bibliography, index.

Levtzion, Nehemia, and Randall L. Pouwels, eds. *The History of Islam in Africa*. Athens: Ohio University Press, 2000. A comprehensive examination of the history of Islam in Africa. Introductory chapter looks at the "Patterns of Islamization and Varieties of Religious Experience Among Muslims of Africa," and Nehemia Levtzion's chapter, "Islam in the Bilad al-Sudan to 1800," touches directly upon the beginnings of Islam in Mali and reveals how many people in Gao and other towns in Mali clung to their animist religious practices. Illustrations, maps, bibliography, index.

SEE ALSO: 630-711: Islam Expands Throughout North Africa; c. 1100: Founding of Timbuktu; 1221-1259: Mai Dunama Dibbalemi Expands Kanem Empire; 1230's-1255: Reign of Sundiata of Mali; 1324-1325: Mansa Mūsā's Pilgrimage to Mecca Sparks Interest in Mali Empire; 1377: Ibn Khaldūn Completes His *Muqaddimah*.

RELATED ARTICLES in *Great Lives from History: The Middle Ages, 477-1453*: Ibn Khaldūn; Mansa Mūsā; Sundiata.

c. 1010-1015
AVICENNA WRITES HIS *CANON OF MEDICINE*

Avicenna's five-book medical encyclopedia, the Canon of Medicine, *served as the authoritative and most influential medical treatise in both the Islamic world and Europe for more than half a millennium.*

LOCALE: Hamadān, Persia (now in Iran)

CATEGORIES: Cultural and intellectual history; health and medicine; literature

KEY FIGURES

Avicenna (980-1037), Islamic scientist and philosopher

ʿAlāʾ al-Dawlah, ruler of Eṣfahān, r. 1008-1042, and last prince served by Avicenna

Shams al-Dawlah (d. 1022), Buyid prince of Hamadān whom Avicenna served as physician and vizier

Gerard of Cremona (c. 1114-1187), scholar who first translated the *Canon of Medicine* into Latin

Nūḥ ibn Manṣūr (d. 997), Sāmānid ruler at Bukhara, r. 976-997, who brought Avicenna to court as a physician

SUMMARY OF EVENT

In 1015, at the age of thirty-five, Avicenna completed the first of five books that would make up his *al-Qānūn fī al-ṭibb* (1010-1015; *Canon of Medicine*, 1930), a task undertaken because he believed that neither the classical nor the Islamic world had produced a book that could teach the practice of medicine as an integral whole. The end result of his efforts was a medical encyclopedia that would become the most influential single work in the history of medicine, remaining the authoritative text for both the Islamic and European worlds for five centuries.

Avicenna was one of the greatest philosophical and scientific minds produced by medieval Islam as well as a highly capable physician and political administrator. He was born near Bukhara, then the capital of the Persian Sāmānid Dynasty, the son of a local governor who opened his house for learned men to meet and discuss theological and philosophical issues. Avicenna, who had a private tutor since early childhood, mastered the Qurʾān and a substantial body of Arabic poetry by the age of ten and then was instructed in Aristotelian logic and metaphysics. He impressed his tutor, Abū ʿAbd Allāh al-Natili, by his independent thought and then soon outgrew his teacher.

In his early teens, while grappling with Aristotle's *Metaphysica* (348-336 B.C.E.; *Metaphysics*, 1801), Avicenna decided to turn to medicine, which he found easy to master by reading the numerous works of Galen translated into Arabic. He found Galen hard to reconcile with some of Aristotle's conclusions, and he continued his intellectual struggles with *Metaphysica*.

At the age of sixteen, Avicenna began the practice of medicine, establishing a reputation for originating his own methods of treatment based on careful observation of symptoms and attention to detail. One year later, when the reigning Sāmānid prince Nūḥ ibn Manṣūr fell ill, Avicenna was invited to court and successfully treated him along with other doctors. He remained at court, receiving permission to use the vast royal library containing numerous Greek works that Avicenna had never imagined to be in existence. His self-education grew by quantum leaps, along with his reputation as a skilled physician.

The fall of the Sāmānids to the Turkish-led Ghazavids forced Avicenna from court, sending him on a journey across central Persia to the courts of Buyid princes where he continued his role as a physician, before finally settling at the court of Shams al-Dawlah at Hamadān in central western Persia. Here he became court physician while also serving as the prince's vizier. Avicenna's nights were spent at Hamadān with a large retinue of students, composing and transcribing what would become the *Canon of Medicine*.

Also finalized was *Kitāb al-shifa* (book of healing; partially translated, 1927), probably the largest philosophic and scientific treatise written by a single individual, an encyclopedic synthesis of Greco-Roman knowledge, both theoretical and practical, with Islamic beliefs.

Following the death of Shams al-Dawlah in 1022, Avicenna fled to Eşfahān, where he was accepted as an esteemed member of the court of ʿAlāʾ al-Dawlah and continued his prolific writing, turning in his later years toward mystical spiritualism. More than one hundred of Avicenna's major works and treatises would survive the ravages of time. He died in 1037, while accompanying his prince on a military campaign at Hamadān. About half a century later, with the first comprehensive Latin translation by Gerard of Cremona, Avicenna's *Canon of Medicine* would be born as a rapidly growing work of authority in Europe.

Avicenna's work consisted of five books that, sharing an Aristotelian penchant for classification, were each subject to three subdivisions by Avicenna. Book 1 would rapidly be adopted on its own as a textbook on medical theory and as a standard setter for the major operating principles underlying the medical profession. Unlike Hippocrates, who viewed

AVICENNA DESCRIBES THE FOUR HUMORS

(Library of Congress)

The humors are the vital essences of the body. These humors affect the function of the body and are themselves influenced by physical functions. . . . Illness results when there is either a quantitative or qualitative change of a humor. . . .

- The sanguineous humor (blood), which is of a balanced nature, is hot and moist, sweet and red, and exceeds the other humors in proportion to quantity. It imparts strength and colour to the body and engenders the drives. Located in the heart. . . .
- The phlegm or serous humor, is next to blood as far as the relative quantity present in the body is concerned. This humor is watery, cold, moist and white and moderates the strength, heat and thickness of the blood, nourishes the brain, and moistens and nourishes the moving parts of the body. . . .
- The bilious humor, is less plentiful in the body than either blood or phlegm. Its quantity is hot and dry, yellow or red and bitter. A part of it passes from the liver to the gallbladder and another part flows from the liver with other humors. This humor moderates moisture and provides a penetrating quality to the blood so that it may enter more readily into every tissue of the body. The bilious humor prevents the body from becoming heavy, sleepy and dull. . . .
- The atrabilious humor's quality is earthy and gross, thick, black and sour. A part of it is separated out by the spleen and a part remains within the blood. This humor feeds the bones, the spleen and other parts of the body which are gross or "melancholy" in nature. . . .

Source: Avicenna, *Canon of Medicine*, quoted at the Traditional Medicine Network, http://www.traditionalmedicine.net.au/canonavi.htm.

A German surgeon from a wood engraving after Hans Holbein. (Frederick Ungar Publishing Co.)

medicine as an art or craft, Avicenna showed it to be a science that used both philosophy and logical reasoning for practical ends. Book 1 was heavily based on Greek sources, particularly Aristotle and Galen. Avicenna pointed out the differences between the two (such as marked differences in defining the function of the heart and brain), and then proceeded to synthesize Galen, Aristotle, and Neoplatonic thought. Basically, Avicenna took Aristotle's thought and updated it with Galen's superior anatomical knowledge and the practical observations of Islamic physicians such as himself. Hence, book 1 contained a lengthy general discussion of the anatomy of the body.

In book 1, Avicenna tried to clarify the causes for both health and sickness that he found, like his Greek predecessors, subject to the laws of nature, a proper balance of hot, wet, cold, and dry, and a balance of four primary humors (blood, phlegm, red bile, and black bile). For Avicenna, imbalances in urine and pulse were also important monitors of the state of health.

In book 2 on *meteria dedica*, Avicenna blended Aristotle and Galen, while opening medical methodology to Stoic logic. Here he expounded on rules for isolating causes of disease, treatments, and means of measuring recurrence.

Book 3 was an analysis of specific diseases that affected twenty-one separate organs or organ systems, along with descriptions about how to treat each, while book 4 analyzed diseases that affect whole systems. Central ideas put forth in book 4 were the concept of crisis in fevers and the effects of toxins and tumors. Also of significance was the recognition that disease could be spread not only by bad air, but by contaminated water and soil as well, the contagious nature of tuberculosis, and the system weakening effects of intestinal worms. Avicenna also stressed the importance of minor surgery to correct whole system maladies, thus considering surgery to be part of the practice of medicine, not separate from it. Similarly, pharmacology was considered an important part of the practice of medicine, not in a world of its own, and book 5 was devoted to this end.

In book 5 on pharmacology, 760 drugs and herbs were discussed, including directions on how to prepare and administer them. In this book, Avicenna made many original contributions to medicine, including discussion of the antiseptic qualities of alcohol, the curative effects of mineral waters, and even the significance of animal experimentation in testing new drugs, along with general rules for experimental use of drugs.

The first Latin translation of the *Canon of Medicine* was made by Gerard of Cremona at a time when universities were beginning to rise in Europe and Scholasticism was orienting students to the ancients. Book 1 of the *Canon of Medicine*, with its heavy reliance on Greek sources, found its way into the universities at Padua and Salerno. By the late 1200's, using the *Canon of Medicine* (although not the total encyclopedia) was a standard part of a university medical education. The text could be found even in both monastic and personal libraries. By the fourteenth century, major parts of the text were translated into a variety of vernacular languages. A major retranslation into Latin was made by Andrea Alpago in the sixteenth century. More than sixty Latin editions would be printed in the sixteenth century, along with a tremendous amount of commentary to modernize the work.

SIGNIFICANCE

Avicenna was the first Islamic thinker to synthesize Islamic thought with that of Western philosophy. The persistent and practical significance of the *Canon of Medicine* fell out of favor only with the increasing use of dissection and the scientific revolution of the second half of the seventeenth century. The five-hundred-year authority of the *Canon of Medicine* would be undermined by the direct observation that Avicenna advocated. While Avicenna would be removed as a current influence in the Western world by 1700, he would remain as one of the most influential figures in the historical evolution of medicine.

—*Irwin Halfond*

FURTHER READING

Afnan, Soheil. *Avicenna: His Life and Works*. London: Allen and Unwin, 1958. A standard treatment of Avicenna for the general reader, with a chapter devoted to his work in medicine and the natural sciences.

Amundsen, Darrel W., ed. *Medicine, Society, and Faith in the Ancient and Medieval Worlds*. Baltimore: Johns Hopkins University Press, 1996. Covers the connections between medicine and religious faith, canon law on medical practice, medical ethics, and more.

Bakar, Osman. *The History and Philosophy of Islamic Science*. Cambridge, England: Islamic Texts Society, 1999. Discusses questions of methodology, doubt, spirituality and scientific knowledge, the philosophy of Islamic medicine, and how Islamic science influenced medieval Christian views of the natural world.

Goodman, Lenn E. *Avicenna*. New York: Routledge, 1992. A thorough philosophical analysis of Avicenna's work viewed within the wider context of his times. Bibliography, index.

Huff, Toby E. *The Rise of Early Modern Science: Islam, China, and the West*. 2d ed. New York: Cambridge University Press, 2003. Provides a strong cross-cultural background for the rise of science and medicine in Avicenna's time. Includes illustrations, a bibliography, and index.

Sirasi, Nancy G. *Avicenna in Renaissance Italy: The Canon and Medical Teaching in Italian Universities After 1500*. Princeton, N.J.: Princeton University Press, 1987. The best English analysis of Avicenna's work and its influence on Western medical education.

Wisnovsky, Robert, ed. *Aspects of Avicenna*. Princeton, N.J.: Markus Wiener, 2001. Chapters explore Avicenna's psychology, epistemology, natural philosophy, metaphysics, and ideas on substance and materiality and intuition and thinking. Bibliography, index.

_______. *Avicenna's Metaphysics in Context*. Ithaca, N.Y.: Cornell University Press, 2003. Chapters cover Avicenna's ideas on perfection and the soul and explore the synthesizing of his philosophy within the work of other his contemporaries. Bibliography, index.

SEE ALSO: c. 950: Court of Córdoba Flourishes in Spain; 1100-1300: European Universities Emerge; c. 1150: Moors Transmit Classical Philosophy and Medicine to Europe.

RELATED ARTICLES in *Great Lives from History: The Middle Ages, 477-1453*: Pietro d'Abano; Saint Albertus Magnus; Alhazen; Arnold of Villanova; Averroës; Avicenna; Roger Bacon; John Duns Scotus; Fakhr al-Dīn al-Rāzī; Jacqueline Félicie; Guy de Chauliac; Ibn Khaldūn; Omar Khayyám; Thomas Aquinas.

1012
RICE IS INTRODUCED INTO CHINA

Trade from Southeast Asia brought rice to China, where it became such a staple crop that the Chinese word for "rice" is virtually synonymous with the word "food."

LOCALE: China
CATEGORY: Agriculture

KEY FIGURE

Zhenzong (Chen-tsung, 968-1022), Song Dynasty emperor, r. 998-1022, who ordered short-season rice imported from Champa to alleviate a famine

SUMMARY OF EVENT

Rice is a cereal grain adapted to life in wetlands and probably evolved in response to the monsoon cycles of Southeast Asia (modern Vietnam, Laos, Cambodia, and Myanmar). Most scientists believe that the original plant species from which domesticated rice developed is now extinct and that the present cultivated varieties arose from it through a process of progressive evolution over several thousand years, speeded by selective propagation by humans. The scientific name of domesticated rice is *Oryza sativa*.

Various primitive types of rice have been cultivated in southern China from prehistorical times. In even the earliest forms of the written language, agriculture is synonymous with the cultivation of rice. This correspondence of terms indicates that rice was already the principal crop of the region as early as the Shang Dynasty (1600-1066 B.C.E.). Rice was so important that a myth arose regarding its discovery after a worldwide flood, a discovery that ended the famine that followed the flood. By contrast, European food myths such as those of Ceres or Demeter deal with the discovery of wheat, Egyptian food myths center on barley, and Mesoamerican myths, including those of the Aztec and Maya, deal with maize. The rice cultivated in early China was a relatively primitive strain that took 180 days, effectively the entire growing season, to mature to the point that it could be harvested.

This situation changed in the first part of the eleventh century, with the introduction of new strains of early-ripening rice from Champa (modern Cambodia and central Vietnam). In 1012, following a severe drought on the lower Yangtze and Huai Rivers, the Song emperor Zhenzong issued a proclamation ordering thirty thousand bushels of these Champa seeds to be shipped to the affected area, particularly Fujian Province. As the local peasants were unfamiliar with the new variety of rice, the emperor also commanded that pamphlets be printed and distributed throughout the area, instructing them on the virtues of the new form of rice.

According to the local histories of Zhejian and southern Jiangsu Provinces, the use of Champa rice shortened the ripening time to less than a hundred days, although later selective breeding and hybridization reduced the growing cycle to a mere sixty days by the twelfth century. As a result, farmers were able to grow two crops instead of one every year, making every acre of cultivated land doubly productive. In addition to growing more rapidly, Champa rice required less water than did earlier varieties. Not only did this feature make Champa rice more resistant to drought but it also enabled farmers to expand the cultivation of rice from the bottomland immediately beside the rivers. Higher ground and even hillsides could be planted in Champa rice and be relied on to produce a crop.

However, Champa rice was not entirely without its negative features. Because of its lower gluten content, it was less tasty and did not store as well as traditional varieties of rice. As a result, imperial taxes and levies continued to be collected in medium-gluten rice varieties.

During this period, the Chinese developed a method of rice farming that enabled them to squeeze every possible day out of the growing season. In sharp contrast to the methods used in planting almost every other grain known to humanity, Chinese peasants did not plant the seeds directly into the fields from which the rice would be harvested. Instead, they would sow the grain in smaller "nursery" fields, with the seedlings coming up as tightly spaced as possible. Once the seedlings were about eight inches tall, they were removed from the nursery field and transplanted into the field in which they were to grow to maturity. In these flooded fields, the seedlings would be individually planted into the soft mud, spaced several inches apart so that they would have sufficient room to finish their growth. As a result, farmers could get a head start on the season's second crop while the first crop was still ripening. However, these techniques were very labor-intensive and tied large numbers of people to the land. (By contrast, the methods used in modern commercial rice farming in the United States, where labor is expensive and land is cheap, are more typical of grain farming; seeds are sown directly into the field in which the rice will mature.)

The Chinese developed a method of sowing rice in "nursery" fields, then transplanting the eight-inch-tall seedlings into the soft mud of flooded fields to finish their growth. In this way, farmers could get a head start on the season's second crop while the first crop was still ripening. (Hulton|Archive by Getty Images)

As the primary staple of the region, rice became associated with various festivals and rites of passage in Chinese culture. Even Buddhist ceremonies imported from India were adapted by the Chinese to include rice. Rice wine became the principal alcoholic beverage of the rice-growing regions of China. Although often connected with Japan, where it is known as *sake*, it was first brewed in China. Because of the revenues associated with the production of rice wine, several dynasties made it an imperial monopoly.

Although most Westerners tend to think of rice primarily in terms of food, the Chinese also made a large number of products from other parts of the rice plant. One of the most notable was paper made from rice straw. Rice paper was very smooth and white, with a fine grain that accepted ink very well, leading to new and more subtle techniques of painting, in particular, the Chinese forms of ink wash and watercolor. As a result, the Song Dynasty (Sung; 960-1279) saw an extraordinary flowering of the art of painting, rarely equaled and never exceeded by later generations of painters.

Chinese farmers also squeezed additional productivity out of limited acreage by taking advantage of the fish that often infiltrated the flooded fields. These fish would eat weeds and aquatic insect pests that would otherwise lower yields and spread diseases. Shortly before the fields were drained, the farmers would harvest the fish, adding protein to diets that were otherwise heavy in starches. Eventually they would deliberately introduce selected species of fish into the rice fields at the beginning of the flooding cycle so they could control pests during the growing season and later harvest the resulting fattened fish.

SIGNIFICANCE

The introduction of rice to China had an effect on Chinese culture that went far beyond agricultural and culinary habits. Intensive rice cultivation using the two-field method and multiple crop seasons per year greatly increased the carrying capacity of the land, enabling the population of China to increase until it would become the most populous country in the world. It also led to the development of a very large class of extremely poor peasants performing intensive stoop labor throughout the year for relatively little return and, as a result, locked Chinese culture into a system of extreme stratification with a large gulf between the wealthy leisured classes and the toiling peasantry.

—Leigh Husband Kimmel

FURTHER READING

Anderson, E. N. *The Food of China*. New Haven, Conn.: Yale University Press, 1988. An overview of the role of food in Chinese culture and history, showing the relationships between agricultural patterns and social change, folkways, and other aspects of the culture.

Ebrey, Patricia Buckley, ed. *Chinese Civilization and Society: A Sourcebook*. New York: Free Press, 1981. A useful overview on Chinese history from ancient times to the present, including excellent bibliographies to help find more in-depth information.

Elvin, Mark. *The Pattern of the Chinese Past*. Stanford, Calif.: Stanford University Press, 1973. This classic ethnological study of the origins of Chinese culture and folkways includes a discussion of the introduction of short-season rice and its social consequences, both short-term and long-term.

Gang Deng. *Development Versus Stagnation: Technological Continuity and Agricultural Progress in Pre-modern China*. Westport, Conn.: Greenwood Press, 1993. Somewhat technical, but the work places agricultural change in a historical context. Also includes a bibliography for further research.

Ho, Ping-ti. *Studies on the Population of China, 1368-1953*. Cambridge, Mass.: Harvard University Press, 1959. Develops the thesis that the introduction of short-season rice was absolutely critical to the growth of the Chinese population and its extreme concentration in the fertile lowlands of the south, which has shaped all its subsequent history. Of particular interest because of Ho's use of Chinese sources often not available to Western scholars.

Roberts, J. A. G. *A Concise History of China*. Cambridge, Mass.: Harvard University Press, 1999. Basic survey of Chinese history, providing an overview of the cultural matrix into which short-season rice was introduced, and the changes throughout society that resulted from its introduction.

Von Glahn, Richard, and Paul Jakov Smith. *The Song-Yuan-Ming Transition in Chinese History*. Cambridge, Mass.: Harvard University Press, 2003. This collection of essays on medieval and early modern China includes some of the latest scholarship on the role of Champa rice in the development of modern China.

SEE ALSO: 618: Founding of the Tang Dynasty; 907-960: Period of Five Dynasties and Ten Kingdoms; 960: Founding of the Song Dynasty; 960-1279: Scholar-Official Class Flourishes Under Song Dynasty; 1115: Foundation of the Jin Dynasty.

RELATED ARTICLES in *Great Lives from History: The Middle Ages, 477-1453*: Ma Yuan; Xia Gui.

April 23, 1014
BATTLE OF CLONTARF

The Battle of Clontarf pitted the Irish forces of Leinster and their Norse allies against the Munster forces of Brian, resulting in Brian's victory on Good Friday and the dismantling of Norse control in Ireland.

LOCALE: Clontarf, Ireland

CATEGORIES: Expansion and land acquisition; wars, uprisings, and civil unrest

KEY FIGURES

Brian (941-1014), leader of the Dál Cais tribe and high king of Ireland, r. 1002-1014

Murchad (d. 1014), son of Brian

Sitric Mac-Aulaffe I (d. 1029), Viking king of Dublin, r. 989-1029

Brodar (d. 1014) and

Ospak (d. 1014), two prominent Viking leaders who had a fleet on the Isle of Man

Sigurd (d. 1014), Viking earl of the Orkneys

SUMMARY OF EVENT

Few battles in Irish history command the fame that has been attached to Brian's victory at Clontarf on Good Friday, April 23, 1014. Since medieval times, the Battle of Clontarf has been presented as a struggle between Irish forces and Norse invaders for the control of Ireland. Correspondingly, the Irish victory has been seen as breaking the power of the Norse in Ireland and as a defining moment in Ireland's progress toward national unity under a single king. Moreover, the fact that Brian, a Christian king, was killed by a pagan Norseman on Good Friday, the day of Christ's death, made for suitable hagiographical comparisons. Most of these claims belong to legend rather than history, however, and originated in a propagandistic Irish work, entitled *Cogadh Gaedhel re Gallaibh* (c. 1100; *The War of the Gaedhil with the Gaill*, 1867), that was designed to glorify Brian.

For a more objective and reliable account of what happened, the primary source is the *Annals of Ulster*, a year by-year chronicle, started in 431 and completed in 1541, of Irish events, whose entry on the battle may be almost contemporaneous. Not only does it detail the military movements in the preceding months, but it also lists the main contestants and fatalities in the battle. Curiously, the *Annals of Inisfallen* (c. 1015 to c. 1318), the chronicle that originated in Munster (the province from which Brian hailed) and might have been expected to provide the fullest and most detailed account, is disappointing on both counts. Next in importance to the annals as a source is *The War of the Gaedhil with the Gaill*. This work, composed during the reign of Brian's great-grandson, was designed to glorify Brian. It is cast in the form of a native saga with heroes and villains, contains much dramatic incident, and is written in a suitably hyperbolic style. Obviously, its propagandistic intent, coupled with its adherence to the conventions of a literary genre, make it suspect as a historical source. At best, it can be described as a "tale with a historical background."

Even more unreliable are the various versions of the Middle Irish saga *Cath Cluana Tarbh* (eleventh century; *The Battle of Clontarf*, 1832), which, among other marvels, has supernatural figures visiting the protagonists before the battle. Yet, if nothing else, these tales bear witness to the extraordinary importance later assumed by the battle among the literate classes in Ireland. A final source is *Njáls Saga* (c. thirteenth century; *The Story of Burnt Njal*, 1861), the most famous of the Icelandic prose sagas, which was probably composed in the thirteenth century. While attesting that the reverberations of the Battle of Clontarf were also felt in the Scandinavian world, this source provides a unique Norse perspective on events. Although its account of the battle is dull, it does provide details about the Norse combatants that may well be genuine.

Brian belonged to the Dál Cais, a minor tribe occupying an area of southwest Ireland roughly equal to eastern County Clare of today. This strategic location guaranteed the tribe's control of the estuary and waterway of the Shannon, Ireland's main river, which provided access to the Midlands. When Brian was growing up early in the second half of the tenth century, this tribe began to emerge as a major player on the local political scene. Taking advantage of a power vacuum in the southern province of Munster, the Dál Cais formed alliances with various Munster parties, including the Norse city of Waterford. On the death of his brother Mathgamain in 976, Brian became the leader and prime mover of Dál Cais expansion. By the end of the tenth century, Brian was well on his way to establishing himself as the foremost king in Ireland. His extraordinary success was partly the result of natural ability and of divisions among his rivals that he was able to exploit.

At the turn of the eleventh century, Ireland was a political conglomerate of numerous petty kingdoms, known as *tuatha*, loosely bound together in five major provinces: Leinster in the east, Munster in the south, Connaught in the west, Ulster in the north, and Meath in north-central Ireland. Each of these provinces had its own over-king. In the thirty years after he became king of the Dál Cais, Brian progressively extended his influence, first over Munster, over the southern part of Ireland by 997, later over Meath, and eventually over Ulster by 1005. His relations with Leinster, however, were more problematic. To assert his authority over the southern part of Ireland, Brian needed to control Leinster, including the independent Norse city of Dublin. Following earlier forays into Leinster in 984 and 991, Brian defeated the Leinstermen at Glen Máma in late 999. Early in 1000, he plundered Dublin and compelled its ruler Sitric Mac-Aulaffe I to submit. (Brian was well aware of the commercial and military advantages found in controlling Viking cities such as Dublin.) A few years later, Brian intervened politically in Leinster affairs by deposing Domhnall mac Donnchada as king of Leinster, replacing him with Máel Mórda mac Murchada, who hailed from a north Leinster tribe.

Nevertheless, Leinster's longstanding resentment against outsider control erupted again in 1013, possibly as a result of an insult suffered by Máel Mórda at the hands of Brian's son Murchad. Máel Mórda not only withdrew his submission to Brian but also encouraged other subject tribes to do the same. In addition, Máel Mórda entered an alliance with the Norse residents of Dublin.

In the meantime, Brian was also gathering his forces. Along with his own army of Munstermen, Brian recruited forces from the southern Connaught kingdoms of the Uí Fiachrach Aidne and the Uí Maine. He advanced eastward through the border territory of Ossory (now southwestern Leinster) at the same time that Murchad proceeded northward through Leinster from the south. The two armies converged on the north side of Dublin, which Brian then besieged all through the autumn of 1013. After failing to take the city, Brian withdrew his forces by Christmas and returned home to Munster.

Realizing that Brian and his forces would return, the Norse of Dublin made preparations. Sitric Mac-Aulaffe visited his Norse allies in western Scotland and the Isle of

Man. He won over Earl Sigurd of the Orkneys and two prominent Viking leaders, Brodar and Ospak, who had a fleet on the Isle of Man. These allies agreed to be in Dublin with their ships by Palm Sunday of 1014. They may have deliberately chosen this date as a time when their Christian enemies would be preoccupied with the observance of Holy Week.

This time, Brian returned with an even larger army, although the advantage of superior numbers was wiped out when his ally, Máelsechlainn II of Meath, withdrew his forces on the eve of the battle. Arriving near Dublin, Brian ravaged the Norse suburbs of Fingal and Howth. The Norse and their Leinster allies marched out of the city to meet Brian. The battle was joined on the plains of Clontarf on the north side of Dublin, where the river Tolka runs into Dublin Bay. By this time an elderly man, Brian remained in his tent and left the conduct of the battle to Murchad.

The battle was fought all day, but by evening the Leinster and Norse armies gave way and fled toward the sea. The victory was marred by the slaughter of Brian in his tent by Brodar during his retreat inland from the battle. Other prominent casualties included Murchad and kings of the subject Munster tribes, as well as a grandson and nephew of Brian; casualties on the other side included Máel Mórda, Sigurd, and Brodar, as well as most of the prominent Leinster leaders. The victorious Munster army, led by Brian's surviving son, Donnchad, returned home, but not without harassment from another Leinster tribe, the Osraige.

SIGNIFICANCE

In no real sense could this battle be described as a decisive conflict between two national armies. Brian's army consisted essentially of men from his own tribe and province; with the exception of Leinster, the rest of Ireland remained unengaged. Likewise, his enemies could not be characterized as Norse invaders as the majority of them were residents of Leinster. The role played by the Norsemen of Dublin was relatively minor, and the majority of these men were residents of Ireland, not invaders. As for the portrayal of Brian as the first real high king of Ireland, it also falls short of being accurate. Brian certainly gave new definition and potential to this notion, but he never achieved a national monarchy and did not establish the institutions and administration normally associated with such an office.

How then does one explain the enormous significance that later time attached to the Battle of Clontarf? The memory of a protracted and bitterly fought battle, the death of a man who had already carved out for himself a special place in Irish history, and the propaganda produced a few decades later by Brian's own people in *The War of the Gaedhil with the Gaill* all ensured a permanent place for the battle in Irish literary and pseudo-historical tradition.

—*Patrick P. O'Neill*

FURTHER READING

Byrne, Francis John. *Irish Kings and High-Kings*. Portland, Oreg.: Four Courts Press, 2001. Discusses the Irish tribes and the rivalries leading up to the Battle of Clontarf.

Loyn, H. R. *The Vikings in Britain*. Rev. ed. Cambridge, Mass.: Blackwell, 1995. The author devotes three chapters to the early raids and subsequent large-scale invasions of Britain by Scandinavians. A highly regarded history of the Viking Age.

Moody, T. W., and F. X. Martin, eds. *The Course of Irish History*. Rev. ed. Lanham, Md.: Roberts Rhinehart, 2001. A scholarly collection of articles that provides a useful introduction to Irish history. Contains illustrations, a chronological table, and an extensive bibliography.

Ó Corráin, Donnchadh. *Ireland Before the Normans*. Vol. 2 in *The Gill History of Ireland*. Dublin: Gill and Macmillan, 1972. Provides insights into events surrounding the Battle of Clontarf.

O Croinin, Daibhi. *Early Medieval Ireland, 400-1200*. New York: Longman, 1995. Discusses the beginnings of Irish history, its politics, and the Irish as a people.

Otway-Ruthven, A. J. *A History of Medieval Ireland*. 2d ed. New York: Barnes and Noble Books, 1993. An overview of medieval Irish history and a good starting point for understanding events during the period before 1496.

SEE ALSO: June 7, 793: Norse Raid Lindisfarne Monastery; 850-950: Viking Era; 878: Alfred Defeats the Danes; 1169-1172: Normans Invade Ireland; 1366: Statute of Kilkenny.

RELATED ARTICLES in *Great Lives from History: The Middle Ages, 477-1453*: Edward I; Edward III; Henry II; Olaf I.

1016
CANUTE CONQUERS ENGLAND

Danish invaders, led by Canute, conquered England and launched the nineteen-year reign of Canute, a period of benign leadership, relative peace, and strengthened bonds between England and the Christian church in Rome.

LOCALE: England
CATEGORIES: Expansion and land acquisition; religion; wars, uprisings, and civil unrest

KEY FIGURES

Sweyn Forkbeard (d. 1014), father of Canute and first Danish king of England, r. 1013-1014
Canute the Great (c. 995-1035), Danish Viking and king of England, r. 1016-1035
Ethelred II, the Unready (c. 968-1016), Saxon king of England, r. 978-1013 and 1014-1016
Emma of Normandy (d. 1052), wife of Ethelred II, the Unready, who married Canute in 1017 after her husband's death
Edmund Ironside (c. 993-1016), son of Ethelred and Saxon king of England who ruled jointly with Canute for seven months, r. 1016

SUMMARY OF EVENT

For more than two hundred years, starting about 789, Viking warriors from Denmark and Norway harassed the peoples of the British Isles. Indeed, a familiar prayer uttered by the hapless Britons petitioned God, "From the fury of the Norsemen, good Lord deliver us!" Adding to the slaughter, warrior earls and would-be kings among the resident Saxons battled for the right to rule Britain. A nineteen-year interlude of peace transformed the country when Canute the Great, a Danish Viking who had been baptized a Christian, became the ruler of all of England in 1016.

Historians are not in full agreement about the meaning of the word "viking." As a verb, the term had been used in the original written sources to mean piracy or a pirate raid; as a noun, it was used to mean a pirate or raider. Whatever the term's exact meaning, the Vikings were bold, bloodthirsty plunderers. Roaming the seas in their well-crafted long boats or dragon ships, they primarily attacked the British Isles. In 793, a Viking raid on the monastery of Lindisfarne, located off the Northumbrian coast, horrified the Christian world. The invaders slaughtered some of the monks, took others to sell as slaves, and looted the monastery of gold and jeweled religious objects. After this raid, Viking attacks increased in fury and frequency.

The east coast of England took the brunt of the raids as the Vikings sailed their dragon ships up the rivers to harass the inland villagers. The invaders frequently found allies among the resident peoples, particularly the Celts, who joined the Danes in battles against the Saxon rulers of England. In 838, a large Danish force landed in Cornwall, where many of the residents joined the Vikings to fight their enemy, Wessex.

For the next century and a half, the battles between the Vikings and the various peoples of the British Isles seesawed across England. In the end, the Vikings occupied large sections of the country and established their headquarters in London. Local British resistance continued, however, and the Vikings, now well organized under a sound Danish government at home, launched their forces for the final conquest of England.

Sweyn Forkbeard, king of Denmark, led a major thrust against England in 994. He was supported in the field by forces from Norway. The battles raged on for nearly twenty years. In 1013, Sweyn's army defeated the disorganized and weary Britons, led by Ethelred II, the Unready. In a curious twist of fate, Sweyn died on February 3, 1014, just as he had secured this total victory. Command of the Danish troops was turned over to Sweyn's younger son, Canute, who was unable to prevail against a counterattack launched by the Britons and fled to Denmark.

Born in Denmark around 994, Canute was the younger son of Sweyn Forkbeard. Little is known of his early years before he accompanied his father on a raid to England in 1013, when he was about nineteen years old. Canute's older brother, Harold, may also have accompanied Sweyn on the raid. In the wake of his success, Sweyn was accepted as king over the Danelaw, the Danish-held part of eastern England, where he collected the Danegeld, an enforced contribution of money, precious metals, and jewels taken from resident Britons to support the needs of the Viking occupation forces. After Sweyn's death in 1014, his followers considered Canute to be heir to their English territory. Believed to be a Viking as able as his father, Canute assembled a fleet and set sail for England in 1015. The ruling structure of England was in shambles, and treachery and distrust prevented effective resistance to the Vikings. After landing his forces, Canute carried the battle to Nottingham and York in the north before moving south to London. After a prolonged siege of London, which ultimately ended in a stalemate, Canute and Edmund Ironside signed a peace settlement in 1016 giving Edmund continued control of Wessex while granting Canute control over the lands north of the Thames River. After Edmund's death later that year, Canute became sole ruler of England.

As king, Canute ushered in a period of peace for his new kingdom, the first the people had enjoyed for several decades. The Saxon English and the Danes managed to live in harmony, although Canute had appointed many Danish officials to govern the land. Saxons and Danes intermarried, and many adopted new names befitting these unions.

Many years of paying the Danegeld had seriously depleted the nation's finances. Canute imposed widespread taxation to replenish the treasury. As a warrior, Canute recognized that England's defenses had to be rebuilt to withstand future attacks, and most of the tax revenue was used to improve the system of walls, bulwarks, and ditches.

Canute also sought to strengthen his standing with the English by marrying into the Saxon royal line. In 1017, he married Emma of Normandy, widow of Ethelred II, the Unready. This shrewd stroke of policy pleased the English and appeared to ensure a sound line of succession to the English throne. Canute's marital arrangements, however, suffered some complications. Canute acknowledged two sons, Sweyn and Harold Harefoot, whom he had fathered by his Anglo-Danish mistress, Ælgifu of Northampton. Of the children Canute later had with Emma, young Harthacnut was in the line of succession to the English throne. Both Harold Harefoot and Harthacnut were to serve briefly as English monarchs after Canute's death.

Canute's governing policy for England lay along two lines. First, he sought to continue a national government that followed that of King Edgar, Anglo-Saxon ruler from 359 to 375, who was considered one of the best of the preceding English monarchs. Second, Canute sought to strengthen relations with the Catholic Church in Rome. Although he had been born a pagan, Canute had been baptized a Christian sometime before he accompanied his father on the 1013 raid against England. Canute gave generous donations to the Catholic Church and traveled to Rome in 1027 to attend the coronation of Emperor Conrad II, whose son Henry had married Canute's daughter Gunhild.

Canute died at Shaftesbury, England, on November 12, 1035. His son Harold Harefoot ruled as regent for his half brother Harthacnut from 1035 to 1037 and then took the kingship for himself and ruled from 1037 to 1040. Canute's legitimate son Harthacnut ruled England from 1040 to 1042. Because Canute's sons lacked their father's strength and popularity, the English soon re-

Canute assembled a fleet and set sail for England in 1015, conquering the north in 1016 and becoming the sole ruler of England by the end of that year. (F. R. Niglutsch)

stored a Saxon heir to the throne. Harthacnut was succeeded by his Anglo-Saxon half brother Edward the Confessor, the son of Ethelred II, the Unready, and Emma of Normandy, who ruled from 1042 to 1066. Edward was succeeded by Harold II, who ruled briefly in 1066. The entire Danish-Saxon dynasty collapsed with the Norman invasion of 1066, led by William the Conqueror.

SIGNIFICANCE

In addition to briefly maintaining peace in England, Canute became king of Denmark in 1018 (after the death of his brother Harold) and king of Norway in 1028. As a result, he brought England into a Scandinavian empire that facilitated healthy commerce among the nations.

Canute ruled wisely and was held in high regard by his English subjects, many of whom believed he was all-powerful and could command anything, including the tides of the sea. According to one story, which may well be apocryphal, Canute had his throne placed at the seashore to demonstrate that he was, after all, only a man. In this story, Canute commanded the sea to fall back. The tide continued to rise, however, dampening both Canute's shoes and the flattery of his courtiers. Their sincere admiration could not be dampened, however, and Canute was extolled as the first Viking king to be ranked as a civilized Christian ruler.

—*Albert C. Jensen*

FURTHER READING

Adams, Phoebe-Lou. "From York to Jorvik: The Viking Past Lives on in England." *Atlantic Monthly* 275 (March, 1995): 46-50. Describes the role of the Vikings not only as plunderers but also as traders who converted the Saxon town of Eoforwic into an international port they named Jorvik (now York).

Christiansen, Eric. "Canute and His World." *History Today* 36 (November, 1986): 34-39. A well-rounded view of Canute that presents him as a good Christian monarch who married into the English nobility despite his previous reputation as a murderous Viking outlaw.

Davies, Wendy, ed. *From the Vikings to the Normans*. New York: Oxford University Press, 2003. Discusses the Anglo-Saxon period from the Norse to the Normans. Includes bibliography and index.

Jones, Gwyn. *A History of the Vikings*. Rev. ed. New York: Oxford University Press, 1984. Provides a detailed, informative history of the Vikings.

Lawson, M. K. *Cnut: The Danes in England in the Early Eleventh Century*. New York: Longman, 1993. A solid survey of Canute's career, with valuable insight into his relations with the Holy Roman Empire and Anglo-Danish government.

May, Robin. *Canute and the Vikings*. New York: Bookwright, 1985. Brief but authoritative account of the Viking king of England written for a young high school audience.

SEE ALSO: June 7, 793: Norse Raid Lindisfarne Monastery; 850-950: Viking Era; 878: Alfred Defeats the Danes; October 14, 1066: Battle of Hastings.

RELATED ARTICLES in *Great Lives from History: The Middle Ages, 477-1453*: Canute the Great; Edward the Confessor; Ethelred II, the Unready; Harold II; William the Conqueror.

c. 1025
SCHOLARS AT CHARTRES REVIVE INTEREST IN THE CLASSICS

Scholars at Chartres revived interest in classical learning, providing the foundation for the twelfth century Renaissance through the use of the seven liberal arts, a program of learning reflected in sculpture and stained glass windows at Chartres Cathedral.

LOCALE: Chartres, France
CATEGORIES: Cultural and intellectual history; education; religion

KEY FIGURES

Saint Fulbert of Chartres (c. 960-1020), bishop of Chartres, led the effort to rebuild the cathedral at Chartres
Gerbert of Aurillac (c. 945-1003), French scholar in charge of the cathedral school at Reims, later archbishop of Reims and Pope Sylvester II, 999-1003

SUMMARY OF EVENT

By the eleventh century, the cathedral at Chartres was already known as an important pilgrimage center. The Carolingian cathedral held the *Sancta Camisia*, the garment that allegedly had been worn by Mary at the time of the Annunciation. As the cult of Mary grew during the High Middle Ages, so did the importance of Chartres Cathedral.

The year 1020 proved to be an ominous one for the cathedral. On September 7, 1020, it was consumed by fire. Fulbert of Chartres, the local bishop, rallied financial support from King Robert of France, King Canute the Great of England, and other sovereigns in a successful effort to rebuild the cathedral. Monetary magnanimity allowed Fulbert to commission the architect Beregar to construct the apse, the ambulatory, and the chapels for the eastern portion of the cathedral. Another fire in 1030 delayed consecration of the rebuilt cathedral until 1037. Fulbert's new cathedral was built in the Romanesque style and was the predecessor of the twelfth century Gothic structure now found at Chartres.

While Fulbert was the decided inspiration for the reconstruction of the cathedral and its restoration as a major pilgrimage site, he is equally important for his revitalization of the classics studied at the Chartres Cathedral school. The eleventh century witnessed the shift of learning from the sometimes remote monastic centers to the urban cathedral schools. Because of the general prosperity resulting from commercial trade in cities and towns, the urban cathedral schools were able to attract the best scholars and the most promising young students. Fulbert laid the cornerstone for the new learning and was the academic coordinator for the curriculum at Chartres. Educated at the cathedral school at Reims under the tutelage of Gerbert of Aurillac, the future Pope Sylvester II, Fulbert came to Chartres in the 980's and established the cathedral school there. Chartres was considered the foremost school in France until the University of Paris and other similar institutions forced the cathedral schools into oblivion during the thirteenth century.

The cathedral school at Chartres fostered the classical tradition through its curriculum. Martianus Capella's fifth century treatise, the *De nuptis philologie et mercurii* (*Marriage of Philology and Mercury*, 1977), provided the pedagogical foundation for learning. Boethius (c. 480-524) later fine-tuned Capella's work and formally activated the *trivium* and *quadrivium* into divisional entities and outlined their specific functions within the ideal curriculum. The *trivium* consisted of grammar, rhetoric, and dialectic (or logic), while the *quadrivium* included arithmetic, geometry, music, and astronomy. The *trivium* allowed the educated person to speak, to communicate, and to persuade clearly and compellingly. The *quadrivium*, on the other hand, provided a theoretical background necessary to understand the workings of the universe. According to the traditions of Plato and Pythagoras, much in evidence at Chartres, mathematics held the key to understanding order in the universe.

Grammar was the foundation for the *trivium*. The texts of Donatus and Priscian were available from the cathedral's vast library. The method of teaching grammar was incessant drilling conducted by underlings and probably not by the major scholars at Chartres. If the later sculpture of Grammar holding a switch, located on the portal of the Gothic cathedral at Chartres, is any indication, flogging assumed a part of the pedagogical methodology through which the student suffered (in addition to the drilling) as he proceeded along the path toward mastering the *trivium*.

Rhetoric and logic emerged triumphant in the eleventh century in response to the growing need to persuade an audience of readers or listeners toward goodness. This persuasion was part of a religious mission for the monks at Chartres. The work of Quintillian served as the basis of oratorical study, but rhetoric was subordinate to logic at this time. Having studied logic with Gerbert at Reims, Fulbert strongly advocated the pursuit of logic. Porphyrys's third century B.C.E. commentary on Aristotle's *Topica* (335-323 B.C.E.; *Topics*, 1812) and Boethius's treatise "Introductio ad syllogismos categoricos" (early 500's; introduction to categoric syllogisms) were starting points for the fledgling subject of logic at Chartres: Aristotle and his rationalism were not to appear in France until the twelfth century. Yet the importance of syllogisms here points directly toward the advent of Scholasticism in the twelfth and thirteenth centuries.

Although the *trivium* was more in evidence than the *quadrivium* at Chartres, the cathedral school still managed to earn an outstanding reputation for mathematics. A rare book on geometry written by Albinus circulated throughout the cathedral school. Fulbert's talents in mathematics attracted Ragimbold of Cologne to come to Chartres and study with Fulbert. Ragimbold's experience, however, was not an entirely happy one. Ragimbold claimed that on one occasion Fulbert was able to demonstrate one geometric problem but not a second one. Ragimbold left Chartres in frustration. Because Ragimbold was to become a major mathematician of the eleventh century, perhaps Fulbert was overmatched by a brilliant student who not only was much better that the other students at Chartres but also may have surpassed Fulbert himself in the study of mathematics. Aside from this one criticism, most students had nothing but praise for the mathematical instruction they received at Chartres.

The Cathedral at Chartres, south transept. The cathedral's Gothic features were added after the fire of 1194. (Hulton|Archive by Getty Images)

Medicine was taught and practiced at Chartres under the watchful eye of Heribrand. Richer, the monk of Saint Remy and a former student of Gerbert of Aurillac, described the process of a long and complicated journey to Chartres in 991. It seemed that the trip was beset by difficulties at every turn. With his perilous travels behind him, Richer recounted that he studied the *Harmony of Hippocrates, Galen and Suranus*, along with the *Aphorisms* of Hippocrates. From his studies with Heribrand and from his readings of the classical texts, Richer recounted that he was prepared to write theoretical analyses of medical problems and surgical procedures. Richer praised the generosity of his teacher and claimed that pharmacy, botany, and surgery were well within Heribrand's range of expertise. Although Richer and Heribrand were thoroughly acquainted with the ancients and the medical manuscripts in the Chartres library, other capable scholars, such as Fulbert, understood the rudiments of home remedies and their application toward healing even though they failed to grasp the more advanced theoretical treatises on medicine. It appears that divisional study and expertise were in evidence at the cathedral school.

From the *quadrivium*, astronomy was another popular subject at

Chartres. Fulbert was responsible for introducing the astrolabe, a device long used by the Muslims to gauge celestial altitudes and to tell time. The Muslims were chiefly responsible for the transmission of ancient Greek astronomical texts. Tenth century contact with the Muslims introduced the astrolabe and astronomy to Christian Europe. Gerbert of Aurillac had traveled to Muslim Spain, where he studied the ancient texts as seen through Muslim eyes. Gerbert himself used the astrolabe and wrote a book about the device. It is likely that Fulbert's knowledge of the astrolabe and astronomy came from his association with Gerbert. Fulbert's interest in astronomy is demonstrated by his writings, which are sprinkled with reference to zodiacal signs and the tabulations of constellations.

One of the three doors of the Royal Portal of Chartres, showing the ancient motif of Christ and the Four Animals but with a humanized Christ. The Apostles are joined by famous scholars from the ancient world, signaling the Scholastics' belief that classical learning could be reconciled with Christian doctrine. (Hulton|Archive by Getty Images)

An eleventh century Vatican inventory of books at Chartres reveals the breadth and the depth of classical sources in the cathedral school library. Martianus Capella accompanies Fortunatus, Juvenal, Ovid, Porphyry, Vergil, and Cicero. An eleventh century monk brought a list of books that he had read to Saint Emneram's monastery in Regensburg. It is not exactly clear whether he had studied either at Chartres or Reims, but the surviving list is instructive about the availability of books at both Reims and Chartres. The student monk mentions works by Cicero, Quintillian, Pliny, and Livy, among others. If this student knew these sources, it is clear that Fulbert and his scholarly circle were thoroughly conversant with the same texts. These books would have formed the backbone of the most important classical Roman literature. It is true that Fulbert, his colleagues, and his students admired the classical tradition and all that it had to offer them.

SIGNIFICANCE

The scholars of Chartres gave proper tribute to the value of the classical tradition for the clergy and their receptive flock. The primary goal of the cathedral school was not to train students in the liberal arts for their use in the secular world, but rather to train educated orthodox and moral clergymen who would temper the vicissitudes of daily life faced by their parishioners who lived in the secular world. The classics, an appropriate background for the study of theology, were used to support Christian principles and ideals.

In the twelfth century, Bernard of Chartres understood the blending of the Christian and classical worlds. He saw no conflict between them when he said, unabashedly, that scholars of his own time were dwarfs standing on the shoulders of the giants from a more glorious past.

Barbara M. Fahy

FURTHER READING

Bolgar, R. R. *The Classical Heritage and Its Beneficiaries*. New York: Cambridge University Press, 1958. This scholarly work, accessible to general readers, serves as an important text on classical learning in the Western world.

Burckhardt, Titus. *Chartres and the Birth of the Cathedral*. Translated by William Stoddart. Ipswich, England: Golgonooza, 1995. A look into the architectural history of the Gothic cathedral of Chartres.

Courtenay, William J., and Jürgen Miethke, eds. *Universities and Schooling in Medieval Society*. Boston: Brill, 2000. A history of universities and schooling during the European Middle Ages. Essays originally presented as conference papers.

MacKinney, Loren C. *Bishop Fulbert and Education at the School of Chartres*. Vol. 6. Notre Dame, Ind.: Mediaeval Institute, 1957. An attempt at balance and comprehensiveness in portraying Fulbert and his role as teacher and mentor at the cathedral school. Recommended for advanced readers familiar with medieval history.

Mann, Nicholas, and Birger Munk Olsen, eds. *Medieval and Renaissance Scholarship: Proceedings of the Second European Science Foundation Workshop on the Classical Tradition in the Middle Ages and the Renaissance*. New York: E. J. Brill, 1997. Essays surveying the history and significance of classical literature, scholarship, and learning during the Middle Ages through the Renaissance.

Sandys, John E. *A History of Classical Scholarship*. 3 vols. Harper and Row, 1964. A standard, comprehensive work on the classics. Essential reading for those who want to understand the evolution of classical scholarship throughout the ages.

Southern, R. W. *Medieval Humanism and Other Studies*. New York: Harper and Row, 1971. This survey of medieval Humanism covers many topics on intellectual history and provides an original presentation of the material.

Wagner, David L. *The Seven Liberal Arts in the Middle Ages*. Bloomington: Indiana University Press, 1986. This collection of superb essays written by key scholars provides an excellent, in-depth guide to the study of the seven liberal arts throughout the Middle Ages.

SEE ALSO: 595-665: Invention of Decimals and Negative Numbers; c. 950: Court of Córdoba Flourishes in Spain; 11th-12th centuries: Building of Romanesque Cathedrals; c. 1100: Arabic Numerals Are Introduced into Europe; 1100-1300: European Universities Emerge; c. 1150: Moors Transmit Classical Philosophy and Medicine to Europe; c. 1150-1200: Development of Gothic Architecture; 1155: Charter of Lorris Is Written; c. 1250: Improvements in Shipbuilding and Navigation; 1328-1350: Flowering of Late Medieval Physics; 1403-1407: *Yonglo Dadian* Encyclopedia Is Compiled; 1410-1440: Florentine School of Art Emerges.

RELATED ARTICLES in *Great Lives from History: The Middle Ages, 477-1453*: Canute the Great; Saint Fulbert of Chartres; Judah ha-Levi; Poggio; Priscian; William of Moerbeke.

1031
CALIPHATE OF CÓRDOBA FALLS

The fall of the caliphate of Córdoba marked the receding political power of Muslim Spain and its loss of cultural influence.

LOCALE: Córdoba, Spain

CATEGORIES: Government and politics; religion; wars, uprisings, and civil unrest; cultural and intellectual history

KEY FIGURES

ʿAbd al-Raḥmān III al-Nāṣir (891-961), emir who proclaimed himself caliph of Córdoba, r. 929-961

al-Hakam II (d. 976), son of ʿAbd al-Raḥmān III and caliph of Córdoba, r. 961-976

Subh (fl. tenth century), concubine, then favored wife of al-Hakam, then queen mother of Hishām II

Hishām II (965-1013), caliph of Córdoba, r. 976-1009 and 1010-1013

Abū ʿĀmir al-Manṣūr (c. 938-1002), prime minister-chancellor of Córdoba, 976-1002

al-Mushafi (fl. tenth century), first minister under al-Hakam II and Hishām II

Ghalib (fl. tenth century), general and military head under al-Hakam II and Hishām II

al-Muẓaffar (d. 1008), son of al-Manṣūr who served as chamberlain, 1002-1008

SUMMARY OF EVENT

The tenth century was the golden age of Muslim Spain, and Córdoba was its political and intellectual center. Yet the roots of the downfall of the Umayyad caliphate in al-Andalus (Andalusia, or Muslim Spain)

The first caliph of Córdoba, ʿAbd al-Raḥman III al-Nāṣir, on horseback, surveying his executioners. Taking the title caliph in 929, he was known for unifying Islamic Spain and maintaining the peace, in part by ruthless suppression of Christians, Jews, and other religious dissidents. (Hulton/Archive by Getty Images)

can be found in the caliphate's rapid rise to power.

On January 16, 929, ʿAbd al-Raḥmān III al-Nāṣir proclaimed himself caliph, an act that separated Córdoba from the caliphate at Baghdad. Córdoba, a city with a population of 100,000, was noted for its extensive markets, the architecture of its mosques, its official residences, palace, industrial zones, baths, and gardens. Beginning in 936, ʿAbd al-Raḥmān built a new palace and administrative headquarters, Madinat az-Zahra, approximately 3 miles (5 kilometers) from the city. Until 961, al-Andalus prospered during his reign. ʿAbd al-Raḥmān quieted the Christian campaigns in the north as well as the Fāṭimid navy that threatened the Mediterranean from North Africa. To maintain this peace, he relied heavily on mercenary soldiers, and he imported Slavs from Europe for his personal protection.

ʿAbd al-Raḥmān was succeeded as caliph by his son al-Hakam II, who continued many of the policies of his father. Always the scholar, he accumulated a library of more than 400,000 books, an impressive collection in its time. Al-Hakam tended, however, to rely more strongly than his father on officials to conduct routine activities of the caliphate. Although he failed to prepare a successor to assume the caliphate on his death, his concubine Subh gave birth to a son, Hishām, who succeeded his father.

Because Hishām was only eleven years old when his father died, there was some difficulty in determining who would assume the position of caliph while several groups, including the Slav bodyguards, attempted to place their own choices. Abū ʿĀmir al-Manṣūr, chancellor under al-Hakam, accepted the guardianship of Hishām until he came of age and was able to serve as caliph. Al-Manṣūr, as Ibn Abū ʿĀmir came to be known, with al-Mushafi, the first minister, and Ghalib, the head of the military, formed a triumvirate to carry out the responsibilities of the young caliph. Unfortunately, Hishām was isolated in the palace for the remainder of his life, however, and others ruled for him. Al-Manṣūr manipulated himself into a position of absolute power; he was aided in his acquiescence of power by Subh who, by that time, held great influence outside of Córdoba. His Madinat az-Zḥira equaled in splendor the palace of ʿAbd al-Raḥmān III. With his administration relocated to the new center, Hishām was left a veritable prisoner within the palace. By 981, al-Manṣūr was named mayor of the palace and ruled until 1002. During his reign, he built extensively, cut taxes, and increased the size of the army by the use of Berbers from Africa. Despite his means of obtaining control of the caliphate, al-Andalus was stable and prosperous under his rule.

Al-Manṣūr not only centralized authority in his own hands but also nominated his son, al-Muẓaffar as chamberlain. After the death of al-Manṣūr, the change in authority was again challenged by several groups, particularly the Slavs. Al-Muẓaffar and al-Manṣūr had both maintained the absolute power bequeathed to them by the caliph, who was left completely unfit to assume the responsibilities of the office. Because al-Muẓaffar and al-Manṣūr had done nothing to harm the caliph nor diminish the respect for the office, the populace generally accepted their rule. When al-Muẓaffar died after only six years of rule, his brother tried to succeed him and, ultimately, gain the title of caliph. These actions quickly led to his downfall and to the end of the dictatorship.

From 1008 until the dissolution of the caliphate in 1031, al-Andalus suffered an ongoing civil war. In the absence of the tight control that al-Manṣūr and his son had maintained, chaos suddenly erupted. Mercenaries who were no longer being paid soon resorted to lawlessness and violence. Various groups, particularly the Slavs and the Berbers as well as the people of Córdoba, again put forward leaders who tried to establish control, but none was successful. Some were in control for only a few months, others for as long as a few years. Madinat az-Zahra, the royal city built by ʿAbd al-Raḥmān, and Madinat az-Ẓhira, the administrative center built by al-Manṣūr, were both destroyed completely in the civil war. Hishām II retained the title of caliph through the early years of the civil war, but remained impotent and was eventually killed in 1013.

Following so many years of war and internal struggles, al-Andalus was eager for the peace and stability it had enjoyed previously. In 1031, the elders of Córdoba met under the leadership of Abn Hazm Ibn Jahwar and abolished the institution of the caliphate. In its place, a governing council was established, which was to rule the region of Córdoba. Shortly thereafter, towns established their own independent rulers, who became known as party kings.

In considering this period of al-Andalus, the historian is left with few primary sources of material. While some caliphs employed professional historians to record the events of the period, much of their writing was destroyed during the civil war. Historians also caution that these writers made no attempt to hide their allegiances in their efforts to explain the reasons for the downfall of the caliphate. Some Muslim writers of the time followed a religious line of thought that claimed that the events were a trial or test for Muslims from God. They were defeated, they believed, because of losing their way from the right path.

Other writers pointed to more political and social causes for the great downfall. Many, for example, pointed to ʿAbd al-Raḥmān's reliance on mercenary soldiers and Slavs, which led to ethnic divisions within Muslim society. In the same way, al-Manṣūr increased the size of the military by importing Berber soldiers and, at the same time, eliminated tribal groupings. Society was unable to assimilate so many new groups, and a great deal of friction resulted. There was also concern that the caliphate did not have the resources to maintain such a large military force.

Another cause for concern was al-Hakam's relinquishment of his authority to various officials of the palace. This action may have enabled al-Manṣūr and others who followed to usurp the power of the caliph and then centralize that power outside of the office of caliph.

SIGNIFICANCE

Despite such reasons, history clearly shows that with the abolishment of the caliphate in 1031, al-Andalus was divided into many independent kingdoms and the glory of the tenth century caliphate was not seen again. It also seems safe to assert that the loss of the Umayyad caliphate marked a shift in the relations between Christian Spanish kings of the north and the Muslims of al-Andalus. The Christian kings' efforts to reconquer Spain from the Muslims gained greater strength and momentum after the fall of Córdoba.

—Donald E. Cellini

FURTHER READING

Chejne, Anwar G. *Muslim Spain: Its History and Culture*. St. Paul: University of Minnesota Press, 1974. The second chapter, "The Caliphate 929-1031," includes a discussion of both the rise and fall of the caliphate of Córdoba.

Fletcher, Richard. *Moorish Spain*. New York: Henry Holt, 1992. While this work deals with various aspects of the Spanish-Islamic state, chapter 4, "The Caliphate of Córdoba," considers the glories of the caliphate as well as its collapse.

García-Ballester, Luis. *Medicine in a Multicultural Society: Christian, Jewish and Muslim Practitioners in the Spanish Kingdoms, 1222-1610*. Aldershot, England: Ashgate, 2001. A look at medical practice and medical practitioners in the Spanish realm after the introduction of Moorish medical knowledge into the region. Includes an index.

Huff, Toby E. *The Rise of Early Modern Science: Islam, China, and the West*. 2d ed. New York: Cambridge University Press, 2003. Provides a strong cross-cultural background for the rise of science and medicine in Moorish Spain. Includes illustrations, a bibliography, and index.

Reilly, Bernard F. *The Medieval Spains*. New York: Cambridge University Press, 1993. The caliphate and its decline is discussed within the general context of medieval Spain.

Scales, Peter C. *The Fall of the Caliphate of Córdoba: Berbers and Andalusis in Conflict*. Leiden, the Netherlands: E. J. Brill, 1994. In this scholarly work, Scales examines the primary sources available in his discussion of the fall of the caliphate.

Watt, W. Montgomery. *A History of Islamic Spain*. Edinburgh: Edinburgh University Press, 1965. This detailed history of Islam in Spain provides extensive background on the events leading up to and following the collapse of the caliphate of Córdoba.

SEE ALSO: April or May, 711: Ṭārik Crosses into Spain; c. 950: Court of Córdoba Flourishes in Spain; c. 1010-1015: Avicenna Writes His *Canon of Medicine*; c. 1150: Moors Transmit Classical Philosophy and Medicine to Europe; 1190: Moses Maimonides Writes *The Guide of the Perplexed*; c. 1265-1273: Thomas Aquinas Compiles the *Summa Theologica*.

RELATED ARTICLES in *Great Lives from History: The Middle Ages, 477-1453*: Pietro d'Abano; ʿAbd al-Raḥmān III al-Nāṣir; Abū Ḥanīfah; Alfonso X; Alhazen; Averroës; Avicenna; Roger Bacon; al-Bīrūnī; Dante; Fakhr al-Dīn al-Rāzī; al-Ghazzālī; al-Ḥallāj; Ibn Gabirol; Judah ha-Levi; Raymond Lull; Moses Maimonides; Moses de León; Naḥmanides; Raymond of Peñafort; Thomas Aquinas.

1040-1055
EXPANSION OF THE SELJUK TURKS

The Oğuz Turkish Seljuks migrated from Central Asia to Khorāsān and later into Persia and Anatolia, where they took Baghdad from the Buyid Dynasty and established an empire that lasted for more than two centuries.

LOCALE: Central Asia and Persia (now Iraq and Iran)
CATEGORY: Expansion and land acquisition

KEY FIGURES

Seljuk (c. tenth century), founder of the Seljuk Dynasty
Toghrïl Beg (c. 990-1063), khan of the Seljuk Turks, r. 1016-1063, and sultan, r. 1055-1063
Chaghrï Beg (c. 990-1060), king of Khorāsān, r. 1040-1060
Masʿūd I (d. 1040), son of Maḥmūd of Ghazna and ruler of the Ghaznavid Empire, r. 1031-1040

SUMMARY OF EVENT

The Xiongnu (Hsiung-nu, or Huns) of the Altai Mountains and Lake Baikal region, mentioned in the Chinese documents of the second century B.C.E., are most likely the ancestors of the Turks. Turkish nomads, the Oğuz or Turkmen, founded the Göktürk Empire in Transoxiania in the sixth century and by the eighth century extended from the Aral Sea to the Hindu Kush. As part of the great migrations of peoples from Central Asia in the first millennium of the common era, in the eighth century, Turkish tribes, including the Oğuz, moved south of the Oxus and into the steppe north of the Black Sea.

One of the military leaders of the Oğuz was the resourceful Duqaq (Iron Bow), a member of the Qiniq tribe, the leading clan of the Oğuz. Duqaq's son Seljuk fled with his family and followers from the Oğuz leader Yabghu, who had become jealous of his popularity and power. When Seljuk became khan, he moved to the lower Jaxartes (Syr Darya) River. In the 990's, the tribe adopted Islam and began fighting against the pagan Turks. Seljuk's son bore biblical names—Mūsā (Moses), Mikail (Michael), and Arslan Israil (Israel). Although this practice was not uncommon among Turkish Muslim leaders, some scholars have suggested that before converting to Islam, the Seljuks had considered Christianity. Seljuk's son moved farther southward to find better grazing lands and herbs.

The Seljuks served as frontier guards for the Turkish Sāmānids of western Turkistan and Maḥmūd of Ghazna in Afghanistan. Seljuk's descendants split, some going to India, others becoming vassals of the ʿAbbāsid caliph of Baghdad, the spiritual Sunni successor of Muḥammad the Prophet. The latter group, led by Mikail's sons, Seljuk's grandsons Toghrïl Beg and Chaghrï Beg, established the empire bearing his name in 1040. Although some individuals had moved into Persia and Egypt earlier, this was the first large-scale migration of Turks from Central Asia into the Middle East, opening a new era of

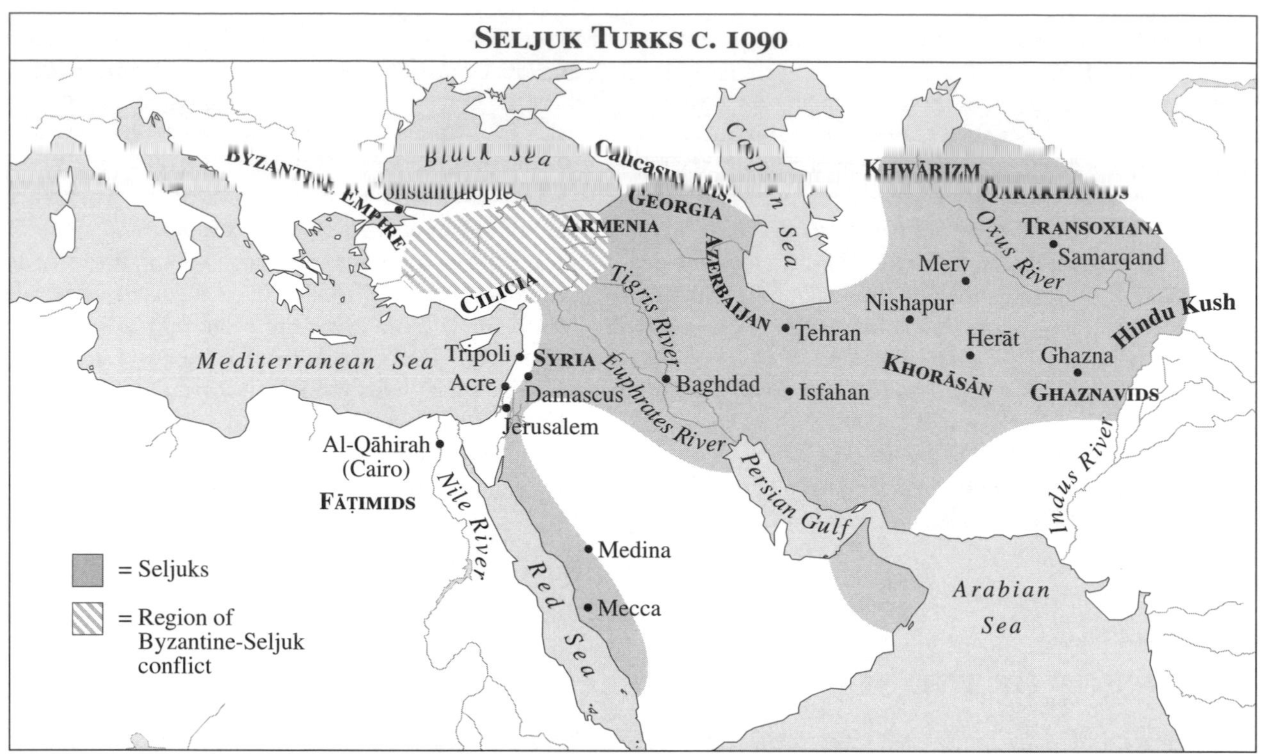

SELJUK TURKS C. 1090

Islamic history. They were fierce warriors, but their contact with the Persians greatly influenced their culture and made them able administrators and promoters of Islamic art and science as well.

In 1038, Toghrïl and Chaghrï defeated Masʿūd I, son of Maḥmūd of Ghazna, at the Battle of Nishapur, and the Seljuks, a pastoral herding people, moved into the Khorāsān grazing grounds of northeastern Persia. The Seljuks used the effective tactics of fire and feigned flight. The light cavalry of the Turks rode close to the enemy, fired at them with their bows and arrows, and then retreated rapidly, drawing the enemy into an encirclement. After this battle, Masʿūd I saw that the Seljuks were a threat to his empire and prepared to defeat them. However, although he won battles in 1039, he was unable to destroy the Seljuk threat. Masʿūd I proposed a peace that would leave the Seljuks the border cities of Nesa, Bevard, and Fevre, while the Turks would leave Nishapur, Serahs, and Merv, and Masʿūd I would concentrate his forces in Herāt. The Seljuks agreed in order to gain time to regroup, but soon they began to invade Ghaznavid territory again. Masʿūd faced the Turks in a series of battles, the greatest of which took place at Dandāngān Castle near Merv on May 24, 1040, where the Seljuk army won a decisive victory over Masʿūd's forces.

Toghrïl declared himself emir of Khorāsān and *sultan al-muazzam* (exalted leader). As was the custom, he also sent a *fetih-name*, a declaration of victory, to neighboring rulers. The Seljuks now were an independent state. The Seljuk leaders met in council at Merv immediately after the battle and declared that they were loyal to the Sunni ʿAbbāsid caliph and that they would administer Khorāsān with justice. According to Turkish custom, the council also announced plans for future conquests and the lands they would administer. Chaghrï Beg, whom the council declared as *melik* (king) of Khorāsān, would expand into Ceyhan and Ghazna. The council assigned Toghrïl Beg to rule over Nishapur and the western regions of Persia. Their uncle, Mūsā Yabghu, was given the command to move south toward Herāt in Persia. The Seljuks carried out their tasks rapidly over the next months.

Later in 1040, Chaghrï Beg drove the Ghaznavids from their last positions in Khorāsān, taking the city of Belh. In 1043, Chaghrï and Toghrïl captured the commercial center Harezm, the city of Shah Melik, who had previously raided into their lands. Chaghrï Beg and his son, the future sultan Alp Arslan, defeated the Qarakhanids and established a border treaty with them. In 1059, Chaghrï also came to agreement with the

Ghaznavid sultan Ibrāhīm, establishing a border at the Hindu Kush Mountains between them. Mūsā Yabghu took Herāt and the Sistan, but in 1064, he rebelled against his great-nephew Alp Arslan (by then sultan) and lost his political positions.

The ʿAbbāsid caliph, al-Qāʾim, organized the Turks under Toghrïl Beg as *ghazi* warriors (defenders of the faith) in tribal bands living on the borders of the empire and defending its territories from invaders, but Toghrïl asked for the task of spreading Islam westward, a task he had been assigned by the Seljuk council. The caliph designated him King of the East and the West, giving the Seljuks great prestige, and they established a well-administered Sunni state with its capital at Isfahan under the nominal authority of the ʿAbbāsid caliphs in Baghdad.

The Sunni ʿAbbāsid caliphs, however, were under the control of the ruling Shīʿite Buyid Dynasty in Persia, and from 1043 to 1055, Toghrïl Beg invaded their territory in northern and eastern Persia. He also raid Armenia and, in 1048, the Byzantine territory of Anatolia. Then, in 1055, Toghrïl Beg led the *ghazis* and his mercenary slaves, mainly Circassians and Kurds, into Baghdad and seized power from the Buyids, beginning the great Seljuk sultanate.

SIGNIFICANCE

The Seljuk Empire revived Islamic political power in the Middle East and established several ruling dynasties—in Iraq, in Kirman (southeast Persia), in Syria, and most famously in Asia Minor, where the Seljuks paved the way for the great Ottoman Empire that succeeded them.

This first large-scale Turkish invasion into the Middle East instigated an age of great cultural achievement, although many of the advances were accomplished by non-Turkish Muslims such as the Persian Niẓām al-Mulk (1018/1019-1092), whose *Siyāsat-nama* (c. 1091; *The Book of Government: Or, Rules for Kings*, 1960) gives insight into the Seljuk state and also the Islamic philosophies of the age. The Seljuks also established hospitals and medical schools. They introduced some Turkish elements into Islamic society, art, and culture such as the use of the horsetail, or *galish*, as the symbol of the van of the army and the sultan's gold embroidered leather saddle as his symbol on public occasions.

Ultimately, the Seljuks' empire proved to be short-lived because of their practice of dividing their land among all their heirs—unlike the later Ottomans, who kept their empire together under one son of the sultan.

—*Frederick B. Chary*

FURTHER READING

Editors of Time-Life Books. *Light in the East: Time Frame A.D. 1000-1100*. Alexandria, Va.: Time-Life Books, 1988. A history designed for the general reading putting the role of the Seljuks in the context of the eleventh century. Bibliography, index.

Lapidus, Ira M. *A History of Islamic Societies*. 2d ed. New York: Cambridge University Press, 2002. A scholarly account containing chapters on the Seljuk Turks. Illustrations, maps, bibliographic references, index.

Leiser, Gary, ed. and trans. *A History of the Seljuks: İbrahim Kafesoğlu's Interpretation and the Resulting Controversy*. Carbondale: Southern Illinois University Press, 1988. An authoritative and indispensable translation of a book-length article by a modern scholar that is not only "a significant Turkish contribution to Seljuk historiography, but . . . also among the most recent surveys of the entire Seljuk period in any language," a claim that remained true to the end of the twentieth century. Genealogical tables, glossary, bibligraphy.

Rāshid al-Dīn ibn Ṭabib. *The History of the Seljuq Turks from the Jāmiʿal-tawārīkh*. Translated and annotated by Kenneth Allin Luther; edited by C. Edmund Bosworth. Richmond, Surrey, England: Curzon, 2001. An annotated English translation of two contemporary works on the Seljuks. Maps.

Richards, D. S. *The Annals of the Saljuq Turks*. London: Routledge/Curzon, 2002. A modern translation of contemporary Turkish documents. Includes bibliographical references and index.

_______, ed. *Islamic Civilization, 950-1150: A Colloquium Published Under the Auspices of the Near Eastern History Group, Oxford, the Near East Center, University of Pennsylvania*. Oxford, England: Cassier, 1973. A scholarly colloquium covering the period of the Seljuks and their impact on the Islamic world. Illustrations, bibliographic references, and index.

SEE ALSO: 744-840: Uighur Turks Rule Central Asia; 956: Oğhuz Turks Migrate to Transoxiana; 997-1030: Reign of Maḥmūd of Ghazna; 1010: Firdusi Composes the *Shahnamah*; 1077: Seljuk Dynasty Is Founded.

RELATED ARTICLES in *Great Lives from History: The Middle Ages, 477-1453*: Alp Arslan; al-Bīrūnī; Maḥmūd of Ghazna; Niẓām al-Mulk; Tamerlane.

c. 1045
BI SHENG DEVELOPS MOVABLE EARTHENWARE TYPE

Bi Sheng's invention of movable type was a significant event in the history of printing. His discovery preceded Johannes Gutenberg's developments in typography by about four centuries.

LOCALE: China

CATEGORIES: Science and technology; cultural and intellectual history; communications

KEY FIGURES

Bi Sheng (Pi Sheng; d. 1051), a Chinese alchemist, who invented movable type

Shen Kuo (Shen K'ua; 1031-1095), Chinese scientist who wrote about movable type

SUMMARY OF EVENT

Printing existed in China by the end of the second century. In the earliest form of printing, moistened paper was pressed against stone inscriptions or carvings of texts, much like stone rubbings. Woodblock printing began to be used during the Tang Dynasty (Tan'g; 618-907). The text or images were carved in relief on a single wood plate, which was then inked. This form of printing continued to be used in China until the end of the nineteenth century. The world's first movable type was created by Bi Sheng, a commoner, during the Northern Song Dynasty (Sung; 960-1126). He made individual ceramic-type pieces for each character or ideogram.

Little is known about Bi Sheng's life. His year of birth is unknown, but the discovery of his tomb in 1990 established that he had lived in Yingshan County, Hubei Province. According to his tombstone, he had four sons and three grandsons and died in 1051.

Bi Sheng's invention of movable-type printing was described in great detail by his contemporary, Shen Kuo, the eminent Song scholar and scientist. After Shen Kuo retired, in about 1088, he wrote his famous thirty-volume encyclopedic work, *Mengxi bitan* (dream pool essays, or brush talks from the dream creek), The work's 609 articles covered such diverse subjects as science, history, politics, philosophy, and technology. *Mengxi bitan* also contained the earliest surviving historical account of movable-type printing. Shen Kuo describes Bi Sheng's method (as translated in Thomas Carter's *The Invention of Printing in China*, 1955):

> He took sticky clay and cut in it characters as thin as the edge of a copper coin. Each character formed as it were a single type. He baked them in the fire to make them hard. He had previously prepared an iron plate and he had covered this plate with a mixture of pine resin, wax, and paper ashes. When he wished to print, he took an iron frame and set it on the iron plate. In this he placed the type, set close together. When the frame was full, the whole made one solid block of type. He then placed it near the fire to warm it. When the paste [at the back] was slightly melted, he took a smooth board and pressed it over the surface, so that the block of type became as even as a whetstone.

Shen Kuo said Bi Sheng could print quite rapidly, partly because he would prepare a second form while the first one was printing to avoid wasting any time. He also made several pieces of type for each character, up to twenty or more pieces for common characters. When he was not using the charters, Bi Sheng "had them arranged with paper labels, one label for words of each rhyme-group, and thus kept them in wooden cases."

In 1313, another historical account of Bi Sheng's invention appeared in Wang Zhen's historical work, *A Guide to Movable-type Printing*. Wang Zhen, a magistrate, experimented with wooden type, cut individually by hand, to print his district's official records in the *Jing de xian zhi* (chronicle of Jingde County) and the *Nong shu* (treatise on agriculture). He invented a rotary typesetting device, a revolving table on which was placed a round bamboo frame holding the type. The type in the compartments were arranged according to a popular book of rhymes. A second table held the most common characters, with a total of more than 30,000 characters on the two tables. The type was taken from the tables to put on a dry block for printing.

SIGNIFICANCE

Bi Sheng's invention was a major revolution in printing technology, but movable-type printing did not flourish or become widespread in China at that time. Although the invention made it possible to print thousands of copies of a book easily, much time and effort were required to set up printing plates with the individual movable characters. In contrast to the twenty-six characters or letters of the English alphabet, there were tens of thousands of individual Chinese characters. Also, in feudal society, reading was limited to a privileged minority, so it was not necessary or economical to print thousands of copies. Traditional woodblock printing, with characters engraved a page at a time, remained the principal printing technology.

However, although movable-type printing was not the dominant technology, printers and others continued to experiment, resulting in numerous improvements. During the Mongol Yuan Dynasty (1279-1368), experiments with tin, the earliest metal type, were conducted. Tin failed to hold the traditional water-based inks well, and wooden types were developed.

Later, during the Ming (1368-1644) and Qing (Ch'ing, 1644-1911) Dynasties, wood-block-letter printing became popular. In 1773, during the reign of Emperor Qianlong (r. 1736-1795), the government produced 253,500 type pieces from date tree wood. China's largest wood-type publication was *Wu ying dian ju zhen ban cong shu* (eighteenth century; books of Wuying Hall), a 2,300-volume compilation of 138 books by various writers. During the reign of Emperor Daoguang (r. 1821-1850), Zhai Jingsheng is recorded as having used more than 100,000 pieces of clay type to print the *Pedigree Records of the Zhais*.

Chinese printers c. 1500. (Hulton|Archive by Getty Images)

Movable-type printing technology also traveled to Korea, Japan, the Middle East, and Europe. Bi Sheng's invention, the world's first block-letter printing, was the precursor of twentieth century lead type printing.

—*Alice Myers*

FURTHER READING

Carter, Thomas. *The Invention of Printing in China and Its Spread Westward*. New York: Ronald Press, 1955. The authoritative, scholarly work on the subject. The chapter, "The Invention of Movable Type in China" includes the author's translation of the entire passage about Bi Sheng's invention, as recorded in Shen Kuo's work. Includes an extensive bibliography, footnotes, and illustrations.

Guppy, Henry, and Bruce Rogers. *Stepping-Stones to the Art of Typography*. Manchester, England: Manchester University Press, 1928. Describes Bi Sheng's invention within its historical context and the difficulties of the method. Includes a bibliography and illustrations.

Institute of the History of Natural Sciences, Chinese Academy of Sciences. *Ancient China's Technology and Science*. Beijing: Foreign Languages Press, 1987. The chapter, "The Invention and Development of Printing and Its Dissemination Abroad," discusses Bi Sheng's invention. Bibliography consists primarily of original source materials.

Liu, Guojun, and Zheng Rusi. Translated by Zhou Yicheng. *The Story of Chinese Books*. Beijing: Foreign Language Press, 1985. The chapter entitled. "The Invention of Movable-Type Printing and Its Development" discusses in detail the history of this invention. Illustrations include a picture of Bi Sheng.

McMurtrie, Douglas C. *The Book: The Story of Printing and Bookmaking*. London: Oxford University Press, 1972. The chapter on "Printing in the Far East" discusses the historical records of the invention of movable type in China and its later development in Korea. Illustrated, with a bibliography for each chapter.

Ross, Frank. *Oracle Bones, Stars, and Wheelbarrows:*

Ancient Chinese Science and Technology. Boston: Houghton Mifflin Company, 1982. Includes a basic, general history of printing in China and a description of Bi Sheng's printing process. Bibliography.

Tsien Tsuen-Hsuin. *Paper and Printing*. Part 1 in *Chemistry and Chemical Technology*, Vol. 5 in *Science and Civilisation in China*, translated and edited by Joseph Needham. New York: Cambridge University Press, 1985. A scholarly and comprehensive study of the invention and technology of printing in China, from the earliest woodcuts to the beginning of the nineteenth century. It discusses the invention of movable type and the resulting spread of printing. Illustrated, with bibliography.

Twitchett, Denis. *Printing and Publishing in Medieval China*. London: Wynkyn de Worde Society, 1983. Informative chapters on printing from movable type in both China and Korea. Includes illustrations, notes, and bibliography.

SEE ALSO: 7th-8th centuries: Papermaking Spreads to Korea, Japan, and Central Asia; 618: Founding of the Tang Dynasty; 713-741: First Newspapers in China; 868: First Book Printed; 960: Founding of the Song Dynasty; 1403-1407: *Yonglo Dadian* Encyclopedia Is Compiled; c. 1450: Gutenberg Pioneers the Printing Press.

RELATED ARTICLE in *Great Lives from History: The Middle Ages, 477-1453*: Mi Fei.

1048
ZĪRIDS BREAK FROM FĀṬIMID DYNASTY AND REVIVE SUNNI ISLAM

The Berber Zīrids broke from the Fāṭimid Dynasty and its Shīʿite Islam, took control of the province it was entrusted to maintain, and started a revival of Sunni Islam in the Maghreb. The Zīrid's control marked the first time in the history of Islamic Africa that the leadership of an Islamic dynasty did not originate out of the east and the first time Berbers headed a dynasty.

LOCALE: North (especially northwest) Africa
CATEGORIES: Expansion and land acquisition; government and politics; religion

KEY FIGURES

al-Muʾizz ibn Bādīs (1007-1062), Zīrid leader and prince, initiated break from the Fāṭimids, r. 1016-1062

Zīrī ibn Manad (d. 971), loyal Fāṭimid soldier selected as commander of the Sanhaja Berbers and ruler of their territory

Yūsuf Buluggīn I ibn Zīrī (d. 984), Zīrī's son, appointed lieutenant of the western Fāṭimid Empire, r. 972-984

SUMMARY OF EVENT

In 1048, the Sanhaja Berber lieutenants of the Fāṭimid Empire relinquished their allegiance to the state, claimed allegiance to the ʿAbbāsids in faraway Baghdad, and eventually formed the Zīrid Dynasty. Before 1048, the Zīrids maintained nominal loyalty, paying tribute to the Fāṭimids, but they constantly pushed the boundaries toward independence without openly renouncing Fāṭimid authority. The Zīrids, it seems, were able to do this because of their past fidelity to the Fāṭimid state.

Three Zīrid rulers followed Zīrī ibn Manad: his son Yūsuf Buluggīn I ibn Zīrī; al-Manṣūr, who reigned from 984 to 995; and Bādīs ibn al-Mansūr, who reigned from 995 to 1016. Al-Manṣūr openly overthrew a Fāṭimid governor in Ifriqiya and tried to impose his control over the lost western Maghreb, focusing on Fès and Sijilmasa in 985, two important trans-Saharan trade centers. The Fāṭimids intervened militarily to rectify the situation, but the Zīrids were able to defeat this effort, although they did not maintain control of the west.

The political affairs in the eastern half of the Fāṭimid Empire kept the leadership occupied to such an extent that the Zīrids were left to make many of their own decisions. In 1048, the Zīrids officially broke away under the leadership of al-Muʾizz ibn Bādīs. The split was on both sociopolitical and religious grounds: political differences and a desire for autonomy, along with the social problems caused by economic stress; and religious differences. The Fāṭimids were Ismāʿīlī Shīʿites, which did not sit well with the primarily Khāijite and Sunni population of Zīrids.

For the lieutenants who came to be the leaders of a new empire known as the Zīrids, the economic collapse of their own territory in Ifriqiya, while Egyptian power and wealth increased, was cause for Zīrid discontent, recalcitrance, and noncooperation with the Fāṭimids. (By the 1060's even the Fāṭimid state was in serious economic difficulty.)

Ifriqiya's troubles were caused by multiple factors. Byzantine presence in the Mediterranean as well as the invasions of the Banū Hilāl Bedouins on behalf of the Egyptian state only exacerbated the problems caused by the increasing aridity of Ifriqiya. Competition from more powerful states diverted trade away from important trade centers in Ifriqiya, rerouting merchants to Morocco and Egypt and depriving the merchants and Ifriqiyan state of an income. Beginning in the early eleventh century, a series of food crises occurred, devastating the economy and social life of Ifriqiya, particularly the capital Kayrawan (Kairwan). For the nonmerchant classes, primarily the pastoralists and agriculturalists, these struggles were addressed by retreating into the western Sahara and the mountain regions. For those in the urban centers—the merchant classes—this was a period of economic hardship.

The Zīrids came to control the entire Maghreb and continued to control Ifriqiya, but lost control of the west to the Almoravids and the central Maghreb between Ifriqiya and the west to the Ḥammādids. In the end, the Zīrid Dynasty stretched from just west of present-day Tunis to just east of present-day Tripoli.

Under the reign of the Zīrids and Almoravids, the Maghreb population came to represent definitively the Sunni Muslim ideology that adhered to the Malikite school of Islamic law (*sharia*). The Maghreb had a strong segment of Khāijite Muslims. Under the Zīrids, this element was forced to accept Sunni Islam in the eleventh century. While the Sunni's believed that Abū Bakr was the rightful successor to the Prophet Muḥammad, the Khāijites, like the Shia, believed that ʿAlī was the rightful successor to the Prophet. With the defeat of Abū Yazīd (d. 947), the primary leader of Khāijites, the Muslims of that branch either converted or withdrew to secluded rural areas. As the Sunnis began to exert violence and massacre many of the Shīʿite of eastern Algeria and Tunisia in 1062, the practice of Shīʿite Islam, which had been advanced by the Fāṭimids, began to recede.

By 1065, the Banū Hilāl sieges on the Zīrid were relentless and shrinking the state. By the early twelfth century the Almohads seized control from the Banū Hilāl and other Arab tribes, but this was the end of Zīrid independence. The Ifriqiyan state was reduced to a small coastal strip, but piracy was so prevalent at that point that the state was in ruins.

SIGNIFICANCE

The Zīrid's political break from the Fāṭimid's was an important signal that the Fāṭimid Empire was losing control of its provinces politically and economically and that the empire was in a state of decline. Thus, with the short-lived rise to power of the Zīrids, a significant and renowned Islamic empire was waning.

Following the Zīrid rise to power, there were a number of Berber dynasties that came into the fore, including the Almoravids, Almohads, Zayyanids, Marinids, and Hafsids. Even in the eastern half of the Fāṭimid Empire, between Libya and Egypt, the Sanhaja Berbers rose to powerful positions for the first time following Zīrid rule.

In the eleventh century, the attempts of the Zīrids to centralize the Maghreb under their rule failed. The Zīrids still had to contend with hostilities from the Zanātah Berbers, even after throwing off their Fāṭimid overlords. As a consequence of the ethnic, religious, and political conflicts of the Zīrids, Zanātahs, and Ḥammādids, the central and western Maghreb became two separate entities. The Zīrids ruled the central region and the Ḥammādids governed the western Maghreb.

As a result of the religious tensions between Ismāʿīlī Shīʿite and Khāijites, Sunni Islam was able to achieve prominence in North Africa. The political struggles of the eleventh century had tremendous religious outcomes for North Africa, particularly in the Maghreb.

—Catherine Cymone Fourshey

FURTHER READING

Bosworth, Clifford Edmund. *The New Islamic Dynasties: A Chronological and Genealogical Manual.* 1967. Rev. ed. New York: Columbia University Press, 1996. A historical and genealogical accounting of the Islamic dynasties, including those in Africa. Bibliography, index.

Brett, Michael. "The Islamisization of Morocco from the Arabs to the Almoravids." *Journal of the Society for Moroccan Studies* 2 (1992): 57-71. A study of North Africa's development into a region with a distinct Islamic character.

Brett, Michael, and Elizabeth Fentress. *The Berbers.* Cambridge, Mass.: Blackwell, 1996. This study focuses on the history of the Berber-speaking peoples. The authors establish the identity of the Berbers and analyze their traditions, while tracing their political and social history. Maps, bibliography, index.

Clancy-Smith, Julia, ed. *North Africa, Islam, and the Mediterranean World: From the Almoravids to the Algerian War.* Portland, Oreg.: Frank Cass, 2001. Explores Islamic influence in North Africa in the century following the beginning of the Zīrid Dynasty. Illustrations, maps, bibliography, index.

Handler, Andrew. *The Zīrids of Granada*. Coral Gables, Fla.: University of Miami Press, 1974. Examines the north African Zīrid administrative system and its influence on Spain. Illustrations, bibliography.

Hrbek, I. "The Emergence of the Fāṭimids." In *Africa from the Seventh to the Eleventh Century*, edited by M. Elfasi and I. Hrbek. Vol. 4. Berkeley: University of California Press, 1995. Chapter 12 elucidates the history of the Fāṭimids as well as the emergence of the Zīrid Dynasty. Maps, plans, bibliography, index.

Oliver, Roland, and J. D. Fage, eds. *The Cambridge History of Africa*. Vols. 2-3. New York: Cambridge University Press, 1975-1986. A historical account of African civilizations before and during the time of the Zīrids. Focuses mostly on dynasties other than the Zīrid. Illustrations, bibliography, index.

Schatzmiller, Maya. *The Berbers and the Islamic State: The Marinid Experience in Pre-protectorate Morocco*. Princeton, N.J.: Markus Wiener, 2000. A detailed study of the history of the Berbers in North Africa and Morocco. Includes discussion of acculturation and its legacy, developing an Islamic state and institutions, and more. Bibliography, index.

SEE ALSO: 630-711: Islam Expands Throughout North Africa; April or May, 711: Ṭārik Crosses into Spain; 969-1171: Reign of the Fāṭimids; 11th century: Expansion of Sunni Islam in North Africa and Iberia; 1062-1147: Almoravids Conquer Morocco and Establish the Almoravid Empire; c. 1075-1086: Hummay Founds the Sefuwa Dynasty; 1076: Almoravids Sack Kumbi.

RELATED ARTICLES in *Great Lives from History: The Middle Ages, 477-1453*: ʿAbd al-Muʾmin; Afonso I; Damia al-Kāhina; Ṭāriq ibn-Ziyād; ʿUmar I.

1054
BEGINNING OF THE ROME-CONSTANTINOPLE SCHISM

The schism between Christians in Rome and Christians in Constantinople intensified and reached its culmination after the conquest of Constantinople by the soldiers of the Fourth Crusade in 1204. The schism later weakened Christianity against the rise of Islam during the Turkish conquests of the fourteenth and fifteenth centuries.

LOCALE: Constantinople, Byzantine Empire
CATEGORIES: Government and politics; organizations and institutions; religion

KEY FIGURES

Michael Cerularius (c. 1000-1059), patriarch of Constantinople, 1043-1058
Leo IX (1002-1054), Roman Catholic pope, 1048-1054
Urban II (c. 1042-1099), Roman Catholic pope, 1088-1099
Constantine IX Monomachus (c. 980-1055), Byzantine emperor, r. 1042-1055
Humbert of Silva Candida (c. 1000-1061), cardinal of Silva Candida and papal legate
Alexius I Comnenus (1048-1118), emperor of Constantinople, r. 1081-1118
Argyros (d. 1058), commander of Italy, Calabria, Sicily, and Paphlagonia, 1051-1058
Bohemond I (c. 1052-1111), Norman adventurer, commander of the Normans against Byzantium

SUMMARY OF EVENT

The gradual alienation between the Eastern and Western Christian churches may be traced as far back as the physical division of the Roman Empire in 395, when the Eastern Church, with its capital in Constantinople, was separated from the Western Roman Church by the Theodosian line, a geographic demarcation that traversed the Balkan peninsula.

Founded in 330 by Emperor Constantine the Great (r. 306-337) and heavily influenced by Hellenic Greek culture, the Eastern Church adopted the Greek language and became the center of an empire in which church and state were equally under the authority of the Byzantine emperor, the representative of God on earth. Doctrinal matters were decided by ecumenical councils called by the emperor, which were attended by the bishops of the five patriarchal cities: Rome, Constantinople, Antioch, Alexandria, and Jerusalem. Of these Rome was considered the most important, since it was the see founded by Saint Peter. Constantinople, the residence of the emperor, was second in importance after Rome.

The weakening of the Latin-speaking Church based in Rome following the barbarian incursions of the fourth century meant that the Byzantines saw themselves as the legitimate heirs of the Roman Empire and the repository of the Christian tradition. As bishop of Rome, however, the pope maintained his primacy because of the apostolic foundation of his see.

Over time, disagreements between the two branches of Christianity developed, in part because of communication difficulties and also because of cultural differences between them. These differences touched on issues both of authority and doctrine. The concept of schism, a split within the Christian community, is distinguished from heresy, which is a division based on doctrinal differences.

Past schisms had developed between the churches, the most noteworthy being the Acacian schism of 483-518, in which Acacius, patriarch of Constantinople (471-489), was excommunicated for making concessions to the Monophysites, and that of 595, when Pope Gregory I (590-604) objected to the title of ecumenical patriarch being applied to the patriarch of Constantinople. Further ill-will developed in Rome when the Byzantines instigated the Iconoclastic Controversy under Emperor Leo III (r. 795-816), which was later condemned at the seventh ecumenical Council of Nicaea in 787. This estrangement was exacerbated by the papal crowning of Charlemagne (r. 800-814) as emperor of the Romans in 800 and subsequently, when attempts were made to substitute the primacy of the pope for that of the emperor.

A more serious doctrinal dispute was occasioned by the insertion of the *filioque* clause into the Nicene Creed, first proposed by the German popes elected after Emperor Otto I (r. 936-972) restored the Western Roman Empire. The *filioque* was inserted into the language approved at the Council of Nicaea concerning the procession of the Holy Spirit, which was believed to come from the Father. The addition of language indicating that it proceeded also from the Son, in Latin *filioque*, was considered heretical by the Eastern Church. A further area of disagreement touched on celibacy of the clergy, an innovation in the Roman Church imposed by the western Franks, and Latin condemnation of the use of leavened bread in the celebration of the eucharist by the Greeks.

Some date the Eastern schism from 1009, when the pope sent a copy of the creed with the *filioque* included to the patriarch Sergius II of Constantinople (1001-1019). From that date, the Byzantines no longer included the pope's name in the diptychs of their Church. Nevertheless, practitioners of the Greek and Roman rites did not feel that the churches were in schism at that time.

The immediate cause of the controversy of 1054 was the refusal of Michael Cerularius, the patriarch of Constantinople, to countenance the use of unleavened bread in the communion ceremony as practiced in Byzantine territory in southern Italy. To the Greeks, the leaven in the bread was symbolic of the life of Christ. So Cerularius closed down churches using the Latin rite in Constantinople in 1052. Leo, the Eastern Orthodox archbishop of Ochrida, dispatched a letter of protest against the use of unleavened bread. The archbishop's action outraged Pope Leo IX, who replied to the letter and demanded the submission of the patriarch to the primacy of Rome. After a further exchange of letters, the pope dispatched legates to Constantinople with a letter to Cerularius that was insulting in tone, as well as a more amicable one to the emperor.

Wishing to avoid controversy, Constantine IX Monomachus, the Byzantine emperor, cordially received the legates, headed by Cardinal Humbert of Silva Candida. Although Constantine proposed a compromise, it was unacceptable to Patriarch Michael Cerularius, who saw the views of the Romans as heretical. The papal legates

Pope Leo IX. (Library of Congress)

Alexius I Comnenus, emperor of Constantinople (r. 1081-1118). (H. Bricher and B. F. Waitt)

composed a bull of excommunication, written in Latin, against the patriarch and all his supporters. After placing this document on the altar of the cathedral of Hagia Sophia in Constantinople, the legates left the city. When it was translated back into Greek, this bull was mistranslated, extending the excommunication against the entire Eastern Church. Cerularius used this pretext to recall the legates to Constantinople and imprison the supporters of Argyros, his archenemy in Italy. Cerularius also had the translators beaten and convened a holy synod to excommunicate the legates and pronounce anathema. His precipitate action outfaced the emperor of Constantinople, who wished to adopt a conciliatory policy toward Rome.

In the meantime, Pope Leo IX had died in 1054, thus invalidating the bull of excommunication. Confusion as to the implications of the actions of Humbert and Cerularius made it unclear whether a state of schism actually existed between the churches of Rome and Constantinople.

While these events were taking place, the Turks of Anatolia were continuing to threaten Christendom. Urban II, who was elected pope in 1088, and Alexius I Comnenus, emperor of Constantinople, were in accord on the need to form a crusade to resist the Turks. Although the emperor was hesitant to throw open the doors of his empire to armed soldiers from the West, he and Pope Urban II decided to pursue a Crusade. For his part, the pope saw a Crusade as a way to repair the rupture between the Eastern and Western churches. The Byzantine emperor reached an understanding that any formerly Byzantine cities captured by the Crusaders should revert to the empire. Unfortunately, this did not happen when Antioch, one of the five patriarch cities, was recovered by the Crusaders. Bohemond I, a Norman adventurer, kept the city in spite of his oath to Emperor Alexius I and nominated a Latin patriarch, exiling the Greek patriarch to Constantinople.

Significance

Nominally intended to recapture the Holy Land but more frequently causing pillage and destruction throughout the imperial realms of the Byzantines, subsequent Crusades only served to deepen the distrust of the Byzantine Greeks toward the adherents of the Latin Church. The Greeks maintained their unwillingness to recognize the primacy of the pope of Rome. This mutual bitterness reached a bloody culmination in 1182, when the Greeks massacred the population of the Latin colony of Constantinople, and again in 1185, when the Greeks of Salonika were in their turn massacred by the Normans. Because they attempted to negotiate with the Turks, the Byzantine Greeks were accused of treachery by the Latins. Bohemond I used this argument as a rationale for diverting the armies of the Fourth Crusade to attack Constantinople in 1204. The Crusaders sacked and plundered the city, massacred many of the inhabitants, destroyed churches, works of art, and architectural monuments, appointed a Latin patriarch, and founded Constantinople as a Latin empire.

Although the Greek rule of Constantinople was restored during the following century, this destruction of their beautiful city by fellow Christians remained in the Greek memory as an unforgivable transgression, and it doomed all subsequent attempts to reunify the Eastern and Western churches.

—*Gloria Fulton*

Further Reading

Angold, Michael. *The Byzantine Empire, 1025-1204: A Political History.* 2d ed. New York: Longman, 1997. This study focuses on political events and discusses the schism within that context. Maps, bibliography, index.

Chadwick, Henry. *East and West: The Making of a Rift in the Church, from Apostolic Times Until the Council of*

Florence. New York: Oxford University Press, 2003. Explores the history of the Christian faith and its schisms from apostolic times—the first two centuries C.E.—through the Council of Florence in 1439, which attempted to unify the Eastern and Western Churches. Bibliography, index.

Hassan bin Talal, El. *Christianity in the Arab World*. New York: Continuum, 1998. A brief look at the schism from the Arab perspective. Also includes chapters on the iconoclastic controversy, the Nicene Creed, and Islamic influences on Christianity. Bibliography, index.

Luscombe, David, and Jonathan Riley-Smith, eds. *The New Cambridge Medieval History*. Vol. 4. New York: Cambridge University Press, 2004. This standard and often reprinted work focuses on the eleventh and twelfth centuries and discusses in part one the schism from the Roman point of view and the reform of the Western Church. Maps, bibliography, index.

Norwich, John Julius. *Byzantium: The Apogee*. New York: Alfred A. Knopf, 1996. A popular, highly readable account of the Byzantine Empire from 800 to 1081. Illustrations, bibliography, index.

_______. *Byzantium: The Decline and Fall*. New York: Alfred A. Knopf, 1996. Continuation of the author's account above, covering the period from the Crusades to the fall of the Byzantine Empire to the Turks in 1453.

Runciman, Steven. *The Eastern Schism: A Study of the Papacy and the Eastern Churches During the Eleventh and Twelfth Centuries*. 1955. Reprint. New York: AMS Press, 1983. The classic work on events leading up to the schism, reasons for the positions of each side, and the aftermath, focusing on the devastating impact of the schism for the Byzantine Empire. This study represents the Greek point of view. Bibliography, index.

SEE ALSO: 532-537: Building of Hagia Sophia; 726-843: Iconoclastic Controversy; 1040-1055: Expansion of the Seljuk Turks; 1077: Seljuk Dynasty Is Founded; November 27, 1095: Pope Urban II Calls the First Crusade; 1204: Knights of the Fourth Crusade Capture Constantinople; 1305-1417: Avignon Papacy and the Great Schism; May 29, 1453: Fall of Constantinople.

RELATED ARTICLES in *Great Lives from History: The Middle Ages, 477-1453*: Anna Comnena; Bohemond I; Charlemagne; Enrico Dandolo; Gregory VII; Justinian I; Leo IX; Nicholas the Great; Otto I; Michael Psellus; Saint Sergius I; Theoleptus of Philadelphia; Urban II.

1062-1147
ALMORAVIDS CONQUER MOROCCO AND ESTABLISH THE ALMORAVID EMPIRE

The Almoravid conquest of Morocco was inspired by the desire to spread a fundamentalist interpretation of the teachings of Islam. The year 1062 marks the founding of Marrakesh, the Almoravid capital city, from which the Almoravids governed Morocco, Algeria, parts of the Sahara Desert region, and Spain.

LOCALE: Morocco, North Africa
CATEGORIES: Expansion and land acquisition; religion; wars, uprisings, and civil unrest

KEY FIGURES

Yaḥyā ibn Ibrāhīm (d. 1058), Sanhaja Berber chief, implemented the Islamic reform movement that led to the establishment of the Almoravid Dynasty

Ibn Yāsīn (d. 1050), holy man and religious advisor to Yaḥyā ibn Ibrāhīm

Yūsuf ibn Tāshufīn (d. 1106), Almoravid leader, r. 1061-1106, led major conquests in north Africa and in Spain and founded the city of Marrakesh

ʿAlī ibn Yūsuf (d. 1143), son and successor of Yūsuf ibn Tāshufīn, r. 1106-1143

SUMMARY OF EVENT

The Islamic Almoravid Dynasty ruled northwestern Africa and parts of southern Spain from 1056 to 1147. In contrast to the eastern Arab dynastics that had dominated these regions in preceding centuries, the Almoravids were Berbers, an ethnic group indigenous to North Africa. They are traditionally considered to have lived in the region since Neolithic times, and were originally from the Sahara region, in what is now Mauritania.

They were converted to Islam at the time of the Arab conquest of North Africa in the seventh century. The Berber tribes retained a common language and some cultural ties, though their political fragmentation and disparate economic interests impeded the unity required for sustained military conquest.

In 1035, the chief of the Sanhaja Berber tribe, Yaḥyā ibn Ibrahim, made a pilgrimage to Mecca (the *hajj*). His experiences on his journey, as well as the influence of the holy man and teacher Ibn Yāsīn, whose acquaintance he made on the trip, inspired him to implement a reform movement among the people of his tribe when he returned home, with the help of Ibn Yāsīn. The two men and their followers emphasized simplicity and asceticism and a return to a strict interpretation of Islamic teaching, in contrast to the perceived incorrect beliefs and lax practices of their fellow Berber Muslims.

Fourteenth century historians report that the converts to the fundamentalist reform movement established a fortress (or *ribat*) on an island in the Senegal River that increasingly attracted followers from the surrounding region. The residents of the fortress became known as the al-Murābitūn or, in Spanish, Almoravids. It is also possible that the Berber warriors were thus named because of their militant religious practices, and the legend of the *ribat* grew out of this reputation.

Fortified by religious zeal and an economic interest in controlling the trans-Saharan trade, the Almoravids set out to proselytize and conquer the inhabitants of the western Sahara and Morocco. The rapid Almoravid advance was made possible by their intense interest in religious reform, because this common religious belief had the effect of uniting the otherwise historically fragmented Berber tribes.

The greatest military successes of the Almoravids took place during the long and prosperous reign of the leader Yūsuf ibn Tāshufīn, who was responsible for the conquest of the Maghreb and southern Spain. (Maghreb is a term derived from the Arabic word for "west"; it describes the region that today comprises Morocco, Algeria, and Tunisia.) Yūsuf founded a new capital city, Marrakesh, in Morocco in 1062. He occupied the city of Fās (Fès) in 1069 and in the 1070's extended his empire to include Algeria.

After the fall of the Spanish city of Toledo to a Christian army from Castile in 1085, the Islamic kings of Al-Andalus (the Islamic-controlled area of Spain) requested the military intervention of the Almoravids. Yūsuf obliged, defeating a Christian army at the Battle of Al-Zallāqah in 1086. By 1090, the rest of Al-Andalus had come under Almoravid control. The Almoravid Dynasty had also amassed great wealth through its control of the western Mediterranean and trans-Sarahan trade routes.

Mosques built under the Almoravids were sober in their decoration, reflecting Almoravid asceticism and an interest in simple piety. Yūsuf was also impressed by the rich traditions of art and culture that he had encountered in Islamic Spain, and he contributed significantly to cultural exchange between the Maghreb and southern Europe through his importation of Andalusian artists to work at his courts in Fās and Marrakesh. In this period Spanish decorative forms such as the horseshoe arch began to appear in architecture of the Maghreb, in, for example, the Great Mosque of Algiers. It has been argued that the Algiers mosque as well the mosque at the city of Tlemcen, both built during the reign of Yūsuf, were modeled after the Great Mosque (built in the late eighth century) in the Spanish city of Córdoba. In addition, the *minbar* (pulpit) intended for an Almoravid mosque at Marrakesh has an inscription that reports that it was constructed in Córdoba.

The Almoravid Empire reached its greatest extent during the reign of Yūsuf's son, ʿAlī ibn Yūsuf, though it was also during his reign that a rebellion by another Berber dynasty, known as the Almohads, set into motion the decline of the Almoravids. The Almohads were also motivated by a desire for religious reform, as they believed the Almoravids had succumbed to the temptations of imperial wealth and luxury. Military setbacks in Spain further weakened the Almoravids, and the capital of Marrakesh fell to the Almohads in 1147.

SIGNIFICANCE

The Almoravids succeeded in uniting the Berber tribes of North Africa under one cause. They were exceptionally successful in a relatively short period of time because this cause, the promotion of a strict interpretation of the principles of Islam, inspired great religious fervor among its followers. The Almoravids were one of the two great Berber reforming dynasties, along with the Almohads, that rose up from origins in the Sahara to rule the Maghreb.

The Berbers had been superficially Islamicized by their Arab conquerors in the preceding centuries, but the Almoravids developed an indigenous Islamic empire in northwestern Africa with an accompanying indigenous north African culture that was increasingly isolated in its interests and cultural practices from the Islamic Arab dynasties in the east.

The Almoravid conquest of Spain created strong cultural ties between the Maghreb and southern Europe. The compelling stylistic relationships between the art, architecture, and literature of southern Spain and the Maghreb as a result of Almoravid rule has meant that the artistic styles of northwestern Africa and southern Europe are much more closely related to each other than either is to any other region.

—*Marguerite Keane*

FURTHER READING

Abun-Nasr, Jamil M. *A History of the Maghrib in the Islamic Period*. New York: Cambridge University Press, 1987. A comprehensive survey of the region from its earliest history to the present day, with a chapter devoted to the Almoravid Empire.

Bloom, Jonathan, et al. *The Minbar from the Kutubiyya Mosque*. New York: Metropolitan Museum of Art, 1998. An in-depth study of one example of artistic exchange between the Maghreb and Islamic Spain: the *minbar* created for the Great Mosque of Marrakesh by artists in Córdoba.

Bosworth, Clifford Edmund. *The New Islamic Dynasties: A Chronological and Genealogical Manual*. 1967. Rev. ed. New York: Columbia University Press, 1996. A historical and genealogical accounting of the Islamic dynasties, including those in Spain and Africa. Bibliography, index.

Brett, Michael. "The Arab Conquest and the Rise of Islam in North Africa." In *The Cambridge History of Africa*, edited by J. D. Fage. Vol. 2. Cambridge, England: Cambridge University Press, 1979. One of the best analyses available of the conquests and their consequences written by the field's leading authority.

_______. "The Islamisization of Morocco from the Arabs to the Almoravids." *Journal of the Society for Moroccan Studies* 2 (1992): 57-71. A study of the process whereby North Africa developed a distinct Islamic character.

Brett, Michael, and Elizabeth Fentress. *The Berbers*. Cambridge, Mass.: Blackwell, 1996. This study focuses on the history of the Berber-speaking peoples. The authors establish the identity of the Berbers and analyze their traditions, while tracing their political and social history up until the twentieth century. The Almoravids are studied as one of the two major Islamic Berber dynasties of the Middle Ages. Maps, bibliography, index.

Clancy-Smith, Julia, ed. *North Africa, Islam, and the Mediterranean World: From the Almoravids to the Algerian War*. Portland, Or.: Frank Cass, 2001. Early chapters explore the Almoravid Empire's influence in North Africa, including Morocco, and Spain. Illustrations, maps, bibliography, index.

Eickelman, Dale F. *Moroccan Islam: Tradition and Society in a Pilgrimage Center*. Austin: University of Texas Press, 1976. The author takes an anthropological approach to the study of the history of Islam in Morocco. Bibliography, index.

Knapp, Wilfrid. *North West Africa: A Political and Economic Survey*. Oxford, England: Oxford University Press, 1977. A chapter is devoted to the history of each of the modern countries in the region: Algeria, Libya, Morocco, Tunisia, and Mauritania. Bibliography, index.

Power, Daniel, and Naomi Standen, eds. *Frontiers in Question: Eurasian Borderlands, 700-1700*. New York: St. Martin's Press, 1999. Chapter 2 explores the conflicts and tensions between the overlapping "borders" and "boundaries" of Muslims and Christians in Muslim-Christian Spain. Bibliography, index.

Reilly, Bernard F. *The Contest of Christian and Muslim Spain, 1031-1157*. Cambridge, Mass.: Blackwell, 1995. This work is a more complete coverage of the rise of Christian Spain and deals extensively with military struggles and dynastic history. Illustrations, maps, bibliography, index.

Schatzmiller, Maya. *The Berbers and the Islamic State: The Marinid Experience in Pre-protectorate Morocco*. Princeton, N.J.: Markus Wiener, 2000. A detailed study of the history of the Berbers in North Africa and Morocco. Includes discussion of acculturation and its legacy, developing an Islamic state and institutions, Jews in the region, and more. Bibliography, index.

SEE ALSO: 630-711: Islam Expands Throughout North Africa; April or May, 711: Ṭārik Crosses into Spain; 969-1171: Reign of the Fāṭimids; 11th century: Expansion of Sunni Islam in North Africa and Iberia; 1076: Almoravids Sack Kumbi; November 1, 1092-June 15, 1094: El Cid Conquers Valencia; 1147-1149: Second Crusade; c. 1150: Moors Transmit Classical Philosophy and Medicine to Europe; 1230: Unification of Castile and León; 1377: Ibn Khaldūn Completes His *Muqaddimah*.

RELATED ARTICLES in *Great Lives from History: The Middle Ages, 477-1453*: ʿAbd al-Muʾmin; Afonso I; Alfonso X; El Cid; Prince Henry the Navigator; Ibn Baṭṭūṭah; Ibn Khaldūn; al-Idrīsī; James I the Conqueror; Damia al-Kāhina; Lalibela; Mansa Mūsā; Ṭāriq ibn-Ziyād.

October 14, 1066
BATTLE OF HASTINGS

The Battle of Hastings, part of the Norman Conquest, marked the defeat of Anglo-Saxon forces by the French-speaking Normans and the decline of the Anglo-Saxon ruling class and its language and culture.

LOCALE: England

CATEGORIES: Cultural and intellectual history; wars, uprisings, and civil unrest

KEY FIGURES

Edward the Confessor (1005-1066), Anglo-Saxon king of England, r. 1043-1066, died without an heir

Harold II (c. 1022-1066), Anglo-Saxon king of England, r. 1066, crowned after Edward the Confessor's death

Harold Hardrada (1015-1066), king of Norway, r. 1047-1066, and claimant to the English throne

William the Conqueror (c. 1028-1087), duke of Normandy, 1035-1087, first Norman king of England, r. 1066-1087

SUMMARY OF EVENT

In 1066, on the death of Edward the Confessor, the childless Anglo-Saxon king, there were three rivals for the throne: Harold Hardrada, king of Norway, who based his claim on his relationship to Canute the Great of Denmark, who had ruled England from 1016 to 1035; Harold II, accepted as heir to the throne by the dying Edward and by the Witan, the Anglo-Saxon assembly of nobles; and William the Conqueror, duke of Normandy, who based his claim on blood relationship as well as on promises from both Edward the Confessor and Harold II that the throne should be his.

William's claim to the throne was no surprise. Edward, although English on his father's side, had been born of a Norman mother and had spent his early years in Normandy. He included many Normans in his court and received frequent Norman visitors, William among them. William maintained that Edward had promised him the English throne when he had visited Edward in England. In addition, William based his claim on a promise he had exacted from Harold II when Harold had been held captive in Normandy after a shipwreck. William also had the support of the pope, who wanted to closen the ties between the English Church and Rome.

To enforce his claim, William assembled a feudal army composed not only of Normans but also of knights from the neighboring duchies of Maine and Brittany and from Flanders, central France, Aquitaine, and the Norman colonies in southern Italy. These mercenary troops consisted mostly of landless men, looking to gain wealth and land in England by fighting for William. Their strength lay in their cavalry tactics and in the leadership of William, who had proven himself an indomitable soldier in the campaigns in Normandy and elsewhere in France. As they waited in Normandy for good sailing weather, William's troops numbered conservatively between five thousand and six thousand men, a massive force by medieval standards.

Harold II's force had two parts: the standing army, made up of housecarls, trained members of the king's bodyguard, and fyrdmen, a part-time force made up of men who owed service to the king. When Harold received news of William's preparations, he marched his army to the coast to wait for William's attack. When

> **WILLIAM OF MALMESBURY ASSESSES THE NORMAN CONQUEST**
>
> This was a fatal day to England, and melancholy havoc was wrought in our dear country during the change of its lords.... Nevertheless, the attention to literature and religion had gradually decreased for several years before the arrival of the Normans.... The monks mocked the ruler of their order by fine vestments and the use of every kind of food. The nobility, given up to luxury and wantonness, went not to church in the morning.... The commonalty, left unprotected became a prey to the most powerful.... Drinking in parties was an universal practice, in which occupation [the people] passed entire nights as well as days ...; hence it came about that when they engaged William [the Conqueror], with more rashness and precipitate fury than military skill, they doomed themselves and their country to slavery by a single, and that an easy, victory. For nothing is less effective than rashness; and what begins with violence quickly ceases or is repelled.
>
> William of Malmesbury, *De gentis regum Anglorum* (*History of the Kings of England*), quoted in *Readings in European History*, edited by James Harvey Robinson, abridged edition (Boston: Ginn & Company, 1906), p. 112.

The Battle of Hastings. (F. R. Niglutsch)

he heard that his brother, Tostig, and the Norwegian Harold Hardrada had attacked England, however, Harold II turned his army northward, engaging the invaders at Stamford Bridge in Yorkshire and defeating them soundly.

Three days later, William landed at Pevensey on the south coast of England on September 28. Still in the north, Harold received word of William's landing after the decisive victory at Stamford Bridge. By a forced march of some two hundred miles (125 kilometers), Harold brought his weary army to meet the fresh enemy. He reached London by October 5-6 with the vanguard of his army. He stayed in London for several days, resting his troops and waiting for the rest of his army to arrive from Yorkshire. Ignoring the advice from his brother Gyrth to wait longer, Harold left London on October 11 with less than his full force to meet William. Had he delayed, time would have proven his best ally, because William needed to fight before his supplies ran out and winter set in. Instead, on a field between Hastings and Senlac in Sussex, the two armies met on October 14, 1066. The famous Bayeux tapestry, a 231-foot piece of linen needlework created to commemorate the battle, provides a graphic representation of the fighting, detailing the Normans and Anglo-Saxons in battle.

The battle started at about 9:00 A.M. and continued throughout the day. For all their disadvantages, the English troops fought tenaciously and almost won the day. They depended on a close phalanx formation, a long line of men shoulder to shoulder with spears raised. This formation held during the early hours of the battle, and the Saxons successfully repulsed William's Breton troops, who were in the lead. As the afternoon wore on, large numbers of both Saxons and Normans were killed, including Leofwin and Gyrth, Harold's brothers. By late afternoon, the Normans began to force their way through the Saxon line. Even then, according to the chronicler William of Malmesbury, the English fought bravely and "by frequently making a stand, they slaughtered their pursuers by heaps." King Harold was killed during the

William the Conqueror lands in England. (F. R. Niglutsch)

last stages of the battle, and without leadership, the Saxon defense crumbled. William had won the day and England.

During the Battle of Hastings, many of the Anglo-Saxon nobility were killed; those who survived had their lands confiscated. The defeat at Hastings led effectively to the end of the Anglo-Saxon ruling class. It took William another seven years to put down all the resistance in the north and in the west.

SIGNIFICANCE

With the Norman Conquest, William fused Norman and Saxon institutions so that England became, much earlier than France, a consolidated monarchy with an efficient central government. He also introduced Norman feudal practices into England and made himself an effective sovereign over his nobles by insisting that they acknowledge him as liege lord. At the same time, he left the machinery of government on the local level much as he found it, keeping the Anglo-Saxon shires with their sheriffs responsible to the king. William also inaugurated a remarkable census when he ordered the Domesday Book (1086), also called the Domesday survey, which recorded properties and their holders at the time of the Norman Conquest. It was this record that enabled the royal government to provide for itself an adequate and consistent income, since officials knew what revenues could be expected from any piece of land.

The Norman Conquest also meant that French, along with Latin, became the language of the upper class, the government, and power for the next three hundred years at the expense of Anglo-Saxon. Ecclesiastical life was greatly affected also, as William repaid the pope for his support by strengthening the ties between the English Church and Rome.

If Duke William had not won the Battle of Hastings, England might have developed an isolated culture or maintained an orientation toward Scandinavia. In the opinion of some historians, the battle constitutes the most important single event in English history. It not only marks the last time that the island was successfully invaded, but, more important, it is also the event that effectively brought England into the European orbit.

—Mary Evelyn Jegen,
updated by Diane Andrews Henningfeld

FURTHER READING

Barber, Malcolm. "The Kingdom of England." In *The Two Cities: Medieval Europe, 1050-1320*. London: Routledge, 1992. Carefully traces the events leading to Hastings as well as the aftermath of the Norman Conquest, paying particular attention to the medieval mentality.

Bradbury, Jim. *The Battle of Hastings*. Stroud, England: Sutton, 1998. Focuses on the tactics and strategies of the battle and discusses the battle in the context of European military events of the eleventh century.

Brown, R. A. "The Battle of Hastings." *The Proceedings of the Battle Conference on Anglo-Norman Studies* 3 (1981): 1-21. Explores military tactics and strategies of Hastings.

Furneaux, Rupert. *Invasion 1066*. Englewood Cliffs, N.J.: Prentice Hall, 1966. Presents a vivid account, complete with maps, diagrams, and a reconstruction of the scene of battle.

Morillo, Stephen, ed. *The Battle of Hastings: Sources and Interpretations*. Rochester, N.Y.: Boydell Press, 1996. Collection discusses the Bayeux tapestry, fyrds, naval logistics in the English Channel, the larger Norman Conquest, and more.

Stenton, F. M. *Anglo-Saxon England*. 3d ed. New York: Oxford University Press, 1989. Hastings is covered in a section on the Norman Conquest.

Walker, David. *The Normans in Britain*. Cambridge, Mass.: Blackwell, 1995. An overview of the Anglo-Norman period in England, Scotland, Ireland, and Wales, beginning with Hastings.

Wright, Peter Poyntz. *The Battle of Hastings*. Salisbury, England: Michael Russell, 1986. Traces the events leading to the battle, its tactics and strategies, and the immediate aftermath. Filled with illustrations and maps.

SEE ALSO: 1016: Canute Conquers England; 1086: Domesday Survey.

RELATED ARTICLES in *Great Lives from History: The Middle Ages, 477-1453*: Edward the Confessor; Harold II; William the Conqueror.

A scene from the twelfth century Bayeux Tapestry showing the funeral of Edward the Confessor, who died in the Battle of Hastings. (Frederick Ungar Publishing Co.)

1069-1072
WANG ANSHI INTRODUCES BUREAUCRATIC REFORMS

As adviser to the emperor Shenzong, Wang Anshi introduced reforms covering finance, the recruiting and training of officials, and the organization and staffing of the military. Though the reforms failed, many historians see them as the beginning of modern China.

LOCALE: Kaifeng, China
CATEGORY: Government and politics

KEY FIGURES

Wang Anshi (Wang An-shih; 1021-1086) councilor to the emperor, 1069-1074, 1075-1076

Shenzong (Shen-tsung; 1049-1085), Song Dynasty emperor, r. 1068-1085

Zhezong (Che-tsung; 1077-1101), Song Dynasty emperor, r. 1086-1101

Xuan Ren (Hsüan-jen; d. 1093), empress dowager, r. 1086-1093

Sima Guang (Ssu-ma Kuang; 1019-1086), historian, prime minister, 1085-1086

SUMMARY OF EVENT

The Song Dynasty (Sung; 960-1279) followed a time of disunion referred to as the Five Dynasties and Ten Kingdoms period (907-960). Bordered on the north by two powerful tribal dynasties, the Khitan Liao Dynasty (907-1125) and the Jurchen Jin Dynasty (Chin; 1115-1234), the Song faced persistent problems with revenue and a weak military. Reforms were proposed by many officials, among them Wang Anshi, who was serving in the area of present-day Nanjing. In a petition known as the "Ten Thousand Word Memorial," Wang discussed the recruitment and training of officials and suggested procedures to restrain abuses by officials of the imperial system. In 1069, Wang was summoned to the capital of Kaifeng by the recently installed emperor, Shenzong. Through edicts issued from 1069 through 1072, Wang Anshi and Emperor Shenzong implemented a series of reforms.

Wang's changes focused on three areas: finance, officials, and the military. In the area of finance, Wang's first act was to reorganize the finance bureau. He created the finance planning commission. Through this commission, the Chinese government became engaged in advance financial planning for the first time. Wang also instituted a government operation that would buy grain at lower prices, store it in government granaries, and then transport it to markets to sell when supplies were short. The intent was to stabilize the market price for grain for commoners and to gain profit for the government. He further created the "green shoots" program, under which the government would extend loans to farmers for seeds and expenses during planting, to be repaid after the next harvest. Although the government's interest rate of 2 percent per month sounds high, it was a lower rate on much easier terms than those offered by private money lenders.

In his reforms pertaining to officials, Wang proposed to increase salaries to raise morale and to reduce the temptation to accept bribes and also to change the examination system by which government officials were chosen. Wang's plan for the examination was to incorporate more questions on policy and practical problems and put less emphasis on esoteric learning. Previously, those taking the exam were judged by how well they wrote poems in two different styles. Wang believed in applying Confucian ideas, which had long been favored by the imperial system, to practical situations, and the new exam reflected that view.

To reduce the standing military force and to make that force more effective, Wang proposed using more local militias made up of conscripts. These troops would train for short periods each year and could be called up as needed. The intent was to have more troops available without the expense of maintaining a large standing army.

These reforms drew criticism from Song officials. Some attacks were personal: One official wrote a petition calling for Wang's impeachment in 1069, clearly before the reforms would have had an effect. The petition was ignored. More serious criticism came from officials such as Sima Guang, who complained that Wang's reforms put too much emphasis on government profit to the detriment of the people. The "green shoots" program, for example, was short-circuited by official corruption. What had been a program based on need became mandatory and a burden to farmers who were forced to borrow whether or not they needed the loans. The criticism grew until Wang was forced to resign in 1074. However, in 1075, the emperor, who felt he could not continue the reforms without Wang, recalled him. Despite opposition from many imperial officials, the reform edicts stayed in effect until the death of Shenzong in 1085.

The emperor Zhezong, under the control of the empress dowager Xuan Ren and with the support of his prime minister Sima Guang, repealed the reforms and exiled Wang Anshi's supporters. However, on the death of Xuan Ren in 1093, the same emperor asserted his authority by recalling many of these officials and reinstituting many of the reforms. This last phase of the reforms ended when the Song were forced to relocate to the south in 1127.

Most Song officials, including Sima Guang, agreed on the need for reforms, but those instituted by Wang were controversial. Wang's reforms were part of a shift in power from the large landholders in the north of China to the middle-sized landholders of the increasingly prosperous south. Wang was born in what is now the southern province of Jiangxi to a family that in three generations produced eight *jinshi* holders (successful candidates who passed the highest level civil service examinations and became eligible for government positions). Part of the opposition to changes to the examination questions came from northern officials who objected that changes in the system would give Wang control over who became officials.

Wang's reforms also touched off philosophical debates within the Confucian community. According to the Confucian ideal, the emperor controls China by his "shining virtue," not by laws, punishment, or statecraft. The point of Confucian teaching and scholarship is to train men in virtue so that they can advise and help polish the virtue of the ruler. Wang's attention to worldly matters such as finance caused many Confucians to feel that he was sacrificing a key Confucian tenet to less important matters and government greed.

SIGNIFICANCE

Shortly after the political career of Wang Anshi, Chinese historians, the most noted being the prime minister and famous Song historian Sima Guang, tended to take a negative view of his reforms. Wang was seen as sincere but misguided. Such early views also tended to focus on his perceived stubbornness and his tendency to listen only to his supporters.

Later historians have focused on questions such as whether the reforms were practical and whether they could have succeeded if given more time. Wang's initial period of reform lasted only sixteen years—probably not enough time to overcome the corruption that had become ingrained in the imperial system. Proper oversight of officials in what had become a complicated and far-flung system had waned during the earlier period of disunion. As a result, many of Wang's efforts such as the "green shoots" program were blunted by inefficient and corrupt local officials.

Other historians have asked whether the reforms can be considered modern in intent and in focus. The reforms do, after all, address what are seen as modern problems such as increasing state revenue, intervening in commerce, and controlling and maintaining a growing bureaucracy. Wang's aims may have overestimated the ability of any government at the time to realize them. Historians have also debated whether Wang's reforms were too radical for his times. Wang believed his ideas were workable and couched all of his proposals in terms taken from philosophers such as Mencius and Confucius. Many of his programs, such as the program in which the government would buy grain, transport it, and sell it in areas of shortage, were not actually new but were already in effect in other forms.

—*David W. Blaylock*

FURTHER READING

Anderson, Greg. "To Change China: A Tale of Three Reformers." *Asia Pacific: Perspectives* 1 (May, 2001): 1-18. An electronic journal article that compares the reform efforts of Wang Mang in the Han Dynasty, Wang Anshi in the Song Dynasty, and Zhang Juzheng in the Ming Dynasty. It contains an interesting perspective on conditions, motives, and results.

Huang, Ray. *China: A Macro History.* Armonk, N.Y.: M. E. Sharpe, 1988. A general history. Huang describes the reform period very well and discusses the historical debates.

Liu, James T. C. *Reform in Sung China: Wang An-shih (1021-1086) and His New Policies.* Cambridge, Mass.: Harvard University Press, 1959. Liu provides a good summary of Wang Anshi's career and policies, describing his reforms as innovation and noting the political problems they caused for Wang.

Meskill, John, ed. *Wang An-shih: Practical Reformer?* Boston: D. C. Heath, 1963. A collection of articles that includes debates about the reforms and translations of documents from the period.

Roberts, J. A. G. *A Concise History of China.* Cambridge, Mass.: Harvard University Press, 2003. Contains a chapter on the Song and Yuan Dynasties with a section on Wang Anshi's reforms.

Williamson, H. R. *Wang An-shih: A Chinese Statesman and Educationalist of the Sung Dynasty.* 2 vols. London: Arthur Probsthain, 1935. Still the most comprehensive source. Williamson bases his work squarely on documents of the period and includes a full translation of the "Ten Thousand Word Memorial."

SEE ALSO: 907-960: Period of Five Dynasties and Ten Kingdoms; 960: Founding of the Song Dynasty; 960-1279: Scholar-Official Class Flourishes Under Song Dynasty; 1115: Foundation of the Jin Dynasty.

RELATED ARTICLES in *Great Lives from History: The Middle Ages, 477-1453*: Sima Guang; Wang Anshi.

August 26, 1071
BATTLE OF MANZIKERT

The Battle of Manzikert, a catastrophic military loss to the Turks, undermined Byzantine control of Asia Minor and launched the Crusades.

LOCALE: Manzikert, Byzantine Empire (now Malazgirt, Turkey)
CATEGORY: Wars, uprisings, and civil unrest

KEY FIGURES

Alp Arslan (c. 1030-1072 or 1073), Seljuk sultan, r. 1063-1072 or 1073 and victor at Manzikert
Romanus IV Diogenes (d. 1071), Byzantine emperor, r. 1068-1071, who was captured at Manzikert
Seljuk (d. 970), Turkish chieftain, r. 956-970
Toghrïl Beg (c. 990-1063), grandson of Seljuk and founder of the Turkish Seljuk Dynasty

SUMMARY OF EVENT

Soon after the Arabs emerged from the Arabian peninsula in the seventh century to extend their conquests eastward and westward, they attempted to conquer the Byzantine Empire by capturing Constantinople. Their repeated failures, however, kept Asia Minor and eastern Europe closed to them. In the middle of the eleventh century, the Seljuk Turks, who were later converts to Islam, arose to restore the power and prestige of the debilitated Muslim caliphate. In turn, they inherited Arab ambitions against Byzantium.

The Seljuks took their name from Seljuk, the chieftain of a tribe of Turkish nomads who wandered from the Kirghiz steppes of Turkistan into the Transoxiana region, settling there about the middle of the tenth century. The true founder of the dynasty was Seljuk's grandson, Toghrïl Beg, who fought his way slowly westward until he came to the gates of Baghdad in 1055. His nephew, Alp Arslan, followed him as sultan and succeeded in extending his empire until it reached from what is now Turkmenistan to the Mediterranean.

Expansion into Armenia caused the decisive Battle of Manzikert in 1071, when Byzantine emperor Romanus IV Diogenes was taken prisoner and Asia Minor was laid open to complete occupation by the Turks. The outcome of the battle had been partially determined by the unexpected desertion of a portion of Romanus's troops who were ethnic Turks to the Turkish enemy. Whether this was done out of ethnic solidarity or because of Romanus's unpopularity is unknown, but the desertion fatally undermined the cohesiveness and confidence of the Byzantine army. Alp Arslan did not take Constantinople, although he did conquer up to the Sea of Marmora.

The conquest of Asia Minor may well have been facilitated by disaffection, especially in Armenian areas, because of high taxes. The Battle of Manzikert itself may have been intended by Alp Arslan merely as a strategic act to guarantee his right flank while he subdued Syria and Egypt and not as a step in the conquest of Asia Minor. Nevertheless, the occupation of the area had far-reaching results, less for the Seljuks than for the Byzantines. Prowess and booty invested Baghdad once again with some of the past glory it had enjoyed under the ʿAbbāsids. With the deaths of Sultan Malik Shāh (r. 1073-1092) and his vizier Niẓām al-Mulk by 1092, the unity of the Seljuks collapsed. Civil wars and dissidence in the provinces caused the empire to break up into petty states. One such Turkish band, which eventually carried on the further investment of Asia Minor by occupying and redistributing the land, established the independent sultanate of Rum, or Roman lands. Members of this band in turn lost their independence when they were conquered by Mongol invaders in 1243. It remained for the Ottomans, cousins of the Seljuks, to bring a stable political regime into the area once more.

The impact of the Battle of Manzikert was far more intense and disastrous to Byzantium. The complete conquest of Asia Minor included even the Asiatic shore of the Sea of Marmora directly across from Constantinople, which dominated commercial routes vital to the Greek capital. The further investment of the peninsula at the hands of Süleyman, one of Alp Arslan's distant cousins, was so thorough that Hellenization of Asia Minor, finally being completed by Byzantium, was wrecked forever. It seems significant and ironic that Süleyman chose Nicaea, a city in western Asia Minor noted for the first Christian ecumenical council, as his capital. Byzantium's loss of food supplies, raw materials, revenues, commerce, and trade routes was serious indeed, and it was never redeemed. Especially disastrous was the loss of Asia Minor as a source of manpower, for the best army recruits of the Byzantine state came from the interior of that peninsula.

It was not immediately clear that Asia Minor would be permanently lost. After all, Byzantine armies had lost considerable territory in the past and much of it had been reconquered. Under the capable Comnenus dynasty of the twelfth century, the Byzantiune Empire, with Crusader assistance, reconquered much of Asia Minor. Yet, after Manzikert, the Turkish presence, in the form of either the Seljuks or their successors, was always there. When Emperor Manuel I Comnenus (r. 1143-1180) suffered a devastating defeat to the Turks at Myriocephalon in 1176, it was clear that the majority of Asia Minor would be permanently Turkish.

SIGNIFICANCE

The Battle of Manzikert had an immediate repercussion of wide significance. When the Byzantine Empire called on Western Christendom for aid, the Crusades were launched. As Italian merchants followed in the wake of the Crusaders and the Latin states were founded, trade routes tended to shift from Byzantium in favor of Syria. The fall of Constantinople to Venetian merchants and soldiers in 1204 wrought such damage to the Byzantine Empire that, even though Emperor Michael VIII Palaeologus (r. 1259-1282) managed to overthrow the Latin domination in 1261, the Byzantine Empire never regained its full strength before its final defeat in 1453 at the hands of the Ottoman Turks in the final fall of Byzantine Constantinople.

Joseph R. Rosenbloom, updated by Nicholas Birns

FURTHER READING

Angold, Michael. *The Byzantine Empire, 1025-1204: A Political History*. London: Longman, 1984. Provides background on both Alp Arslan and Romanus IV Diogenes.

Bryer, Anthony, and Michael Ursinus, eds. *Manzikert to Lepanto: The Byzantine World and the Turks, 1071-1571*. Amsterdam: A. M. Hakkert, 1991. A detailed source on Byzantine-Turkish relations in the wake of the Battle of Manzikert.

Bull, Marcus. "The Pilgrimage Origins of the First Crusade." *History Today* 47, no. 3 (March, 1997). The author explores Pope Urban II's speech in 1095 calling for a Crusade against the Turks and then traces the Crusades from their start as a Christian pilgrimage to a holy war.

Friendly, Alfred. *The Dreadful Day: The Battle of Manzikert, 1071*. London: Hutchinson, 1981. The author provides a thorough and detailed account of the battle and its consequences.

Irwin, Robert. "Muslim Responses to the Crusades." *History Today* 47, no. 4 (April, 1997). Presents a rich overview of the Muslim perspective on the Crusades, including the responses of the Seljuks before the First Crusade in the late eleventh century. Provides photographs and a short list of further readings.

Kafesoglu, Ibrahim. *A History of the Seljuks*. Translated and edited by Gary Leiser. Carbondale: Southern Illinois University Press, 1988. A fine translation of a contemporary Turkish treatment of Seljuk history. Bibliography, index.

Norwich, John Julius. *Byzantium: The Apogee*. New York: Alfred A. Knopf, 1996. The author offers a well-written narrative history that gives a vivid description of the Battle of Manzikert. Illustrations, bibliography, index.

Psellus, Michael. *Fourteen Byzantine Rulers*. Translated by E. R. A. Sewter. Rev. ed. New York: Penguin, 1982. A contemporary translation of the best primary source on the battle. Tables, maps, bibliography, index.

SEE ALSO: 637-657: Islam Expands Throughout the Middle East; 956: Oğhuz Turks Migrate to Transoxiana; 1009: Destruction of the Church of the Holy Sepulchre; 1040-1055: Expansion of the Seljuk Turks; 1054: Beginning of the Rome-Constantinople Schism; 1077: Seljuk Dynasty Is Founded; November 27, 1095: Pope Urban II Calls the First Crusade; c. 1145: Prester John Myth Sweeps Across Europe; 1147-1149: Second Crusade; 1150: Venetian Merchants Dominate Trade with the East; 1189-1192: Third Crusade; 1204: Knights of the Fourth Crusade Capture Constantinople; May 29, 1453: Fall of Constantinople.

RELATED ARTICLES in *Great Lives from History: The Middle Ages, 477-1453*: Alp Arslan; Niẓām al-Mulk; Omar Khayyám; Osman I; Urban II.

c. 1075-1086
HUMMAY FOUNDS SEFUWA DYNASTY

Hummay was a political leader who consolidated Sefuwa power, ousted the Zaghawa rulers, and expanded Islam in central Sudanic Africa. The Sefuwa Dynasty emerged under Hummay.

LOCALE: Lake Chad, Kanem-Bornu, Africa
CATEGORIES: Government and politics; religion

KEY FIGURE

Dunama bin Hummay (d. 1086), key politico-religious leader and founder of the Sefuwa Dynasty

SUMMARY OF EVENT

In the later twelfth century in the central Sudan's heartland, a significant city-state had grown to control the majority of the Lake Chad region. Kanem was an expansionist state that fully incorporated Islamic beliefs into its empire. Dunama bin Hummay, a devout Muslim, is believed to have initiated some of the prominent changes that reshaped Kanem in this era. The fact that Hummay and other inhabitants of Kanem were practicing Muslims at the time of the political changes is made clear in the *Dīwān*, a chronicle of Kanem rulers discovered and published in 1850 by German archaeologist Heinrich Barth. What is less clear is the sequence of historical changes and whether these changes occurred entirely under the leadership of Hummay or whether the political and religious shifts merely correlate with the same general decades in which Hummay ruled.

Hummay's ancestry is linked in accounts to the Sayf bin Dhī Yazan (Yazaniyyun) lineage of Yemen. Based on Arab chroniclers, the dates for the political shift between Zaghawa and Sefuwa can be narrowed to early in Hummay's time in power because his rule marked a new dynastic line (the Banu Hummay); his predecessor had been of the Banu Duku line. The accounts of the rule of the Sefuwa leader typically highlight Hummay's faithfulness to Islam and commitment to the incorporation of his religious values and way of life into the administration of his political kingdom. This reputation stems from the fact that Hummay demonstrated his piety by making pilgrimages to Mecca in the eleventh century and recording his religious journey in written accounts.

The politico-religious movement led by Hummay coincided with other similar types of movements for religious intensification and the "purification" of Islam and the simultaneous attempts at political centralization. For example, the Almoravids were taking control of parts of western Sudanic Africa. While there was a larger climate of religious and political expansion in Sudanic Africa, the Sefuwa project seems to have been an indigenous movement that claimed ties to both external and indigenous populations at various times.

There is some indication that Hummay may have had a Berber cultural background. However, Hummay challenged the status quo of the Zaghawa Berbers who were in power in Kanem. Although Kanem had certainly been exposed to Islam by the ninth century by means of trans-Saharan trade, it was under the rule of Hummay that Islam began to take hold among a wider spectrum of the population, which became more deeply Islamized in this period. The Sefuwa rulers linked themselves to the religious and cultural communities of Yemeni Muslims, particularly the Sayf bin Dhī Yazan. In the thirteenth century, the Sefuwa genealogy was restructured to deemphasize any Yemeni Berber roots. The genealogy of the Sefuwa was then re-created to demonstrate direct links with local ancestry while maintaining ties to Islam and the Prophet Muḥammad. However, it is most likely that Hummay was not of Arabian or Yemeni ancestry, but instead was a devout Muslim Berber or local Kanemite.

Kanem was known internationally through the writings of Arab chroniclers. Chroniclers such as al-Idrīsī (c. 1154), Ibn-Saʿīd (d. 1286), al-ʿUmarī (1301-1349), and al-Maqrīzī (d. 1442) each wrote about Kanem and its populations. An important document for the history of Kanem is the locally maintained record called the *Dīwān*—which has been kept since the thirteenth century—incorporating oral accounts into a written record. Though much remains unanswered and unclear, bits of information from the *Dīwān* and Arab chroniclers' accounts describe the reign of Hummay and demonstrate that his reign was a defining moment in the history of the Lake Chad kingdoms.

An important aim of the Kanem kingdom under the Sefuwa Dynasty, like other kingdoms of this region, was to control trade. The revenues from trade that allowed the state to maintain itself and improve infrastructure in the territory. Unlike the Zaghawa capital, the Sefuwa capital was at Njimi (Djimi), directly northeast of Lake Chad but removed from the caravan route. When Hummay came to power, he quickly shifted the Sefuwa capital to Njimi, displacing Manan to the north. This change signified a much greater political shift that was emerging and by which the capital became more of an administrative seat than a crucial point of trade. While not directly on the trade route, Njimi continued to be a major point for the transshipment of goods from Lake Chad through the Sahara-Sudanic world into the Mediterranean in the north and the forests of the south.

Fertile and economically productive regions such as Kanem, the Kawar, and the Fezzan (Fès), provided fruitful and highly desired lands for the Sefuwa kings. Kanem was a lakeside environment that created many opportunities for economic diversification through fishing and various forms of cultivation. The Kawar provided a river valley niche, and the Fezzan was endowed with the multiple trade routes that crisscrossed the Sahara, tapping into trade from both western Sudanic Africa to Egypt and north-south circuits.

SIGNIFICANCE

Within the Sefuwa Dynasty, the process of change overseen by Hummay is signaled with the formation, by the thirteenth century, of a distinct royal line, the Magomi (Banu Hummay). The Magomi were crucial to the campaigns of expansion conducted after Hummay's rule by the Sefuwa Magomi kings in the thirteenth century. Control of trade was essential for political and military strength, as commerce was the economic backbone of many Sudanic and Saharan states. For Kanem, control of the Fezzan was the critical nexus of trade. It was Hummay who was able to begin this process through his consolidation of Kanem. By providing security for merchants in the Sahara, the Sefuwa created an important alliance that allowed them to expand their power northward from Kanem across the Kawar and into the Fezzan and to gain profitable remuneration from taxing trade.

Through their network of social alliances with nonsedentary Berbers as well as some of the northern kingdoms and through securing caravans against raids, the Sefuwa achieved a position of political authority in the Fezzan. The Sefuwa state profited from the taxation of luxury-item trade as well as fabrics, salt, and metals that were exported to north Africa, the Mediterranean world, the Arabian Peninsula, Europe, and Asia. In return, the state received copper, silk, iron weapons, and horses, which were used to build a sizable cavalry component in the Sefuwa military under the reign of Mai Dunama Dibbalemi (r. 1221-1259).

—*Catherine Cymone Fourshey*

FURTHER READING

Hallam, W. K. R. "Towards a Re-assessment of the Early Kanem Mais." *Annals of Borno*, no. 4 (1987): 33-46. A history of the Zaghawa in Kanem-Borno. Also details political histories of rulers.

Holl, Augustin. *The Dīwān Revisited: Literacy, State Formation and the Rise of Kanuri Domination (A.D. 1200-1600)*. New York: Kegan Paul, 2000. A history of politics in the Kanem-Bornu empires. Description of the sultans of Kanem and the Sefuwa connections. Covers the history of the Kanem-Bornu Empire with special emphasis on politics and government. Contains an excellent bibliography of research on Kanem.

Lange, D. "Society in the Lake Chad Area at the End of the Byzantine Period, Prior to the Introduction of Islam." In *Libya Antiqua*. Paris: UNESCO, 1986. A history of the Zaghawa in the Lake Chad region. In particular, the essay examines the history of commerce in the Sahara.

Lange, D., and B. W. Barkindo. "The Chad Region as a Crossroads." In *Africa from the Seventh to the Twelfth Century*, edited by M. Elfasi and I. Hrbek. Vol. 4. Berkeley: University of California Press, 1988. Chapter 15 elucidates the history of the Zaghawa as well as the emergence of the Sefuwa. Several pages are devoted to the Sefuwa Dynasty.

Levtzion, Nehemia, and Randall L. Pouwels, eds. *The History of Islam in Africa*. Athens: Ohio University Press, 2000. A comprehensive examination of the history of Islam in Africa. Introductory chapter looks at the "Patterns of Islamization and Varieties of Religious Experience Among Muslims of Africa." Illustrations, maps, bibliography, index.

Niane, D. T., ed. "The Kingdoms and Peoples of Chad." *General History of Africa: Africa from the Twelfth to the Sixteenth Century*. Vol. 4. Berkeley: University of California Press, 1984. Chapter 10 contains a twelve-page section on the Sefuwa Dynasty. Gives a detailed history of how the dynasty emerged.

Tobert, Natalie. *The Ethnoarchaeology of the Zaghawa of Darfur (Sudan): Settlement and Transience*. New York: Oxford University Press, 1988. Examines Zaghawa land settlement patterns in the eastern Sudan, Darfur al-Shamaliyah Province. Provides an ethnoarchaeological perspective on Zaghawa.

SEE ALSO: 630-711: Islam Expands Throughout North Africa; 10th-11th centuries: First Hausa State Established; 1048: Zīrids Break from Fāṭimid Dynasty and Revive Sunni Islam; 11th century: Expansion of Sunni Islam in North Africa and Iberia.

1075-c. 1220
EMERGENCE OF MAPUNGUBWE

In the late eleventh century, a centralized state emerged in southeastern Africa. Although other populations had long inhabited this region of Africa, no centralized, commercial, and semiurban focused towns have been uncovered except for Mapungubwe and its successor states.

LOCALE: Limpopo River Valley, Zimbabwe Plateau, and southeastern Africa
CATEGORY: Government and politics

SUMMARY OF EVENT

In the tenth century on the southern riverbank of the Limpopo bend, a political ideology emerged that was focused in the centrality of the chief or king. In southeastern Africa, this was a new political concept that utilized redistribution of wealth, which was a twofold or mutual obligation: The chief had the privilege to collect half of all of the profit made in luxury trade (valuable stones and beads, gold, ivory, and other such commodities)—which those engaged in trade were obligated to remit—but in times of economic stress or political crisis, the chief was also obliged to provide security to the population, which in turn bestowed their loyalty to the chief.

The primary basis for the chief's power, authority, and affluence was the possession of a large quantity of cattle, because cattle could always provide food in times of economic or ecological crisis. Because the soils of Mapungubwe were not the most fertile for agricultural production, the raising of livestock had become a significant component in the Mapungubwe subsistence economy. Thus, the southeast relied on an agropastoral economy with an immense weight placed on pastoralism and particularly the accumulation of large herds.

In the late eleventh century, the new basis of power, which began to build greater wealth concentrated in the hands of the few chiefs, was the catalyst for the appearance by the twelfth century of the Mapungubwe state. By the twelfth century, the Mapungubwe state was drawing its wealth not only from cattle but also from trading gold and ivory to the international markets on Indian Ocean networks. The wealth of the state or the chiefs came not primarily from cattle or even gold but rather from the exploitation of ivory for export to the coast, from where Swahili merchants transported it into the wider world. Ivory was more important than gold because the Mapungubwe state could better control the hunting of elephants but did not control the mining of gold. The Mapungubwe rulers had power over taxation of the precious metal only as it passed through the region; they did not control production. While the wealth of the state was based on the exploitation of gold, cattle, copper, and ivory in international trade, the authority and power of the state were derived more directly from the king's ability to build up wealth in political and social dependents and to acquire livestock to support them.

As Swahili trade expanded in volume, traders explored new sources for commodities farther south, on the Indian Ocean coast. Chibuene, which was just east of Mapungubwe, became a productive port of trade because of this international interest and demand for both gold and ivory. Besides the urban center of Chibuene, the southeastern interior had a town with important significance for trade. This town was the site of Mapungubwe; hence, the commercial center merged with the state as the site of kingship and the exchange of gold, copper, and ivory from three different regions of southern Africa—the regions currently known as the Zimbabwe plateau, the Transvaal, and the Limpopo River Valley—which respectively controlled each of these three commodities of exchange.

Mapungubwe was distinct from the previous political and social units that existed in this corner of southeastern Africa for several important reasons. First, it was established not on the plain, as were Leopard's Kopje and many smaller political entities, but on a hilltop, enclosed by large stone walls around the cattle kraals, grain bins, and households. Second, Mapungubwe's political organization was clearly an attempt to limit economic and political segmentation. Political divisions of small chiefdoms circumscribed the amount of centralization, the concentration of power, and the size or extent that the state was able to achieve. By contrast, the social hierarchy indicated in the layout of Mapungubwe demonstrates that it consisted, not in a multiplicity of chiefs ruling over various different populations and the territories they occupied, but rather in a single chief or king who ruled over subjects and delegated power to subordinate chiefs. Third, the archaeological evidence of Mapungubwe also demonstrates a more privileged elite who enjoyed a greater variety of luxury. Grave wares included gold-plated items and beads in the larger burial sites of individuals presumed to be from the elite classes. The technology of spindle whorls found in

Mapungubwe sites indicates that new categories of work were developing and that cloth was being produced. In addition to cloth, pottery was significant in Mapungubwe's archaeological record beginning in the eleventh century.

Mapungubwe not only was an important locus for orchestrated trade but also served as an important ritual site for adherents of locally based religious ideologies that emerged among the population. In other words, Mapungubwe was of spiritual importance, and even after the collapse of the site politically, it continued to serve as a religious shrine, demonstrating that the religious significance and symbolism of a location cannot always be easily erased in the same manner that its political importance can be eliminated.

Mapungubwe was abandoned in the thirteenth century, most likely because the hilltop settlement became ecologically and environmentally uninhabitable as a result of the density of human and cattle populations and partially because of the economic downturn resulting from a shift in the trade patterns at the coast. In the stead of Mapungubwe, an even larger state emerged at the site of Great Zimbabwe farther to the north.

Significance

Mapungubwe presents the earliest evidence, archaeological or historical, of a centralized state in southern Africa headed by a king. Mapungubwe demonstrates the function of economic wealth in building a centralized state. In the twelfth century, the wealth produced from ivory was tremendous, while by the thirteenth century, the Mapungubwe state had shrunk considerable and virtually collapsed as ivory trade declined and as Swahili merchants abandoned Chibuene and concentrated commercial activities in ports farther north.

Mapungubwe seems to be a political precursor to Great Zimbabwe, which emerged to the north of Mapungubwe in the thirteenth century. Much of the material culture and architecture of Great Zimbabwe demonstrates continuity in style, structure, and function with the culture and institutions that have been identified for Mapungubwe a century earlier to the south.

—*Catherine Cymone Fourshey*

Further Reading

Huffman, Thomas N. "The Mapungubwe Period." *Snakes and Crocodiles: Power and Symbolism in Ancient Zimbabwe*. Johannesburg, South Africa: Witwatersrand University Press, 1996. An archaeological approach to understanding historical, political, and cultural symbols.

Inskeep, R. R. "South Africa." In *African Iron Age*, edited by P. L. Shinnie. Oxford, England: Clarendon Press, 1971. Examines the archaeology and history of southern Africa with attention to Mapungubwe and pottery.

Leslie, Mary, and T. M. O'C Maggs. *African Naissance: The Limpopo Valley One Thousand Years Ago*. Cape Town: South African Archaeological Society, 2000. An archaeological examination of Mapungubwe and the origins of the Zimbabwe culture. Focuses particularly on Iron Age materials.

Voigt, Elizabeth A. *Mapungubwe: An Archaeozoological Interpretation of an Iron Age Community*. Pretoria, South Africa: Transvaal Museum, 1983. Examines the material culture of Mapungubwe in the Iron Age, paying particular attention to animal remains.

See also: c. 500-1000: Rise of Swahili Cultures; 11th-15th centuries: Great Zimbabwe Urbanism and Architecture; 12th century: Coins Are Minted on the Swahili Coast; 12th century: Trading Center of Kilwa Kisiwani Is Founded; 1333: Kilwa Kisiwani Begins Economic and Historical Decline.

Related articles in *Great Lives from History: The Middle Ages, 477-1453*: ʿAbd al-Muʾmin; Ibn Baṭṭūṭah; Ibn Khaldūn; al-Idrīsī; Lalibela; Mansa Mūsā; Sundiata; Ṭāriq ibn-Ziyād.

1076
ALMORAVIDS SACK KUMBI

The incursion of Islamic Almoravid Berbers on the Ghanian city of Kumbi Saleh led to the decline of Ghana's economic power and, by 1080, the effective control by the Almoravids.

LOCALE: Inland Niger Delta, Niger-Senegal junction, and Western Sahel, Africa (now Mali)
CATEGORIES: Expansion and land acquisition; government and politics; trade and commerce

KEY FIGURE

Abū Bakr ibn ʿUmar (d. 1087), leader of the Almoravids

SUMMARY OF EVENT

In the mid- to late first millennium, Kumbi Saleh served as an important political and commercial center in western Africa, located just south of Awdaghust and just north of the alluvial plain between the Niger and Senegal Rivers. Kumbi was ideally situated to exploit medieval trans-Saharan trade and in particular salt and gold trade. Kumbi also served as the political center of the Ghana Empire.

Begun by settled Soninke populations, Ghana was the earliest true empire of western Africa. The state's power emanated from its base in Sudanic sacral chiefship, whereby the political elite were instilled with the right to rule granted by the will of a divine power. Evidence from archaeological excavation reveals that by the fifth century, the ancient empire had emerged as a consequence of environment, population density, and technological developments in the realm of metals, all occurring contemporaneously in the isthmus of land between the Niger and Senegal Rivers.

Prior to the arrival of Islam in the ninth century, the inland Niger Delta, just south of Kumbi, was an urban trading area. Archaeological evidence based on both the material culture and carbon-14 dating reveals that, by the tenth century, many Muslims resided in the town of Kumbi. The forests south of the delta were a source of gold, which was traded via the delta to Kumbi and by the tenth century to Gao, Awdaghust, and the other trans-Saharan markets. After the arrival of Islam, the Ghana state continued cooperative trade relations with Muslim merchants and chiefs in the surrounding territories.

The Ghana state was engaged in trade not only regionally but also as far north as Ifrikiya (Libya) by means of long-distance merchants. Ghana's politico-economic system was well connected laterally to the west as well. Hence, Ghanaians were able to position themselves as brokers in the trade of gold, slaves, rice, dried fish from the river, and ivory from the savannah, which were exchanged for the northern products of copper, salt, and woven textiles. Situated on its interriver peninsula at the critical junction for transshipment between river and desert, the Ghana state could collect taxes or broker fees, which provided the state with surplus wealth to buttress its power. Ghana allowed for the trading of gold dust but not gold bullion (nuggets), thereby preventing the market from becoming flooded with gold.

In the eleventh century, Ghana's economic power fueled the conflicts with the Almoravids, Berber Muslims of the Maliki school who sought to expand the practice of Islam and to enhance religious devotion. The Almoravids sought political and economic control of the region in order to further the aims of religious "purification." The Zanata Berbers at Awdaghust controlled Sijilmasa but lived under Ghanaian political rule. In 1054, the Almoravids, allied with the Sanhaja Berbers, seized control of Awdaghust from the previously dominant Zanatas.

By 1055, Abū Bakr ibn ʿUmar, the leader of the Sanhaja army, had captured Awdaghust. The Almoravids then began the process of full Islamization in Ghana territory just south of Awdaghust. Thus, during the later eleventh century, Ghana underwent a period of defense against the infiltration of Almoravid religious and cultural ideas. The Almoravid infiltration led to the conversion of a large part of the Ghana population. Whether the Almoravids captured Kumbi outright, traditionally in 1076, is contested—but what is certain is that Almoravid presence in the Ghana territory and its control of Sijilmasa and Awdaghust in effect meant that it controlled Kumbi's trade relations and policies.

SIGNIFICANCE

The Almoravid control of the major trade centers (Sijilmasa, Awdaghust, and Kumbi) had several long-term effects. First, the charge of trans-Saharan trade originating from the inter-Niger-Senegal River region shifted away from the Ghana Empire. The economic impact of this shift was ruinous for the political power of the Ghana state, which collapsed completely by the thirteenth century. Second, the role of the Almoravids in this historic moment of change resulted in a new religious landscape as elements of Ghana's population converted to Islam. In particular, many of the Soninke merchants and traders underwent religious conversion. Third, the Almoravid presence encouraged provinces of the Ghana Empire to assert their own independence, which further weakened the centralized power of Ghana. Fourth, the Almoravid control of trans-Saharan trade meant that Ghana's profit from this trade declined immensely. With a new broker in the market, the benefits were divided and cut Ghana's percentage of the market, which—even at a moment when the volume of trade was increasing—significantly reduced Ghana's share of revenues compared with previous times.

Additionally, trade shifted farther north and westward to Walata, Timbuktu, and Gao, which were just at the fringe of Ghana's power. As a result, Ghana no longer served as the southernmost terminus of trans-Saharan trade, nor did it hold a monopoly as the dominant mediator of trade. The Almoravid presence ultimately shifted trade westward onto the Niger River and north into the Sahara. The new political power also had the major religious consequence of spreading Islam farther south.

Almoravid control of Kumbi did not last more than two decades. By the early twelfth century, the Ghana state had reasserted its independence politically, but it never recovered its prior political grandeur or economic wealth. The Almoravid successes had weakened Ghana to the point that several of its vassal states were able in the thirteenth century to defeat the once powerful Ghana military. Without economic wealth, Ghana was prevented from fully upgrading and training its military forces, so that first the Susu and later the Mali states were able to turn Ghana into a province of their own expanding empires.

—*Catherine Cymone Fourshey*

FURTHER READING

Berthier, Sophie. *Recherches archéologiques sur la capitale de l'empire de Ghana: Étude d'un secteur d'habitat à Koumbi Saleh, Mauritanie*. Oxford, England: Archaeopress, 1997. Examines the antiquities of the Ghana Empire and Kumbi. In French.

Conrad, David C., and Humphrey J. Fischer. "The Conquest That Never Was: Ghana and the Almoravids, 1076. II, The Local Oral Sources." *History in Africa* 17, no. 3 (1983): 53-78. An account of Ghana and the Almoravids.

Hrbek, I., and J. Devisse. "The Almoravids." In *Africa from the Seventh to the Eleventh Century*, edited by M. Elfasi and I. Hrbek. Vol. 4. Berkeley: University of California Press, 1988. Chapter 13 elucidates the history of the Almoravid conquest and rule in northwestern and western Africa. Approximately twelve pages are devoted to a discussion of the history of the importance of Kumbi and the Ghana Empire.

McIntosh, Susan Keech, and Roderick J. McIntosh. "The Inland Niger Delta Before the Empire of Mali: Evidence from Jenno-Jeno." *Journal of African History* 22 (1981): 1-22. An examination of trade activity and relations just west of the Ghana Empire.

Masonen, Pekka, and Humphrey J. Fisher. "Not Quite Venus from the Waves: The Almoravid Conquest of Ghana in the Modern Historiography of Western Africa." *History in Africa* 23 (1996): 197-232. Addresses the 1076 conquest of Ghana as "one of the myths which still populate African historiography."

SEE ALSO: c. 1075-1220: Emergence of Mapungubwe.

RELATED ARTICLES in *Great Lives from History: The Middle Ages, 477-1453*: ʿAbd al-Muʾmin; Afonso I; El Cid; al-Idrīsī; Mansa Mūsā; Sundiata.

1077
SELJUK DYNASTY IS FOUNDED

The creation of the Seljuk Dynasty in Asia Minor led to the disintegration of the Byzantine Empire, the European Crusades into the Middle East, and the permanent settlement of the Turkish people in Asia Minor.

LOCALE: Asia Minor (now Turkey)
CATEGORIES: Expansion and land acquisition; government and politics

KEY FIGURES

Süleyman (d. 1086), founder of Seljuk Rum, r. 1077-1086
Alp Arslan (c. 1030-1072 or 1073), Seljuk leader, r. 1063-1072, who won the Battle of Manzikert
Romanus IV Diogenes (d. 1071), Byzantine general and emperor, r. 1068-1071, defeated and captured by the Seljuks
Malik Shāh (1055-1092), Seljuk leader, r. 1073-1092, who conquered Asia Minor
Niẓām al-Mulk (1018 or 1019-1092), Seljuk government administrator

SUMMARY OF EVENT

The Seljuk Turks were one in a line of invaders who swept across the Central Asian plains and into the Middle East during medieval times—creating an empire in 1077 after they defeated the Byzantines in 1071—and who occupied the Anatolia region (Asia Minor) that is now known as Turkey.

The Seljuks were part of the Turkmen tribes that ranged across Central Asia near the Aral Sea. The Seljuks acquired their name from a Turkmen prince named Seljuk (d. 970) who lived near the city of Bukhara. As they moved south and west, they conquered Persia and established a capital in the city of Eşfahān. After Seljuk's death, the empire was ruled by his four sons. Yet it was the descendants of these four, Toghrïl (c. 990-1063) and his nephew Alp Arslan, who led the empire to greater glory.

Toghrïl captured Baghdad and ended the caliph's rule and the ʿAbbāsid Empire in 1055. On Toghrïl's death in 1063, Alp Arslan won a civil war and assumed command of the army. Alp Arslan proved to be a great military leader, building Seljuk strength and using it to hand the Byzantine Empire one of its greatest defeats.

By the eleventh century, the Byzantines, who were heirs to the Roman Empire of the east, were in military, economic, and political decline. Overwhelming bureaucracy had made reform or change impossible and the unending political battles led to a series of leaders who allowed the empire to decay. By the time of the Seljuk's invasion, the Byzantine Empire was limited to the territory of modern Turkey.

Alp Arslan was seeking to capture Syria, Arabia, and what is now called Israel. Before this, however, he moved to shore up his western boundary with the Byzantines. The Turks pushed into Armenia, a kingdom allied with the Byzantines, and camped there. Initially, the Byzantines did not respond. After the death of the Byzantine emperor Constantine X Ducas (r. 1059-1067), his wife, Eudocia Macrembolitissa, married Byzantine general Romanus IV Diogenes, who attempted to reconstruct the army and protect the empire from the Turks. He marched his army from Constantinople to Armenia. Near Lake Van, he directed his army from his headquarters at the city of Manzikert and met Alp Arslan's army of Turkmen in 1071.

Alp Arslan showed his military genius when attacked by the Byzantines. He allowed them to advance, leaving his troops to attack the Byzantines on three sides. The Battle of Manzikert was a military disaster for the Byzantines. The army, made up of mercenaries, fled at the first sign of trouble. The general was unable to rally his troops and was captured. The rest of the army was either killed or disintegrated.

Belying their fierce reputation, the Turks neither killed nor tortured the captured general. Instead, Diogenes was allowed to go free after paying a ransom and agreeing to pay annual tribute. He ceded control over portions of Armenia, then was allowed to return to Byzantine territory. Once there, he was not treated as well. Stripped of his throne, his wife imprisoned, Diogenes had his eyes burned out with hot pokers, then was forced to ride a mule over long stretches of road.

The Battle of Manzikert led to more than the loss of a general; it also destroyed the empire's military power in the east. The entire Anatolia plain, also known as Asia Minor, lay open to the Turks. It was at this point that events turned from bad to worse for the Byzantines.

A few months after the battle, Alp Arslan was assassinated. When the Byzantines refused to pay tribute as required by the treaty with Diogenes, Alp Arslan's son and successor, Malik Shāh, decided to invade. While Malik took his own army into Central Asia to push the empire eastward, he designated his general Süleyman to attack the Byzantines in Anatolia. The Byzantines, under the bumbling leadership of the emperor Michael VII Ducas (r. 1067-1078), proved unable to halt the Turks' advance. Only the desolate Anatolia plains slowed Süleyman's advance, as he swept aside the weak Byzantine forces sent to defeat him.

As Süleyman advanced westward toward Constantinople, Michael VII and the Byzantine government panicked and sought help from European nations, but no help was forthcoming. The Turks' advance included capturing such famous Byzantine cities as Antioch, Tarsus, and Nicaea. Süleyman eventually halted his drive within sight of Constantinople. At that point, Süleyman declared the creation of the sultanate of Rum—derived from the word Rome—with its capital in Konya, previously known as Iconium and a city visited by Paul.

The sultanate, which was the Seljuk Turk nation, lasted a century and half until defeated by the Mongols and broken into smaller kingdoms. Süleyman's declaration also began the golden age of the Seljuk Empire. This was the result of his and Malik Shāh's conquests but also the rule of one of his ministers, Niẓām al-Mulk. A political philosopher, Niẓām wrote *Siyāsat-nāma* (wr. 1091-1092; *The Book of Government: Or, Rules for Kings*, 1978), in which he stated that every state was to be based on religion and that each ruler ruled on the basis of divine right. This was advice the Seljuk rulers and their successors in the Ottoman Empire would take and use.

Niẓām's three decades of rule saw the development of literature and Islamic culture and an efficient administration of a large geographic territory containing many different peoples, religions, and cultures. A series of mosques were built, including several in the capital of Konya. Burial mosques were scattered across the territory and contained the bodies of Alp Arslan and, later, Malik Shāh. Many of these mosques still stand, testifying to the architectural and building skills of the Seljuks. In addition to the construction efforts, Niẓām's administrative abilities allowed Malik Shāh to campaign at the frontiers without fear of chaos or coup. This led to the great expansion of Seljuk territory.

Upon capturing Asia Minor, the Seljuks began to eliminate Greek and Roman influences from the area. One tactic was to change the names of the cities; hence, Iconium became Konya. Another was to spread Islam throughout the region, forcing many Christians to convert or in some cases face death. Islamic culture and literature spread throughout the region with the use of the Turkish language. A century and a half of rule—brief when compared with other empires and dynasties—Islamicized the empire and helped settle the Turks at the borders of Europe.

With the capture of much of Byzantium's Asian territory, Malik Shāh turned his attention to the south. Syria and Jerusalem had been captured, allowing the Turks to advance against the Egyptians and then the Arabs, taking both Mecca and Medina. It was the capture of Jerusalem and the threat posed to Constantinople by Turkish armies that led to the eventual collapse of the Seljuk Empire. The Turks soon found themselves at conflict with most of Europe. Malik Shāh's death also weakened the empire as his successors fought for control.

SIGNIFICANCE

The creation of the Turkish Muslim state in Asia Minor had profound consequences in Europe. The loss of land held by the west for more than one thousand years and the possible defeat of a Christian empire by an Islamic one led to Pope Urban II calling for the First Crusade. The major European nations took up the call. Tens of thousands of European soldiers moved east to defeat the Turks. The Crusades proved to be an exhausting fight for the Seljuk Turks, who initially shouldered much of the burden. The constant battles weakened the Seljuk empires. After the death of their last great emperor, Sinjar, the Turks split up into smaller kingdoms, which were smashed by the invading Mongols in the thirteenth century. One of the kingdoms later became the Ottoman Turks, who developed their own empire in Asia Minor after capturing Constantinople in 1453.

—Douglas Clouatre

FURTHER READING

Armstrong, Karen. *Holy War.* New York: Doubleday, 1991. Describes the Crusades from the perspective of modern times and how the battles of medieval years still resonate.

Bryer, Anthony, and Michael Ursinus, eds. *Manzikert to Lepanto: The Byzantine World and the Turks, 1071-1571.* Amsterdam: A. M. Hakkert, 1991. A detailed source on Byzantine-Turkish relations in the wake of the Battle of Manzikert.

Cahen, Claude. *Pre-Ottoman Turkey: A General Survey of the Material and Spiritual Culture and History, c. 1071-1330.* New York: Taplinger, 1968. This definitive study of the Seljuk period of Turkish history gives a straightforward, scholarly account of the rise of the

Seljuks and their involvement in Anatolia prior to 1071.

Irwin, Robert. "Muslim Responses to the Crusades." *History Today* 47, no. 4 (April, 1997). Presents a rich overview of the Muslim perspective on the Crusades, including the responses of the Seljuks before the First Crusade in the late eleventh century. Provides photographs and a short list of further readings.

Niẓām al-Mulk. *The Book of Government: Or, Rules for Kings*. Translated by Hubert Darke. Richmond, Surrey, England: Curzon Press, 2002. This polished translation of the *Siyāsat-nāma* is essential reading for an understanding of both Niẓām al-Mulk and the workings of government during the Seljuk period. Bibliography, index.

Norwich, John Julius. *A Short History of Byzantium*. New York: Vintage Books, 1997. A concise version of a three-volume work on Byzantium, describing the political, military, religious, and cultural decline of the empire.

Richards, D. S., ed. *The Annals of the Seljuk Turks*. New York: Routledge, 2002. A description of the Seljuk Turks, their leaders, goals, accomplishments, and defeat by the Mongols.

Treadgold, Warren. *A History of the Byzantine State and Society*. Stanford, Calif.: Stanford University Press, 1997. A brief discussion of the Eastern Roman Empire with an emphasis on the causes leading to its destruction.

SEE ALSO: August 15-20, 636: Battle of Yarmūk; 637-657: Islam Expands Throughout the Middle East; 956: Oğhuz Turks Migrate to Transoxiana; 1040-1055: Expansion of the Seljuk Turks; 1054: Beginning of the Rome-Constantinople Schism; August 26, 1071: Battle of Manzikert; November 27, 1095: Pope Urban II Calls the First Crusade; c. 1145: Prester John Myth Sweeps Across Europe; 1147-1149: Second Crusade; 1189-1192: Third Crusade; 1204: Knights of the Fourth Crusade Capture Constantinople; May 29, 1453: Fall of Constantinople.

RELATED ARTICLES in *Great Lives from History: The Middle Ages, 477-1453*: Alp Arslan; Genghis Khan; Niẓām al-Mulk; Omar Khayyám; Osman I; Urban II.

1086
DOMESDAY SURVEY

The Domesday survey provided detailed information about the resources of individual landholders in England for purposes of identification, settling disputed titles, and levying taxes while establishing feudal law and consolidating Norman rule.

LOCALE: England

CATEGORIES: Economics; government and politics; laws, acts, and legal history

KEY FIGURES

Robert of Losinga (fl. eleventh century), bishop of Hereford, 1079-1095

William the Conqueror (c. 1028-1087), first Norman king of England, r. 1066-1087

SUMMARY OF EVENT

During the Christmas court at Gloucester in 1085, William the Conqueror, faced with the threat of armies from Denmark, Norway, and Flanders, met with his advisers in what the *Anglo-Saxon Chronicle* (compiled c. 890 to c. 1150) called "a deep discussion" about the state of the country. The outcome of their deliberations was William's decision to survey his kingdom in order to reveal the resources of the new feudal order he had established. At the same time, he probably announced an increase in the annual tax on land (Danegeld) to what was perceived by his subjects as an exorbitant level.

To carry out the proposed survey, William and his advisers divided the kingdom into seven circuits, each consisting of between three and six counties. The first circuit, for example, included Kent, Sussex, Surrey, Hampshire, and Berkshire. Yorkshire and Lincolnshire may actually have been surveyed separately from their designated circuits. William appointed a team of commissioners, prelates, and barons, assisted by clerks and monks, to visit the circuits and record the responses to a series of questions about every manor and its wealth.

Robert of Losinga, bishop of Hereford, who was most likely present at the Gloucester Council, provides the earliest contemporary reference to this event. According to his account, William

> made a survey of all England; of the land in each of the counties; of the possessions of each of the magnates,

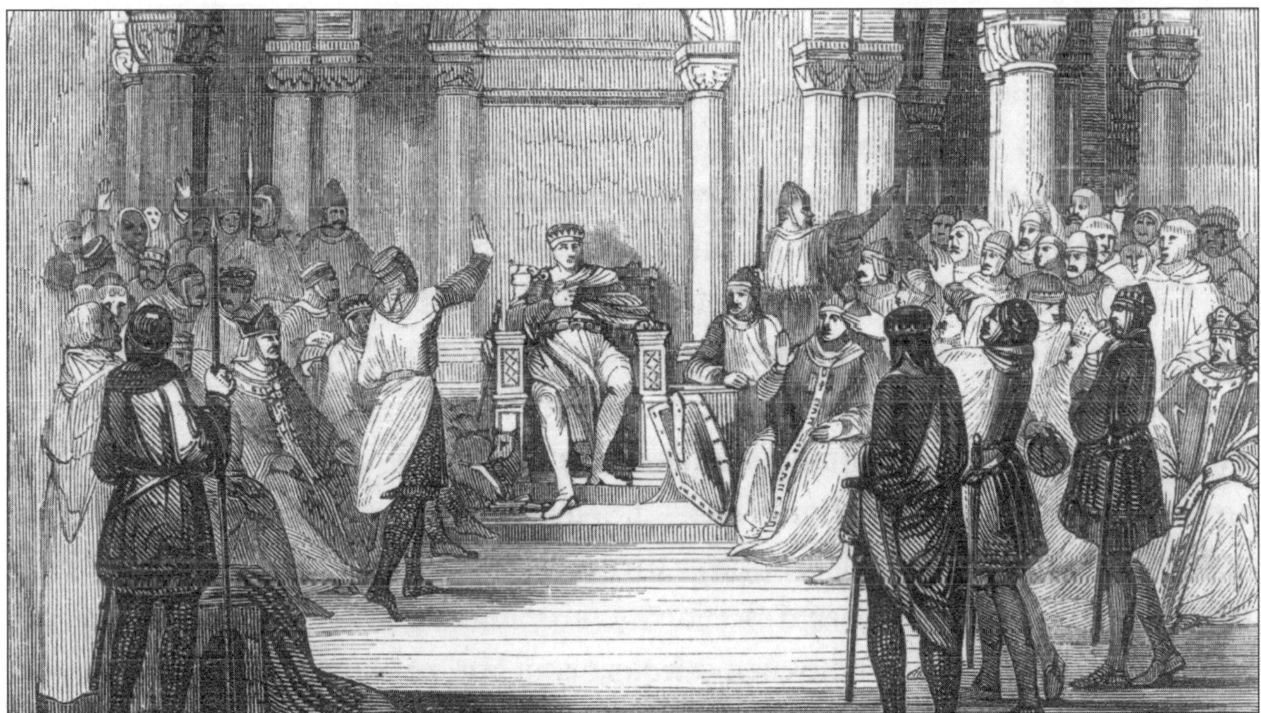

William the Conqueror promising to observe the laws of England. His Domesday survey helped settle title disputes caused by the Norman Conquest and identified the country's resources. (B. F. Waitt)

> their lands, their habitations, their men, both slaves and freemen, living in huts or with their own houses and lands; of plows, horses, and other animals; of the services and payments due from each and every estate.

He also reports that the commissioners were to conduct a second survey in areas where they were not known to the inhabitants to verify the first and check for possible fraud. He corroborates that the survey coincided with a tax levy.

The commissioners began their task as early as January in some counties and probably finished it by August 1, 1086, when William held a court at Salisbury. He had summoned the substantial landowners there to swear oaths of loyalty and obedience shortly before he departed for Normandy. Afterward, he successfully taxed his vassals to support his military ventures and penalized those accused of wrongfully possessing their estates. He could only have accomplished these things if the survey was already complete.

Each commission relied on the existing court structure to assemble their evidence. The sheriff of each county was responsible for collecting information and summoning those holding manors to appear. The king's tenants-in-chief were required to submit their responses in writing, and there is good evidence that the barons and ecclesiastical tenants cooperated. Royal scribes used shorthand to write down the testimony given them in French or English then prepared drafts for delivery to Winchester, site of the treasury and most likely the central gathering place for all reports. At Winchester, the survey was translated into Latin, edited—possibly by one scribe—into 888 richly detailed leaves, and listed by county with individual manors highlighted in red. The leaves were subsequently bound into two books: Little Domesday, encompassing Essex, Norfolk, and Suffolk, and the larger Exchequer Domesday, covering the remainder of the kingdom. Both books, collectively summarized into the Domesday Book, were originally housed at Winchester in a large chest protected with lock and three keys. Later, they were moved to Westminster.

Although the survey is incomplete, omitting London, Winchester, and other places known to have existed in the eleventh century, it is still a magnificent testament to Norman administrative efficiency and a unique medieval document. While the Carolingian surveys of the late eighth century contain some parallels, none matches Domesday in breadth or thoroughness. It is quite literally a survey of the landed wealth of England. There is nothing comparable for the Middle Ages for any European country. It records the estates and manors before the start of the Norman Conquest at the Battle of Hastings (1066) and twenty years later (1086). In many cases, it also reports the value of an estate when it was acquired by its Norman landlord. Thus, the survey was both a land register and rent book for the upper levels of society.

While its sole purpose was not the collection of the land tax or geld, the survey illustrates William's obvious need to revise the tax lists in light of the altered pattern of ownership occasioned by the Norman Conquest and consequent settlement. For example, Domesday includes nearly two hundred landowners who possessed estates yielding one hundred pounds yearly. By 1086, this aggregate included only two Englishmen. Among the lesser magnates, that number was one in fourteen and a single bishopric remained in English hands. There was less transfer of properties further down the social scale; however, the settlement transformed landholdings throughout the country and many who owned lands in 1066 found themselves leasing them twenty years later. Because of the immediate military threat from abroad, William had to know what resources he could draw on to defend his territories. He also understood the advantages of settling disputed land claims held for peace and stability in England. The survey allowed William to accomplish both goals.

SIGNIFICANCE

The immediate significance of the Domesday Book was as an administrative document used to arbitrate disputes between central and local government. It is a precise record of the location and value of lands and, as such, was an essential reference to sheriffs and other royal officials charged with settling tenure disputes for nearly two hundred years. During William's reign, no estate, even those forfeit for rebellion, could be transferred without his approval. The value of the survey in this connection was that it permitted him to know readily which of his vassals was acquiring too many estates and thereby becoming too powerful. Within a century of its completion, its reputation was so profound that the survey had acquired the popular name "Domesday," according to Richard Fitzneale, author of *Dialogus de scaccario* (c. 1179; *The Ancient Dialogue Concerning the Exchequer,* 1758). The reference was to the Day of Judgment, from which there was no appeal.

Although its principal purposes may have been feudal and fiscal, the Domesday Book's enduring importance is found in the comprehensive portrait it provides of English rural life in the eleventh century. It records more than thirteen thousand place-names and permits a reasonably accurate population estimate for England of about two million in 1086. Of that total, there were more than one hundred thousand villeins, peasants tied to the land who owed labor service to the lord of the manor. They also held a share in the common field. This aggregate headed nearly one-third of the households in the country. The south and southwest contained nearly thirty thousand slaves, more than twice the number of free men. The details of mills, ponds, plows, and livestock are similarly full.

The Domesday survey gave William precise knowledge of his kingdom. It facilitated collection of the geld, helped settle title disputes caused by the Norman Conquest, and showed the general resources of England in a compact form useful to royal administrators at the time and ever since.

—*Michael J. Galgano*

FURTHER READING

Darby, H. C. *Domesday England.* New York: Cambridge University Press, 1986. Summary volume to *Domesday Geography,* which was produced earlier in five volumes under Darby's direction. Compares contemporary lists with the Domesday Book, illustrates the feudal purpose of the survey, and includes full statistics.

Douglas, David C. *William the Conqueror: The Norman Impact upon England.* Berkeley: University of California Press, 1964. Standard biography of William. Examines William in Normandy but focuses on the Conquest and the establishment of Norman rule and influence in England.

Fleming, Robin. *Domesday Book and the Law: Society and Legal Custom in Early Medieval England.* New York: Cambridge University Press, 1998. Covers the transmission of legal information, the inquest and justice, and disputes. Includes the text of the "Exchequer Domesday Book" and "Little Domesday Book."

Galbraith, V. H. *The Making of Domesday Book.* New York: Clarendon Press, 1961. Stresses that the purpose of the Domesday was feudal, not fiscal.

Holt, J. C., ed. *Domesday Studies.* Rochester, N.Y.: Boydell Press, 1987. Essays examine range of political, economic, administrative, and structural topics associated with the survey, the making of the Domesday Book, and the times.

Maitland, Frederic William. *Domesday Book and Beyond: Three Essays in the Early History of England.*

New York: Cambridge University Press, 1987. First published in 1897, this work spurred the modern scholarly study of the Domesday. Concentrates on social structure, feudal tenure, and the hides, and emphasizes the survey's fiscal purpose.

Roffe, David. *Domesday: The Inquest and the Book*. New York: Oxford University Press, 2000. Discusses the book's "mystique," land rights, the Domesday inquest, disputes and dispute resolutions, the writing of the book, and more.

Sawyer, Peter, ed. *Domesday Book: A Reassessment*. Baltimore: Edward Arnold, 1985. Collection of articles that illustrate the range of scholarship on the survey, the survey's intent, the paleography of the manuscripts, and the problems executing the survey.

Williams, Anne, and G. H. Martin, eds. *Domesday Book: A Complete Translation*. New York: Penguin Books, 2002. A one-volume translation of the text, which amounts to more than fourteen hundred pages. Includes an index.

SEE ALSO: October 14, 1066: Battle of Hastings.

RELATED ARTICLE in *Great Lives from History: The Middle Ages, 477-1453*: William the Conqueror.

November, 1092-June 15, 1094
EL CID CONQUERS VALENCIA

El Cid conquered Valencia and became its ruler, making use of excellent military strategies and tactics to defeat Muslims from northern Africa who invaded Spain in the eleventh century.

LOCALE: Valencia, Spain

CATEGORIES: Government and politics; wars, uprisings, and civil unrest

KEY FIGURES

El Cid (c. 1043-1099), Spanish military leader who defeated the Almoravids at Valencia

Ferdinand I (1016 or 1018-1065), king of Castile, r. 1035-1065, and king of León, r. 1037-1065

Alfonso VI (1040-1109), younger son of Ferdinand and his successor as king of Léon, r. 1065-1070, later king of reunited León and Castile, r. 1072-1109

Jimena Díaz (fl. eleventh century), wife of El Cid and niece of Alfonso VI

Sancho II (c. 1037-1072), eldest son of Ferdinand and his successor as king of Castile, r. 1065-1072

Urraca (1080 or 1081-1126), daughter of Ferdinand and queen of Castile and Léon, r. 1109-1126

Yūsuf ibn Tāshufīn (d. 1106), emir of the Almoravid Empire, 1061-1106

SUMMARY OF EVENT

Rodrigo Díaz de Vivar, best known as El Cid, is both a historical and a literary figure. Since his death in 1099, this hero's life has been celebrated in several works, particularly the epic poem *El Cantar de mío Cid* (c. 1140; *The Poem of the Cid*, 1879), also known as *Poema de mío Cid*. History and legend have become so entangled that scholars still struggle to determine the exact events of his life.

In 711, thousands of Islamic Berbers from northern Africa crossed into Spain at Gibraltar, and Islam remained in Spain for nearly eight hundred years. Partially because the Christian kingdoms were divided among themselves, there was little resistance to this invasion. In 718, the leader Pelayo was the first to stop these Muslim troops as they attempted to cross the Iberian Peninsula and invade the rest of Europe. Over the next several hundred years, until 1492 when the last Moorish leaders left Spain, Christians and Moors battled what was known as the Reconquest of Spain.

The Reconquista was not a period of continual warfare. Córdoba, Seville, and Granada became powerful political and cultural centers in the southern part of the peninsula under Muslim rule. Evidence of the glories of this culture can still be seen in the architecture that remains in these cities: The Great Mosque at Córdoba, the Alcázar in Seville, and the famous Alhambra in Granada. Boundaries between the Christian north and Muslim south were not fixed, and one group or the other often initiated warfare in an attempt to control territory, while at other times there was relative harmony.

During the Reconquista, El Cid emerged as a Christian military leader and later became a legendary hero. Born in Vivar, near Burgos around 1043, Rodrigo Díaz de Vivar became known more widely as El Cid, a nickname derived from the Arabic *sayyid*, meaning lord or sir.

At the age of seventeen, El Cid was knighted by Sancho II and later appointed commander of the royal army. Following the death of the king Ferdinand I, father of Sancho, a civil war erupted between Alfonso and his sister Urraca against their brother Sancho. When Sancho was murdered, Alfonso VI became king of Castile. For a time, El Cid seemed to have royal favor under this new king. In 1074, Alfonso arranged a marriage between El Cid and his niece, Jimena Díaz of the House of Aragón. His status with Alfonso, however, quickly changed. In 1081, El Cid led a successful raid into the territory of Toledo without the king's approval. El Cid's enemies convinced Alfonso that the leader had taken the action for personal gain. After his wife and children were placed in a monastery for safety, El Cid was exiled from Castile and León. He took with him a small army of trained warriors and served as a mercenary for both Christian and Muslim kings. During this period, El Cid demonstrated his military genius through a series of successful campaigns.

El Cid at Valencia after defeating the Almoravids. (Hulton|Archive by Getty Images)

During the time when El Cid was in exile in the eastern part of Spain, events in the southern part of the country were occupying Alfonso. He had taken the Moorish city of Toledo and extended his reign farther into Moorish territory. He controlled nearly all of Christian and Muslim Spain. Seeing the threat they were under, Muslim rulers eventually sought additional help from the Almoravid Empire in northern Africa.

In June of 1086, Yūsuf ibn Tāshufīn crossed into Spain and was met by Muslim leaders of Seville, Granada, and Málaga. Alfonso VI ceased his attempt to gain control of Zaragoza and marched south with his troops to meet Yūsuf. The two met at Sagrajas, and Alfonso was humiliated in defeat. The military tactics of these North Africans were unlike those of the Spaniards; they were more compact and unified compared with the Spanish one-on-one style combat. Finally, Yūsuf returned to Africa and Alfonso called El Cid out of exile.

Alfonso gave El Cid free reign in large parts of eastern al-Andalus—Muslim-occupied Spain—and even promised El Cid and his heirs all the land that he freed from the Moors. El Cid gained control of several independent kingdoms and demanded tribute from them. He even succeeded in forcing Valencia to pay tribute owed to Alfonso.

In 1089, Yūsuf once again crossed into Spain, and Alfonso demanded that El Cid join him in fighting against the Almoravids. Because of internal struggles between Yūsuf and other Muslim leaders, however, Yūsuf and his army had retreated before Alfonso reached Aledo. It is not clear exactly what occurred, but El Cid failed to meet up with Alfonso. Enraged, the king once again banished El Cid from his kingdom, confiscated his property, and imprisoned El Cid's wife and children, although the family was reunited later.

Exiled for a second time, El Cid again began to demand tribute from several of the independent kingdoms in the east and southeast of al-Andalus. He even persuaded al-Qadir, former ruler of Toledo, then ruler of Valencia to again pay tribute to ensure protection. El Cid remained a nuisance to both Yūsuf and to Alfonso, but became acceptable to many of the Moors. He practiced an authority that permitted tolerance rather than influence by power. Nevertheless, many Muslims resented the taxes imposed on them by Christian rulers.

When Yūsuf began his third campaign into Spain, many Muslim rulers decided they were safer without Yūsuf as an ally. They were prepared to ally themselves with Alfonso instead. This time, however, Yūsuf managed to reclaim several cities and Alfonso lost his control of al-Andalus. Only El Cid remained to exert pressure within the Moorish territory.

At the request of Alfonso's wife, Queen Constanza, El Cid joined the king near Granada. The reconciliation, however, was short lived. The Almoravids did not attack as anticipated, and eventually the royal troops were ordered back to Toledo. In a misunderstanding over protocol, El Cid pitched his tents close to the walls of the city. Alfonso was only too ready to misinterpret El Cid's actions, and El Cid fled and returned safely to Valencia where both Muslim and Christian leaders sought his support against the Almoravids of northern Africa.

During this period, Alfonso was unable to regain control of the south, and Yūsuf reconquered several cities and kingdoms. While El Cid was in Zaragoza, Valencia's ruler al-Qadir was forced to flee the city, and the populace planned to turn the city over to the Almoravids. On his return in the fall of 1092, El Cid began a siege of the city that took nearly nineteen months to complete. When the new ruler refused to honor the previous accord, El Cid cut off food supplies. News of another Almoravid invasion encouraged those in control of Valencia to hold out until the North African troops could arrive. The famine and death caused by the lack of supplies, combined with further news that the Almoravids had eventually returned to Africa, forced Valencia to negotiate a settlement. On June 15, 1094, El Cid took control of Valencia as its unofficial king.

Yūsuf, now aged and perhaps ill, sent his nephew to reconquer Valencia and bring back El Cid alive; his nephew was unsuccessful and Yūsuf never returned to Spain. In the fall of 1094, at the Battle of Cuarte, El Cid again defeated the Almoravids.

El Cid held the city of Valencia for another five years until he died suddenly on July 10, 1099. His widow, Jimena, held Valencia for only a few years before she was forced to withdraw from the city, and Valencia once again fell to Muslim rule in 1102.

SIGNIFICANCE

El Cid managed to persist against repeated attacks against the people of Spain, embodying heroism and living a life of legend. The epic *Poem of the Cid* reflects his legendary life, one filled with strength and determination but also brutality and cruelty. El Cid's leadership in conquering Valencia and defeating the Muslims represents simply his final act recognizing that Spain deserved national unity.

—*Donald E. Cellini*

FURTHER READING

Barton, Simon, and Richard Fletcher, trans. *The World of El Cid: Chronicles of the Spanish Reconquest*. New York: St. Martin's Press, 2000. Translations—with annotations—of four historical works by El Cid's contemporaries, documenting the Reconquest. Includes a bibliography and index.

Fletcher, Richard. *The Quest for El Cid*. New York: Alfred A. Knopf, 1990. Provides a synthesis of research and refutes some earlier assumptions.

Fregosi, Paul. *Jihad in the West: Muslim Conquests from the Seventh to the Twenty-first Centuries*. Amherst, N.Y.: Prometheus Books, 1998. A history of Muslim conquests, including the "occupation" of Valencia during El Cid's time. Includes the chapter, "Mio Cid: Valencia, 1080-1108." Also includes a bibliography and index.

Fuentes, Carlos. "The Reconquest of Spain." In *The Buried Mirror: Reflection on Spain and the New World*. Boston: Houghton Mifflin, 1992. A widely accessible work that discusses El Cid within the context of the Spanish Reconquista and describes its significance on the conquest of the Americas several hundred years later.

Madden, Thomas F., ed. *The Crusades: The Essential Readings*. Malden, Mass.: Blackwell, 2002. An exploration of the Crusades, including the chapter, "Reconquest and Crusade in Spain, c. 1050-1150." Also provides a bibliography and index.

Matthews, John. *El Cid: Champion of Spain*. New York: Sterling Publishing, 1988. This publication provides an easy and concise introduction to El Cid and to Spain of the eleventh century. Includes maps, drawings, and photographs.

Menendez Pidal, Ramón. *The Cid and His Spain*. Translated by Harold Sunderland. Reprint. London: J. Murray, 1971. A well-known scholar provides classic scholarship about El Cid.

O'Callaghan, Joseph F. *Reconquest and Crusade in Medieval Spain*. Philadelphia: University of Pennsylvania Press, 2002. The author argues that the Papacy in the twelfth and thirteenth centuries regarded the conflict in Spain between Muslims and Christians, which continued after El Cid's death, to be a Crusade, and they afforded the same benefits to Crusaders in Spain as to those in the Holy Land. Includes chapters on battles, financing the conflicts, and Crusade warfare in general.

Read, Jan. *The Moors in Spain and Portugal*. Totowa, N.J: Rowman and Littlefield, 1975. Told from the Moorish point of view, this history makes use of many Arabic sources and includes a fine chapter on El Cid.

Smith, Colin. Introduction and notes in *Poema de mío Cid*. Oxford, England: Clarendon Press, 1972. Contains perhaps the definitive edition of the epic poem as well as an exhaustive introduction, a bibliography, and historical footnotes.

SEE ALSO: April or May, 711: Tārik Crosses into Spain; c. 950: Court of Córdoba Flourishes in Spain; c. 1150: Moors Transmit Classical Philosophy and Medicine to Europe; 1230: Unification of Castile and León.

RELATED ARTICLES in *Great Lives from History: The Middle Ages, 477-1453*: Afonso I; El Cid; Saint Isidore of Seville; James I the Conqueror; Raymond of Peñafort; Ṭārik ibn-Ziyād.

November 27, 1095
POPE URBAN II CALLS THE FIRST CRUSADE

Pope Urban II initiated the first in a series of military expeditions from Christian Western Europe to the Middle East by calling the First Crusade, which intended to recapture the Holy Land from the Muslims.

LOCALE: Clermont, France
CATEGORIES: Religion; wars, uprisings, and civil unrest

KEY FIGURES

Urban II (c. 1042-1099), Roman Catholic pope, 1088-1099, who preached the First Crusade

Alexius I Comnenus (1048-1118), Byzantine emperor, r. 1081-1118

Peter the Hermit (c. 1050-1115), French ascetic and preacher of the Peasants' Crusade

Gautier Sans Avoir (d. 1097), French knight and a leader of the Peasants' Crusade

Bohemond I (c. 1052-1111), son of Robert Guiscard of Italy and a leader of the First Crusade

Godfrey of Bouillon (c. 1060-1100), duke of Lower Lorraine and protector of the Holy Sepulchre, 1099

Raymond of Saint-Gilles (1042-1105), count of Toulouse, a leader of the First Crusade

Adhémar de Monteil (d. 1098), papal legate with the First Crusade

Robert II of Jerusalem (c. 1065-1111), count of Flanders, Norman Crusader, and ruler of Jerusalem

THE CRUSADES, 1095-1270

Crusade	*Dates*	*Leaders*	*Destination*
First	1095-1099	Urban II, Bohemond I, Raymond IV	Nicaea, Dorylaeum, Antioch, Jerusalem
Second	1147-1149	Eugenius III, Bernard of Clairvaux, Louis VII, Conrad III	Outremer, Iberian Peninsula, Damascus
Third	1189-1192	Gregory VIII, Richard I, Philip II, Frederick I Barbarossa	Acre, Arsuf
Fourth	1202-1204	Innocent III, Enrico Dandolo	Zara, Constantinople
Fifth	1217-1221	Innocent III, Honorius III, Andrew II, John of Brienne	Damietta in Egypt
Sixth	1227-1230	Honorius III, Frederick II	Sidon, Tyre, Acre, Jerusalem
Seventh (or Sixth)	1248-1254	Louis IX	Damietta and Mansurah in Egypt
Eighth (or Seventh)	1270	Louis IX	Tunis

Pope Urban II, at the Council of Clermont in 1095, calls Christians to the First Crusade (facsimile of a wood engraving from Grand Voyage de Hiérusalem, *1522).* (Frederick Ungar Publishing Co.)

SUMMARY OF EVENT

Fought between 1096 and 1270, the Crusades, or "Wars of the Cross," were defining features of the High Middle Ages in Europe. For almost four centuries, between nine and ten major military expeditions left the West for the Middle East in an effort to achieve two strategic goals. One was to prevent the conquest of the Byzantine Empire, a Christian stronghold, by the Muslim Turks. The other goal, which was more important to the Europeans, was to establish Christian control over the venerated pilgrimage sites in the Holy Land, especially Jerusalem. Ultimately, neither aim was secured permanently.

The Turks conquered Constantinople in 1453, ending forever the Byzantine Empire. By 1515, all the East, including Palestine, had fallen under the control of the Turks. The Crusades, however, represent the West's earliest effort to expand and create what has been rightly called "Europe's first adventure in colonialism."

On Tuesday, November 27, 1095, Pope Urban II preached the First Crusade before the Council of Clermont, an assembly of some two hundred bishops meeting in the south of France. Of French noble birth, Urban had been educated at Soissons and Reims and had served as a prior in the reforming abbey of Cluny before becoming a papal legate and later pope on March 12, 1088, at Terracina. The agenda at Clermont included many items. The council adopted some thirty-two canons on a variety of topics. The main business, however, was the pope's call for a holy war to liberate the East from the Turks. What language Urban used in his speech is not known, since there is no surviving transcript. The response to his speech was immediate and positive. From the congregation came the cry "*Deus volt*" ("God wills it"). The Crusades were launched.

The pope had two primary motives in calling the Crusade. One was his hope for the reunification of the Christian world, which had been rent asunder by a schism between Rome and Constantinople in 1054. Another was his dream of a universal Papacy, with the pope having hegemony over Christendom's three holiest cities—Rome, Constantinople, and Jerusalem. The Crusade he called would facilitate both these visions.

The occasion for the pope's message was also twofold. The Byzantine Empire was in danger of falling under the control of the Turks. In August of 1071, the Seljuk Turks had decisively defeated the Eastern emperor at the

Battle of Manzikert. In the wake of that victory, the Turks advanced across Anatolia, taking Antioch in 1085 and Nicaea in 1092. These reversals prompted the new Byzantine emperor, Alexius I Comnenus, to appeal to the West for help. A parallel problem involved the Turkish occupation of Palestine. The economic and religious revival of the West had resulted in an increased traffic of pilgrims journeying to the Holy Land. Tales of sacrilege, desecrations, and abuse were heard in Europe. Many individuals believed that only a Christian military presence in the East could guarantee the security and the integrity of Christian pilgrims and shrines from Turkish atrocities.

A variety of reasons account for the popularity of Pope Urban II's appeal among all classes—peasants, merchants, warriors, and clergy. Merchants and other residents of Italian towns were eager to secure commercial advantages in the Mediterranean from the Greeks and Arabs. Younger sons of the aristocracy could find fiefs of their own in *Outre Mer* (the land beyond the sea). Epidemic private warfare between Europe's nobility was expected to diminish as aggression was directed toward an external foe.

A precedent for wars of reconquest had been established by Christian advances in Spain, Sardinia, and Sicily. Europe was in an expansive mood as new domains were added in Scandinavia, the Baltic, and the Balkans. An expanding population was seeking space all the way from Iceland to Cyprus. Military science had proved the potential for success of major international expeditions, as seen in the Norman Conquest of England in 1066. Peasants were eager for freedom and adventure in the exotic East. A major religious revival was evident, giving birth to universities, cathedrals, and now the Crusades, a kind of "spiritual journey." Very much a product of his times, Pope Urban II had touched the vibrant energies and the vivid imagination of a rejuvenated Europe.

One facet of the First Crusade was the Peasants' or People's Crusade, led by Gautier Sans Avoir. Here he and his fellow crusaders receive permission from the king of Hungary to pass through his territory. (Frederick Ungar Publishing Co.)

Probably to the pope's surprise, the masses were the first to respond to the call. A French ascetic from Amiens known as Peter the Hermit and a French knight named Gautier Sans Avoir (Walter the Penniless) preached the Peasants' or People's Crusade. This popular movement attracted the innocent as well as the iniquitous, who in undisciplined fashion worked their way down the Balkans to Constantinople. Crossing the straits of Bosporus into Asia, participants in the Peasants' Crusade faced annihilation by the Turks at the Battle of Cibotus (Civetot) in August, 1096.

In Europe that same month, the expected response to the pope's sermon occurred among the nobility. Although no kings took up the cross, many European nobles did. The First Crusade, also known as the Barons' Crusade, set out for the East in four major contingents. One contingent was led by Godfrey of Bouillon, the duke of Lower Lorraine. A second group was headed by Bohemond I, the middle-aged son of Robert Guiscard, a Norman noble with properties in Italy. Leading the third and largest forces was Raymond of Saint-Gilles, the count of Toulouse, who was the oldest and most experienced of the crusaders. Raymond was accompanied by Adhémar de Monteil, a warrior bishop who served as papal legate for the Crusade. A fourth group was directed by Robert II of Jerusalem. Because the French predominated among the Crusader forces, the soldiers of the First Crusade were known in the East as "the Franks" or "the Normans."

Passing through Constantinople, some four thousand mounted knights and twenty-five thousand infantry invaded Anatolia, taking Nicaea on June 19, 1097, and surrendering it to the Byzantine emperor. On June 3, 1098, the Syrian city of Antioch was taken and was retained by Bohemond I as his own. Jerusalem itself was captured on July 15, 1099, with much bloodshed. Within three years, the Crusaders had obtained their goals of pushing the Turks back from Anatolia and securing western sovereignty in Palestine. Godfrey of Bouillon was appointed to remain as defender of the Holy Sepulchre in Jerusalem. Within a few years, a series of Latin feudal principalities were established along the Levantine coast. For Europe, the First Crusade appeared to be a resounding success.

POPE URBAN II'S CALL TO CRUSADE

Although no transcript of the acts of the Council of Clermont survives, several renditions of Pope Urban II's speech—deemed by many to be one of the most rousing in history—have come down to us, including this one from Robert the Monk, in Historia Hierosolymitana, *recorded about twenty-five years after the pope's speech:*

From the confines of Jerusalem and the city of Constantinople a horrible tale has gone forth and very frequently has been brought to our ears, namely, that a race from the kingdom of the Persians, an accursed race . . . has invaded the lands of those Christians and has depopulated them by the sword, pillage and fire. . . . ; it has either entirely destroyed the churches of God or appropriated them for the rites of its own religion. They destroy the altars, after having defiled them with their uncleanness. They circumcise the Christians, and the blood of the circumcision they either spread upon the altars or pour into the vases of the baptismal font. When they wish to torture people by a base death, they perforate their navels, and dragging forth the extremity of the intestines, bind it to a stake. . . . On whom therefore is the labor of avenging these wrongs and of recovering this territory incumbent, if not upon you? You, upon whom above other nations God has conferred remarkable glory in arms, great courage, bodily activity, and strength to humble the hairy scalp of those who resist you. . . .

When Pope Urban had said these and very many similar things in his urbane discourse, he so influenced to one purpose the desires of all who were present, that they cried out, "It is the will of God! It is the will of God!"

Source: Dana C. Munro, "Urban and the Crusaders," in *Translations and Reprints from the Original Sources of European History* 1, no. 2 (Philadelphia: University of Pennsylvania, 1895), pp. 5-8.

SIGNIFICANCE

Appearances were deceptive, however, as Crusader victories occurred because of fragmentation of power in the Muslim East. Once the Turks and other Muslims recovered political control, the tide turned. Maintaining a Western military presence in the Middle East proved difficult, not only because of the proximity of enemies but also because of the distance of these military forces from the European base of power. Within a short time, it became necessary to wage the Second and Third Crusades, leading to a series of religious wars that would terminate in the eventual expulsion of European Crusader forces from the Middle East.

—*C. George Fry*

FURTHER READING

Bridge, Anthony. *The Crusades*. New York: Franklin Watts, 1982. Written for a general audience, this beautifully illustrated text provides a fine introduction to the history of the Crusades. Maps, useful bibliography.

Bull, Marcus. "The Pilgrimage Origins of the First Crusade." *History Today* 47, no. 3 (March, 1997). The author explores Urban II's speech at Clermont and then traces the Crusades from their start as a Christian pilgrimage to a holy war.

Chazan, Robert. "Jerusalem as Christian Symbol During the First Crusade: Jewish Awareness and Response." In *Jerusalem: Its Sanctity and Centrality to Judaism, Christianity, and Islam*, edited by Lee I. Levine. New York: Continuum, 1999. Examines the Jewish response to the presence of Christian Crusaders and the Christian Church in the Holy City.

Foss, Michael. *People of the First Crusade*. Boston: Little, Brown, 1997. This work on the First Crusade focuses on the individuals involved in the holy war. Bibliography and index.

France, John. *Victory in the East: A Military History of the First Crusade*. New York: Cambridge University Press, 1994. A detailed study of the First Crusade, primarily as a military campaign.

Hillenbrand, Carole. *The Crusades: Islamic Perspectives*. New York: Routledge, 2000. Chapters explore Muslim reactions to the Franks of the First Crusade, ethnic and religious stereotyping, daily life, the conduct of war, and more. Bibliography, index.

Irwin, Robert. "Muslim Responses to the Crusades." *History Today* 47, no. 4 (April, 1997). Presents a rich overview of the Muslim perspective on the Crusades, including the responses of the Seljuks before the First Crusade in the late eleventh century. Provides photographs and a short list of further readings.

Madden, Thomas F., ed. *The Crusades: The Essential Readings*. Malden, Mass.: Blackwell, 2002. A collection of previously published articles about the Crusades, including Pope Urban's call for the First Crusade, medieval sources, lay enthusiasm, patronage, Byzantium, and the subjection of Muslims. Bibliography, index.

Phillips, Jonathan, ed. *The First Crusade: Origins and Impact*. New York: St. Martin's Press, 1997. A collection that explores the First Crusade from multiple angles, including its patrons and chroniclers, the Muslim perspective, and property confiscation. Maps, bibliography, index.

Riley-Smith, Jonathan. *The First Crusade and the Idea of Crusading*. Philadelphia: University of Pennsylvania Press, 1986. A scholarly overview of the initial Crusade and its motivations. Maps, excellent bibliography.

_______. *The First Crusaders, 1095-1131*. New York: Cambridge University Press, 1997. The story of the First Crusade, including recruitment, preparation, preaching, the holy war, and the return. Includes an appendix listing the Crusaders, illustrations, maps, and index.

Runciman, Steven. *A History of the Crusades*. 3 vols. New York: Cambridge University Press, 1987. One of the most detailed resources on the Crusader era, by a respected British historian. The first volume provides a good overview of the First Crusade. Illustrations, maps, genealogical table, bibliography, index.

SEE ALSO: August 15-20, 636: Battle of Yarmūk; 11th-12th centuries: Building of Romanesque Cathedrals; 1009: Destruction of the Church of the Holy Sepulchre; 1040-1055: Expansion of the Seljuk Turks; 1054: Beginning of the Rome-Constantinople Schism; October 14, 1066: Battle of Hastings; August 26, 1071: Battle of Manzikert; 1077: Seljuk Dynasty Is Founded; 1100-1300: European Universities Emerge; c. 1120: Order of the Knights Templar Is Founded; c. 1145: Prester John Myth Sweeps Across Europe; 1147-1149: Second Crusade; 1150: Venetian Merchants Dominate Trade with the East; 1189-1192: Third Crusade; c. 1200: Fairs of Champagne; 1204: Knights of the Fourth Crusade Capture Constantinople; 1217-1221: Fifth Crusade; 1227-1230: Frederick II Leads the Sixth Crusade; 1248-1254: Failure of the Seventh Crusade; May 29, 1453: Fall of Constantinople.

RELATED ARTICLES in *Great Lives from History: The Middle Ages, 477-1453*: Alp Arslan; Anna Comnena; Baybars I; Bohemond I; Gregory VII; Henry IV (of Germany); Matilda of Canossa; Melisende; Tancred; Urban II.

March 21, 1098
FOUNDATION OF THE CISTERCIAN ORDER

The Cistercian monastic order adopted more austere practices than the Benedictines in following the Rule—poverty, solitariness, simplicity, labor—returning to its original simplicity in Christianity and antiquity and justifying this "new" way of life.

LOCALE: Burgundy, France
CATEGORIES: Religion; organizations and institutions

KEY FIGURES

Saint Benedict of Nursia (c. 480-c. 547), founder of Benedictine Order
Saint Robert of Molesme (c. 1027-1110), abbot of Cîteaux, 1098-1099
Hugh de Die (1030-1106), archbishop of Lyons and papal legate in France
Saint Alberic (d. 1109), abbot of Cîteaux, 1099-1109
Saint Stephen Harding (c. 1060-1134), abbot of Cîteaux, 1109-1134
Saint Bernard of Clairvaux (1090-1153), abbot of Clairvaux, 1115-1153

SUMMARY OF EVENT

The history of monasticism in the Roman Catholic Church has been said to be an account of a continuing series of internal reformations. The founding of the Order of Cistercians in 1098 is no exception. Reform was in the air during the eleventh century, and the reform of the Cistercians, or White Monks as they were called, changed monasticism during the twelfth century, and the Roman Catholic Church was not the same thereafter.

This reform as well as other reforms of the eleventh and twelfth centuries were reactions to the changing times. The Carolingian reforms around 800 were by the eleventh century out of date. So, too, was the Cluniac reform begun in 909. In broad terms, what was needed at the time was institutional separation of church and state. More narrowly, within monasticism what was needed was a return to following strictly the Rule of Saint Benedict of Nursia that had governed monastic life in western Europe since the sixth century. More specifically, a threefold reform was necessary: a return to poverty, an emphasis on the higher nature of eremetical (solitary) rather than conventional (communal) monastic life, and a desire to imitate the lives of Christ's first apostles as literally as possible, including providing for themselves through their labor while leading a life of poverty and simplicity. A return to the ideals and practices of the earliest hermits and monks also seemed desirable.

The reformers wanted monks to leave the secular world as far behind as possible in order to lead a life of prayer, penance, and mortification. Specifically, the reform included living monastic life according to the literal interpretation of the Benedictine Rule, having an abbot for each house rather than one for the whole order as with the Benedictines and the Cluniacs, having a yearlong novitiate probationary period, and setting a minimum age of fifteen for admission.

The Cistercian order began at Cîteaux, the place known in Latin as Cistercium. An important precursor to Cîteaux was the founding of the monastery of Molesme by Robert in 1075. The son of noble parents, Robert was born about 1027 in Champagne. Robert became a monk

A Cistercian monk tending garden. (Hulton|Archive by Getty Images)

in his youth and rose rapidly to become a prior and abbot. Disillusioned with the practices of contemporary monastic life, he joined a group of hermit monks in the forest of Collan in 1074. The next year, he founded the reform monastery of Molesme. Many new men were called to monastic life because of Molesme, and gifts allowed for about forty daughter monasteries to be founded by 1100. These successes eventually made Molesme similar to the monasteries it had set out to reform. The need for reform and its success eventually begets the need for further reform.

In 1098, Robert and twenty-one other monks set out for another reformed "new monastery" in Burgundy that was to be Cîteaux, about 20 miles (32 kilometers) south of Dijon and about 60 miles (96 kilometers) north of Cluny. Archbishop Hugh de Die of Lyons, papal legate in France, gave permission for this establishment. Robert had told the archbishop that the observance of the Rule of Saint Benedict at Molesme was "lukewarm and negligent." When Robert and his hermit monks arrived at Cîteaux they found a few peasant buildings and perhaps even the remains of an old chapel as the base for their monastery. For several years, the name "Cîteaux" was not used; instead, it was called generically the New Monastery. The date officially given for the founding of the monastery of Cîteaux is March 21, 1098, Palm Sunday that year and appropriately the feast day of Saint Benedict. Exactly when the canonical erection of the abbey, the oath of obedience of Abbot Robert to the local bishop, or the stability vows of the monks to the New Monastery took place is not known. Probably it was during the same year, possibly during the summer.

Meanwhile the monastery of Molesme had fallen even further from the ideals of the Benedictine Rule, and there was a call for Robert to return with the hope that he could bring about reforms. The nobles of the area around Molesme, the pope, the papal legate in France, and a number of bishops were involved in this attempt to get Robert to return. The papal legate Hugh called a synod probably during June, 1099; the abbot of Molesme at the time voluntarily resigned, and Robert was ordered by Hugh to return to Molesme. The monks of Cîteaux were given the option of remaining there or returning with Robert to Molesme. Several returned with him, leaving perhaps just eight monks at Cîteaux. Robert then served as abbot of Molesme until his death in 1110. There was a struggle for survival of the New Monastery at Cîteaux that went on for twenty years. Recruits were hard to come by, and it looked as if this too would be a failed monastic experiment.

Shortly after Robert's departure, Alberic was elected abbot of Cîteaux. Alberic had been prior under Robert and seems to have been one of the founders not only of Cîteaux but also of Molesme earlier. Abbot Alberic, with the material support of Odo, duke of Burgundy, and his son Hugh, consolidated the founding of the monastery of Cîteaux and deserves along with Robert credit for the establishment of the Order of Cistercians. Independence from Molesme and other monasteries was obtained along with papal protection during the tenure of Alberic, who died January 26, 1109.

A group of thirteenth century Cistercian nuns receive the charter to their convent from Maria de Molina, queen of Castile. (Frederick Ungar Publishing Co.)

The monastery's prior, Stephen Harding, an Englishman, was elected abbot. During Stephen's tenure, the new Cistercian order was fully established. Stephen was born about 1060 of noble Anglo-Saxon parents. The Norman Conquest of England ruined his family and resulted in his moving to Scotland and then to France. After studying in Paris and visiting Rome, he joined first the community at Molesme and then at Cîteaux. During his tenure, numerous additional woods and vineyards were added to the monastery holdings.

Also about April of 1112, a monk known later as Bernard of Clairvaux had entered Cîteaux. Bernard brought about thirty new monks with him, many of them his relatives, and the reversal of the seemingly failing experiment was at hand. Bernard is given the credit for setting the New Monastery on a firm base and leading it to a time of impressive growth and influence. The number of monks had grown so that a second monastery was necessary at La Ferté by 1113. This expansion was followed quickly with new houses in 1114 at Pontigny, 1115 at Clairvaux and at Morimond, 1118 at Preuilly, and 1119 at La Cour Dieu, Bouras, Cadouin, and Fontenay. Abbot Stephen secured papal authorization from Pope Callistus II in 1119 for a further independence of Cîteaux and its affiliated monasteries.

SAINT BERNARD'S "NEW MONASTERY"

Bernard of Clairvaux is given the credit for setting the New Monastery at Citeaux on a firm base and leading it to a time of impressive growth and influence. Here William of Saint-Thierry describes the monastery in his biography of his friend Bernard.

[A] silence deep as that of night prevailed. The sounds of labor, or the chants of the brethren in the choral service, were the only exceptions. . . . The solitude, also, of the place—between dense forests in a narrow gorge of neighboring hills—in a certain sense recalled the cave of our father St. Benedict, so that while they strove to imitate his life, they also had some similarity to him in their habitation and loneliness. . . . There the proud are humbled, the rich are made poor, the poor have the Gospel preached to them, and the darkness of sinners is changed into light. . . . Many of [the monks], I hear, are bishops and earls, and many illustrious through their birth or knowledge; but now, by God's grace, all distinction of persons being dead among them, the greater any one thought himself in the world, the more in this flock does he regard himself as less than the least. I see them in the garden with hoes, in the meadows with forks or rakes, in the fields with scythes, in the forest with axes. To judge from their outward appearance, their tools, their bad and disordered clothes, they appear a race of fools, without speech or sense. . . . I knew them proud and puffed up; I see them walking humbly under the merciful hand of God.

Source: William of Saint-Thierry, *Vite prima Bernardi abbatis*, translated in Edward L. Cutts, *Scenes and Characters of the Middle Ages*, as quoted in *A Source Book of Mediæval History*, edited by Frederic Austin Ogg (New York: American Book Company, 1908), pp. 258-260.

SIGNIFICANCE

The Order of Cistercians had indeed become a reality, and it soon spread to nearly every part of western Europe, bringing a much needed renewed vitality to monasticism and, as a side effect of work with the land, major agricultural pioneering advances, most notably with sheep farming in England.

—*Douglas J. McMillan*

FURTHER READING

Berman, Constance Hoffman. *The Cistercian Evolution: The Invention of a Religious Order in Twelfth-century Europe*. Philadelphia: University of Pennsylvania Press, 2000. Discusses Cistercian mythology, the beginnings of the order, religious reform, papal confirmations, and related documents.

Bouchard, Constance Brittain. *Holy Entrepreneurs: Cistercians, Knights, and Economic Exchange in Twelfth-Century Burgundy*. Ithaca, N.Y.: Cornell University Press, 1991. Explores the Cistercian contributions to the economic development of Burgundy.

Brooke, Christopher. *The Age of the Cloister: The Story of Monastic Life in the Middle Ages*. Rev. ed. Mahwah, N.J.: HiddenSpring, 2003. A history of medieval monasticism. Includes an extensive bibliography, index, illustrations, and maps.

_______. "The Cistercians." In *Monasteries of the World*. Ware, England: Omega Books, 1982. Presents the origin and history of the Cistercian order in words and pictures. Includes a map, diagrams, and photographs.

Cosman, Madeleine Pelner. *Women at Work in Medieval Europe*. New York: Facts On File, 2000. A social history with a chapter on women as leaders of medieval European monasteries.

King, Archdale A. *Cîteaux and Her Elder Daughters*. London: Burns and Oates, 1954. The major study of the first physical home of the Cistercians and of four daughter houses.

Lawrence, C. H. "The Cistercian Model." In *Medieval Monasticism: Forms of Religious Life in Western Europe in the Middle Ages*. London: Longman, 1984. Explores the new form of monastic life developed by the Cistercians.

Lekai, Louis J. *The Cistercians: Ideals and Reality*. Kent, Ohio: Kent State University Press. 1977. The definitive study of the Cistercian order from its founding to Vatican II.

This book was later translated into Latin, probably by Adelard of Bath, with the title *Algoritmi de numero Indorum* (c. 1100; "Thus Spake al-Khwārizmī," 1990). The Hindu forms described by al-Khwārizmī were not used by the Arabs. The scholars in Baghdad evidently derived their forms from other sources, possibly from Kabul in Afghanistan in some modified form. The earliest Arabic manuscripts containing the numerals are dated 874 and 888.

In a work written at Shiraz in Persia in 970, the numerals occur again. Close to the Jeremias Monastery in Egypt, they appear on a pillar of the church with the date 961. The oldest definitely dated European manuscript to contain the Hindu-Arabic numerals is the *Codex Vigilanus*, written in the Albelda Cloister in Spain in 976. A Vatican Library manuscript of 1077 also contains the numerals, written similar to modern symbols. The earliest known English manuscripts containing the Hindu-Arabic numerals are contained in the British Museum and date from the thirteenth century.

SIGNIFICANCE

Leonardo of Pisa was the first great mathematician to advocate the adoption of Arabic notation in Europe with his book *Liber abaci* (1202; English translation, 2002). The learned classes readily accepted it, but the merchants and monks in the monasteries adhered to the older forms as late as 1300. Even one hundred years after the publication of *Liber abaci*, the merchants of Florence were forbidden to use Arabic notation in bookkeeping, one reason being the possibility of forging documents by interchanging the numerals 0, 6, and 9. By about 1275, Arabic notation began to be widely used. Roman numerals, however, were widely employed for bookkeeping in European countries until the eighteenth century, mainly because of the facility of using them in addition and subtraction.

—John Francis Daly

FURTHER READING

Ball, W. W. Rouse. *A Short Account of the History of Mathematics*. New York: Dover, 1960. Chapter 9 surveys the history of Arabic mathematics.

Cajori, Florian. *A History of Mathematical Notations*. 2 vols. La Salle. Ill.: Open Court, 1952. A comprehensive text that details the symbols for Arabic numerals and the symbols used in arithmetic, algebra, geometry, and numerical analysis.

________. *A History of Mathematics*. 5th ed. Providence, R.I.: AMS Chelsea, 2000. This book is devoted to the general history of mathematics and attempts to speculate on the origins as well as the variation of Hindu-Arabic numeral forms.

Hill, G. F. *The Development of Arabic Numerals in Europe*. Oxford, England: Oxford University Press, 1915. A still-useful description of the forms of early numerals in Europe.

Ifrah, Georges. *The Universal History of Numbers: From Prehistory to the Invention of the Computer*. Translated by David Bellos et al. New York: J. Wiley, 2000. Comprehensive survey of numerals and numeration throughout history. Includes a chapter on the importation of Indo-Arabic numerals into Western Europe.

Kunitzsch, Paul. "The Transmission of Hindu-Arabic Numerals Reconsidered." In *The Enterprise of Science in Islam: New Perspectives*, edited by Jan P. Hogendijk and Abdelhamid I. Sabra. Cambridge, Mass.: MIT Press, 2003. Explores the development of Eastern Islamic numerals into the Western Islamic numerals that were later introduced into Europe.

Kūshyār ibn Labbān. *Hindu Reckoning*. Translated by M. Levey and M. Petruck. Madison: University of Wisconsin Press, 1965. The oldest surviving Arabic text using the Hindu numerals.

Newman, James R. *The World of Mathematics*. 4 vols. 1956. Reprint. Redmond, Wash.: Tempus Books, 1988. A study of number and numerals may be found in volume 1, part 3, no. 3.

Rotman, Brian. *Mathematics as Sign: Writing, Imagining, Counting*. Stanford, Calif.: Stanford University Press, 2000. A study of the importance, meaning, and effects of written numbers.

Smith, D. E., and L. D. Karpinski. *The Hindu-Arabic Numerals*. Boston: Ginn, 1911. A classic and standard reference book.

SEE ALSO: 595-665: Invention of Decimals and Negative Numbers; c. 950: Court of Córdoba Flourishes in Spain; c. 1025: Scholars at Chartres Revive Interest in the Classics; 1100-1300: European Universities Emerge; 1328-1350: Flowering of Late Medieval Physics.

RELATED ARTICLES in *Great Lives from History: The Middle Ages, 477-1453*: Abul Wefa; Āryabhaṭa the Elder; Brahmagupta; al-Khwārizmī; Leonardo of Pisa; Muḥammad.

c. 1100
FOUNDING OF TIMBUKTU

Timbuktu was a major post for the lively trade in gold and salt between other regions in Africa and in Europe. Timbuktu benefited from being located among military, economic, and religious powers and was strategically situated within several African empires. It was also a center of Islamic learning.

LOCALE: East Africa
CATEGORIES: Cultural and intellectual history; trade and commerce

KEY FIGURE

Mansa Mūsā (c. 1280-1337), leader of the Mali Empire, r. 1312-1337

SUMMARY OF EVENT

One of the most mysterious cities in the world, Timbuktu has acquired a reputation as an exotic and ancient city in the nether reaches of the Sahara Desert. Separating myth from reality about the city is difficult because Timbuktu has been idealized by visitors and even by those who have never been to the city.

Timbuktu is located a few miles north of the Niger River, in the middle of West Africa. The Niger River has nourished several empires in West Africa. Along the great bend of the river were the Songhai, who would come to rule Timbuktu after defeating the Mali Empire. The Songhai capital of Gao was a major trading rival of Timbuktu but also helped develop the city's trade. Near the source of the Niger, as it curls toward the Atlantic Ocean but never quite reaches it, were the Mande people. Tribes within the Mande would challenge the ancient empire of Ghana and eventually become part of Mali. To the south near the Volta River were the Gurs, while to the immediate north of Timbuktu were the Berbers, a group of nomads who ranged from the Niger River to the Mediterranean Sea and what is now Morocco. Other tribes, too, would compete for the lucrative trade routes and economic power would shift up and down the Niger from the thirteenth through the sixteenth centuries.

The Niger River is an important trade route and source of water near one of the most desolate areas on the globe, the Sahara Desert. The river enabled trade from the eastern Sudan to the western Sudan, and from the Sahara and Europe to the gold mines of Ghana and West Africa.

Ghana was the dominant political and military force in West Africa from the sixth through the tenth centuries. It used trade to maintain its power, using taxes assessed on trade caravans for its army. As gold flowed into the capital of Kumbi, the Ghana kings expanded their empire from the Atlantic Ocean into what is now Nigeria. The kings exploited the notion of divine rule, that is, they promoted the idea that they were successors to gods. Yet divine rule led to the tradition of killing the kings when they became ill, for fear their illness would harm the kingdom.

The movement of Islamic armies into North Africa presented a challenge to Ghana, starting in the eleventh century. A nomadic tribe known as the Berbers swept south through the Sahara Desert in the last half of the eleventh century, captured the Ghana capital, and weakened the empire sufficiently to make it vulnerable to attacks from its West African neighbors. Still, the Berbers continued their extensive trade with the area, further enhancing the importance of Timbuktu.

The arrival of the Berber traders and the subsequent rise in the trading cities along the Niger River can be attributed partially to the fall of the Roman Empire during the fifth century. The Romans, suspicious of nomadic tribes crossing in and out of their well-defended borders in North Africa, forced the Berbers in that region to adopt an agricultural rather than trade-oriented way of life. Once Roman power was broken in the area, the Berbers returned to nomadism and moved south, transporting trade goods from Europe into West Africa and making the Niger River Valley a key component of that trade. With trade came the need to establish cities where goods could be exchanged. One of those cities was Timbuktu.

The exact year of the founding of Timbuktu is unknown, but most scholars place it around 1100. Its creation came out of the trading practices of the Tuareg tribe, a group of fierce nomadic and independent tribesmen who traded goods along the Niger River. It is believed that the Tuareg created Timbuktu as a storage place for their goods while they roamed the surrounding desert. However, Timbuktu soon began to grow in population and size, and its central location along trade routes made it strategically important for the various empires jockeying for control of the area.

Timbuktu was one of the nearest overland points for trade routes north to Europe, which was desperate for new sources of gold as its own sources were being diminished. For this reason, traders used Timbuktu as a point of departure north into the Sahara Desert, bringing trade

Ruins at Timbuktu, Mali, Africa, c. 1950. (Hulton|Archive by Getty Images)

goods from Europe to exchange for Ghana's gold. Trade with the Europeans marked Timbuktu—both in fact and as myth—as a place of extraordinary wealth.

Some 500 miles (800 kilometers) north of the city sat the salt mines of Taghaza. The mines had existed since the founding of the city, and the salt trade was part of its commerce. The lack of salt in the Ghana region suddenly made it a valuable commodity, and it was traded for the gold, which was plentiful. Another crop that was valuable to those in the north was the kola nut. Produced widely in the southern portion of West Africa, it was valued in Europe—and became the basis for cola drinks in the twentieth century. Ivory also was plentiful in West Africa, and it was valued all over the world. As the gold became depleted in Ghana, ivory became a kind of coin for those seeking to buy goods from the north.

As it developed, Timbuktu became the last overland leg for goods being brought in from the north. After reaching the city, the goods were transported to the Niger, where they were taken by canoe to the other major trading city of Jenne (Djenné).

Timbuktu, however, did not become known throughout much of the world until after the fall of the Ghana Empire. The empire of Mali, begun by a tribe of the Monde people, not only saw Timbuktu expand beyond a single point along a 2,000-mile (3,200-kilometer) trade route but as a major destination for political and religious figures. Timbuktu became a center of intellectual and religious life during the reign of the Malian king Mansa Mūsā.

Possibly one of the greatest kings in Mali and medieval West Africa, Mansa Mūsā had converted to the Muslim faith. As part of that faith, he began a journey to Mecca in 1324. Arriving in Egypt in 1325, the king, along with his entourage of approximately ten thousand people, began spending the gold in his possession so freely that the Egyptian price of the precious metal plummeted almost 10 percent because of the oversupply. His extraordinary wealth and willingness to spend it created much talk in the Muslim world about the riches to be found in West Africa and Mali. He returned to Mali in 1325 and visited Timbuktu. During that visit, he recruited an Egyptian to build one of the largest mosques in West Africa. It still stands today.

While the mosque might be the most visible result of the king's journey to Timbuktu, his creation of a center of education at the Sankore mosque was his longest lasting, significant achievement. Sankore became a major focus of Islamic learning and scholarship in West Africa. Thousands of students went through the university and many remained to add to the interpretation of Islamic law and culture. It also made Timbuktu a center of Islamic learning in Africa.

SIGNIFICANCE

The founding of Timbuktu saw the creation of a multiethnic and multireligious city within the realms of three different empires. Timbuktu's reputation as a major center of Islamic learning and teaching in Africa made it one of the most cosmopolitan cities on the continent. Even though it was ruled by the Ghana, Mali, and Songhai Empires, it remained independent politically, which was a testament to its importance as a trading center on the southern fringes of the Sahara Desert. Timbuktu declined only after it was sacked by the Berbers in the sixteenth century. Colonization of Africa by Europeans in the eighteenth and nineteenth centuries eventually reduced Timbuktu to the backwater it remains today, clinging only to a reputation as an exotic city.

—Douglas Clouatre

FURTHER READING

Gates, Henry Louis, Jr. *Wonders of the African World.* New York: Knopf, 1999. A work by a well-known scholar of African history. Includes the chapter, "Salt, Gold, and Books: The Road to Timbuktu." Illustrations, maps, bibliography, index.

Insoll, Timothy. "Timbuktu and Europe: Trade, Cities and Islam in 'Medieval' West Africa." In *The Medieval World*, edited by Peter Linehan and Janet L. Nelson. New York: Routledge, 2001. Part of a collection exploring a history of the Middle Ages, this chapter looks at Timbuktu's role in trading with Europe. Bibliography, index.

Oliver, Roland, and Anthony Atmore. *Medieval Africa, 1250-1800*. New York: Cambridge University Press, 2001. A wide-ranging book that describes the various empires and leaders of medieval Africa, with a more limited focus on the advancement of culture within the region. Bibliography, index.

Palumbo, Joe. *Mansa Mūsa, African King of Gold*. Los Angeles: National Center for History in the Schools, University of California, Los Angeles, 1991. A teacher's guide to preparing a unit for grades 7-9 on Mansa Mūsā.

Reader, John. *Africa: A Biography of a Continent*. New York: Alfred Knopf, 1998. An eminently readable book that focuses on both political and cultural issues and also such rarely discussed issues as how disease affected the development of Africa and how colonization interfered with that development. Illustrations, maps, bibliography, index.

Saad, Elias N. *A Social History of Timbuktu: The Role of Muslim Scholars and Notables*. New York: Cambridge University Press, 1995. Focuses on the various peoples and religions of Timbuktu after its founding and during its golden age from 1200 to 1500. Bibliography, index.

SEE ALSO: 630-711: Islam Expands Throughout North Africa; c. 1010: Songhai Kingdom Converts to Islam; 1230's-1255: Reign of Sundiata of Mali; 1324-1325: Mansa Mūsā's Pilgrimage to Mecca Sparks Interest in Mali Empire; 1325-1355: Travels of Ibn Baṭṭūṭah.

RELATED ARTICLES in *Great Lives from History: The Middle Ages, 477-1453*: Prince Henry the Navigator; Ibn Baṭṭūṭah; Mansa Mūsā; Sundiata.

c. 1100
Origins of Swahili in Its Written Form

The origins of written Swahili demonstrates the historical connection between East Africa, the Arabian peninsula, and the Islamic faith. The Swahili language stems from African roots and is a language of the Bantu branch of Niger Congo. There is, however, a notable Arabic influence in elements of the Swahili written vocabulary, and the earliest Swahili texts were recorded with Arabic script.

Locale: East African Coast from Mogadishu to Sofala
Categories: Communications; cultural and intellectual history; literature

Summary of Event

The written form of Swahili developed about four hundred years after the emergence of the spoken form of the language. Whereas written and spoken Swahili did not develop simultaneously, the written form clearly reflects the style and traditions of Swahili oral forms, particularly its poetic style; and whereas the script used to first write Swahili was Arabic, the actual Arabic language influence on Swahili is limited to religious and legal language primarily.

The emergence of Swahili language and culture began with pre-Swahili, coastal east-African fishing communities between 100 and 350. The proto-northeast-coastal-Bantu language developed as Bantu populations migrated farther eastward and formed settlements. Linguistically, the Swahili people are speakers of Bantu languages. The proto-Kiswahili culture developed between 650 and 1000, but by the ninth century, the cultural elements typically associated today with the Swahili had already became distinctly evident (as is reflected in the archaeological record). The basic components of the foundation of Swahili culture include the Swahili language, urban coastal settlements, Islamic influence, a trading economy, and a unique architectural style. Prior to the ninth century, only two trading towns had been identified: Rhapta and Kanbalu. However, many more towns were identified by the ninth century. Thus, while Swahili culture began to develop before the eighth century, the urban nature and heavy trade component of Swahili does not become distinctive in the archaeological record until the ninth century.

The Swahili coastline is defined as a 3,000-mile-long (4,800-kilometer-long) band of land extending from Mogadishu (Somalia) to Sofala (Mozambique), varying from 32 to 321 miles (20 to 200 kilometers) wide. The Swahili coast also encompasses the islands of Mombassa, Pemba, Zanzibar, Mafia, and Kerimba and the archipelagoes of the Comoros and Lamu. Trade expanded in this area, as Swahili towns increasingly received contact with traders from across the Indian Ocean.

The Arab traders were of particular influence, but other important partners in trade were the Persian, Indian, and Chinese merchants. By 1100, overseas trade occurred frequently, and as trade increased in volume and quality, the Swahili economies benefited with material wealth. Iron trade was prevalent in Swahili towns such as Kilwa, Shanga, and Manda. In addition to material commodities, intellectual ideas were also being exchanged between coastal east Africans and their foreign trade partners. Important among these ideas was Islam and the Arabic language.

Between 1100 and 1300, Islamization intensified within the Swahili community. By the end of this period, Mogadishu was a center of Islamic learning with three mosques. Wealthy Swahili merchants incorporated trends they observed among the more affluent Arab merchants by integrating clothing, furniture, designs, and, most important, an Islamic education for children. It is in the era of increased Muslim conversion around 1100 that Swahili began to be captured in written Arabic script.

Because the Swahili communities incorporated elements of Islamic law into their judicial practice and religion in their belief systems, there was an increasing need to be able to read Arabic script to observe religious rights and privileges. In addition, because trade had become so intense in volume since the eighth century, there was a greater need to keep written financial records. Rather than learning both the script and language of Arabic, some enterprising Swahilis sought to use the script to capture their own language. Thus, Swahili was documented with Arabic script. It is clear from scholarly research that these Arabic-script Swahili documents could not be read by literate Arab speakers unless they knew the Swahili language.

Significance

As Islam became more widely followed among the Swahili, the incentive for a written form of Swahili grew. Wealthy and devout African Muslims learned how to read and write in Arabic. Swahili remained the language of daily discourse while Arabic increasingly became the language for religion and often legal correspondence. However, this was not the case for all Swahili, and some people relied instead on Swahili-language Arabic script. The advent of Swahili script led to the flourishing of original Swahili literature and poetry in written form.

Arabic-script Swahili writings are important sources of historical information about medieval Swahili history. While much of the writing was devoted to poetry, literature, and religious subjects, the events of everyday life are captured in the writings as well. From these documents, it is clear that Islam and Arabic culture had a significant, lasting influence on the Swahili.

—Catherine Cymone Fourshey and Blaine Horrocks

Further Reading

Horton, Mark, and John Middleton. *The Swahili: The Social Landscape of a Mercantile Society.* Malden, Mass.: Blackwell, 2000. A survey of the social life, customs, and trade and commerce history of the Swahili-speaking peoples of East Africa. Includes a chapter on the "acceptance of Islam" into Swahili life. Bibliography, index.

Knappert, Jan. *Law Glossary of Islamic Terms in Swahili.* Peramiho, Tanzania: Benedictine Ndanda, 2001. Covers Islamic law in Eastern Africa and its impact on the Swahili culture and Swahili language.

Kusimba, Chapurukha M. *The Rise and Fall of Swahili States.* Walnut Creek, Calif.: AltaMira Press, 1999. A history of the east African coast, particularly the role of the Swahili people and city-states in the Indian Ocean. Bibliography, index.

Mazrui, Alamin M., and Ibrahim Noor Shariff. *The Swahili: Idiom and Identity of an African People.* Trenton, N.J.: Africa World Press, 1994. An in-depth examination of Swahili culture, people, and language. Bibliography, index.

Mazrui, Ali A., and Alamin M. Mazrui. *Swahili State and Society: The Political Economy of an African Language.* London: James Currey, 1995. An exploration of how the Swahili language effects Swahili government and society. Bibliography, index.

Nurse, Derek, and Thomas Spear. *The Swahili: Reconstructing the History and Language of an African Society, 800-1500.* Philadelphia: University of Pennsylvania Press, 1985. A detailed history of Swahili communities and civilization from 800-1500. Also examines Swahili language.

Pouwels, Randall L. *Horn and Crescent: Cultural Change and Traditional Islam on the East African Coast, 800-1900.* New York: Cambridge University Press, 1987. Examines the history of Islam in the eastern African coast between the ninth and twentieth centuries. Part of the African Studies series.

Rosander, Eva Evers, and David Westerlund, eds. *African Islam and Islam in Africa: Encounters Between Sufis and Islamists.* Athens: Ohio University Press, 1997. Examines the effects of Islam in Africa. Includes the chapter, "Translations of the Quʾrān into Swahili, and Contemporary Islamic Revival in East Africa," by Justo Lacunza-Balda. Bibliography, index.

See also: c. 500-1000: Rise of Swahili Cultures; 630-711: Islam Expands Throughout North Africa; 637-657: Islam Expands Throughout the Middle East; 12th century: Coins Are Minted on the Swahili Coast.

c. 1100
Rise of Courtly Love

At the end of the eleventh century, courtly love appeared suddenly and unexpectedly in the south of France, a region historically and culturally distinct from the north. The sentiments that it fostered began a new concept of romantic love that remains embedded in the modern psyche.

Locale: Provence (now in France)

Categories: Literature; cultural and intellectual history

Key Figures

Guillaume de Poitiers (1071-1127), duke of Aquitaine, the earliest known Provençal troubadour

Guiraut Riquier (d. 1294), a troubadour from Narbonne

Summary of Event

The first known record of the sentiment now known as courtly love is in the form of eleven poems left by Guillaume IX, count of Poitiers and duke of Aquitaine, who died in 1127. Many important troubadour love poems were written in the "classic" period of the art, from about 1140 to about 1250. Guiraut Riquier of Narbonne, who died in 1294, saw himself appropriately as the last of the troubadours. In his verse, he deplored the passing of his noble public's interest in his art. He wrote, "In noble courts no vocation is now less appreciated than the fine art of poetry; for men prefer to see and hear frivolities."

Courtly love was, however, far from dead. Though abandoned in the Midi, the theme was carried throughout Europe by courtly singers to become a powerful influence on the Western mind. According to scholar C. S. Lewis, the troubadours

> effected a change which left no corner of our ethics, our imagination, or our daily life untouched, and they erected impassable barriers between us and the classical past or the Oriental present. Compared with this revolution the Renaissance is a mere ripple on the surface of literature.

It is as an aristocratic, aesthetic ideal, a strictly literary phenomenon divorced from visible, observable forms of life, that courtly love first spread throughout Europe. A lofty sentiment, it was refined still further in Italy, to which it was borne by the Provençal troubadours. Guido Cavalcanti and the Florentine writers of the "sweet new style," the *dolce stil nuovo*, underwent its influence and themselves modified it. Dante swelled the chorus of voices raised in praise of love, celebrating the beauty and wisdom of Beatrice in his sonnets and his *canzoni*, *La vita nuova* (c. 1292; *Vita Nuova*, 1861; better known as *The New Life*), and finally in *La divina commedia* (c. 1320; *The Divine Comedy*, 1802).

Eleanor, daughter of the last duke of Aquitaine, helped to popularize courtly love in the north when she married first Louis VII, king of France, and later Henry Plantagenet, who became King Henry II of England. Her daughters, in turn, made the courts of Blois and Reims important centers for courtly poetry. The notion of total service in the name of socially illicit love was assimilated into the romances of Chrétien de Troyes and given its most complete expression in his *Lancelot* (c. 1168; English translation, 1913). The rules of courtship and love, codified by Andreas Capellanus in the early thirteenth century,

Some Rules of Courtly Love

- Marriage is no real excuse for not loving.
- He who is not jealous cannot love.
- No one can be bound by a double love. . . .
- Boys do not love until they arrive at the age of maturity.
- When one lover dies, a widowhood of two years is required of the survivor.
- No one should be deprived of love without the very best of reasons. . . .
- It is not proper to love any woman whom one would be ashamed to seek to marry. . . .
- When made public love rarely endures.
- The easy attainment of love makes it of little value; difficulty of attainment makes it prized. . . .
- When a lover suddenly catches sight of his beloved his heart palpitates. . . .
- Good character alone makes any man worthy of love. . . .
- Love can deny nothing to love.
- A man who is vexed by too much passion usually does not love. . . .
- Nothing forbids one woman being loved by two men or one man by two women.

Source: Andreas Capellanus, *The Art of Courtly Love*, translated by J. J. Parry and quoted in *The Portable Medieval Reader* (New York: Penguin Books, 1977), edited by James Bruce Ross and Mary Martin McLaughlin, pp. 115-117.

form the center around which the first part of the *Romance of the Rose*, the most celebrated allegorical poem of the Middle Ages, revolves. It is out of this tradition that the modern prose novel, with love as its theme, developed.

In the fourteenth century, courtly love was given new life by Petrarch, the first great Renaissance Humanist. As the major theme of lyrical poetry, love spread by way of his sonnets throughout Europe, including England. It now seems "natural" that romantic or passionate love should be one of the two or three principal preoccupations of individuals in their lives and of poets in their work. However, until the appearance of the troubadours, nothing was less likely.

The emergence of true love, or in Provençal *fin amor*, is enveloped in mystery. There seems little precedent for a cult that enshrines a woman at the center of her lover's gaze as the object of his complete and rapt attention. The prototypical cast of characters who acted out the drama of true love remained relatively unchanged in the troubadour love songs. A typical representation is that of a proud lady before whom a noble lover kneels. He pledges his life in service to her. She is for him the supreme embodiment of wisdom and beauty, and his hopes of earthly happiness rest on her. He longs for some reward, some token of recognition or acceptance: a smile, a glance, a touch of the hand, and eventually a kiss. He offers himself, his life and his valor, in complete, perpetual submission to her will and whimsy.

Lancelot and Guinevere, in a miniature from an eleventh century manuscript at the Bibliothèque National de Paris. (Frederick Ungar Publishing Co.)

In contrast to the traditional epic knight, with his boastful, fiery ardor in love and war, the courtly knight lives and languishes with suffering as a constant companion, withdrawn and secretive. Melancholy is the predominant tone of the Provençal *canso*, for, if the martial courage of the noble lover was no more to be doubted than that of one of Charlemagne's paladins, such bravery was no more than a necessary but secondary accessory.

Since the lady was set so high—the most noble, the most exalted, the fairest and wisest of all—there was no guarantee that the *domnei*, or courtship, would be a success. The knight was called on to possess several remarkable qualities in order to be nearly worthy of his loved one. Above all, he had to display a rare degree of self-discipline and inner restraint, or *mezura* in Provençal. Finally, as if these temperamental obstacles were not enough, the lover was confronted by other, outside threats. There was, never far away, the jealous husband, the *gilos*, an uncouth, doltish lout, perhaps, but a dangerous one, necessitating strict silence and secrecy on the part of the lover. In the background, flitting to and fro, an indistinct but real peril, were the *losengiers*, the bearers of tales, or gossipmongers, ready to flatter insincerely, eager to exercise their hypocrisy, waiting for the chance to endanger and defeat the lady and her lover.

The myth of true love clashes curiously with the real situation of woman throughout the Middle Ages and into the time of the Renaissance. It appears alien to the principal traditions concerning woman that have been handed

A trouvère, or troubadour, accompanying himself on an early violin (based on a sculpture on the portico of the Abbey of Saint Denis in France). (Frederick Ungar Publishing Co.)

down from Greece and Rome. The epic tradition completely ignores women. For the philosophers of classical antiquity, love was a form of madness leading the way to crime and ignominy. The patristic writers expressed reservations about both lovc and marriage. Clement of Alexandria saw in woman the agent of Satan, holding open the gates to Hell. He wrote, "Every woman ought to be overwhelmed with shame at the thought that she is a woman." Most of the Humanist writers of the Middle Ages agreed that woman's proper place was comparable to that of a troublesome, albeit valuable, animal. Even Petrarch, his adoration of Laura notwithstanding, presented woman as a source of strife and wickedness, a devil: "Femina verus est diabolus, hostis pacis, fons impatientiae." (Woman is a true devil, the enemy of peace, the source of impatience).

Even if one takes into account a strong sensual component that runs through the troubadours' songs, courtly love remains, in its essence, an enigma. Certainly the picture of lovc as sacred rite and solemn ceremony, a lifelong dance of courtship in which the partners scarcely, if ever, touch, is incomplete. Some of the best known troubadours, such as Guillaume of Poitiers, Bernart de Ventadorn, Bertran de Born, Cercamon, and Marcabrun, were explicit in their anticipation of the sexual delights their ladies could provide. Nonetheless, love was not seen as essentially carnal. Even sexual intercourse, when it took place, was portrayed as no more than the outer sign of spiritual symbiosis, or total acceptance. The pleasures of the flesh were fused into the larger ones of the spirit.

The apparent incompatibility between courtly love, with its adoration of woman, and historical practice, with the denigration of woman, has to be recognized. Such a contradiction is not without parallel in the Middle Ages. Chivalry, for example, with its emphasis on valor, generosity, and courtesy, was held up as an ideal to be imitated. Yet the chronicles of Jean Froissart (1337-c. 1404) and Jean Molinet (1435-1507) leave it aside and speak of acts of greed, self-interest, and cruelty. Rather than being a reflection of a historical situation, courtly love was probably a compensatory image, an ideal fantasy arising in response to a spiritual, social, or psychological inadequacy. It was a reordering of reality after an image of perfection, an ideal of aristocracy based not on the harsh law of the father as expressed in the patriarchal feudal system, but on that of the ability to love, the law of the gentle heart.

Feudal society was the mold or form into which the content of courtly love could be poured. The strength, courage, piety, and loyalty that bound a liegeman to his lord, his church, and his class were the same qualities that the courtly knight was required to present to his lady. Indeed, he often addressed her as *midons*, "my lord." However, as Maurice Valency has suggested, the very substitution of a lady for a man as sovereign lord indicates a fundamental dissatisfaction with or repudiation of the patriarchal structure. In adopting the form and rejecting the substance of the feudal mode, courtly love appears to be an outgrowth of the *decline* of the feudal system. It is perhaps significant that the female archetype was asserting itself in another form at about the same time. After 1100, the cult of the Virgin Mary established itself alongside that of love. It was, moreover, during this period in the north that Louis VI, king of France from 1108 to 1137, was initiating a struggle against the feudal system by undertaking a merciless campaign to break the power of his barons.

Significance

The apostles, the discoverers, or perhaps even the inventors, of true love were the troubadours. Their name, from the verb *trobar*, "to find" or "to invent," reveals their identity as poet-composers. Their art was essentially aural. Unfortunately, the music they composed for their chansons has been handed down in a transcription that is no more than schematic or rudimentary and gives little idea of the true effect achieved. However, the incredible verbal and metric dexterity of the troubadours, admired and translated by Ezra Pound, gives some idea of the technical mastery and inventiveness of these poets. It is especially suggestive of a high degree of sophistication on the part of their audiences, sensitive to the beauty and intricacy of prodigious feats of rhyming skill. They were initiates writing for initiates. In their frequent cult of difficulty-for-its-own-sake, they were elitists writing for an elite, aristocrats (at least by adoption if not always by birth) performing before aristocrats. By comparison, the modern folksinger, to whom the troubadour is often likened, seems positively unlettered.

The troubadours—artists wandering in the south of France from castle to castle, currying favor, singing of an esoteric doctrine—may seem remote and merely picturesque. Yet it is from them that the notion of love as ideal passion, source of joy and suffering, derives. Their recondite songs, in Provençal, a language difficult of access, form the background to some eight and a half centuries of literature in the West.

—*James P. McNab*

Further Reading

De Rougemont, Denis. *Love in the Western World*. New York: Pantheon Books, 1956. A convincing examination of the fundamental conflict between passion and marriage in Western life and literature.

Duby, Georges. *Love and Marriage in the Middle Ages*. Translated by Jane Dunnett. Chicago: University of Chicago Press, 1994. Written by a scholar of everyday life, this text discusses courtly love and the state and history of love in twelfth century France.

Huizinga, Johan. *The Waning of the Middle Ages*. London: Edward Arnold, 1937. Reprint. Mineola, N.Y.: Dover, 1999. Although concerned with a later period than that in which courtly love arose, this classic work provides a brilliant insight into the mental landscape that made the idea of courtly love possible.

Lewis, C. S. *The Allegory of Love: A Study in Medieval Tradition*. London: Oxford University Press, 1936. Traces the growth of the noble sentiment of noble love and the development of the literary form, allegory, and the marriage of the two. One of the greatest merits of this work is its vigorous attempt to escape from the limits of a strictly twentieth century view, in order to look at medieval literature with greater accuracy and justice.

Markale, Jean. *Courtly Love: The Path of Sexual Initiation*. Translated by Jon Graham. Rochester, Vt.: Inner Traditions, 2000. Looks at the tradition of courtly love in the literature of the time, at the theme of adultery, and at the roles of women, goddess figures, and the troubadours.

Pound, Ezra. *The Spirit of Romance*. Norfolk, Conn.: New Directions Books, 1958. The author's temperamental sympathy for the Romance poets and his joyful appreciation of their daring make him a stimulating interpreter and a magnificent translator. He recreates the poems with an awareness of their essentially aural quality.

Press, Alan R., ed. and trans. *Anthology of Troubadour Lyric Poetry*. Austin: University of Texas Press, 1971. To correct the frequently distorted image of the troubadour and his song, this anthology is extremely useful. Provides facing-page translations of the Provençal poems that are accurate and unadorned. There is a brief, cogent introduction to the life and work of each of the troubadours.

Rousselot, Pierre. *The Problem of Love in the Middle Ages: A Historical Contribution*. Translated by Alan Vincelette. Milwaukee, Wis.: Marquette University Press, 2001. Presents a philosophical and religious history of love in the time of courtly love in Europe.

Chapters include discussion of the themes of love as violent and as irrational.

Valency, Maurice. *In Praise of Love: An Introduction to the Love-Poetry of the Renaissance*. New York: Macmillan, 1958. Stresses courtly love as an aesthetic principle and a reflection of an inner psychological or spiritual need.

SEE ALSO: c. 950: Court of Córdoba Flourishes in Spain; c. 1145: Prester John Myth Sweeps Across Europe; c. 1350-1400: Petrarch and Boccaccio Recover Classical Texts; 1387-1400: Chaucer Writes *The Canterbury Tales*.

RELATED ARTICLES in *Great Lives from History: The Middle Ages, 477-1453*. Adam de la Halle; Charles d'Orléans; Geoffrey Chaucer; Chrétien de Troyes; Christine de Pizan; Dante; Eleanor of Aquitaine; Gottfried von Strassburg; Hartmann von Aue; Guillaume de Machaut; Marie de France; Petrarch; Walther von der Vogelweide; Wolfram von Eschenbach.

1100-1300
EUROPEAN UNIVERSITIES EMERGE

The emergence of European universities provided a systematic organization for teaching and made possible the exponential growth and transmission of knowledge across Western civilization.

LOCALE: Europe
CATEGORIES: Cultural and intellectual history; education; organizations and institutions; religion

KEY FIGURES

Peter Abelard (1079-1142), French logician
Thomas Aquinas (c. 1224-1274), Italian-born Scholastic philosopher and theologian
Irnerius (c. 1050-1125), Italian scholar

SUMMARY OF EVENT

The rise of the universities from the abbey and cathedral schools is one of the great achievements of the Middle Ages, making possible the steady increase in education of large numbers of people and the explosion of knowledge on which the modern world is based.

The history of their rise is a complex subject covering the whole of Europe. Some of that history is unreliable, as the early universities attempted to establish a tradition for themselves by claiming to have been founded by famous individuals, such as King Arthur, Charlemagne, or the survivors of Troy. In actuality, the universities arose slowly over time, seldom established by but rather recognized by the pope or a ruler after having reached an established level of growth.

In the Middle Ages, the word *universitas*, or university, had no specific connection with the world of learning. It did not refer to the universe or universality of learning, but rather meant simply an association or group. The term could refer to a guild or group of barbers, carpenters, or students, denoting only that its members were engaged in a common enterprise.

In the early Middle Ages, education was concerned chiefly with the preservation of minimal standards of clerical literacy. Education took place in schools organized in the parishes, abbeys, and cathedrals, and its subjects were the seven liberal arts. These seven were traditionally divided into two categories: the *trivium*, consisting of grammar, logic, and rhetoric, and the *quadrivium*, consisting of arithmetic, geometry, astronomy, and music. In the literature of the Greco-Roman world, sometimes two other liberal arts are mentioned—medicine and architecture—but these two appear already to have started becoming professionalized. In the early Middle Ages, the *trivium* was emphasized, especially grammar, because the ability to read sacred texts and commentaries was the chief need. The only *quadrivium* subject to receive much attention was arithmetic, since it was needed in calculating the date of Easter. The Greek ideal, seconded by Cicero, of the importance of rhetoric and of the other *quadrivium* subjects to educate a person to become a capable citizen, able to engage fully in public life, received scant attention in a society that lacked the same public outlets for participation. Thus, education until about 1100 was primarily concerned with ecclesiastical and administrative needs and chiefly centered on the transmission of the accumulated knowledge of the past.

The change that became known as the Twelfth Century Renaissance was led by logic, of all subjects, and its most famous early embodiment was Peter Abelard, known as "the first academic." A part of Aristotle's writings on logic, preserved by Boethius, had long been known, but Abelard put this "old logic" to work in a new way, testing Scripture and commentaries of the Church

Fathers by reason rather than faith. Abelard is remembered for his bitter dispute with Saint Bernard of Clairvaux over this point, and perhaps even more so for his amorous misadventure with Heloïse, but he was a brilliant teacher, flamboyant and arrogant, who attracted many students to the cathedral school at Paris.

During the twelfth century, the cathedral school at Notre Dame had gathered a number of teaching masters, a large urban student population, and the support of the French monarchy. The school had a continent-wide reputation in the study of logic applied to theology and had developed the institutional framework of the cathedral school. These factors led to its establishment as a permanent center for learning. The development of the school at Notre Dame is an example of one pattern by which the university developed. The Paris model is one of organization by the scholars, or masters, who eventually received a charter from King Philip II (r. 1179-1223) in 1200 and obtained recognition from Pope Innocent III (1198-1216) in 1208 that gave the corporate body or university of masters certain rights of independence against the municipal authorities.

Another pattern of organization is exemplified by the school of law at Bologna, perhaps the earliest "university," which received formal recognition from Emperor Frederick I Barbarossa in 1158. At Bologna, it was students who received the charter after they had organized into an association or university for economic protection against the town and eventually for power in choosing their instructors. As at Paris, however, it was a great teacher, Irnerius (also known as Guarnerius), known as "the father of scientific jurisprudence," who gave the school its initial reputation and impetus. Farther south at Salerno was an even older center of learning whose reputation in the study of medicine was equal to the reputations of Paris in theology and Bologna in law. Despite this reputation, the proto-university at Salerno remained only a center for medicine and never developed the institutional framework to capitalize on its expertise and reputation.

Salerno's early advantage was its location, which placed it in close contact with the Greek East. The great influx of new knowledge from the East served as the primary impetus for the rise of the new learning and of the university organizations that took advantage of this learning. Although much of this knowledge came to Europe from the Greek East by way of Italy, the most important works came chiefly from libraries in the Muslim world through the Arab scholars of Spain. Europe was awash in newly discovered works, chiefly those of Aristotle, with commentaries by Greek, Roman, Arabic, and Jewish scholars. Also included were works of Euclid, Ptolemy, Galen, and Hippocrates, with the new arithmetic expressed in al-Khwārizmī's book on algebra, *Kitāb al-jabr wa al-muqābalah* (c. 820), which used Arab numerals (including the concept of zero) rather than clumsy Roman numerals. In addition, the *Corpus juris civilis* (early sixth century; body of civil law) of Byzantine emperor Justinian I (r. 527-565) helped lead the study of law.

During the thirteenth century, the university system expanded rapidly. In England, masters associations were formed at Oxford in 1214 and at

RULES FOR STUDENTS AT THE UNIVERSITY OF PARIS, THIRTEENTH CENTURY

- [N]o one shall eat in his room except for cause. If anyone has a guest, he shall eat in hall. . . .
- Also, the rule does not apply to the sick. If anyone eats in a private room because of sickness, he may have a fellow with him. . . .
- Also, all shall wear closed outer garments, nor shall they have trimmings of vair or grise or of red or green. . . .
- Also, no one shall have loud shoes or clothing by which scandal might be generated. . . .
- Also, no one shall be received in the house unless he pledges faith that, if he happens to receive books from the common store, he will treat them carefully as if his own. . . .
- Also, let every fellow have his own mark on his clothes. . . .
- Also, for peace and utility we propound that no secular person living in town . . . have frequent conversation in the gardens or hall or other parts of the house, lest the secrets of the house and the remarks of the fellows be spread abroad. . . .
- Also, no fellow shall have a key to the kitchen.
- Also, no fellow shall presume to sleep outside the house in town. . . .
- Also, no women of any sort shall eat in the private rooms.

Source: Robert de Sorbonne, *Chartulary of the University of Paris*, translated by L. Thorndike, *University Records and Life in the Middle Ages* (New York: Columbia University Press, 1944), quoted in *The Portable Medieval Reader* (New York: Penguin Books, 1977), edited by James Bruce Ross and Mary Martin McLaughlin, pp. 82-85.

Cambridge in the 1230's. At Montpellier in the south of France, a faculty of medicine assembled in 1220. Universities arose in France at Orléans and Toulouse that rivaled Paris in the study of law and the study of theology, respectively. For the universities that arose after 1300, the archetypal universities of Paris and Bologna served as the organizing models. In general, the pattern of the student university (Bologna) was followed in southern Europe, and the masters university (Paris) prevailed in northern Europe, with the German universities strongly affected by both models.

Perhaps the greatest scholar of the period was Thomas Aquinas; his career reveals much about the new universities. Born near Naples in about 1224, he became a member of the Dominican order in 1244 and was sent to Paris, where he studied under Albertus Magnus. Aquinas studied biblical exegesis and Peter Lombard's *Sententiarum libri IV* (1148-1151; *The Books of Opinions of Peter Lombard*, 1970; better known as *Sentences*)., and was given a teaching post in theology in 1257. He taught in Paris and Rome and began to write extensively, eventually producing *Summa theologiae* (c. 1265-1273; *Summa Theologica*, 1911-1921) as well as commentaries on all of Aristotle's works. In Aquinas's lifetime, the universities were transnational and attracted students by the fame of their teachers. Most were still connected with religious life and religious orders and emphasized a long program of study—usually four to eight years. Such programs led to a teaching apprenticeship, thus supplying much of the teaching labor force of a university, before one was licensed to enter the guild of masters. On entering this guild, a new master became entitled to the full privileges of his degree, which for practical purposes in theology—the highest of pursuits—meant the freedom to teach and write. Even in these early days, one of the disappointments expressed by faculty members was the preference of students for more lucrative and worldly degrees, such as law and medicine.

Allegorical depiction of the degrees of university instruction, from entry-level ABC's to theology, with Peter Lombard at the top of the tower of learning. From a wood engraving in the 1508 edition of Margarita Philosophica. (Frederick Ungar Publishing Co.)

SIGNIFICANCE

The apparatus that made the universities different from the cathedral schools and from earlier Greek and Roman education are familiar to the modern university—the power to grant degrees, a regulated curriculum, an organized faculty with a rector, the lecture, examinations, and commencements. It is this organizational achievement that constitutes the heart of the medieval invention of the university.

—*James Persoon*

FURTHER READING

Cobban, A. B. *The Medieval Universities: Their Development and Organization*. London: Methuen, 1975. Scholarly, readable account, with emphasis on developments at Salerno, Bologna, Paris, Oxford, and Cambridge.

Haskins, Charles Homer. *The Rise of Universities*. 2d ed. New Brunswick, N.J.: Transaction, 2002. A short introduction for the general reader, covering the earliest universities, the medieval professor, and the medieval student.

Mundy, John H. *Europe in the High Middle Ages, 1150-1309*. London: Longman, 1973. A general history of the years in which the universities arose, placing that movement in larger political, economic, and social contexts.

Pedersen, Olaf. *The First Universities: Studium Generale and the Origins of University Education in Eu-*

This facsimile of a wood engraving, from an edition of Cicero's De Officiis *(Paris National Library), shows a university student receiving a new doctor (professor).* (Frederick Ungar Publishing Co.)

rope. Translated by Richard North. New York: Cambridge University Press, 1997. A survey of the history of European higher learning from its beginnings in antiquity through the end of the Middle Ages. Attributes the transformation of early medieval schools into universities in large part to the European discovery of Islamic scholarship.

Piltz, Anders. *The World of Medieval Learning*. London: Basil Blackwell, 1981. A survey for the general reader, with special attention to the life and academic career of Thomas Aquinas.

Rashdall, H. *The Universities of Europe in the Middle Ages*. New ed. Edited by F. M. Powicke, and A. B. Emden. New York: Oxford University Press, 1987. First published in 1895, this monumental three-volume work provides an excellent foundation for further study of the medieval university.

Van Deusen, Nancy, ed. *The Intellectual Climate of the Early University: Essays in Honor of Otto Gründler*. Kalamazoo: Medieval Institute, Western Michigan University, 1997. An anthology examining the scholarly activity within the first universities. Includes essays on mathematics, physics, music, philosophy, and religion.

SEE ALSO: 529-534: Justinian's Code Is Compiled; 595-665: Invention of Decimals and Negative Numbers; 606: National University Awards First Doctorate; 781: Alcuin Becomes Adviser to Charlemagne; 868: First Book Printed; c. 950: Court of Córdoba Flourishes in Spain; c. 950-1100: Rise of Madrasas; c. 1025: Scholars at Chartres Revive Interest in the Classics; c. 1100: Arabic Numerals Are Introduced into Europe; c. 1150: Moors Transmit Classical Philosophy and Medicine to Europe; c. 1265-1273: Thomas Aquinas Compiles the *Summa Theologica*; 1328-1350: Flowering of Late Medieval Physics; c. 1350-1400: Petrarch and Boccaccio Recover Classical Texts.

RELATED ARTICLES in *Great Lives from History: The Middle Ages, 477-1453*: Peter Abelard; Saint Albertus Magnus; Saint Bernard of Clairvaux; Jacqueline Félicie; Frederick I Barbarossa; Innocent III; Justinian I; Leonardo of Pisa; Philip II; Thomas Aquinas; Vincent of Beauvais; Yaqut.

12th century
Coins Are Minted on the Swahili Coast

The minting of coins on the Swahili coast for purposes of trade began in the twelfth century. International trade on the East African coast, specifically by the Swahili, augmented and diversified the region's economic system.

Locale: East African coast from Mogadishu to Kilwa Kisiwani

Categories: Economics; trade and commerce

Key Figure

ʿAlī bin al-Ḥasan (fl. twelfth century), ruler who minted coins in Kilwa

Summary of Event

Based on both archaeological evidence and the historical record, it seems that the peoples of both Kilwa Kisiwani (located in southeastern Tanzania) and Mogadishu (a seaport at the northern end of the Swahili coast in modern Somalia) minted their own coins and did not simply use coins from foreign mints. The towns of Kilwa, Mafia, and Mogadishu were economic centers for the Swahili because of their resources and locations. Archaeologists have found coins in all of these trade centers as well as on Juani Island and the islands of Zanzibar and Pemba. Coins from Kilwa have also been unearthed in Great Zimbabwe sites.

The Islamic scholar Ibn Baṭṭūṭah declared after his visit to East Africa in the mid-fourteenth century that Mogadishu and Kilwa had elements of Islamic law and were thriving portals of trade. The fact that there were many coins in circulation over a wide territory serves as testament that trade was increasing and spreading geographically.

Kilwa, which began as a small, locally focused economy, serves as an example of how many of the Swahili towns or urban centers emerged over the centuries, starting as small backwaters and then coming of age as distinguished trade centers. According to conclusions drawn by Neville Chittick based on his archaeological excavations, coins in Kilwa came into use during the twelfth century, supplanting or supplementing other media of exchange such as cowrie shells and iron bars. By the late twelfth century, Kilwa had become a central minting center for the Shirazi Dynasty.

Coin minting in Kilwa began under the auspices of ʿAlī bin al-Ḥasan and continued during his successors' reigns. The coins of the late twelfth and early thirteenth centuries became defining characteristics of the Shirazi Dynasty. The coins of Kilwa were undated but typically were inscribed with the name of ʿAlī bin al-Ḥasan, an indication that they were minted during his reign or soon thereafter. The coins minted by al-Ḥasan's ventures were of both copper and silver. Silver was imported from North Africa and was relatively low in exchange value. Gold and copper, on the other hand, were imported from southern areas such as Great Zimbabwe and the Zambian copper belt.

Because of gold's high value, it was generally not worth making it into coins; it was typically used for trade rather than a currency minted for exchange. Until the late twelfth and early thirteenth centuries, Mogadishu had been the main center of the gold trade, but with the ascent of Abū al-Mawāhib (r. 1310-1333) of the Mahdali Dynasty (fourteenth century), who conducted the coin casting for the Shirazi Dynasty on the Swahili coast, the center of the gold trade moved to Kilwa, and prosperity followed. In addition to locating coins from Kilwa, scholars have identified luxury goods most likely obtained through trade. Imported objects, notably Sāsānian glazed pots from the ninth century and Chinese porcelain, accumulated in growing numbers. Such artifacts are consistent with the increasing use of coins for luxury exchanges.

From Mogadishu, the earliest coin bearing a date is stamped 1322. The hundred-year difference between the ages of the earlier coins from Kilwa and those minted in north at Mogadishu may be attributed to the fact that in the north there was greater access to foreign coins minted in nearby regions. Kilwa, however, was far enough south—at the periphery of the Red Sea and Mediterranean trade—that minting may have become necessary earlier, as trade intensified and competition with foreign markets increased.

Significance

As trade grew with Persians, Arabs, and Indians, the need for a common currency increased. The minting of coins demonstrates a qualitative and quantitative intensification of trade. Kilwa, Mafia, and Mogadishu grew from small settlements to major economic centers, as trade flooded into the towns. By the fourteenth century, Mogadishu had become a center of Islamic learning, with three mosques for foreign Muslim merchants as well as locals. Additionally, mosques had been built in Kilwa, Gedi, Kaole, Sanje, and Magoma.

The use of coins in Swahili trade also signals a new era in commerce. As trade volume expanded, new methods of exchange were adopted to increase trade efficiency. With coins, prices could be standardized and commercial exchanges made more expedient across territories separated by oceans.

—*Blaine Horrocks and Catherine Cymone Fourshey*

Further Reading

Allen, James de Vere. *Swahili Origins*. Athens: Ohio University Press, 1994. Discusses the Swahili coast and the origins and culture of its peoples.

Chittick, Neville. *Kilwa: An Islamic Trading City on the East African Coast*. 2 vols. Nairobi, Kenya: British Institute in Eastern Africa, 1974. This two-volume work gives a detailed account of archaeological finds from Kilwa up to 1974. Illustrations, bibliography, index.

_______. "Unguja Ukuu: The Earliest Imported Pottery and an ʿAbbāsid Dinar." *Azania* 1 (1966): 161-163. A short but informative article on pottery and coins in Zanzibar.

Coupland, R. *East Africa and Its Invaders*. Oxford, England: Clarendon Press, 1956. An early and now contested study that sees the Swahili peoples as primarily consisting of the progeny of Arab and Persian settlers.

Fage, J. D., and William Tordoff. *A History of Africa*. 4th ed. New York: Routledge, 2001. A classic general history, now updated through the 1990's.

Freeman-Grenville, G. S. P. *The East African Coast: Select Documents from the First to the Early Nineteenth Century*. Oxford, England: Clarendon Press, 1962. Consists primarily of source documents about the region.

Howgego, Christopher. *Ancient History from Coins*. New York: Routledge, 1995. Although focused on medieval Europe, especially Greece, a good introduction to coinage and its place in the history of trade, commerce, and society. Also discusses the technology of coining, the metals used, the meaning of "mint," and the purpose of "striking" coins. Illustrations, bibliography, index.

Niane, D. T., ed. *General History of Africa: Africa from the Twelfth to the Sixteenth Century*. Berkeley: University of California Press, 1984. Contains a chapter on the Swahili that details their economic history.

Nurse, Derek, and Thomas Spear. *The Swahili: Reconstructing the History and Language of an African Society, 800-1500*. Philadelphia: University of Pennsylvania Press, 1984. A detailed history of Swahili communities and civilization from the ninth through the sixteenth century. Examines economic history and contains a genealogy of the male heads of the Shirazi Dynasty. Bibliography, index.

Sutton, John Edward Giles. "East African Coinage: New Finds and New Work Necessary." *Newsletter of the Regional Centre for Study of Urban Origins in Eastern and Southern Africa*, No. 2 (November, 1991): 18-21. This article looks at the indigenous and foreign coinage of East Africa.

_______. *A Thousand Years of East Africa*. London: British Institute in Eastern Africa, 1990. Presents and discusses East African archaeological findings and gives relative chronologies and calendar dates for events. Also examines material culture, including that of coins. Bibliography, index.

See also: c. 500-1000: Rise of Swahili Cultures; 812: Paper Money First Used in China; c. 1100: Origins of Swahili in Its Written Form; c. 1150: Refinements in Banking.

Related article in *Great Lives from History: The Middle Ages, 477-1453*: Ibn Baṭṭūṭah.

12th century
Trading Center of Kilwa Kisiwani Founded

After its founding by ʿAlī bin al-Ḥasan, Kilwa Kisiwani became the dominant trading center of the Indian Ocean and East African coastal regions. It was supported by a safe and economically strategic geographical location close to abundant natural resources such as gold and was the main endpoint for trade products ready for export from the interior of Africa.

Locale: Kilwa Kisiwani, East African coast (now Tanzania)

Categories: Economics; trade and commerce

Key Figure

ʿAlī bin al-Ḥasan (fl. twelfth century), founder of Kilwa Kisiwani

Summary of Event

Although the exact date for the founding of Kilwa Kisiwani (or, simply, Kilwa) by ʿAlī bin al-Ḥasan remains unknown, scholars of the region accept the twelfth century as a likely time frame in which Kilwa became established as a dominant center in Indian Ocean trade economies.

According to the first chapter of the *Kilwa Chronicles* (c. 1550), which recounts the history of Kilwa from its beginnings until first contact with the Portuguese in the early sixteenth century, ʿAlī bin al-Ḥasan acquired political control of the city by providing a local Swahili chieftain with lengths of colored cloth.

Much legend surrounds the personage of al-Ḥasan and his origins. Popular perceptions hold that he was from a royal family from Shīrāz in Persia. According to most accounts, al-Ḥasan and six of his brothers were ordered to leave Persia by their father after he had a dream of a rat eating through a city wall that he interpreted as the ruin of his family unless they fled Persia. Sailing from Persia, al-Ḥasan landed on the African continent and eventually purchased Kilwa in the twelfth century, while his remaining six brothers established other cities in the same manner in eastern Africa. Whether these oral accounts are exact representations of the course of events in al-Ḥasan's life is debated, but it is accepted that al-Ḥasan was an actual person who existed and ruled in Kilwa.

Al-Ḥasan established Kilwa as one of the premier trading cities on the East African coast. The wealth of the city rested on the trade of primarily ivory and gold. To the south of Kilwa was the state of Great Zimbabwe, which had vast amounts of gold attractive to outsiders. The gold that was mined in the area of Great Zimbabwe was taken from the interior to the coast to the city of Sofala from which it was sent northward to Kilwa. Once it reached Kilwa, the gold was sent to other parts of the world, specifically to the governments and elites of Europe and the Middle East via sailing ships. Kilwa also exported slaves. although they were never as important economically as gold and ivory. Of secondary importance to the sea route was a land route that stretched from the coast of the continent nearest the island of Kilwa down to Lake Nyasa with its terminus at Great Zimbabwe.

In exchange for gold, ivory, and slaves, Kilwa received textiles, jewelry, spices, and some of the gold that came from Great Zimbabwe. By the thirteenth century, all of the wealth that the city accumulated made Kilwa the most powerful city on the East African Coast. It was during Kilwa's golden years that a Moroccan traveler and writer, Ibn Baṭṭūṭah, visited and was so impressed by the city that he considered it one of the most beautiful he had ever seen. So enormous was the wealth of Kilwa when Baṭṭūṭah visited in 1331, it became the first urban center in sub-Saharan Africa to mint and issue coins.

By the beginning of the fourteenth century, the coffers of Kilwa were so full that the city undertook a major renovation of the Great Mosque, its most holy Islamic place of worship. Additions were made to the mosque that increased it to four times its original size. Although major additions or renovations were never again undertaken, the mosque remained the dominant focal point of everyday life in Kilwa until the eventual decline of the city beginning in the sixteenth century.

Like most wealthy cities and societies throughout history, the wealth of Kilwa found its way into the hands of a small percentage of the population. The wealthy citizens of Kilwa could afford large and majestic stone houses, while the vast majority of Kilwa's citizens had homes of wood, earth, and thatch. Buildings made from materials of the earth degrade and require continual repair. On average a commoner's house in Kilwa was completely rebuilt every ten years. Thus the architecture of Kilwa reveals a picture of the social stratification of the urban center during its height of its wealth and power.

Significance

The island and city of Kilwa became an urban center and port of economic and political empowerment during the twelfth century. The city was crucial to the gold, ivory, and textile trade because of its location, which allowed Kilwa to have close connections with the Indian Ocean world. Kilwa's ability to dominate another nearby city, Sofala, afforded it great wealth as it controlled an excess of gold resources. Kilwa was also able to trade with China, which exported glass beads and Chinese porcelain to the western Indian Ocean.

The merchants involved in the Kilwa trade, foreign and internal, made large profits off the high value of the imports. The city of Kilwa worked to bring goods from the interior of the continent out to the coast to ship to other nearby countries. This caused the interior countries to rely heavily on Kilwa for their own trading. Kilwa took advantage of this reliance and imposed and demanded high customs duties and large taxes on the gold trade, becoming not only wealthy but also autonomous in the process.

Kilwa was also involved in the lucrative spice trade. Spices were very important to the region, mainly because they helped preserve foods, and included cloves, ginger, cinnamon, nutmeg, cardamom, and saffron. The Portuguese sought to control the spice trade along the Swahili coast in order to circumvent and undermine the Asian domination of this trade to Europe, leading to Kilwa's decline in the sixteenth century. The once-thriving trade center is now a small village.

—*Travis Hamilton, Elizabeth Leighton, and Daisy Conduah*

Further Reading

Bahn, Paul G. *Lost Cities*. New York: Barnes and Noble Books, 1997. A book about various great cities around the world that have declined or become extinct. Contains a section on Kilwa.

Chittick, Neville. *Kilwa: An Islamic Trading City on the East African Coast*. Nairobi, Kenya: British Institute in Eastern Africa, 1974. A historical reference book that recounts the history of Kilwa's trade as well as the Islamic influence within the area. Also displays maps and floor plans of particular and important buildings.

Ibn Baṭṭūṭah. *Travels of Ibn Baṭṭūṭa*. Translated and edited by H. A. R. Gibb. 4 vols. Cambridge, England: Cambridge University Press, 1958-2000. This careful, amply annotated translation is by far the most important English-language source of information on the man and his milieu. Gibb's introduction and notes offer useful historical background.

Oliver, Roland, and J. D. Fage. *The Cambridge History of Africa*. Cambridge, England: Cambridge University Press, 1977. A historical account of African civilizations from about 1050 to about 1600.

Pearson, Michael N. *Port Cities and Intruders: The Swahili Coast, India, and Portugal in the Early Modern Era*. Baltimore: John Hopkins University Press, 1998. A discussion of the major economic, social, and religious interchanges that took place on the Swahili coast and how Portugal's intrusion affected that interchange.

Pouwels, Randall L. "The East African Coast, c. 780-1900 C.E." In *The History of Islam in Africa*, edited by Nehemia Levzion and Randall Pouwels. Athens: Ohio University Press, 2000. Details the Islamic history of coastal east Africa. Covers the history of commerce, architecture, and culture on the Swahili coast and discusses important dates, persons, and events in Swahili history. Includes maps of Kilwa and photos of Kilwa's Great Mosque.

Sutton, John. *A Thousand Years of East Africa*. Nairobi, Kenya: British Institute in Eastern Africa, 1990. A discussion of Kilwa's history, with special attention paid to religion in Kilwa and the Great Mosque.

See also: c. 500-1000: Rise of Swahili Cultures; 630-711: Islam Expands Throughout North Africa; 11th-15th centuries: Great Zimbabwe Urbanism and Architecture; 12th century: Coins Are Minted on the Swahili Coast.

Related article in *Great Lives from History: The Middle Ages, 477-1453*: Ibn Baṭṭūṭah.

12th century
WANG CHONGYANG FOUNDS QUANZHEN DAOISM

The founding of Quanzhen (Complete Perfection) Daoism by Wang Chongyang helped revitalize Daoism and represented a major religious movement in China. Its impact on Chinese thinking and life can still be felt today.

LOCALE: China
CATEGORIES: Religion; philosophy

KEY FIGURE

Wang Chongyang (Wang Ch'ung-yang; 1113-1170), founder of the Quanzhen (Complete Perfection) school of Daoism

SUMMARY OF EVENT

Quanzhen (Complete Perfection) Daoism was founded by Wang Chongyang (also known as Wang Zhe, or Wang Che) in northern China in the mid-twelfth century, a time characterized by political disunity and wars among the Chinese regime of the Song Dynasty (Sung; 960-1279), the Jurchen state of Jin (Chin; 1115-1234), and the Mongols, as well as ethnic tensions, especially in northern China. Wang's time also was one of religious and intellectual changes, including the decline of Daoist outer alchemy and the growth of Daoist inner alchemy, the prospering of neo-Confucianism, and an increase in the interaction among Daoism, Buddhism, and Confucianism.

Wang Chongyang came from a rich family in Shaanxi Province and was educated in Confucianism during his early years. After repeated failures in pursuing an official career, Wang turned to Daoism, claiming that he had been taught a secret formula by a mystic in 1159. In 1161, he left his family and began to practice Daoism in a cave located in a village on Mount Zhongnan. In 1167, Wang traveled to Shandong peninsula, where he formally started preaching Quanzhen Daoism. He conducted his preaching activities among people of various social strata and often used poetry and songs in his preaching, which proved appealing and persuasive. Wang recruited seven adepts from rich and scholarly backgrounds as disciples; they became the backbone of the Quanzhen Daoist movement. By 1169, Wang had set up five Quanzhen Daoist societies in Shandong peninsula. Wang wrote about one thousand poems and *Jinguan yusuo jue* (twelfth century; formula on the golden bolt and the jade chain), a text in which he enunciated the basic doctrines of Quanzhen Daoism.

After Wang's death, his disciples extended their preaching activities beyond Shandong to the rest of northern China, particularly Hebei, Shaanxi, and Henan Provinces, and established their own schools. Quanzhen Daoism formally gained official recognition in 1187 when the Jin emperor summoned one of Wang's disciples to the imperial court. Quanzhen Daoism reached its peak during the Mongol Yuan Dynasty (1279-1368), when the numbers of its temples and followers increased rapidly. It remains one of the major Daoist schools in present-day China, with its headquarters in the White Cloud Temple in Beijing.

Quanzhen Daoism is generally believed to represent a synthesis of Confucianism, Buddhism, and Daoism. Wang Chongyang stressed that the three schools belonged to the same family, were like three branches of the same tree, and were equal. He made friends with Confucian scholars and Buddhist monks and advised his followers to read the scriptures of all three schools. In addition, Wang integrated some key ideas of Confucianism and the Chan school of Buddhism into Quanzhen Daoism, especially those about cultivation of the mind and one's inner nature.

Despite the influence of Confucianism and Buddhism, Wang remained fundamentally a Daoist adept and Quanchen Daoism a Daoist school, which inherited the basic concepts and beliefs of both philosophical Daoism represented by Laozi (Lao-tzu; 604-sixth century B.C.E.) and Zhuangzi (Chuang-tzu; c. 365-290 B.C.E.)—nothingness, tranquility, abandonment of desires—and religious Daoism—immortality and golden elixir. Quanzhen Daoism evolved directly from inner alchemy (*neidan*), a sect of religious Daoism. Inner alchemy emerged late in the Tang Dynasty (T'ang; 618-907) and matured in the Song Dynasty (Sung; 960-1279). It represented a negation of outer alchemy, another sect of religious Daoism. Outer alchemy focused on taking a specific chemical substance—a golden elixir produced from lead and mercury and other minerals—as the principal technique for achieving immortality. This caused the premature death of many practitioners, including some emperors, because the golden elixirs were often poisonous. Daoist adepts turned instead to inner alchemy, which emphasized physiological and mental training as the way to reach immortality. The materials needed for inner alchemical training do not come from outside but from inside a person's body. Invisible and untouchable, these materials include energy (*jing*), breath (*qi*), and spirit (*shen*). In inner alchemical training, one maneuvers or reorganizes these ingredients through imagination or contemplation. Inner alchemy split into two groups, one giving priority to physiological training (training of the body) and the other underscoring mental training (training of the mind). Quanzhen Daoism belongs to the latter group.

Wang Chongyang and his followers believed in immortality and regarded its achievement as their ultimate goal. They believed that people suffered in life and in hell after death. To avoid suffering, people should try to become immortals through training in Daoism. Every person has the potential to be an immortal, because everyone is endowed with the true inner nature (*zhenxing*), which is associated with the mind. To discover (or illuminate) and maintain this true inner nature is the key to becoming immortal. Training of the mind requires a person to keep his or her mind absolutely "pure and tranquil" (*qing jing*), free from all kinds of defilement and worldly attachments. Eventually, the trainee will reach a point at which his or her true inner nature is illuminated or revealed. This true inner nature was identified by Wang as the golden elixir needed for immortality. Wang insisted that some people got sick and died while still young because they were obsessed with worldly concerns or desires, causing their minds to be impure and not still, and destroying their energy.

Although primarily concerned with training of the mind, Wang also acknowledged the necessity of training the body because he felt it to be closely linked to the training of the mind. The techniques, which include quiet sitting and guiding the movement of breath (*yunqi*) along certain imagined channels within the body, are supposed to strengthen one's internal energy or prevent it from leaking, thus maintaining health and achieving longevity.

Wang and his followers regarded passion and family life as major obstacles to achieving the illumination of one's true inner nature and hence immortality. They viewed the family to be a jail and the husband-wife relationship as chains, and they compared children to wolves, tigers, and leopards. They encouraged people to abandon their families and to pursue and concentrate on Daoism. However, Quanzhen Daoists did not utterly negate ethics related to family and other worldly matters nor did they insist on an absolutely seclusive life. For instance, Wang advised people to observe such Confucian values as loyalty to rulers, obedience to laws, benevolence, filial piety to parents, respect for teachers, and altruism. In Wang's opinion, doing good deeds by following these values is an integral component of the training aimed at achieving immortality. In addition, Wang also asked his followers to study medicine to save people's lives. Many Quanzhen Daoist adepts indeed followed his teachings and worked among lower-class people.

SIGNIFICANCE

The new school of Quanzhen Daoism contributed significantly to the revitalization of Daoism by integrating Buddhist and Confucian beliefs into Daoism, stressing inner alchemical cultivation, and publicizing Daoism among the common people. Since its founding, Quanzhen Daoism has influenced Chinese thought and life. People, particularly scholars and scholar-officials, adopted Quanzhen Daoism's physiological and mental training as a way to improve their health and prevent diseases. Generally, intellectuals proved more interested in mental training, while working people were more fond of physiological training. Quanzhen Daoism probably also affected traditional Chinese medicine, given that they share some basic beliefs, for example, that health depends, among other things, on peace of mind and nourishment of one's internal energy.

—Yunqiu Zhang

FURTHER READING

Kohn, Livia, ed. *Taoist Meditation and Longevity Techniques*. Ann Arbor: Center for Chinese Studies, University of Michigan Press, 1989. Includes some chapters on Daoist techniques for physiological and mental training. Mentions Quanzhen Daoism.

Kuang, Guoqiang. "Quanzhen Daoism's Doctrine on Mind and Inner Nature." In *Study of Daoist Culture*, edited by Chen Guying. Shanghai: Shanghai Ancient Works Press, 1996. Examines Wang's views on inner alchemical cultivation, particularly on training of the mind.

Ren, Jiyu, ed. *A History of Chinese Daoism*. Beijing: Chinese Social Sciences Press, 2001. Contains a chapter about the origins and doctrines of Quanzhen Daoism.

Zhang, Guangbao. *Inner Alchemical Daoism During Tang and Song Dynasties*. Shanghai: Shanghai Cultural Press, 2001. Examines the origins, evolution, and doctrines of inner alchemy, providing valuable information about the background of the rise of Quanzhen Daoism.

SEE ALSO: 907-960: Period of Five Dynasties and Ten Kingdoms; 960: Founding of the Song Dynasty; 960-1279: Scholar-Official Class Flourishes Under Song Dynasty; 1115: Foundation of the Jin Dynasty; 1130: Birth of Zhu Xi; 1153: Jin Move Their Capital to Beijing.

RELATED ARTICLES in *Great Lives from History: The Middle Ages, 477-1453*: Xuangzang; Zhu Xi.

12th-14th centuries
SOCIAL AND POLITICAL IMPACT OF LEPROSY

Although the impact of leprosy was not as great as that of the Black Death two centuries later, its development in Europe did have a serious social and political impact, playing a pivotal role, for example, in the stigmatization of those with the disease and in the Crusaders' loss of Jerusalem in 1187.

LOCALE: Europe
CATEGORY: Health and medicine

KEY FIGURES

Gregory the Great (c. 540-604), pope, 590-604
Baldwin IV (1161-1185), king of the Crusader kingdom of Jerusalem, r. 1174-1185
Henry IV (1367-1413), king of England, r. 1399-1413

SUMMARY OF EVENT

No disease carried more social stigma in the Middle Ages than did leprosy. The term "leper" is synonymous with ostracism and the image of the medieval leper is still strong in the popular imagination.

Lepers were often required to shout "unclean!" or to make noise with a bell, rattle, or clapper so that others would know to give them a wide berth, and they were forbidden to touch or breathe on anyone. With such restrictions, a leper would be unable to work for a living and would be entirely dependent on charity or an allowance from his or her family for survival. The social wretchedness of lepers made their case particularly attractive to those who wished to benefit their own souls by doing exceptional works of charity, but this certainly did not make up for the devastating emotional effects that came from the leper's total social isolation. It seems likely that this isolation frequently broke both body and spirit and greatly hastened the death of the afflicted from causes such as exposure, malnutrition, or diseases unrelated to leprosy.

Leprosy, generally called Hansen's disease, is now treatable and is far better understood than it was in the Middle Ages. It is caused by the bacterium *Mycobacterium leprae* and is manifested by skin lesions, rashes, and damage to nerves and mucous membranes. It is spread primarily through intimate contact with an infected person, and it has a long incubation period, ranging from one to seven years. Over time, it can be disfiguring and debilitating, though physical decay is slow enough that most lepers die of causes unrelated to leprosy.

Leprosy has existed for thousands of years. It is mentioned at least fifty times in the Bible, and there is evidence of its presence in ancient Egypt. It may have reached Rome in the first century, carried by soldiers returning from North Africa. Medieval Europe learned from the Bible how to identify and treat lepers. Leviticus 13:44-46 states,

> Now whosoever shall be defiled with the leprosy, and is separated by the judgment of the priest, shall have his clothes hanging loose, his head bare, his mouth covered with a cloth, and he shall cry out that he is defiled and unclean. All the time that he is infected and unclean, he shall dwell alone without the camp.

Interestingly enough, the Bible and other historical sources mention a whiteness to the skin of lepers, but this is not a symptom of Hansen's disease. While an examination of skeletons would indicate that Hansen's disease was present among the leper population, it would appear that many other diseases of the skin were also classed as leprosy and their sufferers were treated similarly. Those suffering from fungal infection, eczema, pellagra, ringworm, psoriasis, pigment disorders, and even syphilis were labeled lepers.

Data for accurate epidemiology is not present for the Middle Ages, but an examination of the number of establishments created for the housing of lepers suggests that leprosy reached its greatest prevalence during the twelfth and thirteenth centuries and declined in later years. This is, however, disputable evidence. The numbers might indicate a rise in the founding of leper hospitals merely for saving a founder's soul rather than actual need, a concern for lepers and leprosy, or its actual prevalence during this time period.

A leper house as depicted in a thirteenth century manuscript of Miroir Historical, *by Vincent de Beauvais.* (Frederick Ungar Publishing Co.)

Medieval science was ignorant of *Mycobacterium leprae*, so it followed the lead of the Bible and other early writers in faulting the victim for his or her affliction. Sexual excess or perversion was the most commonly cited cause. Pope Gregory the Great felt that leprosy was God's punishment for heresy. Sin was not the only suspect, however.

Leprosy also was believed to be a highly contagious disease requiring the isolation of the afflicted. Breathing and touching were thought to be the prime means of transmitting the disease. Lepers were often required to wear scarves over their mouths and stay downwind of healthy people, as well as carry a stick to point to something they wished to draw attention to or to have or buy.

The violent aversion people had to lepers was most likely caused by the frightening physical appearance of lepers, along with the exaggerated fear of contagion. How a leper was treated in a given society varied tremendously from place to place and over time and also had much to do with the social position of the leper. For a poor man or poor woman to be diagnosed with leprosy meant a sort of living death. For a member of the upper classes, the stigma could be less drastic.

There are at least two instances of medieval kings who had leprosy or something similar (whether it was Hansen's disease cannot be determined). The first, and best known case, is that of Baldwin IV, king of the Crusader kingdom of Jerusalem. While he was described as an able and intelligent young man, his reign was troubled, and the debilitation caused by the disease made it necessary for him to appoint a regent to rule for the second half of his short reign. His lack of a clear successor and the power struggles that broke out in the last years of his reign fractured the kingdom of Jerusalem, just when it was under its greatest threat, and hastened its fall in 1187.

Another leper king may have been Henry IV of England, though the diagnosis was not as clear as with Baldwin IV. He may, in fact, have had syphilis, which would have been more in keeping with the general degeneration of his physical and mental health seen in his later years. However, the distinction between "true" leprosy and some other disfiguring skin disease was not really important in the Middle Ages. Henry's final years were spent in isolation, with effective control of government being exercised by his son and principle supporters.

His condition was not widely discussed in the kingdom and the nobles who had supported him in his seizure of the throne had a vested interest in not allowing his disease to undermine his dynasty.

Clear or probable cases of leprosy in a king did not result in that ruler's immediate removal from power nor result in other drastic social consequences generally associated with leprosy. While it seriously impeded their ability to rule, political and dynastic imperatives made it essential to the nation that they remain on the throne as long as they were able.

For a poor man or poor woman, whose individual fate was not so crucial to society, the results of a diagnosis of leprosy were disastrous personally. The sufferer was frequently considered to have entered an ambiguous legal and social state, that of being virtually dead to the world while being actually alive. Husbands and wives were separated if one was afflicted and the other was not, and a religious ceremony similar to last rites was performed. The leper then renounced all property to the unafflicted members of his or her family and departed to live life as a wandering beggar or a patient of a leper hospital.

SIGNIFICANCE

The impact of leprosy was certainly not as devastating as the Black Death to the fabric of society. It was a slow acting and stubborn disease rather than a fast moving pandemic. Its most serious impact was on the afflicted individual and his or her family.

Although leprosy seems to have been endemic throughout Europe, Asia, and Africa, it never attacked more than a small percentage of a given community. However, when the infected individual was a king, the political and social impact could be severe. The leprosy of King Baldwin IV, and his consequent appointment of Guy de Lusignan in 1183 as his regent, played a pivotal role in the Crusader's eventual loss of Jerusalem in 1187.

—*Walter Nelson*

FURTHER READING

Brody, Saul Nathaniel. *The Disease of the Soul: Leprosy in Medieval Literature.* Ithaca, N.Y.: Cornell University Press, 1974. A history of how leprosy was perceived and then represented in the literature of the Middle Ages.

Cobb, Ivo Geikie. *Through the Leper-Squint: A Study of Leprosy from Pre-Christian Times to the Present.* London: Selwyn and Blount, 1938. A still-useful, important, and sweeping historical study of leprosy.

Covey, Herbert C. "Peoples with Leprosy (Hansen's Disease) During the Middle Ages." *The Social Science Journal* 38, no. 2 (2001): 315-321. Discusses the social consequences of leprosy in medieval times.

Hamilton, Bernard. *The Leper King and His Heirs: Baldwin IV and the Crusader Kingdom of Jerusalem.* New York: Cambridge University Press, 2000. Challenges traditional notions about Baldwin's reign, asserting, for example, that his war with Saladin was necessary rather than ill-advised and that his leprosy did not seriously debilitate either the king or his kingdom.

Lee, Gerard A. *Leper Hospitals in Medieval Ireland: With a Short Account of the Military and Hospitaller Order of St. Lazarus of Jerusalem.* Dublin: Four Courts Press, 1996. In addition to its detailed discussion of the leper hospitals in Ireland and of the Order of Saint Lazarus, which administered them, this study opens with a brief general history of leprosy.

McNiven, Peter. "The Problem of Henry IV's Health." *English Historical Review* 100, no. 397 (1985): 747-772. Explores the ongoing issue of whether Henry IV had leprosy.

Marcombe, David. *Leper Knights: The Order of St. Lazarus of Jerusalem in England, c. 1150-1544.* Rochester, N.Y.: Boydell Press, 2003. Detailed account of the English branch of the order of crusading hospitallers who cared for lepers for four hundred years.

Watts, Sheldon. "Dark Hidden Meanings: Leprosy and Lepers in the Medieval West and in the Tropical World Under the European Imperium." In *Epidemics and History: Disease, Power, and Imperialism.* New Haven, Conn.: Yale University Press, 1997. Discusses leprosy within the context of a sociopolitical and medical history of epidemics from the Middle Ages to the present. Attempts to reveal connections between strategies for disease control and imperialist expansion.

SEE ALSO: 590-604: Reforms of Pope Gregory the Great; 1189-1192: Third Crusade; 1347-1352: Invasion of the Black Death in Europe.

RELATED ARTICLES in *Great Lives from History: The Middle Ages, 477-1453*: Gregory the Great; Guy de Chauliac; Henry IV (of England); Paul of Aegina; Saladin.

MAJOR RULERS OF THE JIN DYNASTY

Reign	*Ruler*
1115-1123	Aguda (Wanyan Min; Taizu)
1123-1135	Taizong (Wanyan Sheng)
1135-1149	Xizong
1150-1161	Wanyan Liang, king of Hailing
1161-1190	Shizong
1190-1209	Zhangzong
1209-1213	Wanyan Yongji, king of Weishao
1213-1224	Xuanzong
1224-1234	Aizong
1234	The Last Emperor

Note: The Jurchen created the Jin Dynasty in 1115. They took over China in 1125, when the Jin Dynasty, as part of the Chinese dynastic line, began.

their place of origin; the Liao had taken their name from the Liao River in Manchuria. *Liao* also means "iron"; therefore, Aguda chose to name his dynasty *jin*, which means "gold," to demonstrate the superiority of his dynasty to that of the Khitans. Chinese emperors traditionally chose a reign name, and Aguda, whose Jin Dynasty (Chin; 1115-1234) would be greatly influenced by Chinese models, took the reign name of Taizu (T'ai-tsu).

In 1120, to further their military campaign against the Liao, the Jin allied with the Song. The Liao, already weakened by dynastic divisions and suffering economic collapse, fell to the Jin-Song alliance in 1125, shortly after Aguda's death in 1123. The surviving Liao retreated to the west, where they formed a new dynasty usually referred to as the Western Liao, and which survived in reduced circumstances until overwhelmed by the Mongols in 1218.

Although the Song and Jin had united against the Liao, when the Song emperor Huizong attempted to recover additional Liao territory, the new Jin emperor Taizong (Wanyan Sheng) invaded the Song in 1125. With their heavily armored cavalry and their increasing mastery of siege machines, the Jin proved to be an almost irresistible force, even against walled cities. The Jin occupied the Song capital, Kaifeng, in 1126, and the Song emperor, Huizong, who had abdicated in 1125, and his son and successor, Qinzong (Ch'in-tsung; r. 1125-1126), were taken as hostages back to Manchuria, where they died in captivity, Huizong in 1135 and Qinzong in 1156. The Jin pressed their advantage, and the surviving Song retreated to China's south, establishing a new capital at Hangzhou. Only in 1142 did the Southern Song and the Jin agree to a peace treaty, leaving the Jin in control of most of China north of the Yangtze River. In becoming a vassal state to the Jin, the Southern Song agreed to pay silver and silk tribute to the Jin emperors, ushering in an era of uneasy coexistence that lasted until the invasion of another nomadic non-Chinese people, the Mongols, in the early thirteenth century.

SIGNIFICANCE

Aguda's proclaiming of the Jin Dynasty in 1115 and his and his successors' military victories over first the Liao and then the Song created a large Jurchen-Jin state that controlled much of northern China. However, as other non-Chinese conquest dynasties had discovered, it proved easier to conquer the Chinese than to permanently rule them. The leadership abilities of Aguda and the military superiority of the Jin cavalry were not automatically conducive to peacetime rule.

The Jin Dynasty adopted many aspects of traditional Chinese culture. The use of Chinese script was widespread; the Jin encouraged Chinese calligraphy, and some of the Jin emperors collected Chinese manuscripts. However, ultimately, the Jin were not Chinese, and although many Chinese accepted the Jin Dynasty, some did not, raising issues of Jin legitimacy. These were challenges faced by all non-Chinese conquest dynasties. More significant, the Jin faced an increasing threat from the nomadic Mongols, led by Genghis Khan and his son Ogatai. When attacked by the Mongols, instead of uniting with the Southern Song against the Mongols (perhaps an impossibility given the conflicts of the past), the Jin attempted, unsuccessfully, to seize Song territory in the south. Ogatai captured the last Jin capital, Caihou, in 1234, bringing an end to the Jin Dynasty after little more than a century of existence.

—*Eugene Larson*

FURTHER READING

Chan, Hok-lam. *Legitimation in Imperial China: Discussions Under the Jurchen-Chin Dynasty.* Seattle: University of Washington, 1984. A study of the Jin Dynasty during the twelfth century.

Tao, Jing-shen. *The Jurchen in Twelfth-Century China: A Study of Sinicization.* Seattle: University of Washington Press, 1976. A readable work on the Jin adoption of and adaption to China's dominant culture.

Tillman, Hoyt Cleveland, and Stephen H. West, eds. *China Under Jurchen Rule: Essays on Chin Intellectual and Cultural History.* Albany: State University of

1115
Foundation of the Jin Dynasty

Aguda, from the Wanyan clan of the Jurchen peoples of Manchuria, led the Jurchen armies into battle in northern China against the Liao Dynasty. He established the Jin Dynasty, placing much of northern China under non-Chinese rule.

Locale: Manchuria and northern China
Categories: Expansion and land acquisition; government and politics

Key Figures

Aguda (A-ku-ta; 1069-1123), first emperor of the Jin Dynasty, r. 1115-1123
Tianzuodi (T'ien-tsu-ti; d. 1125), Khitan Liao Dynasty emperor, r. 1101-1125
Huizong (1082-1135), Song emperor, r. 1101-1125
Taizong (T'ai-tsung; d. 1135), second emperor of the Jin Dynasty, r. 1123-1135

Summary of Event

The non-Chinese Jurchen did not emerge as a separate entity in written historical records until the mid-tenth century. They originated to the north of China in present-day eastern Manchuria. Originally, the Jurchen were hunters in the forested areas of Manchuria. They became expert horsemen, a skill shared by members of other northern conquest dynasties such as the Khitan Liao (907-1125) and the later Mongolian-Yuan (1279-1368) and Manchu-Qing (Ch'ing; 1644-1911) Dynasties. The Jurchen could best be described as seminomadic, and although hunting and horsemanship were central to their culture, they also practiced agriculture, some living in small, walled towns.

The tenth and eleventh centuries had been a confusing period in Chinese history. One of China's most glorious dynasties, the Tang (T'ang), fell in 907, ushering in the Five Dynasties and Ten Kingdoms period (907-960). Unity was restored under the Song Dynasty (Sung; 960-1279), but during those decades, much of northern China had come under the rule of the non-Chinese Khitans, who established the Khitan Liao Dynasty shortly after the fall of the Tang. The Song were unable to dislodge the Liao from the region around modern-day Beijing, and it was not until the early eleventh century that the Song and the Liao agreed to a truce, with the Song paying annual tribute to the Liao, much of it in the form of silk. The Liao rulers were not native Chinese, but like many other of the non-Chinese conquest dynasties, the Liao adopted some of the culture and institutions of imperial China, a process known as sinicization. However, the Liao, who maintained their traditional religion of shamanism and human sacrifice, were less drawn by Chinese culture than the Jin and Qing Dynasties that followed.

The Jurchen clans were under the rule of the Liao Dynasty, whose origins were also in Manchuria. During the tenth century, the Jurchen were forced to pay tribute both to the Liao and to the Southern Song (1127-1279) Dynasties. The tribute was often paid in horses, a reflection of their mastery of horses, which, in the early twelfth century, they used in warfare along with iron weapons.

After a struggle for supremacy between the clans (a not unusual occurrence among seminomadic people), the Wanyan clan achieved dominance over their fellow Jurchens in the early 1100's. Aguda became head of the clan and was known as Wanyan Min (Wan-yen Min). Given the Jurchens' skill in horsemanship and their expertise in weapons, raiding and warfare were central to their culture. When united under the leadership of a strong and charismatic leader and when aided by political and military weakness among potential opponents, the northern nomads frequently emerged as formidable foes. That convergence occurred in the early twelfth century, with the rise of Aguda to Jurchen leadership and a corresponding weaknesses in both the Liao and Song Dynasties.

Among the earliest of Jurchen opponents was the Koryŏ, the dynasty that gave its name to the land of Korea, but the Liao Dynasty of northern China proved to be the primary early victim of Jurchen unity. The Jurche had been tributaries of the Liao, but in 1112, the bal ance between the two peoples shifted significantly. I that year, the Liao emperor, Tianzuodi, visited Ma churia, and during a banquet given by the Liao er peror, Aguda refused to perform a Jurchen tribal dan for the Liao contingent. Whether it was a sudden decisi on the part of the Jurchen leader or part of a calcula ploy to unite the Jurchen against the ruling Liao is known. In any event, the subordinate relationship that Jurchen had long experienced under the Liao came quick end.

War was declared against the Liao in 1114, and Jurchen victories at Ningliang and Chuhedian, A proclaimed himself emperor of the great Jin Dyna 1115. Previous dynasties had often taken the nar

New York Press, 1995. A series of essays on aspects on the era of the Jin Dynasty.

Twitchett, Denis, and Herbert Franke, eds. *Alien Regimes and Border States, 907-1368*. Vol. 6 in *The Cambridge History of China*. New York: Cambridge University Press, 1994. Contains an extensive discussion of the Jin Dynasty.

See also: 907-960: Period of Five Dynasties and Ten Kingdoms; 936: Khitans Settle Near Beijing; 960: Founding of the Song Dynasty; 960-1279: Scholar-Official Class Flourishes Under Song Dynasty; 1153: Jin Move Their Capital to Beijing.

Related articles in *Great Lives from History: The Middle Ages, 477-1453*: Genghis Khan; Kublai Khan.

c. 1120
Order of the Knights Templar Is Founded

The religious-military order of the Knights Templar was founded to protect the holy land and its pilgrims. The presence of the Knights enabled the Roman Catholic Church to gain political, military, and financial power in the Middle East.

Locale: Jerusalem
Categories: Organizations and institutions; religion

Key Figures

Hugues des Payens (c. 1070-1136), French knight and cofounder, with Geoffroi de Saint-Omer, of Knights Templar

Baldwin II (d. 1131), king of Jerusalem, r. 1118-1131

Saint Bernard of Clairvaux (1090-1153), French saint influential in establishing the Knights Templar

Philip IV the Fair (1268-1314), king of France, r. 1285-1314, destroyed Knights Templar

Summary of Event

During the Middle Ages, several orders of knighthood were founded while the Crusades against the Muslims were in progress. Among the first of twelve religious-military orders of knighthood were the Poor Knights of Christ and the Temple of Solomon, popularly known as the Knights Templar, founded around 1120.

A religious-military order dedicated to the protection of the Holy Sepulchre in Jerusalem, which was violently taken against the Turks during the First Crusade on July 15, 1099, the members conformed to both military and religious discipline. They were soldiers with the obliga-ions and training of knighthood, but who also took the onastic vows of poverty, chastity, and obedience. The ights Templar took their name from their headquarters ed in the Temple of Solomon in Jerusalem. De-d as "lions in war, lambs in the house, to the ene- Christ implacable, but to Christians kind and gracious," the Knights built castles and hospitals in Palestine with ancillary branches in Europe.

The Knights Templar grew from a group of pious soldiers who gathered in Jerusalem during the second decade of the twelfth century when the Crusaders controlled only a few strongholds in the Holy Land. An order that followed the rules of Saint Augustine, in groups of eight or nine, they protected pilgrims from marauding Muslim bands on the roads between Jaffa, on the Palestine coast, and Jerusalem and other holy places. They also provided sustenance and medical treatment. The order was founded and led by a French nobleman, Hugues des Payens, who with nine or ten other knights, swore to offer protection to pilgrims. They were welcomed by and given quarters in Jerusalem in King Baldwin II's palace that, it is said, stood on the site of King Solomon's Temple.

At the commencement of the order, the Knights were laymen who promised to follow religious monastic rules. In 1127, Hugues de Payens, traveling in Europe seeking funds, met Bernard, the abbot of Clairvaux (later Saint Bernard), a spiritual leader with a large following. The idea of a military-religious order appealed to Bernard and at the Council of Troyes in 1128, the Poor Knights of the Temple were given official Church status, switching allegiance to Bernard's stricter Cistercian Order's regime of prayer, silence, plainness, simple diet, self denial, and manual labor. The Knights were permitted to wear the white mantle of the Cistercians, to which Pope Eugene III had added the characteristic red cross.

To overcome the discrepancy between the military purpose of the Knights Templar and the Church's idea of a peaceful man of God, sworn to nonviolence, Saint Bernard argued that the Knights fought for Christ's purposes, protecting the Holy Land from unbelievers: "Not without cause does he bear the sword! He is the instrument of God for the punishment of the malefactors and for the defence of the just . . . he is accounted Christ's legal executioner against evildoers." Any land or property taken by the Knights became the property of the Church, and other Church orders tended to look down on the Knights Templar and considered them inferior to the "true," that is, the monks who lived lives of peaceful contemplation within the walls of European abbeys. They were headed by a grand master, and each branch of the order was headed by a commander who swore absolute obedience to the grand master.

Because of their defense of the Holy Land, the Knights Templar gained universal approval in Catholic Europe. Their reputation was constructed in part by the propagandistic writings of Saint Bernard. Immensely successful, they quickly increased their land and power, becoming influential in European political and religious circles. Because men of all classes were accepted into their order, the feudal class came to identify with them and herein lay their primary strength. At their height, they numbered twenty thousand, and by the middle of the twelfth century, they owned estates and castles scattered throughout western Europe, the Mediterranean, and the Holy Land. While the Templar Knights proper had to be from the rank of knights, a lower bourgeoisie class rank of "sergeants," who were armed and wore brown rather then white, were accepted. Other ranks of chaplain and servant were also decreed. They surrendered all their property, joining the order for life, leaving only to join a stricter order.

The seal of the Knights of Christ, an emblem of the Knights Templar. (Frederick Ungar Publishing Co.)

In Paris in 1147, just before the departure of the French king on the Second Crusade, 130 white-robed Templars offered homage to the king and pope. Thousands of estates in England, France, and Spain were given to the Templars, and millions throughout Europe contributed funds to the continuing cause of the Crusades. Templar houses and castles were the strongest and safest buildings. Their membership increased dramatically and their wealth and position grew, until they owned property throughout most of western Europe. At this point, they came to take on the role of international banker, often granting loans to European monarchs. They adopted absolute secrecy to cover all internal activities, and because they were considered "defenders of the Church," they were free from tithes and taxes. With this diversification of roles, they became a vital element in the defense of the Holy Land, where they built numerous castles and garrisoned every town. While the Crusades went on in the East, men and materials were needed in the West and as long as the defense of the Holy Land was in question, political attacks on Templars were unsuccessful.

For more than one hundred years, the Templars maintained their power. Nevertheless, the fall of Jerusalem in 1187 led to the demise of the order. After the Holy Land fell to the Muslims in 1291, the Templars transfigured themselves into an international mercenary force, available to any government that had the funds to pay them. With centers in London and Paris, they retained their international banking status, servicing nobles and commoners alike. Indeed, the king of France deposited the French royal treasury with them.

For at least forty years, rumors had circulated regarding the rites of initiation of the Templars. Because of the complete secrecy of all rituals, however, no proof was available. King Philip IV of France, known as Philip IV the Fair, was said to have manufactured accounts of these rumored sacrilegious and obscene rites, based on magical ritual, and sent them to Pope Clement V.

On October 13, 1307, King Philip had the entire population of some two thousand members of the Knights Templar in France arrested. The king also confiscated all French property belonging to the order. Accusing the Templars of heresy and immorality, Philip blamed them for the loss of the Holy Land.

SIGNIFICANCE

Although the reasons for King Philip's actions are no[t en-]
tirely clear, many scholars believe that he coveted [the]
financial resources. When Philip ascended the th[rone]

A Templar knight in traveling dress, from a woodcut by Jost Amman in Cleri Totius Romanæ ecclesiæ . . . habitus *(Frankfurt, 1585).* (Frederick Ungar Publishing Co.)

1285, the country was near bankruptcy, but the Templars possessed land and money in great quantity.

Philip was not satisfied, however, with halting the activities of the Templars in France. In an effort to destroy the entire order, Philip launched a propaganda campaign that painted the Templars as a rich, corrupt organization that used magic to accumulate power. In July, 1308, the pope approved an investigation of these charges, and Philip began an inquisition that coerced confessions under torture. Although a papal council voted against the abolition of the Templars in December, 1311, Philip ordered Jacques de Molay, the Templar grand master, and other high-ranking Templar officials burned at the stake in March, 1314. At this point, the Knights Templar were dissolved and their guilt remains a historical controversy.

—*M. Casey Diana*

FURTHER READING

Barber, Malcolm. *The New Knighthood: A History of the Order of the Temple*. New York: Cambridge University Press, 1994. A well-known historian of the Knights Templar provides a fresh account of the order, including origins, the concept, their rise in the East, Templar life, and the order's demise. Maps, bibliography, index.

_______. *The Trial of the Templars*. 1978. Rev. ed. New York: Cambridge University Press, 1993. Scholarly account of the latter years of the Templars with an emphasis on the politics surrounding the organization's demise. Bibliography, index.

Barber, Malcolm, and Keith Bate, trans. *The Templars: Selected Sources*. New York: Manchester University Press, 2002. A collection of sources on the Knights Templar, with annotations. Part of the Manchester Medieval Sources series. Maps, bibliography, index.

Curzon, Henry de. *The Rule of the Templars*. Translated and introduced by Judith M. Upton-Ward. Rochester, N.Y.: Boydell Press, 2001. The first English translation of the 1886 text, called the French Rule, on the life of the order. In addition to providing a historical introduction to the order's military-monastic manual or "rule," this text covers details about clothing, armor, equipment, and conduct, all gleaned from three surviving medieval manuscripts. Map, bibliography, index.

Howarth, Stephan. *The Knights Templar*. New York: Atheneum, 1982. Covers in great detail the period from the First Crusade in 1099 to the collapse of the Knights Templar in 1308. Readable account that contains illustrations of significant sites and personages associated with the order. Bibliography, index.

Nicholson, Helen. *The Knights Templar: A New History*. Stroud, England: Sutton, 2001. Explores the history of the order from its origins to its dissolution and downfall. Discusses the Knights' role in banking, their protection of the Holy Land, the accusations that led to their long trial, and the trial itself. Map, bibliography, index.

Partner, Peter. *The Murdered Magicians: The Templars and Their Myth*. New York: Oxford University Press, 1982. Although this book is directed more at the scholar of Masonic mysticism and can be challenging for the layperson, the introduction contains concise historical information on the Knights Templar. Bibliography, index.

Robinson, John J. *Dungeon, Fire, and Sword: The Knights Templar in the Crusades*. New York: M. Evans, 1991. Provides a concise historical account of the Templars' religious-military mission in battling for control of the Holy Land. Contains illustrations and a comprehensive bibliography.

SEE ALSO: 1009: Destruction of the Church of the Holy Sepulchre; November 27, 1095: Pope Urban II Calls the First Crusade; c. 1145: Prester John Myth Sweeps Across Europe; 1147-1149: Second Crusade; c. 1150: Refinements in Banking; 1189-1192: Third Crusade; 1204: Knights of the Fourth Crusade Capture Constantinople; 1217-1221: Fifth Crusade; 1227-1230: Frederick II Leads the Sixth Crusade; 1228-1231: Teutonic Knights Bring Baltic Region Under Catholic Control; 1248-1254: Failure of the Seventh Crusade; April, 1291: Fall of Acre, Palestine.

RELATED ARTICLES in *Great Lives from History: The Middle Ages, 477-1453*: Baybars I; Saint Bernard of Clairvaux; James I the Conqueror; Melisende; Philip IV the Fair; Saladin.

1127-1130
CREATION OF THE KINGDOM OF SICILY

The establishment of the Kingdom of Sicily created a realm that dominated the central Mediterranean.

LOCALE: Sicily and southern Italy
CATEGORY: Government and politics

KEY FIGURES

Robert Guiscard (c. 1015-1085), duke of Apulia, Calabria, and Sicily
Roger I (1031-1101), conqueror of Sicily
Roger II (1095-1154), count of Sicily, 1105-1130, and later king of Sicily, r. 1130-1154

SUMMARY OF EVENT

In the early eleventh century, an increasing number of landless Norman knights found service as mercenaries in the confused struggles in southern Italy and on Sicily. This region was at the crossroads of three cultures—Byzantine, Latin, and Arabic. Apulia and Calabria remained under the power of the Byzantine Empire. The central provinces were governed by Lombard lords. Across the narrow straits of Messina, the island of Sicily was under Muslim control.

Taking service with Lombard princes, the pope, or the Byzantines as circumstances prescribed, the Normans soon made a name for themselves in southern Italy, in 1030 acquiring their first territorial possession. As the family property proved unable to keep pace with the family fertility, increasing numbers of Norman warriors sought their fortunes in southern Italy, including nine of the twelve sons of Tancred d'Hauteville. By the end of 1042, William d'Hauteville was proclaimed count of Apulia and Calabria.

In 1046, the sixth son of old Tancred, Robert, called Guiscard (the foxy or the cunning), arrived and in 1057 effectively succeeded his brothers in Apulia and Calabria. At the synod of Melfi in 1059, Pope Nicholas II formally invested Robert Guiscard with Apulia, Calabria, and Sicily, even though at that time Robert had never set foot on the island and the only claim of the pope to sovereignty was the fictitious Donation of Constantine.

Before acting to enforce his claims to Sicily, Robert strengthened his position on the mainland, restricting the Byzantines to Bari in Apulia and eliminating them from Calabria. On Sicily, three Muslim emirs engaged in fratricidal conflict, while a large part of the population remained Christian, open to the blandishments of the Normans. A Byzantine attack on Apulia called Robert away from Sicily, so it was his youngest brother Roger who became the major force in the island's conquest.

In May, 1061, the Normans captured Messina, giving them an opening to the entire island. In alliance with Emir Ibn at-Timnah of Palermo, they soundly defeated Emir Ibn al-Hawas at Enna. Despite these early successes, limited resources and intermittent internecine quarrels meant that the Norman conquest would not be quick. The Norman victory at Misilmeri in 1068 broke the back of Saracen. Count Roger also built up his fleet, which appeared before Palermo. After a five-month siege, the city surrendered in 1071. Meanwhile, Duke Robert brought Byzantine power in southern Italy to an end with the capitulation of Bari, also in 1071. During the next fifteen years, he successfully fended off rebellions among his vassals, conflicts with other south Italian powers, and the enmity of Pope Gregory VII, expanding his holdings by the conquest of Amalfi and Salerno and becoming the indispensable ally of the pope in his struggle with Emperor Henry IV. Duke Robert also turned his energies against his earliest opponents, the Byzantines, dying in 1085 on Cephalonia. He was succeeded by his son Roger Borsa, who was immediately challenged by a half brother, Bohemond.

Although Robert Guiscard remained the titular overlord of Sicily, he was busy with the defense and enlargement of his possessions on the mainland, and he left control to his brother Roger I. After the capitulation of Palermo, Roger began to incorporate elements of the native Muslim population into his administration and army. In 1075, he concluded a treaty of friendship with the Zirid sultan at Mahdia, thus depriving the Sicilian Muslims of any hope of aid from Africa. In 1085, Syracuse was captured, but it was not until 1091 that Noto, the last Muslim stronghold, surrendered.

Conquest was quickly followed by conciliation, creating a new, multilingual, and multireligious society. Although Muslims and Jews had to pay a special tax, Latins, Greeks, Jews, and Saracens enjoyed the protection of their own laws. The Muslims were granted extensive religious toleration, continued possession of their lands, and inclusion in many military and administrative positions. The Greek Christians had to swallow the bitter pill of Roman primacy; however, they not only kept their own language and liturgy but also gained the rebuilding of their churches and the foundation of fourteen Basilian monasteries. The Latins obtained the Church hierarchy and the choicest fiefs. Court ceremonies were more Byzantine than feudal. Although allied with the Papacy, Roger held firm control of the Sicilian Church, in 1098 receiving from Pope Urban II for himself and his successors the authority of a papal legate. By the time Roger I died in 1101, he had established one of the most remarkable states of medieval Europe, a hybrid of three cultures at the focal point of the Mediterranean world.

Roger I was succeeded by his son, Roger II, under the regency of his widow, Adelaide of Savona. Relying in large part on her Greek and Arab subjects, Adelaide weathered many difficulties, establishing her court at Palermo. By 1113, Roger II was ready to take up the government. The island realm was prosperous and well protected by the strong fleet founded by the Great Count. On the mainland, Roger Borsa and his son William showed none of the abilities of Robert Guiscard. In 1125, the childless Duke William recognized Roger II as his heir and died two years later at the age of thirty. Roger rushed to Salerno, gained possession there, and, after ineffective resistance by the pope and disgruntled barons, in 1128 was invested by Honorius II as duke of Apulia, Calabria, and Sicily. He then held a grand court at Melfi, where the feudal nobility of Apulia and Calabria were required to swear loyalty to himself and his sons, to forswear private warfare, and to surrender criminals to the ducal courts. Thus the foundations were laid for the extension to the mainland of the strong kingly power that his father had established on Sicily. Somewhat later in that same year, the only remaining independent Norman lord in southern Italy, Robert of Capua, submitted to Roger's suzerainty. Taking advantage of a disputed papal election, Roger obtained a bull raising him to the royal dignity. After obtaining the agreement of his vassals at assemblies held at Salerno and Palermo, Roger was crowned the first king of Sicily in Palermo cathedral on Christmas Day, 1130.

Robert Guiscard, whom in 1059 Pope Nicholas II formally invested with Apulia, Calabria, and Sicily. (H. Bricher)

SIGNIFICANCE

King Roger ruled for another twenty-four years, continuing to strengthen his already impressive realm. He was succeeded in 1154 by William the Bad, and he in turn by his son, William the Good, who died in 1198. This period from Roger I to William II was a golden age in Sicilian history, when good government provided peace, some degree of protection against the greed and violence of feudal lords, and more toleration than anywhere else in the contemporary Mediterranean world.

With William II's death in 1198, the throne passed to the Hohenstaufen dynasty, which involved Sicily in the endless struggles between Papacy and empire. This connection was especially strong under Emperor Frederick II (1194-1250), with the southern realm sharing in the glories and the downfall of this enigmatic sovereign, who died in battle against the forces allied with the Papacy. Not long thereafter, Sicily passed under the control of Frederick's illegitimate son, Manfred. In his capacity as feudal suzerain, Pope Urban IV offered the crown to Charles of Anjou, brother of King Louis IX of France, who conquered Sicily in 1266. The harshness of Angevin rule encouraged dissatisfaction, and the island of Sicily rose in a rebellion known as the Sicilian Vespers in 1282. The crown of Sicily was offered to Peter III of Aragon, husband of Manfred's daughter Constance. The Angevins were never able to regain control, so there were two claimants to the Sicilian crown, on the island and on the mainland. In 1504, Ferdinand of Aragon conquered the mainland, after which the two Sicilies remained part of the Spanish monarchy until the extinction of the Spanish Habsburgs. In 1735, both Sicilies were joined under a Bourbon line that, with the exception of the Napoleonic period at Naples, ruled until 1860, when this monarchy, officially called the Kingdom of the Two Sicilies only in the nineteenth century, was united to form the new Italian national state.

—*William C. Schrader*

FURTHER READING

Allibone, Finch. *In Pursuit of the Robber Baron: Recreating the Journeys of Robert Guiscard, Duke of Apulia and "The Terror of the World."* Luton, Beds: Lennard, 1988. An examination of Robert Guiscard and his role in the events surrounding Sicily. Bibliography and maps.

Brown, R. Allen. *The Normans*. 2d ed. Woodbridge, England: Boydell & Brewer, 1995. Emphasizes the capacity of the Normans for leadership and organization.

Houben, Hubert. *Roger II of Sicily: A Ruler Between East and West*. Translated by Graham A. Loud and Diane Milburn. New York: Cambridge University Press, 2002. A biography of Roger II, king of Sicily, that examines his life and world. Illustrations, maps, and index.

Loud, G. A. *The Age of Robert Guiscard: Southern Italy and the Norman Conquest*. New York: Longman, 2000. A biography of Robert Guiscard that examines the world he lived in and the Norman conquest. Bibligraphy and index.

Norwich, John Julius. *The Normans in Sicily: The Normans in the South, 1016-1130, and the Kingdom in the Sun, 1130-1194*. 1967 and 1970. Reprint. London: Penguin, 1992. An examination of the Norman conquest and the establishment of the Kingdom of Sicily. Bibliography and index.

Wolf, Kenneth Baxter. *Making History: The Normans and Their Historians in Eleventh-Century Italy*. Philadelphia: University of Pennsylvania Press, 1995. Begins with an overview of the Norman conquests in Italy and Sicily and examines the Normans' history in the Mediterranean. Bibliography and index.

SEE ALSO: November 27, 1095: Pope Urban II Calls the First Crusade; c. 1120: Order of the Knights Templar Is Founded; 1169-1172: Normans Invade Ireland; 1440: Donation of Constantine Is Exposed.

RELATED ARTICLES in *Great Lives from History: The Middle Ages, 477-1453*: Frederick II; Gregory VII; Henry IV (of Germany); Louis IX; Urban II.

1130
Birth of Zhu Xi

Zhu Xi created a comprehensive system of Confucian ideas, referred to as neo-Confucianism, which has dominated Confucian thought, and to some degree Chinese and East Asian thought, to the present day.

Locale: Fujian Province, China

Categories: Cultural and intellectual history; philosophy

Key Figures

Zhu Xi (Chu Hsi; 1130-1200), Chinese philosopher

Cheng Hao (Ch'eng Hao; 1032-1085), Confucian philosopher

Cheng Yi (Ch'eng I; 1033-1107), Confucian philosopher

Zhou Dunyi (Chou Tun-i; 1017-1073), Confucian philosopher.

Wang Yangming (Wang Yang-ming; 1472-1529), neo-Confucian philosopher

Summary of Event

Zhu Xi was born in what is now Fujian Province after his father retired from a government position there. His early education in Confucianism came from his father, but he later studied with the tutor Li Tong (Li T'ung). Li came out of an intellectual tradition that can be traced back to the Cheng brothers, Cheng Yi and Cheng Hao. The work of these two brothers, particularly Cheng Yi, helped shape Zhu Xi's philosophical views. According to some accounts, Zhu Xi showed his genius at an early age. When he was eighteen, he passed the *jinshi* examination, which made him eligible to serve in government posts.

For the most part, Zhu Xi refused to accept government posts although he did serve as keeper of records in the city of Tongan from 1151 to 1157. Zhu preferred to study and write even though this meant that he led a life of poverty. In 1175, he wrote his most notable work, *Jin si lü* (*Reflections on Things at Hand*, 1967), with Lu Zuqian (Lu Tsu-ch'ien; 1137-1181). In this work, Zhu Xi gave direction to neo-Confucianism by pulling ideas from Confucius (551-479 B.C.E.), Mencius (c. 372-c. 289 B.C.E.), and others and making them into a coherent and comprehensive system. In the course of his life, Zhu Xi rebuilt the White Deer Hollow Academy, helped found or reconstruct many other schools, taught more than four hundred students, and wrote, compiled, and edited more than eighty works.

Before Zhu Xi, Confucian study had been centered on the Five Classics: *Yijing* (eighth to third century B.C.E.; English translation, 1876; also known as *Book of Changes*, 1986), *Shijing* (compiled fifth century B.C.E.; *The Book of Songs*, 1937), *Shujing* (compiled after first century B.c.e.; English translation in *The Chinese Classics*, Vol. 5, Parts 1 and 2, 1872; commonly know as *Classic of History*), *Liji* (compiled fifth century B.C.E.; *The Liki*, 1885; commonly known as *Classic of Rituals*), and *Chunqiu* (fifth century B.C.E.; *The Ch'un Ts'ew with the Tso Chuen*, 1872; commonly known as *Spring and Autumn Annals*). In 1190, Zhu Xi compiled the Four Books—Confucius's *Lunyu* (late sixth-early fifth centuries B.C.E.; *The Analects*, 1861), Mencius's *Mengzi* (first transcribed in the early third century B.C.E.; English translation in *The Confucian Classics*, 1861; commonly known as *Mencius*), the *Da Xue* (fifth-first century B.C.E.; *The Great Learning*, 1861), and the *Zhong yong* (written c. 500 B.C.E.; *The Doctrine of the Mean*, 1861)—into a course of study that became the new foundation for Confucian learning. In Zhu Xi's system, *The Great Learning* provided the pattern of thought, *The Analects* provided the foundation, *Mencius* provided the elaboration of ideas, and *The Doctrine of the Mean* provided subtlety and profundity. In 1313, the Yuan Dynasty (1279-1368) declared Zhu Xi's interpretation of Confucianism and his commentaries on the Four Books the orthodox interpretation for the purposes of the civil service exams. They remained the standard until the exams were abolished in 1905.

Zhu Xi also described what became the accepted direct line of transmission of true Confucian ideas from Confucius through Mencius, to Zhou Dunyi, Cheng Yi, Cheng Hao, and himself. His concept of the evolution of Confucian ideas clarified acceptable views and gave weight to Confucianism as a clear line of developed thought. One result of this line of transmission was that the teachings of important scholars such as Xunzi (Hsün-tzu; c. 307-c. 235 B.C.E.) were no longer part of the mainstream of Confucian thought.

Although many scholars see Zhu Xi as merely synthesizing the ideas of others, he actually added ideas to and clarified certain concepts in Confucianism. Drawing on the work of Cheng Yi and Cheng Hao, Zhu Xi refined what became the central concepts of "principle" (*li*) and "material force" (*chi*). All things, Zhu Xi explained, have principle. In fact, all things have the same basic principle. This principle existed even before

Heaven and Earth. However, principle exists only together with material force because principle needs material force to which to "cling." Material force, concomitantly, needs principle to shape it. The two are inseparable. There is never principle without material force and never material force without principle. One aim of neo-Confucians is to grasp principle (*li*) in themselves by first grasping it outside of themselves through "the investigation of things."

The concepts of principle, material force, and the investigation of things became important when they were applied to self-improvement. Since the earliest ideas of Confucius, the goal of Confucians has been to perfect their virtue in order to serve society. Virtue, in Zhu Xi's view, is equated with principle, which is obscured when material force becomes cloudy because of human desires. By grasping principle within themselves, Confucians can use principle to clarify their material force and allow their virtue to shine forth.

Zhu Xi then linked principle and material force to the idea of the Great Ultimate, the beginning of all things, which was a concept developed by Zhou Dunyi. According to Zhou Dunyi, the Great Ultimate created yin and yang, the two basic forces of the universe. Yin and yang then created the five elements of earth, water, fire, metal, and wood. The interaction of yin and yang and the five elements created all things in the universe. For Zhu Xi, principle became associated with the Great Ultimate. This association gave the Confucians an answer to the origins of Heaven and Earth and supported the concept that principle runs through everything in the universe.

Zhu Xi also clarified the concept of *jen*, which was central to Confucians. Confucius was vague about this term, defining it only as "humanity." Mencius elaborated by including the idea of *jen* as the natural empathy human beings have for one another. Zhu Xi added the idea of love but also equated *jen* with the mind of Heaven and Earth through which Heaven and Earth created things. Thus, *jen* changed from just a description of virtue to an active force in the universe.

Significance

Zhu Xi's metaphysical interpretations helped Confucianism contend with Buddhism during his life and after. Buddhism had gained followers in the years of disunion between the Tang and the Song Dynasties (907-960). With the formulation of his ideas, Zhu Xi provided a view of the universe and its relationship to human virtue that could compete successfully with the ideas of Buddhism. He also provided a means for Confucians to focus on self-improvement outside of government and society, a fundamental idea in Buddhism that had appealed to the Chinese.

Zhu Xi's work served as the foundation for later thinkers and became the basis for debate within Confucianism. When the noted neo-Confucian Wang Yangming challenged Zhu Xi's ideas, he did so in terms proposed by Zhu Xi. Wang argued that Zhu Xi had separated principle and material force, thus separating thought and action. For Wang, thought was connected to principle, while action was connected to material force. To act according to principle, there could be no separation between thought and action just as there could be no separation between principle and material force. Moreover, Wang felt principle should be grasped within the mind rather than in the investigation of things. The debate revolved around what terms such as "principle" and "material force" meant, not whether these fundamental concepts laid out by Zhu Xi were correct or not. The active debate over the theories of Zhu Xi and Wang Yangming spread throughout China and into Korea and Japan. Ultimately, Zhu Xi's ideas were ultimately adopted as part of the ruling ideology by the Yi Dynasty in Korea (1392-1910) and the Tokugawa rulers in Japan (1600-1868).

—*David W. Blaylock*

Further Reading

Chan, Wing-tsit. *Chu Hsi: Life and Thought*. New York: St. Martin's Press, 1987. A compilation of articles by a major scholar of Zhu Xi and neo-Confucianism. Chan discusses Zhu Xi's ideas and his legacy.

________. *A Source Book in Chinese Philosophy*. Princeton, N.J.: Princeton University Press, 1969. An invaluable source in Chinese philosophy. Chan provides an introductory essay, translations of sections of major works, and commentary.

Chu Hsi. *Further Reflections on Things at Hand*. Lanham, Md.: University Press of America, 1991. Allen Wittenburn translated selections from several of Zhu Xi's works, and arranged them by topic. His commentary is complex but good on outlining the wide range of Zhu Xi's ideas.

Chu Hsi and Lu Tsu-ch'ien. *Reflections on Things at Hand: The Neo-Confucian Anthology*. New York: Columbia University Press, 1967. Wing-tsit Chan's translation of a fundamental work that gave direction to neo-Confucianism.

DeBary, William T., Wing-tsit Chan, and Burton Watson, eds. *Sources of Chinese Tradition*. Vol. 1. New York:

Columbia University Press, 1960. This work has short translations from major philosophical works with a general introduction.

Liu Shu-hsien. *Understanding Confucian Philosophy Classical and Sung-Ming*. Westport, Conn.: Greenwood Press, 1998. A discussion of the development of Confucian thought from the viewpoint of a contemporary neo-Confucian. The section on Zhu Xi is very good on the development of Zhu Xi's ideas and the philosophical problems he faced and provides critical commentary on the views of current scholars studying Zhu Xi.

SEE ALSO: 960-1279: Scholar-Official Class Flourishes Under Song Dynasty; 1115: Foundation of the Jin Dynasty; 1368: Establishment of the Ming Dynasty.

RELATED ARTICLE in *Great Lives from History: The Middle Ages, 477-1453*: Zhu Xi.

1130
KARAKITAI EMPIRE ESTABLISHED

Establishment of the Karakitai Empire, founded by a former dynasty of China, marked the rise of a non-Islamic empire in Central Asia. Although its existence was brief, it played a critical role in creating an atmosphere of religious tolerance and influencing administrative practices in a region of mixed nomadic and sedentary populations.

LOCALE: Central Asia (modern Kazakhstan, Uzbekistan, Kyrgyzstan, Tajikistan, Turkmenistan, and parts of Xinjiang Autonomous Region in China)

CATEGORIES: Expansion and land acquisition; government and politics

KEY FIGURES

Yelü Dashi (Yeh-lü Ta-shih; 1087-1143), founder and first gurkhan of Karakitai, r. 1130-1143

Atsiz (d. 1157), ruler of Khwārizm, r. 1127/28-1157

Sanjar (1084/1086-1157), ruler of the Seljuk Empire, r. 1118-1157

Muḥammad II (d. 1221), the last ruler of the Khwārizmian Empire in thirteenth century, r. 1200-1221

Küchlüg (d. 1218), Naiman prince who fled Mongolia and ruled Karakitai after a coup, r. 1211-1218

Genghis Khan (Temüjin; between 1155 and 1162-1227), founder and ruler of the Mongolian Empire, r. 1206-1227

SUMMARY OF EVENT

A refugee from the Liao Dynasty (907-1125) of northern China established the Karakitai Empire (1130-1210) in Central Asia after the Manchurian Jurchen tribes defeated the Liao in 1125. The Jurchen tribes established the Jin Dynasty (1125-1234) of China. Although they ruled northern China (and much of Mongolia), the Liao Dynasty was not native to China but a Mongolian group known as the Khitans. Once they were driven from their empire, Yelü Dashi, a prince of the Liao royal family, continued resistance against the Jurchen from Kedun, located along the Orkhon River in Mongolia.

Although Yelü Dashi's efforts against the Jin were at times effective, the Jin Dynasty continued to grow in strength. Without allies, Yelü Dashi had little choice but to move farther west to elude the Jin. Thus, in 1130, Yelü Dashi moved along with his followers to the region between the Irtysh and Emil Rivers and established a base.

Yelü Dashi's following increased because of the recruitment of various Turkic tribes, and he was elected gurkhan, or universal khan. Despite his title, Yelü Dashi controlled very little territory, although he began to expand it slowly but steadily over the areas of Qayaliq and Almaliq (now in Kazakhstan). His greatest opportunity arrived when the Qarakhanid rulers of the city of Balasaghun (now in Kyrgyzstan), requested Yelü Dashi's assistance against the restless nomadic tribes that threatened his realm.

Yelü Dashi accepted the offer but first took over Balasaghun and usurped the throne there. Then he defeated the nomadic Qarluq and Qangli tribes that had intimidated the Qarakhanids. Thus, by 1134, the Karakitai Empire had increased substantially. After his victories, more nomadic tribes joined his ranks, seeking booty from plundering the cities of Central Asia. By 1137, the Karakitai realm contained the cities of Khotan, Kashgar, and Besh-Baliq, all in the Xinjiang (Sinkiang) region. In addition, the gurkhan marched into the Fergana valley (now divided between Uzbekistan, Kyrgyzstan, and Tajikistan). There he defeated the western Qarakhanids in May, 1137, at the Battle of Khujand along the Oxus River.

Although the gurkhan won a resounding victory there,

THE MYSTERY OF THE KARAKITAI NAME

The meaning of the name Karakitai remains a mystery. The Khitan (Kitai, Khitai, Khitay) who formed the empire were a tribe of Mongolian origin, who lived in eastern Mongolia and Manchuria. After this group conquered much of northern China and established the Liao Dynasty, this part of China was often known as Khitan, or as Marco Polo called it, Cathay. Although the Khitans were driven from power in 1125, the name remained significant: "Khitai" remains the term for China in Russian and in Mongolian.

What is unclear about the name is the appellation of Kara, which means "black" in Turkic. Often in Turkic languages as well as in Chinese, colors have directional designations. Black typically designated "north"; however, Karakitai was certainly not north China. Perhaps the Turks and Muslims viewed them as being north of them, not to the east, where Khitan was located. In any case, the name remains a mystery, and its etymology at this point is mere speculation.

---

he did not follow his victory with the complete subjugation of Mawarannahr (the land between the Oxus River and the Jaxartes River, also known as Transoxiana in antiquity and in the west). Instead, he consolidated his recent conquests.

Soon, however, the attention of the gurkhan once again was drawn to Mawarannahr. One chronicler attributed it to the growing need to provide territory and plunder for the gurkhan's tribal followers. However, most sources indicated that the Karakitai were invited into the territory by Atsiz, ruler of Khwārizm (east of the Caspian Sea and south of the Aral Sea in modern Turkmenistan and Uzbekistan). His invitation to the gurkhan came because of the increasing tension between him and his overlord, Sultan Sanjar, the ruler of the Seljuk Empire. Atsiz had attempted to gain his independence from the Seljuks in 1138, but Sanjar defeated him and ousted Atsiz from his governorship. Although Atsiz eventually regained his position in Khwārizm through a coup, he submitted to Sultan Sanjar again in return for clemency. In addition to the proposition offered to the gurkhan by Atsiz, Sultan Sanjar had other reasons for entering the region. Although Atsiz had proven to be a recalcitrant subject, the Karakitai were infidels in the eyes of the Muslim Seljuk ruler. Indeed, while the overall religiosity of the Khitans may be called into question, they tended toward Buddhism, shamanism, or Nestorian Christianity. In any case, this offered Sanjar an excellent opportunity to raise his status by defeating the infidel hordes.

With the older Seljuk Empire (1040-1194) to the south and the nascent Karakitai Empire to the north, the lands between the two attempted to determine which empire would benefit them the most. Thus, in 1141, at the Battle of Qatwan near Samarqand (now in Uzbekistan), the armies of the two empires met. The sources tend to exaggerate the number of troops that the gurkhan led into battle, but in any case the gurkhan decisively defeated Sanjar.

With the defeat of the Seljuks, Yelü Daishi had secured Mawarannahr for the Karakitai Empire. Furthermore, Atsiz now became the vassal of the gurkhan. Finally, the empire of Karakitai firmly established itself as a considerable power in Central Asia. Although Yelü Daishi died two years later in 1143, he established a strong and flexible empire that ruled over nomadic tribes as well as sedentary mercantile and agricultural regions, including the great cities of Samarqand and Bukhara, Khotan, and Kashgar. Additionally, his empire was not only multiethnic but also a mixture of religions including Islam, Buddhism, and Nestorian Christianity. His empire demonstrated considerable tolerance of all creeds until the early thirteenth century, when the throne was usurped by an interloper from Mongolia.

SIGNIFICANCE

The creation of the Karakitai Empire had a tremendous influence on Central Asia. As Karakitai was the nexus point for the Islamic world, East Asia, and the steppe regions, a great number of influences came to the fore under the empire. Among the most important was religious tolerance. Although the gurkhans of the Karakitai tended to be Buddhist, they did not attempt to convert their subjects, who were predominantly Muslim. Many Muslims preferred the rule of the Karakitai over that of previous Muslim rulers, as the gurkhans tended to be more just in their rule or at least less oppressive. Furthermore, the Karakitai were able to maintain control over the unruly tribes of Qarluqs and Qanglis, both Turkic groups. Thus, agricultural and mercantile interests prospered within the empire. The Karakitai also realized the needs of the nomads and attempted to balance their interests, creating a fairly stable and secure empire among a potentially volatile mixture of groups.

Not until forces beyond its peripheries came into play did the empire of Karakitai begin to rupture. The primary cause was the rise of the Mongol Empire under the leadership of Genghis Khan. As some tribes fled before him, they entered the Karakitai Empire and sowed the seeds of discord, ultimately undermining the empire and causing it to fall in 1210 when the Khwārizm shāh, Muḥammad II, and Küchlüg, the leader of the Naiman tribe of Mongolia and an opponent of Genghis Khan, carved the empire of Karakitai between them.

—*Timothy May*

FURTHER READING

Bartold, V. V. *Four Studies on Central Asia.* Vol. 1. Translated by V. Minorsky and T. Minorsky. Leiden: Brill, 1956. A collection of extended studies on particular regions of Central Asia that includes a brief summary of the empire of Karakitai.

_______. *Turkestan Down to the Mongol Invasion.* 4th ed. Philadelphia: Porcupine Press and E. J. W. Gibb Memorial Trust, 1977. The section on Karakitai is relatively brief; however, it provides a complete and detailed history of Central Asia before and after the empire.

Biran, Michal. *"'Like a Mighty Wall': The Armies of the Qara Khitai, 1124-1218." Jerusalem Studies on Arabic and Islam* 25 (2001): 44-91. The definitive study on the Karakitai military.

Bosworth, C. E. "The Eastern Seljuq Sultanate, 1118-1157, and the Rise and Florescence of the Khwarizm Shahs of Anushtegin's Line up to the Appearance of the Mongols, 1097-1219." In *The Age of Achievement: A.D. 750 to the End of the Fifteenth Century,* edited by M. S. Asimov and C. E. Bosworth. Vol. 4 in *History of Civilizations of Central Asia.* Paris: UNESCO, 1998. Addresses the flourishing of the eastern Seljuk sultanate and the appearance of the Mongols. Discusses their alliance with the Karakitai.

Grousset, René. *The Empire of the Steppes: A History of Central Asia.* Translated by Naomi Walford. New Brunswick, N.J.: Rutgers University Press, 1970. A classic work on Central Asian history. The section on Karakitai is only a summary, but the entire work is highly readable and offers a solid introduction to the study of the Karakitai.

Sinor, Denis. "The Kitan and the Kara Khitay." In *The Age of Achievement: A.D. 750 to the End of the Fifteenth Century,* edited by M. S. Asimov and C. E. Bosworth. Vol. 4 in *History of Civilizations of Central Asia.* Paris: UNESCO, 1998. Covers the rise of the Khitan people in China over two centuries. Addresses military and political issues.

Wittfogel, Karl A., and Fêng Chia-Shêng. *History of Chinese Society: Liao (907-1125).* Philadelphia: American Philosophical Society, 1949. Although the focus is on the Liao Dynasty of northern China, the authors also have included a chapter on the Karakitai, including translations of primary sources.

SEE ALSO: 936: Khitans Settle Near Beijing; 1115: Foundation of the Jin Dynasty; 1153: Jin Move Their Capital to Beijing.

RELATED ARTICLE in *Great Lives from History: The Middle Ages, 477-1453*: Genghis Khan.

1136
HILDEGARD VON BINGEN BECOMES ABBESS

Hildegard's leadership in two German monasteries and her mystical writings expanded her religious and political influence across twelfth century Europe and opened new possibilities for women's religious leadership.

LOCALE: Rhine River area, western Germany
CATEGORIES: Literature; religion; social reform

KEY FIGURES

Hildegard von Bingen (1098-1179), abbess of the Disibodenberg and Rupertsberg monasteries, 1136-1179

Jutta von Spanheim (1092-1136), Hildegard's predecessor and abbess of Disibodenberg

Eugenius III (d. 1153), pope, 1145-1153, who supported Hildegard's visions and encouraged the Church's intellectual renewal

SUMMARY OF EVENT

It was believed that only two venues best suited medieval women: the home and the monastery. Women unattached to either were suspect and thus displaced from a divinely instituted order. Since women were thought particularly culpable in bringing sin into the world—as the biblical story of Adam and Eve was believed to have illustrated—they were considered unlikely conduits for divine revelation. Hence, the church was governed exclusively by male clergy and practically all its teachers and theologians were men.

Women who raised children bore Eve's burden in one sense but atoned for it in another by modeling the maternal virtues associated with Mary, the mother of Jesus. Conversely, nuns reflected Mary's holiness through their physical virginity and spiritual quest for communion with God. [illegible] communion was best achieved in a monastery's communal prayer and solitude. Worldly goods and power were sacrificed and monks and nuns lived dead to the world beyond the monastery walls.

Yet silence and solitude were not wholly constitutive of the lives of all medieval nuns. The monastery afforded them real leadership roles and space in which to exercise spiritual gifts other than maternal love. A few nuns, such as Hildegard von Bingen, spoke publicly, produced treatises on a variety of subjects, and corresponded with clerics, often with persuasive effect. As an abbess, she oversaw her community's daily life and advised her nuns as they sought perfection in the virtues of faith, hope, and love. Some of these women were mystics who claimed close union with God through visions and revelations. In the meditative atmosphere of a monastery a woman could reflect upon her spiritual experiences and think about them in a wider light. Some women received theological training in these settings and so were afforded tools to develop their minds.

Unlike their modern counterparts, medieval nuns performed little social outreach, though a few monasteries provided care for the sick and refuge for the poor. Prayer and contemplation were the norm. Daily activities in a Benedictine foundation such as Hildegard's were punctuated by the canonical hours, or times of worship throughout the day and night. Otherwise, monastics worked their gardens and performed chores with a minimum of conversation and lived on simple meals of bread, water, wine, and vegetables.

Intellectual and mystic met in Hildegard, the Sybil of the Rhine. She was a scientist and an otherworldly mystic, one who revealed the mysteries of the natural world and claimed extraordinary visions. Though a child of baronial wealth, born in 1098 in Bermersheim bei Alzey (now in Germany), she was destined for monastic life. This probably was because she was the tenth child, given by her parents to a holy life in reference to the biblical concept of the tithe, or tenth of one's household income. Her sickly nature also precipitated her being pledged. Jutta von Spanheim, abbess of Disibodenberg, became her superior when Hildegard was eight, beginning a life of female monastic administration brought to fruition when she succeeded Jutta as abbess in 1136.

Hildegard von Bingen. (Hulton|Archive by Getty Images)

Hildegard described her visions as light streaming from above, filling her mind. Hence, she is often depicted with a stream of light from heaven over her. She did not claim that her visions were of real things, but rather, were of light, stars, or great circles visible in her mind and accompanied by knowledge of the Scriptures. They were seen, she explains, by her "interior" eyes in a wakeful state and not in dreams or hallucinations. She wrote down the fruits of her visions in her *Scivias* (1141-1151; English translation, 1986), an abbreviated form of *nosce vias (Domini)*, or "know the ways of the Lord." She tells of being compelled to record her experiences at that time. Her reluctance to obey resulted in illness that subsided when she finally agreed to record them, a process spanning a decade.

The book is a mix of science, philosophy, and theology and gives an account of the universe, the self, and the harmony and order that attends them. Though she claimed this knowledge came through visions, there is much affinity with medieval thinkers with whom she would have been familiar. She continued developing her comprehensive vision in the *De operatione Dei* (1163-1173; *Book of Divine Works*, 1987). The writing of *Scivias* was not the first instance of her unusual gifts. It was reported that, as a child, Hildegard "saw" a calf inside its mother cow and accurately predicted its spots and coloring. This unusual gift for visioning could have won her derision or censure, but it instead received approbation from Pope Eugenius III, who read a portion of the *Scivias* at the Council of Trier in 1147.

Hildegard called herself a "poor little womanly creature." Such humility combined with her physical ailments figured into her visions. Scholars have speculated about the possible psychosomatic causes for her visions, speculating that migraine headaches produced "stars," lights, and blurred vision. Whatever their cause, admirers continue to laud her experiences as spiritually instructive.

Humility, however, did not mean reticence. She was in touch with worldly realities around her. When Pope Eugenius approved her visions, she replied by admonishing him to reform Church abuses. Few other correspondents escaped her review, except Bernard of Clairvaux, the great Cistercian abbot and Crusade leader. She told Emperor Frederick I Barbarossa that his rule was corrupt and that she envisioned storms clouding his career. Henry II of England received a similar admonition. She also made four preaching tours across Europe during her career.

Her own reforming work involved separating the Disibodenberg nuns from their male counterparts in 1148. Such a move scandalized the monks, to whose abbot the nuns were to be obedient. A move meant loss of income for the monks, as well as personal sorrow over sundered friendships. As usual, a divine vision accompanying a bout of illness confirmed the plan, and Hildegard moved her eighteen nuns to Rupertsberg in 1150. As an abbess, she accommodated to some institutional biases, such as choosing only well-bred women as nuns. Highborn women brought wealth and prestige, ensuring the practical survival of her community.

Her closest confidant in the monastery, Richardis von Sade, became abbess of another monastery in 1151, despite Hildegard's opposition. The move crushed Hildegard as much as it advanced her protégé. Nonetheless, Richardis was persuaded by Hildegard's sadness to return to Rupertsberg, where Richardis died shortly thereafter.

An episode from her last years illustrates Hildegard's outspoken leadership. It involved the burial of a man in the Rupertsberg monastery yard whom the Church had excommunicated. The local archbishop considered null the dead man's forgiveness by the Church and ordered the body removed from holy ground. Hildegard refused, arguing her case before a tribunal and disguising the grave. Not until the archbishop died two years later was the issue resolved in Hildegard's favor, and the saying of mass by priests could resume for the Rupertsberg nuns. Months later, she died, satisfied that justice and mercy had met in her leadership.

SIGNIFICANCE

Hildegard's ability to lead was coupled with an appreciation of science, poetry, and music. Among her nonvisionary works is a morality play designed for use in churches, music, a treatise on the human body and disease, and a secret alphabet and language. In all these works, Hildegard understood herself to be a channel of divine revelation. For her, there was no separation between the mystical and the scientific, the known and the sensed. As the *Scivias* described it, the human body with its senses and emotions was a microcosm of the universe, where divinely given form joined matter in creating harmony, order, and beauty. Even her music defied twelfth century conventions with its free verse and rhapsodic melody.

Her fame as a mystic and intellectual have won Hildegard attention in recent scholarship on medieval women. Despite her intriguing spirituality and bold leadership, she is not officially recognized as a saint in the Catholic Church, though scores of faithful study her works, enjoy her music, and laud her example.

—*William P. McDonald*

FURTHER READING

Dronke, Peter. *Women Writers of the Middle Ages*. Cambridge, England: Cambridge University Press, 1984. An in-depth analysis of the literature and religious language of medieval women.

Gies, Frances, and Joseph Gies. *Women in the Middle Ages*. New York: Harper and Row, 1978. An informative social history concerning customs, mores, and the role of women in medieval life.

Hart, Columba, et al., eds. *Hildegard of Bingen: Scivias*. Classics of Western Spirituality Series. Mahwah, N.J.: Paulist Press, 1990. A solid introduction to Hildegard and a translation of her key work.

Hildegard von Bingen. *Eleven Thousand Virgins: Chants for the Feast of St. Ursula*. Harmonia Mundi France, 1997. One of several recordings available of Hildegard's music.

________. *Scivias*. Translated by Bruce Hozeski. Santa Fe, N.Mex.: Bear, 1986. A translated text of Hildegard's major visionary cycle, accompanied by black-and-white illustrations of the text's illuminations. Introductory essays include a biographical sketch, a review of her work, and an analysis of the structure and contents of *Scivias*.

King-Lenzmeier, Anne H. *Hildegard of Bingen: An Integrated Vision*. Collegeville, Minn.: Liturgical Press, 2001. This study treats Hildegard's writing as a coherent body of work. It brings together and analyzes the visionary and nonvisionary writing with the music, and provides biographical and sociological information to place the work in context.

Maddocks, Fiona. *Hildegard of Bingen: The Woman of Her Age*. New York: Doubleday, 2001. A biography of Hildegard emphasizing the wide variety of her accomplishments in many fields and the diverse and contradictory facets of her personality.

Newman, Barbara. *Sister of Wisdom: St. Hildegard's Theology of the Feminine*. Berkeley: University of California Press, 1989. This book examines Hildegard's theological views, placing her within her intellectual milieu.

_______, ed. *Voice of the Living Light: Hildegard of Bingen and Her World*. Berkeley: University of California Press, 1998. Scholars in different fields analyze Hildegard and her realm from varied perspectives.

Petroff, Elizabeth A. *Medieval Women's Visionary Literature*. New York: Oxford University Press, 1986. Anthologizes and analyzes in great detail the varied genres produced by medieval women.

Wilson, Katharina M., ed. *Medieval Women Writers*. Athens: University of Georgia Press, 1984. Another valuable anthology of women's literature, including that of Hildegard.

Zum Brun, Emilie, and Georgette Epiney-Burgard. *Women Mystics in Medieval Europe*. New York: Paragon House, 1989. A chapter on Hildegard links her with other female mystics and provides excerpts from their works.

See also: 735: Christianity Is Introduced into Germany; March 21, 1098: Foundation of the Cistercian Order.

Related articles in *Great Lives from History: The Middle Ages, 477-1453*: Beatrice of Nazareth; Saint Benedict of Nursia; Saint Bernard of Clairvaux; Boethius; Saint Brigit; Saint Catherine of Siena; Christina of Markyate; Saint Clare of Assisi; Dhuoda; Saint Hilda of Whitby; Hildegard von Bingen; Saint Isidore of Seville; Julian of Norwich; Margery Kempe; Mechthild von Magdeburg; Marguerite Porete.

1145
Kim Pu-sik Writes *Samguk Sagi*

In 1145, the Koryŏ statesman and scholar Kim Pu-sik wrote Samguk sagi, *a history of the three kingdoms. As the oldest extant history of Korea and practically the only source of information for the first millennium of Korean history, it is an invaluable work.*

Locale: Korean peninsula
Category: Historiography

Key Figures

Kim Pu-sik (1075-1151), statesman and scholar
Wang Hae (posthumous title King Injong; 1109-1146), king of Koryŏ, r. 1122-1146

Summary of Event

In the mid-twelfth century, the Koryŏ Dynasty (918-1392) seemed to have overcome the contradictions that had beset it since its founding. Though laying claim to the inheritance of the ancient state of Koguryŏ, including its heartland in what is now northeast China, in fact, Koryŏ mainly followed in the footsteps of the Silla Dynasty (668-935), from which its core officials derived. In 1135, under the leadership of the monk Myoch'ŏng, the Koguryŏ faction within the Koryŏ Dynasty made a last stand. Occupying the ancient Koguryŏ capital of P'yŏngyang, they tried to sway King Injong toward a military conquest of the ancient Koguryŏ heartland. However, they were defeated the following year by Kim Pu-sik, who represented the Silla loyalist faction. His victory sealed the supremacy of the Silla tradition and dissipated any illusions that Koryŏ would ever break out of its peninsular confines. It also marked the culmination of a trend toward civil domination over the military. Furthermore, renouncing the Koguryŏ heartland ensured a stable and peaceful relationship with the neighboring Jurchen Jin Dynasty (Chin; 1115-1234) that occupied this territory. It is against this background that the writing of the *Samguk sagi* (1145; history of the Three Kingdoms) should be understood: Its author, Kim Pu-sik, was not a neutral historian but someone with a clear ideological agenda.

Kim Pu-sik was a descendant of the royal dynasty of Silla. He was the third of four brothers, all of whom passed the civil service examination and thus cemented their status as part of the capital elite. However, his was undoubtedly the most illustrious career: He not only attained high office and a reputation for scholarship and writing but also gained the trust of rulers as a royal tutor. An able military strategist, he retired from active government duties in 1142 because of his age and also because he felt isolated after all his brothers and close colleagues had died and a political rival had been reinstated in office.

Kim Pu-sik, however, still had the ear of King Injong, in whom he had inculcated the value of the Confucian classics and history. Kim was a staunch defender of Confucian values: In one famous instance, he rebuked Injong for giving too much power to his father-in-law, arguing that this would violate the cardinal relationship between ruler and subject. The emulation of Confucian values is a recurring theme in some of his other writings, including his poetry and memorials, in which he also shows a profound grasp of Chinese history. Undoubtedly, this expertise led to his involvement in the compilation of the official records of Injong's predecessor, King Yejong (r. 1105-1122), and he was in charge of the national history compilation of the Koryŏ Dynasty. He was therefore uniquely qualified to write a history of the three kingdoms period preceding Koryŏ. Given his background and the circumstances in which the work emerged, it is likely that Kim had suggested the work in the first place, but the royal commission gave it the status of official historiography.

Although compilations of Korean history had been made before his time, Kim Pu-sik's work was the first to be written in complete conformity with the Chinese historiographic tradition. The *Samguk sagi* follows the format established by Sima Qian's *Shiji* (first century B.C.E.; *Records of the Grand Historian of China*, 1960, rev. ed. 1993), dividing the material into four categories: annals, tables, monographs, and biographies. The annals are a chronological account of main events arranged by reign. They consist of twenty-eight chapters: The first twelve deal with Silla (57 B.C.E.-668 C.E.) and unified Silla (668-935), the next ten chapters cover Koguryŏ (37 B.C.E.-668 C.E.), and the last six are dedicated to Paekche (18 B.C.E.-660 C.E.). The tables (chapters 29 to 31) are year-by-year lists of reigns, offering no new information. The monographs describe the basic institutions of the state and its main areas of concern, such as geography or ritual (chapters 32 to 40). The last ten chapters of this fifty-chapter work contain biographies of important personalities.

One of the reasons Chinese historians organized their material in this way was to make a large amount of information more readily accessible. However, in the case of the *Samguk sagi*, the reverse is true: Kim Pu-sik seems to have used it to make a limited amount of information look more impressive. There is a considerable amount of overlap between the different sections: The biographies contain mostly material that can also be found in the annals section, and within the annals section, there is also considerable duplication. For instance, battles that occurred between Silla and Paekche are described in exactly the same terms in the respective chapters of each kingdom. It is obvious that by the time Kim compiled his work, a lot of sources had been irretrievably lost. Although each of the three kingdoms had once compiled its own national history, most of these seem to have been lost by the twelfth century. Kim Pu-sik thus had to rely on a few general histories of Korea (now lost), accounts from Chinese sources, and some fragmentary records and biographies. This lack of sources is especially evident in his coverage of the first centuries. It is generally agreed that the founding dates of the three states are fictitious, and his work becomes reliable only from the fourth century.

Besides borrowing the framework of the Chinese histories, Kim Pu-sik was also indebted to the methodology and mental universe of the Chinese historians. Thus, he worked with a team of ten compilers to gather sources, compare them critically, and use the most reliable parts. He refrained from using his own voice in the text, inserting instead his comments at places where he felt the source material needed to be criticized. These comments reveal that he saw history in moralistic terms and wanted to use precedents as warnings or instructions for present rulers. He was also keen to edit out any legendary narratives or miraculous events. Despite the influence of Chinese models and the fact that he wrote in classical Chinese (Korean officialdom's preferred language for written communication until the end of the Yi Dynasty (Chosŏn; 1392-1910), Kim Pu-sik succeeded in his main aim: to compile an authoritative account of his country's ancient history and thereby justify its status in the world order of the time.

Despite his objectivist methodology, Kim Pu-sik has been taken to task by late Yi and modern Korean historians for his bias toward Silla and his attempts to represent it as the sole rightful source of Koryŏ culture and political legitimacy. Perhaps the main criticism leveled at this work is that it excludes the state of Parhae (698-926), a successor state to Koguryŏ in northeast China, thereby forfeiting any Korean claims to that territory. This is attributed to Kim Pu-sik's excessive respect for Chinese culture and his resultant subservience to China. However, by bringing Korean history in line with the Chinese world order, he also ensured that the peninsula had a clearer and less ambiguous identity within that order, restricted to the peninsula but also firmly implanted on it.

SIGNIFICANCE

Despite Kim Pu-sik's preference for Silla, his work is umistakably a painstaking search to recover the facts of history. Although Kim relied heavily on Chinese sources for the first centuries of the common era, he did not hesitate to reject these in favor of Korean sources when he felt these were more reliable. Thus, he evidently relied heavily on a Koguryŏ source when writing about the first three centuries of that kingdom's history, making his work an invaluable resource for Koguryŏ history. The list of Koguryŏ place-names in the Monographs section allows readers to reconstruct elements of the Koguryŏ language. The Paekche annals are undoubtedly the most meager of the three, but it is not sure whether Kim is to blame for this—the accuracy of the basic facts is confirmed in Japanese sources, and the mistakes may be present in his sources. In the Silla annals, the author shows even-handedness by including material that cast a negative light on his ancestral dynasty, such as the practice of endogamy by some Silla rulers. Even though this work may have been intended to unify the peninsula under a Silla identity, its plurality of voices betrays the inherently pluralist worldview of Koryŏ intellectuals.

—*Sem Vermeersch*

FURTHER READING

Best, Jonathan W. "Redating the Earliest Silla-Related Entries in the 'Paekche Annals' of the *Samguk Sagi*." *Han'guk sanggosa hakpo* 21, no. 4 (1996): 147-171. Shows how some events in the Paekche annals have been antedated to embellish Paekche's early history.

Gardiner, Kenneth H. J. "The *Samguk-sagi* and Its Sources." *Papers on Far Eastern History* 2 (1970): 1-42. A brief but authoritative introduction to the sources at Kim Pu-sik's disposal and how he used them.

Kim Pu-sik. *Samguk sagi*. Translated and edited by Yi Pyŏng-do. Seoul: Ŭryu Munhwasa, 1977. In Korean. Still the standard edition and modern Korean translation of Kim Pu-sik's work.

Sin, Hyong-sik. *Samguk sagi yŏn'gu*. Seoul: Ilchogak, 1981. In Korean, with summary in English. Offers a thorough statistical analysis of all parts of the *Samguk sagi*, and seeks to redeem Kim Pu-sik as a protonationalist historian.

SEE ALSO: 668-935: Silla Unification of Korea; 918-936: Foundation of the Koryŏ Dynasty; 958-1076: Koreans Adopt the Tang Civil Service Model; 1196-1258: Ch'oe Family Takes Power in Korea; July, 1392: Establishment of the Yi Dynasty.

RELATED ARTICLE in *Great Lives from History: The Middle Ages, 477-1453*: Wang Kŏn.

c. 1145

PRESTER JOHN MYTH SWEEPS ACROSS EUROPE

Prester John appeared to be the ideal Christian king and a champion against the Muslims who were ready to retake Jerusalem when reports of him came to Europe in the mid-twelfth century. Even though the reports were later found to be fabricated, his legend grew steadily over the next three centuries.

LOCALE: Europe, Middle East, Africa, India, and Central Asia

CATEGORIES: Cultural and intellectual history; exploration and discovery; literature; religion

KEY FIGURES

Otto of Freising (c. 1111-1158), chronicler and historian

Alexander III (c. 1105-1181), pope, 1159-1181

Marco Polo (c. 1254-1324), Italian explorer and writer

Genghis Khan (between 1155 and 1162-1227), Mongol ruler and empire builder, r. 1206-1227

SUMMARY OF EVENT

Twelfth century Europe saw disillusioning political setbacks that caused widespread anxiety. European princes fought each other, and the Byzantine emperor, the pope, and Holy Roman Emperor were at loggerheads. In addition, the Muslim Saracen armies were poised to retake the territory in Palestine conquered by the First Crusade in 1099 and possibly drive Christians from the Holy Land altogether. It is no wonder, then, that when reports came of a great ruler in the Far East who was coming to the rescue, Europeans were eager to believe in him. He was Prester (or Presbyter) John, a king who was also a priest.

Mandeville's Visit to Prester John

The fourteenth century Travels of Sir John Mandeville, *supposedly by a knight of that name from St. Albans, relates the marvels its author purportedly encountered during his travels through the Middle East, Africa, and Asia. Although little is known of the author (including whether he really existed), the number of manuscripts that survive attests to the work's popularity among fourteenth century readers. One chapter is devoted to Prester John.*

This emperor, Prester John, holds full great land, and hath many full noble cities and good towns in his realm, and many great diverse isles and large. . . . [He] is Christian, and a great part of his country also. But yet, they have not all the articles of our faith as we have. They believe well in the Father, in the Son and in the Holy Ghost. And they be full devout and right true one to another. . . . And he hath under him seventy-two provinces, and in every province is a king. And these kings have kings under them, and all be tributaries to Prester John. And he hath in his lordships many great marvels.

Source: As quoted in *The Travels of Sir John Mandeville*, from *Medieval Sourcebook*, edited by Paul Halsall, http://www.fordham.edu/halsall/sbook.html.

The first reports may have referred to actual events, if imprecisely, but as time passed, Prester John became ever more a figure of fantasy, the subject of hoaxes, literary exaggeration, and wishful thinking. The first recorded mention of him occurs in 1145 in a chronicle by Otto of Freising. Bishop Otto relates the testimony of Hugh, bishop of Jabala in Syria. According to Hugh, a Christian priest and king named John, a descendant of the biblical Magi, led an army against the Persians in a three-day battle. Prester John's forces prevailed, and he intended to lead them on to Jerusalem to preserve the city for Christianity but was unable to cross the Tigris River.

Bishop Otto's report may have been partly propaganda, since Bishop Hugh made it after a scouting mission in support of a second crusade, but modern scholars, such as Charles F. Beckingham, have found supporting evidence in other medieval historians. In 1141, an immense battle took place between forces of the Persian prince Sanjar and those of Korkhan (or Ku-Khan, Corchan) of China. The Chinese obliterated the 100,000-man Persian army, welcome news indeed for the Christian rulers of Palestine.

Bishop Hugh's Prester John belonged to the Nestorian sect, which believed that Christ's human existence on earth was distinct from his divine nature. Although Nestorianism was heresy to the Roman Catholic Church, Prester John was still a Christian and a potentially powerful ally. However, the mysterious Eastern potentate might have remained little more than an encouraging rumor had not a letter from him, written sometime around 1165, reached Pope Alexander III. The letter, addressed to Byzantine emperor Manuel II Comnenus, boasted at length about Prester John's wealth and splendor.

It was an outrageous forgery, yet because of it, the Prester John legend assumed a life of its own and grew. The letter claims that Prester John dominated the "three Indias" where milk and honey flowed and where there was an abundance of gems of every kind and gold; he lived in a palace built of ebony and precious stones, where daily his tables fed 30,000 people and his retainers included 7 kings, 62 dukes, 365 counts and an equal number of abbots and bishops. Prester John, it says, received tribute from 72 kings. When minstrels and storytellers learned the contents of the fabulous letter, they were quick to include Prester John in their performances. Soon his legend expanded in magnificence by incorporating episodes from tales about Alexander the Great and from miracle stories about the Apostle Saint Thomas during his mission in India.

Pope Alexander III was clearly skeptical of the letter. Yet he was so worried about Christianity's political straits that he dispatched an aide, Philippus, to Prester John with a reply. While admonishing Prester John for the irresponsible self-glorification, the pontiff made overtures for an alliance with the Nestorian as if he really existed. Philippus left on his mission in 1177 and vanished from history.

The legend spread. Marco Polo, and others, confidently but wrongly identified Unc-Khan, a rebellious vassal of Genghis Khan who died in battle fighting the great Mongol emperor, as Prester John. Polo's account of his visit to the Mongol court had a wide readership and enhanced the legend's authenticity. So when it eventually became apparent that Prester John could not possibly have been a khan of Central Asia, hopeful Western princes and scholars simply looked elsewhere, sure that his realm existed. To find it, they took clues not only from the letter, which steadily grew longer with embellishments by copyists, but also from reports by other travelers, however doubtful. India was next thought to be Prester John's home, although the exact location was vague. To Europeans "India" denoted a poorly defined region somewhere east of Palestine and west of Cathay (China). Armenia and the Caucasus were also considered.

Finally, based on reports by captured Africans and diplomatic missions from African kings to European princes in the fourteenth and fifteenth centuries, King Henry IV of England, Prince Henry the Navigator, and King John I of Portugal convinced themselves that Prester John was the emperor of Ethiopia, which was believed to be somewhere in sub-Saharan Africa. Expeditions were dispatched to find him during the fifteenth century. However, as explorers made contact with the major kingdoms of Africa, including Ethiopia, it became clear that Prester John had never ruled there either. By the seventeenth century, the legend had lost its attraction.

Significance

The belief in pending help from Prester John had harmful military and political consequences. The fall of Jerusalem to the great Ayyūbid Dynasty general Saladin in 1187 and the failures of the Third Crusade (1191), Fourth Crusade (1199), and Fifth Crusade (1218-1221) to retake it made Christians overeager to look for help. When reports came that a mighty King David, the heir of Prester John (who also styled himself Prester John), was on his way to Palestine, rejoicing spread through Europe. A great army was indeed approaching but not led by any Prester John. It was the army of Ghengis Khan. Rejoicing turned to alarm as the Mongols not only crushed and plundered the Muslims but also Christians, Jews, and everyone else in their way. Soon Europe, lulled by the legend of Prester John and unprepared for common defense, found itself besieged and escaped conquest only because Ghengis Khan died.

Contact with the Mongols disabused many Europeans of their faith in an ideal Eastern Christian monarch, but the legend still held powerful allure, and it led to practical benefits. The Catholic Church renewed its interest in Nestorians and sent missionaries to India and China. Reports from the missionaries greatly increased knowledge of the East, as did the accounts of traders who wanted to profit from Prester John's reportedly vast wealth.

European leaders continued trying to make contact when attention turned to Ethiopia as the site of Prester John's kingdom. The attempts furthered the exploration of Africa and surrounding seas. For example, both Bartolomeu Dias's discovery of the Cape of Good Hope in 1488 and Vasco da Gama's 1498 voyage up the eastern coast of Africa and on to India came in part from the search for Prester John.

The legend found its way into the literature of many lands, not only travelogues like those of Marco Polo and Sir John Mandeville but also great epics. In his *Parzival* (c. 1200-1210; English translation, 1894), the German poet Wolfram von Eschenbach (c. 1170-c. 1217) referred to Prester John, the first such mention in a chivalric romance, and three centuries later, Sir Thomas Malory (d. 1471) made similar use of it in *Le Morte d'Arthur* (1485). In this courtly literature, Prester John represented a perfect blending of the roles of priest and king, bringing modesty, justice, and piety to government. His ideal commonwealth contrasted sharply with the actual European kingdoms of the times. Indeed, some modern scholars, such as Leonardo Olschki, believe that Bishop Otto's 1145 description of Prester John may itself have been an attempt to shame Emperor Frederick I Barbarossa and Pope Alexander III from their bitter power struggles by inventing a virtuous monarch who united spiritual and temporal authority.

—*Roger Smith*

The legendary Prester John is shown as the head of a Tartary tribe in Cesar Vecelli's Degli Habiti Antichi e Moderni *(1560), a book on clothing and fashion.* (Frederick Ungar Publishing Co.)

FURTHER READING

Beckingham, Charles F. "The Quest for Prester John." In *The European Opportunity: The European Impact on World History 1450-1800*. Vol. 2. Brookfield, Vt.: Variorum, 1995. Discusses the sources of erroneous reports of Prester John and the political considerations that led Western rulers to seek him in Asia and Africa.

Beckingham, Charles F., and Bernard Hamilton, eds. *Prester John and the Ten Lost Tribes*. Brookfield, Vt.: Variorum, 1996. This scholarly collection contains two sections: one of ancient texts about Prester John in Latin and German, and one of articles interpreting the texts, with particular attention to historical references and the development of the legend.

Relaño, Francesc. "Prester John: The Migration of a Legend." In *The Shaping of Africa: Cosmographic Discourse and Cartographic Science in Late Medieval and Early Modern Europe*. Burlington, Vt.: Ashgate, 2002. Discusses the role of the Prester John legend in shaping Europe's idea of Africa.

Silverberg, Robert. *The Realm of Prester John*. 1972. Reprint. Athens: Ohio University Press, 1996. A prolific popular author provides a readable, judicious, wide-ranging study of the Prester John legend, its origins, and its historical and cultural milieu, based upon extensive review of original sources and scholarly studies.

Westrem, Scott D. *Broader Horizons: A Study of Johannes Witte de Hese's "Itinerarius" and Medieval Travel Narratives*. Cambridge, Mass.: Medieval Academy of America, 2001. This analysis of travel narratives discusses voyages made in search of Prester John.

SEE ALSO: November 27, 1095: Pope Urban II Calls the First Crusade; 1147-1149: Second Crusade; 1189-1192: Third Crusade; 1204: Genghis Khan Founds Mongol Empire; 1204: Knights of the Fourth Crusade Capture Constantinople; 1217-1221: Fifth Crusade; 1227-1230: Frederick II Leads the Sixth Crusade; 1248-1254: Failure of the Seventh Crusade; 1271-1295: Travels of Marco Polo; 1275: Nestorian Archbishopric Is Founded in Beijing; 1415-1460: Prince Henry the Navigator Promotes Portuguese Exploration.

RELATED ARTICLES in *Great Lives from History: The Middle Ages, 477-1453*: Alexander III; Frederick I Barbarossa; Genghis Khan; Marco Polo; Prince Henry the Navigator; Henry IV (of England); Lalibela; Saladin; Wolfram von Eschenbach.

1147-1149
SECOND CRUSADE

The Second Crusade was launched by Pope Eugenius III and, despite its ultimate failure, provided a model for the preaching of later expeditions. The Second Crusade also expanded the definition of crusade to include holy wars against pagans and other enemies of the Catholic Church.

LOCALE: Outremer (Jerusalem), Portugal, and lands east of the Elbe River (now in the Czech Republic)

CATEGORIES: Religion; wars, uprisings, and civil unrest

KEY FIGURES

Eugenius III (d. 1153), pope, 1145-1153

Louis VII (1120-1180), king of France, r. 1137-1179

Saint Bernard of Clairvaux (1090-1153), abbot of Clairvaux, 1115-1153

Conrad III (1093-1152), king of Germany, r. 1138-1152

Roger II (1095-1154), Norman king of Sicily, r. 1130-1154

Manuel I Comnenus (c. 1122-1180), Byzantine emperor, r. 1143-1180

Eleanor of Aquitaine (c. 1122-1204), queen consort of Louis VII of France, 1137-1152, and Henry II of England, 1152-1204

Raymond of Poitiers (1099-1149), prince of Antioch, r. 1136-1149, and uncle of Eleanor of Aquitaine

SUMMARY OF EVENT

While crusades were preached in Europe after the First Crusade of 1096 and while Europeans continued to send reinforcements to the Latin settlements of the East (commonly known as Outremer), it was not until 1145 that a pope called for a large-scale Crusade. The call was precipitated by the December 24, 1144, capture of Edessa by Caliph Zangī (r. 1127-1146) of the Seljuk Empire. Edessa had been in Christian hands since the

Crusaders depicted in the stained-glass window of a twelfth century French abbey. (Hulton|Archive by Getty Images)

First Crusade, and its fall sent shock waves through Europe.

As a result, in 1145, Pope Eugenius III called for a new Crusade to the East in his encyclical Quantum Praedecessores. This encyclical became the model for the formulation of later papal calls to crusade, including a summary of the threat, a call to take the cross, and a list of privileges granted to the Crusaders.

Louis VII of France was the first to heed the call. Apparently Louis had long planned a pilgrimage to Jerusalem. He announced his plan to take up the cross in December, 1145, to an assembly of nobles gathered for the Christmas Court at Bourges; however, the response to Louis's call for a crusade was lukewarm.

It was not until Pope Eugenius appointed Bernard of Clairvaux to preach the Crusade that Louis received widespread support. Indeed, contemporary chroniclers report that Bernard's preaching so moved the crowd at Vézelay on March 31, 1146, that Bernard ran out of the cloth crosses he had brought with him to give to those pledging themselves to the Crusade.

Although Crusade fever gripped France, the Germans were less enthusiastic. In spite of continued urging from the pope, Conrad III of Germany was reluctant to take up the cross or to commit his men to the Crusade. It was not until Bernard himself traveled to Germany that Conrad acquiesced.

During the two years of planning, the scale of the Second Crusade expanded to include three distinct arenas: Outremer, the Wendish lands beyond the Elbe River, and the Iberian Peninsula. Shortly before the departure of Conrad's German forces for Outremer, a group of Saxons asked to be allowed to crusade against the pagan Wends who lived beyond the Elbe River. The pope granted them permission, and so for the first time, the definition of crusade grew to include war against pagans or enemies of the Church.

The pope also included a call for the reconquest of the Iberian Peninsula, and Crusaders who fought in this arena were accorded the same indulgences that Crusaders headed for the East enjoyed. Consequently, when the Anglo-Flemish forces landed in Portugal on their way east in June of 1147, they were persuaded to participate in the siege of Lisbon. The subsequent Crusader victory was the only real success of the entire Second Crusade.

The main thrust of the Second Crusade was the relief of Outremer. Conrad's forces left Germany in May, 1147, and Louis followed in June. They elected to travel overland, through the Byzantine Empire ruled by Manuel I Comnenus.

Although both armies had been offered sea passage to Outremer by Roger II of Sicily, neither Conrad nor Louis fully trusted him. Conrad was on especially bad terms with Roger and preferred to negotiate with Manuel for safe conduct through the Byzantine Empire. Although the French were on better terms with Roger, they, too, elected the overland route. Significantly, Roger complicated the situation for the European Crusaders by engaging in a war with the Byzantine Empire.

Initially, the Germans had little problem crossing Byzantine territory. Their refusal to bypass Constantinople, however, as well as Crusader plundering, led to problems. After leaving Nicaea, the German army not only ran out of supplies, but also was ambushed by Turkish forces and routed. The survivors, including Conrad, fled to Nicaea to await aid from Louis.

Louis's departure from France was in grand style. Like the Germans, he had many noncombatant pilgrims with him. In addition, Eleanor of Aquitaine and her court traveled with Louis's forces. There are reports that Eleanor and her ladies frequently dressed like a troop of Amazons and rode alongside the troops headed to Outremer.

Louis was on less friendly terms with Manuel than Conrad, and French troops had to pass through territory already plundered by the Crusaders from Germany. Consequently, the French had little support from the Byzantines. Indeed, just as the French neared Constantinople, they received word that Manuel had been negotiating with the Turks.

When the French army reached Nicaea, they met with the remains of Conrad's army and continued eastward. Provisions grew low, and by the time they reached Antalya, they were in serious trouble, both from starvation and from Turkish harassment. Although Manuel promised ships to take the Crusaders on to Antioch, there were too few ships to transport all of Louis's forces, and therefore many Crusaders were stranded in Byzantine territory to find their own way home or to Antioch.

Louis finally arrived in Antioch on March 19, 1148, where his troops remained as guests of Eleanor's uncle, Raymond of Poitiers. In June, Louis, Conrad, and many Christians from the Latin settlements met and decided to attack Damascus. Contemporary writers alleged that Eleanor's impropriety with her uncle spurred Louis on to rashly starting out for Damascus; whatever the case, the combined forces met with disaster when they attacked Damascus, thus ending the Second Crusade that had begun so grandly.

Many scholars have speculated on the causes leading to the failure of the Second Crusade. Some point to the large number of noncombatants who certainly drained critical resources. Others believe that the failure of the European forces to act in unity led to defeat; the strength of the European force in the East was diluted by the war against the Wends in Germany and against the Islamic holdings in the Iberian Peninsula. Still others suggest that the war between Roger of Sicily and Manuel led to fatal political maneuvering that cost the European forces important support in the East. Finally, some believe that Eleanor's alleged dalliance with her uncle, Raymond, led to the disastrous decision to attack Damascus.

Saint Bernard preaches the Second Crusade. (Gihon)